BIOLOGY OF AGGRESSION

BIOLOGY OF AGGRESSION

Edited by

RANDY J. NELSON

2006

OXFORD
UNIVERSITY PRESS

Oxford University Press, Inc., publishes works that further
Oxford University's objective of excellence
in research, scholarship, and education.

Oxford   New York
Auckland   Cape Town   Dar es Salaam   Hong Kong   Karachi
Kuala Lumpur   Madrid   Melbourne   Mexico City   Nairobi
New Delhi   Shanghai   Taipei   Toronto

With offices in
Argentina   Austria   Brazil   Chile   Czech Republic   France   Greece
Guatemala   Hungary   Italy   Japan   Poland   Portugal   Singapore
South Korea   Switzerland   Thailand   Turkey   Ukraine   Vietnam

Published by Oxford University Press, Inc.
198 Madison Avenue, New York, New York 10016

www.oup.com

Oxford is a registered trademark of Oxford University Press

Library of Congress Cataloging-in-Publication Data
Biology of aggression / edited by Randy J. Nelson.
p.   cm.
Includes bibliographical references and index.
ISBN-13 978-0-19-516876-1
ISBN 0-19-516876-3
1. Aggressiveness—Physiological aspects—Handbooks, manuals, etc.
I. Nelson, Randy Joe.
QP401.H26   2005
155.2'32—dc22   2004020382

9 8 7 6 5 4 3 2 1

Printed in the United States of America
on acid-free paper

Preface

The effects of aggression and violence on people can be seen in the news media every day. Whether the story is about the mauling of a woman by an aggressive dog, students attacking their colleagues in school, workers attacking their colleagues at work, or people detonating bombs in response to their ideological beliefs, unchecked aggression and violence exact a significant toll on society. For years, the roles of learning and environmental influences, both social and nonsocial factors, were prominent in discussions of the etiology of human aggression. Biological factors were not thought likely to be important candidates for dealing with human aggression or violence. With recent advances in pharmacology and genetic manipulation techniques, new interests in the biological mechanisms of human aggression have been pursued. Certainly, aggression is a complex social behavior with multiple causes, but pursuit of molecular biological causes may lead to interventions to prevent excess aggressive behaviors.

Aggression has been defined as overt behavior with the intention of inflicting physical damage upon another individual. The possibility for aggressive behavior exists whenever the interests of two or more individuals conflict. Conflicts are most likely to arise over limited resources, including territories, food, and mates. Indeed, the ubiquitous resident-intruder aggression test models rodent territorial aggression. In nature, the social interaction decides which animal gains access to the contested resource. In many cases, a submissive posture or gesture on the part of one animal avoids the necessity of actual combat over a resource. Animals may also participate in psychological intimidation by engaging in threat displays or ritualized combat in which dominance is determined, but no physical damage is inflicted.

Because most aggressive encounters among humans and nonhuman animals represent a male proclivity, studies using the most appropriate murine model (such as testosterone-dependent offensive intermale aggression, which is typically measured in resident-intruder or isolation-induced aggression tests) are discussed. In this book, various molecules that have been linked to aggression by pharmacological or the latest gene targeting techniques are emphasized as well. The evidence continues to point to androgens and serotonin (5-hydroxytryptamine, or 5-HT) as major hormonal and neurotransmitter factors in aggressive behavior, although recent work with gamma-aminobutyric acid (GABA), dopamine, vasopressin, and other factors, such as nitric oxide, has revealed significant interactions with the neural circuitry underlying aggression. The goal of this volume is to summarize and synthesize the recent advances in the biological study of aggression.

Within the past decade a novel and compelling link has been formed between psychology and molecular biology. Molecular biologists have mapped large segments of the mouse genome as part of the ambitious Human Genome Project. As genes have been identified and sequenced, molecular biologists have begun the difficult task of identifying the function of these genes. An increasingly common genetic engineering technique used to discover the function of genes is targeted disruption ("knockout") of a single gene. By selectively disrupting the expression of a single gene, molecular biologists reason that the function of that targeted gene can be determined. In many cases, the phenotypic description of knockout mice includes alterations in aggressive behavior; this genetic approach provides complementary data to pharmacological studies. Another important technology in understanding the biology of aggression is brain imaging. Although advances in imaging, proteomics, gene microarrays, and RNA silencing are contributing directly to understanding the mechanisms of aggression, it is also critical to appreciate the adaptive and evolutionary forces that shape aggressive behavior. The chapters here were chosen to provide distinct perspectives and multiple levels of analysis of aggressive behavior, from genes to social behavior.

In the first chapter, Stephen C. Maxson and Andrew Canastar explore several contextual issues for developing more fully a comparative genetics of aggression in nonhuman animals. After describing the types of aggression in animals, aspects of the evolution and of the development of aggression are related to the study of its genetics; this is followed by a consideration of different species that are being or could be used to begin a comparative genetics of aggression. Each of these points is relevant to developing the genetics of aggression in animals as models for human aggression.

In chapter 2, Daniel M. Blonigen and Robert F. Krueger present an up-to-date review of human quantitative genetic studies of aggression and violence, including twin, adoption, and molecular genetic designs from both the child and adult literature. They begin their chapter by reviewing the behavioral genetic literature on aggression in childhood and early adolescence. Then they highlight systematic differences across studies based on the method of assessing aggression, as well as presenting evidence for both distinct and common etiologies that link aggression with other

childhood behavioral problems. Next, Blonigen and Krueger review behavioral genetic investigations of aggression in adults. Molecular genetic studies of human aggression across a range of psychiatric and developmental disorders are introduced and briefly summarized in this chapter.

The vast majority of nonhuman animal aggression research is conducted on mice. Most laboratory strains of mice are not particularly aggressive, however, and other animal models may be appropriate to understand certain neurochemical and neuroanatomical circuits common in the regulation of aggressive behavior. In chapter 3, Donald H. Edwards and Jens Herberholz provide an extensive review of crustacean models of aggression. In addition to easily observed aggressive behavior patterns, crustaceans have readily accessible nervous systems that contain many large, identifiable neurons that play key roles in mediating these behaviors. Although this effort is only beginning, the role of specific neural circuits, such as those for escape, and specific neurohormones, including monoamines and peptides, in mediating aspects of aggressive behavior have been elucidated in crustaceans.

Stephen B. Manuck, Jay R. Kaplan, and Francis E. Lotrich evaluate the role of 5-HT in the aggressive behavior of humans and nonhuman primates in chapter 4. Because of its primary role in aggression, many chapters in this volume address some aspect of 5-HT signaling. Chapter 4 first provides a brief introduction to the neurobiology of 5-HT, including common methods of investigation and sources of 5-HT-associated genetic variation. Next, the authors briefly provide comparative conceptualizations of aggressive behavior in human and nonhuman primates, including the role of antagonistic interactions in primate social dominance and human psychopathology. Central nervous system (CNS) serotonergic activity as a correlate of aggressive disposition, as well as impulsivity (reported in studies employing neurochemical indices of serotonergic function), neuropharmacologic challenges, functional neuroimaging, and neurogenetic methodologies, are reviewed. Manuck and coauthors conclude the chapter by attempting to integrate observations derived from studies on humans and nonhuman primates to identify implications of these findings for models of serotonergic influences on aggression and speculate briefly regarding possible evolutionary origins of these associations.

Several classical neurotransmitters have been linked to aggression, but the effects of 5-HT are most prominent. In chapter 5, Klaus A. Miczek and Eric W. Fish review the role of 5-HT, as well as norepinephrine and dopamine, on the mediation of aggressive behavior. These authors emphasize that aggression represents diverse behavioral patterns and functions, and that endogenous amino acids, steroids, and peptides may have very different effects on each kind of aggression. They highlight the importance of escalated forms of aggression in an effort to model the harmful acts of aggression and violence in humans. They also note the reciprocal relationship between monoamines and aggression, explaining that the effects of monoamines are likely due to their interactions with other neurotransmitters, such as GABA and glutamate, and neuropeptides, such as vasopressin and opioids.

The contribution of nitric oxide (NO), a signaling molecule in the brain, to aggression is reviewed in chapter 6 by Silvana Chiavegatto, Gregory E. Demas, and Randy J. Nelson. Male neuronal NO synthase knockout (nNOS$^{-/-}$) mice and wild-type (WT) mice in which nNOS is pharmacologically suppressed are highly aggressive. Castration and testosterone replacement studies in both nNOS$^{-/-}$ and WT mice exclude an activational role for gonadal steroids in the elevated aggression. NO also appears to affect aggressive behavior via 5-HT. The excessive aggressiveness and impulsiveness of nNOS knockout mice are caused by selective decrements in 5-HT turnover and deficient 5-HT$_{1A}$ and 5-HT$_{1B}$ receptor function in brain regions regulating emotion. Although precisely how NO interacts with the 5-HT system in vivo remains unspecified, these results indicate an important role for NO in normal brain 5-HT function and might have significant implications for the treatment of psychiatric disorders characterized by aggressiveness and impulsivity.

Craig F. Ferris details the role of neuropeptides on aggression in chapter 7. He and his colleagues have found that brain vasopressin facilitates aggression in Syrian hamsters. An interesting relationship among vasopressin, 5-HT, and aggression has been discovered; in an important series of experiments, Syrian hamsters treated with 5-HT agonists increased 5-HT, decreased vasopressin, and decreased aggression. Ferris reports a positive correlation between vasopressin and aggression, an inverse correlation between 5-HT responsiveness and aggression, and an inverse correlation between vasopressin and 5-HT responsiveness. Similar data were obtained from violent humans. Ferris's chapter not only serves as an example of how animal data inform human research, but also provides an excellent example of an interaction between two different neuro-

chemical systems in the modulation of aggression in humans.

In chapter 8, John C. Wingfield, Ignacio T. Moore, Wolfgang Goymann, Douglas W. Wacker, and Todd Sperry review the biology of aggression from an evolutionary and ethological perspective. The goal of this chapter is to understand the stimuli and situational factors that underlie aggressive behaviors and to place aggressive behaviors in an ecological and evolutionary context. The different types of aggressive behaviors are defined and described, permitting a link from the ethological function and the laboratory assessments of aggression. This is among the first attempts to summarize how aggression is expressed *and* regulated in different contexts, with examples provided from natural settings. The authors initially address the types and contexts of vertebrate aggression and then discuss how it is controlled by the endocrine system. The second part of chapter 8 then addresses hormone-aggression interactions and their possible evolution.

Castration has been known to inhibit aggressive behavior for at least 2,500 years. We now know that the removal of the testes significantly reduces circulating androgens, primarily testosterone and its metabolites, and male-typical aggression is facilitated by androgens. Neal G. Simon and Shi-Fang Lu review the effects of androgens and aggression in chapter 9. Androgens are important mediators of aggression in several ways. During development, androgens guide the organization of the brain into a malelike pattern by inducing or preventing neural cell death. Early exposure to steroid hormones can also affect the distribution of serotonergic neurons, their connectivity, and the distribution and binding capacities of receptor subtypes. Masculinization and defeminization of the brain are often accomplished by estrogens, the aromatized products of androgens; the lack of androgens and estrogens during early development leads to female (feminized and demasculinized) brains and subsequent behavioral patterns. Later, postpubertal testosterone (or estrogenic by-products) stimulates neural circuits that were organized perinatally, presumably by making aggression-inducing stimuli more salient. Importantly, neurons in these aggression-mediating areas are rich in both steroid hormone receptors and 5-HT$_{1A}$ and 5-HT$_{1B}$ receptor subtypes. Taken together, the contribution of androgens to the regulation of aggression is through their actions as modulators of neurochemical function. The *neuromodulator hypothesis* allows the integration of data from endocrine, neurochemical, and peptide systems that are currently recognized as critical factors in the regulation of conspecific aggression.

Estrogen, as an aromatized metabolite of testosterone, facilitates male aggressive behavior in mice. In chapter 10, Sonoko Ogawa, Masayoshi Nomura, Elena Choleris, and Donald Pfaff review the contribution of estrogen receptors in aggression. Their work focuses on the presence of two subtypes of estrogen receptors (ER), ER-α and ER-β, in the brain that bind estrogen. An individual gene can have opposite effects on aggressive behaviors in the two sexes. For example, ER-α knockout males are less aggressive than their control WT littermates, but ER-α knockout females are more aggressive than WT mice. The ER-β gene can show the opposite regulation of aggressive behaviors compared to the ER-α gene. For example, ER-β knockout male mice, tested as either an adolescent or young adult, are more aggressive, but the ER-α knockout males are less aggressive than WT control mice. In female mice, the ER-β gene can have opposite effects according to the type of aggression tested. For example, ER-β knockouts have quantitatively less testosterone-facilitated aggression, but are more sensitive in tests of maternal aggression postpartum. Finally, the interactions among estrogen receptors, 5-HT, and other neurotransmitters contributing to aggressive behavior are also discussed.

Mothers fiercely protect their young. The adaptive function of maternal aggression is to protect the young, which has direct fitness consequences. In chapter 11, Stephen C. Gammie and Joseph S. Lonstein review maternal aggression in the context of other maternal behavior and note that maternal aggression is different both in form and presumably in underlying brain mechanisms from other types of maternal care and from other types of aggression. They provide a review of what is currently known about the neural circuitry and endocrine processes underlying maternal aggression.

Stress can facilitate aggression. D. Caroline Blanchard and Robert J. Blanchard review the underlying mechanisms and environmental factors that interact with the effects of stress on aggression in chapter 12. Social stress is a common and enduring feature of life with important behavioral and physiological effects. Previous work with laboratory rodents indicates that acute stressors (e.g., exposure to a dominant male) can produce several potentially damaging changes, including increased defensive behavior and decreased social and sexual behaviors; higher circulating concentrations of stress hormones and impairment of brain mechanisms that normally limit stress hormone action; impairment of brain and peripheral mechanisms of male sex hormone production; and widespread changes in brain neurochemical systems. The authors review research using a visible burrow system that allows social interactions. Importantly, this system provides an ecologically valid assessment tool of aggressive behavior. They also document dominance relationships, as well as subordination relationships in response to exposure to various stressors. Chapter 12 also focuses on the analysis of the role of previous (early or recent) stressful experience in modulating or exacerbating the response to subordination.

In chapter 13, Kim L. Huhman and Aaron M. Jasnow review the mechanisms underlying "conditioned defeat." Conditioned defeat is a long-lasting and profound behavioral response following a brief defeat in the home cage of a larger, more aggressive opponent. Following the initial defeat, hamsters fail to produce normal territorial aggression, but instead display only submissive and defensive behaviors even though they are now tested in their own home cages and a smaller, nonaggressive intruder is used as the opponent. Both glutamatergic and GABAergic neurotransmission in the amygdala can block the acquisition and expression of conditioned defeat. The role of anxietylike processes in conditioned defeat remains unspecified, but Huhman and Jasnow make this link, as well as a link to 5-HT mechanisms.

The development of aggression is discussed in chapter 14. Yvon Delville, Matt L. Newman, Joel C. Wommack, Kereshmeh Taravosh-Lahn, and M. Catalina Cervantes review the biological factors underlying the ontogeny of aggression using rodent, nonhuman primate, and human studies. For example, in male Syrian hamsters, the development of agonistic behavior during puberty is marked by a transition from play fighting to adult aggression. These behaviors are characterized by two components: the frequency and the type of attacks. First, attack frequency decreases during puberty. Second, the targets of attacks shift from the face to the lower belly and rump. In addition, the development of agonistic behavior is altered by repeated exposure to aggressive adults during puberty; subjugated hamsters develop adultlike attacks at earlier ages. Delville and coauthors also report new data showing how exposure of peripubertal hamsters to aggression or young people to bullying influences the development of aggressive behavior.

The neurobiology of aggression in children is reviewed in chapter 15 by R. James R. Blair, K. S. Peschardt, Salima Budhani, and Daniel S. Pine. They first consider two general perspectives that have received considerable attention with respect to aggression in children: the frontal lobe and fear dysfunction positions. They then describe a fundamental difficulty with these two perspectives of a general account of aggression in children, namely, that they implicitly assume all aggression is mediated by the same neural mechanisms. Blair and coauthors argue that a distinction must be made between reactive and instrumental aggression. Finally, they delineate neurobiological risk factors for reactive and instrumental aggression.

The influence of drugs of abuse on aggressive behaviors is extensively reviewed by Jill M. Grimes, Lesley Ricci, Khampaseuth Rasakham, and Richard H. Melloni, Jr., in chapter 16. They present the effects of both common drugs of abuse and drugs classified as prescribed medications. Throughout the course of their review, they present studies in a systematic fashion beginning with age of drug exposure (i.e., adult, adolescent, gestational), using different experimental aggression paradigms for examining multiple aggression subtypes (i.e., resident/intruder tests for territorial aggression, neutral arena tests for intermale aggression, and maternal aggression tests, to name a few) in several different species and strains of animals.

The psychopharmacology of human aggression is reviewed in chapter 17 by Don R. Cherek, Oleg V. Tcheremissine, and Scott D. Lane. Epidemiological studies of the use of drugs of abuse, such as alcohol, benzodiazepines, CNS stimulants, and opiates, are reviewed, and all seem to increase aggressive behaviors in people. Several laboratory models of human aggression are described, including the authors' clever *point subtraction aggression paradigm*, which unlike other models (that involve electric shocks) allows subtraction of money as the aversive stimulus. The authors then review the effects of several drugs in these laboratory models of aggression.

Finally, psychophysiology and brain mechanisms of human antisocial behavior are reviewed by Angela Scarpa and Adrian Raine in chapter 18. Based on a wide range of approaches, including genetics, biochemistry, neuropsychology, brain imaging, and psychophysiology, it has been found that biological individual differences likely predispose people to antisocial behavior in response to environmental events. The authors review the major psychophysiological findings and theories regarding antisocial behavior, with a specific focus on skin conductance, heart rate, electroencephalogram, and startle blink research. Their goal is to provide evidence of psychophysiological relationships with antisocial behavior and overview theories regarding the meaning of these relationships.

All of the chapters emphasize future directions for research on aggression and reveal important domains that have received comparatively less attention in this literature. Taken together, these chapters provide up-to-date coverage of the biology of aggression by some of the leading authorities currently working in this field. There is much interest, both generally and among behavioral biologists, in the biological mechanisms of aggressive behavior, and during this past decade remarkable advances have been made using pharmacological and genetic approaches to understanding aggression and violence. It is my hope that this book provides both a comprehensive review of previous work in this field and a guide to future research on the biology of aggression.

—*Randy J. Nelson*
June 1, 2005

Contents

Contributors

R. James R. Blair
National Institute of Mental Health
National Institutes of Heath

D. Caroline Blanchard
Department of Psychology
University of Hawaii

Robert J. Blanchard
Pacific Biomedical Research Center
University of Hawaii

Daniel M. Blonigen
Department of Psychology
University of Minnesota

Salima Budhani
National Institute of Mental Health
National Institutes of Heath

Andrew Canastar
Biobehavioral Sciences Graduate Program
Department of Psychology
University of Connecticut

M. Catalina Cervantes
Department of Psychology
University of Texas

Don R. Cherek
Human Psychopharmacology Laboratory
Department of Psychiatry and Behavioral
    Sciences
University of Texas Health Science Center

Silvana Chiavegatto
Department and Institute of Psychiatry,
    and Laboratory of Genetics
    and Molecular Cardiology, Heart
    Institute (InCor)
University of São Paulo Medical School

Elena Choleris
Laboratory of Neurobiology and Behavior
The Rockefeller University

Yvon Delville
Department of Psychology
University of Texas

Gregory E. Demas
Department of Biology, Program in Neural
    Science, and Center for the Integrative Study
    of Animal Behavior
Indiana University

Donald H. Edwards
Department of Biology and Center
  for Behavioral Neuroscience
Georgia State University

Craig F. Ferris
Center for Comparative Neuroimaging
University of Massachusetts Medical School

Eric W. Fish
Department of Psychology
Tufts University

Stephen C. Gammie
Department of Zoology
University of Wisconsin

Wolfgang Goymann
Department of Biological Rhythms and Behavior
Max Planck Institute for Ornithology

Jill M. Grimes
Department of Psychology
Northeastern University

Jens Herberholz
Department of Biology and Center for
  Behavioral Neuroscience
Georgia State University

Kim L. Huhman
Department of Psychology
Georgia State University

Aaron M. Jasnow
Laboratory of Neurobiology and Behavior
The Rockefeller University

Jay R. Kaplan
Department of Pathology
Wake Forest University School of Medicine

Robert F. Krueger
Department of Psychology
University of Minnesota

Scott D. Lane
Human Psychopharmacology Laboratory
Department of Psychiatry and Behavioral
  Sciences
University of Texas Health Science Center

Joseph S. Lonstein
Program in Neuroscience and Department
  of Psychology
Michigan State University

Francis E. Lotrich
Department of Psychiatry
Western Psychiatric Institute and Clinic

Shi-Fang Lu
Department of Biological Sciences
Lehigh University

Stephen B. Manuck
Behavioral Physiology Laboratory
University of Pittsburgh

Stephen C. Maxson
Biobehavioral Sciences Graduate Program
Department of Psychology
University of Connecticut

Richard H. Melloni, Jr.
Department of Psychology
Northeastern University

Klaus A. Miczek
Departments of Psychology, Psychiatry,
  Pharmacology, and Neuroscience
Tufts University

Ignacio T. Moore
Department of Biology
Virginia Polytechnic Institute and State
  University

Randy J. Nelson
Departments of Psychology
  and Neuroscience
The Ohio State University

Matt L. Newman
Department of Psychology
University of Texas

Masayoshi Nomura
Laboratory of Neurobiology and Behavior
The Rockefeller University

Sonoko Ogawa
Laboratory of Neurobiology and Behavior
The Rockefeller University

Karina S. Peschardt
National Institute of Mental Health
National Institutes of Heath

Donald Pfaff
Laboratory of Neurobiology and Behavior
The Rockefeller University

Daniel S. Pine
National Institute of Mental Health
National Institutes of Heath

Adrian Raine
Department of Psychology
University of Southern California

Khampaseuth Rasakham
Department of Psychology
Northeastern University

Lesley Ricci
Department of Psychology
Northeastern University

Angela Scarpa
Department of Psychology
Virginia Polytechnic Institute and State
  University

Neal G. Simon
Department of Biological Sciences
Lehigh University

Todd Sperry
Department of Biology
University of Washington

Kereshmeh Taravosh-Lahn
Department of Psychology
University of Texas

Oleg V. Tcheremissine
Human Psychopharmacology Laboratory
Department of Psychiatry and Behavioral
  Sciences
University of Texas Health Science Center

Douglas W. Wacker
Department of Biology
University of Washington

John C. Wingfield
Department of Biology
University of Washington

Joel C. Wommack
Department of Psychology
University of Texas

PART I

GENES

1

Genetic Aspects of Aggressions in Nonhuman Animals

Stephen C. Maxson & Andrew Canastar

This review could, but does not, consider what is known about the genetics of aggression in different animal species. Rather, it explores several contextual issues for developing more fully a comparative genetics of aggression in animals. After describing the kinds of aggression in animals, we relate aspects of the evolution and development of aggression to the study of its genetics. This is followed by a consideration of species that are being or could be used to begin a comparative genetics of aggression. A comparative genetics of aggression is most relevant to developing animal models for human aggression.

Types of Aggression in Animals

Here, we only consider the types of aggression known as agonistic behavior. Scott (1966) defined agonistic behavior as "behavior patterns having the common functions of adaptations to situations involving physical conflict between members of the same species." These include offensive, defensive, and parental aggression. Thus, this does not include Brain's (1979) categories of predatory aggression or reproductive termination (infanticide).

Blanchard and Blanchard (1984, 1988, and ch. 12 in this volume) have cogently argued that (a) across species, including humans, offensive and defensive motor patterns differ, (b) offense and defense serve different functions, and (c) defensive attack is more likely to cause serious injury than offensive attack. They suggest that defensive behaviors serve the functions of protecting one's self from injury by others and that offensive behaviors serve the functions of obtaining and retaining survival and reproductive resources. Furthermore, it has been proposed that each of these two broad classes of aggressive behavior (at least in mammals) has motivational systems with neural homologies across species (Adams, 1979, 1980; Blanchard & Blanchard, 1988). Parental aggression by female, male, or both parents serves the function of defending progeny from injury by conspecifics and predators. Where appropriate, the genetics of each type of agonistic behavior in both sexes should be, as discussed below, investigated in all animals used in studies of the genetics of aggression.

Evolution of Aggression

For a behavior to evolve by natural selection, its reproductive benefits must exceed its reproductive costs. The potential reproductive benefits of aggression have been discussed above. They are high. The potential reproductive costs are high, too—for many species, these include risk of injury and death. As a consequence, many species have evolved a sequence of interactions during one-on-one agonistic conflict, which can resolve the conflict without escalating to a fight, with the risk of injury and death (Archer, 1988).

For example, male red deer compete with one another during the rutting season for control of female herds (Clutton-Brock, Albon, Gibson, & Guinness, 1979). The male that controls the herd has exclusive mating rights. Agonistic encounters begin with roaring over and over up to 3,000 times a day. This can resolve the dispute, with one male leaving and the other controlling the female herd. If the conflict is not resolved in this way, then it escalates to the two males walking side by side, with each male making himself look as big as possible. If this does not resolve the dispute, then it escalates to a fight, with the males locking horns while pushing and shoving one another. There is a grave potential for injury and even death in this last stage, which will always resolve the conflict. Across species, it appears that two factors are involved in determining whether or not the conflict escalates. These are resource holding power (RHP) and resource value (RV). RHP is essentially fighting ability, and the male with the large RHP usually wins the conflict. Conflicts usually escalate when RHP or RV or both are the same for both contestants.

This has relevance to research on the genetics of aggression. Most of these studies in mice and other animals are concerned with the last phase of an agonistic conflict, the escalated fight (see Miczek, Fish, & DeBold, 2003, and Nyberg, Sandnabba, Schalkwyk, & Sluyter, 2004). We suggest that all phases of the agonistic conflict should be considered in genetic studies and that this should include an assessment of the genetics of RHP and RV and how each animal in the encounter evaluates these. There is one study with mice that incorporates this approach (Parmigiani, Ferrari, & Palanza, 1998). It was proposed that males with and without successful fighting experience differed in RHP and that males mating and cohabiting with females would have higher RV to defend than males that were singly housed.

Development of Aggression

A variety of environmental and experiential factors influence the development of agonistic behaviors. Evidence for these effects and their role in the development of agonistic behaviors across a range of species is discussed in Huntingford and Turner (1987) and in Delville, Newman, Wommack, Taravosh-Lahn, and Cervantes (ch. 14 in this volume). Such environmental factors appear to have more effects on the development of the occurrence and intensity of aggression than on its motor patterns. Regardless, they may have a critical role in adjusting the level of aggressive behavior to local environment conditions. In this context, it would be interesting to know whether they act on RHP, RV, or their assessment.

The effects of genetic variants on aggression are often dependent on environmental or experiential parameters, as has been shown repeatedly for mice. These include effects on aggression of genetic background, maternal environment, peer environment, early experience, sexual experience, wins and defeats, observational learning, type of opponent, and type of test (see reviews by Maxson, 1992, and Maxson & Canastar, 2003). For example, handling affects the aggressive behavior of male mice of the C57BL/10 strain, but has no effect on aggressive behavior of male mice from two other strains (Ginsburg & Allee, 1942; Ginsburg & Jummonville, 1967; Scott, 1942). The study by Ginsburg and Allee also showed that C57BL/10 males were aggressive in the presence but not in the absence of a female mouse. This may reflect a genetic sensitivity to the value of this reproductive resource. Additionally, mice of the aggressive BALB/c strain became pacific after a series of defeats, whereas mice of the C57BL/10 strain became aggressive after a series of wins. This may reflect learned changes in RHP of each strain. We suggest that such interactions of genes and environments may be ways to adjust aggression levels of genetic variants to the local circumstances and that they should be investigated across a range of species.

Comparative Genetics of Aggression

Elsewhere, Maxson (2003) has suggested that we should seek to develop a comparative genetics of adaptive behaviors, with the goal of finding general principles relating genes and environments across animal species. This can and should be done for aggressive behavior.

Such a comparative genetics has several advantages. It will identify (a) genes with effects on aggression across many species and those with effects restricted to a few or even one species, (b) neural mechanisms of aggression based on these genes involved in many species or limited to a few or even one species, (c) interactions of genes and environments that affect the development and expression of aggression across many species and ones that are restricted for a few or even one species, and (d) the role of these genetic and environmental interactions across species in the evolution of adaptive aggressive behaviors. This strategy will also provide a more substantial base for developing hypotheses about human aggression derived from animal models.

As a beginning of a comparative genetics of aggression, here we consider some aspects of the genetics and aggressive behaviors of a few invertebrates (fruit flies and honeybees) and vertebrates (fish [sticklebacks and zebra fish], birds [chickens], and mammals [rodents, carnivores, and primates]). These were chosen on the basis of their potential for genetic analyses and/or because of an existing literature on their aggression.

In general, three approaches are used in research that seeks to identify the genes with effects on one or more types of aggression in males and females of a species. One seeks to map genes with effects on one or more types of aggression in males or females to their chromosomal location. This detects the genetic variants with effects on a type of aggression in males or females that exist in the species. The other mutates a gene, and the variants in this gene are tested for effects on a type of aggression in males or females. Potentially, this can detect all of the genes that affect a type of aggression in males or females. Last, strain or phenotype differences in brain expression of many genes across development can (with gene chips) be assessed in relation to a type of aggression in males or females. This can detect both variant and nonvariant genes, as well as identify systems of interacting gene with effects on the development of aggression.

Invertebrates

It appears that aggressive behavior is widespread across the invertebrate phyla (Huntingford & Turner, 1987). It has been documented in Cniderians, Annelids, Mollusks, Echinoderms, and Arthropods. But only the insects (an Arthropod class) have been the focus of genetic studies. Two of these are considered in more detail.

Fruit Flies

Recently, the aggressive behavior of fruit flies has been detailed (Chen, Lee, Bowens, Huber, & Kravitz, 2002). Here we briefly focus on several important aspects of this work.

First, the aggression test involves competition over resources. The agonistic encounters occur in the presence of food and a female. This should enable the manipulation of RV in these studies.

Second, there is a sequence of well-described interactions that progress from low-intensity behaviors to escalated fight with potential for injury. These steps allow the opponents to acquire information about each other's RHP. This should enable the detection of genetic and environmental effects on the full sequence of the agonistic encounter, not just the escalated fight.

Third, Chan, Nilsen, and Kravitz (2003) have described the agonistic behavior of females. Thus, sex differences in the genetics and development of aggression can be studied.

Fourth, there are at least 471 species of Hawaiian *Drosophila*, and about 1,000 to 2,000 species worldwide. Much is known about the taxonomy, phylogeny, ecology, and behavior of these species (Parsons, 1973). As genes with effects on aggression are identified and characterized for *D. melanogaster*, their role in the aggression of other species can be studied with the goal of understanding the evolutionary genetics of *Drosophila* aggression.

Fifth, there are the well-known genetic advantages of *Drosophila* (Sokolowski, 2001). Its DNA (160 megabases or Mb, on 4 chromosome pairs) was sequenced in 2000. There are many techniques for mapping genes to *Drosophila* chromosomes, and there are many approaches to making and rescuing genetic mutants, as well as to tracing their developmental effects. All of this should lead to the identification of all of the genes that can cause variation in fruit fly aggression and to successfully tracing the gene effects from protein to behavior.

Honeybees

Honeybees are eusocial insects with haplodiplod sex determination. Females are diploid and males are haploid. Females but not males show agonistic behaviors. Aggression occurs in both the reproductive queen and nonreproductive workers. The DNA (200 Mb) of the 32 chromosome pairs of the honeybee is now being sequenced (http://hgsc.bcm.tmc.edu/projects/honeybee/).

Some workers (about 15% of them) specialize at about 15 days of age in guarding the nest from invasion by honeybees from other nests or by various predators and thieves, and some of these guard bees at about 19 days of age sting such intruders. In the act of stinging, they usually die. In crosses of Africanized and European colonies, three quantitative trait loci (QTLs) (chromosomal regions) with effects on stinging behavior have been detected (Aerchavaleta-Velasco, Gregg, & Emore, 2003; Guzman-Novoa, Hunt, Uribe, Smith, & Aerchavaleta-Velasco, 2002). These are Stings 1, 2, and 3. Sting 1 affects both guarding and stinging behaviors and Stings 2 and 3 affect only stinging behaviors. Also, it appears that the role of guard or stinging worker is at least in part genetically determined, as it depends on having appropriate alleles of Stings 1, 2, and 3.

In the spring, a colony usually divides (Gould & Gould, 1995). The old queen leaves with about half the colony. Before that, the workers have prepared several brood cells for raising new queens. When one of these emerges, she kills the others still in the cells and fights to the death any that have already emerged. This behavior may depend on genes expressed in queens and not in workers. This differential gene expression could be assessed with gene chips, as has already been done for the transformation from nurse to foraging worker. It has been shown that there is in foraging workers (as compared to nursing workers) an increase in brain expression of the period (Bloch, Toma, & Robinson, 2001) and the foraging (Ben-Shahar, Robichon, Sokolowski, & Robinson, 2002) genes, among many others (Whitfield, Cziko, & Robinson, 2003).

The high cost and lethal aggression of workers and queens raises some interesting issues about inclusive fitness, kin selection, and aggression (Hamilton, 1964). This is relevant when a gene decreases the fitness of the individual (as occurs in honeybee workers) but increases the fitness of one or more relatives (as occurs in their sister, the queen). In honeybees, the workers are sterile. Moreover, the guard stingers die in defending the nest and the queen. Here, the reproductive cost of aggression to the worker is balanced by benefits to the queen, her sister. In other species, the high cost to the individual of an escalated fight may also be compensated for by a reproductive benefit to relatives.

Inclusive fitness and kin selection theories suggest that fighting among relatives should be attenuated. But this does not happen among queens that share between 75 and 50% of their genes. It may be that when the RV

is very high for both individuals, genetic similarity does not inhibit aggression among relatives. Here only the winner of the fight between queens will reproduce. This may also account for siblicide in some birds and mammals (Dugatkin, 2004). For example, there is siblicide in egrets where the resource is food and in spotted hyena females where the survivor can achieve the mother's clan status.

Aggression among new queens and nest guarding by workers occur in other eusocial hymenoptera, including ants (Holldobler & Wilson, 1994). Many species of ants attack and raid the nests of the same or different species of ants. There are 12,000 known species of eusocial insects, with 11 independent origins in the hymenoptera. As genes are identified with effects on aggression in honeybees, it will be possible to investigate the effects of these across the hymenoptera and other eusocial insects.

Vertebrates

Aggressive behavior is widespread across the vertebrate phyla (Huntingford & Turner, 1987) and has been documented in fish, amphibians, reptiles, birds, and mammals. But to our knowledge no genetic studies have been conducted with amphibians or reptiles.

Fish

Sticklebacks

Both male and female three-spined sticklebacks (*Gasterosteus aculeatus*) are highly aggressive as reproductive adults. Males fight with males for access to females and sometimes females fight with females for access to males. Nonreproductive adults, subadults, and juveniles also can be aggressive. One study has investigated whether the various types of aggression in these sticklebacks are genetically correlated, with some genes causing variation in more than one type of aggression (Baker, 1994).

A series of double or two-way selection studies have been conducted. Fish were selected over 3 generations for one type of aggression and tested each generation for that and another type of aggression. There was selection for high and low levels of juvenile aggressiveness of both sexes, for territorial aggression of adult males and females, and for dominance. A random control line was also maintained. The base population was composed of wild sticklebacks from a stream in the Netherlands. For the aggression test, a same-sex, same-age opponent was placed in a glass tube or plastic chamber in the home tank, and the duration of bumping and biting was recorded for 5 min. Dominance was based on a round-robin paired test among 15 males.

Selection was successful for all but the high line of adult male territorial aggression. This indicates that even with adaptive traits, such as these types of aggression, genetic variability can remain in the population and contribute to individual differences in aggression. Also, there were significant genetic correlations between juvenile and adult aggression of each sex and between territorial aggression and dominance in males. These genetic correlations indicate that variation in two traits is due in part to variation in the same genes. This may constrain the evolution of each kind of aggression. Selective effects on one type of aggression should influence the other types. In other words, because of the genetic correlation among types of aggression, selective effects on one will cause generational changes in another.

We know little or nothing about genetic correlations for different kinds of aggression in other species. However, it is critical to understanding the effects of reproductive costs and benefits on species aggressive behaviors and the underlying genetics.

Zebra Fish

Although selective breeding studies, such as those with stickleback, can show that aggression is heritable in an animal species and that the same genes can affect more than one kind of aggression, it cannot identify the individual genes with effects on aggression. It has been suggested that zebra fish could be used for this purpose (Gerlai, 2003).

Zebra fish have been used to identify genes with effects on neural and brain development. These fish do well in captivity and a single spawning can yield hundreds of progeny. Single gene variants can be and have been produced with the chemical mutagen ethyl nitrosourea (Guo, 2004). Males are exposed to the mutagen. Dominant mutants can be detected in the F1 generation, and the recessive mutants can be identified in the F3 generations.

A test of territorial aggression has been proposed that could be used as a mutant screen. Several aggressive behaviors would be measures in response to seeing the subject's image in a mirror. These are fin erection display (erection of dorsal, caudal, pectoral, and anal fins), undulating body movements, slaps of the caudal fin, and attacks (short bouts of fast swimming directed at an opponent, sometimes accompanied by an open mouth and biting).

A mutagenesis approach can potentially detect all of the genes across the 25 chromosomes of the zebra fish that could affect variation in these measures of aggression. The cell and neural biology of the zebra fish are well developed, which should facilitate tracing the pathway from each gene to behavior.

Once genes are identified with effects on aggression in this teleost fish, the effects of their homologues on aggression in other fish could be studied.

Birds

Surprisingly, there is very little genetic research on aggression in birds. It would be interesting to compare the genetics of aggression in polygynous species with that in polyandrous species. In polygynous species, males fight one another for reproductive access to females, whereas in polyandrous species, females fight one another for reproductive access to males (Dugatkin, 2004). It would also be of interest to know whether the genes involved in song learning of monogamous birds were involved in their territorial aggression. The experience of hearing one's own species song, but not other species songs, increases the expression of genes for transcription factors in zebra finch and in canary brains (Mello, Vicario, & Clayton, 1992). The songs of such birds are the initial part of their sequences of agonistic behaviors toward intruders. But most of the research on the genetics of aggression in birds has been with domestic chickens. In these, there is aggression in males and females to achieve and maintain status in dominance hierarchies. Selective breeding and strain differences in chickens suggest that the aggressive behaviors of female and male chickens are heritable (for a review, see Craig & Muir, 1998). In one study, selection for male aggression and dominance had a correlated effect on female aggression and dominance, suggesting that some of the same genes affect these behaviors in male and female chickens (Craig, Ortman, & Gujl, 1965). Also, there have been some recent studies to map regions of chromosomes (QTLs) that affect variability in the pecking of one bird by another (Buitenhuis et al., 2003; Kjaer & Sorensen, 1997). The search for genes with effects on aggression in domestic chicken will be facilitated by having a genetic map for this species (Burt & Cheng, 1998) and by the DNA sequencing (1,000 Mb across 39 chromosome pairs) of the red jungle fowl, which is the ancestor of the domestic chicken (Burt & Pourquie, 2003; http://www.nhgri.nih.gov/11510730). Once genes with effects on aggression are identified in chickens, effects of their homologues on aggression in other bird species could be studied.

Mammals

Rodents, carnivores, and primates are considered in this section. Some information on the genetics of aggression for horses, cattle, swine, and sheep can be found in Huntingford and Turner (1987) and in Grandin (1998).

Rodents

Mice Both male and female mice show offensive and defensive aggression. Aggression by males is primarily territorial; male mice exclude other males from the territory or deme and dominate males within a deme. Aggression by females is both territorial and parental. They guard food and protect progeny by attacking intruding males and females. In the deme, adult females are usually both lactating and pregnant, both of which conditions facilitate parental aggression against an intruder.

In the laboratory, two paradigms are widely used in genetics research on mouse aggression. These are the resident-intruder test, in which an intruder is placed into the resident's home cage, and the neutral cage test, in which both opponents are placed into a cage other than the home cage. These tests may model encounters in the deme or home territory and outside the deme, respectively. Studies on maternal aggression occur in the home cage with pups present. It is also usual to weight match opponents in these tests, which could facilitate escalation of encounters to fights.

The search for genes with effects on aggression in male and female mice has been and will be greatly facilitated by the sequencing of its DNA (2,600 Mb), a dense gene map of its 20 chromosome pairs, knockout and chemical mutagenesis, and transgenic rescue of mutants (Maxson, 2003).

Male Aggression. The first studies on male aggression of inbred strains of mice were published more than 60 years ago (Ginsburg & Allee, 1942; Scott, 1942). Since 1942, many studies of strain differences in mu-

rine aggression have been published. There have also been three selective breeding studies of male mouse aggression (for a review of the literature on inbred and selected strains, see Miczek, Maxson, Fish, & Faccidomo, 2001). Taken together, these studies provide initial evidence that some aspects of male mouse aggression are heritable, but do not identify the genes that can or do cause variation in male mouse aggression. However, 36 of the genes that contribute to murine aggression by males have been identified to date, mostly using knockout mice (see review by Maxson & Canastar, 2003). Research on several of these is described in detail elsewhere in the volume (see Chiavegatto, Demas, & Nelson, ch. 6 in this volume, and Simon & Lu, ch. 9 in this volume). Here we consider some other aspects of the genetics of mouse aggression, especially some conceptual and methodological issues.

(A) The Y Chromosome (Male-Specific Part or Non-Pseudoautosomal Region) and Aggression. The DBA/1 and C57BL/10 Y chromosomes (male-specific part or non-pseudoautosomal region) differ in effect on offensive aggression. The differential effect of these Y chromosomes depends, at least in part, on the genotype of the opponent. When the congenic strains, DBA/1 and DBA1.C57BL10-Y, are tested in a homogeneous set test, the strains differ in aggressive behavior, but when they are tested against a DBA/1 opponent, they do not differ in aggressive behavior (Maxson, Didier-Erickson, & Ogawa, 1989). Similar effects of the opponent have been reported for the CBA/H and NZB Y chromosome pair (Guillot, Carlier, Maxson, & Roubertoux, 1995). The DBA/1 and C57BL/10 Y chromosomes have differential effects on a urinary odor type. Mice can tell the difference between the urinary odor types of DBA/1 and DBA1.C57BL10-Y males (Monahan, Yamazaki, Beauchamp, & Maxson, 1993). This Y chromosomal effect on odor type is independent of adult testosterone (Schellinck, Monahan, Brown, & Maxson, 1993). Also, DBA/1 but not DBA1.C57BL10-Y males appear to show differential aggressive behavior to these urinary odor types (Monahan & Maxson, 1998). There are at least 12 genes on the mouse Y chromosome (Mitchell, 2000) and some of these are expressed in brain (Xu, Burgoyne, & Arnold, 2002). These are candidates for the Y effect on aggression and the differential response to Y odor types.

These findings on opponent effects raise two general issues: (a) the investigation of the mechanisms and functions of this and other opponent effects and (b) the recognition that effects of other genetic variants on aggression in mice and other species might depend on the type of opponent.

The differential effect of the DBA/1 and C57BL/10 Y chromosomes also depends on strain background. This occurs on a 100 or 50% DBA/1 background but not on a C57BL/10 background (Maxson et al., 1989; Maxson, Ginsburg, & Trattner, 1979). For example, the congenic pair DBA/1 and DBA1.C57BL10-Y differ in aggressive behaviors, but the congenic pair C57BL/10 and C57BL10.DBA1-Y do not. Similar effects of background on aggression are seen for the CBA/H and NZB (Guillot et al., 1995), the CBA/Fa and C57BL/6 (Stewart, Manning, & Batty, 1980), and the SAL and LAL (Sluyter, van Oortmerssen, & Koolhouse, 1994) pairs of Y chromosomes. These findings raise three general issues for research on the genetics of aggression in mice and other species. First, how common are these epistatic interactions? Second, what are the mechanisms of these epistatic interactions? Third, what effects of other genetic variants on aggression in mice and other species might depend on the genetic background?

(B) The Y Chromosome (Recombining or Pseudoautosomal Region) and Aggression. Two groups have shown that there is an effect of the recombining or pseudoautosomal region of the Y chromosome on aggression (Roubertoux et al., 1994; Sluyter, van Oortmerssen, et al., 1994). There is a single gene in this region of the murine Y chromosome, and it codes for the enzyme steroid sulfatase. It is expressed in brain, and it may regulate neurosteroids. For the CBA/H versus NZB Y chromosome, the effect of this region occurs with nonisolated males paired with an A/J opponent in a neutral cage (Le Roy et al., 1999; Roubertoux & Carlier, 2003). There is no effect of variants in this region of the Y chromosome when the mice are isolated before testing, in a resident-intruder test, and the opponent is not an A/J male.

There are similar findings for the strain correlations between the size of the hippocampal mossy fibers and the proportion of attacking males across several strains. The strain correlation is $r = -0.86$ when the test is in the resident's cage, when the resident has been isolated for 13 days, and when the opponent is an A/J male (Guillot, Roubertoux, & Crusio, 1994). This strain correlation becomes zero when the test is in a neutral cage, or when the tested mouse is not isolated or isolated for a day, or when the tested mouse and its opponent are the same strain (Roubertoux, Le Roy, Mortaud, Perez-Diaz, & Tordjman, 1999). Also, in this study, a general factor for initiating attack was not revealed across 11 inbred strains for four groups that differed in one or more of the following: (a) isolated versus nonisolated test males, (b) resident-intruder test versus neutral cage test, and (c) an opponent of the same versus a different strain as the tested male. Also, for the four groups, there were unique strain correlations with measures of neurotransmitters or of gonadal hormones.

These findings raise several general issues. First, genetic effects on aggression in mice and other species depend on several nongenetic parameters. Second, this implies that a gene variant may not have the same effects across these nongenetic parameters. Third, how do genetic effects in laboratory tests for mice or other species relate to genetic effects on aggression in feral conditions, where the nongenetic parameters may differ between the laboratory and the wild?

(C) Short and Long Attack Latency Mice. About 1971, feral *Mus domesticus* were trapped in a mansion near Groningen, the Netherlands. Mice descended from these were the foundation stock for selective breeding for short and long attack latencies (van Oortmerssen & Baker, 1981). After 30 generations of selection, male mice of the long attack latency line (LAL) rarely attacked and male mice of the short attack latency line (SAL) consistently attacked. The opponent was a male of the Mas-Gro strain. The encounters occurred on a familiar, but not the home, part of the test cage. The successful selection for attack latency indicates that, at least in male mice, it is heritable, and that there was genetic variability with effects on attack latency in the wild population.

Studies of feral mice indicated that these occurred in two behavioral morphs, short and long attack latency males (van Oortmerssen & Busser, 1989). It was suggested that this was the result of each morph being adaptive in different phases of the population cycle in wild mice. Within a settled population or deme, selection favors for a while short attack latencies. Males with short attack latencies are more likely to dominate the deme and breed. But as the attack latencies get very short, these males attack not only intruding males but also females and progeny; this results in the collapse of the deme and the dispersion of its members. Now long attack latencies are favored in establishing new demes. Thus, extreme aggression is constrained by its effect on population dynamics, with shifting selective advantage for extreme aggression or extreme pacificity.

It would be of interest to know how many and which genes are involved in this dimorphism, as well as the mechanism of their effect. There is a minor contribution of the two regions of the Y chromosome (Sluyter, van Oortmerssen, et al., 1994). Recent studies using gene chips have found differential expression of 191 genes in the hippocampus of SAL and LAL mice (Feldker, Datson, Veenema, Meulmeester, et al., 2003; Feldker, Datson, Veenema, Proutski, et al., 2003). Some but not all of these genes may be involved in the difference in size of the hippocampal mossy fibers of SALs and LALs (Sluyter, Jamot, van Oortmerssen, & Crusio, 1994). However, artificial selection was too rapid and heritability too modest for variants of all 191 genes to be involved in the difference between SAL and LAL mice in behavior and biology.

There are some general issues raised by these studies. First, whether aggression is adaptive depends on the level of aggression. Second, the same genes can affect both adaptive and nonadaptive aggression.

(D) Competitive Aggression. Most recent studies of the genetics of aggression in males take place in the resident's cage or a neutral cage in the absence of a resource such as food or a female. But earlier, there was research on strain differences for what was called competitive aggression. In these studies, mice were food deprived and a standard pellet of food was placed in the cage. Both male and female mice displayed competitive aggression, and within a strain, there were no sex differences in competitive aggression. This suggests that the same genes can cause variation in this type of offensive aggression for both males and females. In one study the rank order of offensive aggression was compared in a neutral cage test and a competitive test (Hahn, 1983). It was not the same, suggesting that some of the genes causing variation in offense have effects in one test but not in the other. Also, Adams (1980) proposed that the olfactory system is involved in sex recognition-mediated resident-intruder or neutral cage offense by males, but that it has no role in competitive aggression of males and females. This may account for different genetic effects on territorial and competitive aggression in males and for the same genetic effects on competitive aggression of males and females.

To date, the competitive test has not been used with gene knockout mutants. We suggest that it should be, for a more rounded understanding of the genetics of mouse aggression. We also suggest that the competitive test may be of use in studying the role of RV in the escalation of encounters.

(E) Sexual Aggression. Male mice are often characterized as nonaggressive toward females (Mackin-

tosh, 1970; Maxson, 1999; Miczek et al., 2001). However, there are a few reports indicating that female mice can be the targets of male aggression. Male mice of various inbred strains, two sets of lines selected for male aggression, and laboratory-bred wild mice exhibit this behavior that is genotype dependent and can be modified by sexual and aggressive experiences (Benus, Den Daas, Koolhaas, & van Oortmerssen, 1990; Canastar & Maxson, 2003; Mugford & Nowell, 1971; Rowe & Redfern, 1969; Sandnabba & Korpela, 1994). To have a more complete picture of the genetics of aggression in mice, there should be a search for genes with effects on this type in comparison to other types of mouse aggression.

(F) Defensive Aggression. Defensive aggression has the adaptive function of protecting not only against attacks by conspecifics but also from predators. On this basis a Mouse Defense Test Battery was developed (Blanchard, Griebel, & Blanchard, 2001; see also Blanchard & Blanchard, ch. 12). When exposed to a potentially threatening stimulus, such as an anesthetized rat, mice can show risk assessment, defensive threat and attack, freezing, and flight. This battery has been used to study the effects of drugs on defense, but it has not been used in genetic studies to date. We suggest that it should be.

There have been a few studies of the genetics of defense in conspecific encounters. Potentially, one of these is a study of different aggression tests in the Turku Aggressive (TA) and Turku Nonaggressive (TNA) selected lines (Nyberg et al., 2004). As residents or as intruders, the TNA males are more aggressive than TA males in a resident-intruder paradigm. If the attacks by intruders were defensive, then this finding would suggest that some genetic variants enhance both offense and defense. However, knockout mutants of two genes appear to increase offense and decrease defense. These are knockouts of the genes coding for α-calcium calmodulin kinase II (Chen, Rainne, Greene, & Tonegawa, 1994) and Fyn tyrosine kinase (Miyakawa, Yagi, Takao, & Niki, 2001).

Because defense is a significant part of agonistic behavior in mice and other species, we strongly recommend that tests for this be included in chemical and knockout mutagenesis screens.

Female Aggression. Once upon a time it was thought that female mice were not aggressive. But it was subsequently shown that female laboratory mice could be aggressive when pregnant or lactating (see Gammie & Lonstein, ch. 11 in this volume). There are strain differences in maternal aggression, which are mediated by ovarian hormones (Svare, 1989). Additionally, some inbred strain females (Ogawa & Makino, 1981) and some wild female mice (Ebert, 1983) are aggressive against males in resident-intruder tests when the females are neither pregnant nor lactating. Wild mice were a base population for the successful selective breeding of high and low female aggression lines, indicating that there was genetic variation in the wild population for this trait in female mice. There was also a correlated effect of this selective breeding on maternal aggression during lactation against an intruder female (Ebert, 1983). This suggests that some of the same genetic variants affect both kinds of female aggression. Regardless, it has been suggested that maternal aggression in mice is offensive or defensive depending on how likely an intruder is to kill pups (Parmigiani, Palanza, Rodgers, & Ferrari, 1999).

There has been a lively discussion as to whether the same genes cause variation in the territorial aggression of males and females. Two selection studies suggest that they do (Hood & Cairns, 1988; Lagerspetz & Lagerspetz, 1983) and two selection studies suggest that they do not (Ebert, 1983; van Oortmerssen & Baker, 1981). Some knockout mutants cause only male aggression to vary, some cause both to vary in the same direction, and some cause an increase in one and a decrease in the other (see Maxson, 1999, for a review). These suggest that the correlation depends on the gene involved and its variants. Also, it may depend on the opponent. Regardless, it appears, as discussed above, that the same genes cause competitive aggression to vary in male and female mice.

Many of the issues raised for the genetics of male aggression are also relevant to the genetics of female aggression, and the genetics of aggression in females should be as intensively and extensively studied as that in males.

Rats   Both male and female rats show offensive and defensive aggression. Within the colony, there are male and female dominance hierarchies and status is determined by wins and loses in within sex agonistic encounters. Alpha males attack and exclude intruders. Aggression by females is also parental; they protect progeny by attacking intruding males and females. In the colony, adult females are usually both lactating and pregnant. These physiological conditions facilitate maternal aggression against an intruder.

There are two main paradigms for offense and one for defense in rats. For offense, these are the resident-intruder test and the colony model (Wall, Blanchard, & Blanchard, 2003). The resident-intruder test for rats is similar to that for mice. The colony model has both males and females present, and it consists of the burrow and other spaces. One of these is the visible burrow system (see Blanchard & Blanchard, ch. 12). Offense is shown by the resident in the resident-intruder test and by the alpha male in the colony model. Defense in males and females is often studied in the Rat Defense Test Battery. Frequently a cat or cat odor is used as the stimulus (Shepherd, Flores, Rodgers, Blanchard, & Blanchard, 1992). Rats also display risk assessment, defensive threat and attack, freezing, and flight in response to such potentially threatening stimuli.

The physiology, pharmacology, and endocrinology of rat offense and defense have been well studied and characterized (see Miczek & Fish, ch. 5 in this volume, and Blanchard & Blanchard, ch. 12). Except for some strain comparisons, there have been few genetic studies of aggression in rats (see, for example, Berton, Ramos, Chaouloff, & Mormde, 1997; Fujita, Annen, & Kitaoka, 1994; Hendley, Ohlsson, & Musty, 1992). This may be about to change, as the DNA (2,750 Mb across 21 chromosome pairs) of the rat is being sequenced (Gibbs et al., 2004; http://www.hgsc.bcm.tmc.edu; Pennisi, 2004). This and a genetic map of the rat chromosomes (Levan, Stah, Klinga-Levan, Szpirer, & Szpirer, 1998) will facilitate mapping of QTLs with effects on offense and defense. It may also assist in identifying chemically induced mutants with effects on rat agonistic behavior. These genetic research programs should be modeled on those in mice. Regardless, studies could now be conducted to determine whether any of the genes with effects on mouse offense are varying in rat populations and if any of these have effects on rat offense. Also, known physiological, hormonal, and pharmacological effects on rat offense and defense may suggest genes to consider for association analysis (see Blonigen & Krueger, ch. 2 in this volume, for a discussion of this genetic method).

Voles   Prairie (*Microtus ochrogaster*) and pine (*M. pinetorum*) voles are socially monogamous and both males and females exhibit strong partner preference, joint parental care, and selective aggression toward unfamiliar intruders (Curtis & Wang, 2003). Meadow (*M. pennsylvanicus*) and montane (*M. montanus*) voles are socially promiscuous and neither males nor females exhibit much, if any, joint parental care or selective aggression. After mating, pair bonds are formed in prairie and pine voles, as well as establishment of partner preference, parental care, and selective aggression by the male. This can also be induced in male prairie voles by intracerebral ventricular infusion of arginine vasopressin (AVP) and can be blocked by a specific antagonist of the AVP receptor (Young, Wang, & Insel, 1998). The infusion of AVP has no effect on these behaviors in montane voles. Prairie and montane voles differ in the gene for the AVP receptor; there is a 428-bp insert in the promoter of the AVP gene of prairie voles but not montane voles. This insert is also present in the AVP promoter of the monogamous pine but not the promiscuous meadow vole. The insert appears to have a role in directing the distribution of the neuropeptide receptor V1a in the brain. It has been proposed that male prairie voles become, after mating, socially monogamous, parental, and selectively aggressive toward intruders because of the brain regional sensitivity to AVP. Oxytocin and its receptor appear to have a similar role in the social monogamy, parenting, and selective aggression of female prairie voles. The dopamine systems and stress hormones, such as corticosterone, also appear to have a role in the development of these behaviors in prairie voles.

It is of interest that similar neurotransmitter and behavior correlations have been observed in deer mice. *Peromycus californicus* are monogamous and *P. leucopus* are polygamous. The former have lower latencies to attack opponents in resident-intruder and neutral cage tests. But although there are species differences in distribution of AVP receptors between the monogamous and polygamous deer mice, they are not the same as those for the monogamous and promiscuous voles (Bester-Meredith, Young, & Marler, 1999).

These studies raise several issues. First, it is possible to do genetic analysis at the molecular level by species comparisons. Second, it is possible to relate mating systems to aggressive behavior and their genetics by species comparisons. Third, some aspects of behavioral evolution may be primarily due to effects of a single gene. Fourth, it is unfortunate that the vole genome is not being sequenced. This would facilitate genetic analysis within the species. However, there are genetic maps of the chromosomes of some vole species (Nesterova, Mazurok, Rubtsova, Isaenko, & Zakian, 1998). Regardless, studies could now be conducted to determine whether any of the genes with effects on mouse offense are varying in vole populations and if any of these have effects on offense in male or female voles.

Carnivores   There are two large taxonomic groups of carnivores—canids and the felids. Canids tend to be socially monogamous and many, but not all, live in groups. Felids tend to be socially polygamous or promiscuous and territorial, and most are solitary. For each, there is a domestic species in which the genetics of aggression could potentially be studied. The DNA of dogs (about 2,500 Mb across 39 chromosome pairs) is being sequenced (Kirkness et al., 2003). Also, linkage maps are being developed for dogs (Binns, Holmes, & Breen, 1998) and cats (Menotti-Raymond et al., 1999; O'Brien, 1993).

Dogs. Dogs are descended from wolves (Scott & Fuller, 1965), and they were domesticated about 14,000 years ago (Budiansky, 2000). Wolves live in packs with a dominance hierarchy for males and for females. Aggression occurs within sex to obtain and retain status. The alpha male also uses aggression to restrict mating of other males, and the alpha female uses aggression to restrict mating of other females. Much, but not all, of this aggressive behavior involves threat displays rather than physical attacks with bites. However, it has been reported that intraspecific fighting accounts for 35 to 65% of adult mortality (Mech, Adams, Meir, Burch, & Dale, 1998). Since their initial domestication, dogs have been selectively bred to develop the many breeds with differing characteristics, including behavior. There are effects on their social behavior, including aggression. Some dogs were selectively bred to fight other dogs as a sport. Two aspects of the genetics of dog aggression have been studied to at least some degree: (a) the aggressive interactions of dogs mainly as pups or juveniles and (b) attacks against humans.

From 1952 to 1965, a large study was conducted at the Jackson Laboratory on the genetics of dog behavior (Scott & Fuller, 1965). The behaviors of five dog breeds and their F1s and derived generations were studied. The breeds were beagles, cocker spaniels, fox terriers, Shetland sheepdogs, and basenji. Aggression and dominance were mostly investigated in puppy-puppy relationships across development.

In one test, pairs of puppies of the same litter competed for food in the bone-in-pen test from 2 weeks of age. Each puppy was tested with each littermate for control of the bone. Puppies and adults often growl and bark when given a meat-covered bone in the presence of another dog. For all breeds, little dominance had developed at 5 weeks of age; by 11 weeks of age, all breeds had shown an increase in the proportion of fully dominant individuals. After that, there was an increase in the proportion of dominants in the fox terriers, but not in the other breeds. Actual fights, mostly with noise and struggle but no bites, occurred in many of these dominance tests. During the dominance tests, there were very few fights or attacks in fox terriers, Shelties' fighting decreased with age, and basenjis' fighting increased with age. However, outside these tests, the fox terriers were so aggressive by 5 weeks of age that litters had to be separated. This finding suggests that the genetics of aggression in dogs may be different in food competition situations and in social situations. Taken together, these data indicate that situation-specific aggression in dogs is heritable. No genes with effects on this in dogs have been identified.

Dog attacks on humans are a serious problem with legal consequences (Budiansky, 2000). About 5 million people are bitten by dogs in the United States every year, and about 500,000 to 1 million of these bites are serious enough to need medical attention. Some have suggested that there may be breed differences in dogs that attack people. However, there does not exist clear evidence that breed is a reliable predictor of whether a dog will bite a human (Hahn & Wright, 1998). They also discuss the statistical and methodological issues in determining this one way or another. The environmental contributions to dog attacks and bites have recently been reviewed for golden retrievers by van den Berg, Schilder, and Knol (2003).

Much progress has been made in the study of the genetics of the dog. Recently, molecular genetics has been used to classify dog breeds and their genetic distance (Parker et al., 2004). Also, the dog genome is being sequenced (Kirkness et al., 2003). But the study of its aggressive behavior lags. If not already characterized, the offensive and defensive motor patterns of dogs need to be described in the same detail as those for the domestic cat, and the environmental and experiential causes of dog offense and defense need to be analyzed. It then may be possible to identify the contributions of individual genes. These can then be related to these behaviors in other canid species.

Cats. Domestic cats are promiscuous and solitary. Both male and female cats are territorial. The territories of male cats are larger than those of female cats, and the territory of a male cat overlaps that of several female cats; this is known as a sublease territory. (Tigers have this type of territory, too.) Both male and female cats are aggressive in defending their territories against same-sex intruders. Most territorial encounters are avoided by marking the territory with scent from chin glands, food pad glands, and unburied scats and by spraying urine (males), and the use of claw marks. Male cats fight over access to estrous females. There is also maternal aggression: Female cats defend their progeny from lethal attacks by males.

There are distinct motor patterns for offense and defense in cats (Budiansky, 2002; Tabor, 2003). These include ear positions, pupillary size, vocalizations, body posture, hair fluffing or not, and tail position. In territorial disputes, intruders frequently show defensive patterns and the resident offensive patterns. Although territorial disputes are usually settled without a fight, such disputes can escalate to full fights. This usually occurs when both cats show offense patterns and when they are equally matched. Both cats will roll on the ground trying to get a good grasp on the other's chest, while kicking with their hind legs into the belly of the opponent. During courtship, a female may incite her many suitors to fight, and victorious males mate guard the estrous female.

There appears to be very little research on the biology of offense in cats. But there is substantial research on the brain systems and neurotransmitters involved in defense (Gregg, 2003). Most data are consistent with the dorsal rostral periaqueductal gray (PAG) of the midbrain as being the center that organizes, integrates, and controls all of the defensive behaviors. Neurons from the PAG project to brain stem areas involved in each of the motor patterns of defense. Also, the PAG receives input from hypothalamic, limbic, and cortical areas that modulate the intensity of the defensive behaviors. Neurotransmitters thought to be involved in these systems include serotonin (also known as 5-HT), acetylcholine, gamma-aminobutyric acid (GABA), and neurokinin (Siegel, Roeling, Gregg, & Kruk, 1999). This would appear to be an excellent system for studies to find genes with effects on defense. The effects of these genes could be readily related to the known neurobiology of defense in cats and perhaps in other vertebrates. Regrettably, the cat genome (about 2,900 Mb on 19 chromosomes) appears not to be undergoing sequencing at this time. We recommend that it should be, as was done for the dog genome. However, a genetic map of the domestic cat's chromosomes is being developed (Menotti-Raymond et al., 1999; O'Brien, 1993).

Primates There are four main groups of primates. These are the prosimians, the Old World monkeys, the New World monkeys, and the apes. Although aggressive behavior has been studied and documented in all of these four groups, both in the wild and in captivity (deWaal, 1989; Holloway, 1974), most of the genetics research on primate aggression has been on the rhesus macaque. These macaques appear to have very frequent aggressive encounters; in two captive populations, the average aggression rate was 18 acts per monkey per 10 hr of observation (deWaal, 1989). These are social monkeys, with male dispersal and female matrilocality (Strier, 2003). This has a role in the aggression of males and females. In these matrilineal societies, there is a strict female dominance hierarchy, with daughters inheriting their status from their mothers. High-ranking mothers help their juvenile daughters assert and achieve their status in agonistic encounters with other females, and when their daughters reach adult size, they can maintain their place by aggressive displays and attacks. Males usually disperse before they are capable of winning fights. Young males dispersing for the first time are usually at the bottom of the male hierarchy of the joined group. There is often a secondary dispersal when the male has reached physical maturity and can hold his own in a fight, as well as having acquired social skills that attract females. Within-group competition among males for mates inevitably leads to fights. Success in these depends not only on the individual's fighting ability but also on his coalitions with other males. Higher ranking males have larger, stronger coalitions. In the birth season, females also defend infants. The agonistic encounters between females or between males often involve both offensive and defensive displays and threats, such as wide open mouth and staring, usually by dominants, or one with ears flat and chin thrust forward with grunting, usually by subordinates. But they can and do escalate to fights with potential for injury and death. In the wild, many show signs of injury, such as scars, frayed ears, and stumpy fingers (deWaal, 1989). Also, most of the deaths of males on Cayo Santiago Island, Puerto Rico, occur from fights during the breeding season (Wilson & Boelkins, 1970).

Genetic analysis of rhesus aggressive behavior will be facilitated by the development of the genetic map of its 21 chromosome pairs (Rogers & Vandenberg, 1998; http://www.shsu.edu/~org_tgs/abstracts%202004/johnson%20abstract.htm) and by characterization of its DNA (about 3,590 Mb) sequence (http://hgsc.bcm.tmc.edu/projects/ rmacaque/).

Most genetic studies to date on the agonistic behavior of male and female rhesus macaque have focused on the role of serotonin as follows (also see Manuck, Kaplan, & Lotrich, ch. 4 in this volume). (a) Levels of 5-HIAA in cerebrospinal fluid (CSF) are a measure of serotonin turnover. 5-HIAA levels are inversely correlated with individual differences in escalated aggression of male rhesus macaques (Higley, Suomi, & Linnoila, 1996). (b) Female pigtail macaques have higher levels of 5-HIAA in CSF and lower levels of escalated attacks than female rhesus macaques (Westergaard, Suomi, Higley, & Mehlman, 1999). (c) There is a polymorphism in the gene for the serotonin transporter in rhesus macaques (Lesch, 2003). This is a 21-bp repeat polymorphism in its promoter. A long (l) and a short (s) allele of this gene differ in the numbers of this repeat. In mother-reared monkeys, there is no effect of this polymorphism on 5-HIAA concentration in CSF. In peer-raised monkeys, those with the s allele had lower 5-HIAA levels than those with the l/l genotype. (d) There are behavioral effects of this genotype interacting with the environment. Mother-reared monkeys were more likely than peer-reared ones to engage in aggression. However, peer- but not mother-reared monkeys with the s allele were more aggressive than those with the l/l genotype (Barr et al., 2003). There are many other environmental contexts that influence the aggression of primates, including rhesus macaques (Wilson, 2003). It would be of interest to know how these environmental influences interact with genotype.

These studies raise two general issues. First, the effect of the 5-HTT variant depends on the environment. Similarly, genotype-environment interactions were reported recently for human behaviors. The effect of monoamine oxidase A variants on adult antisocial behavior depends on childhood maltreatment (Caspi et al., 2002), and that of serotonin transporter variants on adult depression depends on childhood maltreatment or stressful events (Caspi et al., 2003). Such genotype and environment interactions should be studied for agonistic behaviors across species (see Edwards & Herberholz, ch. 3 in this volume). Second, everything discussed so far on the genetics of aggression fits the individual model (deWaal, 2000) in which factors such as genes act on the individual and thus facilitate or inhibit the probability of aggression. But at least for primates, there is a well-developed social context for aggressive acts, and agonistic encounters are often followed by acts of reconciliation, such a mutual grooming. For this reason, deWaal (2000) suggested a relationship model for aggression in which aggressive behavior is one of several ways of settling conflicts of

interest. This model also proposes that after an agonistic encounter, reconciliation restores cooperation
among individuals with competing interests. So far,
those working in the genetics of aggression have not
considered this model, But we suggest that it should be.

Conclusions and Future Directions

We have already discussed the implications and goals
of a comparative genetics of aggression in the context
of evolution and development. What is needed for now
are intensive genetic studies of the species indicated
above. Eventually, this should be broadened to other
species, both closely and distantly related. Only then
will we have a genetics of aggression with general principles across species that would be a firm basis for understanding the evolution, development, and mechanisms
of aggression.

However, most genetics studies on aggression in
animals are currently directed toward developing and
studying genetic variants in animals as models of escalated aggression in humans (Miczek et al., 2003;
Nyberg et al., 2004). We suggest that the following be
considered in developing and using such models. First,
any animal behavior will be, at best, both similar to and
different than that of humans. For this reason, Scott
(1984, 1989) suggested that no animal species could
serve as an exact model for human aggression. Consequently, he proposed that information should be accumulated on the various types of aggression in a wide
range of animal species. This is a comparative approach
to aggressive behavior in animals as models, an approach that we also recommend for genetic models of
human aggression. A comparative approach can identify genes, mechanisms, gene-environment interactions, and contexts with effects across many species. It
seems to us that these are more likely to have a role in
human aggression than ones limited to one or a few
species. Second, what is discovered about the genetics of aggression in an animal should be viewed as generating hypotheses about human aggression. These
hypotheses would be about what genes are involved,
how these genes have their effect, the interactions of
one gene with others, the interactions of genes and the
environment, such as nonsocial and social context, the
gene-based physiological or hormonal mechanisms,
and much more. Such hypotheses need in some way
to be tested in humans. One cannot simply assume that
what is found in another species will generalize fully
to humans. The generation and testing of these hypotheses will necessitate considerate and knowledge-
able interactions among those working on animal and
human aggression (Blanchard, Wall, & Blanchard,
2003).

References

Adams, D. B. (1979). Brain mechanisms of offense, defense and submission. *Behavioral Brain Science, 2,*
210–241.

Adams, D. B. (1980). Motivational systems of agonistic
behavior: A comparative review and neural model.
Aggressive Behavior, 4, 295–346.

Aerchavaleta-Velasco, M. E., Gregg, J. H., & Emore, C.
(2003). Quantitative trait loci that influence the expression of guarding and stinging behaviors in individual honey bees. *Behavior Genetics, 33,* 357–
364.

Archer, J. (1988). *The behavioural biology of aggression.*
New York: Cambridge University Press.

Baker, T. C. M. (1994). Genetic correlations and the
control of behaviour, exemplified by aggressiveness
in sticklebacks. *Advances in the Study of Behavior,*
23, 135–171

Barr, C. S., Newman, T. K., Becker, M. L., Parker, C. C.,
Champoux, M., Lesch, K. P., et al. (2003). The utility of the non-human primate model for studying
gene by environmental interactions in behavioral research. *Genes, Brain and Behavior, 2,* 336–340.

Ben-Shahar,Y., Robichon, A., Sokolowski, M. B., &
Robinson, G. E. (2002). Influence of gene action
across different time scales on behavior. *Science, 296,*
741–744.

Benus, R. F., Den Daas, S., Koolhaas, J. M., & van
Oortmerssen, G. A. (1990). Routine formation and
flexibility in social and non-social behaviour of aggressive and non-aggressive male mice. *Behaviour,*
112, 176–193.

Berton, O., Ramos, A., Chaouloff, F., & Mormde, P.
(1997). Behavioral reactivity to social and nonsocial
stimulations: A multivariate analysis of six inbred rat
strains. *Behavior Genetics, 27,* 155–166.

Bester-Meredith, J. K., Young, L. J., & Marler, C. A. (1999).
Species differences in paternal behavior and aggression in *peromyscus* and their associations with vasopressin immunoreactivity and receptors. *Hormones
and Behavior, 36,* 25–38.

Binns, M., Holmes, N., & Breen, M. (1998). The dog gene
map. *ILAR Journal, 39,* 177–181.

Blanchard, D. C., & Blanchard, R. J. (1984). Affect and
aggression: An animal model applied to human behavior. In R. J. Blanchard & D. C. Blanchard (Eds.),

Advances in the study of aggression (Vol. 1, pp. 1–63). New York: Academic Press.

Blanchard, D. C., & Blanchard, R. J. (1988). Ethoexperimental approaches to the biology of emotion. *Annual Review of Psychology, 39,* 43–68.

Blanchard, D. C., Griebel, G., & Blanchard, R. J. (2001). Mouse defense behaviors: Pharmacological and behavioral assay for anxiety and panic. *Neuroscience and Biobehavioral Review, 25,* 205–218.

Blanchard, R. J., Wall, P. M., & Blanchard, D. C. (2003). Problems in the study of rodent aggression. *Hormones and Behavior, 44,* 161–170.

Bloch, G., Toma, D. P., & Robinson, G. E. (2001). Behavioral rhythmicity, age, division of labor and *period* expression in the honey bee brain. *Journal of Biological Rhythm, 16,* 444–456.

Brain, P. F. (1979). *Annual research reviews: Vol. 2. Hormones and aggression.* Montreal, Ontario, Canada: Eden Press.

Budiansky, S. (2000). *The truth about dogs.* New York: Penguin.

Budiansky, S. (2002). *The character of cats.* New York: Viking.

Buitenhuis, A. J., Rodenburg, T. B., van Hierden, Y. M., Siwek, M., Cornelissen, S. J., Nieuwland, M. G., et al. (2003). Mapping quantitative trait loci affecting feather pecking behavior and stress response in laying hens. *Poultry Science, 82,* 1215–1222.

Burt, D. W., & Cheng, H. H. (1998). The chicken gene map. *ILAR Journal, 38,* 229–236.

Burt, D. W., & Pourquie, O. (2003). Chicken genome—science nugget to come soon. *Science, 300,* 1669.

Canastar, A., & Maxson, S. C. (2003). Sexual aggression in mice: Effects of strain and estrous state. *Behavior Genetics, 33,* 521–528.

Caspi, A., McClay, J., Moffitt, T. E., Mill, J., Martin, J., Craig, I. W., et al. (2002). Role of genotype in the cycle of violence in maltreated children. *Science, 297,* 851–854.

Caspi, A., Sugden, K., Moffitt, T. E., Taylor, A., Craig, I. W., Harrington, H., et al. (2003). Influence of life stress on depression: Moderation by a polymorphism in the 5–HTT gene. *Science, 301,* 291–293.

Chan, Y., Nilsen, S., & Kravitz, E. A. (2003). Aggression in female *Drosophila melanogaster.* Program No. 839.19. Abstract Viewer/Itinerary. Washington, DC: Society for Neuroscience.

Chen, C., Rainne, D. G., Greene, R. W., & Tonegawa, S. (1994). Abnormal fear response and aggressive behavior in mutant mice deficient for alpha-calcium-calmodulin kinase II. *Science, 266,* 291–294.

Chen, S., Lee, A. Y., Bowens, N. M., Huber, R., & Kravitz, E. A. (2002). Fighting in fruit flies: A model system for the study of aggression. *Proceedings of the National Academy of Sciences USA, 99,* 5664–5668.

Clutton-Brock, T. H., Albon, S., Gibson, R. M., & Guinness, F. (1979). The logical stag: Adaptive aspects of fighting in the red deer. *Animal Behaviour, 27,* 211–225.

Craig, J., & Muir, W. (1998). Genetics and behavior of chickens: Welfare and productivity. In T. Grandin (Ed.), *Genetics and the behavior of domestic animals* (pp. 265–297). New York: Academic Press.

Craig, J. V., Ortman, L. L., & Gujl, A. M. (1965). Genetic selection for social dominance ability in chickens. *Animal Behaviour, 13,* 114–131.

Curtis, J. T., & Wang, Z. (2003). The neurochemistry of pair bonding. *Current Directions in Psychological Science, 12,* 49–53.

DeWaal, F. (1989). *Peacemaking among primates.* Cambridge, MA: Harvard University Press.

DeWaal, F. B. M. (2000). Primates—a natural heritage of conflict resolution. *Science, 289,* 586–590.

Dugatkin, L. A. (2004). *Principles of animal behavior.* New York: Norton

Ebert, P. D. (1983). Selection for aggression in a natural population. In E. C. Simmel, M. E. Hahn, & J. K. Walters (Eds.), *Aggressive behavior: Genetic and neural approaches* (pp. 103–127). Hillsdale, NJ: Erlbaum.

Feldker, D. E., Datson, N. A., Veenema, A. H., Meulmeester, E., De Kloet, E. R., & Vreugdenhil, E. (2003). Serial analysis of gene expression predicts structural differences in hippocampus of long attack latency and short attack latency mice. *European Journal of Neuroscience, 17,* 379–87.

Feldker, D. E., Datson, N. A., Veenema, A. H., Proutski, V., Lathouwers, D., De Kloet, E. R., et al. (2003). Gene chip analysis of hippocampal gene expression profiles of short- and long-attack-latency mice: Technical and biological implications. *Journal of Neuroscience Research, 74,* 701–716.

Fujita, O., Annen, Y., & Kitaoka, A. (1994). Tsukuba high- and low-emotional strains of rats (*Rattus norvegicus*): An overview. *Behavior Genetics, 24,* 389–415.

Gerlai, R. (2003). Zebra fish: An uncharted behavioral model. *Behavior Genetics, 33,* 461–468.

Gibbs, R. A., Weinstock, G. M., Metzker, M. L., Muzny, D. M., Sodergren, E. J., Scherer, S., et al. (Rat Genome Sequencing Project Consortium). (2004). Genome sequence of the Brown Norway rat yields insights into mammalian evolution. *Nature, 428,* 493–521.

Ginsburg, B. E., & Allee, W. C. (1942). Some effects of conditioning on social dominance and subordination in inbred strains of mice. *Physiological Zoology, 15,* 485–506.

Ginsburg, B. E., & Jummonville, J. E. (1967). Genetic

variability in response to early stimulation viewed as an adaptive mechanism in population ecology. *American Zoologist, 7,* 795.

Gould, J. L., & Gould, C. G. (1995). *The honey bee.* New York: Scientific American.

Grandin, T. (1998). *Genetics and the behavior of domestic animals.* New York: Academic Press.

Gregg, T. R. (2003). Cortical and limbic neural circuits mediating aggressive behavior. In M. P. Mattson (Ed.), *Neurobiology of aggression: Understanding and preventing violence* (pp. 1–20). Totowa, NJ: Humana.

Guillot, P.-V., Carlier, M., Maxson, S. C., & Roubertoux, P. L. (1995). Intermale aggression tested in two procedures, using four inbred strains of mice and their reciprocal congenics: Y chromosomal implications. *Behavior Genetics, 25,* 357–360.

Guillot, P.-V., Roubertoux, P. L., & Crusio, W. E. (1994). Hippocampal mossy fiber distribution and intermale aggression in seven inbred mouse strains. *Brain Research, 660,* 167–169.

Guo, S. (2004). Linking genes to brain, behavior and neurological diseases: What can we learn from zebra fish? *Genes, Brain and Behavior, 3,* 63–74.

Guzman-Novoa, G., Hunt, G. J., Uribe, J. L., Smith, C., & Aerchavaleta-Velasco, M. E. (2002). Confirmation of QTL effects and evidence of genetic dominance of honeybee defensive behavior: Results of colony and individual behavioral assays. *Behavior Genetics, 32,* 95–102.

Hahn, M. E. (1983). Genetic "artifacts" and aggressive behavior. In E. C. Simmel, M. E. Hahn, & J. K. Walters (Eds.), *Aggressive behavior: Genetic and neural approaches* (pp. 67–88). Hillsdale, NJ: Erlbaum.

Hahn, M. E., & Wright, J. C. (1998). The influence of genes on social behavior of dogs. In T. Grandin (Ed.), *Genetics and the behavior of domestic animals* (pp. 299–318). New York: Academic Press.

Hamilton, W. D. (1964). The genetical evolution of social behavior I and II. *Journal of Theoretical Biology, 7,* 1–52.

Hendley, E. D., Ohlsson, W. G., & Musty, R. E. (1992). Interstrain aggression in hypertensive and/or hyperactive rats: SHR, WKY, WKHA, WKHT. *Physiology and Behavior, 51,* 1041–1046.

Higley, J. D, Suomi, S. J., & Linnoila, M. (1996). A nonhuman primate model of type II alcoholism? Part 2. Diminished social competence and excessive aggression correlates with low cerebrospinal fluid 5-hydroxyindoleacetic acid concentrations. *Alcoholism: Clinical and Experimental Research, 20,* 643–650.

Holldobler, B., & Wilson, E. O. (1994). *Journey of the ants: A story of scientific exploration.* Cambridge, MA: Belknap Press.

Holloway, R. L. (1974). *Primate aggression, territoriality, and xenophobia: A comparative perspective.* New York: Academic Press.

Hood, K. E., & Cairns, R. B. (1988). A developmental analysis of aggressive behavior in mice. II. Cross-sex inheritance. *Behavior Genetics, 18,* 605–619.

Huntingford, F., & Turner, A. (1987). *Animal conflict.* New York: Chapman Hall.

Kirkness, E. F., Bafna, V., Halpern, A. L., Levy, S., Remington, K., Rusch, D. B., et al. (2003). The dog genome: Survey sequencing and comparative analysis. *Science, 301,* 1898–1903.

Kjaer, J. B., & Sorensen, P. (1997). Feather pecking behaviour in White Leghorns: A genetic study. *British Poultry Science, 38,* 333–341.

Lagerspetz, K. M. J., & Lagerspetz, K. Y. H. (1983). Genes and aggression. In E. C. Simmel, M. E. Hahn, & J. K. Walters (Eds.), *Aggressive behavior: Genetic and neural approaches* (pp. 89–101). Hillsdale, NJ: Erlbaum.

Le Roy, I., Mortaud, S., Tordjman, S., Donsez-Darcel, E., Carlier, M., Degrelle, H., et al. (1999). Genetic correlation between steroid sulfatase concentration and initiation of attack behavior in mice. *Behavior Genetics, 29,* 131–136.

Lesch, K. P. (2003). The serotonergic dimension of aggression and violence. In M. P. Mattson (Ed.), *Neurobiology of aggression: Understanding and preventing violence* (pp. 33–63). Totowa, NJ: Humana.

Levan, G., Stah, F., Klinga-Levan, K., Szpirer, J., & Szpirer, C. (1998). The rat gene map. *ILAR Journal, 39,* 132–137.

Mackintosh, J. H. (1970). Territory formation by laboratory mice. *Animal Behaviour, 18,* 177–183.

Maxson, S. C. (1992). Methodological issues in genetic analyses of an agonistic behavior (offense) in male mice. In D. Goldowitz, D. Wahlsten, & R. E. Wimer (Eds.), *Techniques for the genetic analysis of brain and behavior: Focus on the mouse* (pp. 349–373). Amsterdam: Elsevier.

Maxson, S. C. (1999). Genetic influences on aggressive behavior. In D. W. Pfaff, W. H. Berrettini, T. J. Joh, & S. C. Maxson (Eds.), *Genetic influences on neural and behavioral functions* (pp. 405–416). Boca Raton, FL: CRC Press.

Maxson, S. C. (2003). Behavioral genetics. In M. Gallagher & R. J. Nelson (Eds.), *Handbook of psychology: Vol. 3. Biological psychology* (pp. 35–46). New York: Wiley.

Maxson, S. C., & Canastar, A. (2003). Conceptual and methodological issues in the genetics of mouse agonistic behavior. *Hormones and Behavior, 44,* 258–262.

Maxson, S. C, Didier-Erickson, A., & Ogawa, S. (1989).

The Y chromosome, social signals, and offense in mice. *Behavioral and Neural Biology, 52,* 251–259.

Maxson, S. C., Ginsburg, B. E., & Trattner, A. (1979). Interaction of Y-chromosomal and autosomal gene(s) in the development of intermale aggression in mice. *Behavior Genetics, 9,* 219–226.

Mech, L. D., Adams, L. G., Meir, T. J., Burch, J. W., & Dale, B. W. (1998). *The wolves of Denali.* Minneapolis: University of Minnesota Press.

Mello, C. V., Vicario, D. S., & Clayton, D. F. (1992). Song presentation induces gene expression in the songbird's forebrain. *Proceedings of the National Academy of Sciences USA, 89,* 6818–6822.

Menotti-Raymond, M., David, V. A., Lyons, L. A., Schäffer, A. A., Tomlin, J. F., Hutton, M. K., et al. (1999). A genetic linkage map of microsatellites in the domestic cat (*Felis catus*). *Genomics, 57,* 9–23.

Miczek, K. A., Fish, E. W., & DeBold, J. F. (2003). Neurosteroids, GABA_A receptors, and escalated aggressive behavior. *Hormones and Behavior, 44,* 242–257.

Miczek, K. A., Maxson, S. C., Fish, E. W., & Faccidomo, S. (2001). Aggressive behavioral phenotypes in mice. *Behavioral Brain Research, 125,* 167–181.

Mitchell, M. J. (2000). Spermatogenesis and the mouse Y chromosome: Specialization out of decay. *Results and Problems in Cell Differentiation, 28,* 233–270.

Miyakawa, T. Y., Yagi, T., Takao, K., & Niki, H. (2001). Differential effect of Fyn kinase deletion on offensive and defensive aggression. *Behavioral Brain Research, 122,* 51–56.

Monahan, E. J., & Maxson, S. C. (1998). Y chromosome, urinary chemosignals, and an agonistic behavior (offense) of mice. *Physiology and Behavior, 64,* 123–132.

Monahan, E. J., Yamazaki, K., Beauchamp, G. K., & Maxson, S. C. (1993). Olfactory discrimination of urinary odor types from congenic strains (DBA/1Bg and DBA1.C57BL10–YBg) of mice differing in their Y chromosomes. *Behavior Genetics, 23,* 251–255.

Mugford, R. A., & Nowell, N. W. (1971). The relationship between endocrine status of female opponents and aggressive behaviour of male mice. *Animal Behaviour, 19,* 153–155.

Nesterova, T. B., Mazurok, N. A., Rubtsova, N. V., Isaenko, & Zakian, S. M. (1998). The vole gene map. *ILAR Journal, 39,* 138–144.

Nyberg, J., Sandnabba, K., Schalkwyk, L., & Sluyter, F. (2004). Genetic and environmental (inter)actions in male mouse lines selected for aggressive and nonaggressive behavior. *Gene, Brain, and Behavior, 3,* 101–109.

O'Brien, S. J. (1993). Genetic map of *Felis catus* (domestic cat). In S. J. O'Brien (Ed.), *Genetic maps: Locus maps of complex genomes, nonhuman vertebrates* (6th ed., pp. 4.250–4.253) New York: Cold Spring Harbor Laboratory.

Ogawa, S., & Makino, J. (1981). Maternal aggression in inbred strains of mice: Effects of reproductive state. *The Japanese Journal of Psychology, 52,* 78–84.

Parker, H. G., Kim, L. V., Sutter, N. B., Carlson, S., Lorentzen, T. D., Malek, T. B., et al. (2004). Genetic structure of the purebred domestic dog. *Science, 304,* 1160–1164.

Parmigiani, S., Ferrari, P. F., & Palanza, P. (1998). An evolutionary approach to behavioral pharmacology: Using drugs to understand proximate and ultimate mechanisms of different forms of aggression. *Neuroscience and Biobehavioral Reviews, 23,* 143–153.

Parmigiani, S., Palanza, P. S., Rodgers, J., & Ferrari, P. F. (1999). Selection, evolution of behavior and animal models in behavioral neuroscience. *Neuroscience and Biobehavioral Reviews, 23,* 957–970.

Parsons, P. A. (1973). *Behavioral and ecological genetics: A study in Drosophila.* Glasgow, UK: Clarendon Press.

Pennisi, E. (2004). New sequence boosts tats' research appeal. *Science, 303,* 455–458.

Rogers, J., & Vandenberg, J. L. (1998). Gene maps of nonhuman primates. *ILAR Journal, 38,* 145–152.

Roubertoux, P. L., & Carlier, M. (2003). Y chromosome and antisocial behavior. In M. P. Mattson (Ed.), *Neurobiology of aggression: Understanding and preventing violence* (pp. 119–134). Totowa, NJ: Humana.

Roubertoux, P. L., Carlier, M., Degrelle, H., Haas-Dupertuis, M. C., Phillips, J., & Moutier, R. (1994). Co-segregation of intermale aggression with the pseudoautosomal region of the Y chromosome in mice. *Genetics, 135,* 225–230.

Roubertoux, P. L., Le Roy, I., Mortaud, S., Perez-Diaz, F., & Tordjman, S. (1999). Measuring aggression in the mouse. In W. E. Crusio & R. T. Gerlai (Eds.), *Handbook of molecular-genetic techniques for brain and behavior research* (pp. 696–709). New York: Elsevier.

Rowe, F. P., & Redfern, R. (1969). Aggressive behaviour in related and unrelated wild house mice (*Mus musculus* L.). *Annals of Applied Biology, 64,* 425–431.

Sandnabba, K. N., & Korpela, S. R. (1994). Effects of early exposure to mating on adult sexual behavior in male mice varying in their genetic disposition for aggressive behavior. *Aggressive Behavior, 20,* 429–439.

Schellinck, H. M., Monahan, E., Brown, R. E., & Maxson, S. C. (1993). A comparison of the contribution of the major histocompatibility complex (MHC) and Y chromosomes to the discriminability of individual urine odors of mice by Long-Evans rats. *Behavior Genetics, 23,* 257–263.

Scott, J. P. (1942). Genetic differences in the social behavior of inbred strains of mice. *Journal of Heredity, 33,* 11–15.

Scott, J. P. (1966). Agonistic behavior in mice and rats: A review. *American Zoologist, 6,* 683–701.

Scott, J. P. (1984). The dog as a model for human aggression. In K. J. Flannelly, R. J. Blanchard, & D. C. Blanchard (Eds.), *Biological perspectives on aggression* (pp. 97–107). New York: A. R. Liss.

Scott, J. P. (1989). *The evolution of social systems.* New York: Gordon and Breach.

Scott, J. P., & Fuller, J. L. (1965). *Genetics and social behavior of dogs.* Chicago: University of Chicago Press.

Shepherd, J. K., Flores, T., Rodgers, R. J., Blanchard, R. J., & Blanchard, D. C. (1992). The anxiety/defense test battery: Influences of gender and ritanserin treatment on antipredator defensive behavior. *Physiology and Behavior, 51,* 277–285.

Siegel, A., Roeling, T. A., Gregg, T. R., & Kruk, M. R. (1999). Neuropharmacology of brain-simulation-evoked aggression. *Neuroscience and Biobehavioral Reviews, 23,* 359–389.

Sluyter, F., Jamot, L., van Oortmerssen, G. A., & Crusio, W. E. (1994). Hippocampal mossy fiber distribution in mice selected for aggression. *Brain Research, 646,* 145–148.

Sluyter, F., van Oortmerssen, G. A., & Koolhouse, J. P. (1994). Studies on wild house mice. VI. Differential effects of the Y chromosome on intermale aggression. *Aggressive Behavior, 20,* 379–386.

Sokolowski, M. B. (2001). Drosophila: Genetics meets behaviour. *Nature Reviews Genetics, 2,* 879–90.

Stewart, A. D., Manning, A., & Batty, J. (1980). Effects of Y-chromosome variants on male behavior of the mouse, *Mus musculus. Genetical Research Cambridge, 35,* 261–268.

Strier, K. B. (2003). *Primate behavioral ecology* (2nd ed.). New York: Allyn & Bacon.

Svare, B. (1989). Recent advances in the study of female aggressive behavior in mice. In P. F. Brain, D. Mainardi, & S. Parmigiani (Eds.), *House mouse aggression* (pp. 135–159). New York: Harwood Academic.

Tabor, R. (2003). *Understanding cat behavior.* Newton Abbot, UK: David and Charles.

Van den Berg, L., Schilder, B. H., & Knol, B. W. (2003). Behavior genetics of canine aggression: Behavioral phenotyping of golden retrievers by means of an aggression test. *Behavior Genetics, 33,* 469–483.

Van Oortmerssen, G. A., & Baker, T. C. M. (1981). Artificial selection for short and long attack latencies in wild *Mus musculus domesticus. Behavior Genetics, 11,* 115–126.

Van Oortmerssen, G. A., & Busser, J. (1989). Studies in wild house mice. 3. Disruptive selection of aggression as a possible force in evolution. In P. F. Brain, D. Mainardi, & S. Parmigiani (Eds.), *House mouse aggression* (pp. 87–117). New York: Harwood Academic.

Wall, P. M., Blanchard, D. C., & Blanchard, R. J. (2003). Behavioral and neuropharmacological differentiation of offensive and defensive aggression in experimental and seminaturalistic models. In M. P. Mattson (Ed.), *Neurobiology of aggression: Understanding and preventing violence* (pp. 73–91). Totowa, NJ: Humana.

Westergaard, G. C., Suomi, S. J., Higley, J. D., & Mehlman, P. T. (1999). CSF 5–HIAA and aggression in female macaque monkeys: Species and interindividual differences. *Psychopharmacology, 146,* 440–446.

Whitfield, C. W., Cziko, A.-M., & Robinson, G. E. (2003). Gene expression profiles in the brain predict behavior in individual honey bees. *Science, 302,* 296–299.

Wilson, A. P., & Boelkins, R. C. (1970). Evidence for seasonal variation in aggressive behavior by *Macaca mulatta. Animal Behaviour, 18,* 719–724.

Wilson, M. L. (2003). Environmental factors and aggression in nonhuman primates. In M. P. Mattson (Ed.), *Neurobiology of aggression: Understanding and preventing violence* (pp. 151–165). Totowa, NJ: Humana.

Xu, J., Burgoyne, P. S., & Arnold, A. P. (2002). Sex differences in sex chromosome gene expression in mouse brain. *Human Molecular Genetics, 11,* 1409–1419.

Young, L. J., Wang, Z., & Insel, T. R. (1998). The neuroendocrine bases of monogamy. *Trends in Neuroscience, 21,* 71–75.

2

Human Quantitative Genetics of Aggression

Daniel M. Blonigen & Robert F. Krueger

For some time, psychological science has sought to understand the underlying biological and etiological processes involved in human aggression and violence. Primarily in the latter half of the 20th century, behavioral genetic methodology has contributed substantially to this body of knowledge by providing a means of systematically estimating the relative influence of genes and environments on aggressive traits and behaviors. Quantitative genetic studies of twins and adoptees, as implemented in behavior genetic investigations, present a distinct advantage over other methods because they are able to disentangle the inherently confounded influences of nature and nurture. In this way, behavioral genetic designs provide an important step toward identifying genetic and environmental risk factors for aggression and violence.

In this chapter we present an overview of human quantitative genetic studies of aggression and violence, including twin, adoption, and molecular genetic designs from both the child and adult literature. Our review begins with the behavioral genetic literature on aggression in childhood and early adolescence. We highlight systematic differences across studies based on the method of assessing aggression, as well as present evidence for both distinct and common etiologies that link aggression with other childhood behavioral problems. Next, we review relevant behavioral genetic investigations of aggression in adulthood; in particular, we note results from studies using official statistics and self-report questionnaires, as well as highlight the absence of a consistent operational definition of aggression in this literature. From there, we discuss predominant theories and empirical findings from longitudinal studies of aggression in both childhood and adulthood, as well as highlight various moderating effects on the etiology of these behaviors (i.e., gender differences and gene-environment interactions). Subsequently, we introduce and briefly summarize molecular genetic studies of human aggression across a range of psychiatric and developmental disorders. Last, we discuss future directions for behavioral genetic research on aggression and underscore important domains that have received comparatively less attention in this literature.

Before proceeding, it should be noted that aggression is a heterogeneous phenotype that pervades numerous forms of psychopathology. Importantly, aggression is a criterion in several diagnostic categories, such as conduct disorder and antisocial and borderline personality disorders. In addition, it is common among individuals suffering from mood disorders, psychosis, or dementia. The present review, however, primarily focuses on individual differences in aggressive traits and behaviors rather than these aforementioned diagnostic categories. Such an approach should minimize issues of phenotypic and genotypic heterogeneity that can arise when dealing with heterogeneous diagnostic categories (Alsobrook & Pauls, 2000; Plomin, Nitz, & Rowe, 1990).[1] Nevertheless, when applicable, the degree to which aggressive traits or behaviors are related to these disorders on a genetic level is explored to determine whether there are broader etiologies or vulnerabilities underlying the comorbidity of aggression with specific forms of psychopathology.

Behavioral Genetic Methodology

Prior to reviewing the literature, it is important to discuss some key concepts, assumptions, and limitations in behavioral genetic research. Two models of inheritance are especially relevant. *Monogenic* models assume that a single gene is both necessary and sufficient for the expression of a phenotype. Monogenic models are best suited to explain the inheritance of discontinuous or dichotomous traits. However, with exceptions such as the discovery of a single autosomal dominant gene on Chromosome 4 resulting in the development of Huntington's disease (Gusella et al., 1983), single gene findings in psychopathology research are the exception rather than the norm. Nevertheless, the aggression literature does include a study showing increased rates of antisocial behavior among individuals with an extra Y chromosome (Jacobs, Brunton, Melville, Brittain, & McClement, 1965) and another investigation linking a point mutation in the structural gene for the monoamine oxidase (MAO) enzyme to impulsive aggression in a Dutch pedigree (Brunner, Nelen, Breakefield, Ropers, & van Oost, 1993). The former finding, however, has since been discounted, given that most criminals do not possess the XYY sex chromosome genotype and the vast majority of XYY individuals are not criminal. The latter finding regarding MAO represents a unique intrafamilial mutation that may not necessarily generalize to the larger population. This last point is discussed further in the section on molecular genetic findings.

In contrast to monogenic models, most individual difference traits and forms of psychopathology follow a quantitative, or *polygenic*, pattern of inheritance

(Fisher, 1918; Wright, 1921). In this model, several genetic loci as well as various environmental factors combine in either an additive or nonadditive fashion to form continuously distributed traits. As the number of loci contributing to a trait or disorder increases, the overall distribution of phenotypes begins to approach normality. Aggression is typically conceptualized as a quantitative, normally distributed trait that is dimensional in nature rather than a dichotomous, "either-or" category of pathology. Moreover, pathological expression of quantitative traits is thought to occur at the extreme end points of the trait's distribution. Therefore, unless it is demonstrated that the etiology of the extremes differ from the rest of the distribution, aggressive traits and behaviors lend themselves most readily to quantitative genetic analyses (Plomin et al., 1990).

Though it is seemingly contradictory, single-gene inheritance forms the basis for the transmission of polygenic traits. According to Mendel's law of segregation, each gene in the offspring is inherited as a combination of two alleles. In a Mendelian model, certain alleles are dominant and recessive and, therefore, limit the number of phenotypic outcomes which may occur. For traits that are inherently quantitative or polygenic, alleles are not simply dominant or recessive with respect to the phenotype, but operate in synchrony across multiple loci, with each allele contributing some small effect to the phenotype. In other words, quantitative phenotypes are expressed through the cumulative effect of several genetic loci, each of which is inherited according to Mendelian laws of segregation (Evans, Gillespie, & Martin, 2002; Plomin, DeFries, McClearn, & Rutter, 1997).

Twin Studies

Twin studies offer a powerful means of estimating the degree to which genetic and environmental influences contribute to the etiology of human quantitative traits. Twin designs rely on the difference in genetic relatedness between monozygotic (MZ) and dizygotic (DZ) twin pairs to estimate the degree to which these traits are influenced by genetic as well as environmental factors. Genetic effects are of two sorts: *additive* and *nonadditive*. Additive genetic effects involve the summation of individual alleles across several loci in which each allele in the genotype has a cumulative impact. Given that MZ twins share all of their genes, whereas DZ twins share half on average, additive genetic effects are inferred when MZ twin correlations are roughly twice the magnitude of the DZ twin correlations. Shown below, twice the difference between the identical twin correlation (r_{MZ}) and the fraternal twin correlation (r_{DZ}) can be used to compute additive genetic heritability estimates: $h^2 = 2(r_{MZ} - r_{DZ})$.[2] Some genetic effects do not involve a simple linear summation of genes across loci but rather result from nonadditive genetic mechanisms such as *dominance* and *epistasis* (Plomin et al., 1997). Dominance involves an interaction rather than linear combination of two alleles at a given locus, whereas epistasis results from the interaction of alleles across several genetic loci. Given that MZ twins are genetically identical, they will share all of their genetic effects, including nonadditive influences. However, because these genetic mechanisms deviate from the typical linear pattern seen in additive genetics, DZ twins will share less than half of their nonadditive genetic effects. Specifically, when dominance is relevant to the etiology of a phenotype, DZ twin correlations will be one quarter of the MZ twin correlation, on average. Epistatic effects, on the other hand, are no more likely to occur in fraternal twins than in individuals randomly chosen from the population and, therefore, result in DZ twin correlations of roughly zero.

Twin designs also allow for the quantification of two sorts of environmental effects: *shared* and *nonshared* environmental effects. The shared environment (c^2) consists of factors which both members of a twin pair have in common that serve to increase resemblance between them (e.g., early family environment). Such effects are inferred when MZ and DZ correlations are similar in magnitude. Shared environmental estimates may be computed according to the formula $c^2 = 2(r_{DZ}) - r_{MZ}$. Nonshared environmental effects (e^2) are environmental factors unique and specific to each member of a twin pair (e.g., random accidents) that tend to decrease resemblance between them. To the extent that MZ twins share all of their genetic effects and none of their nonshared environmental effects, e^2 may be computed by subtracting the MZ twin correlation from one: $e^2 = 1 - r_{MZ}$.

Despite their utility, some limitations and assumptions regarding the twin method must be considered. First, this method has been criticized on the grounds that identical and fraternal twins are not representative of the general population and differ from nontwins in important and systematic ways. Though being a twin is certainly a unique experience, findings from the literature suggest that with respect to psychiatric symptoms (Kendler, Martin, Heath, & Eaves, 1995), as well

as normal range personality traits (Johnson, Krueger, Bouchard, & McGue, 2002), twins are not systematically or appreciably different than nontwins in the population. Second, the equal environments assumption, or the equal "trait-relevant" environments assumption (cf. Krueger & Markon, 2002), is also crucial to the twin design. This assumption holds that any imposed environmental differences in terms of how MZ twins are treated compared to DZ twins are not relevant to the etiology of the phenotype under investigation.[3] Although environmental differences may exist between MZ and DZ twins (e.g., mothers may dress identical twins more alike than fraternal twins), these differences have not been shown to be relevant to psychological variables, such as personality (Loehlin & Nichols, 1976) or psychopathology (Kendler, Neale, Kessler, Heath, & Eaves, 1994). A third assumption, assortative mating, holds that individuals mate randomly and not based on their degree of similarity for a specific trait. If nonrandom mating does occur based on the trait in question, DZ twins may share more genes for that trait than expected by chance. DZ twins will be more genotypically similar than they would be given random mating, resulting in an overestimate of shared environmental effects and an underestimate of heritability (see, e.g., Krueger, Moffitt, Caspi, Bleske, & Silva, 1998).

Adoption Studies

Adoption studies provide another powerful method of disentangling confounding causes of familial resemblance. In this method, the correlation between adoptees and their adoptive relatives is compared to the correlation between adoptees and their biological relatives. If a trait is primarily genetic in nature, adopted children should resemble their biological relatives to a greater degree than their adoptive relatives. In turn, any resemblance between individuals and their adoptive relatives is, in theory, due to the family environment. An important assumption in adoption designs is that selective placement has not occurred in the adoption process. That is, adopted-away children are not placed with adoptive families that are systematically related to the biological families on the trait in question. However, if a correlation does exist between these groups, that correlation can be modeled and included in the analyses in order to determine its impact on the findings. Notably, a meta-analytic review of twin and adoption studies of aggression tested the relative fit of models which assumed both perfect selective placement and heritability against the fit of models assuming only the influence of heritability (Miles & Carey, 1997). Though the models assuming perfect selective placement provided an adequate fit to the data, models containing only a heritability parameter provided the best fit across three separate measures of aggression. Furthermore, the heritability estimates from the models assuming perfect selective placement were not appreciably different from the heritabilities of any of the other models (for a more detailed review of the aforementioned behavioral genetic methods and their relevant assumptions and limitations, see Evans et al., 2002, or Plomin et al., 1997).

Genetic and Environmental Influences on Aggression in Childhood and Adolescence

Method of Assessment: Variability in Heritability

In general, findings from behavioral genetic studies in childhood and adolescence suggest that genetic factors play at least some role in the etiology of aggression (DiLalla, 2002). However, heritability estimates vary across these studies depending on the method that is utilized to index aggression. In studies of children, aggression has primarily been assessed via parental reports or independent observational ratings. In terms of parental ratings, the Childhood Behavior Checklist (CBCL; Achenbach & Edelbrock, 1984) is perhaps the most widely employed and validated measure to assess behavioral and psychiatric problems in childhood. The CBCL is a broad range measure consisting of several scales tapping both internalizing (e.g., anxious/depressed) and externalizing (aggression and delinquency) syndromes of childhood. Using this measure, several behavioral genetic studies have demonstrated large genetic contributions to variance in aggression. Ghodsian-Carpey and Baker (1987) obtained maternal ratings of aggression in 4- to 7-year-old twins on the CBCL and found that the vast majority of the variance in these behaviors (94%) could be explained by genetic factors. Also, two other twin studies using parental reports on the CBCL have noted substantial genetic contributions to aggressive behaviors despite using twins across a wide developmental span (ages 7–16; Edelbrock, Rende, Plomin, & Thompson, 1995; Eley, Lichtenstein, & Stevenson, 1999). Largely

parallel findings have also emerged from adoption studies of aggression. Genetic effects accounted for 70% of the variance in the aggression scale of the CBCL among groups of adoptees consisting of either biologically related or unrelated sibling pairs (van den Oord, Boomsma, & Verhulst, 1994). In addition, results from a similar adoption design yielded a heritability estimate of .57 for CBCL aggression (van der Valk, Verhulst, Neale, & Boomsma, 1998).

Other investigations using parental ratings from different indices of childhood behaviors have obtained similar findings. O'Connor, Foch, Sherry, and Plomin (1980) used a revised version of the Connors Parental Symptom Rating form (PSR; Connors, 1970) to measure specific behavioral problems in twins averaging 7 years of age. On the Bullying scale (e.g., hits or kicks others, is mean, fights constantly, picks on other children), DZ twin correlations were roughly half the MZ twin correlations ($r_{MZ} = .72$, $r_{DZ} = .42$), suggesting that genetic influences also play an important role in the etiology of aggression as measured by the PSR. Similarly, a twin design by Scarr (1966) in which parents rated their children's aggression using an adjective checklist yielded a heritability estimate of .40 on this measure.

Although there is variability across these studies in terms of the magnitude of the heritability estimates, investigations using parental reports consistently reveal significant genetic contributions to aggression in childhood. On the other hand, observational studies of childhood aggression have been much less consistent, with some investigations yielding little or no evidence of heritability for these behaviors. In a study of 6- to 14-year-old twins using a projective measure in which subjects sorted a series of pictures into groups based on whether or not they looked "fun," a heritability estimate of .16 was obtained on an aggressivity scale, suggesting minimal evidence of genetic contributions (Owen & Sines, 1970). In a laboratory study, physical aggression was observed in twins who were encouraged to hit a Bobo the Clown doll, as demonstrated by the experimenter (Plomin, Foch, & Rowe, 1981). MZ correlations were not significantly greater than the DZ correlation, indicating that individual differences in this form of aggression in children are not genetically mediated. In addition, one twin design involving observational ratings of parent-adolescent interactions found a heritability estimate of .27 for adolescents' behavior toward fathers on a scale of transactional conflict (i.e., reciprocated anger/hostility; O'Connor,

Hetherington, Reiss, & Plomin, 1995). As a whole, results from observational designs generally demonstrate less evidence for the heritability of childhood aggression than studies using parental ratings. Consistent with this, Miles and Carey (1997) examined mode of assessment as a moderator in their meta-analysis of twin and adoption studies of aggression. Whereas genetic contributions explained a large amount of the variance in studies using parental and self-reports, observational ratings showed significantly less genetic contribution and a greater impact of the shared and nonshared environment.

Several explanations may be posited to explain why heritability estimates vary by mode of assessment. With respect to observational ratings, this method may be inherently less internally consistent than more psychometrically sound parent or self-report measures. If this is the case, measurement error, which is encompassed under the nonshared environmental parameter, will be inflated and, in turn, heritability estimates will be attenuated (DiLalla, 2002). In terms of parental ratings, some scholars have conjectured that contrast effects may explain the larger heritability estimates in these studies (Borkenau, Riemann, Spinath, & Angleitner, 2000; Plomin, 1981; Saudino, 2003; Simonoff et al., 1998). Contrast effects result from parents rating identical twins as more similar than fraternal twins on a certain trait based on the expectation that the former are more alike than the latter. Accordingly, parental reports may introduce some degree of bias in their measurement of childhood behaviors and, thus, may overestimate heritability relative to other informants.

Despite these limitations, specific "biases" from reports by different informants in some cases may actually reflect true differences observed in a child's behavior based on the relationship the informant has with that child. In such cases, differences across raters essentially reflect rater-specific contributions rather than rater biases per se. To account for both of these effects, behavioral genetic designs need to utilize multiple informants to clarify the relative influence of genes and environment in the etiology of childhood aggression. One study utilizing this approach involved a cross-sectional analysis of Dutch twins at ages 3, 7, and 10 years (Hudziak et al., 2003). The authors examined the genetic and environmental contributions to aggression as defined by the CBCL in a multi-informant design by obtaining paternal, maternal, and teacher ratings of each twin. Although mean differences did emerge across the ratings of aggression, the common

variance across all informants was largely due to additive genetic effects (60–79%). Moreover, each informant also provided a small, albeit significant, amount of rater-specific variance that was also genetic in nature. That is, rater differences did not merely reflect measurement error or rater bias, but ultimately further informed the extent to which genes influence aggressive behavior. In effect, the results advocate for the use of multiple informants in behavioral genetic investigations of aggression in order to more reliably measure the genetic and environmental contributions to this construct (Hudziak et al., 2003; Loehlin, 1998).

Aggression and Other Childhood Behavioral Problems: Distinct or Common Etiologies?

There is some evidence to suggest that both distinct and common etiologies may link aggression with other childhood behavioral problems. For instance, some findings have noted that aggression is predominantly influenced by genetic factors, whereas delinquency (i.e., rule breaking) is more determined by the shared environment. Parental ratings of twins on the CBCL yielded significant genetic influences for both the aggression and delinquency subscales (Edelbrock et al., 1995). However, a larger proportion of the variance in aggression was due to heritable factors (60%) than for delinquency (35%), while shared environmental effects were significant for delinquency but not aggression. A similar pattern was reported in male twins (Eley et al., 1999). Heritability estimates were large and significant for aggression (h^2 = .70), but not for delinquency, and the shared environment was substantial for delinquency only (c^2 = .54). Moreover, in a sibling adoption study teacher ratings on the Teacher Report Form (TRF) of the CBCL were moderately heritable for the aggression scale, but not for delinquency (Deater-Deckard & Plomin, 1999).

Other investigations have noted a large degree of covariation between measures of aggression and delinquent behaviors in children (Achenbach & Ruffle, 2000; Deater-Deckard & Plomin, 1999; Verhulst & van der Ende, 1993; Yang, Chen, & Soong, 2001). Moreover, some scholars have posited that the comorbidity of these behaviors may arise from correlated risk factors that are either genetic or environmental in nature (Rutter, 1997). Although the studies are limited, there is some evidence to suggest that the co-occurrence of these behaviors is largely due to shared genetic effects.

For example, Eley (1997) presented data showing that a large amount of covariance between the aggression and delinquency scales of the CBCL was due to genetic factors. As well, a recent twin analysis specifically examined the etiology of the co-occurrence between CBCL aggression and delinquency and reported that roughly 80% of the covariance between these phenotypes was due to additive genetic contributions (Bartels et al., 2003).

These ostensibly incompatible findings regarding the etiology of childhood behavioral problems may be resolved under a hierarchical model (Achenbach & McConaughy, 1997). Such a model posits that the etiology of co-occurring behaviors is due to both a broad or common factor, which may be genetic or environmental in nature, and specific etiologic influences that are unique to each of the disorders in the model. Krueger et al. (2002) delineated such a model in their biometric analysis of externalizing psychopathology (i.e., covariation of child and adult antisocial behavior, substance abuse, and disinhibitory personality traits) in a sample of 17-year-old male twins. The authors demonstrated that although a common latent factor that was highly genetic accounted for a large amount of the covariance among externalizing symptoms, significant and unique genetic and environmental contributions were evident for each of the observed phenotypes. Based on the aforementioned findings, the etiology of aggression and delinquency may be similarly represented by a hierarchical model. As suggested by Eley (1997), "general" genes may confer a propensity to a broad spectrum of externalizing behaviors in childhood. In turn, other unique and specific genetic and environmental factors may determine how this broad vulnerability is ultimately expressed. Future behavioral genetic investigations may need to take this perspective into account and consider expanding the boundaries of the phenotypes they study in order to more precisely delineate the underlying etiology of aggression in childhood and adolescence.

Genetic and Environmental Influences on Aggression in Adulthood: Operational Inconsistency

Somewhat analogous to the childhood literature, behavioral genetic studies of aggression in adulthood have been plagued by inconsistent operational definitions of the construct (DiLalla, 2002). Early twin and adoption studies of criminality approached this issue using official statistics of violent crime. However, the findings from these classic studies are mixed. Cloninger and Gottesman (1987), in their reanalysis of twin data from Christiansen (1977), found both nonviolent and violent crimes to be highly heritable ($h^2 = .78$ and .50, respectively). Conversely, a large investigation of 14,427 adoptees from Denmark (Mednick, Gabrielli, & Hutchings, 1984) reported a significant relationship between adoptees and their biological parents for nonviolent, but not violent criminal convictions, suggesting that the latter are not due to the influence of genes. Similarly, petty, but not violent, crime was heritable in cases in which the adoptee and the biological parent were not alcoholic (Bohman, Cloninger, Sigvardsson, & von Knorring, 1982). Despite these inconsistencies, some caution is warranted in interpreting these findings. First, as previously emphasized (Coccaro & McNamee, 1998), violent crime is much less frequent than property crime and, therefore, is likely to be restricted in terms of its variance. In effect, there will be a limited amount of statistical power to detect a heritable signal for these particular crimes. Second, criminality is a fairly global and heterogeneous construct that relates to an assortment of personality styles and psychopathologies. Given this phenotypic heterogeneity, violent criminal convictions may not be the most appropriate means of operationalizing and investigating the etiology of aggression.

In an effort to overcome the problems of operationalizing aggression via violent crime statistics, other behavioral genetic researchers have turned toward the domain of personality as assessed via self-report to assess the etiologic contributions to the construct. Though self-report questionnaires are more amenable to use in epidemiological samples of twins and adoptees, the findings from these studies are ambiguous, given the variety of constructs and measures that have been employed to index aggression. For example, some investigators have examined the etiology of aggression using traits of hostility and have obtained mixed findings. Genetic and environmental influences on scores on the Cook and Medley Hostility (Ho) scale were examined in a small sample of male twins and significant genetic contributions for the Cynicism subscale, but not for the full Ho scale or the Paranoid Alienation subscale of this measure, were reported (Carmelli, Rosenman, & Swan, 1988). In a follow-up to this study using a larger sample of twins, similar findings were obtained, although there was some evidence of modest heritability to the full Ho scale (Carmelli, Swan, & Rosenman, 1990). Overall though, environmental factors appear to play a greater role in the etiology of hostility as measured by the Cook and Medley Ho scale. Despite these findings, the validity of the Ho scale as an index of aggression appears questionable, as this measure may actually tap social desirability, suspiciousness, resentment, and mistrust rather than overtly aggressive behaviors (Carmelli et al., 1988; Smith & Frohm, 1985).

In contrast to the Ho scale, other investigators have taken a multifaceted approach to exploring the etiology of hostility-related traits and behaviors. Coccaro, Bergeman, Kavoussi, and Seroczynski (1997) obtained scores on the Buss–Durkee Hostility Inventory (BDHI; Buss & Durkee, 1957) in a sample of male twins. The BDHI is composed of four subscales: Direct Assault (i.e., violence against others), Indirect Assault (i.e., covert or relational aggression), Verbal Assault (i.e., arguing, shouting, screaming), and Irritability. Genetic contributions were significant for each subscale of the BDHI (28–47%) and were primarily nonadditive in nature, with the exception of Direct Assault, which was due to additive genetic factors (47%). Contrary to this, in an examination of the heritability of the BDHI scales in a sample of female twins, only verbal and indirect forms of aggression were due to genetic factors, whereas physical aggression and direct assault demonstrated no evidence for genetic influence (Cates, Houston, Vavak, Crawford, & Uttley, 1993). The authors note, however, that socialization may serve to reduce the expression of overt, physical aggression in women, thereby restricting variance and limiting the power to detect a heritable effect for these more extreme behaviors in women (Cates et al., 1993).

Other behavioral genetic studies of aggression have explored slightly different yet related trait dimensions of the construct. For example, Pedersen and colleagues (1989), in a study of twins reared together and apart, found that the majority of the variance in Type A personality, a multidimensional construct characterized by such features as aggression, hostility, and time urgency, was due to nonshared environmental factors, whereas genetic factors accounted for less than 20% of the variance. Gustavsson, Pedersen, Åsberg, and Schalling (1996) examined the etiologic contributions to individual differences in the Aggression-Hostility-Anger dimension of personality (Spielberger et al., 1985) in a sample of male and female twins. The majority of the variance in these traits was due to nonshared envi-

ronmental factors, with genetic contributions significant for only the Anger component of this dimension. Conversely, significant heritabilities were obtained for both an irritable impulsiveness and (lack of) aggression factor in a sample of male twins reared apart (Coccaro, Bergeman, & McClearn, 1993). However, the magnitude of these estimates varied considerably as irritable impulsiveness was due largely to nonadditive genetic effects (44%), whereas lack of aggression was primarily due to nonshared environmental contributions and only a small amount of additive genetic variance (17%).

By and large, these findings demonstrate the considerable variability across these studies in terms of the extent to which genetic factors play a role in the etiology of aggression. Although these differences may be due to small sample sizes or the inclusion of only one gender, the range of operational definitions and measures used to index aggression likely introduced considerable phenotypic heterogeneity across these investigations and, therefore, this makes it difficult to draw any firm conclusions. In contrast to these investigations, other behavioral genetic studies have utilized more explicit self-report indices of trait aggression to assess the relative genetic and environmental contributions to this construct. Rushton, Fulker, Neale, Nias, and Eysenck (1986) examined the heritability of individual differences in aggression in a sample of male and female twins using 23 items from the Interpersonal Behavior Survey (Mauger & Adkinson, 1980). Approximately 50% of the variance in self-reported aggression was due to genetic effects, with no evidence of shared environmental contributions. Other investigations have explored the etiology of aggression using the Multidimensional Personality Questionnaire (MPQ; Tellegen, in press), an omnibus measure of normal range personality variation. The MPQ is composed of 11 lower order primary trait scales that cohere into three higher order personality superfactors. The aggression scale is a primary scale relating to physical aggression and vindictiveness and loads onto the higher order superfactor of negative emotionality (Krueger, 2000; Tellegen, 1985). Using the MPQ, several investigations have also demonstrated substantial genetic effects and minimal influence from the shared environment to the etiology of trait aggression. In an investigation of the heritability of the MPQ subscales in a sample of twins reared together and apart, approximately half the variance in the aggression scale was due to genetic factors (Tellegen et al., 1988). Other twin studies also note significant and substantial genetic contributions to the aggression scale of the MPQ (Finkel & McGue, 1997; McGue, Bacon, & Lykken, 1993). Furthermore, results from each of the aforementioned designs yielded MZ twin correlations more than twice the magnitude of the DZ twin correlations, suggesting that nonadditive genetic factors may be involved in the etiology of these traits.

Given the large amount of variability across twin and adoption studies of aggression in adulthood, it is difficult to assess the degree to which genes and environment actually contribute to expression of these traits and behaviors. Meta-analyses, however, provide a means of summarizing this literature (Miles & Carey, 1997; Rhee & Waldman, 2002). In general, these investigations reported aggression to be largely due to genetic factors in adulthood and to a lesser extent the shared environment. Miles and Carey (1997) reported that approximately 50% of the overall variance was due to genes, whereas Rhee and Waldman (2002) found that 44% of the variance in twin and adoption studies of antisocial behavior (operationalized in terms of aggression) was largely due to genetic contributions. In sum, despite problems in operationally defining aggression in the adult literature, there is sufficient evidence to assert that genetic factors play a significant role in the etiology of these behaviors.

Genes and Environment in the Stability of Aggression: Longitudinal Findings

In investigating the developmental course of aggression, several studies have noted that these traits are relatively stable from childhood to adulthood (Hofstra, van der Ende, & Verhulst, 2000; Koot, 1995; Loeber & Hay, 1997; Pulkkinen & Pitkaenen, 1993; Verhulst & van der Ende, 1995). With regard to this continuity, it is worth inquiring about the extent to which genetic and environmental influences contribute to the persistence of these traits across development. Moreover, what is the pattern of these etiologic effects? If this stability is largely genetic, then are the same genes exerting an influence on the expression of a phenotype throughout development or do new genes "turn on" at specific maturational points? Conversely, do environmental forces contribute to the persistence of these traits or are there critical periods in which environmental factors have their greatest impact and exert change in these behaviors? According to the meta-analyses highlighted earlier (Miles & Carey, 1997; Rhee & Waldman, 2002), the influence of the shared environment

appears to decrease, whereas the relative influence of genes increases from childhood to adulthood, suggesting that genetic factors may represent an important component in the persistence of aggression over time. However, these studies are cross-sectional and cannot directly attest to the role of genes and environment in the stability or change of these behaviors. Instead, other studies have utilized longitudinal (prospective) designs with genetically informative data to answer these questions and elucidate the etiologic contributions to the stability of aggression.

In studies of children and adolescents, several prospective designs suggest that the stability of aggression is largely due to the influence of genetic factors. CBCL data were examined in twins using parental reports when the twins were 2 years old and then again at 7 years of age (Schmitz, Fulker, & Mrazek, 1995). Although the sample was small, all of the covariance in aggression scores across these two time periods was due to genetic effects. In a study of biologically related and unrelated adoptees (van der Valk et al., 1998), parental ratings on the CBCL were obtained when the adoptees were in either early or mid adolescence and again 3 years later. Genetic influences were substantial for aggression at both assessment points (61% and 52%, respectively), with 69% of the covariance in aggression across these time points due to genetic factors. Moreover, 37% of the genetic variance at the second assessment was due to the continuing influence of genes that were important at the first assessment, whereas 15% of the genetic variance at the second assessment was due to the expression of new genetic factors.

In a recent longitudinal twin design, the genetic and environmental contributions to the stability and change of parentally rated CBCL aggression were examined at 3, 5, 7, 10, and 12 years of age (van Beijsterveldt, Bartels, Hudziak, & Boomsma, 2003). To explore the mechanisms involved in both continuity and change in these behaviors, the authors tested the applicability of two developmental models: a *common factor* model and a *simplex* model. The common factor model implies that the same genetic or environmental factors contribute to the stability of a behavior or trait throughout a particular developmental period. In the simplex model, genetic and environmental factors may exert a continuous effect across a period of time but begin to wane as new age-specific genetic and environmental factors emerge. The results indicated that CBCL aggression was highly stable across these age ranges and largely accounted for by genetic influences that followed a simplex model of inheritance. Although shared environmental contributions were fairly modest, these influences were best described by a common factor model, suggesting that the same shared environmental influences underlie the development of aggression from early childhood to the beginning of adolescence. In total, the stability of aggression in childhood and adolescence appears to be largely genetic and follows a dynamic pattern, with the continuous influence of some genes across this developmental epoch combining with the emergence of new genetic factors at specific ages.

Although few studies have explicitly assessed the etiologic contributions to the stability of aggression in adulthood, a few notable exceptions exist. One longitudinal twin design assessed the influence of genes and environment in the stability and change of personality from ages 20 to 30 (McGue et al., 1993). Using the MPQ as their measure of personality, the aggression scale was highly genetic at both time periods and consisted primarily of nonadditive genetic and nonshared environmental contributions. While changes in aggression were largely due to the nonshared environment, genetic factors exerted a substantial influence on the stability of these traits, as roughly 90% of the stable variance was genetic in nature. A recent investigation, however, suggests that the impact of genes on the stability of MPQ aggression may begin to wane in late adulthood (Johnson, McGue, & Krueger, 2005).

Overall, longitudinal findings from both the child and adult literatures suggest that the continuity of aggression across development is largely due to genetic factors. Notably, these findings align with several developmental taxonomies posited in the literature on antisocial behavior. Specifically, both Moffitt's (1993) *life course persistent* and DiLalla and Gottesman's (1989) *continuous antisocials* represent developmentally stable subtypes that are largely constitutional in nature and associated with higher levels of trait aggression (Elkins, Iacono, & Doyle, 1997) and violent criminal offenses (Moffitt, Caspi, Harrington, & Milne, 2002).

Moderating Effects in the Etiology of Aggression

In our review of the behavioral genetic literature thus far, it is apparent that genes play a significant role in the etiology of aggressive traits and behaviors across development. It would be misleading, however, to characterize this as an absolute finding or to suggest that genetic factors are impervious to the moderating influence of other variables. For example, some evidence suggests that gender differences, as well as gene-environment interactions, are significant moderators in the etiology of aggression and violence.

Gender Differences

A thoroughly investigated and fairly consistent finding from both the child and adult literature is that males exhibit higher mean levels of aggression than females (Hudziak et al., 2003; Maccoby & Jacklin, 1980; McGue et al., 1993; Rushton et al., 1986; Verhulst & Koot, 1992). There has been less empirical attention, however, investigating whether there are gender differences in the genetic and environmental contributions to aggressive behavior. Despite the inclusion of both male and female samples, most behavioral genetic studies of aggression have not fit sex-limitation models to the data which specifically test for gender differences in the genetic and environmental contributions to a phenotype. However, a few studies employing such models have noted gender differences in the etiologic contributions to these behaviors.

The relative fit of two sex-limitation models to CBCL data was assessed on 10- to 15-year-old adoptees (van den Oord et al., 1994). A *general* sex-limitation model assuming no differences in the magnitude of the genetic and environmental influences across males and females was compared to a *specific* sex-limitation model in which these estimates were assumed to vary by gender. The specific sex-limitation model fit best for the aggression scale, with significantly larger genetic and smaller shared environmental influences for males than females. Analogous findings were obtained in a longitudinal study of twins ages 3–12 (van Beijsterveldt et al., 2003). Gender differences in terms of the overall magnitude and stability of the genetic effects on CBCL aggression were evident after age 7, with greater genetic contributions for males and larger shared environmental contributions for females.

In a recent investigation of 11- to 12-year-old twins (Vierikko, Pulkkinen, Kaprio, Viken, & Rose, 2003), a different pattern of gender differences was observed. Using parent and teacher reports on a six-item scale of aggression derived from the Multidimensional Peer Nomination Inventory (Pulkkinen, Kaprio, & Rose, 1999), the authors examined two questions: (a) whether the same etiological factors contribute to aggression in males and females (i.e., qualitative sex differences) and (b) whether the magnitude of these contributions differs across gender (i.e., quantitative sex differences). Qualitative sex differences varied by informant. Teacher reports suggested some sex-specific genetic and shared environmental effects, whereas parental reports yielded no such effects. Conversely, quantitative sex differences were evident for both teacher and parent reports, but yielded lower heritabilities and higher shared environmental contributions for males than females, a finding that contrasts with the aforementioned studies observing greater genetic and less shared environmental influences in males.

Contrary to these findings, other studies have failed to detect any significant gender differences in the etiologic contributions to aggression altogether. In two studies (Eley et al., 1999), no gender differences were noted for maternally rated aggression in either a Swedish sample of twins ages 7–9 or a British sample ages 8–16. As well, results from a twin study of personality in adulthood as measured by the MPQ found no evidence for sex differences in the magnitude of the genetic and environmental effects on the aggression trait scale (Finkel & McGue, 1997). As highlighted in previous sections, these inconsistencies may be due to differences in age or the mode of measurement and make any direct comparisons across studies tenuous. After accounting for such factors, Miles and Carey (1997), in their meta-analysis, report gender as a significant moderator in the etiology of aggression. These findings, however, were not very robust and yielded only slightly larger genetic contributions for males and greater shared environmental effects for females. Thus, the extent to which gender may moderate the genetic and environmental effects on aggression warrants further inquiry.

Gene-Environment Interactions

Behavioral genetic studies from the aggression literature have typically assumed that genetic and environmental factors operate independently in the etiology of these behaviors. Twin and adoption studies, however, are not bound to this assumption and have the capability of investigating whether the phenotypic expression of a trait is dependent upon the interaction of a particular genotype with certain environmental factors. Though the studies are limited in the aggression and violence literature, two noteworthy findings have demonstrated significant gene by environment interactions in the etiology of these behaviors.

First, in an adoption study, the effect of an adverse home environment in predicting aggressive and delinquent behavior was examined in adoptees with and without a family history of externalizing disorders (Cadoret, Yates, Troughton, Woodworth, & Stewart, 1995). In this retrospective design, 95 male and 102 female adoptees whose biological parents had a documented history of antisocial personality disorder (ASPD) or alcohol abuse and dependence were interviewed in adulthood and compared to a control sample of adoptees whose biological parents had no known history of psychopathology. In addition, adoptive parents were interviewed to assess for an "adverse environment" in the rearing adoptive families as defined by the presence of marital discord (e.g., divorce or separation), substance abuse or dependence in an adoptive parents, another psychiatric condition in an adoptive parent, or legal problems in an adoptive parent. The findings revealed that the interaction of a biological parent with a diagnosis of ASPD and an adverse home environment was a significant predictor of both child and adolescent aggression. Moreover, the interaction of these factors was a more robust predictor of aggression than the presence of either a negative biological background or an adverse rearing environment alone.

Second, Caspi and colleagues (2002) utilized a molecular genetic design to investigate whether a gene encoding for enzyme activity of monoamine oxidase-A (MAO-A) would moderate the predictability of violence in children with a history of maltreatment. This hypothesis was based on prior evidence suggesting that childhood maltreatment (Luntz & Widom, 1994) and genetic deficiencies in MAO-A (Brunner et al., 1993) are associated with increased aggression in humans. A polymorphism (variants of DNA sequence) affecting the expression of the MAO-A gene was genotyped in male participants from the Dunedin Multidisciplinary Health and Development Study. A significant interaction was observed between MAO-A activity and childhood maltreatment. Specifically, 85% of males with a low-activity MAO-A genotype who had experienced severe maltreatment as children developed some form of antisocial behavior (e.g., convictions for violent offenses, a personality disposition toward violence). In conjunction with the findings from Cadoret et al. (1995), these results illustrate the importance of a genetic disposition interacting with adverse environmental events as key to the phenotypic expression of aggression and violence. Nonetheless, further investigation may be necessary, particularly in light of a recent study which found an increase in shared environmental but not genetic influences to aggression among twins from disadvantaged neighborhoods (Cleveland, 2003).

Molecular Genetic Studies of Aggression in Humans

Methodology

One limitation of behavioral genetic designs is that they are only capable of inferring the role of genes in the etiology of a phenotype and cannot directly identify which genes are relevant to this process. Molecular genetic designs, however, are rapidly advancing and provide methods aimed at elucidating the causal genes in the etiology of a phenotype. In some respects, searching for causal genes for a quantitative (polygenic) trait, such as aggression, may appear misguided given that such traits are thought to be due to the additive influence of several genes which each confer a very small effect size. The search for quantitative trait loci (QTL) offers an alternative method and helps to bridge quantitative and molecular genetic perspectives (see Maxson & Canastar, ch. 1 in this volume). In common with polygenic models, QTL models presume that multiple genes are important to the etiology of a trait or disorder. However, this method further assumes that these genes may have varying effect sizes and that the genes with larger effects can be identified. Molecular genetic investigations for QTL involve the study of variants of DNA sequences known as markers or *polymorphisms* that are found in either the coding (functional) or noncoding regions of genes. Polymorphisms from coding regions (exons) are important in that they may represent mutations in regions of DNA that code for amino acids. Hence, such polymorphisms may have functional significance for certain biological subsystems. In contrast, polymorphisms from noncoding regions (introns), though of no functional significance, may be worth investigating if they are linked with an unknown functional polymorphism on the same gene.

There are two primary approaches to identifying genes relevant to the etiology of a particular trait or behavior: *Linkage analysis* and *allelic association*. In linkage analysis, DNA from large multigenerational pedigrees with a history of family transmission for a particular trait or disorder are assayed to detect genetic markers whose location on a chromosome is known

and sufficiently near a causal gene. The markers themselves which are implicated need not have any known association with a biological function and may simply be in noncoding regions of a gene. However, these markers tend to remain near the causal genes within genetically homogenous families as result of nonrandom segregation of genes. A variant of this method, sibling-pair linkage analysis, obviates the inherent problems of identifying large multigenerational pedigrees and entails an examination of the number of alleles shared by siblings who are either concordant or discordant for a certain trait or disorder. If the number of shared alleles is significantly greater than expected by chance (approximately 50%, on average, for biological siblings), then the causal gene is thought to be close to the marker being examined. Although these methods may be successful at identifying the causal agents for single-gene (monogenic) disorders such as Huntington's disease, they have comparatively less power to detect genetic effects for polygenic traits such as aggression.

Allelic association assesses whether a known polymorphism or allelic variant of a candidate gene is related to a particular phenotype in a sample of unrelated individuals from the population. Unlike linkage analysis, this method requires that the target marker itself cause the association and code for a particular structure or function (e.g., an enzyme or amino acid) or be in close proximity to the candidate gene or QTL. The frequency of the marker or candidate gene is then compared in individuals with and without a disorder or who are high or low on a specific trait. Notably this approach, which is distinctly suited to the investigation of polygenic phenotypes, requires a previously known association between the function of the specific candidate gene and the phenotype under study. With respect to aggression, most candidate genes selected for investigation have been genes directly implicated in the synthesis or metabolism of the neurotransmitters dopamine and serotonin.

Candidate Genes

Dopamine, an important neurotransmitter associated with individual differences in personality traits and various forms of psychopathology, has been previously linked to novelty seeking in humans (Benjamin, Patterson, Greenberg, Murphy, & Hamer, 1996; Ebstein et al., 1996) and approach behavior in animals (Cloninger, 1987). Several molecular genetic studies have yielded significant associations between dopamine receptor genes and aggression across a variety of disorders. For example, 4-year-olds with long allele repeats of the dopamine D4 receptor gene (DRD4) were rated as more aggressive by their mothers on the CBCL than children with short allele repeats of this gene (Schmidt, Fox, Rubin, Hu, & Hammer, 2002). Dopamine receptor genes have also been implicated in studies of aggressive Alzheimer's dementia (AD) patients. Sweet and colleagues (1998) examined whether polymorphisms for several dopamine receptor genes were associated with psychotic and aggressive behaviors in these patients and found aggressive behavior to be significantly prevalent among AD patients who were homozygous for the DRD1 B2 allele. Likewise, Holmes et al. (2001) found variation in the DRD1 receptor gene to be associated with aggression in AD patients. This relationship, however, was observed in heterozygotes as well as homozygotes for the B2 allele.

Related to the investigation of dopamine receptor genes, other studies have observed associations between aggression and a functional polymorphism in the gene for catechol-O-methyltransferase (COMT), a key enzyme in the metabolism of dopamine. Variations of the COMT polymorphism result in either high or low enzyme activity. Associations between the low activity allele of the COMT gene and aggression in schizophrenic patients have been reported (Kotler et al., 1999; Lachman et al., 1996, 1998; Strous, Bark, Parsia, Volavka, & Lachman, 1997). In an effort to replicate these findings, this association was investigated in a larger sample of schizophrenics (Jones et al., 2001). However, the subsequent finding of an association between aggression and schizophrenics who were homozygous for the *high*-activity COMT allele suggests that the specific relationship between the COMT alleles and aggression is equivocal.

Serotonin, a monoamine neurotransmitter, is perhaps the most thoroughly investigated neurobiological substrate in the etiology of aggression. Dysfunctional serotonergic activity is related to impulsive aggression across a variety of populations and phenotypes (Coccaro, 1989) and has generated extensive research seeking possible candidate genes in the pathogenesis of aggression (see New, Goodman, Mitropoulou, & Siever, 2002). A detailed review of the neurobiology and genetics of serotonin and its associations with aggression is given by Manuck, Kaplan, and Lotrich (ch. 4 in this volume) and is not reproduced here. However, a brief précis of this literature is relevant to the present discussion.

A functional polymorphism in the promoter region of the serotonin transporter gene (5-HTLLPR), which regulates the transcription of this gene and results in either high or low transporter production, has been targeted as a candidate gene for aggression but has yielded variable findings. For example, the presence of a short (S) allele was significantly greater among violent suicide attempters than controls (Courtet et al., 2001). Conversely, the long (L) variant of this allele was associated with aggression in a sample of AD patients (Sukonick et al., 2001). A polymorphism in the noncoding region of the gene for tryptophan hydroxylase (TPH), an important rate-limiting enzyme in the synthesis of serotonin, has also been linked to aggression. Again, however, the findings have been inconsistent regarding the U and L alleles of this gene. Although some studies have demonstrated increased aggression in individuals homozygous for the U allele of this polymorphism (cf. Manuck et al., 1999), others have noted a similar association in individuals homozygous for the L allele (New et al., 2002; Nielsen et al., 1994). This discrepancy notwithstanding, the relevant function of this polymorphism is not entirely clear, given that it is found in a noncoding region of the TPH gene. Thus, its significance may lie more as a marker in close proximity to a functional polymorphism directly related to TPH production.

Finally, a polymorphism in the gene for MAO-A, a key enzyme in the metabolism of serotonin, dopamine, and noradrenaline, has generated considerable speculation as a candidate gene of aggression. As noted earlier, Brunner and colleagues (1993) found that a point mutation in the structural gene for MAO-A resulted in complete and selective deficiency of this enzyme's activity in males from a Dutch kindred who exhibited abnormal impulsive behavior including aggression. Although it is debatable whether such a rare mutation leading to complete MAO inactivity would generalize to studies of normal MAO allelic variation in the population, subsequent studies have been promising. This finding was extended to the larger population and a significant association between allelic variation in the promoter region of the MAO-A gene and several indices of aggression was discovered (Caspi et al., 2002; Manuck, Flory, Ferrell, Mann, & Muldoon, 2000). Thus, functional polymorphisms involved in MAO-A activity remain a viable target for future molecular genetic investigations of aggression and violence.

Conclusions, Implications, and Future Directions

In this chapter we have reviewed the human quantitative genetic literature on aggression across the life span. Overall, the findings suggest that genes begin to emerge as a significant factor in the etiology of aggression in early childhood and continue to influence the stability of these traits well into adulthood. Additionally, the influence of genetic factors appears to increase over the course of development and is followed by a concomitant decrease in contributions from the shared environment. Furthermore, genetic effects on aggression do not appear to operate in isolation and may be moderated by gender differences, as well as interactions with adverse environmental factors.

In this chapter we also attempted to highlight important areas in this literature that require further investigation and clarification. These issues most notably include (a) variable findings based on the method of assessing aggression, (b) inconsistent operational definitions of the construct, and (c) the lack of clearly defined boundaries for the aggression phenotype.

First, in the childhood behavioral genetic literature, estimates of the heritability of aggression have varied as a function of the method of assessment (e.g., parent report vs. observational ratings). Additionally, adult behavioral genetic studies of aggression have been dominated by the use of self-report questionnaires, with little attention to comparable observational or laboratory paradigms. As previously advocated by Miles and Carey (1997), these issues suggest that future research on the etiology of aggression would benefit greatly from multitrait-multimethod approaches (cf. Campbell & Fiske, 1959). Specifically, future studies should strive to obtain reports from multiple informants to account for rater bias or rater-specific contributions to variance in these traits (cf. Hudziak et al., 2003). As well, adult behavioral genetic designs should utilize both self-report questionnaires and laboratory paradigms within the same design in order to assess the degree to which genetic and environmental estimates vary by mode of assessment. Though extant laboratory paradigms of aggression have been criticized for lacking construct validity (see Tedeschi & Quigley, 2000), their inclusion in adult behavioral genetic studies could yield worthwhile insights into the etiology of aggression, as well as fill a notable gap in this literature.

Second, inconsistencies in operationalizing or defining aggression, particularly in the adult literature, have made it difficult to integrate findings across behavioral genetic studies of these traits. Moreover, there exists a lack of behavioral genetic studies investigating alternative typologies of aggression (e.g., reactive vs. proactive aggression, Crick & Dodge, 1996; relational vs. physical aggression, Crick & Grotpeter, 1995). Research of this kind could potentially address important questions regarding the etiology of known expressions of this construct. For example, research on the genetic and environmental contributions to both reactive and proactive aggression could address whether there are common or distinct etiologies to these diverse motivations. Moreover, such research may ultimately enhance our understanding about the etiology of broader motivational subsystems that underlie such behavior (Konorski, 1967). In any case, recognition of the multifaceted nature of aggression represents a promising endeavor for future behavioral genetic investigations of the construct.

Third, the inherent difficulty in defining the boundaries of the construct represents another challenge to future research on the etiology of aggression. In some respects, narrow phenotypic definitions of aggressive behavior that ignore the co-occurrence of these behaviors with other externalizing behaviors (e.g., delinquency) may hinder the search for "general" genes that confer a susceptibility to a range of behavioral problems. On the other hand, an overinclusive approach examining the etiology of such multidimensional traits as Type-A personality may create considerable phenotypic and genotypic heterogeneity in these studies and obscure the relevance of the findings. Accordingly, these issues necessitate a model that can address both *bandwidth* and *fidelity* in defining the boundaries of the aggression construct. As described earlier in this chapter, a hierarchical model which delineates both broad (e.g., externalizing) and specific manifestations of the construct (e.g., hostility) may help guide future research by allowing for the estimation of both common and unique etiologic contributions to aggression and related phenotypes (cf. Krueger et al., 2002).

On a final note, our review of molecular genetic studies of aggression illustrates the feasibility of identifying candidate genes in the etiology of these behaviors. It cannot be overstated, however, that aggression is multifactorial and likely due to the influence of several genes. Thus, caution is warranted in interpreting significant associations with candidate genes without further knowledge of the amount of variance in the phenotype accounted for by these genes. Moreover, given the evidence for genetic nonadditivity in some studies of aggression in adulthood (e.g., Tellegen et al., 1988), future molecular genetic investigations are also encouraged to explore whether interactions of genes within and across alleles (i.e., dominance and epistasis) significantly contribute to the etiology of aggression. Last, the preponderance of evidence demonstrating significant genetic contributions is not meant to undermine the importance of nonshared environmental factors to aggressive behavior. Given previous findings (e.g., Caspi et al., 2002), behavioral and molecular genetic studies may also be well served to investigate the interaction of genetic and environmental factors in order to more precisely delineate the etiologic and developmental course of aggression and violence.

Notes

Preparation of this chapter was supported in part by USPHS Grant MH65137. Daniel M. Blonigen was supported by NIMH Training Grant MH17069.

1. Readers interested in the related behavior genetic literature on antisocial behavior and criminality are referred to reviews by Carey and Goldman (1997), Ishikawa and Raine (2002), and McGuffin and Thapar (1998).

2. The equations given for h^2, c^2, and e^2 derive from Falconer (1960) estimates and represent one of the simplest means of computing values for additive genetic, shared, and nonshared environmental parameters. However, modern analysis of twin data utilizes structural modeling approaches involving maximum likelihood estimation to more precisely estimate these parameters (see Neale & Cardon, 1992, for a review of these methods).

3. Of course, MZ twins may experience more similar environments because their genes have led to such an outcome. Consider, for example, a pair of MZ twins with a genetic predisposition toward athletic talent, both of whom succeed in the childhood pursuit of athletic excellence and, as a result, become world-class athletes in adulthood. This type of phenomenon would not logically violate the assumption, but would instead be a form of gene-environment correlation (cf. Scarr & McCartney, 1983).

References

Achenbach, T. M., & Edelbrock, C. S. (1984). Psychopathology of childhood. *Annual Review of Psychology*, 35, 227–256.

Achenbach, T. M., & McConaughy, S. H. (1997). *Developmental clinical psychology and psychiatry: Vol. 13.*

Empirically based assessment of child and adolescent psychopathology: Practical applications (2nd ed.). Thousand Oaks, CA: Sage.

Achenbach, T. M., & Ruffle, T. M. (2000). The child behavior checklist and related forms for assessing behavioral/emotional problems and competencies. *Pediatrics in Review*, 21, 265–271.

Alsobrook, J. P., & Pauls, D. L. (2000). Genetics and violence. *Child and Adolescent Psychiatric Clinics of North America*, 9(4), 765–776.

Bartels, M., Hudziak, J. J., van den Oord, E. J. C. G., van Beijsterveldt, C. E. M., Rietveld, M. J. H., & Boomsma, D. I. (2003). Co-occurrence of aggressive behavior and rule-breaking behavior at age 12: Multi-rater analyses. *Behavior Genetics*, 33(5), 607–621.

Benjamin, J., Li, L., Patterson, C., Greenberg, B. D., Murphy, D. L., & Hamer, D. H. (1996). Population and familial association between D4 dopamine receptor gene and measures of novelty seeking. *Nature Genetics*, 12, 81–84.

Bohman, M., Cloninger, C. R., Sigvardsson, S., & von Knorring, A. L. (1982). Predisposition in petty criminality in Swedish adoptees: I. Genetic and environmental heterogeneity. *Archives of General Psychiatry*, 39, 1233–1241.

Borkenau, P., Riemann, R., Spinath, F. M., & Angleitner, A. (2000). Behaviour genetics of personality: The case of observational studies. In S. E. Hampson (Ed.), *Advances in personality psychology* (Vol. 1, pp. 107–137). Philadelphia: Taylor & Francis.

Brunner, H. G., Nelen, M., Breakefield, X. O., Ropers, H. H., & van Oost, B. A. (1993). Abnormal behavior associated with a point mutation in the structural gene for monoamine oxidase A. *Science*, 262, 578–580.

Buss, A. H., & Durkee, A. (1957). An inventory for assessing different types of hostility. *Journal of Consulting and Clinical Psychology*, 21, 343–349.

Cadoret, R. J., Yates, W. R., Troughton, E., Woodworth, G., & Stewart, M. A. (1995). Gene-environmental interaction in the genesis of aggressivity and conduct disorders. *Archives of General Psychiatry*, 52, 916–924.

Campbell, D. T., & Fiske, D. W. (1959). Convergent and discriminant validation by the multitrait-multimethod matrix. *Psychological Bulletin*, 56, 81–105.

Carey, G., & Goldman, D. (1997). The genetics of antisocial behavior. In D. M. Stoff, J. Breiling, & J. P. Maser (Eds.), *Handbook of antisocial behavior* (pp. 243–254). New York: Wiley.

Carmelli, D., Rosenman, R. H., & Swan, G. E. (1988). The Cook and Medley Ho Scale: A heritability analysis in adult male twins. *Psychosomatic Medicine*, 50, 165–174.

Carmelli, D., Rosenman, R. H., & Swan, G. E. (1990). The heritability of the Cook and Medley Hostility Scale revisited. *Journal of Social Behavior and Personality, 5,* 107–116.

Caspi, A., McClay, J., Moffitt, T. E., Mill, J., Martin, J., Craig, I. W., et al. (2002). Role of genotype in the cycle of violence in maltreated children. *Science, 297,* 851–854.

Cates, D. S., Houston, B. K., Vavak, C. R., Crawford, M. H., & Uttley, M. (1993). Heritability of hostility-related emotions, attitudes, and behaviors. *Journal of Behavioral Medicine, 16*(3), 237–256.

Christiansen, K. O. (1977). A review of studies of criminality among twins. In S. A. Mednick & K. O. Christiansen (Eds.), *Biosocial bases of criminal behavior* (pp. 45–88). New York: Gardner.

Cleveland, H. H. (2003). Disadvantaged neighborhoods and adolescent aggression: Behavioral genetic evidence of contextual effects. *Journal of Research on Adolescence, 13*(2), 211–238.

Cloninger, C. R. (1987). A systematic method for clinical description and classification of personality variants. *Archives of General Psychiatry, 44,* 573–588.

Cloninger, C. R., & Gottesman, I. I. (1987). Genetic and environmental factors in antisocial behavior disorders. In S. A. Mednick, T. E. Moffit, & S. A. Stark (Eds.), *The causes of crime: New biological approaches* (pp. 92–109). New York: Cambridge University Press.

Coccaro, E. F. (1989). Central serotonin and impulsive aggression. *British Journal of Psychiatry, 155*(Suppl. 8), 52–62.

Coccaro, E. F., Bergeman, C. S., Kavoussi, R. J., & Seroczynski, A. D. (1997). Heritability of aggression and irritability: A twin study of the Buss-Durkee aggression scales in adult male subjects. *Biological Psychiatry, 41*(3), 273–284.

Coccaro, E. F., Bergeman, C. S., & McClearn, G. E. (1993). Heritability of irritable impulsiveness: A study of twins reared apart and together. *Psychiatry Research, 48*(3), 229–242.

Coccaro, E. F., & McNamee, B. (1998). Biology of aggression: Relevance to crime. In A. E. Skodol (Ed.), *Psychopathology and violent crime. Review of psychiatry series* (pp. 99–128). Washington, DC: American Psychiatric Association.

Connors, C. K. (1970). Symptom patterns in hyperkinetic, neurotic, and normal children. *Child Development, 41,* 667–682.

Courtet, P., Baud, P., Abbar, M., Boulenger, J. P., Castelnau, D., Mouthon, D., et al. (2001). Association between violent suicidal behavior and the low activity allele of the serotonin transporter gene. *Molecular Psychiatry, 6,* 338–341.

Crick, N. R., & Dodge, K. A. (1996). Social information-processing mechanisms on reactive and proactive aggression. *Child Development, 67,* 993–1002.

Crick, N. R., & Grotpeter, J. K. (1995). Relationship aggression, gender, and social-psychological adjustment. *Child Development, 66,* 710–722.

Deater-Deckard, K., & Plomin, R. (1999). An adoption study of the etiology of teacher and parent reports of externalizing behavior problems in middle childhood. *Child Development, 70*(1), 144–154.

DiLalla, L. F. (2002). Behavior genetics of aggression in children: Review and future directions. *Developmental Review, 22*(4), 593–622.

DiLalla, L. F., & Gottesman, I. I. (1989). Heterogeneity of causes for delinquency and criminality: Lifespan perspectives. *Development and Psychopathology, 1,* 339–349.

Ebstein, R. P., Novick, O., Umansky, R., Priel, B., Osher, Y., Blaine, D., et al. (1996). Dopamine D4 receptor (D4DR) exon III polymorphism associated with the human personality trait of novelty seeking. *Nature Genetics, 12,* 78–80.

Edelbrock, C., Rende, R., Plomin, R., & Thompson, L. A. (1995). A twin study of competence and problem behavior in childhood and early adolescence. *Journal of Child Psychology and Psychiatry, 36,* 775–785.

Eley, T. C. (1997). General genes: A new theme in developmental psychopathology. *Current Directions in Psychological Science, 6*(4), 90–95.

Eley, T. C., Lichtenstein, P., & Stevenson, J. (1999). Sex differences in the etiology of aggressive and non-aggressive antisocial behavior: Results from two twin studies. *Child Development, 70,* 155–168.

Elkins, I. J., Iacono, W. G., & Doyle, A. E. (1997) Characteristics associated with the persistence of antisocial behavior: Results from recent longitudinal research. *Aggression and Violent Behavior, 2*(2), 101–124.

Evans, D. M., Gillespie, N. A., & Martin, N. G. (2002). Biometrical genetics. *Biological Psychology, 61,* 33–51

Falconer, D. S. (1960). *Introduction to quantitative genetics.* New York: Ronald Press.

Finkel, D., & McGue, M. (1997). Sex differences and nonadditivity in heritability of the Multidimensional Personality Questionnaire scales. *Journal of Personality and Social Psychology, 72*(4), 929–938.

Fisher, R. A. (1918). The correlation between relatives on the supposition of Mendelian inheritance. *Transactions of the Royal Society of Edinburgh, 52,* 399–433.

Ghodsian-Carpey, J., & Baker, L. A. (1987). Genetic and environmental influences on aggression in 4- to 7-year-old twins. *Aggressive Behavior, 13,* 173–186.

Gusella, J. F., Wexler, N. S., Conneally, M. P., Naylor, S. L., Anderson, M., Tanzi, R. E., et al. (1983). A polymorphic DNA marker genetically linked to Huntington's disease. *Nature, 306,* 234–238.

Gustavsson, J. P., Pedersen, N. L., Åsberg, M., & Schalling, D. (1996). Exploration into the sources of individual differences in aggression, hostility, and anger-related (AHA) personality traits. *Personality and Individual Differences, 21*(6), 1067–1071.

Hofstra, M. B., van der Ende, J., & Verhulst, F. C. (2000). Continuity and change of psychopathology from childhood into adulthood: A 14-year follow-up study. *Journal of the American Academy of Child and Adolescent Psychiatry, 39,* 850–858.

Holmes, C., Smith, H., Ganderton, R., Arranz, M., Collier, D., Powell, J., et al. (2001). Psychosis and aggression in Alzheimer's disease: The effect of dopamine receptor gene variation. *Journal of Neurology, Neurosurgery, and Psychiatry, 71*(6), 777–779.

Hudziak, J. J., van Beijsterveldt, C. E. M., Bartels, M., Rietveld, M. J. H., Rettew, D. C., Derks, E. M., et al. (2003). Individual differences in aggression: Genetic analyses by age, gender, and informant in 3, 7, and 10-year-old Dutch twins. *Behavior Genetics, 33*(5), 575–589.

Ishikawa, S. S., & Raine, A. (2002). Behavioral genetics of crime. In J. Glicksohn (Ed.), *The neurobiology of criminal behavior. Neurobiological foundation of aberrant behaviors* (pp. 81–110). Dordrecht, Netherlands: Kluwer Academic.

Jacobs, P. A., Brunton, M., Melville, M. M., Brittain, R. P., & McClement, W. F. (1965). Aggressive behaviour, mental sub-normality, and the XYY male. *Nature, 208,* 1351–1352.

Johnson, W., Krueger, R. F., Bouchard, T. J., & McGue, M. (2002). The personalities of twins: Just ordinary folks. *Twin Research, 5*(2), 125–131.

Johnson, W., McGue, M., & Krueger, R. F. (2005). Personality stability in late adulthood: A behavioral genetic analysis. *Journal of Personality, 73*(2), 523–552.

Jones, G., Zammit, S., Norton, N., Hamshere, M. L., Jones, S. J., Milham, C., et al. (2001). Aggressive behaviour in patients with schizophrenia is associated with catechol-O-methyltransferase genotype. *British Journal of Psychiatry, 179,* 351–355.

Kendler, K. S., Martin, N. G., Heath, A. C., & Eaves, L. J. (1995). Self-report psychiatric symptoms in twins and their non-twin relatives: Are twins different? *American Journal of Medical Genetics, 60,* 588–591.

Kendler, K. S., Neale, M. C., Kessler, R. C., Heath, A. C., & Eaves, L. J. (1994). Parental treatment and the equal environment assumption in twin studies of psychiatric illness. *Psychological Medicine, 24,* 579–590.

Konorski, J. (1967). *Integrative activity of the brain: An interdisciplinary approach.* Chicago: University of Chicago Press.

Koot, H. M. (1995). Longitudinal studies of general population and community samples. In F. C. Verhulst & H. M. Koot (Eds.), *The epidemiology of child and adolescent psychopathology* (pp. 337–365). New York: Oxford University Press.

Kotler, M., Barak, P., Cohen, H., Averbuch, I. E., Grinshpoon, A., Gritsenko, I., et al. (1999). Homicidal behavior in schizophrenia associated with a genetic polymorphism determining low catechol-O-methyltransferase (COMT) activity. *American Journal of Medical Genetics, 88*(6), 628–633.

Krueger, R. F. (2000). Phenotypic, genetic, and nonshared environmental parallels in the structure of personality: A view from the Multidimensional Personality Questionnaire. *Journal of Personality and Social Psychology, 79*(6), 1057–1067.

Krueger, R. F., Hicks, B. M., Patrick, C. J., Carlson, S. R., Iacono, W. G., & McGue, M. (2002). Etiologic connections among substance dependence, antisocial behavior, and personality: Modeling the externalizing spectrum. Journal of Abnormal Psychology, 111, 411–424.

Krueger, R. F., & Markon, K. E. (2002). Behavior genetic perspectives on clinical personality assessment. In J. N. Butcher (Ed.), *Clinical personality assessment: Practical approaches* (2nd ed., pp. 40–55). London: Oxford University Press.

Krueger, R. F., Moffitt, T. E., Caspi, A., Bleske, A., & Silva, P. A. (1998). Assortative mating for antisocial behavior: Developmental and methodological implications. *Behavior Genetics, 28*(3), 173–186.

Lachman, H. M., Nolan, K. A., Mohr, P., Saito, T., & Volavka, J. (1998). Association between catechol-O-methyltransferase genotype and violence in schizophrenia and schizoaffective disorder. *American Journal of Psychiatry, 155*(6), 835–837.

Lachman, H. M., Papolos, D. F., Saito, T., Yu, Y. M., Szumlanski, C. L., & Weinshilboum, R. M. (1996). Human catechol-O-methyltransferase pharmacogenetics: Description of a functional polymorphism and its potential application to neuropsychiatric disorders. Pharmacogenetics, 6, 243–250.

Loeber, R., & Hay, D. (1997). Key issues in the development of aggression and violence from childhood to early adulthood. Annual Review of Psychology, 48, 371–410.

Loehlin, J. C. (1998). *Latent variable models: An introduction to factor, path, and structural analysis* (3rd ed.). Mahwah, NJ: Erlbaum.

Loehlin, J. C., & Nichols, R. C. (1976). *Heredity, environment, and personality.* Austin: University of Texas Press.

Luntz, B. K., & Widom, C. S. (1994). Antisocial personality disorder in abused and neglected children grown up. *American Journal of Psychiatry, 151*(5), 670–674.

Maccoby, E. E., & Jacklin, C. N. (1980). Sex differences in aggression: A rejoinder and reprise. *Child Development, 51,* 964–980.

Manuck, S. B., Flory, J. D., Ferrell, R. E., Dent, K. M., Mann, J. J., & Muldoon, M. F. (1999). Aggression and anger-related traits associated with a polymorphism of the tryptophan hydroxylase gene. *Biological Psychiatry, 45,* 603–614.

Manuck, S. B., Flory, J. D., Ferrell, R. E., Mann, J. J., & Muldoon, M. F. (2000). A regulatory polymorphism of the monoamine oxidase-A gene may be associated with variability in aggression, impulsivity, and central nervous system serotonergic activity. *Psychiatry Research, 95,* 9–23.

Mauger, P. A., & Adkinson, D. R. (1980). *Interpersonal behavior survey (IBS) manual.* Los Angeles: Western Psychological Services.

McGue, M., Bacon, S., & Lykken, D. T. (1993). Personality stability and change in early adulthood: A behavioral genetic analysis. *Developmental Psychology, 29,* 96–109.

McGuffin, P., & Thapar, A. (1998). Genetics and antisocial personality disorder. In T. Millon, E. Simonsen, M. Birket-Smith, & R. Davis (Eds.), *Psychopathy: Antisocial, criminal, and violent behavior* (pp. 215–230). New York: Guilford Press.

Mednick, S. A., Gabrielli, W. F., & Hutchings, B. (1984). Genetic influences in criminal convictions: Evidence from an adoption cohort. *Science, 224,* 891–894.

Miles, D. R., & Carey, G. (1997). Genetic and environmental architecture of human aggression. *Journal of Personality and Social Psychology, 72,* 207–217.

Moffitt, T. E. (1993). Adolescence-limited and life-course persistent antisocial behavior: A developmental taxonomy. *Psychological Review, 100,* 674–701.

Moffitt, T. E., Caspi, A., Harrington, H., & Milne B. J. (2002). Males on the life-course-persistent and adolescence-limited antisocial pathways: Follow-up at age 26 years. *Development and Psychopathology, 14*(1), 179–207.

Neale, M. C., & Cardon, L. R. (1992). *Methodology for genetic studies of twins and families.* Dordrecht, Netherlands: Kluwer Academic.

New, A., Goodman, M., Mitropoulou, V., & Siever, L. (2002). Genetic polymorphisms and aggression. In J. Benjamin & B. P. Ebstein (Eds.), *Molecular genetics and the human personality* (pp. 231–244). Washington, DC: American Psychiatric Association.

Nielsen, D. A., Goldman, D., Virkkunen, M., Tokola, R., Rawlings, R., & Linnoila, M. (1994). Suicidality and 5-hydroxyindoleacetic acid concentration associated with a tryptophan hydroxylase polymorphism. *Archives of General Psychiatry, 51,* 34–38.

O'Connor, M., Foch, T., Sherry, T., & Plomin, R. (1980). A twin study of specific behavioral problems of socialization as viewed by parents. *Journal of Abnormal Child Psychology, 8*(2), 189–199.

O'Connor, T. G., Hetherington, E. M., Reiss, D., & Plomin, R. (1995). A twin-sibling study of observed parent-adolescent interactions. *Child Development, 66,* 812–829.

Owen, D. R., & Sines, J. O. (1970). Heritability of personality in children. *Behavior Genetics, 1,* 235–248.

Pedersen, N. L., Lichtenstein, P., Plomin, R., DeFaire, U., McClearn, G. E., & Matthews, K. A. (1989). Genetic and environmental influences for Type A-like measures and related traits: A study of twins reared apart and twins reared together. *Psychosomatic Medicine, 51,* 428–440.

Plomin, R. (1981). Heredity and temperament: A comparison of twin data for self-report questionnaires, parental ratings, and objectively assessed behavior. In L. Gedda, P. Parisi, & W. E. Nance (Eds.), *Twin research 3: Part B. Intelligence, personality, and development* (pp. 269–278). New York: Alan R. Liss.

Plomin, R., DeFries, J. C., McClearn, G. E., & Rutter, M. (1997). *Behavioral genetics* (3rd ed.). New York: Freeman.

Plomin, R., Foch, T. T., & Rowe, D. C. (1981). Bobo clown aggression in childhood: Environment not genes. *Journal of Research in Personality, 15,* 331–342.

Plomin, R., Nitz, K., & Rowe, D. C. (1990) Behavior genetics and aggressive behavior in childhood. In M. Lewis & S. Miller (Eds.), *Handbook of developmental psychopathology: Perspectives in developmental psychology* (pp. 119–133). New York: Plenum.

Pulkkinen, L., Kaprio, J., & Rose, R. (1999). Peers, teachers, and parents as assessors of the behavioural and emotional problems of twins and their adjustment: The Multidimensional Peer Nomination Inventory. *Twin Research, 2,* 274–285.

Pulkkinen, L., & Pitkaenen, T. (1993). Continuities in aggressive behavior from childhood to adulthood. *Aggressive Behavior, 19*(4), 249–263.

Rhee, S. H., & Waldman, I. D. (2002). Genetic and environmental influences on antisocial behavior: A meta-analysis of twin and adoption studies. *Psychological Bulletin, 128*(3), 490–529.

Rushton, J. P., Fulker, D. W., Neale, M. C., Nias, D. K. B., & Eysenck, H. J. (1986). Altruism and aggression: The heritability of individual differences. *Journal of Personality and Social Psychology, 50*(6), 1192–1198.

Rutter, M. (1997). Comorbidity: Concepts, claims, and choices. *Criminal Behaviour and Mental Health, 7,* 265–285.

Saudino, K. J. (2003). Parent ratings of infant temperament: Lessons from twin studies. *Infant Behavior and Development, 26*, 100–107.

Scarr, S. (1966). Genetic factors in activity motivation. *Child Development, 37*, 663–673.

Scarr, S., & McCartney, K. (1983). How people make their own environments: A theory of genotype-environment effects. *Child Development, 54*, 424–435.

Schmidt, L. A., Fox, N. A., Rubin, K. H., Hu, S., & Hamer, D. H. (2002). Molecular genetics of shyness and aggression in preschoolers. *Personality and Individual Differences, 33*(2), 227–238.

Schmitz, S., Fulker, D. W., & Mrazek, D. A. (1995). Problem behavior in early and middle childhood: An initial behavior genetic analysis. *Journal of Child Psychology and Psychiatry, 36*(8), 1443–1458.

Simonoff, E., Pickles, A., Hervas, A., Silberg, J. L., Rutter, M., & Eaves, L. J. (1998). Genetic influences on childhood hyperactivity: Contrast effects imply parental rating bias not sibling interaction. *Psychological Medicine, 28*(4), 825–837.

Smith, T. W., & Frohm, K. D. (1985). What's so unhealthy about hostility? Construct validity and psychosocial correlates of the Cook and Medley HO scale. *Health Psychology, 4*, 503–520.

Spielberger, C. D., Johnson, E. H., Russell, S. F., Crane, R. J., Jacobs, G. A., & Worden, T. J. (1985). The experience and expression of anger: Construction and validation of an anger expression scale. In M. A. Chesney & R. H. Rosenman (Eds.), *Anger and hostility in cardiovascular and behavioral disorders* (pp. 5–30). New York: Hemisphere/McGraw–Hill.

Strous, R. D., Bark, N., Parsia, S. S., Volavka, J., & Lachman, H. M. (1997). Analysis of a functional catechol-O-methyltransferase gene polymorphism in schizophrenia: Evidence for association with aggressive and antisocial behavior. *Psychiatry Research, 69*, 71–77.

Sukonick, D. L., Pollock, B. G., Sweet, R. A., Mulsant, B. H., Rosen, J., Klunk, W. E., et al. (2001). The 5-HTTPR*S/*L polymorphism and aggressive behavior in Alzheimer disease. *Archives of Neurology, 58*(9), 1425–1428.

Sweet, R. A., Nimgaonkar, V. L., Kamboh, M. I., Lopez, O. L., Zhang, F., & DeKosky, S. T. (1998). Dopamine receptor genetic variation, psychosis, and aggression in Alzheimer disease. *Archives of Neurology, 55*(10), 1335–1340.

Tedeschi, J. T., & Quigley, B. M. (2000). A further comment on the construct validity of laboratory aggression paradigms: A response to Giancola and Chermack. *Aggression and Violent Behavior, 5*(2), 127–136.

Tellegen, A. (1985). Structure of mood and personality and their relevance to assessing anxiety, with an emphasis on self-report. In T. A. Hussain & J. D. Maser (Eds.), *Anxiety and anxiety disorders* (pp. 681–706). Hillsdale, NJ: Erlbaum.

Tellegen, A. (in press). *Manual for the Multidimensional Personality Questionnaire.* Minneapolis: University of Minnesota Press.

Tellegen, A., Lykken, D. T., Bouchard, T. J., Jr., Wilcox, K. J., Segal, N. L., & Rich, S. (1988). Personality similarity in twins reared apart and together. *Journal of Personality and Social Psychology, 54*(6), 1031–1039.

Van Beijsterveldt, C. E. M., Bartels, M., Hudziak, J. J., & Boomsma, D. I. (2003). Causes of stability of aggression from early childhood to adolescence: A longitudinal genetic analysis in Dutch twins. *Behavior Genetics, 33*(5), 591–605.

Van den Oord, E. J. C. G., Boomsma, D. I., & Verhulst, F. C. (1994). A study of problem behaviors in 10- to 15-year-old biologically related and unrelated international adoptees. *Behavior Genetics, 24*, 193–205.

Van der Valk, J. C., Verhulst, F. C., Neale, M. C., & Boomsma, D. I. (1998). Longitudinal genetic analysis of problem behaviors in biologically related and unrelated adoptees. *Behavior Genetics, 28*(5), 365–380.

Verhulst, F. C., & Koot, H. M. (1992). *Developmental clinical psychology and psychiatry: Vol. 23. Child psychiatric epidemiology: Concepts, methods, and findings.* Newbury Park, CA: Sage.

Verhulst, F. C., & van der Ende, J. (1993). "Comorbidity" in an epidemiological sample: A longitudinal perspective. *Journal of Child Psychiatry and Psychology, 34*, 767–783.

Verhulst, F. C., & van der Ende, J. (1995). The eight-year stability of problem behavior in an epidemiological sample. *Pediatric Research, 38*, 612–617.

Vierikko, E., Pulkkinen, L., Kaprio, J., Viken, R., & Rose, R. J. (2003). Sex differences in genetic and environmental effects on aggression. *Aggressive Behavior, 29*(1), 55–68.

Wright, S. (1921). Systems of mating. *Genetics, 6*, 111–178.

Yang, H. J., Chen, W. J., & Soong, W. T. (2001). Rates and patterns of comorbidity of adolescent behavioral syndromes as reported by parents and teachers in a Taiwanese nonreferred sample. *Journal of the American Academy of Child and Adolescent Psychiatry, 40*, 1045–1052.

3

Crustacean Models
of Aggression

Donald H. Edwards & Jens Herberholz

In crustaceans, as in other social animals, aggression is used to gain and control access to resources, including shelter, food, and mate choice. The high "resource-holding potential" of some crustaceans (their heavy claws and armor, their mobility and agility, and their aggressive temperament) enables them both to attack and to defend against conspecifics, to obtain or retain these resources. The ability of some crustaceans to recognize other individuals or social dominance cues enables them to establish and maintain a social dominance hierarchy, which then helps to divide scarce resources while reducing aggressive behavior. The recent focus on social behavior has led to an appreciation of the roles that communication and learning play in mediating between dominance and aggression. Olfactory signaling and learning have been shown to be particularly important for the struggle to become or remain socially dominant.

Many species of crustaceans, especially the familiar crabs, lobsters, and crayfish, are equipped with both heavy armor for defense and heavy pincers for attack and defense. Others, such as stomatopods and snapping shrimp, have modified the claws into powerful offensive weapons, while still others, such as barnacles, have forsaken offense and built stout fixed shelters or

found strong mobile shelters, as with hermit crabs. The variety of behaviors displayed both within and across species, as well as their small size and accessibility in the wild, makes crustaceans an excellent model for the study of aggressive behavior.

The same behaviors used in conspecific aggression are used in interspecific competition and in predator/prey interactions, where crustaceans can play both roles. The characteristics of crustaceans that facilitate the study of aggression also facilitate study of competitive and predator/prey behavior and provide an opportunity to study the relationship of both to aggression. What are the similarities and differences between an attack used to assert social dominance and that used to drive a rival species away, or that used in predation? Similarly, what is the relationship between defensive behaviors used to signal social subordination and those used to avoid predation?

Crustaceans have also been a popular choice for neuroethological studies. In addition to easily observed behavior patterns, they have readily accessible nervous systems that contain many large, identifiable neurons that play key roles in mediating these behaviors. Moreover, the hard exoskeleton, open circulation, and hardy constitution together have facilitated many studies on sensory and motor processes, neural circuits, and neuroendocrine systems and their effects on behavior in both dissected and largely intact preparations. Indeed, studies of higher order visual processing, the neural substrates of fixed action patterns, rhythmic pattern generation, postural control, neuromuscular control, GABAergic inhibition, and neuromodulation were first pioneered in crustacean preparations.

This understanding of the neural mechanisms of simple behaviors provides the foundation for understanding mechanisms behind more complex aggressive behavior. Although this effort is only beginning, the role of specific neural circuits, such as those for escape, and specific neurohormones, including monoamines and peptides, in mediating aspects of aggressive behavior have already become apparent. Here we address all of these issues and end by identifying promising future approaches to research on crustacean aggression.

Natural Contexts of Aggression

Intraspecific Competition for Scarce Resources

Many crustaceans live in an environment of limited resources. They compete aggressively for immediate or future access to these resources and once obtained they defend them vigorously. Shelter possession is of great importance for most crustaceans. Shelters are mainly used for predator defense, but are also used by reproductive adults to attract and mate with individuals of the opposite sex. Obtaining and retaining a shelter usually involves aggressive interactions and the number of observed aggressive behaviors correlates with the abundance of shelters. The potential to gain and hold shelter possession depends on size, prior residence, sex, and maternal state.

In crayfish, shelter possession directly influences survival by reducing the risk of predation. In the presence of a predator, crayfish select substrates that afford the most protection (Stein, 1977; Stein & Magnuson, 1976) and survival rates decrease with limitation of shelters (Garvey, Stein, & Thomas, 1994). With decreased shelter, more aggressive interactions take place (Capelli & Hamilton, 1984; Capelli & Munjal, 1982). Juvenile signal crayfish (*Pacifastacus leniusculus*) reside inside shelters during the day and leave for food during the night (Ranta & Lindström, 1992). At daybreak they return to either the burrow they left or a new shelter. Upon return, fights break out and larger intruders usually evict smaller owners from their shelters. If food is presented in a single spot, then large animals occupy shelters nearby, while smaller animals live in shelters farther away from the food source. Studying juveniles of another crayfish species, *Procambarus clarkii*, it was shown that size, but neither sex nor prior residency, is correlated with the outcome of shelter-related competition (Figler, Cheverton, & Blank, 1999). In adult *Pro. clarkii*, however, enhanced territoriality of maternal residents was reported. Maternal female crayfish were much more successful in defending a shelter or burrow against male intruders than nonmaternal females (Figler, Blank, & Peeke, 2001). Moreover, prior residence effects were observed in adults of several crustacean species, but these effects may not emerge until reproductive age is reached.

Possession of a shelter is required for male lobsters to attract and mate with females (Atema, Jacobson, Karnofsky, Oleszko-Szuts, & Stein, 1979; Cowan & Atema, 1990). Males perform pre- and postcopulatory mate guarding, which allows the females to molt inside the shelter and to harden the exoskeleton before it leaves the burrow (Atema, 1986; Atema & Cobb, 1980; Atema et al., 1979; Atema & Voigt, 1995). Consequently, adult male lobsters are very successful in defending their shelters against intruders and have a shelter competition advantage over females. Even juvenile nonreproductive male lobsters were discovered to be successful in winning or holding a shelter against other males, a possible preadaptation for later stages in their lives (Peeke, Figler, & Chang, 1998).

Snapping shrimp are marine crustaceans that live in large populations and occupy shelters as male-female pairs. The females reproduce after each molt and are guarded by the males. Snapping shrimp use a large modified claw to produce fast water jets during intra- and interspecific encounters. The water jets are generated in a ritualized fashion during aggressive encounters with conspecifics (Herberholz & Schmitz, 1998) and are frequently used in the acquisition and defense of shelters. Larger individuals possess larger snapping claws, thus producing faster jets, and readily evict smaller opponents from shelters (Nolan & Salmon, 1970). Pairs usually consist of size-matched males and females and it was found that snapping shrimp prefer to pair according to size (Rahman, Dunham, & Govind, 2002). Males with the same body size and claw size as females produce more powerful water jets, which corresponds to their main function of defending the territory and mate (Herberholz & Schmitz, 1999).

Hermit crabs inhabit gastropod shells and aggressively fight over ownership, sometimes leading to an exchange of shells. During the interactions the attacker raps its own shell against that of the defender in a series of bouts that are interrupted by pauses, during which the initiator tries to pull the opponent out of the shell (Briffa & Elwood, 2000, 2002). As the rapping increases in power, the likelihood of displacing the defender increases; consequently, the probability of a successful eviction is determined by the physical fitness of the attacker. Both the temporal rate and magnitude of rapping are subject to fatigue and only hermit crabs in good condition produce shell rapping attacks sufficiently powerful to evict the opponent (Briffa, Elwood, & Russ, 2003).

Competition for food, another resource that can be limited under certain circumstances, commonly leads to aggressive interactions among crustaceans. Capelli and Hamilton (1984) described the effects of food availability and quality on aggression in the crayfish species *Orconectes rusticus*. They found that the limitation of preferred food results in more aggressive interactions than an abundance of the same food or the limitation of a less preferred food. Furthermore, crayfish are more aggressive and escalate fights more rapidly and fighting lasts longer in the presence of chemical food cues (Stocker & Huber, 2001). Similarly, the intensity of fights among male shore crabs, *Carcinus maenas*, increases in the presence of food, while the duration of encounters decreases (Sneddon, Huntingford, & Taylor, 1997).

No size differences were found in crayfish residing in areas nearby or farther away in a nursery pond experiment with juvenile signal crayfish (*P. leniusculus*) when low-protein food was made available throughout. When high-protein food was introduced in only one spot, large animals occupied areas close by, while small animals were aggressively displaced into areas farther away from the food source (Ranta & Lindström, 1992).

Observation of aggressive behavior in two crayfish species (*O. virilis* and *O. rusticus*) in the field revealed longer and more intense fighting in detritus habitats than in macrophyte habitats, presumably because detritus has a higher nutritional value than macrophytes (Bergman & Moore, 2003).

To guarantee reproductive success, many crustaceans must also compete for receptive mates. Males compete for access to females, which are limited in relation to males. Some crustaceans (e.g., crabs, lobsters, and shrimps) are exceptional in the sense that females are only receptive immediately after molting, when their carapace is soft and they are vulnerable to predation. As a result, males in these species often guard females to enhance their reproductive success prior to and some time after the females' molt inside the shelter. Thus, females need to be attracted, guarded, and often aggressively defended for prolonged time periods. In other crustaceans (e.g., crayfish) females do not molt prior to mating and breed in isolation. Although differently structured, both systems involve highly aggressive behaviors between competitors for mates or between mates themselves.

Pair formation in crayfish starts with aggressive interactions between the male and female, from which the male emerges as the dominant member of the pair (Bovbjerg, 1956; Lowe, 1956). Once the female displays submissive postures, copulation takes place. However, if the female continues to show aggression toward the male mating, mating attempts cease and fights often cause injuries or death in females (Woodlock & Reynolds, 1988). Besides the aggressive behaviors between males and females, intermale competition for a female is also common among different crayfish species. In groups of *Austropotamobius pallipes*, the white-clawed crayfish, larger males kill smaller rival males before any mating is subsequently initiated (Woodlock & Reynolds, 1988), and in a different species (*O. rusticus*) smaller males have fewer copulations than larger ones but intermale aggression ceases when the females are removed (Berrill & Arsenault, 1984).

In lobsters, fighting mainly occurs between males to establish dominance hierarchies. Large dominant animals then occupy preferred shelters and pair formation takes place inside the shelter, which the males defend against intruders (Atema & Voigt, 1995). In groups of mixed-sex lobsters, females are able to stagger the timing of their molting to mate with the dominant male (Cowan & Atema, 1990).

In blue crabs, *Callinectes sapidus*, field observations have shown that large males are more often found paired with a female than are small males (Jivoff, 1997) and large males are also more successful in displacing guarding males from females and in defending a shelter against intruders (Jivoff & Hines, 1998). In green shore crabs, *C. maenas*, larger males outcompete smaller males and have more copulations even when the smaller males are paired with a female before the larger rival is introduced (Berrill & Arsenault, 1982).

When tested during different molt stages and with regard to the effects of these stages on competition for access to receptive females, rock shrimp (*Rhynchocinetes typus*) males of the later molt stages (equipped with chelae) were more successful in a competitive environment, while all male stages have similar mating success in a competition-free environment (Correa, Baeza, Hinojosa, & Thiel, 2003).

Snapping shrimp are socially monogamous and share shelters that are defended by both partners against intruders. Males and females of a pair are usually size matched (Rahman et al., 2002), but males possess a larger snapper claw and produce more powerful water jets (Herberholz & Schmitz, 1999). The water jets are used during agonistic interactions and larger individuals usually dominate smaller ones, which are frequently evicted from shelters (Nolan & Salmon, 1970). In the snapping shrimp species *Alpheus angulatus*, Mathews (2002) recently reported that males that cohabit shelters with receptive females are less likely to be evicted from the burrow than males with low expectations of immediate reproductive success. These results suggest that males invest more in territorial defense when the partner has high reproductive value.

Many crustaceans engage in aggressive encounters without the expectation of immediate access to a resource. In fact, many studies that analyzed the structural and temporal dynamics of agonistic interactions in crustaceans used featureless aquaria for this purpose. After a group of juvenile crayfish with no former social experience was introduced into a water-filled but otherwise empty arena, the members of the group immediately established a social hierarchy through agonistic interactions (Issa, Adamson, & Edwards, 1999). In doing so, the animals displace an innate willingness to fight that may help determine access to future resources.

Although success in retaining and defending a resource is often decided by differences in body size between the contestants, weaponry can be a predictor of competitive success as well. Many crustaceans have developed powerful weapons by modifying the first pair of walking legs into (bilateral asymmetric) chelipeds of different sizes and shapes. Male fiddler crabs use one greatly enlarged claw to attract females and to fight other males, while the smaller claw is used for feeding. Crabs (*Uca annulipes*) that had lost their claw and regenerated a new one that was of less mass, but equal length, are more likely to lose to opponents that possess original claws (Backwell, Christy, Telford,

Jennions, & Passmore, 2000). However, females do not discriminate against males with regenerated claws; thus the disadvantage is restricted to agonistic interactions with competitors. In shore crabs, *C. maenas*, claw size rather than body size predicts the outcome of aggressive encounters (Sneddon et al., 1997). When the differences in claw lengths are small between the opponents, the winners of agonistic contests always have wider claws that give them a mechanical advantage and generate greater force (Sneddon, Taylor, Huntingford, & Orr, 2000). Using males of the freshwater prawn *Macrobrachium rosenbergii*, Barki, Karplus, and Goren (1997) studied the outcome of fights between animals of different body sizes and claw sizes. They found that males with longer claws win most encounters and animals that are much smaller in body size but have claws of equal size win half of the contests. These results suggest that cheliped size is the sole decision maker for fighting success in freshwater prawns. Snapping shrimp of the species *A. heterochaelis* typically have one large chela that is modified to produce water jets during intra- and interspecific encounters. When used at close distance, the water jets are sufficiently powerful to stun and kill small prey but are used at longer distances during ritualized aggressive interactions with conspecifics (Herberholz & Schmitz, 1998). It has been shown that shrimp with removed or immobilized large claws are less successful in acquiring a shelter and less successful in retaining it against opponents, even when larger in body size. However, these impaired shrimp are as likely to pair with the opposite sex (Conover & Miller, 1978). The importance of the large snapper claw for agonistic success has lead to an interesting phenomenon in these animals. Immediately after the large claw is lost (e.g., during fights), the intact smaller pincer claw on the opposite side gradually transforms into a new snapper claw, while a new pincer claw regenerates at the old snapper claw site (Read & Govind, 1997).

Aggression During Maternity and the Molt Cycle

Crustaceans display aggressive behaviors not only in competition for current or future resources, but also, in common with mammals and birds (see Gammie & Lonstein, ch. 11 in this volume), show increased aggression as a result of maternity and molt stage.

Lowe (1956) first noted that female crayfish (*Cambarellus shufeldtii*) carrying eggs are more aggressive than those without. In her study, a single female with eggs dominated an entire group of male and female crayfish without eggs. As soon as a female drops its offspring the aggressiveness ceases. Heightened aggressiveness against adult conspecifics was also reported in ovigerous females of another crayfish species, *P. trowbridgi* (Mason, 1970). More recently, Figler, Twum, Finkelstein, and Peeke (1995) reported that maternal crayfish females (*Pro. clarkii*) are very successful in defending a shelter against male and nonmaternal female intruders. Residents carrying eggs or offspring win more encounters against opponents than nonmaternal residents (Figler, Peeke, & Chang, 1997).

Heightened aggressiveness and contest advantages for maternal females over nonmaternal females were also demonstrated in the American lobster (*Homarus americanus*), where females carrying eggs perform more aggressive behaviors and engage in more intense fighting than nonmaternal females (Figler et al., 1997; Mello, Cromarty, & Kass-Simon, 1999). Moreover, egg-carrying females fail to respond to a visual threat that readily elicits escape behavior in nonmaternal and male lobsters (Cromarty, Mello, & Kass-Simon, 1998).

In stomatopods (*Gonodactylus bredini*) females with eggs are most aggressive during the time of breeding, which increases their success in shelter competition. The effect of increased shelter defense lasts several days after the eggs are removed from females (Montgomery & Caldwell, 1984). However, females and males are able to distinguish between former mates and unfamiliar members of the opposite sex. They remember mates for at least 2 weeks following separation and greatly reduce aggressiveness in encounters with them (Caldwell, 1992).

Changes in aggressiveness were also observed in lobsters during different stages of the molt cycle. Postmolt animals are soft shelled and vulnerable to intra- and interspecific predation. As a consequence, premolt lobsters become extremely aggressive shortly before they molt, most likely to scare away any potential postmolt threats and to acquire or defend a shelter for subsequent molting (Atema et al., 1979; Tamm & Cobb, 1978). The increased aggressiveness is accompanied by and may be linked to an increase of 20-hydroxyecdysone, the active form of the molting hormone ecdysone, in blood titers (Snyder & Chang, 1991; and see below).

Newly molted stomatopods (*G. bredini*) cannot use their raptorial appendages to defend their shelters and instead produce a threat display by raising and later-

ally spreading the appendages. The aggressive display increases after molts and may enhance the chances to defend the shelter by bluffing possible intruders (Steger & Caldwell, 1983).

Interspecific Competition and Displacement

Co-occurrence of different crustacean species in the same geographical locations leads to aggressive competition between them. The agonistic encounters result from competition for shared resources in overlapping ecological ranges. More aggressive species often dominate less aggressive ones, which causes eviction, displacement, and sometimes exclusion of some (often native) species from selected habitats. Unfortunately, few data on interspecific competition among different crustacean species have been collected in the field; most results are obtained form laboratory experiments, which may only be an approximate account of the actual ecological situation in the natural habitat. Moreover, most reports focus on freshwater species (e.g., crayfish) and little is known about interspecific aggressiveness in marine crustaceans.

Bovbjerg (1970) investigated the relationship between two crayfish species, *O. virilis* and *O. immunis*, in field and laboratory experiments and concluded that the exclusion of the pond species *O. immunis* from a nearby stream is a result of direct aggressive interactions between the species, the more aggressive and dominant *O. virilis* prevailing over its counterpart. Capelli and Munjal (1982) studied three different *Orconectes* species (*O. rusticus* and *O. propinquus*, both intruders, and *O. virilis*, a native species in lakes of northern Wisconsin) in the laboratory in the presence and absence of shelters. They reported that *O. rusticus* most aggressively dominates both other species in agonistic encounters and outcompetes both for shelter possession. This result is consistent with field data showing that *O. rusticus* had almost entirely displaced the other species within some years following its introduction. When paired with a predatory fish, *O. virilis* is consumed in large numbers and *O. propinquus* is eaten more often than *O. rusticus* because of its smaller average size. The increased vulnerability of *O. virilis* to predation is a direct result of shelter eviction by both intruder species (Garvey et al., 1994). Tierney, Godleski, and Massanari (2000) provided a detailed comparison of aggressiveness in four different crayfish species, measuring the number and aggressive acts during intra-specific encounters. They reported that *P. leniusculus* displays most aggressive behaviors during agonistic interactions, while *O. rusticus* and *O. propinquus* are similar but less aggressive and *O. immunis* is the least aggressive. Behavior of juveniles from two crayfish species was studied, one native species (*Astacus astacus*) to Swedish lakes that is being replaced by an intruder (*P. leniusculus*) (Söderbäck, 1994). Both were paired with a fish predator in the laboratory and *P. leniusculus* showed clear dominance over similar sized *Ast. astacus* in competition for shelter. Consequently, higher predation rates on the evicted *Ast. astacus* are observed. *P. leniusculus* has been invading several freshwater habitats in Europe and has displaced at least two native crayfish species. Vorburger and Ribi (1999) investigated the effects of the invader *P. leniusculus* on the rare and endangered native species *Aus. torrentium* in Switzerland. They did not find that *P. leniusculus* dominated *Aus. torrentium* in similar sized pairings but the larger average size and faster growing rate gives *P. leniusculus* a competitive advantage. Most important, however, *P. leniusculus* used in their study were infected with crayfish plague and transmitted the disease to the nonresistant *Aus. torrentium*, killing most of the experimental animals within 2 weeks. The role of aggressive interactions and shelter competition was also investigated in the two sympatric North American crayfish species, *Pro. zonangulus* and *Pro. clarkii* (Blank & Figler, 1996). Both species occupy the same ecological niche where replacement of *Pro. zonangulus* by *Pro. clarkii* was observed. The displacement is a direct consequence of overlapping resource competition, with both species preferring and competing for the same shelter type. The more aggressive *Pro. clarkii* initiates fights more often and usually wins encounters against equal sized *Pro. zonangulus* in pairwise encounters.

In competition for food and shelter, the introduced European green crab (*C. maenas*) and the introduced Asian shore crab (*Hemigraspus sanguineus*) interact aggressively with the native North American species *H. oregonensis*. In laboratory trials, Jensen, McDonald, and Armstrong (2002) found an unequal distribution of competitive success for access to food and shelter among the different species. During aggressive competition for access to food, *H. sanguineus* clearly dominated *C. maenas*, which dominated *H. oregonensis*. However, in aggressive contests for shelter both *Hemigraspus* species outcompeted *C. maenas*.

Aggression in Development

Intrinsic Differences and the Effects of Growth

Clawed decapod crustacean mothers typically hatch a few hundred eggs that, after several pelagic larval stages, molt into an adultlike animal and settle to the bottom. There they begin to interact socially. Crayfish have a different developmental sequence and forgo metamorphosis to adopt the form of the adult after the second molt. At that time they are often still in the burrow chamber where their mother retreated to hatch them. Within that confined space, they too begin to interact as they become free swimming. If confined to the burrow (or to a common aquarium), they will prey upon each other, with the larger ones catching, subduing, and eating their smaller siblings. This leads to rapid growth of the larger animals, so that the differences in animal size in the population increase as the numbers drop. If the animals are allowed to leave the burrow, they will quickly disburse to make their way as individuals; most will be taken by predators, including other conspecifics, before adulthood.

In crayfish, the rapid growth and cannibalism among siblings is clearly enhanced by a positive feedback between attacking and winning that exists in juveniles (Issa et al., 1999). However, aggressiveness is also an individual characteristic: crayfish siblings display differences in aggressiveness that are independent of size and experience (Issa et al., 1999). When groups of five crayfish (*Pro. clarkii*) ranging from 1.3 to 1.8 cm in length were formed from siblings that had been isolated since becoming free swimming, one animal quickly emerged as the dominant by attacking and defeating the others. In three of the groups it was the largest that prevailed initially, but in two others, smaller animals were dominant. One of those, the middle sized of its group of five, immediately began to attack the others, making more than 200 separate attacks in the first hour, five times more than any of the others in the group.

Both adult lobsters and crayfish depend primarily on their claws for defense, but as juveniles, they rely on escape. As juveniles, the chelipeds are a small fraction of the body mass, and the abdomen is a large fraction. As adults, the chelipeds are a much larger fraction of the body mass, and the abdomen is proportionately smaller (Fricke, 1986; Lang, Govind, Costello, & Greene, 1977). The change in behavior follows this change in allometry and is also associated with a change in the elements of the escape circuit in the nervous system. In each juvenile animal, increases in axonal diameter exceed the increases in animal (and axon) growth, so that the conduction time for the giant command neurons for escape remains constant. However, when the lobsters reach 5 cm in length and crayfish reach 4 cm, the growth in axonal diameter slows, so that conduction time increases with further increases in length. This slows the reaction time for the escape response and makes it a relatively less assured defense mechanism. Moreover, the allometry changes in the animal also make escape a less attractive mechanism. The relatively smaller abdomen of the adult enables the animal to move fewer body lengths with each tail flip than it did as a juvenile. Insofar as predator size scales with prey size, this change should reduce the adult crayfish's ability to escape predation or an antagonist's attack.

Signaling

A wound sustained in fighting can be fatal, if only because the blood released into the water may attract predators, including cannibalistic conspecifics. Consequently, as noted for vertebrates by Maxson and Canastar (ch. 1 in this volume), agonistic interactions rarely reach the level of intense fighting in the wild and are often decided instead on the basis of signals exchanged by the adversaries. These signals include odors, primarily through urine release, visual postural displays, and tactile stimuli through direct contact.

Chemical Signals

A series of studies conducted by Atema and Breithaupt have shown that for lobsters and crayfish, urine release conveys important information about the identity, sex, and aggressive motivation of the sender (Breithaupt & Atema, 1993, 2000; Breithaupt, Lindstrom, & Atema, 1999). In crayfish, urine is released from the nephropores at the front of the animal below the eyes and can be directed by gill currents and fanning by the exopodites of the maxillipeds (Breithaupt & Eger, 2002). Both future winners and losers release urine during offensive behaviors, and release increases with the level of aggression. Urine release appears necessary to intimidate a blindfolded opponent; aggressive behavior without urine release has no effect. In crayfish, urine appears to convey aggressiveness or dominance status,

but not individual identity (Breithaupt & Eger, 2002; Zulandt Schneider, Schneider, & Moore, 1999), whereas in lobsters, urine facilitates individual recognition (Breithaupt & Atema, 2000). The linkage of urine release to the aggressive behavior may help the losing receiver to remember the dominant individual and avoid future contacts (Karavanich & Atema, 1993).

Visual Signals

An elevated body posture and meral spread are visual signals used by lobsters, crayfish, and crabs to demonstrate aggressiveness and dominance status, while a lowered, extended body posture and claws signal submissiveness (Bruski & Dunham, 1987). In addition to increasing the animal's apparent size, a meral spread display provides maximum exposure of the opponent to the bright underside of the claws. The position of the antennae is highly correlated with the aggressiveness of crayfish, as shown by a study in which the postures and limb positions of winners and losers were correlated with fighting intensity (Heckenlively, 1970). Antennal position appears to provide a threat display to an opponent as it signals the animal's aggressive intent. These visually mediated behaviors depend on adequate light. Bruski and Dunham (1987) found that in crayfish the frequency of visually mediated behaviors decreased in the absence of light, while tactile behaviors (e.g., antennal tap, chela strike, and push) were performed more frequently.

Visual display of large colorful claws also helps determine dominance contests in both freshwater shrimp, *Macrobrachium*, and in male fiddler crabs. The shrimp have three different morphotypes that differ in size and color. The larger blue morphotype is dominant, followed by the smaller yellow adult males. Blue shrimp have much longer and heavier claws than yellow shrimp and dominate the yellows largely through visual display (Grafals, Sosa, Hernandez, & Inserni, 2000). Male fiddler crabs use their major claw by moving it in and out in an aggressive display that deters rival males and attracts females. The importance of this visual stimulus in dominance contests has led to cheating, in which a regenerated major claw is used to the same effect as a normal claw, despite the near uselessness of the regenerated claw as a weapon (Backwell et al., 2000).

Tactile Signals

Tactile signaling plays an important role during fights, as animals lock claws and push and pull on each other, demonstrating their strength while punishing their opponent. This becomes particularly important during offensive tail flips in crayfish, which occur when the two animals are locked together. At later times, bouts of antennal whipping occur, when the animals alternate flailing their opponent about the head with their antennae (Bruski & Dunham, 1987). In lobsters, this is often accompanied by a back-and-forth dancelike movement, where each animal flails the other as it moves forward (Huber & Kravitz, 1995). Antennal contact appears to be necessary for crayfish to engage each other in physical contact. Crayfish with intact antennae had three times as many interactions with other animals as did crayfish without antennae (Smith & Dunham, 1996).

Hermit crabs use an unusual tactile signal, "shell rapping," in their contests over possession of a gastropod shell shelter. Attackers will rap on the defender's shell; the vigor and persistence of the rapping are key indicators of whether the attacker will win and take possession. If the power and persistence of the rapping is high, the resident is more likely to give up and surrender the shell (Briffa & Elwood, 2001, 2002).

Aggressive Behavior

Promoters and Suppressors

The clawed decapods have relatively low thresholds for aggressive behavior; simply the presence of a strange conspecific will often trigger a fight between crayfish (Issa et al., 1999). At other times, sexual rivalry, competition for shelters, or hunger acts to promote aggressive behavior, as is described above. In laboratory aquaria, both crowding and isolation promote aggressive behavior among crayfish, as in many other animals. Fights that break out among crayfish kept at high density spread, especially if one animal is wounded, and ultimately engage most of the population (personal observation). This may result from spread of an alarm substance present in the blood (Gherardi, Acquistapace, Hazlett, & Whisson, 2002; Hazlett, 1994).

Aggression is also suppressed by a variety of factors, including a size disparity between the antagonists, courtship displays between opposing sexes, and the accumulation of lactic acid in vigorous opponents. Animals will only engage in fighting if they are closely matched in size, and fights are usually begun by the larger of the pair of antagonists (Thorpe, Huntingford,

& Taylor, 1994). The aggressive encounter usually begins as the newly met animals demonstrate their size to one another: crayfish and lobsters will raise and extend their claws laterally tip to tip with their opponent's to measure their relative size and reach (Bruski & Dunham, 1987; Guiasu & Dunham, 1997b; Huber & Kravitz, 1995). A significant asymmetry will often lead to retreat and submissive displays by the smaller, avoiding escalation of the aggressive encounter.

Courtship displays suppress aggressive responses by a resident male lobster to the approach of a conspecific to its burrow. Approaches by male lobsters are greeted with aggressive pushes to drive the interloper away, whereas female lobsters are admitted after they display both chemical and postural signals (Bushmann & Atema, 1994). Urine release by the approaching female reduces the frequency and intensity of male aggression. She then often assumes a submissive posture and displays her abdomen to the resident male, which then ceases pushing her away and allows her to enter the burrow.

Stages of Escalation

The most detailed descriptions of fighting in crustaceans are from studies of crayfish and clawed lobsters. Fighting among crayfish was described 50 years ago by Bovbjerg (1953), who found that crayfish fighting included several distinct behavior patterns that occurred at different frequencies, with the greatest being "threat" (39%) and the least frequent being "fight" (6%). The fighting led to formation of linear dominance hierarchies, but he found no differences in the frequencies of these behaviors for different ranks.

Crayfish fights follow a predictable sequence of behaviors (Bruski & Dunham, 1987). A pair of strange animals will begin with an "approach" with a high body posture and "meral spread," presumably to threaten and compare their relative body and major claw (chela) sizes. They then may strike each other with the chelae and lock them onto their opponents ("chela strike, lock"). They will then "push" the other backward and try to turn it over. They might then lower their posture ("body down") and exchange antennal taps: first one animal uses its antennae to deliver a series of vigorous taps of the other's head, followed by a return exchange by the other. The series may then repeat until antennal waving, a lowered posture, and retreat or tail flip signal submission. When socially naïve juvenile crayfish (*Pro. clarkii*) of equal size are paired they rapidly engage in aggressive interactions that include approaches, attacks, claw grasping, chasing, and other offensive behavioral elements (Edwards, Issa, & Herberholz, 2003; Herberholz, Sen, & Edwards, 2003; Issa et al., 1999). During this early part of the encounter the animals are similarly aggressive and frequently use offensive tail flips to demonstrate their physical fitness to the opponent (Herberholz, Issa, & Edwards, 2001).

Adult male crayfish have two reproductive morphotypes, Form 1, which has larger claws and is reproductively able, and Form 2, which has smaller claws and is not reproductively able. Both forms are found in the same populations of C. robustus, suggesting that they may compete for common resources (Guiasu & Dunham, 1998). Winners in both forms display more aggressive behavior patterns, such as "claws raised" and "lunge," than do eventual losers (Guiasu & Dunham, 1997a). Form 1 animals usually won size-matched contests between Form 1 and Form 2 animals. As in intraform contests, eventual winners displayed more aggressive behavior patterns than eventual losers (Guiasu & Dunham, 1998).

Lobsters follow a pattern of aggressive escalation similar to that of crayfish, obeying strict rules of conduct as they display six patterns of behavior in an orderly progression. As with crayfish, they begin with threat displays that grow into ritualized aggressive displays with a restrained use of the claws and culminating in brief bouts of unrestrained combat (Huber, Smith, Delago, Isaksson, & Kravitz, 1997). In dyadic interactions, equally sized opponents initially show aggressive displays and postures. If no decision is reached at this point, then use of the appendages comes into play and both contestants wrestle trying to overturn the opponent. If neither of the two breaks off the fight at this stage, then the next and highest level of intensity follows, with unrestricted use of the claws. The animals grasp each other and produce tail flips in an attempt to dismember the counterpart. By now at the latest, one animal will try to escape and retreat from the emerged dominant, and the social relationship between the two is determined (Atema & Cobb, 1980; Huber & Kravitz, 1995; Kravitz, 2000; Scrivener, 1971). As in crayfish, the full scenario of these agonistic interactions with all stereotyped escalating stages must be prewired in the nervous system of these animals since socially naïve crayfish and lobsters display the same fighting repertoire as socially experienced ones (Kravitz, 2000).

Unlike lobsters and crayfish, fights between female velvet swimming crabs (Necora puber) do not gradually escalate in violence and they are not longer or more intense when between evenly matched opponents (Thorpe et al., 1994). Fights are initiated equally often by the larger and smaller of the two opponents, although the larger is usually victorious.

Winning and Losing

The winner of a fight can often be predicted from its behavior during the fight. Among crayfish, prospective winners display more lunges, strikes, offensive tail flips, and other aggressive behavior patterns than do eventual losers (Guiasu & Dunham, 1998). It is likely that the crayfish and lobster combatants can identify the probable winner from these and other cues, including urine odor signals (Breithaupt & Atema, 1993, 2000; Breithaupt & Eger, 2002; Breithaupt et al., 1999).

At some point during the contest and often following a series of offensive tail flips generated by one animal, the rival will suddenly change its behavior and produce escapes and retreats to end the conflict (Herberholz et al., 2001). The underlying mechanisms that promote these behavioral changes in the new subordinate are still unknown, but sudden changes in the excitability of the neural escape circuits accompany the change in behavioral patterns (Edwards et al., 2003; Herberholz et al., 2001). Moreover, changes in social behavior have been linked to certain neuromodulators (e.g., serotonin [also called 5-HT], octopamine, ecdysone, and crustacean hyperglycemic hormone) that could affect the willingness and ability to continue a fight (Bolingbroke & Kass-Simon, 2001; Chang et al., 1999; Kravitz, 2000; and see below).

Dominance Hierarchy Formation

The Mechanisms of Hierarchy Formation

In crustaceans as in other animals, conflicts over limited resources often lead to the formation of social dominance hierarchies. Distinct social ranks among individuals in a group of crustaceans promote a reduction in aggressiveness and allow access to current or future resources to be decided through less violent agonistic interactions. Dominant and subordinate animals display differences in behaviors that stabilize and maintain the social order. Hierarchies are formed through dyadic relationships within the group and are often linearly organized.

Several authors have reported the formation of stable and linear social hierarchies in small groups of crayfish. Bovbjerg (1953) tested groups of four equally sized crayfish (O. virilis) and found that a clear dominance order is established within 5 days and remains for at least 15 more days. Interestingly, these experiments were carried out in featureless aquaria where no immediate access to resources was provided. Members of the crayfish species Cam. shufeldtii also establish linear dominance hierarchies without the expectation for immediate access to resources. Here, smaller groups form orders with clearer distinction between the ranks than larger groups (Lowe, 1956). The individual social roles of the members in the group are based on the outcome of dyadic agonistic contacts among them. The interactions are initially high in number and of intense aggressiveness, but cease over time and become less intense. Larger animals usually win the individual encounters and emerge at the top of the hierarchy (Lowe, 1956). Copp (1986) investigated the hierarchy formation in groups of four individuals of yet another crayfish species (Pro. clarkii) and found that ranks among them are not equally separated. Instead one animal clearly dominates the other three, while the differences are less established among those lower-ranked animals. The most dominant animal is more aggressive than any of the others and initiates most fights. The stability of the hierarchy is ensured by recognition of aggressive state rather than individual recognition among the members of the group (Copp, 1986). It was recently demonstrated in the same species that within groups of five socially naïve juvenile crayfish one would rapidly emerge and often remain as the "superdominant." This can be the largest animal or the most aggressive one that initiates most fights, which are frequent during the first day but strongly reduced thereafter (Issa et al., 1999). During the formation of linear hierarchies in groups of the crayfish Ast. astacus, winning agonistic encounters influenced subsequent fighting of the winner by reducing its motivation to retreat and increasing its motivation to escalate a fight (Goessmann, Hemelrijk, & Huber, 2000). These behavioral changes are likely to stabilize the social relationships among the members of the group.

Similar mechanisms that regulate hierarchy formation among groups of crustaceans have been demonstrated in lobsters, crabs, and prawns. When lobsters are grouped they quickly form a stable social dominance hierarchy through pairwise aggressive encounters that are initially frequent and violent, but are reduced to fewer and less aggressive interactions after dominants and subordinates are identified (Atema & Voigt, 1995).

The formation of dominance hierarchies was also observed in groups of four hermit crabs (Pagurus longicarpus) over a 7-day period. Groups with higher frequencies of aggressive interactions form hierarchies with more distinctive ranks, and dominant animals initiate most aggressive acts (Winston & Jacobson, 1978).

In freshwater prawn, M. rosenbergii, sexually mature males exist in three different morphological types: small, orange clawed, and blue clawed, the successive stages in male development. Blue-clawed prawns possess the longest claws but can be similar to or smaller in body size than orange-clawed prawns. In groups of six animals from both the orange- and blue-clawed types, smaller blue-clawed males easily dominated larger orange-clawed ones. This indicates that claw size and not body size is the decisive factor in hierarchy formation among these animals (Barki et al., 1992).

The Hierarchy Decision and Its Consequences

Social hierarchies in crustaceans are established through aggressive pairwise encounters from which dominant and subordinate animals emerge. The initial decision on social status is reached when one animal retreats or escapes from the opponent. The abrupt behavioral change in one of the contestant from being aggressive to being defensive marks the decision point of hierarchy formation (Herberholz et al., 2001, 2003). The animal that continuously retreats after this point is the new subordinate and the animal that continues to attack is the new dominant. Once the initial decision is made, subordinates and dominates display very different patterns of agonistic behaviors. The subordinates' aggressiveness is greatly reduced; they display submissive postures, try to avoid the dominant opponent, escape immediately from an approaching rival, and are generally more timid, spending less time in locomotion. On the other hand, dominant animals continue to be aggressive, approach and attack the new subordinate, and often chase it away.

The dominance decision determines the order of access to desirable resources, and it thereby has behavioral consequences for both animals that extend beyond agonistic interactions. Following aggressive interactions that determine relative dominance between pairs of juvenile crayfish (Pro. clarkii), the new subordinates not only reduced the frequency and intensity of aggressive behaviors, but also greatly reduced the time spent in excavating a burrow in the floor substrate. In contrast, their newly identified dominant partners spent more time in shelter construction after their social status was determined than before (Herberholz et al., 2003). The changes in burrowing behavior may be a rapid adaptation by the subordinate to its new social status. It inhibits the subordinate from wasting energy by investing in a resource that would probably be lost to the superior rival and prevents unsuccessful competition over other limited resources with the closely dominant opponent. The strikingly similar changes in agonistic and nonagonistic behaviors immediately following status decision may be controlled by the same neural mechanisms, which are still to be determined (Herberholz et al., 2003).

The Maintenance of Dominance Hierarchy

Once clear social ranks are determined within a group of crustaceans or between two contestants, they are remembered and maintained. Numerous studies have shown that aggressiveness ceases over time in animals that are kept together for prolonged periods. Although physical aggression is common in both contestants during the first pairwise encounters, the animals decide subsequent interactions with less physical and less aggressive behavior. The reduction in aggressive intensity during subsequent confrontations leads to an avoidance of unnecessary fights that could cause (further) physical injuries. The maintenance of these stable relationships between subordinate and dominant animals is likely to be promoted by recognition of the opponents' status or individuality.

Karavanich and Atema (1998a) demonstrated in an elegant study that lobster (*Hom. americanus*) not only remember previous encounters with combatants, but also differentiate between familiar and unfamiliar opponents. In fact, subordinates drastically change their behavior when paired with a familiar dominant but show little behavioral adaptation when confronted with an unfamiliar previous winner. The aggressiveness is greatly reduced in subordinates that fight against an opponent that defeated them in a previous encounter (an adaptation to avoid further damage), but remains high in subsequent fights against established dominants they meet for the first time. In conclusion, lobsters use individual recognition to maintain established social ranks and remember familiar opponents for at least

7 days (Karavanich & Atema, 1998a). The mechanisms of individual recognition among lobsters are still under discussion but chemical signals transmitted by urine release are now considered at least in part responsible. Lobsters always release urine during agonistic encounters (Breithaupt et al., 1999) and perception of urine signals is required for memory of individuals (Karavanich & Atema, 1998b).

Individual recognition was also reported in stomatopods (*G. festae*). In laboratory experiments, the animals showed no behavioral change when exposed to chemical cues from unfamiliar conspecifics. However, when responses to odors from former successful opponents (winner) were compared with responses to odors from former unsuccessful opponents (loser), a drastic change in shelter-related aggression was observed (Caldwell, 1985). Because the presented chemical cues did not include information about the "aggressive state" or social status of the opponent, individual recognition presumably accounts for the reported behavioral changes.

In crayfish, recognition of aggressive state or dominance status rather than individual recognition helps maintain social order. Status recognition does not require prior experience with a specific opponent and can be effective in reducing aggressive interactions between subordinates and familiar or unfamiliar dominants. Crayfish (*Pro. clarkii*) recognize unfamiliar subordinate and dominant individuals through chemical cues (Zulandt Schneider et al., 1999). Fight intensity and duration are greatly reduced in back-to-back encounters between unfamiliar opponents of different social status and information on social state is presumably transmitted through urine release (Zulandt Schneider, Huber, & Moore, 2001).

Status recognition has also been reported in groups of hermit crabs (*Pag. longicarpus*), where the exchange of a member of an established hierarchy with a stranger of the same rank produces no behavioral change in the other members of the group, whereas aggressive activity is greatly enhanced when a stranger with an assigned rank is introduced (Winston & Jacobson, 1978).

In snapping shrimp (*A. heterochaelis*) it was recently demonstrated that status recognition rather than individual recognition is used to stabilize social relationships. A significant decrease in aggressiveness was found in subordinates meeting familiar or unfamiliar dominants and this effect was maintained for several days (Obermeier & Schmitz, 2003).

Taken together these studies suggest that lobsters and stomatopods have the ability to remember a specific previous opponent, but many other crustaceans rely on status recognition to avoid aggression and to maintain an established social hierarchy. This may in part be explained by the different life patterns of lobsters and stomatopods compared to crayfish, crabs, and shrimp. Both lobsters and stomatopods usually live in small distinct groups experiencing little exchange with outside visitors, while crayfish, crabs, and shrimp often live in much larger populations where interactions between unfamiliar conspecifics are common. Remembering each individual within a large colony may therefore exceed the capability of these animals or may have proven unnecessary for successful cohabitation. Unfortunately, our knowledge of the natural behavior in the wild is sparse and more experiments are required to explain why different crustacean species use different mechanisms of recognition for maintaining stable social relationships.

Hormonal Control of Aggressive Behavior

Aggressive behavior linked to sexual rivalry, circadian rhythms, and molt cycle is promoted by hormones in each instance. Many of these hormones are related to those found in vertebrates and have similar effects on crustacean cells and tissues outside the central nervous system (CNS). Unlike vertebrates, hormonal effects in crustaceans are not segregated from neuromodulatory effects, in part because crustaceans lack the highly developed blood-brain barrier of vertebrates and in part because the same neurosecretory cells that release a neurochemical into the hemolymph also release it into ganglionic neuropiles of the CNS. How the hormonal and paracrine effects of neurosecretion are coordinated in the modulation of CNS function is not yet understood.

Monoaminergic Neuromodulation and the Formation of Dominance Hierarchies

Monoamines that have been identified as affecting the social behavior of decapod crustaceans include serotonin and octopamine (Kravitz, 1988, 2000; Livingstone, Harris-Warrick, & Kravitz, 1980; Panksepp, Yue, Drerup, & Huber, 2003), dopamine (Sneddon, Taylor, Huntingford, & Watson, 2000), steroid hormones (Bolingbroke & Kass-Simon, 2001), and peptide stress hormones (Chang et al., 1999; Kravitz, Basu, & Haass, 2001). Serotonin is the best understood of these sub-

stances, although others, including these and as yet unidentified other substances, may play important roles alone and in combination. When injected separately into crayfish, lobsters, squat lobsters, and prawns, serotonin and octopamine released postures that resembled those of dominant and subordinate animals, respectively (Antonsen & Paul, 1997; Livingstone et al., 1980; Sosa & Baro, 2002). Although serotonin injections did not produce behavior patterns that were specifically associated with aggression (Tierney & Mangiamele, 2001), manipulations that altered serotonin levels delayed a subordinate's decision to retreat from an aggressive dominant (Doernberg, Cromarty, Heinrich, Beltz, & Kravitz, 2001; Huber & Delago, 1998; Huber et al., 1997, Huber, Panksepp, Yue, Delago, & Moore, 2001). The effect of increased serotonin on withdrawal was blocked by fluoxetine, which inhibits uptake of serotonin. This result suggests that the delay in withdrawal results from extra serotonin that is taken up and released by serotonergic neurons onto normal targets.

Levels of serotonin in the hemolymph of crayfish are reduced to normal within 10 min of an acute injection into a blood sinus (Panksepp et al., 2003), after which serotonin levels rise along the ventral nerve cord and increase dramatically in the hindgut (B. E. Musolf, personal communication). Levels in the crayfish brain change very little, however. Unlike in crabs, where serotonin, dopamine, and octopamine levels rise in dominant animals following a fight (Sneddon, Taylor, Huntingford, & Watson, 2000), dominance status and fighting in crayfish appear to have little effect on either serotonin or dopamine levels anywhere in the nervous system (Panksepp et al., 2003). This negative result has to be qualified by noting that the measurement procedure would have missed rapid changes in monoamine levels and that increases in one part of the brain or a ganglion could be balanced by decreases elsewhere. All of the monoamines have effects on multiple targets and these effects are not clearly all synergistic, so that a change in dominance status may lead to offsetting changes in serotonin levels in different systems.

Many of the modulatory targets of serotonin have been identified in crayfish and lobster, where serotonin modulates the excitability of abdominal postural circuits (Djokaj, Cooper, & Rathmayer, 2001; Harris-Warrick & Kravitz, 1984, 1985), claw opening (Qian & Delaney, 1997), escape circuits (Glanzman & Krasne, 1983), heart rate (Florey & Rathmayer, 1978), locomotion (Gill & Skorupski, 1996; Glusman & Kravitz, 1982;

Pearlstein, Clarac, & Cattaert, 1998; Rossi-Durand, 1993), swimmeret beating (Barthe, Bevengut, & Clarac, 1993), digestion (Ayali & Harris-Warrick, 1999; Katz & Harris-Warrick, 1990; Tierney, Godleski, & Rattananont, 1999), and gut movements (Musolf & Edwards, 2000). In most of these systems, serotonin acts to increase or decrease the system's "gain" (Kravitz, 1988, 2000; Ma, Beltz, & Kravitz, 1992), to enhance the excitation or inhibition produced by the local transmitter.

Few of the neuromodulatory effects of serotonin have been linked directly to aggression or to changes in social status. Serotonergic neurons promote abdominal postural flexion (Ma et al., 1992), and their own reflex responsiveness depends on the social status of the animal (Drummond, Issa, Song, Herberholz, & Edwards, 2002). The lateral giant command neuron (LG) for escape is also modulated by serotonin (Glanzman & Krasne, 1983), but the sign of this modulation also depends on the social status of the crayfish (Yeh, Fricke, & Edwards, 1996; Yeh, Musolf, & Edwards, 1997). Serotonin facilitates the LG's synaptic response in dominant animals, but inhibits it in subordinates. This difference in effect develops over a 2-week period following a change in social status; this period is about the time needed for a dominance relationship to mature to a low-aggression state (Issa et al., 1999). If serotonin is released during fights, then it should act to affect the excitability of the LG differentially in dominants and subordinates, such that the excitability of the LG in subordinates should be reduced relative to that in dominants. In an imaginative series of experiments using implanted electrodes to stimulate sensory input to the LG electrically, Krasne, Shamsian, and Kulkarni (1997) found that this was true: the LG's excitability was significantly reduced in subordinates during fights, whereas that of dominants was either unaffected or slightly reduced. The LG is excited by tactile stimuli to the abdomen, which is usually facing away from the opponent during a fight. It makes teleological sense that LG excitability should be reduced during a fight, particularly in a subordinate, which is likely to be backing away from the dominant and may experience abdominal collisions with unseen objects. This view is supported by experiments on dominance hierarchy formation in eight pairs of juvenile crayfish, in which an LG-mediated escape occurred only once, whereas medial giant neuron (MG)-mediated tail flips, which are excited by frontal stimuli and pitch the animal backward, occurred at a high frequency in new subordinates (Herberholz et al., 2001).

Pharmacological experiments indicate that the difference in serotonin's effect on the LG in dominant and subordinate animals is likely to result from a difference in serotonin receptors, so that the gradual change in effect would result from a corresponding change in receptors (Yeh et al., 1996, 1997). One of possibly several crustacean serotonin receptors, 5-HT_{1crust}, has been identified in crayfish (Sosa, Spitzer, Edwards, & Baro, 2004), and although CNS expression levels differ in different crayfish, these differences do not correlate with the social status of individual animals (Spitzer, Baro, & Edwards, 2002). The affected escape command neuron, the LG, is in the abdomen, whereas the presumed center of status identification is the brain, raising the question as to how an abdominal neuron recognizes the animal's social status. Arfai and Krasne (1999) addressed this by separating the neural connection between the brain and abdomen by cutting the ventral nerve cord at the thoracic/abdominal joint. This was done in socially isolated animals that were then paired to create dominant-subordinate pairs. The social dominance relationships developed normally in these animals and the differences in serotonin's effect on the LG developed in these cord-cut dominant and subordinate animals in the same manner as in intact animals, suggesting that the dominance signal was carried humorally from the brain to the LG, where it triggered changes in serotonin receptor populations (Arfai & Krasne, 1999).

In addition to apparent changes in serotonin receptors, changes in the patterns of serotonin release also occur following a change in the social status of crayfish. The large identifiable serotonergic neurons in the last thoracic (T5) and first abdominal (A1) ganglia tonically modulate the abdominal postural and thoracic locomotor systems in both crayfish and lobsters. They project unilaterally in their own and more rostral ganglia, and they are neurosecretory, with endings on adjacent ganglionic third nerves (Beltz & Kravitz, 1987; Harris-Warrick & Kravitz, 1984; Ma et al., 1992; Real & Czternasty, 1990). A light touch to one side of the A1 segment of restrained, decapitated dominant crayfish excited ipsilateral serotonergic neurons and inhibited their contralateral homologs; the same touch to subordinates produced either bilateral excitation or bilateral inhibition of the A1 and T5 serotonin neurons (Drummond et al., 2002). When delivered to unsuspecting, freely behaving animals, the same touch always caused a dominant animal to make a rapid turn toward the stimulus source to confront it, whereas subordinate animals consistently moved straight forward or straight backward away from the stimulus source (Song, Herberholz, Drummond, & Edwards, 2000). If the pattern of serotonin release depends on the firing frequency, then the asymmetrical responses of modulatory neurons in dominants increased the amounts of serotonin released ipsilateral to the touch and reduced the amounts released contralaterally. This asymmetric release may help account for the asymmetry of the turning response of dominant animals. In a similar vein, the bilateral increases or decreases in neuronal firing observed in subordinates should produce bilateral increases or decreases in released serotonin. These symmetric changes in release may help account for the symmetrical forward or rearward retreats evoked by the same touch stimulus in these animals.

Molting and Sex

Crayfish and lobsters become more aggressive during the premolt interval, and this increase could be enhanced by injections of 20-hydroxyecdysone into intermolt female lobsters (Bolingbroke & Kass-Simon, 2001). The 20-hydroxyecdysone could be acting directly or through release of crustacean cardioactive peptide, a neuromodulator with widespread effects that experiences dramatic release at the outset of a molt (Phlippen, Webster, Chung, & Dircksen, 2000).

In many animals, testosterone and other androgens have been linked to male behavior patterns, including enhanced aggression (Rubinow & Schmidt, 1996). In crustaceans, the androgenic gland (AG) governs male sexual differentiation and secondary male sexual characteristics, including behavior, as part of the eyestalk–androgenic gland–testis endocrine axis (Khalaila et al., 2002). When the AG was transplanted into immature female crayfish, aggression was reduced between implanted animals and intact females compared to pairs of intact or AG-implanted females (Barki, Karplus, Khalaila, Manor, & Sagi, 2003). Courtship and mating behavior was also disturbed, linking as yet unidentified AG hormones to male patterns of behavior.

Neural Mechanisms

Neural Circuits for Relevant Behavior Patterns

The complex behaviors used in agonistic interactions can often be seen to comprise simpler elements, including escape, postural changes, forward walking, backward walking, and defense. These have been shown to result from activation of discrete neural circuits that can be excited by specific sensory stimuli or by command systems of central neurons. However, with the exception of escape and defense (i.e., meral spread, the distance between the tip of the right and left chelae), little is known about how these circuits are excited in a social context to produce adaptive patterns of behavior (Herberholz et al., 2001).

Escape Tail Flips

Three different neural circuits mediate tail flip escape responses in lobsters (*Homarus*) and crayfish. Crabs also escape, but with a running response (Aggio, Rakitin, & Maldonado, 1996). Two of these circuits have giant interneurons as command elements. The LG interneurons respond to a phasic tactile stimulus on the abdomen with a single spike that activates premotor interneurons and motor neurons in a highly stereotyped manner to produce an equally stereotyped tail flip escape response (Antonsen & Edwards, 2003; Edwards, Heitler, & Krasne, 1999; Herberholz, Antonsen, & Edwards, 2002; Horner, Weiger, Edwards, & Kravitz, 1997; Wine & Krasne, 1982). The tail flip results from a strong, rapid flexion of the anterior abdominal joints and simultaneous promotion of the uropods. This causes the animal to "jackknife" upward and forward, away from the attack. The pair of MG interneurons responds to similar strong, phasic tactile stimuli to the front of the animal or to rapidly looming visual stimuli. A single spike in the MGs moves caudally along both sides of the nerve cord and excites the same premotor interneurons and motor neurons in a different segmental pattern to produce a pattern of rapid flexion at each abdominal joint. This pattern thrusts the animal backward away from the frontal attack. The nongiant circuit is much less understood, but consists of a set of nongiant interneurons that excite sets of abdominal fast flexor motor neurons in a pattern that will carry the animal away from the point of attack. Nongiant tail flips are evoked by more gradually developing noxious stimuli, such as pinching a limb, but can also be produced "voluntarily," in which the animal tail flips in response to no obvious stimulus, and "swimming," a repetitive series of flexions and extensions that propels the animal backward rapidly through the water. Whereas the latencies of the giant-mediated tail flips to unexpected, phasic stimuli are 10–25 ms, depending on the size of the animal, the latency of the nongiant tail flip to similar stimuli is increased 4 to 8 times. This increased latency may be attributed to the time required to determine both the direction of the source of the attack and the motor pattern needed to move the animal in the opposite direction. When an attack is anticipated, however, the latency of the nongiant tail flip is only slightly longer than that of a giant-evoked tail flip (Herberholz, Sen, & Edwards, 2004).

Posture

Body posture depends on the behavioral context. Decapod crustaceans tend to hold themselves high off the substrate, when socially dominant or at the outset of a fight, and more prone and extended when subordinate (Livingstone et al., 1980). When resting, crayfish may lie on their ventral surface, with abdomen flexed or extended. Abdominal postural motor neurons, which are always tonically active in dissected preparations, are silent in freely behaving resting animals, suggesting that the overall level of nervous excitability then is low (Edwards, 1984). The control of body posture is produced by a balance between central commands and local reflex systems (Cattaert, Libersat, & El Manira, 2001; Fields, 1966; Larimer, 2000). Abdominal posture is controlled by a command network of interneurons, subsets of which are activated to produce specific flexed or extended postures (Aggio et al., 1996; Kennedy, Evoy, & Hanawalt, 1966; Jones & Page, 1986; Larimer, 2000; Miall & Larimer, 1982a, 1982b). Overall control of body posture may be held by interneurons in the circumesophageal connectives that activate different body postures, usually in the context of a specific behavior, such as walking or defense (Bowerman & Larimer, 1974). Local control systems include a set of proprioceptors in the limbs, abdominal segments, and ventral nerve cord that mediate both resistance and assistance reflexes and a set of photoreceptors in each abdominal ganglion that excites postural flexion motor neurons locally and in all of the more caudal abdominal ganglia (Clarac, Cattaert, & Le Ray, 2000; Edwards, 1984).

Interestingly, the neural circuits that mediate the flexed and extended abdominal postures typical of dominant and subordinate crayfish are reciprocally inhibitory. Flexion postural interneurons (FPIs) are linked through an excitatory network of connections, as are the extension postural interneurons (EPIs). The two networks are linked through reciprocal inhibition, such that when any one FPI (or EPI) is activated, the others are recruited and the EPIs (FPIs) are inhibited (Larimer, 2000).

Defense

Clawed decapods use their claws offensively and defensively in confrontations with their opponents. Offensive claw use is guided both visually and tactually as the animal strikes its opponent's head, grabs its claws, and strikes the soft underside of the abdomen. Meral spread is part of a defense response that is triggered by visual looming stimuli and consists of an elevation and spread of the claws, a widened stance, and, in crayfish and lobsters, an extended abdomen and a flattened tail. It is a low-threshold response, as anyone who has approached an aquarium containing crayfish has observed. The defense response is guided by visual stimuli, as the direction of the body axis and thrust of the claws will follow the movement of a visually threatening stimulus (Kelly & Chapple, 1990). The defense response of crayfish can also be evoked by stimulation of any one of a set of three to six defense interneurons (DIs) in the circumesophageal connectives (Atwood & Wiersma, 1967; Bowerman & Larimer, 1974; Wiersma, Roach, & Glantz, 1982). Both the DIs and the defense response are subject to facilitation and habituation and to modulation by the "excited state" of the animal. The DIs appear to be monosynaptically excited by "jittery movement detector" (JMD) interneurons found in the optic nerve (Glantz, 1974; Wiersma et al., 1982). Consequently, the defense response appears to be evoked by an ensemble of DIs that are excited by a small group of JMDs as they respond to a looming stimulus. Although it is likely that many of the same elements also mediate offensive use of meral spread displays, the circuitry has not yet been studied in this context.

Walking

Walking provides the primary means of locomotion within small areas along a streambed or lake bed or during overland treks between watersheds. During social interactions between lobsters or crayfish, approaches are mediated by forward walking, whereas retreats are mediated by backward walking, although forward and backward walking can be components of other behaviors as well. Forward walking is usually accompanied by abdominal extension, whereas backward walking is often accompanied by a cyclical pattern of abdominal flexion and extension. Networks of interneurons that promote cyclical patterns of abdominal flexion and extension (Moore & Larimer, 1988, 1993) are tied into the network that produces backward walking in response to central commands, visual looming stimuli, or illumination of the caudal photoreceptor (Kovac, 1974; Miall & Larimer, 1982b; Simon & Edwards, 1990). Motor patterns for either backward or forward walking can be excited by the application of muscarinic cholinergic agonists (Cattaert, Pearlstein, & Clarac, 1995; Chrachri & Clarac, 1990); these rhythms can be entrained by stimulation of proprioceptive afferents (Elson, Sillar, & Bush, 1992; Leibrock, Marchand, & Barnes, 1996). Circuitry mediating both resistance and assistance reflexes has been described and shown to be active in enabling normal walking (Clarac et al., 2000).

Use of Neural Circuits in Dominance Hierarchy Formation

Many of the different patterns of behavior displayed during hierarchy formation can be related directly to those for which neural circuits have been described. Attack and approach behaviors make use of forward walking, whereas retreat relies on backward walking; the neural substrates for these agonistic behaviors are likely to include activation of the appropriate walking command circuits. The cheliped strikes and the defense posture that occurs in response to the approach or attack of another crayfish is likely to result from excitation of the DIs and other postural command elements by the JMDs as they respond to looming stimuli provided by the approach of the other crayfish. The meral spread that accompanies forward walking during an attack may be mediated by some of the DIs that produce the defense response. Defensive behavior can include the three forms of tail flip escape that are released by their respective neuronal command systems, whereas offensive tail flipping is likely to be released by yet another command system.

Activation of the different neural circuits and patterns of behavior is highly coordinated, but the pattern of coordination can change dramatically, as when an animal breaks off the contest and escapes (Herberholz et al., 2001). Offensive behaviors were frequent and defensive behaviors were rare before that point, whereas afterward the reverse was true of the new subordinate. Before this decision, MG and nongiant escapes of the prospective subordinate were rare and

occurred in response to an approach or attack by the prospective dominant as the two animals faced each other. The suddenness of the decision to escape, which often occurs without an obvious stimulus trigger, suggests that the needed circuitry was in some way mobilized in advance, just as the nongiant circuitry is by the frontal approach of a dragonfly (Herberholz et al., 2004). This suggests that the excitability of these defensive circuits suddenly changed from being low before the subordinate's decision to retreat to very high afterward, while the excitability of circuits that mediate offensive action (approaches, attacks, offensive tail flips) changed in the opposite direction. In the dominant animal, the excitability of circuits that evoke defensive behavior remained low throughout, whereas that for offensive behavior remained high (Herberholz et al., 2001, 2003).

The failure of the LG neuron to respond more than once during intraspecific encounters between two juvenile crayfish is consistent with these changes (Herberholz et al., 2001). The animals faced each other throughout these bouts and so provided little opportunity for an attack on the tail that would excite the LG. At the same time, the LG also failed to respond to the inadvertent bump of a retreating animal into a side of the aquarium, suggesting that the LG's excitability is kept low throughout these encounters. This suggestion is supported by results from experiments on established dominant and subordinate adult animals (Krasne et al., 1997), in which the LG's stimulus threshold was shown to rise substantially in subordinates and less in dominants during fighting, but not before or after.

Mechanisms of Circuit Activation and Inhibition

The sudden and persistent shift in the excitability of suites of neural circuits has been seen before in crayfish and occurs when a feeding animal is suddenly challenged by a threatening stimulus (Bellman & Krasne, 1983). If the food was readily portable, then the animal tail flipped quickly away. The normally low excitability of the LG increased during feeding, and the circuit and escape behavior were triggered by relatively weak stimuli directed at the abdomen. If the food was heavy or hard to move, the LG excitability was low, and even strong hits to the abdomen would not evoke escape. These variations in the LG's excitability were attributed to the effects of "tonic inhibition" of the LG (Vu & Krasne, 1993; Vu, Lee, & Krasne, 1993), which is active during the display of behaviors that are mutu-ally exclusive of escape, including restraint, walking, defense, and feeding (Beall, Langley, & Edwards, 1990). Activation of the LG or MGs also inhibits abdominal postural movements (Kuwada, Hagiwara, & Wine, 1980; Kuwada & Wine, 1979). This mutual inhibition provides the animal with control over the release of different discrete patterns of behavior and does not have to be centrally generated by a master decision network. Mutual inhibition among circuits that produce differ-ent behavior patterns provides a mechanism for behav-ioral choice in which the "decision" to display any particular behavior is distributed across the circuits (Edwards, 1991). It may be, then, that the decision to break off aggressive behavior and initiate defensive behavior by the new subordinate reflects such a shift between excitation and inhibition among the circuits that organize different behavior patterns.

Long-Term Adaptations to a Change in Social Status

Longer term changes in social behavior may require corresponding longer term changes in the neuro-modulatory systems and circuits that mediate the dif-ferent components of social behavior. For example, the 2-week decline in agonistic activity among five juve-nile crayfish that occurred following the initial forma-tion of a dominance hierarchy was accompanied by a decline in the frequency of tail flip escape behavior of social subordinates and a rise in the frequency of re-treats (Issa et al., 1999). A similar decline in the ag-gressiveness of paired animals was accompanied by a change in the modulatory effect of serotonin on the LG neuron (Yeh et al., 1996, 1997). Serotonin changed from being facilitatory in newly paired subordinates to being inhibitory after 2 weeks of pairing, whereas se-rotonin remained facilitatory in their dominant part-ners throughout. These changes, which appear to have resulted from changes in the population of serotonin receptors, were readily reversible over the same time course by reisolation of the subordinate or by enabling the subordinate to become dominant to another ani-mal. We do not know how these changes might ap-ply to a mid-ranking animal, nor do we know whether dominance relationships in the wild persist long enough for these changes to develop, although it seems likely. Crayfish cluster in groups along the banks of streams or ponds, where they interact both competi-

tively and cooperatively. It is likely that these groups persist in a stable configuration for the 2 weeks needed to produce changes in receptor populations.

It is likely that other circuits experience similar long-term changes in neuromodulation. The MG and nongiant circuits, which were very active in new sub-ordinates (Herberholz et al., 2001), were rarely excited after animals had been grouped for 2 weeks (Issa et al., 1999). They appear to have experienced long-term changes in neuromodulatory effect similar to those produced by serotonin in the LG. The backward walk-ing circuits that mediate retreat might become more excitable as the crayfish learns to avoid the approach of the dominant animal, whereas the defense circuits may become less excitable.

Such gradual changes require a daily signal that reports to the rest of the nervous system, including the abdominal ganglia where the LG is located, about the current social status of the animal. As described above, that signal appears to be humoral and may be the re-lease of serotonin itself. If the changes in the modula-tory effect of serotonin result from a change in the population of serotonin receptors (Yeh et al., 1997), then these results indicate that a humoral factor re-leased from the anterior nervous system is sufficient to induce changes in the sensitivity of the LG to seroto-nin by changing the population of serotonin receptors in the cell. Given that patterns of serotonin release differ in dominant and subordinate animals (Drum-mond & Edwards, 1998), it may be that the pattern or level of serotonin release tells the LG and other neu-rons which serotonin receptors to display.

Conclusions and Future Directions

It is readily apparent that, as for most animals, our knowledge of crustacean aggressive behavior far ex-ceeds our understanding of the neural and hormonal mechanisms that govern it. The many different con-texts in which aggressive behavior is released, the role of chemical, visual, and tactile signals in signaling ag-gressive intent, and the different stages of an aggressive encounter are well described in more than one clawed decapod. These results provide the essential set of clues needed for an investigation of the neural and hormonal mechanisms of aggressive behavior. Our current un-derstanding of the crustacean nervous system is rich in descriptions of circuits for individual elements of behavior, including escape, posture, walking, leg reflexes, swimmeret beating, control of the stomach, and visual processing. However, we have not yet identified circuits or hormonal signals that directly activate or govern aggressive behavior, although we have some tantalizing hints about them. The immediate aggressive response of juvenile crayfish to the presence of unfamiliar conspecifics is like a fixed action pattern response to a sign stimulus, and it invites us to ask about the neural substrates for recognizing this sign stimulus and for triggering this fixed action pattern. Because the aggressive response entails a transformation of the posture and motivation of the animal, the activity and stimulus thresholds of entire suites of neural circuits must be changed in a coordinated fashion. This suggests that part of the response entails the release of one or more substances that evoke this transformation throughout the nervous system. A similar transformation occurs when one animal gives up a fight with another. Here again, a particular set of external and internal stimuli must combine to trigger the response, which also entails the resetting of activation thresholds across a wide array of circuits. The challenge is to identify the decision mechanism and the elements that serve it and to identify the transformative signal that alerts and conditions the rest of the nervous system.

The behavioral studies also indicate that crustaceans experience longer-term, state-changing effects from aggressive interactions. These are typified by the loss of aggressiveness by both dominant and subordinate animals as a dominance hierarchy matures and confrontations are avoided instead of sought. Again, the neural and hormonal mechanisms for this are obscure, but one example, in which the modulatory effect of serotonin on the crayfish LG escape circuit changes along the same time course as this maturation, is suggestive. Here, changes in the balance of serotonin receptors appear to occur in new subordinates, suggesting a change in gene expression that is promoted daily for as long as the animal's current dominance status quo is maintained. Unfortunately, our ability to measure gene expression changes is compromised by the lack of sequence data for all crustaceans, so that we are forced to rely on a targeted a gene-by-gene approach based on degenerative primers assembled from an analysis of homologous genes in other arthropods, primarily *Drosophila*. Despite this handicap (which, given the economic importance of crustaceans, may soon be remedied), both current and new techniques should make it possible to identify the circuits that are transformed and the agents of transformation.

References

Aggio, J., Rakitin, A., & Maldonado, H. (1996). Serotonin-induced short- and long-term sensitization in the crab Chasmagnathus. *Pharmacology, Biochemistry, and Behavior, 53,* 441–448.

Antonsen, B. L., & Edwards, D. H. (2003). Differential dye coupling reveals lateral giant escape circuit in crayfish. *Journal of Comparative Neurology, 466,* 1–13.

Antonsen, B. L., & Paul, D. H. (1997). Serotonin and octopamine elicit stereotypical behaviors in the squat lobster *Munida quadrispina* (Anomura, Galatheidae). *Journal of Comparative Physiology A, 181,* 501–510.

Arfai, N., & Krasne, F. B. (1999). Social experience-dependent changes in response of crayfish Lateral Giant neurons to 5-HT may be induced by humoral factors. *Society for Neuroscience Abstracts.*

Atema, J. (1986). Review of sexual selection and chemical communication in the lobster, *Homarus americanus. Canadian Journal of Fisheries and Aquatic Sciences, 43,* 2283–2390.

Atema, J., & Cobb, J. S. (1980). Social behavior. In J. S. Cobb & B. F. Philips (Eds.), *The biology and management of lobsters* (pp. 409–449). New York: Academic Press.

Atema, J., Jacobson, S., Karnofsky, E., Oleszko-Szuts, S., & Stein, L. (1979). Pair formation in the lobster, *Homarus americanus. Marine Behavior and Physiology, 6,* 277–296.

Atema, J., & Voigt, R. (1995). Behavior and sensory biology. In J. R. Factor (Ed.), *Biology of the lobster Homarus americanus* (pp. 313–348). New York: Academic Press.

Atwood, H. L., & Wiersma, C. A. G. (1967). Command interneurons in the crayfish central nervous system. *Journal of Experimental Biology, 46,* 249–261.

Ayali, A., & Harris-Warrick, R. M. (1999). Monoamine control of the pacemaker kernel and cycle frequency in the lobster pyloric network. *Journal of Neuroscience, 19,* 6712–6722.

Backwell, P. R., Christy, J. H., Telford, S. R., Jennions, M. D., & Passmore, N. I. (2000). Dishonest signalling in a fiddler crab. *Proceedings of the Royal Society of London, Series B, Biological Science, 267,* 719–724.

Barki, A., Karplus, I., & Goren, M. (1992). Effects of size and morphotype on dominance hierarchies and resource competition in the freshwater prawn *Macrobrachium rosenbergii. Animal Behaviour, 44,* 547–555.

Barki, A., Karplus, I., Khalaila, I., Manor, R., & Sagi, A. (2003). Male-like behavioral patterns and physiological alterations induced by androgenic gland implantation in female crayfish. *Journal of Experimental Biology, 206,* 1791–1797.

Barthe, J. Y., Bevengut, M., & Clarac, F. (1993). In vitro, proctolin and serotonin induced modulations of the abdominal motor system activities in crayfish. *Brain Research, 623,* 101–109.

Beall, S. P., Langley, D. J., & Edwards, D. H. (1990). Inhibition of escape tailflip in crayfish during backward walking and the defense posture. *Journal of Experimental Biology, 152,* 577–582.

Bellman, K. L., & Krasne, F. B. (1983). Adaptive complexity of interactions between feeding and escape in crayfish. *Science, 221,* 779–781.

Beltz, B. S., & Kravitz, E. A. (1987). Physiological identification, morphological analysis, and development of identified serotonin-proctolin containing neurons in the lobster ventral nerve cord. *Journal of Neuroscience, 7,* 533–546.

Bergman, D. A., & Moore, P. A. (2003). Field observations of intraspecific agonistic behavior of two crayfish species, *Orconectes rusticus* and *Orconectes virilis,* in different habitats. *The Biological Bulletin, 205,* 26–35.

Berrill, M., & Arsenault, M. (1982). Mating behavior of the green shore crab *Carcinus maenas. Bulletin of Marine Science, 32,* 632–638.

Berrill, M., & Arsenault, M. (1984). The breeding behaviour of a northern temperate orconectid crayfish, *Orconectes rusticus. Animal Behaviour, 32,* 333–339.

Blank, G. S., & Figler, M. H. (1996). Interspecific shelter competition between the sympatric crayfish species *Procambarus clarkii* (Girard) and *Procambarus zonangulus* (Hobbs and Hobbs). *Journal of Crustacean Biology, 16,* 300–309.

Bolingbroke, M., & Kass-Simon, G. (2001). 20-Hydroxyecdysone causes increased aggressiveness in female American lobsters, *Homarus americanus. Hormones and Behavior, 39,* 144–156.

Bovbjerg, R. V. (1953). Dominance order in the crayfish *Oconectes virilis* (Hagen). *Physiological Zoology, 26,* 173–178.

Bovbjerg, R. V. (1956). Some factors affecting aggressive behavior in crayfish. *Physiological Zoology, 29,* 127–136.

Bovbjerg, R. V. (1970). Ecological, isolation and competitive exclusion in two crayfish (*Orconectes virilis* and *Orconectes immunis*). *Ecology, 51,* 225–236.

Bowerman, R. F., & Larimer, J. L. (1974). Command fibres in the circumoesophageal connectives of crayfish. *Journal of Experimental Biology, 60,* 95–117.

Breithaupt, T., & Atema, J. (1993). Evidence for the use of urine signals in agonistic interactions of the American lobster. *The Biological Bulletin, 185,* 318.

Breithaupt, T., & Atema, J. (2000). The timing of chemical signaling with urine in dominance fights of male lobsters (*Homarus americanus*). *Behavioral Ecology and Sociobiology, 49,* 67–78.

Breithaupt, T., & Eger, P. (2002). Urine makes the difference: Chemical communication in fighting crayfish made visible. *Journal of Experimental Biology, 205,* 1221–1231.

Breithaupt, T., Lindstrom, D. P., & Atema, J. (1999). Urine release in freely moving catheterised lobsters (*Homarus americanus*) with reference to feeding and social activities. *Journal of Experimental Biology, 202,* 837–844.

Briffa, M., & Elwood, R. W. (2000). The power of shell rapping influences rates of eviction in hermit crabs. *Behavioral Ecology, 11,* 288–293.

Briffa, M., & Elwood, R. W. (2001). Decision rules, energy metabolism and vigour of hermit-crab fights. *Proceedings of the Royal Society of London, Series B, Biological Science, 268,* 1841–1848.

Briffa, M., & Elwood, R. W. (2002). Power of shell-rapping signals influences physiological costs and subsequent decisions during hermit crab fights. *Proceedings of the Royal Society of London, Series B, Biological Science, 269,* 2331–2336.

Briffa, M., Elwood, R. W., & Russ, J. M. (2003). Analysis of multiple aspects of a repeated signal: Power and rate of rapping during shell fights in hermit crabs. *Behavioral Ecology, 14,* 74–79.

Bruski, C. A., & Dunham, D. W. (1987). The importance of vision in agonistic communication of the crayfish *Orconectes rusticus.* I: An analysis of bout dynamics. *Behavior, 103,* 83–107.

Bushmann, P., & Atema, J. (1994) Aggression-reducing courtship signals in the lobster, *Homarus americanus. The Biological Bulletin, 187,* 275–276.

Caldwell, R. L. (1979). Cavity occupation and defensive behaviour in the stomatopod *Gonodactylus festai:* Evidence for chemically mediated individual recognition. *Animal Behaviour, 27,* 194–201.

Caldwell, R. L. (1985). A test of individual recognition in the stomatopod *Gonodactylus festae. Animal Behaviour, 33,* 101–106.

Caldwell, R. L. (1992). Recognition, signalling and reduced aggression between former mates in a stomatopod. *Animal Behaviour, 44,* 11–19.

Capelli, G. M., & Hamilton, P. A. (1984). Effects of food and shelter on aggressive activity in the crayfish *Orconectes rusticus* (Girard). *Journal of Crustacean Biology, 4,* 252–260.

Capelli, G. M., & Munjal, B. L. (1982). Aggressive interactions and resource competition in relation to species displacement among crayfish of the genus *Orconectes*. *Journal of Crustacean Biology, 2,* 486–492.

Cattaert, D., Libersat, F., & El Manira, A. A. (2001). Presynaptic inhibition and antidromic spikes in primary afferents of the crayfish: A computational and experimental analysis. *Journal of Neuroscience, 21,* 1007–1021.

Cattaert, D., Pearlstein, E., & Clarac, F. (1995). Cholinergic control of the walking network in the crayfish *Procambarus clarkii*. *Journal of Physiology, Paris, 89,* 209–220.

Chang, E. S., Chang, S. A., Keller, R., Reddy, P., Sr., Snyder, M. J., & Spees, J. L. (1999). Quantification of stress in lobsters: Crustacean hyperglycemic hormone, stress proteins, and gene expression. *American Zoologist, 39,* 487–495.

Chrachri, A., & Clarac, F. (1990). Fictive locomotion in the fourth thoracic ganglion of the crayfish, *Procambarus clarkii*. *Journal of Neuroscience, 10,* 707–719.

Clarac, F., Cattaert, D., & Le Ray, D. (2000). Central control components of a "simple" stretch reflex. *Trends in Neurosciences, 23,* 199–208.

Conover, M. R., & Miller, D. E. (1978). The importance of the large chela in the territorial and pairing behaviour of the snapping shrimp *Alpheus heterochaelis*. *Marine Behavior and Physiology, 5,* 185–192.

Copp, N. H. (1986). Dominance hierarchies in the crayfish *Procambarus clarkii* (Girard, 1852) and the question of learned individual recognition (Decapoda, Astacidea). *Crustaceana, 51,* 9–24.

Correa, C., Baeza, J. A., Hinojosa, I. A., & Thiel, M. (2003). Dominance hierarchy and mating tactics in the rock shrimp *Rhynchocinetes typus* (Decapoda: Caridea). *Journal of Crustacean Biology, 23,* 33–45.

Cowan, D. F., & Atema, J. (1990). Moult staggering and serial monogamy in American lobsters, *Homarus americanus*. *Animal Behaviour, 39,* 1199–1206.

Cromarty, S. I., Mello, J., & Kass-Simon, G. (1998). Comparative analysis of escape behavior in male, and gravid and non-gravid female lobsters. *The Biological Bulletin, 194,* 63–71.

Djokaj, S., Cooper, R. L., & Rathmayer, W. (2001). Presynaptic effects of octopamine, serotonin, and cocktails of the two modulators on neuromuscular transmission in crustaceans. *Journal of Comparative Physiology, 187,* 145–154.

Doernberg, S. B., Cromarty, S. I., Heinrich, R., Beltz, B. S., & Kravitz, E. A. (2001). Agonistic behavior in naïve juvenile lobsters depleted of serotonin by 5,7–dihydroxytryptamine. *Journal of Comparative Physiology A, 187,* 91–103.

Drummond, J., & Edwards, D. H. (1998). Effect of social experience on reflex responses of serotonergic neurons in crayfish. Fifth International Congress on Neuroethology, Abstract No. 208.

Drummond, J., Issa, F. A., Song, C.-K., Herberholz, J., & Edwards, D. H. (2002). Neural mechanisms of dominance hierarchies in crayfish. In K. Wiese & M. Schmidt (Eds.), *The crustacean nervous system* (pp. 124–135). Berlin: Springer-Verlag.

Edwards, D. H. (1984). Crayfish extraretinal photoreception. I. Behavioural and motoneuronal responses to abdominal illumination. *Journal of Experimental Biology, 109,* 291–306.

Edwards, D. H. (1991). Mutual inhibition among neural command systems as a possible mechanism for behavioral choice in crayfish. *Journal of Neuroscience, 11,* 1210–1223.

Edwards, D. H., Heitler, W. J., & Krasne, F. B. (1999). 50 years of a command neuron: The neurobiology of escape behavior in the crayfish. *Trends in Neurosciences, 22,* 153–161.

Edwards, D. H., Issa, F. A., & Herberholz, J. (2003). The neural basis of dominance hierarchy formation in crayfish. *Microscopy Research and Technique, 60,* 369–376.

Elson, R. C., Sillar, K. T., & Bush, B. M. (1992). Identified proprioceptive afferents and motor rhythm entrainment in the crayfish walking system. *Journal of Neurophysiology, 67,* 530–546.

Fields, H. L. (1966). Proprioceptive control of posture in the crayfish abdomen. *Journal of Experimental Biology, 44,* 455–468.

Figler, M. H., Blank, G. S., & Peeke, H. V. S. (2001). Maternal territoriality as an offspring defense strategy in red swamp crayfish (*Procambarus clarkii*, Girard). *Aggressive Behavior, 27,* 391–403.

Figler, M. H., Cheverton, H. M., & Blank, G. S. (1999). Shelter competition in juvenile red swamp crayfish (*Procambarus clarkii*): The influences of sex differences, relative size, and prior residence. *Aquaculture, 178,* 63–75.

Figler, M. H., Peeke, H. V. S., & Chang, E. S. (1997). Maternal aggression in American lobsters (*Homarus americanus* Milne-Edwards): Shelter-related encounters against non-maternal female conspecifics. *Marine and Freshwater Behaviour and Physiology, 30,* 267–274.

Figler, M. H., Twum, M., Finkelstein, J. E., & Peeke, H. V. S. (1995). Maternal aggression in red swamp crayfish (*Procambarus clarkii*, Girard): The relation between reproductive status and outcome of aggressive encounters with male and female conspecifics. *Behaviour, 132,* 108–121.

Florey, E., & Rathmayer, M. (1978). The effects of octopamine and other amines on the heart and on neuromuscular transmission in decapod crustaceans: Further evidence for a role as neurohormone. *Comparative Biochemistry and Physiology C, 61C,* 229–237.

Fricke, R. A. (1986). Structure-function considerations in the development expression of crayfish behavioral plasticity. *IEEE Symposia,* 1–6.

Garvey, J. E., Stein, R. A., & Thomas, H. M. (1994). Assessing how fish predation and interspecific prey competition influence a crayfish assemblage. *Journal of Ecology, 75,* 532–547.

Gherardi, F., Acquistapace, P., Hazlett, B. A., & Whisson, G. (2002). Behavioural responses to alarm odours in indigenous and non-indigenous crayfish species: A case study from Western Australia. *Marine and Freshwater Research, 53,* 93–98.

Gill, M. D., & Skorupski, P. (1996). Modulation of spontaneous and reflex activity of crayfish leg motor neurons by octopamine and serotonin. *Journal of Neurophysiology, 76,* 3535–3549.

Glantz, R. M. (1974). Defense reflex and motion detector responsiveness to approaching targets: The motion detector trigger to the defense reflex pathway. *Journal of Comparative Physiology, 95,* 297–314.

Glanzman, D. L., & Krasne, F. B. (1983). Serotonin and octopamine have opposite modulatory effects on the crayfish's lateral giant escape reaction. *Journal of Neuroscience, 3,* 2263–2269.

Glusman, S., & Kravitz, E. A. (1982). The action of serotonin on excitatory nerve terminals in lobster nerve-muscle preparations. *Journal of Physiology, 325,* 223–241.

Goessmann, C., Hemelrijk, C., & Huber, R. (2000). The formation and maintenance of crayfish hierarchies: Behavioral and self-structuring properties. *Behavioral Ecology and Sociobiology, 48,* 418–428.

Grafals, M., Sosa, M. A., Hernandez, C. M., & Inserni, J. A. (2000). Role of serotonin and octopamine in aggressive behavior in the freshwater prawn *Macrobrachium rosenbergii*. *FASEB Journal, 14,* A546.

Guiasu, R. C., & Dunham, D. W. (1997a). Agonistic interactions in male form II *Cambarus robustus* Girard, 1852 crayfish (Decapoda, Cambaridae) and a comparison between male form I and form II intra-form contests. *Crustaceana, 70,* 720–736.

Guiasu, R. C., & Dunham, D. W. (1997b). Initiation and outcome of agonistic contests in male form I *Cambarus robustus* Girard, 1852 crayfish (Decapoda, Cambaridae). *Crustaceana, 70,* 480–496.

Guiasu, R. C., & Dunham, D. W. (1998). Inter-form agonistic contests in male crayfishes, *Cambarus robustus* (Decapoda, Cambaridae). *Invertebrate Biology, 117,* 144–154.

Harris-Warrick, R. M., & Kravitz, E. A. (1984). Cellular mechanisms for modulation of posture by octopamine and serotonin in the lobster. *Journal of Neuroscience, 4,* 1976–1993.

Harris-Warrick, R. M., & Kravitz, E. A. (1985). Amine modulation of extension command element-evoked motor activity in lobster abdomen. *Journal of Comparative Physiology A, 156,* 875–884.

Hazlett, B. A. (1994). Alarm responses in the crayfish *Orconectes virilis* and *Orconectes propinquus*. *Journal of Chemical Ecology, 20,* 1525–1535.

Heckenlively, D. B. (1970). Intensity of aggression in the crayfish, *Orconectes virilis* (Hagen). *Nature, 225,* 180–181.

Herberholz, J., Antonsen, B. L., & Edwards, D. H. (2002). A lateral excitatory network in the escape circuit of crayfish. *Journal of Neuroscience, 22,* 9078–9085.

Herberholz, J., Issa, F. A., & Edwards, D. H. (2001). Patterns of neural circuit activation and behavior during dominance hierarchy formation in freely behaving crayfish. *Journal of Neuroscience, 21,* 2759–2767.

Herberholz, J., & Schmitz, B. (1998). Role of mechanosensory stimuli in intraspecific agonistic encounters in the snapping shrimp (*Alpheus heterochaelis*). *The Biological Bulletin, 195,* 156–167.

Herberholz, J., & Schmitz, B. (1999). Flow visualisation and high speed video analysis of water jets in the snapping shrimp (*Alpheus heterochaelis*). *Journal of Comparative Physiology A, 185,* 41–49.

Herberholz, J., Sen, M. M., & Edwards, D. H. (2003). Parallel changes in agonistic and non- agonistic behaviors during dominance hierarchy formation in crayfish. *Journal of Comparative Physiology A, 189,* 321–325.

Herberholz, J., Sen, M. M., & Edwards, D. H. (2004). Escape behavior and escape circuit activation in juvenile crayfish during prey-predator interactions. *Journal of Experimental Biology, 207,* 1855–1863.

Horner, M., Weiger, W. A., Edwards, D. H., & Kravitz, E. A. (1997). Excitation of identified serotonergic neurons by escape command neurons in lobsters. *Journal of Experimental Biology, 200,* 2017–2033.

Huber, R., & Delago, A. (1998). Serotonin alters decisions to withdraw in fighting crayfish, *Astacus astacus*: The motivational concept revisited. *Journal of Comparative Physiology A, 182,* 573–583.

Huber, R., & Kravitz, E. A. (1995). A quantitative analysis of agonistic behavior in juvenile American lobsters (*Homarus americanus* L.). *Brain, Behavior and Evolution, 46,* 72–83.

Huber, R., Panksepp, J. B., Yue, Z., Delago, A., & Moore, P. (2001). Dynamic interactions of behavior and amine neurochemistry in acquisition and maintenance of social rank in crayfish. *Brain, Behavior and Evolution, 57,* 271–282.

Huber, R., Smith, K., Delago, A., Isaksson, K., & Kravitz, E. A. (1997). Serotonin and aggressive motivation in crustaceans: Altering the decision to retreat. *Proceedings of the National Academy of Sciences USA, 94,* 5939–5942.

Issa, F. A., Adamson, D. J., & Edwards, D. H. (1999). Dominance hierarchy formation in juvenile crayfish, *Procambarus clarkii. Journal of Experimental Biology, 202,* 3497–3506.

Jensen, G. C., McDonald, P. S., & Armstrong, D. A. (2002). East meets west: Competitive interactions between green crab, *Carcinus maenas,* and native and introduced *Hemigrapsus spp. Marine Ecology Progress Series, 225,* 251–262.

Jivoff, P. (1997). Sexual competition among male blue crab, *Callinectes sapidus. The Biological Bulletin, 193,* 368–380.

Jivoff, P., & Hines, A. H. (1998). Female behavior, sexual competition and mate guarding in the blue crab, *Callinectes sapidus. Animal Behaviour, 55,* 589–603.

Jones, K. A., & Page, C. H. (1986). Postural interneurons in the abdominal nervous system of lobster. III. Pathways mediating intersegmental spread of excitation. *Journal of Comparative Physiology A, 158,* 281–290.

Karavanich, C., & Atema, J. (1993). Agonistic encounters in the American lobster, *Homarus americanus*—do they remember their opponents? *The Biological Bulletin, 185,* 321–322.

Karavanich, C., & Atema, J. (1998a). Individual recognition and memory in lobster dominance. *Animal Behaviour, 56,* 1553–1560.

Karavanich, C., & Atema, J. (1998b). Olfactory recognition of urine signals in dominance fights between male lobster, *Homarus americanus. Behaviour, 135,* 719–730.

Katz, P. S., & Harris-Warrick, R. M. (1990). Neuromodulation of the crab pyloric central pattern generator by serotonergic/cholinergic proprioceptive afferents. *Journal of Neuroscience, 10,* 1495–1512.

Kelly, T. M., & Chapple, W. D. (1990). Kinematic analysis of the defense response in crayfish. *Journal of Neurophysiology, 64,* 64–76.

Kennedy, D., Evoy, W. H., & Hanawalt, J. T. (1966). Release of coordinated behavior in crayfish by single central neurons. *Science, 154,* 917–919.

Khalaila, I., Manor, R., Weil, S., Granot, Y., Keller, R., & Sagi, A. (2002). The eyestalk-androgenic gland-testis endocrine axis in the crayfish *Cherax quadricarinatus. General and Comparative Endocrinology, 127,* 147–156.

Kovac, M. (1974). Abdominal movements during backward walking in crayfish. I. Properties of the motor program. *Journal of Comparative Physiology, 95,* 61–78.

Krasne, F. B., Shamsian, A., & Kulkarni, R. (1997). Altered excitability of the crayfish lateral giant escape reflex during agonistic encounters. *Journal of Neuroscience, 17,* 709–716.

Kravitz, E. A. (1988). Hormonal control of behavior: Amines and the biasing of behavioral output in lobsters. *Science, 241,* 1775–1781.

Kravitz, E. A. (2000). Serotonin and aggression: Insights gained from a lobster model system and speculations on the role of amine neurons in a complex behavior like aggression. *Journal of Comparative Physiology A, 186,* 221–238.

Kravitz, E. A., Basu, A. C., & Haass, F. A. (2001). Crustacean hyperglycemic hormone (CHH)-containing cells in second thoracic roots of the lobster: Intrinsic properties and pharmacological characterization. *Society for Neuroscience Abstracts.*

Kuwada, J. Y., Hagiwara, G., & Wine, J. J. (1980). Postsynaptic inhibition of crayfish tonic flexor motor neurones by escape commands. *Journal of Experimental Biology, 85,* 343–347.

Kuwada, J. Y., & Wine, J. J. (1979). Crayfish escape behaviour: Commands for fast movement inhibit postural tone and reflexes, and prevent habituation of slow reflexes. *Journal of Experimental Biology, 79,* 205–224.

Lang, F., Govind, C. K., Costello, W. J., & Greene, S. I. (1977). Developmental neuroethology: Changes in escape and defensive behavior during growth of the lobster. *Science, 197,* 682–685.

Larimer, J. L. (2000). The interneurons of the abdominal positioning system of the crayfish. How these neurons were established and their use as identified cells and command elements. *Brain, Behavior and Evolution, 55,* 241–247.

Leibrock, C. S., Marchand, A. R., & Barnes, W. J. (1996). Force dependent response reversal mediated by low- and high-threshold afferents from the same mechanoreceptor in a crayfish leg. *Journal of Neurophysiology, 76,* 1540–1544.

Livingstone, M. S., Harris-Warrick, R. M., & Kravitz, E. A. (1980). Serotonin and octopamine produce opposite postures in lobsters. *Science, 208,* 76–79.

Lowe, M. (1956). Dominance-subordinance relationships in the crayfish *Cambarellus shufeldtii. Tulane Studies in Zoology, 4,* 139–170.

Ma, P. M., Beltz, B. S., & Kravitz, E. A. (1992). Serotonin-containing neurons in lobsters: Their role as gain-setters in postural control mechanisms. *Journal of Neurophysiology, 68,* 36–54.

Mason, J. C. (1970). Maternal-offspring behavior of the crayfish, *Pacifastacus trowbridgi* (Stimpson). *American Midland Naturalist, 84,* 463–473.

Mathews, L. M. (2002). Territorial cooperation and social

monogamy: Factors affecting intersexual behaviours in pair-living snapping shrimp. *Animal Behaviour, 63,* 767–777.

Mello, J., Cromarty, S. I., & Kass-Simon, G. (1999). Increased aggressiveness in gravid female American lobsters, *Homarus americanus. Aggressive Behavior, 25,* 451–472.

Miall, R. C., & Larimer, J. L. (1982a). Central organization of crustacean abdominal posture motoneurons: Connectivity and command fiber inputs. *Journal of Experimental Zoology, 224,* 45–56.

Miall, R. C., & Larimer, J. L. (1982b). Interneurons involved in abdominal posture in crayfish: Structure, function and command fiber response. *Journal of Comparative Physiology, 148,* 159–173.

Montgomery, E. L., & Caldwell, R. L. (1984). Aggressive brood defense by females in the stomatopod *Gonodactylus bredini. Behavioral Ecology and Sociobiology, 14,* 247–251.

Moore, D., & Larimer, J. L. (1988). Interactions between the tonic and cyclic postural motor programs in the crayfish abdomen. *Journal of Comparative Physiology A, 163,* 187–199.

Moore, D., & Larimer, J. L. (1993). Cyclic postural behavior in the crayfish, *Procambarus clarkii:* Properties of the pattern-initiating network. *Journal of Experimental Zoology, 267,* 404–415.

Musolf, B. E., & Edwards, D. H. (2000). Crayfish hindgut neurons can take up serotonin from different sources in the terminal ganglion. *Society for Neuroscience Abstracts, 26,* 643.16

Nolan, B. A., & Salmon, M. (1970). The behaviour and ecology of snapping shrimp (Crustacea: *Alpheus heterochelis* and *Alpheus normanni*). *Forma et Functio, 2,* 289–335.

Obermeier, M., & Schmitz, B. (2003). Recognition of dominance in the big-clawed snapping shrimp (*Alpheus heterochaelis* Say 1818). Part I: Individual or group recognition? *Marine Freshwater Behavior and Physiology, 36,* 1–16.

Panksepp, J. B., Yue, Z., Drerup, C., & Huber, R. (2003). Amine neurochemistry and aggression in crayfish. *Microscopy Research and Technique, 60,* 360–368.

Pearlstein, E., Clarac, F., & Cattaert, D. (1998). Neuromodulation of reciprocal glutamatergic inhibition between antagonistic motoneurons by 5-hydroxytryptamine (5-HT) in crayfish walking system. *Neuroscience Letters, 241,* 37–40.

Peeke, H. V. S., Figler, M. H., & Chang, E. S. (1998). Sex differences and prior residence effects in shelter competition in juvenile lobsters, *Homarus americanus* Milne-Edwards. *Journal of Experimental Marine Biology and Ecology, 229,* 149–156.

Phlippen, M. K., Webster, S. G., Chung, J. S., & Dircksen, H. (2000). Ecdysis of decapod crustaceans is associated with a dramatic release of crustacean cardioactive peptide into the haemolymph. *Journal of Experimental Biology, 203,* 521–536.

Qian, S. M., & Delaney, K. R. (1997). Neuromodulation of activity-dependent synaptic enhancement at crayfish neuromuscular junction. *Brain Research, 771,* 259–270.

Rahman, N., Dunham, D. W., & Govind, C. K. (2002). Size-assortative pairing in the big-clawed snapping shrimp, *Alpheus heterochelis. Behaviour, 139,* 1443–1468.

Ranta, E., & Lindström, K. (1992). Power to hold sheltering burrows by juveniles of the signal crayfish, *Pasifastacus leniusculus. Ethology, 92,* 217–226.

Read, A. T., & Govind, C. K. (1997). Regeneration and sex-biased transformation of the sexually dimorphic pincer claw in adult snapping shrimps. *Journal of Experimental Zoology, 279,* 356–366.

Real, D., & Czternasty, G. (1990). Mapping of serotonin-like immunoreactivity in the ventral nerve cord of crayfish. *Brain Research, 521,* 203–212.

Rossi-Durand, C. (1993). Peripheral proprioceptive modulation in crayfish walking leg by serotonin. *Brain Research, 632,* 1–15.

Rubinow, D. R., & Schmidt, P. J. (1996). Androgens, brain, and behavior. *American Journal of Psychiatry, 153,* 974–984.

Scrivener, J. C. E. (1971). Agonistic behaviour of the American lobster *Homarus americanus* (Milne-Edwards). *Fisheries Research Board of Canada: Technical Reports, 235,* 1–128.

Simon, T. W., & Edwards, D. H. (1990). Light-evoked walking in crayfish: Behavioral and neuronal responses triggered by the caudal photoreceptor. *Journal of Comparative Physiology, 166,* 745–755.

Smith, M. R., & Dunham, D. W. (1996). Antennae mediate agonistic physical contact in the crayfish *Orconectes rusticus* (Girard, 1852) (Decapoda, Cambaridae). *Crustaceana, 69,* 668–674.

Sneddon, L. U., Huntingford, F. A., & Taylor, A. C. (1997). Weapon size versus body size as a predictor of winning fights between shore crabs, *Carcinus maenas* (L.). *Behavioral Ecology and Sociobiology, 41,* 237–242.

Sneddon, L. U., Taylor, A. C., Huntingford, F. A., & Orr, J. F. (2000). Weapon strength and competitive success in fights between shore crabs. *Journal of Zoology, 250,* 397–403.

Sneddon, L. U., Taylor, A. C., Huntingford, F. A., & Watson, D. G. (2000). Agonistic behaviour and biogenic amines in shore crabs *Carcinus maenas. Journal of Experimental Biology, 203,* 537–545.

Snyder, M. J., & Chang, E. S. (1991). Metabolism and

excretion of injected [3H]-ecdysone by female lobsters, *Homarus americanus*. *The Biological Bulletin, 180,* 475–484.

Söderbäck, B. (1994). Interactions among juveniles of two freshwater crayfish species and a predatory fish. *Oecologia, 100,* 229–235.

Song, C. K., Herberholz, J., Drummond, J., & Edwards, D. H. (2000). Social experience changes the behavioral response to unexpected touch in crayfish. *Society for Neuroscience Abstracts, 26,* 174.

Sosa, M. A., & Baro, D. J. (2002). The role of amines and aminergic receptors in mediating dominance in the giant tropical freshwater prawn. In K. Wiese & M. Schmidt (Eds.), *Physiology of the crustacean nervous system* (pp. 143–155). Berlin: Springer-Verlag.

Sosa, M. A., Spitzer, N., Edwards, D. H., & Baro, D. J. (2004). A crustacean serotonin receptor: Cloning and distribution in the thoracic ganglia of crayfish and freshwater prawn. *Journal of Comparative Neurology, 473,* 526–537.

Spitzer, N., Baro, D. J., & Edwards, D. H. (2002). Social regulation of serotonin receptor expression in the CNS of crayfish. *Society for Neuroscience Abstracts, 28,* 59.4.

Steger, R., & Caldwell, R. L. (1983). Intraspecific deception by bluffing: A defense strategy of newly molted stomatopods (Arthropoda: Crustacea). *Science, 221,* 558–560.

Stein, R. A. (1977). Selective predation, optimal foraging, and the predator-prey interaction between fish and crayfish. *Ecology, 58,* 1237–1253.

Stein, R. A., & Magnuson, J. J. (1976). Behavioral response of crayfish to a fish predator. *Ecology 57,* 751–761.

Stocker, A. M., & Huber, R. (2001). Fighting strategies in crayfish *Orconectes rusticus* (Decapoda, Cambaridae) differ with hunger state and the presence of food cues. *Ethology, 107,* 727–736.

Tamm, G. R., & Cobb, J. S. (1978). Behavior and the crustacean molt cycle: Changes in aggression of *Homarus americanus. Science, 200,* 79–81.

Thorpe, K. E., Huntingford, F. A., & Taylor, A. C. (1994). Relative size and agonistic behaviour in the female velvet swimming crab, *Necora puber* (L.) (Brachyura, Portunidae). *Behavioural Processes, 32,* 235–246.

Tierney, A. J., Godleski, M. S., & Massanari, J. R. (2000). Comparative analysis of agonistic behavior in four crayfish species. *Journal of Crustacean Biology, 20,* 54–66.

Tierney, A. J., Godleski, M. S., & Rattananont, P. (1999). Serotonin-like immunoreactivity in the stomatogastric nervous systems of crayfishes from four genera. *Cell and Tissue Research, 295,* 537–551.

Tierney, A. J., & Mangiamele, L. A. (2001). Effects of serotonin and serotonin analogs on posture and agonistic behavior in crayfish. *Journal of Comparative Physiology, 187,* 757–767.

Vorburger, C., & Ribi, G. (1999). Aggression and competition for shelter between a native and an introduced crayfish in Europe. *Freshwater Biology, 42,* 111–119.

Vu, E. T., & Krasne, F. B. (1993). Crayfish tonic inhibition: Prolonged modulation of behavioral excitability by classical GABAergic inhibition. *Journal of Neuroscience, 13,* 4394–4402.

Vu, E. T., Lee, S. C., & Krasne, F. B. (1993). The mechanism of tonic inhibition of crayfish escape behavior: Distal inhibition and its functional significance. *Journal of Neuroscience, 13,* 4379–4393.

Wiersma, C. A., Roach, J. L., & Glantz, R. M. (1982). Neural integration in the optic system. In D. C. Sandeman & H. L. Atwood (Eds.), *Neural integration and behavior* (pp. 2–31). New York: Academic Press.

Wine, J. J., & Krasne, F. B. (1982). The cellular organization of crayfish escape behavior. In D. C. Sandeman & H. L. Atwood (Eds.), *The biology of crustacea* (pp. 241–292). New York: Academic Press.

Winston, M. L., & Jacobson, S. (1978). Dominance and effects of strange conspecifics on aggressive interactions in the hermit crab *Pagurus longicarpus* (Say). *Animal Behaviour, 26,* 184–191.

Woodlock, B., & Reynolds, J. D. (1988). Laboratory breeding studies of freshwater crayfish, *Austropotamobius pallipes* (Lereboullet). *Freshwater Biology, 19,* 71–78.

Yeh, S. R., Fricke, R. A., & Edwards, D. H. (1996). The effect of social experience on serotonergic modulation of the escape circuit of crayfish. *Science, 271,* 366–369.

Yeh, S. R., Musolf, B. E., & Edwards, D. H. (1997). Neuronal adaptations to changes in the social dominance status of crayfish. *Journal of Neuroscience, 17,* 697–708.

Zulandt Schneider, R. A., Huber, R., & Moore, P. A. (2001). Individual and status recognition in the crayfish, *Orconectes rusticus:* The effects of urine release on fight dynamics. *Behaviour, 138,* 137–154.

Zulandt Schneider, R. A., Schneider, R. W. S., & Moore, P. A. (1999). Recognition of dominance status by chemoreception in the red swamp crayfish, *Procambarus clarkii. Journal of Chemical Ecology, 25,* 781–794.

PART II

NEUROTRANSMITTERS

4

Brain Serotonin and Aggressive Disposition in Humans and Nonhuman Primates

Stephen B. Manuck, Jay R. Kaplan, & Francis E. Lotrich

To the psychologically minded, serotonin must seem the iconic neurotransmitter, emblematic of brain and behavior in much the way DNA bespeaks genetic design. Popular imagination holds that many emotional ills sprout from brains containing too little serotonin, whereas drugs boosting brain serotonin are sought to relieve anguish, brighten mood, possibly even transform personality (Kramer, 1993). To the psychiatric imagination, dysregulated serotonergic neurotransmission is similarly ubiquitous in the disordered mind and figures prominently in research on such diverse clinical entities as depression, autism, eating disorders, generalized anxiety and obsessive-compulsive disorders, substance abuse, pathological gambling, and antisocial and borderline personality disorders. Other literatures document serotonergic abnormalities among people who have committed or attempted suicide and in persons of aggressive disposition, particularly those prone to aggression of an unpremeditated, impulsive, or irritable nature. The search for a common factor uniting these diverse associations, in turn, has prompted speculation that dimensional variation in central nervous system (CNS) serotonergic activity underlies individual differences in the capacity to restrain impulses and act in the service of long-term goals—abilities also long

known to behavioral scientists as components of ego strength, behavioral inhibition, delayed gratification, self-control, and, to the economist, intertemporal choice (Manuck, Flory, Muldoon, & Ferrell, 2003). In this context, diminished (or dysregulated) central serotonergic function is said to disinhibit normatively constrained behavior, thereby promoting impulsive aggression, suicide, substance abuse, or other impulse-related psychopathologies. The particular manifestation of disinhibited behavior exhibited by a susceptible individual would likely depend, of course, on circumstance or other vulnerability, including the presence of antagonistic motivation in the case of aggression, depression in most instances of suicide, and heightened sensitivity to reward or reinforcement among patients with substance abuse disorders.

Although the explanatory reach assigned this one neurotransmitter by both popular wisdom and much psychiatric writing is exceedingly broad, our charge covers a single province in the territory of serotonin—namely, aggression and then, specifically, associations of brain serotonergic activity with individual differences in the aggressive behaviors of humans and nonhuman primates. Following a short introduction to the neurobiology of serotonin, including common methods of investigation and sources of serotonin-associated genetic variation, we briefly address comparative conceptualizations of aggressive behavior in monkeys and people, including the role of antagonistic interaction in primate social dominance and human psychopathology. We then summarize the now substantial literature on CNS serotonergic activity as a correlate of aggressive disposition, as seen in studies employing neurochemical indices of serotonergic function, neuropharmacologic challenges, functional neuroimaging, and neurogenetic methodologies. Although study results in nonhuman primates sometimes speak directly to issues raised in corresponding human literature (as on whether impulsivity mediates the covariation of serotonin and aggression), these two bodies of research are presented separately below. In concluding sections of the chapter, we attempt to integrate observations derived from studies on monkeys and humans, identify implications of these findings for models of serotonergic influences on aggression, and speculate briefly regarding possible evolutionary origins of these associations.

Neurochemistry of Serotonin

The indoleamine serotonin is classified by molecular structure as one of the principal monoamine neurotransmitters, along with the catecholamines dopamine and norepinephrine. Neurons of the serotonergic system originate in the raphe nuclei of the brain stem and project to diverse areas of the forebrain, including subcortical structures such as the thalamus, basal ganglia, hypothalamus, hippocampus, amygdala, and septum as well as most of the cerebral cortex. Downward projections synapse on sensory and motor neurons of the spinal cord and extend to the intermediolateral cell column, where they can influence patterns of peripheral autonomic (sympathetic) discharge. Serotonergic projections also innervate primary sites of origin for neurons containing both dopamine (the ventral tegmental area and substantia nigra) and norepinephrine (locus coeruleus). In general, serotonin modulates responses evoked by other neurotransmitters, rather than exciting postsynaptic neurons directly, and is thought to exert largely inhibitory (or stabilizing) effects on behavior. The domains of behavior affected by serotonin are diverse, including locomotion, consummatory and sexual behavior, sleep, appetite, mood, and, as discussed in this chapter, aggression. Heightened serotonergic activity typically restrains, rather than facili-

tates, behavioral responding and has been shown to do so in a variety of contexts, including conditions of uncertainty, conflict, and punishment (Depue & Spoont, 1986; Soubrie, 1986; Spoont, 1992). Conversely, diminished serotonergic neurotransmission is said to negate restraints on goal-directed activity and to impair the regulation of behavioral and affective responses activated by other transmitter systems.

Serotonin is synthesized from the essential (diet-derived) amino acid tryptophan, which is carried into the brain competitively with other large neutral amino acids (e.g., phenylalanine, tyrosine) by a common transporter. The synthesis of serotonin is accomplished in two steps, starting with tryptophan's oxidation to 5-hydroxytryptophan (5-HTP) by the enzyme tryptophan hydroxylase. Decarboxylation of 5-HTP to 5-hydroxytryptamine (5-HT, or serotonin) is then catalyzed by a second enzyme, aromatic amino acid decarboxylase, which plays a similar role in dopaminergic and noradrenergic neurons. The first step is clearly the rate-limiting stage in serotonin biosynthesis, as it is uncommon for tryptophan hydroxylase to be saturated with substrate and the availability of tryptophan is critically dependent upon dietary intake and competitive transport across the blood-brain barrier.

Once synthesized, serotonin is transported down the cell axon for storage in synaptic vesicles. When released into the synapse, serotonin binds to specialized 5-HT receptors, which are now known to number 20 or more and comprise at least seven subfamilies. Of these, all but the ionotropic $5-HT_3$ receptor are G-protein coupled (metabotropic) signal transduction molecules that typically either inhibit or activate adenylyl cyclase or, by activation of phospholipase C, increase inositol triphosphate and diacylglycerol in the phosphoinositide system. Because the ascending axons of serotonergic neurons branch extensively, postsynaptic 5-HT receptors can be stimulated nearly simultaneously at multiple sites throughout the brain. Serotonergic neurotransmission is terminated when released serotonin is removed from the synapse and taken back up into the presynaptic (releasing) neuron by a transmitter-specific reuptake pump, the serotonin transporter. The recovered serotonin is then either re-stored in synaptic vesicles or it is metabolized, starting with its oxidation to 5-hydroxyindoleacetaldehyde by the enzyme monoamine oxidase (MAO). Some uncertainty surrounds this initial breakdown, as MAO exists in two forms, MAO-A and MAO-B. Of the two, MAO-A preferentially deaminates serotonin in vitro, but is not located in serotonergic neurons (Arai, Kimura, Nagatsu, & Maeda, 1997; Kitahama, Maeda, Denney, & Jouvet, 1994; Saura et al., 1996; Weslund, Denney, Kochersperger, Rose, & Abell, 1985). The less efficient MAO-B is present in serotonergic neurons, but its role there is unclear since MAO-B inactivation does not appear to alter serotonin turnover (as seen, for instance, in mice lacking the MAO-B gene (MAO-B "knock-outs") or animals administered MAO-B inhibitors) (Grimsby et al., 1997; Kato, Dong, Ishii, & Kine-muchi, 1986; Youdim, & Finberg, 1994). In any case, 5-hydroxyindoleacetaldehyde is subsequently oxidized by aldehyde dehydrogenase to yield a final metabolic product, 5-hydroxyindoleacetic acid (5-HIAA).

Measurement of Serotonergic Activity

Cerebrospinal Fluid (CSF) 5-HIAA

In vivo assessment of neurophysiologic activity is hampered by the brain's inaccessibility and, with respect to individual neurotransmitter systems, by juxtaposition of functionally distinct and interacting neural pathways. As a result, only indirect measurements of neuronal activity are generally feasible. One commonly reported index of central serotonergic function is the CSF concentration of 5-HIAA, which is ordinarily obtained from human subjects by lumbar puncture, and therefore, from the distal end of the spinal cord. Because some portion of CSF 5-HIAA content in the lumbar region also arises from the spinal cord, brain-derived 5-HIAA is both diluted in the CSF sample and displaced in time by its descent through the spinal column. These limitations are typically mitigated in studies of nonhuman primates by withdrawing CSF from the cisterna magna, which lies immediately beneath the raphe and provides a reasonably undiluted reservoir for 5-HIAA. However sampled, CSF 5-HIAA is only interpretable as an index of brain serotonin turnover to the extent that it correlates with brain 5-HIAA concentration. Although this assumption has not been tested extensively, postmortem evaluation of suddenly deceased individuals shows CSF 5-HIAA obtained by lumbar puncture to covary substantially with 5-HIAA in brain, including the frontal cortex (Stanley, Taskman-Bendz, & Doronini-Zis, 1985; Wester et al., 1990). It should be noted, however, that 5-HIAA is not an indicator of serotonergic neurotransmission, but of serotonin metabolism, and that a major portion of neuronally synthesized serotonin may be catabolized without having participated in synaptic transmission. Conversely, synaptic transmission may occur without metabolism when released serotonin is recycled efficiently back into synaptic vesicles. The invasive nature of its sampling also limits the utility of CSF as a source of measurement in investigations involving large samples and studies of healthy, nonpatient volunteers.

Neuroendocrine Challenges

Variation in brain serotonergic responsivity may be inferred from neuroendocrine reactions to drugs that act on serotonin-releasing neurons or neurons expressing serotonin receptors. This inference stems from the role of serotonergic neurotransmission in the release of certain anterior pituitary hormones. In the most frequently reported challenge, administering fenfluramine in either its dextro or racemic form induces the neuronal release of serotonin and inhibits reuptake. Because subsequent activation of serotonin receptors in the hypothalamus stimulates the pituitary to release prolactin into circulation, the resulting rise in plasma prolactin concentration is thought to index serotonergic responsivity in the hypothalamic-pituitary axis. Prolactin responses induced by fenfluramine are dose dependent (Quattrone et al., 1983; Yatham & Steiner, 1993) and correlate positively with CSF 5-HIAA concentrations (Mann, McBride, Brown, et al., 1992, but see also Coccaro, Kavoussi, Cooper, & Hauger, 1997). The prolactin rise is blocked by antagonists of $5-HT_2$ receptors (e.g., Coccaro, Kavoussi, Oakes, Cooper, & Hauger, 1996; DiRenzo et al., 1989; Goodall, Cowen, Franklin, & Silverstone, 1993; Lewis & Sherman, 1985; Quattrone et al., 1983) and, in rodents, by lesioning of the raphe nuclei (Quattrone, Shettini, DiRenzo, Tedeshi, & Preziosi, 1979). Although the utility of fenfluramine as a serotonergic challenge was restricted recently due to toxicities of chronic administration, other pharmacologic agents (or probes) that act presynaptically include the serotonin precursor tryptophan and several of the serotonin reuptake inhibitors (e.g., citalopram, clomiprimine). Postsynaptic mechanisms may also be studied using direct agonists of differing specificity for the various serotonin receptors (e.g., buspirone, ipsapirone, meta-chlorophenylpiperazine (m-CPP) (e.g., Yathem & Steiner, 1993). In addition to this diversity of probes, challenge responses may be indexed by different indices of neuroendocrine response, such as adrenocorticotropic hormone (ACTH), cortisol, and growth hormone, which, along with prolactin, vary somewhat in their relative sensitivities to different serotonergic agents (Yathem & Steiner, 1993).

Neuroimaging

Neuroendocrine challenges are informative only if the serotonergic responsivity they index extends to neural circuitry implicated in aggression. Impaired impulse control and heightened aggressiveness due to brain malignancy or trauma commonly result from lesions to prefrontal areas, such as the ventromedial prefrontal and orbitofrontal cortices (Anderson, Bechara, Damasio, Tranel, & Damasio, 1999; Grafman et al., 1996; Heinrichs, 1989). Analogously, studies of regional metabolic activity by positron emission tomography (PET) show reduced prefrontal activation (less glucose utilization) in forensic samples and psychiatric patients with histories of impulsive aggression (Goyer et al., 1994; Raine et al., 1998; Volkow & Tancredi, 1987). These observations suggest that functional impairments in the prefrontal cortex and allied regions (e.g., anterior cingulate), particularly those governing affect regulation and inhibitory control of behavior, confer liability for some forms of aggression. To examine serotonergic influences on area-specific neural activity, PET imaging may be combined with standard neuroendocrine probes to examine regional metabolic activity under serotonergic stimulation. Here, individuals are administered a serotonin agonist (such as fenfluramine or m-CPP) or placebo, followed by intravenous infusion of the radiolabeled glucose tracer [18]fluorodeoxyglucose ([18]FDG), which is readily taken up into metabolically active cells. A PET scan is then conducted to assess rates of cerebral [18]FDG uptake in regions of interest (e.g., New et al., 2002; Siever et al., 1999; Soloff, Meltzer, Greer, Constantine, & Kelly, 2000). Alternatively, radiolabeled antagonists for specific serotonin receptors may be administered to evaluate receptor number and affinity in various brain areas (Parsey et al., 2002).

Peripheral Measures
of Serotonergic Function

The bulk of serotonin in the body is not present in the brain, but is synthesized by enterochromaffin cells of the gut and deposited into the portal circulation. Serotonin is taken up actively by transporters located on the membranes of circulating blood platelets and is stored within platelets in specialized vesicles (dense granules). In turn, platelets release their stored serotonin in response to endothelial injury, facilitating platelet aggregation and helping to modulate vascular tone. This release may be stimulated by serotonin itself, as when newly released serotonin binds to membrane-bound serotonin receptors on neighboring cells. In addition to promoting platelet aggregation, serotonin affects the tonus of blood vessels by influencing the balance of receptor-mediated constriction and relaxation factors acting on vascular smooth muscle cells (e.g., reduction of endothelium-dependent vasodilation, augmentation of adrenergic- and angiotensin-II-mediated vasoconstriction). Finally, circulating serotonin that is not sequestered within platelet dense granules is ultimately metabolized by monoamine oxidase.

Although the brain and peripheral serotonin systems do not interact directly, they share common features. These include dependence on dietary tryptophan for biosynthesis, identical serotonin transporter and receptor ($5\text{-}HT_{2A}$ receptor) molecules, and enzymatic degradation of serotonin by monoamine oxidase. These similarities have encouraged the use of blood and platelet measurements in some serotonin studies of aggression, particularly in earlier literature and among investigations involving children. In addition to the serotonin content of platelets and whole blood, platelet serotonin transporters and $5\text{-}HT_{2A}$ receptors are often used as models of their neuronal counterparts in radioligand binding studies assessing the affinity and density (number) of these components in tissue. Common processes also can act independently in brain and platelet to modulate aspects of receptor function, including changes in the density of expressed receptors (via internalization) and in their affinity or efficacy (e.g., via phosphorylation of receptors). Although platelets have mechanisms for dynamically regulating receptor expression, affinity, and efficacy, platelet receptor number cannot be regulated via changes in gene transcription. For this reason, central and peripheral serotonin receptor activities do not have entirely comparable determinants, which complicates their interpretation when used as proxies for corresponding responses in brain. Except incidentally, we do not address investigations employing peripheral indices of serotonergic function in the following review, but instead focus on methodologies reflecting CNS processes more directly, such as metabolite concentrations in CSF, neuropharmacologic challenges, neuroimaging, and potential genetic influences on central serotonergic activity.

Genetic Variation in the Serotonergic System

The search for informative genetic variation in the serotonergic system has advanced vigorously with the advent of new molecular technologies. Genetic influences on brain serotonergic function might arise from differences in genes coding for any of the various proteins that support serotonergic neurotransmission, including those involved in serotonin's synthesis, release and reuptake, metabolism, or receptor activation. As noted by Maxson and Canastar (ch. 1 in this volume), there are many forms of common genetic variation, all of which entail differences in the sequence of nucleotides comprising the gene. Any stretch of DNA at which two or more different nucleotide sequences exist with some frequency in a population is said to be polymorphic, and the alternate versions of DNA present at this site (polymorphism) are referred to as alleles. A polymorphism also may be located in any of several regions of the gene. These include areas of DNA that specify the amino acid sequence of the protein that the gene encodes (exons); areas interspersed between exons, which are excised from the RNA transcript prior to translation (introns); and regulatory regions that interact with other genes and binding proteins to control and modulate the gene's transcription. The sequence variation defining a polymorphism typically involves alteration of a single DNA base pair (single nucleotide polymorphism, or SNP) or stretches of DNA that occur repetitively at a given site, with varying numbers of repeat elements present in different individuals. With respect to the latter, units of repetition may be very short (e.g., di- and trinucleotide repeats) or contain longer DNA sequences known as variable number of tandem repeats (VNTRs).

As the amino acid-specifying codons of DNA are each composed of three nucleotides and more than one codon can specify a single amino acid, polymorphisms that occur in coding regions and involve single base pair substitutions may or may not alter the amino acid sequence of the encoded protein. By insertion or deletion of a single nucleotide, other point mutations can alter all succeeding codons ("frameshift" mutations), thereby garbling the assembled protein, or terminate protein assembly entirely by incorporating a premature "stop" codon ("nonsense" mutations). In both of the latter cases, the mutation is likely to prove deleterious and therefore not survive in the population, either failing in transmission to a subsequent generation or suffering removal from the gene pool through selection. On the other hand, some polymorphisms that specify slightly different amino acid sequences may have functional significance for the proteins they encode, yet not markedly disadvantage the reproductive success of individuals carrying alternate alleles. Polymorphisms of this type comprise one significant source of functional genetic variation. A second source stems from DNA sequence variation that lies in regulatory regions and modulates the efficiency with which a gene is transcribed or translated. Unlike amino acid substitutions, such polymorphisms affect the rate of protein synthesis, but not the structure of the assembled protein.

Because polymorphisms of serotonin-regulating genes and their potential role in aggression are addressed later, here we describe only a few frequently reported sites of genetic variation for illustration. To date, over 70 SNPs have been identified in the MAO-A gene on the X chromosome (Xp11.4–11.3) and in nearly all of these the less common allele is also extremely rare. One involves a mutation that causes insertion of a premature stop codon resulting in complete loss of MAO-A activity in men, but has not been found outside of a single Dutch kindred (Brunner, Nelen, van Zandvoort, et al., 1993). There are also at least 13 alleles of a dinucleotide repeat in the second intron of the MAO-A gene; as one might surmise from its location, this variation has no known functional significance. In contrast, a repeat length polymorphism (VNTR) located 1.2 kilobases (kb) upstream of exon 1 in the MAO-A regulatory region contains four widely distributed alleles having either 3, 3.5, 4, or 5 repeats of a common 30-base-pair (bp) sequence (Sabol, Hu, & Hamer, 1998). The 3.5- and 5-repeat variants are rare, with a combined frequency of less than 5% in most populations; in Caucasian samples, the 4- and 3-repeat alleles occur in a ratio of about 2 to 1, whereas their distribution is nearly reversed in African Americans and among Asian/Pacific Islanders (Sabol et al., 1998). In an in vitro assay system (gene fusion and transfection experiments), reporter gene constructs containing the 3.5- and 4-repeat alleles show 2- to 10-fold greater transcriptional activity than constructs having 3 copies of the repetitive element; findings are mixed with respect to the infrequent 5-repeat variant (Sabol et al., 1998; Deckert et al., 1999). That human fibroblast cell cultures hosting the "high-transcription" 4-repeat allele also express substantially greater MAO-A-specific activity than cultures containing the less efficient 3-repeat allele (Denney, Koch, & Craig, 1999) suggests that this common VNTR is a strong determinant of MAO-A activity in normal human cells and may give rise to important individual differences in the rate of oxidation of MAO-A substrates, including serotonin.

As noted previously, the serotonin transporter (5-HTT) is responsible for terminating neurotransmission by removing serotonin from the synaptic cleft and returning it to the presynaptic neuron. As with MAO-A, a number of SNPs have been identified in the 5-HTT gene on chromosome 17 (17q11.2), only a couple of which alter amino acid sequence, and these are either extremely rare or of undetermined frequency. The most commonly studied variation is again a length (repeat) polymorphism in the gene's regulatory region. Having either 14 or 16 repetitions of a 22-bp core repeat located ~1 kb upstream of the gene's coding sequence yields a 44-bp insertion/deletion polymorphism. Relative to the longer variant of this biallelic repeat, the deletion, or short, allele reduces transcriptional efficiency by about twofold in reporter gene constructs (Heils et al., 1996; Lesch, Bengel, et al., 1996); in cultured lymphoblasts, the short allele is associated with lower 5-HTT mRNA production and reduced serotonin uptake (Lesch, Bengel, et al., 1996). The short allele may be associated with reduced central serotonergic responsivity to neuroendocrine challenge, though this relationship may vary among populations of differing sociodemographic attributes (Manuck, Flory, Ferrell, & Muldoon, 2004; Reist, Mazzanti, Vu, Tran, & Goldman, 2001; Whale, Quested, Laver, Harrison, & Cowen, 2000). Interestingly, length variation in the same 5-HTT gene-linked polymorphic region (5-HTTLPR) of rhesus monkeys (*Macaca mulatta*) has been described as well (Lesch, Meyer, et al., 1996; Bennett et al., 2002). Like its human counterpart, the rhesus polymorphism (rh-5-HTTLPR) is biallelic and confers allele-specific variation in 5-HTT gene promoter activity, with the short variant exhibiting lower transcriptional efficiency in an in vitro expression assay (Bennett et al., 2002). Moreover, similarity of the 5-HTT promoter repeat in the hominidae (humans, great apes) and Old World monkeys (represented by the baboon and rhesus monkeys), and its apparent absence in New World monkeys, led to the conclusion that this variation arose at least 40 million years ago (Lesch et al., 1997). Whereas precise dating of the appearance of this repeat element in primate evolution is constrained by limited DNA sequence data, the apparent sequence homology and its possible functional similarity in humans and rhesus monkeys suggest that varia-

tion in the 5-HTTLPR may modulate brain serotonergic activity throughout the catarrhine lineage.

Some uncertainty surrounds previously identified genetic variation in tryptophan hydroxylase, the rate-limiting enzyme in serotonin biosynthesis. A number of SNPs have been described in the commonly recognized tryptophan hydroxylase (TPH) gene on chromosome 11 (11p14–15.3). Most of these reside in introns, with a few occurring in the promoter region of the TPH gene (Nielsen et al., 1994, 1997; Paoloni-Giacobino et al., 2000; Rotondo et al., 1999). Much attention has focused on a pair of adenine-cytosine transversions located at nucleotides 218 and 779 in intron 7. Across individuals, the alternate alleles of these two polymorphisms (labeled A and C) do not segregate independently, a condition termed linkage disequilibrium. Due to their intronic location, the A218C and A779C polymorphisms are not thought to be functional, yet there is some evidence that allelic variation is associated with individual differences in central serotonergic activity, as indexed by CSF 5-HIAA concentrations and fenfluramine-stimulated prolactin release in healthy men (Jonsson et al., 1997; Manuck et al., 1998) and by TPH immunoreactivity in postmortem brain tissue of both suicide victims and controls (Ono et al., 2002). Such evidence suggests that these intronic polymorphisms may be in linkage disequilibrium with yet unknown variation in a coding region or regulatory sequence of the TPH gene (or, less likely, of another gene nearby). However, it was reported recently that deletion of the homologous TPH gene in mice failed to alter brain serotonin, while largely eliminating duodenal serotonin content (Walther et al., 2003). Further, a second TPH gene (TPH2) was identified in both mouse and rat that is active exclusively in brain. These findings are difficult to reconcile with the studies associating functional variation in brain serotonergic activity with intronic polymorphisms of the initial TPH gene (now labeled TPH1) in humans, especially as the human homologue of TPH2 is located on a different chromosome. There is now some evidence, though, that both TPH1 and TPH2 are expressed in human brain (Zill, Buttner, Eisenmenger, Bondy, & Ackenheil, 2003; Zill, Buttner, et al., 2004), but until more is known regarding their respective influences on central serotonergic function the interpretation of prior literature addressing genetic variation in TPH1 will remain equivocal. Meanwhile, a few SNPs have been found in TPH2 (http://www.ncbi.nlm.nkh.gov/SNP) and, while not yet studied in relation to aggression, initial work suggests one site of common variation in TPH2 may be associated with major depression (Zill, Baghai, et al., 2004).

In addition to genetic variation in the presynaptic components of serotonergic function, genes encoding serotonin receptors are also polymorphic. Studied most extensively are genes of the 5-HT$_1$ and 5-HT$_2$ receptor subtypes, in which scores of SNPs have been identified. Although much of this variation involves alleles of rare occurrence, the less frequent variants of some receptor polymorphisms are relatively common, particularly in the 5-HT$_{1B}$, 5-HT$_{2A}$, and 5-HT$_{2C}$ receptors. A few that are located in coding regions also specify amino acid substitutions, although data regarding their functional significance remain scant or inconclusive. The potential association of aggression-related phenotypes with these and other serotonin-regulating polymorphisms is discussed later in the section on neurogenetic studies.

Dimensions of Aggression

Nonhuman Primates

Surviving to reproduce and reproductive success—in evolutionary perspective, the twin aims of any organism—require acquisition and occasionally defense of vital resources, including food, shelter, territory, or mates. The Malthusian dilemma is that most of these resources are in short supply relative to the number of individuals seeking them, so that advancing one's own interests often conflicts with the interests of others. Organisms typically scramble in largely anonymous competition to obtain resources that are scarce but widely scattered. In contrast, animals naturally congregate in proximity to concentrated resources, such as a fruit-bearing tree, and in this circumstance often find it necessary to compete aggressively for access. A highly localized, sometimes seasonal, resource also may be commandeered and defended against use by others, if doing so is feasible and assures control of its exploitation. In fact, living in groups of either temporary or stable union commonly occurs when vital resources are dispersed in defensible patches of limited availability, as well as for collective protection against predators. Such sociality does not spell the end of conflict, however, but only gives it new dimension, as priority of access to resources within a group, whether of space, food, or social partners, may be partitioned in relation

to the relative power of competing group members (Chapais, 1991). Life's opportunities for aggressive encounter, it would seem, are ubiquitous.

Primate societies are no exception. Aside from the great apes (particularly chimpanzees), perhaps the best understood nonhuman primates are the Cercopithecines, a subfamily of the Cercopithedae, or Old World monkeys (Fleagle, 1999). Nearly all nonhuman primate studies of serotonin and aggression also involve research on four Cercopithecine species, three of the genus *Macaca* (rhesus monkeys, *mulatta*; cynomolgus monkeys, *fascicularis*; and pig-tailed monkeys, *nemestrina*) and one of the genus *Chlorocebus* (vervets, also known as African green monkeys, *Chlorocebus aethiops*). These species differ greatly in size (with average adult weights varying between about 5 and 15 kg) and inhabit geographic regions ranging from sub-Saharan Africa (vervets) to the Indian subcontinent (rhesus monkeys) and Southeast Asia (cynomolgus and pig-tailed monkeys). Yet all consume diets composed principally of fruits, which are supplemented by other plant materials, insects, and, in some species, occasional small vertebrate prey. In their natural habitats these species are usually found distributed in social groups of about 15–70 individuals, composed of multiple adult males, females, and their offspring (Falk, 2000; Fleagle, 1999). Females of multiple generations cohabit the same social group throughout life, whereas males emigrate from their natal groups at or around the time of sexual maturity. And unlike females, males lead a fairly transitory social existence, alternating between membership in established heterosexual troops (with mating opportunities) and periods of nomadic bachelorhood, often spent in association with other males (Pusey & Packer, 1987).

The behavioral repertoires of monkeys are defined by elaborated patterns of agonistic and affiliative interaction (Sade, 1973). Disputed access to food and sexual partners occasions most instances of aggression, and monkeys fight for competitive advantage, personal defense, or the protection of kin (Chapais, 1991). Aggression is costly, by both expenditure of energy and risk of injury, but such costs can be reduced if one party to a fight desists on recognition of an inferior position and signals submission to its opponent. Risk is curtailed further if the relative dominance of a more powerful individual is acknowledged without altercation through overt or ritualized signs of deference. In monkeys, these processes engender dyadic relationships of relative dominance and subordination, thereby minimizing bouts of active aggression (Bernstein, 1981; Bernstein & Gordon, 1974). When aggregated across the numerous dyads of a given social group, moreover, such asymmetrical relationships generate a linear hierarchy of social dominance. In the Cercopithecines, determination of dominance ranking is simplified by the transitivity of these relationships: if monkey A is dominant to monkey B, and if B is dominant to monkey C, then A is usually dominant to C as well.

Importantly, social dominance is not a property or trait of an individual, but the expression of a relationship between individuals, and an animal's dominance status cannot be taken as an indicator of its relative aggressiveness (Bernstein, 1981). One monkey may initiate few fights, for instance, yet win nearly all of the contests in which it is engaged; such an animal is clearly dominant, but not particularly aggressive. Conversely, another monkey may provoke a great many fights, yet habitually lose to the majority of its rivals; this individual is subordinate, albeit highly aggressive. Among males, social dominance is largely determined by an animal's social competence, size, and ability to defeat others in fights, but may also reflect the coercive power two or more monkeys acting in coalition against an animal that none could defeat individually (Walters & Seyfarth, 1987). Owing to the strong matrilineal associations characterizing Cercopithecines, dominance hierarchies among females are largely familial, with a mother's rank shared by her daughters. Whereas a mother is generally dominant to her daughter, the latter will typically prove dominant to both mothers and daughters of lesser ranked matrilines. Finally, consistent with the sexual dimorphism of Cercopithecines, females tend to be subordinate to males, although in some species males may be countered effectively by an alliance of females.

The diverse expressions of antagonistic intent and action that characterize primate social behavior afford latitude for individual variation. Monkeys exhibit stereotyped motor patterns denoting affiliation (e.g., groom, passive body contact), aggression (e.g., stare threat, chase, physical assault), and submission (e.g., yield space [displaced], grimace, cower, flee). Acts of aggression and submission are typically highly ritualized, involving distinct gestures and facial expressions, without physical contact (Sade, 1973). Though less frequent, *overt* acts of aggression also occur, often culminating in escalating cycles of reciprocated threat between rivals. Interestingly, the relative frequencies with which monkeys express ritualized (low-intensity)

and contact (high-intensity) aggression differ greatly among individuals. Some monkeys, in particular, seem unable to modulate their aggressive responses to other individuals "appropriately," and in consequence escalate otherwise ordinary altercations into fights of excessive severity and heightened risk of injury (Higley & Linnoila, 1997). In extensive observations on rhesus monkeys, it has been found that animals exhibiting such unrestrained aggression also act imprudently in contexts unrelated to antagonistic behavior, as by leaping long distances at dangerous heights through the forest canopy (Mehlman et al., 1994). Although it is not clear that this pattern of concurrent aggressiveness and impulsive risk taking comprises a behavioral aberration akin to human psychopathology, high rates of escalated aggression predict early mortality among free-ranging, young male rhesus monkeys (Higley, Mehlman, Higley, et al., 1996).

Humans

There is much continuity in the aggressive behaviors of humans and nonhuman primates. In common with monkeys, humans can assault rivals physically or signal their antagonism through facial expressions or gestures meant to convey the coercive power of the aggressor, and individuals may commit acts of aggression either alone or in alliance with others. Similarly too, humans fight in competition over resources, mates, and social status, in self-defense, and for the protection of kin, friends, and sexual partners. In contrast to nonhuman primates, human aggression is abetted by technology (weapons) and may be despotic, as by deliberate exploitation of subordinates (Chapais, 1991). Of course, language adds insult to injury, in a literal sense, by providing a verbal complement (or alternative) to physical violence. It is also only in humans that aggression may be used to commit crimes, to enslave others or compel acquiescence to religious or ideological doctrine, or to pursue wars of national interest. At the individual level, men are universally more aggressive than women, and rates of aggressive confrontation are greatest among those who are young, poor, or unmarried (Daly & Wilson, 1988). Cultural factors moderate human aggression as well, with men's heightened sensitivity to signs of disrespect, challenge, or threat spawning a high frequency of confrontational violence in so-called "cultures of honor" (Nisbett & Cohen, 1996).

A distinction is often made between instrumental and impulsive, or affective, aggression (Best, Williams,

& Coccaro, 2002; Blair, 2001). Instrumental aggression is said to aim at a defined goal, with premeditation and entailing risk proportional to the value of its object. In contrast, impulsive aggression is said to occur without forethought, often in immediate reaction to an actual or perceived threat, in defiance of risk, and fueled by acute emotional arousal (frequently rage). It is tempting to see a parallel between impulsive aggression in humans and the poorly modulated, unrestrained aggressiveness that characterizes certain risk-taking monkeys. Likewise, the measured, low-intensity aggressive behaviors typically used to maintain dominance relationships and stabilize social hierarchies in Old World monkeys might appear to have much in common with instrumental human aggression. As described later in this chapter, these two categories of aggressive act and motivation do seem to correspond meaningfully in humans and nonhuman primates, with possible commonalities of etiology and neurobiological mechanism.

Measures of Aggression and Impulsivity

Aggressive interactions among monkeys are ordinarily documented by trained observers, who may study the same animals over months or years, amassing hundreds of hours of behavioral observation. Naturally occurring interpersonal aggression is rarely recorded directly in human subjects, although study participants may react aggressively when exposed to provocative laboratory procedures; even here, however, data are typically limited to observations obtained on one or, at best, a few occasions. More often, aggressive disposition and associated behavioral traits, such as impulsivity, are inferred from subjects' responses to structured interviews or standardized questionnaires. The most frequently reported index of aggressive behavior in the serotonin literature was developed by Brown and colleagues (Brown et al., 1982; Brown, Goodwin, Ballenger, Goyer, & Major, 1979) as a method of quantifying lifetime histories of aggression (LHA) among military personnel, based on psychiatric and medical history, interview and physical examination, and job performance assessments. The categories of evaluation identified by Brown and colleagues (1979) were later generalized for use in psychiatric and nonpatient populations and formatted as a semistructured interview (Coccaro, Berman, & Kavoussi, 1997). The Brown-Goodwin/Coccaro LHA interview taps diverse aspects of aggressive history, including *aggression* expressed toward others (by verbal

and physical assault), destruction of property, and temper tantrums; *antisocial* behaviors eliciting disciplinary action (in school and workplace) and illicit acts committed with and without police contact; and *self-inflicted injury*. The LHA interview has good psychometric properties, with strong internal consistency and high retest reliability, and has been validated against aggressive responding in laboratory testing of psychiatric and forensic samples (Coccaro, Berman, et al., 1997; Coccaro, Berman, Kavoussi, & Hauger, 1996).

Two other commonly employed measures are the Buss–Durkee Hostility Inventory (BDHI) and the Barratt Impulsiveness Scale (BIS), both self-administered questionnaires. The 75 items of the BDHI comprise eight subscales covering components of hostile behavior and ideation (Buss & Durkee, 1957). Four of these cohere psychometrically within a single factor labeled "motor aggression," which contains subscales measuring irritable temperament and an individual's propensity to express aggressive impulses verbally (verbal hostility), indirectly ("undirected aggression"), and by physical assault. The Barratt Scale, or BIS, contains 30 questions concerning subjects' control of thoughts and behavior (the number of items varies somewhat by version of the scale) (Barratt, 1994). Typical items assess tendencies to act without thinking (motor impulsivity), to make decisions "on the spur of the moment" (cognitive impulsivity), and to fail to plan ahead (nonplanning impulsiveness). Both the BDHI and BIS have adequate internal consistency and retest reliability consistent with stable individual differences. Other, less frequently used, measures of aggressiveness and impulsivity are cited later in discussion of individual studies.

Psychopathologies of Aggression and Impulse Control

Extremes of disorderly behavior may bring individuals to either legal or psychiatric attention. Because judicial entities deal with criminal offenses and the disposition of offenders, they are naturally concerned with issues of premeditation, motive, and remorse, all of which inform judgments relating to an offender's volition and culpability. But not all aggression is criminal. Psychiatric attention focuses more directly on the distress, functional impairments, and potential loss of autonomy experienced by people exhibiting deviant behaviors, cognitions, or affect. Patients suffering from a number of psychiatric conditions frequently act aggressively, and in some disorders such behavior is especially prominent. Persistent hostility and aggression are common symptoms of the "externalizing" disorders of childhood, for example, particularly oppositional defiant disorder (e.g., chronic disobedience, argumentativeness, tantrums, and rule violations) and conduct disorder (e.g., frequent fighting, intimidation and cruelty, property destruction, theft, and truancy) (American Psychiatric Association, *Diagnostic and Statistical Manual of Mental Disorders* [4th ed.], 2000).

Abnormal levels of aggression are also apparent in several of the adult personality disorders. Patients with borderline personality disorder are characterized by a marked instability of mood and interpersonal relationships, poor impulse control, and a fragile sense of self (or self-image). Shifts of mood in these patients can be rapid, often veering to depression or anger, and may occasion outbursts of rage and physical violence directed at either themselves or others. While borderline personality disorder is most common in women, men are more frequently diagnosed with antisocial personality disorder, which subsumes a variety of symptoms involving violations of law and social norms, irritability and aggressiveness (physical assaults), lack of remorse over mistreatment of others, and a pervasive pattern of irresponsibility, recklessness, and impulsivity. One current hypothesis holds that impulsivity actually lies at the root of both of these personality disorders, yielding gendered variants of a common pathology that may arise from a dysregulation of central serotonergic function (Paris, 1997). However, antisocial personality disorder may encompass aggressive and antisocial behaviors of varying etiology. In addition to those whose aggression stems from undercontrolled impulse and affect, others may simply use aggression to obtain what they want (instrumental aggression), unimpeded by conscience or socialization, due to an impaired capacity for emotional learning (Blair, 2003). Reflecting true psychopathy, the latter account for a significant portion (perhaps 30%) of diagnosed antisocial personality disorders and may involve psychological and neural mechanisms different from those of impulsive aggression (Blair, 2001; Hart & Hare, 1997).

Alcohol and other substance use disorders are highly comorbid with antisocial behavior (e.g., Krueger et al., 2002; Slutske et al., 1998), and this relation may be strongest among male alcoholics whose problem drinking begins at an early age (often referred to as type II alcoholism; Cloninger, Sigvardsson, & Bohman, 1996). In intermittent explosive disorder, a patient's inability to resist aggressive impulses occasions serious episodes of physical assault or property destruction that are out of proportion to any precipitating events. A recent study showed patients with this disorder to have cognitive impairments similar to those of persons who are impulsively aggressive due to lesions of the orbitofrontal and ventromedial prefrontal cortices (Best et al., 2002). These deficits included impaired recognition of facial expressions and failure to choose advantageously in a task pitting immediate rewards against the specter of long-term loss. The authors suggest that inhibitory projections between the orbital/medial prefrontal cortex and the amygdala are dysfunctional in intermittent explosive disorder, an abnormality that may reflect deficient serotonergic modulation of this frontal-limbic circuitry. Finally, extensive comorbidity among all of the foregoing disorders has stimulated biometric analyses aimed at identifying their shared and unique etiologies. This work supports a hierarchical model of alcohol and drug dependence, antisocial behavior, and disinhibitory temperament, in which each component retains some specific genetic and/or environmental determinants, yet all are united by a latent, highly heritable "externalizing" factor (Krueger et al., 2002).

Serotonin and Aggression in Nonhuman Primates

Rhesus Monkeys

Numerous studies of rhesus monkeys involve animals housed on Morgan Island (South Carolina), a sea island maintained as a free-ranging breeding resource (e.g., Higley et al., 1992; Mehlman et al., 1994, 1997; Westergaard et al., 2003; Westergaard, Suomi, Higley, & Mehlman, 1999). Colony monkeys are distributed in natural (multimale, multifemale) social groups of about 50 animals each, occupying distinct, but overlapping, home ranges. In most studies, biochemical indices of CNS neurotransmitter function, such as cisternal CSF 5-HIAA, are examined in relation to behaviors observed on subsets of colony animals located in the field by radiotelemetry. Among male rhesus monkeys, the propensity to engage in unrestrained aggression—defined as the frequency of chases and physical assaults (high-intensity aggression), expressed as a proportion of all aggressive acts exhibited by an animal—covaries inversely with individual differences in CSF 5-HIAA concentrations (Higley, Mehlman,

Poland, et al., 1996; Mehlman et al., 1994). Displacements and ritualized threat gestures (low-intensity aggression), which monkeys commonly display in establishing and maintaining social dominance, do not correlate with individuals' CSF 5-HIAA concentrations, nor does the sum of all aggressive behaviors observed (total aggression). The unrestrained, or escalated, aggression of animals with low 5-HIAA concentrations is apparently unrelated to other monoamine neurotransmitters, as the metabolites of dopamine and norepinephrine show no comparable association. We noted previously that animals having high rates of escalated aggression also exhibit impulsive risk taking in contexts divorced from social interaction, as evidenced by their tendency to leap long distances when traversing upper storeys of the forest canopy. The frequency of unprovoked long leaps observed in these monkeys, when calculated as a percentage of all leaping behavior, likewise correlates negatively with animals' CSF 5-HIAA concentrations (Higley, Mehlman, Poland, et al., 1996; Mehlman et al., 1994). Neither leaps of shorter (prudent) distances, nor variation in activity level per se, as reflected in the total number of leaps observed, are associated with differences in serotonergic activity. Interestingly, CSF free testosterone concentrations among male rhesus monkeys correlate positively with individual differences in low- but not high-intensity aggression and do not covary with animals' "long-leap ratio" (Higley, Mehlman, Poland, et al., 1996). Thus, low central serotonergic activity appears to be associated with impulsivity and severe, unrestrained expressions of aggression, whereas high testosterone (also commonly implicated in aggressive behavior) predicts the more ritualized forms of aggression used in negotiating dominance relationships and is unrelated to impulsive risk taking.

Beyond engaging in disproportionately more contact aggression, adolescent rhesus males with low CSF 5-HIAA concentrations tend to have fewer social companions, spend less time in passive affiliation or in bouts of grooming with conspecifics, and emigrate from their natal groups at younger ages than other monkeys (Mehlman et al., 1995; see also Kaplan, Fontenot, Berard, Manuck, & Mann, 1995). The causes of their early emigration remain unclear, but may reflect ostracism or eviction by older males in consequence of their inept sociality and impaired impulse control and the social disruption occasioned by frequent, severe fighting. Because these monkeys are less likely to display the stereotypical gestures of submission that ordi-

narily terminate fights (e.g., lip smacking, fear grimaces), they are often the targets of aggression and, due to their impulsive escalation of antagonistic encounters, they are also more likely to suffer injuries in fights (Higley & Linnoila, 1997). Indeed, a 4-year longitudinal study of 49 free-ranging, young rhesus males showed all but 1 of 11 animals dying over the course of the investigation to have had CSF 5-HIAA concentrations below the sample median when evaluated previously, at 2 years of age (i.e., as juveniles) (Higley, Mehlman, Higley, et al., 1996). Although the cause of death could not be ascertained in some instances, animals known to have died of wounds sustained in fights had lower CSF 5-HIAA concentrations than those alive to the end of follow-up, and as noted previously, the rate of escalated aggression was itself a significant predictor of early mortality.

The social deficits of "low" 5-HIAA animals are equally apparent in the autumn mating season (Mehlman et al., 1997). At this time adult males compete vigorously for access to reproductive females, with whom they often form brief "consort" relationships. Male consort behaviors include remaining near and engaging the female partner in frequent grooming, followed by sexual mounting and ejaculation. CSF 5-HIAA concentrations rise during this period, but interindividual variation in 5-HIAA remains relatively stable between the nonmating and mating seasons. Consistent with their impaired social competence in other settings, males with low CSF 5-HIAA concentrations form fewer consorts, groom less during consort relationships, and achieve fewer heterosexual mounts and inseminations than their high 5-HIAA counterparts. On the other hand, no aspect of aggression has been found to correlate with individual differences in CSF 5-HIAA concentrations during the mating season. Perhaps serotonergic influences on aggressive behavior diminish adaptively under intense male-male competition for sexual partners, because success in this endeavor is the predicate for reproductive success. Whatever its cause, the consistent covariation of (lower) CSF 5-HIAA concentrations with violent aggression in males outside the mating season and its absence during the season suggests that contextual variables moderate relations between central serotonergic activity and aggressive behavior (see Simon & Lu, ch. 9 in this volume).

Observations on female rhesus monkeys also associate variation in serotonergic function with aspects of aggression. In one study, CSF 5-HIAA concentrations of individually caged, adult females were found to covary inversely with spontaneous aggression (typically chases and physical assaults) recorded when animals were later housed together in groups (Higley, King, et al., 1996). In addition, low CSF 5-HIAA monkeys were more likely than those with higher 5-HIAA concentrations to be removed from their social groups for excessive aggression or treatment of wounds. In a subsequent study of young female rhesus and pigtailed macaques living in small, all-female groups, CSF 5-HIAA levels also correlated negatively with rates of escalated aggression (Westergaard et al., 1999). This association was reported for both species, even though rhesus females were more aggressive, suffered more fight-related wounds, and had lower 5-HIAA concentrations than pigtailed monkeys. Thus, central serotonergic activity appears to vary in relation to the aggressive temperaments of two closely related species in a manner analogous to the covariation of serotonin and aggression within each species. In both adult and juvenile females, moreover, CSF 5-HIAA levels predicted social dominance, with high-ranking animals having higher 5-HIAA concentrations than subordinate monkeys. As high 5-HIAA monkeys were least likely to injure other animals in fights or engage in unrestrained aggression, this finding accords with emerging evidence that aggressive disposition per se may be of limited importance in the acquisition of social dominance.

As in male rhesus monkeys, the association between serotonin with aggression is context dependent in females, differing in this case between captive and free-ranging animals. In addition to the studies cited above, juvenile rhesus females have also been studied in a natural habitat (Morgan Island), in families containing a mother and multiple siblings, including an older sister (Westergaard et al., 2003). As in males, females having low CSF 5-HIAA concentrations were those most likely to engage in impulsive risk taking, as suggested by a high frequency of unprovoked, long leaps between the upper branches of forest trees (high long-leap ratio). CSF 5-HIAA concentrations also covaried inversely with these animals' aggressive behavior, but in contrast to captive females and males observed outside the mating season, only with aggression of mild intensity, such as stares and stationary threats. Westergaard and colleagues (2003) suggest that impulsive, high-intensity aggression among young rhesus females is suppressed in natural settings because the aggression of juveniles is likely to be either targeted at relatives or muted by the protective interference of a mother and older sisters. In the latter instance, kin support may prevent the dangerous escalation of fights to which low 5-HIAA animals are otherwise predisposed. In the absence of kin, however, as among captive animals (Higley, King, et al., 1996; Westergaard et al., 1999), central serotonergic activity is associated with violent, unrestrained aggression in a pattern much like that seen in males.

Developmental Influences

Interindividual variability in central serotonergic activity is present at a young age in rhesus monkeys, persists into adulthood, and is reproducible across different social situations and settings. On retesting over intervals of days to years, individual differences in CSF 5-HIAA concentrations are stable (in the range of .45–.77) in both males and females, juveniles and adults, captive and free-ranging monkeys, and animals housed alone and in social groups (e.g., Higley & Linnoila, 1997; Higley, King, et al., 1996; Higley, Suomi, & Linnoila, 1996b; Mehlman et al., 1997; Westergaard et al., 1999, 2003). Regarding the etiology of trait variation in serotonergic function, significant genetic and environmental influences on rhesus CSF 5-HIAA are documented in analyses of paternal half siblings and maternal offspring reared by unrelated mothers (Higley et al., 1993). Environmental effects on both serotonergic function and behavior have also been demonstrated experimentally in studies manipulating conditions of early rearing (Higley, Suomi, & Linnoila, 1996a, 1996b). Compared to mother-reared rhesus monkeys, for instance, animals raised in peer groups without maternal contact show enduring developmental abnormalities. Notably, the CSF 5-HIAA concentrations of monkeys reared with peers are significantly lower in both infancy and adulthood than those of mother-reared animals. As adults too, peer-reared monkeys are more likely to be removed from their social groups for excessive aggression or wounds received in fights, more frequently exhibit immature or infantlike affiliative behaviors (e.g., ventral clinging), and, when provided free access to alcohol, consume to excess. When administered the serotonin reuptake inhibitor sertraline, peer-reared monkeys become less aggressive and consume less alcohol (Higley, Hasert, Suomi, & Linnoila, 1998). This observation suggests that the increased aggression and alcohol intake characteristic of untreated, peer-reared animals may stem from diminished serotonergic neurotransmission, a result of the reduced brain serotonin turnover associated with early maternal deprivation.

We noted earlier that an insertion/deletion polymorphism in the regulatory region of the serotonin transporter gene (5-HTT) moderates activity of the 5-HTT gene promoter in rhesus monkeys and may be homologous with similarly functional variation in the human 5-HTT gene (5-HTTLPR) (Bennett et al., 2002). Among monkeys housed on Cayo Santiago (Puerto Rico), another free-ranging rhesus colony, males possessing the transcriptionally less efficient variant of this polymorphism, the so-called short (or deletion) allele, emigrate from their natal groups at an earlier age than animals carrying two long alleles (Trefilov, Berard, Krawczak, & Schmidtke, 2000). This finding is especially interesting given the earlier reports that low CSF 5-HIAA predicts early emigration on both Cayo Santiago and Morgan Island (Kaplan et al., 1995; Mehlman et al., 1995). CSF 5-HIAA concentrations and other serotonin-associated behavioral phenotypes also vary by genotype of the rhesus 5-HTT gene-linked polymorphic region (rh-5-HTTLPR), yet interestingly, nearly all of these "genetic" effects reflect an interaction of allelic variation and animals' conditions of rearing. For example, the rh-5-HTTLPR short allele is associated with lower CSF 5-HIAA concentrations in adult monkeys, but only among peer-reared (as opposed to mother-reared) animals (Bennett et al., 2002). Allele-specific modulation of alcohol-induced ataxia and sedation is also reported, but again only among peer-reared monkeys (Barr, Newman, Becker, Champoux, et al., 2003). Although a study of infants in the first month of life shows the rh-5-HTTLPR short allele predictive of greater emotionality (e.g., distress, inconsolability) irrespective of rearing status, an association of the short allele with "orientation" scores reflecting possible attentional deficits is specific to peer rearing (Champoux et al., 2002). And finally, preliminary evidence suggests that among juvenile monkeys, peer-reared animals possessing the short allele are more aggressive (engage in more biting, chasing, hitting, slapping) than animals raised under the same conditions but homozygous for the long allele or mother-reared monkeys of either genotype (Barr, Newman, Becker, Parker, et al., 2003). In sum, altered developmental trajectories arising from an adverse rearing environment may be refracted by regulatory variation in the 5-HTT gene promoter, with interactive effects of gene and environment extending to measures of both CNS serotonergic function and aggressive phenotype.

Vervet Monkeys

Studies of vervet monkeys are less extensive, but largely consistent with those conducted on rhesus macaques. Lowering central serotonergic activity by acute dietary depletion of the serotonin precursor tryptophan, for instance, increased the frequency of spontaneous aggression (threat gestures, hitting, chasing, biting), as well as aggressive behavior elicited in competitions over access to food, in socially housed, adult male, but not female, vervet monkeys (Chamberlain, Ervin, Pihl, & Young, 1987). Conversely, increasing serotonergic activity by tryptophan supplementation reduced competitive aggression in both males and females. Although other social behaviors were not altered by these acute manipulations, chronic administration of drugs acting either to increase or decrease serotonergic neurotransmission may affect the behavioral repertoires of vervet monkeys more broadly. In one extensive investigation (Raleigh, McGuire, Brammer, Pollack, & Yuwiler, 1991), the dominant male was removed from each of 12 social groups originally containing three adult males, three adult females, and their immature offspring. One of the two remaining males then received 4-weeks of active treatment by either (a) one of two agents intended to increase serotonergic activity (tryptophan or the serotonin reuptake inhibitor fluoxetine) or (b) one of two drugs acting to decrease serotonergic activity (the serotonin antagonist cyproheptadine or the releasing agent fenfluramine). In a subsequent experimental period, treated animals were administered a drug of the class opposite that received first. Results showed that both fluoxetine and tryptophan decreased aggressive behavior and increased social affiliation (grooming, approaching and remaining in close proximity to others), relative to baseline measurements. Fenfluramine and cyproheptadine, on the other hand, increased aggression and reduced the frequency of affiliative behaviors. In each group, moreover, the monkey administered fluoxetine or tryptophan became dominant over the untreated referent male, but subordinate when given fenfluramine or cyproheptadine. In addition to again showing a dissociation of aggression and social dominance, behavioral observations in this study suggest that fluoxetine- and tryptophan-treated males attained dominance largely by forming affiliative bonds with adult females, whereas these animals failed to do so when treated with fenfluramine or cyproheptadine, possibly because they initiated fights against females more frequently, provoking counterattacks and social ostracism. As striking as these associations appear, however, it remains unclear how robust the serotonergic influence on rank attainment may be among vervet males, as administration of fluoxetine did not facilitate acquisition of social dominance in one recently attempted replication (M. T. McGuire, personal communication, January, 2004).

The studies of rhesus monkeys show low CSF 5-HIAA concentrations to be associated with heightened impulsivity, as well as with aggression and impaired patterns of social affiliation. Although impulsivity was deliberately assessed in a setting devoid of social interaction (unprovoked leaping), presumably to determine whether variation in serotonergic activity may underlie a more general dimension of behavioral inhibition/disinhibition, problems of impulse control often occur in a social context and are elicited by social cues. To index social impulsivity specifically, Fairbanks (2001) devised a laboratory protocol, the Intruder Challenge, for evaluating individual differences in the propensity to approach and interact with a social stranger. Among adolescent and adult male vervets, animals responding impulsively to the introduction of an unfamiliar monkey (the intruder) had lower CSF 5-HIAA concentrations than less impulsive animals (Fairbanks, Melaga, Jorgensen, Kaplan, & McGuire, 2001). In a related experiment, monkeys administered fluoxetine were less impulsive than vehicle-treated controls. Interestingly, high-ranking (dominant) males were more likely to score in the intermediate range of social impulsivity than at either extreme (Fairbanks, 2001).

The Intruder Challenge also yields two correlated components of animals' behavioral responses: latency to approach the intruder and aggressive interactions (threats and assertive displays) (Fairbanks et al., 2001). Whereas both the latency and aggression components correlated inversely with serotonergic activity, individuals' 5-HIAA concentrations predicted approach latency even after adjusting statistically for correlated variation in aggression. Because the aggression component was not similarly associated with differences in 5-HIAA levels after adjusting for approach behavior, the authors propose that dimensional variation in "impulsivity versus inhibition" comprises a key behavioral correlate of central serotonergic function. In this view, aggressiveness (unlike impulsivity) is not a direct consequence of low serotonergic activity, but a category of behavior that uninhibited, impulsive individuals are more likely to exhibit, depending on circumstance and motivation. Because impulsivity and aggression covary in many

social contexts, though, their etiologies may still share common genetic and environmental determinants, even if the behavioral expression of one (aggression) is conditioned by serotonergically mediated variation in the other (impulsivity). In this regard, a quantitative genetic analysis of Challenge responses among pedigreed vervets from the same population (the UCLA/VA Vervet Research Colony) shows significant heritability of the aggregate social impulsivity score, as well as its subscales of approach and aggression. There is also a substantial genetic correlation ($r = .78$) between the approach and aggression components, but notably, no significant influence of maternal environment on either dimension of social impulsivity (Fairbanks et al., 2004). The latter finding may seem surprising, given the strong effect that maternal deprivation (peer rearing) seems to have on serotonergic function and behavior in rhesus monkeys. Perhaps the most likely explanation for this discrepancy is that exclusive peer interaction in infancy is not within the range of normative developmental experience in undisturbed populations and, therefore, did not constitute a component of variance among animals raised in the vervet colony.

Cynomolgus Monkeys

In contrast to the studies of rhesus and vervet monkeys, in which cisternal CSF 5-HIAA concentrations were used to index of brain serotonergic function, studies of cynomolgus monkeys have assessed in vivo CNS serotonergic responsivity by acute fenfluramine challenge. In these investigations, fenfluramine was administered by intramuscular injection in weight-adjusted dosage, and animals' neuroendocrine responses were expressed as the relative rise in plasma prolactin concentration over "baseline" measurements obtained following saline injection on a separate occasion. Among 75 adult, male cynomolgus monkeys living in unisex social groups, animals having the smallest prolactin responses to fenfluramine (i.e., low serotonergic responsivity) were found to be more aggressive than monkeys exhibiting prolactin responses of greater magnitude (Botchin, Kaplan, Manuck, & Mann, 1993). As in many of the studies of rhesus monkeys, only escalated aggression (or the proportion of all aggressive acts expressed as high-intensity aggression) covaried inversely with serotonergic responsivity. Although animals' fenfluramine-stimulated prolactin responses did not correlate with social dominance, low "responders" spent significantly less time in passive affiliation with other animals and more time alone (asocially). Animals' behavioral reactions to photographic slides depicting either threatening or neutral objects were also evaluated individually, in an open-field enclosure (Kyes, Botchin, Kaplan, Manuck, & Mann, 1995). Low prolactin responders reacted to threatening objects more aggressively (e.g., by lunge, growl, or stare threat) than those showing larger prolactin responses to fenfluramine, but did not differ in their reactions to slides of neutral or nonthreatening content. Thus, the heightened aggressiveness of monkeys having low central serotonergic responsivity does not appear to be conditioned by the social setting in which the animal is housed, as it may also be observed in a nonsocial context.

Smaller prolactin responses to fenfluramine were associated with more frequent aggression of all intensities and, surprisingly, with higher social rank (dominance) in an initial study of just eight female cynomolgus monkeys (Shively, Fontenot, & Kaplan, 1995). Neither of these associations replicated on subsequent investigation involving a larger number of females (n = 39) (Shively, 1998) and, in a study of monoamine metabolites in cisternal CSF, 5-HIAA concentrations were *lower* in dominant than subordinate females and unrelated to social dominance among males (Kaplan, Manuck, Fontenot, & Mann, 2002). Interestingly, central dopaminergic function varied significantly by social rank in each of the latter studies, as prolactin responses to the dopamine receptor antagonist haloperidol were greater in dominant than subordinate females (Shively, 1998) and CSF concentrations of the dopamine metabolite homovanillic acid were higher in dominants of both sexes than among their subordinate counterparts (Kaplan et al., 2002). Finally, when the Intruder Challenge was administered to female cynomolgus monkeys, animals that readily approached the intruder were found to have smaller fenfluramine-stimulated prolactin responses than socially "inhibited" animals, which failed to approach at any time during the challenge (Manuck, Kaplan, Rymeski, Fairbanks, & Wilson, 2003). Hence, social impulsivity was associated negatively with serotonergic responsivity in these animals. Unlike with male vervet monkeys, though, aggressive gestures directed at the intruder were relatively infrequent, did not correlate with approach behavior, and were unrelated to the prolactin response to fenfluramine. In sum, these few studies suggest that central serotonergic function in cynomolgus monkeys covaries inversely with unrestrained aggression and social isolation in males and

with impulsivity (but not consistently with aggression) in females; whether social impulsivity is also related to low serotonergic responsivity in males remains to be examined.

Serotonin and Aggression in Humans

Aggression and impulsivity, which figure so prominently in the work on nonhuman primates, give thematic focus to much human research as well. A further area of relevance to humans, but not monkeys, concerns the role of serotonin in suicide and suicidal behavior. Attempted suicide among patients of diverse psychiatric diagnoses, lethality of prior attempts, and increased risk of future suicidal behavior have been widely associated with diminished serotonergic activity, as indexed by a low CSF 5-HIAA concentration or blunted neuroendocrine response to fenfluramine. Because this literature is reviewed extensively elsewhere (e.g., Asberg, 1998; Kamali, Oquendo, & Mann, 2001; Lester, 1995; Mann, Brent, & Arango, 2001; Placidi et al., 2001), here we address suicidality as a correlate of serotonergic function only when incorporated in studies of outwardly directed aggression and aggressive disposition. Hence, the following sections emphasize reported associations between "externalized" human aggression and serotonin, as informed by studies of lumbar CSF 5-HIAA concentration, neuropharmacologic challenges, neuroimaging, and serotonin-related genetic variation.

CSF 5-HIAA

Several investigations have examined CSF 5-HIAA concentrations in relation to sentinel indices of aggression, such as a life history assessment or adjudicated criminal conduct. In an early study of 26 military servicemen having various personality disorders, 5-HIAA levels correlated strongly and inversely with subjects' lifetime histories of aggression (LHA) (r = −.78) (Brown et al., 1979). This finding was replicated in a second series of 12 active-duty servicemen (r = −.58), and in both studies, subjects with a history of suicide attempt had significantly lower 5-HIAA concentrations than those who had not attempted suicide (Brown et al., 1982). In a later study of 36 Finnish men convicted of murder or attempted murder, offenders who had committed more than one violent act had lower CSF 5-HIAA levels than those committing a single offense

(Linnoila et al., 1983). When these men were included in a prospectively studied sample of 58 violent offenders and arsonists, low 5-HIAA concentrations also were found to predict repeat offenses (recidivism) over an average 3-year follow-up (Virkkunen, DeJong, Bartko, Goodwin, & Linnoila 1989). CSF 5-HIAA concentrations did not differ significantly between chronic alcoholics and controls in a fifth study, but correlated negatively with lifetime history of aggression (LHA scores) across all participants ($r = -.31$) and in alcoholics alone ($r = -.40$) (Limson et al., 1991). Other investigations have shown CSF 5-HIAA concentrations to be lower among nonsuicidal psychiatric patients with a high frequency of adulthood aggressive behavior than among less aggressive patients (Stanley et al., 2000) and lower among community residents selected for histories of repeated violence (episodes of physical aggression causing or having potential to cause injury), relative to nonviolent controls from the same population (Hibbeln et al., 1998). Also, in a large sample of unmedicated patients admitted to the hospital for evaluation of current depression ($n = 93$), LHA scores correlated inversely with CSF 5-HIAA levels among all subjects and in patients both with and without comorbid borderline personality disorder (Placidi et al., 2001). History of prior suicide attempt was not associated with serotonergic activity in this study, but among patients who had attempted suicide, those sustaining the greatest medical injury (high-lethality attempters) were found to have the lowest 5-HIAA concentrations.

In contrast to these largely positive studies, some investigations fail to support a relation between sentinel indices of aggression and CSF 5-HIAA. A comparison of convicted murderers, attempted suicides, and control subjects, for instance, showed the mean 5-HIAA concentration of suicide attempters, but not of homicidal offenders, to be lower than that of controls (Lidberg, Tuck, Asberg, Scalia-Tomba, & Bertilsson, 1985). Increasing the number of murderers studied from 15 to 35 did not alter these findings, although a history of attempted suicide was associated with lower 5-HIAA levels within the larger sample of offenders (Lidberg, Belfrage, Bertilsson, Evenden, & Asberg, 2000). A study of 17 women having borderline personality disorder similarly found low 5-HIAA concentrations in patients who had previously attempted suicide, but not among those reporting a history of physical violence against others (Gardner, Lucas, & Cowdry, 1990). Unfortunately, as the method of evaluating patients' aggressive behaviors in this study was not documented, its validity cannot be ascertained. CSF 5-HIAA concentrations also did not correlate significantly with LHA scores in two mixed-gender studies of patients diagnosed with varying personality disorders (Coccaro, Kavoussi, Cooper, & Hauger, 1997; Coccaro, Kavoussi, Hauger, Cooper, & Ferris, 1998), although as described later, serotonergic responsivity assessed by neuropharmacologic challenge did covary inversely in each of these investigations with patient's lifetime aggression histories.

With some exceptions then (particularly the studies of Lidberg and colleagues [1985, 2000], Coccaro, Kavoussi, Cooper, et al. [1997], and Coccaro, Kavoussi, Hauger, et al. [1998]), low CSF 5-HIAA concentrations among adults appear to be associated with heightened aggressiveness, as indexed by criminal conduct or inventory of aggressive episodes, as well as suicidal behavior. These associations are seen in both forensic and psychiatric samples, in alcoholics, personality disordered and depressed patients, and among community residents recruited for a history of physical violence. The magnitude of relationship between metabolite concentrations and aggression varies moderately across studies, though, possibly reflecting a diminished sensitivity of CSF 5-HIAA to associations involving milder manifestations of aggressive disposition (e.g., Coccaro, 1998). For example, Limson and coauthors (1991) suggest that excluding patients having antisocial traits likely to prove disruptive on a research ward may account for the small, albeit still significant, correlation they observed between subjects' LHA scores and 5-HIAA concentrations, compared to the stronger initial reports (Brown et al., 1979, 1982). Additionally, if weaker effects might be expected due to normatively less severe aggression in a study population (or if aggression "scores" are restricted in range), larger samples will be necessary to detect statistical significance. In this context it is noteworthy that the three 5-HIAA studies showing null results among individuals having personality disorders, who were not selected for known aggressive acts, had sample sizes of only 17 to 26 patients (Gardner et al., 1990; Coccaro, Kavoussi, Cooper, et al., 1997; Coccaro, Kavoussi, Hauger, et al., 1998).

Analyses based on self-reported aggressive tendencies or related personality traits yield far more ambiguous results than those involving sentinel indices of aggression. The BDHI, which was administered in four studies of CSF 5-HIAA, showed no association with metabolite concentrations in three investigations (Brown et al., 1982; Coccaro, Kavoussi, Cooper, et al., 1997; Stanley et al., 2000) and covaried inversely with

5-HIAA levels among physically violent community residents ($r = -.42$) in the fourth (Hibbeln et al., 1998). In contrast, three of these studies showed CSF 5-HIAA to correlate negatively with subjects' enumerated lifetime or adulthood histories of aggressive behavior (i.e., sentinel indices) (Brown et al., 1982; Hibbeln et al., 1998; Stanley et al., 2000). The subscale for Psychopathic Deviance from the Minnesota Multiphasic Personality Inventory, which assesses a general antisocial orientation and disregard for moral stricture (Graham, 2000), correlated inversely with 5-HIAA concentrations in one study (Brown et al., 1982), yielded a nonsignificant trend (when adjusted for age) in a second (Faustman et al., 1991), and showed no association in a third (Limson et al., 1991). Among other investigations, CSF 5-HIAA correlated positively with self-reported "inhibition of aggression" on the Karolinska Scales for Personality (Virkkunen, Kallio, et al., 1994) and with "extraverted aggression" on the Kinsey Institute Reaction List (Moller et al., 1996), but as numerous subscale correlations were calculated in both studies it is unlikely these isolated observations exceed experimentwise error. And while 5-HIAA levels covaried inversely with reported "urge to act out hostility" in a small group of normal volunteers, this finding did not survive correction for age-dependent covariation (Roy, Adinoff, & Linnoila, 1988). In sum, hostility scales and components of personality questionnaires purportedly reflecting aspects of aggression show no reliable association with lumbar CSF 5-HIAA concentrations.

The hypothesis that low central serotonergic activity predisposes specifically to impulsive aggression (as opposed to instrumental, or predatory, aggression) was first suggested in the previously cited report of Linnoila et al. (1983). Of the 36 homicidal offenders studied, subjects who murdered or attempted to murder a person unknown to them and did so without planning or significant provocation had lower CSF 5-HIAA levels than offenders who knew their victims and acted from detectable motive. That serotonin's key behavioral correlate might be impulsivity itself, and not aggression, was argued from further data comparing male arsonists to violent offenders and normal controls (Virkkunen, Nuutila, Goodwin, & Linnoila, 1987). The arsonists, who were said to be impulsive, but not notably aggressive, had lower 5-HIAA concentrations than both the control subjects and those incarcerated for violent crimes. As it was later reported that the majority of arsonists had intermittent explosive disorder (Virkkunen, DeJong, Bartko, & Linnoila, 1989), for which episodic impulsive aggression is pathognomonic, the premise of this study—that arsonists are impulsive, but not aggressive—is largely negated (Coccaro, 1998). A subsequent study by the same investigators, in which alcoholic offenders were identified as impulsive or nonimpulsive based on characteristics of their index crime, is similarly ambiguous (Virkkunen, Rawlings, et al., 1994). As predicted, impulsive subjects had lower CSF 5-HIAA concentrations than nonimpulsive offenders, but, unexpectedly, did not differ from healthy controls.

In an early study of 15 convicted murderers, Lidberg et al. (1985) reported that CSF 5-HIAA levels were lowest in the five who had killed sexual partners "in states of emotional turmoil." The authors were agnostic as to whether impulsivity or negative affect mediated this association, and in any case, their finding failed to replicate when reexamined in a larger cohort of homicidal offenders (Lidberg et al., 2000). Among patients who had attempted suicide in another recent report, those who scored "high" on the Impulsivity Rating Scale (IRS) (Lecrubier, Braconnier, Said, & Payan, 1995) had significantly lower 5-HIAA concentrations than less impulsive suicide attempters or healthy, nonsuicidal controls (Cremniter et al., 1999). Here too, though, interpretation is equivocal, as (a) variation in "impulsivity" was confounded by psychiatric diagnosis among suicide attempters (viz., all impulsive attempters were diagnosed with personality disorders, all nonimpulsive attempters with mood or anxiety disorders) and (b) the IRS includes items reflecting "aggressivity" and "irritability," along with common dimensions of impulsivity, such as impatience, persistence, and tolerance for delay. And last, Stanley et al. (2000) assessed impulsivity by subscale of the Schedule for Interviewing Borderlines (Baron, 1980), but found it uncorrelated with CSF 5-HIAA among nonsuicidal psychiatric patients. Thus, although it is widely believed that impaired impulse control underlies the relation of overt aggression to CSF 5-HIAA concentrations in human subjects, we find existing evidence for this assertion unpersuasive. The hypothesis may well be true, and the studies of nonhuman primates certainly provide impressive support in a comparative context, but by failing to cleave impulsivity and aggression unambiguously, either by selection of subjects or in psychometric assessment, most prior attempts to address this issue in humans remain inconclusive.

Not surprisingly, there are few studies of CSF-sampled metabolite concentrations in children. In one, the 5-HIAA levels of 6- to 12-year-old boys with attention-deficit/hyperactivity disorder (ADHD) correlated positively with physician-assessed childhood aggression and parent reports of delinquent and externalizing behaviors (Castellanos et al., 1994). In a somewhat older sample, on the other hand, children and adolescents with various disruptive behavior disorders (attention-deficit, conduct, and oppositional disorders) had CSF 5-HIAA concentrations lower than those of matched controls with obsessive compulsive disorder (Kruesi et al., 1990). CSF 5-HIAA levels covaried inversely with interview-assessed aggressive behavior among those with disruptive behavior disorders and, on 2-year follow-up, predicted the further occurrence of physical aggression (Kruesi et al., 1992). The latter association also persisted after multivariate adjustment for other common predictors of child and adolescent aggression, including subjects' prior antisocial behavior, socioeconomic status, and IQ. Finally, noting that a low CSF 5-HIAA concentration in aggressive individuals might just as logically result from aggression as cause it, other investigators have measured 5-HIAA in "leftover" CSF drawn from infants with minor febrile illnesses (Constantino, Morris, & Murphy, 1997). Newborns having parents with antisocial personality disorder had significantly lower 5-HIAA concentrations than infants without a family history of this disorder, and among all 193 newborns studied, CSF 5-HIAA correlated modestly ($r = .12$) with genetic distance (number of meiotic divisions) to the nearest relative having antisocial personality disorder. In a follow-up of infants from the same cohort, low CSF 5-HIAA was also a significant, and similarly modest, predictor of externalizing behavior problems at 30 months of age (Clarke, Murphy, & Constantino, 1999).

Whole Blood Serotonin

As noted earlier, our review does not encompass studies reporting only peripheral indices of serotonergic function. An important exception, though, is the one available epidemiologic investigation of serotonin and criminal violence conducted on a population sample (Moffitt et al., 1998). In the Dunedin Multidisciplinary Health and Development Study, court records (from ages 13 to 21) and self-reported violent behavior were examined in relation to measures of whole blood serotonin collected on 781 24-year-old men and women. Although no association was observed in women, men who had been convicted of one or more violent crimes

and those who reported physically attacking or threatening others on multiple occasions over the preceding year had higher blood serotonin levels than men not convicted of such crimes and those who did not report engaging in violent behavior. These effects were undiminished by adjustment for nonviolent criminal activity (whether by court conviction or self-report) and were independent of variation in socioeconomic status, IQ, smoking and alcohol dependence, illicit drug use, concomitant psychopathology, platelet number, and plasma tryptophan concentration. That a history of violent behavior might be associated with high blood serotonin, but low CSF 5-HIAA (as reviewed above), may seem paradoxical but is consistent with some related observations. For instance, whole blood serotonin covaries positively with current hostility and lifetime aggression history among adults with major depression (Mann, McBride, Anderson, et al., 1992) and with documented violence in juvenile offenders (Unis et al., 1997), including those arrested at least once for physical or sexual assault, use of a weapon, arson, or attempted homicide (Pliszka, Rogeness, Renner, Sherman, & Broussard, 1988). On the other hand, one recent study shows LHA scores inversely correlated with platelet serotonin content in patients with mixed personality disorder diagnoses (Goveas, Csernansky, & Coccaro, 2004), and measures of platelet and whole blood serotonin yield inconsistent findings among studies employing less definitive indices of violence and aggression (e.g., parent-reported aggressiveness and psychopathologies defined only in part by overtly aggressive behavior) (Cook, Stein, Elison, Unis, & Leventhal, 1995; Gabel, Stadler, Shindledecker, & Bowden, 1993; Hanna, Yuwiler, & Coates, 1995; Rogeness, Hernandez, Macedo, & Mitchell, 1982; Twitchell, Hanna, Cook, Fitzgerald, & Zucker, 2000).

Because the peripheral and CNS serotonergic systems are independent, explaining how serotonin content of whole blood may be high and, at the same time, CSF 5-HIAA concentrations low also requires positing common processes of synthesis, release, reuptake, and metabolic control. Candidate mechanisms for increased whole blood serotonin (nearly all of which is contained in platelets) might include a diminished release of serotonin sequestered within platelet vesicles, more efficient reuptake (again increasing platelet content), and, possibly, reduced oxidative deamination of serotonin outside the platelet by monoamine oxidase. These events—impaired release, increased reuptake, and a lower rate of enzymatic degradation—are also consistent with reduced CSF 5-HIAA concentration. Common genetic variation in the synthetic pathway for central and peripheral serotonin is conceivable too, but clouded by recent evidence that two genes encode tryptophan hydroxylase, both of which may be expressed in brain but only one in gut (Walther et al., 1993; Zill et al., 2003; Zill, Buttner, et al., 2004). Additionally, there is some evidence that platelet serotonin transporter sites may be reduced among individuals reporting high lifetime histories of aggression (Coccaro, Kavoussi, Shelin, Lish, & Czernansky, 1996).

It is unfortunate that not much is known about the covariation of central and peripheral serotonergic indices, as their inverse association would help (albeit not completely) reconcile differences among studies reporting CSF and blood or platelet measurements. Whole blood serotonin did not covary with CSF 5-HIAA concentrations in a previous study of 35 normal adults (Sarrias, Cabre, Martinez, & Artigas, 1990), but observations on 60 adult male cynomolgus monkeys by the present authors revealed a modest, inverse correlation ($r = -.32$, $p < .02$) of whole blood serotonin with cisternal CSF 5-HIAA concentrations.[1] And in a small study of young men with autism, McBride et al. (1989) reported finding a strong negative correlation ($r = -.86$) between whole blood serotonin and CNS serotonergic responsivity, as measured by prolactin response to fenfluramine challenge. Absent more extensive comparison of peripheral and central measurements, however, interpretations of blood or platelet serotonin content as reflections of brain serotonergic function remains speculative in aggression studies.

Neuroendocrine Challenges

Nearly all neuropharmacologic studies of aggression assess central serotonergic responsivity by one of four neuroendocrine challenges: fenfluramine, m-CPP, buspirone, and ipsapirone. Although used for much the same purpose, the four challenges differ in several respects. As a releasing agent and reuptake inhibitor, fenfluramine enhances activation of postsynaptic serotonin receptors by increasing the availability of neurotransmitter within the synapse. The most commonly reported index of neuroendocrine response, the fenfluramine-induced rise in plasma prolactin concentration, is inhibited entirely by the $5\text{-HT}_{2A/2C}$ receptor antagonists ritanserin (Goodall et al., 1993) and amesergide (Coccaro, Kavoussi, Oakes, et al., 1996), but remains unaffected on blockade of either the 5-HT_{1A} receptor (by pindolol) (Park & Cowen, 1995) or the 5-HT_3 receptor (by ondansetron) (Coccaro, Kavoussi, Cooper, & Hauger, 1996a). Thus, it is generally thought that fenfluramine-stimulated prolactin changes result from activation of hypothalamic 5-HT_2 receptors, although variability in the magnitude of the response can reflect variation in presynaptic processes (synthesis, release), postsynaptic receptor sensitivities, or both.

Unlike fenfluramine, m-CPP (the principal metabolite of the antidepressant trazadone) is a direct agonist having in vitro affinity for serotonin receptors of the 5-HT_1 and 5-HT_2 subtypes (Hoyer, 1988; Hoyer et al., 1994; Kahn & Wetzler, 1991). Administration of m-CPP increases plasma prolactin, ACTH, and cortisol concentrations, and blocking studies show m-CPP-induced prolactin and adrenocortical responses to be attenuated by pretreatment with both metergoline, a relatively nonspecific 5-HT receptor antagonist (Kahn et al., 1990), and the $5\text{-HT}_{2A/2C}$ antagonist ritanserin (Seibyl et al., 1991). In contrast, the prolactin, but not cortisol, response to m-CPP may be inhibited by the 5-HT_{1A} antagonist pindolol (Meltzer & Maes, 1995b). Despite different modes of action and the differing role of 5-HT_{1A} receptors in fenfluramine and m-CPP challenges, prolactin changes evoked by the two drugs correlate appreciably across individuals (Coccaro, 1992; Coccaro, Kavoussi, Trestman, et al., 1997).

The two other probes reported in aggression studies, buspirone and ipsapirone, are 5-HT_{1A} receptor agonists that stimulate rises in prolactin, ACTH, cortisol, and, occasionally, growth hormone (Cowen, Anderson, & Grahame-Smith, 1990; Lesch, Sohnle, et al., 1990; Meltzer & Maes, 1994, 1995a; Yatham & Steiner, 1993). That these changes are diminished by pretreatment with pindolol confirms their mediation by 5-HT_{1A} receptors, although findings are mixed with respect to the buspirone-induced prolactin response (Anderson & Cowen, 1992; Lesch, Mayer, Disselkamp-Tietze, Hoh, Schoellnhammer, et al., 1990; Meltzer, Lee, & Nash, 1992; Meltzer & Maes, 1995a). Whereas 5-HT_{1A} receptors act both postsynaptically and as autoreceptors on presynaptic (serotonin releasing) neurons, it is believed that neuroendocrine responses to these challenges result from activation of postsynaptic receptors. Serotonergic challenges affect central body temperature as well, with temperature increasing in response to 5-HT_2 agonists such as m-CPP and decreasing with

5-HT$_{1A}$ agonists (Anderson & Cohen, 1992; Lesch, Mayer, Disselkamp-Tietze, Hoh, Wiesmann, et al., 1990; Meltzer & Maes, 1995a); whether the latter (hypothermic) response stems from pre- or postsynaptic 5-HT$_{1A}$ receptor activation remains unclear (Lesch, Mayer, Disselkamp-Tietze, Hoh, Wiesmann, et al., 1990; Meltzer & Maes, 1995a). Finally, individual differences in the magnitude of prolactin release stimulated by ipsapirone are uncorrelated with the prolactin response to fenfluramine, suggesting that these probes reflect independent dimensions of CNS serotonergic responsivity (Coccaro, Kavoussi, & Hauger, 1995).

A number of factors constrain interpretation of neuroendocrine challenges, including seasonal and circadian influences; demographic attributes of study populations; participant weight, age, and gender; among women, ovarian status or menstrual cyclicity; and, in the absence of plasma drug levels, unknown variability in drug metabolism (e.g., Manuck et al., 1998, 2004; McBride, Tierney, DeMeo, Chen, & Mann, 1990; Muldoon et al., 1996; Yatham & Steiner, 1993). Specificity is also a concern because activity in other monoamine systems may affect neuroendocrine reactions to serotonergic probes. Buspirone is particularly problematic as it binds to dopamine receptors (Eisen & Temple, 1986), and the prolactin response to buspirone may be blocked by the dopamine receptor antagonist metachopramine (Maskall, Zis, Lam, Clark, & Kuan, 1995). In addition, m-CPP shows some affinity for dopamine receptors, and both m-CPP and ipsapirone bind to α_2-adrenergic receptors (Yathan & Steiner, 1993). The frequently administered levorotary isomer of fenfluramine is also known to affect dopaminergic and noradrenergic activity in rodents (Garattini, Bizzi, Caccia, Mennini, & Samanin, 1988), although in humans peak prolactin responses to d,l-fenfluramine correlate highly ($r = .97$) with prolactin changes induced by the more selective d-fenfluramine (Coccaro, Kavoussi, Cooper, & Hauger, 1996b). The possibility that prolactin responses to serotonergic challenges reflect nonserotonergic influences on the secretory capacity of the lactotroph has occasioned some concern as well. Prolactin responses to direct stimulation by thyrotropin-releasing hormone are largely unrelated to those induced by fenfluramine (Coccaro, Klar, & Siever, 1994), however, and adjusting the prolactin change for covariation with baseline (predrug) prolactin concentration further tends to exclude variability in pituitary lactotroph function as an explanation of individual differences in challenge-induced responsivity.

Neuroendocrine Challenge Studies of Aggression and Impulsivity

Several investigators have found sentinel indices of aggression associated with reduced serotonergic responsivity. In one early study, plasma prolactin concentrations increased less in response to fenfluramine in violent offenders with antisocial personality disorder than among healthy, nonviolent control subjects (O'Keane et al., 1992). Interview-assessed lifetime histories of aggression (LHA scores) also covaried inversely with fenfluramine-stimulated prolactin release ($r = -.38$) in men with current or remitted major affective disorder, mixed personality disorders, or no history of psychopathology (Coccaro et al., 1989). This relationship did not generalize to all study participants, however, but was seen only among personality disordered patients (where $r = -.57$). In contrast, histories of attempted suicide and prior alcohol abuse in this study were associated with an attenuated prolactin response across both patient groups, and the mean prolactin response of control subjects was greater than that of patients with either personality or affective disorders. The negative correlation between fenfluramine-induced prolactin changes and LHA scores of patients with differing personality disorders has since been replicated in several other investigations, each involving samples composed entirely or predominantly of men (rs in the range of $-.45$ to $-.58$) (Coccaro, Berman, et al., 1996; Coccaro, Kavoussi, Cooper, et al., 1997; Coccaro, Kavoussi, Hauger, et al., 1998). Also, results of the latter studies suggest that a low prolactin response may be especially sensitive to LHA indicators of confrontational violence or other forms of outwardly expressed aggression, rather than more general antisocial behavior (Coccaro, Kavoussi, Cooper, 1997; Coccaro, Kavoussi, Hauger, et al., 1998).

The one negative study in this series evaluated only eight personality disordered men and was thus probably underpowered to detect an association of credible effect size (Coccaro et al., 1995). In a recent and quite large study of both men and women, patients with borderline personality disorder showed a smaller prolactin response to fenfluramine than healthy control individuals, but only among men (Soloff, Kelly, Strotmeyer, Malone, & Mann, 2003). LHA scores also predicted prolactin changes in the expected (negative) direction in regression models controlling for age, sex, and diagnostic status, although this association was likewise absent when examined in women alone. Interestingly, the difference in prolactin response between men with and without borderline personality disorder persisted on adjustment for comorbid depression or alcohol abuse, yet lost statistical significance when adjusted for concomitant variation in subjects' lifetime aggression histories.

Sex differences were also observed in a nonpatient sample of community volunteers with no history of major psychiatric disorder (excluding personality disorders, which were not assessed) (Manuck et al., 1998). LHA scores covaried inversely with fenfluramine-induced prolactin responses in men ($r = -.33$), but not women ($r = .08$). The rather large nonclinical sample of males ($n = 59$) may explain, in part, why prolactin responses correlated significantly with histories of aggressive behavior here but not in the previously cited study (Coccaro et al., 1989, in which only a small number of nonpatient men were tested ($n = 18$). When the male cohort studied by Manuck and colleagues (1998) was expanded to 118 men by including individuals meeting criteria for a past, but not current, psychiatric diagnosis (principally prior substance use and affective disorders), LHA scores continued to show a modest, but significant, inverse correlation with subjects' prolactin responses ($r = -.32$) (Manuck, Flory, Muldoon, & Ferrell, 2002). Moreover, this correlation remained significant on deletion of subjects comprising either the most aggressive 20% of men or the lowest quintile of prolactin response to fenfluramine. It is therefore unlikely that the overall association of serotonergic responsivity with men's LHA-assessed aggression was confounded by pathologies of personality (e.g., antisocial or borderline personality disorder) among a small subset of low fenfluramine-responsive individuals. Even in the absence of overt psychopathology, though, difficulties of adjustment may be seen in the life histories and associated personality characteristics of "normatively" aggressive men. For instance, men whose LHA scores fell above the sample median in Manuck et al. (2002) not only showed a blunted prolactin response to fenfluramine, but, relative to their less aggressive counterparts, were more than twice as likely to have had a substance-related disorder in the past, earned less income (despite equivalent years of education), divorced at a fourfold higher rate, and scored higher on standardized measures of hostility and impulsive disposition (BDHI, BIS).

Studies using other neuropharmacologic probes are generally consistent with the fenfluramine literature for sentinel indices of aggression. Among men in rehabili-

tation for cocaine addiction, patients with a history of physical assault (e.g., fighting, shooting, murder, or attempted murder) showed diminished cortisol responses to m-CPP, compared to both less aggressive cocaine-dependent patients and control subjects without psychopathology (Buydens-Branchey, Branchey, Fergeson, Hudson, & McKernen, 1997). The prolactin response to m-CPP did not differ by history of aggression, but was smaller among all patients, relative to controls. Although another study of cocaine-dependent men showed patients' LHA scores similarly correlated (i.e., inversely) with elevations in growth hormone induced by buspirone, this result was due largely to a single outlier with antisocial personality disorder (Moeller et al., 1994). Last, buspirone-stimulated prolactin responses were smaller in parolees convicted of violent crimes (e.g., assault, aggravated robbery) than among paroled prisoners convicted only of nonviolent offenses (Cherek, Moeller, Khan-Dawood, Swann, & Lane, 1999). Notably both men and women were included in this study, and findings did not vary by gender. Owing to the disputed specificity of buspirone as a serotonergic probe, however, it is possible that the attenuated prolactin responses of violent parolees reflect variation in dopaminergic responsivity as well (Maskall et al., 1995).

LHA scores covaried inversely with ipsapirone-stimulated hypothermic, but not cortisol, responses among a small sample of personality-disordered men (Coccaro et al., 1995). A later, mixed-gender study of people without major psychopathology failed to replicate this association, although hypothermic responses to ipsapirone varied by level of aggressiveness displayed in a standardized laboratory protocol, the Point Subtraction Aggression Paradigm (PSAP) (Moeller et al., 1998). In the PSAP, individuals are instructed to press either of two buttons (A or B) on each trial of a task performed against a fictitious opponent. Subjects are told that pressing A accrues points exchangeable for cash, whereas pressing B subtracts points from their opponent's total; the experimental subjects are also informed that points can be subtracted from their total as well if their opponent presses B. During the task a certain number of points are subtracted from the participant's account, which acts as provocation for aggressive responding since these point losses are attributed to the subject's ostensible opponent. The most aggressive participants—those who pressed B most frequently—showed a blunted hypothermic response to ipsapirone, compared to individuals who reacted less aggressively (Moeller et al., 1998). This finding did not vary by gender and is consistent with other studies using the same protocol. Thus, PSAP scores also correlated negatively with the buspirone-induced prolactin responses of parolees (Cherek et al., 1999) and with prolactin responses to fenfluramine in men diagnosed with one or more personality disorders (Coccaro, Berman, et al., 1996).

Neuroendocrine challenges are associated somewhat less consistently with self-rated hostility, as recorded on standardized questionnaires. In part, this may be due to uncertainties introduced by inconsistent or incomplete treatment of instruments containing numerous subscales, such as the BDHI, where analyses may be variously applied to a "total" score, factor scores, and all or only selected subscales and where adjustments for multiple testing are rarely reported. Nonetheless, interindividual variability in the prolactin response to fenfluramine correlated inversely with one or more subscales of the BDHI "motor aggression" factor (Assault, Irritability, Indirect Aggression, or Verbal Hostility) among personality-disordered patients in several samples consisting almost entirely of men (Coccaro et al., 1989, 1995; Coccaro, Berman et al., 1996; Coccaro, Kavoussi, Trestman, et al., 1997). In a mixed-gender study of patients with borderline personality disorder and healthy controls, prolactin responses correlated negatively with both BDHI (total) and MMPI-Pd scores in men, but not women (Soloff et al., 2003). In a further study of patients having diverse personality disorders and nonpatient controls, peak prolactin changes correlated inversely (if modestly) with combined BDHI assault and irritability subscales, but again only in men (New, Trestman, et al., 2004), and similarly, no association was observed among women in two other investigations involving nonpatient samples (Cleare & Bond, 1997; Manuck et al., 1998). In the latter studies men's BDHI scores were unrelated to prolactin changes as well, although self-rated hostility did covary inversely with the cortisol response to fenfluramine in men (but again, not in women) (Cleare & Bond, 1997).

Among other challenges, prolactin, but not cortisol, responses to the direct agonist m-CPP correlated negatively with the Assault subscale of the BDHI in antisocial males (Moss, Yao, & Panzak, 1990) and with BDHI (total) Assault and Irritability scores in abstinent alcoholic men (Handelsman et al., 1996). Neither neuroendocrine response to m-CPP was associated with BDHI-assessed hostility among men and women

with major depression or panic disorder (Wetzler, Kahn, Asnis, Korn, & van Praag, 1991). m-CPP-stimulated prolactin responses covaried inversely with BDHI Assault and Irritability scores in an initial study of men having different personality disorder diagnoses (Coccaro, 1992), but not on reexamination in a somewhat larger sample (Coccaro, Kavoussi, Trestman, et al., 1997). In contrast to the several null effects reported previously in females, prolactin responses to m-CPP correlated negatively with BDHI (total) scores among women with borderline personality disorder and matched controls and with the Indirect Aggression subscale of the BDHI among all subjects and in borderline patients alone (Paris et al., 2004). No other subscales correlated with prolactin rise, and in agreement with prior studies, subjects' cortisol responses to m-CPP were unrelated to self-reported hostility.

Findings are likewise mixed among challenge studies of 5-HT$_{1A}$ agonists. Buspirone-stimulated prolactin changes correlated negatively with BDHI Assault and Irritability scores in a small sample ($n = 10$) of men and women with personality disorders (Coccaro, Gabriel, & Siever, 1990), but in a similarly small group of cocaine-dependent men the growth hormone response to buspirone did not covary significantly with the BDHI (Moeller et al., 1994). Ipsapirone-induced neuroendocrine and hypothermic responses also were unrelated to BDHI scores among personality disordered patients (Coccaro et al., 1995) and in one of two studies employing nonpatient samples (Moeller et al., 1998). Nonetheless, healthy adult men who reported high BDHI Irritability showed a lower prolactin and cortisol response to ipsapirone (Cleare & Bond, 2000), and in the same study, ipsapirone-induced rises in cortisol and growth hormone correlated inversely with Trait Anger scores on the Spielberger State–Trait Anger Scale. The disposition to experience anger has been studied occasionally with other challenges as well, though here too results are mixed. Indeed, Trait Anger (also measured by the Spielberger scale) did not vary by prolactin response to fenfluramine among men selected for variation in impulsiveness (Evans, Platts, Lightman, & Nutt, 2000) and correlated positively with m-CPP-stimulated cortisol elevations of 15 mood disordered patients (Klaasen, Riedel, van Praag, Menheere, & Griez, 2002); the latter result is doubtful, however, as significant associations barely exceeded error rate in this investigation. Among other findings, experiences of anger, irritability, and annoyance assessed by diagnostic interview in depressed patients and patients with panic disorder were unrelated to cortisol or prolactin changes evoked by m-CPP (Wetzler et al., 1991), whereas "angry hostility" scores on the NEO personality inventory correlated negatively with prolactin responses to fenfluramine in healthy men, but not women (Manuck et al., 1998). Finally, depressed patients (both men and women) who reported having anger "attacks" (including outwardly expressed aggression and physical signs of autonomic arousal) showed a blunted prolactin response to fenfluramine challenge, relative to patients without anger attacks (Fava et al., 2000). It is notable that externalizing behavior problems, such as delinquency and aggression, among the offspring of depressed patients are greatest in children whose depressed parent also experiences anger attacks (Alpert et al., 2003) and that the frequency of anger attacks in depression can be reduced by treatment with fluoxetine (Fava et al., 1993) or the 5-HT$_{2A}$ receptor antagonist/reuptake inhibitor nefazodone (Mischoulon et al., 2002).

In an early study of men with a prior history of substance abuse, individuals who scored high on the Eysenck impulsiveness scale, and those reporting high levels of aggressiveness, exhibited heightened cortisol and prolactin responses to fenfluramine when compared to their less impulsive or aggressive counterparts (Fishbein, Lozovsky, & Jaffe, 1989). That interindividual variation in aggressiveness might correlate *positively* with central serotonergic responsivity finds little corroboration in the literatures cited above. The same may be concluded for impulsivity, though not surprisingly, results of available studies are again mixed. One likely source of inconsistency is statistical power. Although fenfluramine-stimulated prolactin responses covaried negatively with impulsivity (BIS scores) among men with differing personality disorders (Coccaro et al., 1989), this finding did not replicate in two similar patient samples (Coccaro, Berman, et al., 1996; Coccaro, Kavoussi, Hauger, et al., 1998), among abstinent male alcoholics (Handelsman et al., 1996), or in men with major depression (Coccaro et al., 1989; Mulder & Joyce, 2002). On the other hand, BIS scores covaried inversely with rises in cortisol following administration of the serotonin reuptake inhibitor paroxetine in nonpatient males (Reist, Helmeste, Albers, Chhay, & Tang, 1996), and in a separate study of healthy men selected for high versus low impulsivity scores on the Eysenck Personality Inventory, the more impulsive group showed a diminished prolactin response to fenfluamine (Evans et al., 2000).

With respect to sex differences, BIS scores were found to correlate negatively with fenfluramine-induced prolactin release in men with and without borderline personality disorder, but not among women (Soloff et al., 2003). In a similar study of women only, however, impulsivity correlated inversely with participants' prolactin responses to m-CPP (Paris et al., 2004). Also, this finding obtained among all subjects and among women with borderline personality disorder alone. In addition to employing a different neuroendocrine challenge, in this study all women were tested during the follicular phase of their menstrual cycles. Estrogens are known to modulate prolactin synthesis and release (Ben-Jonathan 1985; Liebenluft, Fiero, & Rubinow, 1994), and prolactin rises stimulated by fenfluramine show threefold variability over the menstrual cycle (with a nadir early in the follicular phase and a peak at midcycle) (O'Keane, O'Hanlon, Webb, & Dinan, 1991). Hence, estrogenic effects associated with menstrual cyclicity may account for a substantial portion of the variance in prolactin-dependent indices of serotonergic activity, thereby obscuring correlational associations with behavioral measurements at sample sizes otherwise adequate to detect such relationships in men (e.g., Soloff et al., 2003) or among women standardized for menstrual phase (e.g., Paris et al., 2004; see Ogawa, Nomura, Cholaris, & Pfaff, ch. 10 in this volume). Consistent with this argument, elevated prolactin induced by fenfluramine again covaried inversely with BIS impulsivity scores in men, but not women, in a nonpatient community sample (Manuck et al., 1998). In this study, women were tested without respect to menopausal status and, in premenopausal women, without regard to menstrual phase. However, analyses conducted separately on women who were uniformly hypoestrogenic due to natural or surgical menopause (without hormone replacement) revealed the same inverse association as seen in men between impulsivity and interindividual variability in the prolactin response to fenfluramine. This comparability of association extended also to an analogous behavioral dimension, conscientiousness, as measured by the NEO personality inventory. Tapping attributes such as persistence, resourcefulness, and self-discipline, and by their absence, impatience, haste, and carelessness, conscientiousness correlated positively with the prolactin responses of both men and postmenopausal women. Unlike men, though, prolactin change among postmenopausal subjects correlated inversely with "attitudinal hostility" on the BDHI, particularly "suspiciousness," and not with more direct indicators of aggressive behavior (e.g., LHA scores). Together with the observation that blunted prolactin responses to m-CPP predict impulsiveness and indirect aggression in women with borderline personality disorder (Paris et al., 2004), these findings suggest two possible conclusions: (a) that low central serotonergic responsivity is associated with heightened impulsivity among women as well as men and (b) that with respect to aggression, serotonergic function may be related more strongly to covert antagonism and hostile attributions in women and to overt expressions of hostile intent in men.

Fenfluramine Challenge Studies of Aggression in Children and Adolescents

Studies using the fenfluramine challenge to evaluate serotonergic involvement in the aggressive behaviors of youth have generated discrepant findings. In the first such study, prolactin and cortisol responses to fenfluramine did not covary with clinician, parent, or self-ratings of aggression among prepubertal and adolescent boys with disruptive behavior disorders, nor were fenfluramine-stimulated neuroendocrine responses in the adolescent sample different than those of normal controls (Stoff et al., 1992). In contrast, prolactin changes correlated positively with parent-reported aggression in prepubertal male siblings of delinquent boys (Pine et al., 1997) and, among boys with ADHD (7–11 years of age), prolactin responses were greatest in children with histories of persistently aggressive behavior (Halperin et al., 1994). The latter finding failed to replicate in an independent sample of ADHD boys (Halperin et al., 1997), and in yet a third study of boys with ADHD, temperature (hyperthermic) responses to fenfluramine covaried inversely with teacher ratings of children's aggressive behavior at school (Donovan, Halperin, Newcorn, & Sharma, 1999). Initial attempts at reconciling these findings focused on differences in sample characteristics, particularly variation in participant age and the inclusion of boys with concomitant ADHD (Halperin et al., 1997). However, subsequent investigation showed no difference in the fenfluramine-induced prolactin responses of aggressive boys with and without ADHD and nonaggressive ADHD children, nor did the interaction of subjects' aggressive behavior and age predict prolactin change (Schulz et al., 2001). Further complicating this litera-

ture is an additional study of older adolescents, both normal controls and individuals having alcohol use disorders (with and without comorbid conduct disorder) (Soloff, Lynch, & Moss, 2000). Across all subjects, fenfluramine-stimulated prolactin responses correlated inversely with impulsivity (BIS scores) and aggressive disposition measured by a common personality inventory, yet cortisol responses to the same challenge covaried *positively* with history of aggression (LHA) and BDHI Assault scores.

Recently, family histories of aggressive and antisocial behavior were assessed via structured interviews administered to parents of prepubertal boys who had participated in several of the preceding studies (Halperin et al., 1994, 1997; Schulz et al., 2001). Using criteria similar to those defining positive LHA responses, individuals were designated "aggressive" for repeated episodes of fighting, property destruction, use of weapons, or injuring others and "antisocial" for significant and persistent violations of law, including theft or arson (Halperin, Schulz, McKay, Sharma, & Newcorn, 2003). The odds of having an aggressive and antisocial first- or second-degree relative were 2 to 5 times greater among boys who were themselves aggressive and exhibited a low (< median) prolactin response to fenfluramine, compared to nonaggressive children, and about twofold greater than in aggressive children with larger prolactin responses. In the latter group the likelihood of having an aggressive or antisocial relative was only slightly greater than that among nonaggressive boys. The authors posit that low serotonergic responsivity among aggressive children reflects a component of the neurobiology underlying a familial predisposition to lifelong patterns of aggressive behavior. By this reasoning, children whose aggression persists into adulthood possess an enduring biologic diathesis that is continuous with the altered central serotonergic function differentiating aggressive and nonaggressive adults, whereas children whose aggression may arise from other causes (e.g., perhaps peer influences of a time-limited nature) are more likely to desist in their disruptive behavior later in life. There is precedent for hypothesizing variation in the etiologies of early aggressive behavior, as in Moffitt's distinction between life-course-persistent and adolescence-limited antisocial behavior (Moffitt, 1993, 2003). Moffitt describes a biologically (and genetically) influenced, stable antisocial pattern that is abetted by environmental adversity and emerges in the first years of childhood. This pattern

SEROTONIN AND AGGRESSION IN HUMANS AND PRIMATES 89

stands in contrast to delinquent behavior that is of limited duration, occasioned by puberty, and linked to "normative" developmental tasks of adolescence. Low serotonergic responsivity may be one biologic marker of life-course-persistent antisocial behavior, although extending this framework to encompass prepubertal children (as in the studies cited above) presumes heterogeneity in the etiology of childhood aggression as well, with alternative causes of preadolescent disruptive behavior akin to Moffit's developmental model of adolescence-limited delinquency. Although not fully articulated by Halperin and colleagues (2003), such a model is at least conceivable given that not all young children troubled by aggression grow into aggressive adolescents and adults (Loeber et al., 1993).

Neuroimaging

The hypothesis that serotonin enhances activation of important prefrontal regions of the brain, promoting activity in neural circuitry underlying impulse control and affect regulation, implies that such activation will be diminished or impaired among impulsively aggressive individuals (Davidson, Putnam, & Larson, 2000). In a small initial test of this hypothesis, changes in regional glucose metabolism following administration of fenfluramine were compared in six patients with "impulsive aggression disorder" (an adaptation of diagnostic criteria for intermittent explosive disorder) and five healthy controls (Siever et al., 1999). Control subjects showed a generalized increase in prefrontal uptake of [18]FDG, whereas impulsive aggressive patients showed blunted metabolic responses in orbital frontal, ventral medial frontal, and cingulate cortex. Subsequently, these investigators challenged another 13 impulsive aggressive patients (here defined by intermittent explosive disorder, impulsivity, and self-damaging behavior) and 13 controls with the 5-HT$_2$ receptor agonist m-CPP (New et al., 2002). Compared to controls, aggressive subjects had an attenuated [18]FDG response to m-CPP in the anterior cingulate, and left medial prefrontal and right lateral frontal cortex and, interestingly, a more pronounced metabolic response in the posterior cingulate and left lateral frontal cortex. These findings suggest that serotonergic responsivity in impulsive aggressive individuals may not be reduced uniformly across all frontal regions, but in a pattern localized to areas modulating aggressive responses. And in a third, also very small, study of patients with borderline personality disorder and controls, patients again showed a blunted [18]FDG response to fenfluramine in several areas, including the medial and orbital prefrontal cortex (Soloff et al., 2000). Conversely, treating impulsive aggressive patients having borderline personality disorder for 12 weeks with the serotonin reuptake inhibitor fluoxetine increased fenfluramine-stimulated [18]FDG uptake in the orbital frontal cortex, and did so in proportion to patients' clinical improvement (i.e., antiaggressive response to fluoxetine) (New et al., in press). These preliminary investigations support the supposition that aggression and impulsivity are associated with a reduced sensitivity to serotonin in key prefrontal areas. Variation in the neuroanatomical pattern of activation seen following serotonergic challenges and in the specification of regions of interest indicates, however, that the neural circuitry implicated in serotonergically regulated aggressive behavior requires further elucidation. Finally, it should be noted that in the two studies specifically targeting impulsive aggressive patients, the prolactin response to fenfluramine or m-CPP did not differentiate aggressive subjects from controls (New et al., 2002; Siever et al., 1999). Because the study samples were quite small, it is possible that aggression-related differences in cerebral metabolic responses are more readily detected than corresponding differences in neuroendocrine reactions to serotonergic challenges.

In another neuroimaging technique, a radiolabeled compound that binds specifically to serotonin receptors is injected and PET scans are used to determine levels of the tracer in various neuroanatomical regions. In this manner, the number and affinity of serotonin receptors in select areas of the brain can be assessed in vivo. For example, WAY-100635, an antagonist with high affinity and selectivity for 5-HT$_{1A}$ receptors, has been used for this purpose. The amount of WAY-100635 in a specific region is related to a combination of the total number and affinity of 5-HT$_{1A}$ receptors in that area, the so-called "binding potential." Consistent with several of the neuropharmacologic studies employing 5-HT$_{1A}$ agonists (Cherek et al., 1999; Cleare & Bond, 2000; Coccaro et al., 1990, 1995; Moeller et al., 1998), LHA-assessed aggression histories of 25 nonpatient volunteers correlated inversely with 5-HT$_{1A}$ binding potential in several brain areas, including the anterior cingulate, and medial and orbital prefrontal cortex, amygdala, and dorsal raphe (Parsey et al., 2002). Moreover, even though men were more aggressive than women in this study, the covariation of participants' LHA scores with 5-HT$_{1A}$ binding potential did not differ by participant gender.

Neurogenetic Studies

There is yet little literature on the heritability of individual differences in CNS serotonergic activity. As noted before, a positive family history of aggressive and antisocial behavior has been associated with low CSF 5-HIAA concentrations among newborns (Constantino et al., 1997) and with attenuated prolactin responses to fenfluramine in prepubertal, aggressive boys (Halperin et al., 2003). Similarly in adults, first-degree relatives of personality disordered patients who show a blunted prolactin response to fenfluramine are more likely to exhibit personality traits indicative of heightened aggressiveness, anger, and impulsivity than relatives of probands showing greater prolactin responsivity (Coccaro, Silverman, Klar, Horvath, & Siever, 1994). These findings are not direct evidence of heritable variation in serotonergic function, but such familiality is consistent with genetic influence. Although heritability estimates derived from biometric family (e.g., twin) analyses are largely lacking in humans (see, for instance, Oxenstierna et al., 1986), we have previously cited the heritability of cisternal CSF 5-HIAA concentrations in young rhesus monkeys (Higley et al., 1993), and similar findings were reported recently in a large pedigreed population of baboons (*Papio hamadryas*) (Rogers et al., 2004). Despite the dearth of quantitative genetic investigations in humans, molecular studies of serotonergic involvement in aggression have followed rapidly on the identification of polymorphic variation in serotonin-regulating genes. In this section we summarize association studies of aggression-related phenotypes and DNA sequence variation (described earlier) in genes encoding TPH, MAO-A, 5-HTT, and selected serotonin receptors.

Tryptophan Hydroxylase

Nearly all studies have examined one of the two adenine-cytosine transversions in intron 7, labeled A218C and A779C, that exist in very strong linkage disequilibrium in populations of European descent (Nielsen et al., 1994, 1997). One early investigation of violent criminals and fire setters showed no difference in the distribution of A218C alleles between impulsive and nonimpulsive offenders (a designation based on the premeditation of index crimes), nor did either of these groups differ significantly from healthy control participants (Nielsen et al., 1994). Nonetheless, the 218C allele was associated with a history of attempted suicide among all offenders and with lower CSF 5-HIAA concentrations in impulsive offenders only. In a replication sample, attempted suicide was associated with the 779C allele in impulsive offenders (which corresponds to 218C in the initial report), but, conversely, with A779 among nonimpulsive offenders (Nielsen et al., 1998). CSF 5-HIAA concentrations did not vary by genotype in this sample, and although criminality itself was unrelated to genotype across all subjects, the A779 allele was more common in nonsuicidal criminal offenders than among nonoffender controls.

In a small study of patients with mixed personality disorder diagnoses ($n = 40$), BDHI scores were unrelated to the A218C polymorphism in women, whereas men homozygous for the 218C allele scored highest on the BDHI Assault and Irritability subscales (New et al., 1998). The 218C allele was also associated with "impulsive tendencies" reported by psychiatric inpatients on an inventory of behaviors that included fighting and unprovoked anger, impulsive self-injury, and various other nonaggressive impulsive acts (Staner et al., 2002). However, 218C did not differ in frequency between impulsive patients and nonimpulsive, nonpatient controls in this study, and neither BDHI nor BIS scores varied by genotype. Among patients with schizophrenia and schizoaffective disorder, histories of violence (multiple physical assaults) showed a modest association with the 779C allele, when compared to nonviolent patients of comparable diagnosis, albeit only in men (Nolan, Volavka, Lachman, & Saito, 2000).

In contrast, lifetime histories of aggression (LHA scores) among 251 community volunteers were found to be greater in individuals having any A218 allele, relative to subjects homozygous for 218C, and this association obtained for both "aggression" and "antisocial" subscales of the LHA interview (Manuck et al., 1999). Although unrelated to BDHI Assault and Irritability scores, the A218 allele further predicted "angry temperament" (a tendency to experience unprovoked anger) and the propensity to express anger outwardly (either verbally or by physical assault) on the Spielberger Anger Expression Inventory. These findings were independent of variability in age and socioeconomic status, were stronger in men than women, and persisted in analyses restricted to individuals without current major psychopathology. In this study too, men having any A218 allele showed an attenuated prolactin response to fenfluramine (reduced central serotonergic responsivity), which is consistent with the lower CSF 5-HIAA concentrations observed elsewhere in healthy men having the corresponding A779 allele (Jonsson et al., 1997). Similarly, self-reported "angry temperament," identically assessed, was associated with both the A218 and A779 alleles in an independent (German) sample of 240 healthy volunteers and psychiatric patients with histories of attempted suicide (Rujescu et al., 2002). The same TPH alleles (A218, A779) predicted other anger-related traits among suicidal patients, including "angry reactions" (the tendency to become angered when criticized or treated unfairly) and "anger-in" (conceptualized as the internalization of angry feelings).

Across all studies these two TPH polymorphisms yield highly mixed results with respect to aggression and anger-related personality traits, some investigators reporting positive findings for the A218/A779 alleles and others for the 218C/779C variants. A lack of known functional genetic variation in TPH, together with the recent discovery of a second TPH gene (TPH2) and evidence that the commonly studied TPH1 gene may not be expressed prominently in the brain (Walther et al., 2003), also cast a long shadow over this literature. At the least, previous findings will need to be reevaluated as more is learned about the genetic control of neuronal tryptophan hydroxylase activity.

Monoamine Oxidase A

Impulsive aggression (including arson and attempted rape) were found to cosegregate among males of a large Dutch kindred with a chain termination mutation in the X-chromosomal MAO-A gene (Brunner, Nelen, Breakefield, Ropers, & van Oost, 1993). Although this mutation is rare and therefore not plausibly predictive of behavior in the general population, common allelic variation at the MAO-A locus has been studied as a potential correlate of aggression in both normal and patient populations. Most of this research has focused on the functional VNTR located in the regulatory region of the MAO-A gene, where variable repeats of a 30-bp sequence yield alleles of "high" and "low" transcriptional activity. Impulsive aggression, as defined by the unit-weighted composite of standardized LHA, BDHI, and BIS scores, was found to be greatest in individuals having high-transcription MAO-A alleles among a community sample of 110 Caucasian men

(Manuck, Flory, Ferrell, Mann, & Muldoon, 2000). Central serotonergic responsivity also varied by MAO-A genotype in a subset of these men administered a standard fenfluramine challenge, with subjects possessing high-activity alleles exhibiting a smaller prolactin response to fenflurmine than those with low-activity alleles. Moreover, adjusting for concomitant variability in fenfluramine-induced prolactin release eroded the effect of MAO-A genotype on LHA-assessed aggression history to nonsignificance (Manuck et al., 2002). This suggests that the MAO-A promoter polymorphism may influence an aggressive phenotype via allele-specific variation in CNS serotonergic function. Also consistent with these findings, persistently aggressive boys (identified by both parent and teacher reports) were more likely to carry the high-activity, four-repeat MAO-A allele than ethnically matched, nonaggressive (adult) controls (Beitchman, Mik, Ehtesham, Douglas, & Kennedy, 2004).

In studies of alcoholism, however, the low activity, three-repeat variant of this length polymorphism was more common in male alcoholics with comorbid antisocial personality disorder than among nonalcoholic controls, non-antisocial alcoholics, or alcoholics with anxious-depressive personality disorders (Samochowiec et al., 1999; Schmidt et al., 2000). Still, more recent investigations have failed to find any association between MAO-A genotype and antisocial alcoholism, whether defined by history of criminal violence and diagnosis of antisocial personality disorder (Saito et al., 2002) or by psychometric indices of aggressiveness and impulsivity (LHA by questionnaire, BDHI, BIS) (Koller, Bondy, Preuss, Bottlender, & Soyka, 2003). In two investigations involving relatively large nonpatient samples, standardized personality questionnaires, some of which contain subscales considered sensitive to individual differences in impulsiveness and aggressive disposition, showed no association with the MAO-A promoter polymorphism (Garpenstrand et al., 2002; Jorm et al., 2000).

Suggesting possible gene × environment interaction, a unique longitudinal study of 442 boys showed childhood maltreatment (as instanced by parental rejection, severe physical punishment, or abuse) to predict multiple indices of violence and antisocial behavior as a function of MAO-A genotype (Caspi et al., 2002). Self-rated aggressiveness, conduct disorder between ages 10 and 18, symptoms of adult antisocial personality disorder, and the commission of a violent crime by age 26 were potentiated by childhood maltreatment among individuals having low-transcription MAO-A alleles. Early adversity did not presage problems of aggression among those having high-activity alleles. Indeed, 44% of all violent convictions occurring in this population sample were attributable to the 12% of study participants who both were maltreated as children and possessed a genotype conferring diminished MAO-A transcriptional activity. This is one of the few existing studies showing social and environmental factors to qualify influences of genetic variation in a neuroregulatory system on complex behavioral phenotypes, a form of interaction that is widely hypothesized but rarely tested. That the study's results are inconsistent with the heightened aggressiveness and reduced serotonergic responsivity described previously in men with high-activity alleles of the MAO-A promoter polymorphism (Manuck et al., 2000, 2002) is perplexing, however, as it seems unlikely these contradictory findings can both reflect true associations.

Adding to this confusion is one additional study that yields an interaction of MAO-A genotype and environment similar to that described by Caspi et al. (2002). In this investigation, it is reported that children and adolescents (all males) having low activity MAO-A alleles were at increased risk for a diagnosis of conduct disorder if they had experienced several adversities of rearing, including neglect, inconsistent discipline, and parental conflict (Foley et al., 2004). However, on controlling for early adversity and its interaction with MAO-A genotype, low transcription MAO-A alleles were associated overall with lower (not higher) risk of conduct disorder. The interaction that suggests replication of Caspi et al. (2002) arose from a very high prevalence of conduct disorder among the few boys who fell in the top two (of five) levels of childhood adversity and also carried low-activity MAO-A alleles. But there were only three such individuals (accounting for 5% of 59 conduct disorder cases among the 514 boys comprising this sample). In addition, the authors' two highest strata of adversity included less than 4% of the study cohort. Thus, one interpretation of this study might be that MAO-A genotypes predicting high transcriptional efficiency are generally associated with an increased risk of conduct disorder (see also Beitchman et al., 2004), whereas low activity alleles confer exceptionally high risk among those exposed to the most egregious rearing environments (as in Caspi et al., 2002). If true, it might be asked whether the nature of conduct problems seen among children reared in extreme adversity differs in any significant way from the aggressiveness of those raised under less onerous circumstances.

Serotonin Transporter

The first study of behavioral factors related to allelic variation in the 5-HTT gene-linked polymorphic region found the 5-HTTLPR "short" allele, which reduces transcriptional efficiency of the transporter gene, associated with several personality traits that might predispose to aggressive behavior. These included disagreeableness (an irritable and antagonistic temperament), neuroticism (heightened emotionality), and, as a component of neuroticism, angry hostility (Lesch, Bengel, et al., 1996). Neuroticism and angry hostility both covary inversely with fenfluramine-stimulated prolactin release in men, and angry hostility loads psychometrically on a common factor with impulsivity and lifetime aggression history (assessed by the BIS and LHA, respectively) (Manuck et al., 1998). These genetic associations replicated subsequently (e.g., Greenburg et al., 2000), but several investigators have failed to find 5-HTTLPR variation related to these personality traits when using the same or similar self-report instruments (e.g., Ebstein et al., 1997; Flory et al., 1999; Gelernter, Kranzler, Coccaro, Siever, & New, 1998; Jorm et al., 1998; Stoltenberg et al., 2002). With respect to impulsivity, the 5-HTTLPR long allele predicted high BIS scores in a mixed sample of incarcerated adolescent offenders and controls (Lee, Kim, & Hyun, 2003), whereas the transporter polymorphism was found unrelated to impulsivity among alcoholics (Preuss et al., 2000), to both BIS and BDHI scores in cocaine-dependent African Americans (Patkar et al., 2002), and to BIS and LHA scores in a large Spanish sample of suicide attempters and controls (Baca-Garcia et al., 2004).

Among other findings, homozygosity for the long allele was associated with "past feelings and acts of violence" reported by suicidal adolescents (Zalsman et al., 2001) and with problems of aggression (e.g., cruelty, frequent fighting, threats, and temper tantrums) identified in maternal ratings of offspring of alcoholic fathers (Twitchell et al., 2001). Interestingly, the latter study also showed the 5-HTTLPR long allele to predict behaviors indicative of anxiety and depression (e.g., sadness, crying, loneliness), suggesting an association with both internalizing and externalizing childhood behavior problems. In a longitudinal adoption study, though, allelic variation in the 5-HTTLPR exerted no direct effects on children, but interacted with attributes of the adoptee's biological parents to predict aggressive phenotypes (Cadoret et al., 2003). For instance, adoptees who were homozygous for the long allele exhibited high levels of adolescent aggression and antisocial behavior (e.g., fighting, theft and vandalism, arson, insolence and verbal abuse) if they also had antisocial biological parents; having any 5-HTTLPR *short* allele predicted adolescent aggression among offspring of alcoholic biological parents. Unlike the previously cited longitudinal study of aggression, maltreatment, and MAO-A variation (Caspi et al., 2002), an adverse (adoptive) home environment in this investigation did not interact with genetic variation in the serotonin transporter to affect adolescent aggressive behavior. Of course, in the prior (MAO-A) study investigators could not partition genetic and environmental effects on development, leaving the interpretation of "maltreatment" as a strictly environmental influence indefinite. Hence, among children raised by biological parents, parental maltreatment and offspring aggressiveness may stem partly from shared genetic influences, whether acting additively or in interaction (epistasis). In severing the confound of biological parentage and rearing environment by studying adoptees, Cadoret and colleagues (2003) suggest that adolescent aggression may be promoted through an interaction of genetic variation in the serotonin transporter and heritable factors underlying the familial transmission of genetic liability for alcoholism or antisocial personality. If so, this might also account for the failure elsewhere to observe a direct association of 5-HTTLPR variation with children's aggressive behavior (e.g., Beitchman et al., 2003). Nonetheless, the relatively small sample studied by Cadoret and colleagues ($n = 87$) and the opposing roles of the 5-HTTLPR short and long alleles in interactions involving parental antisocial behavior and alcoholism make replication of these preliminary findings especially critical.

In one study of alcoholism, the frequency of the 5-HTTLPR short allele and of the short/short genotype were greater in alcoholics who had committed violent offenses (including homicide or attempted homicide, aggravated assault, and arson) than among nonviolent alcoholics or healthy control subjects (Hallikainen et al., 1999). This association was only weakly supported in a second study of antisocial alcoholics (Sander et al., 1998), and in a third, the long allele and long/long genotype predominated among alcoholics with antisocial personality, compared to normal controls (Parsian & Cloninger, 2001). Finally, in each of two studies of Alzheimer disease patients, individuals with histories of aggressive behavior during the course of their dementia were more likely to carry the 5-HTTLPR long allele and long/long genotype than non-aggressive patients with comparable cognitive impairment (Sukonick et al., 2001; Sweet et al., 2001). Although it is unclear whether the physical and verbal aggression seen in these patients reflect behavioral sequelae of Alzheimer's disease or a premorbid aggressive disposition, it is noteworthy that agitation (including aggressiveness) among Alzheimer's patients covaries inversely with the prolactin response to fenfluramine (Mintzer et al., 1998) and may be ameliorated when treated with the selective serotonin reuptake inhibitor citalopram (Pollock et al., 2002).

Serotonin Receptors

The few aggression studies addressing genetic variation in serotonin receptors focus primarily on the 5-HT$_{1B}$ and 5-HT$_{2A}$ receptors. Of several SNPs identified in the gene encoding the 5-HT$_{1B}$ receptor (HTR1B), located on chromosome 6 (6q13–15), the most commonly studied polymorphism is a silent guanine-cytosine substitution at nucleotide 861 (G861C). Antisocial alcoholism was found in linkage to G861C in an initial study of two populations, one composed of Finnish alcoholic criminal offenders and their siblings and the second a large multigenerational Native American family in the southwestern United States (Lappalainen et al., 1998). Among Finns, the G861 allele was also shown by association analysis to be more common in antisocial alcoholics (those having comorbid antisocial personality or intermittent explosive disorder) than among unaffected subjects or non-antisocial alcoholics. However, subsequent investigation failed to replicate allelic association with antisocial alcoholism at G861C among Americans of either European or African descent (Kranzler, Hernandez-Avila, & Gelernter, 2002). Allele frequencies did not differentiate subjects identified as pathologically aggressive (for acts of aggression causing physical injury or occasioning legal action for destruction of property) from nonaggressive controls (Huang, Grailhe, Arango, Hen, & Mann, 1999), and among patients having various personality disorder diagnoses, the G861C polymorphism showed no association with dispositional hostility assessed by the BDHI (New et al., 2001).

Personality-disordered patients scoring high on the Assault subscale of the BDHI have an increased number of 5-HT$_{2A}$ receptors on platelets, relative to less aggressive subjects (Coccaro, Kavoussi, Sheline, Berman & Csernansky, 1997). Because 5-HT$_{2A}$ receptors on both platelets and neurons are encoded by the same gene, this receptor would seem a reasonable candidate for genetic association. The 5-HT$_{2A}$ receptor gene

(HTR2A), located on chromosome 13 (13q14–21), contains common variation at several sites, two of which have been studied frequently. These include a silent thymine-cytosine substitution in the coding region at nucleotide 102 (T102C) and a base change (adenine-cytosine) at position –1438 in the gene's upstream promoter region (A –1438G) (Jonsson et al., 2001). The two polymorphisms are in near perfect disequilibrium in European and Caucasian American populations (Masellis et al., 1998; Spurlock et al., 1998), but neither has known functional significance (Bray, Buckland, Hall, Owen, & O'Donovan, 2004). In a limited sample of patients with alcohol abuse, homozygosity for the 102C allele was found more commonly in men (but not women) reporting antisocial behavior problems in childhood and adolescence (e.g., frequent fighting, use of weapons, property destruction, arson, robbery, or truancy), compared to patients who did not report early antisocial behavior (Hwu & Chen, 2000). Although the frequency of the T102 allele was lower in this group also, allele frequencies did not vary as a function of antisocial background among a similar sample of alcohol-dependent individuals. In a second study, male criminal offenders (most incarcerated for crimes of violence) were more likely than healthy controls to have HTR2A genotypes containing any A –1438 allele (Berggard et al., 2003). As the A –1438 allele corresponds to T102 of the alternate HTR2A polymorphism genotyped by Hwu and Chen (2000), allelic associations with aggression or antisocial behavior appear to be reversed in these two reports. In another study of (mostly male) alcohol-dependent patients, though, BIS impulsivity scores were higher in –1438G/G homozygous subjects than among patients having any A –1438 allele (Preuss, Koller, Bondy, Bahlmann, & Soyka, 2001). And finally, healthy individuals homozygous for the 102C allele were found to make more errors indicative of poor impulse control on a behavioral task requiring sustained attention (the Continuous Performance Test) than subjects of other T102C genotypes (Bjork et al., 2002). As with the several other genes reviewed here, HTR2A yields a mixed literature; in this case, all studies show significant findings in relation to aggression- or impulsivity-related phenotypes, but the direction of allelic association is not consistent across investigations.

Commentary and Conclusions

In historical perspective, biologically informed models of aggression have not faired well. This is perhaps the unsurprising consequence of a premature and sometimes faulty science that often yielded, as among early 20th century eugenicists, to morally suspect temptations of a purblind determinism. A century before eugenics the phrenologists imagined a propensity to violence as the servant of an irascible temperament that could be detected as a bump on the skull a bit behind and above the ear (Combe, 1847). A particularly large protuberance in this area predisposed the affected individual to behave aggressively, unless offset by cautious apprehension, the benevolent sentiments, or intellect—qualities scattered about from parietal to prefrontal cortex. The evidence for this cortically localized aggressiveness was said to derive from a comparison of the skulls of carnivorous animals and herbivores, of murderers and healthy controls. The phrenological framework, with its scaffolding of traits and cortical topography, did not last long, debunked widely by midcentury (e.g., Bain, 1861) and superceded by experimentation and clinical study of patients with lesions involving discrete, ultimately verifiable regions of the brain (e.g., Ferrier, 1876). After Phineas Gage's famous (and horrific) accident in 1848, the seat of impulsivity and irascible temperament moved to the far frontal regions, albeit largely unrecognized until rediscovered in recent decades by a neuroscience newly interested in the neural regulation of impulse and affect (Damasio, 1994; Macmillan, 1992, 2000). The neurochemistry of these same processes has advanced apace, with serotonin one of numerous neurotransmitters that convey evanescent messages over complex neural circuitry, including circuits of frontal-limbic connectivity. The monoamine neuromodulators attracted particular interest, and initial observations suggested an association of some specificity between heightened aggressiveness and low CSF concentrations of the serotonin metabolite 5-HIAA (Brown et al., 1979, 1982). Many related literatures followed, of which we have reviewed only those addressing individual differences in CNS serotonergic activity as a correlate of aggressive disposition in humans and nonhuman primates. In the context of this work, do we stand today closer to a neurobiology of aggression or to a neurochemical neophrenology reminiscent of earlier eras?

The serotonin "hypothesis" of aggression has been reviewed previously, though generally with respect to only one or a few of the literatures summarized here, usually human studies of CSF 5-HIAA concentrations (e.g., Berman, Tracy, & Coccaro, 1997; Roggenbach, Muller-Oerlinghausen, & Franke, 2002; Tuinier,

Verhoeven, & van Praag, 1995). These critiques cite prevalent methodological deficiencies, such as small samples and subject populations of limited generalizability; potential confounding of participant aggressiveness with comorbid psychopathology; recruitment of comparison subjects (controls) from convenience populations; and reliance on indirect measures of aggression, often of unreported psychometric properties. Individual studies vary in their susceptibility to these limitations, however, and more recent investigations have often attempted to surmount one or another interpretive constraint of prior work. Also, we have found it useful to distinguish analyses based on sentinel indices of aggression from those involving the many self-administered questionnaires that tap traits of personality putatively indicative of an aggressive or impulsive disposition. As sentinel indices, we have included events of documented aggression (e.g., adjudicated criminality of a violent nature), clinical entities for which aggressive conduct is pathognomonic (e.g., intermittent explosive disorder, conduct disorder), or enumerated reports of persistent aggression and antisocial behavior elicited by structured interview (LHA). Despite occasional contrary or null findings, we believe that a clear preponderance of evidence associates heightened aggressiveness—whether indexed by violent criminal activity or recidivism, lifetime history of aggression, or aggressive behavior observed in a laboratory setting (PSAP)—with diminished or otherwise dysregulated central serotonergic activity. These associations are seen in forensic, clinical, nonpatient, and community populations and are documented by several measures of serotonergic function, including CSF 5-HIAA concentrations, neuroendocrine challenges, and responsivity to serotonergic stimulation in frontal brain regions thought to modulate aggressive behavior. Self-ratings of aggressiveness (e.g., BDHI scores) and of traits reflecting a likely propensity to aggression (e.g., anger-related traits) yield more ambiguous results, but in studies employing neuroendocrine challenges, these measures, on balance, also covary inversely with CNS serotonergic function. There is some evidence for receptor-specific mediation of these associations, particularly in relation to the 5-HT_{1A} receptor (e.g., Cherek et al., 1999; Cleare & Bond, 2000; Coccaro et al., 1990, 1995; Moeller et al., 1998; Parsey et al., 2002), but much further work will be needed to more adequately characterize pre- and postsynaptic influences on brain serotonergic activity and its covariation with the aggressive potential of individuals.

Across all studies, women are understudied, relative to men, and overall show a weaker pattern of association between serotonergic indices and aggression. It remains for future work to clarify how much this reflects a true sex difference, gender-related differences in the qualities of aggressive disposition covarying with serotonergic function, ovarian influences on measures of serotonergic activity, or simply a need for larger samples when studying women, due to lower base rates of aggressive conduct. One clearly inconsistent literature is that addressing serotonergic activity as a correlate of externalizing behavior problems of children and adolescents. Some studies have found aggressive behavior in youth correlated inversely with CSF 5-HIAA concentrations or responses to pharmacologic challenge, but others have not or have reported associations in the opposite direction, and attempts to reconcile these differences by appeal to sample characteristics (e.g., age, concomitant ADHD) have not been successful (Schulz et al., 2001). It is of interest that there is some evidence that family histories of aggressive and antisocial behavior are associated with low CSF 5-HIAA concentrations in infants (Constantino et al., 1997) and with diminished serotonergic responsivity in prepubertal, aggressive boys (Halperin et al., 2003); preliminary findings also suggest that familial vulnerability to alcoholism and antisocial personality predict adolescent aggression as a function of regulatory variation in the serotonin transporter gene (Cadoret et al., 2003). These intriguing associations notwithstanding, what role serotonin may play in the early development of aggressive behavior remains poorly understood and, therefore, in clear need of more extensive investigation.

Although in this chapter we did not review the behavioral effects of experimental and therapeutic manipulations of serotonergic function, it is worth noting that lowering brain serotonin synthesis by acute tryptophan depletion reduces both CSF 5-HIAA concentrations and central serotonergic responsivity, assessed by fenfluramine challenge (Coccaro, Kavoussi, Cooper, et al., 1998; Moreno et al., 2000; Williams, Shoaf, Hommer, Rawlings, & Linnoila, 1999). Acute tryptophan depletion has been shown also to increase aggressive responding in laboratory paradigms (e.g., PSAP and other competitive tasks) in both men and women, particularly among individuals of aggressive predisposition as indicated on trait measures of hostility (see review by Young & Leyton, 2002; also, e.g., Bjork, Dougherty, Moeller, Cherek, & Swann, 1999; Cleare & Bond, 1995; Dougherty, Bjork, Marsh, & Moeller,

1999; Finn, Young, Pihl, & Ervin, 1998; Pihl et al., 1995). Conversely, administering the serotonin reuptake inhibitor paroxetine decreases aggressive behavior on the PSAP in men with histories of conduct disorder (Cherek, Lane, Pietras, & Steinberg, 2002), and several double-blind, placebo-controlled studies show reuptake inhibitors to reduce aggression among patients with personality disorders, autism, schizophrenia, and dementia (see review by McQuade, Barrnet, & King, 2003; also, e.g., Coccaro & Kavoussi, 1997; McDougle et al., 1996; Pollock et al., 2002; Vartiainen et al., 1995). Preliminary evidence also indicates that metabolic response to serotonergic stimulation increases in orbital frontal cortex in impulsive aggressive patients treated with the reuptake inhibitor fluoxetine and that the magnitude of this response covaries with the extent of clinical improvement (New et al., in press).

Much of the research reviewed here entails subject populations selected for deviance, as represented by a variety of diagnostic entities or a history of criminal activity. That studies conducted on healthy volunteers and in nonpatient community samples have now also shown central serotonergic function to covary inversely with aggression and dispositional hostility suggests that these associations reflect a more general neurobehavioral dimension of individual differences. As noted earlier, it is widely hypothesized that serotonergic activity underlies, in part, interindividual variation in the constraint of impulses, with "deficiencies" of serotonergic function exerting disinhibitory effects on behavior, as evidenced by a disregard for future consequences, actions committed in haste, and a propensity to aggressive expression. The notion that impaired impulse control lies at the root of serotonergically mediated aggression nonetheless preceded speculation regarding normative variability in this domain. This is reflected in the several attempts to distinguish criminal offenders having lower and higher CSF 5-HIAA concentrations based on the inferred impulsiveness of their index crimes (e.g., Linnoila et al., 1983; Virkkunen et al., 1987; Virkkunen, Rawlings, et al., 1994). For reasons cited previously—failure to replicate, confounding psychopathology—the results of these studies are not convincing, yet the premise that "low" serotonin disinhibits otherwise constrained behavior (such as aggression) persists, not least because other observations are consistent with the hypothesis. For instance, psychometric indices of impulsivity (e.g., BIS) have been found to correlate inversely with central serotonergic responsivity, as assessed by neuroendocrine challenge, in sev-

eral, albeit not all, studies (e.g., Coccaro et al., 1989; Manuck et al., 1998; Paris et al., 2004; Reist et al., 1996; Soloff et al., 2003).

Perhaps the most persuasive evidence that aggression and impulsivity are conjoined by serotonin derives from the remarkably consistent studies of nonhuman primates. Overt aggression, and, specifically, severe or unrestrained aggression, was found to be associated with low CSF 5-HIAA concentrations among both free-ranging male rhesus monkeys and socially housed female rhesus and pigtailed monkeys (e.g., Higley, Mehlman, Poland, et al., 1996; Mehlman et al., 1994; Westergaard et al., 1999, 2003). Similarly, male cynomolgus monkeys showing the smallest prolactin responses to fenfluramine exhibited higher rates of escalated aggression when observed in all-male social groups and were more likely to react aggressively to slides of threatening objects in a nonsocial context than animals having prolactin responses of larger magnitude (Botchin et al., 1993; Kyes et al., 1995). Impulsive risk taking, expressed as a tendency to leap long distances at dangerous heights in the forest canopy, also characterized male and female rhesus monkeys with low CSF 5-HIAA (Higley, Mehlman, Poland, et al., 1996; Mehlman et al., 1994). Uninhibited approach to a social stranger (social impulsivity, as assessed by the Intruder Challenge) was found similarly associated with both low 5-HIAA levels in male vervet monkeys (Fairbanks et al., 2001) and a blunted prolactin response to fenfluramine in female cynomolgus monkeys (Manuck, Kaplan, et al., 2003). While vervet males' aggressive behavior during the Intruder Challenge correlated inversely with 5-HIAA concentration, this association disappeared on statistical adjustment for correlated variation in animals' latency of approach to the intruder (impulsivity). But the converse was not also seen, as individual differences in approach behavior covaried with 5-HIAA even after adjustment for aggression. As noted earlier, these findings suggest that dimensional variation in "impulsivity versus inhibition" may represent a primary behavioral correlate of central serotonergic function, with aggression occurring in consequence (or not occurring) depending on circumstance and prevailing motivation (Fairbanks et al., 2001). The observations on rhesus monkeys cited above are consistent with such speculation, inasmuch as low CSF 5-HIAA animals are inclined to impulsive action even outside a context of potential antagonistic interaction.

That serotonin may modulate capacities to inhibit impulsive behavior has been tested more directly in studies of laboratory rats. In a common experimental paradigm, for instance, animals are offered a choice of rewards that differ in value and availability: one to be had immediately but of small worth (e.g., a pellet or two of chow) and the other of greater value (e.g., say eight pellets) but delivered only after some delay. Selecting immediate (or sooner) rewards of lesser preference is referred to as impulsive choice, whereas waiting for the more desired outcome requires the restraint of impulse and is said therefore to reflect inhibitory (or self-) control. Importantly, manipulating serotonergic activity alters the delay preferences (impulsivity) of laboratory animals. Drugs that decrease serotonergic neurotransmission by blocking transmitter synthesis, activating inhibitory autoreceptors, or selectively destroying ascending serotonin neurons heighten impulsive choice (i.e., bias responding toward immediate rewards), and, conversely, increasing serotonergic activity by blocking synaptic reuptake, potentiating the neuronal release of serotonin stores, or inhibiting enzymatic degradation of serotonin enhances animals' preferences for delayed, larger rewards (for review, see Manuck, Flory, et al., 2003). A similar shift in preference to delayed rewards of higher value (decreased impulsivity) has been shown also in analogous laboratory testing among conduct disordered men, both as a dose-dependent response to acute fenfluramine administration (Cherek & Lane, 1999) and following chronic treatment with the serotonin reuptake inhibitor paroxetine (Cherek et al., 2002). Such findings provide support for a model of serotonergically modulated impulsivity in which diminished central serotonergic activity disinhibits goal-directed behavior by impairing an organism's capacity to tolerate delay between impulse and action, or basically, to wait (Soubrie, 1986).

Is impulsivity *the* key behavioral correlate of individual differences in serotonergic function? Aggression is commonly accompanied by emotion (e.g., anger, rage), and what some consider impulsive aggression is called affective aggression by others (Blair & Charney, 2003). Observational studies of nonhuman primates are obviously silent on animals' affective experiences, and correlational research on serotonergic function in humans has rarely addressed the role of affective processes in the instigation of aggression. This neglect is somewhat surprising since serotonin reuptake inhibitors are the principal agents of pharmacotherapy for mood disorders. In addition, acute tryptophan depletion not only increases aggressive responding on competitive laboratory tasks, but also lowers mood (Young

& Leyton, 2002). And in one study of healthy individuals administered paroxetine or placebo over 4 weeks, reductions in hostility (BDHI Assault) among those receiving the reuptake inhibitor were found to be mediated by more general changes in negative affect (Knutson et al., 1998). It is not difficult either to conceptualize interactions of emotion and impulse, with negative affects fueling antagonistic intent or disrupting inhibitory processes that might otherwise abort an aggressive impulse (Krakowski, 2003).[2]

Perhaps, too, there are essential similarities to impulses and affects, the two entwined in origin but one expressed externally (as motivated action) and the other internally (as subjective experience). Notably, the regulation of impulse and affect are thought to involve common neural structures, including the inhibitory circuitry of medial frontal, anterior cingulate, and orbitofrontal cortices (Blair & Charney, 2003; see Grimes, Ricci, Rasakham, & Melloni, ch. 16 in this volume). It has been argued also that serotonergic neurotransmission modulates behavioral and affective responses activated by other transmitter systems—for example, locomotion, sexual activity, sensitivity to environmental cues of threat, punishment, or reward—but does not itself underlie particular motivational systems or instantiate valenced affect (Depue & Collins, 1999; Spoont, 1992; Zald & Depue, 2001). On this view, diminished serotonergic activity may potentiate aggression (perhaps enhancing reactivity to instigating stimuli), but could equally facilitate rewarded behaviors of a prosocial nature. In one recent study, for example, a blunted prolactin response to fenfluramine predicted greater *positive*, as well as greater negative, affect in self-ratings aggregated over numerous measurements from daily life (Zald & Depue, 2001). Uncertainties persist, however, and in the end the literatures reviewed in this chapter do not seem uniquely informative regarding serotonin's broader role in the regulation of behavior, impulse, and affect. Yet even if these "higher" functions of serotonin remain elusive, accumulated findings on aggression and impulsivity advance our understanding of the behavioral correlates of interindividual variation in central serotonergic activity. Until a more comprehensive integration of clinical and experimental literatures is achieved, serotonin will likely remain reminiscent of the proverbial elephant described by blind men, each acquainted by touch with a different part of the animal.

Undoubtedly, heritable variation underlies much phenotypic variability in serotonergic function. Although the heritability of CNS serotonergic activity has rarely been studied in humans (Oxenstierna et al., 1986), there is evidence of genetic influence on the CSF 5-HIAA concentrations of rhesus monkeys and baboons (Higley et al., 1993; Rogers et al., 2004). In addition, a number of common polymorphisms, some of apparent functional significance, have been identified in components of the serotonergic system, and among these, aggression-related phenotypes have been found associated with allelic variation in genes encoding TPH, the serotonin transporter, MAO-A, and the 5-HT_{1B} and 5-HT_{2A} receptors. Unfortunately, there is yet little or no consistency in the pattern of reported genetic associations for any individual gene, and indeed, self-ratings or sentinel indices of aggression have been predicted by each of the alternate alleles of every polymorphism studied to date. Perhaps the least charitable interpretation is that the existing literature reflects tails of a sampling distribution of random study outcomes, with the bulk of nonsignificant findings remaining unpublished. However, this may overstate the problem, as available studies vary greatly in size and adequacy of design. Few investigators have employed family-based methodologies or other genetic designs that mitigate confounding by cryptic sources of population substructure, but some have restricted their genetic analyses to ethnically homogenous samples, while others have not or do not fully report the nature of their study cohort. Statistical power is also a major concern because the proportion of heritable variation that can be attributed to the distribution of alleles of a single polymorphism is expected to be small for any polygenic trait (and even smaller as a proportion of total variation in the phenotype). "Positive" findings reported in the many studies containing samples of 50 or 100 subjects must be viewed skeptically, therefore, as the magnitude of genetic association needed to attain statistical significance in these investigations may far exceed credible effect sizes for single loci. Moreover, problems of statistical power are compounded where genetic associations exist in interaction with environmental factors or other genes. In one notable study, regulatory variation in the MAO-A gene predicted later violence and antisocial behavior in men who had been maltreated in childhood, yet only 12% of participants carried the vulnerability alleles of MAO-A *and* had histories of maltreatment (Caspi et al., 2002). Any investigator attempting to replicate this finding will obviously need to both assess rearing environments and obtain a similarly robust sample of many hundreds of participants. In sum, identifying reliable genetic associa-

tions for phenotypes of relevance to aggression may not pose an intractable problem, but will likely prove fruitful only when study samples and methodologies are routinely scaled to the standards of genetic epidemiology.

Finally, we may ask why interindividual variability in central serotonergic activity (variability of partly heritable origin) should persist in covariation with aggression and impaired impulse control when the clinical and forensic sequelae of a serotonergic "deficiency" seem so patently maladaptive. It cannot just be argued that modernity or culturally defined social structures conducive to deviance hijacked a neurobiology of otherwise benign behavioral manifestation, as the many studies of nonhuman primates show analogously aberrant behavior in monkeys exhibiting low CSF 5-HIAA concentrations or a blunted prolactin response to fenfluramine. Interestingly, low serotonin turnover among male rhesus monkeys is associated not only with impulsive aggression, heightened risk of fight-inflicted injury, and premature mortality, but also with social isolation and less competent reproductive behavior (Mehlman et al., 1997). In the mating season, for instance, these animals form fewer consort relationships with receptive females and achieve fewer inseminations than males of higher 5-HIAA concentration. This would seem to confer reproductive disadvantage on low 5-HIAA animals and, by selection, presage their ultimate decline in populations (or at least the loss of whatever genetic variation may help sustain such behavior). However, consorts do not guarantee exclusive sexual access to females, and furtive copulations "stolen" by nonconsorting males comprise an alternative reproductive tactic—one that was found responsible for fully 45% of offspring sired in a study of free-ranging rhesus monkeys on Cayo Santiago (Berard, Nurnberg, Epplen, & Schmidtke, 1994). Also informative are recent observations on captive rhesus monkeys (Gerald et al., 2002). Among males with higher CSF 5-HIAA concentrations, animals that successfully sired offspring tended to be older than those that did not. But the reverse held for low 5-HIAA monkeys, where reproductively successful males were younger than those failing to sire offspring (Gerald et al., 2002). Considering also the younger age at which low 5-HIAA males emigrate from their natal groups (Kaplan et al., 1995; Mehlman et al., 1995), it might be thought that these monkeys follow a life history strategy in which prominent features include an early pursuit of sexual opportunities, a propensity for impulsive behavior and confrontational violence (which may abet competition for mates), and increased risk of premature mortality ("live fast, die young") (Gerald & Higley 2002).[3]

It is tempting, though risky, to contemplate corresponding behavioral adaptations in humans. Promiscuous sexual exploitation has been proposed previously as a variant reproductive strategy accounting for the persistence of antisocial personality and, by its association with aggressiveness and impulsivity, contributing to delinquency and criminal violence (MacMillan & Kofoed, 1984; Mealey, 1995; Rowe, 1996). Mating tactics and reproductive fitness have not been studied in relation to central serotonergic function in humans, although we noted earlier that the more aggressive men in a nonpatient community sample—men who also showed diminished serotonergic responsivity on fenfluramine challenge—divorced at a fourfold higher rate than their less aggressive counterparts (Manuck et al., 2002). Similarly, higher rates of marital instability and divorce have been reported among men with antisocial personalities, compared to controls (Robins, 1966). In this study also, antisocial men appeared more variable than controls in the number of offspring they had fathered, with a somewhat greater proportion of antisocial men either childless or fathering more than four children. Consistent with a life history of aggressive competition, promiscuity, unstable marital relations, and depreciated parenting, these variable reproductive outcomes might conceivably yield offspring equivalent in number, when averaged over all antisocial men, to the normative reproductive outcomes of males leading lives of marital constancy and high parental investment (MacMillan & Kofoed, 1984). It is often argued that this high-risk strategy of antisocial exploitation could be sustained in a population by frequency-dependent selection if it is rare and thereby eludes easy detection (Mealey, 1995). It is also possible that people vary quantitatively in traits predisposing to infidelity and sexual opportunism (a "cheating" strategy) and that these traits cohere with variation in competitive antagonism (aggressiveness) and regard for future consequences (impulsivity) as correlated manifestations of a broad, neurobiologically influenced distribution of individual differences (Rowe, 1996). Whether sculpted by selection or an emergent property of social environments affording diverse behavioral niches, interindividual variability in CNS serotonergic activity would seem one likely candidate for a neurobiologic mechanism underlying an externalizing spectrum of functionally covarying behavioral propensities.

Notes

Preparation of this chapter was supported in part by National Institutes of Health Grants P01 HL40962 and R01 HL65137.

1. Monkeys used in this analysis had been imported from Indonesia and placed in social groups following a 1-month quarantine. Cisternal CSF samples were obtained at the end of the first and fifth months of social housing, and measurements of 5-HIAA concentration were averaged over these two evaluations; animals were sampled for whole blood serotonin on a single occasion in the sixth month of social housing. Although the latter samples were offset in time from CSF collection, previous studies in our laboratory have shown whole blood serotonin to correlate highly over repeated measurements ($rs > .90$ for samples collected at monthly intervals) (Shively, Brammer, Kaplan, Raleigh, & Manuck, 1991).

2. Some recent experimental research suggests that many individuals engage in aggression as a means of regulating (ameliorating) negative affect, particularly people who are inclined to outward expressions of anger or who believe angry feelings are dissipated by their expression (Bushman, Baumeister, & Phillips, 2001).

3. Relatedly, allelic variation in the rhesus 5-HTTLPR was noted earlier to modulate age at emigration, with homozygosity for the short allele predicting the earliest dispersal and homozygosity for the long allele associated with the latest emigration (Trefilov et al., 2000). Citing reproductive disadvantages of late dispersal, Trefilov et al. postulate an optimal age of emigration that is associated with heterozygosity for the rh-5-HTTLPR long and short alleles. A trend toward higher reproductive success among heterozygotes further suggests that intermediate aged dispersal might be maintained by balancing selection. Of course, this line of argument assumes that variation in the rh-5-HTTLPR substantially influences central serotonergic activity, which other work suggests may obtain only among rhesus monkeys exposed to an adverse rearing environment (Bennett et al., 2002).

References

Alpert, J. E., Petersen, T., Roffi, P. A., Papakostas, G. I., Freed, R., Smith, M. M., et al. (2003). Behavioral and emotional disturbances in the offspring of depressed parents with anger attacks. *Psychotherapy and Psychosomatics, 72,* 102–106.

American Psychiatric Association. (2000). *Diagnostic and statistical manual of mental disorders* (4th ed., text rev.). Washington, DC: Author.

Anderson, I. M., & Cowen, P. J. (1992). Effect of pindolol

on endocrine and temperature responses to buspirone in healthy volunteers. *Psychopharmacology, 106*, 428–432.

Anderson, S. W., Bechara, A., Damasio, H., Tranel, D., & Damasio, A. R. (1999). Impairment of social and moral behavior related to early damage in human prefrontal cortex. *Nature Neuroscience, 2*, 1032–1037.

Arai, R., Kimura, H., Nagatsu, I., & Maeda, T. (1997). Preferential localization of monoamine oxidase type A activity in neurons of the locus coeruleus and type B activity in neurons of the dorsal raphe nucleus of the rate: A detailed enzyme histochemical study. *Brain Research, 745*, 352–356.

Asberg, M. (1998). Neurotransmitters and suicidal behavior: The evidence from cerebrospinal fluid studies. *Annals of the New York Academy of Sciences, 836*, 158–181.

Baca-Garcia, E., Vaquero, C., Diaz-Sastre, C., Garcia-Resa, E., Saiz-Ruiz, J., Fernandez-Piqueras, J., et al. (2004). Lack of association between the serotonin transporter promoter gene polymorphism and impulsivity or aggressive behavior among suicide attempters and health volunteers. *Psychiatry Research, 126*, 99–106.

Bain, A. (1861). *On the study of character*. London: Parker, Son, and Bourn.

Baron, M. (1980). *The schedule for interviewing borderlines (SIB)*. New York: New York State Psychiatric Institute.

Barr, C. S., Newman, T. K., Becker, M. L., Champoux, M., Lesch, K. P., Suomi, S. J., et al. (2003). Serotonin transporter gene variation is associated with alcohol sensitivity in rhesus macaques exposed to early-life stress. *Alcoholism: Clinical and Experimental Research, 27*, 812–817.

Barr, C. S., Newman, T. K., Becker, M. L., Parker, C. C., Champoux, M., Lesch, K. P., et al. (2003). The utility of the non-human primate model for studying gene by environment interactions in behavioral research. *Genes, Brain and Behavior, 2*, 336–340.

Barratt, E. S. (1994). Impulsiveness and aggression. In J. Monahan & H. J. Steadman (Eds.), *Violence and mental disorder: Developments in risk assessment* (pp. 61–79). Chicago: University of Chicago Press.

Beitchman, J. H., Davidge, K. M., Kennedy, J. L., Atkinson, L., Lee, V., Shapiro, S., et al. (2003). The serotonin transporter gene in aggressive children with and without ADHD and nonaggressive matched controls. *Annals of the New York Academy of Sciences, 1008*, 248–251.

Beitchman, J. H., Mik, H. M., Ehtesham, S., Douglas, L., & Kennedy, J. L. (2004). MAOA and persistent, pervasive childhood aggression. *Molecular Psychiatry, 9*, 546–547.

Ben-Jonathan, N. (1985). Dopamine: A prolactin-inhibiting hormone. *Endocrinology Review, 6*, 564–589.

Bennett, A., Lesch, K. P., Heils, A., Long, J. C., Lorenz, J. G., Shoaf, S. E., et al. (2002). Early experience and serotonin transporter gene variation interact to influence primate CNS function. *Molecular Psychiatry, 7*, 118–122.

Berard, J. D., Nurnberg, P., Epplen, J. T., & Schmidtke, J. (1994). Alternative reproductive tactics and reproductive success in male rhesus macaques. *Behaviour, 129*, 177–201.

Berggard, C., Damberg, M., Longato-Stadler, E., Hallman, J., Oreland, L., & Garpenstrand, H. (2003). The serotonin 2A -1438 G/A polymorphism in a group of Swedish male criminals. *Neuroscience Letters, 247*, 196–198.

Berman, M. E., Tracy, J. I., & Coccaro, E. F. (1997). The serotonin hypothesis of aggression revisited. *Clinical Psychology Review, 17*, 651–665.

Bernstein, I. S. (1981). Dominance: The baby and the bathwater. *Behavioural and Brain Sciences, 4*, 419–458.

Bernstein, I. S., & Gordon, T. P. (1974). The function of aggression in primate societies. *American Scientist, 62*, 304–311.

Best, M., Williams, J. M., & Coccaro, E. F. (2002). Evidence for a dysfunctional prefrontal circuit in patients with an impulsive aggressive disorder. *Proceedings of the National Academy of Sciences USA, 99*, 8448–8453.

Bjork, J. M., Dougherty, D. M., Moeller, F. G., Cherek, D. R., & Swann, A. C. (1999). The effects of tryptophan depletion and loading on laboratory aggression in men: Time course and a food-restricted control. *Psychopharmacology, 142*, 24–30.

Bjork, J. M., Moeller, F. G., Dougherty, D. M., Swann, A. C., Machado, M. A., & Hanis, C. L. (2002). Serotonin 2a receptor T102C polymorphism and impaired impulse control. *American Journal of Medical Genetics (Neuropsychiatric Genetics), 114*, 336–339.

Blair, R. J. R. (2001). Neurocognitive models of aggression, the antisocial personality disorders, and psychopathy. *Journal of Neurology, Neurosurgery and Psychiatry, 71*, 727–731.

Blair, R. J. R. (2003). Neurobiological basis of psychopathology. *British Journal of Psychiatry, 182*, 5–7.

Blair, R. J. R., & Charney, D. S. (2003). Emotion regulation: An affective neuroscience approach. In M. P. Mattson (Ed.), *Neurobiology of aggression* (pp. 21–32). Totowa, NJ: Humana.

Botchin, M. B., Kaplan, J. R., Manuck, S. B., & Mann, J. J. (1993). Low versus high prolactin responders to fenfluramine challenge: Marker of behavioral differences in adult male cynomolgus macaques. *Neuro-psychopharmacaology*, 9, 93–99.

Bray, N. M. Buckland, P. R., Hall, H., Owen, M. J., & O'Donovan, M. C. (2004). The serotonin-2A receptor gene locus does not contain common polymorphism affecting mRNA levels in adult brain. *Molecular Psychiatry*, 9, 109–114.

Brown, G. L., Ebert, M. H., Goyer, P. F., Jimerson, D. C., Klein, W. J., Bunney, W. E., et al. (1982). Aggression, suicide, and serotonin: Relationships to CSF amine metabolites. *American Journal of Psychiatry*, 139, 741–746.

Brown, G. L., Goodwin, F. K., Ballenger, J. C., Goyer, P. F., & Major, L. F. (1979). Aggression in humans correlates with cerebrospinal fluid amine metabolites. *Psychiatry Research*, 1, 131–139.

Brunner, H. G., Nelen, M., Breakefield, X. O., Ropers, H. H., & van Oost, B. A. (1993). Abnormal behavior associated with a point mutation in the structural gene for monoamine oxidase. *Science*, 262, 578–580.

Brunner, H. G., Nelen, M. R., van Zandvoort, P., Abeling, N. G., van Gennip, A. H., Wolters, E. C., et al. (1993). X-linked borderline mental retardation with prominent behavioral disturbance: Phenotype, genetic localization, and evidence for disturbed monoamine metabolism. *American Journal of Human Genetics*, 52, 1032–1039.

Bushman, B. J., Baumeister, R. F., & Phillips, C. M. (2001). Do people aggress to improve their mood? Catharsis beliefs, affect regulation opportunity, and aggressive responding. *Journal of Personality and Social Psychology*, 81, 17–32.

Buss, A. H., & Durkee, A. (1957). An inventory for assessing different kinds of hostility. *Journal of Consulting Psychology*, 21, 343–348.

Buydens-Branchey, L., Branchey, M., Fergeson, P., Hudson, J., & McKernen, C. (1997). The meta-chlorophenylpiperazine challenge test in cocaine addicts: Hormonal and psychological responses. *Biological Psychiatry*, 41, 1071–1086.

Cadoret, R. J., Langbehn, D., Caspers, K., Troughton, E. P., Yucuis, R., Sandhu, H. K., et al. (2003). Associations of the serotonin transporter promoter polymorphism with aggressivity, attention deficit, and conduct disorder in an adoptee population. *Comprehensive Psychiatry*, 44, 88–101.

Caspi, A., McClay, J., Moffitt, T. E., Mill, J., Martin, J., Craig, I. W., et al. (2002). Role of genotype in the cycle of violence in maltreated children. *Science*, 297, 851–854.

Castellanos, F. X., Elia, J., Kruesi, M. J. P., Gulotta, C. S., Mefford, I. N., Potter, W. Z., et al. (1994). Cerebrospinal fluid monoamine metabolites in boys with attention-deficit hyperactivity disorder. *Psychiatry Research*, 52, 305–316.

Chamberlain, B., Ervin, F. R., Pihl, R. O., & Young, S. N. (1987). The effect of raising or lowering tryptophan levels on aggression in vervet monkeys. *Pharmacology, Biochemistry and Behavior*, 28, 503–510.

Champoux, M., Bennett, A., Shannon, C., Higley, J. D., Lesch, K. P., & Suomi, S. J. (2002). Serotonin transporter gene polymorphism, differential early rearing, and behavior in rhesus monkey neonates. *Molecular Psychiatry*, 7, 1058–1063.

Chapais, B. (1991). Primates and the origins of aggression, power, and politics among humans. In J. D. Loy & C. B. Peters (Eds.), *Understanding behavior: What primate studies tell us about human behavior* (pp. 190–228). New York: Oxford University Press.

Cherek, D. R., & Lane, S. D. (1999). Effects of D,l-fenfluramine on aggressive and impulsive responding in adult males with a history of conduct disorder. *Psychopharmacology*, 146, 473–481.

Cherek, D. R., Lane, S. D., Pietras, C. J., & Steinberg, J. L. (2002). Effects of chronic paroxetine administration on measures of aggressive and impulsive responses of adult males with a history of conduct disorder. *Psychopharmacology*, 159, 266–274.

Cherek, D. R., Moeller, F. G., Khan-Dawood, F., Swann, A., & Lane, S. D. (1999). Prolactin response to buspirone was reduced in violent compared to non-violent parolees. *Psychopharmacology*, 142, 144–148.

Clarke, R. A., Murphy, D. L., & Constantino, J. N. (1999). Serotonin and externalizing behavior in young children. *Psychiatry Research*, 86, 29–40.

Cleare, A. J., & Bond, A. J. (1995). The effect of tryptophan depletion and enhancement on subjective and behavioural aggression in normal male subjects. *Psychopharmacology*, 118, 82–81.

Cleare, A. J., & Bond, A. J. (1997). Does central serotonergic function correlate inversely with aggression? A study using d-fenfluramine in healthy subjects. *Psychiatry Research*, 69, 89–95.

Cleare, A. J., & Bond, A. J. (2000). Ipsapirone challenge in aggressive men shows an inverse correlation between 5-HT$_{1A}$ receptor function and aggression. *Psychopharmacology*, 148, 344–349.

Cloninger, C. R., Sigvardsson, S., & Bohman, M. (1996). Type I and type II alcoholism: An update. *Alcohol Health and Research World*, 20, 18–23.

Coccaro, E. F. (1992). Impulsive aggression and central serotonergic system function in humans: An example of a dimensional brain-behavior relationship. *International Clinical Psychopharmacology*, 7, 3–12.

Coccaro, E. F. (1998). Central neurotransmitter function in human aggression and impulsivity. In M. Maes & E. F. Coccaro (Eds.), *Neurobiology and clinical views on aggression and impulsivity* (pp. 143–168). New York: Wiley.

Coccaro, E. F., Berman, M. E., & Kavoussi, R. J. (1997). Assessment of life history of aggression: Development and psychometric characteristics. *Psychiatry Research, 73*, 147–157.

Coccaro, E. F., Berman, M. E., Kavoussi, E. J., & Hauger, R. L. (1996). Relationship of prolactin response to d-fenfluramine to behavioral and questionnaire assessments of aggression in personality-disordered men. *Biological Psychiatry, 40*, 157–164.

Coccaro, E. F., Gabriel, S., & Siever, L. J. (1990). Buspirone challenge: Preliminary evidence for a role for central 5-HT$_{1a}$ receptor function in impulsive aggressive behavior in humans. *Psychopharmacology Bulletin, 26*, 393–405.

Coccaro, E. F., & Kavoussi, R. J. (1997). Fluoxetine and impulsive aggressive behavior in personality-disordered subjects. *Archives of General Psychiatry, 54*, 1081–1087.

Coccaro, E. F., Kavoussi, R. J., Cooper, T. B., & Hauger, R. L. (1996a). 5-HT$_3$ receptor antagonism by ondansetron does not attenuate the prolactin response to d-fenfluramine challenge in healthy male subjects. *Psychopharmacology, 127*, 108–112.

Coccaro, E. F., Kavoussi, R. J., Cooper, T. B., & Hauger, R. L. (1996b). Hormonal responses to d- and d,l-fenfluramine in healthy human subjects. *Neuropsychopharmacology, 15*, 595–607.

Coccaro, E. F., Kavoussi, R. J., Cooper, T. B., & Hauger, R. L. (1997). Central serotonin activity and aggression: Inverse relationship with prolactin response to d-fenfluramine, but not CSF 5-HIAA concentration, in human subjects. *American Journal of Psychiatry, 154*, 1430–1435.

Coccaro, E. F., Kavoussi, R. J., Cooper, T. B., & Hauger, R. (1998). Acute tryptophan depletion attenuates the prolactin response to d-fenfluramine challenge in healthy human subjects. *Psychopharmacology, 138*, 9–15.

Coccaro, E. F., Kavoussi, R. J., & Hauger, R. L. (1995). Physiological responses to d-fenfluramine and ipsapirone challenge correlate with indices of aggression in males with personality disorders. *International Clinical Psychopharmacology, 10*, 177–179.

Coccaro, E. F., Kavoussi, R. J., Hauger, R. L., Cooper, T. B., & Ferris, C. F. (1998). Cerebrospinal fluid vasopressin levels: Correlates in aggression and serotonin function in personality-disordered subjects. *Archives of General Psychiatry, 55*, 708–714.

Coccaro, E. F., Kavoussi, R. J., Oakes, M., Cooper, T. B., & Hauger, R. (1996). 5-HT$_{2a/2c}$ receptor blockade by amesergide fully attenuates prolactin response to d-fenfluramine challenge in physically healthy human subjects. *Psychopharmacology, 126*, 24–30.

Coccaro, E. J., Kavoussi, R. J., Sheline, Y. I., Berman, M. E., & Csernansky, J. G. (1997). Impulsive aggression in personality disorder correlates with platelet 5-HT$_{2A}$ receptor binding. *Neuropsychopharmacology, 16*, 211–216.

Coccaro, E. F., Kavoussi, R. J., Sheline, Y. I., Lish, J. D., & Csernansky, J. G. (1996). Impulsive aggression in personality disorder correlates with tritiated paroxetine binding in the platelet. *Archives of General Psychiatry, 53*, 531–536.

Coccaro, E. F., Kavoussi, R. J., Trestman, R. L., Gabriel, S. M., Cooper, T. B., & Siever, L. J. (1997). Serotonin function in human subjects: Intercorrelations among central 5-HT indices and aggressiveness. *Psychiatry Research, 73*, 1–14.

Coccaro, E. F., Klar, H., & Siever, L. J. (1994). Reduced prolactin response to fenfluramine challenge in personality disorder patients is not due to deficiency of pituitary lactotrophs. *Biological Psychiatry, 36*, 344–346.

Coccaro, E. F., Siever, L. J., Klar, H. M., Maurer, G., Cochrane, K., Cooper, T. B., et al. (1989). Serotonergic studies in patients with affective and personality disorders. *Archives of General Psychiatry, 46*, 587–599.

Coccaro, E. F., Silverman, J. M., Klar, H. M., Horvath, T. B., & Siever, L. J. (1994). Familial correlates of reduced central serotonergic system function in patients with personality disorders. *Archives of General Psychiatry, 51*, 318–324.

Combe, G. (1847). *The constitution of man* (8th ed.). Edinburgh, UK: Maclachlan, Stewart.

Constantino, J. N., Morris, J. A., & Murphy, D. L. (1997). CSF 5–HIAA and family history of antisocial personality disorder in newborns. *American Journal of Psychiatry, 154*, 1771–1773.

Cook, E. H., Stein, M. A., Ellison, T., Unis, A. S., & Leventhal, B. L. (1995). Attention deficit hyperactivity disorder and whole-blood serotonin levels: Effects of comorbidity. *Psychiatry Research, 57*, 13–20.

Cowen, P. J., Anderson, I. M., & Grahame-Smith, D. G. (1990). Neuroendocrine effects of azapirones. *Journal of Clinical Psychopharmacology, 10*, 21S–25S.

Cremniter, D. Jamain, S., Kollenbach, K., Alvarez, J.-C., Lecubier, Y., Gilton, A., et al. (1999). CSF 5-HIAA levels are lower in impulsive as compared to non-impulsive suicide attempters and control subjects. *Biological Psychiatry, 45*, 1572–1579.

Daly, M., & Wilson, M. (1988). *Homicide*. New York: de Gruyter.

Damasio, A. R. (1994). *Descartes' error*. New York: Putnam.

Davidson, R. J., Putnam, K. M., & Larson, C. L. (2000). Dysfunction in the neural circuitry of emotion regulation: A possible prelude to violence. *Science, 289*, 591–593.

Deckert, J., Catalano, M., Syagailo, Y. V., Bosi, M., Okladnova, O., Di Bella, D., et al. (1999). Excess of high activity monoamine oxidase A gene promoter alleles in female patients with panic disorder. *Human Molecular Genetics, 8*, 621–624.

Denney, R. M., Koch, H., & Craig, I. W. (1999). Association between monoamine oxidase A activity in human male skin fibroblasts and genotype of the MAOA promoter-associated variable number tandem repeat. *Human Genetics, 105*, 542–551.

Depue, R. A., & Collins, P. F. (1999). Neurobiology of the structure of personality: Dopamine, facilitation of incentive motivation, and extraversion. *Behavioral and Brain Sciences, 22*, 491–569.

Depue, R. A., & Spoont, M. R. (1986). Conceptualizing a serotonin trait: A behavioral dimension of constraint. *Annals of the New York Academy of Sciences, 487*, 47–62.

DiRenzo, G., Amoroso, S., Taglialatela, M., Canzoniero, L., Basile, V., Fatatis, A., et al. (1989). Pharmacological characterization of serotonin receptors involved in the control of prolactin secretion. *European Journal of Pharmacology, 162*, 371–373.

Donovan, A. M., Halperin, J. M., Newcorn, J. H., & Sharma, V. (1999). Thermal response to serotonergic challenge and aggression in attention deficit hyperactivity disorder children. *Journal of Child and Adolescent Psychopharmacology, 9*, 85–91.

Dougherty, D. M., Bjork, J. M., Marsh, D. M., & Moeller, F. G. (1999). Influence of trait hostility on tryptophan depletion-induced laboratory aggression. *Psychiatry Research, 88*, 227–232.

Ebstein, R. P., Gritsenko, I., Nemanov, L., Frisch, A., Osher, Y., & Belmaker, R. H. (1997). No association between the serotonin transporter gene regulatory region polymorphism and the Tridimensional Personality Questionnaire (TPQ) temperament of harm avoidance. *Molecular Psychiatry, 2*, 224–226.

Eisen, A. S., & Temple, D. L., Jr. (1986). Buspirone: Review of its pharmacology and current perspectives on its mechanism of action. *American Journal of Medicine, 80*, 1–9.

Evans, J., Platts, H., Lightman, S., & Nutt, D. (2000). Impulsiveness and the prolactin response to d-fenfluramine. *Psychopharmacology, 149*, 147–152.

Fairbanks, L. A. (2001). Individual differences in response to a stranger: Social impulsivity as a dimension of temperament in vervet monkeys (*Cercopithecus aethiops sabaeus*). *Journal of Comparative Psychology, 115*, 22–28.

Fairbanks, L. A., Melaga, W. P., Jorgensen, M. J., Kaplan, J. R., & McGuire, M. T. (2001). Social impulsivity inversely associated with CSF 5-HIAA and fluoxetine

exposure in vervet monkeys. *Neuropsychopharmacology, 24*, 370–378.

Fairbanks, L. A., Newman, T. K., Bailey, J. N., Jorgensen, M. J., Breidenthal, S. E., Ophoff, R. A., et al. (2004). Genetic contributions to social impulsivity and aggressiveness in vervet monkeys. *Biological Psychology, 55*, 642–647.

Falk, D. (2000). *Primate diversity.* New York: Norton.

Faustman, W. O., King, R. J., Faull, K. F. Moses, J. A., Jr., Benson, K. L., Zarcone, V. P., et al. (1991). MMPI measures of impulsivity and depression correlate with CSF 5-HIAA and HVA in depression but not schizophrenia. *Journal of Affective Disorders, 22*, 235–239.

Fava, M., Rosenbaum, J. F., Pava, J. A., McCarthy, M. K., Steingard, R. J., & Bouffides, E. (1993). Anger attacks in unipolar depression. Part 1: Clinical correlates and response to fluoxetine treatment. *American Journal of Psychiatry, 150*, 1158–1163.

Fava, M., Vuolo, R. D., Wright, E. C., Nierenberg, A. A., Alpert, J. E., & Rosenbaum, J. F. (2000). Fenfluramine challenge in unipolar depression with and without anger attacks. *Psychiatry Research, 94*, 9–18.

Ferrier, D. (1876). *The functions of the brain.* London: Smith, Elder.

Finn, P. R., Young, S. N., Pihl, R. O., & Ervin, F. R. (1998). The effects of acute plasma tryptophan manipulation on hostile mood: The influence of trait hostility. *Aggressive Behavior, 24*, 173–185.

Fishbein, D. H., Lozovsky, D., & Jaffe, J. H. (1989). Impulsivity, aggression, and neuroendocrine responses to serotonergic stimulation in substance abusers. *Biological Psychiatry, 25*, 1049–1066.

Fleagle, J. G. (1999). *Primate adaptation and evolution* (2nd ed.). New York: Academic Press.

Flory, J. D., Manuck, S. B., Ferrell, R. E., Dent, K. M., Peters, D. G., & Muldoon, M. F. (1999). Neuroticism is not associated with the serotonin transporter (5-HTTLPR) polymorphism. *Molecular Psychiatry, 4*, 93–96.

Foley, D. L., Eaves, L. J., Wormley, B., Silberg, J. L., Maes, H. H., Kuhn, J., et al. (2004). Childhood adversity, monoamine oxidase A genotype, and risk for conduct disorder. *Archives of General Psychiatry, 61*, 738–744.

Gabel, S., Stadler, J., Bjorn, J., Shindledecker, R., & Bowden, C. (1993). Dopamine-beta-hydroxylase in behaviorally disturbed youth. *Biological Psychiatry, 34*, 434–442.

Garattini, S., Bizzi, Z., Caccia, S., Mennini, T., & Samanin, R. (1988). Progress in assessing the role of serotonin in the control of food intake. *Clinical Neuropharmacology, 11*, S8–S32.

Gardner, D. L., Lucas, P. B., & Cowdry, R. W. (1990). CSF metabolites in borderline personality disorder compared with normal controls. *Biological Psychiatry, 28,* 247–254.

Garpenstrand, H., Norton, N., Damberg, M., Rylander, G., Forslund, K., Mattila-Evenden, M., et al. (2002). A regulatory monoamine oxidase A promoter polymorphism and personality traits. *Neuropsychobiology, 46,* 190–193.

Gelernter, J., Kranzler, H., Coccaro, E. F., Siever, L. J., & New, A. S. (1998). Serotonin transporter protein gene polymorphism and personality measures in African American and European American subjects. *American Journal of Psychiatry, 155,* 1332–1338.

Gerald, M. S., & Higley, J. D. (2002). Evolutionary underpinnings of excessive alcohol consumption. *Addiction, 97,* 415–425.

Gerald, M. S., Higley, S., Lussier, I. D., Westergaard, G. C., Suomi, S. J., & Higley, J. D. (2002). Variation in reproductive outcomes for captive male rhesus macaques (*Macaca mulatta*) differing in CSF 5-hydroxyindoleacetic acid concentrations. *Brain, Behavior and Evolution, 60,* 117–124.

Goodall, E. M., Coewn, P. J., Franklin, M., & Silverstone, T. (1993). Ritanserin attenuates anorectic, endocrine and thermic responses to d-fenfluramine in human volunteers. *Psychopharmacology, 112,* 461–466.

Goveas, J. S., Csernansky, J. G., & Coccaro, E. F. (2004). Platelet serotonin content correlates inversely with life history of aggression in personality-disordered subjects. *Psychiatry Research, 126,* 23–32.

Goyer, P. F., Andreason, P. J., Semple, W. E., Clayton, A. H., King, A. C., Compton-Toth, B. A., et al. (1994). Positron-emission tomography and personality disorders. *Neuropsychopharmacology, 10,* 21–28.

Grafman, J., Schwab, K., Warden, D., Pridgen, A., Brown, H., & Salazar, A. (1996). Frontal lobe injuries, violence, and aggression: A report of the Vietnam head injury study. *Neurology, 46,* 1231–1238.

Graham, J. R. (2000) *MMPI-2: Assessing personality and psychopathology* (3rd ed.). New York: Oxford University Press.

Greenberg, B. D., Li, Q., Lucas, F. R., Hu, S., Sirota, L. A., Benjamin, J., et al. (2000). Association between the serotonin transporter promoter polymorphism and personality traits in a primarily female population sample. *American Journal of Medical Genetics (Neuropsychiatric Genetics), 96,* 202–216.

Grimsby, J., Toth, M., Chen, K., Kumazawa, T., Klaidman, L., Adams, J. D., et al. (1997). Increased stress response and beta-phenylethylamine in MAOB-deficient mice. *Nature Genetics, 17,* 206–210.

Hallikainen, T., Saito, T., Lachman, H. M., Volavka, J., Pohjalainen, T., Ryynanen, O.-P., et al. (1999). Association between low activity serotonin transporter promoter genotype and early onset alcoholism with habitual impulsive violent behavior. *Molecular Psychiatry, 4,* 385–388.

Halperin, J. M., Newcorn, J. H., Schwartz, S. T., Sharma, V., Siever, L. J., Koda, V. H., et al. (1997). Age-related changes in the association between serotonergic function and aggression in boys with ADHD. *Biological Psychiatry, 41,* 682–689.

Halperin, J. M., Schulz, K. P., McKay, K. E., Sharma, V., & Newcorn, J. H. (2003). Familial correlates of central serotonin function in children with disruptive behavior disorders. *Psychiatry Research, 119,* 205–216.

Halperin, J. M., Sharma, V., Siever, L. J., Schwartz, S. T., Matier, K., Wornell, G., et al. (1994). Serotonergic function in aggressive and nonaggressive boys with attention deficit hyperactivity disorder. *American Journal of Psychiatry, 151,* 243–248.

Handelsman, L., Holloway, K., Kayn, R. S., Sturiano, C., Rinaldi, P. J., Bernstein, D. P., et al. (1996). Hostility is associated with a low prolactin response to *meta*-chlorophenylpiperazine in abstinent alcoholics. *Alcoholism: Clinical and Experimental Research, 20,* 824–829.

Hanna, G. L., Yuwiler, A., & Coates, J. K. (1995). Whole blood serotonin and disruptive behaviors in juvenile obsessive-compulsive disorder. *Journal of the American Academy of Child and Adolescent Psychiatry, 34,* 28–35.

Hart, S. D., & Hare, R. D. (1997). Psychopathy: Assessment and association with criminal conduct. In D. M. Stoff, J. Breiling, & J. D. Maser (Eds.), *Handbook of antisocial behavior* (pp. 22–35). New York: Wiley.

Heils, A., Teufel, A., Petri, S., Stober, G., Riederer, P., Bengel, D., et al. (1996). Allelic variation in human serotonin transporter gene expression. *Journal of Neurochemistry, 66,* 2621–2624.

Heinrichs, W. (1989). Frontal cerebral lesions and violent incidents in chronic neuropsychiatric patients. *Biological Psychiatry, 25,* 174–178.

Hibbeln, J. R., Umhau, J. L., Linnoila, M., George, D. T., Ragan, P. W., Shoaf, S. E., et al. (1998). A replication study of violent and nonviolent subjects: Cerebrospinal fluid metabolites of serotonin and dopamine are predicted by plasma essential fatty acids. *Biological Psychiatry, 44,* 243–249.

Higley, J., Hasert, M., Suomi, S., & Linnoila, M. (1998). The serotonin reuptake inhibitor sertraline reduces excessive alcohol consumption in nonhuman primates: Effect of stress. *Neuropsychopharmacology, 18,* 431–443.

Higley, J. D., King, S. T., Hasert, M. J., Champoux, M., Suomi, S. J., & Linnoila, M. (1996). Stability of interindividual differences in serotonin function and its relationship to severe aggression and competent social behavior in rhesus macaque females. *Neuropsychopharmacology, 14,* 67–76.

Higley, J. D., & Linnoila, M. (1997). Low central nervous system serotonergic activity is traitlike and correlates with impulsive behavior: A nonhuman primate model investigating genetic and environmental influences on neurotransmission. *Annals of the New York Academy of Sciences, 836,* 39–56.

Higley, J. D., Mehlman, P. T., Higley, S. B., Fernald, B., Vickers, J., Lindell, S. G., et al. (1996). Excessive mortality in young fee-ranging male nonhuman primates with low cerebrospinal fluid 5-hydroxyindoleacetic acid concentrations. *Archives of General Psychiatry, 53,* 537–542.

Higley, J. D., Mehlman, P. T., Poland, R. E., Taub, D. M., Vickers, J., et al. (1996). CSF testosterone and 5-HIAA correlate with different types of aggressive behaviors. *Biological Psychiatry, 40,* 1067–1082.

Higley, J. D., Mehlman, P. T., Taub, D. M., Higley, S. B., Suomi, S. J., Linnoila, M., et al. (1992). Cerebrospinal fluid monoamine and adrenal correlates of aggression in free-ranging rhesus monkeys. *Archives of General Psychiatry, 49,* 436–441.

Higley, J. D., Suomi, S. J., & Linnoila, M. (1996a). A nonhuman primate model of Type II excessive alcohol consumption? Part 1. Low cerebrospinal fluid 5-hydroxyindoleacetic acid concentrations and diminished social competence correlate with excessive alcohol consumption. *Alcoholism: Clinical and Experimental Research, 20,* 629–642.

Higley, J. D., Suomi, S. J., & Linnoila, M. (1996b). A nonhuman primate model of Type II alcoholism? Part 2. Diminished social competence and excessive aggression correlates with low cerebrospinal fluid 5-hydroxyindoleacetic acid concentrations. *Alcoholism: Clinical and Experimental Research, 20,* 643–650.

Higley, J. D., Thompson, W. W., Champoux, M., Goldman, D., Hasert, M. F., Kraemer, G. W., et al. (1993). Paternal and maternal genetic and environmental contributions to cerebrospinal fluid monoamine metabolites in rhesus monkeys (*Macaca mulatta*). *Archives of General Psychiatry, 50,* 615–623.

Hoyer, D. (1988). Functional correlates of serotonin 5-HT₁ recognition sites. *Journal of Receptor Research, 8,* 59–81.

Hoyer, D., Clarke, E. D. E., Fozard, J. R., Hartig, P. R., Martin, G. R., Mylecharane, E. J., et al. (1994). VII. International Union of Pharmacology classification of receptors for 5-hydroxytryptamine (serotonin). *Pharmacological Reviews, 46,* 158–203.

Huang, Y., Grailhe, R., Arango, V., Hen, R., & Mann, J. J. (1999). Relationship of psychopathology to the human serotonin$_{1B}$ genotype and receptor binding kinetics in postmortem brain tissue. *Neuropsychopharmacology, 21,* 238–246.

Hwu, H.-G., & Chen, C.-H. (2000). Association of 5HT2A receptor gene polymorphism and alcohol abuse with behavior problems. *American Journal of Medical Genetics (Neuropsychiatric Genetics), 96,* 797–800.

Jonsson, E. G., Goldman, D., Spurlock, G., Gustavsson, J. P., Nielsen, D. A., Linnoila, M., et al. (1997). Tryptophan hydroxylase and catechol-O-methyltransferase gene polymorphisms: Relationships to monoamine metabolite concentrations in CSF of healthy volunteers. *European Archives of Psychiatry and Clinical Neuroscience, 247,* 297–302.

Jonsson, E. G., Nothen, M. M., Gustavsson, J. P., Berggard, C., Bunzel, R., Forslund, K., et al. (2001). No association between serotonin 2A receptor gene variants and personality traits. *Psychiatric Genetics, 11,* 11–17.

Jorm, A. F., Henderson, A. S., Jacomb, P. A., Christensen, H., Korten, A. E., Rodgers, B., et al. (1998). An association study of a functional polymorphism of the serotonin transporter gene with personality and psychiatric symptoms. *Molecular Psychiatry, 3,* 449–451.

Jorm, A. F., Henderson, A. S., Jacomb, P. A., Christensen, H., Korten, A. E., Rodgers, B., et al. (2000). Association of a functional polymorphism of the monoamine oxidase A gene promoter with personality and psychiatric symptoms. *Psychiatric Genetics, 10,* 87–90.

Kahn, R. S., Kalus, O., Wetzler, S., Cahn, W., Asnis, G. M., & van Praag, H. M. (1990). Effects of serotonin antagonists on *m*-chlorophenylpiperazine-mediated responses in normal subjects. *Psychiatry Research, 33,* 189–198.

Kahn, R. S., & Wetzler, S. (1991). m-Chlorophenylpiperazine as a probe of serotonin function. *Biological Psychiatry, 30,* 1139–1166.

Kamali, M., Oquendo, M. A., & Mann, J. J. (2001). Understanding the neurobiology of suicidal behavior. *Depression and Anxiety, 14,* 164–176.

Kaplan, J. R., Fontenot, M. B., Berard, J., Manuck, S. B., & Mann, J. J. (1995). Delayed dispersal and elevated monoaminergic activity in free-ranging rhesus monkeys. *American Journal of Primatology, 35,* 229–234.

Kaplan, J. R., Manuck, S. B., Fontenot, M. B., & Mann, J. J. (2002). Central nervous system monoamine correlates of social dominance in cynomolgus monkeys (*Macaca fascicularis*). *Neuropsychopharmacology, 26,* 431–443.

Kato, T., Dong, B., Ishii, K., & Kinemuchi, H. (1986). Brain dialysis: *In vivo* metabolism of dopamine and serotonin by monoamine oxidase A but not B in the striatum of unrestrained rats. *Journal of Neurochemistry, 46,* 1277–1282.

Kitahama, K., Maeda, T., Denney, R. M., & Jouvet, M. (1994). Monoamine oxidase: Distribution in the cat brain studied by enzyme- and immunohistochemistry. Recent progress. *Progress in Neurobiology, 42,* 53–78.

Klaasen, T., Riedel, W. J., van Praag, H. M., Menheere, P. P. C. A., & Griez, E. (2002). Neuroendocrine response to meta-chlorophenylpiperazine and ipsapirone in relation to anxiety and aggression. *Psychiatry Research, 113,* 29–40.

Knutson, B., Wolkowitz, W. M., Cole, S. W., Chan, T., Moore, E. A., Johnson, R. C., et al. (1998). Selective alteration of personality and social behavior by serotonergic intervention. *American Journal of Psychiatry, 155,* 373–379.

Koller, G., Bondy, B., Preuss, U. W., Bottlender, M., & Soyka, M. (2003). No association between a polymorphism in the promoter region of the MAOA gene with antisocial personality traits in alcoholics. *Alcohol and Alcoholism, 38,* 31–34.

Krakowski, M. (2003). Violence and serotonin: Influence of impulse control, affect regulation, and social functioning. *Journal of Neuropsychiatry and Clinical Neuroscience, 15,* 294–305.

Kramer, P. D. (1993). *Listening to Prozac.* New York: Viking.

Kranzler, H. R., Hernandez-Avila, C. A., & Gelernter, J. (2002). Polymorphism of the 5-HT1B receptor gene (HTR1B): Strong within-locus linkage disequilibrium without association to antisocial substance dependence. *Neuropsychopharmacology, 26,* 115–122.

Krueger, R. F., Hicks, B. M., Patrick, C. J., Carlson, S. R., Iacono, W. G., & McGue, M. (2002). Etiological connections among substance dependence, antisocial behavior, and personality: Modeling the externalizing spectrum. *Journal of Abnormal Psychology, 111,* 411–424.

Kruesi, M. J. P., Hibbs, E. D., Zahn, T. P., Keysor, C. S., Hamburger, S. D., Bartko, J. J., et al. (1992). A 2-year prospective follow-up study of children and adolescents with disruptive behavior disorders. *Archives of General Psychiatry, 49,* 429–435.

Kruesi, M. J. P., Rapoport, J. L., Hamburger, S., Hibbs, E., Potter, W. Z., Nenane, M., et al. (1990). Cerebrospinal fluid monoamine metabolites, aggression, and impulsivity in disruptive behavior disorders of children and adolescents. *Archives of General Psychiatry, 47,* 419–422.

Kyes, R. C., Botchin, M. B., Kaplan, J. R., Manuck, S. B., & Mann, J. J. (1995). Aggression and brain serotonergic responsivity: Response to slides in male macaques. *Physiology and Behavior, 57,* 205–208.

Lappalainen, J., Long, J. C., Eggert, M., Ozaki, N., Robin, R. W., Brown, G. L., et al. (1998). Linkage of antisocial alcoholism to the serotonin 5-HT1B receptor gene in 2 populations. *Archives of General Psychiatry, 55,* 989–994.

Lecrubier, Y., Braconnier, A., Said, S., & Payan, C. (1995). The impulsivity rating scale (IRS): Preliminary results. *European Psychiatry, 10,* 331–338.

Lee, J.-H., Kim, H.-T., & Hyun, D.-S. (2003). Possible association between serotonin transporter promoter region polymorphism and impulsivity in Koreans. *Psychiatry Research, 118,* 19–24.

Lesch, K. P., Bengel, D., Heils, A., Sabol, S. Z., Greenberg, B. D., Petri, S., et al. (1996). Association of anxiety-related traits with a polymorphism in the serotonin transporter gene regulatory region. *Science, 274,* 1527–1531.

Lesch, K. P., Mayer, S., Disselkamp-Tietze, J., Hoh, A., Schoellnhammer, G., & Schulte, H. M. (1990). Subsensitivity of the 5-hydroxytryptamine 1A (5-HT$_{1A}$) receptor-mediated hypothermic response to ipsapirone in unipolar depression. *Life Sciences, 46,* 1271–1277.

Lesch, K. P., Mayer, S., Disselkamp-Tietze, J., Hoh, A., Wiesmann, M., Osterheider, M., et al. (1990). 5-HT$_{1A}$ receptor responsivity in unipolar depression: Evaluation of ipsapirone-induced ACTH and cortisol secretion in patients and control. *Biological Psychiatry, 28,* 620–628.

Lesch, K. P., Meyer, J., Glatz, K., Flugge, G., Hinney, A., Hebebrand, J., et al. (1996). The 5-HT transporter gene-linked polymorphic region (5-HTTLPR) in evolutionary perspective: Alternative biallelic variation in rhesus monkeys. *Journal of Neural Transmission, 104,* 1259–1266.

Lesch, K. P., Sohnle, K., Poten, B., Schoellnhammer, G., Rupprecht, R., & Schulte, H. M. (1990). Corticotropin and cortisol secretion after central 5-hydroxytryptamine-1A (5-HT1A) receptor activation: Effects of 5-HT receptor and a$_2$-adrenoreceptor antagonists. *Journal of Clinical Endocrinology and Metabolism, 70,* 670–674.

Lester, D. (1995). The concentration of neurotransmitter metabolites in the cerebrospinal fluid of suicidal individuals: A meta-analysis. *Pharmacopsychiatry, 28,* 45–50.

Lewis, D. A., & Sherman, B. M. (1985). Serotonergic regulation of prolactin and growth hormone secretion in man. *Acta Endocrinologica, 110,* 152–157.

Lidberg, L., Belfrage, H., Bertilsson, L., Evenden, M. M., & Asberg, M. (2000). Suicide attempts and impulse control disorder are related to low cerebrospinal fluid 5-HIAA in mentally disordered violent offenders. *Acta Psychiatrica Scandinavica, 101,* 395–402.

Lidberg, L., Tuck, J. R., Asberg, M., Scalia-Tomba, P., & Bertilsson, L. (1985). Homicide, suicide and CSF 5-HIAA. *Acta Psychiatrica Scandinavica*, 71, 230–236.

Liebenluft, E., Fiero, P. L., & Rubinow, D. R. (1994). Effects of the menstrual cycle on dependent variables in mood disorder research. *Archives of General Psychiatry*, 51, 761–781.

Limson, R., Goldman, D., Roy, A., Lamparski, D., Ravitz, B., Adinoff, B., et al. (1991). Personality and cerebrospinal fluid monoamine metabolites in alcoholics and controls. *Archives of General Psychiatry*, 48, 437–441.

Linnoila, M., Virkkunen, M., Scheinin, M., Nuutila, A., Rimon, R., & Goodwin, F. K. (1983). Low cerebrospinal fluid 5-hydroxyindoleacetic acid concentration differentiates impulsive from nonimpulsive violent behavior. *Life Sciences*, 33, 2609–2614.

Loeber, R., Wung, P., Keenan, K., Giroux, B., Stouthamer-Loeber, M., van Kammen, W. B., et al. (1993). Developmental pathways in disruptive child behavior. *Development and Psychopathology*, 5, 103–133.

MacMillan, J., & Kofoed, L. (1984). Sociobiology and antisocial personality: An alternative perspective. *The Journal of Nervous and Mental Disease*, 172, 701–706.

Macmillan, M. (1992). Inhibition and the control of behavior: From Gall to Freud via Phineas Gage and the frontal lobes. *Brain and Cognition*, 19, 72–104.

Macmillan, M. (2000). *An odd kind of fame*. Cambridge, MA: MIT Press.

Mann, J. J., Brent, D. A., & Arango, V. (2001). The neurobiology and genetics of suicide and attempted suicide: A focus on the serotonergic system. *Neuropsychopharmacology*, 24, 467–477.

Mann, J. J., McBride, P. A., Anderson, G. M., & Mieczkowski, T. A. (1992). Platelet and whole blood serotonin content in depressed inpatients: Correlations with acute and life-time psychopathology. *Biological Psychiatry*, 32, 243–257.

Mann, J. J., McBride, P. A., Brown, R. P., Linnoila, M., Leon, A. C., DeMeo, M., et al. (1992). Relationship between central and peripheral serotonin indexes in depressed and suicidal psychiatric inpatients. *Archives of General Psychiatry*, 49, 442–446.

Manuck, S. B., Flory, J. D., Ferrell, R. E., Dent, K. M., Mann, J. J., & Muldoon, M. F. (1999). Aggression and anger-related traits associated with a polymorphism of the tryptophan hydroxylase gene. *Biological Psychiatry*, 45, 603–614.

Manuck, S. B., Flory, J. D., Ferrell, R. E., Mann, J. J., & Muldoon, M. F. (2000). A regulatory polymorphism of the monoamine oxidase-A gene may be associated with variability in aggression, impulsivity, and central nervous system serotonergic responsivity. *Psychiatry Research*, 95, 9–23.

Manuck, S. B., Flory, J. D., Ferrell, R. E., & Muldoon, M. F. (2004). Socio-economic status covaries with central nervous system serotonergic responsivity as a function of allelic variation in the serotonin transporter gene-linked polymorphic region. *Psychoneuroendocrinology*, 29, 651–668.

Manuck, S. B., Flory, J. D., McCaffery, J. M., Matthews, K. A., Mann, J. J., & Muldoon, M. F. (1998). Aggression, impulsivity, and central nervous system serotonergic responsivity in a nonpatient sample. *Neuropsychopharmacology*, 19, 287–299.

Manuck, S. B., Flory, J. D., Muldoon, M. F., & Ferrell, R. E. (2002). Central nervous system serotonergic responsivity and aggressive disposition in men. *Physiology and Behavior*, 77, 705–709.

Manuck, S. B., Flory, J. D., Muldoon, M. F., & Ferrell, R. E. (2003). A neurobiology of intertemporal choice. In G. Loewenstein, D. Read, & R. Baumeister (Eds.), *Time and decision: Economic and psychological perspective on intertemporal choice* (pp. 139–172). New York: Sage.

Manuck, S. B., Kaplan, J. R., Rymeski, B. A., Fairbanks, L. A., & Wilson, M. E. (2003). Approach to a social stranger is associated with low central nervous system serotonergic responsivity in female cynomolgus monkeys (*Macaca fascicularis*). *American Journal of Primatology*, 61, 187–194.

Masellis, M., Basile, V., Meltzer, H. Y., Liverman, J. A., Sevy, S., Macciardi, F. M., et al. (1998). Serotonin subtype 2 receptor genes and clinical response to clozapine in schizophrenia patients. *Neuropsychopharmacology*, 10, 123–132.

Maskall, D. D., Zis, A. P., Lam, R. W., Clark, C. M., & Kuan, A. J. (1995). Prolactin response to buspirone challenge in the presence of dopaminergic blockade. *Biological Psychiatry*, 38, 235–239.

McBride, P. A., Anderson, G. M., Hertzig, M. E., Sweeney, J. A., Kream, J., Cohen, D. J., et al. (1989). Serotonergic responsivity in male young adults with autistic disorder. *Archives of General Psychiatry*, 46, 213–221.

McBride, P. A., Tierney, H., DeMeo, M., Chen, J.-S., & Mann, J. J. (1990). Effects of age and gender on CNS serotonergic responsivity in normal adults. *Biological Psychiatry*, 27, 1143–1155.

McDougle, C. J., Naylor, S. T., Cohen, D. J., Volkmar, F. R., Heninger, G. R., & Price, L. H. (1996). A double-blind, placebo-controlled study of fluvoxamine in adults with autistic disorder. *Archives of General Psychiatry*, 63, 1001–1008.

Mealey, L. (1995). The sociobiology of sociopathy: An

integrated evolutionary model. *Behavioral and Brain Sciences, 18,* 523–542.

Mehlman, P. T., Higley, S. D., Faucher, I., Lilly, A. A., Taub, D. M., Vickers, J., et al. (1994). Low CSF 5-HIAA concentrations and severe aggression and impaired impulse control in nonhuman primates. *American Journal Psychiatry, 151,* 1485–1491.

Mehlman, P. T., Higley, J. D., Faucher, I., Lilly, A. A., Taub, D. M., Vickers, J., et al. (1995). Correlation of CSF 5-HIAA concentration with sociality and the timing of emigration in free-ranging primates. *American Journal of Psychiatry, 152,* 907–913.

Mehlman, P. T., Higley, J. D., Fernald, B. J., Sallee, F. R., Suomi, S. J., & Linnoila, M. (1997). CSF 5-HIAA, testosterone, and sociosexual behaviors in free-ranging male rhesus macaques in the mating season. *Psychiatry Research, 72,* 89–102.

Meltzer, H. Y., Lee, H. S., & Nash, J. F., Jr., (1992). Effects of buspirone on prolactin secretion is not mediated by 5-HT-1a receptor stimulation. *Archives of General Psychiatry, 49,* 163–164.

Meltzer, H. Y., & Maes, M. (1994). Effects of buspirone on plasma prolactin and cortisol levels in major depressed and normal subjects. *Biological Psychiatry, 35,* 316–325.

Meltzer, H. Y., & Maes, M. (1995a). Effects of ipsapirone on plasma cortisol and body temperature in major depression. *Biological Psychiatry, 38,* 450–457.

Meltzer, H. Y., & Maes, M. (1995b). Pindolol pretreatment blocks stimulation by meta-chlorophenyl-piperazine of prolactin but not cortisol secretion in normal men. *Psychiatry Research, 58,* 89–98.

Mintzer, J., Brawman-Mintzer, O., Mirski, D. F., Unger, R., Nietert, P., Meeks, A., et al. (1998). Fenfluramine challenge test as a marker of serotonin activity in patients with Alzheimer's dementia and agitation. *Biological Psychiatry, 44.* 918–921.

Mischoulon, D., Dougherty, D. D., Bottonari, K. A., Gresham, R. L., Sonawalla, S. B., Fischman, A. J., et al. (2002). An open pilot study of nefazodone in depression with anger attacks: Relationship between clinical response and receptor binding. *Psychiatry Research, 116,* 151–161.

Moeller, F. G., Allen, T., Cherek, D. R., Dougherty, D. M., Lane, S., & Swann, A. C. (1998). Ipsapirone neuroendocrine challenge: Relationship to aggression as measured in the human laboratory. *Psychiatry Research, 81,* 31–38.

Moeller, F. G., Steinberg, J. L., Petty, F., Fulton, M., Cherek, D. R., Kramer, G., et al. (1994). Serotonin and impulsive/aggressive behavior in cocaine dependent subjects. *Progress in Neuropsychopharmacology and Biological Psychiatry, 18,* 1027–1035.

Moffitt, T. E. (1993). "Life-course-persistent" and "adolescence-limited" antisocial behavior: A developmental taxonomy. *Psychological Bulletin, 100,* 674–701.

Moffitt, T. E. (2003). Life-course-persistent and adolescence-limited antisocial behavior: A 10-year review and a research agenda. In B. B. Lahey, T. E. Moffitt, & A. Caspi (Eds.), *Causes of conduct disorder and juvenile delinquency* (pp. 49–75). New York: Guilford Press.

Moffitt, T. E., Brammer, G. L., Caspi, A., Fawcett, J. P., Raleigh, M., Yuwiler, A., et al. (1998). Whole blood serotonin relates to violence in an epidemiological study. *Biological Psychiatry, 43,* 446–457.

Moller, S. E., Mortensen, E. L., Breum, L., Alling, C., Larsen, O. G., Boge-Rasmussen, T., et al. (1996). Aggression and personality: Association with amino acids and monoamine metabolites. *Psychological Medicine, 26,* 323–331.

Moreno, F. A., McGavin, C., Malan, T. P., Gelenberg, A. J., Heninger, G. R., Mathe, A. A., et al. (2000). Tryptophan depletion selectively reduces CSF 5-HT metabolites in healthy young men: Results from single lumbar puncture sampling technique. *International Journal of Neuropsychopharmacology, 3,* 277–283.

Moss, H. B., Yao, J. K., & Panzak, G. L. (1990). Serotonergic responsivity and behavioral dimensions in antisocial personality disorder with substance abuse. *Biological Psychiatry, 28,* 325–338.

Mulder, R. T., & Joyce, P. J. (2002). Relationship of temperament and behaviour measures to the prolactin response to fenfluramine in depressed men. *Psychiatry Research, 109,* 221–228.

Muldoon, M. F., Manuck, S. B., Jansma, C. L., Moore, A. L., Perel, J., & Mann, J. J. (1996). D,l-fenfluramine challenge test: Experience in nonpatient sample. *Biological Psychiatry, 39,* 25–338.

New, A. S., Buchsbaum, M. S., Hazlett, E. A., Goodman, M., Koenigsberg, H. W., Lo, J., et al. (2004). Fluoxetine increases relative metabolic rate in prefrontal cortex in impulsive aggression. *Psychopharmacology, 176,* 451–458.

New, A. S., Gelernter, J., Goodman, M., Mitropoulou, V., Koenigsberg, H., Silverman, J., et al. (2001). Suicide, impulsive aggression, and HTR1B genotype. *Biological Psychiatry, 50,* 62–65.

New, A. S., Gelernter, J., Yovell, Y., Trestman, R. L., Nielsen, D. A., Silverman, J., et al. (1998). Tryptophan hydroxylase genotype is associated with impulsive-aggression measures: A preliminary study. *American Journal of Medical Genetics (Neuropsychiatric Genetics), 81,* 13–17.

New, A. S., Hazlett, E. A., Buschsbaum, M. S., Goodman, M., Reynolds, D., Mitropoulou, V., et al. (2002). Blunted prefrontal cortical [18]flurodeoxyglucose positron emission tomography response to meta-chlorophenylpiperazine in impulsive aggression. *Archives of General Psychiatry, 59,* 621–629.

New, A. S., Trestman, R. F., Mitropoulou, B., Godman, M., Koenigsberg, H. H., Silverman, J., et al. (2004). Low prolactin response to fenfluramine in impulsive aggression. *Journal of Psychiatric Research, 38,* 223–230.

Nielsen, D. A., Goldman, D., Virkkunen, M., Tokola, R., Rawlings, R., & Linnoila, M. (1994). Suicidality and 5-hydroxyindoleacetic acid concentration associated with a tryptophan hydroxylase polymorphism. *Archives of General Psychiatry, 61,* 34–38.

Nielsen, D. A., Jenkins, G. L., Stefanisko, K. M., Jefferson, K. K., & Goldman, D. (1997). Sequence, splice site and population frequency distribution analyses of the polymorphic human tryptophan hydroxylase intron 7. *Molecular Brain Research, 45,* 145–148.

Nielsen, D. A., Virkkunen, M., Lappalainen, J., Eggert, M., Brown, G. L., Long, J. C., et al. (1998). A tryptophan hydroxylase gene marker for suicidality and alcoholism. *Archives of General Psychiatry, 55,* 593–602.

Nisbett, R. E., & Cohen, D. (1996). *Culture of honor: The psychology of violence in the South.* Boulder, CO: Westview.

Nolan, K. A., Volavka, J., Lachman, H. M., & Saito, T. (2000). An association between a polymorphism of the tryptophan hydroxylase gene and aggression in schizophrenia and schizoaffective disorder. *Psychiatric Genetics, 10,* 109–115.

O'Keane, V., O'Hanlon, M., Webb, M., & Dinan, T. (1991). D-Fenfluramine/prolactin response throughout the menstrual cycle: Evidence for an oestrogen-induced alteration. *Clinical Endocrinology, 34,* 289–292.

O'Keane, V. O., Moloney, E., O'Neill, H., O'Connor, A., Smith, R., & Dinan, T. G. (1992). Blunted prolactin responses to d-fenfluramine in sociopathy: Evidence for subsensitivity of central serotonergic function. *British Journal of Psychiatry, 160,* 643–646.

Ono, H., Shirakawa, O., Kitamura, N., Hashimoto, T., Nishiguchi, N., Nishimura, A., et al. (2002). Tryptophan hydroxylase immunoreactivity is altered by the genetic variation in postmortem brain samples of both suicide victims and controls. *Molecular Psychiatry, 7,* 1127–1132.

Oxenstierna, G., Edman, G., Iselius, L., Oreland, L., Ross, S. B., & Sedvall, G. (1986). Concentrations of monoamine metabolites in the cerebrospinal fluid of twins and unrelated individuals—a genetic study. *Journal of Psychiatric Research, 20,* 19–29.

Paoloni-Giacobino, A., Mouthon, D., Lambercy, C., Vessaz, M., Soutant-Zimmerli, S., Rudolph, W., et al. (2000). Identification and analysis of new sequence variants in the human tryptophan hydroxylase (TpH) gene. *Molecular Psychiatry, 5,* 49–55.

Paris, J. (1997). Antisocial and borderline personality: Two separate disorders or two aspects of the same psychopathology? *Comprehensive Psychiatry, 38,* 237–242.

Paris, J., Zweig-Frank, H., Ng Ying Kin, N. M. K., Schwartz, G., Steiger, H., & Nair, N. P. V. (2004). Neurobiological correlates of diagnosis and underlying traits in patients with borderline personality disorder compared with normal controls. *Psychiatry Research, 121,* 239–252.

Park, S. B. G., & Cowen, P. J. (1995). Effect of pindolol on the prolactin response to d-fenfluramine. *Psychopharmacology, 118,* 471–474.

Parsey, R. V., Oquendo, M. A., Simpson, N. R., Ogden, R. T., VanHeertum, R., Arango, V., et al. (2002). Effects of sex, age, and aggressive traits in men on brain serotonin 5-HT$_{1A}$ receptor binding potential measured by PET using [C-11]WAY-100635. *Brain Research, 954,* 173–182.

Parsian, A., & Cloninger, C. R. (2001). Serotonergic pathway genes and subtypes of alcoholism: Association studies. *Psychiatry Genetics, 11,* 89–94.

Patkar, A. A., Berrettinin, W. H., Hoehe, M., Thornton, C. C., Gottheil, E., Hill, K., et al. (2002). Serotonin transporter polymorphisms and measures of impulsivity, aggression, and sensation seeking among African-American cocaine-dependent individuals. *Psychiatry Research, 110,* 103–110.

Pihl, R. O., Young, S. N., Harden, P., Plotnick, S., Chamberlain, B., & Ervin, F. R. (1995). Acute effect of altered tryptophan levels and alcohol on aggression in normal human males. *Psychopharmacology, 119,* 353–360.

Pine, D. S., Coplan, J. D., Wasserman, G. A., Miller, L. S., Fried, J. E., Davies, M., et al. (1997). Neuroendocrine response to fenfluramine challenge in boys: Associations with aggressive behavior and adverse rearing. *Archives of General Psychiatry, 54,* 839–846.

Placidi, G. P. A., Oquendo, M. A., Malone, K. M., Huang, Y.-Y., Ellis, S. P., & Mann, J. J. (2001). Aggressivity, suicide attempts, and depression: Relationship to cerebrospinal fluid monoamine metabolite levels. *Biological Psychiatry, 50,* 783–791.

Pliszka, S. R., Rogeness, G. A., Renner, P., Sherman, J., & Broussard, T. (1988). Plasma neurochemistry in juvenile offenders. *Journal of the American Academy of Child and Adolescent Psychiatry, 27,* 588–594.

Pollock, B. G., Mulsant, B. H., Rosen, J., Sweet, R. A., Mazumdar, S., Bharucha, A., et al. (2002). Comparison of citalopram, perphenazine, and placebo for the acute treatment of psychosis and behavioral disturbances in hospitalized, demented patients. *American Journal of Psychiatry, 159,* 460–165.

Preuss, U. W., Koller, G., Bondy, B., Bahlmann, M., & Soyka, M. (2001). Impulsive traits and 5-HT2A receptor promoter polymorphism in alcohol dependents: Possible association but no influence on personality disorders. *Neuropsychobiology, 43,* 186–191.

Preuss, U. W., Soyka, M., Bahlmann, M., Wenzel, K., Behrens, S., de Jonge, S., et al. (2000). Serotonin transporter gene regulatory region polymorphism (5-HTTLPR), [³H]paroxetine binding in healthy control subjects and alcohol-dependent patients and their relationships to impulsivity. *Psychiatry Research, 96,* 51–61.

Pusey, A. E., & Packer, C. (1987). Dispersal and philopatry. In B. B. Smuts, D. L. Cheney, R. M. Seyfarth, R. W. Wrangham, & T. T. Struhsaker (Eds.), *Primate societies* (pp. 250–266). Chicago: University of Chicago Press.

Quattrone, A., Schettini, G., DiRenzo, G. F., Tedeshi, G., & Preziosi, P. (1979). Effect of midbrain raphe lesion or 5,7-dihydroxytryptamine treatments on the prolactin-releasing action of quipazine and d-fenfluramine in rats. *Brain Research, 174,* 71–79.

Quattrone, A., Tedeschi, G., Aguglia, U., Scopacasa, F., DiRenzo, G. F., & Annunziato, L. (1983). Prolactin secretion in man, a useful tool to evaluate the activity of drugs on central 5–hydroxytryptaminergic neurons: Studies with fenfluramine. *British Journal of Pharmacology, 16,* 471–475.

Raine, A., Meloy, J. R., Bihrle, S., Stoddard, J., LaCasse, L., & Buschsbaum, M. S. (1998). Reduced prefrontal and increased subcortical brain functioning assessed using positron emission tomography in predatory and affective murderers. *Behavioral Sciences and the Law, 16,* 319–332.

Raleigh, M. J., McGuire, M. T., Brammer, G. L., Pollack, D. B., & Yuwiler, A. (1991). Serotonergic mechanisms promote dominance acquisition in adult male vervet monkeys. *Brain Research, 559,* 181–190.

Reist, C., Helmeste, D., Albers, L., Chhay, H., & Tang, S. W. (1996). Serotonin indices and impulsivity in normal volunteers. *Psychiatry Research, 60,* 177–184.

Reist, C., Mazzanti, C., Vu, R., Tran, D., & Goldman, D. (2001). Serotonin transporter promoter polymorphism is associated with attenuated prolactin response to fenfluramine. *American Journal of Medical Genetics, 105,* 363–368.

Robins, L. N. (1966). *Deviant children grown up.* Baltimore: Williams & Wilkins.

Rogeness, G. A., Hernandez, J. M., Macedo, C. A., & Mitchell, E. L. (1982). Biochemical differences in children with conduct disorder socialized and undersocialized. *American Journal of Psychiatry, 139,* 307–311.

Rogers, J., Martin, L. J., Comuzzie, A. G., Mann, J. J., Manuck, S. B., Leland, M., et al. (2004). Genetics of monoamine metabolites in baboons: Overlapping sets of genes influence levels of 5-hydroxyindoleacetic acid, 3-hydroxy-4-methoxyphenylglycol, and homovanillic acid. *Biological Psychiatry, 55,* 739–744.

Roggenbach, J., Muller-Oerlinghausen, B., Franke, L. (2002). Suicidality, impulsivity and aggression—is there a link to 5HIAA concentration in the cerebrospinal fluid? *Psychiatry Research, 113,* 193–206.

Rotondo, A., Schuebel, K. E., Bergen, A. W., Aragon, R., Virkkunen, M., Linnoila, M., et al. (1999). Identification of four variants in the tryptophan hydroxylase promoter and association to behavior. *Molecular Psychiatry, 4,* 360–368.

Rowe, D. C. (1996). An adaptive strategy theory of crime and delinquency. In J. D. Hawkins (Ed.), *Delinquency and crime* (pp. 268–314). New York: Cambridge University Press.

Roy, A., Adinoff, B., & Linnoila, M. (1988). Acting out hostility in normal volunteers: Negative correlation with levels of 5HIAA in cerebrospinal fluid. *Psychiatry Research, 24,* 187–194.

Rujescu, D., Giegling, I., Bondy, B., Gietl, A., Zill, P., & Moller, H.-J. (2002). Association of anger-related traits with SNPs in the TPH gene. *Molecular Psychiatry, 7,* 1023–1009.

Sabol, S. Z., Hu, S., & Hamer, D. (1998). A functional polymorphism in the monoamine oxidase A gene promoter. *Human Genetics, 103,* 273–279.

Sade, D. S. (1973). An ethogram for rhesus monkeys: I. Antithetical contrasts in posture and movement. *American Journal of Physical Anthropology, 38,* 537–542.

Saito, T., Lachman, H. M., Diaz, L., Hallikainen, T., Kauhanen, J., Salonen, J. T., et al. (2002). Analysis of monoamine oxidase A (MAOA) promoter polymorphism in Finnish male alcoholics. *Psychiatry Research, 109,* 113–119.

Samochowiec, J., Lesch, K.-P., Rottmann, M., Smolka, M., Syagailo, Y. V., Ookladnova, O., et al. (1999). Association of a regulatory polymorphism in the promoter region of the monamine oxidase A gene with antisocial alcoholism. *Psychiatry Research, 86,* 67–72.

Sander, T., Harms, H., Dufeu, P., Kuhn, S., Hoehe, M., Lesch, K.-P., et al. (1998). Serotonin transporter gene variants in alcohol-dependent subjects with dissocial personality disorder. *Biological Psychiatry, 43,* 908–912.

Sarrias, M. J., Cabre, P., Martinez, E., & Artigas, F. (1990). Relationship between serotonergic measures in blood and cerebrospinal fluid simultaneously obtained in humans. *Journal of Neurochemistry, 54,* 783–786.

Saura, J., Bleuel, Z., Ulrich, J., Mendelowitsch, A., Chen, K., Shih, J. C., et al. (1996). Molecular neuroanatomy of human monoamine oxidases A and B revealed by quantitative enzyme radioautography and *in situ* hybridization histochemistry. *Neuroscience, 70,* 755–774.

Schmidt, L. G., Sander, T., Kuhn, S., Smolka, M., Rommelspacher, H., Samochowiec, J., et al. (2000). Different allele distribution of a regulatory MAOA gene promoter polymorphism in antisocial and anxious-depressive alcoholics. *Journal of Neural Transmission, 107,* 681–689.

Schulz, K. P., Newcorn, J. H., McKay, K. E., Himelstein, J., Koda, V. H., Siever, L. J., et al. (2001). Relationship between central serotonergic function and aggression in prepubertal boys: Effect of age and attention-deficit/hyperactivity disorder. *Psychiatry Research, 101,* 1–10.

Seibyl, J. P., Krystal, J. H., Price, L. H., Woods, S. W., D'Amico, C., et al. (1991). Effects of ritanserin on the behavioral, neuroendocrine, and cardiovascular responses to meta-chlorophenylpiperazine in healthy human subjects. *Psychiatry Research, 38,* 227–236.

Shively, C. A. (1998). Social subordination stress, behavior, and central monoaminergic function in female cynomolgus monkeys. *Biological Psychiatry, 44,* 882–891.

Shively, C. A., Brammer, G. L., Kaplan, J. R., Raleigh, M. J., & Manuck, S. B. (1991). The complex relationship between behavioral attributes, social status, and whole blood serotonin in male *Macaca fascicularis. American Journal of Primatology, 23,* 99–112.

Shively, C. A., Fontenot, M. B., & Kaplan, J. K. (1995). Social status, behavior, and central serotonergic responsivity in female cynomolgus monkeys. *American Journal of Primatology, 37,* 333–330.

Siever, L. J., Buchsbaum, M. S., New, A. S., Spiegel-Cohen, J., Wei, T., Hazlett, E. A., et al. (1999). D,l-fenfluramine response in impulsive personality disorder assessed with [18F]fluorodeoxyglucose positron emission tomography. *Neuropsychopharmacology, 20,* 413–423.

Slutske, W. S., Health, A. C., Dinwiddie, S. H., Madden, P. A. F., Bucholz, K. K., Dunne, M. P., et al. (1998). Common genetic risk factors for conduct disorder and alcohol dependence. *Journal of Abnormal Psychology, 107,* 363–374.

Soloff, P. H., Kelly, T. M., Strotmeyer, S. J., Malone, K. M., & Mann, J. J. (2003). Impulsivity, gender, and response to fenfluramine challenge in borderline personality disorder. *Psychiatry Research, 199,* 11–24.

Soloff, P. H., Lynch, K. G., & Moss, H. B. (2000). Serotonin, impulsivity, and alcohol use disorders in the older adolescent: A psychobiological study. *Alcoholism: Clinical and Experimental Research, 24,* 1609–1619.

Soloff, P. H., Meltzer, C. C., Greer, P. J., Constantine, D., & Kelly, T. M. (2000). A fenfluramine-activated FDG-PET study of borderline personality disorder. *Biological Psychiatry, 47,* 540–547.

Soubrie, P. (1986). Reconciling the role of central serotonin neurons in humans and animal behavior. *Behavioral and Brain Sciences, 9,* 319–364.

Spoont, M. R. (1992). Modulatory role of serotonin in neural information processing: Implication for human psychopathology. *Psychological Bulletin, 112,* 330–350.

Spurlock, G., Heils, A., Holmans, P., Williams, J., D'Souza, U. M., Cardno, A., et al. (1998). A family based association study of T102C polymorphism in 5HT2A and schizophrenia plus identification of new polymorphisms in the promoter. *Molecular Psychiatry, 3,* 42–49.

Staner, L., Uyanik, G., Correa, H., Tremeau, F., Monreal, J., Crocq, M.-A., et al. (2002). A dimensional impulsive-aggressive phenotype is associated with the A218C polymorphism of the tryptophan hydroxylase gene: A pilot study in well-characterized impulsive inpatients. *American Journal of Medical Genetics (Neuropsychiatric Genetics), 114,* 553–557.

Stanley, B., Molcho, A., Standley, M. Winchel, R., Gameroff, M. J., Parsons, B., et al. (2000). Association of aggressive behavior with altered serotonergic function in patients who are not suicidal. *American Journal of Psychiatry, 157,* 609–614.

Stanley, M., Taskman-Bendz, L., & Doronini-Zis, K. (1985). Correlations between aminergic metabolites simultaneously obtained from CSF and brain. *Life Sciences, 37,* 1279–1286.

Stoff, D. M., Pasatiempo, A. P., Yeung, J., Cooper, T. B., Bridger, W. H., & Rabinovich, H. (1992). Neuroendocrine responses to challenge with *dl*-fenfluramine and aggression in disruptive behavior disorders of children and adolescents. *Psychiatry Research, 43,* 263–276.

Stoltenberg, S. F., Twitchell, G. R., Hanna, G. L., Cook, E. H., Fitzgerald, H. E., Zucker, R. A., et al. (2002). Serotonin transporter promoter polymorphism, peripheral indexes of serotonin function, and personality measures in families with alcoholism. *American Journal of Medical Genetics (Neuropsychiatric Genetics), 114,* 230–234.

Sukonick, D. L., Pollock, B. G., Sweet, R. A., Mulsant, B. H., Rosen, J., Klunk, W. E., et al. (2001). The 5-HTTLPR*S/*L polymorphism and aggressive behavior in Alzheimer disease. *Archives of Neurology, 58,* 1425–1428.

Sweet, R. A., Pollock, B. G., Sukonick, D. L., Mulsant, B. H., Rosen, J., Klunk, W. E., et al. (2001). The 5-HTTLPR polymorphism confers liability to a combined phenotype of psychotic and aggressive behavior in Alzheimer disease. *International Psychogeriatrics, 13*, 401–409.

Trefilov, A., Berard, J., Krawczak, M., & Schmidtke, J. (2000). Natal dispersal in rhesus macaques is related to serotonin transporter gene promoter variation. *Behavior Genetics, 3*, 295–301.

Tuinier, S., Verhoeven, W. M. A., & van Praag, H. M. (1995). Cerebrospinal fluid 5-hydroxyindoleacetic acid and aggression: A critical reappraisal of the clinical data. *International Clinical Psychopharmacology, 10*, 147–156.

Twitchell, G. R., Hanna, G. L., Cook, E. H., Fitzgerald, H. E., & Zucker, R. A. (2000). Serotonergic function, behavioral disinhibition, and negative affect in children of alcoholics: The moderating effects of puberty. *Alcohol: Clinical and Experimental Research, 24*, 972–929.

Twitchell, G. R., Hanna, G. L., Cook, E. H., Stoltenberg, S. F., Fitzgerald, H. E., & Zucker, R. A. (2001). Serotonin transporter promoter polymorphism genotype is associated with behavioral disinhibition and negative affect in children of alcoholics. *Alcoholism: Clinical and Experimental Research, 25*, 953–959.

Unis, A. S., Cook, E. H., Vincent, J. G., Gjerde, D. K., Perry, B. D., Mason, C., et al. (1997). Platelet serotonin measures in adolescents with conduct disorder. *Biological Psychiatry, 42*, 553–559.

Vartiainen, H., Tiihonen, J., Putkonen, A., Koponen, H., Virkkunen, M., Hakola, P., et al. (1995). Citalopram, a selective serotonin reuptake inhibitor, in the treatment of aggression in schizophrenia. *Acta Psychiatrica Scandinavica, 91*, 348–351.

Virkkunen, M., DeJong, J., Bartko, J., Goodwin, F. K., & Linnoila, M. (1989). Relationship of psychobiological variables to recidivism in violent offenders and impulsive fire setters: A follow-up study. *Archives of General Psychiatry, 46*, 600–603.

Virkkunen, M., DeJong, J., Bartko, J., & Linnoila, M. (1989). Psychobiological concomitants of history of suicide attempts among violent offenders and impulsive fire setters. *Archives of General Psychiatry, 46*, 604–606.

Virkkunen, M., Kallio, E., Rawlings, R., Tokola, R., Poland, R. E., Guidotti, A., et al. (1994). Personality profiles and state aggressiveness in Finnish alcoholic, violent offenders, fire setters, and healthy volunteers. *Archives of General Psychiatry, 51*, 28–33.

Virkkunen, M., Nuutila, A., Goodwin, F. K., & Linnoila, M. (1987). Cerebrospinal fluid monoamine metabolite levels in male arsonists. *Archives of General Psychiatry, 44*, 241–247.

Virkkunen, M., Rawlings, R., Tokola, R., Poland, R. E., Guidotti, A., Nemeroff, C., et al. (1994). CSF bio-

chemistries, glucose metabolism, and diurnal activity rhythms in alcoholic, violent offenders, fire setters, and healthy volunteers. *Archives of General Psychiatry, 51*, 20–27.

Volkow, N. D., & Tancredi, L. (1987). Neural substrates of violent behavior: A preliminary study with positron emission tomography. *British Journal of Psychiatry, 151*, 668–673.

Walters, J. R., & Seyfarth, R. M. (1987). Conflict and cooperation. In B. B. Smuts, D. L. Cheney, R. M. Seyfarth, R. W. Wrangham, & T. T. Struhsaker (Eds.), *Primate societies* (pp. 306–317). Chicago: University of Chicago Press.

Walther, D. J., Peter, J.-U., Bashammakh, S., Hortnagl, H., Voits, M., Fink, H., et al. (2003). Synthesis of serotonin by a second tryptophan hydroxylase isoform. *Science, 299*, 76.

Wester, P., Bergstrom, U., Eriksson, A., Gezelius, C., Hardy, J., & Winblad, B. (1990). Ventricular cerebrospinal fluid monoamine transmitter and metabolic concentrations reflect human brain neurochemistry in autopsy cases. *Journal of Neurochemistry, 54*, 1148–1156.

Westergaard, G. C., Suomi, S. J., Chavanne, T. J., Houser, L., Hurley, A., Cleveland, A., et al. (2003). Physiological correlates of aggression and impulsivity in free-ranging female primates. *Neuropsychopharmacology, 28*, 1045–1055.

Westergaard, G. C., Suomi, S. J., Higley, J. D., & Mehlman, P. T. (1999). CSF 5-HIAA and aggression in female macaque monkeys: Species and individual differences. *Psychopharmacology, 145*, 440–446.

Westlund, K. N., Denney, R. M., Kochersperger, L. M., Rose, R. M., & Abell, C. W. (1985). Distinct monoamine oxidase A and B populations in primate brain. *Science, 230*, 181–183.

Wetzler, S., Kahn, R. S., Asnis, G. M., Korn, M., & van Praag, H. M. (1991). Serotonin receptor sensitivity and aggression. *Psychiatry Research, 37*, 271–279.

Whale, R., Quested, D. J., Laver, D., Harrison, P. J., Cowen, P. J. (2000). Serotonin transporter (5-HTT) promoter genotype may influence the prolactin response to clomipramine. *Psychopharmacology, 150*, 120–122.

Williams, W. A., Shoaf, S. E., Hommer, D., Rawlings, R., & Linnoila, M. (1999). Effects of acute tryptophan depletion on plasma and cerebrospinal fluid tryptophan and 5-hydroxyindoleacetic acid in normal volunteers. *Journal of Neurochemistry, 72*, 1641–1647.

Yatham, L. N., & Steiner, M. (1993). Neuroendocrine probes of serotonergic function: A critical review. *Life Sciences, 53*, 447–463.

Youdim, M. B., & Finberg, J. P. (1994). Pharmacological actions of l-deprenyl (selegiline) and other selective monoamine oxidase B inhibitors. *Clinical Pharmacology and Therapeutics, 56,* 725–733.

Young, S. N., & Leyton, M. (2002). The role of serotonin in human mood and social interaction: Insight from altered tryptophan levels. *Pharmacology, Biochemistry and Behavior, 71,* 857–865.

Zald, D. H., & Depue, R. A. (2001). Serotonergic functioning correlates with positive and negative affect in psychiatrically healthy males. *Personality and Individual Differences, 30,* 71–86.

Zalsman, G., Frisch, A., Bromberg, M., Gelernter, J., Michaelovsky, E., Campino, A., et al. (2001). Family-based association study of serotonin transporter promoter in suicidal adolescents: No association with suicidality but possible role in violence traits. *American Journal of Medical Genetics (Neuropsychiatric Genetics), 105,* 239–245.

Zill, P., Baghai, T. C., Zwanzger, P., Schule, C., Eser, D., Rupprecht, R., et al. (2004). SNP and haplotype analysis of a novel tryptophan hydroxylase isoform (TPH2) gene provide evidence for association with major depression. *Molecular Psychiatry, 9,* 1030–1036.

Zill, P., Buttner, A., Eisenmenger, W., Bondy, B., & Ackenheil, M. (2003). Regional mRNA expression of a second tryptophan ydroxylase isoform in postmortem tissue samples of two human brains. *European Neuropsychopharmacology, 14,* 282–284.

Zill, P., Buttner, A., Eisenmenger, W., Moller, H.-J., Bondy, B., & Ackenheil, M. (2004). Single nucleotide polymorphism and haplotype analysis of a novel tryptophan hydroxylase isoform (TPH2) gene in suicide victims. *Biological Psychiatry, 56,* 581–586.

5

Monoamines, GABA, Glutamate, and Aggression

Klaus A. Miczek & Eric W. Fish

After half a century of research on the neurochemical mechanisms subserving different kinds of aggressive behavior, early attempts to assign a specific role for each of the canonical monoaminergic neurotransmitters, the excitatory and inhibitory amino acid transmitters, and the steroid and peptide modulators have been supplanted by theories of interacting neural circuits and subcellular mechanisms for different kinds of aggressive behavior. Historically, dualistic concepts of noradrenergic excitation and cholinergic inhibition of behavior were derived from the sympathetic and parasympathetic activity of autonomic functions (Hendley, Moisset, & Welch, 1973; Hoebel, 1968). The classic portrayal of the "fight-flight" phenomenon relied on postulated imbalances in cholinergic-adrenergic mechanisms (Cannon, 1934). At present, this dualistic framework persists in the proposal that brain serotonergic deficiency characterizes violence-prone individuals and that dopaminergic receptor blockade effectively calms violent individuals.

By now, a neural circuit view of aggressive behavior accommodates evidence of a more intricate nature (e.g., Gregg & Siegel, 2001). Ascending mesocorticolimbic aminergic projections and descending glutamatergic and gamma-aminobutyric acidergic (GABAergic) feedback, as well as peptidergic modulation of these circuits, have emerged as the substrate for aggressive and defensive acts and postures in rodent and feline species. For example, converging pharmacological evidence reveals that positive allosteric modulation of selected pools of $GABA_A$ receptors can heighten aggression, and it is likely that GABA interacts with other neurotransmitters to produce this effect. Positive modulation of $GABA_A$ receptors can alter the impulse flow in serotonergic presynaptic terminals that are juxtaposed to dopaminergic cells projecting from ventral tegmental soma to prefrontal cortical terminals (Soderpalm & Engel, 1991). The resulting dopamine (DA) increase in the prefrontal cortex then inhibits glutamate projections from the prefrontal cortex to central and basolateral nuclei of the amygdala, which normally function to suppress aggression. Once disinhibited, information from the basolateral and central amygdaloid nuclei activates hypothalamic and brain stem circuits for intense aggressive behavior.

One of the conceptual sources for studying the neurochemical basis of social behavior derives from the endocrine research paradigm that was introduced in 1849. Arnold Berthold removed the gland of interest (testes) that secreted the source of the endogenous substance (testosterone) that he suspected to be necessary for the display of a specific behavior (aggressive displays) and consequently that behavior disappeared. Thereafter he replaced the glandular material and recorded the return of the behavior (Berthold, 1849). Ever since this demonstration, depletion and repletion have served as a model for characterizing endogenous chemical systems (figure 5.1).

In replication and extension of the Berthold experiments, male lizards, snakes, fish, and birds decline in their aggressive displays and fighting after castration, and administration of testosterone propionate restores this behavior effectively, highlighting the *obligatory* role of androgens in aggressive behavior in these species (Crews & Moore, 1986; Wingfield, Ball, Dufty, Hegner, & Ramenofsky, 1987). In mammalian species, the obligatory effects of androgens depend largely on experience. Castrated mice and rats without prior aggressive experience rarely fight when confronted by a male conspecific (Beeman, 1947; Christie & Barfield, 1979). However, when aggressive behavior is fully established in the behavioral repertoire, castration gradually reduces but does not prevent aggression against a conspecific male (Christie & Barfield, 1979; DeBold & Miczek, 1981, 1984). Instead of being obligatory in their function, as in invertebrates, fish, and avian species, androgens exert a *modulatory* effect on mammalian aggressive behavior. The fact that experiential factors are sufficiently powerful to attenuate and even obliterate the effects of castration highlights the importance of understanding how multiple mechanisms enable aggressive behavior.

This endocrine research paradigm has been applied to the neuropharmacological study of brain monoamines and aggressive behavior. The canonical neurotransmitter substances are readily depleted by selective neurotoxic interventions and the depletion can be reversed by the administration of the specific precursors (e.g., Seiden & Carlsson, 1964). For example, the effects of neurotoxic depletion of DA by 6-hydroxydopamine can be reversed by the administration of the immediate DA precursor, *l*-DOPA, and similarly, the serotonin (5-hydroxytryptamine, or 5-HT)-depleting effects of 5,7-dihydroxytryptamine can be reversed by the administration of the 5-HT precursor 5-hydroxytryptamine. The effects of neurotoxic insults on aggressive behavior are effectively reversed by precursor treatment, implicating the monoamines in the mediation of aggressive behavior (Kantak, Hegstrand, & Eichelman, 1981).

The endocrine strategy of depletion and then repletion of an endogenous mechanism that is suspected to be of significance in the mechanisms mediating aggressive behavior has been extended to gene manipulations. Once aggressive behavior is established in an adult mouse, so-called knockdown techniques allow the expression of a gene to be suppressed and subsequently expressed again by the tetracycline-gene regulation system (Chen, Kelz, Hope, Nakabeppu, & Nestler, 1997).

A more clinically oriented research strategy relies on neurobiological measurements that are *correlated* with aggressive behavior that either occurred relatively recently or reflects measures of aggression in the individual's past. An early example is the correlation between reduced 5-HT turnover in the brain stem of mice that had been previously subjected to isolated housing, which rendered most of them aggressive (Giacalone, Tansella, Valzelli, & Garattini, 1968). Subsequent clinical studies correlated measures of cerebrospinal fluid (CSF) 5-HIAA or blood platelet 5-HT binding or blood tryptophan levels with a life history of violent behavior (e.g. Brown, Goodwin, Ballenger,

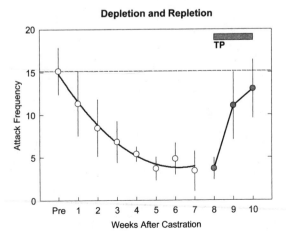

FIGURE 5.1 Aggressive behavior of castrated male rats during weekly confrontations with male intruders. The residents were castrated 7 weeks before hormone treatment began and then treated with testosterone propionate (TP, 500 μg/day) for 3 weeks. Based on "Sexual Dimorphism in the Hormonal Control of Aggressive Behavior of Rats," by J. F. DeBold and K. A. Miczek, 1981, *Pharmacology, Biochemistry and Behavior*, 14(Suppl. 1), p. 90. Copyright 1981 by Elsevier. Reprinted with permission.

Goyer, & Major, 1979; Linnoila et al., 1983; Maes, Cosyns, Meltzer, De Meyer, & Peeters, 1993).

In the following sections we summarize the evidence that describes the roles that monoamines, specifically 5-HT, norepinephrine (NE), and DA, exert in the mediation of aggressive behavior. Aggression is diverse in its behavioral patterns and functions, and endogenous amines, acids, steroids, and peptides may have very different effects on each kind of aggression. We highlight the importance of escalated forms of aggression in an effort to model the harmful acts of aggression and violence in humans. Monoamines have powerful modulatory effects on aggression, and reciprocally, aggression alters monoamines. It is important to delineate the specific conditions and behaviors, when 5-HT appears to be inhibitory, and when NE and DA are aggression stimulating. The effects of monoamines are likely to be due to their interactions with other neurotransmitters, such as GABA and glutamate, and neuropeptides, such as vasopressin and opioids.

Diverse Aggressive Behavior Patterns

A prerequisite for outlining neurobiological mechanisms of aggression is an understanding of the distal and proximal antecedents and consequences of different kinds of aggressive behavior. It is helpful to recall that a psychiatric perspective focuses on escalated and pathological forms of aggressive behavior (Eichelman, 1992), whereas ethological studies emphasize species-typical kinds of aggressive behavior. Conceptually, these approaches should be complementary and reciprocal because the ethological approach provides the framework for dominance, territorial, maternal aggression, or even predatory behavior, which when escalated can become problems in veterinary and human medicine.

Dominance Aggression

In socially organized species ranging from invertebrates, birds, and fish to mammals, the formation of a dominance hierarchy and the maintenance of social status within the group are the key determinants for the display of aggressive behavior. The behavioral repertoire comprises sequences of offensive and defensive acts, postures, and displays that are often summarily referred to as agonistic behavior (Scott & Fredericson, 1951). The ritualized character of so-called dominance

displays (*Imponiergehabe*) has been hypothesized to reduce the probability of tissue-damaging attacks (Lorenz, 1966). Each animal species has evolved an elaborate repertoire of pursuits, threat displays, and attacks that are responded to with defensive, evasive, submissive, and flight reactions. In colonial rodent species such as rats (*Rattus norvegicus*) aggressive confrontations may occur between rival males within an existing colony or between a resident member of the colony, usually the dominant one, and an intruder male (Barnett, Evans, & Stoddart, 1968).

Probably the most serious form of aggressive behavior within socially organized species is the account of "killing parties," as described in chimpanzees that pursue members of a neighboring troupe (Nishida, Haraiwa-Hasegawa, & Takahata, 1985; Wrangham, 1999). Although these events are rare, they cannot be dismissed as accidental or abnormal. They are associated with many physiological and behavioral expressions of anticipatory excitement, and the actual killing of the victims shows many signs of pleasurable vocalizations and postural displays, in parallel to human psychopathologies (Farrington, 1993; McElroy, Soutullo, Beckman, Taylor, & Keck, 1998).

Territorial Aggression

Murine species such as *Mus musculus* mark, patrol, and defend territories against other males. It is worth pointing out that it is only under laboratory conditions that groups of adult males will live together. After growing up in the deme (breeding unit) or "Grossfamilie," males disperse upon puberty and form an itinerant population (van Oortmerssen & Bakker, 1981). Resident breeding males exclude other males from the marked and patrolled territory ("exclusive territory") or dominate other males ("dominance territory") by engaging in attack bites, sideways threats, and pursuits (Eibl-Eibesfeldt, 1950; Sluyter, van Oortmerssen, & Koolhaas, 1996). Under controlled experimental conditions, this latter type of aggressive behavior has become the most frequently employed test protocol, most often referred to as *resident-intruder* or *intermale aggression* (figure 5.2). When an adult male mouse is housed singly for a period of time (ranging from 1 day to 8 weeks), it displays aggressive behavior very much akin to that seen by a territorial breeding male (Brain, 1975), and this particular arrangement engenders *isolation-induced aggression*. Depending on mouse strain, the proportion of animals that becomes aggressive rather than displaying timidlike

FIGURE 5.2 The most salient acts and postures characteristic of fighting between resident and intruder mice. (A) Attack bite and leap by resident and escape leap by intruder; (B) offensive sideways threat by resident (right) and defensive upright posture by intruder (left); (C) anogenital contact by resident; (D) pursuit by resident; and (E) mutual upright posture by resident and intruder. From "Intruder-Evoked Aggression in Isolated and Non-Isolated Mice: Effects of Psychomotor Stimulants and L-Dopa," by K. A. Miczek and J. M. O'Donnell, 1978,

behavior varies considerably (30–90% of isolates become aggressive; Krsiak, 1975).

The current focus on aggressive behavior in transgenic mice relies on embryonic stem cells that are harvested most often from the 129 Sv strain of mice, a strain without the pugnacious characteristics of other *M. musculus* strains. It is not surprising that many gene deletions have been found to result in the emergence of some aggressive behavior in mice whose genetic background provides poorly for fundamental acts and postures of social intercourse.

Maternal Aggression

Dominant female mice and rats, like members of many mammalian species, fight in order to defend safe nesting sites against intruding males and females (Hurst, 1987). The breeding success of the lactating female is enhanced via successfully attacking males and females that may threaten the survival of the litter, and fending off potential infanticide increases the relative fitness of the dominant female (see Gammie & Lonstein, ch. 11 in this volume). In female rodents, the repertoire of aggressive behavior includes predominately bites that are directed at the snout and head of the opponent, in addition to the typical pursuits and sideways threats (Svare & Gandelman, 1973, 1976). It is difficult to extrapolate maternal aggression in rodents to the human condition, because intense aggressive outbursts in human females are relatively rare in the postpartum period.

Escalated Aggression: Frustration, Social Instigation, and Anticipation

Studies on animal aggression become particularly relevant to clinical concerns when they focus on escalated aggressive behavior that far exceeds the species-typical patterns. Escalated aggression is characterized by rapid initiation, very high frequency, and intensity of occurrence, often with injurious consequences, lengthy bouts that are uninhibited by signals of submission (Miczek, Fish, & DeBold, 2003). It is conceivable that escalated aggressive behavior is based on neurobiological mechanisms that also mediate the species-typical patterns, but

Psychopharmacology, 57, p. 49. Copyright 1978 by Springer-Verlag. Reprinted with permission.

it may also be the case that new mechanisms are recruited to engender escalated forms of aggressive behavior. For example, the proposed human hostile-affective subtype of aggressive behavior may relate to animal aggression that is readily provoked by frustrative experiences, whereas the human subtype of controlled-proactive-instrumental-predatory aggression may have its counterpart in killing behavior by animals (Vitiello & Stoff, 1997).

Frustration-Heightened Aggressive Behavior

Heightened aggressive behavior is triggered by frustrative experiences that result from sudden omission of scheduled reinforcement or reward, and this type of escalated aggression has the widest cross-species generality and validity. The link between frustration and aggression has been studied in humans and various other species under rigorously controlled conditions since 1939 (Dollard, Doob, Miller, Mowrer, & Sears, 1939). Experimental procedures have been designed to identify the conditions of extinction or intermittent reinforcement that engender high levels of aggressive behavior toward an opponent or even an inanimate object. Initial studies focused on birds, the avian symbol of peace, and demonstrated that the more infrequent conditioned responses were reinforced, the more likely it was for the pigeon to attack a target bird (Azrin, Hutchinson, & Hake, 1966). The basic principle of omitting a scheduled reinforcement has been implemented in mice, and the rate of attacks toward an opponent escalated after the mice were subjected to extinction of a reinforced operant conditioning task (figure 5.3; de Almeida & Miczek, 2002).

Social Instigation-Heightened Aggressive Behavior

A particularly effective variant of frustrating experiences is the presence in the home cage of a provocative opponent that cannot be removed. When certain species of fish, mice, rats, or hamsters are exposed to an adult

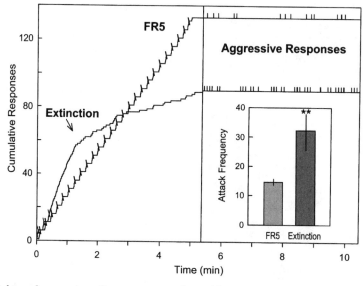

FIGURE 5.3 Heightened aggression after exposure to the sudden omission of scheduled reinforcement of responding ("frustration-induced" aggression). (Left) Cumulative responses under the control of a fixed ratio 5 schedule of positive reinforcement, with each reinforced response denoted by a slash. In the extinction condition, reinforcement is stopped after the third delivery. (Right) Time line with vertical deflections indicating the resident mouse's aggressive responses when an intruder mouse was presented at the end of the conditioning session. (Inset) The frequency of attack bites (mean ± *SEM*) in nonextinction (light gray bar) and extinction (dark gray bar) tests; **$p < .01$. From "Social and Neural Determinants of Aggressive Behavior: Pharmacotherapeutic Targets at Serotonin, Dopamine and γ-Aminobutyric Acid Systems," by K. A. Miczek, E. W. Fish, J. F. DeBold, and R. M. M. de Almeida, 2002, *Psychopharmacology, 163*, p. 437. Copyright 2002 by Springer-Verlag. Reprinted with permission.

breeding male in their home cage for a brief interval and this male is protected behind a screen, then the resident escalates its rate of attacks and threats significantly in a subsequent aggressive confrontation (Fish, Faccidomo, & Miczek, 1999; Heiligenberg, 1974; Potegal & Tenbrink, 1984). In experimental protocols with mice, the olfactory, auditory, and visual cues from a shielded opponent instigate the resident, presumably activating "aggressive arousal," so that the resident subsequently attacks and threatens an intruding male incessantly and intensely (figure 5.4; de Almeida & Miczek, 2002; Fish et al., 1999; Kudryavtseva, 1991). The neurobiological basis of the putative aggressive arousal that engenders the escalated rates of attack in instigated animals remains to be identified.

Aggressive Behavior as a Reinforcer or Anticipation of Aggressive Behavior

The opportunity to fight can serve as a reinforcer or reward, and experimental protocols have been designed to establish how animals emit large and persistent patterns of operant behavior that is reinforced by an aggressive bout (Connor, 1974; Potegal, 1979; Thompson & Schuster, 1964). When implementing this fundamental phenomenon in mice, the opportunity to attack effectively rein-

forced operant responding according to a fixed ratio or interval requirement (Fish, DeBold, & Miczek, 2002; Fish et al., in preparation). Mice that gradually accelerate their responding during a fixed interval are reinforced by the opportunity to fight and do so very intensely and frequently (figure 5.5). Under conditions of anticipating and responding to a fight, mice become very aroused, as indicated by their gradually increasing rate of operant responding, elevated levels of plasma corticosterone, and escalated levels of aggressive behavior.

Neural Systems of Aggression

During aggressive confrontations insects, reptiles, amphibians, fish, birds, and mammals engage in acts and postures that injure their opponent or defend themselves from injury (Huber & Kravitz, 1995; Kravitz & Huber, 2003). The intricate pattern of central and peripheral activity in ascending and descending systems of epinephrine, NE, DA, and 5-HT cells sets in motion changes in body temperature, glucose metabolism, and cardiovascular and endocrine activity that are necessary for these behaviors. Even after the confrontation has terminated, these monoamines continue to shape and coordinate the long-lasting consequences of aggression, consequences

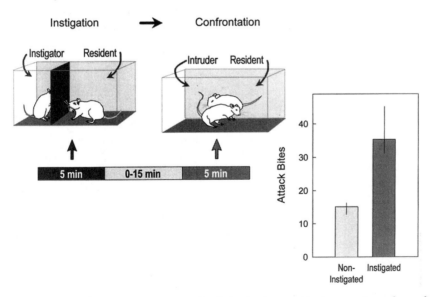

FIGURE 5.4 Effects of social instigation on aggressive behavior by a resident mouse toward a male intruder. The resident mouse is exposed to another male behind a protective screen for 5 min; after a specific interval, the resident is then confronted by an intruder. Bars represent the frequency (mean ± SEM) of attack bites under control (light gray) and instigated (dark gray) conditions.

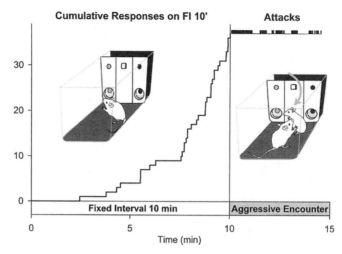

FIGURE 5.5 The opportunity to engage in aggressive behavior can reinforce operant responding. The left panel shows the cumulative number of responses (solid line) by a single mouse over a 10-min fixed interval schedule of reinforcement. The right panel shows attack bites toward an intruder that is subsequently introduced into the resident's cage for 5 min. Each *deflection* on the time line represents an attack bite. From "Social and Neural Determinants of Aggressive Behavior: Pharmacotherapeutic Targets at Serotonin, Dopamine and γ-Aminobutyric Acid Systems," by K. A. Miczek, E. W. Fish, J. F. DeBold, and R. M. M. de Almeida, 2002, *Psychopharmacology, 163*, p. 440. Copyright 2002 by Springer-Verlag. Reprinted with permission.

that determine the individual's future behavior. Winners are more likely to be victorious in future confrontations; losers are more likely to flee or submit to defeat (Scott & Marston, 1953).

5-HT as an Inhibitor of Aggression

5-HT Levels

Among all neurotransmitters, 5-HT is the monoamine most consistently linked to aggressive behavior (Lesch & Merschdorf, 2000; Miczek, Fish, DeBold, & de Almeida, 2002; Nelson & Chiavegatto, 2001). From the early work of Valzelli and colleagues showing that isolated, aggressive mice have lower brain levels of 5-HT and 5-HIAA than do nonaggressive, group-housed mice (Giacalone et al., 1968) to the findings that certain human patients with a history of violent and impulsively aggressive behavior have reduced CSF levels of 5-HIAA (Brown et al., 1979; figure 5.6), it has been proposed that 5-HT exerts a strong inhibitory effect on aggression (Coccaro, Kavoussi, Cooper, & Hauger, 1997; Mann, 1999). Early studies relied on postmortem tissue measurements in mice, hamsters, rats, or tree shrews that had previously engaged in aggressive acts and subsequently shown a complex pattern of changes

in 5-HT and 5-HIAA (Karczmar, Scudder, & Richardson, 1973; Lasley & Thurmond, 1985; Payne, Andrews, & Wilson, 1985; Raab, 1970; Welch & Welch, 1968). Reduced 5-HT function, as measured by low CSF 5-HIAA levels, has emerged as one of the few relatively consistent biological markers for trait characteristics of certain aggressive behaviors, impulsivity, risk taking, and alcoholism (Fairbanks et al., 1999; Fairbanks, Melega, Jorgensen, Kaplan, & McGuire, 2001; Higley & Bennett, 1999; Kruesi et al., 1990; Linnoila et al., 1983; Manuck et al., 1998; Manuck, Kaplan, Rymeski, Fairbanks, & Wilson, 2003; Mehlman et al., 1994; Placidi et al., 2001; van der Vegt, Lieuwes, Cremers, de Boer, & Koolhaas, 2003; Virkkunen & Linnoila, 1993).

As intriguing as these findings appear, two significant limitations must be reiterated. First, the measurement of CSF 5-HIAA is temporally separated from the execution of the behavior, making it difficult to establish causal relationship between 5-HT and the display of aggressive acts. Second, CSF measurements reflect the activity of several brain regions, particularly those near the ventricles, in which 5-HT may function differently than it does in other corticolimbic structures. However, the prefrontal cortex, which has been identified as an important brain region for the inhibition of

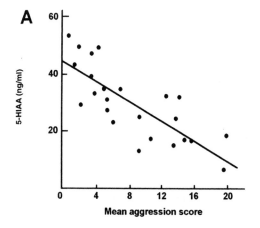

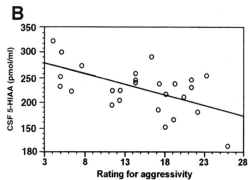

FIGURE 5.6 Aggression and cerebrospinal fluid 5-hydroxy-indoleacetic acid (CSF 5-HIAA) in young men with personality disorders (A) and in young vervet monkeys (B). (A) From "Aggression in Humans Correlates With Cerebrospinal Fluid Amine Metabolites," by G. L. Brown, F. K. Goodwin, J. C. Ballenger, P. F. Goyer, and L. F. Major, 1979, *Psychiatry Research, 1*, p. 134. Copyright 1979 by Elsevier. Reprinted with permission. (B) From "Cerebrospinal Fluid Monoamine and Adrenal Correlates of Aggression in Free-Ranging Rhesus Monkeys," by J. D. Higley et al., 1992, *Archives of General Psychiatry, 49*, p. 439. Copyright 1992 by the American Medical Association. Reprinted with permission.

and terminates the fight, and finally recovers from the confrontation. These studies reveal the temporal pattern of 5-HT release in specific terminal regions. Microdialysis data also confirm some of the clinical findings, namely, lower 5-HT values in aggressive individuals, but importantly only *after* the confrontation has already been initiated and when it is terminated. As an individual resident rat attacks an intruder, levels of 5-HT in the prefrontal cortex decline (Van Erp & Miczek, 2000), but do not change in the nucleus accumbens (Ferrari, Van Erp, Tornatzky, & Miczek, 2003; Van Erp & Miczek, 2000). Even after the confrontation ends, cortical 5-HT remains suppressed for more than 1 hr (Van Erp & Miczek, 2000; figure 5.7). Aggressive acts themselves are not necessary to reduce 5-HT; rats that have been entrained to regularly occurring daily confrontations show a decline in accumbal 5-HT even when the confrontation never occurs (Ferrari et al., 2003). These data reveal that merely anticipating aggression is sufficient to reduce 5-HT, and these data are consistent with the hypothesis that 5-HT is lowered in individuals who are primed for aggression.

The microdialysis data are most informative on 5-HT activity after aggression, but they reveal less about what occurs during the actual episode. A sample taken 10 min after the start of a fight reflects the net effect of the aggressive interaction but not the moment-to-moment variation within the interaction. It would be instructive to compare 5-HT levels in the initial moments of an aggressive encounter, when aggressive acts are most intense, to extracellular concentrations as the encounter progresses and the animal spends more time in static postures and self-grooming. Reduced 5-HT may facilitate the expression of aggression or, alternatively, the recovery from aggression and the return to stasis. Only when it is possible to measure 5-HT neurotransmission more precisely in the most intense phases of an encounter will we be able to assess the function of 5-HT during aggression.

aggressive and impulsive behavior (Best, Williams, & Coccaro, 2002; Raine, Buchsbaum, & LaCasse, 1997; Raine et al., 1998), is thought to contribute to the CSF serotonergic levels that are obtained from lumbar punctures (Doudet et al., 1995).

Studies using in vivo microdialysis in rats have begun to provide a more detailed analysis of the dynamic changes in 5-HT as an individual rests, prepares for an aggressive confrontation, initiates an attack, prevails

Receptor-Selective Agonists and Antagonists

A new era of research on 5-HT and aggression began with the molecular identification of distinctively separate families of 5-HT receptors and the genes that code for these receptor proteins. However, so far only the 5-HT transporter (SERT) and the 5-HT_1, 5-HT_2, and

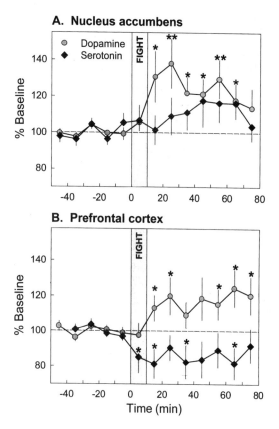

FIGURE 5.7 Increased accumbal dopamine (DA) and decreased serotonin (5-HT) during and following a resident's attack on an intruder rat. (A) Samples collected from the nucleus accumbens and (B) samples collected from the prefrontal cortex are shown. Gray circles and filled diamonds represent the mean ± *SEM* (vertical lines) extracellular DA and 5-HT concentrations, respectively. All data are expressed as percentages of baseline. Ten-minute samples were collected 50 min before, during, and 80 min after a confrontation with a smaller male intruder. The vertical bar indicates the 10-min period of actual physical confrontation. Asterisks denote a significant change from baseline levels as assessed by planned *t* test (*$p < .05$, **$p < .01$). The dashed line indicates baseline levels. From "Aggressive Behavior, Increased Accumbal Dopamine and Decreased Cortical Serotonin in Rats," by A. M. M. Van Erp and K. A. Miczek, 2000, *Journal of Neuroscience, 20*, p. 9322. Copyright 2000 by the Society for Neuroscience. Reprinted with permission.

$5-HT_3$ receptor families have been studied for their roles in aggressive behavior. These experiments using receptor-selective agonists and antagonists, as well as gene knockout or overexpression, reveal the complexity of the 5-HT modulation of aggressive behavior.

The $5-HT_1$ Receptor Family

The $5-HT_{1A}$ Receptor

The $5-HT_1$ family of receptors consists of subtypes 1A, 1B, and 1D (Barnes & Sharp, 1999; Hoyer, Hannon, & Martin, 2002). In humans, there is evidence for impaired function of $5-HT_{1A}$ receptors in aggressive individuals. When compared to nonaggressive populations, aggressive individuals have a blunted prolactin increase and hypothermia after administration of partial agonists (Cleare & Bond, 2000; Coccaro, Gabriel, & Siever, 1990; Coccaro, Kavoussi, & Hauger, 1995). Consistent with these observations, drugs that act on 1A receptors, such as the full agonist 8-OH-DPAT, alnespirone, or the partial agonist buspirone have been consistently shown to reduce fighting across several species and

experimental methods (figure 5.8; Bell & Hobson, 1994; Blanchard, Rodgers, Hendrie, & Hori, 1988; de Almeida & Lucion, 1997; de Boer, Lesourd, Mocaer, & Koolhaas, 1999, 2000; Dompert, Glaser, & Traber, 1985; Haug, Wallian, & Brain, 1990; Joppa, Rowe, & Meisel, 1997; Lindgren & Kantak, 1987; McMillen, DaVanzo, Scott, & Song, 1988; Miczek, Hussain, & Faccidomo, 1998; Muehlenkamp, Lucion, & Vogel, 1995; Nikulina, Avgustinovich, & Popova, 1992; Sanchez, Arnt, Hyttel, & Moltzen, 1993; Sanchez & Hyttel, 1994; Tompkins, Clemento, Taylor, & Perhach, 1980; Van der Vegt et al., 2001). Prevention of these effects by the antagonist WAY 100635 indicates that the 1A receptor is the relevant site of action for these agents.

There are, however, inconsistencies between the pharmacology studies that indicate an inhibitory role of the $5-HT_{1A}$ receptor on aggression and the measurement of $5-HT_{1A}$ receptor function in laboratory rodents. First, "knocking out" the $5-HT_{1A}$ receptor reportedly decreases aggressive behavior (Zhuang et al., 1999). Second, $5-HT_{1A}$ receptor mRNA and 5-HT receptor binding in the prefrontal cortex and hippocampal regions is higher in mice that have been selectively bred for short latencies to initiate a first attack (Korte et al., 1996). These mice are also more sensitive to the hypothermic effects of the 5-HT$_{1A}$ agonist alnespirone (Van der Vegt et al., 2001). Moreover, aggressive wild rats show a similar enhanced hypothermia compared to nonaggressive wild rats, though receptor binding itself does not differ (Van der Vegt et al., 2001). When evaluating these inconsistencies it is important to consider the extent to which developmental and experiential adaptations can interact with the density and function of 5-HT$_{1A}$ receptors.

The key limitation of the antiaggressive effect of 5-HT$_{1A}$ receptor agonists is the concurrent effects on a range of other nonaggressive types of behavior, that is, the limited behavioral specificity. For example, in rats administration of very low doses of 5-HT$_{1A}$ agonists can facilitate male copulatory performance by shortening the postejaculatory interval (Ahlenius, Larsson, & Wijkstroem, 1991) and increase alimentary behavior and alcohol consumption (McKenzie-Quirk & Miczek, 2003; Tomkins, Higgins, & Sellers, 1994). Of all the behavioral effects of 5-HT$_{1A}$ agonists, changes in motor activity interact most significantly with aggressive behavior. At

higher doses, 5-HT$_{1A}$ agonists can induce the so-called serotonin syndrome, which in rats consists of resting tremor, rigidity, forepaw treading, hind limb abduction, Straub tail, lateral head weaving, head shaking, hyperreactivity, hyperactivity, and salivation (Jacobs, 1976), and these effects are thought to be mediated by postsynaptic receptors (Millan, Bervoets, & Colpaert, 1991).

Whether the antiaggressive effects of 5-HT$_{1A}$ agonists rely on postsynaptic receptor activation rather than somatodendritic autoreceptor stimulation needs to be investigated in more detail. Destruction of presynaptic 5-HT terminals, by injecting the neurotoxin 5,7-DHT, does not affect the antiaggressive effects of 8-OH-DPAT, suggesting a postsynaptic action (Sijbesma et al., 1991). However, the compound S-15535 is thought to act as an agonist primarily at pre- rather than postsynaptic 5-HT$_{1A}$ receptors and it reduces aggression with considerably more behavioral specificity than do other 5-HT$_{1A}$ agonists (de Boer et al., 1999, 2000). The generation of 5-HT$_{1A}$ agonists that discretely target pre- versus postsynaptic receptors may lead to the development of efficacious and behaviorally selective antiaggressive treatments.

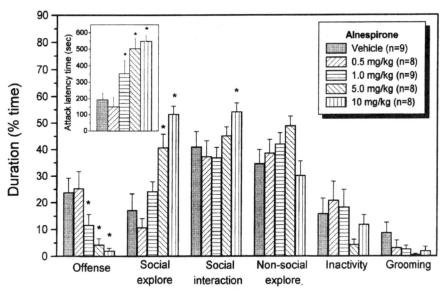

FIGURE 5.8 Effect of alnespirone on the attack latency (inset) and the behavior of resident rats in an offensive aggression test; $*p < .05$ compared to vehicle. From "Selective Antiaggressive Effects of Alnespirone in Resident-Intruder Test Are Mediated via (5-Hydroxytryptamine)1A Receptors: A Comparative Pharmacological Study With 8-Hydroxy-2-Dipropylaminotetralin, Ipsapirone, Buspirone, Eltoprazine, and WAY-100635," by S. F. De Boer, M. Lesourd, E. Mocaer, and J. M. Koolhaas, 1999, *Journal of Pharmacology and Experimental Therapeutics*, 288, p. 1128. Copyright 1999 by the American Society for Pharmacology and Experimental Therapeutics. Reprinted with permission.

The 5-HT$_{1B}$ Receptor

The 5-HT$_{1B}$ receptor has a more selective effect on aggression than does the 1A receptor. The agonists CP-94,253, anpirtoline, and zolmitriptan all reduce aggressive behaviors in resident mice and rats (figure 5.9; de Almeida & Miczek, 2002; de Almeida, Nikulina, Faccidomo, Fish, & Miczek, 2001; Fish, Faccidomo, & Miczek, 1999) and likewise, mice lacking the 5-HT$_{1B}$ receptor gene are more aggressive than the wild-type (WT) counterparts (Bouwknecht et al., 2001; Saudou et al., 1994). Unlike most other compounds that reduce aggressive behavior, 5-HT$_{1B}$ agonists do not reduce concurrently motor activity. However, in contexts that do not elicit aggression, 5-HT$_{1B}$ receptor agonists have been shown to reduce feeding (Lee & Simansky, 1997) and sexual performance (Ahlenius & Larsson, 1998), increase or decrease measures of stimulant self-

administration (Fletcher, Azampanah, & Korth, 2002; Fletcher & Korth, 1999; Parsons, Weiss, & Koob, 1998; Rocha et al., 1998), have antidepressantlike effects (O'Neill & Conway, 2001), and are motor stimulating (O'Neill & Parameswaran, 1997). When given before an aggressive interaction, the behavioral specificity of these agonists, particularly CP-94,253, depends on the level of aggression that is measured. When mice fight at heightened levels, such as after alcohol administration, social instigation, or in anticipation of a fight, rather than stimulating motor activity, CP-94,253 actually reduces locomotion.

These context-dependent effects of CP-94,253 highlight the interplay between the intensity of aggressive behavior and the actions of 5-HT at its receptors. This may occur as a result of changes in 5-HT neurotransmission. If heightened aggression occurs on a background of reduced 5-HT transmission, there should be

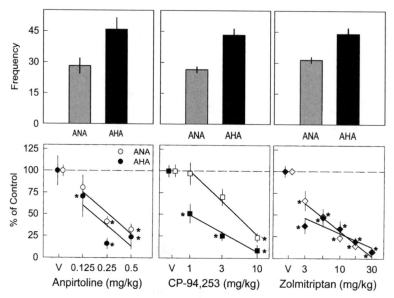

FIGURE 5.9 (Top) Certain mice are more aggressive than others following experimenter-administered oral alcohol (center and right panels) or orally self-administered alcohol (1.0 g/kg). Bars represent the mean frequency of attack bites ± *SEM* (vertical lines) toward an intruder for the subset of mice identified as alcohol-nonheightened aggressors (ANAs, light gray bars) and alcohol-heightened aggressors (AHAs, dark gray bars). (Bottom) Reduction of aggressive behavior in ANAs (light gray symbols) and AHAs (dark gray symbols) that were exposed to 1.0 g/kg of alcohol and subsequently treated with the 5-HT$_{1B}$ agonist anpirtoline (left panel, circles), CP-94,253 (center panel, squares), or zolmitriptan (right panel, diamonds). Data are expressed as a percentage of vehicle baseline. Symbols represent the mean number of attack bites ± *SEM* (vertical lines). Asterisks denote statistical significance relative to vehicle ($p < .05$). From "Social and Neural Determinants of Aggressive Behavior: Pharmacotherapeutic Targets at Serotonin, Dopamine and γ-Aminobutyric Acid Systems," by K. A. Miczek, E. W. Fish, J. F. DeBold, and R. M. M. de Almeida, 2002, *Psychopharmacology, 163,* p. 443. Copyright 2002 by Springer-Verlag. Reprinted with permission.

less competition between a pharmacological agonist and the endogenous ligand for a given receptor. Under these conditions, agonists should be more effective, as indicated by leftward shifts in dose-response curves. Consistent with this scenario, CP-94,253 reduces alcohol-heightened, instigated, and schedule-heightened aggression at doses lower than those that reduce species-typical levels of aggression.

The 5-HT$_2$ Receptor Family

Several newly developed neuroleptic drugs with significant affinity for the 5-HT$_{2A}$ receptor have proven to be effective in the clinical management of aggressive patients (Fava, 1997). The characterization of the 5-HT$_{2A}$ receptor as a critical site for effecting increases and decreases in aggressive behavior remains incomplete in the absence of selectively acting agonists at this receptor. Substituted phenylisopropylamines, such as DOI, act on both 5-HT$_{2A}$ and 5-HT$_{2C}$ receptors and TFMPP, which acts as agonist at 5-HT$_{2C}$ receptors, also has significant affinity for the 5-HT$_{1B}$ receptor. These less than perfect pharmacological tools decrease aggressive behavior in male and female rats and in male mice with concurrent suppression of motor activity (Baxter, Kennett, Blaney, & Blackburn, 1995; Bonson, Johnson, Fiorella, Rabin, & Winter, 1994; de Almeida & Lucion, 1994; Groenink, van der Gugten, Mos, Maes, & Olivier, 1995; Muehlenkamp et al., 1995; Olivier, Mos, Van Oorschot, & Hen, 1995; Sanchez et al., 1993). Intracerebral DOI microinjections facilitate defensive hissing that is elicited by electrical stimulation of the medial hypothalamus in cats (Shaikh, De Lanerolle, & Siegel, 1997), and this effect may be related to the anxietylike effects that can be generated by stimulation of these receptors (Lucki & Wieland, 1990; Nogueira & Graeff, 1995).

Risperidone and similar atypical neuroleptics that act as antagonists at 5-HT$_{2A}$ receptors effectively reduce aggressive behavior in children, adolescents, and middle-aged and elderly patients diagnosed with schizophrenia, dementia, depression, or posttraumatic stress disorder (Buckley et al., 1997; Buitelaar, van der Gaag, Cohen-Kettenis, & Melman, 2001; Czobor, Volavka, & Meibach, 1995; De Deyn et al., 1999; Keck, Strakowski, & McElroy, 2000; McCracken et al., 2002; Zarcone et al., 2001). In isolated mice, risperidone and related neuroleptics decrease aggressive behavior, but only at doses that also reduce motor activity (Rodriguez-Arias, Minarro, Aguilar, Pinazo, & Simon, 1998). Similarly, ketanserin effectively reduces the aggressive behavior of monoamine oxidase-A-deficient mice (Shih et al., 1999). It is clear, however, that antagonism of 5-HT$_{2A}$ receptors is an effective means to inhibit aggressive behavior only concurrent with reductions in a range of behavioral activities.

The 5-HT Transporter

Ever since the introduction of the selective serotonin reuptake inhibitors (SSRIs) in the early 1980s there have been periodic reports of aggressive outbursts and suicidal tendencies in some individuals undergoing SSRI treatments (Troisi, Vicario, Nuccetelli, Ciani, & Pasini, 1995). In the meantime, large-scale meta-analysis clearly demonstrated that significantly fewer patients who are treated with fluoxetine engaged in aggressive behavior than did placebo-treated controls (Heiligenstein, Beasley, & Potvin, 1993; Walsh & Dinan, 2001). The transporter molecule in the presynaptic terminal and in the vesicular membrane of serotonergic cells continues to be an important target for blocking the uptake process of 5-HT, and this mechanism is one of the targets for the pharmacotherapeutic management of aggressive patients (Swann, 2003).

Acute administration of SSRIs to several animal species reduces aggressive behavior (see, e.g., Dodman et al., 1996; Ferris & Delville, 1994; Huber, Smith, Delago, Isaksson, & Kravitz, 1997; Olivier, Mos, Van der Heyden, & Hartog, 1989; Pinna, Dong, Matsumoto, Costa, & Guidotti, 2003). Long-term administration of fluoxetine has been reported to increase in aggressive behavior in rats (Mitchell & Redfern, 1997), but decreased aggression in male prairie voles (Villalba, Boyle, Caliguri, & DeVries, 1997). The interpretation of the antiaggressive effects of SSRIs being due to the increased concentration of extracellular 5-HT is consistent with the inverse correlation between 5-HT levels and aggression. Interestingly, these effects, at least in aggression naive mice, could also involve a nonserotonergic mechanism that increases levels of the GABA$_A$ receptor-positive modulator allopregnanolone (Pinna et al., 2003). Whether this mechanism also occurs in aggression experienced mice requires further study (see GABA section below).

Several studies have linked the 5-HT transporter gene with aggressive behavior. In mice the effect of missing the 5-HTT gene is reduced aggressive behavior during initial encounters, as well as after repeated experience (Holmes, Murphy, & Crawley, 2002). The postulated association between a polymorphism in the

5-HTTT gene and aggressive behavior in autistic children, Type II alcoholics, and antisocial personality, and
other disorders with heightened aggressive behavior
has been reported, but these findings are difficult to
replicate (Klauck, Poustka, Benner, Lesch, & Poustka,
1997; Sander et al., 1998).

Monoamine Oxidase (MAO)

Enzymatic inactivation of 5-HT via monoamine oxidase A (MAO-A) has attracted attention since a rare deficiency in the gene coding for this enzyme has been
associated with increased impulsive aggressive behavior in the male members of a Dutch family, among
other abnormalities (Brunner, Nelen, Breakefield,
Ropers, & van Oost, 1993). Male transgenic mice missing the gene for MAO-A exhibited heightened aggressive behavior and 5-HT levels that were elevated
throughout most of the life span (Cases et al., 1995;
Shih, 2004; Holschneider, Chen, Seif, & Shih, 2001).
These suggestive, but inconclusive, data prompted an
important investigation into the interaction between experiences in the early developmental period in the form
of maltreatment, the expression of MAO-A, and antisocial behavior during adolescence and young adulthood (Caspi et al., 2002). The evidence indicated that
a polymorphism exists at the promoter region of the
MAO-A gene that leads to differential expression. Individuals with low MAO-A gene expression had a
higher likelihood of developing adult antisocial and
aggressive behavior when severely maltreated in childhood, and conversely, high MAO-A activity protected
against engendering adult antisocial behavior after severe maltreatment in early life. This type of study on
gene-early environment interactions promises to be
informative as to developmental scenarios for neurobiological mechanisms mediating aggressive behavior.

NE as a Permissive System

Agonistic confrontations are characterized by increased
central and peripheral NE activity, and this catecholaminergic activation has been confirmed in many species
(Gerra et al., 1997; Sgoifo, de Boer, Haller, & Koolhaas,
1996; Summers & Greenberg, 1994; Welch & Welch,
1965). Elevations in NE are pervasive across a range of
intensely arousing situations that command attention;
they are not specific to agonistic interactions. Fighting
constitutes a potent stressor, and catecholamines are ac-

tivated as part of the physiological responses to many stressors (Bell & Hepper, 1987). However, despite these observations a consistent relationship between aggressive
behavior and NE has yet to be established.

High aggressivity does not reliably correlate with
CSF levels or brain levels of NE or its metabolite
3-methoxy-4-hydroxyphenylethylene glycol across several species. Though positive correlations have been
reported (Brown et al., 1979; Higley et al., 1992; Kaplan,
Manuck, Fontenot, & Mann, 2002; Placidi et al., 2001;
Traskman-Bendz et al., 1992; Van der Vegt, Lieuwes,
Cremers, de Boer, & Koolhaas, 2003), so have the
inverse (Bernard, Finkelstein, & Everett, 1975; Virkkunen, Eggert, Rawlings, & Linnoila, 1996) and the
absent correlations (Brown et al., 1982; Higley et al.,
1992; Höglund, Balm, & Winberg, 2000; Kim et al.,
2000; Linnoila et al., 1983; Reisner, Mann, Stanley,
Huang, & Houpt, 1996). These inconsistencies may
reflect the interval between the measurements and the
preceding aggressive act, as well as the specific patterns
of aggressive behavior.

Pharmacological manipulations of NE or specific
noradrenergic receptors suggest that NE can facilitate
the expression of aggressive behaviors. Decreasing levels of NE can attenuate offensive aggressive patterns
(Crawley & Contrera, 1976) and facilitate some forms
of defensive aggression (Thoa, Eichelman, Richardson,
& Jacobowitz, 1972). Conversely, increasing synaptic
levels of NE, using low doses of antidepressants that
inhibit NE reuptake by blocking the norepinephrine
transporter (NET), can increase the aggressive behavior of isolated mice confronting each other (Cai, Matsumoto, Ohta, & Watanabe, 1993; Cutler, Rodgers,
& Jackson, 1997; Matsumoto, Cai, Satoh, Ohta, &
Watanabe, 1991). Similarly, increased defensive responses were seen when NE was injected into the hypothalamic area from which feline "affective defense"
is electrically elicited (Barrett, Edinger, & Siegel, 1990;
Barrett, Shaikh, Edinger, & Siegel, 1987).

The importance of NE levels to aggressive behavior is further supported by the findings from two types
of "knockout" mice that have altered NE systems and
that display increased aggressive behavior. Disruption
of the gene encoding for NET increases levels of NE,
and these mice are more likely to retaliate when attacked by a larger, aggressive resident mouse (Haller
et al., 2002). Elevated NE, as well as 5-HT, levels also
occur in mice lacking MAO-A (Cases et al., 1995).
Similar to humans with a point mutation in the MAO-
A gene (Brunner et al., 1993), these mice are more

aggressive than are those that express the MAO-A gene. It is unclear whether the aggressive phenotype is more associated with the NE or 5-HT levels. NE remains elevated in the knockout (KO) mice throughout adulthood, whereas 5-HT deficiencies are largest during early development, suggesting a more likely contribution of NE. On the other hand, the heightened aggressive behavior in the MAO-A KO mice is reduced by 5-HT_{2A} but not β receptor antagonists (Shih et al., 1999), indicating the potential importance of 5-HT mechanisms. However, many β-blockers also have substantial affinity for 5-HT_{1A} receptors (Barnes & Sharp, 1999), and this mechanism of action may be relevant for their antiaggressive effects.

The α and β adrenergic receptors appear to contribute differentially to the regulation of aggressive behavior. Species differences in the NE system and the lack of particularly selective agonists and antagonists make interpreting these findings difficult (Bell & Hepper, 1987; Haller, Makara, & Kruk, 1998). Drugs such as propanolol that block the postsynaptic β-adrenergic receptor have long been successfully used to treat aggressive behavior disorders (Elliott, 1977; Ratey & Gordon, 1993; Sorgi, Ratey, & Polakoff, 1986; Yudofsky, Williams, & Gorman, 1981). Acutely, β-blockers reduce aggression in preclinical studies as well, though their effects are often accompanied by sedation (Bell & Hobson, 1993; Gao & Cutler, 1992; Hegstrand & Eichelman, 1983; Matsumoto et al., 1991).

The role for α_2 receptors in aggressive behavior may depend on the species and also whether the receptor is located pre- or postsynaptically. Yohimbine and similar α_2 antagonists seem to shift mice from behaving offensively to behaving defensively (Haller, Makara, & Kovacs, 1996; Kemble, Behrens, Rawleigh, & Gibson, 1991). In rats, however, α_2 receptor antagonists have a biphasic effect on aggressive behavior; low doses increase and high doses decrease both low and high baseline rates of aggression (Haller, 1995; Haller, Barna, & Kovacs, 1994). As is similar for the DA receptors, α_2 receptor agonists exert the same behavioral effect as the antagonists. Such an apparently perplexing receptor pharmacology may be caused by the relative activation of pre- versus postsynaptic α_2 receptors (Haller & Kruk, 2003). Evidence for an inhibitory role of the α_{2c} receptor subtype comes from the finding that isolated mice lacking this receptor attacked an intruder faster than did the WT mice, while mice overexpressing this receptor had the opposite phenotype (Sallinen, Haapalinna, Viitamaa, Kobilka, & Scheinin, 1998). However,

the α_{2c} receptor did not appear to contribute to the attack behavior once it was initiated.

The evidence suggests that NE plays a significant permissive role in aggressive behavior. The basal activity of the NE system, unlike that of the 5-HT system, does not consistently differentiate aggressive *from* nonaggressive individuals. Therefore, it may be productive to question how NE changes in response to an aggressive challenge and then prepare an individual to fight rather than to flee. For example, there is a larger activation in the locus coeruleus of hamsters that have experienced several defeats compared to hamsters that have experienced several victories (Kollack-Walker, Watson, & Akil, 1997), suggesting that the relative amount of activation in this brain region may contribute to the eventual fight or flight response. It will also be important to understand how aggression-facilitating β receptors interact with aggression-*inhibiting* α adrenoreceptors at the time of the encounter and how these receptors are regulated with repeated victory or defeat.

DA: Anticipatory and Enabling Systems

Aggressive behavior depends on intact DA neurons in the mesocorticolimbic pathways. In particular, the ascending dopaminergic projections from the ventral tegmental area, to the ventral striatum, including the nucleus accumbens, and to the prefrontal cortex are critical for initiating different kinds of aggressive behavior (Redmond, Maas, Kling, & Dekirmenjian, 1971; Redmond, Maas, Kling, Graham, & Dekirmenjian, 1971). Destroying these dopaminergic systems by injecting the neurotoxin 6-OHDA decreases offensive aggression and exaggerates defensive, ragelike reactions (Eichelman, Thoa, & Ng, 1972; Pucilowski, Kostowski, Bidzinski, & Hauptmann, 1982; Reis & Fuxe, 1968). Interestingly, these same neurons are also essential for other adaptive behaviors, including sexual and maternal behaviors, feeding, and drug taking, as well as higher cognitive functions (Hansen, Harthon, & Wallin, 1991; Koob, Riley, Smith, & Robbins, 1978; Robbins, Cador, Taylor, & Everitt, 1989; Roberts & Koob, 1982).

Measurements of elevated DA activity in postmortem tissue assays of aggressive mice and rats established an important link between aggression and DA in the frontal cotex, ventral striatum, and nucleus accumbens (Hadfield, 1983; Haney, Noda, Kream, & Miczek, 1990; Mos & Van Valkenburg, 1979; Puglisi-Allegra & Cabib, 1990). Much like the correlations of 5-HT and impulsively aggressive humans, these early studies could not dissociate the DA changes prior to an aggressive encounter from those that follow the encounter, and the causality remained uncertain.

In vivo microdialysis studies have identified temporally distinct DA changes in brain areas during the initiation, execution, and termination of aggressive confrontations. Extracellular DA levels are increased in the prefrontal cortex and nucleus accumbens in aggressive resident rats, as well as in defensive and submissive intruder rats (figure 5.7; Van Erp & Miczek, 2000). When intruder rats are protected from the aggressor by a wire mesh screen, they react with defensive upright postures and show 50–60% increases in extracellular DA that persist even after the termination of the threat (Tidey & Miczek, 1996). In contrast, no significant changes were seen in the striatum despite the large amount of motor activity during the confrontation.

There is also evidence that DA, like 5-HT, can change in anticipation of an aggressive encounter (Ferrari et al., 2003). The first confrontation is intensely arousing and is characterized by a very great tachycardia, as assessed via telemetry, and a rise in extracellular DA levels in the nucleus accumbens that outlasted the confrontation. Significantly, once resident rats experienced these confrontations for 10 consecutive days at precisely the same time, DA levels rose on the 11th day in advance of the anticipated confrontation. These data reveal entrainment or conditioning of monoamine release. The role of such conditioned release is not entirely clear, but could serve to prepare an individual for action.

Elevated DA levels are not specific to agonistic behavior. In fact, elevated DA occurs during many experiences that are ostensibly stressful (e.g., inescapable novel environments, foot shock, or restraint) (Abercrombie, Keefe, DiFrischia, & Zigmond, 1989; Thierry, Tassin, Blanc, & Glowinski, 1976) or pleasurable (e.g., feeding, sexual behavior, or maternal behavior) (Champagne et al., 2004; Pfaus et al., 1990; Wilson, Nomikos, Collu, & Fibiger, 1995). These similarities question the often reiterated interpretation of the mesocorticolimbic DA pathway as a pure reward system. It appears that activation of this pathway is more of a general response to a salient, biologically significant event. In the case of aggression, these could be the pheromonal, vocal, and/or postural cues provided by the opponent. There is an additional issue of functional specificity, namely, what is the specific role for DA to specifically coordinate attack behavior when a resident rat confronts an intruder? Presumably, because DA increases in response to either a male intruder or a sexually receptive female, DA could activate either attack or sexual behavior. Which mechanisms confer the appropriate behavioral response to the appropriate stimulus?

Functional specificity is particularly relevant for pharmacotherapies that target the DA system in aggressive patients. The introduction of neuroleptics in the 1950s fundamentally changed how clinicians managed aggression in psychotics, depressives, schizophrenics, mentally retarded, nonpsychotic character disordered delinquents, amphetamine abusers, alcoholics, or patients suffering from organic brain syndrome (Citrome & Volavka, 1997a, 1997b). The effectiveness of chlorpromazine and haloperidol in reducing aggressive behavior continues to serve as benchmark in the evaluation of novel compounds (Connor, Boone, Steingard, Lopez, & Melloni, 2003; Humble & Berk, 2003; Itil, 1981; Itil & Wadud, 1975; Leventhal & Brodie, 1981; Poeldinger, 1981; Sheard, 1988; Tupin, 1985). Although the first-generation neuroleptics were critiqued as a form of "chemical restraint," subsequently developed compounds increasingly improved the profile of action, and most importantly, reduced the incidence of tardive dyskinesia and extrapyramidal symptoms in the course of continued treatment (Swann, 2003). Still, as effective as dopaminergic antagonists are, their effects, especially in laboratory animals, appear largely sedative and generally behaviorally disruptive.

There is some evidence that pharmacologically induced DA increases are associated with increased aggressive behavior. Low to moderate doses of amphetamine or apomorphine can heighten aggression of isolated mice or rats after omission of a scheduled reward. Higher doses of amphetamine also increase the defensive responses of rats reacting to electric shock or to the attacks by an opponent—behavioral changes which are likely to be due to changes in general stimulus reactivity or arousal (Crowley, 1972; Hasselager, Rolinski, & Randrup, 1972; Miczek, 1974; Puech, Simon, Chermat, & Boissier, 1974; Ray, Sharma, Alkondon, & Sen, 1983; Senault, 1968, 1971). When undergoing withdrawal from morphine, a state with profound neurochemical sequelae, including suppressed dopaminergic activity (Diana, Pistis, Muntoni, & Gessa, 1995; Nowycky, Walters, & Roth, 1978), amphetamines enhance aggression in mice and rats (Gianutsos & Lal, 1978; Kantak & Miczek, 1988; Tidey & Miczek, 1992b). Amphetamines can also increase aggressive behavior secondarily, by preventing fatigue, particularly during extended fights (Winslow & Miczek, 1983). However, these agents can actually reduce both aggressive and social behavior in animals with a prior history of extensive aggressive experiences (Hodge & Butcher, 1975; Miczek & Haney, 1994; Miczek & O'Donnell, 1978; Miczek & Yoshimura, 1982).

The behavioral and pharmacological histories of the individual have emerged as critical determinants of psychomotor stimulant effects on aggressive behavior, and it can be hypothesized that these experiential factors are based on molecular changes in dopaminergic neurons. It will be significant to identify how these experiential factors regulate not only DA release concurrent with the initiation of an aggressive episode, but prompt up- and down-regulation of DA receptor subtypes and alter second messenger function and phosphorylation. There is evidence that brief defeat experiences in an aggressive confrontation profoundly increase the expression of c-fos in brain stem and limbic structures, and these changes persist for several months (Martinez, Calvo-Torrent, & Herbert, 2002; Miczek, Covington, Nikulina, & Hammer, 2004; Nikulina, Covington, Ganshow, Hammer, & Miczek, 2004; Nikulina, Hammer, Miczek, & Kream, 1999; Nikulina, Marchand, Kream, & Miczek, 1998).

The role of the two DA receptor families in aggressive behavior is only beginning to be delineated, with the exception of D2 receptor antagonists, which have been studied for decades. One of the hallmark features of behavioral pharmacological studies of aggressive behavior is the concurrent assessment of the specificity of antiaggressive effects. The sedative and motor-incoordinating effects of neuroleptics indicate the nonselective nature of their antiaggressive effects, which highlights the urgency to develop superior pharmacotherapeutic alternatives.

From a pharmacological perspective it is troubling that in many animal species, including mice, D2 receptor agonists, such as quinpirole, and antagonists, such as raclopride, both decrease aggressive and motor behaviors (Aguilar, Minarro, Perez-Iranzo, & Simon, 1994; Rodriguez-Arias, Pinazo, Minarro, & Stinus, 1999; Tidey & Miczek, 1992a, 1992c). Agents that act on D1 receptors (SKF 38393 and SCH 23390) are equally perplexing (Rodriguez-Arias, Pinazo, Minarro, & Stinus, 1999; Tidey & Miczek, 1992a). More comprehensive and detailed behavioral analyses are required to distinguish the agonist and antagonist antiaggressive effects. It appears that D2 receptor antago-

nists slow motor activities, including those that are part of the aggressive behavioral repertoire (Fowler & Liou, 1998), whereas D2 agonists fragment and disrupt complex behavioral sequences (Paulus & Geyer, 1991) as required for aggressive behavior patterns. It will be important to study the effects of DA receptor agonists and antagonists in procedures that distinguish the behaviors during the initiation phase of a fight from the actual execution of aggressive acts itself in order to dissociate the role of functionally separate DA receptor pools in the striatal, limbic, and cortical terminal regions.

"Atypical" neuroleptic drugs, such as clozapine and olanzapine, have emerged as an effective treatment for aggressive and nonaggressive schizophrenic and geriatric patients (Bhana, Foster, Olney, & Plosker, 2001; Chalasani, Kant, & Chengappa, 2001; Glazer & Dickson, 1998; Hector, 1998; Kennedy et al., 2001; Rabinowitz, Avnon, & Rosenberg, 1996; Spivak et al., 1998; Volavka, 1999). However, it is not clear whether these antiaggressive effects are due to their actions at DA receptors or 5-HT or histaminergic receptors. For example, olanzapine has a much greater affinity for the $5\text{-}HT_{2A}$ receptor than for the D2 receptors and also binds to muscarinic and H1 receptors.

DA changes in mesocorticolimbic neural circuits that are relevant for aggressive behavior. However, a specific role of DA and its receptor families in mediating aggressive behavior remains to be determined. The clinical success in managing violent patients with neuroleptic drugs that target the D2 receptor family is compromised by the sedative side effects. "Atypical" neuroleptics are currently a more desirable treatment, but their antiaggressive effects likely involve nondopaminergic receptors. The impact of repeated aggressive or submissive experiences on patterns of gene expression in dopaminergic cells could reveal which interactions between DA and other neurochemical systems are critical for specific behavioral outputs.

Focus on Amines and Acids

Glutamate

Glutamate excites neural circuits that are critical for aggressive behavior. In humans suffering from seizure disorders glutamate dysfunction is hypothesized to underlie the association of seizure disorders and aggressive acts (Monroe, 1978; Siegel & Mirsky, 1994). The strongest evidence for glutamate's role in aggression comes from studies examining defensive patterns of aggression, particularly in cats. Pharmacological manipulations of glutamate, however, have contradictory results, perhaps due to the variety of effects that these agents have on glutamate receptors.

Several psychiatric disorders, such as schizophrenia and temporal lobe epilepsy, have correlated symptoms of altered glutamate activity and aggressive behavior (Bear & Fedio, 1977; Mirsky & Harman, 1974; Weiger & Bear, 1988). Treatment of aggressive patients with anticonvulsant drugs (i.e., valproate, carbamazepine, phenytoin) has been effective (Barratt, 1993; Lindenmayer & Kotsaftis, 2000; Pabis & Stanislav, 1996). In animal models of seizure disorder, there are long-lasting changes in emotional reactivity and particularly defensive aggression following repeated periodic stimulation of the amygdala or hippocampus (i.e., kindling) (Adamec, 1990, 1993; Adamec & Young, 2000; Kalynchuk, Dalal, Mana, & Pinel, 1992; Pinel, Treit, & Rovner, 1977). Similar defensive reactions and seizure susceptibility occur after glutamate neurotransmission is increased due to exposure to the neurotoxin trimethyltin (Dawson, Patterson, & Eppler, 1995; Ishida et al., 1997; Lipe, Ali, Newport, Scallet, & Slikker, 1991; Naalsund, Allen, & Fonnum, 1985; Patel, Ardelt, Yim, & Isom, 1990). These studies suggest that excessive glutamatergic activity in critical limbic regions, such as the amygdala, increases the probability of an exaggerated response toward threatening stimuli.

One function of glutamate may be to exaggerate the excitability of the neural systems responsible for aggressive behavior, particularly when aggression is intense. Support for this comes from studies on the threshold to elicit electrically stimulated "defensive rage" in cats. A glutamatergic pathway from the amygdala and the hypothalamus to the periaqueductal gray (PAG) has been proposed to mediate the electrical stimulation of defensive rage (Siegel, Roeling, Gregg, & Kruk, 1999). Whereas microinjection of N-methyl-D-aspartate (NMDA) receptor antagonists dizocilpine (MK-801) and AP-7 into several brain regions increases the amount of current needed to elicit the affective defense reaction (Schubert, Shaikh, & Siegel, 1996; Shaikh, Barrett, & Siegel, 1987; Siegel et al., 1999), NMDA receptor stimulation by itself is not sufficient to elicit the reaction, except in the PAG (Bandler, Depaulis, & Vergnes, 1985). These results suggest that the function of glutamate is to increase the sensitivity of the defensive rage pathway, leading to an exaggerated re-

sponse to stimulation. Experiments comparing the effects of glutamate receptor antagonists on species-typical versus heightened or escalated aggressive behaviors could help address whether glutamate preferentially mediates the escalated form of the response.

Targeting excessive glutamatergic activity has been proposed as a pharmacotherapy for psychiatric disorders associated with aggression. Of glutamate's ionotrophic (i.e., NMDA, AMPA, and kainate) and metabotrophic (mGluR1–8) receptors, the NMDA receptors are the most promising targets for the pharmacotherapeutic management of aggressive behavior.

In preclinical studies, however, NMDA receptor antagonists have mixed effects on aggression and can be quite sedative. The individual's prior history and baseline of aggression is a further consideration for understanding the effects of these antagonists. When the NMDA receptor antagonists phencyclidine (PCP) and MK-801 are given to individuals with very little fighting experience, they tend to increase levels of aggression. These increases occurred when isolated mice confronted an intruder for the first time or fought at low levels and when rats were sleep deprived (Burkhalter & Balster, 1979; Krsiak, 1974; McAllister, 1990; Musty & Consroe, 1982; Rewerski, Kostowski, Piechocki, & Rylski, 1971; Wilmot, Vander Wende, & Spoerlein, 1987). The same agents appear to have the opposite effect in mice and rats with a robust repertoire of aggressive behavior. Individuals that fight at very high, escalated levels are calmed by PCP and MK-801 administration (Belozertseva & Bespalov, 1999; Lang et al., 1995; Miczek & Haney, 1994; Tyler & Miczek, 1982).

The therapeutic potential of a low-affinity NMDA receptor channel blocker is evident from two studies on mouse aggression. When given to isolated, aggression-experienced male mice, the only effect of memantine (1–30 mg/kg) and MRZ 2/579 (0.3–10 mg/kg) was motor impairment at the highest memantine dose (Belozertseva & Bespalov, 1999). However, these drugs dose dependently reduced aggression that had been heightened by morphine withdrawal at doses that were two- to threefold lower than those that impaired motor activity (Sukhotina & Bespalov, 2000). In a preliminary study, another very low-affinity receptor antagonist that also affects the DA system, amantadine, reduced symptoms of impulsivity, aggression, and/or hyperactivity in hospitalized children (King et al., 2001).

Despite the overwhelming evidence for a key role of glutamate in disease states, such as dementia, neurotoxicity, seizure susceptibility, and psychosis (Calabresi,

Pisani, Mercuri, & Bernardi, 1996; Carlsson et al., 2001; Kalivas & McFarland, 2003; Starr, 1998), it is surprising that more is not known about a specific role of glutamate in aggressive behavior. The data from electrical brain stimulation and kindling studies strongly suggest that glutamate is important for the genesis of defensive reactions, but the contribution of glutamate to species-typical and escalated offensive aggressive behaviors awaits detailed ethopharmacological studies. The few studies using antagonists at the NMDA receptor indicate that these compounds may be useful for managing aggressive outbursts. However, early studies with the high-affinity NMDA receptor antagonists PCP and MK-801 reveal antiaggressive effects as part of nonspecific changes in motor activity and suggest that an individual's behavioral history can interact with the actions of glutamatergic drugs. The low-affinity NMDA receptor antagonists, such as memantine, may offer more behaviorally specific effects on aggression by modifying escalated, rather than basal, levels of excitation.

Aggressive confrontations are correlated with profound neuroadaptive changes for the offensively aggressive and for the defensive animal. The neural changes in rats that have been sensitized by repeated defeat experiences include glutamatergic mechanisms, as evidenced by the protective effects of NMDA and mGluR5 receptor antagonists (Yap, Covington, Gale, Datta, & Miczek, 2005). It is feasible that escalating offensive aggressive experiences may also be based on neuroadaptive changes involving glutamatergic mechanisms. Glutamate's most dramatic role in aggression may actually occur in laying down the consequences of aggression that promote its future occurrence.

GABA

As with glutamate, GABA is widely distributed in about one third of all neurons, acting primarily on the A receptor subtype, although $GABA_B$ receptors are important regulators as autoreceptors. $GABA_A$ receptors are heteropentameric glycoproteins and the many variants of their subunit composition suggest anatomical and functional diversity. Allosteric modulators of the $GABA_A$ receptors, such as benzodiazepines, barbiturates, and alcohol, or endogenous modulators, such as allopregnanolone, share a common profile of effects on aggressive behavior. This profile is characterized by a bidirectional dose-effect curve, with administration of low doses of these compounds increasing aggressive behavior and higher doses reducing this behavior (fig-

ure 5.10; Miczek, DeBold, & Van Erp, 1994; Miczek et al., 2002).

Inhibition of Aggressive Behavior

Early postmortem studies provided evidence that brain levels of GABA and of glutamic acid decarboxylase (GAD), especially in the striatum and olfactory bulb, are low in rats and mice that had exhibited aggressive behavior (Clement et al., 1987; Early & Leonard, 1980; Guillot & Chapouthier, 1996, 1998; Haug, Simler, Ciesielski, Mandel, & Moutier, 1984; Potegal, Perumal, Barkai, Cannova, & Blau, 1982). These correlative data have been interpreted to indicate that GABA inhibits aggressive behavior. When GABA transmission is pharmacologically altered, such as by blocking GABA transaminase with sodium n-dipropylacetate or valproate, or when reuptake is blocked by diaminobutyric acid or nipecotic acid amide, aggressive behavior by isolated or irritated mice and defensive aggression in rats are inhibited (DaVanzo & Sydow, 1979; Krsiak et al., 1981; Poshivalov, 1981; Puglisi-Allegra & Mandel, 1980; Puglisi-Allegra, Mack, Oliverio, & Mandel, 1979; Puglisi-Allegra, Simler, Kempf, & Mandel, 1981; Rodgers & Depaulis, 1982).

Some clinical success is documented with anticonvulsant agents that act on GABAergic neurons. Valproate, phenytoin, and carbamazapine have been effective in reducing aggressive outbursts in patients with impulse disorders and various other diagnoses (Barratt, 1993; Barratt, Stanford, Felthous, & Kent, 1997; Lindenmayer & Kotsaftis, 2000; Neppe, 1988; Pabis & Stanislav, 1996; Tariot et al., 1998). The most promising evidence was obtained with phenytoin in prisoners with a history of impulsive aggression and in men with obsessive compulsive, antisocial, or narcissistic personality disorders (Barratt et al., 1997; Stanford et al., 2001). These findings point to the need of defining the specific types of aggressive behavior that are responsive to anticonvulsant treatment by conducting large-scale studies.

Enhancement of Aggressive Behavior Through Positive Modulation

In contrast to the findings on the inhibitory role of GABA in the neural control of aggressive behavior, evidence accumulates that shows how direct or indirect activation of $GABA_A$ receptors increases several types of aggressive behavior. Although the focus is mostly on the aggression-

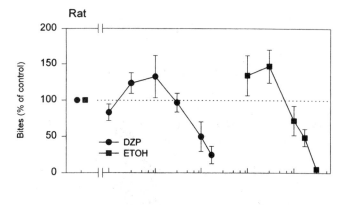

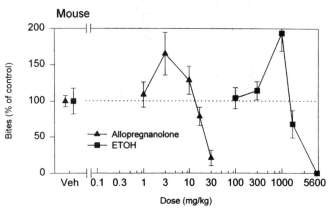

FIGURE 5.10 Changes in the mean frequency of attack bites, expressed as percentages of control, as a function of dose of diazepam (DZP) and ethanol (ETOH) in resident rats confronting an intruder (top) and of allopregnanolone and ethanol in resident mice confronting an intruder (bottom). Dashed horizontal line indicates control (100%), and data points denote means ± *SEM*. From "Alcohol, GABAA-Benzodiazepine Receptor Complex, and Aggression," by K. A. Miczek, J. F. DeBold, A. M. M. Van Erp, and W. Tornatzky. In M. Galanter (Ed.), *Alcoholism and Violence: Recent Developments in Alcoholism* (13th ed., p. 161), 1997, New York: Plenum. Copyright 1997 by Plenum Press. Reprinted with permission.

heightening effects of positive allosteric modulators of GABA$_A$, direct stimulation of the GABA$_A$ receptor with the agonist 4,5,6,7-tetrahydroisoxazolo[5,4-c]pyridine-3-ol (THIP) via the intraventricular route or directly into the septal forebrain area can increase aggressive and defensive behavior of placid laboratory rats (Depaulis & Vergnes, 1983; Potegal, Yoburn, & Glusman, 1983). Even systemic administration of THIP can facilitate moderately aggressive behavior of resident rats toward an intruder (Gourley, DeBold, Yin, Cook, & Miczek, 2005). When the gene that codes for the rate-limiting synthetic enzyme GAD$_{65}$ is deleted, the mutant mice display less aggressive behavior than their WT counterparts (Stork et al., 2000). More substantial and reliable increases in aggressive behavior are seen after the administration of most positive allosteric modulators of the GABA$_A$ receptors in various animal species and conditions.

The clinical observations that benzodiazepine treatment can sometimes result in paradoxical violent and hostile outbursts are relatively infrequent, particularly when these drugs are given in "calming doses" (Dietch

& Jennings, 1988; DiMascio, Shader, & Harmatz, 1969). Systematic experimental studies in human and non-human subjects delineated clear dose-dependent bidirectional effects on aggressive behavior by chlordiazepoxide, diazepam, and midazolam, with administration of high doses reducing aggressive behavior and low doses engendering aggression-heightening effects. Even before the discovery of the mechanism and site of action of benzodiazepines (Braestrup & Squires, 1977), the aggression-heightening effects of benzodiazepine doses on the ascending limb of the dose-effect curve began to be characterized in mice, rats, pigs, monkeys, and humans (Arnone & Dantzer, 1980; Bond, Curran, Bruce, O'Sullivan, & Shine, 1995; Christmas & Maxwell, 1970; Cole & Wolf, 1970; DiMascio, 1973; Ferrari, Parmigiani, Rodgers, & Palanza, 1997; Gourley et al., 2005; Miczek, 1974; Miczek & O'Donnell, 1980; Mos, Olivier, & van der Poel, 1987; Weerts & Miczek, 1996; Weerts, Tornatzky, & Miczek, 1993a; Weisman, Berman, & Taylor, 1998). The antagonism by flumazenil and beta-carboline derivatives point to the benzodiazepine receptor as the critical site for these benzodiazepine effects (figure 5.11; Gourley et al., 2005; Olivier, Mos, & Miczek, 1991).

New insights into the molecular biology of GABA$_A$ receptors promise to help us to understand why not all positive modulators of the GABA$_A$ receptors heighten aggressive behavior in every individual. The role of the α and γ subunits of the GABA$_A$ receptor and their reciprocal interactions are being defined in terms of their functional significance for the anxiolytic, anticonvulsant, and sedative actions of benzodiazepines (Collinson et al., 2002; Löw et al., 2000; Rudolph et al., 1999). Several benzodiazepines do not exert aggression-heightening effects at all; even at low doses, oxazepam, clorazepate, and zolpidem consistently produce antiaggressive effects (Bond & Lader, 1988; de Almeida, Rowlett, Cook, Yin, & Miczek, 2004; Martin-Lopez & Navarro, 2002; Weisman, Berman, & Taylor, 1998), and triazolam fails to increase aggressive behavior in various experimental protocols (Cherek, Spiga, Roache, & Cowan, 1991; de Almeida, Rowlett, Cook, Yin, & Miczek, 2004; Kruk, 1991). It has been hypothesized that a specific subunit composition of the GABA$_A$

receptors is required for the aggression-heightening effects of allosteric-positive modulators to emerge (Miczek et al., 2002). This hypothesis derives from the findings that the sedative and anxiolytic-like effects of diazepam depend upon the presence of certain α subunits (McKernan & Whiting, 1996; Löw et al., 2000; Rudolph et al., 1999). In addition to point mutation data, pharmacological studies suggest that certain α subunits of the GABA$_A$ receptor can selectively target anxiolytic-like and sedative effects. Beta-carboline derivatives have been designed with selectivity for subunits of the GABA$_A$ receptor, and early data point to the α$_1$ subunit as one of the sites where the aggression-heightening effects of positive modulators such as alcohol and midazolam can be attenuated (de Almeida et al., 2004; Gourley et al., 2005).

One of the most effective and serious forms of escalated aggression is triggered by alcohol (Murdoch, Pihl, & Ross, 1990; Pihl, Paylan, Gentes-Hawn, & Hoaken, 2003; Roizen, 1997), and a key facet of the neurobiological mechanism for alcohol-heightened aggression is the allosteric modulation of the GABA$_A$ receptor (Miczek, DeBold, Van Erp, & Tornatzky, 1997; Miczek et al., 1993, 2002). Alcohol increases the frequency and duration of Cl$^-$ channel openings and thereby facilitates GABA-mediated Cl$^-$ flux (Mehta & Ticku, 1988; Suzdak, Schwartz, Skolnick, & Paul, 1986). Although the actions of alcohol have not been localized to a specific subunit of the GABA$_A$ receptor complex, positive modulators of the GABA$_A$ receptor, such as benzodiazepines or allopregnanolone, can enhance the aggression-heightening and aggression-suppressant effects of alcohol in mice (figure 5.12; Fish, Faccidomo, et al., 2001; Miczek & O'Donnell, 1980). Conversely, blockade of the benzodiazepine receptor with broad spectrum antagonists, such as flumazenil or the beta-carboline derivative ZK93426, prevents the aggression-heightening effects of alcohol, but not sedation in rats and squirrel monkeys (Weerts, Tornatzky, & Miczek, 1993b). Heightened aggressive behavior in resident mice confronting an intruder after voluntary consumption of 1 g/kg of alcohol is attenuated by administration of the beta-carboline derivative β-CCt, which acts preferentially at GABA$_A$ receptors with α$_1$ subunits (figure 5.13; de Almeida et al., 2004).

Individual differences in aggression-heightening effects are characteristic of several positive modulators of GABA$_A$ receptors and are most apparent after alcohol intake (Higley, 2001; Linnoila, De Jong, & Virkkunen, 1989; Miczek, Barros, Sakoda, & Weerts, 1998;

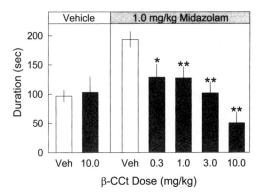

FIGURE 5.11 The effects of β-CCt on the duration of aggressive acts and postures in resident rats confronting an intruder for 5 min. On the left, the effects of β-CCt are shown in vehicle-treated animals and on the right in midazolam-treated (1.0 mg/kg) animals. The vertical lines in each bar identify ±1 SEM. Asterisks indicate statistically significant differences between a specific drug treatment and the corresponding vehicle control (*$p < .05$, **$p < .01$). From "Benzodiazepines and Heightened Aggressive Behavior in Rats: Reduction by GABA$_A$/α$_1$ Receptor Antagonists," by S. L. Gourley, J. F. DeBold, W. Yin, J. Cook, and K. A. Miczek, 2005, *Psychopharmacology*, 178, pp. 232–240. Copyright 2005 by Springer-Verlag. Reprinted with permission.

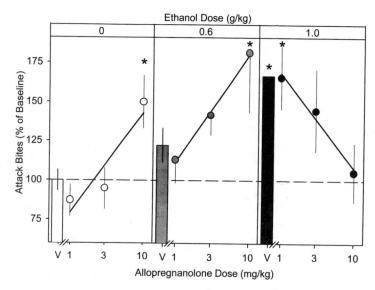

FIGURE 5.12 Effects of the interaction between alcohol and allopregnanolone on the frequency of aggressive behavior, expressed as a percentage of baseline, in resident mice that show alcohol-heightened aggressive behavior. Open circles represent the mean for allopregnanolone when administered with a simultaneous oral injection with water (left panel). Filled, light gray circles represent the mean for allopregnanolone when administered with a simultaneous oral injection with 0.6 g/kg of alcohol (middle panel). Filled, dark gray circles represent the mean for allopregnanolone when administered with a simultaneous oral injection with 1.0 g/kg alcohol (right panel). Bars represent the mean for alcohol after administration of the allopregnanolone vehicle. Vertical lines represent *SEM*. The allopregnanolone dose–effect data are fitted with a regression line. A dashed line is drawn to indicate baseline. Asterisks denote significance from vehicle control levels ($p < .05$). From "Alcohol, Allopregnanolone and Aggression in Mice," by E. W. Fish, S. Faccidomo, J. F. DeBold, and K. A. Miczek, 2001, *Psychopharmacology, 153*, p. 477. Copyright 2001 by Springer-Verlag. Reprinted with permission.

Van Erp & Miczek, 1997; Virkkunen et al., 1994; Weerts et al., 1993b). In mice, rats, and squirrel monkeys a significant minority of animals consistently engages in escalated levels of aggressive behavior after alcohol intake, and the persistent nature of this suggests this alcohol effect to be a trait characteristic (figure 5.14). As a matter of fact, the proportion of individuals displaying alcohol-heightened aggressive behavior can be substantially increased by repeated prior experience with alcohol. Mice that have been behaviorally sensitized by repeated alcohol injections are twice as likely to engage in alcohol-heightened aggressive behavior than are mice receiving the saline vehicle (Fish, DeBold, & Miczek, 2001). It is tempting to hypothesize that the specific GABA$_A$ subunit composition contributes to the individual vulnerability or resilience to the aggression-heightening effects of alcohol. Similarly, expression and suppression of the genes that encode for the specific α, β, and γ subunits may be influenced by the repeated experience with alcohol and aggressive behavior.

Conclusions

The affective dimension of aggressive behavior relative to its instrumentality differentiates several kinds of aggression, necessitating feedback and feed-forward neural circuitry. The temporal and sequential patterning of species-typical offensive and defensive acts and postures requires elaborate neural mechanisms of integrating sensory, motivational, and motor signals. To label 5-HT simply an inhibitory, NE a permissive, or DA an enabling system conveys neither the distinctive roles of pre- and postsynaptic receptor subtypes and transporter molecules nor the chain of intracellular mechanisms. Converging evidence points to the prominent role of 5-HT synthesis, release, and interaction with receptor and uptake sites in affective aggressive behavior. Mesocorticolimbic DA systems are critical for the more calculating instrumental types of aggressive behavior, such as dominance, territorial, maternal, and predatory aggression. Both dopaminergic and seroton-

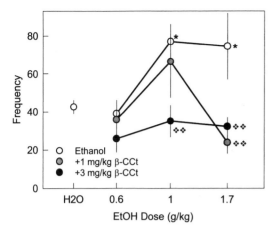

FIGURE 5.13 Frequency of aggressive behaviors (attack bites, sideways threats, and pursuits) as a function of self-administered ethanol dose in male resident mice confronting an intruder. The measurements were obtained from the AHA mice ($n = 8$) after they had self-administered various doses of ethanol only and then confronted an intruder (clear circles) or after ethanol self-administration and treatment with 1 mg/kg of β-CCt (ip; gray circles) or 3 mg/kg of β-CCt (black circles). For comparison, the level of attack bites and sideways threats after water self-administration, as determined in the initial experiment, is shown. The asterisks denote significant differences between the values from tests after alcohol self-administration and after water vehicle consumption ($p < .05$), and diamonds indicate significant differences ($p < .01$) between the values from alcohol effects in the presence and absence of β-CCt. From "GABAA/Alpha1 Receptor Agonists and Antagonists: Effects on Species-Typical and Heightened Aggressive Behavior After Alcohol Self-Administration in Mice," by R. M. M. de Almeida, J. K. Rowlett, J. M. Cook, W. Yin, and K. A. Miczek, 2004, *Psychopharmacology, 172*, p. 259. Copyright 2004 by Springer-Verlag. Reprinted with permission.

ergic systems are critical in the rewarding aspects of aggressive behavior, which can develop into a significant psychopathology.

The interaction within monoaminergic systems and their interactions with amino acid and peptidergic systems offer multiple targets for intervention. Several currently used pharmacotherapeutic agents target these monoaminergic sites, and they have proven effective, although still lacking specificity.

A cascade of genomic and nongenomic events is triggered by the experience of attacking an adversary or by being the target of attacks. Persistent neuro-

adaptations, as evidenced by intracellular changes in the mesocorticolimbic projections, characterize individuals who engage repeatedly in aggressive and defensive behavior (Miczek, Covington, Nikulina, & Hammer, 2004). Increased understanding of these regulatory mechanisms for gene expression and protein synthesis that are triggered by aggressive experiences promise to identify targets for specific pharmacotherapeutic interventions.

References

Abercrombie, E. D., Keefe, K. A., DiFrischia, D. S., & Zigmond, M. J. (1989). Differential effect of stress on in vivo dopamine release in striatum, nucleus accumbens, and medial frontal cortex. *Journal of Neurochemistry, 52*, 1655–1658.

Adamec, R. E. (1990). Does kindling model anything clinically relevant? *Biological Psychiatry, 27*, 249–279.

Adamec, R. E. (1993). Lasting effects of FG-7142 on anxiety, aggression and limbic physiology in the cat. *Journal of Psychopharmacology, 7*, 232–248.

Adamec, R. E., & Young, B. (2000). Neuroplasticity in specific limbic system circuits may mediate specific kindling induced changes in animal affect-implications for understanding anxiety associated with epilepsy. *Neuroscience and Biobehavioral Reviews, 24*, 705–723.

Aguilar, M. A., Minarro, J., Perez-Iranzo, N., & Simon, V. M. (1994). Behavioral profile of raclopride in agonistic encounters between male mice. *Pharmacology, Biochemistry and Behavior, 47*, 753–756.

Ahlenius, S., & Larsson, K. (1998). Evidence for an involvement of 5-HT1B receptors in the inhibition of male rat ejaculatory behavior produced by 5-HTP. *Psychopharmacology, 137*, 374–382.

Ahlenius, S., Larsson, K., & Wijkstroem, A. (1991). Behavioral and biochemical effects of the 5-HT1A receptor agonists flesinoxan and 8-OH-DPAT in the rat. *European Journal of Pharmacology, 200*, 259–266.

Arnone, M., & Dantzer, R. (1980). Effects of diazepam on extinction induced aggression in pigs. *Pharmacology, Biochemistry and Behavior, 13*, 27–30.

Azrin, N. H., Hutchinson, R. R., & Hake, D. F. (1966). Extinction-induced aggression. *Journal of the Experimental Analysis of Behavior, 9*, 191–204.

Bandler, R., Depaulis, A., & Vergnes, M. (1985). Identification of midbrain neurons mediating defensive behaviour in the rat by microinjections of excitatory amino acids. *Behavioural Brain Research, 15*, 107–119.

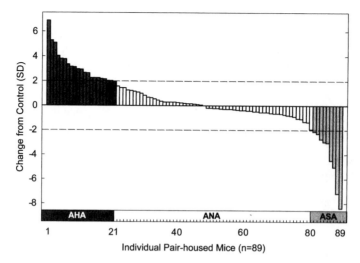

FIGURE 5.14 Effects of a 1.0 g/kg p.o. ethanol challenge on attack bite frequency by individual pair-housed male mice confronted by an intruder. Each bar denotes the standardized data for one mouse, ordered according to the magnitude of the change due to ethanol treatment compared to the individual's vehicle control level. The change is expressed in standard deviations, and the horizontal dotted lines depict the ±2 SD cutoffs that were used to identify individuals exhibiting alcohol-heightened aggression (AHA) or alcohol-suppressed aggression (ASA) versus those who did not show a significant change (alcohol-nonheightened aggression, ANA).

Barnes, N. M., & Sharp, T. (1999). A review of central 5-HT receptors and their function. *Neuropharmacology*, 38, 1083–1152.

Barnett, S. A., Evans, C. S., & Stoddart, R. C. (1968). Influence of females on conflict among wild rats. *Journal of Zoology*, 154, 391–396.

Barratt, E. S. (1993). The use of anticonvulsants in aggression and violence. *Psychopharmacology Bulletin*, 29, 75–81.

Barratt, E. S., Stanford, M. S., Felthous, A. R., & Kent, T. A. (1997). The effects of phenytoin on impulsive and premeditated aggression: A controlled study. *Journal of Clinical Psychopharmacology*, 17, 341–349.

Barrett, J. A., Edinger, H., & Siegel, A. (1990). Intrahypothalamic injections of norepinephrine facilitate feline affective aggression via a2-adrenoceptors. *Brain Research*, 525, 285–293.

Barrett, J. A., Shaikh, M. B., Edinger, H., & Siegel, A. (1987). The effects of intrahypothalamic injections of norepinephrine upon affective defense behavior in the cat. *Brain Research*, 426, 381–384.

Baxter, G., Kennett, G., Blaney, F., & Blackburn, T. (1995). 5-HT2 receptor subtypes: A family re-united? *Trends in Pharmacological Sciences*, 16, 105–110.

Bear, D. M., & Fedio, P. (1977). Quantitative analysis of interictal behavior in temporal lobe epilepsy. *Archives of Neurology*, 34, 454–467.

Beeman, E. (1947). The effect of male hormone on aggressive behavior in mice. *Physiological Zoology*, 20, 393–405.

Bell, R., & Hepper, P. G. (1987). Catecholamines and aggression in animals. *Behavioural Brain Research*, 23, 1–21.

Bell, R., & Hobson, H. (1993). Effects of (-)-pindolol and SDZ 216–525 on social and agonistic behavior in mice. *Pharmacology, Biochemistry and Behavior*, 46, 873–880.

Bell, R., & Hobson, H. (1994). 5-HT(1A) receptor influences on rodent social and agonistic behavior: A review and empirical study. *Neuroscience and Biobehavioral Reviews*, 18, 325–338.

Belozertseva, I. V., & Bespalov, A. Y. (1999). Effects of NMDA receptor channel blockade on aggression in isolated male mice. *Aggressive Behavior*, 25, 381–396.

Bernard, B. K., Finkelstein, E. R., & Everett, G. M. (1975). Alterations in mouse aggressive behavior and brain monoamine dynamics as a function of age. *Physiology and Behavior*, 15, 731–736.

Berthold, A. A. (1849). Transplantation der Hoden. *Archiv fuer Anatomie, Physiologie und Wissenschaftliche Medicin*, 16, 42–46.

Best, M., Williams, J. M., & Coccaro, E. F. (2002). Evidence for a dysfunctional prefrontal circuit in patients with an impulsive aggressive disorder. *Proceedings of the National Academy of Sciences USA*, 99, 8448–8453.

Bhana, N., Foster, R. H., Olney, R., & Plosker, G. L. (2001). Olanzapine: An updated review of its use in the management of schizophrenia. *Drugs, 61,* 111–161.

Blanchard, D. C., Rodgers, R. J., Hendrie, C. A., & Hori, K. (1988). "Taming" of wild rats (*Rattus rattus*) by 5HT1A agonists buspirone and gepirone. *Pharmacology, Biochemistry and Behavior, 31,* 269–278.

Bond, A., & Lader, M. (1988). Differential effects of oxazepam and lorazepam on aggressive responding. *Psychopharmacology, 95,* 369–373.

Bond, A. J., Curran, H. V., Bruce, M. S., O'Sullivan, G., & Shine, P. (1995). Behavioural aggression in panic disorder after 8 weeks' treatment with alprazolam. *Journal of Affective Disorders, 35,* 117–123.

Bonson, K. R., Johnson, R. G., Fiorella, D., Rabin, R. A., & Winter, J. C. (1994). Serotonergic control of androgen-induced dominance. *Pharmacology, Biochemistry and Behavior, 49,* 313–322.

Bouwknecht, J. A., Hijzen, T. H., van der, Gugten J., Maes, R. A., Hen, R., & Olivier, B. (2001). Absence of 5-HT(1B) receptors is associated with impaired impulse control in male 5-HT(1B) knockout mice. *Biological Psychiatry, 49,* 557–568.

Braestrup, C., & Squires, R. F. (1977). Brain specific benzodiazepine receptors in rats characterized by high affinity 3H-diazepam binding. *Proceedings of the National Academy of Sciences USA, 74,* 3805.

Brain, P. F. (1975). What does individual housing mean to a mouse? *Life Sciences, 16,* 187–200.

Brown, G. L., Ebert, M. H., Goyer, P. F., Jimerson, D. C., Klein, W. J., Bunney, W. E., et al. (1982). Aggression, suicide, and serotonin-relationships to CSF amine metabolites. *American Journal of Psychiatry, 139,* 741–746.

Brown, G. L., Goodwin, F. K., Ballenger, J. C., Goyer, P. F., & Major, L. F. (1979). Aggression in humans correlates with cerebrospinal fluid amine metabolites. *Psychiatry Research, 1,* 131–139.

Brunner, H. G., Nelen, M., Breakefield, X. O., Ropers, H. H., & van Oost, B. A. (1993). Abnormal behavior associated with a point mutation in the structural gene for monoamine oxidase A. *Science, 262,* 578–580.

Buckley, P. F., Ibrahim, Z. Y., Singer, B., Orr, B., Donenwirth, K., & Brar, P. S. (1997). Aggression and schizophrenia: Efficacy of risperidone. *Journal of the American Academy of Psychiatry and the Law, 25,* 173–181.

Buitelaar, J. K., van der Gaag, R. J., Cohen-Kettenis, P., & Melman, T. M. (2001). A randomized controlled trial of risperidone in the treatment of aggression in hospitalized adolescents with subaverage cognitive abilities. *Journal of Clinical Psychiatry, 62,* 239–248.

Burkhalter, J. E., & Balster, R. L. (1979). The effects of phencyclidine on isolation-induced aggression in mice. *Psychological Reports, 45,* 571–576.

Cai, B., Matsumoto, K., Ohta, H., & Watanabe, H. (1993). Biphasic effects of typical antidepressants and mianserin, an atypical antidepressant, on aggressive behavior in socially isolated mice. *Pharmacology, Biochemistry and Behavior, 44,* 519–525.

Calabresi, P., Pisani, A., Mercuri, N. B., & Bernardi, G. (1996). The corticostriatal projection: From synaptic plasticity to dysfunctions of the basal ganglia. *Trends in Neurosciences, 19,* 19–24.

Cannon, W. B. (1934). Stresses and strains of homeostasis. *American Journal of the Medical Sciences, 189,* 1–14.

Carlsson, A., Waters, N., Holm-Waters, S., Tedroff, J., Nilsson, M., & Carlsson, M. L. (2001). Interactions between monoamines, glutamate, and GABA in schizophrenia: New evidence. *Annual Review of Pharmacology and Toxicology, 41,* 237–260.

Cases, O., Seif, I., Grimsby, J., Gaspar, P., Chen, K., Pournin, S., et al. (1995). Aggressive behavior and altered amounts of brain serotonin and norepinephrine in mice lacking MAOA. *Science, 268,* 1763–1766.

Caspi, A., McClay, J., Moffitt, T. E., Mill, J., Martin, J., Craig, I. W., et al. (2002). Role of genotype in the cycle of violence in maltreated children. *Science, 297,* 851–854.

Chalasani, L., Kant, R., & Chengappa, R. (2001). Clozapine impact on clinical outcomes and aggression in severely ill adolescents with childhood-onset schizophrenia. *Canadian Journal of Psychiatry, 46,* 965–968.

Champagne, F. A., Chretien, P., Stevenson, C. W., Zhang, T. Y., Gratton, A., & Meaney, M. J. (2004). Variations in nucleus accumbens dopamine associated with individual differences in maternal behavior in the rat. *Journal of Neuroscience, 24,* 4113–4123.

Chen, J. S., Kelz, M. B., Hope, B. T., Nakabeppu, Y., & Nestler, E. J. (1997). Chronic Fos-related antigens: Stable variants of Delta FosB induced in brain by chronic treatments. *Journal of Neuroscience, 17,* 4933–4941.

Cherek, D. R., Spiga, R., Roache, J. D., & Cowan, K. A. (1991). Effects of triazolam on human aggressive, escape and point-maintained responding. *Pharmacology, Biochemistry and Behavior, 40,* 835–839.

Christie, M. H., & Barfield, R. J. (1979). Effects of castration and home cage residency on aggressive behavior in rats. *Hormones and Behavior, 13,* 85–91.

Christmas, A. J., & Maxwell, D. R. (1970). A comparison of the effects of some benzodiazepines and other drugs on aggressive and exploratory behaviour in mice and rats. *Neuropharmacology, 9,* 17–29.

Citrome, L., & Volavka, J. (1997a). Psychopharmacology of violence: Part I. Assessment and acute treatment. *Psychiatric Annals, 27,* 691–695.

Citrome, L., & Volavka, J. (1997b). Psychopharmacology of violence: Part II. Beyond the acute episode. *Psychiatric Annals, 10,* 696–703.

Cleare, A. J., & Bond, A. J. (2000). Ipsapirone challenge in aggressive men shows an inverse correlation between 5-HT1A receptor function and aggression. *Psychopharmacology, 148,* 344–349.

Clement, J., Simler, S., Ciesielski, L., Mandel, P., Cabib, S., & Puglisi-Allegra, S. (1987). Age-dependent changes of brain GABA levels, turnover rates and shock-induced aggressive behavior in inbred strains of mice. *Pharmacology, Biochemistry and Behavior, 26,* 83–88.

Coccaro, E. F., Gabriel, S., & Siever, L. J. (1990). Buspirone challenge: Preliminary evidence for a role for central 5-HT1a receptor function in impulsive aggressive behavior in humans. *Psychopharmacology Bulletin, 26,* 393–405.

Coccaro, E. F., Kavoussi, R. J., Cooper, T. B., & Hauger, R. L. (1997). Central serotonin activity and aggression: Inverse relationship with prolactin response to d-fenfluramine, but not CSF 5-HIAA concentration, in human subjects. *American Journal of Psychiatry, 154,* 1430–1435.

Coccaro, E. F., Kavoussi, R. J., & Hauger, R. L. (1995). Physiological responses to d-fenfluramine and ipsapirone challenge correlate with indices of aggression in males with personality disorder. *International Clinical Psychopharmacology, 10,* 177–179.

Cole, H. F., & Wolf, H. H. (1970). Laboratory evaluation of aggressive behavior of the grasshopper mouse (*Onychomys*). *Journal of Pharmaceutical Sciences, 59,* 969–971.

Collinson, N., Kuenzi, F. M., Jarolimek, W., Maubach, K. A., Cothliff, R., Sur, C., et al. (2002). Enhanced learning and memory and altered GABAergic synaptic transmission in mice lacking the alpha 5 subunit of the GABA(A) receptor. *Journal of Neuroscience, 22,* 5572–5580.

Connor, D. F., Boone, R. T., Steingard, R. J., Lopez, I. D., & Melloni, R. H. (2003). Psychopharmacology and aggression: II. A meta-analysis of nonstimulant medication effects on overt aggression-related behaviors in youth with SED. *Journal of Emotional and Behavioral Disorders, 11,* 157–168.

Connor, J. L. (1974). Waning and recovery of conspecific aggression in the house mouse (*Mus musculus* L). *Journal of Comparative and Physiological Psychology, 87,* 215–227.

Crawley, J. N., & Contrera, J. F. (1976). Intraventricular 6-hydroxydopamine lowers isolation-induced fighting behavior in male mice. *Pharmacology, Biochemistry and Behavior, 4,* 381–384.

Crews, D., & Moore, M. C. (1986). Evolution of mechanisms controlling mating behavior. *Science, 231,* 121–125.

Crowley, T. J. (1972). Dose-dependent facilitation or suppression of rat fighting by methamphetamine, phenobarbital, or imipramine. *Psychopharmacologia, 27,* 213–222.

Cutler, M. G., Rodgers, R. J., & Jackson, J. E. (1997). Behavioural effects in mice of subchronic buspirone, ondansetron, and tianeptine: I. Social interactions. *Pharmacology, Biochemistry and Behavior, 56,* 287–293.

Czobor, P., Volavka, J., & Meibach, R. C. (1995). Effect of risperidone on hostility in schizophrenia. *Journal of Clinical Psychopharmacology, 15,* 243–249.

DaVanzo, J. P., & Sydow, M. (1979). Inhibition of isolation-induced aggressive behavior with GABA transaminase inhibitors. *Psychopharmacology, 62,* 23–27.

Dawson, R., Jr., Patterson, T. A., & Eppler, B. (1995). Endogenous excitatory amino acid release from brain slices and astrocyte cultures evoked by trimethyltin and other neurotoxic agents. *Neurochemical Research, 20,* 847–858.

De Almeida, R. M. M., & Lucion, A. (1994). Effects of intracerebroventricular administration of 5-HT receptor agonists on the maternal aggression of rats. *European Journal of Neuroscience, 264,* 445–448.

De Almeida, R. M. M., & Lucion, A. B. (1997). 8-OH-DPAT in the median raphe, dorsal periaqueductal gray and corticomedial amygdala nucleus decreases, but the medial septal area it can increase maternal aggressive behavior in rats. *Psychopharmacology, 134,* 392–400.

De Almeida, R. M. M., & Miczek, K. A. (2002). Aggression escalated by social instigation or by discontinuation of reinforcement ("frustration") in mice: Inhibition by anpirtoline—a 5-HT1B receptor agonist. *Neuropsychopharmacology, 27,* 171–1.

De Almeida, R. M. M., Nikulina, E. M., Faccidomo, S., Fish, E. W., & Miczek, K. A. (2001). Zolmitriptan—a 5-HT1B/D agonist, alcohol, and aggression in mice. *Psychopharmacology, 157,* 131–141.

De Almeida, R. M. M., Rowlett, J. K., Cook, J. M., Yin, W., & Miczek, K. A. (2004). GABAA/alpha1 receptor agonists and antagonists: Effects on species-typical and heightened aggressive behavior after alcohol self-administration in mice. *Psychopharmacology, 172,* 255–263.

De Boer, S. F., Lesourd, M., Mocaer, E., & Koolhaas, J. M. (1999). Selective antiaggressive effects of alnespirone in resident-intruder test are mediated via (5-hydroxytryptamine)1A receptors: A comparative pharmacological study with 8-hydroxy-2-dipropylaminotetralin, ipsapirone, buspirone, eltoprazine, and WAY-100635. *Journal of Pharmacology and Experimental Therapeutics, 288,* 1125–1133.

De Boer, S. F., Lesourd, M., Mocaer, E., & Koolhaas, J. M. (2000). Somatodendritic 5-HT(1A) autoreceptors mediate the anti-aggressive actions of 5-HT(1A) receptor agonists in rats: An ethopharmacological study with S-15535, alnespirone, and WAY-100635. *Neuropsychopharmacology, 23,* 20–33.

DeBold, J. F., & Miczek, K. A. (1981). Sexual dimorphism in the hormonal control of aggressive behavior of rats. *Pharmacology, Biochemistry and Behavior, 14*(Suppl. 1), 89–93.

DeBold, J. F., & Miczek, K. A. (1984). Aggression persists after ovariectomy in female rats. *Hormones and Behavior, 18,* 177–190.

De Deyn, P. P., Rabheru, K., Rasmussen, A., Bocksberger, J. P., Dautzenberg, P. L., Eriksson, S., et al. (1999). A randomized trial of risperidone, placebo, and haloperidol for behavioral symptoms of dementia. *Neurology, 53,* 946–955.

Depaulis, A., & Vergnes, M. (1983). Induction of mouse-killing in the rat by intraventricular injection of a GABA-agonist. *Physiology and Behavior, 30,* 383–388.

Diana, M., Pistis, M., Muntoni, A., & Gessa, G. (1995). Profound decrease of mesolimbic dopaminergic neuronal activity in morphine withdrawn rats. *Journal of Pharmacology and Experimental Therapeutics, 272,* 781–785.

Dietch, J. T., & Jennings, R. K. (1988). Aggressive dyscontrol in patients treated with benzodiazepines. *Journal of Clinical Psychiatry, 49,* 184–188.

DiMascio, A. (1973). The effects of benzodiazepines on aggression: Reduced or increased? *Psychopharmacologia, 30,* 95–102.

DiMascio, A., Shader, R. I., & Harmatz, J. (1969). Psychotropic drugs and induced hostility. *Psychosomatics, 10,* 46–47.

Dodman, N. H., Donnelly, R., Shuster, L., Mertens, P., Rand, W., & Miczek, K. A. (1996). Use of fluoxetine to treat dominance aggression in dogs. *Journal of the American Veterinary Medical Association, 209,* 1585–1587.

Dollard, J., Doob, L., Miller, N., Mowrer, O., & Sears, R. (1939). *Frustration and aggression.* New Haven, CT: Yale University Press.

Dompert, W. U., Glaser, T., & Traber, J. (1985). 3H-TVX Q 7821: Identification of 5-HT1 binding sites as target for a novel putative anxiolytic. *Naunyn-Schmiedeberg's Archives of Pharmacology, 328,* 467–470.

Doudet, D., Hommer, D., Higley, J. D., Andreason, P. J., Moneman, R., Suomi, S. J., et al. (1995). Cerebral glucose metabolism, CSF 5-HIAA levels, and aggressive behavior in rhesus monkeys. *American Journal of Psychiatry, 152,* 1782–1787.

Early, C. J., & Leonard, B. E. (1980). The effect of testosterone and cyproterone acetate on the concentration of γ-aminobutyric acid in brain areas of aggressive and non-aggressive mice. *Pharmacology, Biochemistry and Behavior, 12,* 189–193.

Eibl-Eibesfeldt, I. (1950). Beiträge zur biologie der haus—und der ährenmaus nebst einigen beobachtungen an anderen nagern. *Zeitschrift für Tierpsychologie, 7,* 558–587.

Eichelman, B. (1992). Aggressive behavior: From laboratory to clinic. *Archives of General Psychiatry, 49,* 488–492.

Eichelman, B. S. J., Thoa, N. B., & Ng, K. Y. (1972). Facilitated aggression in the rat following 6-hydroxydopamine administration. *Physiology and Behavior, 8,* 1–3.

Elliott, F. A. (1977). Propanolol for the control of belligerent behavior following acute brain damage. *Annals of Neurology, 1,* 489–491.

Fairbanks, L. A., Fontenot, M. B., Phillips-Conroy, J. E., Jolly, C. J., Kaplan, J. R., & Mann, J. J. (1999). CSF monoamines, age and impulsivity in wild grivet monkeys (*Cercopithecus aethiops aethiops*). *Brain Behavior and Evolution, 53,* 305–312.

Fairbanks, L. A., Melega, W. P., Jorgensen, M. J., Kaplan, J. R., & McGuire, M. T. (2001). Social impulsivity inversely associated with CSF 5-HIAA and fluoxetine exposure in vervet monkeys. *Neuropsychopharmacology, 24,* 370–378.

Farrington, D. P. (1993). Motivations for conduct disorder and delinquency. *Development and Psychopathology, 5,* 225–241.

Fava, M. (1997). Psychopharmacologic treatment of pathologic aggression. *Anger, Aggression, and Violence, 20,* 427–451.

Ferrari, P. F., Parmigiani, S., Rodgers, R. J., & Palanza, P. (1997). Differential effects of chlordiazepoxide on aggressive behavior in male mice: The influence of social factors. *Psychopharmacology, 134,* 258–265.

Ferrari, P. F., Van Erp, A. M. M., Tornatzky, W., & Miczek, K. A. (2003). Accumbal dopamine and serotonin in anticipation of the next aggressive episode in rats. *European Journal of Neuroscience, 17,* 371–378.

Ferris, C. F., & Delville, Y. (1994). Vasopressin and serotonin interactions in the control of agonistic behavior. *Psychoneuroendocrinology, 19,* 593–601.

Fish, E. W., DeBold, J. F., & Miczek, K. A. (2001). Repeated alcohol: Behavioral sensitization and alcohol-heightened aggression in mice. *Psychopharmacology, 160,* 39–48.

Fish, E. W., DeBold, J. F., & Miczek, K. A. (2002). Aggressive behavior as a reinforcer in mice: Activation by allopregnanolone. *Psychopharmacology, 163,* 459–466.

Fish, E. W., Faccidomo, S., DeBold, J. F., & Miczek, K. A. (2001). Alcohol, allopregnanolone and aggression in mice. *Psychopharmacology, 153,* 473–483.

Fish, E. W., Faccidomo, S., & Miczek, K. A. (1999). Aggression heightened by alcohol or social instigation in mice: Reduction by the 5-HT1B receptor agonist CP-94,253. *Psychopharmacology, 146,* 391–399.

Fletcher, P. J., Azampanah, A., & Korth, K. M. (2002). Activation of 5-HT1B receptors in the nucleus accumbens reduces self-administration of amphetamine on a progressive ratio schedule. *Pharmacology, Biochemistry and Behavior, 71,* 717–725.

Fletcher, P. J., & Korth, K. M. (1999). RU-24969 disrupts d-amphetamine self-administration and responding for conditioned reward via stimulation of 5-HT1B receptors. *Behavioural Pharmacology, 10,* 183–193.

Fowler, S. C., & Liou, J. R. (1998). Haloperidol, raclopride, and eticlopride induce microcatalepsy during operant performance in rats, but clozapine and SCH 23390 do not. *Psychopharmacology, 140,* 81–90.

Gao, B., & Cutler, M. G. (1992). Effects of acute and subchronic administration of propranolol on the social behaviour of mice—an ethopharmacological study. *Neuropharmacology, 31,* 749–756.

Gerra, G., Zaimovic, A., Avanzini, P., Chittolini, B., Giucastro, G., Caccavari, R., et al. (1997). Neurotransmitter-neuroendocrine responses to experimentally induced aggression in humans: Influence of personality variable. *Psychiatry Research, 66,* 33–43.

Giacalone, E., Tansella, M., Valzelli, L., & Garattini, S. (1968). Brain serotonin metabolism in isolated aggressive mice. *Biochemical Pharmacology, 17,* 1315–1327.

Gianutsos, G. & Lal, H. (1978). Narcotic analgesics and aggression. In L. Valzelli (Ed.), *Modern problems of pharmopsychiatry: Psychopharmacology of aggression* (13th ed., pp. 114–138). New York: Karger.

Glazer, W. M., & Dickson, R. A. (1998). Clozapine reduces violence and persistent aggression in schizophrenia. *Journal of Clinical Psychiatry, 59*(Suppl. 3), 8–14.

Gourley, S. L., DeBold, J. F., Yin, W., Cook, J., & Miczek, K. A. (2005). Benzodiazepines and heightened aggressive behavior in rats: Reduction by GABA(A)/α(1) receptor antagonists. *Psychopharmacology, 178,* 232–240.

Gregg, T. R., & Siegel, A. (2001). Brain structures and neurotransmitters regulating aggression in cats: Implications for human aggression. *Progress in Neuro-Psychopharmacology and Biological Psychiatry, 25,* 91–140.

Groenink, L., van der Gugten, J., Mos, J., Maes, R. A. A., & Olivier, B. (1995). The corticosterone-enhancing effects of the 5-HT{-1A} receptor antagonist, (S)-UH301, are not mediated by the 5-HT{-1A} receptor. *European Journal of Pharmacology, 272,* 177–183.

Guillot, P. V., & Chapouthier, G. (1996). Intermale aggression and dark preference in ten inbred mouse strains. *Behavioural Brain Research, 77,* 211–213.

Guillot, P. V., & Chapouthier, G. (1998). Intermale aggression, GAD activity in the olfactory bulbs and Y chromosome effect in seven inbred mouse strains. *Behavioural Brain Research, 90,* 203–206.

Hadfield, M. G. (1983). Dopamine: Mesocortical versus nigrostriatal uptake in isolated fighting mice and controls. *Behavioural Brain Research, 7,* 269–281.

Haller, J. (1995). Alpha-2 adrenoceptor blockade and the response to intruder aggression in Long-Evans rats. *Physiology and Behavior, 58*(1), 101–106.

Haller, J., Bakos, N., Rodriguiz, R. M., Caron, M. G., Wetsel, W. C., & Liposits, Z. (2002). Behavioral responses to social stress in noradrenaline transporter knockout mice: Effects on social behavior and depression. *Brain Research Bulletin, 58,* 279–284.

Haller, J., Barna, I., & Kovacs, J. L. (1994). Alpha2-adrenoceptor blockade, pituitary-adrenal hormones, and agonistic interactions in rats. *Psychopharmacology, 115,* 478–484.

Haller, J., & Kruk, M. R. (2003). Neuroendocrine stress responses and aggression. In *Neurobiology of aggression: Understanding and preventing violence* (1st ed., pp. 93–118). Totowa, NJ: Humana.

Haller, J., Makara, G. B., & Kovacs, J. L. (1996). The effect of alpha-3 adrenoceptor blockers on aggressive behavior in mice: Implications for the actions of adrenoceptor agents. *Psychopharmacology, 126,* 345–350.

Haller, J., Makara, G. B., & Kruk, M. R. (1998). Catecholaminergic involvement in the control of aggression: Hormones, the peripheral sympathetic, and central noradrenergic systems. *Neuroscience and Biobehavioral Reviews, 22,* 85–97.

Haney, M., Noda, K., Kream, R., & Miczek, K. A. (1990). Regional serotonin and dopamine activity: Sensitivity to amphetamine and aggressive behavior in mice. *Aggressive Behavior, 16,* 259–270.

Hansen, S., Harthon, C., & Wallin, E. (1991). Mesotelencephalic dopamine system and reproductive behavior in the female rat: Effects of ventral tegmental 6-hydroxydopamine lesions on maternal and sexual responsiveness. *Behavioral Neuroscience, 105,* 588–598.

Hasselager, E., Rolinski, Z., & Randrup, A. (1972). Specific antagonism by dopamine inhibitors of items of amphetamine induced aggressive behaviour. *Psychopharmacologia, 24*, 485–495.

Haug, M., Simler, S., Ciesielski, L., Mandel, P., & Moutier, R. (1984). Influence of castration and brain GABA levels in three strains of mice on aggression towards lactating intruders. *Physiology and Behavior, 32*, 767–770.

Haug, M., Wallian, L., & Brain, P. F. (1990). Effects of 8-OH-DPAT and fluoxetine on activity and attack by female mice towards lactating intruders. *General Pharmacology, 21*, 845–849.

Hector, R. I. (1998). The use of clozapine in the treatment of aggressive schizophrenia. *Canadian Journal of Psychiatry, 43*, 466–472.

Hegstrand, L. R., & Eichelman, B. (1983). Increased shock-induced fighting with supersensitive beta-adrenergic receptors. *Pharmacology, Biochemistry and Behavior, 19*, 313–320.

Heiligenberg, W. (1974). Processes governing behavioral states of readiness. *Advances in the Study of Behavior, 5*, 173–200.

Heiligenstein, J. H., Beasley, C. M., Jr., & Potvin, J. H. (1993). Fluoxetine not associated with increased aggression in controlled clinical trials. *International Clinical Psychopharmacology, 8*, 277–280.

Hendley, E. D., Moisset, B., & Welch, B. L. (1973). Catecholamine uptake in cerebral cortex: Adaptive change induced by fighting. *Science, 180*, 1050–1052.

Higley, J. D. (2001). Individual differences in alcohol-induced aggression. A nonhuman-primate model. *Alcohol Research and Health, 25*, 12–19.

Higley, J. D., & Bennett, A. J. (1999). Central nervous system serotonin and personality as variables contributing to excessive alcohol consumption in non-human primates. *Alcohol and Alcoholism, 34*, 402–418.

Higley, J. D., Mehlman, P. T., Taub, D. M., Higley, S. B., Suomi, S. J., Vickers, J. H., et al. (1992). Cerebrospinal fluid monoamine and adrenal correlates of aggression in free-ranging rhesus monkeys. *Archives of General Psychiatry, 49*, 436–441.

Hodge, G. K., & Butcher, L. L. (1975). Catecholamine correlates of isolation-induced aggression in mice. *European Journal of Pharmacology, 31*, 81–93.

Hoebel, B. G. (1968). Inhibition and disinhibition of self-stimulation and feeding: Hypothalamic control and postingestional factors. *Journal of Comparative and Physiological Psychology, 66*, 89–100.

Höglund, E., Balm, P. H., & Winberg, S. (2000). Skin darkening, a potential social signal in subordinate arctic charr (*Salvelinus alpinus*): The regulatory role of brain monoamines and pro-opiomelanocortin-derived peptides. *Journal of Experimental Biology, 203 Pt 11*, 1711–1721.

Holmes, A., Murphy, D. L., & Crawley, J. N. (2002). Reduced aggression in mice lacking the serotonin transporter. *Psychopharmacology, 161*, 160–167.

Holschneider, D. P., Chen, K., Seif, I., & Shih, J. C. (2001). Biochemical, behavioral, physiologic, and neurodevelopmental changes in mice deficient in monoamine oxidase A or B. *Brain Research Bulletin, 56*, 453–462.

Hoyer, D., Hannon, J. P., & Martin, G. R. (2002). Molecular, pharmacological and functional diversity of 5-HT receptors. *Pharmacology, Biochemistry and Behavior, 71*, 533–554.

Huber, R., & Kravitz, E. A. (1995). A quantitative analysis of agonistic behavior in juvenile American lobsters (*Homarus americanus* L.). *Brain, Behavior and Evolution, 46*, 72–83.

Huber, R., Smith, K., Delago, A., Isaksson, K., & Kravitz, E. A. (1997). Serotonin and aggressive motivation in crustaceans: Altering the decision to retreat. *Proceedings of the National Academy of Sciences USA, 94*, 5939–5942.

Humble, F., & Berk, M. (2003). Pharmacological management of aggression and violence. *Human Psychopharmacology, 18*, 423–436.

Hurst, J. L. (1987). Behavioral variation in wild house mice *Mus domesticus* Rutty: A quantitative assessment of female social organization. *Animal Behaviour, 35*, 1846–1857.

Ishida, N., Akaike, M., Tsutsumi, S., Kanai, H., Masui, A., Sadamatsu, M., et al. (1997). Trimethyltin syndrome as a hippocampal degeneration model: Temporal changes and neurochemical features of seizure susceptibility and learning impairment. *Neuroscience, 81*, 1183–1191.

Itil, T. M. (1981). Drug therapy in the management of aggression. In P. F. Brain (Ed.), *Multidisciplinary approaches to aggression research* (pp. 489–501). New York: Elsevier/North-Holland Biomedical.

Itil, T. M., & Wadud, A. (1975). Treatment of human aggression with major tranquilizers, antidepressants and newer psychotropic drugs. *Journal of Nervous and Mental Disease, 160*, 83–99.

Jacobs, B. L. (1976). An animal behavior model for studying central serotonergic synapses. *Life Sciences, 19*, 777–786.

Joppa, M. A., Rowe, R. K., & Meisel, R. L. (1997). Effects of serotonin 1A or 1B receptor agonists on social aggression in male and female Syrian hamsters. *Pharmacology, Biochemistry and Behavior, 58*, 349–353.

Kalivas, P. W., & McFarland, K. (2003). Brain circuitry and the reinstatement of cocaine-seeking behavior. *Psychopharmacology, 168*, 44–56.

Kalynchuk, L. E., Dalal, S., Mana, M. J., & Pinel, J. P. (1992). Nifedipine blocks the development of tolerance to the anticonvulsant effects of ethanol. *Annals of the New York Academy of Sciences, 654*, 459–460.

Kantak, K. M., Hegstrand, L. R., & Eichelman, B. (1981).

Dietary tryptophan reversal of septal lesion and 5,7-DHT lesion elicited shock-induced fighting. *Pharmacology, Biochemistry and Behavior, 15*, 343–350.

Kantak, K. M., & Miczek, K. A. (1988). Social, motor, and autonomic signs of morphine withdrawal: Differential sensitivities to catecholaminergic drugs in mice. *Psychopharmacology, 96*, 468–476.

Kaplan, J. R., Manuck, S. B., Fontenot, M. B., & Mann, J. J. (2002). Central nervous system monoamine correlates of social dominance in cynomolgus monkeys (*Macaca fascicularis*). *Neuropsychopharmacology, 26*, 431–443.

Karczmar, A. G., Scudder, C. L., & Richardson, D. L. (1973). Interdisciplinary approach to the study of behavior in related mice types. *Neuroscience Research, 5*, 159–245.

Keck, P. E., Jr., Strakowski, S. M., & McElroy, S. L. (2000). The efficacy of atypical antipsychotics in the treatment of depressive symptoms, hostility, and suicidality in patients with schizophrenia. *Journal of Clinical Psychiatry, 61*(Suppl. 3), 4–9.

Kemble, E. D., Behrens, M., Rawleigh, J. M., & Gibson, B. M. (1991). Effects of yohimbine on isolation-induced aggression, social attraction, and conspecific odor preference in mice. *Pharmacology, Biochemistry and Behavior, 40*, 781–785.

Kennedy, J. S., Bymaster, F. P., Schuh, L., Calligaro, D. O., Nomikos, G., Felder, C. C., et al. (2001). A current review of olanzapine's safety in the geriatric patient: From pre-clinical pharmacology to clinical data. *International Journal of Geriatric Psychiatry, 16*, S33–S61.

Kim, D. H., Jung, J. S., Yan, J. J., Suh, H. W., Son, B. K., Kim, Y. H., et al. (2000). Increased plasma corticosterone, aggressiveness and brain monoamine changes induced by central injection of pertussis toxin. *European Journal of Pharmacology, 409*, 67–72.

King, B. H., Wright, D. M., Handen, B. L., Sikich, L., Zimmerman, A. W., McMahon, W., et al. (2001). Double-blind, placebo-controlled study of amantadine hydrochloride in the treatment of children with autistic disorder. *Journal of the American Academy of Child and Adolescent Psychiatry, 40*, 658–665.

Klauck, S. M., Poustka, F., Benner, A., Lesch, K. P., & Poustka, A. (1997). Serotonin transporter (5-HTT) gene variants associated with autism? *Human Molecular Genetics, 6*, 2233–2238.

Kollack-Walker, S., Watson, S. J., & Akil, H. (1997). Social stress in hamsters: Defeat activates specific neurocircuits within the brain. *Journal of Neuroscience, 17*, 8842–8855.

Koob, G. F., Riley, S. J., Smith, S. C., & Robbins, T. W. (1978). Effects of 6-hydroxydopamine lesions of the nucleus accumbens septi and olfactory tubercle on

feeding, locomotor activity, and amphetamine anorexia in the rat. *Journal of Comparative and Physiological Psychology, 92*, 917–927.

Korte, S. M., Meijer, O. C., De Kloet, E. R., Buwalda, B., Keijser, J., Sluyter, F., et al. (1996). Enhanced 5-HT1A receptor expression in forebrain regions of aggressive house mice. *Brain Research, 736*, 338–343.

Kravitz, E. A., & Huber, R. (2003). Aggression in invertebrates. *Current Opinion in Neurobiology, 13*, 736–743.

Krsiak, M. (1974). Behavioral changes and aggressivity evoked by drugs in mice. *Research Communications in Chemical Pathology and Pharmacology, 7*, 237–257.

Krsiak, M. (1975). Timid singly-housed mice: Their value in prediction of psychotropic activity of drugs. *British Journal of Pharmacology, 55*, 141–150.

Krsiak, M., Sulcova, A., Tomasikova, Z., Dlohozkova, N., Kosar, E., & Masek, K. (1981). Drug effects on attack, defense and escape in mice. *Pharmacology, Biochemistry and Behavior, 14*, 47–52.

Kruesi, M. J. P., Rapoport, J. L., Hamburger, S., Hibbs, E., Potter, W. Z., Lenane, M., et al. (1990). Cerebrospinal fluid monoamine metabolites, aggression, and impulsivity in disruptive behavior disorders of children and adolescents. *Archives of General Psychiatry, 47*, 419–426.

Kruk, M. R. (1991). Ethology and pharmacology of hypothalamic aggression in the rat. *Neuroscience and Biobehavioral Reviews, 15*, 527–538.

Kudryavtseva, N. N. (1991). A sensory contact model for the study of aggressive and submissive behavior in male mice. *Aggressive Behavior, 17*, 285–291.

Lang, A., Harro, J., Soosaar, A., Koks, S., Volke, V., Oreland, L., et al. (1995). Role of N-methyl-D-aspartic acid and cholecystokinin receptors in apomorphine-induced aggressive behaviour in rats. *Naunyn-Schmiedeberg's Archives of Pharmacology, 351*, 363–370.

Lasley, S. M., & Thurmond, J. B. (1985). Interaction of dietary tryptophan and social isolation on territorial aggression, motor activity, and neurochemistry in mice. *Psychopharmacology, 87*, 313–321.

Lee, M., & Simansky, K. (1997). CP-94,253: A selective serotonin 5-HT1B agonist that promotes satiety. *Psychopharmacology, 131*, 264–270.

Lesch, K. P., & Merschdorf, U. (2000). Impulsivity, aggression, and serotonin: A molecular psychobiological perspective. *Behavioral Sciences and the Law, 18*, 581–604.

Leventhal, B. L., & Brodie, H. K. H. (1981). The pharmacology of violence. In D. A. Hamburg (Ed.), *Biobehavioral aspects of aggression* (pp. 85–106). New York: A. R. Liss.

Lindenmayer, J. P., & Kotsaftis, A. (2000). Use of sodium valproate in violent and aggressive behaviors: A critical review. *Journal of Clinical Psychiatry, 61,* 123–128.

Lindgren, T., & Kantak, K. M. (1987). Effects of serotonin receptor agonists and antagonists on offensive aggression in mice. *Aggressive Behavior, 13,* 87–96.

Linnoila, M., De Jong, J., & Virkkunen, M. (1989). Family history of alcoholism in violent offenders and impulsive fire setters. *Archives of General Psychiatry, 46,* 613–616.

Linnoila, M., Virkkunen, M., Scheinin, M., Nuutila, A., Rimon, R., & Goodwin, F. K. (1983). Low cerebrospinal fluid 5-hydroxyindoleacetic acid concentration differentiates impulsive from nonimpulsive violent behavior. *Life Sciences, 33,* 2609–2614.

Lipe, G. W., Ali, S. F., Newport, G. D., Scallet, A. C., & Slikker, W., Jr. (1991). Effect of trimethyltin on amino acid concentrations in different regions of the mouse brain. *Pharmacology and Toxicology, 68,* 450–455.

Lorenz, K. (1966). *On aggression.* London: Methuen.

Löw, K., Crestani, F., Keist, R., Benke, D., Brünig, I., Benson, J. A., et al. (2000). Molecular and neuronal substrate for the selective attenuation of anxiety. *Science, 290,* 131–134.

Lucki, I., & Wieland, S. (1990). 5-Hydroxytryptamine-1A receptors and behavioral responses. *Neuropsychopharmacology, 3,* 481–493.

Maes, M., Cosyns, P., Meltzer, H. Y., De Meyer, J., & Peeters, D. (1993). Seasonality in violent suicide but not in nonviolent suicide or homicide. *American Journal of Psychiatry, 150,* 1380–1385.

Mann, J. J. (1999). Role of the serotonergic system in the pathogenesis of major depression and suicidal behavior. *Neuropsychopharmacology, 21,* 99S–105S.

Manuck, S. B., Flory, J. D., McCaffery, J. M., Matthews, K. A., Mann, J. J., & Muldoon, M. F. (1998). Aggression, impulsivity, and central nervous system serotonergic responsivity in a nonpatient sample. *Neuropsychopharmacology, 19,* 287–299.

Manuck, S. B., Kaplan, J. R., Rymeski, B. A., Fairbanks, L. A., & Wilson, M. E. (2003). Approach to a social stranger is associated with low central nervous system serotonergic responsivity in female cynomolgus monkeys (*Macaca fascicularis*). *American Journal of Primatology, 61,* 187–194.

Martin-Lopez, M., & Navarro, J. F. (2002). Antiaggressive effects of zolpidem and zopiclone in agonistic encounters between male mice. *Aggressive Behavior, 28,* 416–425.

Martinez, M., Calvo-Torrent, A., & Herbert, J. (2002). Mapping brain response to social stress in rodents with c-fos expression: A review. *Stress, 5,* 3–13.

Matsumoto, K., Cai, B., Satoh, T., Ohta, H., & Watanabe, H. (1991). Desipramine enhances isolation-induced aggression behavior in mice. *Pharmacology, Biochemistry and Behavior, 39,* 167–170.

McAllister, K. H. (1990). Ethological analysis of the effects of MK-801 upon aggressive male mice: Similarity to chlordiazepoxide. *Pharmacology, Biochemistry and Behavior, 37,* 101–106.

McCracken, J. T., McGough, J., Shah, B., Cronin, P., Hong, D., Aman, M. G., et al. (2002). Risperidone in children with autism and serious behavioral problems. *New England Journal of Medicine, 347,* 314–321.

McElroy, S. L., Soutullo, C. A., Beckman, D. A., Taylor, P., & Keck, P. E. (1998). DSM-IV intermittent explosive disorder: A report of 27 cases. *Journal of Clinical Psychiatry, 59,* 203–210.

McKenzie-Quirk, S. D., & Miczek, K. A. (2003). 5-HT1A agonists: Alcohol drinking in rats and squirrel monkeys. *Psychopharmacology, 167,* 145–152.

McKernan, R. M., & Whiting, P. J. (1996). Which GABA(A)-receptor subtypes really occur in the brain? *Trends in Neurosciences, 19,* 139–143.

McMillen, B. A., DaVanzo, E. A., Scott, S. M., & Song, A. H. (1988). N-alkyl-substituted aryl-piperazine drugs: Relationship between affinity for serotonin receptors and inhibition of aggression. *Drug Development Research, 12,* 53–62.

Mehlman, P. T., Higley, J. D., Faucher, I., Lilly, A. A., Taub, D. M., Vickers, J., et al. (1994). Low CSF 5-HIAA concentrations and severe aggression and impaired impulse control in nonhuman primates. *American Journal of Psychiatry, 151,* 1485–1491.

Mehta, A. K., & Ticku, M. K. (1988). Ethanol potentiation of GABAergic transmission in cultured spinal cord neurons involves gamma-aminobutyric acid A-gated chloride channels. *Journal of Pharmacology and Experimental Therapeutics, 246,* 558–564.

Miczek, K. A. (1974). Intraspecies aggression in rats: Effects of d-amphetamine and chlordiazepoxide. *Psychopharmacologia, 39,* 275–301.

Miczek, K. A., Barros, H. M., Sakoda, L., & Weerts, E. M. (1998). Alcohol and heightened aggression in individual mice. *Alcoholism, Clinical and Experimental Research, 22,* 1698–1705.

Miczek, K. A., Covington, H. E., Nikulina, E. A., & Hammer, R. P. (2004). Aggression and defeat: Persistent effects on cocaine self-administration and gene expression in peptidergic and aminergic mesocorticolimbic circuits. *Neuroscience and Biobehavioral Reviews, 27,* 787–802.

Miczek, K. A., DeBold, J. F., & Van Erp, A. M. M. (1994). Neuropharmacological characteristics of individual differences in alcohol effects on aggression in rodents and primates. *Behavioural Pharmacology, 5,* 407–421.

Miczek, K. A., DeBold, J. F., Van Erp, A. M. M., & Tornatzky, W. (1997). Alcohol, GABAA-benzodiazepine receptor complex, and aggression. In M. Galanter (Ed.), *Alcoholism and violence: Recent developments in alcoholism* (13th ed., pp. 139–171). New York: Plenum.

Miczek, K. A., Fish, E. W., & DeBold, J. F. (2003). Neurosteroids, GABAA receptors, and escalated aggressive behavior. *Hormones and Behavior, 44,* 242–257.

Miczek, K. A., Fish, E. W., DeBold, J. F., & de Almeida, R. M. M. (2002). Social and neural determinants of aggressive behavior: Pharmacotherapeutic targets at serotonin, dopamine and γ-aminobutyric acid systems. *Psychopharmacology, 163,* 434–458.

Miczek, K. A., & Haney, M. (1994). Psychomotor stimulant effects of d-amphetamine, MDMA and PCP: Aggressive and schedule-controlled behavior in mice. *Psychopharmacology, 115,* 358–365.

Miczek, K. A., Hussain, S., & Faccidomo, S. (1998). Alcohol-heightened aggression in mice: Attenuation by 5-HT1A receptor agonists. *Psychopharmacology, 139,* 160–168.

Miczek, K. A., & O'Donnell, J. M. (1978). Intruder-evoked aggression in isolated and nonisolated mice: Effects of psychomotor stimulants and l-dopa. *Psychopharmacology, 57,* 47–55.

Miczek, K. A., & O'Donnell, J. M. (1980). Alcohol and chlordiazepoxide increase suppressed aggression in mice. *Psychopharmacology, 69,* 39–44.

Miczek, K. A., Weerts, E. M., & DeBold, J. F. (1993). Alcohol, benzodiazepine-GABA{-A} receptor complex and aggression: Ethological analysis of individual differences in rodents and primates. *Journal of Studies on Alcohol, 11*(Suppl.), 170–179.

Miczek, K. A., & Yoshimura, H. (1982). Disruption of primate social behavior by d-amphetamine and cocaine: Differential antagonism by antipsychotics. *Psychopharmacology, 76,* 163–171.

Millan, M. J., Bervoets, K., & Colpaert, F. C. (1991). 5-Hydroxytryptamine (5-HT)1A receptors and the tail-flick response: I. 8-Hydroxy-2-(di-n-propylamino) tetralin HBr-induced spontaneous tail-flicks in the rat as an in vivo model of 5-HT1A receptor-mediated activity. *Journal of Pharmacology and Experimental Therapeutics, 256,* 973–982.

Mirsky, A. F., & Harman, N. (1974). On aggressive behavior and brain disease-some questions and possible relationships derived from the study of men and monkeys. In R. F. Whalen (Ed.), *The neuropsychology of aggression* (12th ed., pp. 185–210). New York: Plenum.

Mitchell, P. J., & Redfern, P. H. (1997). Potentiation of the time-dependent, antidepressant-induced changes in the agonistic behaviour of resident rats by the 5-HT(1A)

receptor antagonist, WAY-100635. *Behavioural Pharmacology, 8,* 585–606.

Monroe, R. R. (1978). *Brain dysfunction in aggressive criminals.* Lexington: Heath.

Mos, J., Olivier, B., & van der Poel, A. M. (1987). Modulatory actions of benzodiazepine receptor ligands on agonistic behaviour. *Physiology and Behavior, 41,* 265–278.

Mos, J., & Van Valkenburg, C. F. M. (1979). Specific effect on social stress and aggression on regional dopamine metabolism in rat brain. *Neuroscience Letters, 15,* 325–327.

Muehlenkamp, F., Lucion, A., & Vogel, W. H. (1995). Effects of selective serotonergic agonists on aggressive behavior in rats. *Pharmacology, Biochemistry and Behavior, 50,* 671–674.

Murdoch, D., Pihl, R. O., & Ross, D. (1990). Alcohol and crimes of violence: Present issues. *International Journal of the Addictions, 25,* 1065–1081.

Musty, R. E., & Consroe, P. F. (1982). Phencyclidine produces aggressive behavior in rapid eye movement sleep-deprived rats. *Life Sciences, 30,* 1733–1738.

Naalsund, L. U., Allen, C. N., & Fonnum, F. (1985). Changes in neurobiological parameters in the hippocampus after exposure to trimethyltin. *Neurotoxicology, 6,* 145–158.

Nelson, R. J., & Chiavegatto, S. (2001). Molecular basis of aggression. *Trends in Neurosciences, 24,* 713–719.

Neppe, V. M. (1988). Carbamazepine in nonresponsive psychosis. *Journal of Clinical Psychiatry, 49*(Suppl.), 22–30.

Nikulina, E. M., Avgustinovich, D. F., & Popova, N. K. (1992). Role of 5HT1A receptors in a variety of kinds of aggressive behavior in wild rats and counterparts selected for low defensiveness towards man. *Aggressive Behavior, 18,* 357–364.

Nikulina, E. M., Covington, H. E., III, Ganshow, R. P., Hammer, R. P., Jr., & Miczek, K. A. (2004). Long-term behavioral and neuronal cross-sensitization to amphetamine induced by repeated brief social defeat stress: Fos in the ventral tegmental area and amygdala. *Neuroscience, 123,* 857–865.

Nikulina, E. M., Hammer, R. P., Jr., Miczek, K. A., & Kream, R. M. (1999). Social defeat stress increases expression of mu-opioid receptor mRNA in rat ventral tegmental area. *NeuroReport, 10,* 3015–3019.

Nikulina, E. M., Marchand, J. E., Kream, R. M., & Miczek, K. A. (1998). Behavioral sensitization to cocaine after a brief social stress is accompanied by changes in fos expression in the murine brainstem. *Brain Research, 810,* 200–210.

Nishida, T., Haraiwa-Hasegawa, M., & Takahata, Y. (1985). Group extinction and female transfer in wild chimpanzees in the Mahale National Park, Tanzania. *Zeitschrift für Tierpsychologie, 67,* 284–301.

Nogueira, R. L., & Graeff, F. G. (1995). Role of 5HT receptor subtypes in the modulation of dorsal periaqueductal gray generated aversion. *Pharmacology, Biochemistry and Behavior, 52,* 1–6.

Nowycky, M. C., Walters, J. R., & Roth, R. H. (1978). Dopaminergic neurons—effect of acute and chronic morphine administration on single cell activity and transmitter metabolism. *Journal of Neural Transmission, 42,* 99–116.

Olivier, B., Mos, J., & Miczek, K. A. (1991). Ethopharmacological studies of anxiolytics and aggression. *European Neuropsychopharmacology, 1,* 97–100.

Olivier, B., Mos, J., Van der Heyden, J., & Hartog, J. (1989). Serotonergic modulation of social interactions in isolated male mice. *Psychopharmacology, 97,* 154–156.

Olivier, B., Mos, J., Van Oorschot, R., & Hen, R. (1995). Serotonin receptors and animal models of aggressive behavior. *Pharmacopsychiatry, 28,* 80–90.

O'Neill, M. F., & Conway, M. W. (2001). Role of 5-HT(1A) and 5-HT(1B) receptors in the mediation of behavior in the forced swim test in mice. *Neuropsychopharmacology, 24,* 391–398.

O'Neill, M. F., & Parameswaran, T. (1997). RU24969-induced behavioural syndrome requires activation of both 5HT{-1A} and 5HT{-1B} receptors. *Psychopharmacology, 132,* 255–260.

Pabis, D. J., & Stanislav, S. W. (1996). Pharmacotherapy of aggressive behavior. *Annals of Pharmacotherapy, 30,* 278–287.

Parsons, L. H., Weiss, F., & Koob, G. F. (1998). Serotonin(1B) receptor stimulation enhances cocaine reinforcement. *Journal of Neuroscience, 18,* 10078–10089.

Patel, M., Ardelt, B. K., Yim, G. K., & Isom, G. E. (1990). Interaction of trimethyltin with hippocampal glutamate. *Neurotoxicology, 11,* 601–608.

Paulus, M. P., & Geyer, M. A. (1991). A scaling approach to find order parameters quantifying the effects of dopaminergic agents on unconditioned motor activity in rats. *Progress in Neuro-Psychopharmacology and Biological Psychiatry, 15,* 903–919.

Payne, A. P., Andrews, M. J., & Wilson, C. A. (1985). The effects of isolation, grouping and aggressive interactions on indole and catecholamine levels and apparent turnover in the hypothalamus and midbrain of the male golden hamster. *Physiology and Behavior, 34,* 911–916.

Pfaus, J. G., Damsma, G., Nomikos, G. G., Wenkstern, D. G., Blaha, C. D., Phillips, A. G., et al. (1990). Sexual behavior enhances central dopamine transmission in the male rat. *Brain Research, 530,* 345–348.

Pihl, R. O., Paylan, S. S., Gentes-Hawn, A., & Hoaken, P. N. (2003). Alcohol affects executive cognitive functioning differentially on the ascending versus descending limb of the blood alcohol concentration curve. *Alcoholism, Clinical and Experimental Research, 27,* 773–779.

Pinel, J. P. J., Treit, D., & Rovner, L. I. (1977). Temporal lobe aggression in rats. *Science, 197,* 1088–1089.

Pinna, G., Dong, E., Matsumoto, K., Costa, E., & Guidotti, A. (2003). In socially isolated mice, the reversal of brain allopregnanolone down-regulation mediates the anti-aggressive action of fluoxetine. *Proceedings of the National Academy of Sciences USA, 100,* 2035–2040.

Placidi, G. P. A., Oquendo, M. A., Malone, K. M., Huang, Y. Y., Ellis, S. P., & Mann, J. J. (2001). Aggressivity, suicide attempts, and depression: Relationship to cerebrospinal fluid monoamine metabolite levels. *Biological Psychiatry, 50,* 783–791.

Poeldinger, W. (1981). Pharmakotherapie der aggressivitaet. *Schweizer Archiv für Neurologie, Neurochirurgie und Psychiatrie, 129,* 147–155.

Poshivalov, V. P. (1981). Pharmaco-ethological analysis of social behaviour of isolated mice. *Pharmacology, Biochemistry and Behavior, 14, S1,* 53–59.

Potegal, M. (1979). The reinforcing value of several types of aggressive behavior: A review. *Aggressive Behavior 5(4),* 353–373.

Potegal, M., Perumal, A. S., Barkai, A. I., Cannova, G. E., & Blau, A. D. (1982). GABA binding in the brains of aggressive and non-aggressive female hamsters. *Brain Research, 247,* 315–324.

Potegal, M., & Tenbrink, L. (1984). Behavior of attack-primed and attack-satiated female golden hamsters (*Mesocricetus auratus*). *Journal of Comparative Psychology, 98,* 66–75.

Potegal, M., Yoburn, B., & Glusman, M. (1983). Disinhibition of muricide and irritability by intraseptal muscimol. *Pharmacology, Biochemistry and Behavior, 19,* 663–669.

Pucilowski, O., Kostowski, W., Bidzinski, A., & Hauptmann, M. (1982). Effect of 6-hydroxydopamine-induced lesions of A10 dopaminergic neurons on aggressive behavior in rats. *Pharmacology, Biochemistry and Behavior, 16,* 547–551.

Puech, A. J., Simon, P., Chermat, R., & Boisseir, J. R. (1974). Profil neuropsychopharmacologique de l'apomorphine. *Journal of Pharmacology, 5,* 241–254.

Puglisi-Allegra, S., & Cabib, S. (1990). Effects of defeat experiences on dopamine metabolism in different brain areas of the mouse. *Aggressive Behavior, 16,* 271–284.

Puglisi-Allegra, S., Mack, G., Oliverio, A., & Mandel, P. (1979). Effects of apomorphine and sodium di-npropylacetate on the aggressive behaviour of three strains of mice. *Progress in Neuro-Psychopharmacology*, 3, 491–502.

Puglisi-Allegra, S., & Mandel, P. (1980). Effects of sodium n-dipropylacetate, muscimol hydrobromide and (R, S)nipecotic acid amide on isolation-induced aggressive behavior in mice. *Psychopharmacology*, 70, 287–290.

Puglisi-Allegra, S., Simler, S., Kempf, E., & Mandel, P. (1981). Involvement of the GABAergic system on shock-induced aggressive behavior in two strains of mice. *Pharmacology, Biochemistry and Behavior*, 14, S1, 13–18.

Raab, A. (1970). Der serotoninstoffwechsel in einzelnen hirnteilen von *Tupaia* (*Tupaia belangeri*) bei soziopsychischem stress. *Internationale Zeitschrift für Angewandte Physiologie, Einschliesslich Arbeitsphysiologie*, 72, 54–66.

Rabinowitz, J., Avnon, M., & Rosenberg, V. (1996). Effect of clozapine on physical and verbal aggression. *Schizophrenia Research*, 22, 249–255.

Raine, A., Buchsbaum, M., & LaCasse, L. (1997). Brain abnormalities in murderers indicated by positron emission tomography. *Biological Psychiatry*, 42, 495–508.

Raine, A., Meloy, J. R., Bihrle, S., Stoddard, J., LaCasse, L., & Buchsbaum, M. S. (1998). Reduced prefrontal and increased subcortical brain functioning assessed using positron emission tomography in predatory and affective murderers. *Behavior Sciences and the Law*, 16, 319–332.

Ratey, J. J., & Gordon, A. (1993). The psychopharmacology of aggression: Toward a new day. *Psychopharmacology Bulletin*, 29, 65–73.

Ray, A., Sharma, K. K., Alkondon, M., & Sen, P. (1983). Possible interrelationship between the biogenic amines involved in the modulation of footshock aggression in rats. *Archives Internationales de Pharmacodynamie et de Therapie*, 265, 36–41.

Redmond, D. E., Jr., Maas, J. W., Kling, A., & Dekirmenjian, H. (1971). Changes in primate social behavior after treatment with alpha-methyl-para-tyrosine. *Psychosomatic Medicine*, 33, 97–113.

Redmond, D. E., Jr., Maas, J. W., Kling, A., Graham, C. W., & Dekirmenjian, H. (1971). Social behavior of monkeys selectively depleted of monoamines. *Science*, 174, 428–431.

Reis, D. J., & Fuxe, K. (1968). Depletion of noradrenaline in brainstem neurons during sham rage behaviour produced by acute brainstem transection in cat. *Brain Research*, 7, 448–451.

Reisner, I. R., Mann, J. J., Stanley, M., Huang, Y. Y., & Houpt, K. A. (1996). Comparison of cerebrospinal fluid monoamine metabolite levels in dominant-

aggressive and non-aggressive dogs. *Brain Research*, 714, 57–64.

Rewerski, W., Kostowski, W., Piechocki, T., & Rylski, M. (1971). The effects of some hallucinogens on aggressiveness of mice and rats. I. *Pharmacology*, 5, 314–320.

Robbins, T. W., Cador, M., Taylor, J. R., & Everitt, B. J. (1989). Limbic-striatal interactions in reward-related processes. *Neuroscience and Biobehavioral Reviews*, 13, 155–162.

Roberts, D. C., & Koob, G. F. (1982). Disruption of cocaine self-administration following 6-hydroxydopamine lesions of the ventral tegmental area in rats. *Pharmacology, Biochemistry and Behavior*, 17, 901–904.

Rocha, B. A., Scearce-Levie, K., Lucas, J. J., Hiroi, N., Castanon, N., Crabbe, J. C., et al. (1998). Increased vulnerability to cocaine in mice lacking the serotonin-1B receptor. *Nature*, 393, 175–178.

Rodgers, R. J., & Depaulis, A. (1982). GABAergic influences on defensive fighting in rats. *Pharmacology, Biochemistry and Behavior*, 17, 451–456.

Rodriguez-Arias, M., Minarro, J., Aguilar, M. A., Pinazo, J., & Simon, V. M. (1998). Effects of risperidone and SCH 23390 on isolation-induced aggression in male mice. *European Neuropsychopharmacology*, 8, 95–103.

Rodriguez-Arias, M., Pinazo, J., Minarro, J., & Stinus, L. (1999). Effects of SCH 23390, raclopride, and haloperidol on morphine withdrawal-induced aggression in male mice. *Pharmacology, Biochemistry and Behavior*, 64, 123–130.

Roizen, J. (1997). Epidemiological issues in alcohol-related violence. In M. Galanter (Ed.), *Alcohol and violence: Recent developments in alcoholism* (13th ed., pp. 7–41). New York: Plenum.

Rudolph, U., Crestani, F., Benke, D., Brünig, I., Benson, J. A., Fritschy, J. M., et al. (1999). Benzodiazepine actions mediated by specific gamma-aminobutyric acid-A receptor subtypes. *Nature*, 401, 796–800.

Sallinen, J., Haapalinna, A., Viitamaa, T., Kobilka, B. K., & Scheinin, M. (1998). Adrenergic alpha2c receptors modulate the acoustic startle reflex, prepulse inhibition, and aggression in mice. *Journal of Neuroscience*, 18, 3035–3042.

Sanchez, C., Arnt, J., Hyttel, J., & Moltzen, E. K. (1993). The role of serotonergic mechanisms in inhibition of isolation-induced aggression in male mice. *Psychopharmacology*, 110, 53–59.

Sanchez, C., & Hyttel, J. (1994). Isolation-induced aggression in mice: Effects of 5-hydroxytryptamine uptake inhibitors and involvement of postsynaptic 5-HT(1A) receptors. *European Journal of Pharmacology*, 264, 241–247.

Sander, T., Harms, H., Dufeu, P., Kuhn, S., Hoehe, M., Lesch, K. P., et al. (1998). Serotonin transporter gene variants in alcohol-dependent subjects with dissocial personality disorder. *Biological Psychiatry, 43,* 908–912.

Saudou, F., Amara, D. A., Dierich, A., Lemeur, M., Ramboz, S., Segu, L., et al. (1994). Enhanced aggressive behavior in mice lacking 5-HT{-1B} receptor. *Science, 265,* 1875–1878.

Schubert, K., Shaikh, M. B., & Siegel, A. (1996). NMDA receptors in the midbrain periaqueductal gray mediate hypothalamically evoked hissing behavior in the cat. *Brain Research, 762,* 80–90.

Scott, J. P., & Fredericson, E. (1951). The causes of fighting in mice and rats. *Physiological Zoology, 24,* 273–309.

Scott, J. P., & Marston, M. V. (1953). Nonadaptive behavior resulting from a series of defeats in fighting mice. *Journal of Abnormal and Social Psychology, 48,* 417–428.

Seiden, L. S., & Carlsson, A. (1964). Brain and heart catecholamine levels after L-DOPA administration in reserpine-treated mice: Correlations with a conditioned avoidance response. *Psychopharmacologia, 13,* 178–181.

Senault, B. (1968). Syndrome agressif induit par l'apomorphine chez le rat. *Journal of Physiology, 60,* 543–544.

Senault, B. (1971). Influence de l'isolement sur le comportement d'agressivit, intrasp,cifique induit par l'apomorphine chez le rat. *Psychopharmacologia, 20,* 389–394.

Sgoifo, A., de Boer, S. F., Haller, J., & Koolhaas, J. M. (1996). Individual differences in plasma catecholamine and corticosterone stress responses of wild-type rats: Relationship with aggression. *Physiology and Behavior, 60*(6), 1403–1407.

Shaikh, M. B., Barrett, J. A., & Siegel, A. (1987). The pathways mediating affective defense and quiet biting attack behavior from the midbrain central gray of the cat: An autoradiographic study. *Brain Research, 437,* 9–25.

Shaikh, M. B., De Lanerolle, N. C., & Siegel, A. (1997). Serotonin 5-HT1A and 5-HT2/1C receptors in the midbrain periaqueductal gray differentially modulate defensive rage behavior elicited from the medial hypothalamus of the cat. *Brain Research, 765,* 198–207.

Sheard, M. H. (1988). Clinical pharmacology of aggressive behavior. *Clinical Neuropharmacology, 11,* 483–492.

Shih, J. C. (2004). Cloning, after cloning, knock-out mice, and physiological functions of MAO A and B. *Neurotoxicology, 25,* 21–30.

Shih, J. C., Ridd, M. J., Chen, K., Meehan, W. P., Kung, M. P., Seif, I., et al. (1999). Ketanserin and tetrabenazine aggression in mice lacking monoamine oxidase A. *Brain Research, 835,* 104–112.

Siegel, A., & Mirsky, A. F. (1994). The neurobiology of violence and aggression. In A. J. Reiss, Jr. (Ed.), *Understanding and preventing violence. Biobehavioral influences* (2nd ed., pp. 59–172). Washington, DC: National Academy Press.

Siegel, A., Roeling, T. A. P., Gregg, T. R., & Kruk, M. R. (1999). Neuropharmacology of brain-stimulation-evoked aggression. *Neuroscience and Biobehavioral Reviews, 23,* 359–389.

Sijbesma, H., Schipper, J., De Kloet, E. R., Mos, J., Van Aken, H., & Olivier, B. (1991). Postsynaptic 5-HT{-1} receptors and offensive aggression in rats: A combined behavioural and autoradiographic study with eltoprazine. *Pharmacology, Biochemistry and Behavior, 38,* 447–458.

Sluyter, F., van Oortmerssen, G. A., & Koolhaas, J. M. (1996). Genetic influences on coping behaviour in house mouse lines selected for aggression: Effects of the Y chromosome. *Behaviour, 133,* 117–128.

Soderpalm, B., & Engel, J. A. (1991). Involvement of the GABAA/benzodiazepine chloride ionophore receptor complex in the 5,7-DHT induced anticonflict effect. *Life Sciences, 49,* 139–153.

Sorgi, P. J., Ratey, J. J., & Polakoff, S. (1986). Beta-adrenergic blockers for the control of aggressive behaviors in patients with chronic schizophrenia. *American Journal of Psychiatry, 143,* 775–776.

Spivak, B., Roitman, S., Vered, Y., Mester, R., Graff, E., Talmon, Y., et al. (1998). Diminished suicidal and aggressive behavior, high plasma norepinephrine levels, and serum triglyceride levels in chronic neuroleptic-resistant schizophrenic patients maintained on clozapine. *Clinical Neuropharmacology, 21,* 245–250.

Stanford, M. S., Houston, R. J., Mathias, C. W., Greve, K. W., Villemarette-Pittman, N. R., & Adams, D. (2001). A double-blind placebo-controlled crossover study of phenytoin in individuals with impulsive aggression. *Psychiatry Research, 103,* 193–203.

Starr, M. S. (1998). Antagonists of glutamate in the treatment of Parkinson's disease: From the laboratory to the clinic. *Amino Acids, 14,* 41–42.

Stork, O., Ji, F. Y., Kaneko, K., Stork, S., Yoshinobu, Y., Moriya, T., et al. (2000). Postnatal development of a GABA deficit and disturbance of neural functions in mice lacking GAD65. *Brain Research, 865,* 45–58.

Sukhotina, I. A., & Bespalov, A. Y. (2000). Effects of the NMDA receptor channel blockers memantine and MRZ 2/579 on morphine withdrawal-facilitated aggression in mice. *Psychopharmacology, 149,* 345–350.

Summers, C. H., & Greenberg, N. (1994). Somatic correlates of adrenergic activity during aggression in the lizard, *Anolis carolinensis. Hormones and Behavior, 28,* 29–40.

Suzdak, P. D., Schwartz, R. D., Skolnick, P., & Paul, S. M. (1986). Ethanol stimulates gamma-aminobutyric acid receptor-mediated chloride transport in rat brain synaptoneurosomes. *Proceedings of the National Academy of Sciences USA, 83,* 4071–4075.

Svare, B., & Gandelman, R. (1973). Postpartum aggression in mice: Experiential and environmental factors. *Hormones and Behavior, 4,* 323–334.

Svare, B., & Gandelman, R. (1976). A longitudinal analysis of maternal aggression in Rockland-Swiss albino mice. *Developmental Psychobiology, 9,* 437–446.

Swann, A. C. (2003). Neuroreceptor mechanisms of aggression and its treatment. *Journal of Clinical Psychiatry, 64,* 26–35.

Tariot, P. N., Erb, R., Podgorski, C. A., Cox, C., Patel, S., Jakimovich, L., et al. (1998). Efficacy and tolerability of carbamazepine for agitation and aggression in dementia. *American Journal of Psychiatry, 155,* 54–61.

Thierry, A. M., Tassin, J. P., Blanc, G., & Glowinski, J. (1976). Selective activation of the mesocortical DA system by stress. *Nature, 263,* 242–243.

Thoa, N. B., Eichelman, B., Richardson, J. S., & Jacobowitz, D. (1972). 6-Hydroxydopa depletion of brain norepinephrine and the facilitation of aggressive behavior. *Science, 178,* 75–77.

Thompson, T., & Schuster, C. R. (1964). Morphine self-administration, food-reinforced and avoidance behaviors in rhesus monkeys. *Psychopharmacologia, 5,* 87–94.

Tidey, J. W., & Miczek, K. A. (1992a). Effects of SKF38393 and quinpirole on patterns of aggressive, motor and schedule-controlled behaviors in mice. *Behavioural Pharmacology, 3,* 553–565.

Tidey, J. W., & Miczek, K. A. (1992b). Heightened aggressive behavior during morphine withdrawal: Effects of d-amphetamine. *Psychopharmacology, 107,* 297–302.

Tidey, J. W., & Miczek, K. A. (1992c). Morphine withdrawal aggression: Modification with D1 and D2 receptor agonists. *Psychopharmacology, 108,* 177–184.

Tidey, J. W., & Miczek, K. A. (1996). Social defeat stress selectively alters mesocorticolimbic dopamine release: An in vivo microdialysis study. *Brain Research, 721,* 140–149.

Tomkins, D. M., Higgins, G. A., & Sellers, E. M. (1994). Low doses of the 5-HT1A agonist 8-hydroxy-2-(di-n-propylamino)-tetralin (8-OH DPAT) increase ethanol intake. *Psychopharmacology, 115,* 173–179.

Tompkins, E. C., Clemento, A. J., Taylor, D. P., & Perhach, J. L., Jr. (1980). Inhibition of aggressive behavior in rhesus monkeys by buspirone. *Research Communications in Psychology, Psychiatry and Behavior, 5,* 337–352.

Traskman-Bendz, L., Alling, C., Oreland, L., Regnell, G., Vinge, E., & Ohman, R. (1992). Prediction of suicidal behavior from biologic tests. *Journal of Clinical Psychopharmacology, 12,* 21S–26S.

Troisi, A., Vicario, E., Nuccetelli, F., Ciani, N., & Pasini, A. (1995). Effects of fluoxetine on aggressive behavior of adult inpatients with mental retardation and epilepsy. *Pharmacopsychiatry, 28,* 1–4.

Tupin, J. P. (1985). Psychopharmacology and aggression. In L. H. Roth (Ed.), *Clinical treatment of the violent person* (pp. 83–99). Rockville, MD: U.S. Department of Health and Human Services.

Tyler, C. B., & Miczek, K. A. (1982). Effects of phencyclidine on aggressive behavior in mice. *Pharmacology, Biochemistry and Behavior, 17,* 503–510.

Van der Vegt, B. J., de Boer, S. F., Buwalda, B., de Ruiter, A. J., de Jong, J. G., & Koolhaas, J. M. (2001). Enhanced sensitivity of postsynaptic serotonin-1A receptors in rats and mice with high trait aggression. *Physiology and Behavior, 74,* 205–211.

Van der Vegt, B. J., Lieuwes, N., Cremers, T. I. F. H., de Boer, S. F., & Koolhaas, J. M. (2003). Cerebrospinal fluid monoamine and metabolite concentrations and aggression in rats. *Hormones and Behavior, 44,* 199–208.

Van Erp, A. M. M., & Miczek, K. A. (1997). Increased aggression after ethanol self-administration in male resident rats. *Psychopharmacology, 131,* 287–295.

Van Erp, A. M. M., & Miczek, K. A. (2000). Aggressive behavior, increased accumbal dopamine and decreased cortical serotonin in rats. *Journal of Neuroscience, 20,* 9320–9325.

Van Oortmerssen, G. A., & Bakker, T. C. M. (1981). Artificial selection for short and long attack latencies in wild {I mus} (*Imusculus domesticus*). *Behavior Genetics, 11,* 115–126.

Villalba, C., Boyle, P. A., Caliguri, E. J., & DeVries, G. J. (1997). Effects of the selective serotonin reuptake inhibitor fluoxetine on social behaviors in male and female prairie voles (*Microtus ochrogaster*). *Hormones and Behavior, 32,* 184–191.

Virkkunen, M., Eggert, M., Rawlings, R., & Linnoila, M. (1996). A prospective follow-up study of alcoholic violent offenders and fire setters. *Archives of General Psychiatry, 53,* 523–529.

Virkkunen, M., Kallio, E., Rawlings, R., Tokola, R., Poland, R. E., Guidotti, A., et al. (1994). Personality profiles and state aggressiveness in Finnish alcoholic, violent offenders, fire setters, and healthy volunteers. *Archives of General Psychiatry, 51,* 28–33.

Virkkunen, M., & Linnoila, M. (1993). Brain serotonin, Type II alcoholism and impulsive violence. *Journal of Studies on Alcohol, Supplement 11,* 163–169.

Vitiello, B., & Stoff, D. M. (1997). Subtypes of aggression

and their relevance to child psychiatry. *Journal of the American Academy of Child and Adolescent Psychiatry, 36*, 307–315.

Volavka, J. (1999). The effects of clozapine on aggression and substance abuse in schizophrenic patients. *Journal of Clinical Psychiatry, 60*(Suppl. 12), 43–46.

Walsh, M. T., & Dinan, T. G. (2001). Selective serotonin reuptake inhibitors and violence: A review of the available evidence. *Acta Psychiatrica Scandinavica, 104*, 84–91.

Weerts, E. M., & Miczek, K. A. (1996). Primate vocalizations during social separation and aggression: Effects of alcohol and benzodiazepines. *Psychopharmacology, 127*, 255–264.

Weerts, E. M., Tornatzky, W., & Miczek, K. A. (1993a). "Anxiolytic" and "anxiogenic" benzodiazepines and beta-carbolines: Effects on aggressive and social behavior in rats and squirrel monkeys. *Psychopharmacology, 110*, 451–459.

Weerts, E. M., Tornatzky, W., & Miczek, K. A. (1993b). Prevention of the proaggressive effects of alcohol by benzodiazepine receptor antagonists in rats and in squirrel monkeys. *Psychopharmacology, 111*, 144–152.

Weiger, W. A., & Bear, D. M. (1988). An approach to the neurology of aggression. *Journal of Psychiatric Research, 22*, 85–98.

Weisman, A. M., Berman, M. E., & Taylor, S. P. (1998). Effects of clorazepate, diazepam, and oxazepam on a laboratory measurement of aggression in men. *International Clinical Psychopharmacology, 13*, 183–188.

Welch, B. L., & Welch, A. S. (1965). Effect of grouping on the level of brain norepinephrine in white Swiss mice. *Life Sciences, 4*, 1011–1018.

Welch, B. L., & Welch, A. S. (1968). Rapid modification of isolation-induced aggressive behavior and elevation of brain catecholamines and serotonin by the quick-acting monoamine-oxidase inhibitor pargyline. *Communications in Behavioral Biology, 1*, 347–351.

Wilmot, C. A., Vander Wende, C., & Spoerlein, M. T. (1987). The effects of phencyclidine on fighting in differentially housed mice. *Pharmacology, Biochemistry and Behavior, 28*, 341–346.

Wilson, C., Nomikos, G. G., Collu, M., & Fibiger, H. C. (1995). Dopaminergic correlates of motivated behavior: Importance of drive. *Journal of Neuroscience, 15*, 5169–5178.

Wingfield, J. C., Ball, G. F., Dufty, A. M., Jr., Hegner, R. E., & Ramenofsky, M. (1987). Testosterone and aggression in birds. *American Scientist, 75*, 602–608.

Winslow, J. T., & Miczek, K. A. (1983). Habituation of aggression in mice: Pharmacological evidence of catecholaminergic and serotonergic mediation. *Psychopharmacology, 81*, 286–291.

Wrangham, R. W. (1999). Evolution of coalitionary killing. *American Journal of Physical Anthropology, 29*(Suppl.), 1–30.

Yap, J. J., Covington, H. E., Gale, M. C., Datta, R., & Miczek, K. A. (2005). Behavioral sensitization due to social defeat stress in mice: Antagonism at mGluR5 and NMDA receptors. *Psychopharmacology, 179*, 230–239.

Yudofsky, S., Williams, D., & Gorman, J. (1981). Propranolol in the treatment of rage and violent behavior in patients with chronic brain syndromes. *American Journal of Psychiatry, 138*, 218–220.

Zarcone, J. R., Hellings, J. A., Crandall, K., Reese, R. M., Marquis, J., Fleming, K., et al. (2001). Effects of risperidone on aberrant behavior of persons with developmental disabilities: I. A double-blind crossover study using multiple measures. *American Journal on Mental Retardation, 106*, 525–538.

Zhuang, X., Gross, C., Santarelli, L., Compan, V., Trillat, A. C., & Hen, R. (1999). Altered emotional states in knockout mice lacking 5-HT{-1A} or 5-HT{-1B} receptors. *Neuropsychopharmacology, 21*, S52–S60.

6

Nitric Oxide and Aggression

Silvana Chiavegatto, Gregory E. Demas, & Randy J. Nelson

Nitric oxide (NO), a by-product of the conversion of L-arginine to L-citrulline, is a gaseous free radical at body temperature that serves as an endogenous signaling molecule. NO is involved in many physiological functions. According to the scientific database PubMed, approximately 3,000 papers per year are published on NO. It was named Molecule of the Year in 1992 by the journal *Science*, a Nitric Oxide Society was founded in 1996, and a scientific journal, *Nitric Oxide: Biology and Chemistry*, devoted entirely to nitric oxide research, was soon created. Subsequently, the 1998 Nobel Prize in Physiology or Medicine was awarded to Ferid Murad, Robert Furchgott, and Louis Ignarro for the discovery of the signaling properties of NO.

The first biological function of NO was revealed in the circulatory system. The effectiveness of nitroglycerin and other organic nitrates in alleviating the pain of angina pectoralis was discovered in the 19th century; however, the mechanisms by which nitrates worked were not discovered until 1980. Relaxation of blood vessels in response to acetylcholine requires the endothelium to secrete an additional factor, initially named endothelial-derived relaxing factor, but later discovered to be NO. Further research determined that NO is also the active metabolite of nitroglycerin, as well as other nitrates, and stimulates blood vessel dilation by activating guanylyl cyclase, which induces cGMP formation.

Thus, NO is an important endogenous mediator of blood vessel tone, a function that is important in regulating several neuroendocrine and behavioral functions.

Another biological function of NO emerged in the late 1970s from an independent line of research documenting the carcinogenic risk of dietary nitrosamines. The discovery that both humans and nonhuman animals produce urinary nitrates in greater amounts than consumed, and that this production increases during bacterial infections, led to the hypothesis that an endogenous source of nitrates existed. In the process of converting L-arginine to L-citrulline, macrophages produce a reactive species that kills tumor cells in vitro, namely NO. Thus, NO plays an important role in immune function. It has not yet been determined if NO from macrophages plays a significant role in behavior, but the possibility certainly exists.

It was soon discovered that NO was also released when cerebellar cultures were stimulated with glutamate. Pharmacological inhibition of the synthetic enzyme NO synthase (NOS) blocked the elevation of cGMP levels in brain slices coincident with activation of the N-methyl-D-aspartate subtype of glutamate receptor. Since then, many studies of NO effects on neural function have been reported. By acting on neurons and endothelial cells in the circulatory system, NO exerts profound effects on neuroendocrine function and behavior. The goal of this chapter is to review the effects of NO on aggressive behavior.

Three distinct isoforms of NOS have been identified: (a) in the endothelial tissue of blood vessels (eNOS; type III), (b) as an inducible form acting from macrophages (iNOS; type II), and (c) in neural and glial tissue (nNOS; type I) (figure 6.1). Suppression of NO formation by either elimination of arginine or the use of N-methyl-arginine (N-NOARG) or L-N-nitroarginine (NMA), potent NOS inhibitors, affects all three isoforms of NOS. Although drugs that inhibit specific isoforms of NOS have not yet been perfected, their use paired with mice with targeted disruption of the genes encoding the specific isoforms of NOS is beginning to clarify the precise role of each isoform of NOS in aggressive behavior. The dual approach of using drugs that block synthesis of NO and knockout mice that lack one of the various isoforms of NOS has revealed several intriguing behavioral effects of NO.

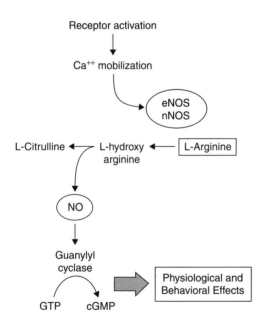

FIGURE 6.1 Biosynthesis of nitric oxide (NO). Upon receptor activation, the synthetic enzymes endothelial nitric oxide synthase (eNOS) and neuronal NOS (nNOS) are activated and facilitate the conversion of L-arginine to L-hydroxyarginine. L-hydroxyarginine is, in turn, converted stoichiometrically to L-citrulline and nitric oxide. The gaseous neurotransmitter NO is necessary for the conversion of guanine triphosphate (GTP) to cyclic guanine monophosphate (cGMP), an important second messenger responsible for the regulation of a variety of physiological and behavioral responses.

NO and Aggressive Behavior

nNOS

A specific role for nNOS-derived NO in aggression was first addressed in mice in which the nNOS gene was deleted by homologous recombination (nNOS$^{-/-}$), thus inhibiting NOS production in neurons (Huang et al., 1995). Among a battery of behavioral tests performed in our laboratory, we conducted a systematic evaluation of aggressive behavior, because students and caretakers informally observed high levels of aggression among male cage mates when these males were moved from individual shipping containers to group housing conditions. In the resident-intruder test of aggression, male nNOS$^{-/-}$ residents displayed more aggressive encounters than wild-type (WT) mice (Nelson et al., 1995). The nNOS$^{-/-}$ animals initiated approximately 90% of the aggressive behavior in dyadic or group encounters occurring in a neutral arena. In all test situations, male nNOS$^{-/-}$ mice were significantly more aggressive and rarely displayed submissive behaviors (Nelson et al., 1995).

In order to investigate whether the increased aggressive behavior of the mutants was due to the missing gene during the development of the brain, with subsequent activation of compensatory mechanisms (Nelson, 1997), WT male mice were treated with 7-nitroindazole (7-NI) (50 mg/kg ip), a relatively specific drug that blocks nNOS activity in vivo (Demas et al., 1997). Indeed, a marked reduction of NOS activity in brain homogenates of 7-NI-treated animals was revealed by immunocytochemical staining for citrulline, an indirect marker for NO synthesis (Demas et al., 1997). Immunocytochemistry for citrulline is generally a more accurate assessment of NO production because NOS staining does not necessarily correspond to NO production. NO itself is labile and not readily detectable in tissues. Male mice treated with 7-NI exhibited substantially increased aggressive behavior in two different tests compared to control animals, with no alteration in other locomotor activities, implying an specific effect on aggression and ruling out the contribution of strain differences in the knockout mice in the aggressive behavioral phenotype (Demas et al., 1997). These pharmacological data extend the behavioral results obtained in nNOS$^{-/-}$ mice and confirm a role of NO in aggression.

As highlighted by Simon and Lu (ch. 9 in this volume), plasma androgen concentrations directly influence aggression. nNOS$^{-/-}$ and WT mice do not differ in blood testosterone concentrations either before or after agonistic encounters (Nelson et al., 1995). Data on castrated nNOS$^{-/-}$ males, however, suggest that testosterone is necessary, if not sufficient, to promote increased aggression in these mutants (Kriegsfeld, Dawson, Dawson, Nelson, & Snyder, 1997). Castrated nNOS$^{-/-}$ mice displayed low levels of aggression that were equivalent to the reduced aggression observed among castrated WT males. Androgen replacement therapy restored the elevated levels of aggression in nNOS$^{-/-}$ mice. Additional studies using perinatal castration on males and androgen treatment on females are required to sort out the organizational effects of androgens on NO-related aggression in males.

Importantly, inappropriate aggressiveness was never observed among female nNOS$^{-/-}$ mice in these test situations; however, when aggressive behavior was examined in female nNOS$^{-/-}$ mice in the context of maternal aggression, during which WT females are highly aggressive toward an intruder, nNOS$^{-/-}$ dams were very docile (Gammie & Nelson, 1999). All other components of maternal care were normal in nNOS$^{-/-}$ females (see below).

Because the specific deficits in maternal aggression in the nNOS$^{-/-}$ mice suggested a possible role for NO in maternal aggression, immunohistochemistry for citrulline was examined after behavioral testing of WT mice to indirectly examine NO synthesis during maternal aggression. A significant increase in the number of citrulline-positive cells was identified in the medial preoptic nucleus, the suprachiasmatic nucleus, and the subparaventricular zone regions of the hypothalamus in aggressive lactating females relative to control mice (Gammie & Nelson, 1999). No changes in the number of citrulline-positive cells were observed across either groups or treatments in other brain regions. These results provide two indirect lines of evidence that NO release is associated with maternal aggression.

Mus fathers did not display alterations in citrulline-positive cells when tested with intruders. In contrast to mice, in which males do not display parental aggression and nest defense, prairie voles (*Microtus ochrogaster*) are socially monogamous and both partners display aggressive nest defense (Gammie & Nelson, 2000). The number of citrulline-positive cells was elevated in the paraventricular nucleus (PVN) of the hypothalamus in aggressive lactating females compared with unstimulated lactating females. A significant increase in the number of citrulline-positive cells was also observed in the PVN of aggressive mated males compared with nonaggressive unmated males and unstimulated mated males (Gammie & Nelson, 2000). Both nonaggressive unmated males and unstimulated mated males show similar levels of citrulline immunoreactivity in the PVN. In other regions of the brain, no changes in the number of citrulline-positive cells were observed. These results suggest that NO is released specifically in the PVN during both maternal and mating-induced aggression in prairie voles and emphasize the need for comparative studies to characterize the role of specific mechanisms underlying aggressive behaviors.

There were no discernable sensorimotor deficits among the mutant mice of either sex to account for the changes in aggressive behavior. Taken together, these results suggest that NO from neurons has important, but opposite, effects in the mediation of aggression in male and female mice. Although there are no sex differences in NOS activity in the cortex, cerebellum, amygdala, or hypothalamus, androgens generally inhibit, whereas estrogens generally increase, NOS activity in the brain (Singh, Pervin, Shryne, Gorski, & Chaudhuri, 2000; Weiner et al., 1994).

An apparent exception to this general rule can be seen in Siberian hamsters (*Phodopus sungorus*). These animals show an "atypical" seasonal pattern of aggressive behavior. Males that have undergone gonadal regression after exposure to short, winterlike days have low circulating testosterone concentrations, but display elevated aggression compared with animals with large functional gonads and relatively high testosterone values (Jasnow, Huhman, Bartness, & Demas, 2000). Male reproductive and aggressive behaviors are both generally regulated by androgens, presumably because defense of resources and competition are critical for reproductive success (see Wingfield, Moore, Goymann, Wacker, & Sperry, ch. 8 in this volume). However, nongonadal mechanisms may have evolved to regulate aggression in animals living in habitats that require competition outside of the breeding season (see, e.g., Soma & Wingfield, 2001).

In a recent study, nNOS expression in the brains of Siberian hamsters housed in either short or long days was examined after aggressive behavior (Wen, Hotchkiss, Demas, & Nelson, 2004). The reproductive response to short days is not uniform (Prendergast, Kriegsfeld, & Nelson, 2001). Short-day-responsive hamsters inhibit reproductive function and have undetectable testosterone concentrations, whereas short-day-nonresponsive hamsters display fully functional gonads and long-day-like testosterone blood concentrations. Regardless of gonadal response to short days, all hamsters housed in short photoperiods were more aggressive than long-day animals. These results replicate previous studies (Jasnow et al., 2000; Jasnow, Huhman, Bartness, & Demas, 2002), as well as indicate that the short-day-induced increases in aggression are not mediated by testosterone, because the short-day nonresponders had testis size and testosterone concentrations similar to those of long-day animals. Short-day Siberian hamsters, again regardless of reproductive response, also displayed significantly fewer nNOS-immunoreactive cells in several parts of the amygdala than long-day animals. Together, these results suggest that seasonal aggression in male Siberian hamsters is regulated by photoperiod, probably independently of gonadal steroid hormones, and may be regulated by nNOS.

eNOS

The contribution of NO derived from eNOS in aggressive behavior was investigated in male and female eNOS$^{-/-}$ mice (Demas et al., 1999). In sharp contrast to the nNOS$^{-/-}$ mice, the eNOS$^{-/-}$ mice were very docile. Male mice were experimentally tested using both the resident-intruder test and a neutral arena with a WT stimulus male mouse. In both tests, male eNOS$^{-/-}$ mice displayed severely reduced aggressive behavior, represented by decreased attacks and a greatly increased latency to attack the stimulus male, in the rare instances of aggressive behavior (Demas et al., 1999). These effects do not likely reflect nonspecific, or general, behavioral disruptions because an extensive sensorimotor repertoire did not find notable abnormalities (Demas et al., 1999). The absence of aggression in male eNOS$^{-/-}$ mice does not seem to be due to the known hypertension of these animals (Huang et al., 1995), because pharmacological normalization of blood pressure with hydralazine did not affect their aggressive behavior (Demas et al., 1999).

Female aggression was investigated in the context of maternal aggressive behavior of eNOS$^{-/-}$ and WT dams. There was no difference in terms of the percentage displaying aggression, the average number of attacks against a male intruder, or the total amount of time spent attacking the male intruder (Gammie, Huang, & Nelson, 2000). Thus, the lack of eNOS decreases the expression of male aggressive behavior, but does not appear to interfere with female aggression in

mice. NO from the endothelia may regulate neuroendocrine events, such as the secretion of releasing hormones from the hypothalamus into the pituitary portal system (Nelson, Kriegsfeld, Dawson, & Dawson, 1997).

The combination of both the nNOS$^{-/-}$ and eNOS$^{-/-}$ behavioral data suggest that NO can have divergent effects on aggression depending on its source. The two isoforms of NOS may normally act to increase (i.e., eNOS$^{-/-}$) and decrease (i.e., nNOS$^{-/-}$) male aggressive behavior in vivo. Thus, male WT mice with balanced NO concentrations from both isoforms of NOS display only moderate levels of aggression. Examination of double eNOS$^{-/-}$/nNOS$^{-/-}$ mice is necessary to test this hypothesis.

iNOS

Although the expression of iNOS in the brain is well characterized in astrocytes, microglia, and, to a lesser extent, in endothelial cells, neurons are capable of expressing iNOS under certain circumstances (reviewed in Heneka & Feinstein, 2001). Mice lacking the iNOS gene have been developed for some time (Laubach, Shesely, Smithies, & Sherman, 1995; MacMicking et al., 1995; Wei et al., 1995), but most of the work on these animals has been directed to the known role of iNOS in inflammatory processes. Consequently, most of the studies using these knockout animals or pharmacological inhibition of iNOS have focused on infection, disease, or tissue damage models. Thus, the behavioral role of iNOS-derived NO remains unspecified.

NO and Aggression in Down Syndrome and Affective Disorders

Several NO-related behaviors have been reported in both Down syndrome (DS) patients and in Ts65Dn mice, a valuable mouse model of DS (reviewed in Dierssen et al., 2001; Galdzicki & Siarey, 2003). The mouse chromosome 16 carries the most homologous sequences to those on the so-called "obligate region" of human chromosome 21. Because mice with total trisomy of chromosome 16 die in utero (Lacey-Casem & Oster-Granite, 1994), a partially trisomic mouse was developed in which only the segment of mouse chromosome 16 syntenic to human chromosome 21 was triplicated (Ts65Dn) (Davisson, Schmidt, & Akeson, 1990). Ts65Dn mice have several behavioral alterations resembling those observed in DS patients, including deficits in learning and memory (Demas, Nelson, Krueger, & Yarowsky, 1996, 1998; Escorihuela et al., 1998; Reeves et al., 1995), equilibrium and motor co-ordination (Costa, Walsh, & Davisson, 1999), and hyperactivity (Coussons-Read & Crnic, 1996; Escorihuela et al., 1995), as well as altered sexual and aggressive behaviors (Klein et al., 1996), suggesting deficits in behaviors that may be modulated by the NO system.

Recently, the distribution of nNOS protein and activity by immunocytochemistry and NADPH-d activity, respectively, were compared in different regions of the basal forebrain in Ts65Dn mice. The mutant animals displayed both reduction in nNOS protein and an additional decrease in its activity in the hypothalamic PVN, the nucleus of the diagonal band of Broca, and the medial septum, associated with aggressive behavior (Gotti et al., in press). These reductions were not observed in the striatum, suggesting that this area is not directly involved with aggressive behavior modulated by nNOS-derived NO. Thus, the partial trisomy of chromosome 16 in Ts65Dn mice (homologous to chromosome 21 in humans) markedly disturbs the neuronal NO system in selected brain areas. It may be possible that the NO alteration is a direct consequence of the aberrant production of SOD-1 protein, due to the triplication of the Sod-1 gene in both DS patients and Ts65Dn mice (Holtzman et al., 1996), which could potentially affect the catabolism or synthesis of NO (Schmidt et al., 1996). Although additional work is necessary to elucidate the molecular mechanisms and to investigate the contribution of the impaired neuronal NO system in specific phenotypes of DS patients, these results are suggestive of an involvement of NO in the aggressive behavior of Ts65Dn male mice and a possible contribution to the poor adaptive behavior in DS.

Aggressive behavior is frequently observed in mentally ill patients. More than 50% of all psychiatric patients and 10% of schizophrenic patients show aggressive symptoms at various levels (Arseneault, Moffitt, Caspi, Taylor, & Silva, 2000; Brieden, Ujeyl, & Naber, 2002; Hodgins, Hiscoke, & Freese, 2003). Correlations of reduced nNOS immunoreactivity in some hypothalamic nuclei of humans are reported in affective disorders (Bernstein et al., 1998, 2002). Reduced calcium-dependent constitutive NOS enzymatic activity was found in the prefrontal cortex of postmortem brains of patients with schizophrenia and depression (Xing, Chavko, Zhang, Yang, & Post, 2002). Furthermore, schizophrenics had significantly lower numbers of

NADPH-d neurons in the hippocampal formation and in the neocortex of the lateral temporal lobe (Akbarian et al., 1993). Epidemiological evidence suggests that prenatal viral infection is a potential etiological factor in the genesis of brain disorders such as schizophrenia and autism (Adams, Kendell, Hare, & Munk-Jorgensen, 1993; Mednick, Machon, Huttunen, & Bonett, 1988; Takei et al., 1996). Accordingly, influenza virus exposure at Day 9 of pregnancy in mice induces subsequent down-regulation of nNOS protein in several brain regions in adulthood (Fatemi, Cuadra, El-Fakahany, Sidwell, & Thuras, 2000). In rats, NO dysfunction during the early postnatal period mimics some aspects of schizophrenia in an animal model (Black, Selk, Hitchcock, Wettstein, & Sorensen, 1999). Aggressive behavior and psychosis are common manifestations of dementia with Lewy bodies and the amygdala is one of the most vulnerable regions for this pathology (Marui et al., 2002). The expression of nNOS was reduced in the amygdala of patients with this type of dementia, suggesting that Lewy pathology causes neuronal dysfunction reducing the expression of nNOS (Katsuse, Iseki, & Kosaka, 2003). Taken together, these data strongly support a role for nNOS-derived NO in the expression of inappropriate aggression of patients suffering from mental disorders and warrant further investigation.

Interaction With Serotonin

As described in several chapters of this book, numerous studies have implicated serotonin (5-hydroxytryptamine, or 5-HT) as a key neurotransmitter involved in aggression and impulsivity. Gene targeting strategies in mice that either directly or indirectly affect the functional integrity of the 5-HT system have generally strengthened the influence of 5-HT on aggression (reviewed in Miczek, Maxson, Fish, & Faccidomo, 2001; Nelson & Chiavegatto, 2001). Accordingly, we investigated the participation of 5-HT in the aggressive phenotype of male nNOS$^{-/-}$ mice as a possible explanation for the excessive aggressiveness of these mutants.

Indeed, the 5-HT metabolism analyzed by the ratio of the metabolite 5-HIAA and the 5-HT levels by HPLC was significantly reduced in several brain regions, including the cortex, hypothalamus, midbrain, and cerebellum of male nNOS$^{-/-}$ in comparison to the WT (Chiavegatto et al., 2001). Unexpectedly, the alterations in 5-HT turnover were due to increased levels of 5-HT, with no changes in its metabolite in most brain regions studied. The 5-HT immunocytochemistry performed in male nNOS$^{-/-}$ mouse brain slices did not reveal significant alteration in the density or distribution of 5-HT axon terminals (Chiavegatto et al., 2001). The elevated aggressive phenotype in nNOS male knockout mice could be ameliorated by pharmacological increases in 5-HT metabolism using its precursor 5-hydroxytryptophan (5-HTP). Conversely, the same increased level of aggressive behavior was induced in WT mice after a regimen of pCPA injections (a 5-HT synthesis inhibitor) that dramatically reduced 5-HT turnover in the brains of WT mice (Chiavegatto et al., 2001). These data demonstrated that, among other downstream effects, the absence of nNOS disturbs 5-HT metabolism associated with increased male aggressive behavior.

Alterations in 5-HT metabolism can reflect or lead to adjustments in 5-HT receptor function. Because both 5-HT$_{1A}$ and 5-HT$_{1B}$ receptors function as auto- as well as heteroreceptors, and are reported to be involved in aggressive behavior, they were investigated in male nNOS$^{-/-}$ and WT mice. Although the 5-HT$_{1A}$ agonist 8-OH-DPAT and the 5-HT$_{1B}$ agonist CP-94,253 dose dependently decreased aggression in both genotypes, significantly higher concentrations of both agonists were necessary to reduce the aggressive behavior of nNOS knockouts (Chiavegatto et al., 2001). Although the effects of pharmacological inhibition of nNOS on 5-HT neurotransmission remain to be determined, our results suggest hypofunction of the 5-HT$_{1A}$ and 5-HT$_{1B}$ receptors in the brain of the male nNOS$^{-/-}$ mouse, thus revealing a requirement for the neuronal isoform of NOS in the integrity of the brain 5-HT system.

5-HT turnover was also determined in mice lacking the endothelial isoform of NOS (Frisch et al., 2000). These mutant mice exhibit an accelerated 5-HT turnover in the frontal cortex and ventral striatum; the 5-HT metabolite is increased in the cerebellum. The increased activity of the brain 5-HT system in eNOS$^{-/-}$ mice is in agreement with the decreased aggression phenotype reported in these animals (Demas et al., 1999), thus strengthening the suggested relationship between NO and 5-HT in aggression (see Chiavegatto & Nelson, 2003, for a review).

Depending on whether it is synthesized from nNOS or eNOS, NO can have opposite effects on 5-HT and therefore opposite effects on male aggressive behavior. It seems that differences in the localization of the source of NO and/or subcellular sites may account for the distinctive alterations in the brain 5-HT system.

Additionally, regarding the putative role of NO in the aggression related to mental disabilities, a possible link with the 5-HT system may also be envisaged, because 5-HT dysfunction has been reported in DS (Gulesserian, Engidawork, Cairns, & Lubec, 2000; Mann, Yates, Marcyniuk, & Ravindra, 1985; Seidl et al., 1999; Whitaker-Azmitia, 2001), autism (Chugani, 2002; Posey & McDougle, 2001), depression, and schizophrenia (Lee & Meltzer, 2001; Meltzer, 1989; Meltzer, Li, Kaneda, & Ichikawa, 2003).

Interaction With the HPA Axis

Despite a growing amount of research, the precise role of NO in regulation of the hypothalamopituitary-adrenal (HPA) axis remains equivocal (Givalois, Li, & Pelletier, 2002). NOS is present in discrete hypothalamic areas (i.e., the supraopic nucleus) and the PVN, which regulate neuroendocrine responses (Huang, Dawson, Bredt, Snyder, & Fishman, 1993), and a variety of stimuli that affect pituitary hormone release (e.g., stress, food deprivation, gonadectomy, exposure to endotoxin) can up-regulate nNOS expression. HPA activity is regulated primarily by the actions of the hypothalamic peptide corticotropin releasing hormone (CRH), which acts on the pituitary to trigger the release of the tropic hormone ACTH. ACTH, in turn, regulates the release of glucocorticoids (GCs) from the adrenal cortex. Numerous factors act at the level of the hypothalamus or pituitary to affect the release of CRH or ACTH, respectively. For example, the cytokines interleukin-1 (IL-1), IL-1β, IL-2, and IL-6 increase CRH release both in vitro and in vivo (McCann et al., 2000). Furthermore, several recent studies have implicated NO in cytokine modulation of hypothalamic CRH. For example, IL-2 injections increase CRH release in incubated hypothalami and IL-2-mediated release of CRH is augmented by the addition of the NO precursor L-arginine in vitro (Karanth, Lyson, & McCann, 1993). In contrast, incubation of hypothalami with the NOS inhibitor NMMA suppresses IL-2-induced CRH release (Karanth et al., 1993). In vivo treatment with IL-1β increases hypothalamic CRH release, as well as plasma ACTH and corticosterone concentrations; IL-1β-induced activation of the HPA can be attenuated, however, by pretreatment with the NOS inhibitor L-NAME (Rivier & Shen, 1994).

In addition to the effects of cytokines on HPA activity, several neurotransmitters/neurohormones (e.g., acetylcholine, norepinephrine, prostaglandins) are capable of affecting CRH secretion and NO has been implicated as a potential mediator of these actions. For example, carbachol, a muscarinic receptor agonist, increases IL-2β-induced CRH release; however, the IL-2β potentiation of CRH release can be blocked by NMMA administration (Karanth et al., 1993). Furthermore, pharmacological inhibition of NOS can either increase or decrease IL-1-induced CRH release in vitro (Costa, Trainer, Besser, & Grossman, 1993; Sandi & Guaza, 1995). Despite these contradictory results, more recent evidence suggests that NO serves a tonic inhibitory role on HPA activity.

In addition to the effects of NO on CRH discussed above, NO also appears to play an important role in mediating ACTH release at the level of the pituitary. For example, icv or peripheral injections of the non-specific NOS inhibitor L-NAME attenuate stress-induced ACTH release (Kim & Rivier, 2000). In contrast, endotoxin-induced increases in plasma ACTH and corticosterone are actually enhanced by pretreatment with L-NAME centrally (Harada, Imaki, Chikada, Naruse, & Demura, 1999; Rivier & Shen, 1994). Specifically, pharmacological inhibition of NOS via icv injections of NMMA or HP-228 increases expression of CRH mRNA in the PVN, as well as plasma ACTH (Givalois et al., 2002). Given the contradictory results regarding the specific effects of NO on HPA activity, NO clearly plays a significant role at the level of the HPA, and its has been suggested that NO may have a differential modulatory in CRH release depending on whether the stressor is environmental/physical or immunological (Bilbo, Hotchkiss, Chiavegatto, & Nelson, 2003).

Collectively, the results above suggest an important role of NO in mediating HPA activity. Furthermore, considerable evidence exists demonstrating HPA regulation of stress responses and aggression and these interactions in rodents have recently been reviewed (Haller & Kruk, 2003). For example, both increased and decreased activity of the HPA axis can affect aggressive behavior. Circadian and seasonal rhythms in HPA activity correlate with fluctuations in aggression in a range of species. In addition, the neuroendocrine stress response resulting from an aggressive encounter can have important implications for subsequent behavioral responses (Haller & Kruk, 2003). As discussed above, glucocorticoids (e.g., cortisol, corticosterone) are released from the adrenal glands and serve as the end product of HPA activation in response to stress. In

addition to mediating a wide range of physiological and metabolic responses throughout the body, GCs can easily penetrate the blood-brain barrier, where they can activate central mineralocorticoid (low affinity) and glucocorticoid (high affinity) receptors and, in turn, affect behavioral responses, including aggression. In general, chronic activation of the HPA axis and the subsequent release of GCs appears to act as a "brake" on aggressive behavior (Haller & Kruk, 2003). For example, animals experiencing a prolonged stress response display chronically elevated circulating corticosterone concentrations and decreased aggression (Haller & Kruk, 2003). Furthermore, animals that demonstrate GC hypofunction demonstrate high levels of pathological aggression (Haller & Kruk, 2003). In contrast, acute activation of the HPA axis can actually increase aggression in rodents. For example, stimulation of hypothalamic brain regions can evoke aggression in addition to rapid activation of the HPA axis (Kruk et al., 1998). Local injections of corticosterone into the hypothalamus also increase the frequency and duration of aggression and decrease the latency to attack in rodents (Brain & Haug, 1992; Haller, Albert, & Makara, 1997). Given the effects of NO on the HPA axis discussed above, along with the effects of the HPA axis on aggressive behavior, it is logical to assume that NO may play an important role in mediating aggression via its actions on the HPA axis. Surprisingly, no research has been conducted to date to test this idea. Because of the evidence suggesting that pharmacological inhibition of nNOS attenuates the stress response, coupled with the fact that prolonged HPA activation reduces aggression, we would predict that the increase in aggression in animals with attenuated nNOS previously reported (e.g., Demas et al., 1997; Kriegsfeld et al., 1997; Nelson et al., 1995) would be mediated, at least in part, via the up-regulation of HPA activity. For instance, male nNOS$^{-/-}$ mice have higher basal concentrations of corticosterone than WT mice (Bilbo et al., 2003). Although this prediction is inconsistent with the chronic effects of GCs on aggression, it is consistent with the acute effects of HPA activity on aggressive behavior (Haller & Kruk, 2003) and the basal corticosterone values in nNOS$^{-/-}$ mice (Bilbo et al., 2003). Considerably more research is needed, however, to delineate the precise role of the HPA axis in mediating NO regulation of aggression.

There are a number of other phenotypic changes in nNOS$^{-/-}$ mice that may be associated with the HPA axis. As mentioned, despite elevated corticosterone concentrations, nNOS knockout mice are less "anxious" or "fearful" than WT mice, which may contribute to their aggressiveness. For example, male nNOS$^{-/-}$ mice spend more time in the center of an open field than WT mice (Bilbo et al., 2003). Furthermore, nNOS knockout mice also show increased sensitivity to painful stimuli, which may also prolong aggressive interactions (M. Rivera & R. J. Nelson, unpublished observations). Aggressive behavior is not a unitary process, but is the result of complex interactions among several physiological, motivational, and behavioral systems, with contributions from the social and physical environment. The multiple, and often unanticipated, effects of targeted gene disruption on aggressive behavior must be considered when phenotyping a gene manipulation.

Environmental Contributions to NO-Mediated Aggression

Isolation and Aggression

It is well documented that social isolation induces aggressive behavior in laboratory strains of rodents. Based on the classic work of Ginsburg and Allee (1942) and Seward (1946), a lab model of isolation-induced aggression has been developed in mice (Yen, Stanger, & Millman, 1959). Isolation-induced aggression is correlated to changes with 5-HT turnover (Garattini, Giacalone, & Valzelli, 1967; Giacalone, Tansella, Valzelli, & Garattini, 1968; Hodge & Butcher, 1974). Several 5-HT drugs, such as 5-HT$_{1A, 1B}$ agonists or 5-HT uptake blockers, ameliorate isolation-induced aggression in mice (Olivier, Mos, van der Heyden, & Hartog, 1989). On the other hand, depletion of 5-HT by pCPA increases isolation-induced aggressiveness in mice (Chiavegatto et al., 2001; Valzelli, 1974). The addition of another individual also somewhat ameliorates the aggressive phenotype; females are more effective than males. NNOS$^{-/-}$ males that are housed together from weaning are less aggressive than cohorts that are individually housed (R. J. Nelson, unpublished observations). The extent to which amelioration of isolation-induced aggression by social interventions is mediated by 5-HT remains unspecified.

Maternal Influences

Maternal behavior can significantly affect subsequent adult behavior in offspring. Because all knockout animals typically have parents with gene knockouts, the altered behavior in the mutant offspring could be due to the effects of the missing gene or could be induced by altered maternal care evoked by the missing gene in the dam (see Francis, Szegda, Campbell, Martin, & Insel, 2003).

Although maternal aggression is classified as one phenotypic component of maternal behavior due to its protective benefits to the offspring (see Lonstein & Gammie, 2002), the hormonal conditions for maternal aggression are somewhat different than those required for maternal behavior in female rodents. Hypophysectomy delays the onset of maternal behavior in hormone-treated females, but has no effect on the onset of maternal aggression. Also, the terminal decline in progesterone, which is necessary for maternal behavior, is not necessary for maternal aggression (Mayer, Ahdieh, & Rosenblatt, 1990; Mayer, Monroy, & Rosenblatt, 1990). The different components of maternal behavior involve specific neural circuits and are affected by different genes (Leckman & Herman, 2002). Accordingly, mice lacking the gene for nNOS$^{-/-}$ exhibit dramatic deficiencies in the production of maternal aggression, although other components of maternal behavior, such as pup retrieval, are normal (Gammie & Nelson, 1999). As mentioned, eNOS$^{-/-}$ females also displayed normal pup retrieval behavior (Gammie et al., 2000).

Disruption in the mother-infant relationship can affect brain function and plasticity in the offspring as they become adults (Cirulli, Berry, & Alleva, 2003). Therefore, studies on maternal behavior in mutant animals are always necessary when assigning a functional role for a gene, in order to preclude an eventual effect due to inadequate maternal behavior. Accordingly, the absence of nNOS- or eNOS-derived NO does not interfere with the normal mother-infant interaction, suggesting that a participation of NO in aggressive behavior is not due to an early environmental disturbance in the animals.

Conclusions and Future Directions

Although many other molecules can affect aggressive behavior (Nelson & Chiavegatto, 2001), most agents likely influence aggression via the signaling properties of 5-HT. Androgens, or their metabolic byproducts, interact with 5-HT receptors to facilitate aggression. Exposure to androgens early during ontogeny influences the expression and binding affinity of specific

5-HT receptor subtypes; postpubertal androgens also modulate 5-HT and its receptors.

NO interacts strongly with the HPA axis, as well as 5-HT mechanisms. Future studies must consider the environmental (social and physical), hormonal, cellular, and molecular contributions to aggressive behavior, as well as abstract psychological conceptual states, including fear, hunger, anxiety, and depressed affect. A variety of subtle adjustments in 5-HT concentrations, turnover, and metabolism or slight changes in receptor subtype activation, density, and binding affinity alone or in combination can influence aggression in different ways by affecting inputs into aggression circuitries. Because aggressive behavior is not a unitary process, it is likely that multiple changes in 5-HT signaling are associated with different types of aggression (see Maxson & Canastar, ch. 1 in this volume). Importantly, manipulations of signaling proteins can also dramatically affect aggression. Activation of specific 5-HT receptors evokes cascades of different signal transduction molecules via distinct, but highly interacting, second messenger systems and via multiple effectors. The integrity of this complex pathway seems necessary for normal expression and termination of aggressive behavior (Chiavegatto & Nelson, 2003).

Understanding the interactions of 5-HT receptor subtypes should lead to novel insights into the molecular mechanisms underlying aggression. Pursuit of gene arrays, inducible gene knockouts and "knockins," and RNA silencing techniques may be necessary to untangle the multiple influences of various molecules on aggressive behavior. Multiple levels of analysis, as well as comparative research approaches, are necessary to completely reveal the contributions of NO to aggressive behavior.

Note

S.C. credits FAPESP–BRAZIL (01/01637-5 and 01/09079-1) for financial support. Preparation of this review was also supported by NIH Grants MH 66144 and MH 57760 (R.J.N.).

References

Adams, W., Kendell, R. E., Hare, E. H., & Munk-Jorgensen, P. (1993). Epidemiological evidence that maternal influenza contributes to the aetiology of schizophrenia. An analysis of Scottish, English, and Danish data. British Journal of Psychiatry, 163, 522–534.

Akbarian, S., Bunney, W. E., Jr., Potkin, S. G., Wigal, S. B., Hagman, J. O., Sandman, C. A., et al. (1993). Altered distribution of nicotinamide-adenine dinucleotide phosphate-diaphorase cells in frontal lobe of schizophrenics implies disturbances of cortical development. Archives of General Psychiatry, 50(3), 169–177.

Arseneault, L., Moffitt, T. E., Caspi, A., Taylor, P. J., & Silva, P. A. (2000). Mental disorders and violence in a total birth cohort: Results from the Dunedin Study. Archives of General Psychiatry, 57(10), 979–986.

Bernstein, H. G., Heinemann, A., Krell, D., Mawrin, C., Bielau, H., Danos, P., et al. (2002). Further immunohistochemical evidence for impaired NO signaling in the hypothalamus of depressed patients. Annals of the New York Academy of Sciences, 973, 91–93.

Bernstein, H. G., Stanarius, A., Baumann, B., Henning, H., Krell, D., Danos, P., et al. (1998). Nitric oxide synthase-containing neurons in the human hypothalamus: Reduced number of immunoreactive cells in the paraventricular nucleus of depressive patients and schizophrenics. Neuroscience, 83(3), 867–875.

Bilbo, S. D., Hotchkiss, A. K., Chiavegatto, S., & Nelson, R. J. (2003). Blunted stress responses in delayed type hypersensitivity in mice lacking the neuronal isoform of nitric oxide synthase. Journal of Neuroimmunology, 140(1–2), 41–48.

Black, M. D., Selk, D. E., Hitchcock, J. M., Wettstein, J. G., & Sorensen, S. M. (1999). On the effect of neonatal nitric oxide synthase inhibition in rats: A potential neurodevelopmental model of schizophrenia. Neuropharmacology, 38(9), 1299–1306.

Brain, P. F., & Haug, M. (1992). Hormonal and neurochemical correlates of various forms of animal "aggression." Psychoneuroendocrinology, 17(6), 537–551.

Brieden, T., Ujeyl, M., & Naber, D. (2002). Psychopharmacological treatment of aggression in schizophrenic patients. Pharmacopsychiatry, 35(3), 83–89.

Chiavegatto, S., Dawson, V. L., Mamounas, L. A., Koliatsos, V. E., Dawson, T. M., & Nelson, R. J. (2001). Brain serotonin dysfunction accounts for aggression in male mice lacking neuronal nitric oxide synthase. Proceedings of the National Academy of Sciences USA, 98(3), 1277–1281.

Chiavegatto, S., & Nelson, R. J. (2003). Interaction of nitric oxide and serotonin in aggressive behavior. Hormones and Behavior, 44(3), 233–241.

Chugani, D. C. (2002). Role of altered brain serotonin mechanisms in autism. Molecular Psychiatry, 7(Suppl. 2), S16–S17.

Cirulli, F., Berry, A., & Alleva, E. (2003). Early disruption of the mother–infant relationship: Effects on brain plasticity and implications for psychopathology. *Neuroscience and Biobehavioral Reviews, 27*(1–2), 73–82.

Costa, A., Trainer, P., Besser, M., & Grossman, A. (1993). Nitric oxide modulates the release of corticotropin-releasing hormone from the rat hypothalamus in vitro. *Brain Research, 605*(2), 187–192.

Costa, A. C., Walsh, K., & Davisson, M. T. (1999). Motor dysfunction in a mouse model for Down syndrome. *Physiology and Behavior, 68*(1–2), 211–220.

Coussons-Read, M. E., & Crnic, L. S. (1996). Behavioral assessment of the Ts65Dn mouse, a model for Down syndrome: Altered behavior in the elevated plus maze and open field. *Behavior Genetics, 26*(1), 7–13.

Davisson, M. T., Schmidt, C., & Akeson, E. C. (1990). Segmental trisomy of murine chromosome 16: A new model system for studying Down syndrome. *Progress in Clinical and Biological Research, 360,* 263–80.

Demas, G. E., Eliasson, M. J., Dawson, T. M., Dawson, V. L., Kriegsfeld, L. J., Nelson, R. J., et al. (1997). Inhibition of neuronal nitric oxide synthase increases aggressive behavior in mice. *Molecular Medicine, 3*(9), 610–616.

Demas, G. E., Kriegsfeld, L. J., Blackshaw, S., Huang, P., Gammie, S. C., Nelson, R. J., et al. (1999). Elimination of aggressive behavior in male mice lacking endothelial nitric oxide synthase. *Journal of Neuroscience, 19*(19), RC30.

Demas, G. E., Nelson, R. J., Krueger, B. K., & Yarowsky, P. J. (1996). Spatial memory deficits in segmental trisomic Ts65Dn mice. *Behavioural Brain Research, 82*(1), 85–92.

Demas, G. E., Nelson, R. J., Krueger, B. K., & Yarowsky, P. J. (1998). Impaired spatial working and reference memory in segmental trisomy (Ts65Dn) mice. *Behavioural Brain Research, 90*(2), 199–201.

Dierssen, M., Fillat, C., Crnic, L., Arbones, M., Florez, J., & Estivill, X. (2001). Murine models for Down syndrome. *Physiology and Behavior, 73*(5), 859–871.

Escorihuela, R. M., Fernandez-Teruel, A., Vallina, I. F., Baamonde, C., Lumbreras, M. A., Dierssen, M., et al. (1995). A behavioral assessment of Ts65Dn mice: A putative Down syndrome model. *Neuroscience Letters, 199*(2), 143–146.

Escorihuela, R. M., Vallina, I. F., Martinez-Cue, C., Baamonde, C., Dierssen, M., Tobena, A., et al. (1998). Impaired short- and long-term memory in Ts65Dn mice, a model for Down syndrome. *Neuroscience Letters, 247*(2–3), 171–174.

Fatemi, S. H., Cuadra, A. E., El-Fakahany, E. E., Sidwell,

R. W., & Thuras, P. (2000). Prenatal viral infection causes alterations in nNOS expression in developing mouse brains. *Neuroreport, 11*(7), 1493–1496.

Francis, D. D., Szegda, K., Campbell, G., Martin, W. D., & Insel, T. R. (2003). Epigenetic sources of behavioral differences in mice. *Nature Neuroscience, 6*(5), 445–446.

Frisch, C., Dere, E., Silva, M. A., Godecke, A., Schrader, J., & Huston, J. P. (2000). Superior water maze performance and increase in fear-related behavior in the endothelial nitric oxide synthase-deficient mouse together with monoamine changes in cerebellum and ventral striatum. *Journal of Neuroscience, 20*(17), 6694–6700.

Galdzicki, Z., & Siarey, R. J. (2003). Understanding mental retardation in Down's syndrome using trisomy 16 mouse models. *Genes, Brain, and Behavior, 2*(3), 167–178.

Gammie, S. C., Huang, P. L., & Nelson, R. J. (2000). Maternal aggression in endothelial nitric oxide synthase-deficient mice. *Hormones and Behavior, 38*(1), 13–20.

Gammie, S. C., & Nelson, R. J. (1999). Maternal aggression is reduced in neuronal nitric oxide synthase-deficient mice. *Journal of Neuroscience, 19*(18), 8027–8035.

Gammie, S. C., & Nelson, R. J. (2000). Maternal and mating-induced aggression is associated with elevated citrulline immunoreactivity in the paraventricular nucleus in prairie voles. *Journal of Comparative Neurology, 418*(2), 182–192.

Garattini, S., Giacalone, E., & Valzelli, L. (1967). Isolation, aggressiveness and brain 5–hydroxytryptamine turnover. *Journal of Pharmacy and Pharmacology, 19*(5), 338–339.

Giacalone, E., Tansella, M., Valzelli, L., & Garattini, S. (1968). Brain serotonin metabolism in isolated aggressive mice. *Biochemical Pharmacology, 17*(7), 1315–1327.

Ginsburg, B., & Allee, W. C. (1942). Some effects of conditioning on social dominance and subordination in inbred strains of mice. *Physiological Zoology, 15,* 485–506.

Givalois, L., Li, S., & Pelletier, G. (2002). Central nitric oxide regulation of the hypothalamic-pituitary-adrenocortical axis in adult male rats. *Brain Research. Molecular Brain Research, 102*(1–2), 1–8.

Gotti, S., Chiavegatto, S., Sica, M., Viglietti-Panzica, C., Nelson, R., & Panzica, G. (in press). Alteration of NO-producing system in the basal forebrain and hypothalamus of Ts65Dn mice: An immunohistochemical and histochemical study of a murine model for Down syndrome. *Neurobiology of Disease.*

Gulesserian, T., Engidawork, E., Cairns, N., & Lubec, G.

(2000). Increased protein levels of serotonin transporter in frontal cortex of patients with Down syndrome. *Neuroscience Letters, 296*(1), 53–57.

Haller, J., Albert, I., & Makara, G. B. (1997). Acute behavioural effects of corticosterone lack specificity but show marked context-dependency. *Journal of Neuroendocrinology, 9*(7), 515–518.

Haller, J., & Kruk, M. R. (2003). Neuroendocrine stress responses and aggression. In M. P. Mattson (Ed.), *Neurobiology of aggression: Understanding and preventing violence* (pp. 93–118). Totowa, NJ: Humana.

Harada, S., Imaki, T., Chikada, N., Naruse, M., & Demura, H. (1999). Distinct distribution and time-course changes in neuronal nitric oxide synthase and inducible NOS in the paraventricular nucleus following lipopolysaccharide injection. *Brain Research, 821*(2), 322–332.

Heneka, M. T., & Feinstein, D. L. (2001). Expression and function of inducible nitric oxide synthase in neurons. *Journal of Neuroimmunology, 114*(1–2), 8–18.

Hodge, G. K., & Butcher, L. L. (1974). 5-Hydroxytryptamine correlates of isolation-induced aggression in mice. *European Journal of Pharmacology, 28*(2), 326–337.

Hodgins, S., Hiscoke, U. L., & Freese, R. (2003). The antecedents of aggressive behavior among men with schizophrenia: A prospective investigation of patients in community treatment. *Behavior Sciences and the Law, 21*(4), 523–546.

Holtzman, D. M., Santucci, D., Kilbridge, J., Chua-Couzens, J., Fontana, D. J., Daniels, S. E., et al. (1996). Developmental abnormalities and age-related neurodegeneration in a mouse model of Down syndrome. *Proceedings of the National Academy of Sciences USA, 93*(23), 13333–13338.

Huang, P. L., Dawson, T. M., Bredt, D. S., Snyder, S. H., & Fishman, M. C. (1993). Targeted disruption of the neuronal nitric oxide synthase gene. *Cell, 75*(7), 1273–1286.

Huang, P. L., Huang, Z., Mashimo, H., Bloch, K. D., Moskowitz, M. A., Bevan, J. A., et al. (1995). Hypertension in mice lacking the gene for endothelial nitric oxide synthase. *Nature, 377*(6546), 239–242.

Jasnow, A. M., Huhman, K. L., Bartness, T. J., & Demas, G. E. (2000). Short-day increases in aggression are inversely related to circulating testosterone concentrations in male Siberian hamsters (*Phodopus sungorus*). *Hormones and Behavior, 38*(2), 102–110.

Jasnow, A. M., Huhman, K. L., Bartness, T. J., & Demas, G. E. (2002). Short days and exogenous melatonin increase aggression of male Syrian hamsters (*Mesocricetus auratus*). *Hormones and Behavior, 42*, 13–20.

Karanth, S., Lyson, K., & McCann, S. M. (1993). Role of nitric oxide in interleukin 2–induced corticotropin-releasing factor release from incubated hypothalami. *Proceedings of the National Academy of Sciences USA, 90*(8), 3383–3387.

Katsuse, O., Iseki, E., & Kosaka, K. (2003). Immunohistochemical study of the expression of cytokines and nitric oxide synthases in brains of patients with dementia with Lewy bodies. *Neuropathology, 23*(1), 9–15.

Kim, C. K., & Rivier, C. L. (2000). Nitric oxide and carbon monoxide have a stimulatory role in the hypothalamic-pituitary-adrenal response to physicoemotional stressors in rats. *Endocrinology, 141*(6), 2244–2253.

Klein, S. L., Kriegsfeld, L. J., Hairston, J. E., Rau, V., Nelson, R. J., & Yarowsky, P. J. (1996). Characterization of sensorimotor performance, reproductive and aggressive behaviors in segmental trisomic 16 (Ts65Dn) mice. *Physiology and Behavior, 60*(4), 1159–1164.

Kriegsfeld, L. J., Dawson, T. M., Dawson, V. L., Nelson, R. J., & Snyder, S. H. (1997). Aggressive behavior in male mice lacking the gene for neuronal nitric oxide synthase requires testosterone. *Brain Research, 769*(1), 66–70.

Kruk, M. R., Westphal, K. G., Van Erp, A. M., van Asperen, J., Cave, B. J., Slater, E., et al. (1998). The hypothalamus: Cross-roads of endocrine and behavioural regulation in grooming and aggression. *Neuroscience and Biobehavioral Reviews, 23*(2), 163–177.

Lacey-Casem, M. L., & Oster-Granite, M. L. (1994). The neuropathology of the trisomy 16 mouse. *Critical Reviews in Neurobiology, 8*(4), 293–322.

Laubach, V. E., Shesely, E. G., Smithies, O., & Sherman, P. A. (1995). Mice lacking inducible nitric oxide synthase are not resistant to lipopolysaccharide-induced death. *Proceedings of the National Academy of Sciences USA, 92*(23), 10688–10692.

Leckman, J. F., & Herman, A. E. (2002). Maternal behavior and developmental psychopathology. *Biological Psychiatry, 51*(1), 27–43.

Lee, M. A., & Meltzer, H. Y. (2001). 5-HT(1A) receptor dysfunction in female patients with schizophrenia. *Biological Psychiatry, 50*(10), 758–766.

Lonstein, J. S., & Gammie, S. C. (2002). Sensory, hormonal, and neural control of maternal aggression in laboratory rodents. *Neuroscience and Biobehavioral Reviews, 26*(8), 869–888.

MacMicking, J. D., Nathan, C., Hom, G., Chartrain, N., Fletcher, D. S., Trumbauer, M., et al. (1995). Altered responses to bacterial infection and endotoxic shock in mice lacking inducible nitric oxide synthase. *Cell, 81*(4), 641–650.

Mann, D. M., Yates, P. O., Marcyniuk, B., & Ravindra, C. R. (1985). Pathological evidence for neurotransmitter deficits in Down's syndrome of middle age. *Journal of Mental Deficiency Research*, 29(Pt. 2), 125–135.

Marui, W., Iseki, E., Nakai, T., Miura, S., Kato, M., Ueda, K., et al. (2002). Progression and staging of Lewy pathology in brains from patients with dementia with Lewy bodies. *Journal of Neurological Sciences*, 195(2), 153–159.

Mayer, A. D., Ahdieh, H. B., & Rosenblatt, J. S. (1990). Effects of prolonged estrogen-progesterone treatment and hypophysectomy on the stimulation of short-latency maternal behavior and aggression in female rats. *Hormones and Behavior*, 24(2), 152–173.

Mayer, A. D., Monroy, M. A., & Rosenblatt, J. S. (1990). Prolonged estrogen-progesterone treatment of non-pregnant ovariectomized rats: Factors stimulating home-cage and maternal aggression and short-latency maternal behavior. *Hormones and Behavior*, 24(3), 342–364.

McCann, S. M., Kimura, M., Karanth, S., Yu, W. H., Mastronardi, C. A., & Rettori, V. (2000). The mechanism of action of cytokines to control the release of hypothalamic and pituitary hormones in infection. *Annals of the New York Academy of Sciences*, 917, 4–18.

Mednick, S. A., Machon, R. A., Huttunen, M. O., & Bonett, D. (1988). Adult schizophrenia following prenatal exposure to an influenza epidemic. *Archives of General Psychiatry*, 45(2), 189–192.

Meltzer, H. (1989). Serotonergic dysfunction in depression. *British Journal of Psychiatry*, 8(Suppl.), 25–31.

Meltzer, H. Y., Li, Z., Kaneda, Y., & Ichikawa, J. (2003). Serotonin receptors: Their key role in drugs to treat schizophrenia. *Progress in Neuro-Psychopharmacology and Biological Psychiatry*, 27(7), 1159–1172.

Miczek, K. A., Maxson, S. C., Fish, E. W., & Faccidomo, S. (2001). Aggressive behavioral phenotypes in mice. *Behavioural Brain Research*, 125(1–2), 167–181.

Nelson, R. J. (1997). The use of genetic "knockout" mice in behavioral endocrinology research. *Hormones and Behavior*, 31(3), 188–196.

Nelson, R. J., & Chiavegatto, S. (2001). Molecular basis of aggression. *Trends in Neurosciences*, 24(12), 713–719.

Nelson, R. J., Demas, G. E., Huang, P. L., Fishman, M. C., Dawson, V. L., Dawson, T. M., et al. (1995). Behavioural abnormalities in male mice lacking neuronal nitric oxide synthase. *Nature*, 378(6555), 383–386.

Nelson, R. J., Kriegsfeld, L. J., Dawson, V. L., & Dawson, T. M. (1997). Effects of nitric oxide on neuroendocrine function and behavior. *Frontiers in Neuroendocrinology*, 18(4), 463–491.

Olivier, B., Mos, J., van der Heyden, J., & Hartog, J. (1989). Serotonergic modulation of social interac-

tions in isolated male mice. *Psychopharmacology*, 97(2), 154–156.

Posey, D. J., & McDougle, C. J. (2001). The pathophysiology and treatment of autism. *Current Psychiatry Reports*, 3(2), 101–108.

Prendergast, B. J., Kriegsfeld, L. J., & Nelson, R. J. (2001). Photoperiodic polyphenisms in rodents: Neuroendocrine mechanisms, costs, and functions. *Quarterly Review of Biology*, 76(3), 293–325.

Reeves, R. H., Irving, N. G., Moran, T. H., Wohn, A., Kitt, C., Sisodia, S. S., et al. (1995). A mouse model for Down syndrome exhibits learning and behaviour deficits. *Nature Genetics*, 11(2), 177–184.

Rivier, C., & Shen, G. H. (1994). In the rat, endogenous nitric oxide modulates the response of the hypothalamic-pituitary-adrenal axis to interleukin-1 beta, vasopressin, and oxytocin. *Journal of Neuroscience*, 14(4), 1985–1993.

Sandi, C., & Guaza, C. (1995). Evidence for a role of nitric oxide in the corticotropin-releasing factor release induced by interleukin-1 beta. *European Journal of Pharmacology*, 274(1–3), 17–23.

Schmidt, H. H., Hofmann, H., Schindler, U., Shutenko, Z. S., Cunningham, D. D., & Feelisch, M. (1996). NO from NO synthase. *Proceedings of the National Academy of Sciences USA*, 93(25), 14492–14497.

Seidl, R., Kaehler, S. T., Prast, H., Singewald, N., Cairns, N., Gratzer, M., et al. (1999). Serotonin (5-HT) in brains of adult patients with Down syndrome. *Journal of Neural Transmission. Supplementum*, 57, 221–232.

Seward, J. P. (1946). Aggressive behavior in the rat. IV. Submission as determined by conditioning, extinction and disuse. *Journal of Comparative and Physiological Psychology*, 39, 51–57.

Singh, R., Pervin, S., Shryne, J., Gorski, R., & Chaudhuri, G. (2000). Castration increases and androgens decrease nitric oxide synthase activity in the brain: Physiologic implications. *Proceedings of the National Academy of Sciences USA*, 97(7), 3672–3677.

Soma, K. K., & Wingfield, J. C. (2001). Dehydroepiandrosterone in songbird plasma: Seasonal regulation and relationship to territorial aggression. *General and Comparatove Endocrinology*, 23, 144–155.

Takei, N., Mortensen, P. B., Klaening, U., Murray, R. M., Sham, P. C., O'Callaghan, E., et al. (1996). Relationship between in utero exposure to influenza epidemics and risk of schizophrenia in Denmark. *Biological Psychiatry*, 40(9), 817–824.

Valzelli, L. (1974). 5-Hydroxytryptamine in aggressiveness. *Advances in Biochemical Psychopharmacology*, 11(0), 255–263.

Wei, X. Q., Charles, I. G., Smith, A., Ure, J., Feng, G. J., Huang, F. P., et al. (1995). Altered immune responses in mice lacking inducible nitric oxide synthase. *Nature*, 375(6530), 408–411.

Weiner, C. P., Lizasoain, I., Baylis, S. A., Knowles, R. G., Charles, I. G., & Moncada, S. (1994). Induction of calcium-dependent nitric oxide synthases by sex hormones. *Proceedings of the National Academy of Sciences USA, 91*(11), 5212–5216.

Wen, J. C., Hotchkiss, A. K., Demas, G. E., & Nelson, R. J. (2004). Photoperiod affects neuronal nitric oxide synthase and aggressive behavior in male Siberian hamsters *(Phodopus sungorus). Journal of Neuroendocrinology, 16,* 916–921.

Whitaker-Azmitia, P. M. (2001). Serotonin and brain development: Role in human developmental diseases. *Brain Research Bulletin, 56*(5), 479–485.

Xing, G., Chavko, M., Zhang, L. X., Yang, S., & Post, R. M. (2002). Decreased calcium-dependent constitutive nitric oxide synthase (cNOS) activity in prefrontal cortex in schizophrenia and depression. *Schizophrenia Research, 58*(1), 21–30.

Yen, C. Y., Stanger, R. L., & Millman, N. (1959). Ataractic suppression of isolation-induced aggressive behavior. *Archives Internationales de Pharmacodynamie et de Therapie, 123*(1–2), 179–185.

7

Neuroplasticity and Aggression: An Interaction Between Vasopressin and Serotonin

Craig F. Ferris

Aggression is a normal part of mammalian behavior as animals fight to defend territory, acquire resources, compete for mates, and protect young (Huntingford & Turner, 1987). However, fighting is not "hardwired," a simple reflex in response to provocative stimuli in the environment. Instead, aggressive behavior is adaptive, modified by a changing environment and previous life experience. Indeed, winning or losing an agonist encounter has a dramatic impact on future aggressive behavior. Winners are more likely to initiate attacks against unknown opponents, whereas losers are more circumspect and likely to retreat from unfamiliar conspecifics, adopting an opportunistic strategy, picking and choosing their fights. In the worst case scenario, animals socially subjugated by constant threat and attack from dominant conspecifics develop a submissive phenotype, showing little or no aggressive behavior, essentially eliminating themselves from the gene pool. How does winning or losing fights alter the neurobiology of the brain to favor aggressive or submissive behavioral phenotypes? This chapter focuses on two neurochemical signals controlling aggression—serotonin (5-hydroxytryptamine, or 5-HT) and vasopressin. Data are discussed linking environment and social experience to changes in glucocorticoids and testosterone and how these transcription factors alter the neurobiology of the 5-HT and vasopressin systems.

Neurochemical Control of Aggression

5-HT

Several neurochemical signals are reported to facilitate and inhibit aggressive behavior (for review, see Ferris & DeVries, 1997). One in particular, 5-HT, appears to have a critical role in reducing aggression in numerous mammals, including humans (Coccaro & Kavoussi, 1997, Cologer-Clifford, Simon, Lu, & Smoluk, 1997; Dalta, Mitra, & Bhattacharya, 1991; Delville, Mansour, & Ferris, 1995; Ferris et al., 1997; Joppa, Rowe, & Meisel, 1997; Molina, Ciesielski, Gobailles, Insel, & Mandel, 1987; Nelson & Chiavegatto, 2001; Ogren, Holm, Renyi, & Ross, 1980; Olivier, Mos, Van der Heyden, & Hartog, 1989; Sanchez & Hyttel, 1994; Villalba, Boyle, Caliguri, & De Vries, 1997). For example, elevation in brain levels of 5-HT following treatment with 5-HT reuptake inhibitors, such as fluoxetine, reduce multiple measures of aggression in a wide range of animals. Mice lacking the 5-HT transporter gene display reduced aggression and less activity overall than control mice (Holmes, Murphy, & Crawley, 2002). Conversely, male rats depleted of brain 5-HT by treatment with neurotoxins are highly aggressive and assume dominant positions when housed with control animals (Ellison, 1976) and enhanced biting attacks toward intruders (Vergnes,

163

Depaulis, Boehrer, & Kempf, 1988). 5-HT appears to reduce aggression by binding to $5-HT_{1A}$ and $5-HT_{1B}$ receptors. Several $5-HT_{1A}$ and $5-HT_{1B}$ receptor agonists produce a dose-dependent decrease in aggressive behavior (Sijbesma et al., 1991). Mutant mice lacking the $5-HT_{1B}$ receptor (Saudou et al., 1994) are exceedingly aggressive toward intruders and appear to be more impulsive (Bouwknecht et al., 2001). Mice and rats bred for high and low aggressive behavior show phenotypic differences in $5-HT_{1A}$ receptors (Korte et al., 1996; van der Vegt et al., 2001).

The relationship between low 5-HT function and high impulsivity has also been reported in nonhuman primates (Mehlman et al., 1994). Adolescent monkeys with the highest aggression and greatest risk taking show the lowest levels of 5-HT metabolite 5-hydroxyindoleacetic acid (5-HIAA) concentrations in the cerebrospinal fluid (CSF). Only monkeys with the most severe forms of aggression and risk taking are correlated with low levels of the 5-HT metabolite 5-HIAA in CSF. These same highly aggressive, high-risk phenotypes were discovered to have a variation in the 5-HT transporter associated with decreased serotonergic function (Bennett et al., 2002). In vervet monkeys, impulsivity in response to unfamiliar male intruders is inversely correlated with 5-HIAA levels in cerebrospinal fluid (Fairbanks, Melega, Jorgensen, Kaplan, & McGuire, 2001). Treatment with a 5-HT reuptake inhibitor reduces the impulsivity of male vervets toward intruders. Rhesus monkeys treated with fenfluramine show an inverse correlation between aggression and prolactin release, a neuroendocrine measure of reduced 5-HT activity in the brain (Tiefenbacher, Davenport, Novak, Pouliot, & Meyer, 2003).

There is compelling evidence from human studies demonstrating an inverse relation between 5-HT function and impulsivity and aggression. The metabolite 5-HIAA is lower in CSF in violent men compared to men assigned to control groups (Brown et al., 1982; Linnoila et al., 1983). Children with conduct disorder and operational defiant disorder have low 5-HIAA compared to other control adolescents (Kruesi, Rapoport, Hamburger, Hibbs, & Potter, 1990). Reduced 5-HT function is inversely correlated with impulsivity in personality disorder adults (Dolan, Anderson, & Deakin, 2001). Treatment with 5-HT reuptake inhibitors reduces inappropriate aggressive behavior in children (Zubieta & Alessi, 1992) and adults with personality disorders characterized by a history of excessive aggressive behavior (Coccaro, Astill, Herbert, & Schut, 1990).

Men with a history of conduct disorder show reduced measures of aggression and impulsivity when treated with a 5-HT reuptake inhibitor or the 5-HT releasing agent fenfluramine (Cherek & Lane, 2001; Cherek, Lane, Pietras, & Steinberg, 2002).

Vasopressin

Studies on rodents indicate a role for vasopressin (VP) in the modulation of aggression. In hamsters, a VP receptor antagonist, microinjected into the anterior hypothalamus, causes a dose-dependent inhibition of aggression of a resident male toward an intruder (Ferris & Potegal, 1988). Treatment with VP receptor antagonist prolongs the latency to bite an intruder, reduces the number of bites, but does not alter other social or appetitive behaviors. Conversely, microinjection of VP into the anterior hypothalamus of resident hamsters significantly increases the number of biting attacks on intruders (Ferris, 1996; Ferris et al., 1997). Vasopressin receptor antagonist also blocks aggression associated with the development of dominant/subordinate relationships (Potegal & Ferris, 1990). Treating adolescent hamsters with anabolic steroids increases the density of VP-immunoreactive fibers and neuropeptide content in the anterior hypothalamus and enhances their VP-mediated aggression as adults (Harrison, Connor, Nowak, Nash, & Melloni, 2000). The ability of VP to modulate offensive aggression is not limited to the anterior hypothalamus. Microinjecting VP into the ventrolateral hypothalamus of the hamster facilitates offensive aggression (Delville et al., 1995). Infusion of VP into the amygdala or lateral septum facilitates offensive aggression in castrated rats (Koolhaas, Moor, Hiemstra, & Bohus, 1991; Koolhaas, Van den Brink, Roozendal, & Boorsma, 1990). In prairie voles, intracerebroventricular injection of VP increases aggressive behavior (Winslow, Hastings, Carter, Harbaugh, & Insel, 1993). Early postnatal exposure to VP increases aggressive behavior in adult male prairie voles (Stribley & Carter, 1999). Bester-Meredith, Young, and Marker (1999) compared VP immunostaining between two species of Peromyscus with high and low aggressive phenotypes. The highly aggressive California mouse had greater VP staining in the bed nucleus of the stria terminalis and VP receptor density in the lateral septum than the less aggressive white-footed mouse. Moreover, when California mice are cross-fostered with white-footed parents they show a reduction in aggression in a resident-intruder paradigm and lower levels of VP in the bed nucleus than their unfostered siblings (Bester-Meredith & Marker, 2001). These studies show that environmental conditions associated with pup rearing can affect VP neurotransmission and behavior. Data from rats and humans show that high indexes of aggressivity correlate with high concentrations of VP in CSF (Cocarro, Kavoussi, Hauger, Cooper, & Ferris, 1998; Haller et al., 1996). The ability of VP to affect aggression at multiple sites in the CNS and in various mammalian species is evidence that this neurochemical system may have a broad physiological role enhancing arousal and attack behavior during agonistic interactions.

Vasopressin/5-HT Interactions

Defining the mechanisms and anatomical substrates underlying interactions between functionally opposed neurotransmitter systems is critical for understanding aggressive behavior. One working hypothesis is that VP promotes aggression and dominant behavior by enhancing the activity of the neural network controlling agonistic behavior that is normally restrained by 5-HT. The anterior hypothalamus, the primary site of VP regulation of aggression, has a high density of 5-HT binding sites and receives a dense innervation of 5-HT fibers and terminals (Ferris et al., 1997). The VP neurons in the anterior hypothalamus implicated in the control of aggression appear to be preferentially innervated by 5-HT (Ferris, Irvin, Potegal, & Axelson, 1990; Ferris, Pilapi, Hayden-Hixson, Wiley, & Koh, 1991; Ferris, Stolberg, & Delville, 1999). Intraperitoneal injection of fluoxetine blocks aggression facilitated by the microinjection of VP in the hypothalamus (Delville et al., 1995; Ferris, 1996; Ferris et al., 1997). Fluoxetine elevates 5-HT and reduces VP levels in hypothalamic tissue in hamsters (Ferris, 1996) and rats (Altemus, Cizza, & Gold, 1992). Kia and coworkers (1996) reported intense immunocytochemical staining for 5-HT_{1A} receptors in the VP system of rats, supporting the notion that activation of 5-HT_{1A} receptors can influence the activity of VP neurons. However, data suggest that 5-HT can also block the activity of VP following its release in the hypothalamus, as evidenced by the dose-dependent diminution of aggression with injections combining VP and 5-HT_{1A} receptor agonist. Enhanced aggression caused by activation of AVP V_{1A} receptors in the hypothalamus is suppressed by the simultaneous activation of 5-HT_{1A} receptors in the same

site. It is not clear whether a common neuronal phenotype in the hypothalamus shares both receptor subtypes or VP and 5-HT act on separate neurons in the hypothalamus.

These animal studies examining the interaction between VP and 5-HT are particularly relevant because Cocarro and coworkers (1998) reported a similar reciprocal relationship in human studies. Personality disordered people with a history of fighting and assault show a negative correlation for prolactin release in response to fenfluramine challenge, an indication of a hyposensitive 5-HT system. Moreover, these same individuals show a positive correlation between CSF levels of VP and aggression. Thus, in humans, a hyposensitive 5-HT system may result in enhanced CNS levels of VP and the facilitation of aggressive behavior.

Steroid Hormones as Transducers of Environmental Stimuli

Adrenal and gonadal steroid hormones can induce changes in brain neurobiology that alter an animal's aggressive predisposition. The levels of these steroid hormones are affected by a brain/environment interaction contributing to a physiological and behavioral strategy most appropriate for the environmental condition. The brain is linked to the environment through multiple sensory modalities impinging on the limbic system, integrating past life experience with present environmental conditions. The hypothalamus sits as a key neural substrate integrating information from the limbic system with feedback from the endocrine milieu to regulate the release of pituitary hormones and ultimately blood levels of glucocorticoids and testosterone. These steroid hormones give feedback to the brain to affect neuronal morphology, synaptic connectivity, neurotransmission, and a host of behaviors, including learning and memory, stress, fear, and aggression.

In many species, defeat and subjugation are associated with changes in plasma concentrations of adrenal and gonadal steroid hormones. In both combatants, aggressive encounters produce an elevation of corticosteroid concentrations, possibly as a response to the stress caused by the confrontation (Schuurman, 1980). Following the encounter, glucocorticoid concentrations return to basal values. During subsequent aggressive encounters, higher concentrations of glucocorticoids are observed in the defeated, submissive animal, and these levels remain elevated for a longer period of time

(Bronson & Eleftheriou, 1964; Eberhart, Keverne, & Meller, 1983; Ely & Henry, 1978; Huhman, Moore, Ferris, Mougey, & Meyerhoff, 1991; Louch & Higgenbotham, 1967; Raab et al., 1986). Furthermore, changes in testosterone concentrations coincide with the changes in glucocorticoids. Elevated concentrations of testosterone are observed in victorious animals, and low levels in defeated males (Coe, Mendoza, & Levine, 1979; Eberhart, Keverne, & Meller, 1980; Rose, Berstein, & Gordon, 1975; Sapolsky, 1985). Below is a discussion of the role of testosterone and glucocorticoids in the control of aggression and how these steroid hormones affect the 5-HT and VP systems.

Testosterone

In many mammals, including nonhuman primates, there is a strong correlation between testosterone concentrations in the blood and aggressive behavior (see Simon & Lu, ch. 9 in this volume). Castration reduces attacks and bites in intermale aggression in mice, rats, and hamsters, while testosterone replacement restores aggressiveness (Barfield, Busch, & Wallen, 1972; Beeman, 1947; Brain & Kamis, 1985; Payne, 1973; Vandenbergh, 1971; Van Oortmessen, Dijk, & Schuurman, 1987). Testosterone implanted into the septum and medial preoptic area can enhance attack behavior in castrated male mice (Owen, Peters, & Bronson, 1974) and rats (Albert, 1987). Testosterone concentrations also correlate with social dominance and aggressive behavior in rhesus monkeys (Rose et al., 1975).

The relationship between testosterone and aggression in human males is far less robust than that shown in other mammalian species. In many cases the data are equivocal. For example, plasma testosterone concentrations in male prisoners with chronic aggressive behavior are significantly higher than testosterone values in nonaggressive inmates (Ehrenkranz, Bliss, Sheard, 1974). Normal young men show a significant relationship between circulating testosterone concentrations on self-ratings of hostility and aggression indices (Perskey, Smith, & Basu, 1971). Serum and salivary testosterone levels in healthy young men are positively correlated with self-ratings of spontaneous aggression (Christiansen & Knussmann, 1987). Conversely, there are other studies reporting no correlation between testosterone and aggressive behavior in criminal and normal populations of men (Kreuz & Rose, 1972; Meyer-Bahlburg, Boon, Sharma, & Edwards, 1974). In a sample of 4,591 men, including men with sex chromosome XYY, presenting with elevated testosterone concentrations there was no correlation between hormone levels and data from psychological interviews assessing aggressive behavior (Schiavi, Theilgaard, Owen, & White, 1984). In contrast, a sample of 1,709 men aged 39 to 70, measures of testosterone correlated with a dominant personality profile with some aggression (Gray, Jackson, & McKinlay, 1991). In self-reports from adolescent males, testosterone had a causal influence on provoked aggression and indirectly affected aggression by increasing impulsivity (Olweus, Mattsson, Schalling, & Low, 1980, 1988). A meta-analysis by Archer (1991) showed a low but positive relationship between circulating testosterone concentrations and associated measures of aggressive behavior in 230 males scored over five studies.

There is considerable evidence showing that testosterone affects the limbic VP signaling pathway. The level of immunoreactive VP in neurons of the bed nucleus of the stria terminalis and amygdala and their fiber projections to the septum are dramatically reduced following castration (De Vries & Al-Shamma, 1990; De Vries, Buijs, & Swaab, 1981; De Vries, Buijs, Van Leeuwen, Caffe, & Swaab, 1985). Accompanying the fall in VP is a reduction in VP mRNA in the bed nucleus (Miller, Urban, & Dorsa, 1989). Following castration, testosterone replacement increases levels of nuclear primary transcripts in the bed nucleus and amygdala within 3 hr of treatment (Szot & Dorsa, 1994) and restores VP to levels to that noted in gonad-intact animals (Zhou, Blaustein, & De Vries, 1994). In Syrian hamsters, chronic anabolic steroid treatment increases VP immunostaining in the anterior hypothalamus (Harrison et al., 2000). Vasopressin receptor binding within the ventrolateral hypothalamus of the hamster is androgen dependent (Delville et al., 1995). Castration essentially eliminates VP binding sites in this area of the hamster brain, raising the possibility that the diminished aggression noted in castrated hamsters (Ferris, Azelson, Martin, Roberge, 1989; Payne & Swanson, 1972; Vandenbergh, 1971; Whitsett, 1975) is caused by a loss of VP responsiveness in this hypothalamic area.

It is important to note that the behavioral and molecular effects of testosterone are primarily mediated through its androgenic and estrogenic metabolites, 5-α-dihydrotestosterone (5-DHT) and estrogen. Restoration of VP immunostaining and expression of VP mRNA in the limbic VP system is fully restored in castrated animals treated with a combination of 5-DHT and estrogen (Brot, De Vries, & Dorsa, 1993; De Vries, Duetz, Buijs, van Heerikhuize, & Vreeburg, 1986; De Vries, Wang, Bullock, & Numan, 1994; Wang & De Vries, 1995). In knockout mice lacking the aromatase enzyme needed for converting testosterone to estrogen, there is a significant depletion of VP staining in the bed nucleus and amygdala (Plumari et al., 2002). These results and a recent study by Scordalakes and Rissman (2004) using knockout mice lacking either one or both of the α-estrogen and androgen receptors show that these receptors play a role in VP gene expression and consequently aggression. Immunostaining has colocalized androgen and estrogen receptors to VP neurons in the bed nucleus and amygdala (Axelson & Van Leeuwen, 1990; Zhou et al., 1994), evidence that 5-DHT and estrogen act directly on limbic VP neurons. An estrogen response element sensitive to both the α- and β-estrogen receptors is present on the VP gene promoter (Shapiro, Xu, & Dorsa, 2000). Mice lacking the α-estrogen receptor are less aggressive in the resident-intruder paradigm (Ogawa, Lubahn, Korach, & Pfaff, 1997; Scordalakes & Rissman, 2004).

Although testosterone has a clear role in promoting VP neurotransmission and aggression, its involvement in 5-HT neurotransmission is less obvious. In a series of studies, Bethea and colleagues demonstrated a role for estrogen in promoting 5-HT neurotransmission in monkeys via a direct action on 5-HT neurons (Bethea, Mirkes, Shively, & Adams, 2000; Gundlah, Lu, Mirke, & Bethea, 2001; Gundlah, Pecins-Thompson, Schutzer, & Bethea, 1999; Pecins-Thompson & Bethea, 1999; Pecins-Thompson, Brown, & Bethea, 1998). Hence, in nonhuman primates the aromatization of testosterone to estrogen might be expected to reduce aggression. However, in rodents there is no evidence of colocalization of the estrogen receptors on 5-HT neurons (Alves, Weiland, Hayashi, & McEwen, 1998). Prolonged testosterone treatment in rats reduces 5-HT levels and increases 5-HT_{1A} receptor binding in the hypothalamus and hippocampus (Bonson, Johnson, Fiorella, Rabin, & Winter, 1994; McMillen, Scott, William, & Sanghera, 1987; Mendelson & McEwen, 1990). The heightened aggression and dominance status noted with anabolic steroid treatment in rats can be reduced with treatment of 5-HT_{1A} and 5-HT_{1B} agonists (Bonson et al., 1994). More recent studies report anabolic steroids alter 5-HT_{1B} receptor density in limbic and striatal areas of the rat brain (Kindlundh, Lindblom, Bergatrom, & Nyberg, 2003). Testosterone also has a significant effect on 5-HT_{1A} and 5-HT_{1B} re-

ceptor sensitivity in the mouse, altering aggressive responding (Cologer-Clifford, Simon, Richter, Smoluk, & Lu, 1999). Serotonergic agonists are most effective in reducing aggression in the presence of 5-DHT compared to estrogen.

Glucocorticoids

The role of the stress hormones, glucocorticoids, in rodent aggression is less predictable and more concentration and context dependent than that of testosterone. Glucocorticoid administration in intact and adrenalectomized rodents can increase aggressiveness or increase submissive behavior dependent upon the context of the social interaction (Brain, 1979). Isolation, a condition that exacerbates aggression in rodents, is reduced with adrenalectomy (Harding & Leshner, 1971). Hamsters are most aggressive during the dark phase of the light/dark cycle, a rhythm that can be disrupted by adrenalectomy (Landau, 1975). Defeat in mice results in elevated corticosterone concentrations that appear to promote submissive behavior (Louch & Higginbotham, 1967). Basal corticosteroid concentrations are inversely correlated with aggressive behavior in mice (Politch & Leshner, 1977). High and low circulating concentrations of glucocorticoids in mice encourage avoidance behavior in agonistic encounters compared to that in mice with intermediate concentrations of stress hormone (Leshner, Moyer, & Walker, 1975). In male golden hamsters, cortisol exerts site-, context-, and dose-dependent effects on agonistic behavior (Hayden-Hixson & Ferris, 1991a, 1991b). In dominant hamsters, cortisol implanted in the anterior hypothalamus facilitates the display of submissive behavior in the presence of other dominant animals, while promoting high levels of aggressive behavior in the presence of submissive animals. Corticosteroid hypofunction in rats caused by adrenalectomy and replacement with low blood corticosterone concentrations causes inappropriate attack behavior more akin to that observed in fear and stress situations than normal intermale aggression (Halázs, Liposits, Kruk, & Haller, 2002).

Unlike the positive correlation between testosterone and aggressive responding in male humans, there appears to be a negative correlation between glucocorticoids and aggression in most clinical studies. For example, habitually violent offenders with antisocial personality present with low urinary cortisol concentrations (Virkkunen, 1985). Salivary cortisol levels in preadolescent boys diagnosed with conduct disorder are lower than those measured in control boys (Van-yukov et al., 1993). Conduct disordered children have reduced autonomic nervous system activity and stress responsivity, despite high levels of emotional arousal (van Goozen et al., 2000). Low salivary cortisol in adolescent males is associated with persistence and early onset of aggression (McBurnett, Lahey, Rathouz, & Loeber, 2000). Male offenders with personality disorder show 5-HT function inversely correlated with impulsivity. Moreover, offenders have lower initial cortisol and higher testosterone than controls (Dolan et al., 2001). Dabbs, Jurkovic, and Frady (1991) measured salivary testosterone and cortisol levels in 113 late-adolescent male offenders and reported a positive correlation between testosterone and violent behavior. Moreover, it was noted that cortisol had no effect of its own but moderated the correlation between testosterone and violence.

Glucocorticoids affect VP and 5-HT neurotransmission. There are several reports that hypothalamic VP gene expression is under tonic inhibition by glucocorticoids (Kovács, Foldes, & Sawchenko, 2000; Kovács, Kiss, & Makarar, 1986; Sawchenko, 1987). This inhibition may be indirectly mediated through synaptic inputs (Baldino, O'Kane, Fitzpatrick-McElligott, & Wolfson, 1988) because it is still uncertain whether the VP promoter contains glucocorticoid response elements (Burke et al., 1997; Iwasaki, Oiso, Saito, & Majzoub, 1997). A recent study by Kuwahara using a rat hypothalamic organotypic culture reported that VP gene transcription is inhibited and mRNA stability decreased by glucocorticoids (Kuwahara et al., 2003). In contrast, VP receptor expression is increased with glucocorticoids. Blocking corticosteroid receptor in a VP receptor expressing cell line reduces receptor mRNA and membrane binding (Watters, Wilkinson, & Dorsa, 1996). Adrenalectomy in rats reduces VP receptor density in the septum and bed nucleus of the rat brain, an effect that can be reversed by dexamethasone (Watters et al., 1996).

Glucocorticoids also facilitate the synthesis and release of 5-HT (Kudryautsena & Bakshtanouskaya, 1989). Nursing rat pups exposed to elevated corticosterone levels show reduced 5-HT_{1A} binding in the hippocampus as adults (Meerlo et al., 2001). Expression of 5-HT_{1A} receptors in the hippocampus and cortex of adult male rats is reduced with chronic corticosteroid treatments (Chalmers, Kwak, Mansour, Akil, & Watson, 1993; Fernandes, McKittrick, File, & McEwen, 1997; Meijer & De Kloet, 1994; Mendelson &

McEwen, 1992). Increased blood concentrations of glucocorticoids are associated with an increase in hypothalamic levels of 5-HT (Kudryautsena & Bakshtanouskaya, 1989). Furthermore, chronic stress activates corticosteroid receptors in 5-HT neurons within the dorsal raphe nucleus (Kitayama et al., 1989).

Social Subjugation and Neural Plasticity

Social subjugation is a very significant and natural stressor with long-term biological and behavioral consequences in the animal kingdom. In a laboratory setting, an individually housed hamster will routinely attack and bite an equal or smaller sized intruder placed into its home cage (Ferris & Potegal, 1988). However, following repeated defeat by a dominant conspecific, a resident hamster will be defensive or fearful of equal sized nonaggressive intruders (Potegal, Huhman, Moore, & Meyerhoff, 1993). The generalization of submissive behavior toward nonthreatening, novel stimulus animals is an example of "conditioned defeat" (Potegal et al., 1993; see Huhman & Jasnow, ch. 13 in this volume). Conditioned defeat in adult hamsters is not permanent as the flight and defensive behaviors disappear over many days. This disappearance of overt conditioned defeat appears time dependent and not a function of repeated exposure to novel nonaggressive intruders. Defeated mice display less offensive aggression and more submissive behavior (Frishknecht, Seigfried, & Waser, 1982; Williams & Lierle, 1988). Rats consistently defeated by more aggressive conspecifics show a behavioral inhibition characterized by less social initiative and offensive aggression, as well as an increase in defensive behavior (Van de Poll, De Jong, Van Oyen, & Van Pelt, 1982).

Adult male rhesus monkeys will fight for dominance status when forming a social group with breeding females. When two such established groups are brought together to form one, the dominant or alpha male from each will fight for dominance. The loser is relegated to the lowest social rank in the male hierarchy, displaying highly submissive behavior (Rose et al., 1975). Chronic social subjugation in male talapoin monkeys reduces social activity and sexual behavior even in the absence of dominant conspecifics (Eberhart, Yodying-yuad, & Keverne, 1985).

Could social subjugation, (i.e., repeated defeat by more aggressive opponents) result in plastic changes in the VP and 5-HT systems that could predispose sub-jugated animals to be less aggressive in subsequent social encounters? The stress of socially intermixing three strains of male mice over extended periods alters aggressive behavior and 5-HT levels. The most aggres-sive animals present with the lowest levels of 5-HT in the supraoptic nuclei of the hypothalamus (Serri & Ely, 1984). Conversely, development of submissive behav-ior is accompanied by an increase in the activity of the 5-HT system in monkeys (Yodyingyuad, De la Riva, Abbott, Herbert, & Keverne, 1985). Stress is associated with an activation of 5-HT release and/or turnover in the brain (Adell, Garcia-Marquez, Armario, & Gelpi, 1988; Blanchard, Sakai, McEwen, Weiss, & Blanchard, 1993; De Souza & Van Loon, 1986). Conversely, the increase in the density of 5-HT-immunoreactive boutons in the anterior hypothalamus (Delville, Melloni, & Ferris, 1998) may suggest an increased release of this neurochemical signal. With more 5-HT release there is a down-regulation of the 5-HT$_{1A}$ receptor (Serres et al., 2000). The down-regulation of 5-HT receptors in response to social stress has been reported previously (Bolanos-Jimenez et al., 1995; McKrittick, Blanchard, Blanchard, McEwen, & Sakai, 1995). In addition, a decrease in VP immunoreactivity has been observed within select populations of neurons in the anterior hypothalamus in continuously defeated, castrated ham-sters (Ferris et al., 1989). Subordinate hamsters exposed to daily bouts of threat and attack by dominant conspe-cifics present with lower levels of VP and fewer VP neurons in the anterior hypothalamus (Ferris et al., 1989). This depletion of VP immunoreactivity in sub-jugated animals is associated with a decrease in fight-ing and flank marking. However, changes in the AVP system are only observed in subjugated animals; no effect was recorded in dominant animals.

Summary and Conclusions

5-HT and VP appear to play significant roles in the regulation of impulsivity and aggression. 5-HT reduces aggressive responding, while VP enhances arousal and aggression in a context-dependent manner. There are compelling neuroanatomical, pharmacological, and molecular data supporting an interaction between 5-HT and VP in the control of aggression. 5-HT may act by reducing the activity of the VP system. The in-teraction between the brain and the environment is regulated, in part, by changes in gonadal and adrenal

steroids. The stress of social subjugation—winning and losing fights—alters the levels of testosterone and stress hormones, affecting gene transcription and translation. Indeed, the VP/5-HT systems are sensitive to changes in these steroid hormones linking the neurochemical regulation of aggression to environmental events.

Note

These experiments were supported by Grant MH 52280 from the NIMH. The contents of this review are solely the responsibility of the author and do not necessarily repre-sent the official views of the NIMH.

References

Adell, A., Garcia-Marquez, C., Armario, A., & Gelpi, E. (1988). Chronic stress increases serotonin and no-radrenaline in rat brain and sensitize their responses to a further acute stress. *Journal of Neurochemistry, 50,* 1678–1681.

Albert, D. J. (1987). Intermale social aggression: Reinstate-ment in castrated rats by implants of testosterone proprionate in the medial hypothalamus. *Physiology and Behavior, 39,* 555–560.

Altemus, M., Cizza, G., & Gold, P. W. (1992). Chronic fluoxetine treatment reduces hypothalamic vaso-pressin secretion in vitro. *Brain Research, 593,* 311–313.

Alves, S. E., Weiland, N. G., Hayashi, S., & McEwen, B. S. (1998). Immunocytochemical localization of nuclear estrogen receptors and progestin receptors within the rat dorsal raphe nucleus. *Journal of Com-parative Neurology, 391,* 322–334.

Archer, J. (1991). The influence of testosterone on human aggression. *British Journal of Psychology, 82,* 1–28.

Axelson, J. F., & Van Leeuwen, F. W. (1990). Differen-tial localization of estrogen receptors in various va-sopressin synthesizing nuclei of the rat brain. *Journal of Neuroendocrinology, 2,* 209–216.

Baldino, F., Jr., O'Kane, T. M., Fitzpatrick-McElligott, S. & Wolfson, B. (1988). Coordinate hormonal and synaptic regulation of vasopressin messenger RNA. *Science, 241,* 978–981.

Barfield, R. J., Busch, D. E., & Wallen, K. (1972). Go-nadal influence on agonistic behavior in the male domestic rat. *Hormones and Behavior, 3,* 247–259.

Beeman, E. A. (1947). The effect of male hormone on aggressive behavior in mice. *Physiological Zoology, 20,* 373–405.

Bennett, A. J., Lesch, K. P., Heils, A., Long, J. C., Lorenz, J. G., Shoaf, S. E., et al. (2002). Early experience and serotonin transporter gene variation interact to influence primate CNS function. *Molecular Psychiatry,* 7, 118–122.

Bester-Meredith, J. K., & Marker, C. A. (2001). Vasopressin and aggression in cross-fostered California mice (*Peromyscus californicus*) and white-footed mice (*Peromyscus leucopus*). *Hormones and Behavior, 40,* 51–64.

Bester-Meredith, J. K., Young, L. J., & Marker, C. A. (1999). Species differences in paternal behavior and aggression in *Peromyscus* and their associations with vasopressin immunoreactivity and receptors. *Hormones and Behavior, 36,* 25–38.

Bethea, C. L., Mirkes, S. J., Shively, C. A., & Adams, M. R. (2000). Steroid regulation of tryptophan hydroxylase protein in the dorsal raphe of macaques. *Biological Psychiatry, 47,* 562–576.

Blanchard, D. C., Sakai, R. R., McEwen, B., Weiss, S. M., & Blanchard, R. J. (1993). Subordination stress: Behavioral, brain and neuroendocrine correlates. *Behavioural Brain Research, 58,* 113–121.

Bolanos-Jimenez, F., Manhaes de Castro, R. M., Cloez-Tarayani, I., Monneret, V., Drieu, K., & Fillion, G. (1995). Effects of stress on the functional properties of pre- and postsynaptic 5-HT$_{1B}$ receptors in the rat brain. *European Journal of Pharmacology, 294,* 531–540.

Bonson, K. R., Johnson, R. G., Fiorella, D., Rabin, R. A., & Winter, J. C. (1994). Serotonergic control of androgen-induced dominance. *Pharmacology, Biochemistry and Behavior, 49,* 313–322.

Bouwknecht, J. A., Hijzen, T. H., van der Gugten, J., Maes, R. A. A., Hen, R., & Olivier, B. (2001). Absence of 5-HT1B receptors is associated with impaired impulse control in male 5-HT1B knockout mice. *Biological Psychiatry, 49,* 557–568.

Brain, P. F. (1979). Effects of the hormones of the pituitary–adrenal axis on behavior. In K. Brown & S. J. Cooper (Eds.), *Chemical influences on behavior* (pp. 331–372). New York: Academic Press.

Brain, P. F., & Kamis, A. B. (1985). How do hormones change aggression? The example of testosterone. In J. M. Ramirez & P. F. Brain (Eds.), *Aggression: Functions and causes* (pp. 84–115). Seville, Spain: Publicaciones de la Universidad de Sevilla.

Bronson, H., & Eleftheriou, B. F. (1964). Chronic physiological effects of fighting in mice. *General and Comparatove Endocrinology, 4,* 9–14.

Brot, M. D., De Vries, G. J., & Dorsa, D. M. (1993). Local implants of testosterone metabolites regulate vasopressin mRNA in sexually dimorphic nuclei of the rat brain. *Peptides, 14,* 933–940.

Brown, G. L., Ebert, M. H., Goyer, P. F., Jimerson, D. C., Klein, W. J., Bunney, W. E., et al. (1982). Aggression, suicide, and serotonin: Relationship to CSF amine metabolites. *American Journal of Psychiatry, 139,* 741–746.

Burke, Z. D., Ho, M. Y., Morgan H., Smith M., Murphy, D. & Carter, D. (1997). Repression of vasopressin gene expression by glucocorticoids in transgenic mice: Evidence of a direct mechanism mediated by proximal 5' flanking sequence. *Neuroscience, 78,* 1177–1185.

Chalmers, D. T., Kwak, S. P., Mansour, A., Akil, H., & Watson, S. J. (1993). Glucocorticoids regulate brain hippocampal 5-HT$_{1A}$ receptor mRNA expression. *Journal of Neuroscience, 13,* 914–923.

Cherek, D. R., & Lane, S. D. (2001). Acute effects of D-fenfluramine on simultaneous measures of aggressive escape and impulsive responses of adult males with and without a history of conduct disorder. *Psychopharmacology, 157,* 221–227.

Cherek, D. R., Lane, S. D., Pietras, C. J., & Steinberg, J. L. (2002). Effects of chronic paroxetine administration on measures of aggressive and impulsive responses of adult males with a history of conduct disorder. *Psychopharmacology, 159,* 266–274.

Christiansen, K., & Knussmann, R. (1987). Androgen levels and components of aggressive behavior in men. *Hormones and Behavior, 21,* 170–180.

Coccaro, E. F., Astill, J. L., Herbert, J. L., & Schut, A. G. (1990). Fluoxetine treatment of impulsive aggression in DSM-III-R personality disorder patients. *Journal of Clinical Psychopharmacology, 10,* 373–375.

Coccaro, E. F., & Kavoussi, R. J. (1997). Fluoxetine and impulsive aggressive behavior in personality-disordered subjects. *Archives of General Psychiatry, 54,* 1081–1088.

Coccaro, E. F., Kavoussi, R. J., Hauger, R. L., Cooper, T. B., & Ferris, C. F. (1998). Cerebrospinal fluid vasopressin levels correlates with aggression and serotonin function in personality-disordered subjects. *Archives of General Psychiatry, 55,* 708–714.

Coe, C. L., Mendoza, S. P., & Levine, S. (1979). Social status constrains the stress response in the squirrel monkey. *Physiology and Behavior, 23,* 633–638.

Cologer-Clifford, A., Simon, N. G., Lu, S.-F., & Smoluk, S. A. (1997). Serotonin agonist-induced decreases in intermale aggression are dependent on brain region and receptor subtype. *Pharmacology, Biochemistry and Behavior, 58,* 425–430.

Cologer-Clifford, A., Simon, N. G., Richter, M. L., Smoluk, S. A., & Lu, S.-F. (1999). Androgens and estrogens modulate 5-HT$_{1A}$ and 5-HT$_{1B}$ agonist effects on aggression. *Physiology and Behavior, 65,* 823–828.

Dabbs, J. M., Jr., Jurkovic, G. L., & Frady, R. L. (1991). Salivary testosterone and cortisol levels among late adolescent male offenders. *Journal of Abnormal Child Psychology, 19*, 469–478.

Dalta, K. P., Mitra, S. K., & Bhattacharya, S. K. (1991). Serotonergic modulation of footshock induced aggression in paired rats. *Indian Journal of Experimental Biology, 29*, 631–635.

Delville, Y., Mansour, K. M., & Ferris, C. F. (1995). Serotonin blocks vasopressin-facilitated offensive aggression: Interactions within the ventrolateral hypothalamus of golden hamsters. *Physiology and Behavior, 59*, 813–816.

Delville, Y., Melloni, R. H., Jr., & Ferris, C. F. (1998). Behavioral and neurobiological consequences of social subjugation during puberty in golden hamsters. *Journal of Neuroscience, 18*, 2667–2672

De Souza, E. B., & Van Loon, G. R. (1986). Brain serotonin and catecholamine responses to repeated stress in rats. *Brain Research, 367*, 77–86.

DeVries, G. J., & Al-Shamma, H. A. (1990). Sex differences in hormonal responses of vasopressin pathways in the rat brain. *Journal of Neurobiology, 21*, 686–693.

DeVries, G. J., Buijs, R. M., & Swaab, D. F. (1981). Ontogeny of the vasopressinergic neurons of the suprachiasmatic nucleus and their extrahypothalamic projections in the rat brain—presence of a sex difference in the lateral septum. *Brain Research, 218*, 67–78.

DeVries, G. J., Buijs, R. M., Van Leeuwen, F. W., Caffe, A. R., & Swaab, D. F. (1985). The vasopressinergic innervation of the brain in normal and castrated rats. *Journal of Comparative Neurology, 233*, 236–254.

DeVries, G. J., Duetz, W., Buijs, R. M., van Heerikhuize, J., & Vreeburg, J. T. (1986). Effects of androgens and estrogens on the vasopressin and oxytocin innervation of the adult rat brain. *Brain Research, 399*, 296–302.

DeVries, G. J., Wang, Z., Bullock, N. A., & Numan, S. (1994). Sex differences in the effects of testosterone and its metabolites on vasopressin messenger RNA levels in the bed nucleus of the stria terminalis of rats. *Journal of Neuroscience, 14*, 1789–1794.

Dolan, M., Anderson, I. M., & Deakin, J. F. (2001). Relationship between 5-HT function and impulsivity and aggression in male offenders with personality disorders. *British Journal of Psychiatry, 178*, 352–359.

Eberhart, J. A., Keverne, E. B., & Meller, R. E. (1980). Social influences on plasma testosterone levels in male talapoin monkeys. *Hormones and Behavior, 14*, 247–266.

Eberhart, J. A., Keverne, E. B., & Meller, R. E. (1983). Social influences on circulating levels of cortisol and prolactin in male talapoin monkeys. *Physiology and Behavior, 30*, 361–369.

Eberhart, J. A., Yodyingyuad, U., & Keverne, E. B. (1985). Subordination in male talapoin monkeys lowers sexual behaviour in the absence of dominants. *Physiology and Behavior, 35*, 673–677.

Ehrenkranz, J., Bliss, E., & Sheard, M. H. (1974). Plasma testosterone: Correlation with aggressive behavior and social dominance in man. *Psychosomatic Medicine, 36*, 469–475.

Ellison, G. (1976). Monoamine neurotoxins: Selective and delayed effects on behavior in colonies of laboratory rats. *Brain Research, 103*, 81–92.

Ely, D. L., & Henry, J. P. (1978). Neuroendocrine response patterns in dominant and subordinate mice. *Hormones and Behavior, 10*, 156–169.

Fairbanks, L. A., Melega, W. P., Jorgensen, M. J., Kaplan, J. R., & McGuire, M. T. (2001). Social impulsivity inversely associated with CSF 5-HIAA and fluoxetine exposure in vervet monkeys. *Neuropsychopharmacology, 24*, 370–378.

Fernandes, C., McKittrick, C. R., File, S. E., & McEwen, B. S. (1997). Decreased 5-HT$_{1A}$ and increased 5-HT$_{2A}$ receptor binding after chronic corticosterone associated with behavioural indication of depression but not anxiety. *Psychoneuroendocrinology, 22*, 477–491.

Ferris, C. F. (1996). Serotonin inhibits vasopressin facilitated aggression in the Syrian hamster. In C. F. Ferris & T. Grisso (Eds.), *Understanding aggressive behavior in children* (Vol. 794, pp. 98–103). New York: New York Academy of Sciences.

Ferris, C. F., Axelson, J. F., Martin, A. M., & Roberge, L. R. (1989). Vasopressin immunoreactivity in the anterior hypothalamus is altered during the establishment of dominant/subordinate relationships between hamsters. *Neuroscience, 29*, 675–683.

Ferris, C. F., & DeVries, G. J. (1997). Ethological models for examining the neurobiology of aggressive and affiliative behaviors. In D. Stoff, J. Breiling, & J. D. Maser (Eds.), *Handbook of antisocial behavior* (ch. 24, pp. 255–268). New York: Wiley.

Ferris, C. F., Irvin, R. W., Potegal, M., & Axelson, J. F. (1990). Kainic acid lesion of vasopressinergic neurons in the hypothalamus disrupts flank marking behavior in golden hamsters. *Journal of Neuroendocrinology, 2*, 123–129.

Ferris, C. F., Pilapi, C. G., Hayden-Hixson, D., Wiley, R., & Koh, E. T. (1991). Evidence for two functionally and anatomically distinct populations of magnocellular neurons in the golden hamster. *Journal of Neuroendocrinology, 4*, 193–205.

Ferris, C. F., Melloni, R. H., Jr., Koppel, G., Perry, K. W., Fuller, R. W., & Delville, Y. (1997). Vasopressin/serotonin interactions in the anterior hypothalamus control aggressive behavior in golden hamsters. *Journal of Neuroscience, 17*, 4331–4340.

Ferris, C. F., & Potegal, M. (1988). Vasopressin receptor blockade in the anterior hypothalamus suppresses aggression in hamsters. *Physiology and Behavior, 44,* 235–239.

Ferris, C. F., Stolberg, T., & Delville, Y. (1999). Serotonin regulation of aggressive behavior in male golden hamsters (*Mesocricetus auratus*). *Behavioral Neuroscience, 113,* 804–815.

Frishknecht, H. R., Seigfreid, B., & Waser, P. G. (1982). Learning of submissive behavior in mice: A new model. *Behavioral Processes, 7,* 235–245.

Gray, A., Jackson, D. N., & McKinlay, J. B. (1991). The relation between dominance, anger, and hormones in normally aging men: Results from the Massachusetts male aging study. *Psychosomatic Medicine, 53,* 375–385.

Gundlah, C., Lu, N. Z., Mirke, S. J., & Bethea, C. L. (2001). Estrogen receptor beta (ERbeta) mRNA and protein in serotonin neurons of macaques. *Brain Research. Molecular Brain Research, 91,* 14–22.

Gundlah, C., Pecins-Thompson, M., Schutzer, W. E., & Bethea, C. L. (1999). Ovarian steroid effects on serotonin 1A, 2A and 2C receptor mRNA in macaque hypothalamus. *Molecular Brain Research, 63,* 325–339.

Halázs, J., Liposits, A., Kruk, M. R., & Haller, J. (2002). Neural background of glucocorticoid dysfunction-induced abnormal aggression in rats: Involvement of fear- and stress-related structures. *European Journal of Neuroscience, 15,* 561–569.

Haller, J., Makara, G. B., Barna, I., Kovacs, K., Nagy, J., & Vecsernyes, M. (1996). Compression of the pituitary stalk elicits chronic increases in CSF vasopressin, oxytocin as well as in social investigation and aggressiveness. *Journal of Neuroendocrinology, 8,* 361–365.

Harding, C. F., & Leshner, A. I. (1972). The effects of adrenalectomy on the aggressiveness of differently housed mice. *Physiology and Behavior, 8,* 437–440.

Harrison, R. J., Connor, D. F., Nowak, C., Nash, K., & Melloni, R. H., Jr. (2000). Chronic anabolic-androgenic steroid treatment during adolescence increases anterior hypothalamic vasopressin and aggression in intact hamsters. *Psychoneuroendocrinology, 25,* 317–338.

Hayden-Hixson, D. M., & Ferris, C. F. (1991a). Cortisol exerts site-, context-, and dose-specific effects on the agonistic behaviors of male golden hamsters. *Journal of Neuroendocrinology, 3,* 613–622.

Hayden-Hixson, D. M., & Ferris, C. F. (1991b). Steroid-specific regulation of agonistic responding in the anterior hypothalamus of male hamsters. *Physiology and Behavior, 50,* 793–799.

Holmes, A., Murphy, D. L., & Crawley, J. N. (2002). Reduced aggression in mice lacking the serotonin transporter. *Psychopharmacology, 161,* 160–167.

Huhman, K. L., Moore, T. O., Ferris, C. F., Mougey, E. H., & Meyerhoff, J. L. (1991). Acute and repeated exposure to social conflict in male golden hamsters: Increases in plasma POMC-peptides and cortisol and decreases in plasma testosterone. *Hormones and Behavior, 25,* 206–216.

Huntingford, F. A., & Turner, A. K. (1987). *Animal conflict.* New York: Chapman & Hall.

Iwasaki, Y., Oiso, Y., Saito, H., & Majzoub, J. A. (1997). Positive and negative regulation of the rat vasopressin gene promoter. *Endocrinology, 138,* 5266–5274.

Joppa, M. A., Rowe, R. K., & Meisel, R. L. (1997). Effects of serotonin 1A or 1B receptor agonists on social aggression in male and female Syrian hamsters. *Pharmacology, Biochemistry and Behavior, 58,* 349–353.

Kia, H. K., Miquel, M. C., Brisorgueil, M. J., Daval, G., Riad, M., El Mestikawy, S., et al. (1996). Immunocytochemical localization of serotonin 1A receptors in the rat central nervous system. *Journal of Comparative Neurology, 365,* 289–305.

Kindlundh, A. M., Lindblom, J., Bergstrom, L., & Nyberg, F. (2003). The anabolic-androgenic steroid nandrolone induces alterations in the density of serotonergic 5–HT1B and 5–HT2 receptors in the male rat brain. *Neuroscience, 119,* 113–120.

Kitayama, I., Cintra, A., Janson, A. M., Fuxe, K., Agnati, L. F., Eneroth, P., et al. (1989). Chronic immobilization stress: Evidence for decreases of 5-hydroxytryptamine immunoreactivity and for increases of glucocorticoid receptor immunoreactivity in various brain regions of the male rat. *Journal of Neural Transmission, 77,* 93–130.

Koolhaas, J. M., Moor, E., Hiemstra, Y., & Bohus, B. (1991). The testosterone-dependent vasopressinergic neurons in the medial amygdala and lateral septum: Involvement in social behaviour of male rats. In S. Jard & R. Jamison (Eds.), *Vasopressin* (pp. 213–219). London: Is. NSERM/John Libbey Eurotext.

Koolhaas, J. M., Van den Brink, T. H. C., Roozendal, B., & Boorsma, F. (1990). Medial amygdala and aggressive behavior: Interaction between testosterone and vasopressin. *Aggressive Behavior, 16,* 223–229.

Korte, S. M., Meijer, O. C., De Kloet, E. R., Buwalda, B., Keijser, J., Sluyter, F., et al. (1996). Enhanced 5-HT$_{1a}$ receptor expression iforebrain regions of aggressive house mice *Brain Research, 736,* 338–343.

Kovács, K., Kiss, J. Z., & Makara, G. B. (1986). Glucocorticoid impolants around the hypothalamic paraventricular nucleus prevent the increase of corticotrophin-releasing factor arginine vasopressin immunostaining induced by adrenalectomy. *Neuroendocrinology, 44,* 229–234.

Kovács, K. J., Foldes, A., & Sawchenko, P. E. (2000). Glucocorticoid negative feedback selectively targets vasopressin transcription in parvocellular neurosecretory neurons. *Journal of Neuroscience, 20,* 3843–3852.

Kreuz, L. E., & Rose, R. M. (1972). Assessment of aggressive behavior and plasma testosterone in young criminal population. *Psychosomatic Medicine, 34,* 331–332.

Kruesi, M. J., Rapoport, J. L., Hamburger, S., Hibbs, E., & Potter, W. Z. (1990). Cerebrospinal fluid monoamines metabolites, aggression and impulsivity in disruptive behavior disorders of children and adolescents *Archives of General Psychiatry, 47,* 419–426.

Kudryautsena, N. N., & Bakshtanouskaya, I. V. (1989). *Influence of aggression or submission experience on the state of neurotransmitter systems in different brain regions of mice.* Novosibirsk, Russia: Institute of Cytology and Genetics.

Kuwahara, S., Arima, H., Banno, R., Sato, I., Kondo, N., & Oiso, Y. (2003). Regulation of vasopressin gene expression by cAMP and glucocorticoids in parvocellular neurons of the paraventricular nucleus in rat hypothalamic organotypic cultures. *Journal of Neuroscience, 23,* 10231–10237.

Landau, I. T. (1975). Light-dark rhythms in aggressive behavior of the male golden hamster. *Physiology and Behavior, 14,* 767–774.

Leshner, A. I., Moyer, J. A., & Walker, W. A. (1975). Pituitary-adrenocortical activity and avoidance-of-attack in mice. *Physiology and Behavior, 15,* 689–693.

Linnoila, M., Virkkunen, M., Scheinin, M., Nuutila, A., Rimon, R., & Goodwin, F. K. (1983). Low cerebrospinal fluid 5-hydroxyindoleacetic acid concentration differentiates impulsive from nonimpulsive violent behavior. *Life Sciences, 33,* 2609–2614.

Louch, C. D., & Higginbotham, M. (1967). The relation between social rank and plasma corticosterone levels in mice. *General and Comparatove Endocrinology, 8,* 441–444.

McBurnett, K., Lahey, B. B., Rathouz, P. J., & Loeber, R. (2000). Low salivary cortisol and persistent aggression in boys referred for disruptive behavior. *Archives of General Psychiatry, 57,* 38–43.

McKittrick, C. R., Blanchard, D. C., Blanchard, R. J., McEwen, B. S., & Sakai, R. R. (1995). Serotonin receptor binding in a colony model of chronic social stress. *Biological Psychiatry, 37,* 383–393.

McMillen, B. A., Scott, S. M., William, H. L., & Sanghera, M. K. (1987). Effects of gepirone, an arylpiperazine anxiolytic drug, on aggressive behavior and brain monoaminergic neurotransmission *Naunyn-Schmiedeberg's Archives of Pharmacology, 335,* 454–464.

Meerlo, P., Horvath, K. M., Luiten, P. G. M., Angelucci, L., Catalani, A., & Koolhaas, J. M., (2001). Increase maternal corticosterone levels in rats: Effects on brain 5-HT1A receptors and behavioral coping with stress in adult offspring. *Behavioral Neuroscience, 115,* 1111–1117.

Mehlman, P. T., Higley, J. D., Faucher, I., Lilly, A. A., Taub, D. M., Vickers, J., et al. (1994). Low CSF 5-HIAA concentration and severe aggression and impaired impulse control in nonhuman primates. *American Journal of Psychiatry, 151,* 1485–1491.

Meijer, O., & De Kloet, E. R. (1994). Corticosterone suppresses the expression of 5-HT$_{1A}$ receptor mRNA in rat dentate gyrus. *European Journal of Pharmacology. Molecular Pharmacology, 266,* 255–261.

Mendelson, S., & McEwen, B. S. (1990). Testosterone increases the concentration of [^{3}H]8-hydroxy-2-(di-n-propylamino) binding at 5-HT$_{1A}$ receptors in the medial preoptic nucleus of the castrated male rat. *European Journal of Pharmacology, 181,* 329–331.

Mendelson, S., & McEwen, B. S. (1992). Autoradiographic analysis of the effects of adrenalectomy and corticosterone on 5-HT$_{1A}$ and 5-HT$_{1B}$ receptors in the dorsal hippocampus and cortex of the rat. *Neuroendocrinology, 55,* 444–450.

Meyer-Bahlburg, H. F., Boon, D. A., Sharma, M., & Edwards, F. A. (1974). Aggressiveness and testosterone measures in man. *Psychosomatic Medicine, 36,* 269–274.

Miller, M. A., Urban, J. H., & Dorsa, D. M. (1989). Steroid dependency of vasopressin neurons in the bed nucleus of the stria terminalis by *in situ* hybridization. *Endocrinology, 125,* 2335–2340.

Molina, V., Ciesielski, L., Gobailles, S., Insel, F., & Mandel, P. (1987). Inhibition of mouse killing behavior by serotonin mimetic drugs: Effects of partial alteration of serotonin neurotransmission. *Pharmacology, Biochemistry and Behavior, 27,* 123–131.

Nelson, R. J. & Chiavegatto S. (2001). Molecular basis of aggression. *Trends Neuroscience, 24,* 713–719.

Ogawa, S., Lubahn, D. B., Korach, K. S., & Pfaff, D. W. (1997). Behavioral effects of estrogen receptor gene disruption in male mice. *Proceedings of the National Academy of Sciences USA, 94,* 1476–1481.

Ogren, S. O., Holm, A. C., Renyi, A. L., & Ross, S. B. (1980). Anti-aggressive effect of zimelidine in isolated mice. *Acta Pharmacologica Toxicologica, 47,* 71–74.

Olivier, B., Mos, J., Van der Heyden, J., & Hartog, J. (1989). Serotonergic modulation of social interactions in isolated male mice. *Psychopharmacology, 97,* 154–156.

Olweus, D., Mattsson, A., Schalling, D., & Low, H. (1980). Testosterone, aggression, physical, and personality dimensions in normal adolescent males. *Psychosomatic Medicine, 42,* 253–269.

Olweus, D., Mattsson, A., Schalling, D., & Low, H. (1988). Circulating testosterone levels and aggression in adolescent males: A causal analysis. *Psychosomatic Medicine, 50,* 261–272.

Owen, K., Peters, P. J., & Bronson, F. H. (1974). Effects of intracranial implants of testosterone proprionate on intermale aggression in the castrated male mouse. *Hormones and Behavior, 5,* 83–92.

Payne, A. P. (1973). A comparison of the aggressive behavior of isolated intact and castrated male den hamsters towards intruders introduced into the home cage. *Physiology and Behavior, 10,* 629–631.

Payne, A. P., & Swanson, H. H. (1972). The effect of sex hormones on the agonistic behavior of the male golden hamster (*Mesocricetus auratus* Waterhouse). *Physiology and Behavior, 8,* 687–691.

Pecins-Thompson, M., & Bethea, C. L. (1999). Ovarian steroid regulation of serotonin-1A autoreceptor messenger RNA expression in the dorsal raphe of rhesus macaques. *Neuroscience, 89,* 267–277.

Pecins-Thompson, M., Brown, N. A., & Bethea, C. L. (1998) Regulation of serotonin re-uptake transporter mRNA expression by ovarian steroids in rhesus macaques. *Brain Research. Molecular Brain Research, 53,* 120–129.

Persky, H., Smith, K. D., & Basu, G. K. (1971). Relation of psychologic measures of aggression and hostility to testosterone production in man. *Psychosomatic Medicine, 33,* 265–277.

Plumari, L., Viglietti-Panzica, C., Allieri, F., Honda, S., Harada, N., Absil, P., et al. (2002). Changes in the arginine-vasopressin immunoreactive systems in male mice lacking a functional aromatase gene. *Journal of Neuroendocrinology, 14,* 971–978.

Politch, J. A., & Leshner, A. I. (1977). Relationship between plasma corticosterone levels and levels of aggressiveness in mice. *Physiology and Behavior, 19,* 775–780

Potegal, M., & Ferris, C. (1990). Intraspecific aggression in male hamsters is inhibited by vasopressin receptor antagonists. *Aggressive Behavior, 15,* 311–320.

Potegal, M., Huhman, K., Moore, T., & Meyerhoff, J. (1993). Conditioned defeat in the Syrian golden hamster (*Mesocricetus auratus*). *Behavioral and Neural Biology, 60,* 93–102.

Raab, A., Dantzer, R., Michaud, B., Mormede, P., Taghzouti, K., Simon, H., et al. (1986). Behavioral, physiological and immunological consequences of social status and aggression in chronically coexisting resident-intruder dyads of male rats. *Physiology and Behavior, 36,* 223–228.

Rose, R. M., Berstein, I. S., & Gordon, T. P. (1975). Consequences of social conflict on plasma testosterone levels in rhesus monkeys. *Psychosomatic Medicine, 37,* 50–61.

Sanchez, C., & Hyttel, J. (1994). Isolation-induced aggression in mice: Effects of 5-hydroxytryptamine uptake inhibitors and involvement of postsynaptic 5-HT$_{1A}$ receptors. *European Journal of Pharmacology, 264,* 241–247.

Sapolsky, R. M. (1985). Stress-induced suppression of testicular function in the wild baboon: Role of glucocorticoids. *Endocrinology, 116,* 2273–2278.

Saudou, F., Amara, D. J., Dierich, A., LeMeur, M., Ramboz, S., Segu, A., et al. (1994). Enhanced aggressive behavior in mice lacking 5-HT$_{1B}$ receptor. *Science, 265,* 1875–1878.

Sawchenko, P. E. (1987). Evidence for a local site of action for glucocorticoids in inhibiting CRF and vasopressin expression in the paraventricular nucleus. *Brain Research, 403,* 213–223.

Schiavi, R. C., Theilgaard, A., Owen, D. R., & White, D. (1984). Sex chromosome anomalies, hormones and aggressivity. *Archives of General Psychiatry, 41,* 93–99.

Schuurman, T. (1980). Hormonal correlates of agonistic behavior in adult male rats. *Progress in Brain Research, 53,* 415–420.

Scordalakes, E. M., & Rissman, E. F. (2004). Aggression and arginine vasopressin immunoreactivity regulation by androgen receptor and estrogen receptor alpha. *Genes, Brain, and Behavior, 3,* 20–26.

Serres, F., Muma, N. A., Raap, D. K., Garcia, F., Battaglia, G., & Van de Kar, L. D. (2000). Coadministration of 5-hydroxytryptamine(1A) antagonist WAY-100635 prevents fluoxetine-induced desensitization of postsynaptic 5-hydroxytryptamine(1A) receptors in hypothalamus. *Journal of Pharmacology and Experimental Therapeutics, 294,* 296–301.

Serri, G. A., & Ely, D. L. (1984). A comparative study of aggression related changes in brain serotonin in CBA, C57BL and DBA mice. *Behavioural Brain Research, 12,* 283–289.

Shapiro, R. A., Xu, C., & Dorsa, D. M. (2000). Differential transcriptional regulation of rat vasopressin gene expression by estrogen receptor α and β. *Endocrinology, 141,* 4056–4064

Sijbesma, H., Schipper, J. J., de Kloet, E., Mos, J., Van Aken, H., & Olivier, B. (1991). Postsynaptic 5-HT1 receptors and offensive aggression in rats: A combined behavioral and autoradiographic study with eltoprazine. *Pharmacology, Biochemistry and Behavior, 38,* 447–458.

Stribley, J. M., & Carter, C. S. (1999). Developmental exposure to vasopressin increases aggression in adult prairie voles. *Proceedings of the National Academy of Sciences USA, 96,* 12601–12604.

Szot, P., & Dorsa, D. M. (1994). Expression of cytoplasmic and nuclear vasopressin RNA following castration and testosterone replacement: Evidence for transcriptional regulation. *Molecular and Cellular Neurosciences, 5,* 1–10.

Tiefenbacher, S., Davenport, M. D., Novak, M. A., Pouliot, A. L., & Meyer, J. S. (2003). Fenfluramine challenge, self-injurious behavior, and aggression in rhesus monkeys. *Physiology and Behavior, 80,* 327–331.

Vandenbergh, J. G. (1971). The effects of gonadal hormones on the aggressive behaviour of adult golden hamsters. *Animal Behaviour, 19,* 589–594.

Van de Poll, N. E., De Jonge, F., Van Oyen, H. G., & Van Pelt, J. (1982). Aggressive behaviour in rats: Effects of winning or losing on subsequent aggressive interactions. *Behavioral Processes, 7,* 143–155.

Van der Vegt, B. J., de Boer, S. F., Bulwalda, B., de Ruiter, A. J. H., De Jong, J. G., & Koolhaas, J. M. (2001). Enhanced sensitivity of postsynaptic serotonin-1A receptors in rats and mice with high trait aggression. *Physiology and Behavior, 74,* 205–211.

Van Goozen, S. H., Matthys, W., Cohen-Kettenis, P. T., Buitelaar, J. K., & van Engeland, H. (2000). Hypothalamic-pituitary-adrenal axis and autonomic nervous system activity in disruptive children and matched controls. *Journal of the American Academy of Child and Adolescent Psychiatry, 39,* 1438–1445.

Van Oortmessen, G. A., Dijk, D. J., & Schuurman, T. (1987). Studies in wild house mice. II. Testosterone and aggression. *Hormones and Behavior, 21,* 139–152.

Vanyukov, M. M., Moss, H. B., Plial, J. A., Blackson, T., Mezzich, A. C., & Tarter, R. E. (1993). Antisocial symptoms in preadolescent boys and in their parents: Associations with cortisol. *Psychiatry Research, 46,* 9–17.

Vergnes, M., Depaulis, A., Boehrer, A., & Kempf, E., (1988). Selective increase of offensive behavior in the rat following intrahypothalamic 5,7-DHT-induced serotonin depletion. *Behavioural Brain Research, 29,* 85–91.

Villalba, C., Boyle, P. A., Caliguri, E. J., & De Vries, G. J. (1997). Effects of the selective serotonin reuptake inhibitor fluoxetine on social behaviors in male and female prairie voles (*Microtus ochrogaster*). *Hormones and Behavior, 32,* 184–191.

Virkkunen, M. (1985). Urinary free cortisol secretion in habitually violent offenders. *Acta Psychiatrica Scandinavica, 72,* 40–44.

Wang, Z., & De Vries, G. J. (1995). Androgen and estrogen effects on vasopressin messenger RNA expression in the medial amygdaloid nucleus in male and female rats. *Journal of Neuroendocrinology, 7,* 827–831.

Watters, J. J., Wilkinson, C. W., & Dorsa, D. M. (1996). Glucocorticoid regulation of vasopressin V1A receptors in rat forebrain. *Brain Research. Molecular Brain Research, 38,* 276–284.

Whitsett, J. M. (1975). The development of aggressive and marking behavior in intact and castrated male hamsters. *Hormones and Behavior, 6,* 47–57.

Williams, J., & Lierle, D. M. (1988). Effects of repeated defeat by a dominant conspecific on subsequent pain sensitivity, open-field activity, and escape learning. *Animal Learning and Behavior, 16,* 477–485.

Winslow, J., Hastings, N., Carter, C. S., Harbaugh, C., & Insel, T. (1993). A role for central vasopressin in pair bonding in monogamous prairie voles. *Nature, 365,* 545–548.

Yodyingyuad, U., De la Riva, C., Abbott, D. H., Herbert, J., & Keverne, E. B. (1985). Relationship between dominance hierarchy, cerebrospinal fluid levels of amine transmitter metabolites (5-hydroxyindole acetic acid and homovanillic acid) and plasma cortisol in monkeys. *Neuroscience, 16,* 851–858.

Zhou, L., Blaustein, J. D., & De Vries, G. J. (1994) Distribution of androgen receptor immunoreactivity in vasopressin- and oxytocin-immunoreactive neurons in the male rat brain. *Endocrinology, 134,* 2622–2627.

Zubieta, J. A., & Alessi, N. E. (1992). Acute and chronic administration of trazodone in the treatment of disruptive behavior disorders in children. *Journal of Clinical Psychopharmacology, 12,* 346–351.

PART III

HORMONES

8

Contexts and Ethology of Vertebrate Aggression: Implications for the Evolution of Hormone-Behavior Interactions

John C. Wingfield, Ignacio T. Moore, Wolfgang Goymann, Douglas W. Wacker, & Todd Sperry

In any habitat configuration, morphology, physiology, and behavior must be regulated to maximize fitness in response to changing environments. An animal's environment can be predictable (e.g., night and day, the seasons, low tide/high tide, etc.) or unpredictable (e.g., severe storms, predators, human disturbance). Individuals must be able to anticipate predictable events in the environment and also respond in a facultative way to unpredictable events (Wingfield, 1988; Wingfield, Doak, & Hahn, 1993; Wingfield , Hahn, Levin, & Honey, 1992; Wingfield & Kenagy, 1991). These adjustments require varying degrees of phenotypic flexibility (i.e., the capacity of an individual to change morphology, physiology, and behavior) depending upon the extent to which the environment may change (Piersma & Drent, 2003). Phenotypic flexibility of behavior is particularly important. An example is aggression, especially for maintaining a territory/home range to defend specific resources or for maintaining social status within a group for access to resources. Thus, aggressive behavior features prominently in just about everything an individual does throughout its life cycle. There have been several excellent reviews and analyses of diversity and the context of aggression, such as territoriality (particularly in birds, e.g., Brown, 1964,

1969), and aggression in general (especially in mammals, including humans e.g., Brain, 1979; Leshner, 1978; Monaghan & Glickman, 1992). However, as far as we are aware, there has been no attempt to summarize how aggression is expressed *and* regulated in different contexts with examples given in natural settings. Here we first address the types and contexts of vertebrate aggression and then how it is controlled by the endocrine system. The second part of the chapter then addresses hormone-aggression interactions and their possible evolution.

Types and Contexts of Aggression

There have been numerous attempts to define aggression and still there is no general consensus. This is not surprising given the tremendous diversity of vertebrates themselves and the enormous variety of contexts in which aggression is expressed. For example, songbirds may use a broad spectrum of behavioral traits when expressing aggression. These include song rate, song stereotypy, number of points (with wing droops and elevated tail), trill vocalizations and wing waves, flights (around the intruder), grass/substrate pulling, bill wipes, closest approach to intruder, attacks, fights, and persistence of aggression after removal of an intruder (Sperry, Thompson, & Wingfield, 2003; Welty & Baptista, 1988; Wingfield, 1985b). Note that many of these traits involve a mixture of auditory and postural signals likely utilizing very different neuronal circuits. In other vertebrates additional sensory modalities may also be used (see below), adding greatly to the complexity of signals and neuronal circuits involved. It is now possible to compare the hormone mechanisms underlying neural circuits for song in birds (Brenowitz, 1997) with auditory signaling in midshipman fish (Bass, 1996) or electrical signaling in weakly electric fish (Zakon & Smith, 2001) and social signaling in amphibians (Wilczynski, Allison, & Marler, 1993). In the future we may be able to explore in much greater detail the evolution of hormonal control systems in aggressive signaling through the vertebrates.

Despite the almost overwhelming diversity of aggressive behaviors in vertebrates, some definitions do provide useful insights for a theoretical framework of potential regulatory mechanisms. For example, Moyer (1968) suggested that the term aggression be applied to behavior "which leads to, or appears to an observer to lead to, the damage or destruction of some goal entity." He defined seven types of aggression and we have modified them in relation to an organism in its environment as follows:

1. *Spatial aggression (territoriality)*: May actually be a continuum in which space can be defined as anything from individual space to large multiple territories
2. *Aggression over food or other ingestive resources*: This would also include the predatory aggression of Moyer (1968)
3. *Aggression over dominance status* (that may influence many other forms of aggression as well)
4. *Sexual aggression* (mate acquisition and mate guarding)
5. *Parental aggression* (both maternal and paternal)
6. *Antipredator aggression (and interspecific aggression)*: This includes the fear-induced aggression of Moyer (1968)
7. *Irritable aggression*

This classification is useful because it points out the breadth of contexts in which aggression may be expressed. It should also be emphasized that although aggressive behavioral traits expressed across taxa vary tremendously, *within* an individual these traits may be

very similar in these different contexts and probably result from identical or similar neural motor circuits (see Wingfield, Whaling, & Marler, 1994). This could have considerable implications for endocrine control mechanisms because hormonal activation of aggression in one context may not be appropriate in another, even though the neural circuitry involved may be the same (Wingfield, Lynn, & Soma, 2001; Wingfield, Soma, Wikelski, Meddle, & Hau, 2001b).

Other classification schemes have addressed an equally important issue—defensive as well as offensive aggression. Brain (1979) plotted aggression types on a continuum (figure 8.1) beginning with avoidance of conflict and ending in acquisition of a resource. The consequences of this continuum range from "fear" at the avoidance end of the spectrum to "competitiveness" at the acquisition end. Brain (1979) also ranked examples of aggression along similar continuums, including self-defense, maternal, predatory, reproductive, social, and termination. Within each category there are subgroups such as mate selection-related aggression, rank-related aggression, and territorial aggression in the social aggression category (Brain, 1979). This complex array can be compared with Moyer's (1968) definitions (above) and together they provide heuristic classifications for considering regulation mechanisms and their evolution. Although we make no attempt here to define and classify aggression, we do not consider predation. It is our view that although a predator may show some behavioral traits associated with aggression in other contexts, we feel that a predator, such as a lion killing a zebra, is engaged in foraging behavior in the same context as a cow grazing on grass or a sparrow cracking a seed.

The defensive versus offensive (Brain, 1979) strategies can be summarized (figure 8.2) as follows. The defensive mode begins with a warning or broadcast of social status (figure 8.2). If an intruder persists then threats may be expressed, increasing in intensity until the intruder or challenger leaves. If the intruder persists then the next level is an attack, often followed by a chase. If at this point the intruder still does not leave, then a fight with physical contact may follow, or the defender may submit and leave (figure 8.2). In the offensive mode, an individual perceives an opportunity to acquire a resource and then threatens other individuals that are already defending the resource. This is followed by a similar cascade of events that may escalate to fights and chases with an outcome of a win (acquire the resource) or defeat (failure, figure 8.2). Consider-

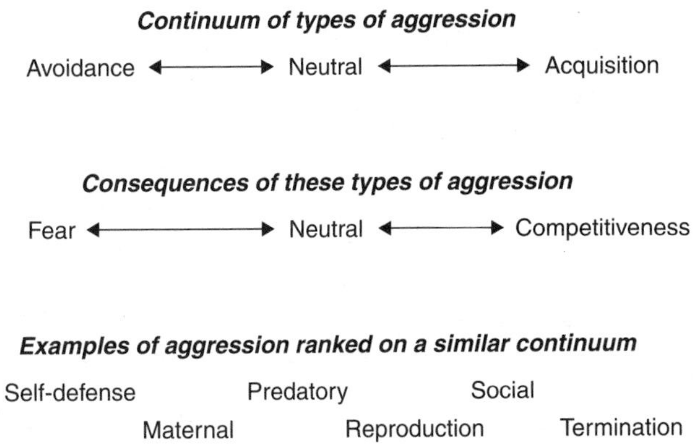

Continuum of types of aggression

Avoidance ←——————→ Neutral ←——————→ Acquisition

Consequences of these types of aggression

Fear ←——————————→ Neutral ←——————→ Competitiveness

Examples of aggression ranked on a similar continuum

Self-defense   Predatory   Social

    Maternal   Reproduction   Termination

FIGURE 8.1 The continuum of types of aggression from defensive to offensive and their consequences. Examples of each are given in the lower lines. From "Hormones, Drugs and Aggression," by P. Brain, 1979, *Annual Research Review, 3,* pp. 1–38. Copyright 1979 by Eden Press. Reprinted with permission.

ing endocrine control systems and aggression, it is unlikely that a single hormone regulates all aspects of this flow chart, or if it does, then there will likely be multiple mechanisms. Clearly, warning and threat behaviors involve very different neural circuits than those of attack, chase, and fight. The hormonal implications of winning and defeat are also different (e.g., Leshner, 1978).

Behavioral traits associated with vertebrate aggression can be expressed in many different ways, depend-ing upon species. Acoustic, visual, chemical, electrical, tactile, and vibrational signals can all be used to communicate in an aggressive context (e.g., Wingfield et al., 1994). The escalating scale of aggression (figure 8.2) can be expressed in a myriad of ways, with different types of sensory modalities employed to transmit (and receive) the signals (table 8.1). It is becoming more and more clear that no one specific signal can transmit the full spectrum of aggression, but a suite of behaviors is involved. Recently, Narins, Hödl,

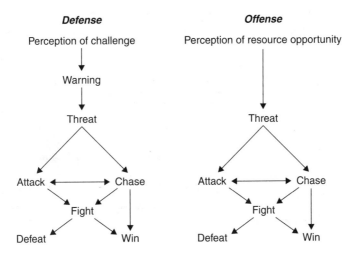

FIGURE 8.2 A possible flowchart of aggressive interactions. First, in the defensive mode, a challenge or potential competitor is perceived and if considered serious, a warning signal may be given. If the intruder does not move away then a threat may follow. At this point, serious escalation of the interaction can occur, with complex interactions of chases, attacks, and fights. These result in a win or defeat. Second, in the offensive mode, perception of an opportunity to acquire a resource results in a threat and then a similar escalation of events resulting in winning the resource or defeat. A point to be made here is that a single hormone is unlikely to regulate all aspects of this flowchart, or if it does, then there will likely be multiple mechanisms. For example, warning and threat behaviors involve very different neural circuits than attack, chase, and fight. The hormonal implications of winning and defeat are also separate processes.

TABLE 8.1 Modes of Communication in Aggression

Communication	Method
Warning	Vocal (e.g., song), visual (display), electrical, chemical (e.g., marking), vibration
Threat	Vocal (e.g., song and other vocalizations), visual, electric chemical (immediate), vibration, tactile
Attack	Visual, tactile, chemical, vocal, electrical
Chase	Visual, tactile, chemical, vocal, electrical
Fight	Tactile, chemical

Each component of the flowchart of aggression may involve different sensory modalities by which information is transmitted between the defender and challenger. An example of vocal communication is bird song. Visual cues include various displays, such as baring of teeth, and include "props," such as thrashing vegetation. Electrical communication is used for territoriality, etc., in weakly electric fish. Chemical cues include marking etc. It is possible that vibrational communication could also occur (e.g., thumping the substrate).

and Grabul (2003) showed that physical attacks by territorial male poison dart frogs, *Epipedobates femoralis*, are evoked only by a combination of vocal and visual signals received from an intruding male. This combination of stimuli may also apply to neuroendocrine responses to aggressive interactions. In the song sparrow, *Melospiza melodia*, simulation of a conspecific intruder by vocal or visual stimuli alone elicited strong territorial aggression, but only a combination of vocal and visual stimuli resulted in a neuroendocrine response leading to an increase in circulating testosterone (Wingfield & Wada, 1989).

The type and context of aggression and the sensory modalities used to communicate may thus have had profound influences on the evolution of mechanisms underlying hormone-behavior interactions. Behavioral ecologists have identified many contexts in which different types of aggression may be used (e.g., Brown, 1964, 1969). These contexts are distinct from types of aggression, because any one type can be expressed in different stages of the life cycle (i.e., contexts). For example, resource defense aggression may be expressed in reproductive and nonreproductive contexts. However, sexual aggression is displayed strictly in a reproductive context. Contexts of aggression can be split into two major categories: narrow and broad. A narrow context involves an acutely malleable condition, for instance, whether an animal is physically in its territory

or not. A broad context involves the physiological, morphological, and behavioral state of the animal, as associated with its current life history stage.

Although expression of aggressive behavior is ubiquitous, the sheer complexity of contexts in which aggression is displayed, and the enormous literature indicating the many hormones and neurotransmitters involved in its control, have been major barriers in the development of a common framework that could be applied to basic biology as well as biomedicine and possibly the foundation of violence in human society. Here we take an approach that considers the contexts and types of aggression displayed in different life history stages of vertebrates and their control mechanisms. This may be one heuristic way of exploring possible common bases for future studies of the evolution of hormone-behavior interactions.

Finite State Machine Theory and Ethology of Aggression

Predictable components of the annual cycle of vertebrates can be divided into a series of life history stages (LHSs), each with a characteristic set of substages. These are expressed in combinations to give a finite number of states (morphological, physiological, and behavioral characteristics) at any point in the individual's life cycle (Jacobs & Wingfield, 2000; Wingfield & Jacobs, 1999). Changes in gene expression regulate transitions from one stage to the next, e.g., development of the reproductive system and its termination in seasonally breeding organisms. This includes regulation of aggressive behavior as contexts and competition for resources change throughout the year. Throughout the life cycle, transition from one LHS to the next and adjustments within a LHS are also influenced by social interactions—even in species that may spend much of their lives in isolation (Wingfield et al., 1994). Although environmental signals may result in the activation, or deactivation, of appropriate behaviors (e.g., during the breeding LHS), it is also clear that social interactions can influence responsiveness to other environmental cues and hormone secretions (e.g., Balthazart, 1983; Harding, 1981; Wingfield et al., 1994). Despite the complexity of social systems and environmental change there is a clear interaction of environmental signals and expression of behavior through neuroendocrine and endocrine secretions. In many cases the mechanisms involved remain obscure partly because of a lack of integration of field studies and laboratory experimentation.

There are limits to the number of LHSs that can be expressed within a single annual cycle (Jacobs & Wingfield, 2000; Wingfield & Jacobs, 1999) and to the number of combinations of substages expressed within a LHS, so that a finite number of states are possible throughout the individual's life cycle. This finite state machine (FSM) of the individual has a number of properties that allow us to make predictions about the individual, including those about control mechanisms at the endocrine level. If the state of the machine (individual) is known (i.e., the LHS and the suite of substages expressed), then it is possible to predict the response of the individual to a set of environmental inputs (both physical and social stimuli). We know that aggression can be expressed throughout an individual's life cycle, i.e., in different LHSs, such as breeding, nonbreeding, migration, molt, etc. Thus we can look at the expression of different types of aggression modified from Moyer (1968, see above) across contexts such as LHSs (figure 8.3) and substages (table 8.2). It should be pointed out that three forms of aggression may occur at all times regardless of stage in life history. Antipredator aggression (i.e., "fight or flight" response— distinct from parental aggression), aggression over food, and irritable aggression are not linked to any particular season or stage (figure 8.3). Many of the behavioral traits used in these types of aggression may be similar or even identical to those used for reproductive aggression. This can be confusing, especially when considering hormonal control mechanisms (below).

Some species are territorial for only very short periods during the breeding season, such as highly seasonal arctic breeding birds and explosively breeding amphibians, or are continuously territorial, as in many tropical vertebrates. Others may be territorial during the breeding season, migrate in nonterritorial groups, and then become territorial again in the nonbreeding season (see Wingfield et al., 1997). Note that the context of territorial aggression may change within a LHS even though the behaviors expressed appear similar (e.g., multiple purpose territorial aggression versus mate-guarding aggression, table 8.2; Wingfield, Jacobs, & Hillgarth, 1997).

We tend to assume that because the behavioral traits are similar or identical at each LHS the control mechanisms will also be similar or identical. FSM theory suggests that this may not be the case. Three predictions stemming from this theoretical approach are the following:

1. Apparently identical physiological processes and behavior expressed in different LHSs may not have the same hormone control mechanisms.
2. When LHSs are expressed for long periods (i.e., if there are few LHSs in an annual cycle), there are dramatic costs to prolonged high circulating levels of hormones that regulate physiology and behavior characteristic of that stage. Many novel mechanisms may have evolved to minimize these costs.
3. The neural pathways by which environmental signals are perceived and transduced into neuroendocrine and endocrine secretions may not be the same among different phases of the LHS, or among different LHSs, even though the environmental factors that regulate these processes may be similar.

The endocrine control of types of territorial aggression in different contexts can be used to test the three predictions. Although it is likely that defense of a resource such as a territory will be expressed regardless of stage in the life cycle and hormonal milieu, offense, involving an individual's actually going out and forcibly taking over a resource, may be entirely different and driven by other mechanisms. Leshner (1978, 1981) has also pointed out that the behaviors of defeat are regulated differently again, whereas winning is more testosterone dependent. Clearly, great care must be taken when defining type, context, defense/offense, LHS, winning, or losing. Furthermore, it is becoming clear that maternal effects, and experiences during development, can result in distinct reactive and proactive coping styles in many vertebrates (Koolhaas et al., 1999). These can have particular influence on the aggressive patterns shown by individuals.

Next, current information on the regulation of aggression is summarized and we then go on to discuss possible tests of the three predictions derived from FSM theory. Selected examples are used rather than an attempt to cover the whole field exhaustively. It is hoped that these examples and future tests will be of heuristic value in determining whether FSM theory in general is applicable to behavioral biology and, if so, whether we can indeed predict how individuals will respond. Only then we will be able to attempt a mean-

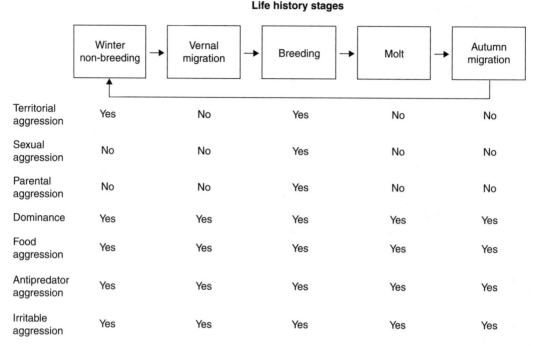

FIGURE 8.3 A finite state machine approach to the classification of types and contexts of aggression in verte-brates (following Jacobs & Wingfield, 2000; Wingfield & Jacobs, 1999). This specific example is of a migratory bird that has five distinct life history stages. Each has a period of development resulting in mature capability when the substages characteristic of that stage can be expressed. For example, in the breeding stage these would be territorial aggression, courtship, copulation, parental behavior, etc. Transitions from one stage to the next are key points for hormonal regulation of morphology, physiology, and behavior. Note here that four of the types of aggression defined by Moyer (1968) can be expressed in all life history stages (dominance, resource aggression such as for food, antipredator aggression and other interspecific aggression, and irritable aggression). Others are specific to life history stages. In this example, sexual and parental aggressive behaviors are expressed only in the breeding stage. Please note that in other examples territorial aggression may be expressed in other life history stages. Some types of aggression may therefore be expressed in varying life history stages determined by the natural history of the population. The number and timing of life history stages can also vary among popu-lations. Some may have as many as seven stages, whereas others, humans and many primates, only have one. Thus the number of life history stages (i.e., the finite state machine) may have a great influence on the degree of regulation of types of aggression.

ingful analysis of how hormone-behavior interactions in relation to aggression evolved.

Hormonal Control of Aggression

Much has been published on the regulation of aggres-sion from neural circuits to endocrine responses. Here we offer only a summary, with emphasis on type and context where possible. Catecholamines regulate rapid expression of aggression in specific agonistic encoun-ters (e.g., adrenalin in the "fight or flight" response,

Axelrod & Reisine, 1984; Sapolsky, 2002), but more long-term changes associated with type and context, such as establishment of a territory or position in a hi-erarchy, are regulated by several hormones. The actions of hormones on behavior in general have been classi-fied as organizational (i.e., during development, ontog-eny or a developmental phase of a LHS) or activational (i.e., within an individual at a specific stage in the life history, Arnold & Breedlove, 1985). Although there are many variants of this scheme, as far as aggression is concerned, these studies have been limited to repro-ductive or associated situations, while many potential mechanisms at other stages in the life history remain largely unexplored. A third type of control exists—suppression—in which aggression may be "turned off" under some conditions (see Wingfield, 1994c; Wingfield & Silverin, 1986).

Organizational Effects of Hormones

It is generally thought that hormones can act on the development of neural circuits, but once they mature the presence of those hormones is not required for the function of those circuits and the subsequent expression of related behavior. An example is the effects of testosterone and its metabolites 5-α-dihydrotestosterone and estradiol-17β on the development of song control nuclei in the brain of male zebra finches, *Poephila guttata* (Gurney & Konishi, 1980; Konishi & Gurney, 1982; Pohl-Apel & Sossinka, 1984). This effect occurs within a few days after hatching and enables the males to respond to the activational effects of testosterone as an adult. Arnold (1975) found that castration in adult male zebra finches reduced singing and courtship, as well as pecking and chasing of other males, whereas injections of testosterone restored these behaviors (see also Harding, Walters, Collado, & Sheridan, 1988). In contrast, injections of testosterone to adult female zebra finches do not induce song (Arnold & Breedlove, 1985). Whether male zebra finches actually use song in aggressive interactions (as do males of many other passerine species) is not exactly clear,

but this example illustrates the phenomenon of organizational effects very well. More recent evidence indicates that a hormone-independent mechanism, probably genetic, is important as well (Agate et al., 2003; Arnold, 2004).

In mice there is a sensitive period for early hormone actions. Male mice that were castrated between Days 0 and 2 after birth were less aggressive than sham-operated mice when treated with testosterone as adults. Animals castrated later in life showed no difference in aggression, suggesting that the sensitive period for the organizational effects of testosterone ends after Day 2 (Peters, Bronson, & Whitsett, 1972). Similar results were obtained with early neonatal exposure to testosterone in female mice (Bronson & Desjardins, 1970). Recent studies on alternative reproductive tactics in tree lizards, *Urosaurus ornatus*, suggest that early exposure to sex steroids can also act to organize individual differences in behavior and physiology within each sex. In these lizards, testosterone and progesterone during early ontogeny appear to determine future reproductive tactics in males (Moore, Hews, & Knapp, 1998). Males exposed to progesterone or testosterone early after hatching develop into the aggressive morph, while those that are castrated develop into the satellite morph. Interestingly, it appears that while testosterone is of gonadal origin, progesterone is of adrenal origin (Jennings, Painter, & Moore, 2004). These results indicate that different organs and hormones are working in concert to organize individual differences in the brain for future adult behavior, morphology, and physiology.

TABLE 8.2 Substages Within the Breeding Life History Stage

	Territory Formation and Maintenance	Pair Bond	Courtship and Copulation	Nest Building	Incubation	Feeding young
Territorial aggression	Yes	Yes	Yes	Yes	Yes	Yes
Sexual aggression	No	Yes	Yes	Yes	No	No
Parental aggression	No	No	No	No	Yes	Yes

Continuing with the finite state machine approach and using the breeding life history stage of the migratory bird example, there are several substages characteristic of breeding (Wingfield & Jacobs, 1999). Here we can see how types of aggression can be used in different contexts within the breeding stage. In this example, territorial aggression is expressed in many species throughout the breeding stage. However, other species may be territorial during the sexual phase and not when parental. Others may show male mate-guarding behavior by males during the sexual phase, but not spatial aggression per se, and then become territorial during the parental phase. Parental aggression, however, is only expressed when eggs and young are present. Similarly, sexual aggression, in this case mate-guarding behavior, will likely be limited to two or three substages when paternity is at stake and/or when sexual competition is most intense. Transition from one type of aggression to another in these contexts may be extremely rapid within the breeding life history stage. It is here that hormonal control of aggression may be much less clear-cut than it is in transition from one life history stage to another.

Activational Effects of Hormones

During both development and the adult life cycle, hormones can activate the expression of behavior. Activational actions of hormones generally require the immediate presence of the hormone for the behavior to be expressed in response to appropriate releasers (Arnold & Breedlove, 1985; Balthazart, 1983; Harding, 1981). If secretion of the hormone declines, it follows that the frequency and intensity of the specific behavior will wane. An example of the activational effects of hormones on aggressive behavior include the expression of territorial aggression early in the breeding season of birds that is accompanied by an increase in circulating levels of androgens (Wingfield & Farner, 1993). Note that there are many interactions of organizational and activational effects.

Suppressional Effects of Hormones

There is accumulating evidence that hormone secretions may actually suppress expression of certain behaviors. For example, it has been shown in birds that elevated levels of corticosterone may suppress the expression of territorial aggression and sexual and parental behavior (e.g., Silverin, 1986; Wingfield & Silverin, 1986). Similar suppressional effects of corticosterone on reproductive behavior have been described in reptiles and amphibians (Moore & Mason, 2001; Moore & Miller, 1984). It is well known throughout vertebrates that elevated (e.g., "stress-induced") levels of glucocorticoids can inhibit the reproductive system, resulting in a decrease in circulating testosterone levels (see Greenberg & Wingfield, 1987; Moore & Jessop, 2003; Sapolsky, 2002; and Sapolsky, Romero, & Munck, 2001, for reviews). Thus expression of any behaviors activated by testosterone would tend to decline. However, under conditions of short-term elevation of glucocorticoid secretion there appears to be a more direct suppressional effect that is independent of inhibition of the reproductive system (Wingfield & Silverin, 1986). For example, implants of corticosterone decreased expression of intermale aggression in the side-blotched lizard, Uta stansburiana, but did not affect courtship and copulation behavior when these males were exposed to females made sexually receptive by implants of estradiol (DeNardo & Licht, 1993). Furthermore, it appeared that simultaneous implants of corticosterone and testosterone also suppressed expression of aggression, suggesting that corticosterone was not acting solely by the inhibition of testosterone secretion (DeNardo & Licht, 1993). Whether this action is directly at the level of testosterone-sensitive neurons or through a different mechanism deserves further investigation. In the high latitude breeding white-crowned sparrow, Zonotrichia leucophrys gambelii, central injection of corticotropin releasing factor rapidly decreased territorial aggression (Romero, Dean, & Wingfield, 1998).

"Interference" Actions of Hormones

A fourth possible mechanism by which hormones may influence behavior involves activation of alternate behavioral patterns that override expression of other behaviors. Leshner (1978) and Leshner and Politch (1979) have shown that corticosterone can activate submissive behavior in agonistic encounters among mice. A decline in testosterone was irrelevant for this effect of corticosterone on submission. Androgens and glucocorticosteroids may polarize the direction of agonistic behaviors toward dominance or submission (Leshner, 1981). Thus it is possible that if corticosterone levels rise as a result of defeat, then expression of submissive behaviors could take precedence. Schuurman (1980) found that both winning and losing male rats showed an increase in plasma corticosterone, but that losers showed a greater increase and took longer to return to a baseline level. Leshner, Korn, Mixon, Rosenthal, and Besser (1980) found that corticosterone treatment had little effect on the submissiveness of male mice in an aggressive encounter, but when that treatment was combined with the experience of defeat in such a paradigm, it increased submissive behavior significantly. Another example is the influence of testosterone on expression of male parental behavior in birds. Males of many passerine species provide considerable parental care, but high levels of testosterone (experimentally induced by implants) resulted in a significant decline in the rate at which they fed their young (Hegner & Wingfield, 1987). High circulating concentrations of testosterone do not suppress or deactivate parental care, but the activation of aggression appears to take precedence over expression of parental care, with a decline of expression of the latter. In Texas bobwhite quail, Colinus virginianus texanus, males with low circulating levels of testosterone showed alloparental care when exposed to chicks. Those males with higher levels of testosterone did not show any alloparental care (Vleck & Dobrott, 1993). However, males given implants of antiandrogens, such as flutamide, showed reduced aggression directed at intruding males in their pens, but there was no effect on sexual behavior or expression of alloparental care (Vleck & Dobrott, 1993).

These data suggest that high levels of testosterone do not simply suppress parental behavior in males but may activate aggressive behavior so that it is expressed in precedence over parental behavior. The etiology of this phenomenon still requires much work, but it is important to bear in mind that hormonal activation of one behavioral pattern could take precedence over expression of another at some stages of the life cycle. This could be an important additional mode of control or just a version of suppressive actions.

There may also be a relation to breeding strategy, at least in birds. Lynn and Wingfield (2003) showed that male parental care is essential for reproductive success in chestnut-collared longspurs, *Calcarius ornatus*, in north central Montana. As a result, it is possible that this dependence on paternal care led to the evolution of behavioral insensitivity to testosterone. Male longspurs did not show increased aggression or reduced parental care with supplemental testosterone, suggesting an insensitivity to that steroid as it relates to those behaviors (Lynn, Hayward, Benowitz-Fredericks, & Wingfield, 2002; see also Hunt, Hahn, & Wingfield, 1999).

Maternal Effects

More recently, evidence is building in egg-laying vertebrates that females may influence the expression of aggression in their offspring by increasing the deposition of testosterone into egg yolk. This maternally derived testosterone may then influence the development of aggressive traits in the chick (e.g., canaries, *Serinus canarius*, Schwabl, 1996). However, in green anoles, *Anolis carolinensis*, it appears that incubating eggs are capable of producing sex steroids and there is not a correlation between maternal testosterone and estradiol levels and those measured in eggs (Lovern & Wade, 2003). A recent study in Japanese quail, *Coturnix japonica*, suggests that only a small proportion of steroids from the maternal circulation (ca. 0.1%) enters quail eggs and that the majority of steroid content in the yolk reflects the production of follicular cells at the time of yolk production (Hackl, Bromundt, Daisley, Kotrschal, & Möstl, 2003). Thus, the mechanisms at play to determine the exact nature and magnitude of maternal effects may be complicated.

General Relationships of Testosterone and Aggression

There can be few hormone-behavior mechanisms that have been more controversial than the interaction of testosterone and aggression. This interrelationship has been well studied throughout the vertebrates and particularly in birds (e.g., Balthazart, 1983; Harding, 1981; Wingfield & Ramenofsky, 1985; Wingfield et al., 1994). It is clear that in many (but not all) taxa social interactions can also influence testosterone secretion and subsequent expression of aggression (e.g., Wingfield et al., 1997). Oliveira (1998) points out that studies of testosterone (androgens) and dominance/aggression, particularly in primates and humans, are oversimplified. Nonetheless, in vertebrates in general there is evidence for and against an effect of androgens on aggression (e.g., castration in fish—Francis, Jacobson, Wingfield, & Fernald, 1992). The effects on dominance are not always obvious and for this reason the challenge hypothesis was put forward (Wingfield, Hegner, Duffy, & Ball, 1990) to explain some of these differences. Testosterone may be a mediator of social status and other male traits associated with dominance. Furthermore, metabolic conversions of testosterone to active, and in some species inactive forms, could be critical in the relationship of testosterone and aggression.

Monaghan and Glickman (1992) and Snowdon (1998) point out that developmental, social, and cognitive effects are important influences on aggression especially in nonhuman primates and appear independent of hormones—or at least few activational or organizational effects have been shown. Snowdon (1998) notes also that females show aggression and dominance widely and have low testosterone (but see Wingfield, 1994b, and Wingfield, Jacobs, et al., 1999, for examples in which females of some species may have as much as or even more testosterone than males). Snowdon (1998) cites cases in which other types of aggression were provoked (e.g., parental or antipredator aggression) but elicited no change in testosterone. This may be based in part on interpretation, particularly of the human literature. Mazur and Booth (1998) assert that in human males, testosterone appears to promote behavior intended to dominate other people. This behavior can be expressed aggressively, even violently, as well as nonaggressively. Testosterone levels, even a single baseline measurement, correlate well with dominance behavior, that is, testosterone not only affects dominance behavior but also responds to it. Others (e.g.,

Archer, 1998; Snowdon, 1998) say that this link is correlative, with little empirical evidence for a causal link. Additional factors are certainly involved, such as neurotransmitters (e.g., Brain, 1998). The fact that testosterone and social environment interact in complex ways to influence behavior and target tissue sensitivity is also an important consideration (Chambers, 1998). Caldwell and colleagues (Caldwell, Glickman, & Smith, 1984) showed that castrated male dusky-footed wood rats, *Neotoma fuscipes*, are equally aggressive as intact controls in open field situations. However, when wood rats were permitted to construct and defend individual houses, intact males had a clear advantage over castrated males, suggesting that testosterone was effective if aggression involved a true territorial or reproductive context (Monaghan & Glickman, 1992). Thus appreciation of the context and types of aggression and the need to consider ecological factors underlying the interrelationships of testosterone, aggression, and other physiological components, such as energetics, are extremely important (Bribiescas, 1998; Wikelski, Lynn, Breuner, Wingfield, & Kenagy, 2001; Wingfield et al., 1997; Wingfield, Ramos-Fernandez, Nuñez-de la Mora, & Drummond, 1999).

All these studies have important points, but they also underscore the lack of a framework to put all these scenarios in context. FSM theory may provide a working base to develop an evolutionary framework that can be tested widely through vertebrate taxa, acting as an alternative to lumping together all types of aggression, and to come up with a universal set of mechanisms. It is possible that because humans and most primates probably only have one LHS, once puberty has passed, there may be no need for further activational/organizational effects of testosterone or other hormones. Most other vertebrates have only one, or sometimes as many as seven, LHSs, making the types and contexts of aggression very complex. Here hormonal control may be more relevant and easier to demonstrate.

In birds, for example, testosterone has well-known effects on the development of many secondary sex characteristics, particularly sperm transport structures such as the vas deferens and the copulatory organ (see Lofts & Murton, 1973, for review). Circulating testosterone levels may also regulate development of bright nuptial plumage, specialized plumes, color, and the shape and size of skin appendages (e.g., Witschi, 1961), all of which may be used in both sexual and aggressive displays. Note, however, that not all secondary sex char-

acteristics derived from the integument are regulated by testosterone (see Owens & Short, 1995; Witschi, 1961). Testosterone also affects brain structures through its role in seasonal plasticity of the neural song control system in songbirds (Tramontin & Brenowitz, 2000; Tramontin, Hartman, & Brenowitz, 2000). Additionally, testosterone acts on neuronal circuits in the brain to regulate sexual behavior and reproductive aggression (see Balthazart, 1983, and Harding, 1981, for reviews). Many experiments have shown that removal of the testes, a major source of testosterone, may result in a decline in the spontaneous expression of aggression. Transplant of a testis into a castrate or injections of testosterone restore expression of aggression in many species studied (see Balthazart, 1983, and Harding, 1981, for reviews). The actions of testosterone on song control nuclei in the avian brain have provided a fertile focus of research on brain, behavior, and hormone interactions (e.g., Brenowitz, 1997).

Testosterone may be converted in target cells to 5-α-dihydrotestosterone and/or estradiol metabolites (e.g., Archawaranon & Haven Wiley, 1988; Harding et al., 1988; Schlinger, 1994, 1987) that then have their effects by binding to genomic receptors. Aromatase, the enzyme that converts testosterone to estradiol, is found throughout the brain of birds, including areas implicated in the control of aggression (Schlinger, 1994, 1987; Schlinger, Slotow, & Arnold, 1992). In the Lapland longspur, *C. lapponicus*, there is a decrease in aromatase activity in the telencephalon and rostral hypothalamus as breeding progresses (Soma, Bindra, Gee, Wingfield, & Schlinger, 1999). Thus regulation of aromatase and reductases may be an additional level of regulation of aggressive behavior.

There are wide-ranging additional effects of testosterone that may have indirect relationships to aggression. For example, resting metabolic rate (RMR) during night- and daytime was measured in castrated and intact male white-crowned sparrows under short-day (8:16 LD) and long-day (20:4 LD) conditions. Photostimulation increased RMR, food intake, hopping activity, and body mass in castrates and intact males. Implantation of testosterone increased activity and food intake, but decreased body mass and RMR in both groups (Wikelski et al., 2001). RMR differs between closely related species of stonechats. RMR is low in tropical stonechats (*Saxicola torquata axillaris*) and higher in migratory populations of Austrian (*S. t. rubicola*) and Kazakhstan (*S. t. maura*) stonechats (Wikelski, Spinney, Schelski,

Scheuerlein, & Gwinner, 2003). Similarly, testosterone concentrations are lowest in tropical stonechats compared to birds from Austria or Kazakhstan (Rödl, Goymann, Schwabl, & Gwinner, in press).

It is clear that the actions of testosterone are diverse and should be considered carefully when relating control of testosterone secretion to activation of reproductive aggression. This point is stressed later when relating temporal patterns of testosterone levels in blood to life histories, mating systems, and breeding strategies.

Control of Aggression in Tropical Vertebrates

The majority of research on endocrine function in tropical vertebrates has been conducted on birds. Recently there has been increased interest in the control of reproduction in tropical birds, as the environmental cues they experience may be more representative, because > 80% of passerines are tropical (Hau, 2001; Stutchbury & Morton, 2001). One of the predictions of the FSM theory was that when LHS are expressed for long periods, there are dramatic costs to prolonged high circulating levels of hormones that regulate the physiology and behavior characteristic of that stage. Many bird species in the tropics are territorial year round and/or have a long breeding season, i.e., the breeding LHS is extended compared to that of most birds that breed in more temperate regions. These year-round territorial species with extended breeding seasons typically have low levels of testosterone throughout the year, generating the impression that male tropical birds have low concentrations of testosterone in general (Dittami & Gwinner, 1990; Hau, Wikelski, Soma, & Wingfield, 2000; Levin & Wingfield, 1992; Stutchbury & Morton, 2001; Wikelski, Hau, Robinson, & Wingfield, 2003a). However, we now know that there are tropical birds with testosterone levels that are well in the range of that of northern temperate species (e.g., Goymann & Wingfield, 2004; Moore, Perfito, Wada, Sperry, & Wingfield, 2002; Moore, Wada, Perfito, Busch, & Wingfield, 2004; Wikelski, Hau, et al., 2003). In a recent phylogenetic comparison of 31 tropical bird species, we showed that tropical bird species with high levels of testosterone are characterized by short breeding seasons and typically establish temporary territories only for the short period of breeding (Goymann et al., 2005). Thus, it seems that some tropical birds follow the predictions of FSM theory and avoid prolonged elevated levels of testosterone. These tropical birds with extended breeding seasons may exhibit territorial aggression that is not regulated by testosterone or may be more sensitive to low concentrations of this hormone (Levin & Wingfield, 1992; Hau et al., 2000). However, in tropical species with short breeding seasons, testosterone may increase to high levels, just as in northern temperate birds, and may be involved in the regulation of breeding season aggression.

From a few studies we are now beginning to understand some of the diversity in hormone-behavior relationships in tropical birds. Spotted antbirds, *Hylophylax naevoides,* in Panama tend to have very low levels of testosterone during the breeding season, but these levels can increase in response to extended periods of social instability (Wikelski, Hau, & Wingfield, 1999). Blocking testosterone during the breeding season results in decreased aggression in this species (Hau et al., 2000). During the nonbreeding season testosterone levels of spotted antbirds are undetectable, but like the northern temperate breeding song sparrow, *M. melodia morpha,* concentrations of dehydroepiandrosterone (DHEA), an androgen precursor that can be converted into testosterone, are detectable and related to behavioral measures of territorial aggressiveness (Hau, Stoddard, & Soma, 2004). Thus, in this bird species with an extended breeding season circulating testosterone does seem to be involved in territorial aggression. In contrast, rufous-collared sparrows, *Z. capensis,* in Ecuador have levels of testosterone that are equal to or higher than those of closely related northern species (Moore et al., 2002). But in rufous-collared sparrows, testosterone levels do not increase in response to territorial challenges, and testosterone levels above breeding baseline do not appear to be related to aggression in any way (Moore et al., 2004; Moore, Bentley, Wingfield, & Brenowitz, 2004). It is possible that, in this system, male-female interactions have more of an effect on testosterone levels than do male-male interactions.

Regulation of Aggression in Territorial Contexts

There is an extensive and historic literature showing that testosterone is involved with the regulation of territorial aggression, at least in reproductive contexts (e.g., Balthazart, 1983; Hinde, 1965; Lehrman, 1965). Testosterone has been implicated in the activation of territorial aggression during ontogeny, during the development of the breeding LHS, in mate-guarding aggression, and in dominance-subordinance relationships in reproductively active birds (Balthazart, 1983; Harding, 1983; Wingfield & Ramenofsky, 1985). The correlation of circulating levels of testosterone with expression of territorial aggression has been more controversial, but evidence suggests that aggressive interactions among males as they compete for territories and mates can result in an increase in testosterone that in turn enhances persistence of aggression in the face of challenges. Furthermore, the degree to which males show such facultative increases in testosterone secretion when challenged tend to be related to the mating system (Hirschenhauser, Winkler, & Oliveira, 2003; Wingfield et al., 1990). This generalization also appears to hold from fish (Oliveira, 1998; Ros, Canario, Couto, Zeilstra, & Oliveira, 2003) to mammals (Goymann, East, & Hofer, 2003; Woodroffe, Macdonald, & Cheeseman, 1997), including primates (Cavigelli & Pereira, 2000; Ostner, Kappeler, & Heistermann, 2002). However, there are exceptions to this rule, such as in dwarf mongooses, *Helogale parvula* (Creel, Wildt, & Monfort, 1993).

There is also growing evidence that central paracrine secretions, such as arginine vasotocin (AVT), vasoactive intestinal peptide (VIP), and serotonin (5-hydroxytryptamine, or 5-HT) modulate aggressive behavior. In golden hamsters (*Mesocricetus auratus*), microinjections of arginine vasopressin (AVP, the mammalian homolog of AVT) increased offensive aggression in a resident intruder paradigm; pretreatment with fluoxetine, a 5-HT reuptake inhibitor, abolished these effects (Ferris et al., 1997). This strongly suggests that the two systems interact to modulate aggressive behavior. Castration eliminated vasopressin type 1 receptor binding as assessed by autoradiography in the ventrolateral hypothalamus (VLH), a nucleus associated with mammalian aggression. Concomitant testosterone treatment prevented this decrease. Furthermore, microinjections of AVP into the VLH decreased the latency to bite in intact, but not castrated, animals (Delville, Mansour, & Ferris, 1996). Kimura, Okanoya, and Wada (1999) noted a sexual dimorphism in AVT-ir in the zebra finch, with the male showing greater AVT-ir in the lateral septum (LS) and bed nucleus of the stria terminalis (BST), two nuclei that may play a role in aggression. Testosterone treatment (implant) increased the number AVT-ir cell bodies in females to the level seen in males in the BST. Castration of male Japanese quail resulted in reduced AVT-

ir fiber density in the BST and LS. Treatment with estradiol, but not 5-a-dihydrotestosterone (DHT), rescued the normal phenotype, indicating an estrogen receptor- rather than androgen receptor-mediated regulation of these changes (Viglietti-Panzica et al., 2001).

This suggests that at least in mammals there is a direct pathway linking steroids, AVT, and 5-HT in the control of aggression (Ferris et al., 1997). In birds, AVT and VIP have been shown to differentially affect aggressive behavior in species with different social structures (Goodson, 1998a, 1998b). Administration of AVT into the LS increased male aggressive behavior in colonial bird species, but decreased such behavior in territorial bird species. VIP tended to elicit the opposite response. For instance, LS administration of AVT increased aggression in the colonial zebra finch, while administration of an AVT antagonist decreased agonistic behavior (Goodson & Adkins-Regan, 1999). However, in the violet-eared waxbill *Uraeginthus granatinus* (Goodson, 1998b) and field sparrow, *spizella pusilla* (Goodson, 1998a), both territorial birds, LS administration of AVT reduced aggression. Alternatively, LS administration of VIP decreased aggression in the colonial zebra finch, but increased aggressive behavior in the territorial violet-eared waxbill (Goodson & Adkins-Regan, 1999). AVT also appears to play an important role in mediating context-dependent aggressive behaviors.

Bluehead wrasse, *Thalassoma bifasciata*, are female-to-male sex changing fish, with males demonstrating three behaviorally and two morphologically distinct phenotypes. Injections of AVT (ip) increased offensive aggression in nonterritorial, but not territorial, terminal phase males toward initial phase males, suggesting that the regulation of offensive aggression is context dependent in this species (Semsar, Kandel, & Godwin, 2001). There have been numerous studies that have examined 5-HT's role in the regulation of vertebrate aggression. For instance, in wild-caught male song sparrows, injections of both fluoxetine, a 5-HT reuptake inhibitor, and 8-OH-DPAT, a 5-HT$_{1A}$ receptor agonist, resulted in reduced aggression compared to saline-injected controls as assessed by a laboratory-based simulated territorial intrusion (Sperry et al., 2003). 5-HT has also been shown to play a role in dominance interactions. Raleigh, McGuire, Brammer, Pollak, and Yuwiler (1991) showed that pharmacologically induced increased serotonergic function was associated with dominance and decreased serotonergic function with subordinance in male adult vervet monkeys. In light of 5-HT's interaction with AVP in the regulation of aggression in the hamster, as well as both 5-HT's and AVT's effects on avian aggression, future studies should determine if and how these neurochemicals interact to fine-tune aggressive responses in territorial songbirds.

Although these data have provided much provocative information on the control mechanisms of territorial aggression and their possible ecological bases, how territorial aggression is regulated in LHSs other than breeding have received much less attention. This is particularly pertinent because FSM theory makes the three predictions (above) concerning these potential mechanisms.

Crews (1984) and Crews and Moore (1986) have pointed out that hormonal control of sexual behavior, including related aggression, may vary according to whether expression of the behavior is associated with gonadal development or is dissociated from it. In some species gametogenesis and sexual behavior are directly associated, and activation of sexual behavior is regulated by secretion of sex steroids such as testosterone and estradiol. However, in other species, gametes may be stored and sexual behavior expressed at a time when gametogenesis is minimal. In these cases activation of sexual behavior may be regulated by hormones other than the classical sex steroids. Similarly, for the expression of aggression, territorial and sexual aggression during the breeding season may be activated by testosterone (e.g., Balthazart, 1983; Harding et al., 1988; Wingfield & Ramenofsky, 1985) because secreted levels of testosterone are high during breeding and thus would be an appropriate signal for activation of aggression at that time. Much work on the control of aggression has focused on reproductively active individuals and the role of testosterone. However, expression of aggression in nonreproductive contexts is often not accompanied by elevated secretion of testosterone, so other cues must be important (e.g., Burger & Millar, 1980; Logan & Wingfield, 1992; Wingfield & Hahn, 1993; Wingfield, 1994a, 1994b, 1994c). Thus the regulation of aggression by sex hormones may depend upon its association with reproduction itself, as suggested for sexual behavior by Crews (1984) and Crews and Moore (1986).

Because the context of aggression can vary but the behaviors expressed are similar, and because hormonal control of aggression can also vary markedly, it is not surprising that there could be considerable confusion over the regulation of aggression in general. It may be advantageous to first discuss the stages in the life cycle as an indicator of why the context of aggression may vary. Developmental stages begin with embryonic de-

velopment within the egg. Here hormonal changes (e.g., Adkins-Regan, Abdelnabi, Mobarak, & Otinger, 1990; Schumacher, Sulon, & Balthazart, 1988; Tanabe, Saito, & Nakamura, 1986; Woods & Brazzil, 1981) may have profound effects on sex differentiation and thus later behavior (e.g., Adkins-Regan, 1987; Konishi & Gurney, 1982). Additionally, it is possible that androgens of maternal origin may be deposited in yolk and then released during development (Lovern & Wade, 2003; Schwabl, 1993, 1996). Whether steroids deposited in yolk may influence future aggressive behavior in the adult remains to be determined. After birth, there are fluctuations in sex steroid levels in blood that may be associated with organization of neural circuits that determine future behavior or even sensitivity to reproductive hormones that activate behavior in the adult (e.g., Gurney & Konishi, 1980; Hutchison, Steiner, & Jaggard, 1986; Marler, Peters, & Wingfield, 1987; Marler, Peters, Ball, Dufty, & Wingfield, 1989; Pröve, 1983; Tanabe et al., 1986). During posthatching development, aggression among siblings is well known and includes siblicide or dominance/subordinance interactions over access to food during growth (e.g., Golla, Hofer, & East, 1999; Mock, 1984; Mock & Parker, 1998; O'Connor, 1978; Ramos-Fernandez, Nuñez-de la Mora, Wingfield, & Drummond, 2000; Trillmich, 1990, 1986). The time course of these developmental events varies markedly with species, but may be as short as 5–6 weeks in some birds and rodents to 10 years or more in some large seabirds and mammals. Developmental changes in hormone secretions, especially as they are affected by these social interactions, may yield major differences in later behavior.

Fluctuations in the context and type of aggression may be complex in adult vertebrates. For example, in white-crowned sparrow, the breeding period begins with onset of gonadal recrudescence—often while still on the winter (or nonbreeding) grounds. This may be followed by a vernal migration to breeding grounds and some species may hold temporary feeding territories en route (e.g., Wingfield et al., 1990). However, as the breeding season approaches, and as gonadal recrudescence progresses, males (and sometimes females also) establish breeding territories, that is, a period of intense territorial aggression. Further competition may occur among males for mates and, in some cases, among females for their mates. In the nesting phase we may see continued territorial aggression, as well as two other kinds of aggressive interaction, male-male competition as males mate guard their sexually receptive mates when copulation, ovulation, and oviposition occur, and parental aggression when both males and females protect eggs and young from predators or other conspecifics. These latter types of aggression occur in the sexual and parental substages of the nesting phase, respectively. Both mate-guarding aggression and parental aggression may recur several times if the individual raises several broods within a season (Wingfield & Farner, 1993).

Correlates of Aggression and Testosterone: Social Interactions

Over the past 25 years, many studies have attempted to correlate circulating testosterone concentrations, and its metabolites, with social interactions of all kinds. These have included a growing number of investigations in the field or in seminatural conditions in captivity. There are now extensive data for all of the major vertebrate groups and selected examples are summarized below.

Challenge Hypothesis

It is well known that testosterone activates aggression associated with male-male competition over territories and mates (Balthazart, 1983; Harding, 1983), although the correlation of plasma levels of testosterone with expression of territorial aggression when breeding is frequently unclear (Wingfield & Ramenofsky, 1985; Wingfield et al., 1990; Wingfield, Soma, et al., 2001). It is thought that baseline levels of testosterone during the breeding season result in development and maintenance of morphological, physiological, and behavioral components of the male reproductive system. However, these baseline levels do not necessarily correlate with actual expression of territorial aggression. Superimposed on this breeding baseline of circulating testosterone level are transient surges to much higher concentrations that are tightly correlated with periods of heightened male-male competition, especially when establishing a territory, when being challenged by another male, or when mate guarding. This is the "challenge hypothesis"—high plasma levels of testosterone occur during periods of social instability in the breeding season, but are at a lower breeding baseline in stable social conditions (Wingfield, Hegner, Dufty, & Ball, 1990; Wingfield et al., 1999).

Territorial aggression associated with reproductive maturity appears to be mediated, with few exceptions, by androgens resulting from gonadal maturation in all vertebrate classes and there is widespread evidence of the interaction of circulating androgens and outcomes of social interactions (Oliveira & Almada, 1998). Urinary androgens increased as dominance relations were formed in several species of cichlid and the demoiselle fish, *Chromis dispilus* (Pankhurst & Barnett, 1993). In the stoplight parrotfish, *Sparisoma viride*, androgens regulate development of male coloration, especially in terminal phase males (Cardwell & Liley, 1991b). Territorial males showed increased plasma levels of androgens when taking over a territory or when experimentally challenged by another male (Cardwell & Liley, 1991a). Indeed, in a well-controlled study, it was shown that just observing fights can raise androgen levels in *O. mossambicus* (Oliveira, Lopes, Carneiro, & Canario, 2001). At the other end of the vertebrate spectrum, interesting studies of humans found that during the soccer world cup in 1994 testosterone levels of Italian and Brazilian fans varied markedly before and after the game (Brazil won). The testosterone concentrations of the Italians decreased, whereas the testosterone concentrations of the Brazilians increased. It is interesting, though, that the initial levels of the Italians were in the range of the final levels of the Brazilians (Bernhardt, Dabbs, Fielden, & Lutter, 1998).

In weakly electric fish from the family Mormyridae, *Brienomyrus brachyistius*, top-ranking males undergo a large increase in electric organ discharges. Second-ranking males show a more modest increase and lower ranking males may actually decrease electric organ discharges (EODs). These changes were correlated with circulating levels of 11-ketotestosterone but not testosterone (Carlson, Hopkins, & Thomas, 2000). Weakly electric fish of the family Apteronotidae show EODs in aggressive contexts. Nonaromatizable androgens raise EODs in a species, *Apteronotus leptorhynchus*, in which males produce high-frequency EODs, while females do not, and lower EODs in a species, *A. albifrons*, in which there is no sexual dimorphism in EODs. Thus dimorphism of EODs may be related to sensitivity to androgens (Zakon & Dunlap, 1999). Together, these investigations shed light on the evolution of communication behavior, especially aggressive interactions. They must be considered in contexts of communication networks rather than dyads. Oliveira and coworkers (Oliveria, McGregor, & Latruffe, 1998) show that male

Siamese fighting fish, *Betta splendens*, appear to monitor aggressive interactions among neighbors. Information on relative fighting ability may then be used in future aggressive interactions with those individuals.

Effects of Mating Systems and Breeding Strategies

One of the more remarkable and consistent results of field investigations is the relationship of patterns of testosterone levels with mating systems and breeding strategies. This is potentially important and may provide insight into the evolution of hormone-behavior interrelationships. Some examples are given below.

Tree Lizards

Two male phenotypes of tree lizards, *U. ornatus*, are associated with alternative male reproductive tactics, one being territorial and the other being nonterritorial (Hews, Thompson, Moore, & Moore, 1997; Thompson & Moore, 1991). In response to winning territorial encounters on the previous day, the nonterritorial males display elevated plasma corticosterone and depressed plasma testosterone levels. In contrast, the territorial males show no change in plasma hormone levels the day after winning an encounter (Knapp & Moore, 1996). It appears that one of the physiological differences between the morphs is the plasma steroid binding globulin capacity. These lizards have a plasma steroid binding globulin that binds both androgens and corticosterone and the binding capacity in territorial males is significantly greater than that in nonterritorial males (Jennings, Moore, Knapp, Matthews, & Orchinik, 2000). This difference in binding capacity between the morphs likely results in higher plasma concentrations of unbound corticosterone in the nonterritorial males. This would be especially evident when plasma corticosterone levels are elevated and free corticosterone could then trigger a decrease in plasma testosterone. The difference in free versus bound corticosterone potentially explains the morph difference in testosterone response to similar increases in corticosterone.

The Energetics–Hormone Vocalization (EHV) Model.

The role of hormones in advertisement calling in anuran amphibians has recently received increased attention. Calling is very important for males of most anuran species and serves as both an advertisement to females

and a warning involved in territory defense from other males. For species that call, the time spent calling is positively associated with male mating success (e.g., Ryan, 1985). In addition, calling behavior is often considered one of the most energetically expensive activities for anurans (Bucher, Ryan, & Bartholomew, 1982). Data from a variety of species suggests that plasma levels of both testosterone and corticosterone are elevated during bouts of calling. Across species analysis suggests that corticosterone is positively correlated to both the calling rate and the rank of relative energy in the call (Emerson & Hess, 2001). Thus, sexual selection arguments would describe calling behavior as an honest signal (Emerson, 2001). However, in the Tungara frog, *Physalaemus pustulosus*, it appears that endogenous plasma corticosterone levels are maintained below a threshold level. Exogenous corticosterone raises plasma corticosterone above the threshold and calling behavior and plasma testosterone levels are reduced (Marler & Ryan, 1996).

Emerson (2001) has proposed an extension of the challenge hypothesis (Wingfield et al., 1990), termed the EHV model, to explain the reported relationships between calling behavior and testosterone and corticosterone levels in male anuran amphibians. This model proposes that calling behavior drives an increase in plasma testosterone that is accompanied by an increase in plasma corticosterone levels due to the energetic demands of the behavior. Thus, over time, levels of both hormones increase until plasma corticosterone triggers a short-term stress response. Plasma testosterone levels then decline, resulting in a negative association between the two hormones (Emerson, 2001). This appears to follow the transition from normal, seasonally variable glucocorticoid levels (level B) to an emergency LHS (level C) modeled by Wingfield and Ramenofsky (1999). The EHV model can probably be extended to explain the apparently paradoxical differences in the relationship between testosterone, corticosterone, and aggression in a variety of taxa, especially reptiles and amphibians (Moore & Jessop, 2003; Romero, 2002). In many species, it appears that when mating or courtship is energetically costly there can be a positive relationship between testosterone and corticosterone levels.

Song Control System

Singing is a critical aspect of reproduction in songbirds. Song is used to defend territories against conspecific males (reviewed by Catchpole & Slater, 1995) and influence female mate choice (reviewed by Searcy, 1996; see also Catchpole & Slater, 1995). The song control system is a series of interconnected brain nuclei that mediate learning and production of song in songbirds. Testosterone plays a crucial role in the seasonal growth of the song control system and thus the seasonal learning and expression of song behavior (Smith, Brenowitz, Beecher, & Wingfield, 1997; Smith, Brenowitz, Wingfield, & Baptista, 1995; Tramontin & Brenowitz, 2000; Tramontin et al., 2000). This is probably the best described example of neural plasticity in the adult brain. Testosterone is probably the crucial endocrine cue that male songbirds are using to translate environmental cues into growth of the song system in the spring. Photoperiod is thought to be that environmental cue for high latitude species. However, plasticity in the song system has been described in tropical birds, independent of photoperiod (Moore, Bentley, et al., 2004).

The exact timing of growth and regression of the song control system has not been well defined for free-living birds, especially those that defend territories in the fall nonbreeding period. It might be predicted that the timing of growth of the song system would differ between species and populations that defend territories during the fall versus spring and migratory versus resident individuals.

Testosterone and Aggression in Females. Since the "challenge hypothesis" was published (Wingfield et al., 1990) many other studies that have looked at the relationship of testosterone and aggression related to the defense of resources, primarily in male vertebrates. It is also known that females compete for resources in a wide array of taxa (reviewed by Floody, 1983), but surprisingly little is known about the relationship of testosterone and aggression related to resource defense in females. There are few studies that actually tested such a relationship using simulated territorial intrusions (STI). Kriner and Schwabl (1991) did not find an effect of testosterone implants on aggression in wintering female European robins (*Erithacus rubecula*) and also treatment with an antiandrogen (Schwabl & Kriner, 1991) or the combination of an antiandrogen and an aromatase inhibitor (W. Goymann, unpublished observations) did not show any effect. In female song sparrows testosterone levels did not increase after an STI (Elekonich & Wingfield, 2000). Interestingly, in

this study passively caught control females had higher levels of androgens (testosterone and DHT) than females caught during the STI experiment. The STI elicited the strongest aggressive response during the prebreeding period, but there was no relationship with testosterone concentrations or any other steroid measured (DHT, progesterone, estradiol, and corticosterone). In contrast to these results from free-ranging birds, implants of testosterone increased aggressive behaviors in captive female song sparrows (Wingfield, 1994b). In male and female spotted antbirds, territorial aggression during the nonbreeding season appears to be related to levels of DHEA, an androgen precursor that can be converted into testosterone (Hau et al., 2004). In males, DHEA concentrations positively correlated with the duration of the STI; data were too few to conduct a similar correlation for females. In female mountain spiny lizards (*Sceloporus jarrowi*) ovariectomy reduced aggressive behavior in staged territorial encounters. Aggressive behavior could be restored by implanting testosterone, suggesting that testosterone (most likely via conversion to estradiol) is involved in the regulation of territorial aggression in female mountain spiny lizards (Woodley & Moore, 1999).

Wingfield (1994b) and Wingfield, Jacobs, et al. (1999) reported that the ratio of male to female levels of testosterone is smaller in bird species in which females are more similar to males in plumage and behavior. However, it appears that the levels of testosterone may be decreased in males rather than increased in females. Also, in classically polyandrous birds, in which sex roles are reversed and females are the more competitive sex, there is not reversal in sex steroid levels. In all polyandrous species investigated so far, males had higher levels of testosterone than females and the pattern resembled those of socially monogamous bird species (Fivizzani, Colwell, & Oring, 1986; Fivizzani & Oring, 1986; Goymann & Wingfield, 2004; Gratto-Trevor, Fivizzani, Oring, & Cooke, 1990; Oring, Fivizzani, Colwell, & El Halawani, 1988; Rissman & Wingfield, 1984). The only exception are moorhens (*Gallinula chloropus*), which showed a partial reversal in sex roles and in which females were more competitive than males (Petrie, 1983). In this species, testosterone concentrations were similar in males and females (Eens & Pinxten, 2000; Eens, Van Duyse, Berghman, & Pinxten, 2000), but again it seems as if testosterone concentrations were decreased in males rather than increased in female moorhens.

A similar pattern emerges from recent studies on mammals. The most famous example is the spotted hyena (*Crocuta crocuta*). The unusual features of female dominance and virilization in this species and the (so far untested) assumption that female spotted hyenas are more aggressive than other female mammals led to the hypothesis that female dominance in spotted hyenas evolved due to selection favoring large androgenized females that can monopolize access to food resources in competitive feeding situations (e.g., Frank, 1996; Glickman, Frank, Licht, et al., 1992; Gould, 1981; Hamilton, Tilson, & Frank, 1986). High levels of androgens during ontogeny are likely to have organizational effects on aggressive behavior of female spotted hyenas (Glickman, Frank, Pavgi, & Licht, 1992; Licht, Frank, Yalcinkaya, Siiteri, & Glickman, 1992; Licht et al., 1998), but female dominance in this species is most likely a function of (a) matrilineal association, (b) coalitions between related females, (c) the inheritance of maternal rank, and (d) the general lack of aggressiveness in males, resulting in habitual male submission toward females (Goymann et al., 2001). The patterns of androgen concentrations of adult spotted hyenas support this view: testosterone levels of female spotted hyenas were significantly lower than those of males (reviewed in Goymann et al., 2001) and similar to those of female brown or striped hyenas (van Jaarsveld & Skinner, 1987). Also, the concentrations of DHT or androstenedione of free-ranging females were well in the range of those of other nonvirilized mammals. The only difference compared to other hyenids was that the ratio of male to female levels of testosterone was smaller in spotted hyenas than in brown or striped hyenas (Goymann et al., 2001; van Jaarsveld & Skinner, 1987). But again this difference was caused by lower levels of testosterone in male spotted hyenas than in brown or striped hyenas and not by an elevation of testosterone in females.

In bonobos (*Pan paniscus*) also, in which females are dominant over males, the ratio of adult male to adult female levels of androgens was smaller than that in chimpanzees (*P. troglodytes*), in which males are dominant over females (Sannen, Heistermann, Van Elsacker, Möhle, & Eens, 2003). But again, the levels of androgens in female bonobos and chimpanzees were quite similar and the difference between the species stems from the fact that male chimpanzees express much higher levels of androgens than male bonobos. It thus appears as if there are limitations to an increase

in testosterone concentrations in female vertebrates and that changes in sex roles are accompanied by a decrease in absolute testosterone concentrations in adult males rather than by an increase in testosterone in adult females. If testosterone is involved in territorial or resource defense aggression in females, then regulation is more likely to occur on the cellular level, for example, through changes in the number or sensitivity of androgen receptors. Alternatively, females may use different hormonal mechanisms than males to regulate this kind of aggression. For example, female California mice (*Peromyscus californicus*) defend territories and aggressively respond to STI. During such STI, Davis and Marler (2003) reported a decrease in progesterone and the progesterone/testosterone ratio, but no changes in testosterone or estradiol. Thus, in female California mice the decrease in progesterone or the decrease in the progesterone/testosterone ratio may mediate aggression in such a challenge situation. Similarly, in parthenogenetic whiptail lizards (*Cnemidophorus uniparens*) malelike mounting behavior occurs mainly in the postovulatory phase, when concentrations of progesterone are high (Crews, 1987).

Phylogenetic Considerations.   A major confound in all of the investigations comparing patterns of testosterone to aggression in life history contexts is phylogeny. In other words, some, if not most, of the differences may be due to phylogenetic reasons rather than being a result of ecological factors per se. Hirschenhauser et al. (2003) conducted an analysis of all avian investigations in relation to the challenge hypothesis. This hypothesis predicts a "trade-off" of male-male interactions resulting in an increase in testosterone secretion with expression of male parental care that requires a decrease in testosterone (Wingfield et al., 1990). The latter phenomenon appears to be widespread in fish (e.g., Sikkel, 1993), as well as in tetrapods. One analysis (Hirschenhauser et al., 2003) revealed that after adjustment for phylogeny, the effect of male paternal care disappeared, but the effects of mating system and male-male interactions and possibly male participation in incubation persisted. Similarly, in a phylogenetic analysis of patterns of testosterone in birds in relation to latitude, very diverse patterns in the tropics were related to environmental factors, such as short breeding seasons, rather than to phylogeny per se (Goymann et al., in press). As the numbers of species and populations studied under natural conditions increases, analyses of this sort will be critical to tease apart phylogeny and ecological constraints, leading to insight into how hormone-behavior interrelationships developed.

The Same Behavior in Different LHSs: The Context of Territorial Aggression

Three predictions were made stemming from FSM theory (see above) and these are applicable to hormonal bases of aggression. The first supposes that apparently identical territorial aggression expressed in different LHSs may not have the same hormone control mechanisms. Several studies have now tested this prediction as follows. The song sparrow, of western Washington State and southwestern British Columbia, is territorial year round and in some populations breeding pairs may stay on their territory for more than 1 year (e.g., Arcese, 1989; Nordby, Campbell, & Beecher, 1999). High levels of territorial response to STI were maintained throughout the breeding LHS, but declined markedly when they were in molt (Wingfield & Hahn, 1994). Males remained on their territories during molt, but did not respond to STI, and then began to sing and defended territories in late September and October (Arcese, 1989). Note that song stereotypy in autumn was less than that in spring (Smith et al., 1997), although all other measures of aggression during STI appeared identical (Wingfield & Hahn, 1994).

In some localities both males and females moved territories between breeding and nonbreeding seasons (Wingfield & Monk, 1992; Wingfield, 1994a). This may be because some territories were exposed to inclement weather in winter, resulting in local movement to more sheltered locations. In other localities pairs of song sparrows remain on the same territory throuhout the year. In contrast, those that move appear to form alliances with one or several individuals (Wingfield, 1994a; Wingfield & Monk, 1992).

Territoriality in Different LHSs

Avian species with autumn territories in nonreproductive contexts tend not to have high testosterone and/or LH. Plasma levels of testosterone were elevated in breeding, territorial, lesser sheathbills, *Chionis minor*, but not in nonbreeding territorial birds (Burger & Millar, 1980). Northern mockingbirds, *Mimus polyglottos*, showed no increase in LH or testosterone in autumn despite using the same territories year round (Logan

& Wingfield, 1990). In European robins, *E. rubecula*, circulating levels of reproductive hormone levels did not change in autumn, when males and females established independent winter feeding territories (Schwabl & Kriner, 1991). Wintering stonechats in Israel established territories as apparent male and female "pairs," but they did not leave on spring migration together nor did pair bonds appear to be stable in winter. Territorial aggression was expressed by both sexes, but testosterone levels remained very low during this period (Canoine & Gwinner, 2002; Gwinner, Rödl, & Schwabl, 1994). Tropical birds, territorial throughout their reproductive life of several years, showed similar patterns (Wikelski et al., 1999).

It is also possible that the challenge hypothesis is in operation in autumn and that socially modulated increases in testosterone secretion do occur at this time. When male song sparrows were removed from their territories in autumn, replacement males and their neighbors had undetectable plasma levels of testosterone, unlike when the experiment was conducted in spring (Wingfield, 1985b, 1994a, 1994c). Similarly, STIs in autumn had no effect on LH and testosterone levels, again unlike in spring (Soma & Wingfield, 2001; Wingfield, 1994a, 1994b; Wingfield & Hahn, 1994). Sexual behavior of female songbirds can also elevate testosterone secretion in males (e.g., Moore, 1982, 1983). Estrogenized female song sparrows in autumn had no effect on territorial aggression in males and did not increase plasma testosterone levels (Wingfield & Monk, 1994). However, as day length increased in late winter, resulting in reproductive development, plasma levels of testosterone in males were elevated when they associated with estrogen-treated females compared to controls (Wingfield & Monk, 1994). Finally, even castrated male song sparrows were able to defend territories and respond to STI in autumn equally well as sham-operated males (Wingfield, 1994a, 1994c).

The next question then is whether high levels of testosterone in spring have any role in territorial aggression if castrated males are capable of maintaining a territory. Field experiments in song sparrows showed that testosterone appears to increase persistence of aggression following an intrusion rather than activate it per se. Enhanced persistence of aggression in the breeding season may maximize reproductive success, but would not be adaptive in autumn, when other territories are less fixed (Wingfield, 1994a, 1994b). Because testosterone also has marked effects on sexual behavior, the morphology of reproductive accessory organs, and other traits, secretion of this hormone outside of the breeding season would likely be inappropriate (Wingfield et al., 1997, 1999).

The Same Behavior in Different Contexts: The Same Control Mechanisms?

It is now well known that in the breeding season territorial aggression is mediated by aromatization of testosterone to estradiol in target neurons of the brain (Balthazart, Foidart, Baillen, & Silverin 1999; Foidart, Silverin, Baillen, Havada, & Balthazart, 1998; Schlinger & Callard, 1990). To determine whether this is the case in the nonbreeding season, free-living European robins were treated with an antiandrogen (flutamide) in autumn and winter. There was no effect on territorial aggression, suggesting that androgen receptors are not primarily involved at this time (Schwabl & Kriner, 1991). In European stonechats, although territorial aggression was reduced by antiandrogen and an aromatase inhibitor (ATD) in spring, this treatment had no effect in winter, suggesting that territorial aggression is regulated differently (Canoine & Gwinner, 2002). Field experiments with male song sparrows gave different results. A combination of flutamide and ATD reduced territorial behavior in autumn and winter (Soma, Sullivan, & Wingfield, 1999). Fadrozole (a potent aromatase inhibitor) alone also dramatically reduced territorial aggression in the nonbreeding season (Soma, Sullivan, et al., 1999). Clearly, blocking aromatase activity, but not androgen receptors, reduced autumn territorial aggressive behavior and thus estrogens are an important component of the regulation of territorial behavior outside the breeding season. Furthermore, if fadrozole-treated male song sparrows were given estradiol implants, territorial aggression in response to STI was restored (Soma, Sullivan, et al., 1999). However, as mentioned above, these results are not universal (Canoine & Gwinner, 2002; Moore, Walker, & Wingfield, 2004).

The actions of testosterone are multiple and include regulation of sexual displays, song and aggressive behavior, development of secondary sex characteristics and accessory organs, spermatogenesis, and muscle hypertrophy. We now also know that prolonged elevation of circulating testosterone levels may incur "costs," such as injury and depredation, reduced fat stores, etc. (Beletsky, Gori, Freeman, & Wingfield, 1995; Dufty, 1989; Ketterson, Nolan, Cawthorn, Parker, & Ziegenfus, 1996; Ketterson, Nolan, Wolf, & Ziegenfus, 1990). Moreover, elevated plasma testosterone may interfere with parental care (Hegner & Wingfield, 1987; Silverin, 1980) and may impair the immune system in some species (Hillgarth & Wingfield, 1997). Such costs associated with extended high levels of testosterone may have had a profound influence on the evolution of hormone-behavior mechanisms (Wingfield et al., 1997; Wingfield, Jacobs, et al., 1999), including mechanisms to avoid those costs.

Avoiding the Costs of Testosterone

Several hypotheses have been put forward to explain how the potential costs of testosterone in the nonbreeding season could be ameliorated. These include the following: the no avoidance hypothesis—social modulation; the decreased sensitivity hypothesis—target neurons in the central nervous system may become highly sensitized to low testosterone levels; the neurosteroid hypothesis—steroid synthesis may occur de novo from cholesterol within the brain; and the circulating precursor hypothesis (Wingfield & Soma, 2002; Wingfield, Soma, et al., 2001).

The first hypothesis (the null hypothesis) is possible in species that have a circulating binding globulin that essentially deactivates circulating sex steroids. This would buffer the animal from high blood levels. However, birds generally lack specific sex steroid binding proteins in blood, suggesting that the null hypothesis is not true for songbirds (Wingfield, Soma, et al., 2001). Increased sensitivity of the brain to extremely low concentrations of sex steroids during the nonbreeding season is also unlikely because many other traits attributable to testosterone do not develop and because castration in autumn had no effect on territorial aggression (Wingfield, 1994c), although it is possible that low levels of androgens could be secreted by the adrenals. Actually the reverse may be true, because there was a decrease in the number of androgen receptors (AR), indicated by a decrease in the efficacy of testosterone to activate postbreeding singing, and a reduction in hypothalamic aromatase activity (e.g., Ball, 1999; Gahr & Metzdorf, 1997; Hutchison et al., 1986; Nowicki & Ball, 1989; Schlinger & Callard, 1990; Soma, Sullivan, et al., 1999). Alternatively, in the song sparrow, aromatase activity in the ventromedial telencephalon correlates with the expression of aggression, with similar levels in the breeding and nonbreeding seasons and significantly lower levels during the molt, when aggression is lowest (Soma et al., 1999). Expression of estrogen receptor (ER) in the telencephalon of canaries was higher in November than in April. Similarly, aromatase mRNA expression was also higher in November, whereas AR mRNA expression did not change (Fusani, Hutchison, & Gahr, 2001). Investigations of expression of ERα and ERβ are needed before this hypothesis can be tested fully.

It is becoming more evident that the brain is able to synthesize steroids de novo from cholesterol (Baulieu, 1998). High local concentrations of steroids in brain that were independent of changes in circulating levels support this concept (Baulieu, 1998; Mensah-Nyagan et al., 1996; Robel & Baulieu, 1995; Tsutsui & Yamakazi, 1995; Ukena et al., 1999). Furthermore, it is now clear that steroidogenic enzymes (protein and mRNA activity) are expressed in brain tissues, although the presence of the enzyme P450c17 in adult brain remains unclear in mammals (Compagnone & Mellon, 2000). Recent reports do, however, suggest that it may be expressed in brains of adult birds (Nomura, Nishimori, Nakabayashia, Yasue, & Mizano, 1998). More recently, the key enzymes, protein, and mRNA have been specifically localized in the brain (Schlinger, Lane, Grisham, & Thompson, 1999; Soma et al., 1999; Ukena et al., 1999; Vanson, Arnold, & Schlinger, 1996). Thus it is possible that high levels of sex steroids can be generated in the brain independently of the gonads and other peripheral tissues.

The presence of steroidogenic enzymes in the brain will also be critical for the circulating precursor hypothesis. Biologically inert sex steroid precursor may be produced by, for example, the adrenals and then converted to an active hormone in the brain (Labrie, Bélanger, Simard, Luuthe, & Labrie, 1995). DHEA is an example of such a circulating precursor that could be converted to testosterone or estrogens by enzymatic activity in brain (Labrie et al., 1995; Ukena et al., 1999; Vanson et al., 1996). Plasma levels of DHEA in free-living male song sparrows were elevated during breeding, declined when they were molting, and then increased again in during a resurgence of territorial aggression in autumn (Soma & Wingfield, 2001). Moreover, DHEA treatment of male song sparrows in autumn increased singing and the growth of the HVc, a song control nucleus in the telencephalon (Soma, Wissman, Brenowitz, & Wingfield, 2002). However, DHEA implants also increased plasma testosterone levels slightly. DHEA may also decrease aggression, possibly by decreasing levels of pregnenolone sulfate, a neurosteroid that is thought to negatively modulate GABA$_A$ receptors and lead to increased aggression (re-

viewed in Simon, 2002). However, a sulfated form of DHEA, DHEAS, also negatively modulates GABA$_A$ receptors. Administration of DHEAS leads to increased intermale mouse aggression and this effect is observable at lower doses of DHEAS when an inhibitor of steroid sulfatase enzyme, the enzyme that catalyzes the conversion of DHEAS to DHEA, is injected simultaneously (Nicolas et al., 2001). It is unclear whether song sparrows implanted with DHEA were more aggressive due to elevated DHEA or DHEAS levels or both. Regardless, DHEA's nongenomic effects on aggressive behavior warrant additional study.

Regulation of Aggression in Response to Environmental and Social Stresses

Unpredictable events (labile perturbation factors) potentially disrupt the life cycle and can occur at any time. Mechanisms have evolved by which individuals survive such perturbations in the best condition possible— called collectively the "emergency LHS." There are four major components: the fight or flight response, proactive and reactive coping styles, sickness behavior, and facultative behavioral and physiological strategies (McEwen & Wingfield, 2003; Sapolsky, Romero, & Munck, 2000; Wingfield, 2005). The fight or flight response is a well known rapid mechanism to avoid predators, dominant conspecifics, and other immediate threatening perturbations. Proactive and reactive coping styles allow vertebrates to deal with psychosocial stress among conspecifics. Coping styles have been classified in various ways, but a recent review by Koolhaas et al. (1999) suggests a grouping that is applicable to vertebrates in general. The proactive coping style is an active response to a social challenge involving aggression, whereas the reactive coping style is characterized by behavioral immobility and low aggression (Koolhaas et al., 1999). Sickness behavior is a suite of responses to wounding and infection that are regulated by cytokines of the immune system. Additionally, there are several physiological and behavioral strategies that animals responding to perturbations in the field can adopt to redirect them away from the normal LHSs (e.g., breeding, migrating) into survival mode. In general, these components of the emergency LHS allow the individual to respond to a perturbation and avoid chronic stress (Wingfield, 2004; Wingfield & Ramenofsky, 1999). Aggressive behavior is frequently expressed even when in an emergency LHS (figure 8.4).

Life history stages

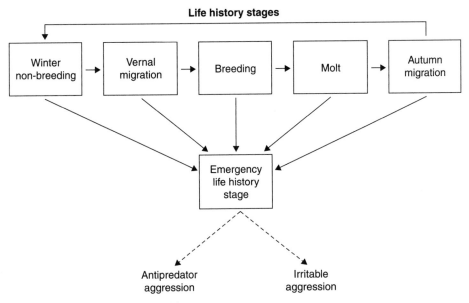

FIGURE 8.4 At any point in the predictable life cycle of life history stages, unpredictable events, perturbation factors (with the potential for stress), can trigger the emergency life history stage. This facultative stage is critical in promoting survival of the individual in the face of potential stress (e.g., Wingfield et al., 1998; Wingfield & Romero, 2000). Thus far, it appears that all vertebrates express the emergency life history stage at some point in their life cycle. This stage can be triggered by environmental perturbations at any time or life history stage and suppresses expression of the normal life history stage to promote survival strategies designed to avoid the effects of chronic stress. It is when in this stage that antipredator and irritable aggression can be expressed. That is, these two types of aggression tend to be facultative and associated with perturbations of the life cycle. Clearly, the context of these two types of aggression may be very different from the other types expressed in the normal life cycle.

Antipredator aggression (or against a dominant conspecific) is well known under such circumstances in many vertebrates (e.g., Sapolsky, 2002). Also, irritable aggression (as defined earlier) may also be expressed (figure 8.4), especially in relation to food shortages, competition for shelter, etc.

Competition in the Face of Food Shortages

Few environmental situations induce such intense aggression as a shortage of food. However, control of aggression under such circumstances has received scant attention, at least on a comparative scale. In a pelagic seabird, the black-legged kittiwake, *Rissa tridactyla*, breeding in the Bering Sea and off the Alaska coast, plasma levels of corticosterone increase in relation to shortage of food (fish) in both adults and chicks (Kitaysky, Wingfield, & Piatt, 1999). Experimental implantation of corticosterone pellets to mimic this increase in

chicks resulted in elevated begging behavior and competition among siblings or paired chicks in a feeding experiment (Kitaysky, Wingfield, & Piatt, 2001). In tropical breeding blue-footed boobies, *Sula nebouxii*, competition between siblings in a nest resulted in elevated corticosterone in the subordinate (Ramos-Fernandez et al., 2000), but food shortage in general had little effect on adults (Wingfield, Jacobs, et al., 1999), suggesting that food was perhaps sufficient for the adults but not for feeding chicks as well. Whether corticosterone facilitates aggression over food in this species remains to be determined.

It is possible that maternal effects may be important in some species in which young compete with their siblings, or even kill them, in response to food shortage. In breeding cattle egrets, *Bubulcus ibis*, dominant siblings hatched from eggs with higher plasma levels of testosterone in yolk (Schwabl & Mock, 1997), and neonatal siblicidal spotted hyenas, *Crocuta crocuta*, have elevated levels of androgens that stem from maternal precursor hormones (Glickman, Frank, Pavgi, et al., 1992; Licht et al., 1992, 1998). Furthermore, in canaries, chicks hatching from eggs with higher testosterone concentrations in yolk grew faster, presumably by being more competitive in begging for food from the parents (Schwabl, 1993, 1996). Mechanisms underlying the effects of corticosterone and testosterone on aggression over food remain to be determined.

Allostasis and Hormone-Behavior Interactions

The concept of allostasis, maintaining stability through change, has been introduced to explain how individuals adjust to both predictable and unpredictable events on a continuum (McEwen, 2000; McEwen & Wingfield, 2003). The allostasis concept has some useful terms that are relevant to expression of aggression. Allostatic load refers to the cumulative cost to the body of allostasis, with allostatic overload (accompanied by elevated plasma levels of glucocorticoids) being a state in which daily food intake and/or body reserves cannot fuel the cumulative cost. It is at this point that glucocorticoid levels surge and an emergency LHS may be triggered (McEwen & Wingfield, 2003). Aggression during competition for food and shelter is known to occur, though the mechanisms remain poorly known, but likely include a role for glucocorticoids (see above). The normal life cycle (appropriate LHS) can be resumed when the perturbation passes.

Social Status, Aggression, and Perturbations of the Environment

Cooperation and social support provide many advantages when living in social groups, but social conflict and competition may introduce disadvantages. Social conflicts elevate allostatic load, followed by increased levels of glucocorticoids. Individuals in groups experience different levels of allostatic load according to status that in turn may predict relative glucocorticoid levels of dominant and subordinate individuals. An analysis of the available data from free-ranging animals using phylogenetic-independent contrasts of allostatic load and relative levels of glucocorticoids shows that the relative allostatic load of social status predicts whether dominant or subordinate members of a social unit express higher or lower levels of glucocorticoids

(Goymann & Wingfield, 2004). If the allostatic load of dominance rank (the sum of acquisition and maintenance) is higher than the allostatic load of being subordinate, then dominants are significantly more likely to have elevated levels of glucocorticoids. Conversely, if the allostatic load of social status is greatest in subordinates, then they are significantly more likely to express higher levels of glucocorticoids (Goymann & Wingfield, 2004).

Conclusions

It is clear from the literature summarized here that the varied types of aggression can be expressed in multiple contexts, both narrow and broad, throughout the life cycle of an individual. It is intriguing that in most species the behavioral traits associated with aggression, both defensive and offensive, are similar regardless of stage in the life cycle. This suggests that neural circuits may indeed be conserved, but the mechanisms by which hormones regulate expression of aggression may vary. The majority of work on endocrine correlates of aggression has been performed on vertebrates during breeding, or at least when mature, and much more work will be required to determine how aggression of other types in nonbreeding situations is regulated. It is important to bear in mind that the hormonal regulation of submissive behavior is also important and appears to involve a separate suite of control mechanisms. Given the state of our knowledge at present, and that we are only beginning to explore control mechanisms of aggression expressed in natural settings, is it possible to conclude anything about the evolution of hormone-behavior interactions?

Evolution of Hormone-Behavior Interactions

Aggression expressed in very similar ways within an individual across a wide spectrum of contexts and types suggests that similar or common neural circuits are involved. Thus some types of aggression may always be expressed, whereas others only occur at specific times of year or in characteristic situations. Hormones regulate the specificity (type) of the response, not necessarily whether aggression is expressed per se. The latter may be entirely neural. Examples are the role of peripheral sex steroids on territorial aggression, when breeding, and centrally synthesized steroids (neuro-steroids), when not breeding. Another example is the inhibition of aggression in social subordinance by glucocorticoids, or they may interfere with aggression by promoting subordinance. In other situations glucocorticoids may promote aggression over food. What other factors are involved remains obscure. Nonetheless, certain behavioral traits may be common to many types of aggression, and hormones influence type and context. Thus evolutionary trends are probably in relation to the latter and not to aggression per se.

FSM theory describes the organization of LHSs in the life cycle of individuals and can be used to investigate how the endocrine system regulates changes in behavior, particularly aggression, characteristic of each LHS (Jacobs & Wingfield, 2000). Three predictions stem from this theory that have direct relevance to the evolution of hormone-aggression interactions. First, aggression expressed in different LHSs may appear to be identical in terms of postures, vocalizations, etc., but the control mechanisms may be different. This is because hormone control in one LHS may be inappropriate in another. An example is the androgenic control of territorial aggression in breeding and nonbreeding seasons. It turns out that the cellular mechanisms at the neuron level appear to be conserved and that the way the hormone message gets to the target cell is different in the two LHSs. In this case sex steroids are produced locally in relevant brain areas in the non-breeding season, thus avoiding effects of high blood levels of testosterone at the wrong time. Second, if a LHS is prolonged throughout the year, then chronic exposure to high circulating levels of hormones, such as sex steroids, could be detrimental. These result in "costs," such as increased injury, decreased parental care, energetic overload, etc. Many mechanisms may have evolved by which organisms avoid these costs and comparative studies on other vertebrate taxa will reveal how widespread such mechanisms are. Third, the neural pathways by which environmental signals are perceived and transduced into neuroendocrine and endocrine secretions that regulate aggression may not be the same among different phases of the LHS or among different LHSs, even though the environmental factors that regulate these processes may be similar. In other words, the social cues that trigger territorial aggression when breeding may be different from those in the nonbreeding season. An example is the observation that male song sparrows respond to sexually receptive females by in-creasing testosterone secretion and persistence of aggression in the breeding season, but not in the nonbreeding season. How these pathways are turned on and off and what others may exist remain to be determined.

Finally, it must be pointed out that field and laboratory investigations are essential to determine how animals use the endocrine system to orchestrate their life cycles. Field investigations reveal ecological bases of patterns of behavior and the costs associated with prolonged high levels of sex steroids. Although it is possible that these perspectives could have been realized in laboratory experiments on "conventional" animal models, many will likely only be revealed by animals interacting with their real world. Ecological bases of hormone actions have undoubtedly had a strong influence on the evolution of mechanisms, including, paradoxically, ways to preserve one action of a hormone in different LHSs but avoid potential costs that may accompany it. Given the diversity of behavioral patterns expressed within a population of animals from season to season, as well as among different populations, the possible mechanisms underlying hormone-behavior interactions are probably numerous and many remain to be discovered.

Note

Preparation of this chapter and many of the investigations cited were supported by grants from the National Science Foundation, Division of Integrative Biology and Neuroscience, the Office of Polar Programs, to J.C.W. He also acknowledges a Benjamin Meaker Fellowship (University of Bristol, United Kingdom), a John Simon Guggenheim Fellowship, and the Russell F. Stark University Professorship (University of Washington). We are also grateful to Lynn Erckman for expert help with animal care and hormone assays. I.T.M. was supported by NSF Minority Postdoctoral Fellowship DBI-9904144 and a Society for Neuroscience Postdoctoral Fellowship. W.G. acknowledges support from a postdoctoral grant from the Deutsche Forschungsgemeinschaft (Go 985/2–1).

References

Adkins-Regan, E. (1987). Sexual differentiation in birds. *Trends in Neurosciences, 10*, 517–522.

Adkins-Regan, E., Abdelnabi, M., Mobarak, M., & Ottinger, M. A. (1990). Sex steroid levels in developing and adult male and female zebra finches (*Poephila guttata*). *General and Comparative Endocrinology, 78*, 93–109.

Agate, R. J., Grisham, W., Wade, J., Mann, S., Wingfield, J. C., Schanen, C., et al. (2003). Neural not gonadal origin of brain sex differences in a gynandromorphic finch. *Proceedings of the National Academy of Sciences USA, 100*, 4873–4878.

Arcese, P. (1989). Territory acquisition and loss in male song sparrows. *Animal Behaviour, 37*, 45–55.

Archawaranon, M., & Haven Wiley, R. (1988). Control of aggression and dominance in white-throated sparrows by testosterone and its metabolites. *Hormones and Behavior, 22*, 497–517.

Archer, J. (1998). Problems with the concept of dominance and lack of empirical support for a testosterone-dominance link. *Behavioral and Brain Sciences, 21*, 363–363.

Arnold, A. P. (1975). The effects of castration and androgen replacement on song, courtship and aggression in zebra finches (*Poephila guttata*). *Journal of Experimental Zoology, 191*, 309–325.

Arnold, A. P. (2004). Sex chromosones and brain gender. *Nature Reviews Neuroscience, 5*, 701–708.

Arnold, A. P., & Breedlove, S. M. (1985). Organizational and activational effects of sex steroids on brain and behavior: A re analysis. *Hormones and Behavior, 19*, 469–498.

Axelrod, J., & Reisine, T. D. (1984). Stress hormones: Their interaction and regulation. *Science, 224*, 452–459.

Ball, G. F. (1999). Neuroendocrine basis of seasonal changes in vocal behavior among songbirds. In M. Hauser & M. Konishi (Eds.), *The design of communication* (pp. 213–254). Cambridge, MA: MIT Press.

Balthazart, J. (1983). Hormonal correlates of behavior. In D. S. Farner, J. R. King, & K. S. Parkes (Eds.), *Avian biology* (Vol. 7, pp. 221–365). New York: Academic Press.

Balthazart, J., Foidant, A., Baillen, M., & Silverin, B. (1999). Brain aromatase in laboratory and free-living songbirds: Relationships with reproductive behavior. In *Proceedings of the 22nd International Ornithology Congress, Durban* (pp. 1257–1289). Johannsburg: Birdlife South Africa.

Bass, A. H. (1996). Shaping brain sexuality. *American Scientist, 84*, 352–363.

Baulieu, E. (1998). Neurosteroids: A novel function of the brain. *Psychoneuroendocrinology, 23*, 963–987.

Beletsky, L. D., Gori, D. F., Freeman, S., & Wingfield, J. C. (1995). Testosterone and polygyny in birds. *Current Ornithology, 12*, 1–41.

Bernhardt, P. C., Dabbs, J. M., Jr., Fielden, J. A., & Lutter, C. D. (1998). Testosterone changes during vicarious experiences of winning and losing among fans at sporting events. *Physiology and Behavior, 65*, 59–62.

Brain, P. (1979). Hormones, drugs and aggression. *Annual Research Review, 3*, 1–38.

Brain, P. F. (1998). Androgens and human behavior: A complex relationship. *Behavioral and Brain Sciences, 21*, 363–364.

Brenowitz, E. (1997). Comparative approaches to study of the avian song control system. *Journal of Neurobiology, 33*, 517–531.

Bribiescas, R. G. (1998). Testosterone and dominance: Between-population variance and male energetics. *Behavioral and Brain Sciences, 21*, 364–365.

Bronson, S. H., & Desjardins, C. (1970). Neonatal androgen administration and adult aggressiveness in female mice. *General and Comparative Endocrinology, 15*, 320–325.

Brown, J. L. (1964). The evolution of diversity in avian territorial systems. *Wilson Bulletin, 76*, 160–169.

Brown, J. L. (1969). Territorial behavior and population regulation in birds: A review and re-evaluation. *Wilson Bulletin, 81*, 293–329.

Bucher, T., Ryan, M., & Bartholomew, G. (1982). Oxygen consumption during resting, calling, and nest building in the frog, *Physalaemus pustulosus*. *Physiological Zoology, 55*, 10–22.

Burger, A. E., & Millar, R. P. (1980). Seasonal changes of sexual and territorial behavior and plasma testosterone levels in male lesser sheathbills (*Chionis minor*). *Zeitschrift fur Tierpsychologie, 52*, 397–406.

Caldwell, G. S., Glickman, S. E., & Smith, E. R. (1984). Seasonal aggression independent of seasonal testosterone in wood rats. *Proceedings of the National Academy of Sciences USA, 81*, 5255–5257.

Canoine, V., & Gwinner, E. (2002). Seasonal differences in the hormonal control of territorial aggression in free-living European stonechats. *Hormones and Behavior, 41*, 1–8.

Cardwell, J. R., & Liley, N. R. (1991a). Androgen control of social status in males of a wild population of stoplight parrotfish, *Sparisoma viride* (Scaridae). *Hormones and Behavior, 25*, 1–18.

Cardwell, J. R., & Liley, N. R. (1991b). Hormonal control of sex and color change in the stoplight parrotfish, *Sparisoma viride*. *General and Comparative Endocrinology, 81*, 7–20.

Catchpole, C. K., & Slater P. J. (1995). *Bird song: Biological theme and variation*. Cambridge: Cambridge University Press.

Carlson, B. A., Hopkins, C. D., & Thomas, P. (2000). Androgen correlates of socially induced changes in the electric organ discharge waveform of a mormyrid fish. *Hormones and Behavior, 38*, 177–186.

Cavigelli, S. A., & Pereira, M. E. (2000). Mating season aggression and fecal testosterone levels in male ring-tailed lemurs (*Lemur catta*). *Hormones and Behavior, 37,* 246–255.

Chambers, K. C. (1998). Target tissue sensitivity, testosterone-social environment interactions, and lattice hierarchies. *Behavioral and Brain Sciences, 21,* 366–367.

Compagnone, N. A. & Mellon, S. H. (2000). Neurosteroids: Biosynthesis and function of these novel neuromodulators. *Frontiers in Neuroendocrinology, 21,* 1–56.

Creel, S., Wildt, D. E., & Monfort, S. L. (1993). Aggression, reproduction, and androgens in wild dwarf mongooses: A test of the challenge hypothesis. *American Naturalist, 141,* 816–825.

Crews, D. (1984). Gamete production, sex hormone secretion, and mating behavior uncoupled. *Hormones and Behavior, 18,* 22–28.

Crews, D. (1987). Diversity and evolution of behavioral controlling mechanisms. In D. Crews (Ed.), *Psychobiology of reproductive behavior* (pp. 88–119). Englewood Cliffs, NJ: Prentice Hall.

Crews, D., & Moore, M. C. (1986) Evolution of mechanisms controlling mating behavior. *Science, 231,* 121–125.

Davis, E. S., & Marler, C. A. (2003). The progesterone challenge: Steroid hormone changes following a simulated territorial intrusion in female *Peromyscus californicus. Hormones and Behavior, 44,* 185–198.

Delville, Y., Mansour, K. M., & Ferris, C. F. (1996). Testosterone facilitates aggression by modulating vasopressin receptors in the hypothalamus. *Physiology and Behavior, 60,* 25–29.

DeNardo, D. F., & Licht, P. (1993). Effects of corticosterone on social behavior of lizards. *Hormones and Behavior, 27,* 184–199.

Dittami, J., & Gwinner, E. (1990). Endocrine correlates of seasonal reproduction and territorial behavior in some tropical passerines. In M. Wada (Ed.), *Endocrinology of birds: Molecular to behavioral* (pp. 225–233). Tokyo: Japan Science Society Press/Berlin: Springer-Verlag.

Dufty, A. M., Jr. (1989). Testosterone and survival. *Hormones and Behavior, 23,* 185–193.

Eens, M., & Pinxten, R. (2000). Sex-role reversal in vertebrates: Behavioural and endocrinological accounts. *Behavioural Processes, 51,* 135–147.

Eens, M., Van Duyse, E., Berghman, L., & Pinxten, R. (2000). Shield characteristics are testosterone-dependent in both male and female moorhens. *Hormones and Behavior, 37,* 126–134.

Elekonich, M. M., & Wingfield, J. C. (2000). Seasonality and hormonal control of territorial aggression in female song sparrows (*Melospiza melodia;* Passeriformes, Emberizidae). *Ethology, 106,* 493–510.

Emerson, S. B. (2001). Male advertisement calls: Behavioral variation and physiological processes. In M. J. Ryan (Ed.), *Anuran communication* (pp. 36–44). Washington, DC: Smithsonian Institution Press.

Emerson, S. B., & Hess, D. L. (2001). Glucocorticoids, androgens, testis mass, and the enrgetics of vocalization in breeding male frogs. *Hormones and Behavior, 39,* 59–69.

Ferris, C. F., Melloni, R. H. J., Koppel, G., Perry, K. W., Fuller, R. W., & Delville, Y. (1997). Vasopressin/serotonin interactions in the anterior hypothalamus control aggressive behavior in golden hamsters. *Journal of Neuroscience, 17,* 4331–4340.

Fivizzani, A. J., Colwell, M. A., & Oring, L. W. (1986). Plasma steroid hormone levels in free-living Wilson's phalaropes, *Phalaropus tricolor. General and Comparative Endocrinology, 62,* 137–144.

Fivizzani, A. J., & Oring, L. W. (1986). Plasma steroid hormones in relation to behavioral sex role reversal in the spotted sandpiper, *Actitis macularia. Biology of Reproduction, 35,* 1195–1201.

Floody, O. R. (1983). Hormones and aggression in female mammals. In B. B. Svare (Ed.), *Hormones and aggressive behavior* (pp. 39–89). New York: Plenum.

Foidart, A., Silverin, B., Baillen, M., Havada, N., & Balthazart, J. (1998). Neuroanatomical distribution and variations across the reproductive cycles of aromatase activity and aromatase-immunoreactive cells in the pied fly catcher (*Ficedula hypoleuca*). *Hormone Behavior, 33,* 180–196.

Francis, R. C., Jacobson, B., Wingfield, J. C., & Fernald, R. D. (1992). Castration lowers aggression but social dominance in male *Haplochromis burtoni* (Cichlidae). *Ethology, 90,* 247–255.

Frank, L. G. (1996). Female masculinization in the spotted hyaena: Endocrinology, behavioral ecology, and evolution. In J. L. Gittleman (Ed.), *Carnivore behavior, ecology, and evolution* (pp. 78–131). Ithaca, NY: Cornell University Press.

Fusani, L., Hutchison, J. B., & Gahr, M. (2001). Testosterone regulates the activity and expression of aromatase in the canary neostinatum. *Journal of Neurobiology, 49,* 1–8.

Gahr, M., & Metzdor, F. R. (1997). Distribution and dynamics in the expression of androgen and estrogen receptors in vocal control system of birds. *Brain Research Bulletin, 44,* 509–517.

Glickman, S. E., & Caldwell, G. S. (1993). Studying natural behaviors in artificial environments: The problems of salient elements. In E. F. Gibbons, Jr., E. J. Wyers, E. Waters, & E. W. Menzel (Eds.), *Naturalistic environments in captivity for animal behavior research.* Albany: State University of New York Press.

Glickman, S. E., Frank, L. G., Licht, P., Yalcinkaya, T.,

Siiteri, P. K., & Davidson, J. (1992). Sexual differentiation of the female spotted hyaena. One of nature's experiments. *Annals of the New York Academy of Sciences, 662,* 135–159.

Glickman, S. E., Frank, L. G., Pavgi, S., & Licht, P. (1992). Hormonal correlates of "masculinization" in female spotted hyaenas (*Crocuta crocuta*). 1. Infancy to sexual maturity. *Journal of Reproduction and Fertility, 95,* 451–462.

Golla, W., Hofer, H., & East, M. L. (1999). Within-litter sibling aggression in spotted hyaenas: Effect of maternal nursing, sex and age. *Animal Behaviour, 58,* 715–726.

Goodson, J. L. (1998a). Territorial aggression and dawn song are modulated by septal vasotocin and vasoactive intestinal peptide in male field sparrows (*Spizella pusilla*). *Hormones and Behavior, 34,* 67–77.

Goodson, J. L. (1998b). Vasotocin and vasoactive intestinal polypeptide modulate aggression in a territorial songbird, the violet-eared waxbill (Estrildidae: *Uraeginthus granatina*). *General and Comparative Endocrinology, 111,* 233–244.

Goodson, J. L., & Adkins-Regan, E. (1999). Effect of intraseptal vasotocin and vasoactive intestinal polypeptide infusions on courtship song and aggression in the male zebra finch (*Taeniopygia guttata*). *Journal of Neuroendocrinology, 11,* 19–25.

Gould, S. J. (1981). Hyena myths and realities. *Natural History, 90,* 16–24.

Goymann, W., East, M. L., & Hofer, H. (2003). Defense of females, but not social status, predicts plasma androgen levels in male spotted hyenas. *Physiological and Biochemical Zoology, 76*(4), 586–593.

Goymann, W., East, M. L., Wachter, B., Höner, O. P., Möstl, E., Van'thof, T. J., & Hofer, H. (2001). Social, state dependent and environmental modulation of fecal corticosteroid levels in free-ranging female spotted hyenas. *Proceedings of the Royal Society of London, Series B., 268,* 2453–2459.

Goymann, W., Moore, I. T., Scheuerlein, A., Hirschenhauser, K., Grafen, A., & Wingfield, J. C. (in press). Testosterone in tropical birds: Effects of environmental and social factors. *American Naturalist.*

Goymann, W., & Wingfield, J. C. (in press). Allostatic load, social status and stress hormones—the costs of social status matter. *Animal Behavior.*

Gratto-Trevor, C. L., Fivizzani, A. J., Oring, L. W., & Cooke, F. (1990). Seasonal changes in gonadal steroids of a monogamous versus a polyandrous shorebird. *General and Comparative Endocrinology, 80,* 407–418.

Greenberg, N., & Wingfield, J. C. 1987. Stress and reproduction: Reciprocal relationships. In D.O. Norris & R.E. Jones (Eds.), *Reproductive endocrinology of fishes, amphibians and reptiles* (pp. 389–426). New York: Wiley.

Gurney, M. E., & Konishi, M. (1980). Hormone-induced sexual differentiation of brain and behavior in zebra finches. *Science, 208,* 1380–1382.

Gwinner, E., Rödl, T., & Schwabl, H. (1994). Pair territoriality of wintering stonechats: Behavior, function & hormones. *Behavior Ecology and Sociobiology, 34,* 321–327.

Hackl, R., Bromundt, V., Daisley, J., Kotrschal, K., & Möstl, E. (2003). Distribution and origin of steroid hormones in the yolk of Japanese quail eggs (*Coturnix coturnix japonica*). *Journal of Comparative Physiology, B, 173,* 327–331.

Hamilton, W. J., Tilson, R. L., & Frank, L. G. (1986). Sexual monomorphism in spotted hyaenas, *Crocuta crocuta*. *Ethology, 71,* 63–73.

Harding, C. F. (1981). Social modulation of circulating hormone levels in the male. *American Zoologist, 21,* 223–232.

Harding, C. F. (1983). Hormonal influences on avian aggressive behavior. In B. Svare (Ed.), *Hormones and aggressive behavior* (pp. 435–467). New York: Plenum.

Harding, C. F., Walters, M. J., Collado, D., & Sheridan, K. (1988). Hormone specificity and activation of social behavior in male red-winged blackbirds. *Hormones and Behavior, 22,* 402–418.

Hau, M. (2001). Timing of breeding in variable environments: Tropical birds as model systems. *Hormones and Behavior, 40,* 281–290.

Hau, M., Stoddard, S. T., & Soma, K. K. (2004). Territorial aggression and hormones during the non-breeding season in a tropical bird. *Hormones and Behavior, 45.* 40–49.

Hau, M., Wikelski, M., Soma, K. K., & Wingfield, J. C. (2000). Testosterone and year-round territorial aggression in a tropical bird. *General and Comparative Endocrinology, 117,* 20–33.

Hegner, R., & Wingfield, J. C. (1987). Effects of experimental manipulation of testosterone levels on parental investment and breeding success in male house sparrows. *Auk, 104,* 462–469.

Hews, D. K., Thompson, C. W., Moore, I. T., & Moore, M. C. (1997). Population frequencies of alternative male phenotypes in tree lizards: Geographic variation and common-garden rearing studies. *Behavioral Ecology and Sociobiology, 41,* 371–380.

Hillgarth, N., & Wingfield, J. C. (1997). Parasite sexual selection: Endocrine aspects. In D. H. Clayton & J. Moore (Eds.), *Host-parasite evolution* (pp. 78–104). Oxford: Oxford University Press.

Hinde, R. A. (1965). Interaction of internal and external factors in integration of canary reproduction. In

F. A. Beach (Ed.), *Sex and behavior* (pp. 381–415). New York: Wiley.

Hirschenhauser, K., Winkler, H., & Oliveira, R. F. (2003). Comparative analysis of male androgen responsiveness to social environment in birds: The effects of mating system and paternal incubation. *Hormones and Behavior, 43*, 508–519.

Hunt, K. E., Hahn, T. P., & Wingfield, J. C. (1999). Endocrine influences on parental care during a short breeding season: Testosterone and male parental care in Lapland longspurs (*Calcarius lapponicus*). *Behavioral Ecology and Sociobiology, 45*, 360–369.

Hutchison, J. B., Steiner, T., & Jaggard, D. (1986). Effects of photoperiod on formation of estradiol-17β in the dove brain. *Journal Endocrinology, 109*, 371–377.

Jacobs, J. D., & Wingfield, J. C. (2000). Endocrine control of life-cycle stages: A constraint on response to the environment? *Condor, 102*, 35–51.

Jennings, D. H., Moore, M. C., Knapp, R., Matthews, L., & Orchinik, M. (2000). Plasma steroid-binding globulin mediation of differences in stress reactivity in alternative male phenotypes in tree lizards, *Urosaurus ornatus*. *General and Comparative Endocrinology, 120*, 289–299.

Jennings, D. H., Painter, D. L., & Moore, M. C. (2004). Role of the adrenal gland in early post-hatching differentiation of alternative male phenotypes in the tree lizard (*Urosaurus ornatus*). *General and Comparative Endocrinology, 135*, 81–89.

Ketterson, E. D., Nolan, V., Jr., Cawthorn, M. J., Parker, P. G., & Ziegenfus, C. (1996). Phenotypic engineering: Using hormones to explore the mechanistic and functional bases of phenotypic variation in nature *Ibis, 138*, 70–86.

Ketterson, E. D., Nolan, V., Jr., Wolf, L., & Ziegenfus, C. (1990). Testosterone and avian life histories: Effects of experimentally elevated testosterone on behavior and correlates of fitness in the dark-eyed junco (*Junco hyemalis*) *American Naturalist, 140*, 980–999.

Kimura, T., Okanoya, K., & Wada, M. (1999). Effect of testosterone on the distribution of vasotocin immunoreactivity in the brain of the zebra finch, *Taeniopygia guttata castanotis*. *Life Sciences, 65*, 1663–70.

Kitaysky, A. S., Wingfield, J. C., & Piatt, J. F. (1999). Dynamics of food availability, body condition and physiological stress response in breeding black-legged kittiwakes. *Functional Ecology, 13*, 577–584.

Kitaysky, A. S., Wingfield, J. C., & Piatt, J. F. (2001). Corticosterone facilitates begging and affects resource allocation in the black-legged kittiwake. *Behavioral Ecology, 12*, 619–625.

Knapp, R., & Moore, M. C. (1996). Male morphs in tree lizards, *Urosaurus ornatus*, have different delayed

responses to aggressive encounters. *Animal Behaviour 52*, 1045–1055.

Konishi, M., & Gurney, M. E. (1982). Sexual differentiation of brain and behavior. *Trends in Neurosciences, 5*, 20–23.

Koolhaas, J. M., Korte, S. M., Boer, S. F., Van Der Vegt, B. J., Van Renen, C. G., Hopster, H., et al. (1999). Coping styles in animals: Current status in behavior and stress-physiology. *Neuroscience and Biobehavioral Reviews, 23*, 925–935.

Kriner, E., & Schwabl, H. (1991). Control of winter song and territorial aggresion of female robins (*Erithacus rubecula*) by testosterone. *Ethology, 87*, 37–44.

Labrie, F., Bélanger, A., Simard, J., Luuthe, V., & Labrie, C. (1995). DHEA and peripheral androgen and estrogen formation: Intracrinology. *Annals of the New York Academy of Sciences, 774*, 16–28.

Lehrman, D. S. (1965). Interaction between internal and external environments in the regulation of the reproductive cycle of the ring dove. In F. A. Beach (Ed.), *Sex and behavior* (pp. 355–380). New York: Wiley.

Leshner, A. I. (1978). *An introduction to behavioral endocrinology.* New York: Oxford University Press.

Leshner, A. I. (1981). The role of hormones in the control of submissiveness. In P. F. Brain & D. Denton (Eds.), *Multidisciplinary approaches to aggression research* (pp. 302–322). Amsterdam: Elsevier/North-Holland.

Leshner, A. I., Korn S. J., Mixon, J. F., Rosenthal, C., & Besser, A. K. (1980). Effects of corticosterone on submissiveness in mice: Some temporal and theoretical considerations. *Physiology and Behavior, 24*, 283–288.

Leshner, A. I., & Politch, J. A. (1979). Hormonal control of submissiveness in mice: Irrelevance of the androgens and relevance of pituitary-adrenal hormones. *Physiology and Behavior, 22*, 531–534.

Levin, R. N., & Wingfield, J. C. (1992). Control of territorial aggression in tropical birds. *Ornis Scandinavica, 23*, 259–270.

Licht, P., Frank, L. G., Yalcinkaya, T. M., Siiteri, P. K., & Glickman, S. E. (1992). Hormonal correlates of "masculinization" in female spotted hyaenas (*Crocuta crocuta*). 2. Maternal and fetal steroids. *Journal of Reproduction and Fertility, 95*, 463–474.

Licht, P., Hayes, T., Tsai, P., Cunha, G., Kim, H., Golbus, M., et al. (1998). Androgens and masculinization of genitalia in the spotted hyena (*Crocuta crocuta*)—1. Urogenital morphology and placental androgen production during fetal life. *Journal of Reproduction and Fertility, 113*, 105–116.

Logan, C. A., & Wingfield, J. C. (1990). Autumnal territorial aggression is independent of plasma testosterone in mockingbirds. *Hormones and Behavior, 24,* 568–581.

Lofts, B., & Murton, P. K. (1973. Reproduction in birds. *Avian Biology, 3,* 1–107.

Lovern, M. B., & Wade, J. (2003). Sex steroids in green anoles (*Anolis carolinensis*): Uncoupled maternal plasma and yolking follicle concentrations, potential embryonic steroidogenesis, and evolutionary implications. *General and Comparative Endocrinology, 134,* 109–115.

Lynn, S. E., Hayward, L. S., Benowitz-Fredericks, Z. M., & Wingfield, J. C. (2002). Behavioral insensitivity to supplementary testosterone during the parental phase in the chestnut-collared longspur (*Calcarius ornatus*). *Animal Behaviour, 63,* 795–803.

Lynn, S. E., & Wingfield, J. C. (2003). Male chestnut-collared longspurs are essential for nestling survival: A removal study. *Condor, 105,* 154–158.

Marler, P., Peters, S., Ball, G. F., Dufty, A. M., Jr., & Wingfield, J. C. (1989). The role of sex steriods in the acquisition and production of birdsong. *Nature, 336,* 770–771.

Marler, P., Peters, S., & Wingfield, J. C. (1987). Correlations between song acquisition, song production, and plasma levels of testosterone and estradiol in sparrows. *Journal of Neurobiology, 18,* 531–548.

Marler, C., & Ryan, M. (1996). Energetic constraints and steroid hormone correlates of male calling behavior in the tungara frog. *Journal of Zoology, 240,* 397–409.

Mazur, A., & Booth, A. (1998). Testosterone and dominance in men. *Behavioral and Brain Sciences, 21,* 353–363.

McEwen, B. S. (2000). Allostasis and allostatic load: implications for neuropsychopharmacology. *Neuropsychopharmacology 22,* 108–124.

McEwen, B. S., & Wingfield, J. C. (2003). The concept of allostasis in biology and biomedicine. *Hormones and Behavior, 43,* 2–15.

Mensah-Nyagan, A., Feuilloley, M., Do-Rego, J., Marcual, A., Lange, C., et al. (1996). Localization of 17β-hydroxysteroid dehydrogenase and characterization of testosterone in the brain of the male frog. *Proceedings of the National Academy of Science USA, 93,* 1423–1428.

Mock, D. W. (1984). Siblicidal aggression and resource monopolization in birds. *Science, 225,* 731–733.

Mock, D. W., & Parker, G. A. (1998). Siblicide, family conflict and the evolutionary limits of selfishness. *Animal Behaviour, 56,* 1–10.

Monaghan, E. P., & Glickman, S. E. (1992). Hormones and aggressive behavior. In J. B. Becker, S. M. Breedlove, & D. Crews (Eds.), *Behavioral endocrinology* (pp. 261–285). Cambridge, MA: MIT Press.

Moore, F. L., & Miller, L. J. (1984). Stress-induced inhibition of sexual behavior: Corticosterone inhibits

courtship behaviors of a male amphibian (*Taricha granulosa*). *Hormones and Behavior, 18,* 400–410.

Moore, I. T., Bentley, G. E., Wingfield, J. C., & Brenowitz, E. A. (2004). Plasticity of the avian song control system in response to localized environmental areas in an equatorial song bird. *Journal of Neuroscience, 24,* 10182–10185.

Moore, I. T., & Jessop, T. S. (2003). Stress, reproduction, and adrenocortical modulation in amphibians and reptiles. *Hormones and Behavior, 43,* 39–47.

Moore, I. T., & Mason, R. T. (2001). Behavioral and hormonal responses to corticosterone in the male red-sided garter snake, *Thamnophis sirtalis parietalis. Physiology and Behavior, 72,* 669–674.

Moore, I. T., Perfito, N., Wada, H., Sperry, T. S., & Wingfield, J. C. (2002). Latitudinal variation in plasma testosterone levels in birds of the genus *Zonotrichia. General and Comparative Endocrinology, 129,* 13–19.

Moore, I. T., Wada, H., Perfito, N., Busch, D. S., & Wingfield, J. C. (2004). Territoriality and testosterone in an equatorial population of Rufous-collared sparrows, *Zonotrichia capensis. Animal Behavior, 67,* 411–420.

Moore, I. T., Walker, B. G., & Wingfield, J. C. (2004). The effects of combined aromatase inhibitor and anti-androgen on male territorial aggression in a tropical population of rufous-collared sparrows, *Zonotrichia capensis. General and Comparative Endocrinology, 135,* 223–229.

Moore, M. C., Hews, D. K., & Knapp, R. (1998). Hormonal control and evolution of alternative male phenotypes: Generalizations of models for sexual differentiation. *American Zoologist, 38,* 133–151.

Moyer, K. E. (1968). Kinds of aggression and their physiological basis. *Communications in Behavioral Biology, Part A, 2,* 65–87.

Narins, P. M., Hödl, W., & Grabul, D. S. (2003). Bimodal signal requisite for agonistic behavior in a poison dart frog *Epipedobates femoralis. Proceeding of the National Academy of Sciences USA, 100,* 577–580.

Nicolas, L. B., Pinoteau, W., Papot, S., Routier, S., Guillaumet, G. & Mortaud, S. (2001). Aggressive behavior induced by the steriod sulfatase inhibitor COUMATE and by DHEAs in CBA/H mice. *Brain Research, 922,* 216–222.

Nomura, O., Nishimori, K., Nakabayashi, O., Yasue, H. & Mizano, S. (1998). Determination by modified RT-PCR of transcript amounts from genes involved in sex steriod synthesis in chicken organs including brain. *Journal of Steroid Biochemistry and Molecular Biology, 67,* 143–148.

Nordby, J. C., Campbell, S. E., & Beecher, M. D. (1999). Ecological correlates of song learning in song sparrows. *Behavioral Ecology, 10,* 287–297.

Nowicki, S., & Ball, G. F. (1989). Testosterone induction of song in photosensitive and photorefractory male sparrows. *Hormones and Behavior, 23,* 514–525.

O'Connor, R. J. (1978). Brood reduction in birds: Selection for fratricide, infanticide, and suicide? *Animal Behaviour, 26,* 79–96.

Oliveira, R. F. (1998). Of fish and men—a comparative approach to androgens and social dominance. *Behavioral and Brain Sciences, 21,* 383.

Oliveira, R. F., & Almada, V. C. (1998). Androgenization of dominant males in a cichlid fish: Androgens mediate the social modulation of sexually dimorphic traits. *Ethology, 104,* 841–858.

Oliveira, R. F., Lopes, M., Carneiro, L. A., & Canario, A. V. M. (2001). Watching fights raises fish hormone levels. *Nature (London), 409,* 475.

Oliveira, R. F., McGregor, P. K., & Latruffe, C. (1998). Know thine enemy: Fighting fish gather information from observing conspecific interactions. *Proceedings of the Royal Society of London, Series B, 265,* 1045–1049.

Oring, L. W., Fivizzani, A. J., Colwell, M. A., & El Halawani, M. E. (1988). Hormonal changes associated with natural and manipulated incubation in the sex-role reversed Wilson's phalarope. *General and Comparative Endocrinology, 72,* 247–256.

Ostner, J., Kappeler, P. M., & Heistermann, M. (2002). Seasonal variation and social correlates of androgen excretion in male redfronted lemurs (*Eulemur fulvus rufus*). *Behavioral Ecology and Sociobiology, 52,* 485–495.

Owens, I. P. F., & Short, R. V. (1995). Hormonal basis of sexual dimorphism in birds: Implications for new theories of sexual selection. *Trends in Ecology and Evolution, 10,* 44–47.

Pankhurst, N. W., & Barnett, C. W. (1993). Relationship of population density, territorial interaction and plasma levels of gonadal steroids in spawning male demoiselles *Chromis dispilus* (Pisces, Pomacentridae). *General and Comparative Endocrinology, 90,* 168–176.

Peters, P. J., Bronson, F. H., & Whitsett, J. M. (1972). Neonatal castration and intermale aggression in mice. *Physiology and Behavior, 8,* 265–268.

Petrie, M. (1983). Female moorhens compete for small fat males. *Science, 220,* 413–415.

Piersma, T., & Drent, J. (2003). Phenotypic flexibility and the evolution of organismal design. *Trends in Ecology and Evolution, 18,* 228–233.

Pohl-Apel, G., & Sossinka, R. (1984). Hormonal determination of song capacity in females of the zebra finch. *Zeitschrift für Tierpsychologie, 64,* 330–336.

Pröve, E. (1983). Hormonal correlates of behavioral development in male zebra finches. In J. Balthazart, E. Pröve, & R. Gilles (Eds.), *Hormones and behavior in higher vertebrates* (pp. 368–374). Berlin: Springer-Verlag.

Raleigh, M. J., McQuire, M. T., Brammer, G. L., Pollak, D. B., & Yuwiler, A. (1991). Serotonergic mechanisms promote dominance acquisition in adult male vervet monkeys. *Brain Research, 559,* 181–190.

Ramos-Fernandez G., Nuñez-de-la Mora, A., Wingfield, J. C., & Drummond, H. (2000). Endocrine correlates of dominance in chicks of the blue-footed booby (*Sula nebouxii*): Testing the challenge hypothesis. *Ethology, Ecology, and Evolution, 12,* 27–34.

Robel, P., & Baulieu, E. (1995). Dehydroepiandrosterone (DHEA) is a neuroactive neurosteroid. *Annals of the New York Academy of Sciences, 774,* 82–110.

Rödl, T., Goymann, W., Schwabl, I., & Gwinner, E. (in press). Comparative analysis of excremental androgen metabolite levels and gonad sizes in male Stonechats (Saxicola torquata ssp.) from temperate and tropical latitudes. *General and Comparative Endocrinology.*

Rissman, E. F., & Wingfield, J. C. (1984). Hormonal correlates of polyandry in the spotted sandpiper, *Actitis macularia. General and Comparative Endocrinology, 56,* 401–405.

Romero, L. M. (2002). Seasonal changes in plasma glucocorticoid concentrations in free-living vertebrates. *General and Comparative Endocrinology, 128,* 1–24.

Romero, L. M., Dean, S. C., & Wingfield, J. C. (1998). Neurally active peptide inhibits territorial defense in wild birds. *Hormones and Behavior, 34,* 239–247.

Ros, A. F. H., Canario, A. V. M., Couto, E., Zeilstra, I., & Oliveira, R. F. (2003). Endocrine correlates of intra-specific variation in the mating system of the St. Peter's fish (*Sarotherodon galilaeus*). *Hormones and Behavior, 44,* 365–373.

Ryan, M. (1985). *The Tungara frog.* Chicago: University of Chicago Press.

Sannen, A., Heistermann, M., Van Elsacker, L., Möhle, U., & Eens, M. (2003). Urinary testosterone metabolite levels in bonobos: A comparison with chimpanzees in relation to social system. *Behaviour, 140,* 683–696.

Sapolsky, R., Romero, L. M., & Munck, A. U. (2000). How do glucocorticosteroids influence stress responses? Integrating permissive, suppressive, stimulatory and preparative actions. *Endocrine Reviews, 21,* 55–89.

Sapolsky, R. M. (2002). Endocrinology of the stress response. In J. B. Becker, S. M. Breedlove, D. Crews, & M. M. McCarthy (Eds.), *Behavioral endocrinology* (2nd ed., pp. 409–450). Cambridge, MA: MIT Press.

Schlinger, B. A. (1987). Plasma androgens and aggressiveness in captive winter white-throated sparrows (*Zonotrichia albicollis*). *Hormones and Behavior, 21,* 203–210.

Schlinger, B. A. (1994). Estrogens to song: Picograms to sonograms. *Hormones and Behavior, 28,* 191–198.

Schlinger, B. A., & Callard, G. V. (1990). Aromatization mediates aggressive behavior in quail. *General and Comparative Endocrinology, 79,* 39–53.

Schlinger, B. A., Lane, N., Grisham, W., & Thompson, L. (1999). Androgen synthesis in a songbird: A study of Cyp17 (17a-hydroxylase/C17,20-lyase) activity in the Zebra finch. *General and Comparative Endocrinology, 113,* 46–58.

Schlinger, B. A., Slotow R. H., & Arnold A. P. (1992). Plasma estrogens and brain aromatase in winter white-crowned sparrows. *Ornis Scandinavica, 23,* 292–297.

Schumacher, M., Sulon, J., & Balthazart, J. (1988). Changes in serum concentrations of steroids during embryonic and post-hatching development of male and female Japanese quail (*Coturnix coturnix japonica*). *Journal of Endocrinology, 127,* 127–134.

Schuurman, T. (1980). Hormonal correlates of agonistic behavior in adult male rats. *Progress in Brain Research, 53,* 415–420.

Schwabl, H. (1993). Yolk is a source of maternal testosterone for developing birds. *Proceedings of the National Academy of Sciences USA, 90,* 11446–11450.

Schwabl, H. (1996). Environment modifies the testosterone levels of a female bird and its eggs. *Journal of Experimental Zoology, 276,* 157–163.

Schwabl, H., & Kriner, E. (1991). Territorial aggression and song of male European robins (*Erithacus rubecula*) in autumn and spring: Effects of antiandrogen treatment. *Hormones and Behavior, 25,* 180–194.

Schwabl, H., & Mock, D. (1997). A hormonal mechanism for parental favoritism. *Nature, 386,* 231.

Searcy, W. A. (1996). Sound-pressure levels and song preference in female redwing blackbirds (Agelauis phoeniceus) (Aves Emberizidae). *Ethology, 102,* 187–196.

Semsar, K., Kandel, F. L. M., & Godwin, J. (2001). Manipulations of the AVT system shift social status and related courtship and aggressive behavior in the Bluehead Wrasse. *Hormones and Behavior, 40,* 21–31.

Sikkel, P. C. (1993). Changes in plasma androgen levels associated with changes in male reproductive behavior in a brood cycling marine fish. *General and Comparative Endocrinology, 89,* 229–237.

Silverin, B. (1980). Effects of long acting testosterone treatment on free-living pied flycatchers, *Ficedula hypoleuca,* during the breeding period. *Animal Behavior, 28,* 906–912.

Silverin, B. (1986). Corticosterone binding proteins and behavioral effects of high plasma levels of corticosterone during the breeding period in the pied flycatcher. *General and Comparative Endocrinology, 64,* 67–74.

Simon, N. (2002). Hormonal processes in the development and expression of aggressive behavior. In D. Pfaff, A. Arnold, A. Etgen, S. Fahrbach, & R. Rubin (Eds.), *Hormones, brain and behavior* (Vol. 1, pp. 339–392). New York: Academic Press.

Smith, G. T., Brenowitz, E. A., Beecher, M. D., & Wingfield, J. C. (1997). Seasonal changes in testosterone, neural attributes of song control nuclei, and song structure in wild songbirds. *Journal of Neuroscience, 17,* 6001–6010.

Smith, G. T., Brenowitz, E. A., Wingfield, J. C., & Baptista, L. F. (1995). Seasonal changes in song nuclei and song behavior in Gambel's white-crowned sparrows. *Journal of Neurobiology, 28,* 114–125.

Snowdon, C. T. (1998). The nurture of nature: Social, developmental, and environmental controls of aggression. *Behavioral and Brain Sciences, 21,* 384–385.

Soma, K. K., Bindra, R. K., Gee, J., Wingfield, J. C., & Schlinger, B. A. (1999). Androgen-metabolizing enzymes show region-specific changes across the breeding season in the brain of a wild songbird. *Journal of Neurobiology, 41,* 176–88.

Soma, K. K., Sullivan, K., & Wingfield, J. C. (1999). Combined aromatase inhibitor and antiandrogen treatment decreases territorial aggression in a wild songbird during the nonbreeding season. *General and Comparative Endocrinology, 115,* 442–453.

Soma, K. K., & Wingfield, J. C. (2001). Dehydroepiandrosterone in songbird plasma: Seasonal regulation and relationship to territorial aggression. *General and Comparative Endocrinology, 123,* 144–155.

Soma, K. K., Wissman, A. M., Brenowitz, E. A., & Wingfield, J. C. (2002). Dehydroepiandrosterone (DHEA) increases male aggression and the size of an associated brain region. *Homones and Behavior, 41,* 203–212.

Sperry, T. S., Thompson, C. K., & Wingfield, J. C. (2003). Effects of acute treatment with 8-OH-DPAT and fluoxetine on aggressive behavior in male song sparrows (*Melospiza melodia morphna*). *Journal of Neuroendocrinology, 15,* 150–160.

Stutchbury, B. J. M., & Morton, E. S. (2001). *Behavioral ecology of tropical birds.* San Diego: Academic Press.

Tanabe, Y., Saito, N., & Nakamura, T. (1986). Onotgenetic steroidogenesis by testes, ovary and adrenals and embryonic and postembryonic development in chickens (*Gallus domesticus*). *General and Comparative Endocrinology, 63,* 456–463.

Thompson, C. W., & Moore, M. C. (1991). Throat color reliably signals status in male tree lizards, *Urosaurus ornatus. Animal Behaviour, 42,* 745–753.

Tramontin, A. D., & Brenowitz, E. A. (2000). Seasonal plasticity in the adult brain. *Trends in Neurosciences, 23,* 251–258.

Tramontin, A. D., Hartman, V. N., & Brenowitz, E. A. (2000). Breeding conditions induce rapid and sequential growth in adult avian song control circuits:

A model of seasonal plasticity in the brain. *Journal of Neuroscience, 20,* 854–861.

Trillmich, F. (1986). Attendance behavior of Galapagos fur seals. In R. L. Gentry & G. L. Koyman (Eds.), *Fur seals. Maternal strategies on land and at sea* (pp. 34–51). Princeton, NJ: Princeton University Press.

Trillmich, F. (1990). The behavioral ecology of maternal effort in fur seals and sea lions. *Behaviour, 114,* 1–4.

Tsutsui, K., & Yamazaki, T. (1995). Avian neurosteroids. 1. Pregnenolone synthesis in the quail brain. *Brain Research, 78,* 1–9.

Ukena, K., Honda, Y., Inai, Y., Kohchi, C., Lea, R., & Tsustui, K. (1999). Expression and activity of 3β-hydroxysteroid dehydrogenase/Δ^5-Δ^4-isomevase in different regions of the avian brain. *Brain Research, 818,* 536–542.

Van Jaarsveld, A. S., & Skinner, J. D. (1987). Spotted hyaena monomorphism: An adaptive "phallusy"? *South African Journal of Science, 83,* 612–615.

Vanson, A., Arnold, A. P., & Schlinger, B. A. (1996). 3α-hydroxysteroid dehydrogenase isomerase and aromatase activity in primary cultures of developing zebra finch telencephalon: Dehydroepiandrosterone as substrate for synthesis of androstenedione and estrogens *General Comparative Endrocrinology, 102,* 342–350.

Viglietti-Panzica, C., Balthazart, J., Plumari, L., Fratesi, S., Absil, P., & Panzica, G. (2001). Estradiol mediates effects of testosterone on vasotocin immunoreactivity in the adult quail brain. *Hormones and Behavior, 40,* 445–461.

Vleck, C. M., & Dobrott, S. J. (1993). Testosterone, anti-androgen and alloparental behavior in bobwhite quail foster fathers. *Hormones and Behavior, 27,* 92–107.

Welty, J., & Baptista, L. (1988). *The life of birds* (4th ed.). New York: Saunders College.

Wikelski, M., Hau, M., Robinson, W. D., & Wingfield, J. C. (2003). Reproductive seasonality of seven neotropical passerine species. *Condor, 105,* 683–695.

Wikelski, M., Hau, M., & Wingfield, J. C. (1999). Social instability increases plasma testosterone in a year-round territorial neotropical bird. *Proceedings of the Royal Society of London, Series B, 266,* 551–556.

Wikelski, M., Hau, M., & Wingfield, J. C. (2000). Seasonality of reproduction in a neotropical rain forest bird. *Ecology, 81,* 2458–2472.

Wikelski, M., Lynn, S., Breuner, C., Wingfield, J. C., & Kenagy, G. J. (2001). Metabolic rates, testosterone and corticosterone in white-crowned sparrows. *Comparative Biochemistry and Physiology* A, 185, 463–470.

Wikelski, M., Spinney, L., Schelski, W., Scheuerlein, A., & Gwinner, E. (2003). Slow pace of life in tropical sedentary birds: A common-garden experiment on four stonechat populations from different latitudes.

Proceedings of the Royal Society of London, Series B, 270, 2383–2388.

Wilczynski, W., Allison, J. D., & Marler, C. A. (1993). Sensory pathways linking social and environmental cues to endocrine regions of amphibian forebrains. *Brain Behavior and Evolution, 42,* 252–264.

Wingfield, J. C. (1985a). Environmental and endocrine control of territorial behavior in birds. In B. K. Follett, S. Ishii, & A. Chandola (Eds.), *The endocrine system and the environment* (pp. 265–277). Tokyo: Japan Science Society Press/Berlin: Springer-Verlag.

Wingfield, J. C. (1985b). Short term changes in plasma levels of hormones during establishment and defense of a breeding territory in male song sparrows, *Melospiza melodia. Hormones and Behavior, 19,* 174–187.

Wingfield, J. C. (1988). Changes in reproductive function of free-living birds in direct response to environmental perturbations. In M. H. Stetson (Ed.), *Processing of environmental information in vertebrates* (pp. 121–148). Berlin: Springer-Verlag.

Wingfield, J. C. (1994a). Control of territorial aggression in a changing environment. *Psychoneuroendocrinology, 19,* 709–721.

Wingfield, J. C. (1994b). Hormone-behavior interactions and mating systems in male and female birds. In R.V. Short & E. Balaban (Eds.), *The difference between the sexes* (pp. 303–330). Cambridge: Cambridge University Press.

Wingfield, J. C. (1994c). Regulation of territorial behavior in the sedentary song sparrow, *Melospiza melodia morphna. Hormones and Behavior, 28,* 1–15.

Wingfield, J. C. (2005). Allostatic load and life cycles. Implications for neuroendocrine control mechanisms. In J. Schulkin (ed.), *Allostasis.* Cambridge, MA: MIT Press.

Wingfield, J. C., Breuner, C., Jacobs, J., Lynn, S., Maney, D., Ramenofsky, M., et al. (1998). Ecological bases of hormone-behavior interactions: The "emergency life history stage." *American Zoologist, 38,* 191–206.

Wingfield, J. C., Doak, D., & Hahn, T. P. (1993). Integration of environmental cues regulating transitions of physiological state, morphology and behavior. In P. J. Sharp (Ed.), *Avian endocrinology* (pp. 111–122). Bristol, UK: Journal of Endocrinology, Inc.

Wingfield, J. C., & Farner, D. S. (1993). The endocrinology of wild species. In D. S. Farner, J. R. King, & K. C. Parkes (Eds.), *Avian biology* (Vol. 9, pp. 163–327). New York: Academic Press.

Wingfield, J. C., & Hahn, T. P. (1994). Testosterone and territorial behavior in sedentary and migratory sparrows. *Animal Behaviour, 47,* 77–89.

Wingfield, J. C., Hahn, T. P., Levin, R., & Honey, P. (1992). Environmental predictability and control of gonadal cycles in birds. *Journal of Experimental Zoology, 261,* 214–231.

Wingfield, J. C., Hegner, R. E., Dufty, A. M., Jr., & Ball, G. F. (1990). The "Challenge Hypothesis": Theoretical implications for patterns of testosterone secretion, mating systems, and breeding strategies. *American Naturalist, 136,* 829–846.

Wingfield, J. C., & Jacobs, J. D. (1999). The interplay of innate and experiential factors regulating the life history cycle of birds. In N. Adams & R. Slotow (Eds.), *Proceedings of the 22nd International Ornithological Congress* (pp. 2417–2443). Johannesburg: BirdLife South Africa.

Wingfield, J. C., Jacobs, J., & Hillgarth, N. (1997). Ecological constraints and the evolution of hormone-behavior interrelationships. In C. S. Carter, I. I. Lederhendler, & B. Kirkpatrick (Eds.), *The integrative neurobiology of affiliation* (Vol. 807, pp. 22–41). New York: New York Academy of Science.

Wingfield, J. C., Jacobs, J. D., Tramontin, A. D., Perfito, N., Meddle, S., Maney, D. L., et al. (1999). Toward an ecological basis of hormone-behavior interactions in reproduction of birds. In K. Wallen & J. Schneider (Eds.), *Reproduction in context* (pp. 85–128). Cambridge, MA: MIT Press.

Wingfield, J. C., & Kenagy, G. J. (1991). Natural regulation of reproductive cycles. In M. Schreibman & R. E. Jones (Eds.), *Vertebrate endocrinology: Fundamentals and biomedical implications* (Vol. 4, Pt. B, pp. 181–241). New York: Academic Press.

Wingfield, J. C., Lynn, S. E., & Soma, K. K. (2001). Avoiding the "costs" of testosterone: Ecological bases of hormone-behavior interactions. *Brain Behavior and Evolution, 57,* 239–251.

Wingfield, J. C., & Monk, D. (1992). Control and context of year-round territorial aggression in the nonmigratory song sparrow, *melospiza melodia morphna. Omis Scandinavica, 23,* 298–303.

Wingfield, J. C., & Monk, D. (1994). Behavioral and hormonal responses of male song sparrows to estrogenized females during the non-breeding season. *Hormones and Behavior, 28,* 146–154.

Wingfield, J. C., & Ramenofsky, M. (1985). Hormonal and environmental control of aggression in birds. In R. Gilles & J. Balthazart (Eds.), *Neurobiology* (pp. 92–104). Berlin: Springer-Verlag.

Wingfield, J. C., & Ramenofsky, M. (1999). Hormones and the behavioral ecology of stress. In P. H. M. Balm (Ed.), *Stress physiology in animals* (pp. 1–51). Sheffield, UK: Sheffield Academic Press.

Wingfield, J. C., Ramos-Fernandez, G., Nuñez-de la Mora, A., & Drummond, H. (1999). The effects of an "El Niño" Southern Oscillation event on reproduction in male and female blue-footed boobies, *Sula nebouxii. General and Comparative Endocrinology, 114,* 163–172.

Wingfield, J. C., & Romero, L. M. (2000). Adrenocortical responses to stress and their modulation in free-living vertebrates. In B. S. McEwen (Ed.), *Handbook of physiology, section 7: The endrocrine system, volume 4: Coping with the environment: Neural and endocrine mechanisms* (pp. 211–236). Oxford: Oxford University Press.

Wingfield, J. C., & Silverin, B. (1986). Effects of corticosterone on territorial behavior of free-living song sparrows, *Melospiza melodia. Hormones and Behavior, 20,* 405–417.

Wingfield, J. C., & Soma, K. K. (2002). Spring and autumn territoriality: Same behavior different mechanisms? *Integrative and Comparative Biology, 42,* 11–20.

Wingfield, J. C., Soma, K. K., Wikelski, M., Meddle, S. L., & Hau, M. (2001). Life cycles, behavioral traits and endocrine mechanisms. In A. Dawson & C. M. Chaturvedi (Eds.), *Avian endocrinology* (pp. 3–17). New Delhi, India: Narosa.

Wingfield, J. C., & Wada, M. (1989). Male-male interactions increase both luteinizing hormone and testosterone in the song sparrow, *Melospiza melodia*: Specificity, time course and possible neural pathways. *Journal of Comparative Physiology, A, 166,* 189–194.

Wingfield, J. C., Whaling, C. S., & Marler, P. R. (1994). Communication in vertebrate aggression and reproduction: The role of hormones. In E. Knobil & J. D. Neill (Eds.), *The physiology of reproduction* (2nd ed.). New York: Raven Press.

Witschi, E. (1961). Sex and secondary sexual characters. In A. J. Marshall (Ed.), *Biology and comparative physiology of birds* (Vol. 2, pp. 115–168). New York: Academic Press.

Woodley, S. K., & Moore, M. C. (1999). Ovarian hormones influence territorial aggression in free-living female mountain spiny lizards. *Hormones and Behavior, 35,* 205–214.

Woodroffe, R., Macdonald, D. W., & Cheeseman, C. L. (1997). Endocrine correlates of contrasting male mating strategies in the European badger (*Meles meles*). *Journal of Zoology, 241,* 291–300.

Woods, J. E., & Brazzil, D. M. (1981). Plasma 17ß-estradiol levels in the chick embryo. *General and Comparative Endocrinology, 44,* 37–43.

Zakon, H. H., & Dunlap, K. D. (1999). Sex hormones and communication signals: A tale of two species. *Brain Behavior and Evolution, 54,* 61–69.

Zakon, H. H., & Smith, G. T. (2001). Hormones, behavior, and electric fish. In D. Pfaff, A. Arnold, A. Etgen, S. Fahrbach, & R. Rubin (Eds.), *Hormones, brain and behavior.* New York: Academic Press.

9

Androgens and Aggression

Neal G. Simon & Shi-Fang Lu

Androgens contribute to the expression of aggressive behavior. Although this is one of the most widely recognized and oft-cited relationships in behavioral endocrinology, the characterization of precisely how androgens influence aggression remains a work in progress. Factors contributing to this state of affairs are bidirectional. On the one hand, rapid advances in our understanding of molecular, cellular, and biochemical processes that mediate androgenic effects (e.g., Lee & Chang, 2003) continue to drive revisions in increasingly sophisticated models of behavioral regulation. In contrast, studies with clinical populations that attempt to discern hormonal contributions often face significant methodological limitations that, when combined with a lack of specificity in defining forms of aggression, often yield equivocal results (Archer, 1988, 1991). Fortunately, recent trends in this area are improving as subtypes of aggression, including hostility, irritability, impulsivity, and dominance, are increasingly recognized in the literature rather than "aggression" as a global construct (reviewed in Simon, 2002).

This chapter utilizes conspecific, offensive aggression in males and females as model systems to exemplify androgenic influences on aggressive behavior. This form of aggression is a productive behavior exhibited between same-sex conspecifics; its effects are reflected in dominance status and access to resources.

The rationale for using offensive aggression in males as a model is straightforward because its dependence on testosterone (T), the principle testicular androgen, is well established (Nelson, 2000). Although including females may seem surprising, several studies conducted over the past 20 years have shown that females housed in small group settings regularly displayed aggression toward other females, juvenile males, or gonadectomized adult males (Brain & Haug, 1992) and that dehydroepiandrosterone (DHEA), an androgenic neurosteroid synthesized in the brains of humans and other mammals (Baulieu, 1997; Compagnone & Mellon, 2000), played a substantive role in the regulation of this form of aggression. Interestingly, recent studies of seasonal variation in aggression in several avian species suggested that DHEA also may contribute to the display of male-typical aggression outside the breeding season (Hau, Stoddard, & Soma, 2004; Soma & Wingfield, 2001; see Wingfield, Moore, Goymann, Wacker, & Sperry, ch. 8 in this volume).

In considering male-typical and female-typical aggression, a systems perspective is utilized to frame the relationship between androgens and conspecific offensive aggression (figure 9.1). This perspective relies on a robust behavioral end point, aggression, and draws on recent developments in biochemistry, cell biology, and molecular biology to allow the framing of integrative

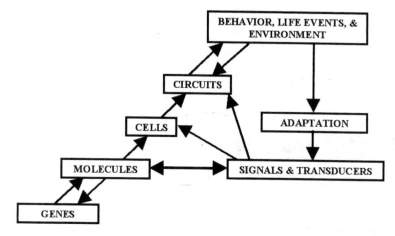

FIGURE 9.1 A summary of the kinds of data required to characterize hormonal processes involved in the regulation of sex-typical aggression with a systems framework. Progress in developing this type of model likely will require a multidisciplinary approach to the analysis of aggression, including drawing on molecular and cell biology, bioinformatics, physiology, ethology, ecology, and evolutionary biology. The application of a systems analysis to the relationship between androgens and offensive aggression should yield a model that integrates events from the gene level to behavioral expression and adaptation based on experience.

regulatory models that span gene function through behavioral expression (Nelson & Chiavegatto, 2001). Ultimately, it is likely that advances in proteomics (see discussions in Collins & Jegalian, 1999, and Vukmirovic & Tilghman, 2000) will be an essential element in comprehensive models of behavioral regulation, although this line of research is in its formative stages with regard to aggression and other behaviors.

Environmental influences on behavior and adaptive responses to these events represent an important feature of the systems approach. In this context, it is important to recognize that factors including, but not limited to, cognition, age, diet, experience, and culture can influence signaling pathways.

Regulatory Models in Males and Females: Common Elements

Neuromodulator Hypothesis

An important theoretical question is whether a construct that bridges androgenic influences on aggressive behavior in both males and females can be advanced. Our position is that such a construct can be put forward based on the premise that the contribution of androgens to the regulation of aggression is through their actions as modulators of neurochemical function.

The *neuromodulator hypothesis* allows the integration of data from endocrine, neurochemical, and peptide systems that are currently recognized as critical factors in the regulation of conspecific aggression. The potential strengths of this model are that (a) it is integrative and (b) it may help bridge basic and clinical considerations related to androgen function and aggression. The neuromodulator hypothesis is illustrated by considering androgenic processes that regulate aggression in adulthood and how these processes interact with representative neurochemical systems.

Metabolism

Any consideration of the effect of T on conspecific aggression in males requires including its major metabolites estradiol (E_2), a product of aromatization, and 5α-dihydrotestosterone (DHT), derived through the action of 5α-reductase. Whereas aromatization is widely recognized as an important step in the promotion of aggression by T (Balthazart, Baillien, Charlier, Cornil, & Ball, 2003; Simon, McKenna, Lu, & Cologer-Clifford, 1996), a small, substantive body of evidence has demonstrated that androgens can directly induce male-typical fighting behavior (e.g., Luttge & Hall, 1973; Simon, Whalen, & Tate, 1985). Embedded in the process of defining the contributions of each metabolite are related questions about enzyme distribution

(Celloti, Negri-Cesi, & Poletti, 1997; Melcangi et al., 1998; Naftolin, Horvath, & Balthazart, 2001; Silverin, Baillien, Foidart, & Balthazart, 2000) and their relationship to neural sites implicated in male-typical aggression. A number of approaches have been employed to address the role of T metabolites. These investigations have generally used rodents in the resident-intruder test paradigm and included behavioral assessments in mice with naturally occurring mutations (e.g., Tfm), disruptions of specific steroid receptor genes (ERα, ERβ), pharmacological manipulations (enzymatic inhibitors), and comparisons among outbred strains in the postcastration response to specifically acting androgens and estrogens after gonadectomy.

Interestingly, a parallel situation can be found concerning the modulatory effect of DHEA on female-typical aggression in that multiple metabolites also may be involved. The biosynthesis and metabolism of DHEA have been studied extensively (Baulieu, 1997; Compagnone & Mellon, 2000; Labrie, 2003) and are shown in figure 9.2. In the context of aggression, the 3β-hydroxysteroid dehydrogenase (3β-HSD), hydroxysteroid sulfotransferase (HST), steroid sulfatase

(SST), and CYP7B pathways all merit attention. The formation of androstenedione in response to 3β-HSD activity can lead to the formation of more potent androgens and potentially estrogens; the relative activity of HST and SST determine the potential contributions of DHEA sulfate (DHEA-S) versus DHEA, and CYP7B family activity leads to the production of 7α- and 7β-hydroxy DHEA, with the former representing the major metabolite of DHEA in both hippocampus and hypothalamus (Cui, Lin, & Belsham, 2003; Jellinck, Lee, & McEwen, 2001). Although substantially less is known about the potential contribution of these metabolites to female-typical aggression, both genomic and nongenomic effects may be involved. Support for genomic effects comes from the demonstration of direct androgenic effects of DHEA itself and the observation that more potent androgens are formed from DHEA in peripheral tissues (Labrie, 2003; Lu, Mo, Hu, Garippa, & Simon, 2003; Mo, Lu, Hu, & Simon, 2004). In relation to nongenomic effects of DHEA, metabolism is important because there are differences in the potency of DHEA versus DHEA-S as negative modulators of the GABA$_A$ receptor (Majewska, Demirgoren, Spivak, & London, 1990).

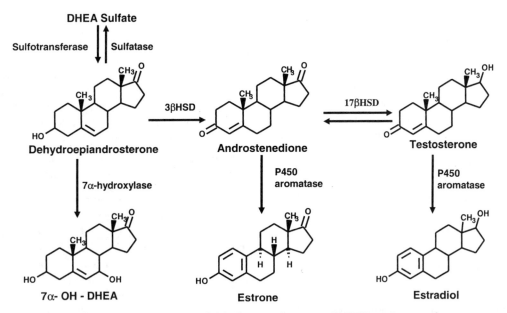

FIGURE 9.2 A summary of the metabolism of dehydroepiandrosterone (DHEA) in the central nervous system. Three pathways have been identified with DHEA as the initial substrate: (1) to DHEA sulfate, a reversible path involving hydroxysteroid sulfotransferase and steroid sulfatase, (2) from 7α or 7β-hydroxyl DHEA, which involves CYP7B pathways, and (3) to androstenedione, which involves 3β-hydroxysteroid dehydrogenase and provides the possibility for the formation of more potent androgens and estrogens.

Males

The ability of T to facilitate the display of intermale aggressive behavior has been extensively documented in a broad range of species. This was demonstrated clearly and unequivocally through castration–hormone replacement experiments and studies of seasonal effects on testicular function and behavior (Nelson, 2000). With the establishment of this fundamental relationship, the focus of research shifted to a mechanistic orientation. Although rodent models have been a principal tool in these investigations, a number of contributing studies have employed species ranging from fish to lizards and, increasingly, birds (Elofsson, Mayer, Damsgard, & Winberg, 2000; Godwin & Crews, 2002; Rhen & Crews, 2000; Wingfield, Jacobs, & Hillgarth, 1997). These studies characterized pathways in the adult central nervous system (CNS) through which T promoted the display of aggressive behavior. Comparisons of sex and strain differences in the response to this testicular hormone and its major metabolites, E_2 and DHT, as well as studies using enzymatic inhibitors and receptor antagonists, were important steps in elaborating these pathways (Simon, 2002).

The biobehavioral findings led to the development of hypotheses about steroid receptor function and cellular mechanisms involved in the hormonal regulation of aggression. The overarching goal was to integrate biochemical, immunochemical, and behavioral results to describe the cell and molecular processes that regulate sensitivity to the aggression-promoting property of gonadal steroids. We believe that achieving this objective will require more than a strict consideration of only hormonal systems. Progress will be tied to defining interactions between steroidal and relevant neurochemical systems. The most extensive studies of hormonal modulation to this point have been on serotonin (5-hydroxytryptamine, or 5-HT) function in males, while the modulation of $GABA_A$ receptor function by DHEA has been a major focus of studies in females. These relationships are presented to exemplify the neuromodulator hypothesis.

Regulation in the Adult

Testosterone can promote the display of aggression in adult males through four distinct pathways (Simon, 2002; Simon et al., 1996):

1. Androgen-sensitive, which responds to T itself or its 5α-reduced metabolite, DHT

2. Estrogen-sensitive, which uses E_2 derived by aromatization of T
3. Synergistic or combined, in which both the androgenic and estrogenic metabolites of T are used to facilitate behavioral expression
4. Direct T-mediated, which utilizes T itself

All of these steroid-sensitive systems are not necessarily present in every male. Rather, the functional pathway appears to be determined by genotype. The most common system uses E_2 as the active agent, which supports a key role for aromatization and the importance of the estrogen receptor. Regardless of the functional system, in males these pathways share the basic feature of high sensitivity. After the postcastration decline in fighting behavior in rats or mice, it takes an average of only 2 to 3 days of hormone treatment with the appropriate steroid at physiological doses to restore aggression to levels seen in intact males.

Neural Steroid Receptors

Pharmacological methods, including the use of specifically acting androgens and estrogens, allowed characterization of multiple neuroendocrine pathways through which T promotes aggressive behavior. Findings in these studies provide a basis for investigating the functions of androgen receptor (AR) and estrogen receptor (ER) in the regulation of aggression. The time frame for the hormonal activation of aggressive behavior in gonadectomized male mice and other rodents following castration (2 to 3 days) is generally consistent with a genomic effect. Our understanding of these processes in relation to the steroidal regulation of aggression, however, is not as well developed in comparison to, for example, reproductive behaviors.

Androgen Receptor

Autoradiographic and immunocytochemical methods have permitted the construction of detailed AR distribution maps. Major regions exhibiting positive immunoreactivity in rodents include the bed nucleus of the stria terminalis (BNST), lateral septum (LS), medial preoptic area (MPOA), and medial amygdala (MAMYG), regions that constitute part of the neuroanatomical substrate for conspecific aggression based on lesion and implant studies (reviewed in Simon, Lu, McKenna, Chen, & Clifford, 1996; Simon et al., 1993). Although, these descriptive findings are valuable for defining functional circuitry, they do not reveal how the regulation of AR itself contributes to behavioral expression. One possibility is that neural AR regulation might differ between males and females, which could be a contributing mechanism to variation in behavioral sensitivity. Among possible studies on this question are assessments of AR mRNA regulation, which potentially provide direct indices of changes in transcriptional activity, or an examination of alterations in the level of AR protein under differing hormonal conditions, which would provide a more direct measure (Ross, 1996).

The effects of castration with or without testosterone propionate (TP) replacement on AR protein regulation in several brain regions were compared in adult male and female CF-1 mice, a strain that has an androgen-sensitive system and is highly aggressive. The results for BNST, which were typical of all regions studied, are shown as an example of the findings (figure 9.3). Gonadectomy led to a rapid loss of immunostaining, while TP replacement led to nearly a twofold increase in AR density in both sexes. Western blot analyses confirmed these results.

Common regulation of AR in both male and female neural tissue strongly indicates that the observed rapid increase in AR protein level by itself is not sufficient to produce parallel changes in behavioral responsiveness. This is because the activation of male-typical aggression in ovariectomized females requires 16–21 days of androgen treatment, while the AR level increased dramatically within 24 hr. These findings suggest that increased cellular AR content probably triggers enhanced (or suppressed) transcription of other androgen-regulated genes, which in combination leads to the expression of aggression. The extended time frame required to induce malelike aggression in females raises interesting possibilities, with one being that the receptor complex promotes elaboration of an androgen-dependent circuit through interactions with or the regulation of growth factors (Bimonte-Nelson, et al., 2003; Yang & Arnold, 2000; Yang, Verhovshek, & Sengelaub, 2004). A comparable view of a complex relationship between AR immunoreactivity and responsiveness to the masculine sexual behavior-promoting effect of T has been put forward based on findings in hamsters (Meek, Romeo, Novak, & Sisk, 1997). The concept of AR-induced circuit remodeling is roughly analogous to that which has been described in the adult male canary brain, where a testosterone-dependent increase in BDNF appears to play an important role in the viability of neurons in the high vocal center

(Rasika, Alveraz-Buylla, & Nottebohm, 1999). Also consistent with the possibility of AR-induced circuitry are the pronounced sexual dimorphisms in neural pathways mediating reproductive behaviors (Hutton, Guibao, & Simerly, 1998; Simerly, 1998). Several of these structures, including the vomeronasal organ, accessory olfactory bulbs, medial and posterior nuclei of the amygdala, and BNST, are part of circuits that process pheromonal and other olfactory stimuli (Segovia & Guillamon, 1993; Simerly, 1998; Van den Bergh, 1994). Because intermale aggression is triggered by a pheromonal stimulus, androgenic stimulation may function to establish this pathway in females and maintain it in normal males.

Estrogen Receptor

Defining the potential role of ER in the regulation of aggression became more complicated when a novel form of the receptor, ERβ, was cloned from rat and human cDNA libraries (Giguere, Tremblay, & Tremblay, 1998; Kuiper, Enmark, Pelto-Huikko, Nilsson, & Gustafsson, 1996; Kuiper, Shughure, Merchenthaler, & Gustafsson, 1998). It differs from ERα in two important aspects. First, many synthetic or naturally occurring ligands, including estradiol, exhibit different relative affinities for ERα versus ERβ (Kuiper et al., 1997; Sun et al., 1999). Second, both the pattern and level of ERα and ERβ mRNA expression differ in relative tissue distribution and cellular localization (Shughrue, Lane, & Merchenthaler, 1997; Shughrue, Lane, Scrimo, & Merchenthaler, 1998).

Studies by Ogawa et al. (Ogawa, Lubahn, Korach, & Pfaff, 1997; Ogawa, Washburn, Lubahn, Korach & Pfaff, 1998; Ogawa et al., 1999; see Ogawa, Nomura, Choleris, & Pfaff, ch. 10 in this volume) in male mice demonstrated a primary role for ERα in male-typical aggression. Initially, aggressive behavior by intact ERα knockout (ERKO) males in the resident-intruder and homogeneous set designs was assessed (for descriptions of these paradigms, see Simon, 1979). Offensive attacks were rarely displayed by ERKO males, whereas wild-type (WT) and heterozygous males showed significantly greater attack durations.

Next, castration–hormone replacement data were developed (Ogawa et al., 1998). These results showed that daily TP injections were ineffective in promoting aggression in ERKO males and highly effective in gonadectomized WT males. This confirmed that ERKO males only have an estrogen-responsive regulatory sys-

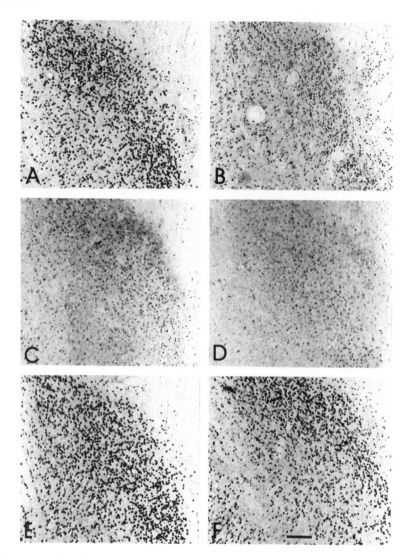

FIGURE 9.3 Representative immunocytochemical sections showing androgen receptor (AR) immunoreactivity in the bed nucleus of the stria terminalis-posterior aspect (BNSTp) in groups of male and female mice that were intact, gonadectomized (GDX), or gonadectomized and treated with TP (GDX + TP). (A) Intact male, (B) intact female, (C) GDX male, (D) GDX female, (E) GDX + TP male, (F) GDX female + TP. This pattern of group differences in AR regulation was seen in all regions examined. Bar, 100 µm. From "Neural Androgen Receptor: Sex Differences and Similarities in Autoregulation," by S. Lu, N. Simon, S. McKenna, G. Nau, and A. Cologer-Clifford, 1998, *Endocrinology, 139*, p. 1597. Copyright 1998 by The Endocrine Society. Reprinted with permission.

tem. The third report examined aggression in ERβ knockout (βERKO) mice. In accord with a model that views ERα as the active primary receptor in aggression, these animals exhibited normal or enhanced attack behavior compared to WT males (Ogawa et al., 1999).

This is not to say that ERβ is without influence on male-typical aggression. A recent investigation in cynomolgus monkeys (Simon, Kaplan, Hu, Register, & Adams, 2004) raised several potential ways that ERβ could effect aggressive behavior. Males were fed diets containing high or low levels of soy phytoestrogens for 15 months. Those on the high soy diet exhibited significantly higher levels of agonistic behavior than monkeys fed a control diet. Soy estrogens preferentially bind to ERβ and are less active than estradiol-ERβ complexes in transcriptional activity in reporter assays

(Jefferson, Padilla-Banks, Clark, & Newbold, 2002; Kuiper et al., 1997). Potential mechanisms underlying the more extreme agonism include decreased 5-HT function in dorsal raphe, where ERβ is the sole subtype thus far detected in primates, or decreased modulation of ERα:ERβ heterodimers, leading to enhanced ERα activity. These concepts are supported by in vitro assays, available immunochemical findings, and results with βERKO mice (Alves et al., 2000; An, Tzagarakis-Foster, Scharschmidt, Lomri, & Leitman, 2001; Bethea, Lu, Gundlah, & Streicher, 2002; Liu et al., 2002; Nomura, McKenna, Korach, Pfaff, & Ogawa, 2002; Weihua, et al., 2000; Yi, Bhagat, Hilf, Bambara, & Muyan, 2002), but remain speculative pending experimental tests. A more detailed consideration of ER subtypes and aggression can be found elsewhere in this volume (see Ogawa et al., ch. 10).

Hormonal Modulation of 5-HT Function

Although virtually every known neurotransmitter system has been implicated at some point in the regulation of aggression, a compelling body of pharmacological and molecular biological studies indicates that 5-HT, via its action at the 5-HT_{1A} and 5-HT_{1B} receptors, represents a major neurochemical regulatory signal in numerous species (Birger et al., 2003; Ferris, 2000; Kravitz, 2000; Panskepp, Yue, Drerup, & Huber, 2003; Simon, Cologer-Clifford, Lu, McKenna, & Hu, 1998). A basic conclusion of this research is that diminished or reduced serotonergic function is associated with increased aggression, while elevated serotonergic tone is associated with reduced levels of aggressive behavior. These relationships have been demonstrated in species ranging from crustaceans to rodents to primates, including humans (Birger et al., 2003; Kravitz, 2000; Simon et al., 1998).

Concerning 5-HT function in intermale aggression, findings have consistently demonstrated that drugs with selective affinity for 5-HT_1 receptors, particularly mixed 5-HT_{1A} and 5-HT_{1B} agonists, specifically and selectively reduced offensive aggression (Olivier, Mos, Raghoebar, de Koning, & Mak, 1994; Olivier, Mos, Van Oorschot, & Hen, 1995). Gonadal hormones may promote behavioral activation by modulating 5-HT function in one or more brain regions that are part of the neuroanatomical substrate for intermale aggression. This aspect of the neuromodulator hypothesis is supported by autoradiographic and in situ hybridization studies that demonstrated overlapping distributions of androgen-,

estrogen-, and 5-HT-concentrating neurons and receptor gene expression in these regions (e.g., Herbison, 1995; Lu, Simon, McKenna, Nau, & Cologer-Clifford, 1998; Mengod et al., 1996; Palacios, Waeber, Hoyer, & Mengod, 1990; Simerly, Chang, Muramatsu, & Swanson, 1990; Wright, Seroogy, Lundgren, Davis, & Jennes, 1995). These observations do not, however, directly test how 5-HT function is affected by gonadal steroids in the context of offensive intermale aggression. This requires delineating whether androgens or estrogens differentially affect the ability of 5-HT_{1A}, 5-HT_{1B}, or combined agonist treatments to modulate offensive intermale aggression, identifying sites in the brain where these effects are produced, and whether androgen or estrogens influence 5-HT_{1A} or 5-HT_{1B} function in these regions by altering any of several aspects of 5-HT function.

Androgenic and estrogenic effects on 5-HT_{1A} and 5-HT_{1B} function in the context of offensive aggression have been described in two investigations (Cologer-Clifford, Simon, & Smoluk, 1997; Cologer-Clifford, Smoluk, Lu, & Simon, 1999). Experiments using systemic administration constituted an initial step in defining the relationship between functional hormonal pathways and the modulation of serotonergic effects on offensive intermale aggression. The findings demonstrated that serotonergic agents, in the presence of androgen, were far more effective in reducing the display of fighting behavior than estrogen. The results showed that if estrogens are present, either alone or as a product of aromatization, there are restrictive conditions for the inhibition of male-typical offensive aggression by 5-HT_{1A} and 5-HT_{1B} agonists. In contrast, when aggression is promoted by a direct androgenic effect, 5-HT_{1A} and 5-HT_{1B} agonists are very effective in decreasing the expression of offensive attacks and threats.

A second question involved the potential location in the brain where these effects occurred. Likely sites for modulatory actions on 5-HT_{1A} or 5-HT_{1B} agonist effects of gonadal steroids include the LS, MPOA, MAMYG, and dorsal raphe nucleus (DR) based on receptor distribution and our understanding of neuroanatomical substrates for intermale aggression. In comparisons between LS and MPOA, there were pronounced differences between the two regions in the effects of microinjections. In LS, the presence of DES blocked inhibitory effects of either 5-HT_{1A} or 5-HT_{1B} agonists. When gonadectomized males were implanted with DHT, aggressive behavior was decreased with CGS12066B alone or in combination with 8-OH-DPAT; the 5-HT_{1A} agonist alone was ineffective. The effects of CGS12066B treatment appear to be specific because motor behavior was unaffected in these conditions. These findings demonstrate that at the level of the LS, the androgen-sensitive pathway that facilitates aggression can be attenuated by the action of 5-HT at 5-HT$_{1B}$ receptor sites.

In the MPOA, effects were more pronounced. Both 5-HT$_{1A}$ and 5-HT$_{1B}$ agonist microinjections significantly reduced offensive aggression in the presence of either androgen or estrogen without altering motor behavior. These findings suggest that the MPOA may be a major integrative site for hormone–5-HT interactions in the regulation of T-dependent aggression.

Modulation of the ability of serotonergic agents to effect T-dependent intermale aggression is consistent with the neuromodulator hypothesis. These types of interactions have been well documented in other systems, particularly reproductive behavior (Etgen, 2002; Etgen, Chu, Fiber, Karkanias, & Morales, 1999; Fink, Sumner, Rosie, Wilson, & McQueen, 1999; Hull et al., 1999; McCarthy, 1995; Melton, 2000; Trevino, Wolf, Jackson, Price, & Uphouse, 1999; Uphouse, 2000), anxiety, and mood disorders (Bethea, Mirkes, Shively, & Adams, 2000; Bethea et al., 2002; Fink, Sumner, McQueen, Wilson, & Rosie, 1998; Fink et al., 1999; Pecins-Thompson & Bethea, 1998). The differences in the ability of estrogens and androgens to attenuate the aggression-inhibiting effects of 5-HT$_{1A}$ and 5-HT$_{1B}$ agonists, and the regional variation in these effects, appear to be the most interesting feature of these experiments.

Studies that build on these results might focus on the mechanisms involved in steroidal enhancement or

repression of the ability of 5-HT$_{1A}$ and 5-HT$_{1B}$ agonists to attenuate the display of offensive intermale aggression. Estrogens can affect 5-HT$_{1A}$ function, for example, by altering 5-HT$_{1A}$ gene expression, exerting nongenomic effects on the receptor, or indirectly influencing ligand availability through effects on synthesis, reuptake, or metabolism (Bethea et al., 2000; Chang & Chang, 1999; Gundlah, Lu, & Bethea, 2002; Lu, Eshleman, Janowsky, & Bethea, 2003; McQueen, Wilson, Sumner, & Fink, 1999; Mize & Alper, 2002; Osterlund, Halldin, & Hurd, 2000; Raap et al., 2000; Sumner et al., 1999). Definitive evidence for a direct effect on 5-HT$_{1A}$ gene function requires the identification of an ERE in the promoter region of the 5-HT$_{1A}$ receptor gene. Interestingly, both the mouse and the human 5-HT$_{1A}$ receptor genes appear to contain the classic ERE, as shown in table 9.1.

The difference between the postulated motifs and the consensus sequence is in the spacer element, which is five nucleotides rather than three. However, nonconsensus EREs with varying spacers can effectively regulate transcription of target genes (Berry, Nunez, & Chambon, 1989; Hall, McDonnell, & Korach, 2002; Klungland, Anderson, Kisen, Alestrom, & Tora, 1994; Shupnik & Rosenzweig, 1990; Sohrabji, Miranda, & Toran-Allerand, 1995). The salmon GnRH and BDNF genes have ERE motifs with eight- or nine-nucleotide spacers and can bind activated estrogen receptors in vitro (Klungland et al., 1994; Sohrabji et al., 1995). Regarding indirect influences, estrogen treatment altered 5-HT$_{1A}$ receptor binding and ligand availability (Osterlund et al., 2000). The latter can be produced through several effects, including changes in tryp-

TABLE 9.1 Estrogen Response Elements With Variable Spacers

Species and Gene	Starting Position	DNA Sequence
Traditional spacer ($n = 3$)		
Xenopus vitellogenin A2	−331	GGTCACAGTGACC
Chicken vitellogenin II	−625	GGTCAGCGTGACC
Chicken ovalbumin	−177	GGTAACAATGTGT
Human c-fos	−1209	CGGCAGCGTGACC
Rat prolactin	−1572	TGTCACTATGTCC
Nontraditional spacer ($n > 3$)		
Rat LH-β	−1173	GGACA[N]$_5$TGTCC
Rat BDNF	−1045	GGTGA[N]$_9$TGACC
Salmon GnRH	−1501	GGTCA[N]$_8$TGTCC
Salmon GnRH	−1569	ACTCA[N]$_9$TGACC
Putative human 5-HT1A motif	−429	GGTCA[N]$_5$TGACC
Putative mouse 5-HT1A motif	−426	

tophan hydroxylase activity or transporter gene expression (Bethea et al., 2000; McQueen et al., 1999; Pecins-Thompson & Bethea, 1998). However, to the extent that these effects have been demonstrated in vivo, they have been defined in females. Extrapolating from these studies about mechanisms related to intermale aggression should be done very cautiously. In addition, ERβ potentially may have direct effects on serotonergic function in DR (Alves et al., 2000; Bethea et al., 2002) and, as suggested earlier, may modulate the regulatory actions of ERα.

Females

Studies of a potential relationship between T and female-typical aggression have been motivated by a perspective that aggressive behavior exhibited by females toward conspecifics, other than during lactation, has the same hormonal determinants that had been identified in males. This model, which can be termed the *common path hypothesis*, has produced results with mixed to markedly negative outcomes (e.g., Albert, Walsh, & Jonik, 1993; Stavisky, Register, Watson, Weaver, & Kaplan, 1999; von Engelhardt, Kappeler, & Heistermann, 2000). It appears reasonable to conclude that a different conceptual approach to hormone function in female-typical offensive aggression is needed. A model that focuses on the effects and mechanism of action of the neurosteroid DHEA may have utility. This neurosteroid inhibits female-typical aggression when administered chronically (Baulieu, 1997; Perché, Young, Robel, Simon, & Haug, 2000; Young et al., 1995, 1996).

When housed in triads or other small groups, intact or ovariectomized females reliably display intense attack behavior toward intruder females that are intact, ovariectomized, or lactating (Brain & Haug, 1992; Simon, 2002). This type of aggression appears to be under GABAergic control and is modulated by DHEA (Perché et al., 2000; Young et al., 1991, 1995, 1996), a neurosteroid synthesized by local, in situ mechanisms in the CNS (Baulieu, 1997; Compagnone & Mellon, 2000). Interest in DHEA came from studies that showed extended treatment with this neurosteroid significantly reduced attack behavior by gonadectomized or intact females toward females or lactating females. In addition to modulating GABA function, recent studies suggest that additional processes may contribute to the antiaggressive effect of DHEA. More specifically,

DHEA exerts androgenic effects through the androgen receptor and also may be metabolized to more potent androgenic and estrogenic compounds (Labrie, 2003; Lu et al., 2003; Mo et al., 2004; see figure 9.2).

Neurosteroid DHEA

DHEA and other neurosteroids are modulators of GABA$_A$, N-methyl-D-aspartate (NMDA), and σ$_1$ receptors (Compagnone & Mellon, 2000). The dominant focus of the neurosteroid literature has been on effects exerted at the GABA$_A$ receptor complex (see reviews by Baulieu, 1997, and Rupprecht & Holsboer, 1999). The emphasis on modulation of GABA$_A$ receptor function in the context of female-typical aggression has been supported by several observations. For example, numerous studies have shown pronounced, specific GABAergic effects on offensive aggression (see reviews by Miczek, DeBold, van Erp, & Tornatzky, 1997; Miczek, Fish, & DeBold, 2003; Siegel, Roeling, Gregg, & Kruk, 1999; see Miczek & Fish, ch. 5 in this volume). Second, a smaller number of studies (approximately 30) have examined NMDA receptor involvement in aggression (e.g., Adamec, 1997; Blanchard et al., 1995; Blanchard, McKittrick, Hardy, & Blanchard, 2002; Gould & Cameron, 1997); these studies have demonstrated that the receptor is linked to defensive behavior. Third, there is no evidence, to the best of our knowledge, linking the σ$_1$ receptor to aggression.

Mechanism of Action

The finding of a robust antiaggressive effect of DHEA generated efforts to elucidate underlying mechanisms. There has been a singular emphasis on DHEA-induced alterations in brain levels of pregnenolone sulfate (PREG-S), a neurosteroid that is a negative modulator of the GABA$_A$ receptor and reduces GABAergic effects (Majewska & Schwartz, 1987). DHEA decreases PREG-S levels in whole brain, an action that leads to enhanced GABA function via the GABA$_A$ receptor complex (Robel & Baulieu, 1995). The increased GABA function then inhibits offensive aggression, a premise strongly supported by numerous studies that demonstrated specific inhibitory effects of GABA on attack behavior (Miczek et al., 1997, 2003; Siegel et al., 1999).

Additional process may be involved. One is the upregulation of AR by DHEA in mouse brain and GT1–7 cells, as shown in figure 9.4 (Lu et al., 2003). Western analysis of brain extracts containing LS, BNST, and

MPOA exhibited a dose-dependent increase in AR content in response to DHEA treatment. A similar regulatory effect also was seen in an AR-expressing hypothalamic cell line. This AR upregulation by DHEA was not blocked by trilostane, an inhibitor of 3β-hydroxysteroid dehydrogenase activity responsible for the conversion of DHEA to androstenedione, a more potent androgen. The direct upregulation of AR by DHEA represents a novel mechanistic finding that also may be a potential component of an antiaggressive mechanism. Intact and T-treated GDX males do not exhibit aggression toward female targets and a 15-day treatment course is required for DHEA to reduce aggression (Simon, 2002).

Neurosteroids such as DHEA exert profound effects on the GABA$_A$ receptor. This effect involves multiple sites on the receptor and can be produced by direct action at the membrane level in a time frame from minutes (a nongenomic effect) to longer term processes that involve neurosteroid metabolites, steroidal effects, or both on gene function, which, through alterations in protein synthesis, in turn influence membrane receptor function (a genomic effect).

The structure and function of the GABA$_A$ receptor are reviewed by Barnard et al. (1998) and Mehta and Ticku (1999). The most salient feature is that it is a ligand-gated chloride channel that can be modulated through neurosteroid effects on the GABA site, the benzodiazepine (BZ) site, the Cl$^-$ ionophore (TBPS) site, the barbiturate site, the antagonist site, and an as yet unidentified neurosteroid binding site, as well as by ethanol. For female-typical aggression, however, prevailing models have emphasized an indirect action of DHEA tied to a reduction in the level of PREG-S, another neurosteroid that is a potent negative modulator of GABA$_A$. It has been argued that by reducing PREG-S, possibly via competition for HST, DHEA enhances GABAergic tone and thus decreases aggression. Effects at GABA$_A$ then would involve sites modulated by PREG-S. Fortunately, PREG-S modulates binding at three sites: the Cl$^-$ ionophore, the BZ site, and the GABA agonist site (Majewska, 1995; Majewska, Demirgoren, & London, 1990; Majewska & Schwartz, 1987). DHEA-induced changes in binding need to be assessed at each site in regard to effects at the membrane level, as well as in the context of genomic modulation. Changes in GABA$_A$ receptor gene expression that affect subunit structure, for example, represent another possible pathway for steroidal modulation (Canonaco, Tavolaro, & Maggi, 1993; Herbison & Fenelon, 1995; Mehta & Ticku, 1999; Rupprecht,

et al., 1993). The direct androgenic effects of DHEA and its metabolites thus may represent a cross-talk cellular signaling system (Katzenellenbogen, 1996, 2000; Rupprecht & Holsboer, 1999) linked to its antiaggressive effect. Overall, these observations demonstrate the importance of defining the potential interrelationship among DHEA, its androgenic effects, the subunit structure of GABA$_A$ receptor, and attendant changes in function to fully understand the mechanism of action of this neurosteroid and how it modulates the expression of female-typical aggression.

Even if progress is made in characterizing the mechanisms involved in the modulatory effects of DHEA on the function of GABA$_A$ receptor, establishing their functional significance in relation to female-typical aggression requires additional steps. First, the neuroanatomical circuitry for this form of aggression needs to be defined. Because DHEA modulation of GABA$_A$ can occur through multiple mechanisms that may differ by brain region, this is a complex question. For example, GABA$_A$ receptor subunit structure is a constraint on steroidal effects and varies regionally (Mehta & Ticku, 1999). In addition, AR distribution and the GABA system only partially overlap. Thus, a cross-talk system may be important in some regions, whereas a DHEA-induced reduction in PREG-S may be a key modulatory effect elsewhere.

Humans

Progress in defining the hormonal contribution to human aggressive behavior has been limited by methodological and conceptual considerations. For example, studies have employed concurrent or near-concurrent fluid sampling through attempts to identify relationships between current hormone profiles and past violent acts (e.g., Brooks & Reddon, 1996; Dabbs & Jurkovic, 1991; Gladue, Boechler, McCaul, 1989; Olweus, Mattsson, Schalling, & Low, 1988; Salvador, Suay, Martinez-Sanchis, Simon, & Brain, 1999; van Honk, et al., 1999). Second, systemic T assays are assumed to reflect effects in the brain without an appreciation for the role of intracellular events. There also has been variation in experimental models, from paper and pencil assessments to athletic and staged competitions through criminal histories (e.g., Gonzalez-Bono, Salvador, Serrano, & Ricarte, 1999; McCaul, Claude, & Joppa, 1992; Soler, Vinayak, & Quadagno, 2000; Suay et al., 1999; Thiblin, Runeson, & Rajs, 1999) to an empha-

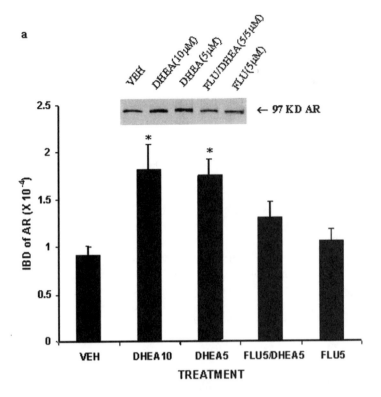

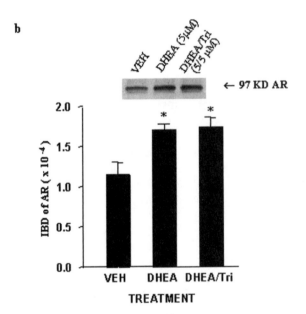

FIGURE 9.4 Cultured GT1–7 cells were treated with 5 μM DHEA with or without flutamide (5 μM) for 48 hr. Cell lysates were analyzed for relative AR concentration. The resulting integrated density of the 97-kDa AR bands was quantified. Concurrent flutamide treatment inhibited the effect of DHEA on AR augmentation (a). In a similar experiment, concurrent trilostane treatment did not block DHEA induced AR upregulation (b). Data shown are mean IBD + *SEM* of 97-kDa AR bands; *significantly different than controls ($p < .05$). From "Dehydroepiandrosterone Upregulates Neural Androgen Receptor and Transcriptional Activity," by S. Lu, Q. Mo, S. Hu, C. Garippa, and N. G. Simon, 2003, *Journal of Neurobiology, 57*, p. 167. Copyright 2003 by Wiley Interscience. Reprinted with permission.

sis on violent, assaultive behavior as an end point (e.g., Banks & Dabbs, 1996; Brooks & Reddon, 1996; Choi & Pope, 1994; Studer, Reddon, Siminoski, 1997; Virkkunen, Goldman, & Linnoila, 1996), rather than on forms of aggressive behavior, such as dominance, that may be facilitated by T (Gray, Jackson, & McKinlay, 1991; Mazur & Booth, 1998). Finally, there is the inherent complexity that results when cognitive, social, cultural, economic, and experiential factors interact with physiological systems. Even with these constraints, there has been progress in assessing how gonadal hormones may influence aggression in human males. This becomes evident when advances in conceptual frameworks are emphasized rather than mechanistic considerations. Hostility, irritability, impulsiveness, and dominance are now used as correlates of T level rather than a global "aggression" construct. As noted in previous chapters, in terms of mechanism, molecular genetics has identified polymorphisms in several genes, including tryptophan hydroxylase, the 5-HT transporter, certain 5-HT receptor subtypes, and monoamine oxidase A (MAO-A), that may be associated with inappropriate or impulsive aggression in some individuals (Arango, Huang, Underwood, & Mann, 2003; Barr et al., 2003; Gorwood, Batel, Ades, Hamon, & Boni, 2000; Manuck, Flory, Ferrell, Mann, & Muldoon, 2000; Shih, Chen, & Ridd, 1999; Veenstra-VanderWeele, Anderson, & Cook, 2000). At the same time, other groups have not found these relationships or have raised issues that temper these findings (Furlong, Rubenstein, Walsh, Paykel, & Rubenstein, 1998; Huang, Grailhe, Argano, Hen, & Mann, 1999; Miczek, 1999). The value of caution in assessing these results is worth emphasizing because molecular biological findings related to aggression, when initially identified, are sometimes interpreted as a definitive cause of inappropriate aggression and violent behavior (e.g., Angier, 1995; summarized chronologically in Enserink, 2000).

It seems premature to directly assess the effects of T or its metabolites in terms of the neuromodulator hypothesis. In humans, there is a need to identify forms of aggression where T has a contributory role. This is likely a controversial issue given the range of T-aggression relationships that have been assessed (see reviews by Albert et al., 1993; Mazur & Booth, 1998; Rubinow & Schmidt, 1996; Rubinow, Schmidt, Roca, & Daly, 2002). Sharpened behavioral definitions, recognition that the effects of T in the CNS are affected by processes not necessarily reflected in systemic measure-

ments (except perhaps in extreme cases, such as large doses of anabolic steroids), and recognition that hormonal effects on behavior in humans may be quite subtle due to factors such as experience are important for progress. For example, it seems reasonable to suggest that dominance interactions and status in males may be influenced by T (Mazur & Booth, 1998). In addition to the aforementioned considerations, the dynamics of T secretion, specifically changes seen in anticipation of and in response to an aggressive interaction and the subsequent effects produced by these changes, may be more important than absolute levels in circulation. This reinforces the need for attention to subtle changes in T secretion as a potentially important influence in human males. One strength of this concept is that it can incorporate normal physiological function in adult males across a range of systemic T values.

Males

Competitive interactions, with or without physical contact, induce a fairly consistent pattern of T secretion—it rises in anticipation and then diverges when the outcome is determined (e.g., McCaul et al., 1992; Gladue et al., 1989). T levels are transiently elevated in winners (i.e., dominance) and significantly lowered in losers (i.e., subordinates). Nonhuman primate studies extend these observations. When dominance status was established through actual contests, for example, changes in T similar to those seen in humans have been observed (Clarke, Kaplan, Bumsted, & Koritnik, 1986; Rose, 1975). In stable group structures, T secretion is suppressed in subordinates (e.g., Kraus, Heistermann, & Kappeler, 1999). Male baboons that shift from subordinate to dominant status begin to show elevated T levels (Virgin & Spolsky, 1997). These findings support the idea that changes in T in response to anticipated or experienced competitive interactions may be most important in primates. Within the frame of the neuromodulator hypothesis, it can be proposed that alterations in T level following dominance interactions or competition produce neuroendocrine changes that modulate neurochemical systems, with attendant effects on mood and behavior. Although speculative pending direct experimental evidence, it is known that estrogen level influences serotonergic tone in rhesus dorsal raphe and chronic stress perturbs both vasopressin and 5-HT function in hamsters (Bethea et al., 2000, 2002; Ferris, 2000).

Females: An Alternative Perspective

Identifying a systematic relationship between T and various forms of aggression in women has been an elusive goal (Bloch, Schmidt, Su, Tobin, & Rubinow, 1998; Cashdan, 1995; Mazur & Booth, 1998; van Goozen, Wiegant, Endert, Helmond, & van de Poll, 1997). Although positive results were sometimes obtained (e.g., Dabbs & Hargrove, 1997), the mixed to negative results should not be surprising because the behaviors assessed ranged from delinquency, self-regard, assertiveness, and various competitive situations to feelings of hostility or irritability over the course of the menstrual cycle. Although a focus on dominance-related behaviors might provide some insights, this more restrictive perspective is uninformative. Women do not exhibit changes in T dynamics comparable to those seen in men in competitive settings (Booth, Shelley, Mazur, & Tharp, 1989; Mazur, Susman, & Edelbrock, 1997) and changes in T concentrations over the menstrual cycle are not positively correlated with mood states associated with aggression (Bloch et al., 1998; van Goozen et al., 1997; although see Eriksson, Sundblad, Lisjo, Modigh, & Andersch, 1992). Nonhuman primate studies largely support the absence of a systematic relationship between androgens and dominance or aggression in females. Even in ring-tailed lemurs, where females are the dominant sex, individual rates of aggression by females toward same-sex individuals were not correlated with circulating androgens (von Engelhardt et al., 2000). A chronic 24-month anabolic steroid treatment regimen also failed to increase aggression in cynomolgus females (Stavisky et al., 1999).

The equivocal to negative results in human and nonhuman primate studies raise several questions about the role of androgens in aggression by human females. A different approach to the relationship between hormones and offensive aggression in women may be needed. Earlier, it was argued that sex-typical aggression in female mice was modulated by DHEA. Whether this pertains to human or nonhuman primates is undetermined, but it suggests that an emphasis on the GABA system and its modulation by neurosteroids might be useful.

Conclusions

Any summary of our understanding of hormonal processes involved in the development and expression of conspecific offensive aggression requires three components: concepts that have been clearly established, areas where there are gaps in knowledge, and issues still needing experimental analysis.

Knowledge is most fully developed in relation to hormonal processes and the expression of conspecific aggression during adulthood in males. The importance of hormone metabolism has been demonstrated; aromatization and 5α-reduction of T in males are critical steps. The intrinsic androgenicity of DHEA and the contribution of its metabolites also may represent important mechanistic steps in females, although this remains an open issue. A critical role for steroid receptors is obvious. Although several target neurochemical systems have been identified, substantial work is needed to identify the full range of cellular processes that are affected, as well as the genomic and nongenomic mechanisms that mediate these effects. Progress in this area is essential for understanding the modulation of neurochemical function by gonadal hormones and neurosteroids. It is an essential step in developing a systems model that eventually should encompass gene regulation, functional circuitry, behavioral expression, and adaptation.

The neuromodulator hypothesis provides an integrative conceptual framework that broadly accounts for the hormonal contribution to sex-typical offensive aggression. Although an emphasis on neuromodulation provides an overarching construct, an interesting feature of the model is that key hormonal systems seem to produce different effects in each sex. In males the net effect of gonadal steroids is neutral or facilitative, while in females it is inhibitory.

Gaps exist concerning neuroanatomical circuitry in males, a subject that could not be addressed due to space limitations. An understanding of neuroanatomical substrates in females is essentially nonexistent and characterization of cell/molecular mechanisms is in its early stages. In males, critical studies defining the molecular interface between T, its metabolites, and components of the 5-HT (and no doubt other) systems are needed. In females, the nongenomic and genomic processes through which DHEA modulates $GABA_A$ receptor function require characterization. This is only a partial list based on the representative systems discussed in this chapter. Efforts to fully characterize hormonal contributions to the expression of offensive aggression will require defining multiple effects covering both genomic and membrane-level actions.

Finally, we could not cover other important aspects of hormone function in offensive aggression. We chose to focus on gonadal steroids in males and one neuro-steroid in females. Other areas of interest, for example, are the effects of corticosteroids and subsequent inter-actions with the 5-HT and vasopressin systems (Ferris, 2000; Haller, Millar, et al., 2000; Haller Halasz, Mikics, Kruk, & Makara, 2000).

Research with animal models demonstrates the com-plex nature of hormonal modulation and the need for increasingly refined models when assessing endocrine contributions to human behavior. There has been progress in classifications. Parsing out hostility, irritabil-ity, impulsivity, and other attributes, for example, is an improvement over grouping very different behaviors under "aggression." Basic research also indicates that focusing on a single genetic or physiological marker as a cause of aggression is very difficult. A systems perspec-tive is required, one that recognizes when hormones may have a role, that the physiological effects are modula-tory, and that social structure, life events, and subsequent adaptations are reflected in alterations in cellular signal-ing pathways and neuroanatomical circuits.

Note

The preparation of this chapter was supported in part by Grant 1 R01 MH59300 from the NIH to N.G.S. and by the H. F. Guggenheim Foundation.

References

Adamec, R. E. (1997). Transmitter systems involved in neural plasticity underlying increased anxiety and defense—implications for understanding anxiety fol-lowing traumatic stress. *Neuroscience and Biobehav-ioral Reviews, 21,* 755–765.

Albert, D. J., Walsh, M. L., & Jonik, R. H. (1993). Aggres-sion in humans: What is its biological foundation? *Neuroscience and Biobehavioral Reviews, 17,* 405–425.

Alves, S. E., McEwen, B. S., Hayashi, S., Korach, K. S., Pfaff, D. W., & Ogawa, S. (2000). Estrogen-regulated progestin receptors are found in the midbrain raphe but not hippocampus of estrogen receptor alpha (ERα) gene-disrupted mice. *Journal of Comparative Neurology, 427,* 185–195.

An, J., Tzagarakis-Foster, C., Scharschmidt, T. C., Lomri, N., and Leitman, D. C. (2001). Estrogen receptor β-selective transcriptional activity and recruitment of coregulators by phytoestrogens. *Journal of Biological Chemistry, 276,* 17808–17814.

Angier, N. (1995). Gene defect tied to violence in male mice. *New York Times,* November 23, pp. A16.

Arango, V., Huang, Y. Y., Underwood, M. D., & Mann, J. J. (2003). Genetics of the serotonergic system in suicidal behavior. *Journal of Psychiatric Research, 37,* 375–386.

Archer, J. (1988). *The behavioral biology of aggression.* Cambridge: Cambridge University Press.

Archer, J. (1991). The influence of testosterone on human aggression. *British Journal of Psychology, 82,* 1–28.

Balthazart, J., Baillien, M., Charlier, T. D., Cornil, C. A., & Ball, G. F. (2003). The neuroendocrinology of reproductive behavior in Japanese quail. *Domestic Animal Endocrinology Review, 25,* 69–82.

Banks, T., & Dabbs, J. M., Jr. (1996). Salivary testoster-one and cortisol in a delinquent and violent urban subculture. *Journal of Social Psychology, 136,* 49–56.

Barnard, E. A., Skolnick, P., Olsen, R. W., Mohler, H., Sieghart, W., Biggio, G., et al. (1998). International union of pharmacology. XV. Subtypes of gaba-aminobutyric acid/A receptors: Classification on the basis of subunit structure and receptor function. *Pharmacological Reviews, 50,* 291–297.

Barr, C. S., Newman, T. K., Becker, M. L., Parker, C. C., Champoux, M., Lesch, K. P., et al. (2003) The util-ity of the non-human primate model for studying gene by environment interactions in behavioral re-search. *Genes, Brain, and Behavior, 2,* 336–340.

Baulieu, E. E. (1997). Neurosteroids: Of the nervous sys-tem, by the nervous system, for the nervous system. *Recent Progress in Hormone Research, 52,* 1–32.

Berry, M., Nunez, A. M., & Chambon, P. (1989). Estro-gen responsive element of the human pS2 gene is an imperfectly palindromic sequence. *Proceedings of the National Academy of Sciences USA, 86,* 1218–1222.

Bethea, C. L., Lu, N. Z., Gundlah, C., & Streicher, J. M. (2002). Diverse actions of ovarian steroids in the serotonin neural system. *Frontiers in Neuroendocri-nology, 23,* 41–100.

Bethea, C. L., Mirkes, S. J., Shively, C. A., & Adams, M. R. (2000). Steroid regulation of tryptophan hy-droxylase protein in the dorsal raphe of macaques. *Biological Psychiatry, 47,* 562–576.

Bimonte-Nelson, H. A., Singleton, R. S., Nelson, M. E., Eckman, C. B., Barber, J., Scott, T. Y., et al. (2003). Testosterone, but not nonaromatizable dihydrotes-tosterone, improves working memory and alters nerve growth factor levels in aged male rats. *Experi-mental Neurology, 181,* 301–312.

Birger, M., Swartz, M., Cohen, D., Alesh, Y., Grishpan, C., & Kotelr, M. (2003). Aggression: The testoster-one-serotonin link. *Israel Medical Association Jour-nal, 5,* 653–658.

Blanchard, D. C., McKittrick, C. R., Hardy, M. P., &

Blanchard, R. (2002). Effects of social stress on hormones, brain, and behavior. In D. W. Pfaff, A. P. Arnold, A. M. Etgen, S. E. Fahrbach, & R. T. Rubin (Eds.), *Hormones, brain and behavior* (pp. 735–772). San Diego: Academic Press.

Blanchard, D. C., Spencer, R. L., Weiss, S. M., Blanchard, R. J., McEwen, B., & Sakai, R. R. (1995). Visible burrow system as a model of chronic social stress: Behavioral and neuroendocrine correlates. *Psychoneuroendocrinology, 20,* 117–134.

Bloch, M., Schmidt, P. J., Su, T. P., Tobin, M. B., & Rubinow, D. R. (1998). Pituitary-adrenal hormones and testosterone cycle in women with premenstrual syndrome and controls. *Biological Psychiatry, 15,* 897–903.

Booth, A., Shelley, G., Mazur, A., & Tharp, G. (1989). Testosterone, and winning and losing in human competition. *Hormones and Behavior, 23,* 556–571.

Brain, P., and Haug, M. (1992). Hormonal and neurochemical correlates of various forms of animal aggression. *Psychoneuroendocrinology, 17,* 537–551.

Brooks, J. H., & Reddon, J. R. (1996). Serum testosterone in violent and nonviolent young offenders. *Journal of Clinical Psychology, 52,* 475–483.

Canonaco, M., Tavolaro, R., and Maggi, A. (1993). Steroid hormones and receptors of the GABA$_A$ supramolecular complex. *Neuroendocrinology 57,* 974–984.

Cashdan, E. (1995). Hormones, sex, and status in women. *Hormones and Behavior, 29,* 354–366.

Celloti, F., Negri-Cesi, P., and Poletti, A. (1997). Steroid metabolism in the mammalian brain: 5alpha-reduction and aromatization. *Brain Research Bulletin, 44,* 365–75.

Chang, A. S., and Chang, S. M. (1999). Nongenomic steroidal modulation of high-affinity serotonin transport. *Biochimica et Biophysica Acta, 1417,* 157–66.

Choi, P. Y., and Pope, H. G., Jr. (1994). Violence toward women and illicit androgenic-anabolic steroid use. *Annals of Clinical Psychiatry, 6,* 21–25.

Clarke, M. R., Kaplan, J. R., Bumsted, P. T., & Koritnik, D. R. (1986). Social dominance and serum testosterone concentration in dyads of male *Macaca fascicularis. Journal of Medical Primatology, 15,* 419–432.

Collins, F., & Jegalian, K. G. (1999). Deciphering the code of life. *Scientific American, 28,* 86–91.

Cologer-Clifford, A., Simon, N., & Smoluk, S. (1997). Serotonin agonist-induced decreases in intermale aggression are dependent on brain region and receptor subtype. *Pharmacology, Biochemistry and Behavior, 58,* 425–430.

Cologer-Clifford, A., Smoluk, S., Lu, S., & Simon, N. G. (1999). Androgens and estrogens modulate 5HT1A and 5HT1B agonist effects on aggression. *Physiology and Behavior, 65,* 823–828.

Compagnone, N. A., & Mellon, S. H. (2000). Neuro-steroids: Biosynthesis and function of these novel neuromodulators. *Frontiers in Neuroendocrinology, 21,* 1–56.

Cui, H., Lin, S. Y., & Belsham, D. D. (2003). Evidence that deyhydroepiandrosterone, DHEA, directly inhibits GnRH gene expression in GT1–7 hypothalamic neurons. *Molecular and Cellular Endocrinology, 203,* 13–23.

Dabbs, J. M., Jr., and Hargrove, M. F. (1997). Age, testosterone, and behavior among female prison inmates. *Psychosomatic Medicine, 59,* 477–480.

Dabbs, J. M., Jr., & Jurkovic, G. (1991). Salivary testosterone and cortisol among late adolescent male offenders. *Journal of Abnormal Child Psychology, 19,* 469–478.

Elofsson, U. O., Mayer, I., Damsgard, B., and Winberg, S. (2000). Intermale competition in sexually mature arctic charr: effects on brain monoamines, endocrine stress responses, sex hormone levels, and behavior. *General and Comparative Endocrinology, 118,* 450–60.

Enserink, M. (2000). Searching for the mark of Cain. *Science, 28,* 575–579.

Eriksson, E., Sundblad, C., Lisjo, P., Modigh, K., & Andersch, B. (1992). Serum levels of androgens are higher in women with premenstrual irritability and dysphoria than in controls. *Psychoneuroendocrinology, 17,* 195–204.

Etgen, A. (2002). Estrogen regulation of neurotransmitter and growth factor signaling in the brain. In D. W. Pfaff, A. P. Arnold, A. M. Etgen, S. E. Fahrbach, & R. T. Rubin (Eds.), *Hormones, brain and behavior* (pp. 381–440). San Diego: Academic Press.

Etgen, A. M., Chu, H. P., Fiber, J. M., Karkanias, G. B., & Morales, J. M. (1999). Hormonal integration of neurochemical and sensory signals governing female reproductive behavior. *Behavioural Brain Research, 105,* 93–103.

Ferris, C. F. (2000). Adolescent stress and neural plasticity in hamsters: A vasopressin-serotonin model of inappropriate aggressive behaviour. *Experimental Physiology, 85,* 85S–90S.

Fink, G., Sumner, B. E., McQueen, J. K., Wilson, H., & Rosie, R. (1998). Sex steroid control of mood, mental state and memory. *Clinical and Experimental Pharmacology and Physiology, 25,* 764–775.

Fink, G., Sumner, B. E., Rosie, R., Wilson, H., & McQueen, J. K. (1999). Androgen actions on central serotonin neurotransmission: Relevance for mood, mental state and memory. *Behavioural Brain Research, 105,* 53–68.

Furlong, R., Ho, L., Rubenstein, J. S., Walsh, L., Paykel, E. S., & Rubenstein, D. C. (1998). No association of the tryptophan hydroxylase gene with bipolar affective disorder, unipolar affective disorder, or suicidal behaviour in major affective disorder. *American Journal of Medical Genetics, 81,* 245–247.

Giguere, V., Tremblay, A., & Tremblay, G. B. (1998). Estrogen receptor β: Re-evaluation of estrogen and antiestrogen signaling. *Steroids, 63,* 335–339.

Gladue, B. A., Boechler, M., & McCaul, D. K. (1989). Hormonal response to competition in human males. *Aggressive Behavior, 15,* 409–422.

Godwin, J., & Crews, D. (2002). Hormones, brain, and behavior in reptiles. In D. W. Pfaff, A. P. Arnold, A. M. Etgen, S. E. Fahrbach, & R. T. Rubin (Eds.), *Hormones, brain and behavior* (pp. 545–586). San Diego: Academic Press.

Gonzales-Bono, E., Salvador, A., Serrano, M. A., & Ricarte, J. (1999). Testosterone, cortisol, and mood in a sports team competition. *Hormones and Behavior, 35,* 55–62.

Gorwood, P., Batel, P., Ades, J., Hamon, M., & Boni, C. (2000). Serotonin transporter gene polymorphisms, alcoholism, and suicidal behavior. *Biological Psychiatry, 48,* 259–264.

Gould, E., & Cameron, H. A. (1997). Early NMDA receptor blockade impairs defensive behavior and increases cell proliferation in the dentate gyrus of developing rats. *Behavioral Neuroscience, 111,* 49–56.

Gray, A., Jackson, D., & McKinlay, J. B. (1991). The relation between dominance, anger, and hormones in normally aging men: Results from the Massachusetts male aging study. *Psychosomatic Medicine, 53,* 375–385.

Gundlah, C., Lu, N. Z., & Bethea, C. L. (2002). Ovarian steroid regulation of monoamine oxidase-A and -B mRNAs in the macaque dorsal raphe and hypothalamic nuclei. *Psychopharmacology, 160,* 271–282.

Hall, J. M., McDonnell, D. P., & Korach, K. S. (2002). Allosteric regulation of estrogen receptor structure, function, and coactivator recruitment by different estrogen response elements. *Molecular Endocrinology, 16,* 469–86.

Haller, J., Halasz, J., Mikics, E., Kruk, M. R., & Makara, G. (2000). Ultradian corticosterone rhythm and the propensity to behave aggressively in male rats. *Journal of Neuroendocrinology, 12,* 937–940.

Haller, J., Millar, S., van de Schraaf, K., de Kloet, R. E., & Kruk, M. R. (2000). The active phase-related increase in corticosterone and aggression are linked. *Journal of Neuroendocrinology, 12,* 431–436.

Hau, M., Stoddard, S. T., & Soma, K. K. (2004). Territorial aggression and hormones during the non-breeding season in a tropical bird. *Hormones and Behavior, 45,* 40–49.

Herbison, A. E. (1995). Sexually dimorphic expression of androgen receptor immunoreactivity by somatostatin neurons in rat hypothalamic periventricular

nucleus and bed nucleus of the stria terminalis. *Journal of Neuroendocrinology, 7,* 543–553.

Herbison, A. E., & Fenelon, V. (1995). Estrogen regulation of GABA-A receptor subunit mRNA expression in preoptic area and bed nucleus of the stria terminalis of female rat brain. *Journal of Neuroscience, 15,* 2328–2337.

Huang, Y. Y., Grailhe, R., Argano, V., Hen, R., & Mann, J. J. (1999). Relationship of psychopathology to the human serotonin 1B genotype and receptor binding kinetics in postmortem brain tissue. *Neuropsychopharmacology, 21,* 238–246.

Hull, E. M., Lorrain, D. S., Du, J., Matuszewich, L., Lumley, L. A., Putnam, S. K., & Moses, J. (1999). Hormone-neurotransmitter interactions in the control of sexual behavior. *Behavioural Brain Research, 105,* 105–116.

Hutton, L., Guibao, G., & Simerly, R. (1998). Development of a sexually dimorphic projection form the bed nuclei of the stria teminalis to the anteroventral periventricular nucleus in the rat. *Journal of Neuroendocrinology, 18,* 3003–3013.

Jefferson, W. N., Padilla-Banks, E., Clark, G., Newbold, R. R. (2002). Assessing estrogenic activity of phytochemicals using transcriptional activation and immature mouse uterotrophic responses. *Journal of Chromatography B—Analytical Technologies in the Biomedical and Life Sciences, 777,* 179–189.

Jellinck, P. H., Lee, S. J., & McEwen, B. S. (2001). Metabolism of dehydroepiandrosterone by rat hippocampal cells in culture: possible role of aromatization and 7-hydroxylation in neuroprotection. *Journal of Steroid Biochemistry and Molecular Biology, 78,* 313–317.

Katzenellenbogen, B. S. (1996). Estrogen receptors: Bioactivities and interactions with cell signaling pathways. *Biology of Reproduction, 54,* 287–293.

Katzenellenbogen, B. S. (2000). Mechanism of action and cross-talk between estrogen receptor and progesterone receptor pathways. *Journal of the Society for Gynecological Investigation, 7,* S33–S37.

Klungland, H., Anderson, O., Kisen, G., Alestrom, P., & Tora, L. (1994). Estrogen receptor binds to the salmon GnRH gene in a region with long palindromic sequences. *Molecular and Cellular Endocrinology, 95,* 147–154.

Kraus, C., Heistermann, M., & Kappeler, P. M. (1999). Physiological suppression of sexual function of subordinate males: A subtle form of intrasexual competition among male sifakas *(Propithesuc verreauxi). Physiology and Behavior, 66,* 855–861.

Kravitz, E. A. (2000). Serotonin and aggression: Insights gained from a lobster model system and speculations on the role of amine neurons in a complex behavior *Journal of Comparative Physiology, 186,* 221–238.

Kuiper, G. G. J. M., Carlson, B., Grandien, K., Enmark, E., Haggblad, J., Nilsson, S., et al. (1997). Comparison of the ligand binding specificity and transcript tissue distribution of estrogen receptors α and β. *Endocrinology, 138,* 863–870.

Kuiper, G. G. J. M., Enmark, E., Pelto-Huikko, M., Nilsson, S., & Gustaffson, J.-A. (1996). Cloning of a novel estrogen receptor expressed in rat prostate and ovary. *Proceedings of the National Academy of Sciences USA, 93,* 5925–5930.

Kuiper, G. G. J. M., Shughrue, P. J., Merchenthaler, I., & Gustaffson, J.-A. (1998). The estrogen receptor â subtype: A novel mediator of estrogen action in neuroendocrine systems. *Frontiers in Neuroendocrinology, 19,* 253–286.

Labrie, F. (2003). Extragonadal synthesis of sex steroids: Intracrinology. *Annales d'Endocrinologie, 64,* 95–107.

Lee, H. J., & Chang, C. (2003). Recent advances in androgen receptor action. *Cellular and Molecular Life Sciences, 60,* 1613–1622.

Liu, S., Sugimoto, Y., Kulp, S. K., Jiang, J., Chang, H. L., Park, K. Y., et al. (2002). Estrogenic down-regulation of protein tyrosine phosphatase gamma (PTP gamma) in human breast is associated with estrogen receptor alpha. *Anticancer Research, 22,* 3917–3923.

Lu, N. Z., Eshleman, A. J., Janowsky, A., & Bethea, C. L. (2003). Ovarian steroid regulation of serotonin reuptake transporter (SERT) binding, distribution, and function in female macaques. *Molecular Psychiatry, 8,* 353–360.

Lu, S., Mo, Q., Hu, S., Garippa, C., & Simon, N. G. (2003). Dehydroepiandrosterone upregulates neural androgen receptor and transcriptional activity. *Journal of Neurobiology, 57,* 163–171.

Lu, S., Simon, N., McKenna, S., Nau, G., & Cologer-Clifford, A. (1998). Neural androgen receptor: Sex differences and similarities in autoregulation. *Endocrinology, 139,* 1594–1601.

Luttge, W. G., & Hall, N. R. (1973). Androgen induced agonistic behavior in castrate male Swiss-Webster mice: Comparison of our naturally occurring androgens. *Behavioral Biology, 8,* 725–732.

Majewska, M. D. (1995). Neuronal actions of dehydroepiandrosterone. Possible roles in brain development, aging, memory, and affect. *Annals of the New York Academy of Sciences, 774,* 111–120.

Majewska, M. D., Demirgoren, S., & London, E. D. (1990). Binding of pregnenolone sulfate to rat brain membranes suggests multiple sites of steroid action at the GABAA receptor. *European Journal of Pharmacology, 189,* 307–315.

Majewska, M. D., Demirgoren, S., Spivak, C. E., & London, E. D. (1990). The neurosteroid dehydroepiandrosterone sulfate is an allosteroid antagonist of the GABAA receptor. *Brain Research, 526,* 143–146.

Majewska, M. D., & Schwartz, R. D. (1987). Pregnenolone sulfate: An endogenous antagonist of the gamma-aminobutyric acid receptor complex in brain? *Brain Research, 404,* 355–360.

Manuck, S. B., Flory, J. D., Ferrell, R. E., Mann, J. J., & Muldoon, M. F. (2000). A regulatory polymorphism of monoamine oxidase-A gene may be associated with variability in aggression, impulsivity, and central nervous system serotonergic responsivity. *Psychiatry Research, 95,* 9–23.

Mazur, A., & Booth, A. (1998). Testosterone and dominance in men. *Behavioral and Brain Sciences, 21,* 353–363.

Mazur, A., Susman, E., & Edelbrock, S. (1997). Sex differences in testosterone response to a video game competition. *Evolution and Human Behavior, 18,* 317–326.

McCarthy, M. M. (1995). Functional significance of steroid modulation of GABAergic neurotransmission: Analysis at the behavioral, cellular, and molecular levels. *Hormones and Behavior, 29,* 131–140.

McCaul, K. D., Claude, B. A., & Joppa, M. (1992). Winning, losing, mood, and testosterone. *Hormones and Behavior, 26,* 486–504.

McQueen, J. K., Wilson, H., Sumner, B. E. H., & Fink, G. (1999). Serotonin transporter (SERT) mRNA and binding site densities in male rat brain affected by sex steroids. *Brain Research. Molecular Brain Research, 63,* 241–247.

Meek, L. R., Romeo, R. D., Novak, C. M., & Sisk, C. L. (1997). Actions of testosterone in prepubertal and postpubertal male hamsters: Dissociation of effects on reproductive behavior and androgen receptor immunoreactivity. *Hormones and Behavior, 31,* 75–88.

Mehta, A. K., & Ticku, M. K. (1999). An update on GABA-A receptors. *Brain Research, 29,* 196–217.

Melcangi, R. C., Poletti, A., Cavarretta, I., Celotti, F., Colciago, F., Magnaghi, V., et al. (1998). The 5alpha-reductase in the central nervous system: Expression and modes of control. *Journal of Steroid Biochemistry and Molecular Biology, 65,* 295–299.

Melton, L. (2000). Sex is all in the brain: Report of a Novartis Foundation Symposium on the Neuronal and Cognitive Effects of Oestrogens, London, UK, 7–9 September 1999. *Trends in Endocrinology and Metabolism, 11,* 69–71.

Mengod, G., Vilaro, T., Raurich, A., Luopez-Gimuenez, F., Cortues, R., & Palacios, J. (1996). 5-HT receptors in mammalian brain: Receptor autoradiography and in situ hybridization studies of new ligands and newly identified receptors. *Histochemical Journal, 11,* 747–758.

Miczek, K. A. (1999). Aggressive and social stress responses in genetically modified mice: From horizontal to vertical strategy. *Psychopharmacology, 147,* 17–19.

Miczek, K. A., DeBold, J. F., van Erp, A. M., & Tornatzky, W. (1997). Alcohol, GABA-A benzodiazepine receptor complex, and aggression. *Recent Developments in Alcoholism, 13,* 139–171.

Miczek, K. A., Fish, E. W., & DeBold, J. F. (2003). Neurosteroids, GABA-A receptors, and escalated aggressive behavior. *Hormones and Behavior, 44,* 242–257.

Mize, A. L., & Alper, R. H. (2002). Rapid uncoupling of serotonin-1A receptors in rat hippocampus by 17beta-estradiol in vitro requires protein kinases A and C. *Neuroendocrinology, 76,* 339–47.

Mo, Q., Lu, S., Hu, S., & Simon, N. G. (2004). DHEA and DHEA sulfate differentially regulate androgen receptor and its transcriptional activity. *Molecular Brain Research, 126,* 165–172.

Naftolin, F., Horvath, T. L., & Balthazart, J. (2001). Estrogen synthetase (aromatase) immunohistochemistry reveals concordance between avian and rodent limbic systems and hypothalami. *Experimental Biology and Medicine, 226,* 717–25.

Nelson, R. J. (2000). *An introduction to behavioral endocrinology* (2nd ed.). Sunderland, MA: Sinauer.

Nelson, R. J., & Chiavegatto, S. (2001). Molecular basis of aggression. *Trends in Neuroscience, 24,* 713–719.

Nomura, M., McKenna, E., Korach, K. S., Pfaff, D. W., & Ogawa, S. (2002). Estrogen receptor-beta regulates transcript levels for oxytocin and arginine vasopressin in the hypothalamic paraventricular nucleus of male mice. *Molecular Brain Research, 109,* 84–94.

Ogawa, S., Chan, J., Chester, A. E., Gustafsson, J., Korach, K., & Pfaff, D. (1999). Survival of reproductive behaviors in estrogen receptor β gene-deficient (βERKO) male and female mice. *Neurobiology, 96,* 12887–12892.

Ogawa, S., Lubahn, D. B., Korach, K. S., & Pfaff, D. W. (1997). Behavioral effects of estrogen receptor gene disruption in male mice. *Proceedings of the National Academy of Sciences USA, 94,* 1476–1481.

Ogawa, S., Washburn, T. F., Lubahn, D. B., Korach, K. S., & Pfaff, D. W. (1998). Modifications of testosterone-dependent behaviors by estrogen receptor-alpha gene disruption in male mice. *Endocrinology, 139,* 5058–5069.

Olivier, B., Mos, J., Raghoebar, M., de Koning, P., & Mak, M. (1994). Serenics. *Progress in Drug Research, 42,* 169–248.

Olivier, B., Mos, J., Van Oorschot, R., & Hen, R. (1995). Serotonin receptors and animal models of aggressive behavior. *Pharmacopsychiatry, 28,* 80–90.

Olweus, D., Mattsson, A., Schalling, D., & Low, H. (1988). Circulating testosterone levels and aggression in adolescent males: A causal analysis. *Psychosomatic Medicine, 50,* 261–272.

Osterlund, M. K., Halldin, C., & Hurd, Y. L. (2000). Effects of chronic 17beta-estradiol treatment on the serotonin 5-HT(1A) receptor mRNA and binding levels in the rat brain. *Synapse, 35,* 39–44.

Palacios, J., Waeber, C., Hoyer, D., & Mengod, G. (1990). Distribution of serotonin receptors. *Annals of the New York Academy of Sciences, 600,* 36–52.

Panksepp, J. B., Yue, Z., Drerup, C., & Huber, R. (2003). Amine neurochemistry and aggression in crayfish. *Microscopy Research and Technique, 60,* 360–368.

Pecins-Thompson, M., & Bethea, C. L. (1998). Ovarian steroid regulation of 5-HT1A autoreceptor messenger ribonucleic acid expression in the dorsal raphe of rhesus macaques. *Neuroscience, 89,* 267–277.

Perché, F., Young, J., Robel, P., Simon, N. G., & Haug, M. (2000). Prenatal testosterone treatment potentiates the aggression suppressive effect of the neurosteroid dehydroepiandrosterone in female mice. *Aggressive Behavior, 27,* 130–138.

Raap, D. K., DonCarlos, L., Garcia, F., Muma, N., Wolf, W. A., Battaglia, G., et al. (2000). Estrogen desensitizes 5-HT1A receptors and reduces levels of GZ, Gi1 and Gi3 proteins in the hypothalamus. *Neuropharmacology, 39,* 1823–1832.

Rasika, S., Alveraz-Buylla, A., & Nottebohm, F. (1999). BDNF mediates the effects of testosterone on the survival of new neurons in an adult brain. *Neuron, 22,* 53–62.

Rhen, T., & Crews, D. (2000). Organization and activation of sexual and agonistic behavior in the leopard gecko, *Eublepharis mascularius. Neuroendocrinology, 71,* 252–261.

Robel, P., & Baulieu, E. E. (1995). Dehydroepiandrosterone (DHEA) is a neuroactive neurosteroid. *Annals of the New York Academy of Sciences, 774,* 82–110.

Rose, R. M. (1975). Consequences of social conflict on plasma testosterone levels in rhesus monkeys. *Psychosomatic Medicine, 37,* 50.

Ross, J. (1996). Control of messenger RNA stability in higher neuroactive steroids. *Trends in Genetics, 12,* 171–175.

Rubinow, D. R., & Schmidt, P. J. (1996). Androgens, brain, and behavior. *American Journal of Psychiatry, 153,* 974–984.

Rubinow, D. R., Schmidt, P. J., Roca, C. A., & Daly, R. C. (2002). Gonadal hormones and behavior in women: Concentrations versus context. In D. W. Pfaff, A. P. Arnold, A. M. Etgen, S. E. Fahrbach, & R. T. Rubin (Eds.), *Hormones, brain and behavior* (pp. 37–74). San Diego: Academic Press.

Rupprecht, R., & Holsboer, F. (1999). Neuroactive steroids: Mechanisms of action and neuropsychopharmacological perspectives. *Trends in Neurosciences, 22,* 410–416.

Rupprecht, R., Reul, J. M., Trapp, T., van Steensel, B., Wetzel, C., Damm, K., et al. (1993). Progesterone receptor-mediated effects of neuroactive steroids. *Neuron, 11,* 523–530.

Salvador, A., Suay, F., Martinez-Sanchis, S., Simon, V. M., & Brain, P. F. (1999). Correlating testosterone and fighting in male participants in judo contests. *Physiology and Behavior, 68,* 205–209.

Segovia, S., & Guillamon, A. (1993). Sexual dimorphism in the vomeronasal pathway and sex differences in reproductive behaviors. *Brain Research. Brain Research Reviews, 18,* 51–74.

Shih, J. C., Chen, K., & Ridd, M. J. (1999). Monoamine oxidase: From genes to behavior. *Annual Review of Neuroscience, 22,* 197–217.

Shughrue, P. J., Lane, M. V., & Merchenthaler, I. (1997). Comparative distribution of estrogen receptor-alpha and -beta mRNA in the rat central nervous system. *Journal of Comparative Neurology, 388,* 507–525.

Shughrue, P. J., Lane, M. V., Scrimo, P. J., & Merchenthaler, I. (1998). Comparative distribution of estrogen receptor-α (ER-α) and β (ER-β) mRNA in the rat pituitary, gonad and reproductive tract. *Steroids, 63,* 498–504.

Shupnik, M. A., & Rosenzweig, B. J. (1990). Identification of an estrogen-responsive element in the rat LH beta gene. DNA-estrogen receptor interactions and functional analysis. *Biological Chemistry, 266,* 17084–17091.

Siegel, A., Roeling, T. A., Gregg, T. R., & Kruk, M. R. (1999). Neuropharmacology of brain-stimulation-evoked aggression. *Neuroscience and Biobehavioral Reviews, 23,* 359–389.

Silverin, B., Baillien, M., Foidart, A., & Balthazart, J. (2000). Distribution of aromatase activity in the brain and peripheral tissues of passerine and nonpasserine avian species. *General and Comparative Endocrinology, 117,* 34–53.

Simerly, R. B. (1998). Organization and regulation of sexually dimorphic neuroendocrine pathways. *Behavioural Brain Research, 92,* 195–203.

Simerly, R. B., Chang, C., Muramatsu, M., & Swanson, L. W. (1990). Distribution of androgen and estrogen receptor mRNA-containing cells in the rat brain: An in situ hybridization study. *Journal of Comparative Neurology, 294,* 76–95.

Simon, N. G. (1979). The genetics of intermale aggression in mice: Recent research and alternative strategies. *Neuroscience and Biobehavioral Reviews, 3,* 97–106.

Simon, N. G. (2002). Hormonal processes in the development and expression of aggressive behavior. In D. W. Pfaff, A. E. Arnold, A. M. Etgen, S. E. Fahrbach, & R. T. Rubin (Eds.), *Hormones, brain and behavior* (pp. 339–391). San Diego: Academic Press.

Simon, N. G., Cologer-Clifford, A., Lu, S. F., McKenna, S. E., and Hu, S. (1998). Testosterone and its metabolites modulate 5HT1A and 5HT1B agonist effects on intermale aggression. *Neuroscience and Biobehavioral Reviews, 23,* 325–336.

Simon, N. G., Kaplan, J. R., Hu, S., Register, T. C., & Adams, M. R. (2004). Increased aggressive behavior and decreased affiliative behavior in adult male monkeys after long-term consumption of diets rich in soy protein and isoflavones. *Hormones and Behavior, 45,* 278–284.

Simon, N. G., Lu, S. F., McKenna, S. E., Chen, X., & Clifford, A. C. (1993). Sexual dimorphisms in regulatory systems for aggression. In M. Haug et al. (Eds.), *The development of sex differences and similarities in behavior* (pp. 389–408). Amsterdam: Kluwer Academic.

Simon, N. G., McKenna, S., Lu, S., & Cologer-Clifford, A. (1996). Development and expression of hormonal systems regulating aggression. *Annals of the New York Academy of Sciences, 794,* 8–17.

Simon, N. G., Whalen, R. E., & Tate, M. P. (1985). Induction of male-like aggression by androgens but not by estrogens in adult female mice. *Hormones and Behavior, 19,* 204–212.

Sohrabji, F., Miranda, R. C. G., & Toran-Allerand, C. D. (1995). Identification of a putative estrogen response element in the gene encoding brain-derived neurotrophic factor. *Proceedings of the National Academy of Sciences USA, 92,* 11110–11114.

Soler, H., Vinayak, P., and Quadagno, D. (2000). Biosocial aspects of domestic violence. *Psychoneuroendocrinology, 25,* 721–739.

Soma, K. K., & Wingfield, J. C. (2001). Dehydroepiandrosterone in songbird plasma: Seasonal regulation and relationship to territorial aggression. *General and Comparative Endocrinology, 123,* 144–155.

Stavisky, R. C., Register, T. C., Watson, S. L., Weaver, D. S., & Kaplan, J. R. (1999). Behavioral responses to ovariectomy and chronic anabolic steroid treatment in female cynomolgus macaques. *Physiology and Behavior, 66,* 95–100.

Studer, L. H., Reddon, J. R., & Siminoski, K. G. (1997). Serum testosterone in adult sex offenders: A comparison between Caucasians and North American Indians. *Journal of Clinical Psychology, 53,* 375–385.

Suay, F., Salvador, A., Gonzalez-Bono, E., Sanchýs, C., Martinez-Sanchis, S., Simon, V. M., et al. (1999). Effects of competition and its outcome on serum testosterone, cortisol and prolactin. *Psychoneuroendocrinology, 24,* 551–566.

Sumner, B. E. H., Grant, K. E., Rosie, R., Hegele-Hartung, C., Fritzemeier, K. H., & Fink, G. (1999). Effects of tamoxifen on serotonin transporter and 5-hydroxytryptamine 2A receptor binding sites and mRNA levels in the brain of ovariectomized rats with or without acute estradiol replacement. *Molecular Brain Research, 73,* 119–128.

Sun, J., Meyers, M., Fink, B. E., Rajendran, R., Katzenellenbogen, J. A., & Katzenellenbogen, B. S. (1999). Novel ligands that function as selective estrogens or antiestrogens for estrogen receptor-α or estrogen receptor-β. *Endocrinology, 140,* 800–804.

Thiblin, I., Runeson, B., & Rajs, J. (1999). Anabolic androgenic steroids and suicide. *Annals of Clinical Psychiatry, 11,* 223–231.

Trevino, A., Wolf, A., Jackson, A., Price, T., & Uphouse, L. (1999). Reduced efficacy of 8-OH-DPAT's inhibition of lordosis behavior by prior estrogen treatment. *Hormones and Behavior, 35,* 215–223.

Uphouse, L. (2000). Female gonadal hormones, serotonin, and sexual receptivity. *Brain Research. Brain Research Reviews, 33,* 242–257.

Van den Bergh, J. G. (1994). Pheromones and mammalian reproduction. In E. Knobil & J. D. Neill (Eds.), *The physiology of reproduction* (pp. 343–349). New York: Raven Press.

Van Goozen, S. H.,Wiegant, V. W., Endert, E., Helmond, F. A., & van de Poll, N. E. (1997). Psychoendocrinological assessment of the menstrual cycle: The relationship between hormones, sexuality, and mood. *Archives of Sexual Behavior, 26,* 359–382.

Van Honk, J., Tuiten, A., Verbaten, R., van den Hout, M., Koppeschaar, H., Thijsen, J., and de Haan, E. (1999). Correlations among salivary testosterone, mood, and selective attention to threat in humans. *Hormones and Behavior, 36,* 17–24.

Veenstra-VanderWeele, J., Anderson, G. M., & Cook, E. H., Jr. (2000). Pharmacogenetics and the serotonin system: Initial studies and future directions. *European Journal of Pharmacology, 410,* 165–181.

Virgin, C. E., Jr., & Sapolsky, R. M. (1997). Styles of male social behavior and their endocrine correlates among low-ranking baboons. *American Journal of Primatology, 42,* 25–39.

Virkkunen, M., Goldman, D., & Linnoila, M. (1996). Serotonin in alcoholic violent offenders. *CIBA Foundation Symposium, 194,* 168–177.

Von Engelhardt, N., Kappeler, P. M., & Heistermann, M. (2000). Androgen levels and female social dominance in *Lemur catta. Proceedings of the Royal Society of London, Series B, 267,* 1533–1539.

Vukmirovic, O. G., & Tilghman, S. M. (2000). Exploring genome space. *Nature Insight, 405,* 820–822.

Weihua, Z., Saji, S., Makinen, S., Cheng, G., Jensen, E. V., Warner, M., et al. (2000). Estrogen receptor (ER) beta, a modulator of ERalpha in the uterus. *Proceedings of the National Academy of Sciences USA, 97,* 5936–5941.

Wingfield, J. C., Jacobs, J., and Hillgarth, N. (1997). Ecological constraints and the evolution of hormone-behavior interrelationships. *Annals of the New York Academy of Sciences, 807,* 22–41.

Wright, D. E., Seroogy, K. B., Lundgren, K. H., Davis, B. M., & Jennes, L. (1995). Comparative localization of serotonin 1A, 1C and 2 receptor subtype mRNAs in rat brain. *Journal of Comparative Neurology, 351,* 357–373.

Yang, L. Y., & Arnold, A. P. (2000). Interaction of BDNF and testosterone in the regulation of adult perineal motoneurons. *Journal of Neurobiology, 44,* 308–319.

Yang, L. Y., Verhovshek, T., & Sengelaub, D. R. (2004). Brain-derived neurotrophic factor and androgen interact in the maintenance of dendritic morphology in a sexually dimorphic rat spinal nucleus. *Endocrinology, 145,* 161–168.

Yi, P., Bhagat, S., Hilf, R., Bambara, R. A., & Muyan, M. (2002). Differences in the abilities of estrogen receptors to integrate activation functions are critical for subtype-specific transcriptional responses. *Molecular Endocrinology, 16,* 1810–1827.

Young, J., Corpechot, C., Haug, M., Gobaille, S., Baulieu, E. E., and Robel, P. (1991). Suppressive effects of dehydroepiandrosterone and 3β-methyl-androst-5-en-17-one on attack towards lactating female intruders by castrated male mice. II. Brain neurosteroids. *Biomedical and Biophysical Research Communications, 174,* 892–897.

Young, J., Corpechot, C., Perché, F., Eychenne, B., Haug, M., Baulieu, E. E., et al. (1996). Neurosteroids in the mouse brain: Behavioral and pharmacological effects of a 3α-hydroxysteroid dehydrogenase inhibitor. *Steroids, 61,* 144–149.

Young, J., Corpechot, C., Perché, F., Haug, M., Baulieu, E. E., & Robel, P. (1995). Neurosteroids: Pharmacological effects of a 3α-hydroxy-steroid dehydrogenase inhibitor. *Endocrine, 2,* 505–509.

10

The Role of Estrogen Receptors in the Regulation of Aggressive Behaviors

Sonoko Ogawa, Masayoshi Nomura, Elena Choleris, & Donald Pfaff

Aggression as Hormone-Controlled Behavior in Mice

Regulation of aggressive behaviors by gonadal steroid hormones has been extensively studied during the past 30 years (reviewed in Simon & Lu, ch. 9 in this volume). It is well established that testosterone is a major hormone that controls expression of aggressive behavior not only in males, but also in androgenized females. Testosterone affects neural functions by (a) acting through androgen receptors (AR), in its original chemical form or as the 5α-reduced form (dihydrotestosterone), or (b) acting through estrogen receptors (ER) after aromatization to estradiol (E$_2$). There is accumulating evidence that ER-dependent mechanisms may play a crucial role in the regulation of aggressive behavior in adulthood, as well as influencing the neural mechanisms underlying adult aggression during perinatal development. It is assumed that ERs act as ligand-dependent transcription factors to regulate several downstream gene products, which may be directly or indirectly involved in the induction (or suppression) of behavior. Discovery of the second form of ER, ER-β, in addition to the previously known classical form of ER, ER-α, however, forced us to reconsider the roles of

neural ERs in the estrogenic regulation of aggressive behavior. Furthermore, the complexity and multidimensional nature of aggressive behaviors often generates more new questions to solve, rather than answers. For instance, evidence from a number of studies demonstrates that both adult and developmental effects of estrogen treatment on the levels of aggression are different in male than in female mice. Furthermore, gonadal steroid regulation of aggression in cycling and pre- and postpartum females is not necessarily the same. Our main focus in this chapter is to summarize our current knowledge of the possible differential roles played by two types of ERs in the expression of aggressive behavior. We also discuss potential brain mechanisms of ER-mediated regulation of aggression.

A brief summary of ER-α and ER-β in the central nervous system is in order. To date, at least two types of ER, the classical ER-α and the more recently identified ER-β (Kuiper, Enmark, Peltohuikko, & Nilsson, 1996; Tremblay et al., 1997), have been localized in the central nervous system. ER-α and ER-β are very similar estrogen binding proteins that act as ligand-dependent transcription factors (Kuiper et al., 1997). Although somewhat overlapping, brain distributions of ER-α and ER-β are not identical (Laflamme, Nappi,

Drolet, Labrie, & Rivest, 1998; Mitra et al., 2003; Nomura, Korach, Pfaff, & Ogawa, 2003; Osterlund, Kuiper, Gustafsson, & Hurd, 1998; Shughrue, Lane, Scrimo, & Merchenthaler, 1998). ER-β mRNA and protein are localized in a number of brain areas not particularly ER-α rich, such as the paraventricular nucleus and midbrain dorsal raphe nuclei. Furthermore, ER-β is highly concentrated in limbic areas, such as the medial amygdala and bed nucleus of the stria terminalis, which are implicated in the regulation of emotional behaviors, including aggressive behaviors. These anatomical findings lead us to hypothesize that ER-β may also play a role in estrogenic control of aggressive behavior by regulating expression of downstream gene products. It is also assumed that ER-β-mediated actions of estrogen may not necessarily be of the same magnitude and/or direction as those caused by ER-α-mediated mechanisms. Some in vitro transfection studies indeed revealed that ER-α and ER-β exert differential regulatory actions on neuroendocrine-related promoter activity (Shapiro, Xu, & Dorsa, 2000; Vasudevan, Davidkova et al., 2001; Vasudevan, Kia, Inoue, Muramatsu, & Pfaff, 2002; Vasudevan, Koibuchi, Chin, & Pfaff, 2001). Through a series of behavioral studies using knockout mice for either ER-α (αERKO; Lubahn et al., 1993) or ER-β (βERKO; Krege et al., 1998) genes, as well as those that lack both genes (αβERKO; Couse et al., 1999), it was discovered that activation of the two types of ERs may have differential roles in the regulation of aggressive behaviors and several other reproduction-related behaviors (sexual and parental), as well as anxiety-related and social preference behaviors (for reviews, see Ogawa, Korach, & Pfaff, 2002; Rissman, Wersinger, Fugger, & Foster, 1999; Rissman, Wersinger, Taylor, & Lubahn, 1997).

Differential Roles of ER-α and ER-β in Male Aggressive Behaviors

Studies from the 1970s and 1980s demonstrated that aggressive behaviors in male mice might be regulated in adulthood by both AR- and ER-mediated neural mechanisms (Simon & Whalen, 1986). Evidence for the involvement of estrogen-dependent mechanisms in male aggressive behaviors has been obtained by comparing the relative efficiencies of testosterone, dihydrotestosterone, and estrogen (Brain, Haug, & Kamis, 1983; Nyby, Matochik, & Barfield, 1992) and by concurrent injection of an aromatase inhibitor with testosterone

(Bowden & Brain, 1978; Clark & Nowell, 1979). These findings, however, do not provide direct evidence for the role of the ER gene product itself. Furthermore, the antiestrogen tamoxifen gave inconsistent behavioral effects; both inhibitory (Hasan, Brain, & Castano, 1988) and facilitatory (Simon & Perry, 1988) effects of tamoxifen on male aggression in mice have been reported. Until recently, no direct technique existed to manipulate endogenous steroid receptor function in order to determine the behavioral role of ERs. This became possible through the development of specific gene knockout mice, first with classical ER-α gene (Lubahn et al., 1993) and then with the more recently cloned ER-β gene (Krege et al., 1998), both by the use of homologous recombination techniques.

We first examined the effects of ER-α gene disruption on the expression of male aggressive behaviors using three different behavioral paradigms frequently used for the assessment of aggressiveness in male mice (Ogawa, Lubahn, Korach, & Pfaff, 1997; Ogawa, Washburn, et al., 1998). In resident-intruder aggression tests with standard opponents of olfactory bulbectomized male mice, αERKO male (gonadally intact) mice showed greatly reduced levels of aggression compared to wild-type (αWT) or heterozygous (αHZ) littermates (figures 10.1A and 10.1B). In particular, the male-typical aggressive behavioral pattern of continuous biting, wrestling, and vigorous lateral attacks was almost completely abolished in αERKO mice (figure 10.1B). When two mice from the same genotype were tested against each other in a neutral area (homogeneous set test), αERKO male mice showed more social interaction than they showed toward olfactory bulbectomized opponents (which reliably elicited aggression in the resident mice, because their gonads were intact and secreted male pheromone, but failed to exhibit active social behaviors, including aggression). This led to a display of active social investigation (genital licking), chasing, and lunging behaviors in αERKO male mouse pairs (figure 10.1C). However, αERKO mouse pairs rarely showed male-typical aggressive behavior patterns (figure 10.1D). Finally, mice were tested in a behavioral paradigm which enabled us to measure both offensive and defensive components of male aggressive behavior. Specifically, experimental mice (αERKO, αWT, and αHZ) were introduced into the home cages of singly housed C57BL/6J mice, which were trained to be aggressive toward intruder mice. As expected, C57BL/6J resident mice showed vigorous aggressive behavior toward intruder mice, although some of the

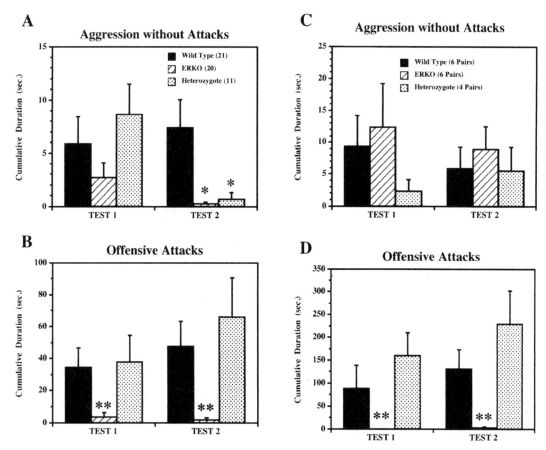

FIGURE 10.1 Effects of ER gene disruption on aggressive behaviors tested in two different paradigms, resident–intruder tests (A and B) and homogeneous set tests (C and D). Cumulative durations of aggressive bouts with (B and D) and without (A and C) offensive attacks are shown separately with different scales. αERKO (indicated as ERKO) mice showed very few aggressive behaviors even without attacks in resident–intruder tests (A; *significantly different than WT mice at α = .05), while in the homogeneous set tests, there were no differences between the three genotypes (C). On the other hand, in both tests, the cumulative durations of offensive attacks (B, D) were greatly reduced in αERKO mice compared to both WT and HZ mice (**α = .05). From "Behavioral Effects of Estrogen Receptor Gene Disruption in Male Mice," by S. Ogawa, D. B. Lubahn, K. S. Korach, & D. W Pfaff, 1997, *Proceedings of the National Academy of Sciences USA*, 94, p. 1478 Copyright 1997 by the National Academy of Sciences. Reprinted with permission.

intruder mice were dominant in certain aggressive bouts (figure 10.2). The levels of these offensive bouts were significantly lower in αERKO mice than in αWT and αHZ mice (figure 10.2A). In contrast, αERKO mice were normal in their ability to elicit aggressive behavior in opponent male mice, suggesting that their aggression-promoting olfactory properties (e.g., male pheromone production) were not disrupted (figure 10.2B). These findings from three different behavioral tests all suggest that ER-α gene expression is necessary for male mice to maintain the propensity to initiate

offensive attacks in response to aggression-promoting olfactory cues from male opponents.

Reduced levels of aggression in gonadally intact αERKO male mice are not due to differences in plasma concentrations of testosterone and/or estradiol, which are known to be either equivalent (estradiol) or slightly higher (testosterone) in αERKO male mice than in αWT mice (Eddy et al., 1996). A study which examined the effects of gonadectomy and subsequent testosterone replacement on aggressive behavior further confirmed the insensitivity of αERKO male mice to

(A) Offensive Bouts

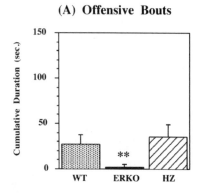

(B) Defensive Bouts

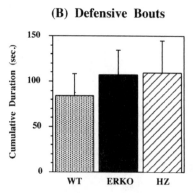

FIGURE 10.2 Results of aggression tests against C57BL/6J resident male mouse. Wild-type (WT; $N = 11$), ERKO ($N = 12$), and heterozygous (HZ; $N = 15$) male mice, which had been singly housed since weaning, were used. Genotype differences were detected (Kruskal–Wallis one-way ANOVA) only in the levels of offensive bouts, but not those of defensive bouts. Posthoc pairwise comparisons with Mann–Whitney U test revealed that αERKO (indicated as ERKO) mice were significantly less aggressive than both WT and HZ mice (**$p < .05$). From "Modifications of Testosterone-Dependent Behaviors by Estrogen Receptor-α Gene Disruption in Male Mice," by S. Ogawa, T. F. Washburn, et al., 1998, *Endocrinology, 139*, p. 5076. Copyright 1998 by The Endocrine Society. Reprinted with permission.

estrogen, as an aromatization product of testosterone (Ogawa, Washburn, et al., 1998). We found that daily injection of testosterone propionate (TP) successfully restored aggressive behavior, suppressed by gonadectomy, in αWT mice, but completely failed to induce any aggression in αERKO mice. It is assumed that multiple processes induced by ER-α gene disruption may also be involved in the almost complete disappearance of male-type offensive attacks in αERKO mice. Lack of ER-α activation may have a cascade effect on several genetic and neural processes involved in the regulation of aggressive behavior in male mice. For example, appropriate ER activation by testosterone, after being aromatized to estradiol during perinatal periods, is essential for normal sexually dimorphic development of the central nervous system. Therefore, a lack of such stimulation in αERKO male mice due to a lack of ER-α, but not necessarily testosterone itself, may severely affect the development of brain substrates regulating aggression.

It is also possible that an important part of the underlying mechanism for the behavioral effects of ER-α gene disruption depends on altered processing of chemosensory information. Male αERKO mice had not attacked any type of male opponent mice so far tested, which were all gonadally intact (i.e., olfactory bulbectomized male intruders in the resident-intruder paradigm, opponent mice from the same genotype in homogeneous set tests, or C57BL/6J resident mice).

On the other hand, a recent study revealed that αERKO male mice exhibited aggression toward sexually receptive female mice (Scordalakes & Rissman, 2003). Therefore, it is possible that the ability to recognize opponents as a proper target of intermale aggression (elicited by olfactory cues from male opponents) is disrupted in αERKO male mice.

In contrast to the facilitatory role of ER-α on male aggression, the role of ER-β activation is an inhibitory one, because ER-β gene disruption generally resulted in the potentiation of aggressive behavior in male mice. In our first behavioral characterization study of βERKO male mice, we found that not only did βERKO males exhibit normal male-typical aggressive behavior, including offensive attacks, but they also showed higher levels of aggression than βWT mice under certain conditions of social experience (Ogawa et al., 1999). Specifically, during the very first aggressive behavioral test, βERKO males showed higher frequencies and lower latencies of aggression than βWT control mice (figure 10.3), although these genotype differences disappeared with repetition of aggressive behavior tests. The hypothesis that ER-β activation may inhibit aggressive behavior was tested further by examining the effects of estrogen replacement on the levels of aggressive behavior in male βERKO mice (Nomura et al., 2001). Overall, βERKO mice showed higher sensitivity to estrogen and the levels of aggression in estrogen-treated βERKO mice were higher than those of βWT mice. On the

(A) Any Aggression Duration (sec)

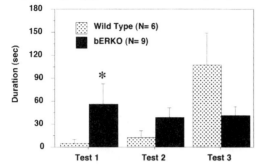

(B) Number of Bouts with Attacks

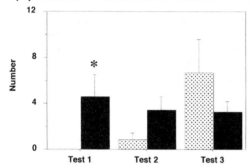

FIGURE 10.3 Effects of ER-β gene disruption on (A) the cumulative duration of aggression and (B) the number of attacks during resident–intruder tests. βERKO male mice showed higher levels of aggression in the first tests than WT male mice, whereas there were no genotype differences in the levels of aggression in the second and third tests (see text for details of statistical analyses); $^*p < .05$ vs. WT. From "Survival of Reproductive Behaviors in Estrogen Receptor β Gene-Deficient (βERKO) Male and Female Mice," by S. Ogawa et al., 1999, *Proceedings of the National Academy of Sciences USA, 96,* p. 12889. Copyright 1999 by the National Academy of Sciences. Adapted with permission.

other hand, the effects of estradiol benzoate (EB) on male sexual behavior did not differ between βERKO and βWT mice regardless of the dose of estrogen. These findings support the notion that ER-β activation may exert an inhibitory action on male aggression, which was induced by estrogen through ER-α-mediated brain mechanisms; thus, ER-β plays a significant role in preventing excessive aggressiveness.

We also determined the effects of ER-β gene disruption on the development of aggressive behavior across puberty in male mice (Nomura, Durbak, et al., 2002). Aggressive behaviors of gonadally intact naïve βERKO and βWT mice were examined in three independent age groups, that is, 5 (puberty), 12 (young adult), or 19 (adult) weeks old. In these studies, βERKO mice were significantly more aggressive than βWT during puberty to young adult age (figures 10.4A and 10.4B). On the other hand, the disinhibitory behavioral effects of ER-β gene disruption were not apparent in the adult age group, when βWT male mice became much more aggressive compared to mice of younger age groups. Increased aggression in βERKO mice in the pubertal age group may be partly due to elevated testosterone concentrations in this group of mice (figure 10.4C). However, there was no genotype difference in testosterone values in the young adult age groups, in which βERKO mice were still significantly more aggressive than βWT mice. Furthermore, calculations based on individual animals' results did not reveal significant correlations between aggression (duration of total aggressive behavior) and serum testosterone concentrations, regardless of age and genotype groups. Therefore, it is hypothesized that the lack of ER-β activation during the prepubertal period may advance the onset of puberty-related behavioral and endocrine functions. In other words, ER-β activation may be necessary to fine-tune the timing of these puberty-related events.

To further delineate the behavioral effects of ER-β gene disruption, which may be related to its modulatory action on aggression, we tested βERKO male mice in a different behavioral paradigm. Because (a) aggressive behaviors of young βERKO mice were very impulsive and (b) adult βERKO mice were more aggressive than βWT in the very fist aggression test, we hypothesized that reactivity to social stimuli may be altered in βERKO male mice compared to βWT mice. To more precisely control and measure their behavioral responses at the first encounter with an opponent mouse, we presented an intruder mouse in a protective shield (a clear perforated Plexiglas cylinder) placed in the center of the home cage for 30 min (social instigation procedure) prior to regular 15-min aggression tests. Mice in control groups were presented with an empty cylinder. Social instigation potentiated the levels of aggression in βERKO mice, but had no effects on βWT mice. We also found that βERKO mice in the instigated group showed elevated levels of social investigation (i.e., sniffing toward the holes of the cylinder) than instigated βWT mice, as well as

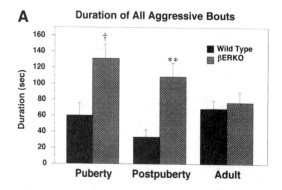

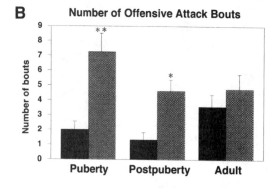

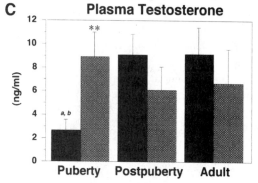

FIGURE 10.4 Effects of ER-β gene disruption on (A) cumulative duration, (B) number of offensive attack bouts, and (C) plasma levels of testosterone. There were overall significant genotype differences in both measurements. βERKO mice showed significantly higher levels of aggression than WT mice in the puberty and young adult groups, but not in the adult group. In WT mice, the serum levels of testosterone in the puberty group were significantly lower than those of the other two age groups. The serum levels of testosterone in pubertal βERKO mice were increased significantly compared to those of pubertal WT; †$p < .1$ vs. WT; *$p < .05$ vs. WT; **$p < .01$ vs. WT; a, $p < .05$ vs. adult mice; b, $p < .05$ vs. young adult mice. All data are presented as means ± SEM. Puberty: WT, $n = 17$; βERKO, $n = 13$; young adult: WT, $n = 11$; βERKO, $n = 17$; adult: WT, $n = 15$; βERKO, $n = 13$. From "Geno-type/Age Interactions on Aggressive Behavior in Gonadally Intact Estrogen Receptor β Knockout (βERKO) Male Mice," by M. Nomura, L. Durbak, et al., 2002, *Hormones and Behavior*, 41, p. 292. Copyright 2002 by Elsevier. Adapted with permission.

noninstigated control βERKO mice. These results suggest that βERKO male mice may be hyper-reactive to social stimuli. Instigated βERKO mice also showed higher levels of c-fos induction than instigated βWT mice, as well as noninstigated control βERKO mice, in a number of brain areas, including the medial amygdala, bed nucleus of stria terminalis, and medial preoptic area, which are known to be involved in the regulation of aggressive behavior (see Simon & Lu, ch. 9).

Finally, male mice lacking both ER-α and ER-β genes (αβERKO) display reduced aggression (figure

10.5). During resident-intruder paradigm tests, the aggressive behaviors of both αERKO and αβERKO male mice were greatly reduced compared to those of βERKO and αβWT mice (Ogawa et al., 2000). βERKO mice also displayed the highest levels of aggression among the four genotypes in the first test. These findings further support the hypothesis that ER-α activation, either during perinatal brain development and/or at the time of testing in adult, is necessary for the induction of aggressive behavior in male mice. On the other hand, the role of ER-β activation on male aggression is more of a modulatory one.

Potential Roles of ER-α and ER-β in Female Aggressive Behaviors

Unlike those in male aggression, the roles of the two types of ERs in the regulation of female aggressive behavior are not as well defined. This reflects, in part, that the effects of gonadal steroid hormones on female aggressive behavior are much more complicated than those on male aggression and possibly may vary depending on animals' reproductive states. In mice, gonadally intact females of most inbred strains (e.g., C57BL/6J, DAB/2J, C3H/He, etc.) rarely show aggressive behavior toward male mice regardless of the day of the estrous cycle (Ogawa & Makino, 1984). In the studies with αERKO and βERKO mice, as well as their WT littermates, female mice, regardless of genotype, were not aggressive toward olfactory bulbectomized male mouse opponents (figure 10.6A). Against female opponents, however, both αERKO and αWT mice exhibited aggression, and the levels of these aggressive behaviors were much higher in αERKO mice than αWT mice (Ogawa, Eng, et al., 1998; Ogawa, Taylor, Lubahn, Korach, & Pfaff, 1996). Elevated testosterone

concentrations reported in gonadally intact αERKO female mice (Lindzey & Korach, 1997; Rissman et al., 1997) might contribute only partially, if at all, to heightened levels of aggression, because aggressive behavior persisted even long after gonadectomy (figure 10.6B), when circulating concentrations of testosterone became nondetectable and male-type sexual behavior was completely abolished (figure 10.6C; Ogawa, Eng, et al., 1998). Rather, it is also possible that ER-α gene deletion might affect developmental processes essential for the subsequent expression of aggressive behavior in adult female mice. For instance, ER-α gene disruption might affect testosterone concentrations during early development and thus modify brain substrates for aggression in αERKO female mice. Interestingly, we have found that estrogen tended to decrease the levels of aggression in gonadectomized females of both αERKO and αWT lines (Ogawa, Eng, et al., 1998; Quinlan, Shibata, Mirasol, Pfaff, & Ogawa, 2003), suggesting that this type of aggressive behavior may also be inhibited by ER-β activation. Because βERKO and βWT female were not aggressive either before or after gonadectomy, whether inhibitory regulation of aggressive behavior by

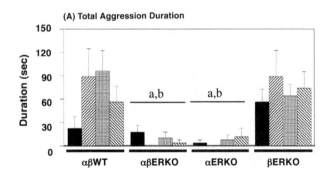

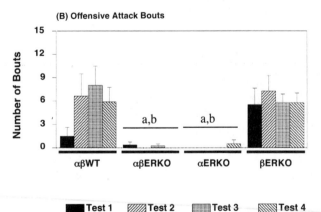

FIGURE 10.5 Effects of ER-α and/or ER-β gene disruption on (A) the cumulative duration of all aggressive bouts and (B) the number of offensive attack bouts during resident–intruder tests. There were significant genotype differences in both measurements, throughout the four tests (p < .01). Post hoc comparisons for the main effects of genotype revealed that both αβERKO and αERKO mice were significantly less aggressive than αβWT, as well as βERKO mice; a, p < .05 vs. αβWT; b, p < .05 vs. βERKO. From "From the Cover: Abolition of Male Sexual Behaviors in Mice Lacking Estrogen Receptors α and β (αβERKO)," by S. Ogawa et al., 2000, Proceedings of the National Academy of Sciences USA, 97, p. 14470. Copyright 2000 by the National Academy of Sciences. Adapted with permission.

(A) Aggression in Gonadally Intact Females

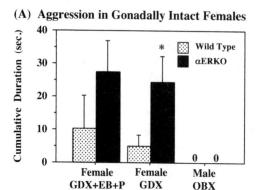

(B) Effects of Gonadectomy on Aggression

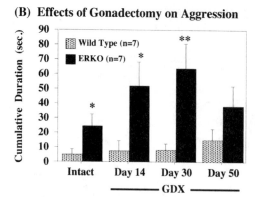

(C) Effects of Gonadectomy on Male-Type Sexual Behavior

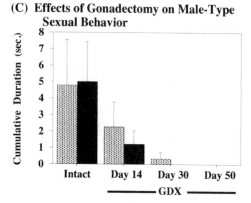

FIGURE 10.6 (A) Genotype differences and effects of opponents on aggressive behavior in female mice measured as cumulative durations of total aggressive behavior bouts during resident–intruder tests. Gonadally intact αERKO (indicated as ERKO) females showed higher levels of aggression than WT females toward female intruder mice (i.e., gonadectomized [GDX] or gonadectomized and treated with estrogen [EB] and progesterone [P]), whereas they did not show any aggression toward male intruder mice (i.e., olfactory bulbectomized [OBX]). (B and C) Gonadectomy (GDX) did not abolish aggressive behavior toward female intruder mice in either αERKO or WT female mice, and αERKO mice were consistently more aggressive than WT mice. In contrast, αERKO and WT females showed similar levels of male-type sexual behavior toward female intruder mice, which was markedly reduced by gonadectomy during the aggression test. Two-way ANOVA for repeated measurements revealed that there were overall significant genotype differences in the mean duration of aggression (B; $^*p < .05$, $^{**}p < 0.01$), but not in the mean duration of male-type sexual behavior (C). Because interactions between genotype and test days were also significant in the former, genotype differences were analyzed in each test ($^*p < .05$ vs. WT). From "Roles of Estrogen Receptor-α Gene Expression in Reproduction-Related Behaviors in Female Mice," by S. Ogawa, V. Eng, et al., 1998, *Endocrinology*, 139, p. 5064. Copyright 1998 by The Endocrine Society. Adapted with permission.

estrogen in gonadectomized female mice may be abolished by ER-β gene disruption could not be tested.

Elevated testosterone concentrations in αERKO female mice, as a by-product of ER-α gene disruption, did not induce aggressive behavior toward male mice, but had a great impact on their social role during male-female behavioral interaction. Gonadally intact αERKO female mice were not only completely sexually nonreceptive, but also vigorously attacked by stud male mice during mating tests (Ogawa et al., 1996). After gonadectomy, however, they were no longer attacked

by male mice (Ogawa, Eng, et al., 1998), suggesting involvement of elevated concentrations of testosterone in this phenomenon.

It is well known that female mice of most inbred strains become very aggressive during pregnancy (Ogawa & Makino, 1984; Svare, 1988) and postpartum (Broida & Svare, 1981; Ogawa & Makino, 1981) periods, in response to both male and female opponent mice (see Gammie & Lonstein, ch. 11 in this volume). Testosterone and estrogen treatment in the postpartum period decreased the levels of aggression in Rockland-Swiss albino mice (Svare, 1980; Svare & Gandelman, 1975), suggesting that ER-mediated mechanisms may be involved in the regulation of postpartum aggression. Our recent studies revealed that postpartum βERKO mice were significantly more aggressive than βWT mice. βERKO mice displayed higher numbers of lunge and bite attacks with shorter latency, and they also exhibited vigorous fighting episodes with continuous chase, biting, and lateral attacks (figure 10.7A; Le, Mirasol, Pfaff, & Ogawa, 2002). Furthermore, βERKO females showed a number of behavioral characteristics suggesting higher levels of anxiety or social reactivity: they (a) more frequently moved between two compartments (a

(A) Number of Attacks

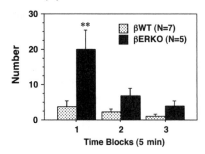

(B) Number of Transitions

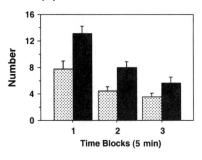

FIGURE 10.7 Effects of ER-β gene disruption on the levels of postpartum aggression. Female βERKO and βWT mice were tested against olfactory bulbectomized male intruder mice during Postpartum Days 1–8. Females were tested in their home cages, which were divided into two compartments, a smaller nest area and a larger area where food, water, and nest material were provided. Mean numbers of attacks (A) and transitions between the two compartments (B) were calculated in each of three 5-min blocks. βERKO female mice not only showed significantly higher levels of aggression than βWT female, but also more frequently went back and forth between two compartments during aggression tests. $^{*}p < .05$, $^{**}p < .01$ vs. βWT.

smaller nest area and a larger area where food, water, and nest material were provided) in their home cages (figure 10.7B), (b) displayed more stretching-sniff postures, and (c) more often attacked intruders that invaded the nest area than WT mice. These findings suggest that ER-β may play a role in the regulation of postpartum aggression, although its neural mechanism needs to be determined.

Although not a naturally occurring aggressive behavior, it is possible to induce "male-type" aggressive behavior (i.e., triggered by olfactory cues from gonadally intact male opponents) in female mice. A number of studies have shown that gonadectomized female mice show vigorous aggressive behavior toward male opponents in response to testosterone or dihydrotestosterone administration (Gandelman, 1980; Simon & Masters, 1987; Simon, Whalen, & Tate, 1985). According to these studies, however, the levels of aggression were generally lower than those seen in male mice with similar treatment, suggesting a sex difference in sensitivity. Furthermore, unlike in male mice, estrogen did not induce aggression in gonadectomized female mice (Simon & Masters, 1987; Simon & Whalen, 1987; Simon et al., 1985), unless females were treated neonatally with estrogen (Klein & Simon, 1991). Therefore, it is assumed that activation of AR plays a more critical role than ER activation in the induction of male-type aggressive behavior in gonadectomized female mice by testosterone. It remains possible, however, that activation of ER by estradiol, as an aromatized metabolite of testosterone, may modulate expression of aggressive behavior induced by testosterone via AR stimulation (even though insufficient by itself to induce male-type aggression in female mice). Because an inhibitory action of ER-β is implicated in a number of different types of aggression as we have described them (e.g., intermale aggression, postpartum aggression, etc.), we have examined whether testosterone-inducible aggression in female mice might also be modulated by an ER-β-mediated mechanism (figure 10.8). In this study, gonadectomized βERKO and βWT female mice, treated with different doses of testosterone (0, 1.5, or 5 mg/21days), were tested with an olfactory bulbectomized male intruder mouse (Durbak, Pfaff, & Ogawa, 2002). Higher doses and longer duration of testosterone treatment were necessary to induce aggression in βERKO compared to βWT females. These results suggest that sensitivity to testosterone-inducible aggression is reduced, instead of increased as originally expected, in female mice lacking the ER-β gene. This markedly

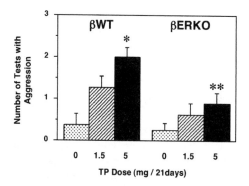

FIGURE 10.8 Effects of ER-β gene disruption on the levels of testosterone-inducible aggression in female mice. Female βERKO and βWT mice were tested gonadectomized and treated with testosterone propionate containing (TP; 1.5 or 5 mg/21 days) or placebo pellets. Mice were tested every 3 days for a total of six times against olfactory bulbectomized male intruder mice. The number of tests in which each female showed aggressive behavior during the last three tests after implants was calculated. βWT female mice showed higher levels of aggression in response to TP treatment than βERKO female mice; *$p < .05$ vs. placebo group of the same genotype, **$p < .05$ vs. βWT of the same treatment group.

contrasts with the effects of ER-β gene deletion on postpartum aggression in female mice, suggesting that regulation of female aggression via ER-β may be dependent on the type of aggression. Although the exact mechanisms of inhibition of testosterone-inducible aggression by the lack of the ER-β gene need to be determined in further studies, it is possible that ER-β gene disruption may indirectly affect the AR-dependent neural system of aggression. A number of studies in rats have demonstrated that the levels of brain AR mRNA are regulated by estrogen both in adulthood (Handa, Kerr, DonCarlos, McGivern, & Hejna, 1996) and during postnatal development (McAbee & DonCarlos, 1999a, 1999b) in the medial preoptic area and bed nucleus of the stria terminalis, which are known to be involved in the regulation of aggressive behavior (Lisciotto, DeBold, Haney, & Miczek, 1990; Owen, Peters, & Bronson, 1974). Although it has not yet been determined which type of ER is responsible for the regulation of AR gene expression, these findings lead us to hypothesize that the hormonal regulation of brain AR might be modified in βERKO female mice.

Potential Brain Mechanisms of ER-Mediated Estrogenic Regulation of Aggressive Behavior in Male Mice

Behavioral studies to date, as described above, collectively suggest that ER-α and ER-β activations have opposite effects on male aggression and that ER-β may inhibit aggressive behavior induced by activation of ER-α (either alone or in combination with the activation of androgen receptors). The accumulating evidence led to the hypothesis that ER-β plays a critical role in fine-tuning the final outcome of aggressive behavior, in contrast to the "all or none" type of regulation by ER-α. There are a number of possible brain mechanisms that may contribute to an inhibitory action of ER-β on aggressive behavior. One such mechanism would include the ascending midbrain raphe nuclei, consisting of the dorsal (DRN) and median/paramedian raphe. In this brain region, abundant ER-β expression is identified at both the mRNA and protein levels in several species (Mitra et al., 2003; Nomura et al., 2003; Shughrue, Lane, & Merchenthaler, 1997). Detailed anatomical studies in male mouse brains have also demonstrated that ER-β is a predominant form of ER widely distributed in the DRN, especially in the ventral and dorsal subdivisions (Nomura et al., 2005). The total number of ER-β-immunoreactive cells was nearly twice that of ER-α in the ventral subdivision of the DRN, whereas in the adjacent periaqueductal gray, it was about one third of that of ER-α. The functional significance of the differential distributions of the two types of ERs in the DRN is shown in terms of estrogenic regulation of progestin receptors (PR), one of the downstream gene products of ER-mediated action. Studies using αEKRO and βERKO mice revealed that estrogen treatment induced PR in the DRN of αERKO mice to the same extent as in αWT mice (Alves et al., 2000), whereas PR induction was greatly reduced in βERKO mice compared to that in βWT mice (Alves et al., 2001).

The DRN comprises the largest population of serotonin (5-hydroxytryptamine; 5-HT) synthesizing neurons. 5-HT is one of the most well characterized neurotransmitters for its inhibitory effect on aggressive behavior (Hen, 1996; Miczek, Maxson, Fish, & Faccidomo, 2001; Olivier, Mos, van Oorschot, & Hen, 1995). Recent studies in male rats and mice also demonstrate that the presynaptic 5-HT$_{1A}$ autoreceptor in the DRN may also be involved in the regulation of aggressive behavior (de Boer, Lesourd, Mocaer, & Koolhaas, 1999, 2000; Veenema, Meijer, de Kloet, & Koolhaas, 2003). In species such as macaques and rats, it is well established that estrogen modulates the serotonergic system in the DRN by affecting mRNA or protein levels of tryptophan hydroxylase (TPH), the rate-limiting enzyme for 5-HT synthesis (Pecins-Thompson, Brown, Kohama, & Bethea, 1996), as well as serotonin transporter mRNA (McQueen, Wilson, & Fink, 1997; McQueen, Wilson, Sumner, & Fink, 1999; Pecins-Thompson, Brown, & Bethea, 1998) and the autoreceptor, 5-HT$_{1A}$ (Pecins-Thompson & Bethea, 1999). In these species, it has also been shown that TPH colocalizes with ER-β in the DRN (Alves et al., 2001; Gundlah, Lu, Mirkes, & Bethea, 2001; Lu, Ozawa, Nishi, Ito, & Kawata, 2001). Using dual-label immunocytochemistry for ER-α or ER-β with TPH, we also found in male mouse brains that over 90% of ER-β-immunoreactive cells exhibited TPH immunoreactivity in all subdivisions of the DRN, whereas on average, only 23% of ER-β-immunoreactive cells contained TPH (Nomura et al., 2005). In addition, there was a small, but significant, decrease in the levels of TPH mRNA expression in the ventral DRN of βERKO mice compared to βWT mice, whereas TPH mRNA levels were not affected in αERKO mice. Therefore, it is conceivable that ER-β activation may contribute to the estrogenic regulation of neuroendocrine and behavioral functions, including aggression, in part by acting directly on 5-HT neurons in the midbrain raphe nuclei.

It is also possible that ER-β-mediated estrogenic actions on neuropeptides, such as oxytocin and vasopressin, as well as gonadotropin releasing hormone (GnRH), may also play a role in the modulation of aggressive behavior in male mice. ER-β is coexpressed in neurons expressing these neuropeptides in a number of hypothalamic, as well as limbic, brain area. In our recent studies, estrogenic up- or down-regulation of oxytocin and vasopressin mRNA levels, as well as developmental changes in GnRH expression, are either abolished or modified in βERKO male mice (figure 10.9; Nomura, McKenna, Korach, Pfaff, & Ogawa, 2002; Ogawa, Mirasol, Mesola, Pfaff, & Parhar, 2002; Soga et al., 2003).

Aggression, Social Living, and Social Recognition

Most mammalian species live in groups, with group composition, social organization, and quality of inter-

actions varying greatly among species. The degree of mammalian social living ranges from highly solitary species (e.g., tigers) to species that live in crowded groups whose life is often ruled by complex social interactions (e.g., chimpanzees). In solitary mammals, elevated intolerance and aggression toward other individuals spaces the animals apart and results in few social interactions. In highly solitary species tolerance to conspecifics is often limited to mating and, in the case of females, tolerance is extended during parental care. Other mammalian species tolerate other individuals and share at least part of their lives with them. In most species with a monogamous social system, where one male and one female spend at least part of the reproductive season together, not only do they tolerate each other, but also they can develop pair bonds (Carter & Keverne, 2002). Increasing levels of tolerance of others may result in groups of various sizes. As humans are highly social mammals with a complex social structure, it is important for us to gain an understanding of the neurobiological mechanisms that are associated with social living. We need to understand not only the proximal mechanisms of sociality, but also their functional and evolutionary implications (Tang-Martinez, 2003). In this section we lean heavily on a recently considered review (Choleris et al., 2004) to summarize mechanisms for social recognition which are important, in turn, for the control of aggression.

Most laboratory research on the neurobiological mechanisms of social interactions has focused on the mechanisms underlying sexual behavior and aggression (Nelson, 2000). As sexual behaviors occur in both solitary and social mammals, the understanding of its neural and genetic (Pfaff, 1999) hormonal substrates provides only limited information on the neurobiology of social life, especially in animals that have complex social structures. As for aggression, it can hardly be considered a prosocial behavior (Parmigiani, Ferrari, & Palanza, 1998). Actually, in order for sociality to develop, intraspecific aggression needs to be either eliminated, with the social interactions being turned into affiliative, bonding interactions, or constrained through the development of rituals that limit both the occurrence and the often lethal consequences of open aggression (de Waal, 2000; Nelson, 2000). For these reasons, the analysis of the mechanisms regulating open and ritualized aggression is important for the understanding of several components of group living. Significant advances have been made in laboratory

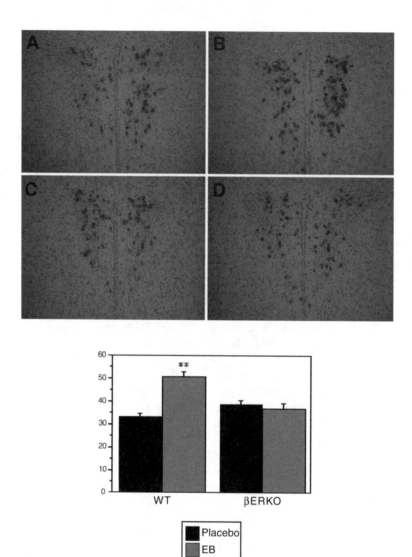

FIGURE 10.9 Abolition of estrogenic up-regulation of oxytocin (OT) mRNA expression in the paraventricular nucleus (PVN) by ER-β gene disruption in gonadectomized male mice. (Top) Representative bright-field photomicrographs of emulsion-dipped sections showing the genotype differences in the effects of estrogen treatment on the OT gene expression in the middle anterior/posterior levels of the PVN. Sections were hybridized to a ^{35}S-labeled oligodeoxynecleotide probe complementary to mRNA for OT and counterstained using cresyl violet. (A) and (B) are sections from placebo- and estrogen-treated WT mice, respectively. (C) and (D) are sections from placebo- and estrogen-treated βERKO mice, respectively. The scale bar represents 100 μm. (Bottom) Quantitative analyses of the effects of estrogen on OT transcript prevalence in the middle anterior/posterior levels (Bregma, 0.70 to –0.82 mm). Values represent the mean ± SEM; **$p < .01$ compared to mice from the placebo-treated group of the same genotype. From "Estrogen Receptor-β Regulates Transcript Levels for Oxytocin and Arginine Vasopressin in the Hypothalamic Paraventricular Nucleus of Male Mice," by M. Nomura, E. McKenna, K. S. Korach, D. W. Pfaff, and S. Ogawa, 2002, *Molecular Brain Research, 109*, p. 91. Copyright 2002 by Elsevier. Adapted with permission.

research in this field (Blanchard & Blanchard, 2003; Miczek et al., 2001; Nelson & Chiavegatto, 2001).

Social recognition, in which animals identify and recognize other individual conspecifics, is an essential prerequisite for the existence of many social behaviors. It allows for the development of bonds between individual animals, as well as for the establishment of hierarchies that limit aggressive interactions and allow group living (Halpin, 1986). Social recognition, by allowing animals to recognize and avoid conspecifics infected with parasites, is also important for coping with the increased risk of exposure to parasites and infection that is consequent to life in a group (Møller, Dufva, & Allander, 1993). Unique modifications in the behavior that an animal directs toward another individual are based on past experiences with that same and other individual animals and are considered evidence of true individual recognition (Lai & Johnston, 2002). To date, true individual recognition has been shown in various species of rodents, such as mice, rats, gerbils, and hamsters, that are commonly used in laboratory studies on social behavior (Choleris & Kavaliers, 1999; Halpin, 1986).

The Interplay of Oxytocin and Estrogens in the Regulation of Social Recognition in Female Mice

The neuroendocrine systems involved in social recognition in rodents include at least two neuropeptides, oxytocin and vasopressin (Young, 2002). Vasopressin is more abundant in male, than female, brains and various studies have implicated it in the mediation of social recognition in male, but not female, rats and mice, where its effects depend upon androgenic hormones (Bluthe & Dantzer, 1993). Oxytocin (OT), instead, is equally expressed in female and male brains and modulates social recognition in both sexes. In female rodents estrogenic regulation of social behavior has been studied in mice whose genes for ER-α or ER-β had been disrupted (αERKO and βERKO) (e.g., Imwalle, Scordalakes, & Rissman, 2002; Ogawa et al., 1999; Ogawa, Eng, et al., 1998; Ogawa, Korach, et al., 2002; Ogawa et al., 1996; Rissman et al., 1999). Estrogens directly regulate the production of OT in the hypothalamus of rats (de Kloet, Voorhuis, Boschma, & Elands, 1986; Dellovade, Zhu, & Pfaff, 1999) and the expression of the gene for the oxytocin receptor (OTR) in various areas of the brains of rats (Quinones-Jenab et al., 1997). Estrogens also regulate OT's mediation

of social recognition in females, with estrogen treatment improving social recognition in ovariectomized female rats (Hlinak, 1993) and mice (A. C. Tang, personal communication; Tang et al., submitted for publication).

A series of functional genomic studies has recently provided new information on the interplay of OT and estrogens in the mediation of social recognition. Male mice deficient in the gene for OT (OT knockout mice, OTKO) showed impaired social recognition (Ferguson et al., 2000) and this deficit could be rescued by infusion of OT in the medial amygdala, whereas the infusion of an OT antagonist blocked social recognition in WT mice (Ferguson, Aldag, Insel, & Young, 2001). The social amnesia of OTKO mice was specific for social recognition, in that these mice were not impaired in other types of learning or in olfactory sensitivity and discrimination (Ferguson et al., 2000). We have recently demonstrated a similar deficit in social recognition in OTKO, αERKO, and βERKO female mice (Choleris, Gustafsson, et al., 2003). We used the habituation/dishabituation procedure (Gheusi, Bluthe, Goodall, & Dantzer, 1994), in which social recognition is inferred from changes in the behavior of animals in subsequent tests. This behavioral test is based on the natural propensity of mice to investigate (e.g., sniffing aimed at the anogenital region or other parts of the body) another mouse placed in their home cage. When the same intruder mouse is presented in subsequent tests, the social response of the resident mouse shows habituation, that is, it declines to very low levels. The initial level of social investigation can be reinstated (dishabituation) in the resident mouse, if a different, novel, conspecific animal is presented. We showed (Choleris, Gustafsson, et al., 2003) that female OTKO, αERKO, and βERKO mice were all similarly impaired in the classic social recognition test, in that in contrast to their WT littermates, the KO females showed neither a habituation response to a repeatedly presented female individual mouse nor a dishabituation response when given a new female mouse. A detailed ethological analysis of the behavior of the mice during testing showed that the three KO mice were not, overall, impaired in various other activities (e.g., self-grooming, digging, and nonsocial investigation). This suggests that the behavioral changes observed in our studies were specific for social behavior rather than deriving from a generalized behavioral impairment. Our studies confirmed, and extended to females, previous results with male OTKO and αERKO mice

(Ferguson et al., 2000; Imwalle et al., 2002), as well as involving for the first time the ER-β gene.

We have recently confirmed and extended these results using both a different genetic manipulation and a different behavioral paradigm. In a first study we used antisense oligodeoxynucleotides and directly demonstrated the involvement of OTR in the medial amygdala in social recognition in female mice. We bilaterally injected antisense DNA targeted against the OTR gene in the medial amygdala and showed that OT wild-type (OTWT) female mice became as impaired in social recognition as their littermate OTKO mice (Choleris, Little, Mong, Langer, & Pfaff, 2003). In a second series of experiments, using a more sensitive binary choice discrimination test (Beauchamp & Yamazaki, 2003; Engelmann, Wotjak, & Landgraf, 1995), we confirmed that OTKO, αERKO, and βERKO mice are all impaired in the identification of individual mice when presented with a direct choice between a familiar and a novel conspecific (Choleris, Pfaff, & Ogawa, 2003).

We have recently identified an important ecologically and evolutionarily significant context in which OTKO, αERKO, and βERKO mice were also impaired in the identification of social chemical signals. OTKO, αERKO, and βERKO males and females were similarly and specifically impaired in their recognition of, and display of aversive responses to, the odors of infected male mice (Kavaliers, Choleris, et al., 2003; Kavaliers, Colwell, et al., 2003). These studies demonstrated that the genes for OT, ER-α and ER-β are involved in the recognition, active avoidance of, and mediation of aversive responses to the odors of male mice infected with either endo- or ectoparasites.

Based on these results, we have proposed a novel gene micronet that forms the core around which increasingly complex genetic, hormonal, and neural interactions can be organized in the regulation of social recognition. This model described a four-gene micronet involving the four genes coding for ER-α, ER-β, OT, and the OTR in the control of social recognition in the central nervous system. In this model circulating estrogens affect OT regulation of social recognition at two levels and in two areas of the mouse brain: through ER-β they regulate OT production in the paraventricular nucleus (PVN) of the hypothalamus and through ER-α they control the expression of the OTR gene in the amygdala (Choleris, Gustafsson, et al., 2003). The model also includes processing of individual-specific olfactory chemical information that is crucial for rodents' social interactions (Dulac & Torello, 2003; Johnston,

2003). In our model, signals from the main and accessory olfactory bulbs converge in the amygdala (Dulac & Torello, 2003), where they are processed for the identification and recognition of individual-specific olfactory information. This model brings together behavioral, genetic, and molecular information.

At the behavioral level, the model is supported by our own and others' studies showing that social recognition depends upon OT (Choleris, Gustafsson, et al., 2003; Ferguson et al., 2001, 2000), ER-α (Choleris, Gustafsson, et al., 2003; Imwalle et al., 2002), ER-β (Choleris, Gustafsson, et al., 2003), and OTR in the amygdala (Choleris, Little, et al., 2003; Ferguson et al., 2000) and is improved by estrogens (de Kloet et al., 1986; Hlinak, 1993). Other behavioral studies have shown impaired social recognition in OTKO, αERKO, and βERKO male and female mice in the ecologically and evolutionarily relevant context of the recognition and avoidance of parasitized individuals (Kavaliers, Choleris, et al., 2003; Kavaliers, Colwell, et al., 2003). The gene micronet model is further supported by genetic and molecular studies showing that although ER-α is almost absent in the mouse PVN, ER-β is highly expressed there (Mitra et al., 2003). In further agreement with our four-gene micronet model are studies showing the lack of estrogen induction of OT in βERKO male (Nomura, McKenna, et al., 2002) and female (Patisaul, Scordalakes, Young, & Rissman, 2003) mice and the high expression of ER-α in the amygdala (Mitra et al., 2003), where its crucial role for the induction of OTR has been shown (Young, Wang, Donaldson, & Rissman, 1998). Very recently, other studies with female βERKO mice have further confirmed that OT production is regulated by ER-β in the PVN, whereas OTR binding in the medial amygdala seems to be independent of ER-β (Patisaul et al., 2003). Together, as reviewed (Choleris et al., submitted for publication), these behavioral, genetic, and molecular studies support the micronet model in the regulation of social recognition.

Conclusions and Summary of Three Lessons From the Mouse Data, and Their Possible Contribution to Understanding Human Aggression

In addition to the specific mechanisms influencing the aggressive behavior of mice, as reviewed in this chapter, three significant general "lessons" are to be learned:

1. An individual gene can have opposite effects on aggressive behaviors in the two sexes. For example, αERKO males are less aggressive than their control WT littermates, but αERKO females are more aggressive than WT mice.
2. The ER-β gene can show the opposite regulation of aggressive behaviors compared to the ER-α gene. For example, βERKO male mice, tested as either adolescents or young adults, are more aggressive, but the αERKO male is less aggressive than WT control mice.
3. In female mice, the ER-β gene can have opposite effects according to the type of aggression tested. For example, βERKO mice have quantitatively less TP-facilitated aggression (figure 10.8), but are more sensitive in tests of maternal aggression postpartum (figure 10.7).

All of these findings point to a great deal of specificity in the functional genomics of aggression, even in mice: Specificity according to (a) the gene examined, (b) the gender of the mouse tested, and (c) the type of aggression assayed.

Speculating about the future of research in this field, at least three guesses can be ventured. First, we will delve much more deeply into mechanisms of the relevant hormone effects at the level of the neuronal membrane, in terms of signal transduction pathways, and, of course, at the level of transcriptional changes. Second, these different routes of hormonal mechanisms will no longer be thought of as alternatives exclusive of each other. Already, with respect to estrogen action, Vasudevan in our lab has shown that membrane-limited estrogen effects can potentiate the hormone's later transcriptional effects. Third, the field will graduate from its emphasis on the individual behavioral response to the consideration (a) of long chains of responses and (b) of CNS states of arousal that affect large numbers of emotional behaviors. Controls over the predisposition to aggression would be an excellent example of this.

Is it possible that genomic differences contribute to individual differences in aggression and violence exhibited by humans? From one point of view this seems likely. Because different species of fish, mice, horses, and dogs all show strain-dependent levels of aggressive behavior, we would have to assume that natural selection discarded all of these behavior regulatory genomic mechanisms in order to conclude that there is absolutely no role for genetic influences on human aggression. On the other hand, it would be impossible at this

time to estimate the percentage of variance accounted for by any given genetic alteration for any particular form of human aggression (see Blonigen & Krueger, ch. 2 in this volume). Instead we emphasize that there are several levels of causation of aggressive behavior by humans and therefore, correspondingly, there are many types of tactics that can help in the reduction of violence exhibited by individual men or women (Devine, Gilligan, Miczek, & Pfaff, 2005). Socioeconomic differences associated with their consequent psychological conditions, cultural influences, rearing differences, alcohol use, and emotional mood states can codetermine violent behavior by young humans. Although genetic predispositions figure in the large number and enduring influence of all of these factors, other causative factors prevent simple-minded extrapolations from well-controlled mouse studies to human social behaviors.

References

Alves, S. E., McEwen, B. S., Hayashi, S., Korach, K. S., Pfaff, D. W., & Ogawa, S. (2000). Estrogen-regulated progestin receptors are found in the midbrain raphe but not hippocampus of estrogen receptor alpha (ER alpha) gene-disrupted mice. *Journal of Comparative Neurology, 427,* 185–195.

Alves, S., McEwen, B. S., Hoskin, E., Gustafsson, J. A., Korach, K. S., Pfaff, D. W., et al. (2001). Regional differences in estrogen regulation of the progestin receptor: Evidence from the estrogen receptor β gene disrupted mouse. *Society for Neuroscience Abstracts.*

Beauchamp, G. K., & Yamazaki, K. (2003). Chemical signalling in mice. *Biochemical Society Transactions, 31,* 147–151.

Blanchard, D. C., & Blanchard, R. J. (2003). What can animal aggression research tell us about human aggression? *Hormones and Behavior, 44,* 171–177.

Bluthe, R. M., & Dantzer, R. (1993). Role of the vomeronasal system in vasopressinergic modulation of social recognition in rats. *Brain Research, 604,* 205–210.

Bowden, N. J., & Brain, P. F. (1978). Blockade of testosterone-maintained intermale fighting in albino laboratory mice by an aromatization inhibitor. *Physiology and Behavior, 20,* 543–546.

Brain, P. F., Haug, M., & Kamis, A. B. (1983). Hormones and different tests for aggression with particular reference to the effects of testosterone metabolites. In J. Balthazart, E. Prove, & R. Gilles (Eds.), *Hormones and behaviour in higher vertebrates* (pp. 290–304). Berlin: Springer-Verlag.

Broida, J., & Svare, B. (1981). Postpartum aggression in C57BL/6 and DBA/2J mice: Experiential and environmental influences. *Behavioral and Neural Biology*, 35, 76–83.

Carter, S. C., & Keverne, E. B. (2002). The neurobiology of social affiliation and pair bonding. In D. W. Pfaff, A. P. Arnold, A. M. Etgen, S. E. Fahrbach, & R. T. Rubin (Eds.), *Hormones, brain and behavior* (Vol. 1, pp. 299–337). San Diego: Academic Press.

Choleris, E., Gustafsson, J. A., Korach, K. S., Muglia, L. J., Pfaff, D. W., & Ogawa, S. (2003). An estrogen-dependent four-gene micronet regulating social recognition: A study with oxytocin and estrogen receptor-alpha and -beta knockout mice. *Proceedings of the National Academy of Sciences USA*, 100, 6192–6197.

Choleris, E., & Kavaliers, M. (1999). Social learning in animals: Sex differences and neurobiological analysis. *Pharmacology, Biochemistry and Behavior*, 64, 767–776.

Choleris, E., Little, S. R., Mong, J. A., Langer, R., & Pfaff, D. W. (2003). Antisense DNA against oxytocin receptor mRNA from microspheres in the medial amygdala blocked social recognition in female mice. *Society for Neuroscience Abstracts*.

Choleris, E., Pfaff, D. W., & Ogawa, S. (2003). Similar impairments of social discrimination in estrogen receptor alpha, beta and oxytocin knockout female mice: A detailed behavioral analysis. *Hormones and Behavior*, 44, 42.

Clark, C. R., & Nowell, N. W. (1979). The effects of the antiestrogen CI-628 on androgen-induced aggressive behavior in castrated male mice. *Hormones and Behavior*, 12, 205–210.

Couse, J. F., Hewitt, S. C., Bunch, D. O., Sar, M., Walker, V. R., Davis, B. J., et al. (1999). Postnatal sex reversal of the ovaries in mice lacking estrogen receptors alpha and beta. *Science*, 286, 2328–2331.

De Boer, S. F., Lesourd, M., Mocaer, E., & Koolhaas, J. M. (1999). Selective antiaggressive effects of alnespirone in resident-intruder test are mediated via 5-hydroxytryptamine 1A receptors: A comparative pharmacological study with 8-hydroxy-2-dipropylaminotetralin, ipsapirone, buspirone, eltoprazine, and WAY-100635. *Journal of Pharmacology and Experimental Therapeutics*, 288, 1125–1133.

De Boer, S. F., Lesourd, M., Mocaer, E., & Koolhaas, J. M. (2000). Somatodendritic 5-HT(1A) autoreceptors mediate the anti-aggressive actions of 5-HT(1A) receptor agonists in rats: An ethopharmacological study with S-15535, alnespirone, and WAY-100635. *Neuropsychopharmacology*, 23, 20–33.

De Kloet, E. R., Voorhuis, D. A., Boschma, Y., & Elands, J. (1986). Estradiol modulates density of putative "oxytocin receptors" in discrete rat brain regions. *Neuroendocrinology*, 44, 415–421.

Dellovade, T. L., Zhu, Y. S., & Pfaff, D. W. (1999). Thyroid hormones and estrogen affect oxytocin gene expression in hypothalamic neurons. *Journal of Neuroendocrinology*, 11, 1–10.

Devine, J., Gilligan, J., Miczek, K., & Pfaff, D. W. (2005). Scientific approaches to youth violence prevention. *Annals of the New York Academy of Science*.

De Waal, F. B. (2000). Primates—a natural heritage of conflict resolution. *Science*, 289, 586–590.

Dulac, C., & Torello, A. T. (2003). Molecular detection of pheromone signals in mammals: From genes to behaviour. *Nature Reviews Neuroscience*, 4, 551–562.

Durbak, L., Pfaff, D. W., & Ogawa, S. (2002). Role of the estrogen receptor b gene in testosterone-inducible aggression in female mice. *Abstract for Society for Neuroscience*.

Eddy, E. M., Washburn, T. F., Bunch, D. O., Goulding, E. H., Gladen, B. C., Lubahn, D. B., et al. (1996). Targeted disruption of the estrogen receptor gene in male mice causes alteration of spermatogenesis and infertility. *Endocrinology*, 137, 4796–4805.

Engelmann, M., Wotjak, C. T., & Landgraf, R. (1995). Social discrimination procedure: An alternative method to investigate juvenile recognition abilities in rats. *Physiology and Behavior*, 58, 315–321.

Ferguson, J. N., Aldag, J. M., Insel, T. R., & Young, L. J. (2001). Oxytocin in the medial amygdala is essential for social recognition in the mouse. *Journal of Neuroscience*, 21, 8278–8285.

Ferguson, J. N., Young, L. J., Hearn, E. F., Matzuk, M. M., Insel, T. R., & Winslow, J. T. (2000). Social amnesia in mice lacking the oxytocin gene. *Nature Genetics*, 25, 284–288.

Gandelman, R. (1980). Gonadal hormones and the induction of intraspecific fighting in mice. *Neuroscience and Biobehavioral Reviews*, 4, 133–140.

Gheusi, G., Bluthe, R. M., Goodall, G., & Dantzer, R. (1994). Ethological study of the effects of tetrahydroaminoacridine (THA) on social recognition in rats. *Psychopharmacology*, 114, 644–650.

Gundlah, C., Lu, N. Z., Mirkes, S. J., & Bethea, C. L. (2001). Estrogen receptor beta (ERbeta) mRNA and protein in serotonin neurons of macaques. *Molecular Brain Research*, 91, 14–22.

Halpin, Z. T. (1986). Individual odors among mammals: Origins and functions. *Advances in the Study of Behavior*, 16, 39–70.

Handa, R. J., Kerr, J. E., DonCarlos, L. L., McGivern, R. F., & Hejna, G. (1996). Hormonal regulation of androgen receptor messenger RNA in the medial preoptic area of the male rat. *Molecular Brain Research*, 39, 57–67.

Hasan, S. A., Brain, P. F., & Castano, D. (1988). Studies of effects of tamoxifen (ICI 46474) on agonistic encounters between pairs of intact mice. *Hormones and Behavior, 22,* 178–185.

Hen, R. (1996). Mean genes. *Neuron, 16,* 17–21.

Hlinak, Z. (1993). Social recognition in ovariectomized and estradiol-treated female rats. *Hormones and Behavior, 27,* 159–166.

Imwalle, D. B., Scordalakes, E. M., & Rissman, E. F. (2002). Estrogen receptor alpha influences socially motivated behaviors. *Hormones and Behavior, 42,* 484–491.

Johnston, R. E. (2003). Chemical communication in rodents: From pheromones to individual recognition. *Journal of Mammalogy, 84,* 1141–1162.

Kavaliers, M., Choleris, E., Ågmo, A., Gustafsson, J.-Å., Korach, K. S., Muglia, L. J., et al. (2003). Impaired recognition of and aversion to parasitized mice by oxytocin and knockout and estrogen receptor α and β knockout male mice. Manuscript submitted for publication.

Kavaliers, M., Colwell, D. D., Choleris, E., Ågmo, A., Muglia, L. J., Ogawa, S., et al. (2003). Impaired discrimination of and aversion to parasitized male odors by female oxytocin knockout mice. *Genes Brain and Behavior, 2,* 220–230.

Klein, W. P., & Simon, N. G. (1991). Timing of neonatal testosterone exposure in the differentiation of estrogenic regulatory systems for aggression. *Physiology and Behavior, 50,* 91–93.

Krege, J. H., Hodgin, J. B., Couse, J. F., Enmark, E., Warner, M., Mahler, J. F., et al. (1998). Generation and reproductive phenotypes of mice lacking estrogen receptor beta. *Proceedings of the National Academy of Sciences USA, 95,* 15677–15682.

Kuiper, G. G. J. M., Carlsson, B., Grandien, K., Enmark, E., Haggblad, J., Nilsson, S., et al. (1997). Comparison of the ligand binding specificity and transcript tissue distribution of estrogen receptor alpha and beta. *Endocrinology, 138,* 863–870.

Kuiper, G. G. J. M., Enmark, E., Peltohuikko, M., & Nilsson, S. (1996). Cloning of a novel estrogen receptor expressed in rat prostate and ovary. *Proceedings of the National Academy of Sciences USA, 93,* 5925–5930.

Laflamme, N., Nappi, R. E., Drolet, G., Labrie, C., & Rivest, S. (1998). Expression and neuropeptidergic characterization of estrogen receptors (ERalpha and ERbeta) throughout the rat brain: Anatomical evidence of distinct roles of each subtype. *Journal of Neurobiology, 36,* 357–378.

Lai, W. S., & Johnston, R. E. (2002). Individual recognition after fighting by golden hamsters: A new method. *Physiology and Behavior, 76,* 225–239.

Le, T. M., Mirasol, E. G., Pfaff, D. W., & Ogawa, S. (2002). Role of the estrogen receptor b gene in postpartum aggression in mice. *Society for Neuroscience Abstracts, 288,* 283.

Lindzey, J., & Korach, K. S. (1997). Developmental and physiological effects of estrogen receptor gene disruption in mice. *Trends in Endocrinology and Metabolism, 8,* 137–145.

Lisciotto, C. A., DeBold, J. F., Haney, M., & Miczek, K. A. (1990). Implants of testosterone into the septal forebrain activate aggressive behavior in male mice. *Aggressive Behavior, 16,* 249–258.

Lu, H., Ozawa, H., Nishi, M., Ito, T., & Kawata, M. (2001). Serotonergic neurones in the dorsal raphe nucleus that project into the medial preoptic area contain oestrogen receptor beta. *Journal of Neuroendocrinology, 13,* 839–845.

Lubahn, D. B., Moyer, J. S., Golding, T. S., Couse, J. F., Korach, K. S., & Smithies, O. (1993). Alternation of reproductive function but not prenatal sexual development after insertional disruption of the mouse estrogen receptor gene. *Proceedings of the National Academy of Sciences USA, 90,* 11162–11166.

McAbee, M. D., & DonCarlos, L. L. (1999a). Estrogen, but not androgens, regulates androgen receptor messenger ribonucleic acid expression in the developing male rat forebrain. *Endocrinology, 140,* 3674–3681.

McAbee, M. D., & DonCarlos, L. L. (1999b). Regulation of androgen receptor messenger ribonucleic acid expression in the developing rat forebrain. *Endocrinology, 140,* 1807–1814.

McQueen, J. K., Wilson, H., & Fink, G. (1997). Estradiol-17 beta increases serotonin transporter (SERT) mRNA levels and the density of SERT-binding sites in female rat brain. *Molecular Brain Research, 45,* 13–23.

McQueen, J. K., Wilson, H., Sumner, B. E., & Fink, G. (1999). Serotonin transporter (SERT) mRNA and binding site densities in male rat brain affected by sex steroids. *Molecular Brain Research, 63,* 241–247.

Miczek, K. A., Maxson, S. C., Fish, E. W., & Faccidomo, S. (2001). Aggressive behavioral phenotypes in mice. *Behavioral Brain Research, 125,* 167–181.

Mitra, S. W., Hoskin, E., Yudkovitz, J., Pear, L., Wilkinson, H. A., Hayashi, S., et al. (2003). Immunolocalization of estrogen receptor beta in the mouse brain: Comparison with estrogen receptor alpha. *Endocrinology, 144,* 2055–2067.

Møller, A. P., Dufva, R., & Allander, K. (1993). Parasites and the evolution of host social behaviour. *Advances in the Study of Behavior, 22,* 65–102.

Nelson, R. J. (2000). Affiliative and aggressive behavior. In *An introduction to behavioral endocrinology* (2nd ed., pp. 395–445). Sunderland, MA: Sinauer.

Nelson, R. J., & Chiavegatto, S. (2001). Molecular basis of aggression. *Trends in Neuroscience, 24,* 713–719.

Nomura, M., Akema, K. T., Alves, S. E., Korach, K. S., Gustafsson, J.-Å., Pfaff, D. W., et al. (2004). Differential distribution of estrogen receptor (ER)-α and

ER-β in the midbrain raphe nucleus and peri-aqueductal gray in male mouse: Predominant role of ER-β in midbrain serotonergic system. Manuscript submitted for publication.

Nomura, M., Durbak, L., Chan, J., Smithies, O., Gustafsson, J. A., Korach, K. S., et al. (2002). Genotype/age interactions on aggressive behavior in gonadally intact estrogen receptor β knockout (βERKO) male mice. *Hormones and Behavior, 41*, 288–296.

Nomura, M., Durbak, L., Korach, K. S., Weihua, Z., Gustafsson, J. A., Pfaff, D. W., et al. (2001). An inhibitory role of ER-β in the regulation of aggressive behavior by estrogen in male mice. *Society of Neuroscience Abstracts*, 856.857.

Nomura, M., Korach, K. S., Pfaff, D. W., & Ogawa, S. (2003). Estrogen receptor beta (ERbeta) protein levels in neurons depend on estrogen receptor α (ERα) gene expression and on its ligand in a brain region-specific manner. *Molecular Brain Research, 110*, 7–14.

Nomura, M., McKenna, E., Korach, K. S., Pfaff, D. W., & Ogawa, S. (2002). Estrogen receptor-β regulates transcript levels for oxytocin and arginine vasopressin in the hypothalamic paraventricular nucleus of male mice. *Molecular Brain Research, 109*, 84–94.

Nyby, J., Matochik, J. A., & Barfield, R. J. (1992). Intracranial androgenic and estrogenic stimulation of male-typical behaviors in house mice (*Mus domesticus*). *Hormones and Behavior, 26*, 24–45.

Ogawa, S., Chan, J., Chester, A. E., Gustafsson, J. A., Korach, K. S., & Pfaff, D. W. (1999). Survival of reproductive behaviors in estrogen receptor β gene-deficient (βERKO) male and female mice. *Proceedings of the National Academy of Sciences USA, 96*, 12887–12892.

Ogawa, S., Chester, A. E., Hewitt, S. C., Walker, V. R., Gustafsson, J. A., Smithies, O., et al. (2000). From the cover: Abolition of male sexual behaviors in mice lacking estrogen receptors α and β (αβERKO). *Proceedings of the National Academy of Sciences USA, 97*, 14737–14741.

Ogawa, S., Eng, V., Taylor, J. A., Lubahn, D. B., Korach, K. S., & Pfaff, D. W. (1998). Roles of estrogen receptor-α gene expression in reproduction-related behaviors in female mice. *Endocrinology, 139*, 5070–5081.

Ogawa, S., Korach, K. S., & Pfaff, D. W. (2002). Differential roles of two types of estrogen receptors in reproductive behavior. *Current Opinion of Endocrinology and Diabetes, 9*, 224–229.

Ogawa, S., Lubahn, D. B., Korach, K. S., & Pfaff, D. W. (1997). Behavioral effects of estrogen receptor gene disruption in male mice. *Proceedings of the National Academy of Sciences USA, 94*, 1476–1481.

Ogawa, S., & Makino, J. (1981). Maternal aggression in inbred strains of mice: Effects of reproductive states. *The Japanese Journal of Psychology, 52*, 78–84.

Ogawa, S., & Makino, J. (1984). Aggressive behavior in inbred strains of mice during pregnancy. *Behavioral and Neural Biology, 40*, 195–204.

Ogawa, S., Mirasol, E. G., Mesola, R., Pfaff, D. W., & Parhar, I. S. (2002). Existence of multiple GnRH forms and their co-localization with estrogen receptor β in the male mouse brains. *Society for Neuroscience Abstracts*.

Ogawa, S., Taylor, J. A., Lubahn, D. B., Korach, K. S., & Pfaff, D. W. (1996). Reversal of sex roles in genetic female mice by disruption of estrogen receptor gene. *Neuroendocrinology, 64*, 467–470.

Ogawa, S., Washburn, T. F., Taylor, J., Lubahn, D. B., Korach, K. S., & Pfaff, D. W. (1998). Modifications of testosterone-dependent behaviors by estrogen receptor-α gene disruption in male mice. *Endocrinology, 139*, 5058–5069.

Olivier, B., Mos, J., van Oorschot, R., & Hen, R. (1995). Serotonin receptors and animal models of aggressive behavior. *Pharmacopsychiatry, 28*(Suppl. 2), 80–90.

Osterlund, M., Kuiper, G. G., Gustafsson, J. A., & Hurd, Y. L. (1998). Differential distribution and regulation of estrogen receptor-alpha and -beta mRNA within the female rat brain. *Molecular Brain Research, 54*, 175–180.

Owen, K., Peters, P. J., & Bronson, F. H. (1974). Effects of intracranial implants of testosterone propionate on intermale aggression in the castrated male mouse. *Hormones and Behavior, 5*, 83–92.

Parmigiani, S., Ferrari, P. F., & Palanza, P. (1998). An evolutionary approach to behavioral pharmacology: Using drugs to understand proximate and ultimate mechanisms of different forms of aggression in mice. *Neuroscience and Biobehavioral Reviews, 23*, 143–153.

Patisaul, H. B., Scordalakes, E. M., Young, L. J., & Rissman, E. F. (2003). Oxytocin, but not oxytocin receptor, is regulated by oestrogen receptor beta in the female mouse hypothalamus. *Journal of Neuroendocrinology, 15*, 787–793.

Pecins-Thompson, M., & Bethea, C. L. (1999). Ovarian steroid regulation of serotonin-1A autoreceptor messenger RNA expression in the dorsal raphe of rhesus macaques. *Neuroscience, 89*, 267–277.

Pecins-Thompson, M., Brown, N. A., & Bethea, C. L. (1998). Regulation of serotonin re-uptake transporter mRNA expression by ovarian steroids in rhesus macaques. *Molecular Brain Research, 53*, 120–129.

Pecins-Thompson, M., Brown, N. A., Kohama, S. G., & Bethea, C. L. (1996). Ovarian steroid regulation of tryptophan hydroxylase mRNA expression in rhesus macaques. *Journal of Neuroscience, 16*, 7021–7029.

Pfaff, D. W. (1999). *Drive: Neurobiological and molecular mechanisms of sexual motivation*. Cambridge, MA: MIT Press.

Quinlan, M. G., Shibata, M., Mirasol, E. G., Pfaff, D. W.,

& Ogawa, S. (2003). Effects of estrogen on socio-sexual behaviors in estrogen receptor a and b knock-out female mice. *Society for Neuroscience Abstracts*.

Quinones-Jenab, V., Jenab, S., Ogawa, S., Adan, R. A., Burbach, J. P., & Pfaff, D. W. (1997). Effects of estrogen on oxytocin receptor messenger ribonucleic acid expression in the uterus, pituitary, and forebrain of the female rat. *Neuroendocrinology*, 65, 9–17.

Rissman, E. F., Wersinger, S. R., Fugger, H. N., & Foster, T. C. (1999). Sex with knockout models: Behavioral studies of estrogen receptor alpha. *Brain Research*, 835, 80–90.

Rissman, E. F., Wersinger, S. R., Taylor, J. A., & Lubahn, D. B. (1997). Estrogen receptor function as revealed by knockout studies: Neuroendocrine and behavioral aspects. *Hormones and Behavior*, 31, 232–243.

Scordalakes, E. M., & Rissman, E. F. (2003). Aggression in male mice lacking functional estrogen receptor alpha. *Behavioral Neuroscience*, 117, 38–45.

Shapiro, R. A., Xu, C., & Dorsa, D. M. (2000). Differential transcriptional regulation of rat vasopressin gene expression by estrogen receptor alpha and beta. *Endocrinology*, 141, 4056–4064.

Shughrue, P. J., Lane, M. V., & Merchenthaler, I. (1997). Comparative distribution of estrogen receptor-alpha and -beta mRNA in the rat central nervous system. *Journal of Comparative Neurology*, 388, 507–525.

Shughrue, P. J., Lane, M. V., Scrimo, P. J., & Merchenthaler, I. (1998). Comparative distribution of estrogen receptor-alpha (ER-alpha) and beta (ER-beta) mRNA in the rat pituitary, gonad, and reproductive tract. *Steroids*, 63, 498–504.

Simon, N. G., & Masters, D. B. (1987). Activation of male-typical aggression by testosterone but not its metabolites in C57BL/6J female mice. *Physiology and Behavior*, 41, 405–407.

Simon, N. G., & Perry, M. (1988). Medroxyprogesterone acetate and tamoxifen do not decrease aggressive behavior in CF-1 male mice. *Physiology and Behavior*, 30, 829–833.

Simon, N. G., & Whalen, R. E. (1986). Hormonal regulation of aggression: Evidence for a relationship among genotype, receptor binding, and behavioral sensitivity to androgen and estrogen. *Aggressive Behavior*, 12, 255–266.

Simon, N. G., & Whalen, R. E. (1987). Sexual differentiation of androgen-sensitive and estrogen-sensitive regulatory systems for aggressive behavior. *Hormones and Behavior*, 21, 493–500.

Simon, N. G., Whalen, R. E., & Tate, M. P. (1985). Induction of male-typical aggression by androgens but not by estrogen in adult female mice. *Hormones and Behavior*, 19, 204–212.

Soga, T., Shibata, M., Hadjimarkou, M. M., Pfaff, D. W.,

Nomura, M., & Ogawa, S. (2003). Roles of estrogen receptor (ER)-α and ER-α in the regulation of arginine vasopressin gene expression in the bed nucleus of stria terminalis and medial amygdala. *Society for Neuroscience Abstracts*.

Svare, B. (1980). Testosterone propionate inhibits maternal aggression in mice. *Physiology and Behavior*, 24, 435–439.

Svare, B. (1988). Genotype modulates the aggression-promoting quality of progesterone in pregnant mice. *Hormones and Behavior*, 22, 90–99.

Svare, B., & Gandelman, R. (1975). Postpartum aggression in mice: Inhibitory effects of estrogen. *Physiology and Behavior*, 14, 31–35.

Tang, A. C., Nakazawa, M., Romeo, R. D., Reeb, B., Sisti, H., & McEwen, B. S. Effects of long term estrogen replacement on social recognition memory, emotional reactivity, and HPA function in the mouse. Manuscript submitted for publication.

Tang-Martinez, Z. (2003). Emerging themes and future challenges: Forgotten rodent, neglected questions. *Journal of Mammalogy*, 84, 1212–1227.

Tremblay, G. B., Tremblay, A., Copeland, N. G., Gilbert, D. J., Jenkins, N. A., Labrie, F., et al. (1997). Cloning, chromosomal localization, and functional analysis of the murine estrogen receptor β. *Molecular Endocrinology*, 11, 353–365.

Vasudevan, N., Davidkova, G., Zhu, Y. S., Koibuchi, N., Chin, W. W., & Pfaff, D. (2001). Differential interaction of estrogen receptor and thyroid hormone receptor isoforms on the rat oxytocin receptor promoter leads to differences in transcriptional regulation. *Neuroendocrinology*, 74, 309–324.

Vasudevan, N., Kia, H. K., Inoue, S., Muramatsu, M., & Pfaff, D. (2002). Isoform specificity for oestrogen receptor and thyroid hormone receptor genes and their interactions on the NR2D gene promoter. *Journal of Neuroendocrinology*, 14, 836–842.

Vasudevan, N., Koibuchi, N., Chin, W. W., & Pfaff, D. W. (2001). Differential crosstalk between estrogen receptor (ER)alpha and ERbeta and the thyroid hormone receptor isoforms results in flexible regulation of the consensus ERE. *Molecular Brain Research*, 95, 9–17.

Veenema, A. H., Meijer, O. C., de Kloet, E. R., & Koolhaas, J. M. (2003). Genetic selection for coping style predicts stressor susceptibility. *Journal of Neuroendocrinology*, 15, 256–267.

Young, L. J. (2002). The neurobiology of social recognition, approach, and avoidance. *Biological Psychiatry*, 51, 18–26.

Young, L. J., Wang, Z., Donaldson, R., & Rissman, E. F. (1998). Estrogen receptor alpha is essential for induction of oxytocin receptor by estrogen. *Neuroreport*, 9, 933–936.

11

Maternal Aggression

Stephen C. Gammie & Joseph S. Lonstein

The Adaptive Role of Maternal Aggression

Despite relatively little scientific research on the topic, it is widely accepted and appreciated that human mothers are extremely vigilant over their children and will actively protect their offspring when necessary, and even sometimes when not necessary. This perception may be based on direct experience or many cultural references to the archetypal "protective mother." In Greek mythology there is the story of how Demeter, the goddess of harvest, threatened to kill all humans by shutting down the harvest to coerce the other gods to return her abducted daughter Persephone. More recently, the plot in the first two *Terminator* movies centers around a single mother who heroically battles cyborgs whose sole mission is to destroy her son.

The fierce protection of offspring by parents is a behavior with great adaptive significance that is expressed in a wide range of chordate species ranging from fish (Crawford & Balon, 1996) to humans (Ledesma, de Luis, Montejo, Llorca, & Perez-Urdaniz, 1988). The colloquialism suggesting that one does not want to "get between a mother bear and her cubs" reflects our understanding that fierce protection of offspring is not limited to humans. Further, the news reporting of how

Scarlett, a cat, ran repeatedly into a burning house in Brooklyn to rescue her kittens (at great pain and harm to herself) (Martin & Suares, 1997) reaffirms our understanding of how self-sacrificing mothers can be. Most of the scientific research on the protective behavior of parents, termed *maternal* or *parental aggression*, has been performed in rodents, especially rats and mice. In rodents, where infanticide by nonparental conspecifics is quite common (Agrell, Wolff, & Ylonen, 1998; Wolff, 1985, 1993), the term maternal aggression is appropriate because a lactating female will attack males that approach her offspring. Lactating humans do not typically use violence as a normal form of child protection, although it certainly can be provoked. Because maternal aggression can bring harm to the mother, it can be viewed as an evolutionary trade-off: expression of the behavior can dramatically increase the fitness of the offspring, but also decrease the life expectancy of the mother.

The high levels of aggression during lactation in rodents serve to protect offspring from harm (Agrell et al., 1998; Wolff, 1985, 1993; Wolff & Peterson, 1998). For example, an increase in maternal aggression in lactating hamsters is positively correlated with a decrease in infanticide committed by intruders (Giordano, Siegel, & Rosenblatt, 1984), and lowered pup mortality in common voles (*Microtus arvalis*) correlates with increased maternal wounding of intruders (Heise & Lippke, 1997). In strains of mice where males are highly infanticidal (such as wild house mice and outbred mice), lactating females exhibit higher levels of maternal aggression (Parmigiani, Palanza, Rogers, & Ferrari, 1999), suggesting levels of aggression are flexible and evolve to meet the protection needs of offspring. In bank voles (*Clethrionomys glareolus*), artificially increasing the size of a litter increases the dam's maternal aggression (Koskela, Juutistenaho, Mappes, & Oksanen, 2000), indicating that in some rodent species, the level of parental investment may influence levels of maternal aggression and be a source of individual differences in this behavior.

Maternal aggression most typically occurs around the familiar nest environment (Calhoun, 1963; Paul, Gronek, & Politch, 1981; St. John & Corning, 1973) and thus could be compared to territorial defense by male rodents (Blanchard & Blanchard, 1990; Blanchard, Fukunaga-Stinson, Takahashi, Flannelly, & Blanchard, 1984; Mos, Olivier, van Oorschot, van Aken, & Zethof, 1989). It is possible, then, that in animals that have a stable home site, such as rodents, maternal aggression is a form of elevated territorial defense in the dam. For animals from species that are not stationary, though, such as ungulates and many primates, linking offspring defense to heightened territorial defense is more difficult. Further, given that maternal aggression is highly conserved across species and that only a subset of species exhibit territorial defense, it is also possible that territorial defense in females could have evolved from maternal aggression. However, it is also possible that these two forms of aggression evolved separately.

Maternal aggression in animals is under the control of a wide variety of factors. These include the dramatic fluctuations in hormones that mothers undergo prior to and after giving birth and the neurochemical changes these hormones produce, as well as the cues provided by infants, intruders, and the general environment.

Hormonal Control of Maternal Aggression

Because of the spectacular changes in ovarian and pituitary hormone secretion during gestation, parturition, and lactation, these hormones have been extensively studied for a function in the control of both maternal responsiveness toward pups and aggression toward in-

truders. Aggressive behavior in rats increases markedly during the last week of gestation, is very high during the first week postpartum, and then declines (Albert, Walsh, Zalys, & Dyson, 1988; Erskine, Barfield, & Goldman, 1980b; Flannelly & Flannelly, 1987; Flannelly, Flannelly, & Lore, 1986; Mayer, Carter, et al., 1987; Mayer & Rosenblatt, 1980, 1984). Levels of aggression in mice show a somewhat different pattern, being low during pregnancy and immediately after parturition, but rising to high levels within hours after the birth of pups and remaining there for about 2 more weeks (Ghiraldi, Plonsky, & Svare, 1993; St. John & Corning, 1973) (figure 11.1). Other studies in mice demonstrate that aggression in some strains begins to rise during late pregnancy (Hedricks & Daniels, 1981; Mann & Svare, 1982; Noirot, Goyens, & Buhot, 1975). The onset of maternal responsiveness toward pups depends on elevations of progesterone, estrogen, and prolactin during pregnancy, followed by progesterone withdrawal at parturition (for reviews, see Bridges, 1996; Numan, 1994; Stern, 1989). The onset of maternal aggression has somewhat different hormonal determinants.

Estradiol, Progesterone, and Steroid Hormone Interactions

Rats, hysterectomized and ovariectomized on Gestational Day 16, show changes in circulating estrogen and progesterone that occur immediately prior to parturition (Rosenblatt, Mayer, & Siegel, 1985). Estradiol treatment of these rats made them highly aggressive toward male intruders, even without pup contact (Mayer & Rosenblatt, 1987). Subsequent pup exposure further elevated their aggressive behavior. Maternal aggression can also be induced in virgin rats by treating them with exogenous estrogen and progesterone in a pattern that mimics late pregnancy and then exposing them to pups (Gandelman & Simon, 1980; Rosenblatt, Hazelwood, & Poole, 1996), the latter process termed sensitization (Rosenblatt, 1969; Weisner & Sheard, 1933). Not all regimens of progesterone and estrogen that induce maternal responsiveness, however, increase aggression in virgin rats (Hansen & Ferreira, 1986b), indicating that the required timing and/or dose of these hormones differs between the two behaviors. Estrogen may be more critical than progesterone for the onset of rat maternal aggression because treatment of virgin females with estrogens alone can stimulate aggression in some (Mayer, Monroy, & Rosenblatt,

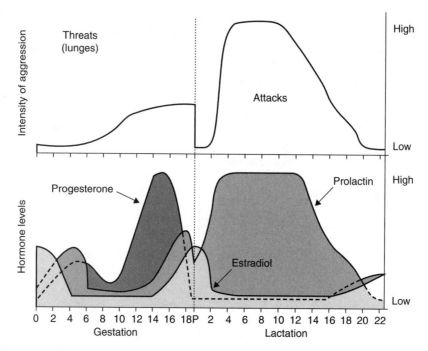

FIGURE 11.1 Profile of relative hormone concentrations and aggression through gestation and lactation in mice. From "Maternal Aggression: Hormonal, Genetic, and Developmental Determinants," by B. Svare. In N. A. Krasnegor and R. S. Bridges (Eds.), *Mammalian Parenting: Biochemical, Neurobiological, and Behavioral Determinants*, 1990, New York: Oxford University Press, p. 119. Copyright 1990 by Oxford University Press. Adapted with permission.

1990b), but not in all cases (van de Poll, van Zanten, & De Jong, 1986). The combination of estradiol and testosterone can also promote maternal aggression (Albert, Jonik, & Walsh, 1992b).

Drawing from their earlier work on the sensory control of maternal aggression in mice, Gandelman and Simon (1980) suggested that the ovarian hormone regimens that successfully promote aggression in female rats also promote nipple development, and that subsequent suckling stimulation provided by pups might actually control the onset of aggression in their dam. This is unlikely, because similar hormone administration also stimulates aggression in virgin male rats (Rosenblatt et al., 1996) that do not have nipples, estrogen- and progesterone-treated virgin females do not require pup exposure to be aggressive (Albert et al., 1992b; Gandelman & Simon, 1980; Mayer, Ahdieh, & Rosenblatt, 1990; Mayer, Monroy, et al., 1990), and lactating female rats without nipples (i.e., thelectomized) remain aggressive (Mayer, Carter, et al., 1987; Stern & Kolunie, 1993).

Even though nulliparous female rats treated with ovarian hormones do not necessarily require interac-

tions with pups to be aggressive, the converse is also sometimes true — virgin rats do not always require exogenous hormones to show maternal aggression and in some cases are more aggressive than nonmaternal virgin controls simply as a result of continuous pup exposure (Mayer & Rosenblatt, 1993b), although other studies do not support this result (Erskine et al., 1980b; Gandelman & Simon, 1980; Krehbiel & LeRoy, 1979). It should be noted that the levels of aggression displayed by these sensitized females is often inferior to that of lactating dams (Erskine et al., 1980b; Krehbiel & LeRoy, 1979; Mayer, Ahdieh, et al., 1990). An interaction between hormonal priming and pup experience contributes to the full display of maternal aggression.

The specific role of progesterone in the control of maternal aggression in rats is unclear. Under many circumstances, progesterone inhibits maternal responsiveness toward pups (Bridges, 1996; Numan et al., 1999) and also inhibits estrogen- and testosterone-induced aggression in virgin female rats (Albert et al., 1992b). Others have found, however, that progesterone has no effect on aggression in virgin female rats when given alone (Mayer, Monroy, et al., 1990) or that it can stimulate aggression when given with estrogen (Mayer, Monroy, et al., 1990). In fact, to do so, the levels of progesterone administered must be relatively high to induce aggression (see (Hansen & Ferreira, 1986b; Mayer, Monroy, et al., 1990). The ability of progesterone to synergize with estrogen to produce high levels of aggression in virgin females also may depend on the length of hormone treatment, enhancing the effects of estradiol if the hormone regimen is provided over a 16-day period, but not if the hormones are only given for 1 week (Mayer, Monroy, et al., 1990). Withdrawal of progesterone during such a hormone regimen is necessary for the onset of maternal responsiveness to pups (Numan et al., 1999), but not for the onset of aggression (Mayer, Monroy, et al., 1990), and females are aggressive even when progesterone treatment continues. Ovarian secretions apparently have no function during the maintenance of maternal aggression in rats and ovariectomy after parturition does not affect their aggression when compared to that of gonadally intact lactating controls (Albert, Jonik, & Walsh, 1992a, 1992c).

Estrogen influences maternal aggression in mice in a dramatically different manner than that in rats. Circulating estrogens in mice markedly rise immediately prior to parturition (Barkley, Geschwind, & Bradford, 1979) and fall immediately afterward (Dewsbury, Evans, & Webster, 1979; Svare, 1990 [figure 11.1]), so unlike in rats, elevated estrogens cannot explain the postpartum increase in aggression in mice. Although the decline in circulating estrogens in postpartum mice may temporarily decrease aggression toward males to allow for mating to occur during postpartum estrus (Dewsbury, 1979), this decrease in circulating estrogens may also facilitate the onset of maternal aggression. Ovariectomizing pregnant mice hastens the onset of maternal aggression, while estrogen replacement delays it (Ghiraldi et al., 1993). Exogenous estrogen also inhibits aggression in lactating mice (Svare & Gandelman, 1975). Estrogen can reduce aggression even before females interact with pups (Ghiraldi et al., 1993), indicating that sensory cues from pups are not absolutely necessary for the initiation of this process if estrogen levels are relatively low. Nonetheless, the fact that maternally sensitized virgin female mice can be highly agonistic indicates that normal pregnancy and parturition are inconsequential for the onset of this behavior (McDermott & Gandelman, 1979). Termi-

nation of pregnancy early (but not late) in gestation does reduce maternal aggression in female mice presented with foster pups, though. This reduction is probably not due to insufficient hormonal stimulation of the nervous system, but rather to the fact that these females cannot receive the necessary appropriate sensory stimuli from pups (Svare, Mann, & Samuels, 1980). Before it needs to be withdrawn for the onset of maternal aggression after parturition, estradiol seems to have a role in promoting postpartum attacks by acting in the periphery. During late pregnancy, estradiol and other ovarian hormones promote adequate development of nipples on which pups can suckle. As will be detailed below, suckling provides maternal female mice with the critical sensory stimulation necessary for their increased aggression and these peripheral effects might be the primary way that ovarian hormones influence the onset and maintenance of this behavior.

Progesterone has no effect on maternal aggression in mice when administered during lactation (Svare & Gandelman, 1975), but it does influence the less intense threat behaviors they display during late pregnancy (Mann, Konen, & Svare, 1984). Levels of threat behavior during pregnancy are highest when circulating progesterone concentrations are high and progesterone administration to virgin female mice produces some threat behavior, while progesterone removal in these virgins eliminates it (Mann et al., 1984). Hysterectomy during midpregnancy reduces circulating progesterone levels (Bridges, Rosenblatt, & Feder, 1978; Critser, Savage, Rutledge, & French, 1982), as well as pregnancy-induced threat behavior in mice (Svare, Miele, & Kinsley, 1986).

Unlike its enhancing effects on aggression in virgin male and female mice (Gleason, Michael, & Christian, 1979), administration of testosterone reduces maternal aggression in ovariectomized mice (Svare, 1980), as well as suppresses other maternal behaviors (Gandelman, 1972, 1973). Because exogenous estrogen also reduces postpartum aggression in mice (Svare & Gandelman, 1975), the inhibitory effects of testosterone on maternal aggression may be mediated by its aromatization to estradiol. The difference between virgin and lactating mice in the effects of testosterone on aggression suggests that the hormonal changes during pregnancy alter the neuronal substrates underlying aggression and render them differentially responsive to testosterone depending on the female's reproductive state.

Sensory Control
of Maternal Aggression

For most social interactions in animals, a variety of sensory cues are normally utilized in order for the participants to display the appropriate behaviors. Many of these behavioral responses are under the control of multiple sensory modalities, such that elimination of any one does not completely eliminate the behavior (Beach & Jaynes, 1956; Stern, 1990). The same is true for maternal aggression in rats and mice, and a variety of cues provided by the pups and intruder are necessary.

Sensory Input From Pups

Although the pups do not need to be present during the actual aggressive interaction for rat and mouse dams to be highly aggressive (Flannelly & Kemble, 1988; Paul et al., 1981; however, see Erskine et al., 1980b), dams require recent exposure to pups to maintain their heightened attack behavior. Separation from the pups for as little as 4 to 5 hr significantly reduces or eliminates maternal attacks (Erskine, Barfield, & Goldman, 1978; Flannelly & Kemble, 1988; Gandelman, 1972; Gandelman & Simon, 1980; Stern & Kolunie, 1993; Svare, Betteridge, Katz, & Samuels, 1981) and elevated aggression can be reinstated in separated rat dams by reexposing them to pups for as little as 1 hr, and in mouse dams for just 5–10 min (Erskine, Barfield, et al., 1978; Gandelman & Simon, 1980; Svare & Gandelman, 1973).

Somatosensory and olfactory cues provided by pups have been the most extensively studied for their role in maternal aggression. Early hypotheses suggested that the critical tactile stimulation from pups necessary for maternal aggression in rats and mice was from suckling and that dams separated from their pups for long periods of time became nonaggressive because of a lack of suckling inputs and mammary nerve activity (Gandelman & Simon, 1980). Later experiments demonstrated that this was not the case in rats because pre- or postmating removal of the nipples (thelectomy) did not reduce maternal aggression in parturient or pregnancy-terminated females (Mayer, Carter, et al., 1987; Stern & Kolunie, 1993). Some type of ventral somatosensory stimulation that dams receive from pups is necessary, though, because complete anesthetization of the dam's nipples and surrounding skin during interactions with pups reduces her aggressiveness (Stern & Kolunie, 1993). It should be noted that these results

do not exclude a role for mammary nerve stimulation in the maintenance of maternal aggression, because innervation of the nipples extends into the mammary glands and overlying ventral skin (Findlay, 1966) and thelectomy alone, therefore, does not prevent the pups from mechanically stimulating the mammary nerves. Thelectomy combined with full mammary gland removal would be necessary to evaluate any functional significance of mammary nerve stimulation in the maintenance of maternal aggression in rats.

In contrast to rats, mouse dams require suckling from the young for the onset and maintenance of their maternal aggression. Parturient mice that are thelectomized prepartum or immediately postpartum are not particularly aggressive (Svare & Gandelman, 1976). It is not necessary that this suckling stimulation is received immediately after parturition, and mice interacting with pups for the first time 1–3 weeks after parturition show heightened aggression similar to dams not separated from their young at birth (Svare et al., 1980). The duration of suckling necessary for the initiation of maternal aggression in mice is relatively brief and can be obtained with as little as 48 hr of contact with pups (Svare & Gandelman, 1976). Once sufficient suckling initiates maternal aggression, it is not absolutely required for its maintenance and females can be thelectomized after only 2 days of suckling and remain highly aggressive for at least another 5 to 7 days (Garland & Svare, 1988; Svare & Gandelman, 1976). During this time, maternal aggression can be maintained by exteroceptive cues provided by young pups, and dams separated from pups by a wire mesh barrier so that they cannot touch the pups but can only see, hear, and smell them will remain highly aggressive (Svare, 1977, 1979; Svare & Gandelman, 1973). Evidence that nonsuckling cues influence the dam's aggression at this time is also apparent from the fact that the reduction of maternal aggression that occurs after a 5-hr separation from the litter can be reinstated after only a 5- to 10-min reunion with the litter, which is likely too short a time for much suckling to occur (Svare & Gandelman, 1973). Maternally sensitized virgin female mice are also more aggressive, but only if the females show adequate development of the nipples upon which pups can suckle (McDermott & Gandelman, 1979).

Suckling suppresses gonadotropin release (e.g., Smith, 1978) and tonically inhibits ovarian function. As noted above, reduced circulating estradiol concentrations facilitate maternal aggression in mice. It is possible that the onset of maternal aggression after normal parturition, and its maintenance during the end of lactation, could largely be due to suckling-induced inhibition of ovarian release of estrogens. Estrogen treatment also changes the pattern, but not total duration, of nursing in ovariectomized maternally sensitized female mice (Ghiraldi et al., 1993), and changes in aggressive behavior in these females may be consequent only to the altered suckling inputs they receive.

Although not critical for its maintenance during midlactation, suckling modulates the decline in maternal aggression that normally occurs during late lactation. Mice thelectomized on Day 5 postpartum showed elevated levels of agonistic behavior when tested through Day 12, as previously reported, but that the rate of decline in maternal aggression between Days 12 and 21 of lactation was significantly accelerated in thelectomized dams (Garland & Svare, 1988). Furthermore, this rapid decline in postpartum aggression in thelectomized dams was seen on Day 12 postpartum even if dams were thelectomized only 24 hr prior. It should be noted that in some of these studies, the control group of sham-thelectomized females showed only a very small decline in aggression over the course of lactation, in contrast to previous data from lactating mice of the same or different strains that showed a much larger decline (Gandelman, 1972; St. John & Corning, 1973; Svare et al., 1981). Nonetheless, Garland and Svare (1988) proposed that postpartum aggression in mice can be divided into three phases: (a) an "initiation phase," in which an acute period of suckling stimulation is necessary for the initiation of maternal aggression, whether it is received immediately postpartum or delayed; (b) a "midlactational" phase, in which continued suckling stimulation is unnecessary for the expression of maternal aggression, and either nonsuckling or distal stimulation from the litter is sufficient to maintain the dam's behavior; and (c) the "late lactational phase" during the final week of lactation, which is characterized by a decline in maternal aggression that can be accelerated in the absence of suckling. The mechanisms controlling the shifts between the suckling-dependent and suckling-independent phases are unknown. It is possible that some neuroendocrine or neurotransmitter fluctuations occur during exposure to distal cues from pups in a manner that maintains maternal aggression during the suckling-independent midlactational phase.

In addition to ventral somatosensory cues, olfactory cues from pups contribute to the maintenance of maternal aggression in lactating rats and mice. Indeed, as long as the dams receive olfactory stimulation from the litter, even without direct physical contact with them, maternal aggression is maintained (Ferreira & Hansen, 1986). Not surprisingly, then, complete surgical removal of the olfactory epithelium and mucosa dramatically reduces maternal aggression in rats (Ferreira, Dahlof, & Hansen, 1987), as does removal of the olfactory bulbs (Kolunie & Stern, 1995). The effects of olfactory bulbectomy on attack behavior in lactating mice is apparently unknown, but it drastically interferes with their maternal care (Gandelman, Zarrow, & Denenberg, 1972; Vandenbergh, 1973). Therefore, it would be difficult to distinguish between the effects of bulbectomy on aggression per se versus a secondary effect on aggression due to the lack of interactions with pups. Olfactory cues from pups can be either volatile or nonvolatile (i.e., pheromonal), and removal of the olfactory epithelium and mucosa or olfactory bulbectomy cannot distinguish between these two types of inputs because these manipulations disrupt both volatile and nonvolatile inputs. The relative importance of these different olfactory cues for maternal aggression has been addressed in rats. Disruption of volatile inputs with $ZnSO_4$ has little effect on aggression if subjects are tested early in lactation (Kolunie & Stern, 1995), but decreases aggression if subjects are tested later in lactation (Mayer & Rosenblatt, 1993a). Mayer and Rosenblatt (1993a, 1993b) argue that these results indicate that aggression is maintained primarily by other factors during early lactation, such as lingering effects of gestational hormones and ventral somatosensory inputs, but becomes more dependent on chemosensory cues from pups after other factors wane during mid to late lactation. Rat dams made anosmic with $ZnSO_4$ are also more aggressive than controls after having their litters removed (Mayer & Rosenblatt, 1993a), suggesting that aggression is normally inhibited by some olfactory cues. It is unknown whether these manipulations in volatile olfactory cues could alter aggression because of the inability to detect olfactory cues from the pups, the intruder, or both. Removal of the vomeronasal organ has little effect on maternal aggression in lactating rats (Kolunie & Stern, 1995; Mayer & Rosenblatt, 1993a). Lactating mice differ from rats in this regard, and vomeronasal organ removal prior to mating or after parturition eliminates later maternal aggression (Bean & Wysocki, 1989), but does not affect their maternal behavior (Lepri, Wysocki, & Vandenbergh, 1985). Disruption of the genes that code for pheromone receptor expression in the vomeronasal organ also impairs maternal aggression in lactating mice (Del Punta et al., 2002).

Other sensory inputs that dams receive from pups, including visual and auditory cues, cannot maintain maternal aggression in rats (Ferreira & Hansen, 1986), and surgical deprivation of these inputs does not affect the dam's aggressive behavior (Kolunie, Stern, & Barfield, 1994). It is not known what effects blinding has on aggression in lactacting mice, although deafening reduces their attacked behavior—although apparently not due to the inability to hear the pups, but instead due to an inability to hear vocalization made by the intruder (see below).

It is clear that both tactile and olfactory cues from pups contribute to the display of maternal aggression in rats and mice, but aggression is not elevated throughout all of lactation in either species and declines as lactation progresses (Flannelly, & Flannelly, 1987; Mayer, 1987; Svare & Gandelman, 1976). The changes in sensory cues that pups provide as they get older appear to mediate this decline. Exteroceptive cues provided by young pups are particularly effective in maintaining high levels of aggression in lactating mice when compared to the cues provided by older pups (Svare, 1977, 1979), and rat dams in early lactation (Day 8) can be rendered less aggressive if they are allowed to freely interact with pups 10 days older than their natural litter for the 5 days prior to testing. Further, rat dams in late lactation (Day 18) show more aggressive behavior if they interact with 8-day-old pups prior to testing (Giovenardi, Consiglio, Barros, & Lucion, 2000). Although these results may be due to differences in the olfactory or tactile cues that are provided by older and younger pups, pups of different ages may produce similar sensory cues, but dams may receive these cues less frequently because of the natural decrease in the time that they spend with their pups as lactation ensues (Grota, 1969; Noirot, 1964). In contrast to the results of one study (Giovenardi et al., 2000), another report examining this question found that the age of the pups does not influence aggressive responding in rat dams during late lactation (Albert & Walsh, 1995). In this study, dams were allowed only 48 hr of contact with the younger pups prior to aggression testing, and Giorvenardi et al. (2000) suggest that this may not have been an adequate amount of time for the age of the pups to influence the dams' behavior.

Less is known about the sensory control of maternal aggression in other species. Olfactory bulbectomy impairs maternal aggression in hamsters (Leonard, 1972), as does a 24-hr, but not a 6-hr, separation from the litter (Giordano et al., 1984; Siegel, Giordano, Mallafre, & Rosenblatt, 1983). Similar to the case in rats, this decline after separation from the litter can be reinstated by as little as 30 min of contact with the pups prior to testing (Giordano et al., 1984). It is not clear whether changes in sensory cues from the pups as they age affect maternal aggression in hamsters, because hamsters may (Wise, 1974; Wise & Pryor, 1977) or may not (Siegel et al., 1983) show a decline in aggression as lactation progresses. Mongolian gerbils without fighting experience are more aggressive during early lactation than virgin females (Stockman, 1983), but it is not known if this is influenced by physical contact with pups.

Sensory Input From Intruders

Sensory cues dams receive from intruding males also modulate aggression in lactating rats and mice (figure 11.2). Immediately prior to attack, a lactating rat spends a considerable amount of time sniffing an intruder (Kolunie & Stern, 1990), which provides not only olfactory stimulation that may be important for attacks, but also trigeminal nerve stimulation during deflection of her vibrissae. It is not clear if olfactory input during this sniffing is important because, as noted above, the effects of manipulating the olfactory system on maternal aggression may be due to the loss of either pup-related olfactory cues or those from the intruder. Nonetheless, trigeminal input received while sniffing the intruder is absolutely critical and acute anesthesia of the dam's mystacial pads prior to testing decreases sniffing of the intruder and markedly reduces her attacks. Dams that do attack only do so after significantly increased sniffing (Kolunie & Stern, 1990; Stern & Kolunie, 1989, 1991). Interestingly, this loss of aggressiveness is not due to an inability to bite the intruder because aggressive behaviors not involving the mouth, such as kicks, are also absent or reduced (Stern & Kolunie, 1989). Perioral somatosensory input is necessary not only for maternal aggression, but also for intermale aggression (Bugbee & Eichelman, 1972) and nonaggressive maternal behaviors (Stern & Johnson, 1989; Stern & Kolunie, 1989).

It is unknown if perioral somatosensory inputs during investigation of the intruder are also necessary for maternal aggression in mice, but the role of olfactory inputs provided by intruders has been studied. The ability of the mouse dam to recognize the intruder is

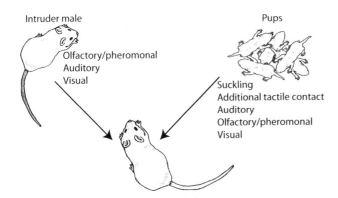

Intruder male

Olfactory/pheromonal
Auditory
Visual

Pups

Suckling
Additional tactile contact
Auditory
Olfactory/pheromonal
Visual

FIGURE 11.2 Diagram of sensory cues from both the intruder and offspring that influence maternal aggression.

critical because males rendered familiar to the female by being housed with them in the same cage, but separated from them by a wire barrier, are not attacked (Svare & Gandelman, 1973). Urinary cues may assist in this recognition and females will not attack unfamiliar males that are doused in the test female's own urine, but they will attack males scented with the urine of an unfamiliar female (Lynds, 1976). Olfactory cues may also influence how dams respond to the intruder's age, sex, and reproductive status. Lactating Rockland–Swiss mice can discriminate between preweaning intruders of different ages, with unfamiliar 14- to 20-day-old males attacked more readily than 1- to 10-day-old intruders (Svare, 1973). Possibly, older preweanlings are less likely to elicit maternal responses and, therefore, receive higher levels of aggression. Although there are data demonstrating that lactating Rockland–Swiss mice attack prepubescent and adult females and males with equal ferocity (Gandelman, 1972; Svare et al., 1981), others report using different mouse strains that intruding mothers of 3- to 8-day-old pups are not attacked, while mothers of 20-day-old pups are (Rosenson & Asheroff, 1975), that gonadally intact males are more readily attacked than castrated males or ovariectomized females (Rosenson & Asheroff, 1975), and that smaller adult male mice elicit higher levels of aggression than larger males (White, Mayo, & Edwards, 1969). Some of the discrepancies between these studies may be due to the methods of the behavioral observations. Lactating Swiss mice can discriminate the sex of their intruder and the topography of attacks is different toward intruding virgin males and females (Parmigiani, Brain, Mainardi, & Brunoni, 1988), with males receiving more attacks in vulnerable body regions. Identification of intruder sex could be ethologically important because in some strains of mice, virgin males are highly infanticidal and represent a greater threat to the litter

than the rarely infanticidal virgin female mouse (Gandelman & vom Saal, 1977; Lonstein & De Vries, 2000). There might be olfactory cues coming from intruders that influence maternal aggression in rats, because Erskine, Denenberg, and Goldman (1978) found that rats during the first week of lactation display higher levels of aggression toward older male intruders (53 or 108 days old) compared to younger, prepubertal intruders (34 or 44 days old). Because these groups of males differ in their circulating concentrations of testosterone, a pheromonal cue emanating from postpubescent males may elicit the dam's aggressive behaviors. This may be particularly important because older male rats are more likely to be infanticidal than younger ones (Erskine, Denenberg, et al., 1978). However, size could be the more important factor because even among postpubescent intruders that presumably produce the same olfactory cues, larger ones are attacked less often than smaller ones (Flannelly & Flannelly, 1985).

It has been proposed that ultrasonic vocalizations emitted by a male while intruding on a lactating female inhibit her maternal aggression, potentially allowing for mating and fertilization during a postpartum estrus (Nyby & Whitney, 1978). Empirical data do not support this hypothesis, at least for rats, and lactating rats attack surgically devocalized males as intensely as vocalizing males (Kolunie et al., 1994). Also, lactating rats are more likely to attack when a male produces a 22-kHz vocalization (Kolunie et al., 1994). This may occur because the male's vocalizations enhance the dam's ability to detect and locate him, similar to the facilitatory effects of ultrasonic vocalizations produced by pups on their mother's retrieval behavior (Smotherman, Bell, Starzec, Elias, & Zachman, 1974). In contrast, vocalizations from male intruders increase maternal aggression in lactating mice, and surgically devocalized males or males with naturally low vocalization rates receive fewer attacks than intruder males that vocalize frequently (Bean, Nunez, & Wysocki, 1986).

The Neural Circuitry of Maternal Aggression

Brain Regions Implicated in Maternal Aggression by Either Lesions or Site-Directed Pharmacological Injections

Olfactory Regions

As detailed previously, olfactory information contributes to maternal aggression in rats, and, not surprisingly, lesions of brain regions that process higher order olfactory information (e.g., the mediodorsal thalamus or prefrontal insular cortex) decrease maternal aggression (Ferreira et al., 1987). Because these lesions do not create anosmia, but rather disrupt olfactory discriminations (Eichenbaum, Shedlack, & Eckmann, 1980), the decrease in aggression could result from an inability either to determine whether the intruder is a potential threat or to process olfactory input from pups. Also, as described above, selective removal (via gene deletion) of either a subset of pheromone receptors or an ion channel linked to pheromonal perception decreases maternal aggression in mice (Del Punta et al., 2002; Stowers, Holy, Meister, Dulac, & Koentges, 2002), indicating an important role for accessory olfactory regions in this behavior.

Septum

Large lesions of the septum inhibit maternal aggression in rats, but also impair responsiveness toward pups (Flannelly, Kemble, Blanchard, & Blanchard, 1986). Hence, reduced maternal aggression could result indirectly from reduced sensory input from offspring. However, infusion of a 5-HT$_{1A}$ receptor agonist into the medial septum elevates maternal attacks in rats (De Almeida & Lucion, 1997), suggesting a specific, excitatory role for the septum in this behavior.

Amygdala

Injection of a 5-HT$_{1A}$ receptor agonist into the corticomedial amygdala reduces maternal attacks (De Almeida & Lucion, 1997). Infusions of a gamma aminobutyric acid-A (GABA$_A$) receptor antagonist into the amygdala also reduce maternal aggression (Hansen & Ferreira, 1986a), but it is not known which specific subregions trigger the behavioral response. Oddly, injection of an oxytocin (OT) antagonist into the central nucleus of the amygdala (CeAMY) elevates aggression in female rats (Lubin, Elliott, Black, & Johns, 2003), whereas infusion of OT itself produces the same effects in lactating female Syrian hamsters (*Mesocricetus auratus*) (Ferris et al., 1992). Why the OT agonist and antagonist elicit the same behavioral response when infused into the same region is unclear, but may simply reflect a species difference in the neural regulation of this behavior. Alternatively, it may be that a particular level of OTergic activity in the CeAMY is required for maternal aggression and that either too much or too little OTergic activity is detrimental.

Medial Preoptic Area (mPOA)

The mPOA is critical for some maternal behaviors in rats, including retrieval of pups and nest construction (Numan, 1994). Lesions of the mPOA reduce aggression in nonlactating female hamsters (Hammond & Rowe, 1976), as well as male rats and mice (Albert, Walsh, Gorzalka, Mendelson, & Zalys, 1986; Edwards, Nahair, & Wright, 1993). However, there has been no examination of maternal aggression following mPOA lesions. One obvious problem with doing so is that dams with mPOA lesions do not behave normally toward pups, and although any reduction in maternal aggression after POA lesions in lactating dams might be due to direct effects on maternal aggression, it could simply be a by-product of the insufficient sensory cues received from the pups (see above).

Periaqueductal Gray (PAG)

Lesions of the ventrolateral caudal area of the PAG (cPAG$_{vl}$) of lactating dams decrease their latency to attack and elevate their attack frequency on a male intruder (Lonstein & Stern, 1997), suggesting that this region tonically inhibits maternal aggression. Further, these lesions appear to be specific to maternal aggression. Lesioned dams do not exhibit elevated aggression toward a relatively nonthreatening stimulus and they are not aggressive if the pups are removed for 24 hr (Lonstein & Stern, 1998), demonstrating that this behavior is coupled to the sensory cues dams receive from pups. Manipulations of serotonergic activity in the rostral dorsal PAG also modulate maternal aggression in rats (see below).

Paraventricular Nucleus of the Hypothalamus (PVN)

Based on a range of studies, it appears that the role of PVN in maternal aggression is complex. In one study, cell-body lesions on Day 2 postpartum did not alter attacks when dams were tested 2 days later (Olazabal & Ferreira, 1997). In another, small cell-body lesions also on Day 2 postpartum increased the number of bites (but not total attacks) 3 days later (Giovenardi, Padoin, Cadore, & Lucion, 1998), but had little effect during later tests (Giovenardi, Padoin, Cadore, & Lucion, 1998). In contrast, small PVN lesions made 5 days after parturition reduced aggression when the females were tested during the second week of lactation (Consiglio & Lucion, 1996). It is possible that early postpartum PVN lesions increase some aspects of maternal aggression, but that later lesions reduce attacks. Although infusion of antisense oligonucleotides to OT in the PVN elevates some aspects of maternal aggression (Giovenardi et al., 1998), OT is released in the PVN during maternal defense (Bosch, Kromel, Brunton, & Neumann, 2004). How OT interacts with the PVN to modulate this behavior is still unclear.

Peripeduncular Nucleus (PPN)

As described above, somatosensory inputs that dams receive from pups help maintain maternal aggression. The PPN of the lateral midbrain transmits mammary inputs to sites such as the hypothalamus, limbic structures, and midbrain—areas that support aggression in other contexts (Albert & Walsh, 1984). Lesions of the PPN also impair maternal aggression (Factor, Mayer, & Rosenblatt, 1993; Hansen & Ferreira, 1986b), but it depends on when the lesions are performed. Lesioning the PPN on or after the fourth day postpartum inhibit maternal attacks (Factor et al., 1993), whereas lesioning prior to that has little effect. Therefore, mammary inputs to the PPN do not support maternal aggression during early lactation in rats.

Ventromedial Hypothalamus (VMH)

The PPN projects to the VMH and lesions of this region, including the ventral VMH (or knife cuts along its lateral borders) inhibit maternal aggression in rats (Hansen,

1989). Injection of a $GABA_A$ receptor antagonist into the VMH impairs maternal aggression (Hansen & Ferreira, 1986a), suggesting that the behavior is facilitated by tonic release of GABA within this site. Electrical stimulation of regions just adjacent to the VMH elicits maternal attacks (Mos, Olivier, Lammers, et al., 1987a), but that behavioral response could also result from unintentional stimulation of axons projecting to or from the VMH.

Neurotransmitters and Neuropeptides Implicated in Maternal Aggression

The roles of neurotransmitters and neuropeptides in maternal aggression have been examined using a range of techniques. General approaches have involved peripheral and central administration of receptor agonists or antagonists, followed by aggression testing. For the neurotransmitter and neuropeptide studies detailed below, specific pharmacological agents are not detailed by name, but rather a broader description of the presumed action (e.g., increased serotonin, inhibited $GABA_A$ receptor) is provided. The reader is referred elsewhere to a more detailed review of the effects of specific pharmacological agents and their effects on maternal aggression (Lonstein & Gammie, 2002). An overview of various treatments that decrease maternal aggression is shown in figure 11.3.

Serotonin

A large number of serotonin (also known as 5-hydroxytryptamine, or 5-HT) receptor subtypes are distributed heterogeneously through the central nervous system (CNS) and specific receptor agonists or antagonists do not exist for all of these subtypes. Further, most available pharmacological agents affect more than one receptor subtype, making interpretation of results sometimes unclear. Given the complex nature of serotonin signaling, it should not be surprising that maternal aggression can be either elevated or reduced by both increasing and decreasing serotonergic activity. In support of serotonin inhibiting maternal aggression, systemic injections that should elevate serotonin synthesis reduce aggression in mice (Ieni & Thurmond, 1985). Also, a $5-HT_1$ receptor agonist impairs maternal aggression in mice, particularly if the intruder is female (Parmigiani, Rodgers, Palanza, Mainardi, & Brain, 1989; Racine & Flannelly, 1986). Similarly, maternal aggression in rats is diminished by systemic injections that either raise serotonin levels (Olivier, Mos, van Oorschot, & Hen, 1995) or activate

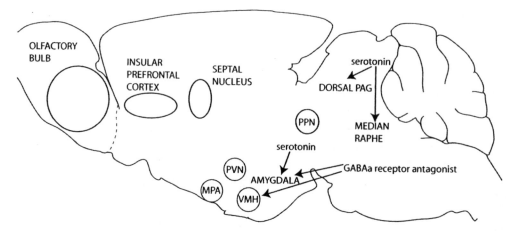

FIGURE 11.3 Schematic sagittal section of the rodent central nervous system highlighting either sites of lesions (open circle) or direct injections (arrow) that trigger *decreases* in maternal aggression.

the 5-HT$_{1A}$ receptor (Ferreira, Picazo, Uriarte, Pereira, & Fernandez-Guasti, 2000; Olivier, Mos, & van Oorschot, 1985, 1986; Olivier et al., 1995). However, because some 5-HT agonists also produce a reduction in general activity, it can be unclear whether they have a specific effect on aggression (Olivier et al., 1995). Further, intracerebroventricular (icv) injections of a 5-HT$_{1A}$ receptor agonist decrease aggression in rats (De Almeida & Lucion, 1994), and these same agonists produce similar effects when injected into the median raphe, corticomedial amygdala, or dorsal cPAG (De Almeida & Lucion, 1997).

Conversely, inhibition of serotonin signaling inhibits the behavior in mice (Ieni & Thurmond, 1985) and elevations of serotonin in the medial septum actually enhance maternal aggression rats (De Almeida & Lucion, 1997).

Sometimes, few or no effects of systemic alteration of serotonin on maternal aggression are found (De Almeida & Lucion, 1994; Ferreira et al., 2000; Olivier et al., 1995). For example, chronic elevation of serotonin in the biparental prairie vole (*M. ochrogaster*) does not alter their maternal aggression (Villalba, Boyle, Caliguri, & De Vries, 1997). Site-directed injections of specific 5-HT receptor agonists and antagonists will probably be the best method to discern all the routes by which serotonin controls aggression in lactating females.

GABA

Increased GABA neurotransmission may be fundamental for maternal aggression in rodents because virgin female rats administered GABA agonists behave very

much like lactating females, and antagonism of GABA reduces aggression in lactating females (Hansen, Ferreira, & Selart, 1985). Contact with pups elevates cerebrospinal GABA concentrations in lactating rats (Qureshi, Hansen, & Sodersten, 1987) and contributes to maternal aggression (see above), suggesting a link between the neurotransmitter and aggressive behavior. Additionally, systemic application of low doses of GABA agonists elevates aggression in lactating rats (Mos & Olivier, 1989; Olivier et al., 1985, 1986), and in some cases the agonists are most effective in elevating aggression in naturally less aggressive females and increasing attacks against larger intruders (Mos, Olivier, & van der Poel, 1987; Mos, Olivier, & van Oorschot, 1987). In mice, some GABA agonists elevated aggression toward male intruders, but inhibited it toward female intruders, if dams were experienced fighters (Laviola, de Acetis, Bignami, & Alleva, 1991; Palanza, Rodgers, Ferrari, & Parmigiani, 1996), which suggests that GABA can be associated with decreases in aggression. Injection of a GABA$_A$ receptor antagonist into either the VMH or mAMY decreases attacks (Hansen & Ferreira, 1986a), suggesting that GABA can elevate this behavior in these regions.

An inhibitory effect of GABA on maternal aggression has also been found, such that GABA agonists decreased attacks against males in dams without fighting experience, but did not affect their attacks on females (Palanza et al., 1996). Further, others have found a dose-dependent decrease in maternal aggression (Ferreira et al., 2000) using the same doses and GABA agonists used by others (cited above) to demonstrate an increase in aggression. Others have found a lack of effect of GABA antagonists on maternal aggression in rats entirely (Mos & Olivier, 1986).

Dopamine

Relatively little work has examined the relationship between dopamine and maternal aggression. Systemic injections that elevate dopamine during pregnancy increase maternal aggression, but acute treatment postpartum decreases it (Johns et al., 1998; Johns, Noonan, Zimmerman, Li, & Pedersen, 1994), suggesting that timing of changes in dopamine neurotransmission is important. Consistent with the idea that dopamine inhibits maternal aggression, destruction of dopamine synthesizing neurons throughout the CNS (Sorenson & Gordon, 1975) or just within the ventral tegmental area (Hansen, Harthon, Wallin, Lofberg, & Svensson, 1991b) elevates attacks in rats. Destruction of dopamine neurons in either the dorsal or ventral striatum, though, does not significantly affect aggression (Hansen, Harthon, Wallin, Lofberg, & Svensson, 1991a). Contrary to an inhibitory effect of dopamine on maternal aggression, systemic injection of a dopamine receptor antagonist decreases maternal aggression, but nonspecific decreases in locomotion may be involved (Yoshimura & Ogawa, 1989). An overview of some of the treatments that elevate maternal aggression is shown in figure 11.4.

Oxytocin

RNA antisense manipulations that decrease OT expression in the PVN elevate maternal aggression in rats (Giovenardi et al., 1998), suggesting an inhibitory role for this peptide. Further, manipulations that elevate dopamine and decrease maternal aggression (Johns et al., 1998) have later been shown to elevate OT in the amygdala (Elliott, Lubin, Walker, & Johns, 2001). Also, an OT receptor antagonist injected into the CeAMY in rats elevates aggression (Lubin et al., 2003), also suggesting an inhibitory role for OT in this behavior. However, maternal aggression is not affected by either icv injection of an OT antagonist (Neumann, 2001; Neumann, Toschi, Ohl, Torner, & Kromer, 2001) or midbrain lesions that impair suckling- induced increases in OT (Factor, Mayer, & Rosenblatt, 1992). Also, injections of OT into the CeAMY in hamsters increases maternal aggression (Ferris et al., 1992). Because OT release in the amygdala is essential for social recognition in mice (Ferguson, Aldag, Insel, & Young, 2001) and identification of an intruder is a critical step in eliciting maternal aggression, it is possible the peptide can play roles in both facilitating and inhibiting maternal aggressive behavior

Vasopressin

Despite an identified positive link of vasopressin to intermale aggression (described in previous chapters), no work has directly examined whether or how vasopressin influences maternal aggression. Infusion of vasopressin promotes parental behaviors in relatively nonparental male voles (Wang, Ferris, & De Vries, 1994) and aggression in pair-bonded male prairie voles has similarities to maternal aggression (Villalba et al.,

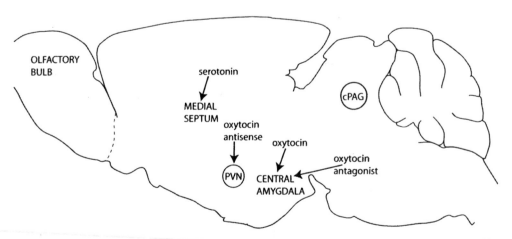

FIGURE 11.4 Schematic sagittal section of the rodent central nervous system highlighting either sites of lesions (open circle) or direct injections (arrow) that trigger *increases* in maternal aggression.

1997). Because the onset of parenting in male voles is linked with elevated aggression, it is possible vasopressin plays a role in this change. However, direct studies of the role of vasopressin on maternal aggression still need to be performed.

Prolactin

Prolactin plays a critical role in maternal care directed to pups (Bridges, 1996), but its role in maternal aggression is unclear. Based only on the profile of prolactin release during lactation, which covaries closely with levels of aggression (figure 11.1), it would be tempting to speculate that prolactin plays a critical, excitatory role in the behavior. Also, circulating prolactin in lactating rats decreases quickly with removal of the litter and at the same time points that decreases in maternal aggression are observed (Amenomori, Chen, & Meites, 1970). In support of an excitatory role for prolactin, in lactating hamsters, maternal aggression levels are reduced after systemic treatments that decrease prolactin and are restored by treatments with prolactin (Wise & Pryor, 1977).

Removal of the pituitary source of prolactin does not affect aggression in rats (Erskine, Barfield, & Goldman, 1980a), suggesting that circulating prolactin may have little role in maternal aggression. Further, other evidence suggests that circulating prolactin is not necessary for maternal aggression in mice because plasma levels of prolactin do not correlate with levels of aggression (Broida, Michael, & Svare, 1981); neither removal of the pituitary (Broida et al., 1981; Svare, Mann, Broida, & Michael, 1982) nor drug-induced decreases in prolactin affect aggression (Mann, Michael, & Svare, 1980), and females that interact with pups, but are not lactating, are aggressive (Svare et al., 1980). However, neurons within the CNS also synthesize prolactin (Emanuele et al., 1992; Paut-Pagano, Roky, Valatx, Kitahama, & Jouvet, 1993; Wilson, Emanuele, Jurgens, & Kelley, 1992). Receptors for prolactin are found in numerous areas of the hypothalamus and amygdala that are associated with aggression (Bakowska & Morrell, 1997) and the expression of prolactin receptors is increased by physical contact with the litter (Pi & Voogt, 2001). Therefore, it remains possible that centrally released prolactin may contribute to the control of maternal aggression.

Corticotropin Releasing Hormone (CRH)

Central release of CRH is a potent activator of indices of fear and anxiety (Liang et al., 1992; Stenzel-Poore,

Heinrichs, Rivest, Koob, & Vale, 1994). As is detailed below, lactating female rodents exhibit decreased fear and anxiety that coincides with their increased aggression. It has been hypothesized that decreases in fear and anxiety (and CRH) may be necessary for a dam to attack a normally fear-evoking stimulus. CRH neurotransmission decreases during lactation occur such that both CRH mRNA (Walker, Toufexis, & Burlet, 2001) and adrenergic input to certain CRH neurons are diminished (Toufexis et al., 1998). Recent work indicates that icv injection of CRH dose dependently decreases maternal aggression (Gammie, Negron, Newman, & Rhodes, 2004). It is possible, but not likely, that CRH inhibits maternal aggression indirectly via activation of either ACTH or glucocorticoids, because injections of neither ACTH nor the synthetic glucocorticoid dexamethasone affect this behavior (Al-Maliki, 1980). Thus, CRH may play a critical in allowing the expression of maternal aggression via decreased neurotransmission during lactation.

Opioids

Opioids appear to inhibit maternal aggression. Systemic injections of opioid agonists decrease maternal aggression (Haney, 1989). Further, concurrent injections of an antagonist with an agonist prevent this effect and injection of the antagonist alone has no effect on aggression (Kinsley & Bridges, 1986). It is possible that decreased opioid activity is critical for maternal aggression, but maternal aggression begins to appear before parturition (Mayer, 1987), when opioid levels are actually increased in brain areas compared to those during lactation (Petraglia et al., 1985; Wardlaw & Frantz, 1983). Opioid effect on aggression could also be nonspecific, because many opioid agonists suppress many types of agonistic behaviors in rodents (Miczek & DeBold 1983). Other mechanisms for opioids to affect aggression could be via altering pain sensitivity (Haney & Miczek, 1989) or disrupting olfactory discriminatory abilities between conspecifics (Kinsley, Morse, Zoumas, Corl, & Billack, 1995).

Nitric Oxide (NO)

NO is a fast-acting, gaseous neuromodulator that is produced by the enzyme neuronal nitric oxide synthase (nNOS). Removal of the nNOS gene in mice reduces maternal aggression, but not other maternal behaviors (Gammie & Nelson, 1999), suggesting that NO may help to activate aggression. Because deletion of the endothelial form of NOS that controls blood vessel vasodilation has no effect on maternal aggression (Gammie, Huang, & Nelson, 2000), it is thought that only NO from neurons plays a role in controlling the behavior. In further support of a role for NO in maternal aggression, lactating mice show significant increases in immunoreactivity to citrulline, a by-product of NO synthesis, in three areas of the hypothalamus only in association with actual defense of offspring (Gammie & Nelson, 1999). Also, prairie voles show similar elevations in citrulline immunoreactivity in association with maternal aggression (Gammie & Nelson, 2000) and maternal aggression is impaired by an nNOS inhibitor in both prairie voles (Gammie, Olaghere-da Silva, & Nelson, 2000) and rats (Popeski & Woodside, 2004).

Specifically how NO affects maternal aggression remains unknown, but NO can increase or decrease target cell excitability and can trigger changes in gene expression (Amir, Rackover, & Funk, 1997; Lee, Kim, & Rivier, 1999). Further, NO can both inhibit (Costa, Trainer, Besser, & Grossman, 1993) and promote (Karanth, Lyson, & McCann, 1993) CRH release. Thus, one possibility is that NO helps to activate maternal aggression by inhibiting CRH release (see above). Changes in male aggression in mice missing the nNOS gene appear to result from an alteration in serotonin levels (Chiavegatto et al., 2001) and it is possible that NO affects maternal aggression indirectly by altering serotonin signaling (see Manuck, Kaplan, & Lotrich, ch. 4, and Miczek & Fish, ch. 5, in this volume).

Indirect Markers of Neuronal Activity

Comparisons of brain regions between lactating mice that either did or did not exhibit maternal aggression during a test were conducted using indirect markers for neuronal activity. In aggressive dams, activity of the immediate-early gene cFOS was increased in the claustrum, bed nucleus of the stria terminalis (BNST), medial preoptic nucleus, PVN, medial amygdala (mAMY), and cortical amygdala. Expression of the transcription factor pCREB, also an indirect marker of neural activity, increased in the ventrolateral septum and cPAG. In a similar study, rats showed elevated cFOS in the BNST, PVN, mAMY, and cPAG in association with maternal aggression (Stern, 1998). Because most of these sites are neuroanatomically connected, it is likely that their interrelated activity is necessary for maternal aggression.

Some limitations to the use of indirect markers of activity are that increased activity could relate to the activation of the circuitry controlling this behavior or could simply passively reflect the change in motor output necessary for the behavior. Regions that are identified as being involved in maternal aggression by more than one approach (e.g., indirect markers, lesion studies, direct injections) are the best candidates for future research on the neural control of maternal aggression.

Similarities and Differences in the Neural Control of Maternal and Intermale Aggression

The current understanding of the neural control of aggression in males has been detailed throughout many chapters of this book. The overlap of some brain regions involved in both intermale and maternal aggression (e.g., mAMY, LS) is intriguing. Indeed, an approach that systematically examines similarities and differences in the neural control of different forms of aggression would be useful in understanding aggression as a whole.

In terms of general differences, intermale aggression in most rodents is orchestrated by brain changes resulting from testosterone or its aromatization to estradiol (Compaan, Wozniak, De Ruiter, Koolhaas, & Hutchison, 1994). In contrast, estradiol release during pregnancy coordinates the onset of maternal aggression, whereas sensory inputs from pups maintain it (see above). These differences do not indicate necessary differences in neuronal circuitry between the sexes, but at the very least, it indicates that activation of the circuitry occurs through different pathways.

Additionally, neuromodulators may have different effects on intermale and maternal aggression. NO appears to facilitate maternal aggression (described above), but it appears to inhibit intermale aggression (Nelson et al., 1995). Further, the same dose of a serotonin agonist significantly reduces intermale aggression, but does not affect maternal aggression in outbred mice (Parmigiani, Ferrari, & Palanza, 1998). In prairie voles, injections that elevate serotonin reduced aggression by sires, but did not affect maternal aggression (Villalba et al., 1997). Interestingly, while central serotonin is inversely correlated with aggression in human males (described in previous chapters), it is not in females (Cleare & Bond, 1997).

Relationship of Fear and Anxiety During Lactation With Maternal Aggression

In addition to the elevations in maternal responsiveness toward pups and maternal aggression emerges around parturition, the parturient rat or mouse also undergoes a change in emotional state. In many experimental paradigms, lactating dams show reduced fear and anxiety when compared to cycling virgins and freeze less after being startled by an acoustic stimulus (Hansen et al., 1985; Hard & Hansen, 1985; Toufexis, Rochford, & Walker, 1999), are more active in an open field (Fleming & Luebke, 1981; Toufexis et al., 1999), enter the open arms of an elevated plus maze more often and for longer durations of time (Bitran, Hilvers, & Kellogg, 1991; Fernandez-Guasti, Ferreira, & Picazo, 2001; Ferreira, Pereira, Agrati, Uriarte, & Fernandez-Guasti, 2002; Kellogg & Barrett, 1999; Lonstein, Simmons, & Stern, 1998), show less defensive burying (Picazo & Fernandez-Guasti, 1993), accept more shocks in a punished drinking paradigm (Ferreira, Hansen, Nielsen, Archer, & Minor, 1989), and are less anxious in a light/dark choice test (Maestripieri, Badiani, & Puglisi-Allegra, 1991; Maestripieri & D'Amato, 1991). Not only do aggression and fear and/or anxiety covary as a function of reproductive state, but inter- and intra-strain (i.e., individual) differences in aggression within groups of lactating mice and rats are negatively correlated with their levels of anxiety (Lonstein et al., 1998; Maestripieri & D'Amato, 1991; Parmigiani et al., 1999). Furthermore, individual differences in maternal aggression and anxiety in rats may result from differences in their early interactions with their own dams (Boccia & Pedersen, 2001). The negative relationship between fearfulness or anxiety and aggression is not exclusive to parental rats and mice and may be a general phenomenon in parental vertebrates—such a relationship can even be found in some species of fish (Budaev, Zworykin, & Mochek, 1999)!

There are many similarities between the mechanisms of aggression and fear or anxiety during lactation. In rats, the time course of increased aggression and reduced anxiety are almost identical, both peaking around the end of the first week postpartum and then waning (J. S. Lonstein, unpublished data), and appear to be similar, because although recent physical contact with pups is necessary for both changes in postpartum behavior (Erskine et al., 1978; Fernandez-Guasti et al., 2001; Fernandez-Guasti, Picazo, & Ferreira,

1998; Ferreira et al., 1989; Gandelman & Simon, 1980; Hard & Hansen, 1985; Stern & Kolunie, 1993), suckling by pups is not necessary for either, and thelectomized dams are just as aggressive and fearless as dams with intact nipples (Mayer, Monroy, et al., 1987). The neural determinants of these behaviors also partly overlap because lesions of the cPAG not only increase maternal aggression, but also further reduce postpartum anxiety, as measured in an elevated plus maze (Lonstein et al., 1998).

Although the above research supports the hypothesis that heightened aggression during lactation requires a concomitant reduction in fear and anxiety, other studies do not. For example, some studies report that lactating females are similarly as fearful and anxious as (Fernandez-Guasti et al., 2001, 1998; Hansen & Ferreira, 1986b; Picazo & Fernandez-Guasti, 1993; Sibolboro Mezzacappa, Tu, & Myers, 2003; Stern, Erskine, & Levine, 1973) or are even more so (Silva, Bernardi, Nasello, & Felicio, 1997) than cycling virgins. However, many of the discrepancies can be partly explained by methodological details, such as when during lactation testing occurred (J. S. Lonstein, unpublished data) and/or whether the dams were in physical contact with pups during or immediately prior to testing (J. S. Lonstein, unpublished data). It has also been found that mid- and late-pregnant rats are more anxious in an elevated plus maze than virgin females (Neumann, 2001), even though maternal aggression begins to emerge at this time (Erskine et al., 1978; Flannelly & Flannelly, 1987; Mayer, Reisbick, Siegel, & Rosenblatt, 1987; Mayer & Rosenblatt, 1984). As noted above, treatment of lactating females with diazepam can reduce maternal aggression even at doses that also reduce fear and anxiety (Ferreira et al., 2000), and some neural manipulations that reduce maternal aggression, such as lesions of the hypothalamic PVN, do not necessarily affect fear or anxiety in the dams (Olazabal & Ferreira, 1997). Last, the process of sensitization without exogenous hormone treatment can increase aggressive behavior in nulliparous female rats (Erskine et al., 1980b; Krehbiel & LeRoy, 1979; Mayer, Ahdieh, et al., 1990), but does not necessarily reduce their fearfulness and anxiety (Bridges, Zarrow, Gandelman, & Denenberg, 1972; Hansen, 1990; Stern & Mackinnon, 1976). When sensitization is shown to reduce fear or anxiety in virgin rats, the reduction is much less than that observed in a naturally parturient dam (Ferreira et al., 2002; Hansen & Ferreira, 1986b). These results indicate that although lactating females are in many cases observed to be both less fearful and more aggressive, the association between these behaviors can be rather complex.

The neurochemical basis underlying changes in fear or anxiety during lactation is not well understood, but seems to involve a variety of neurochemicals, including norepinephrine, OT, prolactin, vasopressin, and CRH. Details of the mechanisms are somewhat beyond the scope of this review, and readers are referred to other sources for more information on this topic (Lightman et al., 2001; Neumann, 2001; Walker et al., 2001). It should be noted that although some of these neurochemicals (e.g., CRH) are also involved in maternal aggression (Gammie et al., 2004), others (e.g., prolactin) are not (Broida et al., 1981; Erskine et al., 1980a; Mayer, Ahdieh, et al., 1990; Svare et al., 1982).

Summary and Conclusions

Human violence is a serious social problem and studies of the biological basis of intermale aggression using a rodent model provide an important foundation for understanding aggression. However, aggression takes a number of forms in humans that may not be easily modeled in rodents. One form of violence in humans that has been of particular interest recently is suicide bombings. It has been suggested that the basis for suicide attacks has an origin linked most closely to the normal expression of maternal aggression (Atran, 2003b), insomuch that it is often performed by individuals who consider it a form of defense of their immediate or very extended family group (Atran, 2003a). It is not implausible that activation of maternal aggression circuitry could best model this behavior. If this is the case, then an understanding of the biological basis of maternal aggression could be the best model for examining interventions. Further, some postpartum human mothers display pathological patterns of aggression that result in the harm or death of children (Haapasalo & Petaja, 1999; Hein & Honeyman, 2000) and an understanding of the controls of maternal aggression in rodents may prove beneficial for determining treatments that prevent unnecessary violence and death in humans. At the very least, understanding the similarities and differences in both the biological basis and the production of different forms of aggression will be a critical part of the use of research to help provide answers for social violence.

References

Agrell, J., Wolff, J. O., & Ylonen, H. (1998). Counter-strategies to infanticide in mammals: Costs and consequences. *Oikos, 83*(3), 507–517.

Albert, D. J., Jonik, R. H., & Walsh, M. L. (1992a). Hormone-dependent aggression in male and female rats: Experiential, hormonal, and neural foundations. *Neuroscience and Biobehavioral Reviews, 16*(2), 177–192.

Albert, D. J., Jonik, R. H., & Walsh, M. L. (1992b). Interaction of estradiol, testosterone, and progesterone in the modulation of hormone-dependent aggression in the female rat. *Physiology and Behavior, 52*(4), 773–779.

Albert, D. J., Jonik, R. H., & Walsh, M. L. (1992c). Ovariectomy does not attenuate aggression by primiparous lactating female rats. *Physiology and Behavior, 52*(6), 1043–1046.

Albert, D. J., & Walsh, M. L. (1984). Neural systems and the inhibitory modulation of agonistic behavior: A comparison of mammalian species. *Neuroscience and Biobehavioral Reviews, 8*(1), 5–24.

Albert, D. J., & Walsh, M. L. (1995). Aggression in the lactating female rat: The normal decline is not dependent on the physical development of the pups. *Physiology and Behavior, 58*(3), 477–481.

Albert, D. J., Walsh, M. L., Gorzalka, B. B., Mendelson, S., & Zalys, C. (1986). Intermale social aggression: Suppression by medial preoptic area lesions. *Physiology & Behavior, 38*(2), 169–173.

Albert, D., Walsh, M., L., Zalys, C., & Dyson, E. M. (1988). Maternal aggression and intermale social aggression: A behavioral comparison. *Behavioural Processes, 14*, 267–276.

Al-Maliki, S. (Ed.). (1980). *Influences of stress-related hormones on a variety of attack behaviour in laboratory mice* (Vol. 53). Amsterdam: Elsevier.

Amenomori, Y., Chen, C. L., & Meites, J. (1970). Serum prolactin levels in rats during different reproductive states. *Endocrinology, 86*(3), 506–510.

Amir, S., Rackover, M., & Funk, D. (1997). Blockers of nitric oxide synthase inhibit stress activation of c-fos expression in neurons of the hypothalamic paraventricular nucleus in the rat. *Neuroscience, 77*(3), 623–627.

Atran, S. (2003a). Genesis of suicide terrorism. *Science, 299*(5612), 1534–1539.

Atran, S. (2003b). The surprises of suicide terrrorism: It's not a new phenomenon, and natural selection may play a role in producing it. *Discover, 24*, 21–22.

Bakowska, J. C., & Morrell, J. I. (1997). Atlas of the neurons that express mRNA for the long form of the prolactin receptor in the forebrain of the female rat. *Journal of Comparative Neurology, 386*(2), 161–177.

Barkley, M. S., Geschwind, I. I., & Bradford, G. E. (1979). The gestational pattern of estradiol, testosterone and progesterone secretion in selected strains of mice. *Biology of Reproduction, 20*(4), 733–738.

Beach, F. A., & Jaynes, J. (1956). Studies of maternal retrieving in rats. III. Sensory cues involved in the lactating females' responses to her young. *Behaviour, 10*, 104–125.

Bean, N. J., Nunez, A. A., & Wysocki, C. J. (1986). 70-kHz vocalizations by male mice do not inhibit aggression in lactating mice. *Behavioral and Neural Biology, 46*(1), 46–53.

Bean, N. J., & Wysocki, C. J. (1989). Vomeronasal organ removal and female mouse aggression: The role of experience. *Physiology and Behavior, 45*(5), 875–882.

Bitran, D., Hilvers, R. J., & Kellogg, C. K. (1991). Ovarian endocrine status modulates the anxiolytic potency of diazepam and the efficacy of gamma-aminobutyric acid-benzodiazepine receptor-mediated chloride ion transport. *Behavioral Neuroscience, 105*(5), 653–662.

Blanchard, D. C., & Blanchard, R. J. (1990). Behavioral correlates of chronic dominance–subordination relationships of male rats in a seminatural situation. *Neuroscience and Biobehavioral Reviews, 14*(4), 455–462.

Blanchard, D. C., Fukunaga-Stinson, C., Takahashi, L. K., Flannelly, K. J., & Blanchard, R. J. (1984). Dominance and aggression in social groups of male and female rats. *Behavioural Processes, 9*, 31–48.

Boccia, M. L., & Pedersen, C. A. (2001). Brief vs. long maternal separations in infancy: Contrasting relationships with adult maternal behavior and lactation levels of aggression and anxiety. *Psychoneuroendocrinology, 26*(7), 657–672.

Bosch, O. J., Kromer, S. A., Brunton, P. J., & Neumann, I. D. (2004). Release of oxytocin in the hypothalamic paraventricular nucleus, but not central amygdala or lateral septum in lactating residents and virgin intruders during maternal defence. *Neuroscience, 124*(2), 439–448.

Bridges, R. (1996). Biochemical basis of parental behavior in the rat. In J. Rosenblatt & C. T. Snowdon (Eds.), *Parental care: Evolution, mechanisms, and adaptive significance* (Vol. 25, pp. 215–242). New York: Academic Press.

Bridges, R. S., Rosenblatt, J. S., & Feder, H. H. (1978). Serum progesterone concentrations and maternal behavior in rats after pregnancy termination: Behavioral stimulation after progesterone withdrawal and inhibition by progesterone maintenance. *Endocrinology, 102*(1), 258–267.

Bridges, R. S., Zarrow, M. X., Gandelman, R., & Denenberg, V. H. (1972). Differences in maternal responsiveness between lactating and sensitized rats. *Developmental Psychobiology, 5*(2), 123–127.

Broida, J., Michael, S. D., & Svare, B. (1981). Plasma prolactin levels are not related to the initiation, maintenance, and decline of postpartum aggression in mice. *Behavioral and Neural Biology, 32*(1), 121–125.

Budaev, S. V., Zworykin, D. D., & Mochek, A. D. (1999). Individual differences in parental care and behaviour profile in the convict cichlid: A correlation study. *Animal Behaviour, 58*, 195–202.

Bugbee, N. M., & Eichelman, B. S., Jr. (1972). Sensory alterations and aggressive behavior in the rat. *Physiology and Behavior, 8*(6), 981–985.

Calhoun, J. (1963). *The ecology and sociology of the Norway rat.* (U.S. Public Health Service Publication Vol. No. 1008). Washington, DC: U.S. Government Printing Office.

Chiavegatto, S., Dawson, V. L., Mamounas, L. A., Koliatsos, V. E., Dawson, T. M., & Nelson, R. J. (2001). Brain serotonin dysfunction accounts for aggression in male mice lacking neuronal nitric oxide synthase. *Proceedings of the National Academy of Sciences USA, 98*(3), 1277–1281.

Cleare, A. J., & Bond, A. J. (1997). Does central serotonergic function correlate inversely with aggression? A study using d-fenfluramine in healthy subjects. *Psychiatry Research, 69*, 89–95.

Compaan, J. C., Wozniak, A., De Ruiter, A. J., Koolhaas, J. M., & Hutchison, J. B. (1994). Aromatase activity in the preoptic area differs between aggressive and nonaggressive male house mice. *Brain Research Bulletin, 35*(1), 1–7.

Consiglio, A. R., & Lucion, A. B. (1996). Lesion of hypothalamic paraventricular nucleus and maternal aggressive behavior in female rats. *Physiology and Behavior, 59*(4–5), 591–596.

Costa, A., Trainer, P., Besser, M., & Grossman, A. (1993). Nitric oxide modulates the release of corticotropin-releasing hormone from the rat hypothalamus in vitro. *Brain Research, 605*(2), 187–192.

Crawford, S., & Balon, E. K. (1996). Cause and effect of parental care in fishes: An epigenetic perspective. In J. Rosenblatt & C. T. Snowdon (Eds.), *Parental care: Evolution, mechanisms, and adaptive significance* (Vol. 25, pp. 53–108). New York: Academic Press.

Critser, E. S., Savage, P. J., Rutledge, J. J., & French, L. R. (1982). Plasma concentrations of progesterone and 13,14-dihydro-15-keto prostaglandin F-2 alpha in pregnant, pseudopregnant and hysterectomized pseudopregnant mice. *Journal of Reproduction and Fertility, 64*(1), 79–83.

De Almeida, R. M., & Lucion, A. B. (1994). Effects of intracerebroventricular administration of 5-HT receptor agonists on the maternal aggression of rats. *European Journal of Pharmacology, 264*(3), 445–448.

De Almeida, R. M., & Lucion, A. B. (1997). 8-OH-DPAT in the median raphe, dorsal periaqueductal gray and corticomedial amygdala nucleus decreases, but in the medial septal area it can increase maternal aggressive behavior in rats. *Psychopharmacology, 134*(4), 392–400.

Del Punta, K., Leinders-Zufall, T., Rodriguez, I., Jukam, D., Wysocki, C. J., Ogawa, S., et al. (2002). Deficient pheromone responses in mice lacking a cluster of vomeronasal receptor genes. *Nature, 419*(6902), 70–74.

Dewsbury, D. (1979). Pregnancy and copulatory behavior in random-bred house mice mated in postpartum estrus. *Bulletin of the Psychonomic Society, 13,* 320–322.

Dewsbury, D. A., Evans, R. L., & Webster, D. G. (1979). Pregnancy initiation in postpartum estrus in three species of muroid rodents. *Hormones and Behavior, 13*(1), 1–8.

Edwards, D. A., Nahai, F. R., & Wright, P. (1993). Pathways linking olfactory bulbs with the medial preoptic anterior hypothalamus are important for intermale aggression in mice. *Physiology & Behavior, 53*(3), 611–615.

Eichenbaum, H., Shedlack, K. J., & Eckmann, K. W. (1980). Thalamocortical mechanisms in odor-guided behavior. I. Effects of lesions of the mediodorsal thalamic nucleus and frontal cortex on olfactory discrimination in the rat. *Brain, Behavior and Evolution, 17*(4), 255–275.

Elliott, J. C., Lubin, D. A., Walker, C. H., & Johns, J. M. (2001). Acute cocaine alters oxytocin levels in the medial preoptic area and amygdala in lactating rat dams: Implications for cocaine-induced changes in maternal behavior and maternal aggression. *Neuropeptides, 35*(2), 127–134.

Emanuele, N. V., Jurgens, J. K., Halloran, M. M., Tentler, J. J., Lawrence, A. M., & Kelley, M. R. (1992). The rat prolactin gene is expressed in brain tissue: Detection of normal and alternatively spliced prolactin messenger RNA. *Molecular Endocrinology, 6*(1), 35–42.

Erskine, M. S., Barfield, R. J., & Goldman, B. D. (1978). Intraspecific fighting during late pregnancy and lactation in rats and effects of litter removal. *Behavioral Biology, 23*(2), 206–218.

Erskine, M. S., Barfield, R. J., & Goldman, B. D. (1980a). Postpartum aggression in rats: I. Effects of hypophysectomy. *Journal of Comparative and Physiological Psychology, 94*(3), 484–494.

Erskine, M. S., Barfield, R. J., & Goldman, B. D. (1980b). Postpartum aggression in rats: II. Dependence on

maternal sensitivity to young and effects of experience with pregnancy and parturition. *Journal of Comparative and Physiological Psychology, 94*(3), 495–505.

Erskine, M. S., Denenberg, V. H., & Goldman, B. D. (1978). Aggression in the lactating rat: Effects of intruder age and test arena. *Behavioral Biology, 23*(1), 52–66.

Factor, E. M., Mayer, A. D., & Rosenblatt, J. S. (1992). Preventing suckling-induced release of oxytocin does not inhibit maternal aggression in lactating rats. *Annals of the New York Academy of Sciences, 652,* 423–424.

Factor, E. M., Mayer, A. D., & Rosenblatt, J. S. (1993). Peripeduncular nucleus lesions in the rat: I. Effects on maternal aggression, lactation, and maternal behavior during pre- and postpartum periods. *Behavioral Neuroscience, 107*(1), 166–185.

Ferguson, J. N., Aldag, J. M., Insel, T. R., & Young, L. J. (2001). Oxytocin in the medial amygdala is essential for social recognition in the mouse. *Journal of Neuroscience, 21*(20), 8278–8285.

Fernandez-Guasti, A., Ferreira, A., & Picazo, O. (2001). Diazepam, but not buspirone, induces similar anxiolytic-like actions in lactating and ovariectomized Wistar rats. *Pharmacology, Biochemistry and Behavior, 70*(1), 85–93.

Fernandez-Guasti, A., Picazo, O., & Ferreira, A. (1998). Blockade of the anxiolytic action of 8-OH-DPAT in lactating rats. *Pharmacology, Biochemistry and Behavior, 59*(1), 45–50.

Ferreira, A., Dahlof, L. G., & Hansen, S. (1987). Olfactory mechanisms in the control of maternal aggression, appetite, and fearfulness: Effects of lesions to olfactory receptors, mediodorsal thalamic nucleus, and insular prefrontal cortex. *Behavioral Neuroscience, 101*(5), 709–717, 746.

Ferreira, A., & Hansen, S. (1986). Sensory control of maternal aggression in *Rattus norvegicus. Journal of Comparative Psychology, 100*(2), 173–177.

Ferreira, A., Hansen, S., Nielsen, M., Archer, T., & Minor, B. G. (1989). Behavior of mother rats in conflict tests sensitive to antianxiety agents. *Behavioral Neuroscience, 103*(1), 193–201.

Ferreira, A., Pereira, M., Agrati, D., Uriarte, N., & Fernandez-Guasti, A. (2002). Role of maternal behavior on aggression, fear and anxiety. *Physiology and Behavior, 77*(2–3), 197–204.

Ferreira, A., Picazo, O., Uriarte, N., Pereira, M., & Fernandez-Guasti, A. (2000). Inhibitory effect of buspirone and diazepam, but not of 8-OH-DPAT, on maternal behavior and aggression. *Pharmacology, Biochemistry and Behavior, 66*(2), 389–396.

Ferris, C. F., Foote, K. B., Meltser, H. M., Plenby, M. G.,

Smith, K. L., & Insel, T. R. (1992). Oxytocin in the amygdala facilitates maternal aggression. *Annals of the New York Academy of Sciences, 652,* 456–457.

Findlay, A. (1966). Sensory discharges from lactating mammary nerves. *Nature, 211,* 1183–1184.

Flannelly, K. J., & Flannelly, L. (1985). Opponents' size influences maternal aggression. *Psychological Reports, 57*(3, Pt. 1), 883–886.

Flannelly, K. J., & Flannelly, L. (1987). Time course of postpartum aggression in rats (*Rattus norvegicus*). *Journal of Comparative Psychology, 101,* 101–103.

Flannelly, K. J., Flannelly, L., & Lore, R. (1986). Postpartum aggression against male conspecifics in Sprague–Dawley rats. *Behavioral Processes, 13,* 279–186.

Flannelly, K. J., & Kemble, E. D. (1988). The effect of pup presence and intruder behavior on maternal aggression in rats. *Bulletin of the Psychonomic Society, 25,* 133–135.

Flannelly, K. J., Kemble, E. D., Blanchard, D. C., & Blanchard, R. J. (1986). Effects of septal-forebrain lesions on maternal aggression and maternal care. *Behavioral and Neural Biology, 45*(1), 17–30.

Fleming, A. S., & Luebke, C. (1981). Timidity prevents the virgin female rat from being a good mother: Emotionality differences between nulliparous and parturient females. *Physiology and Behavior, 27*(5), 863–868.

Gammie, S. C., Huang, P. L., & Nelson, R. J. (2000). Maternal aggression in endothelial nitric oxide synthase-deficient mice. *Hormones and Behavior, 38*(1), 13–20.

Gammie, S. C., Negron, A., Newman, S. M., & Rhodes, J. S. (2004). Corticotropin-releasing factor inhibits maternal aggression in mice. *Behavioral Neuroscience, 118,* 805–814.

Gammie, S. C., & Nelson, R. J. (1999). Maternal aggression is reduced in neuronal nitric oxide synthase-deficient mice. *Journal of Neuroscience, 19,* 8027–8035.

Gammie, S. C., & Nelson, R. J. (2000). Maternal and mating-induced aggression is associated with elevated citrulline immunoreactivity in the paraventricular nucleus in prairie voles. *Journal of Comparative Neurology, 418,* 182–192.

Gammie, S. C., Olaghere-da Silva, U. B., & Nelson, R. J. (2000). 3-Bromo-7-nitroindazole, a neuronal nitric oxide synthase inhibitor, impairs maternal aggression and citrulline immunoreactivity in prairie voles. *Brain Research, 870*(1–2), 80–86.

Gandelman, R. (1972). Mice: Postpartum aggression elicited by the presence of an intruder. *Hormones and Behavior, 3*(1), 23–28.

Gandelman, R. (1973). Reduction of maternal nest building in female mice by testosterone propionate treatment. *Developmental Psychobiology, 6*(6), 539–546.

Gandelman, R., & Simon, N. G. (1980). Postpartum fighting in the rat: Nipple development and the presence of young. *Behavioral and Neural Biology, 28*(3), 350–360.

Gandelman, R., & vom Saal, F. (1977). Exposure to early androgen attenuates androgen-induced pup-killing in male and female mice. *Behavioral Biology, 20*(2), 252–260.

Gandelman, R., Zarrow, M. X., & Denenberg, V. H. (1972). Reproductive and maternal performance in the mouse following removal of the olfactory bulbs. *Journal of Reproduction and Fertility, 28*(3), 453–456.

Garland, M., & Svare, B. (1988). Suckling stimulation modulates the maintenance of postpartum aggression in mice. *Physiology and Behavior, 44*(3), 301–305.

Ghiraldi, L. L., Plonsky, M., & Svare, B. B. (1993). Postpartum aggression in mice: The role of ovarian hormones. *Hormones and Behavior, 27*(2), 251–268.

Giordano, A. L., Siegel, H. I., & Rosenblatt, J. S. (1984). Effects of mother–litter separation and reunion on maternal aggression and pup mortality in lactating hamsters. *Physiology and Behavior, 33*(6), 903–906.

Giovenardi, M., Consiglio, A. R., Barros, H. M., & Lucion, A. B. (2000). Pup age and aggressive behavior in lactating rats. *Brazilian Journal of Medical and Biological Research, 33*(9), 1083–1088.

Giovenardi, M., Padoin, M. J., Cadore, L. P., & Lucion, A. B. (1998). Hypothalamic paraventricular nucleus modulates maternal aggression in rats: Effects of ibotenic acid lesion and oxytocin antisense. *Physiology and Behavior, 63*(3), 351–359.

Gleason, P. E., Michael, S. D., & Christian, J. J. (1979). Effects of gonadal steroids on agonistic behavior of female Peromyscus leucopus. *Hormones and Behavior, 12*(1), 30–39.

Grota, L. J., & Ader, R.,(1969). Continuous recording of maternal behavior in *Rattus norvegicus*. *Animal Behaviour, 17,* 722–729.

Haapasalo, J., & Petaja, S. (1999). Mothers who killed or attempted to kill their child: Life circumstances, childhood abuse, and types of killing. *Violence and Victims, 14,* 219–239.

Hammond, M. A., & Rowe, F. A. (1976). Medial preoptic and anterior hypothalamic lesions: Influences on aggressive behavior in female hamsters. *Physiology and Behavior, 17*(3), 507–513.

Haney, M., & Miczek, K. A. (1989). Morphine effects on maternal aggression, pup care and analgesia in mice. *Psychopharmacology, 98*(1), 68–74.

Hansen, S. (1989). Medial hypothalamic involvement in maternal aggression of rats. *Behavioral Neuroscience, 103*(5), 1035–1046.

Hansen, S. (1990). Mechanisms involved in the control of punished responding in mother rats. *Hormones and Behavior, 24*(2), 186–197.

Hansen, S., & Ferreira, A. (1986a). Effects of bicuculline infusions in the ventromedial hypothalamus and amygdaloid complex on food intake and affective behavior in mother rats. *Behavioral Neuroscience, 100*(3), 410–415.

Hansen, S., & Ferreira, A. (1986b). Food intake, aggression, and fear behavior in the mother rat: Control by neural systems concerned with milk ejection and maternal behavior. *Behavioral Neuroscience, 100*(1), 64–70.

Hansen, S., Ferreira, A., & Selart, M. E. (1985). Behavioural similarities between mother rats and benzodiazepine-treated non-maternal animals. *Psychopharmacology, 86*(3), 344–347.

Hansen, S., Harthon, C., Wallin, E., Lofberg, L., & Svensson, K. (1991a). The effects of 6-OHDA-induced dopamine depletions in the ventral or dorsal striatum on maternal and sexual behavior in the female rat. *Pharmacology, Biochemistry and Behavior, 39*(1), 71–77.

Hansen, S., Harthon, C., Wallin, E., Lofberg, L., & Svensson, K. (1991b). Mesotelencephalic dopamine system and reproductive behavior in the female rat: Effects of ventral tegmental 6-hydroxydopamine lesions on maternal and sexual responsiveness. *Behavioral Neuroscience, 105*(4), 588–598.

Hard, E., & Hansen, S. (1985). Reduced fearfulness in the lactating rat. *Physiology and Behavior, 35*(4), 641–643.

Hedricks, C., & Daniels, C. E. (1981). Agonistic behavior between pregnant mice and male intruders. *Behavioral and Neural Biology, 31*(2), 236–241.

Hein, D., & Honeyman, T. (2000). A closer look at the drug abuse-maternal aggression link. *Journal of Interpersonal Violence, 15*, 503–522.

Heise, S., & Lippke, J. (1997). Role of female aggression in prevention of infanticide in male common voles, *Microtus arvalis*. *Aggressive Behavior, 23*, 293–298.

Ieni, J. R., & Thurmond, J. B. (1985). Maternal aggression in mice: Effects of treatments with PCPA, 5-HTP and 5-HT receptor antagonists. *European Journal of Pharmacology, 111*(2), 211–220.

Johns, J. M., Nelson, C. J., Meter, K. E., Lubin, D. A., Couch, C. D., Ayers, A., et al. (1998). Dose-dependent effects of multiple acute cocaine injections on maternal behavior and aggression in Sprague–Dawley rats. *Developmental Neuroscience, 20*(6), 525–532.

Johns, J. M., Noonan, L. R., Zimmerman, L. I., Li, L., & Pedersen, C. A. (1994). Effects of chronic and acute cocaine treatment on the onset of maternal behavior and aggression in Sprague–Dawley rats. *Behavioral Neuroscience, 108*(1), 107–112.

Karanth, S., Lyson, K., & McCann, S. M. (1993). Role of nitric oxide in interleukin 2-induced corticotropin-releasing factor release from incubated hypothalami. *Proceedings of the National Academy of Sciences USA, 90*(8), 3383–3387.

Kellogg, C. K., & Barrett, K. A. (1999). Reduced progesterone metabolites are not critical for plus-maze performance of lactating female rats. *Pharmacology, Biochemistry and Behavior, 63*(3), 441–448.

Kinsley, C. H., & Bridges, R. S. (1986). Opiate involvement in postpartum aggression in rats. *Pharmacology, Biochemistry and Behavior, 25*(5), 1007–1011.

Kinsley, C. H., Morse, A. C., Zoumas, C., Corl, S., & Billack, B. (1995). Intracerebroventricular infusions of morphine, and blockade with naloxone, modify the olfactory preferences for pup odors in lactating rats. *Brain Research Bulletin, 37*(1), 103–107.

Kolunie, J. M., & Stern, J. M. (1990). Maternal aggression: Disruption by perioral anesthesia in lactating Long–Evans rats (*Rattus norvegicus*). *Journal of Comparative Psychology, 104*(4), 352–360.

Kolunie, J. M., & Stern, J. M. (1995). Maternal aggression in rats: Effects of olfactory bulbectomy, ZnSO4-induced anosmia, and vomeronasal organ removal. *Hormones and Behavior, 29*(4), 492–518.

Kolunie, J. M., Stern, J. M., & Barfield, R. J. (1994). Maternal aggression in rats: Effects of visual or auditory deprivation of the mother and dyadic pattern of ultrasonic vocalizations. *Behavioral and Neural Biology, 62*(1), 41–49.

Koskela, E., Juutistenaho, P., Mappes, T., & Oksanen, T. A. (2000). Offspring defence in relation to litter size and age: Experiment in the bank vole *Clethrionomys glareolus*. *Evolutionary Ecology, 14*(2), 99–109.

Krehbiel, D. A., & LeRoy, L. M. (1979). The quality of hormonally stimulated maternal behavior in ovariectomized rats. *Hormones and Behavior, 12*(3), 243–252.

Laviola, G., de Acetis, L., Bignami, G., & Alleva, E. (1991). Prenatal oxazepam enhances mouse maternal aggression in the offspring, without modifying acute chlordiazepoxide effects. *Neurotoxicology and Teratology, 13*(1), 75–81.

Ledesma, J., de Luis, J. M., Montejo, A. L., Llorca, G., & Perez-Urdaniz, A. (1988). Maternal aggression in human beings. *New Trends in Experimental and Clinical Psychiatry, 4*, 223–228.

Lee, S., Kim, C. K., & Rivier, C. (1999). Nitric oxide stimulates ACTH secretion and the transcription of the genes encoding for NGFI-B, corticotropin-releasing factor, corticotropin-releasing factor receptor type 1, and vasopressin in the hypothalamus of the intact rat. *Journal of Neuroscience, 19*(17), 7640–7647.

Leonard, C. M. (1972). Effects of neonatal (day 10) olfactory bulb lesions on social behavior of female golden hamsters (*Mesocricetus auratus*). *Journal of Comparative and Physiological Psychology, 80*(2), 208–215.

Lepri, J. J., Wysocki, C. J., & Vandenbergh, J. G. (1985). Mouse vomeronasal organ: Effects on chemosignal production and maternal behavior. *Physiology and Behavior, 35*(5), 809–814.

Liang, K. C., Melia, K. R., Miserendino, M. J., Falls, W. A., Campeau, S., & Davis, M. (1992). Corticotropin-releasing factor: Long-lasting facilitation of the acoustic startle reflex. *Journal of Neuroscience, 12*(6), 2303–2312.

Lightman, S. L., Windle, R. J., Wood, S. A., Kershaw, Y. M., Shanks, N., & Ingram, C. D. (2001). Peripartum plasticity within the hypothalamo-pituitary-adrenal axis. *Progress in Brain Research, 133*, 111–129.

Lonstein, J. S., & De Vries, G. J. (2000). Sex differences in the parental behavior of rodents. *Neuroscience and Biobehavioral Reviews, 24*(6), 669–686.

Lonstein, J. S., & Gammie, S. C. (2002). Sensory, hormonal, and neural control of maternal aggression in laboratory rodents. *Neuroscience and Biobehavioral Reviews, 26*(8), 869–888.

Lonstein, J. S., Simmons, D. A., & Stern, J. M. (1998). Functions of the caudal periaqueductal gray in lactating rats: Kyphosis, lordosis, maternal aggression, and fearfulness. *Behavioral Neuroscience, 112*(6), 1502–1518.

Lonstein, J. S., & Stern, J. M. (1997). Role of the midbrain periaqueductal gray in maternal nurturance and aggression: c-Fos and electrolytic lesion studies in lactating rats. *Journal of Neuroscience, 17*(9), 3364–3378.

Lonstein, J. S., & Stern, J. M. (1998). Site and behavioral specificity of periaqueductal gray lesions on postpartum sexual, maternal, and aggressive behaviors in rats. *Brain Research, 804*(1), 21–35.

Lubin, D. A., Elliott, J. C., Black, M. C., & Johns, J. M. (2003). An oxytocin antagonist infused into the central nucleus of the amygdala increases maternal aggressive behavior. *Behavioral Neuroscience, 117*(2), 195–201.

Lynds, P. G. (1976). Olfactory control of aggression in lactating female house mice. *Physiology and Behavior, 17*(1), 157–159.

Maestripieri, D., Badiani, A., & Puglisi-Allegra, S. (1991). Prepartal chronic stress increases anxiety and decreases aggression in lactating female mice. *Behavioral Neuroscience, 105*(5), 663–668.

Maestripieri, D., & D'Amato, F. R. (1991). Anxiety and maternal aggression in house mice (*Mus musculus*): A look at interindividual variability. *Journal of Comparative Psychology, 105*(3), 295–301.

Mann, M. A., Konen, C., & Svare, B. (1984). The role of progesterone in pregnancy-induced aggression in mice. *Hormones and Behavior, 18*(2), 140–160.

Mann, M. A., Michael, S. D., & Svare, B. (1980). Ergot drugs suppress plasma prolactin and lactation but not aggression in parturient mice. *Hormones and Behavior, 14*(4), 319–328.

Mann, M. A., & Svare, B. (1982). Factors influencing pregnancy-induced aggression in mice. *Behavioral and Neural Biology, 36*(3), 242–258.

Martin, J., & Suares, J.-C. (1997). *Scarlett saves her family: The heart-warming true story of a homeless mother cat who rescued her kittens from a raging fire.* New York: Simon & Schuster.

Mayer, A. D., Ahdieh, H. B., & Rosenblatt, J. S. (1990). Effects of prolonged estrogen-progesterone treatment and hypophysectomy on the stimulation of short-latency maternal behavior and aggression in female rats. *Hormones and Behavior, 24*(2), 152–173.

Mayer, A. D., Carter, L., Jorge, W. A., Mota, M. J., Tannu, S., & Rosenblatt, J. S. (1987). Mammary stimulation and maternal aggression in rodents: Thelectomy fails to reduce pre- or postpartum aggression in rats. *Hormones and Behavior, 21*(4), 501–510.

Mayer, A. D., Monroy, M. A., & Rosenblatt, J. S. (1990). Prolonged estrogen-progesterone treatment of nonpregnant ovariectomized rats: Factors stimulating home-cage and maternal aggression and short-latency maternal behavior. *Hormones and Behavior, 24*(3), 342–364.

Mayer, A. D., Reisbick, S., Siegel, H. I., & Rosenblatt, J. S. (1987). Maternal aggression in rats: Changes over pregnancy and lactation in a Sprague–Dawley strain. *Aggressive Behavior, 13*, 29–43.

Mayer, A. D., & Rosenblatt, J. S. (1980). Hormonal interaction with stimulus and situational factors in the initiation of maternal behavior in nonpregnant rats. *Journal of Comparative and Physiological Psychology, 94*(6), 1040–1059.

Mayer, A. D., & Rosenblatt, J. S. (1984). Prepartum changes in maternal responsiveness and nest defense in *Rattus norvegicus. Journal of Comparative Psychology, 98*(2), 177–188.

Mayer, A. D., & Rosenblatt, J. S. (1987). Hormonal factors influence the onset of maternal aggression in laboratory rats. *Hormones and Behavior, 21*(2), 253–267.

Mayer, A. D., & Rosenblatt, J. S. (1993a). Contributions of olfaction to maternal aggression in laboratory rats (*Rattus norvegicus*): Effects of peripheral deafferentation of the primary olfactory system. *Journal of Comparative Psychology, 107*(1), 12–24.

Mayer, A. D., & Rosenblatt, J. S. (1993b). Persistent effects on maternal aggression of pregnancy but not of estrogen/progesterone treatment of nonpregnant ovariectomized rats revealed when initiation of maternal behavior is delayed. *Hormones and Behavior*, 27(1), 132–155.

McDermott, N. J., & Gandelman, R. (1979). Exposure to young induces postpartum-like fighting in virgin female mice. *Physiology and Behavior*, 23(3), 445–448.

Miczek, K., & DeBold, J. (1983). Hormone–drug interactions and their influence on aggressive behavior. In B. Svare (Ed.), *Hormones and aggressive behavior*. New York: Plenum.

Mos, J., & Olivier, B. (1986). RO 15–1788 does not influence postpartum aggression in lactating female rats. *Psychopharmacology*, 90(2), 278–280.

Mos, J., & Olivier, B. (1989). Quantitative and comparative analyses of pro-aggressive actions of benzodiazepines in maternal aggression of rats. *Psychopharmacology*, 97(2), 152–153.

Mos, J., Olivier, B., Lammers, J. H., van der Poel, A. M., Kruk, M. R., & Zethof, T. (1987). Postpartum aggression in rats does not influence threshold currents for EBS-induced aggression. *Brain Research*, 404(1–2), 263–266.

Mos, J., Olivier, B., & van der Poel, A. M. (1987). Modulatory actions of benzodiazepine receptor ligands on agonistic behaviour. *Physiology and Behavior*, 41(3), 265–278.

Mos, J., Olivier, B., & van Oorschot, R. (1987). Maternal aggression towards different sized male opponents: Effect of chlordiazepoxide treatment of the mothers and d-amphetamine treatment of the intruders. *Pharmacology, Biochemistry and Behavior*, 26(3), 577–584.

Mos, J., Olivier, B., van Oorschot, R., van Aken, H. H., & Zethof, T. (1989). Experimental and ethological aspects of maternal aggression in rats: Five years of observations. In R. Blanchard, P. R. Brain, D. C. Blanchard, & S. Parmigiani (Eds.), *Etho-experimental approaches to the study of behavior* (pp. 385–398). Dordrecht, Netherlands: Kluwer.

Nelson, R. J., Demas, G. E., Huang, P. L., Fishman, M. C., Dawson, V. L., Dawson, T. M., et al. (1995). Behavioural abnormalities in male mice lacking neuronal nitric oxide synthase. *Nature*, 378(6555), 383–386.

Neumann, I. D. (2001). Alterations in behavioral and neuroendocrine stress coping strategies in pregnant, parturient and lactating rats. *Progress in Brain Research*, 133, 143–152.

Neumann, I. D., Toschi, N., Ohl, F., Torner, L., & Kromer, S. A. (2001). Maternal defence as an emotional stressor in female rats: Correlation of neuroendocrine and behavioural parameters and involvement of brain oxytocin. *European Journal of Neuroscience*, 13(5), 1016–1024.

Noirot, E. (1964). Changes in the responsiveness to young in the adult mouse. I. The problematic effect of hormones. *Animal Behaviour* 12(52–58).

Noirot, E., Goyens, J., & Buhot, M. C. (1975). Aggressive behavior of pregnant mice toward males. *Hormones and Behavior*, 6(1), 9–17.

Numan, M. (1994). Maternal behavior. In E. Knobil & J. D. Neill (Eds.), *Physiology of reproduction* (2nd ed., Vol. 2, pp. 221–302). New York: Raven Press.

Numan, M., Roach, J. K., del Cerro, M. C., Guillamon, A., Segovia, S., Sheehan, T. P., et al. (1999). Expression of intracellular progesterone receptors in rat brain during different reproductive states, and involvement in maternal behavior. *Brain Research*, 830(2), 358–371.

Nyby, J., & Whitney, G. (1978). Ultrasonic communication of adult mymorph rodents. *Neuroscience and Biobehavioral Reviews*, 2, 1–14.

Olazabal, D. E., & Ferreira, A. (1997). Maternal behavior in rats with kainic acid-induced lesions of the hypothalamic paraventricular nucleus. *Physiology and Behavior*, 61(5), 779–784.

Olivier, B., Mos, J., & van Oorschot, R. (1985). Maternal aggression in rats: Effects of chlordiazepoxide and fluprazine. *Psychopharmacology*, 86(1–2), 68–76.

Olivier, B., Mos, J., & van Oorschot, R. (1986). Maternal aggression in rats: Lack of interaction between chlordiazepoxide and fluprazine. *Psychopharmacology*, 88(1), 40–43.

Olivier, B., Mos, J., van Oorschot, R., & Hen, R. (1995). Serotonin receptors and animal models of aggressive behavior. *Pharmacopsychiatry*, 28(Suppl. 2), 80–90.

Palanza, P., Rodgers, R. J., Ferrari, P. F., & Parmigiani, S. (1996). Effects of chlordiazepoxide on maternal aggression in mice depend on experience of resident and sex of intruder. *Pharmacology, Biochemistry and Behavior*, 54(1), 175–182.

Parmigiani, S., Brain, P. F., Mainardi, D., & Brunoni, V. (1988). Different patterns of biting attack employed by lactating female mice (*Mus domesticus*) in encounters with male and female conspecific intruders. *Journal of Comparative Psychology*, 102(3), 287–293.

Parmigiani, S., Ferrari, P. F., & Palanza, P. (1998). An evolutionary approach to behavioral pharmacology: Using drugs to understand proximate and ultimate mechanisms of different forms of aggression in mice. *Neuroscience & Biobehavioral Reviews*, 23(2), 143–153.

Parmigiani, S., Palanza, P., Rogers, J., & Ferrari, P. F. (1999). Selection, evolution of behavior and animal models in behavioral neuroscience. *Neuroscience and Biobehavioral Reviews*, 23(7), 957–969.

Parmigiani, S., Rodgers, R. J., Palanza, P., Mainardi, M., & Brain, P. F. (1989). The inhibitory effects of fluprazine on parental aggression in female mice are dependent upon intruder sex. *Physiology and Behavior*, 46(3), 455–459.

Paul, L., Gronek, J., & Politch, J. (1981). Maternal aggression in mice: Protection of young is a by-product of attacks at the home site. *Aggressive Behavior*, 6, 19–29.

Paut-Pagano, L., Roky, R., Valatx, J. L., Kitahama, K., & Jouvet, M. (1993). Anatomical distribution of prolactin-like immunoreactivity in the rat brain. *Neuroendocrinology*, 58(6), 682–695.

Petraglia, F., Baraldi, M., Giarre, G., Facchinetti, F., Santi, M., Volpe, A., et al. (1985). Opioid peptides of the pituitary and hypothalamus: Changes in pregnant and lactating rats. *Journal of Endocrinology*, 105(2), 239–245.

Pi, X., & Voogt, J. L. (2001). Mechanisms for suckling-induced changes in expression of prolactin receptor in the hypothalamus of the lactating rat. *Brain Research*, 891(1–2), 197–205.

Picazo, O., & Fernandez-Guasti, A. (1993). Changes in experimental anxiety during pregnancy and lactation. *Physiology and Behavior*, 54(2), 295–299.

Popeski, N., & Woodside, B. (2004). Central nitric oxide synthase inhibition disrupts maternal behavior in the rat. *Behavioral Neuroscience*, 118(6), 1305–1316.

Qureshi, G. A., Hansen, S., & Sodersten, P. (1987). Offspring control of cerebrospinal fluid GABA concentrations in lactating rats. *Neuroscience Letters*, 75(1), 85–88.

Racine, M., & Flannelly, K. J. (1986). The offensive nature of maternal aggression in mice: Effects of fluprazine hydrochloride. *Aggressive Behavior*, 12, 417–424.

Rosenblatt, J. (1969). Non-hormonal basis of maternal behavior the rat. *Science*, 156, 1512–1514.

Rosenblatt, J., Mayer, A. D., & Siegel, H. I. (1985). Maternal behavior among non-primate mammals. In N. Adler, D. Pfaff, & R. W. Goy (Eds.), *Handbook of behavioral neurobiology*. New York: Plenum.

Rosenblatt, J. S., Hazelwood, S., & Poole, J. (1996). Maternal behavior in male rats: Effects of medial preoptic area lesions and presence of maternal aggression. *Hormones and Behavior*, 30(3), 201–215.

Rosenson, L. M., & Asheroff, A. K. (1975). Maternal aggression in CD-l mice: Influence of the hormonal condition of the intruder. *Behavioral Biology*, 15(2), 219–224.

Sibolboro Mezzacappa, E., Tu, A. Y., & Myers, M. M. (2003). Lactation and weaning effects on physiological and behavioral response to stressors. *Physiology and Behavior*, 78(1), 1–9.

Siegel, H. I., Giordano, A. L., Mallafre, C. M., & Rosenblatt, J. S. (1983). Maternal aggression in hamsters: Effects of stage of lactation, presence of pups, and repeated testing. *Hormones and Behavior*, 17(1), 86–93.

Silva, M. R., Bernardi, M. M., Nasello, A. G., & Felicio, L. F. (1997). Influence of lactation on motor activity and elevated plus maze behavior. *Brazilian Journal of Medical and Biological Research*, 30(2), 241–244.

Smith, M. S. (1978). The relative contribution of suckling and prolactin to the inhibition of gonadotropin secretion during lactation in the rat. *Biology of Reproduction*, 19(1), 77–83.

Smotherman, W. P., Bell, R. W., Starzec, J., Elias, J., & Zachman, T. A. (1974). Maternal responses to infant vocalizations and olfactory cues in rats and mice. *Behavioral Biology*, 12(1), 55–66.

Sorenson, C. A., & Gordon, M. (1975). Effects of 6-hydroxydopamine on shock-elicited aggression, emotionality and maternal behavior in female rats. *Pharmacology, Biochemistry and Behavior*, 3(3), 331–335.

Stenzel-Poore, M. P., Heinrichs, S. C., Rivest, S., Koob, G. F., & Vale, W. W. (1994). Overproduction of corticotropin-releasing factor in transgenic mice: A genetic model of anxiogenic behavior. *Journal of Neuroscience*, 14(5, Pt. 1), 2579–2584.

Stern, J. M. (1989). Maternal behavior: Sensory, hormonal and neural determinants. In F. Brush & S. Levine (Eds.), *Psychoneuroendocrinology* (pp. 105–226). New York: Academic Press.

Stern, J. M. (1990). Multisensory regulation of maternal behavior and masculine sexual behavior: A revised view. *Neuroscience and Biobehavioral Reviews*, 14(2), 183–200.

Stern, J. M. (1998). Pattern of brain activation of c-fos after maternal aggression in lactating Long–Evans rats. *Society for Behavioral Neuroendocrinology Abstracts*, 68.

Stern, J., M. Erskine, M. S., & Levine, S. (1973). Dissociation of open-field behavior and pituitary–adrenal function. *Hormones and Behavior*, 4, 149–162.

Stern, J. M., & Johnson, S. K. (1989). Perioral somatosensory determinants of nursing behavior in Norway rats (*Rattus norvegicus*). *Journal of Comparative Psychology*, 103(3), 269–280.

Stern, J. M., & Kolunie, J. M. (1989). Perioral anesthesia disrupts maternal behavior during early lactation in Long–Evans rats. *Behavioral and Neural Biology*, 52(1), 20–38.

Stern, J. M., & Kolunie, J. M. (1991). Trigeminal lesions and maternal behavior in Norway rats: I. Effects of cutaneous rostral snout denervation on maintenance of nurturance and maternal aggression. *Behavioral Neuroscience*, 105(6), 984–997.

Stern, J. M., & Kolunie, J. M. (1993). Maternal aggression of rats is impaired by cutaneous anesthesia of the ventral trunk, but not by nipple removal. *Physiology and Behavior, 54*(5), 861–868.

Stern, J. M., & Mackinnon, D. A. (1976). Postpartum, hormonal, and nonhormonal induction of maternal behavior in rats: Effects on T-maze retrieval of pups. *Hormones and Behavior, 7*(3), 305–316.

St. John, R. D., & Corning, P. A. (1973). Maternal aggression in mice. *Behavioral Biology, 9*(5), 635–639.

Stockman, E. R. (1983). Aggressive experience and maternal aggression in the Mongolian gerbil. *Physiology and Behavior, 30*(2), 319–321.

Stowers, L., Holy, T. E., Meister, M., Dulac, C., & Koentges, G. (2002). Loss of sex discrimination and male-male aggression in mice deficient for TRP2. *Science, 295*(5559), 1493–1500.

Svare, B. (1977). Maternal aggression in mice: Influence of the young. *Biobehavioral Reviews, 1,* 151–164.

Svare, B. (1979). Maternal aggression in mice: The nonspecific nature of the exteroceptive maintenance by young. *Aggressive Behavior, 5*(417–424).

Svare, B. (1980). Testosterone propionate inhibits maternal aggression in mice. *Physiology and Behavior, 24*(3), 435–439.

Svare, B. (1990). Maternal aggression: Hormonal, genetic, and developmental determinants. In N. A. Krasnegor & R. S. Bridges (Eds.), *Mammalian parenting: Biochemical, neurobiological, and behavioral determinants* (pp. 118–132). New York: Oxford University Press.

Svare, B., Betteridge, C., Katz, D., & Samuels, O. (1981). Some situational and experiential determinants of maternal aggression in mice. *Physiology and Behavior, 26*(2), 253–258.

Svare, B., & Gandelman, R. (1973). Postpartum aggression in mice: Experiential and environmental factors. *Hormones and Behavior, 4,* 323–324.

Svare, B., & Gandelman, R. (1975). Postpartum aggression in mice: Inhibitory effect of estrogen. *Physiology and Behavior, 14*(1), 31–35.

Svare, B., & Gandelman, R. (1976). A longitudinal analysis of maternal aggression in Rockland-Swiss albino mice. *Developmental Psychobiology, 9*(5), 437–446.

Svare, B., Mann, M. A., Broida, J., & Michael, S. D. (1982). Maternal aggression exhibited by hypophysectomized parturient mice. *Hormones and Behavior, 16*(4), 455–461.

Svare, B., Mann, M., & Samuels, O. (1980). Mice: Suckling stimulation but not lactation important for maternal aggression. *Behavioral and Neural Biology, 29*(4), 453–462.

Svare, B., Miele, J., & Kinsley, C. (1986). Mice: Progesterone stimulates aggression in pregnancy-terminated females. *Hormones and Behavior, 20*(2), 194–200.

Toufexis, D. J., Rochford, J., & Walker, C. D. (1999). Lactation-induced reduction in rats' acoustic startle is associated with changes in noradrenergic neurotransmission. *Behavioral Neuroscience, 113*(1), 176–184.

Toufexis, D. J., Thrivikraman, K. V., Plotsky, P. M., Morilak, D. A., Huang, N., & Walker, C. D. (1998). Reduced noradrenergic tone to the hypothalamic paraventricular nucleus contributes to the stress hyporesponsiveness of lactation. *Journal of Neuroendocrinology, 10*(6), 417–427.

Vandenbergh, J. G. (1973). Effects of central and peripheral anosmia on reproduction of female mice. *Physiology and Behavior, 10*(2), 257–261.

Van de Poll, N., van Zanten, S., & De Jonge, F. H. (1986). Effects of testosterone, estrogen, and dihydrotestosterone upon aggressive and sexual behavior of female rats. *Hormones and Behavior, 20,* 418–431.

Villalba, C., Boyle, P. A., Caliguri, E. J., & De Vries, G. J. (1997). Effects of the selective serotonin reuptake inhibitor fluoxetine on social behaviors in male and female prairie voles (*Microtus ochrogaster*). *Hormones and Behavior, 32*(3), 184–191.

Walker, C. D., Toufexis, D. J., & Burlet, A. (2001). Hypothalamic and limbic expression of CRF and vasopressin during lactation: Implications for the control of ACTH secretion and stress hyporesponsiveness. *Progress in Brain Research, 133,* 99–110.

Wang, Z., Ferris, C. F., & De Vries, G. J. (1994). Role of septal vasopressin innervation in paternal behavior in prairie voles (*Microtus ochrogaster*). *Proceedings of the National Academy of Sciences USA, 91*(1), 400–404.

Wardlaw, S. L., & Frantz, A. G. (1983). Brain beta-endorphin during pregnancy, parturition, and the postpartum period. *Endocrinology, 113*(5), 1664–1668.

Weisner, B., & Sheard, N. M. (1933). *Maternal behaviour in the rat.* London: Oliver and Boyd.

White, M., Mayo, S., & Edwards, D. A. (1969). Fighting in female mice as a function of the size of the opponent. *Psychonomic Science, 16,* 14–15.

Wilson, D. M., III, Emanuele, N. V., Jurgens, J. K., & Kelley, M. R. (1992). Prolactin message in brain and pituitary of adult male rats is identical: PCR cloning and sequencing of hypothalamic prolactin cDNA from intact and hypophysectomized adult male rats. *Endocrinology, 131*(5), 2488–2490.

Wise, D. A. (1974). Aggression in the female golden hamster: Effects of reproductive state and social isolation. *Hormones and Behavior, 5*(3), 235–250.

Wise, D. A., & Pryor, T. L. (1977). Effects of ergocornine and prolactin on aggression in the postpartum golden hamster. *Hormones and Behavior, 8*(1), 30–39.

Wolff, J. O. (1985). Maternal aggression as a deterrent to infanticide in *Peromyscus leucopus* and *P. maniculatus. Animal Behaviour 33*, 117–123.

Wolff, J. O. (1993). Why are female small mammals territorial? *Oikos, 68*(2), 364–370.

Wolff, J. O., & Peterson, J. A. (1998). An offspring-defense hypothesis for territoriality in female mammals. *Ethology, Ecology, and Evolution, 10*(3), 227–239.

Yoshimura, H., & Ogawa, N. (1989). Acute and chronic effects of psychotropic drugs on maternal aggression in mice. *Psychopharmacology, 97*(3), 339–342.

12

Stress and Aggressive Behaviors

D. Caroline Blanchard & Robert J. Blanchard

There are many aspects to the complex relationship between aggression and stress. One component of this complexity reflects that both aggression and stress have been defined in many different ways and that the relationship between the two concepts may vary with the specific definitions used. In physiological research, stress is often defined in terms of activity of the hypothalamic-pituitary-adrenal (HPA) axis, effecting release of stress hormones such as adrenocorticotropic hormone (ACTH), corticosterone, or cortisol. Stress may also be evaluated in terms of sympathetic activity, conceptually linked to aggression via the "fight or flight" activities that sympathetic arousal promotes. However, much research on stress as it relates to aggression does not evaluate HPA or sympathetic activity, leaving these specific definitions difficult to apply. Thus this chapter utilizes the related, though imperfect, definition of stress as the response to threat, a definition that can be applied through analysis of threat capabilities of stimuli applied to responding subjects or through the behavioral responses of those subjects.

Offensive and Defensive Aggression

The situation with aggression is even more complicated. Aggression is not a monolithic category, and the various behavioral phenomena that are typically included under the rubric of aggression may have very different relationships to stress. Defining aggression loosely as any focused and motivated harm directed at another individual (typically but not always) of the same species, its major forms are offensive aggression, directly or indirectly motivated by resource control and particularly elicited by challenge to such control, and defensive aggression, directly motivated by danger of harm or death to the individual itself.

Other behaviors and categorizations for aggression have been suggested. Hunting or predation (of nonconspecifics) is generally excluded on the basis that it is aimed at the acquisition of food, not harm per se, and because it does not appear to be influenced by a history of either successful or unsuccessful conspecific fighting (e.g., Kemble, Flannelly, Salley, & Blanchard, 1985), whereas play "fighting" during early ontogeny is not aimed at harm (see Pellis & Pellis, 1998, for a review), although harmful attacks can sometimes occur in relatively young animals (e.g., Golla, Hofer, & East, 1999; Wommack & Delville, 2003; see Delville, Newman, Wommack, Taravosh-Lahn, & Cervantes, ch. 14 in this volume). Schema for categorizing aggression have also focused on categories related to offense and defense, but based largely on specific antecedents (e.g., male-male fighting, isolation-induced aggression, etc.;

see Moyer, 1976, for some specific categories). Most of these categories defined in terms of specific antecedents or eliciting stimuli turn out to be included in offensive aggression.

Finally, it is important to recognize that most instances of aggression are dynamic events, in which initial offensive attack may turn to defensive behavior (sometimes including defensive attack) as, and if, a combatant is defeated or vice versa, although the effects of defeat are likely more lasting (e.g., Potegal, Huhman, Moore, & Meyerhoff, 1993). In both nature and laboratory situations, many mixtures of offense and defense are possible, and these may or may not change within a given encounter. One very common scenario involves two animals disputing over an important resource, both with initially high levels of offensive aggressive motivation. Though common, this is typically an unstable situation, with one of the combatants gaining an advantage such that the behavior of the other quickly becomes defensive. Another situation that appears to be common, particularly among animals that live in small groups, involves a dominant animal and a subordinate. In this case considerable polarization has already occurred and fights are usually only initiated by the dominant (if the subordinate initiates a fight it may reflect an animal that is attempting to move up in the dominance hierarchy, suggesting considerable offensive motivation despite the subordinate status). These mixed motivations may also occur in laboratory tests, depending on the specific conditions. A particularly salient example is "maternal aggression" as it is characterized in rodents. In this, attacks by postparturient female mice on intruder females are typically offensive (and respond to antiaggressive drugs), whereas attacks on adult male intruders are more defensive in terms of behavior and less responsive to drugs that are specifically effective against offensive attack (Parmigiani, Ferrari, & Palanza, 1998; Parmigiani, Rodgers, Palanza, Mainardi, & Brain, 1989).

Thus, whereas laboratory situations designed to polarize offensive and defensive aggression, and to keep them relatively "pure," that is, uncontaminated by other motivations or action tendencies during the course of a trial, are important in understanding the differences between them, this polarization should not be taken to imply that they will typically occur as polarized events in nature. This situation is hardly unique to offensive and defensive aggression; hunger and thirst often occur together, as may sexual and aggressive moti-

vations, etc., but this reflects that the situations that produce one may often produce the other as well and should not call into question the existence of separate motivation and action systems for the two.

Differentiation of Offensive and Defensive Aggression

The differences between offensive and defensive aggression can be described in terms of four categories: different antecedents, different behaviors, different biology, and different functions, the last of these evidenced by typical outcomes as they occur under natural and normal circumstances (see Blanchard & Blanchard, 1984, and Blanchard, Hebert, & Blanchard, 1999, for reviews; also see Miyakawa, Yagi, Takao, & Niki, 2001; Parmigiani et al., 1998).

Offensive Aggression

With reference to antecedents, offensive aggression occurs in the context of a resource, including territorial and dominance disputes. Territoriality and dominance hierarchies are believed to have evolved because they are adaptive in reducing fights over specific resources; they are thus, themselves, highly desirable and defensible "super-resources." Territoriality involves a space that is typically marked and patrolled such that (generally same sex) conspecifics are denied entry (see Stamps & Buechner, 1985, for a review). This exclusion obviously eliminates the need for fighting over specific resources within that territory. Dominance hierarchies may take many forms (and be effected by a number of different mechanisms, see Abbot et al., 2003), but dominant animals usually have enhanced access to some or many resources.

The most potent aggression-eliciting resource or rights threat is one that directly reflects the action of a conspecific or other habitual resource challenger. Conspecific challenge to a resource is certainly the more likely of the two, as conspecifics tend to utilize the same habitats and resources, making challenges common when such resources are in limited supply (which they almost always are) and sequesterable. Conspecifics of the same sex are the near-exclusive challengers for one extremely potent resource, an opposite sex conspecific in breeding condition. Typically this involves male-male aggression over females, as male access to a breeding condition female mammal promotes the successful male's extended fitness more than does equivalent access of a female to a male.

An increasing number of reports of common and systematic two-way aggression involving animals that are not conspecifics make it clear that offensive aggression is tied to resource competition and specifically elicited by resource challenge, regardless of whether the challenger is a member of the same species. Thus predators coexisting in the same habitats may fight over prey, especially if the prey are sufficiently large to be worth fighting over. Lions and hyenas are notorious for their interest in each other's kills, leading to agonistic encounters after a successful hunt by either species. Occasionally, this is also reflected in attacks by one species on the other (or by lions on cheetahs) even when no specific resources are in dispute (Durant, 2000). These agonistic encounters in the absence of prey appear to reflect territoriality (albeit with territories that shift with the flow of game), as is characteristic of all of these large predators. Such behavior appears to be adaptive in potentially reducing the number of non-conspecific resource competitors in the aggressors' territory.

With reference to behavior, in lower mammals and potentially in some higher mammalian species as well, offensive aggression involves, in addition to actions that actually deliver harm (e.g., bites, blows, etc.), a set of species-typical behaviors that facilitate the aggressive animal's approach to and contact with particular body sites on the opponent where bites or blows are delivered (e.g., Blanchard, Blanchard, Takahashi, & Kelley, 1977; Pellis & Pellis, 1992). In many species these sites for offensive attack tend to be areas of the opponent's body where wounds are less likely to result in death or reproductive incapacity, a factor that may be particularly important in colonial animals in which the two combatants are likely to be closely related (Blanchard & Blanchard, 1984). Offensive threat may precede offensive attack, but it tends to involve a fairly subtle set of behaviors, such as the direct eye gaze that indicates challenge in a number of primate and canid species (e.g., Kalin, Shelton, & Takahashi, 1991). In rats, piloerection invariably precedes offensive attack, serving as a very reliable indication as to which animal in a group or pair is preparing to attack (Blanchard & Blanchard, 1977).

The function of offensive aggression is closely tied to the outcomes of all of these behaviors. Bites or blows to relatively invulnerable areas of a conspecific opponent may produce pain, but are unlikely to kill the opponent. This pattern facilitates a successful outcome of offensive attack: Termination of the resource/dominance dispute, usually involving flight by the opponent or the appearance of behaviors indicating that this animal has been defeated, but with little danger of killing or reproductively damaging a conspecific opponent that may share the attacker's genes. The best outcome, of course, is to terminate challenge to one's resources or dominance without any offensive attack. This happy state of affairs is not infrequently achieved by the response to offensive threat, particularly in established groups where animals are individually known to each other (see Sapolsky, 1990).

An additional outcome factor for offensive aggression that will serve to differentiate it from defensive attack is that the former is exquisitely sensitive to the fighting capabilities of the opponent. These appear to be evaluated through assessment of structures that will actually be used if a fight ensues, such as the horns and antlers of ungulates or the open mouth and teeth of hippopotami; the value of developing such structures beyond their actual usefulness in battle may be related to this effect (Gonzales, Kitchener, & Lister, 2000). A similar effect for predation has been thoroughly documented, that is, fear strongly inhibits predation (e.g., Pellis et al., 1988). Such fear reflects that damage by prey on a predator can prove disastrous to the predator, in terms either of direct wounding or infection or by reducing the success of its further hunting attempts. Thus, the inhibition of offensive attack by fear is a highly adaptive response on the part of the attacker.

Defensive Aggression

Defensive attack involves a comparatively simple antecedent, immediate threat to the life or body of the subject. In terms of behavior, it is one component of a complex defense pattern that involves many other behaviors, including flight, freezing, and risk assessment (see Blanchard, 1997, for a review). Whereas all of these behaviors are in response to bodily threat, they are complexly modulated by features of the attacker and of the environment that determine whether or not specific defenses will be successful in the short run and adaptive in the long run. Moreover, different species may be particularly adapted to display specific types of defense, reflecting their own evolutionary history and the habitats in which they have evolved. Thus it is usually safe to predict that species with long legs that have evolved in open plains areas will show flight as their primary defense, whereas fossorial species will tend to hide in a burrow.

Within the defense pattern, defensive attack is seldom the primary response to a predator. In rodents, defensive attack is typically elicited only by near-contact proximity with an attacker (hence the term "circa-strike defense"; Fanselow & Lester, 1988). However, the degree of proximity and pain necessary to elicit defensive attack (and defensive threat) may vary considerably for different species. Those that are large or otherwise competent relative to their predators may show defensive threat (and attack if the threat is not effective) as early components of the threat pattern, obviating the remaining defenses. Thus an animal such as an elephant or rhinoceros utilizes less flight/freezing and more threat/attack as antipredator strategies (note that of 21 documented attacks by animals on tourists in South Africa, between 1988 and 1997, 15 were by herbivores, including hippopotami, elephants, rhinoceros, and cape buffalos; Durrheim & Leggat, 1999). Defensive attack behaviors are so effective in such species that adults have relatively little to fear from predators, and the major use of any defense by these animals is in protection of young or in response to conspecific aggression.

Defensive threats are highly salient and generally impossible to ignore. They tend to include loud vocalizations, body orientations that enhance the animal's apparent size, and display of weapons such as teeth or claws, actions useful in displaying the defensive capabilities of the defending animal. However, recent game theory analyses (Szamado, 2003) are concordant with a view that mammalian threat is more than a "display." In addition to providing information on the capabilities of the defensive animals to its opponent, these actions present weapon systems in a state of readiness and more or less set the stage for the species-typical fighting techniques that will be used if the display itself is not effective.

With reference to the actual behaviors constituting defensive attack, in the rodents that remain the most thoroughly investigated animals in this context (see Blanchard, 1997, for a review) defensive bites or blows tend to be directed toward different body sites on the opponent than those contacted during offensive attacks. Rather than the low-vulnerability sites for offensive attack, defensive animals aim bites or blows at sites

that are highly vulnerable, such as the face and eyes of the attacker. In addition to the deterrent effect of a suddenly looming stimulus aimed at the eyes (for which there may be specific neural circuitry; see Comoli et al., 2003), damage to such structures may seriously handicap the subsequent hunting prowess of the predator. This lack of consideration of defensive attack for the level of damage it may cause to the opponent reflects the immediacy and seriousness of this behavior. Unsuccessful defense, particularly against predation, is typically a disaster for the animal, resulting in death or disability, and defensive attack is usually the "last ditch" and most serious component of the defense pattern for most species. It occurs if and only if less dangerous and more effective defenses such as flight, freezing, and defensive threat are impossible or have not been effective, such that the attacker has achieved close proximity or actual attack contact. Especially in predation situations, there may be time for only a single bite or blow, putting a huge premium on aiming that bite or blow at the attacker's most vulnerable site.

Defensive attack to conspecifics is different than that seen to predators in several respects. First, mammalian species vary considerably in the extent to which they show conspecific attack and, thus, conspecific defense. In particular, for species that commonly utilize nonsequesterable or scattered resources, for example, plains ungulates, fighting within the group would waste more time and energy than could be gained in effecting control of the resource. As will be discussed later, the exception to this involves reproduction: a suitable partner in breeding condition is a potentially sequesterable resource of immense evolutionary importance for a mammal of any species. Second, as noted earlier, many mammals have relatively invulnerable (re serious damage) target sites for offense, such that offensive attack is likely to be less lethal than predator attack even if the conspecific defense is not successful. The conspecific defenses that are used in addition to those of antipredator defense comprise a pattern of behaviors that act to conceal those of the defender's body sites that are the specific targets of conspecific attack. They include (in rats) actions such as standing upright and pivoting to continue to maintain a frontal orientation to the attacker or lying on the back, both of which serve to keep the vulnerable back target out of the attacker's reach (Blanchard et al., 1977). Insofar as such actions are successful, defensive attack may be unnecessary.

Despite these differences of defense to a predator or a conspecific, in both cases the defensive animal is responding to an attack that is potentially very dangerous. Defensive behaviors that can reduce this danger while it is still relatively distant, such as freezing, flight, or defensive threat, are far superior strategies if the situation permits them to be effective. However, once contact or a near-contact defensive distance of attacker to victim has been achieved, there is little alternative (aside from the death feigning seen in a few species) to defensive attack. It is thus relatively insensitive to the potential danger in its use, as the alternative (nonuse) is even more likely to be disastrous. In short, defensive attack is generally lacking in the sensitivity to agonistic capability that is so marked a feature of offensive attack.

These conspecific defenses may underlie an early, influential but mistaken view of aggression in nonhuman mammals, that this is never lethal due to the existence of displays that terminate intraspecies aggression. These "submission" displays (defined as actions that reduce the aggression of the opponent by signaling that the displaying animal is accepting a submissive position) have often turned out to be the above-described target site protecting actions (Blanchard & Blanchard, 1977). This is not to say that submission signals are impossible or that they do not occur, but at least in rodents there is relatively little evidence that the specific actions typically regarded as submission signals actually function in this fashion rather than serving to protect targets of attack.

Although not directly relevant to the differentiation of offense and defense, it might be noted that the influential view that nonhuman animals do not show lethal intraspecies aggression is simply incorrect. Indeed, analyses based on detailed observation of specific nonhuman mammalian groups and individuals over long periods of time have made it clear that many nonhuman species show considerably higher rates of lethal intraspecies violence than do humans (compare Wrangham, 1999, with World Health Organization statistics on human death rates involving murder or armed conflicts [WHO, 2002]).

The Offense-Defense Distinction in People

Offensive attack is a response to a certain type of threat, threat to the subject's resources. Resource control has been conceptualized as having evolved in more cognitively complex mammals, particularly humans, to include a system of socially constructed, but biologically modulated *rights* (Blanchard & Blanchard, 1984; Blanchard et al., 1999), suggesting that disputes involving issues of rights may also involve offensive aggression. Otherwise, the distinction between offensive and defensive aggression has been relatively little researched in people. Indeed there have been relatively few studies seeking to determine what actual events (as opposed to theoretical concepts) incite human aggression. However, if the factors that have been described as eliciting anger/aggression in people are examined in terms of the antecedents of offensive and defensive aggression, it is clear that most such instances show a closer relationship to the conditions that produce offensive, rather than defensive, aggression (summarized in Blanchard & Blanchard, 2003).

One study is particularly relevant because it applies to a community sample, rather than violent criminals (Averill, 1982). The focus of this study was on what caused each respondent's last episode of anger. Anger is typically regarded as the emotional concomitant of aggression (e.g., Potegal, 1994), and, indeed, Averill's correspondents did describe aggression as accompanying some of these anger episodes. For each such anger episode, Averill analyzed situational causes, or instigations, and the specific motivations of the angry individual were also assessed. The resulting analyses indicated that actions of another that were seen as voluntary and unjustified, or careless, were particularly effective instigators of anger, relevant to nearly 90% of the episodes evaluated (Averill, 1982, p. 211). Although this outcome is completely consonant with the notion that aggression is elicited by conspecific challenge (i.e., actions of others) it says only a little about exactly what sorts of actions were involved. Nonetheless, that little bit of information is suggestive. The notion that some actions are justified whereas others are not ("careless" also indicating disregard of important modulatory factors in the situation), implies a link to conceptions that individuals have some type of rights that should be recognized by others, such that violations of these represent unjustified behaviors. This interpretation is reinforced by the most commonly selected motive associated with these episodes of anger, which was "to assert your authority or independence, or improve your image" (Averill, 1982), all of which appear to be aimed at reassertion of just the sorts of rights that the instigating individual's actions have called into question.

As these studies were done some years ago, with no conceptual or analytic connection to views of offensive aggression that have emerged largely from animal research, interpretations of the relationship between the instigations and motives Averill reported to be associated with anger and the analysis of offense are necessarily somewhat tenuous. However, the Averill material is important, in part because it deals with a relatively representative range of people, not the typically more restricted array of participants used in research projects, and because it taps reactions to events that occur in the real world. The effectiveness of such events—voluntary, unjustified, or careless actions that provoke the desire to assert one's authority, etc.—in eliciting both anger and aggression can, moreover, be seen in the types of provocations that have proved to be highly effective in eliciting aggression in people in laboratory situations. These "provocations" are always designed to suggest that they represent the actions of another individual, and they typically involve challenge to either resources (directly or indirectly, money) or some type of insult to the subject. Their effectiveness (e.g., Rule & Leger, 1976), and the fact that the subsequent aggressive actions are so clearly directed at the (often unseen) provocateur rather than at other features of the situation (e.g., occurring in response to provocation rather than generally; Cherek & Dougherty, 1995), are both consonant with the description of offensive aggression as representing a challenge to resources and (in humans) to the rights that represent more conceptual aspects of resource control in people. Finally, mitigating circumstances for the provocation, including information on possible provocations received by the provocateur himself or herself, appear to be capable of reducing the anger/aggression expressed by the subject receiving the provocation (e.g., Johnson & Rule, 1986).

If anger and offensive aggression represent the most common forms of aggression in people, then what has happened to defensive attack? In attempting to determine if there is some connection between defensive attack in nonhuman animals and people, it is useful to recall that defensive attack is only one, and sometimes a relatively rare one, of the various behaviors that make up the defense pattern. Moreover, science fiction and fantasy films notwithstanding, attack by a predator on a person is an extremely rare event in most contemporary societies. Finally, such societies put a strong premium on the protection of individuals from potentially damaging physical attack by others. Thus the conditions that elicit defensive threat/attack—a proximal confrontation involving a threat to the subject's life or of serious bodily injury, especially when pain is involved—are much less common than the resource/rights challenges that elicit anger and offensive aggression. Such events do, however, occur. In interviews with over 800 students of varying ages and cultural backgrounds, we have elicited descriptions of a few of these (e.g., Blanchard & Blanchard, 1984). An overwhelming level of fear was a common feature described, as was the subject's claim that his defensive threat/attack actions were unpremeditated and a considerable surprise to himself. "Something snapped" was the description given by one youth, of being held down and beaten by a gang, just prior to his own (quite damaging) retaliatory attack.

However, several potential exceptions to these general differentiators between offensive and defensive aggression may occur in primates, and particularly humans. First, with the development of higher cognitive functions and interpersonal communications, the relationship between animals and their principal predators may show something of a reversal, with the prey beginning to show effective group actions to attack and kill predators of that group. Thus Hiraiwa-Hasegawa, Byrne, Takasaki, and Byrne (1986) reported the killing of leopard cubs by wild Mahale mountain chimpanzees; leopards are predators on chimpanzees (Zuberbuhler, 2000). To be fair, this particular case may be somewhat ambiguous. Chimpanzees and leopards both predate monkeys (Mitani & Watts, 1999; Zuberbuhler 2000), so that chimpanzee attacks on leopards could conceivably be related to resource competition. However, the tendency for current and historic humans to specifically hunt human predators such as lions, that are, in the main, not eaten, suggests actions that are based on defense rather than competition. Early 20th century records from rural Uganda suggest that agropastoralists regularly scavenged lion and leopard kills, suggesting that from a resource/subsistence perspective these animals may have been useful to early humans rather than important resource competitors (Treves & Naughton-Treves, 1999). Notably, hunting of predators and other dangerous animals has also come to serve as an index of courage and strength, contributing to male prestige within many human cultures in much the same sense as does success in conspecific fighting (O'Connell, Hawkes, Lupo, & Blurton Jones, 2002). In this context, in which the human seeks out the predator to kill it, the distinction between offensive and defensive attack is blurred.

An additional blurring of this distinction has resulted from the development of language and its use to present concepts that are advantageous to the user. People show a complex mixture of counterfactual thinking, selective attributions, and other cognitive devices to deflect blame; what is most interesting, however, is that these cognitions may be as effective in shaping the attributions of the thinker as in altering the views of significant others (Branscombe, N'gbala, & Kobrynowicz, 1997; Williams, Lees-Haley, & Brown, 1993). Particularly relevant to present considerations is the explanation of offensive aggression in terms of "defense." To defend something has the strong connotation of protecting it from harm, a virtuous activity when only a certain level of abstraction is considered. Parenthetically, that is often the level of abstraction on which people operate. We once asked a Chinese friend what the thousands of soldiers of the "buried army" in the tomb of Emperor Qin shi Huang di were supposed to be protecting him from. "Evil" was his succinct but perhaps inadequately specific reply.

In fact offensive aggression typically involves protecting the aggressor's rights to something, not protecting the thing itself. Establishment of one's rights to a resource is usually followed by utilization of that resource, a procedure that is no more or less harmful to the resource than would be its similar utilization by someone else. This stands in contrast to defensive attack, in which the genuine motive of the individual is to protect himself or herself from harm. Even in those cases where offensive attack may legitimately be described as protecting something from harm, this may involve a particularly felicitous manner of describing a phenomenon that can be explained in blunter terms; for example, defending my honor, rather than responding to an insult.

We present also a speculation that the virtually universal human tendency to present justifications for offensive aggression in terms of defense may in some cases actually come to involve motivations somewhat similar to those associated with defensive attack. As noted earlier, offensive aggression is very sensitive to the possibility of losing encounters, and when the possibility of death or disability becomes imminent, offensive attack usually terminates. When this sensitivity is lost, and a person is willing to die in "defense" of something, it often signifies that the society in which that person lives has succeeded in convincing him that the goal is more important than his life and that he should pursue and protect it with the same vigor and distain of consequences.

Such considerations (here very briefly outlined; see Blanchard, Hebert, & Blanchard, 1999, for a fuller discussion) suggest several points of blurring of the offense/defense distinction as it applies to people. Nonetheless, the distinction appears to be generally valid for human, as well as nonhuman mammalian behavior. It is insufficient analysis, not some sort of essential disconnect between animal and human behavior, that has led to a failure to recognize this distinction in people.

Stress Hormone Differentiation of Offensive and Defensive Aggression

As other chapters in this volume take up issues of neural and neurotransmitter control of aggression, these are not treated here (see chs. 4–7 in this volume). However, recent studies by Joszef Haller and his associates of the relationship between stress hormones and aggression has suggested some additional factors that may be involved in the differentiation of offensive and defensive attack. Offensive aggression (resident attack on an intruder) in residents housed with females and given repeated exposure to smaller intruders was virtually abolished by injection of the mineralocorticoid blocker spironolactone (Haller, Millar, & Kruk, 1998). Haller, Millar, van de Schraaf, de Kloet, and Kruk (2000) replicated this finding and additionally reported positive correlations between plasma corticosterone levels, such as would result in high mineralocorticoid receptor occupancy, with aggressive behavior of male territorial rats. These animals showed only a decrease in offensive aggression, with no apparent alteration of defensive attack propensities (note, however, that levels of defensive attack in these animals were essentially zero, such that only increments could be seen.)

When adrenalectomy was accompanied by implantation of low-release glucocorticoid pellets, to produce glucocorticoid hypofunctioning (i.e., both low glucocorticoid levels and no glucocorticoid responsivity to situational and social stimuli and events), it failed to produce an overall change in attack levels, but evoked a shift in the target of aggression, with high levels of attack toward the opponent's head (and sometimes the abdomen), in conjunction with reductions in attack targeted toward the usual targets of offense (dorsum). When corticosterone injections were given, to produce concentrations similar to those seen in intact, attacking rats, this shift pattern was abolished (Haller, van de Schraaf, & Kruk, 2001). This finding was repeated by Halasz, Liposits, Kruk, and Haller (2002), who additionally measured c-fos expression during aggression in these animals. Results indicated activation of a number of brain areas similar to those showing activation during attack on intruders by intact animals, with additional activation in the parvocellular part of the hypothalamic paraventricular nucleus and the central nucleus of the amygdala, areas associated with stress and fearful behaviors.

These studies suggest that acute reductions in mineralocorticoid receptor occupancy simply reduce offensive attack, whereas chronic glucocorticoid hypofunctioning appears to produce a switch from offensive aggression to something that, in terms of targeting, looks more like defensive aggression. The interpretation that adrenalectomy alters defense is consonant with findings that it facilitates shock-induced aggression (Sever'ianova, 1981). It is somewhat dissonant, however, with failures to find changes in defensive behaviors per se, with adrenalectomy (personal observations; also J. Haller, personal communication). Nonetheless, these and other studies (e.g.,Calvo & Volosin, 2001; McNaughton, Panickar, & Logan, 1996) do make the point that stress hormones, via the HPA axis, may have strong, and potentially complex, effects on the differentiation of offensive and defensive aggression.

This conclusion, from work on manipulations of the HPA axis, is broadly in agreement with the behavioral phenomenon noted earlier, that offensive aggression and predation are both extremely sensitive to the capabilities of the opponent to respond effectively, that is, that they are powerfully modulated by fear of the opponent's ability to retaliate.

Stress and Aggression

This brief set of definitions and descriptions has outlined certain differences between offensive and defensive aggression, indicating that rather different "threats" are antecedents for the two. An additional way of looking at these threats as stressors is to examine their relationships to a conventional homeostatic stress mechanism, in which the stressor involves a significant departure from homeostasis and the response to it is one that returns the organism to a homeostatic condition.

Antecedents and Short-Term Stress Effects of Offensive Attack

The stressors involved in offensive attack may involve two separate components. One of these is resource deprivation or motivation, a condition that may act to increase the value of a disputed resource. As an example, conventional laboratory chow appears not to be a particularly valuable resource in only lightly deprived laboratory rats, in that access to such food is poorly related to more conventional indices of dominance (Baenninger, 1966). However, rats that show high levels of food motivation (i.e., eat more food) are more aggressive in a situation in which successful aggression is reward by enhanced food access (Albert, Petrovic, Jonik, & Walsh, 1991).

The second stress component of an offensive attack incitement is the challenge to the resource. Like any other evolved biobehavioral system, offensive aggression has to be, in the main, functional. It is generally not directed against threats against which it would be ineffective, such as those stemming from inanimate forces or from nonchallenging animals. (A note: In seeming contradiction to this dictum, offensive aggression is not infrequently directed against a third party, an "innocent bystander." However, such aggression may actually be useful to the attacker. Thus in olive baboons, *Papio anubis*, defeated males that then attack a third party may enjoy significantly lower basal glucocorticoid concentrations [Virgin & Sapolsky, 1997], not to mention that bystanders may have served as witnesses to the defeat, in which case it may pay the defeated male to remind the bystander that it is still capable of an effective attack.) The dependence of offensive attack on challenge is well illustrated in findings that dominant colony males do not attack prepubescent males in their colonies, although they readily attack males only slightly larger who are pubescent (Blanchard, Fukunaga-Stinson, Takahashi, Flannelly, & Blanchard, 1984)

The centrality of challenge to reproductive resources for mammalian aggression is interesting in that it clearly does not fit a homeostatic model. First, while sexual deprivation, per se, might be regarded as a type of stress, Flannelly, Blanchard, Muraoka, and Flannelly (1982) reported that male rats that have just copulated to ejaculation show higher levels of attack on male conspecifics. In addition, the result of successful male-male challenge in the context of access to breeding females is likely to be copulation with the female. Glucocorticoids rise with copulatory behavior, compared to levels seen in non-copulating males (Borg, Esbenshade, Johnson, Lunstra, & Ford, 1992). Thus the successful male is, in the near term, enabling and facilitating an HPA axis-activating event for itself, while denying this to his unsuccessful rival. Similarly, dominant males of many species initiate fights with familiar male subordinates. When, as may be common (e.g., Abbott et al., 2003; Blanchard, Yudko, Dulloog, & Blanchard, 2001), the subordinates are not aggressive among themselves nor to the dominant, it is clear that the dominant is not only initiating all the fights, but is engaged in many more fights than other males in the group, thus, at least sporadically and possibly chronically, elevating its own stress hormone concentrations. Such findings make it clear that the resource challenge situation leading to offensive aggression is better understood in the context of evolutionary mechanisms than with reference to specific changes in stress hormones, even though some instances of successful aggression may result in resource utilization that may fit a stress reduction model.

Longer Term Effects of Aggression on Stress Levels of the Aggressor

Views of the effects of aggression on the aggressor's own stress level have changed substantially in recent years. The classic view (e.g., Schuurman, 1980), and one that remains valid, so far as is known, for many mammalian species, is that successful aggression, whether offensive or defensive, has the effect of reducing stress, as indexed by stress hormones (notwithstanding that subsequent actions facilitated by successful aggression, such as copulation, may elevate stress hormone concentrations again). As described by Virgin and Sapolsky (1990), the aggressive response may be successful in this regard even when it is directed at a third party.

However, victory over a conspecific does not necessarily involve long-term reductions in the autonomic activation that accompanies aggression. Bartolomucci and colleagues have recently (2003) reported on stress changes for winning and losing mice in a resident-intruder paradigm involving 15 days of sensory contact with intermittent (daily) physical interactions. Animals that became dominants and those that became subordinate both showed strong autonomic reactions during encounters, and the tachycardia associated with encounters failed to habituate over the 15-day period for either group. Though behavioral responses (depression of activity) did habituate only for dominants, subordinates but not dominants showed some habituation of the initial hyperthermia associated with agonistic encounters.

Moreover, a developing literature on "reconciliation" strongly suggests that in some species, and under some circumstances, aggression may promote a long-lasting behavioral stress response in the successful animal, the winner of the agonistic encounter. The basis of this stress is the potential damage to interindividual cooperative relationships of animals/persons within a group, for species with certain characteristics (Aureli, Cords, & van Schaik, 2002). These include stable and individualized social relationships, in which post-conflict hostility (reflected in enhanced agonism following a conflict) threatens to jeopardize the benefits associated with these relationships.

These characteristics are found in a number of primate species, including humans (e.g., Aureli et al., 2002; Butovskaya & Kozintsev, 1999; Verbeek & de Waal, 2001), and some nonprimate species as well (e.g., domesticated goats, Aureli et al., 2002). Enhanced stress following agonistic interactions may be manifest by enhanced rates of displacement activities (e.g., enhancement of irrelevant activities) or self-directed behaviors (e.g., touching one's own hand or face or self-grooming). Both displacement and self-directed behaviors have been validated as indices of emotional arousal (Maestripieri, Schino, Aureli, & Troisi, 1992; Troisi et al., 2000), and both increase in aggressors following an agonistic interaction and decline with reconciliation (Aureli & van Schiak, 1991; Ljungberg, Westlund, & Foresberg, 1999). Thus reconciliation is seen as an attempt by the aggressor (and/or by the recipient) to counter the stress of potential damage to a relationship that is of value to both.

Although the list of species in which reconciliation has been demonstrated is expanding rapidly, it is by no means clear that this expansion will include the majority of mammals, as the conditions that combine to make it adaptive may be relatively rare. In addition to solitary species, and herd species in which large groups and migratory habits combine to reduce individual relationships, many species of relatively primitive mammals appear to have little by way of cooperative relationships that might be damaged by within-group agonistic behavior. If these predictions from analyses such as those of Aureli and colleagues (2002) turn out to be correct, it will serve as additional confirmation of the importance of evolutionary adaptive values of specific aggression-related behaviors and the role of specific social factors in fine-tuning their antecedent and modulatory control.

Stress and Defensive Aggression

The stressor that produces defensive aggression is much more straightforward and closer to the traditional views of both stress and threat. The stress of a focused threat to the subject's life and body, typically from predator or conspecific attack, involves a very potent activation of the HPA axis and the sympathetic nervous system (Cohen, Zohar, & Matar, 2003; Schuurman, 1980) and may profoundly alter circadian rhythms (see Meerlo, Sgoifo, & Turek, 2002, for a review). When animals are maintained in colonies in which male-male encounters are common, colony subordinates show persistently elevated glucocorticoid levels (Blanchard et al., 1995).

While these physiological indices of stress appear to be relatively consistent across species, occurring in humans even to less intense social threats such as interviews (Sgoifo et al., 2003), the specific behavior of defensive attack is only one component of the defense pattern and, moreover, one that typically occurs at the end of a defense sequence as the "highest level" of defensive behavior (Blanchard, Blanchard, & Hori, 1989). Although it is typically evaluated in the context of other defenses, making specific relationships between defensive attack and stress hormones difficult to evaluate, this position as the ultimate defense for many species strongly suggests that defensive attack is associated with particularly strong HPA axis and sympathetic activation.

A particularly important factor in research on the relationship between stress/threat and defensive aggression in laboratory research is that laboratory animals are (variably but often strongly) domesticated. A core feature of domestication is selection for breeding of animals that show relatively little defense to human approach and handling. For animals of a size and ability to do significant damage to their human handler, the defensive behavior that is of greatest interest in this selection process is defensive threat/attack. However, the selection process is seldom stringently applied to attack, and reductions in other defensive behaviors usually appear (Blanchard et al., 1994). Comparisons of wild rats with the laboratory animals that have resulted from this domestication process have a long history in psychology. However, early interpretations of these differences (e.g., Yerkes, 1913, and Stone, 1932) that the wild rats were exhibiting "savageness" or "rage" have given way to the recent recognition that offensive aggressive, and even a number of conspecific defensive, behaviors have changed relatively little in these animals (Takahashi & Blanchard, 1982). It appears that it is their active defensive behaviors to humans that are most profoundly reduced (see Blanchard, 1997, for a

review), and this difference appears not to be importantly dependent on early experience (Blanchard, Flannelly, & Blanchard, 1986). Although threat/attacks are hard to elicit in laboratory rats in response to approach, contact, and handling by researchers they still may occur quickly in response to pain (Blanchard, Kleinschmidt, Fukunaga-Stinson, & Blanchard, 1980). This was the phenomenon underlying "pain-elicited aggression" or "shock-elicited aggression" paradigms that were widely used prior to the recognition (Blanchard, Blanchard, & Takahashi, 1978) that the "aggression" elicited was defensive and not representative of a monolithic aggressive behavior pattern.

The process and some of its physiological concomitants are particularly well illustrated by studies of selection of "tame" silver foxes and mink, as well as of wild rats, over multiple generations at the Institute for Cytology and Genetics in Novosibirsk (e.g., Naumenko et al., 1989). After a score or so of generations of such selection, the selected lines show widespread reductions in defensiveness, as well as additional fear-related measures (Popova, Barykina, Pliusnina, Alekhina, & Kolpakov, 1999); widespread changes in serotonin systems (Popova, Voitenko, Kulikov, & Avgustinovich, 1991); and altered HPA axis response to restraint stress; but less change in response to physiological stressors (Shikhevich, Os'kina, & Pliusnina, 2002). Whereas defensiveness in these animals has clearly been down-regulated, the mechanisms underlying this down-regulation have not been clearly conceptualized. These may involve changes in the intrinsic activity of basic emotional systems, or it may be that the basic emotionality systems are intact, but that selection has favored development of inhibitory systems that strongly modulate their expression under certain circumstances. Even in animals that seem to manifest little or none of a given response under normal circumstances, increasing relevant stimulus input may elicit a well-focused and effective behavior, for example, the previously mentioned findings that pain will quickly produce defensive biting in lab rats in which this response is otherwise very difficult to elicit (Blanchard et al., 1980).

Both domestication of laboratory animals and the common practice of studying fear and defense-related behaviors in small test chambers in which flight is useless have promoted the view that freezing is the major (only?) defensive behavior that must be considered by the psychobiologist. This view is likely to be modified as increasing numbers of mouse models and procedures are developed in response to enhanced interest and improved technologies for studying the genetics of aggression and defense, as freezing is a much less prominent defense in the mouse repertoire.

Defeat and Subordination: Long-Term Effects of Aggression on Stress Levels of the Victim

Conspecific aggression is one of the major stressors for individuals of most mammalian species. In primates, and particularly in humans, conspecific interactions—social stressors—probably constitute the most frequent and protracted form of stress in most individual lives (Blanchard, McKittrick, Hardy, & Blanchard, 2002). On a human level, social stress has major effects on physiological phenomena such as male (e.g., McGrady, 1984) and female (Wasser & Barash, 1983) reproduction, immune functioning (Ader, Felten, & Cohen, 1999), heart disease (Hemingway & Marmot, 1998), and the like. It is viewed as an important factor in the etiology of a variety of psychopathologies, such as depression and anxiety (e.g., Kessler, 1997; Mineka & Zinbarg, 1996). Social status, in both humans and nonhuman mammals, is strongly associated with the number of stressful events that are likely to be experienced, and recent studies of subordination effects have indicated that both behavioral and physiological changes may be characteristic of subordinates (see Blanchard et al., 2002, for a review).

There are a number of laboratory models of social stress (reviewed in Blanchard et al., 2002). In one of these, social defeat, animals are defeated during specific, generally brief, encounters with an experienced conspecific, sometimes involving somewhat longer but still nonchronic additional periods in which the subject is left in a protected site but within sound, sight, and smell of the victorious animal (see Huhman & Jasnow, ch. 13 in this volume). In colony or chronic defeat models, animals are maintained in groups, often in an enriched habitat. Inclusion of females and larger and more natural habitats facilitate fighting and enhance stress levels within such groups. Intermittent defeat models (e.g., Fuchs & Flugge, 2002; Kudryavtseva, Bakshtanovskaya, & Koryakina, 1991) incorporate features of both, providing chronic sensory exposure of animals to experienced conspecifics but with contact exposure limited to brief intermittent periods.

All three of these models utilize conditions that are known to facilitate aggression between the animals of a group or dyad, and they specifically measure this aggression, discarding or discounting pairs or groups

(typically few) in which it does not occur. In contrast, crowding and social instability models tend to present social situations believed to be stressful, but do not focus on agonistic behaviors and may or may not measure these. Predictably, such models tend to have more variable effects. In general, when weights do not decline for animals subjected to "social stress" it is unlikely that other major signs of stress will appear. However, even this relatively consistent phenomenon has exceptions. Syrian hamsters (*Mesocricetus auratus*) are solitary animals, but when females are housed in groups of two, rather than singly, both animals gain substantial amounts of weight, although showing aggression and other signs of stress (Fritzsche, Riek, & Gattermann, 2000).

In studies of subordination or defeat among laboratory or captive animals, findings of HPA axis activation for the loser or subordinate animal are very common (e.g., Blanchard et al., 1995; Louch & Higginbotham, 1967; von Holst, 1977), as are weight loss, thymus involution and/or adrenal hypertrophy (Raab et al., 1986; Sachser & Lick, 1989; von Holst, 1977), disruption of the immune system (Stefanski & Hendrichs, 1996), and other forms of pathophysiology, such as atherosclerosis (see Kaplan & Manuck, 1999, for a review). Effects of long-term exposure to a predator (cat) appear to be considerably similar (Figueiredo, Bodie, Tauchi, Dolgas, & Herman, 2003), reinforcing a view that the long-term effects of social defeat/subordination are parallel to those of other strong body-threat stressors.

Behavior changes include enhanced defensiveness, both in the immediate defeat situation and later (Blanchard & Blanchard, 1989; Blanchard et al., 2001; Meerlo et al., 1996), anxietylike or depressionlike behaviors in commonly used tests such as the elevated plus maze and Porsolt's test (e.g., Avgustinovich, Gorbach, & Kudryavtseva, 1997; Heinrichs, Pich, Miczek, Britton, & Koob, 1992), decreases in locomotion, exploration, and celerity of movement (Blanchard, & Blanchard, 1989; Fuchs, Kramer, Hermes, Netter, & Hiemke, 1996; Meerlo, Overkamp, Benning, Koolhaas, & Van den Hoofdakker, 1996; Tornatzky & Miczek, 1994), memory deficits (Ohl & Fuchs, 1998), and enhanced alcohol and drug intake (e.g., Blanchard, Hori, Tom, & Blanchard, 1987; Haney, Maccari, Le Moal, Simon, & Piazza, 1995; Higley, Hasert, Suomi, & Linnoila, 1991, 1998; Hilakivi-Clarke & Lister, 1992; Weisinger, Denton, & Osborne, 1989). These findings appear to depend on the duration and/or degree of stress involved in the specific procedures used. For example, studies using social defeat procedures, which are generally less intense and prolonged than colony models, have often failed to find enhanced alcohol intake (e.g., Keeney & Hogg, 1999; van Erp & Miczek, 2001).

Most laboratory studies of social stress involve rodents or captive (largely undisturbed) primate groups. Field studies of social stress utilize a larger array of species, but have tended to focus on primates or social canids or felids. While many of these studies have reported results similar to those obtained in laboratory or captive groups, some differences have also appeared. In particular, increased secretion of stress hormones in subordinates compared to dominants appears to be a very variable phenomenon. Analyses by Abbott and colleagues (2003) suggest that subordinate stress hormone levels are related to the degree to which subordinates receive a great deal of stress and have few opportunities for kin support. These factors differ for the various primate species evaluated, ranging from those in which dominance is closely tied to victory and defeat for individual male dyads to those in which ingroup fighting is seldom seen.

Finally, female animals have received comparatively little attention in the context of stress and aggression (and in aggression research generally). However, in many primate groups dominant females show higher glucocorticoid secretion than do subordinate females. Although this occurs most often in species where reproduction is limited to only a single dominant female (see Blanchard et al., 2002, for a review), it may also occur in species such as ring-tailed lemurs (*Lemur catta*) in which breeding is not restricted to the dominant (Cagivelli, Dubovick, Levash, Jolly, & Pitts, 2003). In ringtails glucocorticoid concentrations in dominant females are positively related to the degree to which the dominant individuals initiate attacks on other females, whereas in subordinates they are related to the magnitude of attacks received. These brief considerations, taken in the context of findings that adult females of many mammalian species may be more tolerant of each other than are males (e.g., Brown & Grunberg, 1995), suggest that the dynamics of relationships between social behaviors, stress, and aggression may be at least partly gender differentiated.

Some Conclusions

These considerations of some relationships of stress to offensive and defensive aggression, while brief and sketchy, do suggest several points. First, stress defined in terms of HPA axis activity is relatively uninformative with reference to either the antecedents or the consequences of aggression. Stress defined in terms of threat is also insufficiently specific for understanding the two types of aggression. In general, analyses in terms of stressors and stress response provide a less precise understanding of the causes and consequences of aggression than do views that seek to relate aggression to its evolutionary functions, with a focus on precise description and analysis of the events that elicit, modulate, and maintain patterns of aggression and defense.

These studies also indicate that the incidence and specific elicitors of offensive aggression may be very different for mammalian species, depending on their social and physical environments. Similarly, the prevalence of defensive threat/attack and their position in the defense pattern change systematically with group social structure, environmental constraints, and the size and defensive capabilities of the animal relative to major predators for each species.

The importance of such organismic, social, and environmental factors in instigating and modulating offensive and defensive aggression across species highlights the need to analyze aggression in as wide a range of species as possible, both for an enhanced understanding of this particular behavioral phenomenon and for a more accurate and detailed view of how behavior generally is controlled by evolutionary forces. In particular, human linguistic and organizational abilities and the social establishments to which they give rise represent factors that may both introduce complications in the analysis of aggression and contribute to its hyperexpression. The continuity of aggressive behaviors from nonhuman mammalian species to humans deserves and needs further research. In turn, this research needs to be based in a more comprehensive analysis of the interactions of cognitive and emotional factors that impact aggression and serve as a major source of stress in human life.

Note

This work was supported by a grant from the Harry Frank Guggenheim Foundation.

References

Abbott, D. H., Keverne, E. B., Bercovitch, F. B., Shively, C. A., Mendoza, S. P., Saltzman, W., et al. (2003). Are subordinates always stressed? A comparative analysis of rank differences in cortisol levels among primates. *Hormones and Behavior, 43,* 67–82.

Ader, R., Felten, D. L., & Cohen, N. (Eds.). (1999). *Psychoneuroimmunology* (3rd ed.). New York: Academic Press.

Albert, D. J., Petrovic, D. M., Jonik, R. H., & Walsh, M. L. (1991). Enhanced defensiveness and increased food motivation each contribute to aggression and success in food competition by rats with medial hypothalamic lesions. *Physiology and Behavior, 49,* 13–9.

Aureli, F., Cords, M., & van Schaik, C. P. (2002). Conflict resolution following aggression in gregarious animals: A predictive framework. *Animal Behaviour, 64,* 25–343.

Aureli, F., & van Schiak, C. P. (1991). Post-conflict behaviour in long-tailed macaques (*Macaca fascicularis*): Coping with the uncertainty. *Ethology, 89,* 101–114.

Averill, J. R. (1982). *Anger and aggression: An essay on emotion.* New York: Springer-Verlag.

Avgustinovich, D. F., Gorbach, O. V., & Kudryavtseva, N. N. (1997). Comparative analysis of anxiety-like behavior in partition and plus-maze tests after agonistic interactions in mice. *Physiology and Behavior, 61,* 37–43.

Baenninger, L. P. (1966). The reliability of dominance orders in rats. *Animal Behaviour, 14,* 367–371.

Bartolomucci, A., Palanza, P., Costoli, T., Savani, E., Laviola, G., Parmigiani, S., et al. (2003). Chronic psychosocial stress persistently alters autonomic function and physical activity in mice. *Physiology and Behavior, 80,* 57–67.

Blanchard, D. C. (1997). Stimulus and environmental control of defensive behaviors. In M. Bouton & M. Fanselow (Eds.), *The functional behaviorism of Robert C. Bolles: Learning, motivation and cognition* (pp. 283–305). Washington, DC: American Psychological Association.

Blanchard, D. C., & Blanchard, R. J. (1984). Affect and aggression: An animal model applied to human behavior. In R. J. Blanchard & D. C. Blanchard (Eds.), *Advances in the study of aggression* (Vol. I). New York: Academic Press.

Blanchard D. C., & Blanchard, R. J. (2003). What can animal aggression research tell us about human aggression? *Hormones and Behavior, 44,* 171–177.

Blanchard, D. C., Fukunaga-Stinson, C., Takahashi, L. K., Flannelly, K. J., & Blanchard, R. J. (1984). Dominance and aggression in social groups of male and female rats. *Behavioural Processes, 9,* 31–48.

Blanchard, D. C., Hebert, M. A., & Blanchard, R. J. (1999). Continuity versus (political) correctness: Animal models and human aggression. In M. Haug & R. Whalen (Eds.), *Animal models of human psychopathology* (pp. 297–316). Washington, DC: American Psychological Association.

Blanchard, D. C., McKittrick, C. R., Hardy, M. P., & Blanchard, R. J. (2002). Social stress effects on hormones, brain and behavior. In D. Pfaff, A. Arnold, A. Etgen, S. Fahrbach, & R. Rubin (Eds.), *Hormones and behavior* (pp. 735–772). San Diego: Academic Press.

Blanchard, D. C., Popova, N. K., Plyusnina, I. Z., Velichko, I. V., Campbell, D., Blanchard, R. J., et al. (1994). Defensive behaviors of "wild-type" and "domesticated" wild rats in a Fear/Defense Test Battery. *Aggressive Behavior, 20,* 387–398.

Blanchard, D. C., Spencer, R., Weiss, S. M., Blanchard, R. J., McEwen, B. S., & Sakai, R. R. (1995). The visible burrow system as a model of chronic social stress: Behavioral and neuroendocrine correlates. *Psychoendocrinology, 20,* 117–134.

Blanchard, R. J., & Blanchard, D. C. (1977). Aggressive behavior in the rat. *Behavioral Biology, 21,* 197–224.

Blanchard, R. J., & Blanchard, D. C. (1989). Anti-predator defensive behaviors in a visible burrow system. *Journal of Comparative Psychology, 103,* 70–82.

Blanchard, R. J., Blanchard, D. C., & Hori, K. (1989). Ethoexperimental approaches to the study of defensive behavior. In R. J. Blanchard, P. F. Brain, D. C. Blanchard, & S. Parmigiani (Eds.), *Ethoexperimental approaches to the study of behavior* (pp. 114–136). Dordrecht, Netherlands: Kluwer Academic.

Blanchard, R. J., Blanchard, D. C., & Takahashi, L. K. (1978). Pain and aggression in the rat. *Behavioral Biology, 23,* 291–305.

Blanchard, R. J., Blanchard, D. C., Takahashi, T., & Kelley, M. (1977). Attack and defensive behavior in the albino rat. *Animal Behaviour, 25,* 622–634.

Blanchard, R. J., Flannelly, K. J., & Blanchard, D. C. (1986). Defensive behaviors of laboratory and wild *Rattus norvegicus. Journal of Comparative Psychology, 100,* 101–107.

Blanchard, R. J., Hori, K., Tom, P., & Blanchard, D. C. (1987). Social structure and ethanol consumption in the laboratory rat. *Pharmacology, Biochemistry and Behavior, 28,* 437–442.

Blanchard, R. J., Kleinschmidt, C. F., Fukunaga-Stinson, C., & Blanchard, D. C. (1980). Defensive attack behavior in male and female rats. *Animal Learning and Behavior, 8,* 177–183.

Blanchard, R. J., Yudko, E., Dulloog, L., & Blanchard, D. C. (2001). Defense changes in stress-nonresponsive subordinate males in a visible burrow system. *Physiology and Behavior, 72,* 635–642.

Borg, K. E., Esbenshade, K. L., Johnson, B. H., Lunstra, D. D., & Ford, J. J. (1992). Effects of sexual experience, season, and mating stimuli on endocrine concentrations in the adult ram. *Hormones and Behavior, 26,* 87–109.

Branscombe, N. R., N'gbala, A., & Kobrynowicz, D.

(1997). Self and group protection concerns influence attributions but they are not determinants of counterfactual mutation focus. *British Journal of Social Psychology, 36*, 387–404.

Brown, K. J., & Grunberg, N. E. (1995). Effects of housing on male and female rats: Crowding stresses males but calms females. *Physiology and Behavior, 58*, 1085–1089.

Butovskaya, M. L., & Kozintsev, A. G. (1999). Aggression, friendship, and reconciliation in Russian primary schoolchildren. *Aggressive Behavior, 25*, 125–139.

Calvo, N., & Volosin, M. (2001). Glucocorticoid and mineralocorticoid receptors are involved in the facilitation of anxiety-like response induced by restraint. *Neuroendocrinology, 73*, 261–271.

Cavigelli, S. A., Dubovick, T., Levash, W., Jolly, A., & Pitts, A. (2003). Female dominance status and fecal corticoids in a cooperative breeder with low reproductive skew: Ring-tailed lemurs (*Lemur catta*). *Hormones and Behavior, 43*, 166–179.

Cherek, D. R., & Dougherty, D. M. (1995). Provocation frequency and its role in determining the effects of smoked marijuana on human aggressive responding. *Behavioural Pharmacology, 6*, 405–412.

Cohen, H., Zohar, J., & Matar, M. (2003). The relevance of differential response to trauma in an animal model of posttraumatic stress disorder. *Biological Psychiatry, 53*, 463–73.

Comoli, E., Coizet, V., Boyes, J., Bolam, J. P., Canteras, N. S., Quirk, R. H, et al. (2003). A direct projection from superior colliculus to substantia nigra for detecting salient visual events. *Nature Neuroscience, 6*, 974–80.

Durant, S. M. (2000). Predator avoidance, breeding experience and reproductive success in endangered cheetahs, *Acinonyx jubatus*. *Animal Behaviour, 60*, 121–130.

Durrheim, D. N., & Leggat, P. A. (1999). Risk to tourists posed by wild mammals in South Africa. *Journal of Travel Medicine, 6*, 172–179.

Fanselow, M. S., & Lester, L. S. (1988). A functional behavioristic approach to aversively motivated behavior: Predatory imminence as a determinant of the topography of defensive behavior. In R. C. Bolles & M. D. Beecher (Eds.), *Evolution and learning* (pp. 185–211). Hillsdale, NJ: Erlbaum.

Figueiredo, H. F., Bodie, B. L., Tauchi, M., Dolgas, C. M., & Herman, J. P. (2003). Stress integration after acute and chronic predator stress: Differential activation of central stress circuitry and sensitization of the hypothalamo-pituitary-adrenocortical axis. *Endocrinology, 144*, 5249–5258.

Flannelly, K. J., Blanchard, R. J., Muraoka, M. Y., & Flannelly, L. (1982). Copulation increases offensive attack in male rats. *Physiology and Behavior, 29*, 381–385.

Fritzsche, P., Riek, M., & Gattermann, R.(2000). Effects of social stress on behavior and corpus luteum in female golden hamsters (*Mesocricetus auratus*). *Physiology and Behavior, 68*, 625–630.

Fuchs, E., & Flugge, G. (2002). Social stress in tree shrews: Effects on physiology, brain function, and behavior of subordinate individuals. *Pharmacology, Biochemistry and Behavior, 73*, 247–258.

Fuchs, E., Kramer, M., Hermes, B., Netter, P., & Hiemke, C. (1996). Psychosocial stress in tree shrews: Clomipramine counteracts behavioral and endocrine changes. *Pharmacology, Biochemistry and Behavior, 54*, 219–228.

Golla, W., Hofer, H., & East, M. L.(1999). Within-litter sibling aggression in spotted hyaenas: Effect of maternal nursing, sex and age. *Animal Behaviour, 58*, 715–726.

Gonzalez, S., Kitchener, A. C., & Lister, A. M. (2000). Survival of the Irish elk into the Holocene. *Nature, 405*, 753–754.

Halasz, J., Liposits, Z., Kruk, M. R., & Haller, J. (2002). Neural background of glucocorticoid dysfunction-induced abnormal aggression in rats: Involvement of fear- and stress-related structures. *European Journal of Neuroscience, 15*, 561–569.

Haller, J., Millar, S., & Kruk, M. R. (1998). Mineralocorticoid receptor blockade inhibits aggressive behaviour in male rats. *Stress, 2*, 201–207.

Haller, J., Millar, S., van de Schraaf, J., de Kloet, R. E., & Kruk, M. R. (2000). The active phase-related increase in corticosterone and aggression are linked. *Journal of Neuroendocrinology, 12*, 431–436.

Haller, J., van de Schraaf, J., & Kruk, M. R. (2001). Deviant forms of aggression in glucocorticoid hypo-reactive rats: A model for "pathological" aggression? *Journal of Neuroendocrinology, 13*, 102–107.

Haney, M., Maccari, S., Le Moal, M., Simon, H., & Piazza, P. V. (1995). Social stress increases the acquisition of cocaine self-administration in male and female rats. *Brain Research, 98*, 46–52.

Heinrichs, S. C., Pich, E. M., Miczek, K. A., Britton, K. T., & Koob, G. F. (1992). Corticotropin-releasing factor antagonist reduces emotionality in socially defeated rats via direct neurotropic action. *Brain Research, 581*, 190–197.

Hemingway, H., & Marmot, M. (1998). Psychosocial factors in the primary and secondary prevention of coronary heart disease: A systematic review. In S. Yusuf, J. A. Cairns, A. J. Camm, E. L. Fallen, & B. J. Gersh (Eds.), *Evidence based cardiology* (pp. 269–285). London: BMJ Books.

Higley, J. D., Hasert, M., Suomi, S., & Linnoila, M. (1991).

Nonhuman primate model of alcohol abuse: Effects of early experience, personality, and stress on alcohol consumption. *Proceedings of the National Academy of Sciences USA, 88,* 7261–7265.

Higley, J. D., Hasert, M., Suomi, S., & Linnoila, M. (1998). The serotonin uptake inhibitor sertraline reduces excessive alcohol consumption in nonhuman primates: Effect of stress. *Neuropsychopharmacology, 18,* 431–443.

Hilakivi-Clarke, L., & Lister, R. G. (1992). Social status and voluntary alcohol consumption in mice: Interaction with stress. *Psychopharmacology, 108,* 276–282.

Hiraiwa-Hasegawa, M., Byrne, R. W., Takasaki, H., & Byrne, J. M. (1986). Aggression toward large carnivores by wild chimpanzees of Mahale Mountains National Park, Tanzania. *Folia Primatologica, 47,* 8–13.

Johnson, T. E., & Rule, B. G. (1986). Mitigating circumstance information, censure, and aggression. *Journal of Personality and Social Psychology, 50,* 537–542.

Kalin, N. H., Shelton, S. E., & Takahashi, L. K. (1991). Defensive behaviors in infant rhesus monkeys: Ontogeny and context-dependent selective expression. *Child Development, 62,* 1175–1183.

Kaplan, J. R., & Manuck, S. B. (1999). Status, stress, and atherosclerosis: The role of environment and individual behavior. *Annals of the New York Academy of Sciences, 896,* 145–161.

Keeney, A. J., & Hogg, S. (1999). Behavioural consequences of repeated social defeat in the mouse: Preliminary evaluation of a potential animal model of depression. *Behavioural Pharmacology, 10,* 753–764.

Kemble, E. D., Flannelly, K. J., Salley, H., & Blanchard, R. J. (1985). Mouse killing, insect predation, and conspecific attack by rats with differing prior aggressive experience. *Physiology and Behavior, 34,* 645–648.

Kessler, R. C. (1997). The effects of stressful life events on depression. *Annual Review of Psychology, 48,* 191–214.

Kudryavtseva, N. N., Bakshtanovskaya, I. V., & Koryakina, L. A. (1991). Social model of depression in mice of C57/BLBL/6J strain. *Pharmacology, Biochemistry and Behavior, 38,* 315–320.

Ljungberg, T., Westlund, K., & Foresberg, A. J. L. (1999). Conflict resolution in 5-year-old boys: Does postconflict affiliative behaviour have a reconciliatory role? *Animal Behaviour, 58,* 1007–1025.

Louch, C. D., & Higginbotham, M. (1967). The relation between social rank and plasma corticosterone levels in mice. *General and Comparative Endocrinology, 8,* 441–444.

Maestripieri, D., Schino, G., Aureli, F., & Troisi, A. (1992).

A modest proposal: Displacement activities as an indicator of emotions in primates. *Animal Behaviour, 44,* 967–979.

McGrady, A. V. (1984). Effects of psychological stress on male reproduction: A review. *Archives of Andrology, 13,* 1–7.

McNaughton, N., Panickar, K. S., & Logan, B. (1996). The pituitary-adrenal axis and the different behavioral effects of buspirone and chlordiazepoxide. *Pharmacology, Biochemistry and Behavior, 54,* 51–56.

Meerlo, P., Overkamp, G. J., Benning, M. A., Koolhaas, J. M, Van den Hoofdakker, R. H. (1996). Long-term changes in open field behaviour following a single social defeat in rats can be reversed by sleep deprivation. *Physiology and Behavior, 60,* 115–119.

Meerlo, P., Sgoifo, A., & Turek, F. W. (2002). The effects of social defeat and other stressors on the expression of circadian rhythms. *Stress, 5,* 15–22.

Mineka, S., & Zinbarg, R. (1996). Conditioning and ethological models of anxiety disorder: Stress-in-dynamic-context anxiety models. In D. A. Hope (Ed.), *Nebraska Symposium on Motivation: Perspectives on anxiety, panic, and fear* (Vol. 43, pp. 135–210). Lincoln: University of Nebraska Press.

Mitani, J. C., & Watts, D. P. (1999). Demographic influences on the hunting behavior of chimpanzees. *American Journal of Physical Anthropology, 109,* 439–454.

Miyakawa, T., Yagi, T., Takao, K., & Niki, H. (2001). Differential effect of Fyn tyrosine kinase deletion on offensive and defensive aggression. *Behavioural Brain Research, 122,* 51–56.

Moyer, K. E. (1976). *The psychobiology of aggression.* New York: Harper & Row.

Naumenko, E. V., Popova, N. K., & Nikulina, W. M., et al. (1989). Behavior, adrenocortical activity, and brain monoamines in Norway rats selected for reduced aggressiveness towards man. *Pharmacology, Biochemistry and Behavior, 33,* 85–91.

O'Connell, J. F., Hawkes, K., Lupo, K. D., & Blurton Jones, N. G. (2002). Male strategies and Plio-Pleistocene archaeology. *Journal of Human Evolution, 43,* 831–872.

Ohl, F., & Fuchs, E. (1998). Memory performance in tree shrews: Effects of stressful experiences. *Neuroscience and Biobehavioral Reviews, 23,* 319–323.

Parmigiani, S., Ferrari, P. F., & Palanza, P. (1998). An evolutionary approach to behavioral pharmacology: Using drugs to understand proximate and ultimate mechanisms of different forms of aggression in mice. *Neuroscience and Biobehavioral Reviews, 23,* 143–153.

Parmigiani, S., Rodgers, R. J., Palanza, P., Mainardi, M., & Brain, P. F. (1989). The inhibitory effects of fluprazine on parental aggression in female mice are dependent upon intruder sex. *Physiology and Behavior, 46*, 455–459.

Pellis, S. M., O'Brien, D. P., Pellis, V. C., Teitelbaum, P., Wolgin, D. L., & Kennedy, S. (1988). Escalation of feline predation along a gradient from avoidance through "play" to killing. *Behavioral Neuroscience, 102*, 760–777.

Pellis, S. M., & Pellis, V. C. (1992). Analysis of the targets and tactics of conspecific attack and predatory attack in northern grasshopper mice *Onychomys leucogaster*. *Aggressive Behavior, 18*, 301–316.

Pellis, S. M., & Pellis, V. C. (1998). Play fighting of rats in comparative perspective: A schema for neurobehavioral analyses. *Neuroscience and Biobehavioral Reviews, 23*, 87–101.

Popova, N. K., Barykina, N. N., Pliusnina, I. Z., Alekhina, T. A., & Kolpakov, V. G. (1999). Manifestation of fear response in rats genetically predisposed to various kinds of defense behavior. *Rossiiskii Fiziologicheskii Zhurnal Imeni I. M. Sechenova, 85*, 99–104.

Popova, N. K., Voitenko, N. N., Kulikov, A. V., & Avgustinovich, D. F. (1991). Evidence for the involvement of central serotonin in mechanism of domestication of silver foxes. *Pharmacology, Biochemistry and Behavior, 40*, 751–756.

Potegal, M. (1994). Aggressive arousal: The amygdala connection. In M. Potegal & J. F. Knutson (Eds.), *The dynamics of aggression: Biological and social processes in dyads and groups* (pp. 73–105). Hillsdale, NJ: Erlbaum.

Potegal, M., Huhman, K., Moore, T., & Meyerhoff, J. (1993). Conditioned defeat in the Syrian golden hamster (*Mesocricetus auratus*). *Behavioral and Neural Biology, 60*, 93–102.

Raab, A., Dantzer, R., Michaud, B., Mormede, P., Taghzouti, K., Simon, H., et al. (1986). Behavioural, physiological and immunological consequences of social status and aggression in chronically coexisting resident-intruder dyads of male rats. *Physiology and Behavior, 36*, 223–228.

Rule, B. G., & Leger, G. J. (1976). Pain cues and differing functions of aggression. *Canadian Journal of Behavioural Science, 8*, 213–223.

Sachser, N., & Lick, C. (1989). Social stress in guinea pigs. *Physiology and Behavior, 46*, 137–144.

Sapolsky, R. M. (1990). A. E. Bennett Award paper: Adrenocortical function, social rank, and personality among wild baboons. *Biological Psychiatry, 28*, 862–878.

Schuurman, T. (1980). Hormonal correlates of agonistic behavior in adult male rats. *Progress in Brain Research, 53*, 415–420.

Sever'ianova, L. A. (1981). [Role of ACTH and corticosteroids in the aggressive-defensive behavior of rats].

Fiziologicheskii Zhurnal SSSR Imeni I. M. Sechenova, 67, 1117–1122.

Sgoifo, A., Braglia, F., Costoli, T., Musso, E., Meerlo, P., Ceresini, G., et al. (2003). Cardiac autonomic reactivity and salivary cortisol in men and women exposed to social stressors: Relationship with individual ethological profile. *Neuroscience and Biobehavioral Reviews, 27*, 179–188.

Shikhevich, S. G., Os'kina, I. N., & Pliusnina, I. Z. (2002). [Effect of stress and immune stimulus on the pituitary-adrenal axis in gray rats selected for behavior]. *Rossiiskii Fiziologicheskii Zhurnal Imeni I. M. Sechenova, 88*, 781–789.

Stamps, J. A., & Buechner, M. (1985). The territorial defense hypothesis and the ecology of insular vertebrates. *Quarterly Review of Biology, 60*, 155–181.

Stefanski, V., & Hendrichs, H. (1996). Social confrontation in male guinea pigs: Behavior, experience, and complement activity. *Physiology and Behavior, 60*, 235–241.

Stone, C. P. (1932). Wildness and savageness in rats of different strains. In K. S. Lashley (Ed.), *Studies in the dynamics of behavior* (pp. 3–55). Chicago: University of Chicago Press.

Szamado, S. (2003). Threat displays are not handicaps. *Journal of Theoretical Biology, 221*, 327–348.

Takahashi, L. K., & Blanchard, R. J. (1982). Attack and defense in laboratory and wild Norway and black rats. *Behavioral Processes, 7*, 49–62.

Tornatzky, W., & Miczek, K. A. (1994). Behavioral and autonomic responses to intermittent social stress: Differential protection by clonidine and metoprolol. *Psychopharmacology, 16*, 346–56.

Treves, A., & Naughton-Treves, L. (1999). Risk and opportunity for humans coexisting with large carnivores. *Journal of Human Evolution, 36*, 275–282.

Troisi, A., Belsanti, S., Bucci, A. R., Mosco, C., Sinti, F., & Verucci, M. (2000). Affect regulation in alexithymia—an ethological study of displacement behavior during psychiatric interviews. *Journal of Nervous and Mental Disease, 188*, 12–18.

Van Erp, A. M., & Miczek, K. A. (2001). Persistent suppression of ethanol self-administration by brief social stress in rats and increased startle response as index of withdrawal. *Physiology and Behavior, 73*, 301–11.

Verbeek, P., & de Waal, F. B. M. (2001). Peacemaking among preschool children. *Journal of Peace Psychology, 7*, 5–28.

Virgin, C. E., Jr., & Sapolsky, R. M. (1997). Styles of male social behavior and their endocrine correlates among low-ranking baboons. *American Journal of Primatology, 42*, 25–39.

Von Holst, D. V. (1977). Social stress in tree shrews: Problems, results and goals. *Journal of Comparative and Physiological Psychology, 120*, 71–86.

Wasser, S. K., & Barash, D. P. (1983). Reproductive suppression among female mammals: Implications for biomedicine and sexual selection theory. *Quarterly Review of Biology, 58,* 513–538.

Weisinger, R. S., Denton, D. A., & Osborne, P. G. (1989). Voluntary ethanol intake of individually or pair-housed rats: Effect of ACTH or dexamethasone treatment. *Pharmacology, Biochemistry and Behavior, 33,* 335–341.

Williams, C. W., Lees-Haley, P. R., & Brown, R. S. (1993). Human response to traumatic events: An integration of counterfactual thinking, hindsight bias, and attribution theory. *Psychological Reports, 72,* 483–494.

Wommack, J. C., & Delville, Y. (2003). Repeated social stress and the development of agonistic behavior: Individual differences in coping responses in male golden hamsters. *Physiology and Behavior, 80,* 303–308.

Wrangham, R. W. (1999). Evolution of coalitionary killing. *American Journal of Physical Anthropology, 29*(Suppl.), 1–30.

World Health Organization (WHO). (2002). *World Report on Violence and Health.* Geneva: Author.

Yerkes, R. M. (1913). The heredity of savageness and wildness in rats. *Journal of Animal Behaviour, 3,* 286–296.

Zuberbuhler, K. (2000). Causal knowledge of predators' behaviour in wild Diana monkeys. *Animal Behaviour, 59,* 209–220.

PART IV

DEVELOPMENT

13

Conditioned Defeat

Kim L. Huhman & Aaron M. Jasnow

It is perhaps surprising to find a chapter on submission in a book about aggression. In fact, this "flip side" of aggression receives comparatively little attention in the scientific literature. For example, a recent Medline search using the query "aggression AND neurobiology" (and related permutations) yielded 287 references, whereas a search using the query "submission OR subordinate AND neurobiology" (again with related searches) yielded 34 relevant references. Aggression is a relational phenomenon that is usually observed in groups of two or more individuals. Such groupings generally result in a "winner" and a "loser," and although the factors that lead to, underlie, and result from an individual becoming dominant (a "winner") have received considerable attention, the factors associated with becoming subordinate (a "loser") have been largely overlooked. In studies in which subordinate individuals have been examined, the work is often framed from the perspective of stress rather than agonistic behavior. This perspective may have been adopted because numerous scientists have found that their work was considered more acceptable in terms of publication or funding if it was perceived as stress research (i.e., "social stress") rather than research on agonistic behavior. Alternatively, many of these scientists may have determined that the constructs of stress or fear were more useful in generating testable hypotheses about the neurobi-

ology of submission than were aggression or agonistic behavior.

In our laboratory, we are studying the effects of social defeat on physiology and behavior, and we have tended to use the framework of stress/fear when generating scientific questions. We view social defeat as an ethologically relevant stressor that can be used as a valuable addition to more traditional stressors, such as foot shock or immobilization. Although these latter stressors may be highly controllable, it is not as clear what relevance they have to events that naturally occur in the lives of most organisms. Social conflict, though more difficult to quantify and control, is clearly a relevant and often driving force in the lives of most organisms, including humans (Bjorkqvist, 2001). Examination of both types of stressors is probably necessary to continue to advance our understanding of the immediate and long-term effects of stress on physiology and behavior. Similarly, a consideration of subordination from the perspectives of both stress/fear and agonistic behavior should lead to greater advances in our understanding of the neurobiological correlates of subordination or submissiveness. This chapter reviews some of the literature pertaining to stress/fear and defense in an attempt to illustrate how both perspectives are useful in the pursuit of an understanding of the neurobiological correlates of social defeat or subordination.

It is important to note that we are not including "defensive aggression" when we discuss defensive behavior (see Blanchard, Wall, & Blanchard, 2003, and Blanchard & Blanchard, ch. 12 in this volume, for excellent discussions of defensive aggression). In our laboratory, the defensive behaviors that are measured (i.e., upright and side defensive postures) are not associated with any elements of attack or offense, such as biting, but are instead coupled with other submissive behaviors (e.g., tail lift, full submissive posture, and flight). Philosophically, it is also important to consider whether dominance and subordination are to be seen as "two sides of the same coin," so that if one increases the other necessarily decreases, or whether they are viewed as separate, albeit reciprocally connected, processes that can change to some extent independently. Some of our recent data have implications for this question, and these data are discussed later in the chapter.

Effects of Stress on Physiology and Behavior

Individuals of most species are exposed to a wide range of potential stressors during their lifetimes. These stressors can be social in nature (e.g., territorial conflict or competition between males for access to females) or can be the result of environmental perturbations (e.g., reduced ambient temperature or reduced food availability). Regardless of their nature, exposure to stressors leads to marked physiological and behavioral changes in virtually all species examined to date. In vertebrates, one such response observed following exposure to a fearful or stressful situation, including social defeat, is increased activation of the hypothalamic-pituitary-adrenal (HPA) axis. The resulting elevations in circulating glucocorticoids occur in a variety of vertebrate species, including nonhuman primates (Fuchs & Flugge, 2002; Sapolsky, 1992), cats (Kojima et al., 1995), reptiles (Knapp & Moore, 1997; Moore, Thompson, & Marler, 1991), rats (Blanchard et al., 1995), and humans (Biondi & Picardi, 1999; Morgan et al., 2000). The HPA response stimulates physiological changes that support the organism's response to the stressor and may also feed back to alter that organism's ongoing or future behavior (Leshner, 1975, 1983).

A wide range of behavior is altered following exposure to stressors such as social conflict, and, in general, it is the subordinate individual that is more affected.

For example, food and water intake is reduced in subordinates following an agonistic encounter (Meerlo, Overkamp, Daan, Van den Hoofdakker, & Koolhaas, 1996). In addition, exposure to either nonsocial or social stressors disrupts reproductive behavior in several species, including mice (D'Amato, 1988), rats (Blanchard & Blanchard, 1989), snakes (Schuett, Harlow, Rose, Van Kirk, & Murdoch, 1996), birds (Wingfield, Ramos-Fernandez, Nunez-de la Mora, & Drummond, 1999), and fish (Fox, White, Kao, & Fernald, 1997). Another commonly observed effect of social stress is a decrease in general activity (Blanchard & Blanchard 1989; Carere, Welink, Drent, Koolhaas, & Groothuis, 2001; Flugge, Kramer, Rensing, & Fuchs, 1998; Meerlo, de Boer, Koolhaas, Daan, & Van den Hoofdakker, 1996; Meerlo, Overkamp, & Koolhaas, 1997; Shively, Grant, Ehrenkaufer, Mach, & Nader, 1997), although there is evidence that activity may actually increase in hamsters in response to defeat stress (Petrulis, Weidner, & Johnson, 2004). Defeated animals are less affiliative than are nondefeated animals (Meerlo et al., 1996; Shively, 1998). Defeated rodents also typically display increased anxietylike behaviors as assessed by a variety of experimental models, including the elevated plus maze, defensive withdrawal, and defensive burying (Fendt, Koch, & Schnitzler, 1997; Heinrichs, Pich, Miczek, Britton, & Koob, 1992; Lundkvist et al., 1996; Mansbach, Brooks, & Chen, 1997; Martins, Marras, & Guimaraes, 1997; Menzaghi et al., 1994; Smagin, Harris, & Ryan, 1996). Finally, stress exposure results in increased expression of additional defensive behaviors, such as risk assessment following exposure to novel conspecific odors (Garbe & Kemble, 1994; Petrulis et al., 2004).

Why Study Hamsters?

Syrian hamsters (*Mesocricetus auratus*) are a particularly valuable species to use in studies of agonistic behavior and social stress for a number of reasons. First, they are thought to be solitary individuals that naturally defend their home territories against intruders (Nowack & Paradiso, 1983). In the laboratory when housed individually, a resident hamster will rapidly and reliably attack and defeat an intruder placed in its home cage. No complex housing procedures are necessary to induce aggression, as is usually the case with laboratory rats. Additionally, the agonistic behavior of hamsters is ritualized and typically does not result in wounding, as is observed in many aggressive mouse strains. Hamster social behavior is easily observed and quantified and has been described in detail in both males and females (Albers, Huhman, & Meisel, 2002; Floody & Pfaff, 1977; Grant & Mackintosh, 1962; Lerwill & Makings, 1971; Payne & Swanson, 1970). In hamsters, unlike other commonly used laboratory rodents, both males and females are highly aggressive (Lerwill & Makings, 1971; Payne & Swanson, 1970). The lack of aggression exhibited by most female rodents has previously been cited as a major weakness of animal models of aggression/social stress (Bjorkqvist, 2001), and Syrian hamsters nicely overcome this limitation. In fact, when they are not sexually receptive, female hamsters often defeat males even if the pairs are matched for weight (Brain, 1972; Payne & Swanson, 1970).

Physiological Responses to Social Defeat in Hamsters

Exposure to social defeat in Syrian hamsters results in a pronounced stress response in the defeated, but not in the victorious, animal. Defeated hamsters display increased HPA axis activity, as evidenced by elevations in plasma adrenocorticotropin (ACTH), β-endorphin, β-lipotropin, cortisol, and corticosterone (Huhman, Bunnell, Mougey, & Meyerhoff, 1990; Huhman, Moore, Ferris, Mougey, & Meyerhoff, 1991), and decreases in plasma testosterone and prolactin (Huhman et al., 1991; Huhman, Mougey, Moore, & Meyerhoff, 1995). Importantly, this hormonal stress response is not dependent upon physical contact between the animals because previously defeated hamsters will continue to display increased HPA activity when paired with a dominant animal even when they are separated by a physical barrier (Huhman, Moore, Mougey, & Meyerhoff, 1992). This finding emphasizes that the observed changes in physiology and behavior are not merely a response to physical exertion or pain, but are a response to the psychological effects of social defeat. Social defeat has also been shown to have marked effects on humoral immune responses, splenocyte proliferation, and immune cell distribution in hamsters and other rodents (Fleshner, Laudenslager, Simons, & Maier, 1989; Jasnow et al., 2001; Raab et al., 1986; Stefanski, 2000). Exposure to social stress in hamsters during puberty, a time when the pattern of agonistic behavior is shifting

from a juvenile to an adult pattern, alters the types and amounts of agonistic behavior that these individuals will later exhibit (Delville, Melloni, & Ferris, 1998).

Behavioral Response to Social Defeat in Hamsters: Conditioned Defeat

There are distinct behavioral responses to social defeat in hamsters and other rodents. Exposure to social stress has been shown to result in reduced aggression and in increased defensive and submissive behaviors, as well as avoidance of conspecifics (Blanchard et al., 1995; Jasnow, Banks, Owens, & Huhman, 1999; Jasnow & Huhman, 2001; Lai & Johnston, 2002; Potegal, Huhman, Moore, & Meyerhoff, 1993; Scott, 1966; Siegfried, Frischknecht, & Waser, 1984; Van de Poll, Smeets, van Oyen, & van der Zwan, 1982). Over the last several years, our lab has been examining the mechanisms underlying the abrupt and prolonged change in social behavior, called conditioned defeat, that is observed following single or repeated exposure to social defeat in hamsters. As noted before, male Syrian hamsters are naturally aggressive animals that readily defend their home territory (their home cage) against intruding conspecifics. However, if these animals are placed in an agonistic encounter in which they experience a social defeat by a larger, more aggressive animal, then they subsequently become highly submissive and are virtually unable to reverse their subordinate social status. Following the initial defeat experience, these hamsters do not defend their home cage, even against a smaller, nonaggressive animal that they would previously have attacked and defeated. Instead of attacking the intruding animal, previously defeated hamsters vigorously avoid social interaction and display submissive behavior in response to, or flee from, the intruder without provocation. We conclude that a hamster is exhibiting conditioned defeat if that hamster emits only submissive and defensive agonistic behavior in response to a nonaggressive stimulus animal. If during testing with the nonaggressive intruder, the previously defeated hamster produces any aggressive behavior, then we do not consider that animal as demonstrating conditioned defeat. It is interesting that this behavior is emitted in the hamster's own home cage, whereas the initial defeat occurred in another hamster's cage, and the stimulus animal (the nonaggressive intruder) differs from the initial opponent in terms of age, size, and behavior. It is not the case, however, that hamsters are not capable of remembering who defeated them because hamsters have been shown to avoid preferentially for at least 7 days hamsters that have previously defeated them (Lai & Johnston, 2002; Petrulis et al., 2004).

The profound behavioral change observed following social defeat in hamsters can persist for at least 1 month despite the fact that the hamster is being paired repeatedly with a nonaggressive intruder, a situation in which one might expect the response to habituate (Huhman et al., 2003). To examine the duration of the behavioral response to defeat in male hamsters, we exposed subjects to four 5-min defeats on Day 1 by a larger, aggressive male. The next day, and every 3 to 6 days thence until we reached 33 days, we exposed these males for 5 min to a novel, smaller, nonaggressive male. More than half of the previously defeated males continued to exhibit conditioned defeat (defined as an animal that produces only submissive/defensive agonistic behavior with no aggressive behavior emitted) for at least 33 days (figure 13.1).

We have also demonstrated that conditioned defeat can be induced with a single 15-min defeat (Jasnow et al., 2001; Jasnow, Cooper, & Huhman, 2004). This is important for studies in which pharmacological manipulations are to be given either before defeat training (for examining the acquisition of conditioned defeat) or some time after the initial defeat training (for examining the consolidation of conditioned defeat). In these cases, defeating the hamsters four times over 1 day would make the experimental design extremely unwieldy. In other studies, we have used initial defeats of 5 min (so-called "suboptimal training") for examining treatments that are hypothesized to enhance conditioned defeat (Faruzzi & Huhman, 2002; Jasnow, Shi, Israel, Davis, & Huhman, 2002).

Several other points about our experimental design warrant comment. First, we routinely quantify the duration of all behaviors emitted by our experimental animals, as well as our aggressive trainers and nonaggressive stimulus animals (see Albers et al. 2000, for a detailed description of these behaviors and their possible functions).

Measuring all behavior emitted by each of the animals is particularly important in studies in which pharmacological manipulations are used because it allows us to determine if the drug treatment induces nonspecific effects (i.e., ataxia) in the experimental subjects or if the treatment indirectly alters the behavior of the aggressive trainers or the nonaggressive stimulus ani-

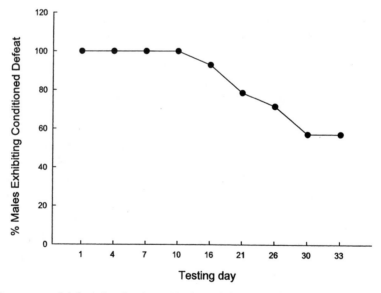

FIGURE 13.1 Percentage of defeated males (N = 14) that exhibited conditioned defeat (only submissive and defensive agonistic behavior with no aggression) during subsequent generalization tests when paired with a nonaggressive intruder. From "Conditioned Defeat in Male and Female Syrian Hamsters," by K. L. Huhman, M. B. Solomon, M. Janicki, A. C. Harmon, S. M. Lin, J. E. Israel, et al., 2003, *Hormones and Behavior, 44,* 293–299. Reprinted with permission from Elsevier.

mals. We can also examine whether a particular treatment affects both submissive and aggressive behavior or only one and not the other. This distinction is important for assessing the question posed above about the interdependence of the mechanisms controlling dominance versus submission.

Another important point about our model is that we do not prescreen our animals or exclude individuals based on preexisting tendencies for submissiveness or aggressiveness but, instead, include all subjects in the experimental design. We singly house the subjects for 1 to 2 weeks before the beginning of an experiment. Thus, these animals have previous social experience and presumably have preexisting submissive or aggressive tendencies. Nonetheless, our aggressive trainers ("resident aggressors") generally defeat all of the experimental animals and then most, if not all, of these animals then exhibit conditioned defeat upon testing with the nonaggressive intruder.

Finally, it is also important to note that there appears to be a striking sex difference in the behavioral response to social defeat in hamsters (Huhman et al., 2003), with female hamsters exhibiting a much less significant behavioral response to social defeat. We have recently obtained data indicating that submissive behavior in female hamsters may be suppressed by estrogen, and it also appears that there is a clear variation over the estrous cycle in the susceptibility of female hamsters to acquiring conditioned defeat. This chapter, however, focuses on what we have discovered about the neurobiological concomitants of conditioned defeat in male Syrian hamsters.

Working Hypothesis and Organization of This Chapter

As mentioned earlier, there is a relative paucity of information on the neural mechanisms and neurochemical signals that regulate defensive and submissive behaviors. There is, by contrast, an enormous literature on the neural circuitry that regulates fear learning, and there are some intuitive parallels between traditional fear conditioning and conditioned defeat. Both phenomena result from a very brief exposure to an aversive stimulus, and both can be quite long lasting. We have used the literature from both agonistic behavior and fear conditioning to guide our initial working hypotheses on the neurobiological concomi-

tants of conditioned defeat, and we briefly review each topic here. Based on these data, we have initially tested the general hypothesis that the amygdala and the bed nucleus of the stria terminalis (BNST) are critical for the acquisition and expression of conditioned defeat.

Neuroanatomy of Defense and Fear: Roles of the Amygdala and BNST

Neuroanatomy of the "Extended Amygdala"

The amygdala is a multinuclear structure located in the temporal lobe of the mammalian brain. Although the amygdala has been considered a functional unit of the brain for many years, it is composed of various subnuclei that differ structurally, embryologically, immunohistochemically, and functionally. Some authors suggest that the amygdala is best conceptualized as a heterogeneous set of nuclei, each with distinct functions, rather than a single functional unit (Swanson & Petrovich, 1998); however, other evidence suggests that the subnuclei of the amygdala have distinct roles that contribute to different aspects of a number of common functions, such as in fear conditioning. Furthermore, it is probably the case that our conception of the amygdala should be "extended" to include parts of the BNST because some subnuclei of these brain areas share similar cell morphology, neurotransmitter content, and efferent connections (Alheid & Heimer, 1988; McDonald, 1992). In fact, parts of the lateral BNST are derived embryologically from the same cells that eventually form the central amygdala (Johnston, 1923), and it is connected to similar brain areas (Gray, Carney, & Magnusun, 1989), suggesting that these two nuclei may serve similar functions. In addition, both the BNST and central amygdala are intricately connected with reciprocal projections, and the BNST is a major target of central amygdalar outputs.

The amygdala has extensive intra- and extraamygdaloid inputs and outputs that allow it to monitor the internal and external environment and to modulate autonomic function and behavior (Pitkanen, 2000). In general, the amygdala receives sensory information from all sensory systems via the lateral and basolateral nuclei, which then project to the central nucleus of the amygdala (LeDoux, Cicchetti, Xagoraris, & Romanski,

1990; McDonald, 1998; Pitkanen, 2000; Pitkanen et al., 1995). The central nucleus, in turn, projects to areas of the hypothalamus and brainstem that regulate autonomic functioning and behavior, including defensive behavior. Electrical or chemical stimulation of the central amygdala increases blood pressure and heart rate (Galeno & Brody, 1983; Ohta, Watanabe, & Ueki, 1991; Stock, Schlor, Heidt, & Buss, 1978), increases plasma corticosterone (Feldman & Weidenfeld, 1998; Weidenfeld, Itzik, & Feldman, 1997), and facilitates the startle reflex (Rosen & Davis, 1988), as well as immobility (Applegate, Kapp, Underwood, & McNall, 1983; Roozendaal, Koolhaas, & Bohus, 1992). Direct projections from the central amygdala to the paraventricular nucleus of the hypothalamus are sparse (Prewitt & Herman, 1998); however projections through the BNST to the paraventricular nucleus appear to influence activity of the HPA axis during times of stress (Cecchi, Khoshbouei, Javors, & Morilak, 2002; Herman & Cullinan, 1997; Zhu, Umegaki, Suzuki, Miura, & Iguchi, 2001). Direct connections of the central amygdala to the locus coeruleus regulate increased vigilance and attention during times of stress and may be responsible for the release of norepinephrine (Van Bockstaele, Chan, & Pickel, 1996; Van Bockstaele, Colago, & Valentino, 1998). Finally, connections to the nucleus reticularis pontis caudalis are involved in the potentiation of the startle reflex (Fendt, Koch, & Schnitzler, 1994).

Neuroanatomy of Defensive Behavior

The data on brain mechanisms of defense are somewhat limited compared to data on offensive aggression or fear conditioning (see next section), and nearly all of the studies have used cats or rats as subjects (for review, see Graeff, 1994; Siegel, Roeling, Gregg, & Kruk, 1999; Siegel, Schubert, & Shaikh, 1997). These studies have employed localized electrical stimulation, tract tracing, and pharmacological manipulations to identify neuroanatomical and neurochemical substrates that mediate or modulate defensive behavior. There is a medial hypothalamic/dorsal periaqueductal gray (dPAG) circuit that appears to control the actual production of defensive behaviors (Bandler, 1988; Schmitt et al., 1986), but this circuit is not thought to be responsible for the "motivational states" that ultimately trigger these behaviors. Instead, the amygdala and possibly the BNST appear to subserve this function. In cats, electrical stimulation of parts of the amygdala fa-

cilitate defensive rage and suppress predatory attack (Kaada, 1967; Siegel et al., 1999). The BNST, as the amygdala, projects to the hypothalamus and appears to be involved in the modulation of defense (Graeff, 1994; Siegel et al., 1999). In rats, defensive reactions can be obtained following electrical stimulation of the amygdala and the stria terminalis (Zbrozyna, 1972). This response differs from that obtained following stimulation of the hypothalamic/dPAG circuit in that it builds up more slowly and persists after the cessation of stimulation. This phenomenon has been interpreted to indicate that the amygdala modulates the defensive behaviors that are mediated by the hypothalamic/PAG circuit (Zbrozyna, 1972). Aggleton and Mishkin (1985) have hypothesized that the amygdala, which receives sensory information about the external and internal environment, evaluates this information for its emotional content. Based on this evaluation (particularly if the stimuli are aversive), the amygdala influences the hypothalamus and PAG (both directly and indirectly through projections to the BNST) so that appropriate behavioral and physiological responses are produced (Davis, 1992b; Fanselow, 1991).

There are data that support a role for the amygdala and the BNST in the modulation of defeat-related behaviors in hamsters. Lesions of the amygdala that encompass the basal, lateral, and central nuclei have been shown to suppress submissive and defensive behavior produced by defeated hamsters (Bunnell, Sodetz, & Shalloway, 1970). These animals are capable, however, of producing defensive and submissive behaviors when they are attacked, indicating that the amygdala is not necessary for the actual organization of the motor patterns but instead influences when or how often they are produced. Shipley and Kolb (1977) performed lesions in various cortical and limbic regions, including the cingulate cortex, septum, hippocampus, and amygdala, and found that only amygdala lesions consistently altered the behavior of hamsters in a social interaction test. Recently, Agrawal, Mayeaux, Johnston, and Adkins-Regan (2000) demonstrated that subordinate hamsters with amygdala lesions do not avoid their dominant partners in a Y maze. This deficit may indicate that lesioned animals either are not fearful of the dominant opponent or simply cannot recognize them. Finally, c-fos mRNA, one marker for cellular activation, has been compared in dominant and subordinate hamsters (Kollack-Walker & Newman, 1995; Kollack-Walker, Watson, & Akil, 1997). Some brain areas, including the medial amygdala, which receives chemosensory inputs, are activated in both dominants and subordinates. Other areas, including the medial preoptic area, anterior hypothalamus, dPAG, lateral septum, BNST, locus coeruleus, and central amygdala, exhibit significantly greater activation in subordinate males. The neuronal activation observed in the hypothalamus and dPAG is consistent with the putative role of these areas in the control of defensive behaviors, while many of the other areas selectively activated in subordinates (e.g., the BNST, locus coeruleus, and central amygdala) are known to be involved in physiological and behavioral responses to stressful stimuli (Bremner, Krystal, Southwick, & Charney, 1996; Graeff, 1994; Jellestad, Markowska, Bakke, & Walther, 1986). In summary, data from cats, rats, and hamsters support an important role for the amygdala and BNST in the mediation or modulation of defensive and submissive behavior.

Neuroanatomy of Fear and Fear Conditioning

There is a great deal of evidence that the amygdala is necessary for the experience of emotion, particularly fear, in rodents, nonhuman primates, and humans (Adolphs & Tranel, 2001; Davis, 2001; LeDoux, 1992, 2001). Lesion, electrical stimulation, and infusion studies have indicated that the extended amygdala is involved in behavioral plasticity observed following exposure to a variety of stressful or aversive stimuli (Davis, 2001; Gallagher, 2001; Kluver & Bucy, 1937; Maren, Aharonov, & Fanselow, 1996). One model system that has been used extensively to study the neural substrates of aversive learning is Pavlovian fear conditioning. In these studies, a neutral stimulus such as a light, tone or an environmental context is paired with an aversive stimulus such as foot shock. Following such pairings, the initially neutral stimulus now elicits a conditioned response such as potentiated startle or freezing.

The importance of the amygdala in fear learning is evidenced by the fact that electrolytic or chemical lesions, as well as chemical inactivation of the amygdala, disrupt conditioned fear responses in animals. For instance, pre- or posttraining lesions of the central, lateral, or basolateral amygdala decrease conditioned freezing to shock or to a context paired with a shock (Helmstetter, 1992; LeDoux, 1992; LeDoux et al., 1990; Roozendaal, Koolhaas, & Bohus, 1991a, 1991b). In addition, freezing and fear-potentiated startle can be attenuated even when lesions of the basolateral amygdala are made up to 1 month after training (Cousens & Otto, 1998; Lee, Walker, & Davis, 1996; Maren, Aharonov, & Fanselow, 1996), suggesting that the amygdala has a lasting role in the expression of fear conditioned responses. Posttraining lesions of the central or basolateral amygdala block expression of fear-potentiated startle (Campeau & Davis, 1995; Hitchcock & Davis, 1986; Lee et al., 1996; Sananes & Davis, 1992), and pretraining chemical or electrolytic lesions of the basolateral or central nucleus of the amygdala block both acquisition and expression of fear-potentiated startle (Kim & Davis, 1993; Sananes & Davis, 1992). Other studies have examined fear learning in more complex paradigms involving operant behaviors such as inhibitory avoidance, and these studies indicate that the amygdala also plays an important role in fear-motivated learning of instrumental tasks (Liang et al., 1982; Wilensky, Schafe, & LeDoux, 2000), although it has been suggested that the actual memory for these tasks may be stored, at least partially, in other brain areas (Liang et al., 1982; Parent & McGaugh, 1994). So, although there is some debate over whether the amygdala is the actual site wherein fear learning is stored or whether the amygdala modulates the strength of memory storage that occurs in other brain areas, there is general agreement that the amygdala plays a critical role in the behavioral changes that occur in response to aversive stimulation.

Whereas the amygdala is involved in regulating both conditioned and unconditioned fear responses, the BNST appears to be preferentially involved in regulating unconditioned fear responses. Lesions of the BNST do not block fear-potentiated startle or conditioned changes in autonomic activity or freezing (Gewirtz, McNish, & Davis, 1998; Hitchcock & Davis, 1991; LeDoux, Iwata, Cicchetti, & Reis, 1988; Lee & Davis, 1997), but they do block responses such as corticotropin releasing factor (CRF)-enhanced startle and light-enhanced startle (Gewirtz et al., 1998; Lee & Davis, 1997; Walker & Davis, 1997a). These data suggest that in addition to the amygdala, the BNST is important for regulating behavioral responses to aversive stimuli.

In summary, the literature investigating the neuroanatomical correlates of defensive/submissive behavior and conditioned fear have implicated subnuclei of the amygdala and BNST in the mediation or modulation of a variety of physiological and behavioral responses to aversive stimuli.

Neurochemistry of Defense and Fear

Glutamate and γ-Aminobutyric Acid (GABA)

There are data indicating that glutamate and GABA are involved in the regulation of defensive behavior, conditioned fear, and anxiety. Infusion of the GABA$_A$ antagonist bicuculline into the basolateral amygdala increases anxiety in rats in a social interaction test, an effect that is blocked by a microinjection of a glutamate antagonist (Sajdyk & Shekhar, 1997). GABA$_A$ antagonists infused into the basolateral amygdala in rats increase heart rate, blood pressure, and anxiety as measured in social interaction tests, while muscimol, a GABA$_A$ agonist, has the opposite effect (Sanders & Shekhar, 1995a, 1995b). Infusion of benzodiazepines into the basolateral amygdala decreases shock probe avoidance (Pesold & Treit, 1994), an effect that can be blocked by the administration of benzodiazepine antagonists or GABA$_A$ antagonists (Scheel-Kruger & Petersen, 1982).

Glutamate appears to act on both N-methyl-D-aspartate (NMDA) and non-NMDA receptors in the central or basolateral amygdala to affect the acquisition and/or expression of fear conditioning. NMDA antagonists infused into the basolateral amygdala block the acquisition but not expression of fear-potentiated startle (Campeau, Miserendino, & Davis, 1992; Lee & Kim, 1998; Miserendino, Sananes, Melia, & Davis, 1990; Walker & Davis, 1997b), whereas NMDA antagonists and the GABA$_A$ agonist muscimol block both the acquisition and expression of contextual fear and conditioned freezing (Fanselow & Kim, 1994; Helmstetter & Bellgowan, 1994; Maren, Aharonov, & Fanselow, 1996; Maren, Aharonov, Stote, & Fanselow, 1996). By contrast, non-NMDA antagonists infused in the central amygdala appear to block only the expression of conditioned fear (Kim, Campeau, Falls, & Davis, 1993; Walker & Davis, 1997b). Numerous infusion studies indicate that it is possible to dissociate the effect of these drugs on amygdaloid subnuclei, even with relatively large injection volumes (200–500 nl) (Campeau et al., 1992; Parent & McGaugh, 1994; Roozendaal & McGaugh, 1997; Silva & Tomaz, 1995). For example, local infusion of DL-2-amino-5-phosphopentanoic acid (AP5), a NMDA antagonist, into the basolateral amygdala, but not into the central amygdala, blocked the acquisition of conditioned fear (Fanselow & Kim, 1994). Together, these data indicate that glutamatergic and

GABAergic neurotransmission in the amygdala is critical in regulating behavioral responses to fear-producing stimuli (Rainnie, Asprodini, & Shinnick-Gallagher, 1991; Smith & Dudek, 1996).

Conditioned Defeat: Corticotropin Releasing Factor (CRF)

Background

CRF is a 41-amino-acid peptide that was first isolated and sequenced from ovine hypothalamus in 1981 (Vale, Spiess, Rivier, & Rivier, 1981). Although the structure of CRF is species specific, CRF from any species will induce the release of ACTH from the pituitary of virtually all species studied to date. Several CRF-related peptides have also been characterized, including amphibian sauvagine, fish urotensin, mammalian urocortin, urocortin II, and urocortin III (Lewis et al., 2001; Reyes et al., 2001; Vaughan et al., 1995). Since its discovery, the role of CRF in regulation of the HPA axis has been well documented. Briefly, activity of the HPA axis is regulated by the release of CRF into the median eminence of the hypothalamus, where it enters the hypophyseal portal system. CRF then stimulates corticotroph cells within the anterior pituitary to initiate the release of ACTH into the general circulation. ACTH stimulates the synthesis and secretion of glucocorticoids from the adrenal cortex (Koob, 1992). A large body of evidence also indicates that CRF mediates behavioral, autonomic, and immune responses to stressors that are independent of HPA axis function.

The distribution of CRF synthesizing neurons outside the hypothalamus is consistent with a role in regulating affective behaviors, as well as autonomic and immune functions. CRF-immunoreactive cells are found in the central, lateral, basolateral, medial, cortical, and basomedial nuclei of the amygdala (Swanson, Sawchenko, Rivier, & Vale, 1983). This distribution suggests that CRF may play an important role in regulating behavioral and autonomic responses to stressful and fearful stimuli. CRF neurons within the central amygdala project to the paraventricular nucleus of the hypothalamus, BNST, midbrain central gray, parabrachial nucleus, mesencephalic nucleus of the trigeminal nerve, locus coeruleus, dorsal vagal nucleus, and nucleus of the solitary tract (Gray & Magnuson, 1992; Marcilhac & Siaud, 1997; Sakanaka, Shibasaki, & Lederis, 1986), suggesting that this system is important for modulating behavioral and autonomic responses to stressors. CRF neurons are also located in areas, such as the BNST, nucleus accumbens, and the septal area (Sawchenko & Swanson, 1985), that are associated with regulating the endocrine, autonomic, and behavioral responses to stress. Finally, CRF is also synthesized in moderate concentrations within the cortex, thalamus, basal ganglia, brain stem, and spinal cord (Swanson et al., 1983).

Two CRF receptor subtypes (CRF_1 and CRF_2) have been cloned from a wide variety of species and are members of the G-protein coupled receptor superfamily which stimulate adenylate cyclase (Chang, Pearse, O'Connel, & Rosenfeld, 1993; Chen, Lewis, Perrin, & Vale, 1993; Dautzenberg, Wille, Lohmann, & Spiess, 1997; Liaw, Grigoriadis, Lovenberg, De Souza, & Maki, 1997; Myers, Trinh, & Myers, 1998; Palchaudhuri et al., 1998; Yu, Xie, & Abou-Samra, 1996). CRF receptors have a heterogeneous distribution throughout the brain and periphery suggesting that each receptor may have distinct functions. These distinctive roles, however, are not yet clearly understood. In general, the distribution of CRF_1 receptors suggests that they play a large role in regulating HPA axis function, as well as some cognitive and sensory functions. The distribution of CRF_2 receptors suggests that they mediate autonomic and behavioral functions. CRF_1 receptors are largely distributed throughout the cortex, amygdala, cerebellum, parts of the hippocampus, and olfactory bulbs; however, the highest abundance of CRF_1 receptors is within the pituitary (Chalmers, Lovenberg, & De Souza, 1995; Sanchez, Young, Plotsky, & Insel, 1999). In the periphery, CRF_1 receptors are located in the testis, ovary, and adrenal glands (Nappi & Rivest, 1995; Palchaudhuri et al., 1998; Vita et al., 1993). Distribution of CRF_2 receptor splice variants have a very different distribution throughout the brain and periphery than CRF_1 receptors. Within the central nervous system, CRF_2 receptors are found in the hypothalamus, lateral septum, hippocampus, amygdala, olfactory bulbs, brainstem, cerebellum, cortex, and retina (Chalmers et al., 1995; Lovenberg, Chalmers, Liu, & De Souza, 1995; Palchaudhuri, Hauger, Wille, Fuchs, & Dautzenberg, 1999). Thus, the distribution of CRF_2 receptors is consistent with a role in the regulation of behavior.

CRF and Behavioral Responses to Aversive Stimuli

CRF gene expression is primarily regulated by glucocorticoids, although several other endogenous substances or external stimuli can influence CRF gene expression as well. For example, restraint stress stimulates expression of CRF mRNA within the central nucleus of the amygdala, as well as within the paraventricular nucleus (Hsu, Chen, Takahashi, & Kalin, 1998), while foot shock and social stress elevate CRF mRNA within the central and medial amygdala, respectively, but not within the paraventricular nucleus (Albeck et al., 1997; Makino et al., 1999). This differential activation may indicate that the CRF system responds to stress in a stimulus- or site-specific manner.

The physiological and behavioral effects of exogenous administration of CRF or its related peptides are similar to those of exposure to a natural stressor (Brown et al., 1982; Brown & Fisher, 1983; Dunn & Berridge, 1990; Jones, Kortekaas, Slade, Middlemiss, & Hagan, 1998; Koob et al., 1984; Moreau, Kilpatrick, & Jenck, 1997; Sherman & Kalin, 1987). Many of these CRF-dependent effects are *independent* of the HPA axis, as they occur following hypophysectomy or adrenalectomy (Britton, Varela, Garcia, & Rosenthal, 1986; Eaves, Thatcher-Britton, Rivier, Vale, & Koob, 1985; Pavcovich & Valentino, 1997). These data indicate that CRF has the capacity to act within the central nervous system to directly modulate behavior independently of ACTH or the glucocorticoids. Also, central infusion of CRF antagonists blocks the behavioral effects of exposure to stressors and to exogenously administered CRF (Fendt et al., 1997; Korte, Korte-Bouws, Bohus, & Koob, 1994; Lundkvist et al., 1996; Mansbach et al., 1997; Martins et al., 1997; Menzaghi et al., 1994).

In our laboratory, the role of central CRF in behavioral responses to social defeat was assessed using the conditioned defeat model. In the first experiment in this series of studies, peripheral administration of a nonpeptide, specific CRF_1 receptor antagonist (CP-154,526) had no effect on submissive/defensive behaviors displayed by previously defeated hamsters (Jasnow et al., 1999). The CRF_1 receptor antagonist did, however, block the ACTH response to defeat during testing (figure 13.2), indicating that the drug was effective in blocking CRF_1 receptors in the pituitary. This experiment also demonstrated that conditioned defeat is not dependent on the pituitary adrenal response. We have subsequently examined another specific CRF_1 receptor antagonist, R121,919 (K. L. Huhman, unpublished data), and this drug also failed to alter conditioned defeat at doses that were effective in blocking CRF_1 receptor binding in hamster brain (as determined by receptor autoradiography).

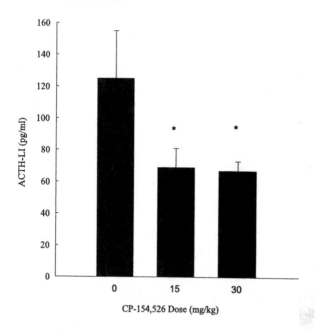

FIGURE 13.2 Plasma ACTH-like immunore-activity (ACTH-LI) in conditioned defeated hamsters that received an ip injection (0, 15, or 30 mg/kg) of CP-154,526, a nonpeptide CRF_1 receptor antagonist. Values are reported in means ± SEM of ACTH-LI. Animals that received either dose of CP-154,526 had a significant reduction in plasma ACTH-LI response compared to animals that received a vehicle control (*$p < .05$). From "Differential Effects of Two Corticotrophin-Releasing Factor Antagonists on Conditioned Defeat in Male Syrian Hamsters (*Mesocricetus auratus*)," by A. M. Jasnow, M. C. Banks, E. C. Owens, and K. L. Huhman, 1999, *Brain Research*, *846*, 122–128. Reprinted with permission from Elsevier.

In another experiment, we demonstrated that intra-cerebroventricular (icv) administration of the non-selective CRF receptor antagonist D-Phe $CRF_{(12-41)}$ attenuated submissive/defensive behaviors displayed by previously defeated animals when they were exposed to a nonaggressive stimulus animal (Figure 13.3). These data suggest that CRF is involved in modulating many of the physiological and behavioral responses to social defeat, possibly through its interaction with a CRF_2-like receptor. However, the specific anatomical sites respon-sible for these behavioral actions of CRF in conditioned defeat were not addressed by these initial experiments.

There is some evidence that the amygdala may be involved in the behavioral actions of CRF. As discussed earlier, it is well known that the amygdala plays a role in emotional responses to aversive stimuli (Davis, 1992a, 1997, 2000; LeDoux, 2000; Maren & Fanselow, 1996). In particular, the central amygdala has been implicated in coordinating the actions of CRF in some behavioral measures of fear and anxiety (Heinrichs et al., 1992; Rassnick, Heinrichs, Britton, & Koob, 1993; Swiergiel, Takahashi, & Kalin, 1993). The BNST also plays an important role in the behavioral effects of CRF. Infu-sion of CRF into the BNST significantly increases startle amplitude and foot shock-induced reinstatement of co-caine seeking, and CRF antagonists administered into the BNST block both of these responses (Erb & Stewart, 1999; Lee & Davis, 1997). In addition, lesions of the BNST block the ability of CRF given icv to enhance

startle (Lee & Davis, 1997). Interestingly, infusion of a CRF antagonist into the central amygdala in both of these studies had no effect on CRF-enhanced startle (Lee & Davis, 1997) or on foot-shock-induced reinstate-ment of cocaine seeking (Erb & Stewart, 1999). Davis and colleagues (Gewirtz et al., 1998; Lee & Davis, 1997) have found dissociations between the behavioral effects of CRF in the BNST and amygdala and have suggested that CRF in the BNST may be important in the modu-lation of responses to unconditioned or less predictable aversive events, whereas the amygdala may play a greater role in conditioned fear responses or the response to highly predictable aversive events (Walker & Davis, 1997b). Although some recent studies demonstrated that the BNST might be more important in the actions of CRF on behavioral responses to stress, the involvement of the amygdala cannot be discounted.

The BNST is a major target site for an ipsilateral CRF projection of the central amygdala (Sakanaka et al., 1986). Erb, Salmaso, Rodaros, and Stewart (2001) demonstrated that functional interruption of this pathway, with infusions of tetrodotoxin into the central amygdala on one side of the brain and infu-sions of a CRF antagonist into the contralateral BNST, could greatly attenuate foot shock-induced re-instatement of cocaine seeking. These data suggest that the CRF-containing pathway from the central amygdala to the BNST is involved in mediating the effects of CRF on foot shock-induced reinstatement of

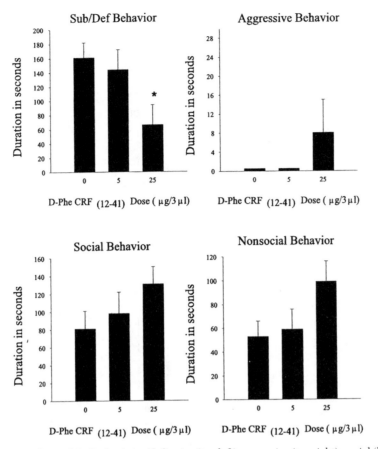

FIGURE 13.3 Duration (seconds) of submissive/defensive (top left), aggressive (top right), social (bottom left) and nonsocial (bottom right) behavior produced by CD hamsters that received an icv injection (0, 5, or 25 μg) of D-Phe CRF. No significant differences in the duration of aggressive, social, and nonsocial behaviors were detected. In contrast, the duration of submissive/defensive behavior was significantly lower in hamsters that received the 25-μg dose of D-Phe CRF (*$p < .05$). From "Differential Effects of Two Corticotrophin-Releasing Factor Antagonists on Conditioned Defeat in Male Syrian Hamsters (*Mesocricetus auratus*)," by A. M. Jasnow, M. C. Banks, E. C. Owens, and K. L. Huhman, 1999, *Brain Research, 846*, 122–128. Reprinted with permission from Elsevier.

cocaine seeking and may be involved in mediating behavioral responses to other stressors as well.

In light of this evidence, we next assessed whether the amygdala and BNST are important components of a neural circuit modulating conditioned defeat in male Syrian hamsters (Jasnow, Huhman, & Davis, 2004). First, we demonstrated that submissive behavior measured during testing was significantly reduced following local infusion of the CRF receptor antagonist D-Phe CRF$_{(12-41)}$ into the BNST (figure 13.4). In contrast, local infusion D-Phe CRF$_{(12-41)}$ into the central nucleus of the amygdala did not reduce conditioned defeat (figure 13.5). Next, we showed that animals with unilateral lesions of the central nucleus of the amygdala combined with local infusion of D-Phe CRF$_{(12-41)}$

into the contralateral BNST displayed greatly attenuated amounts of submissive behavior compared with sham-vehicle, sham-drug, and lesion-vehicle controls (figure 13.6). These data suggest that CRF may be acting within an ipsilateral neural circuit including a projection from the amygdala to the BNST that modulates behavioral responses to social defeat.

One of the questions remaining to be answered is whether CRF$_1$ and CRF$_2$ receptors have separate or overlapping functions in regard to behavioral responses to stressors, including social defeat. A large body of evidence certainly suggests that CRF$_1$ receptors play an important role in stress-induced behaviors. For instance, CRF$_1$ receptor knockout mice exhibit anxiolytic responses on a variety of behavioral tests, including

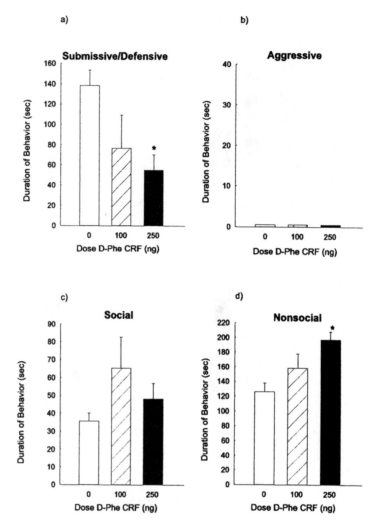

FIGURE 13.4 Total duration (mean ± *SEM* in seconds) of submissive/defensive (a), aggressive (b), social (c), and nonsocial (d) behavior displayed by defeated hamsters during a 5-min test with a nonaggressive intruder. Animals received a bilateral infusion of 0.0, 100, or 250 ng of D-Phe CRF$_{(12-41)}$ into the BNST immediately before testing. *Significantly different ($p < .05$) than vehicle control. From "Involvement of Central Amygdalar and Bed Nucleus of the Stria Terminalis Corticotropin Releasing Factor in Behavioral Responses to Social Defeat," by A. M. Jasnow, M. Davis, and K. L. Huhman, 2004, *Behavioral Neuroscience, 118*, 1052–1061. Copyright 2004 by the American Psychological Association. Reprinted with permission.

the open field, light-dark box, defensive-withdrawal, and elevated plus maze (Contarino et al., 1999; Smith et al., 1998; Timpl et al., 1998). These CRF$_1$ knockout mice also show reduced plasma ACTH and corticosterone levels following stress exposure (Smith et al., 1998; Timpl et al., 1998). Studies using CRF$_1$ receptor antagonists also indicate that this receptor subtype is involved in stress-induced anxiety. For example, administration of CRF$_1$ antagonists to rats produces anxiolytic responses, as measured on acoustic startle

(Schulz et al., 1996) and shock-induced freezing tests (Deak et al., 1999). Studies thus far in our laboratory, however, have not directly observed a role for CRF$_1$ receptors in conditioned defeat (Jasnow et al., 1999), suggesting that the behavioral change observed following social defeat in hamsters may be regulated, at least in part, through CRF$_2$ receptors.

The recent development of the selective CRF$_2$ receptor antagonist anti-sauvagine-30 (anti-Svg-30) has allowed for a more complete investigation of the function of CRF$_2$ in fear and anxiety (Higelin et al., 2001; Ruhmann, Bonk, Lin, Rosenfeld, & Spiess, 1998). In mice, intraseptal infusion of anti-Svg-30 has no effect on open arm activity in the elevated plus maze, but is effective in blocking anxiogenic effects produced by immobilization, as well as by administration of rat/human CRF (Radulovic, Ruhmann, Liepold, & Spiess, 1999). Relatedly, icv administration of anti-Svg-30 produces anxiolytic responses on conditioned freezing, elevated plus maze, and defensive-withdrawal tests in rats (Takahashi, Ho, Livanov, Graciani, & Arneric,

2001). Other studies have reported anxiolytic effects of CRF$_2$ receptor agonists (Risbrough, Hauger, Pelley-mounter, & Geyer, 2003). Thus, the data indicate that CRF$_2$ receptors are involved in modulating stress-induced behavior; however, their exact role remains to be elucidated. It may be that activation of CRF$_2$ receptors can result in either anxiolysis or anxiogenesis depending on what measures are used or where the receptors are activated (Penalva et al., 2002). We have used anti-Svg-30 to investigate the role CRF$_2$ receptors in conditioned defeat (Cooper & Huhman, 2004). In

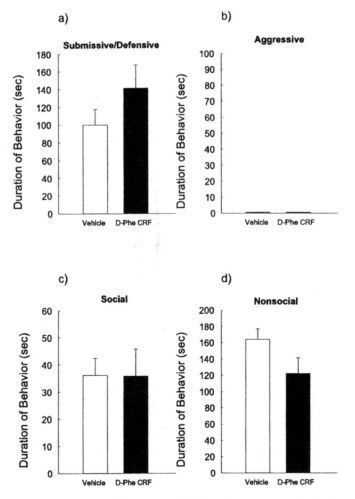

FIGURE 13.5 Total duration (mean ± *SEM*) of submissive/defensive (a), aggressive (b), social (c), and nonsocial (d) behavior displayed by defeated hamsters during a 5-min test with a nonaggressive intruder. Animals received a bilateral infusion of 250 ng of D-Phe CRF$_{(12-41)}$ or vehicle control into the central amygdala immediately before testing. There were no significant effects of the CRF receptor antagonist microinjected into the amygdala. From "Involvement of Central Amygdalar and Bed Nucleus of the Stria Terminalis Corticotropin Releasing Factor in Behavioral Responses to Social Defeat," by A. M. Jasnow, M. Davis, and K. L. Huhman, 2004, *Behavioral Neuroscience, 118,* 1052–1061. Copyright 2004 by the American Psychological Association. Reprinted with permission.

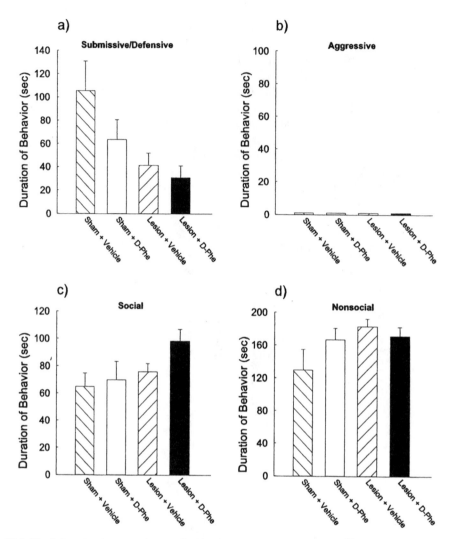

FIGURE 13.6 Total duration (mean ± *SEM*) of submissive/defensive (a), aggressive (b), social (c), and nonsocial (d) behavior displayed by defeated hamsters during a 5-min test with a nonaggressive intruder. Animals received either a unilateral electrolytic lesion of the central nucleus of the amygdala (CeA) or a sham lesion combined with infusions of D-Phe CRF$_{(12–41)}$ or vehicle into the BNST contralateral to the lesioned amygdala. Each of the treatments significantly decreased the duration of submissive/defensive behavior, with the combined amygdala lesion + contralateral D-Phe CRF$_{(12–41)}$ having the greatest effect. From "Involvement of Central Amygdalar and Bed Nucleus of the Stria Terminalis Corticotropin Releasing Factor in Behavioral Responses to Social Defeat," by A. M. Jasnow, M. Davis, and K. L. Huhman, 2004, *Behavioral Neuroscience, 118,* 1052–1061. Copyright 2004 by the American Psychological Association. Reprinted with permission.

previously defeated Syrian hamsters, we demonstrated that icv infusions of anti-Svg-30 significantly reduced the display of submissive/defensive behaviors in response to nonaggressive intruders compared to hamsters injected with vehicle (figure 13.7).

We have previously shown that the BNST rather than the central nucleus of the amygdala is the neuroanatomical location wherein CRF receptors, in least in part, regulate conditioned defeat; however we did

not determine which receptor subtype was responsible for this effect because we were infusing a nonselective CRF receptor antagonist. We next demonstrated that local infusion of anti-Svg-30 into the BNST reduces submissive/defensive behavior with a similar effect size as D-Phe CRF$_{(12–41)}$, suggesting that CRF$_2$ receptors within the BNST may play a role in the profound behavioral change observed in conditioned defeat (figure 13.8). Whereas this study does not rule out a role for

CRF$_1$ receptors in conditioned defeat, it highlights the involvement of CRF$_2$ receptors. It is important to note that both icv and local infusions of CRF antagonists reduce, but do not completely block, conditioned defeat, suggesting that additional neurotransmitter and/or neuromodulator systems are involved.

To conclude, CRF plays an important role in the regulation of behavioral responses to aversive stimuli (Deak et al., 1999; Dunn & Berridge, 1990; Fendt et al., 1997; Gray, 1993; Hammack et al., 2002; Heinrichs et al., 1992; Jasnow et al., 1999; Koob et al., 1993). Both the central amygdala and the BNST have been implicated in the actions of CRF on behavior (Erb & Stewart, 1999; Heinrichs et al., 1992; Lee & Davis, 1997; Rassnick et al., 1993; Swiergiel et al., 1993). It appears, however, that CRF receptors in the BNST, rather than the central nucleus of the amygdala, may be preferentially involved in the actions of CRF on several stress-induced behaviors, including CRF-enhanced startle, stress-induced reinstatement of cocaine seeking, and conditioned defeat (Lee & Davis, 1997; Erb & Stewart,

1999). Furthermore, CRF may be acting within an ipsilateral neural circuit that includes the amygdala and the BNST to modulate behavioral responses to social defeat. We are continuing our work to determine which CRF receptor subtypes mediate the actions of CRF on conditioned defeat in hamsters.

Conditioned Defeat: The Role of GABA and Glutamate in the Amygdala

As stated previously, the consistent ability of icv injections and local infusion of CRF receptor antagonists into the BNST to reduce, but not completely block, conditioned defeat suggest that additional neurotransmitter systems and neuroanatomical sites are involved in regulating conditioned defeat. Data from a number of studies discussed earlier suggest that both GABA and glutamate in the amygdala play an important role in regulating conditioned fear and defensive behavior.

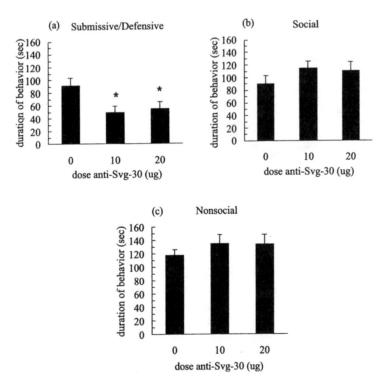

FIGURE 13.7 Total duration (mean ± *SEM*) of submissive/defensive (a), social (b), and nonsocial behavior (c) shown by previously defeated hamsters in a 5-min test with a nonaggressive intruder. None of the experimental animals displayed aggressive behavior during testing. Animals received icv antisauvagine-30 infusions of 0 µg (*n* = 11), 10 µg (*n* = 12), or 20 µg (*n* = 10) 30 min prior to testing. *Significantly different from vehicle control (*p* < .05).

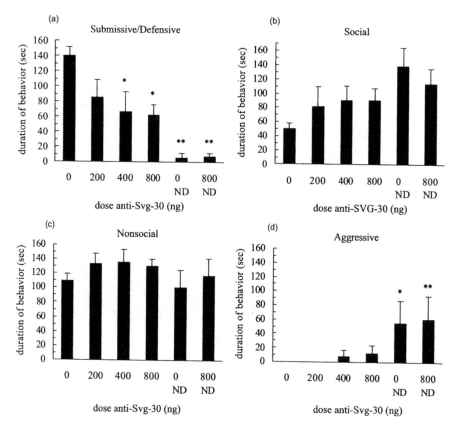

FIGURE 13.8 Total duration (mean ± *SEM*) of submissive/defensive (a), social (b), nonsocial (c), and aggressive behavior (d) shown by previously defeated or nondefeated (ND) hamsters in a 5-min test with a nonaggressive intruder. Previously defeated animals received a bilateral infusion of vehicle (200 nl of saline; $n = 10$) or antisauvagine-30 (200, 400, or 800 ng in 200 nl of saline; $n = 7, 7,$ and 13, respectively) in the BST 15 min prior to testing. Likewise, nondefeated animals received a bilateral infusion of vehicle (200 nl of saline; $n = 6$) or antisauvagine-30 (800 ng in 200 nl of saline; $n = 6$) in the BST 15 min prior to testing. *Significantly different from vehicle control in (a) and significantly different from vehicle control and 200 ng (d) $(p < .05)$; **significantly different from vehicle control and 200 ng $(p < .05)$.

In our laboratory, we tested the hypothesis that infusion of the GABA$_A$ agonist muscimol into the amygdala would block the acquisition and expression of conditioned defeat (Jasnow et al., 2001). Animals that received infusions of muscimol before defeat training displayed significantly less submissive/defensive behavior and significantly more social behavior when tested with a nonaggressive intruder compared with controls (figure 13.9). In our next experiment, bilateral infusions of muscimol into the amygdala immediately before previously defeated hamsters were exposed to a nonaggressive intruder again significantly decreased submissive/defensive behaviors when animals were paired with a nonaggressive intruder (figure 13.10)

We were able to demonstrate that muscimol's effects were not mediated by a change in the responsiveness of the subjects to the initial defeat, to altered sensitivity to painful stimuli, or to a change in the behavior of the aggressive trainers or nonaggressive stimulus animals. The results of this experiment are consistent with the finding that pretraining infusions of muscimol impair Pavlovian fear conditioning and provide the first evidence that the neural circuitry mediating conditioned fear in highly controlled, but largely artificial, models also appears to mediate stress-induced behavioral plasticity in more ecologically relevant models, such as conditioned defeat.

Substantial evidence implicates glutamate as a critical neurochemical signal involved in regulating several forms of fear conditioning. Infusion of the NMDA receptor antagonist AP5 blocks the acquisition, but not expression, of fear-potentiated startle to a visual cue (Miserendino et al., 1990) or an auditory cue (Campeau et al., 1992), as well as the acquisition of freezing to a contextual cue (Fanselow & Kim, 1994). In addition, infusion of non-NMDA glutamate antagonists into the amygdala blocks the expression of fear-potentiated startle to a visual or auditory cue (Kim et al., 1993; Walker & Davis, 1997a), as well as the facilitation of eyeblink conditioning by prior stress (Shors & Mathew, 1998). Collectively, these data strongly suggest that NMDA receptors are essential for plasticity to occur within the amygdala. Other investigations, however,

have demonstrated that NMDA receptors are necessary for normal synaptic transmission within the amygdala, suggesting that NMDA receptors could also be involved in the expression of fear learning. Consistent with this, a number of studies have observed that antagonism of NMDA receptors within the amygdala also blocks the expression of conditioned fear (Fendt, 2001; Kim, Fanselow, DeCola, & Landeira-Fernandez, 1992; Lee, Choi, & Kim, 2001; Lee & Kim, 1998; Maren, Aharonov, Stote, et al., 1996).

In another study, we examined whether bilateral infusion of the NMDA antagonist AP5 into the amygdala would block the acquisition and expression of conditioned defeat (Jasnow, Cooper, et al., 2004). Animals receiving bilateral infusions of AP5 into the amygdala immediately before being exposed to defeat

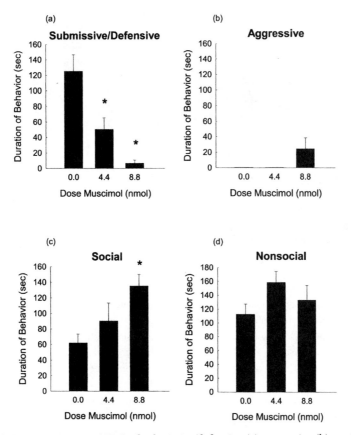

FIGURE 13.9 Total duration (mean ± *SEM*) of submissive/defensive (a), aggressive (b), social (c), and nonsocial (d) behavior displayed by defeated hamsters during a 5-min test with a nonaggressive intruder. Animals received a bilateral infusion of 0.0 ($n = 7$), 4.4 ($n = 5$), or 8.8 ($n = 7$) nmol of muscimol into the amygdala immediately before defeat training on the previous day. *Significantly different ($p < .05$) than vehicle control. From "Activation of GABA(A) Receptors in the Amygdala Blocks the Acquisition and Expression of Conditioned Defeat in Syrian Hamsters," by A. M. Jasnow and K. L. Huhman, 2001, *Brain Research, 920*, 142–150. Reprinted with permission from Elsevier.

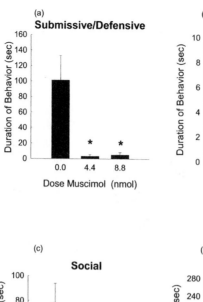
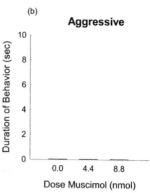
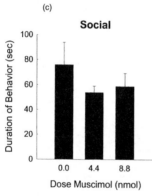
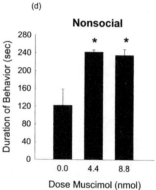

FIGURE 13.10 Total duration (mean ± *SEM*) of submissive/defensive (a), aggressive (b), social (c), and nonsocial (d) behavior displayed by defeated hamsters during a 5-min test with a nonaggressive intruder. Animals received a bilateral infusion of 0.0 ($n = 5$), 4.4 ($n = 5$), or 8.8 ($n = 6$) nmol of muscimol into the amygdala immediately before the 5-min testing session. *Significantly different ($p < .05$) than vehicle control. From "Activation of GABA(A) Receptors in the Amygdala Blocks the Acquisition and Expression of Conditioned Defeat in Syrian Hamsters," by A. M. Jasnow and K. L. Huhman, 2001, *Brain Research, 920,* 142–150. Reprinted with permission from Elsevier.

(acquisition experiment) displayed significantly less submissive/defensive behavior than did animals receiving vehicle control when they were later tested with a nonaggressive intruder (figure 13.11). In addition, infusion of AP5 into the amygdala immediately before testing (expression experiment) with a nonaggressive intruder also significantly reduced the display of submissive/defensive behavior (figure 13.12). Injection of AP5 4 hr after the initial defeat did not alter conditioned defeat observed the next day.

We are currently examining if ifenprodil, a drug that selectively blocks one of the subunits of the NMDA receptor and thus blocks synaptic plasticity but not constitutive synaptic transmission, will block the acquisition, but not expression, of conditioned defeat. The preliminary data indicate that ifenprodil blocks acquisition, but not expression of conditioned defeat.

Data from these experiments suggest that conditioned defeat is dependent, at least in part, upon the presence of a functional amygdala. Disruption of neurotransmission within the amygdala has profound effects on both the acquisition and expression of conditioned defeat. Infusion of the $GABA_A$ agonist muscimol or the NMDA receptor antagonist AP5 into the amygdala greatly attenuates or blocks the submissive/defensive behavior that characterizes conditioned defeat. It is interesting to note, however, that territorial aggression, which is readily exhibited by nondefeated hamsters in this same situation, is not restored in previously defeated hamsters following treatment with muscimol, AP5, or CRF antagonists. This finding suggests that the circuits controlling submissive and defensive behavior are separate from those mediating aggression and that pharmacological treatments can act on one without affecting the other. It also appears that the broad effect of the initial defeat on both systems (i.e., aggression is blocked while submission is facilitated) is not similarly affected by the pharmacological treatments. In other words, it appears that there is some "savings" of the effect of defeat on aggression that would be missed if only submission and defense were measured.

Conditioned Defeat: The Role of the cAMP Response Element Binding Protein (CREB) in the Amygdala

While the amygdala is widely accepted as an essential neural structure in the formation and perhaps storage of fear memories, the synaptic and molecular processes that

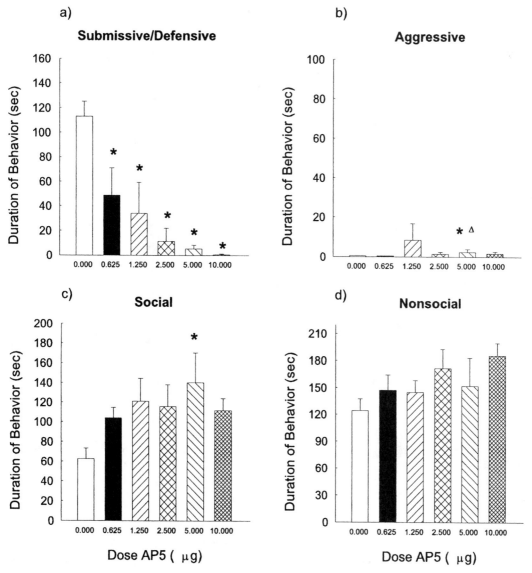

FIGURE 13.11 Total duration (mean ± SEM) of submissive/defensive (a), aggressive (b), social (c), and nonsocial (d) behavior displayed by defeated hamsters during a 5-min test with a nonaggressive intruder 24 hrs earlier. Animals received a bilateral infusion of 0.0, 0.625, 1.25, 2.5, 5.0, or 10 μg of AP5 into the basolateral amygdala immediately before being defeated for 15 min. *Significantly different ($p < .05$) than vehicle control; (Δ) significantly different ($p < .05$) than 0.625 μg. From "N-Methyl-D-aspartate Receptors in the Amygdala Are Necessary for the Acquisition and Expression of Conditioned Defeat," by A. M. Jasnow, M. A. Cooper and K. L. Huhman, 2004, *Neuroscience, 123*, 625–634. Reprinted with permission from Elsevier.

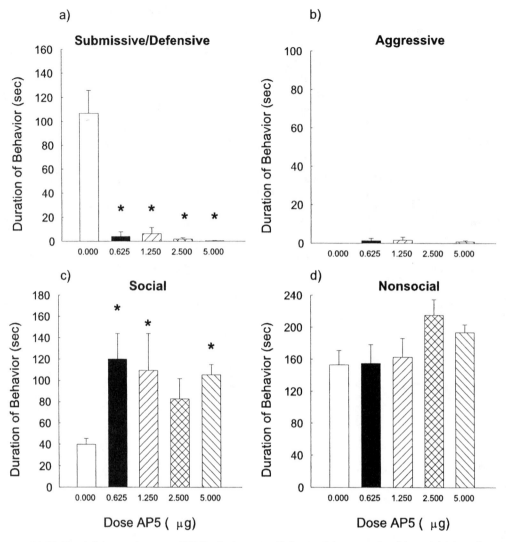

FIGURE 13.12 Total duration (mean ± *SEM*) of submissive/defensive (a), aggressive (b), social (c), and nonsocial (d) behavior displayed by defeated hamsters during a 5-min test with a nonaggressive intruder. Animals received a bilateral infusion of 0.0, 0.625, 1.25, 2.5, or 5.0 μg of AP5 into the basolateral amygdala immediately before being tested with a nonaggressive intruder for 5 min. *Significantly different ($p < .05$) than vehicle control. From "N-Methyl-D-aspartate Receptors in the Amygdala Are Necessary for the Acquisition and Expression of Conditioned Defeat," by A. M. Jasnow, M. A. Cooper and K. L. Huhman, 2004, *Neuroscience, 123,* 625–634. Reprinted with permission from Elsevier.

underlie this learning are not as well understood. A leading candidate for the cellular mechanism mediating learning, including fear learning, is long-term potentiation (LTP), a long-lasting, NMDA-dependent form of synaptic plasticity (Bliss & Collingridge, 1993; Huang & Kandel, 1998; Maren, 1999; Maren & Fanselow, 1995). LTP is observed in the amygdala, as well as in each of the sensory afferent pathways conveying essential information to the amygdala (Huang & Kandel, 1998; Huang,

Martin, & Kandel, 2000; Rogan & LeDoux, 1995). LTP and fear conditioning are RNA (Bailey, Kim, Sun, Thompson, & Helmstetter, 1999) and protein synthesis dependent (Davis & Squire, 1984; Schafe & LeDoux, 2000) processes that require cAMP-dependent protein kinase and extracellular-regulated kinase/mitogen-activated protein kinase, both of which are thought to translocate to the cell nucleus, where they activate transcription factors such as CREB (for a review see Schafe,

Nader, Blair, & LeDoux, 2001). CREB, when phosphorylated, induces the transcription of CREB-mediated genes (such as early growth response gene 1 (ERG1 or zif286) (Malkani & Rosen, 2001) and the subsequent translation of proteins that are thought to mediate the plasticity underlying LTP. The synthesis of CREB is induced in the amygdala and hippocampus by fear conditioning (Impey et al., 1998), and mice with a targeted mutation of CREB exhibit impairments in fear conditioning (Bourtchuladze, Frenguelli, Cioffi, Schutz, & Silvia, 1994). Recently, Josselyn and colleagues (2001) have demonstrated that increasing CREB levels in the basolateral amygdala of rats using herpes simplex virus (HSV) vector-mediated gene transfer enhances long-term memory formation in a fear-potentiated startle task. Together, these data support the hypothesis that the CREB family of proteins is important in the formation of long-term memory and behavioral plasticity.

Although a large number of studies have investigated the mechanisms underlying aversive learning tasks, very little is known about the mechanisms underlying learning in a social context. Given that social conflict is one of the most pervasive forms of stress experienced by most animal species, including humans, we examined the hypothesis that increased CREB levels within the basolateral amygdala would stimulate the acquisition of conditioned defeat (Jasnow, Huhman, Bartness, & Demas, 2002). In these experiments, we used a defeat procedure involving a suboptimal, 5-min defeat that generally does not produce a robust change in social behavior. Animals were infused with HSV vectors encoding the CREB protein or a control protein (β-galactosidase) into the basolateral amygdala. Other control subjects received an HSV-CREB infusion into a nearby control region (the caudate nucleus). Animals infused with HSV-CREB into the basolateral amygdala before testing displayed increased submissive/defensive behavior compared with animals infused with HSV-LacZ in the basolateral amygdala or animals infused with HSV-CREB within the caudate nucleus (figure 13.13).

If CREB is a transcription factor important for the synthesis of proteins necessary for memory formation, then overexpression of CREB should not affect the expression of conditioned defeat. To examine whether increasing CREB levels within the amygdala affects the expression of submissive/defensive behavior associated with conditioned defeat, we exposed animals to the same 5-min social defeat session described above. One day following defeat, HSV-CREB or HSV-LacZ was infused into the basolateral complex of the amygdala. Two days later, animals were tested in their own home cage, with a nonaggressive intruder. No differences were observed in submissive/defensive behavior between animals receiving HSV-CREB and animals receiving HSV-LacZ (figure 13.14).

The present data provide some of the first evidence that increasing CREB levels within a specific brain region enhances memory formation within a social context. These data indicate that increasing CREB levels specifically within the basolateral complex of the amygdala facilitates the acquisition, but not the expression, of conditioned defeat. Thus, CREB may be involved in aversive learning within a social context. In addition, overexpression of CREB within the basolateral amygdala has no effect on the production of submissive/defensive behaviors, themselves, but appears to be specifically involved in the memory formation and not the memory retrieval of social defeat.

Conclusions

Our work has shown that conditioned defeat in Syrian hamsters is elicited in most males following a single or multiple exposures to social defeat. Conditioned defeat is not dependent on the context in which the initial defeat occurred, because animals are defeated in another hamster's cage and then they are tested their own home cages. Conditioned defeat is also not dependent on the subject being paired with the same opponent that initially defeated it. In fact, we test animals for conditioned defeat with a smaller, nonaggressive opponent that the subject would normally be expected to attack. This striking behavioral change is long lasting in many hamsters and is often characterized by a high frequency and duration of fleeing behavior.

We initially began to explore the neurobiological mechanisms of conditioned defeat by adopting the working hypothesis that conditioned defeat is an ecologically relevant example of fear conditioning. This hypothesis has turned out to be productive. We have demonstrated that many brain areas (e.g., the amygdala and the BNST) and neurochemical signals (e.g., glutamate, GABA, CRF, and CREB) that have been shown to be important in fear conditioning in artificial, but highly controllable, situations are also involved in a similar fashion in the mediation or modulation of conditioned defeat. We are continuing to define the neural circuitry and neurochemical signals that lead to

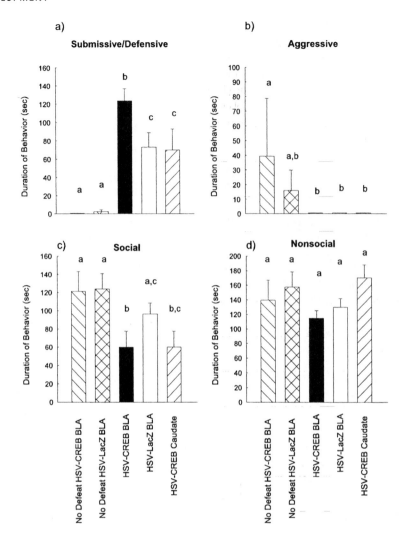

FIGURE 13.13 Effect of infusion of HSV vectors into the basolateral amygdala and caudate nucleus on total duration (mean ± SEM) of submissive/defensive (a), aggressive (b), social (c), and nonsocial (d) behavior displayed by defeated hamsters during a 5-min test with a nonaggressive intruder. Animals received an infusion of either HSV-CREB or HSV-LacZ into the basolateral complex of the amygdala or HSV-CREB into the caudate nucleus 2 days before being defeated. *Significantly different ($p < .05$) than animals receiving HSV-LacZ in the amygdala and HSV-CREB in the caudate. Bars with dissimilar letters are significantly different from one another.

conditioned defeat in both male and female Syrian hamsters.

It is interesting to speculate on the possible adaptive significance of conditioned defeat. One might think that the behavior could actually be maladaptive if a defeated hamster subsequently flees from any conspecific it encounters. On the other hand, conditioned defeat might simply reflect a change in coping strat-

egy by a hamster that learns that it is a poor fighter. This might be an effective way for such an animal to avoid physical injury. We have examined whether there is any difference in sexual behavior between defeated and nondefeated hamsters when they are subsequently exposed to a receptive female, but we have not observed any changes in sexual behavior in terms of latencies or frequencies of mounting, intromission, or ejaculation, supporting the idea that conditioned defeat might be an effective coping strategy for some males.

Dominance and submission appear to be controlled by two separate neural circuits that are mutually inhibitory. In general, offensive aggression is not emitted by a submissive animal, and submissive behavior is not emitted by a dominant animal. We have shown, however, that manipulations that decrease conditioned defeat, as evidenced by a decrease in submissive behavior produced in response to a nonaggressive intruder, do not necessarily restore typical territorial aggression. Instead, it appears that social defeat, to some extent, affects the aggressive and submissive systems independently (thus, they are not "two sides of the same coin"). It is important to define the mechanism whereby a manipulation,

such as a blockade of NMDA receptors, can affect the memory of defeat as assessed by a decrease in submissive and defensive behavior, but can appear to leave intact the "memory" that inhibits territorial aggression.

References

Adolphs, R., & Tranel, D. (2001). Emotion, recognition, and the human amygdala. In J. P. Aggleton (Ed.), *The amygdala: A functional analysis* (pp. 587–630). New York: Oxford University Press.

Aggleton, J. P., & Mishkin, M. (1985). Mamillary-body lesions and visual recognition in monkeys. *Experimental Brain Research*, 58, 190–197.

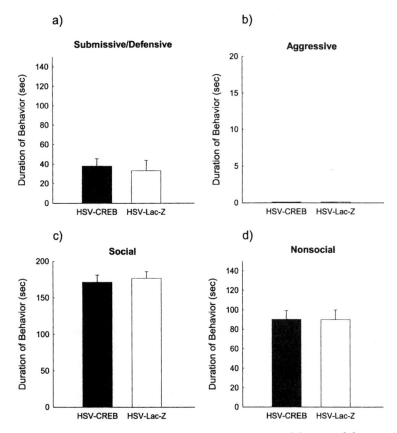

FIGURE 13.14 Effect of infusion of HSV vectors into the basolateral amygdala on total duration (mean ± *SEM*) of submissive/defensive (a), aggressive (b), social (c), and nonsocial (d) behavior displayed by defeated hamsters during a 5-min test with a nonaggressive intruder. Animals received infusion of either HSV-CREB or HSV-LacZ into the basolateral complex of the amygdala 2 days before being tested with a nonaggressive intruder.

Agrawal, P., Mayeaux, D. J., Johnston, R. E., & Adkins-Regan, E. (2000). Combined lesions of basolateral and central amygdala eliminate avoidance of opponent after social defeat in male hamsters. *Society for Neuroscience Abstracts, 26,* 2021.

Albeck, D. S., McKittrick, C. R., Blanchard, D. C., Blandchard, R. J., Nikulina, J., McEwan, B. S., et al. (1997). Chronic social stress alters levels of corticotropin-releasing factor and arginine vasopressin mRNA in rat brain. *Journal of Neuroscience, 17,* 4895–4903.

Albers, H. E., Huhman, K. L., & Meisel, R. L. (2002). Hormonal basis of social conflict and communication. In D. W. Pfaff, A. P. Arnold, A. M. Etgen, S. E. Fahrbach, & R. T. Rubin (Eds.), *Hormones, brain and behavior* (pp. 393–433). San Diego: Academic Press.

Alheid, G. F., & Heimer, L. (1988). New perspectives in basal forebrain organization of special relevance for neuropsychiatric disorders: The striatopallidal, amygdaloid, and corticopetal components of substantia innominata. *Neuroscience, 27,* 1–39.

Applegate, C. D., Kapp, B. S., Underwood, M. D., & McNall, C. L. (1983). Autonomic and somatomotor effects of amygdala central nucleus stimulation in awake rabbits. *Physiology and Behavior, 1983,* 353.

Bailey, D. J., Kim, J. J., Sun, W., Thompson, R. F., & Helmstetter, F. J. (1999). Acquisition of fear conditioning in rats requires the synthesis of mRNA in the amygdala. *Behavioral Neuroscience, 113,* 276–282.

Bandler, R. (1988). Brain mechanisms of aggression as revealed by electrical and chemical stimulation: Suggestion of a central role for the midbrain periaqueductal grey region. *Progress in Psychobiology and Physiological Psychology, 13,* 67–154.

Biondi, M., & Picardi, A. (1999). Psychological stress and neuroendocrine function in humans: The last two decades of research. *Psychotherapy and Psychosomatics, 68,* 114–150.

Bjorkqvist, K. (2001). Social defeat as a stressor in humans. *Physiology and Behavior, 73,* 435–442.

Blanchard, D. C., Spencer, R. L., Weiss, S. M., Blanchard, R. J., McEwen, B., & Sakai, R. R. (1995). Visible burrow system as a model of chronic social stress: Behavioral and neuroendocrine correlates. *Psychoneuroendocrinology, 20,* 117–134.

Blanchard, R. J., & Blanchard, D. C. (1989). Antipredator defensive behaviors in a visible burrow system. *Journal of Comparative Psychology, 103,* 70–82.

Blanchard, R. J., Wall, P. M., & Blanchard, D. C. (2003). Problems in the study of rodent aggression. *Hormones and Behavior, 44,* 161–170.

Bliss, T. V., & Collingridge, G. L. (1993). A synaptic model of memory: Long-term potentiation in the hippocampus. *Nature, 361,* 31–39.

Bourtchuladze, R., Frenguelli, B., Cioffi, D., Schutz, G., & Silvia, A. J. (1994). Deficient long-term memory in mice with a targeted mutation of the cAMP responsive element-binding protein. *Cell, 79,* 59–68.

Brain, P. F. (1972). Effects of isolation/grouping on endocrine function and fighting behavior in male and female golden hamsters. (*Mesocricetus auratus* Waterhouse). *Behavioral Biology, 7,* 349–357.

Bremner, J. D., Krystal, J. H., Southwick, S. M., & Charney, D. S. (1996). Noradrenergic mechanisms in stress and anxiety: I. Preclinical studies. *Synapse, 23,* 28–38.

Britton, D. R., Varela, M., Garcia, A., & Rosenthal, M. (1986). Dexamethasone suppresses pituitary–adrenal but not behavioral effects of centrally administered CRF. *Life Sciences, 38,* 211–216.

Brown, M. R., & Fisher, L. A. (1983). Central nervous system effects of corticotropin releasing factor in the dog. *Brain Research, 280,* 75–79.

Brown, M. R., Fisher, L. A., Rivier, J., Spiess, J., Rivier, C., & Vale, W. (1982). Corticotropin-releasing factor: Effects on the sympathetic nervous system and oxygen consumption. *Life Sciences, 30,* 207–210.

Bunnell, B. N., Sodetz, F. J., Jr., & Shalloway, D. I. (1970). Amygdaloid lesions and social behavior in the golden hamster. *Physiology and Behavior, 5,* 153–161.

Campeau, S., & Davis, M. (1995). Involvement of the central nucleus and basolateral complex of the amygdala in fear conditioning measured with fear-potentiated startle in rats trained concurrently with auditory and visual conditioned stimuli. *Journal of Neuroscience, 15,* 2301–2311.

Campeau, S., Miserendino, M. J., & Davis, M. (1992). Intra-amygdala infusion of the N-methyl-D-aspartate receptor antagonist AP5 blocks acquisition but not expression of fear-potentiated startle to an auditory conditioned stimulus. *Behavioral Neuroscience, 106,* 569–574.

Carere, C., Welink, D., Drent, P. J., Koolhaas, J. M., & Groothuis, T. G. (2001). Effect of social defeat in a territorial bird (*Parus major*) selected for different coping styles. *Physiology and Behavior, 73,* 427–433.

Cecchi, M., Khoshbouei, H., Javors, M., & Morilak, D. A. (2002). Modulatory effects of norepinephrine in the lateral bed nucleus of the stria terminalis on behavioral and neuroendocrine responses to acute stress. *Neuroscience, 112,* 13–21.

Chalmers, D. T., Lovenberg, T. W., & De Souza, E. B. (1995). Localization of novel corticotropin-releasing factor receptor (CRF$_2$) mRNA expression to specific subcortical nuclei in rat brain: Comparison with CRF1 receptor mRNA expression. *Journal of Neuroscience, 15,* 6340–6350.

Chang, C. P., Pearse, R. V., II, O'Connel, S., & Rosenfeld, M. G. (1993). Identification of a seven transmembrane helix receptor for corticotropin-releasing factor and sauvagine in mammalian brain. *Neuron, 11,* 1187–1195.

Chen, R., Lewis, K. A., Perrin, M. H., & Vale, W. W. (1993). Expression cloning of a human corticotropin-releasing factor receptor. *Proceedings of the National Academy of Sciences USA, 90,* 8967–8971.

Contarino, A., Dellu, F., Koob, G. F., Smith, G. W., Lee, K. F., Vale, W., et al. (1999). Reduced anxiety-like and cognitive performance in mice lacking the corticotropin-releasing factor receptor 1. *Brain Research, 835,* 1–9.

Cooper, M. A., & Huhman, K. L. (2004). *Corticotropin-releasing hormone type 2 (CRH2) receptors in the bed nucleus of the stria terminalis modulate conditioned defeat in male Syrian hamsters.* Unpublished manuscript.

Cousens, G., & Otto, T. (1998). Both pre- and posttraining excitotoxic lesions of the basolateral amygdala abolish the expression of olfactory and contextual fear conditioning. *Behavioral Neuroscience, 112,* 1092–1103.

D'Amato, F. R. (1988). Effects of male social status on reproductive success and on behavior in mice (*Mus musculus*). *Journal of Comparative Psychology, 102,* 146–151.

Dautzenberg, F. M., Wille, S., Lohmann, R., & Spiess, J. (1997). Identification of two corticotropin-releasing factor receptors with high ligand selectivity from *Xenopus laevis:* Unusual pharmacology of type 1 receptor. *Journal of Neurochemistry, 69,* 1640–1649.

Davis, H. P., & Squire, L. R. (1984). Protein synthesis and memory: A review. *Psychological Bulletin, 96,* 518–559.

Davis, M. (1992a). The role of the amygdala in fear and anxiety. *Annual Review of Neuroscience, 15,* 353–375.

Davis, M. (1992b). The role of the amygdala in fear-potentiated startle: Implications for animal models of anxiety. *Trends in Pharmacological Science, 13,* 35–41.

Davis, M. (1997). Neurobiology of fear responses: The role of the amygdala. *Neuropsychiatry and Clinical Neuroscience, 9,* 382–402.

Davis, M. (2000). The role of the amygdala in conditioned and unconditioned fear and anxiety. In J. P. Aggleton (Ed.), *The amygdala* (pp. 213–287). Oxford: Oxford University Press.

Davis, M. (2001). The role of the amygdala in conditioned and unconditioned fear and anxiety. In J. P. Aggleton (Ed.), *The amygdala: A functional analysis* (pp. 213–288). New York: Oxford University Press.

Deak, T., Nguyen, K. T., Ehrlich, A. L., Watkins, L. R., Spencer, R. L., Maier, S. F., et al. (1999). The impact of the nonpeptide corticotropin-releasing hormone antagonist antalarmin on behavioral and endocrine responses to stress. *Endocrinology, 140,* 79–86.

Delville, Y., Melloni, R. H., Jr., & Ferris, C. F. (1998). Behavioral and neurobiological consequences of social subjugation during puberty in golden hamsters. *Journal of Neuroscience, 18,* 2667–2672.

Dunn, A. J., & Berridge, C. W. (1990). Physiological and behavioral responses to corticotropin-releasing factor administration: Is CRF a mediator of anxiety or stress responses? *Brain Research. Brain Research Reviews, 15,* 71–100.

Eaves, M., Thatcher-Britton, K., Rivier, J., Vale, W., & Koob, G. F. (1985). Effects of corticotropin releasing factor on locomotor activity in hypophysectomized rats. *Peptides, 6,* 923–926.

Erb, S., Salmaso, N., Rodaros, D., & Stewart, J. (2001). A role for the CRF-containing pathway from central nucleus of the amygdala to bed nucleus of the stria terminalis in the stress-induced reinstatement of cocaine seeking in rats. *Psychopharmacology, 158,* 360–365.

Erb, S., & Stewart, J. (1999). A role for the bed nucleus of the stria terminalis, but not the amygdala, in the effects of corticotropin-releasing factor on stress-induced reinstatement of cocaine seeking. *Journal of Neuroscience, 19,* RC35.

Fanselow, M. S. (1991). The midbrain periaqueductal gray as a coordinator of action in response to fear and anxiety. In A. Depaulis & R. Bandler (Eds.), *The midbrain periaqueductal gray matter: Functional, anatomical and neurochemical organization* (pp. 151–173). New York: Plenum.

Fanselow, M. S., & Kim, J. J. (1994). Acquisition of contextual Pavlovian fear conditioning is blocked by application of an NMDA receptor antagonist D,L-2-amino-5-phosphonovaleric acid to the basolateral amygdala. *Behavioral Neuroscience, 108,* 210–212.

Faruzzi, A. N., & Huhman, K. L. (2002). The role of corticotropin releasing hormone in behavioral responses to defeat in Syrian hamsters. *Society for Neuroscience Abstracts, 28.*

Feldman, S.. & Weidenfeld . J. (1998). The excitatory effects of the amygdala on hypothalamic norepinephrine, serotonin, and CRF-41. *Brain Research Bulletin, 45,* 389–393.

Fendt, M. (2001). Injections of the NMDA receptor antagonist aminophosphonopentanoic acid into the lateral nucleus of the amygdala block the expression of fear-potentiated startle and freezing. *Journal of Neuroscience, 21,* 4111–4115.

Fendt, M., Koch, M., & Schnitzler, H. U. (1994). Lesions of the central gray block the sensitization of the acoustic startle response in rats. *Brain Research, 661,* 163–173.

Fendt, M., Koch, M., & Schnitzler, H. U. (1997). Corticotropin-releasing factor in the caudal pontine reticular nucleus mediates the expression of fear-potentiated startle in the rat. *European Journal of Neuroscience, 9,* 299–305.

Fleshner, M., Laudenslager, M. L., Simons, L., & Maier, S. F. (1989). Reduced serum antibodies associated with social defeat in rats. *Physiology and Behavior, 45,* 1183–1187.

Floody, O. R., & Pfaff, D. W. (1977). Aggressive behavior in female hamsters: The hormonal basis for fluctuations in female aggressiveness correlated with estrous state. *Journal of Comparative and Physiological Psychology, 91,* 443–464.

Flugge, G., Kramer, M., Rensing, S., & Fuchs, E. (1998). 5HT1A-receptors and behaviour under chronic stress: Selective counteraction by testosterone. *European Journal of Neuroscience, 10,* 2685–2693.

Fox, H. E., White, S. A., Kao, M. H., & Fernald, R. D. (1997). Stress and dominance in a social fish. *Journal of Neuroscience, 17,* 6463–6469.

Fuchs, E., & Flugge, G. (2002). Social stress in tree shrews: Effects on physiology, brain function, and behavior of subordinate individuals. *Pharmacology, Biochemistry and Behavior, 73,* 247–258.

Galeno, T. M., & Brody, M. J. (1983). Hemodynamic responses to amygdaloid stimulation in spontaneously hypersensitive rats. *American Journal of Physiology, 245,* R281–R286.

Gallagher, M. (2001). The amygdala and associative learning. In J. P. Aggleton (Ed.), *The amygdala: A functional analysis* (pp. 311–330). New York: Oxford University Press.

Garbe, C. M. & Kemble, E. D. (1994). Effects of prior agonistic experience on risk assessment and approach behavior evoked by familiar or unfamiliar conspecific odors. *Aggressive Behavior, 20,* 143–149.

Gewirtz, J. C., McNish, K. A., & Davis, M. (1998). Lesions of the bed nucleus of the stria terminalis block sensitization of the acoustic startle reflex produced by repeated stress, but not fear-potentiated startle. *Progress in Neuro-Psychopharmacology and Biological Psychiatry, 22,* 625–648.

Graeff, F. G. (1994). Neuroanatomy and neurotransmitter regulation of defensive behaviors and related emotions in mammals. *Brazilian Journal of Medical and Biological Research, 27,* 811–829.

Grant, E. C., & Mackintosh, J. H. (1962). A comparison of the social postures of some common laboratory rodents. *Behaviour, 21,* 246–251.

Gray, T. S. (1993). Amygdaloid CRF pathways. Role in autonomic, neuroendocrine, and behavioral responses to stress. *Annals of the New York Academy of Science, 697,* 53–60.

Gray, T. S., Carney, M. E., & Magnusun, D. J. (1989). Direct projections from the central amygdaloid nucleus to the hypothalamic paraventricular nucleus: Possible role in stress-induced adrenocorticotropin release. *Neuroendocrinology, 50,* 433–446.

Gray, T. S., & Magnuson, D. J. (1992). Peptide immunoreactive neurons in the amygdala and the bed nucleus of the stria terminalis project to the midbrain central gray in the rat. *Peptides, 13,* 451–460.

Hammack, S. E., Richey, K. J., Schmid, M. J., LoPresti, M. L., Watkins, L. R., & Maier, S. F. (2002). The role of corticotropin-releasing hormone in the dorsal raphe nucleus in mediating the behavioral consequences of uncontrollable stress. *Journal of Neuroscience, 22,* 1020–1026.

Heinrichs, S. C., Pich, E. M., Miczek, K. A., Britton, K. T., & Koob, G. F. (1992). Corticotropin-releasing factor antagonist reduces emotionality in socially defeated rats via direct neurotropic action. *Brain Research, 581,* 190–197.

Helmstetter, F. J. (1992). Contribution of the amygdala to learning and performance of conditional fear. *Physiology and Behavior, 51,* 1271–1276.

Helmstetter, F. J., & Bellgowan, P. S. (1994). Effects of muscimol applied to the basolateral amygdala on acquisition and expression of contextual fear conditioning in rats. *Behavioral Neuroscience, 108,* 1005–1009.

Herman, J. P., & Cullinan, W. E. (1997). Neurocircuitry of stress: Central control of the hypothalamo-pituitary-adrenocortical axis. *Trends in Neurosciences, 20,* 78–84.

Higelin, J., Py-Lang, G., Paternoster, C., Ellis, G. J., Patel, A., & Dautzenberg, F. M. (2001). 125I-Antisauvagine-30: A novel and specific high-affinity radioligand for the characterization of corticotropin-releasing factor type 2 receptors. *Neuropharmacology, 40,* 114–122.

Hitchcock, J., & Davis, M. (1986). Lesions of the amygdala, but not of the cerebellum or red nucleus, block conditioned fear as measured with the potentiated startle paradigm. *Behavioral Neuroscience, 100,* 11–22.

Hitchcock, J. M., & Davis, M. (1991). Efferent pathway of the amygdala involved in conditioned fear as measured with the fear-potentiated startle paradigm. *Behavioral Neuroscience, 105,* 826–842.

Hsu, D. T., Chen, F. L., Takahashi, L. K., & Kalin, N. H. (1998). Rapid stress-induced elevations in corticotropin-releasing hormone mRNA in rat central amygdala nucleus and hypothalamic paraventricular nucleus: An in situ hybridization analysis. *Brain Research, 788,* 305–310.

Huang, Y. Y., & Kandel, E. R. (1998). Postsynaptic induction and PKA-dependent expression of LTP in the lateral amygdala. *Neuron, 21,* 169–178.

Huang, Y. Y., Martin, K. C., & Kandel, E. R. (2000). Both protein kinase A and mitogen-activated protein kinase are required in the amygdala for the macromolecular synthesis-dependent late phase of long-term potentiation. *Journal of Neuroscience, 20,* 6317–6325.

Huhman, K. L., Bunnell, B. N., Mougey, E. H., & Meyerhoff, J. L. (1990). Effects of social conflict on POMC-derived peptides and glucocorticoids in male golden hamsters. *Physiology and Behavior, 47,* 949–956.

Huhman, K. L., Moore, T. O., Ferris, C. F., Mougey, E. H., & Meyerhoff, J. L. (1991). Acute and repeated exposure to social conflict in male golden hamsters: Increases in plasma POMC-peptides and cortisol and decreases in plasma testosterone. *Hormones and Behavior, 25,* 206–216.

Huhman, K. L., Moore, T. O., Mougey, E. H., & Meyerhoff, J. L. (1992). Hormonal responses to fighting in hamsters: Separation of physical and psychological causes. *Physiology and Behavior, 51,* 1083–1086.

Huhman, K. L., Mougey, E. H., Moore, T. O., & Meyerhoff, J. L. (1995). Stressors, including social conflict, decrease plasma prolactin in male golden hamsters. *Hormones and Behavior, 29,* 581–592.

Huhman, K. L., Solomon, M. B., Janicki, M., Harmon, A. C., Lin, S. M., Israel, J. E., et al. (2003). Conditioned defeat in male and female Syrian hamsters. *Hormones and Behavior, 44,* 293–299.

Impey, S., Smith, D. M., Obrietan, K., Donahue, R., Wade, C., & Storm, D. R. (1998). Stimulation of cAMP response element (CRE)-mediated transcription during contextual learning. *Nature Neuroscience, 1,* 595–601.

Jasnow, A. M., Banks, M. C., Owens, E. C., & Huhman, K. L. (1999). Differential effects of two corticotropin-releasing factor antagonists on conditioned defeat in male Syrian hamsters (*Mesocricetus auratus*). *Brain Research, 846,* 122–128.

Jasnow, A. M., Cooper, M. A., & Huhman, K. L. (2004). N-methyl-D-aspartate receptors in the amygdala are necessary for the acquisition and expression of conditioned defeat. *Neuroscience, 123,* 625–634.

Jasnow, A. M., Drazen, D. L., Huhman, K. L., Nelson, R. J., & Demas, G. E. (2001). Acute and chronic social defeat suppresses humoral immunity of male Syrian hamsters (*Mesocricetus auratus*). *Hormones and Behavior, 40,* 428–433.

Jasnow, A. M., & Huhman, K. L. (2001). Activation of GABA(A) receptors in the amygdala blocks the acquisition and expression of conditioned defeat in Syrian hamsters. *Brain Research, 920,* 142–150.

Jasnow, A. M., Huhman, K. L., Bartness, T. J., & Demas, G. E. (2002). Short days and exogenous melatonin increase aggression of male Syrian hamsters (*Mesocricetus auratus*). *Hormones and Behavior, 42,* 13–20.

Jasnow, A. M., Huhman, K. L., & Davis, M. (2004). A corticotropin-releasing hormone pathway from the central amygdala to the bed nucleus of the stria terminalis involved in behavioral responses to social defeat. Unpublished manuscript.

Jasnow, A. M., Shi, C., Israel, J. E., Davis, M., & Huhman, K. L. (2002). Overexpression of CREB within the amygdala facilitates the acquisition of conditioned defeat. *Society for Neuroscience Abstracts, 28.*

Jellestad, F. K., Markowska, A., Bakke, H. K., & Walther, B. (1986). Behavioral effects after ibotenic acid, 6-OHDA and electrolytic lesions in the central amygdala nucleus of the rat. *Physiology and Behavior, 37,* 855–862.

Johnston, J. B. (1923). Further contributions to the study of the evolution of the forebrain. *Journal of Comparative Neurology, 35,* 337–481.

Jones, D. N., Kortekaas, R., Slade, P. D., Middlemiss, D. N., & Hagan, J. J. (1998). The behavioural effects of corticotropin-releasing factor-related peptides in rats. *Psychopharmacology, 138,* 124–132.

Josselyn, S. A., Shi, C., Carlezon, W. A., Jr., Neve, R. L., Nestler, E. J., & Davis, M. (2001). Long-term memory is facilitated by cAMP response element-binding protein overexpression in the amygdala. *Journal of Neuroscience, 21,* 2404–2412.

Kaada, B. (1967). Brain mechanisms related to aggressive behavior. *UCLA Forum in Medical Sciences, 7,* 95–133.

Kim, J. J., Fanselow, M. S., DeCola, J. P., & Landeira-Fernandez, J. (1992). Selective impairment of long-term but not short-term conditional fear by the N-methyl-D-aspartate antagonist APV. *Behavioral Neuroscience, 106,* 591–596.

Kim, M., Campeau, S., Falls, W. A., & Davis, M. (1993). Infusion of the non-NMDA receptor antagonist CNQX into the amygdala blocks the expression of fear-potentiated startle. *Behavioral and Neural Biology, 59,* 5–8.

Kim, M., & Davis, M. (1993). Electrolytic lesions of the amygdala block acquisition and expression of fear-potentiated startle even with extensive training but do not prevent reacquisition. *Behavioral Neuroscience, 107,* 580–595.

Kluver, H., & Bucy, P. C. (1937). "Psychic blindness" and other symptoms following bilateral temporal lobectomy in rhesus monkeys. *American Journal of Physiology, 119,* 353.

Knapp, R., & Moore, M. C. (1997). Male morphs in tree lizards have different testosterone responses to elevated levels of corticosterone. *General and Comparative Endocrinology, 107,* 279.

Kojima, K., Maki, S., Hirata, K., Higuchi, S., Akazawa, K., & Tashiro, N. (1995). Relation of emotional behaviors to urine catecholamines and cortisol. *Physiology and Behavior, 57,* 445–449.

Kollack-Walker, S., & Newman, S. W. (1995). Mating and agonistic behavior produce different patterns of Fos immunolabeling in the male Syrian hamster brain. *Neuroscience, 66,* 721–736.

Kollack-Walker, S., Watson, S. J., & Akil, H. (1997). Social stress in hamsters: Defeat activates specific neurocircuits within the brain. *Journal of Neuroscience, 17,* 8842–8855.

Koob, G. F. (1992). The behavioral neuroendocrinology of corticotropin-releasing factor, somatostatin, and gonadotropin-releasing hormone. In C. B. Nemeroff (Ed.), *Neuroendocrinology* (pp. 353–396). Ann Arbor, MI: CRC Press.

Koob, G. F., Heinrichs, S. C., Pich, E. M., Menzaghi, F., Baldwin, H., Miczek, K., et al. (1993). The role of corticotropin-releasing factor in behavioural responses to stress. *CIBA Foundation Symposium, 172,* 277–289.

Koob, G. F., Swerdlow, N., Seeligson, M., Eaves, M., Sutton, R., Rivier, J., et al. (1984). Effects of alpha-flupenthixol and naloxone on CRF-induced locomotor activation. *Neuroendocrinology, 39,* 459–464.

Korte, S. M., Korte-Bouws, G. A., Bohus, B., & Koob, G. F. (1994). Effect of corticotropin-releasing factor antagonist on behavioral and neuroendocrine responses during exposure to defensive burying paradigm in rats. *Physiology and Behavior, 56,* 115–120.

Lai, W. S., & Johnston, R. E. (2002). Individual recognition after fighting by golden hamsters: A new method. *Physiology and Behavior, 76,* 225–239.

LeDoux, J. E. (1992). Emotion and amygdala. In J. P. Aggleton (Ed.), *The amygdala* (pp. 339–351). New York: Wiley-Liss.

LeDoux, J. E. (2000). Emotion circuits in the brain. *Annual Review of Neuroscience, 23,* 155–184.

LeDoux, J. E. (2001). The amygdala and emotion: A view through fear. In J. P. Aggleton (Ed.), *The amygdala: A functional analysis* (pp. 289–310). New York: Oxford University Press.

LeDoux, J. E., Cicchetti, P., Xagoraris, A., & Romanski, L. M. (1990). The lateral amygdaloid nucleus: Sensory interface of the amygdala in fear conditioning. *Journal of Neuroscience, 10,* 1062–1069.

LeDoux, J. E., Iwata, J., Cicchetti, P., & Reis, D. J. (1988). Different projections of the central amygdaloid nucleus mediate autonomic and behavioral correlates of conditioned fear. *Journal of Neuroscience, 8,* 2517–2529.

Lee, H. J., Choi, J. S., & Kim, J. J. (2001). Amygdalar NMDA receptors are critical for the expression of multiple conditioned fear responses. *Journal of Neuroscience, 21,* 4116–4124.

Lee, H. J., & Kim, J. J. (1998). Amygdalar NMDA receptors are critical for new fear learning in previously fear-conditioned rats. *Journal of Neuroscience, 18,* 8444–8454.

Lee, Y., & Davis, M. (1997). Role of the hippocampus, the bed nucleus of the stria terminalis, and the amygdala in the excitatory effect of corticotropin-releasing hormone on the acoustic startle reflex. *Journal of Neuroscience, 17,* 6434–6446.

Lee, Y., Walker, D., & Davis, M. (1996). Lack of temporal gradient of retrograde amnesia following NMDA-induced lesions of the basolateral amygdala assessed with the fear-potentiated startle paradigm. *Behavioral Neuroscience, 110,* 836–839.

Lerwill, C. J., & Makings, P. (1971). The agonistic behavior of the golden hamster *Mesocricetus auratus* (Waterhouse). *Animal Behaviour, 19,* 714–721.

Leshner, A. I. (1975). Theoretical review: A model of hormones and agonistic behavior. *Physiology and Behavior, 15,* 225–235.

Leshner, A. L. (1983). The hormonal responses to competition and their behavioral significance. In B. B. Svare (Ed.), *Hormones and aggressive behavior* (pp. 393–404). New York: Plenum.

Lewis, K., Li, C., Perrin, M. H., Blount, A., Kunitake, K., Donaldson, C., et al. (2001). Identification of urocortin III, an additional member of the corticotropin-releasing factor (CRF) family with high affinity for the CRF2 receptor. *Proceedings of the National Academy of Sciences USA, 98,* 7570–7575.

Liang, K. C., McGaugh, J. L., Martinez, J. L., Jr., Jensen, R. A., Vasquez, B. J., & Messing, R. B. (1982). Post-training amygdaloid lesions impair retention of an inhibitory avoidance response. *Behavioural Brain Research, 4,* 237–249.

Liaw, C. W., Grigoriadis, D. E., Lovenberg, T. W., De Souza, E. B., & Maki, R. A. (1997). Localization of ligand-binding domains of human corticotropin-releasing factor receptor: A chimeric receptor approach. *Molecular Endocrinology, 11,* 980–985.

Lovenberg, T. W., Chalmers, D. T., Liu, C., & De Souza, E. B. (1995). CRF2 alpha and CRF2 beta receptor mRNAs are differentially distributed between the rat central nervous system and peripheral tissues. *Endocrinology, 136,* 4139–4142.

Lundkvist, J., Chai, Z., Teheranian, R., Hasanvan, H., Bartfai, T., Jenck, F., et al. (1996). A non peptidic corticotropin releasing factor receptor antagonist attenuates fever and exhibits anxiolytic-like activity. *European Journal of Pharmacology, 309,* 195–200.

Makino, S., Shibasaki, T., Yamauchi, N., Nishioka, T., Mimoto, T., Wakabayashi, I., et al. (1999). Psychological stress increased corticotropin-releasing hormone mRNA and content in the central nucleus of the amygdala but not in the hypothalamic paraventricular nucleus in the rat. *Brain Research, 850,* 136–143.

Malkani, S., & Rosen, J. B. (2001). N-Methyl-D-aspartate receptor antagonism blocks contextual fear conditioning and differentially regulates early growth response-1 messenger RNA expression in the amygdala: Implications for a functional amygdaloid circuit of fear. *Neuroscience, 102,* 853–861.

Mansbach, R. S., Brooks, E. N., & Chen, Y. L. (1997). Antidepressant-like effects of CP-154,526, a selective CRF1 receptor antagonist. *European Journal of Pharmacology, 323,* 21–26.

Marcilhac, A., & Siaud, P. (1997). Identification of projections from the central nucleus of the amygdala to the paraventricular nucleus of the hypothalamus which are immunoreactive for corticotrophin-releasing hormone in the rat. *Experimental Physiology, 82,* 273–281.

Maren, S. (1999). Long-term potentiation in the amygdala: A mechanism for emotional learning and memory. *Trends in Neurosciences, 22,* 561–567.

Maren, S., Aharonov, G., & Fanselow, M. S. (1996). Retrograde abolition of conditional fear after excitotoxic lesions in the basolateral amygdala of rats: Absence of a temporal gradient. *Behavioral Neuroscience, 110,* 718–726.

Maren, S., Aharonov, G., Stote, D. L., & Fanselow, M. S. (1996). N-methyl-D-aspartate receptors in the basolateral amygdala are required for both acquisition and expression of conditional fear in rats. *Behavioral Neuroscience, 110,* 1365–1374.

Maren, S., & Fanselow, M. S. (1995). Synaptic plasticity in the basolateral amygdala induced by hippocampal formation stimulation in vivo. *Journal of Neuroscience, 15,* 7548–7564.

Maren, S., & Fanselow, M. S. (1996). The amygdala and fear conditioning: Has the nut been cracked? *Neuron, 16,* 237–240.

Martins, A. P., Marras, R. A., & Guimaraes, F. S. (1997). Anxiogenic effect of corticotropin-releasing hormone in the dorsal periaqueductal grey. *Neuroreport, 8,* 3601–3604.

McDonald, A. J. (1992). Projection neurons of the basolateral amygdala: A correlative Golgi and retrograde tract tracing study. *Brain Research Bulletin, 28,* 179–185.

McDonald, A. J. (1998). Cortical pathways to the mammalian amygdala. *Progress in Neurobiology, 55,* 257–332.

Meerlo, P., de Boer, S. F., Koolhaas, J. M., Daan, S., & Van den Hoofdakker, R. H. (1996). Changes in daily rhythms of body temperature and activity after a single social defeat in rats. *Physiology and Behavior, 59,* 735–739.

Meerlo, P., Overkamp, G. J., Daan, S., Van den Hoofdakker, R. H., & Koolhaas, J. M. (1996). Changes in behaviour and body weight following a single or double social defeat in rats. *Stress, 1,* 21–32.

Meerlo, P., Overkamp, G. J., & Koolhaas, J. M. (1997). Behavioural and physiological consequences of a single social defeat in Roman high- and low-avoidance rats. *Psychoneuroendocrinology, 22,* 155–168.

Menzaghi, F., Howard, R. L., Heinrichs, S. C., Vale, W., Rivier, J., & Koob, G. F. (1994). Characterization of a novel and potent corticotropin-releasing factor antagonist in rats. *Journal of Pharmacology and Experimental Therapeutics, 269,* 564–572.

Miserendino, M. J., Sananes, C. B., Melia, K. R., & Davis, M. (1990). Blocking of acquisition but not expression of conditioned fear-potentiated startle by NMDA antagonists in the amygdala. *Nature, 345,* 716–718.

Moore, M. C., Thompson, C. W., & Marler, C. A. (1991). Reciprocal changes in corticosterone and testosterone levels following acute and chronic handling stress in the tree lizard, *Urosaurus ornatus. General and Comparative Endocrinology, 81,* 217–226.

Moreau, J. L., Kilpatrick, G., & Jenck, F. (1997). Urocortin, a novel neuropeptide with anxiogenic-like properties. *Neuroreport, 8,* 1697–1701.

Morgan, C. A., III, Wang, S., Mason, J., Southwick, S. M., Fox, P., Hazlett, G., et al. (2000). Hormone profiles in humans experiencing military survival training. *Biological Psychiatry, 47,* 891–901.

Myers, D. A., Trinh, J. V., & Myers, T. R. (1998). Structure and function of the ovine type 1 corticotropin releasing factor receptor (CRF1) and a carboxyl-terminal variant. *Molecular and Cellular Endocrinology, 144,* 21–35.

Nappi, R. E., & Rivest, S. (1995). Stress-induced genetic expression of a selective corticotropin-releasing factor-receptor subtype within the rat ovaries: An effect dependent on the ovulatory cycle. *Biology of Reproduction, 53,* 1417–1428.

Nowack, R. M., & Paradiso, J. L. (1983). *Walker's mammals of the world.* Baltimore, MD: Johns Hopkins University Press.

Ohta, H., Watanabe, S., & Ueki, S. (1991). Cardiovascular changes induced by chemical stimulation of the amygdala in rats. *Brain Research Bulletin, 26,* 575–581.

Palchaudhuri, M. R., Hauger, R. L., Wille, S., Fuchs, E., & Dautzenberg, F. M. (1999). Isolation and pharmacological characterization of two functional splice variants of corticotropin-releasing factor type 2 receptor from *Tupaia belangeri*. *Journal of Neuroendocrinology*, 11, 419–428.

Palchaudhuri, M. R., Wille, S., Mevenkamp, G., Spiess, J., Fuchs, E., & Dautzenberg, F. M. (1998). Corticotropin-releasing factor receptor type 1 from *Tupaia belangeri* cloning, functional expression and tissue distribution. *European Journal of Biochemistry*, 258, 78–84.

Parent, M. B., & McGaugh, J. L. (1994). Posttraining infusion of lidocaine into the amygdala basolateral complex impairs retention of inhibitory avoidance training. *Brain Research*, 661, 97–103.

Pavcovich, L. A., & Valentino, R. J. (1997). Regulation of a putative neurotransmitter effect of corticotropin-releasing factor: Effects of adrenalectomy. *Journal of Neuroscience*, 17, 401–408.

Payne, A. P., & Swanson, H. H. (1970). Agonistic behaviour between pairs of hamsters of the same and opposite sex in a neutral observation area. *Behaviour*, 36, 260–269.

Penalva, R. G., Flachskamm, C., Zimmermann, S., Wurst, W., Holsboer, F., Reul, J. M., et al. (2002). Corticotropin-releasing hormone receptor type 1-deficiency enhances hippocampal serotonergic neurotransmission: An in vivo microdialysis study in mutant mice. *Neuroscience*, 109, 253–266.

Pesold, C., & Treit, D. (1994). The septum and amygdala differentially mediate the anxiolytic effects of benzodiazepines. *Brain Research*, 638, 295–301.

Petrulis, A., Weidner, M., & Johnson, R. E. (2004). Recognition of competitors by male golden hamsters. *Physiology and Behavior*, 81, 629–638.

Pitkanen, A. (2000). Connectivity of the rat amygdaloid complex. In J. P. Aggleton (Ed.), *The amygdala: A functional analysis* (pp. 31–115). New York: Oxford University Press.

Pitkanen, A., Stefanacci, L., Farb, C. R., Go, G. G., LeDoux, J. E., & Amaral, D. G. (1995). Intrinsic connections of the rat amygdaloid complex: Projections originating in the lateral nucleus. *Journal of Comparative Neurology*, 356, 288–310.

Potegal, M., Huhman, K., Moore, T., & Meyerhoff, J. (1993). Conditioned defeat in the Syrian golden hamster (*Mesocricetus auratus*). *Behavioral and Neural Biology*, 60, 93–102.

Prewitt, C. M. F., & Herman, J. P. (1998). Anatomical interactions between the central amygdaloid nucleus and the hypothalamic paraventricular nucleus of the rat-a dual tract-tracing analysis. *Journal of Chemical Neuroanatomy*, 15, 173–185.

Raab, A., Dantzer, R., Michaud, B., Mormede, P., Taghzouti, K., Simon, H., et al. (1986). Behavioural, physiological and immunological consequences of social status and aggression in chronically coexisting

resident-intruder dyads of male rats. *Physiology and Behavior*, 36, 223–228.

Radulovic, J., Ruhmann, A., Liepold, T., & Spiess, J. (1999). Modulation of learning and anxiety by corticotropin-releasing factor (CRF) and stress: Differential roles of CRF receptors 1 and 2. *Journal of Neuroscience*, 19, 5016–5025.

Rainnie, D. G., Asprodini, E. K., & Shinnick-Gallagher, P. (1991). Excitatory transmission in the basolateral amygdala. *Journal of Neurophysiology*, 66, 986–998.

Rassnick, S., Heinrichs, S. C., Britton, K. T., & Koob, G. F. (1993). Microinjection of a corticotropin-releasing factor antagonist into the central nucleus of the amygdala reverses anxiogenic-like effects of ethanol withdrawal. *Brain Research*, 605, 25–32.

Reyes, T. M., Lewis, K., Perrin, M. H., Kunitake, K. S., Vaughan, J., Arias, C. A., et al. (2001). Urocortin II: A member of the corticotropin-releasing factor (CRF) neuropeptide family that is selectively bound by type 2 CRF receptors. *Proceedings of the National Academy of Sciences USA*, 98, 2843–2848.

Risbrough, V. B., Hauger, R. L., Pelleymounter, M. A., & Geyer, M. A. (2003). Role of corticotropin releasing factor (CRF) receptors 1 and 2 in CRF-potentiated acoustic startle in mice. *Psychopharmacology*, 170, 178–187.

Rogan, M. T., & LeDoux, J. E. (1995). LTP is accompanied by commensurate enhancement of auditory-evoked responses in a fear conditioning circuit. *Neuron*, 15, 127–136.

Roozendaal, B., Koolhaas, J. M., & Bohus, B. (1991a). Attenuated cardiovascular, neuroendocrine, and behavioral responses after a single footshock in central amygdaloid lesioned male rats. *Physiology and Behavior*, 50, 771–775.

Roozendaal, B., Koolhaas, J. M., & Bohus, B. (1991b). Central amygdala lesions affect behavioral and autonomic balance during stress in rats. *Physiology and Behavior*, 50, 777–781.

Roozendaal, B., Koolhaas, J. M., & Bohus, B. (1992). Central amygdaloid involvement in neuroendocrine correlates of conditioned stress responses. *Journal of Neuroendocrinology*, 4, 489.

Roozendaal, B., & McGaugh, J. L. (1997). Glucocorticoid receptor agonist and antagonist administration into the basolateral but not central amygdala modulates memory storage. *Neurobiology of Learning and Memory*, 67, 176–179.

Rosen, J. B., & Davis, M. (1988). Enhancement of acoustic startle by electrical stimulation of the amygdala. *Behavioral Neuroscience*, 102, 102–324.

Ruhmann, A., Bonk, I., Lin, C. R., Rosenfeld, M. G., & Spiess, J. (1998). Structural requirements for peptidic antagonists of the corticotropin-releasing factor receptor (CRFR): Development of CRFR2beta-selective antisauvagine-30. *Proceedings of the National Academy of Sciences USA, 95,* 15264–15269.

Sajdyk, T. J., & Shekhar, A. (1997). Excitatory amino acid receptors in the basolateral amygdala regulate anxiety responses in the social interaction test. *Brain Research, 764,* 262–264.

Sakanaka, M., Shibasaki, T., & Lederis, K. (1986). Distribution and efferent projections of corticotropin-releasing factor-like immunoreactivity in the rat amygdaloid complex. *Brain Research, 382,* 213–238.

Sananes, C. B., & Davis, M. (1992). N-methyl-D-aspartate lesions of the lateral and basolateral nuclei of the amygdala block fear-potentiated startle and shock sensitization of startle. *Behavioral Neuroscience, 106,* 72–80.

Sanchez, M. M., Young, L. J., Plotsky, P. M., & Insel, T. R. (1999). Autoradiographic and in situ hybridization localization of corticotropin-releasing factor 1 and 2 receptors in nonhuman primate brain. *Journal of Comparative Neurology, 408,* 365–377.

Sanders, S. K., & Shekhar, A. (1995a). Anxiolytic effects of chlordiazepoxide blocked by injection of GABAA and benzodiazepine receptor antagonists in the region of the anterior basolateral amygdala of rats. *Biological Psychiatry, 37,* 473–476.

Sanders, S. K., & Shekhar, A. (1995b). Regulation of anxiety by GABAA receptors in the rat amygdala. *Pharmacology, Biochemistry and Behavior, 52,* 701–706.

Sapolsky, R. M. (1992). Cortisol concentrations and the social significance of rank instability among wild baboons. *Psychoneuroendocrinology, 17,* 701–709.

Sawchenko, P. E., & Swanson, L. W. (1985). Localization, colocalization, and plasticity of corticotropin-releasing factor immunoreactivity in rat brain. *Federation Proceedings, 44,* 221–227.

Schafe, G., E. & LeDoux, J. E. (2000). Memory consolidation of auditory Pavlovian fear conditioning requires protein synthesis and protein kinase A in the amygdala. *Journal of Neuroscience, 20,* RC96.

Schafe, G. E., Nader, K., Blair, H. T., & LeDoux, J. E. (2001). Memory consolidation of Pavlovian fear conditioning: A cellular and molecular perspective. *Trends in Neurosciences, 24,* 540–546.

Scheel-Kruger, J., & Petersen, E. N. (1982). Anticonflict effect of the benzodiazepines mediated by a GABAergic mechanism in the amygdala. *European Journal of Pharmacology, 82,* 115–116.

Schmitt, P., Carrive, P., Di Scala, G., Jenck, F., Brandao, M., Bagri, A., et al. (1986). A neuropharmacological study of the periventricular neural substrate involved in flight. *Behavioural Brain Research, 22,* 181–190.

Schuett, G. W., Harlow, H. J., Rose, J. D., Van Kirk, E. A., & Murdoch, W. J. (1996). Levels of plasma corticosterone and testosterone in male copperheads (*Agkistrodon contortrix*) following staged fights. *Hormones and Behavior, 30,* 60–68.

Schulz, D. W., Mansbach, R. S., Sprouse, J., Braselton, J. P., Collins, J., Corman, M., et al. (1996). CP-154,526: A potent and selective nonpeptide antagonist of corticotropin releasing factor receptors. *Proceedings of the National Academy of Sciences USA, 93,* 10477–10482.

Scott, J. P. (1966). Agonistic behavior of mice and rats: A review. *American Zoologist, 6,* 683–701.

Sherman, J. E., & Kalin, N. H. (1987). The effects of ICV-CRH on novelty-induced behavior. *Pharmacology, Biochemistry and Behavior, 26,* 699–703.

Shipley, J. E., & Kolb, B. (1977). Neural correlates of species-typical behavior in the Syrian golden hamster. *Journal of Comparative Psychology, 91,* 1056–1073.

Shively, C. A. (1998). Social subordination stress, behavior, and central monoaminergic function in female cynomolgus monkeys. *Biological Psychiatry, 44,* 882–891.

Shively, C. A., Grant, K. A., Ehrenkaufer, R. L., Mach, R. H., & Nader, M. A. (1997). Social stress, depression, and brain dopamine in female cynomolgus monkeys. *Annals of the New York Academy of Sciences, 807,* 574–577.

Shors, T. J., & Mathew, P. R. (1998). NMDA receptor antagonism in the lateral/basolateral but not central nucleus of the amygdala prevents the induction of facilitated learning in response to stress. *Learning and Memory, 5,* 220–230.

Siegel, A., Roeling, T. A., Gregg, T. R., & Kruk, M. R. (1999). Neuropharmacology of brain-stimulation-evoked aggression. *Neuroscience and Biobehavioral Reviews, 23,* 359–389.

Siegel, A., Schubert, K. L., & Shaikh, M. B. (1997). Neurotransmitters regulating defensive rage behavior in the cat. *Neuroscience and Biobehavioral Reviews, 21,* 733–742.

Siegfried, B., Frischknecht, H. R., & Waser, P. G. (1984). Defeat, learned submissiveness, and analgesia in mice: Effect of genotype. *Behavioral and Neural Biology, 42,* 91–97.

Silva, M. A., & Tomaz, C. (1995). Amnesia after diazepam infusion into basolateral but not central amygdala of *Rattus norvegicus*. *Neuropsychobiology, 32,* 31–36.

Smagin, G. N., Harris, R. B., & Ryan, D. H. (1996). Corticotropin-releasing factor receptor antagonist infused into the locus coeruleus attenuates immobilization stress-induced defensive withdrawal in rats. *Neuroscience Letters, 220,* 167–170.

Smith, B. N., & Dudek, F. E. (1996). Amino acid-mediated regulation of spontaneous synaptic activity patterns in the rat basolateral amygdala. *Journal of Neurophysiology, 76,* 1958–1967.

Smith, G. W., Aubry, J. M., Dellu, F., Contarino, A., Bilezikjian, L. M., Gold, L. H., et al. (1998). Corticotropin releasing factor receptor 1-deficient mice display decreased anxiety, impaired stress response, and aberrant neuroendocrine development. *Neuron*, 20, 1093–1102.

Stefanski, V. (2000). Social stress in laboratory rats: Hormonal responses and immune cell distribution. *Psychoneuroendocrinology*, 25, 389–406.

Stock, G., Schlor, K. H., Heidt, H., & Buss, J. (1978). Psychomotor behaviour and cardiovascular patterns during stimulation of the amygdala. *Pflugers Archiv*, 376, 177–184.

Swanson, L. W., & Petrovich, G. D. (1998). What is the amygdala? *Trends in Neurosciences*, 21, 323–331.

Swanson, L. W., Sawchenko, P. E., Rivier, J., & Vale, W. W. (1983). Organization of ovine corticotropin-releasing factor immunoreactive cells and fibers in the rat brain: An immunohistochemical study. *Neuroendocrinology*, 36, 165–186.

Swiergiel, A. H., Takahashi, L. K., & Kalin, N. H. (1993). Attenuation of stress-induced behavior by antagonism of corticotropin-releasing factor receptors in the central amygdala in the rat. *Brain Research*, 623, 229–234.

Takahashi, L. K., Ho, S. P., Livanov, V., Graciani, N., & Arneric, S. P. (2001). Antagonism of CRF(2) receptors produces anxiolytic behavior in animal models of anxiety. *Brain Research*, 902, 135–142.

Timpl, P., Spanagel, R., Sillaber, I., Kresse, A., Reul, J. M., Stalla, G. K., et al. (1998). Impaired stress response and reduced anxiety in mice lacking a functional corticotropin-releasing hormone receptor 1. *Nature Genetics*, 19, 162–166.

Vale, W., Spiess, J., Rivier, C., & Rivier, J. (1981). Characterization of a 41-residue ovine hypothalamic peptide that stimulates secretion of corticotropin and beta-endorphin. *Science*, 213, 1394–1397.

Van Bockstaele, E. J., Chan, J., & Pickel, V. M. (1996). Input from central nucleus of the amygdala efferents to pericoerulear dendrites, some of which contain tyrosine hydroxylase immunoreactivity. *Journal of Neuroscience Research*, 45, 289–302.

Van Bockstaele, E. J., Colago, E. E., & Valentino, R. J. (1998). Amygdaloid corticotropin-releasing factor targets locus coeruleus dendrites: Substrate for the co-ordination of emotional and cognitive limbs of the stress response. *Journal of Neuroendocrinology*, 10, 743–757.

Van de Poll, N. E., Smeets, J., van Oyen, H. G., & van der Zwan, S. M. (1982). Behavioral consequences of agonistic experience in rats: Sex differences and the effects of testosterone. *Journal of Comparative and Physiological Psychology*, 96, 893–903.

Vaughan, J., Donaldson, C., Bittencourt, J., Perrin, M. H., Lewis, K., Sutton, S., et al. (1995). Urocortin, a mammalian neuropeptide related to fish urotensin I and to corticotropin-releasing factor. *Nature*, 378, 287–292.

Vita, N., Laurent, P., Lefort, S., Chalon, P., Lelias, J. M., Kaghad, M., et al. (1993). Primary structure and functional expression of mouse pituitary and human brain corticotrophin releasing factor receptors. *FEBS Letters*, 335, 1–5.

Walker, D. L., & Davis, M. (1997a). Anxiogenic effects of high illumination levels assessed with the acoustic startle response in rats. *Biological Psychiatry*, 42, 461–471.

Walker, D. L., & Davis, M. (1997b). Double dissociation between the involvement of the bed nucleus of the stria terminalis and the central nucleus of the amygdala in startle increases produced by conditioned versus unconditioned fear. *Journal of Neuroscience*, 17, 9375–9383.

Weidenfeld, J., Itzik, A., & Feldman, S. (1997). Effect of glucocorticoids on the adrenocortical axis responses to electrical stimulation of the amygdala and the ventral noradrenergic bundle. *Brain Research*, 754, 187–194.

Wilensky, A. E., Schafe, G. E., & LeDoux, J. E. (2000). The amygdala modulates memory consolidation of fear-motivated inhibitory avoidance learning but not classical fear conditioning. *Journal of Neuroscience*, 20, 7059–7066.

Wingfield, J. C., Ramos-Fernandez, G., Nunez-de la Mora, A., & Drummond, H. (1999). The effects of an "El Nino" southern oscillation event on reproduction in male and female blue-footed boobies, *Sula nebouxii*. *General and Comparative Endocrinology*, 114, 163–172.

Yu, J., Xie, L. Y., & Abou-Samra, A. B. (1996). Molecular cloning of a type A chicken corticotropin-releasing factor receptor with high affinity for urotensin I. *Endocrinology*, 137, 192–197.

Zbrozyna, A. W. (1972). The organization of the defense reaction elicited from the amygdala. In B. E. Eleptheriou (Ed.), *The neurobiology of the amygdala* (pp. 597–605). New York: Plenum.

Zhu, W., Umegaki, H., Suzuki, Y., Miura, H., & Iguchi, A. (2001). Involvement of the bed nucleus of the stria terminalis in hippocampal cholinergic system-mediated activation of the hypothalamo-pituitary-adrenocortical axis in rats. *Brain Research*, 916, 101–106.

14

Development of Aggression

*Yvon Delville, Matt L. Newman, Joel C. Wommack,
Kereshmeh Taravosh-Lahn, & M. Catalina Cervantes*

Development of Agonistic Behavior

Scent Marking and
Olfactory Communication

In mammals, agonistic behavior is not limited to fighting, but also includes scent marking (Bradbury & Vehrencamp, 1998). Mammals use a variety of olfactory communications for indicating territoriality or sexual readiness. In an agonistic setup, scent marking has two functions. The first is to advertise territoriality and thus prevent an aggressive interaction. The second occurs after an aggressive encounter. In this case, the winner of the fight (i.e., the dominant individual) will initiate a bout of scent marking, as the loser retreats (Johnston, 1975, 1985). This type of behavior can be easily studied in a laboratory setting using golden (Syrian) hamsters (*Mesocricetus auratus*) (Johnston, 1985). Golden hamsters are solitary animals that readily attack intruders placed in their home cage (Dieterlen, 1959; Festing, 1986; Johnston, 1985). Golden hamsters have scent glands located on their flanks (Johnston, 1985). They spread these scents by licking their flanks and rubbing them against vertical surfaces. The behavior, called flank marking, is often displayed after a successful attack

against an individual (Johnston, 1975, 1985). Over repeated encounters between two males, dominant hamsters will substitute flank marking for overt aggression (Ferris, Axelson, Shinto, & Albers, 1987). Interestingly, both scent marking and offensive aggression of intruders are controlled by a common neural substrate, an interaction between vasopressin and serotonin within the anterior hypothalamus (Ferris & Delville, 1994). Both behaviors are activated by vasopressin and inhibited by serotonin injections within the anterior hypothalamus (Albers, Huhman, & Meisel, 2002; Ferris, Albers, Wesoloswki, Goldman, & Leeman, 1984; Ferris et al., 1997; Ferris, Stolberg, & Delville, 1999). This association between scent marking and offensive aggression can be observed developmentally. Hamsters initiate flank marking and fighting simultaneously before weaning. As soon as they are capable of coordinated movements, hamsters engage in play fighting activity (Goldman & Swanson, 1975; Schoenfeld & Leonard, 1985). At the same time, hamsters also start flank marking their cages (Ferris et al., 1996; Johnston, 1985). These observations suggest that a common neural substrate is responsible for the control and developmental onset of flank marking and fighting.

Flank marking is only one of several types of scent marking in hamsters. These rodents have other scent glands (Johnston, 1985). For instance, female hamsters have vaginal scent glands (Deanesly, 1938) and perform vaginal marking by dragging their genital area on the floor of their cages during estrous (Dieterlen, 1959; Johnston, 1977). These markings appear to indicate sexual receptivity (Johnston, 1977; Lisk, Ciacco, & Catanzaro, 1983). Hamsters also have Harderian glands located just behind their eyes (Christensen & Dam, 1953). Rodents spread the products of their Harderian glands on their face and head during grooming (Thiessen, Clancy, & Goodwin, 1976). These glands are also sexually dimorphic and appear to play a role in aggressive and sexual behavior in hamsters (Christensen & Dam, 1953; Clabough & Norvell, 1973; Johnston, 1985; Payne, 1977).

Play Fighting

As noted above, hamsters engage in play fighting as soon as they are capable of coordinated activity. This type of behavior is common in mammals and typically precedes adultlike aggressive behavior (Blanchard, Wall, & Blanchard, 2003; Delville, David, Taravosh-Lahn, & Wommack, 2003; Pellis, 2002; Pellis, Field, Smith, & Pellis, 1997; Pellis & Uwaniuk, 2000). Play fighting is typically associated with agonistic behavior and has been interpreted as a juvenile form of agonistic behavior. However, it is not clear whether play fighting and adult aggression involve similar neural systems. In addition, play fighting appears to change during juvenile development and may undergo several stages (Delville et al., 2003; Pellis, 2002). Nevertheless, play fighting by juveniles can be studied as aggression in adults: separated into offensive responses (attacks) and defensive responses (defense) (Delville et al., 2003; Pellis & Pellis, 1988a, 1988b). Of course, the degree of complexity and the number of developmental sequences vary greatly between species. In addition, play fighting is not necessarily associated with prepubescence. In some species, such as rats, play fighting sequences remain well into adulthood (Pellis & Pellis, 1990; Smith, Fantella, & Pellis, 1999).

In rodents, the maturation of play fighting into adultlike aggression has been well documented in rats and hamsters. However, the expression of the behavior and its developmental sequence differ between these two species. In rats, the development of agonistic behavior appears to include three separate phases: first, a period of rough play before weaning, followed by pure play after weaning, followed again by rough play during puberty, which matures into adultlike aggression (Pellis, 2002). In hamsters, rough play appears first before weaning and matures into adultlike aggression during puberty (Delville et al., 2003).

These distinctions are based on differences in attack and defense during development. In rats, the target site of attack changes during development. Play fighting attacks are directed at the nape of the neck (Pellis & Pellis, 1987; Siviy & Panksepp, 1987b), whereas adult attacks during offensive aggression are directed at the back (Blanchard et al., 2003). At first, social behavior is limited to huddling in rat litters. As infant rats become more active around Postnatal Day 15 (P-15), they start engaging in allogroming (Bolles & Woods, 1964; Pellis & Pellis, 1997). This behavior is directed at the head of partners. This behavior is also the preponderant form of social interaction in rats between P-15 and P-20 (Meaney & Stewart, 1981a; Pellis & Pellis, 1997). It is not entirely clear whether allogroming can be excluded from agonistic behavior in rats. Indeed, on some occasions, individuals will attempt to hold the head of a partner to lick it, while the targeted animal will attempt to do the same, resulting in mutual allogroming. On occasion, forcibly groomed rats attempt to disengage (Pellis & Pellis, 1997). However, during that time, rats start engaging in clearly agonistic interactions. These include tail manipulation (such as biting or grabbing the tail of a littermate) and play fighting attacks (attacking and nuzzling the nape of the neck of a littermate) (Pellis & Pellis, 1987, 1997). The three types of behavior appear to be separate, as they are associated with different behavioral sequences (Pellis & Pellis, 1997). Tail manipulations involve biting. Allogroming involves licking. Play fighting attacks of the nape of the neck involve only nuzzling. Between P-15 and P-20, these three behaviors can succeed each other in various sequences, but always with separate outcomes (biting the tail, licking the face, nuzzling the nape of the neck).

After P-20, play fighting attacks on the nape of the neck become the preponderant form of social and agonistic activity in rats (Panksepp, 1981; Pellis & Pellis, 1997). After that time, these play fighting attacks represent more than 80% of all social activities between littermates. The frequency of play fighting attacks peaks between P-30 and P-40 and then declines as the animals undergo puberty (Beanninger, 1967; Meaney & Stewart, 1981a; Panksepp, 1981; Takahashi & Lore,

1983; Thor & Holloway, 1984). Tail manipulations remain until P-30, but never become preponderant (Pellis & Pellis, 1997). Later, as the animal undergoes puberty, attacks become focused on the back and involve biting, not nuzzling (Pellis & Pellis, 1991; Takahashi & Lore, 1983). These differences in body targets (the back vs. the nape of the neck) and follow-up action (biting vs. nuzzling) suggest that these behaviors are separate.

Analyses of defensive postures have allowed the establishment of a more detailed understanding of play fighting in rats. To date, the most extensive studies of defensive behavior in juveniles have been performed in rats by the laboratory of Sergio Pellis (Pellis, 2002; Pellis et al., 1997; Pellis & Pellis, 1987, 1990, 1991, 1992, 1997). These studies include changes in behavioral sequences and postures. Analyses of the transitions in defensive behavior suggest three separate phases in the development of agonistic behavior in rats. When attacked, juvenile and infant rats have two main responses: evade or face the attacker (defense) (Pellis, Pellis, & Whishaw, 1992). The proportion of attacks followed by either evasions or defense does not appear to change significantly during peripubertal development (Pellis & Pellis, 1997). However, the nature of the defensive postures varies greatly during development. Between P-15 and P-25, infant rats subjected to attacks targeting their neck are most likely to prevent contact to their neck by standing up while turning their upper body partially to face the attacker (*partial rotation*) (Pellis, 2002; Pellis et al., 1992; Pellis & Pellis, 1997). Such defense often leads to an upright defensive posture where animals use their forepaws to block the attacker. This type of defense leads to "rougher" interactions. After P-25 and until puberty, juvenile rats prevent contact to their necks, turning themselves by rotating their bodies along the longitudinal axis to a supine position (*complete rotation*) (Pellis, 2002; Pellis et al., 1992; Pellis & Pellis, 1990, 1997). From this position, rats use all their limbs to block the attacker. This type of defense leads to more "playful" interactions. During puberty, rats shift back to a partial rotation defense (Pellis, 2002), which leads again to "rougher" interactions, eventually maturing into adult aggression (Meaney & Stewart, 1981a; Pellis & Pellis, 1987; Takahashi & Lore, 1983). These three types of defense indicate three different periods: infant (P-15 to P-25), juvenile (P-25 to P-40), and adult (P-40 and afterward) (Pellis, 2002).

These three periods have been further characterized through additional analyses of behavioral sequences and postures through Laban movement analysis (Foroud & Pellis, 2003). This method was originally developed as a form of language for choreography. This analysis was adapted to play fighting interactions when an attacker ends up pinning down its partner. The movement analysis is subdivided into four elements: body, effort, shape, and space. The first element analyzes body postures and movements. The second element determines the intensity of a movement. The third element describes how body postures change during movement. The fourth element determines how a body interacts with the environment. In addition, this analysis quantifies the percentages of pins along the Motif method, a simplified version of Laban movement analysis. In this case, the authors compared the frequencies of four different types of *effort factors* during pinning between animals at P-30 and P-70. These effort factors were separated into *indulging effort quality* (gentle, maintained, multifocal, less tense) and *condensing effort quality* (strong, direct, focal, tense). The relative proportion of condensing and indulging efforts were also compared during pinning between animals at P-30 and P-70. This analysis showed strong differences between pinning by juveniles and adults. In male versus male interactions, over 70% of efforts were of indulging quality during pinning on P-30. As the animals grew, the percentage of indulging efforts decreased, while the proportion of condensing effort increased. By P-50, 50% of efforts had a condensing quality. In this study, indulging efforts were rated as "playful," and condensing efforts as "rough." The study thus revealed a "playful" nature for interactions between males between P-30 and P-40, switching to a "rougher" type of interactions by P-50 and P-60. This analysis, along with the description of defensive postures, shows strong differences between agonistic interactions in rats as infants, juveniles, and adults. This analysis also confirms previous descriptions of agonistic interactions between P-25 and P-40 as fully playful and totally distinct from early play fighting and adult aggression (Meaney & Stewart, 1981a; Pellis, 2002; Pellis & Pellis, 1990; Thor & Holloway, 1985).

It is difficult to remove all forms of anthropomorphism from descriptions of play in rats. The use of the Laban movement analysis and the Motif method provide the most rigorous arguments supporting the hypothesis of a play period in this species. Recent data about vocalizations further support the hypothesis of a play period in rats (Panksepp & Burgdorf, 2003). During play, juvenile rats emit a specific and brief ultrasonic vocalization at 50 kHz (Knutson, Burgdorf, &

Panksepp, 1998). Rats are capable of ultrasonic vocalizations in the 20- and 50-kHz ranges. Typically, vocalizations in the 50-kHz range are associated with sexual encounters (Barfield, Auerbach, Geyer, & McIntosh, 1979; Sales, 1972). In such a context, some vocalizations include frequency modulations between 45 and 80 kHz (Sales, 1972). Ultrasonic vocalization in the 20-kHz range have been associated with negative stimuli (Panksepp & Burgdorf, 2003), although some have also been associated with sexual encounters (Brown, 1979). The short 50-kHz vocalization is frequently emitted in association with play (Knutson et al., 1998) and is highly stereotyped (Brudzynski & Pniak, 2002). In fact, the vocalization was even more frequent in anticipation of play (Knutson et al., 1998). Interestingly, the same vocalization can be reliably evoked in juvenile rats by gentle tickling of the nape of the neck, specifically (Panksepp & Burgdorf, 2003). This part of the skin is nuzzled by successful attackers during play (Pellis & Pellis, 1987; Siviy & Panksepp, 1987b). This 50-kHz chirp has been interpreted as playful and somewhat reminiscent of human laughter in response to tickling (Panksepp & Burgdorf, 2003). Nevertheless, just as play activity decreases during puberty (Panksepp, 1981), the frequency of call response to tickling also decreases during peripubertal development (Panksepp & Burgdorf, 2003). In addition, tickling has been found to be rewarding for individuals performing high levels of 50-kHz chirping. Together, these data support the concept of a unique developmental period in juvenile rats dedicated to play.

Observations made in rats are not necessarily applicable to other species. No such play period has been described in hamsters. Instead, play fighting in hamsters is "rough" throughout juvenile development (Delville et al., 2003; Goldman & Swanson, 1975). Hamsters are capable of ultrasonic vocalizations, particularly during sexual encounters (Floody & Pfaff, 1977; Floody, Pfaff, & Lewis, 1977; Sales, 1972). However, ultrasonic chirps have never been detected during play fights in hamsters in our laboratory. In addition, early agonistic interactions in hamsters do not include tail manipulations. As noted above hamsters start initiating play fighting attacks as soon as they are capable of coordinated movement (Goldman & Swanson, 1975; Schoenfeld & Leonard, 1985). Play fighting attacks start occurring in hamsters between P-15 and P-20 (Goldman & Swanson, 1975). These attacks are targeted at the face and cheeks of the littermates (Pellis & Pellis, 1988a, 1988b; Wommack,

Taravosh-Lahn, David, & Delville, 2003). These attacks are followed by small bites or nibbles, although not necessarily on the body parts initially targeted. Juvenile hamsters will defend themselves and protect their faces (Pellis & Pellis, 1988b). As attackers are pushed away from the face and cheeks, they can end up biting or nibbling another body part (Delville et al., 2003; Pellis & Pellis, 1988b; Romeo, Schulz, Nelson, Menard, & Sisk, 2003). This type of behavior lasts until puberty, around P-40. At this time, hamsters shift their attacks to the flanks and later (by P-50) to the lower belly and rump (Pellis & Pellis, 1988a, 1988b; Wommack et al., 2003) (figure 14.1). As previously, defense also shifts to the protection of the flanks, lower belly, and rump (Pellis & Pellis, 1988b). By P-70, hamsters engage in fully adult aggression (Pellis & Pellis, 1988a, 1988b; Wommack et al., 2003). As such, it is possible to separate a play fighting period (marked by attacks directed at the face) from a period characterized as adultlike (marked by attacks directed at the lower belly and flanks) (figure 14.1). The presence of a third period around midpuberty would be marked by attacks directed at the flanks but would not be comparable to the play period observed in juvenile rats before puberty.

Analyses of defensive behavior in hamsters have not been as extensive as those in rats. Hamsters use defensive strategies similar to those of rats. These strategies include avoidance, facing the attacker through a partial rotation, followed by upright defensive posture, or a complete rotation into a supine position (on-back defense) (Pellis & Pellis, 1988b). As hamsters are defending themselves, they remain active attempting to block the attacker (Pellis & Pellis, 1988b). The frequency of on-back defense changes during peripubertal development in hamsters, as juveniles are more likely to use this defense during play fights than adults during aggressive encounters (Pellis & Pellis, 1988b). In contrast, avoidance and upright defense were also more frequent in adults than juveniles (Pellis and Pellis, 1988b). These data suggest changes in patterns of defense during peripubertal development, in a manner reminiscent of rats. However, it is important to acknowledge two additional factors. First, defense is adapted to attacks. If the targets of attacks change during development, so would the type of defense. The simplest way to prevent an attack targeting the lower belly or rump is a retreat or an upright defense trying to block the advance of the attacker. In addition, during play fighting, the attacker often ends up pushing and pinning its partner on its back (Pellis & Pellis,

Male Offensive Responses

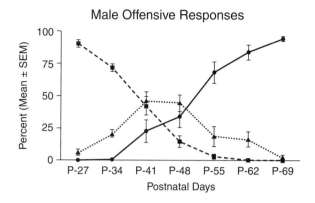

Female Offensive Responses

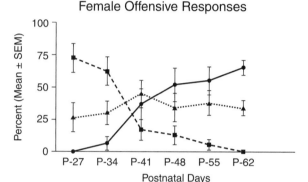

- ■ - Frontal Attack   ···▲··· Side Attack   —●— Rear/belly Attack

FIGURE 14.1 Comparison of the proportion of attacks (offensive responses) that were directed at the face and cheeks (frontal attacks), side/flanks (side attacks), and lower belly and rear (rear attacks) in male and female golden hamsters tested for offensive responses during peripubertal development from Postnatal Days 27 (P-27) to P-69 (males) and P-27 to P-52 (females). Tests were performed for 10-min periods in the presence of a smaller and younger intruder.

1988b). Second, as pinning seems to be preponderant during play fighting (Panksepp, 1981; Taravosh-Lahn & Delville, 2004), the frequency of on-back defense would also be preponderant during play fighting.

In hamsters, the frequency of agonistic interactions also varies greatly during juvenile development in hamsters (figure 14.2). In male hamsters, the frequency of attacks and pins increases after weaning, reaching a peak around P-35 (Goldman & Swanson, 1975; Pellis & Pellis, 1988b; Wommack et al., 2003). These frequencies decrease gradually during puberty from P-35 to P-50. Afterward, attacks frequencies level to a low frequency (relative to P-35), while pins keep disappearing (Taravosh-Lahn & Delville, 2004). These data support the assumption that pinning is a component of play fighting (Panksepp, 1981). It is interesting to note that the frequency of attacks decreases gradually during puberty as testes grow and testosterone levels rise (Vomachka & Greenwald, 1979; Wommack et al., 2003, Wommack, Salinas, Melloni, & Delville, 2004) (figure 14.3). This decrease may be associated with changes in the nature of agonistic interactions during that time.

The decline in attack frequency has also been associated with increased flank marking activity during agonistic encounters (Taravosh-Lahn & Delville, 2004). It is possible that as hamsters mature and become more likely to bite their opponents rather than nibble them, they also develop stereotyped behaviors, such as flank marking, which may decrease the probability of serious injuries.

Transition Into Adult Aggression

In rats, the behavioral characteristics of the play period are clearly different from the early and late rough play fighting (Panksepp & Burgdorf, 2003; Pellis, 2002). Consequently, it is likely that play in rats is controlled by a separate neural system. In comparison, the distinctions in hamsters are much less clear. Instead, play fighting by juvenile hamsters matures gradually into adultlike aggression (Wommack et al., 2003). Slowly, the frequency of attacks and the targets of attacks observed in juveniles develop into an adult form of offensive aggression.

Social Behaviors

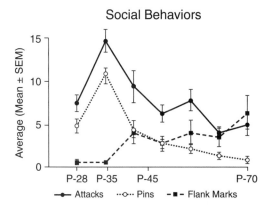

Gonadal Development

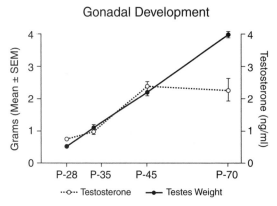

FIGURE 14.2 Frequencies of attacks, pins, and flank marks performed by male hamsters during aggression tests on P-28 through P-70 (social behaviors). Behavioral tests were performed for 10-min periods in the presence of a smaller and younger intruder. Testes weights and serum testosterone levels increase gradually during this developmental period (gonadal development).

Previous research on the transition from play fighting behavior to adult aggression in hamsters has led to the development of two different hypotheses. Some researchers have suggested a gradual transition from one behavior to the other, marked by an increased severity of agonistic interactions (Hole & Heinon, 1984). In this case, the offensive components of adult aggression would be comparable to the offensive components of play fighting. In support of this hypothesis, we have often observed occurrences of flank marking behavior after successful attacks by juveniles, as observed during aggressive encounters between adults (Johnston, 1975). This hypothesis suggests that a common neural substrate controls both the type of rough play fighting and adult aggression in hamsters. This neural substrate is discussed later in this review.

Pins

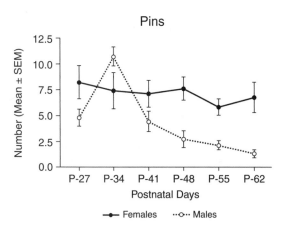

FIGURE 14.3 Comparison of the frequency of pins in male and female golden hamsters tested for offensive responses during peripubertal development from P-27 to P-62. Tests were performed for 10-min periods in the presence of a smaller and younger intruder.

Alternatively, it has been suggested that play fighting and adult aggression are separate behaviors (Goldman & Swanson, 1975; Pellis & Pellis, 1988a, 1988b). This hypothesis is based on the differing targets of attacks and location of following bites between juveniles and adults. During play fighting, most bites are targeted and located at the face and cheeks of the opponent, while they are targeted and located at the rump and belly in adults (Pellis & Pellis, 1988a, 1988b). In addition, the difference in impulsivity (attack frequency and flank marking) between juvenile and adult may also be used to separate the two behaviors. Play fighting is marked by intense and continued activity, including many attacks, bites, or role reversals performed by both partners. Adult aggression is marked by severe attacks and bites, but these typically last for a short time (Goldman & Swanson, 1975; Pellis & Pellis, 1988a, 1988b). This hypothesis would favor separate neural systems for each type of behavior.

Nevertheless, these two opposing hypotheses can possibly be reconciled. While a common neural system may be responsible for the initiation of offensive responses (either play or adultlike fighting), this neural system and/or associated networks may be regulated by neuroendocrine events associated with puberty, resulting in differing intensity and control of the fights (Delville et al., 2003). Furthermore, the transition from attacks targeting the cheeks to the flanks to the lower belly and rump could involve a maturation in olfactory processing. Hamsters have flank glands and Harderian glands (Johnston, 1985). As noted above both types of glands are sexually dimorphic and testosterone dependent (Christensen & Dam, 1953; Clabough & Norvell, 1973; Hamilton & Montagna, 1950; Vandenbergh, 1973). It is possible that play fighting attacks are oriented at secretions from the Harderian glands spread over the face and cheeks during grooming. It is also possible that attacks focused on the flanks around midpuberty are the result of an increased interest in secretions from the flank glands. The change in interest from the face to the flanks would then be caused by a maturation of the neural systems mediating olfaction in hamsters. Finally, the shift from the flanks to the lower belly and rump could also be caused by further maturation of olfactory systems. These interesting possibilities deserve careful testing. Alternatively, it is also possible that the targeting of the lower belly and rump is the result of a learned experience for fighting individuals protecting their flanks. Admittedly, there is presently little evidence supporting this last possibil-

ity; we have observed adult hamsters isolated from their peers since weaning immediately attempt to engage the lower belly or rump of their opponents (unpublished data).

The Adaptive Value of Play and Play Fighting

Comparative Studies

Most mammals perform play fighting behavior as juveniles. Of course, each species has unique sequences and postures. In Djungarian hamsters, the target of a play fight is to lick and nuzzle the mouth (Pellis & Pellis, 1989). In mice, play fighting attacks are focused on the rump and nape of the neck, and defense is mostly limited to retreats (Pellis & Pasztor, 1999). In this species, play fighting includes allogroming, tail manipulations, and locomotor play, where individuals are chasing each other or they are running in tandem (Laviola & Alleva, 1995; Pellis & Pasztor, 1999; Terranova, Laviola, & Alleva, 1993). Through these comparisons, it may be possible to determine a primitive form of play fighting by comparing related species (Pellis & Uwaniuk, 1999, 2000). Such types of study have been undertaken among rodents. One study correlated the degree of complexity of play fighting in relation to phylogeny (Pellis & Uwaniuk, 1999). Unfortunately, this study failed to show an association between phylogeny and the complexity of play fighting. These findings suggest that various factors may be critical for the evolution of the complexity of play fighting in rodents as quantified in this study. A broader analysis was later performed by the same group and involved comparison of rodents and primates (Pellis & Uwaniuk, 2000). In this study, the degree of complexity of play fighting behavior was correlated with prenatal development. It was predicted that play would be most apparent in species with the greatest degree of postnatal development. Indeed, such animals would take a longer time to reach adulthood. The data supported this hypothesis, as up to 60% of the variance between primate species was associated with prenatal brain development. Similarly, in rodents, up to 30% of the variability between species was explained by prenatal body growth.

Another factor associated with play fighting is the degree or type of socialization of the species. The development of rat agonistic behavior includes a period dedicated to play (Panksepp & Burgdorf, 2003; Pellis, 2002). Such a period has not been identified in hamsters. Interestingly, hamsters are solitary animals, while rats are fairly social.

Social Adaptation and Play

The role of play in the development of social relationships has been studied in rats. When males are raised in groups they develop dominant/subordinate relationships (Pellis, Pellis, & McKenna, 1993; Smith et al., 1999). As adults, subordinate males attempt play interactions with the dominants (Pellis & Pellis, 1992). The dominant's response to a playful contact consists mostly of adultlike partial rotations (Pellis et al., 1993; Smith et al., 1999). In contrast, subordinates respond to play contact with juvenile (playful) complete rotations (Pellis et al., 1993; Pellis & Pellis, 1992; Smith et al., 1999). However, when paired with an unknown individual, both dominant and subordinate animals respond to contact with adultlike partial rotations (Smith et al., 1999). Over time, once reestablished as subordinates, they again use complete rotations (Smith et al., 1999). These data suggest that subordinates use play as a form of submissive behavior or to diffuse tensions in a social hierarchy. This possibility has been further supported by studies with triads of rats (Pellis et al., 1993). As they develop their social relationships, one individual will become dominant, while the remaining ones will become subordinates. Each subordinate will be more likely to initiate play contact with the dominant than with the other subordinates. The dominant animal will also be less likely to initiate play contact with any of the subordinates. Interestingly, one of the subordinates will be more likely than the others to initiate play contact with the dominant. The question is, Who is Number Two? After removal of the dominant, which of the subordinates will become the next dominant? In the majority of cases, the individual least likely to initiate play contact with the previous dominant will become the next dominant. In addition, the remaining subordinate will also modify its behavior and start initiating play contacts with the new dominant. These data reinforce the role for play for the maintenance of social relationships in rats.

The importance of play in the development of social relationships is further supported by studies involving play deprivation. Rats isolated at weaning around P-20 develop abnormal social behaviors (Gerall, Ward, & Gerall, 1967; Gruendel & Arnold, 1969; Meaney & Stewart, 1979). However, it could be argued that these effects are not necessarily associated with play deprivation, but rather with isolation. A better experiment would be to isolate animals temporarily during the period of play. Then, the animals would be resocialized and tested later in adulthood. In one study, rats were isolated between P-22 and P-35 (van den Berg et al., 1999). Then they were resocialized and tested as adults. In this study, play-deprived rats showed enhanced anxiety (including elevated corticosterone and adrenaline release) and maladapted behavior in an aggressive setup. In addition, play-deprived animals were quite capable of sexual activity, but showed impaired anogenital exploration.

A different role for play fighting has been observed in hamsters (Pellis & Pellis, 1993). In this species, subordinates avoid contact with the dominant (Potegal, Huhman, Moore, & Meyerhoff, 1993; Wommack et al., 2004). In hamsters, social subjugation inhibits social investigation of the dominant (Pellis & Pellis, 1993; Potegal et al., 1993; Wommack et al., 2004). In juvenile hamsters, dominant hamsters are most likely to initiate play fighting contacts (cheek attacks) (Pellis & Pellis, 1993). In such case, it can be argued that hamsters establish dominant/subordinate relationships early during peripubertal development through play fighting attacks. This conclusion reinforces the differences between rats and hamsters and the lack of playful interactions in juvenile hamsters.

Sex Differences and Hormonal Control of Play Fighting

Sex Differences in Play Fighting

Play fighting or play is performed by both sexes. However, in both rats and hamsters there are a number of differences between the sexes. These differences are quantitative (frequency of behaviors) and qualitative (types of postures and behavioral sequences) (Meaney, Stewart, & Beatty, 1985; Pellis, 2002; Pellis et al., 1997).

Considering quantitative differences first, male rats are more likely to initiate attacks and pin their opponents than females throughout development (Meaney, Stewart, et al., 1985; Olioff & Stewart, 1978; Pellis & Pellis, 1990; Thor & Holloway, 1984). Similarly, in hamsters, as play fighting activity peaks around P-35 in males, females are less likely to attack or pin their opponents on that day (Guerra, Vieiria, Takase, &

Gasparetto, 1992). However, studies on sex differences in hamsters require a longitudinal perspective, as female hamsters are reputed to be more aggressive than males as adults (Siegel, 1985). Indeed, more complex differences have been recently uncovered between sexes through a more detailed analysis of peripubertal development in hamsters (Taravosh-Lahn & Delville, 2004) (figures 14.1 and 14.3). In this species, the sexes show similar levels of play fighting activity earlier in development around P-25. However, as play fighting activity (attack and pin frequency) peaks in males around P-35, it remains stable in females. Afterward, attack and pin frequency decreases as males undergo puberty, while still remaining stable in females. By the end of puberty, females become more likely than males to attack and pin intruders placed in their home cages. The lasting frequency of pins in early adulthood in females suggests that they maintain elements of play into adulthood.

Analyses of the qualitative development of agonistic behavior have also shown sex differences in both rats and hamsters (Pellis, 2002; Pellis et al., 1997; Taravosh-Lahn & Delville, 2004). In rats, these differences are focused on the maturation of defensive tactics (Pellis, 2002; Pellis et al., 1997). These differences have been noted on the types and timing of defensive strategies used by males and females. First, females respond earlier and faster to an approach by a littermate than males (Pellis, Pellis, & McKenna, 1994). This earlier response gives them more time to turn around and face the attacker with a defensive posture. In males, a delayed response will lead to more physical contacts and favors counterattacks, thus leading to a higher frequency of pins. This sex difference has been viewed as sensory or motivational in nature (Pellis et al., 1997). Another difference relates to evasion (Pellis et al., 1997). When attacked and when protecting their food from a robber, females will be more likely to attempt evasion and dodging by rotating their entire body away from the attacker, the pivoting point being close to the pelvis (Field, Whishaw, & Pellis, 1996; Pellis, Field, & Whishaw, 1999; Pellis & Pellis, 1987). In contrast, evasion and dodging attempts in males are more likely to involve a rotation of the upper body away from the attacker, while the pelvis turns toward the attacker. In males, the pivoting point is located midbody. These sex differences are more likely to lead to successful evasion in females, while promoting physical contacts and counterattacks in males, reinforcing the sex differences in play fighting frequency (Pellis et al., 1997).

The most interesting sex difference in the development of agonistic behavior in rats relates to the periods of development. As explained above, three separate periods of development can be identified in rats based on partial and complete rotational defense (Pellis, 2002). In males, puberty is marked by a return to partial rotation and "rougher" play fighting. However, females never abandon complete rotations and do not return to partial rotation (Pellis & Pellis, 1990; Smith, Forgie, & Pellis, 1998a). Consequently, female rats maintain elements of play into adulthood, just as female hamsters maintain elements of play fighting into adulthood (Taravosh-Lahn & Delville, 2004). In addition, this difference in defensive strategies in later puberty may participate in the enhanced "roughness" of play fighting reported in male rats (Meaney & Stewart, 1981b; Pellis, 2002; Takahashi & Lore, 1983; Taylor, 1980).

In hamsters, no such sex differences have yet been reported. However, sex differences have been recently noted in the development of attack types (Taravosh-Lahn & Delville, 2004) (figure 14.1). In females, as in males, play fighting attacks are focused on the face and cheeks, while adult attacks are focused on the lower belly and rump. In males, a period has been recognized with attack focused on the flanks around midpuberty. This period was absent in females, as females were equally likely to attack flanks throughout peripubertal development (figure 14.1). In addition, females appeared to mature faster than males, as their play fighting attacks decreased earlier and as they initiated adultlike attacks earlier in development (figure 14.1). By P-40, females were less likely to target the face and cheeks and more likely to target the lower belly and rump.

Role of Gonadal Hormones

In adults, male sex hormones have been clearly associated with offensive responses (Albers, Karom, & Smith, 2002; Simon, 2002). In hamsters, castration inhibits offensive aggression (Delville, Mansour, & Ferris, 1996b; Payne, 1973). Treatment with testosterone or anabolic steroids enhances offensive aggression toward intruders (Melloni, Connor, Hang, Harrison, & Ferris, 1997; Payne, 1974). However, it is important to note that the association between offensive aggression and gonadal steroids is not necessarily absolute (Albers, Karom, et al., 2002). Certain physiological conditions that include lower testosterone levels have also been associated with increased aggression, even offensive aggression. Hamsters kept under short photoperiods have decreased testosterone levels, but are also more aggressive toward intruders (Jasnow, Huhman, Bartness, & Demas, 2002). These data show that plasma testosterone levels do not necessarily predict aggressive behavior or offensive aggression; instead, testosterone appears to have a permissive role.

As juveniles engage in play fighting well before sexual maturity (Bolles & Woods, 1964; Goldman & Swanson, 1975; Pellis & Pellis, 1997), it is clear that there is no association between plasma levels of sex hormones and the activation of play fighting. However, the preweaning onset of play fighting coincides with adrenarche, the activation of the hypothalamic-pituitary-adrenal (HPA) axis (Cutler et al., 1978). It could be argued that androgens released at that time by the adrenals (Cutler et al., 1978) have an activational effect on play fighting. This hypothesis has not been tested. In rats, castration at weaning has little effect on the decrease in play fighting frequency and on the decrease in the likelihood of complete rotations outside a dominant/subordinate hierarchy (Beatty, Dodge, Traylor, & Meaney, 1981; Pellis, 2002; Smith, Field, Forgie, & Pellis, 1996). However, in the context of a dominant/subordinate relationship, males castrated at weaning will be more likely to become subordinate (Albert, Walsh, Gorzalka, Siemens, & Louie, 1996) and therefore more likely to keep performing complete rotations (Pellis & Pellis, 1993; Smith et al., 1996, 1999). Similarly, in hamsters, castration at weaning seems to have little effect on the development of play fighting behavior in the following weeks (Romeo et al., 2003). Together, these data suggest that although play fighting matures into adult aggression during puberty, increased androgen release around that time has little to do with the transitions in agonistic behavior.

The lack of a role for androgens in the maturation of agonistic behavior around puberty does not mean an absence of function for androgens in play fighting behavior nor for gonadal steroid hormones around weaning (Pellis, 2002; Pellis et al., 1997). Several of the sex differences noted in rats are modulated by perinatal manipulations of sex steroid hormones. The sex differences in play fighting frequency can be altered by standard perinatal treatment (Beatty et al., 1981; Meaney & Stewart, 1981b; Meaney, Stewart, Poulin, & McEwen, 1983; Pellis & McKenna, 1992; Taylor, Frechmann, & Royalty, 1986; Thor & Holloway, 1985; Tonjes, Docke, & Dorner, 1987). Males castrated at birth develop a play fighting frequency similar to that of females. Females treated with testosterone at birth have a play fighting frequency similar to that of males. Some of the sex differences in avoidance and defense are also modulated by perinatal manipulations of steroid hormones. As noted above, females are faster to react to an approach than males (Pellis et al., 1994). Perinatal testosterone treatment of females not only enhances their play fighting frequency but also delays their reaction to approaches, in a manner similar to that of males (Pellis et al., 1994).

However, a somewhat nontraditional hormonal dependence has been noted in the sex difference in the return to partial rotation during puberty (Pellis, 2002). As explained above, females do not return to partial rotation during puberty, therefore maintaining the play period into adulthood (Pellis & Pellis, 1990; Smith et al., 1998a). Just as with females, males castrated at birth keep using complete rotations outside dominant/subordinate relationships (Smith, Forgie, & Pellis, 1998b). However, perinatal testosterone treatment alone is not sufficient to alter the female phenotype for this behavior. Females receiving testosterone treatment around birth, while having a malelike frequency of play fighting activity, maintain complete rotations (and the play period) well into adulthood, even outside dominant/subordinate relationship (Smith et al., 1998a, 1998b). In females, the appearance of a male phenotype for this behavior requires ovariectomy either at birth or after weaning (Pellis 2002; Smith et al., 1998a). This finding shows a role for ovarian hormones in the maturation of play fighting during puberty.

Role of Adrenal Hormones

The hypothalamopituitary-gonadal (HPG) axis is not the only neuroendocrine system maturing during puberty. As explained above, the HPA axis starts becoming active before weaning, but it does not reach maturity until the end of puberty (Elmlinger, Kuhnel, & Ranke, 2002; Gomez, Houshyar, Dallman, 2002; Jonetz-Mentzel & Wiedemann, 1993; Meaney, Sapolski, & McEwen, 1985; Van Kampen & Fuchs, 1998; Wommack et al., 2004). In male hamsters, basal cortisol levels start rising significantly after P-35, as the animals undergo puberty (Wommack et al., 2004). In hamsters, as well as in rats, tree shrews, and humans, the HPA axis reaches adult levels of cortisol or corticosterone release only toward the end of puberty, paralleling the development of the HPG axis (Elmlinger et al., 2002;

Gomez et al., 2002; Jonetz-Metzel & Wiedemann, 1993; Van Kampen & Fuchs, 1998; Wommack et al., 2004). Thus, the development of agonistic behavior coincides with the development of the HPA axis as much as with the HPG axis. Better, adrenarche precedes the onset of preweaning play fighting activity by just a few days (Cutler et al., 1978). Consequently, an association between the onset and the development of agonistic behavior is much more likely to occur with adrenal hormones than gonadal hormones.

This possibility was recently tested in hamsters through treatment with dexamethasone (a type II receptor agonist) around P-35 (Wommack & Delville, manuscript in preparation) (figure 14.4). At that time, repeated treatment with dexamethasone accelerated the development of agonistic behavior away from play fighting and into adultlike aggression. The role of glucocorticoids in the development of agonistic behavior is being further tested through treatment with RU 486 (a type II glucocorticoid receptor antagonist in hamsters [Gray & Leavitt, 1987]). Repeated injections of RU 486 around P-45 could delay the onset of adultlike attacks and maintain the use of play fighting attacks. As these treatments have no effect on other variables, such as growth and body weight, these data support the hypothesis that the peripubertal development of agonistic behavior from play fighting into adultlike aggression is controlled by enhanced activity of the HPA axis.

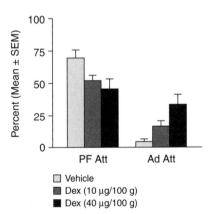

FIGURE 14.4 Juveniles injected with dexamethasone, a glucocorticoid receptor type II agonist, performed fewer play fighting attacks (attacks targeted the face and cheeks, PF Att) at and more adult aggression (attacks targeted at the lower belly and rump, Ad Att) than vehicle-treated animals. Tests were performed for 10-min periods in the presence of a smaller and younger intruder around midpuberty.

Neural Control of Play Fighting

Unlike with adult aggression, few studies have been dedicated to uncovering the neural systems controlling play or play fighting. The distinction between play and play fighting is important to make at this point. These two behaviors should be studied separately, as they probably involve separate neural systems. Most studies in rats have so far focused on the play period; consequently most of these data probably have little to do with rough play fighting as observed in hamsters. Pharmacological studies performed on play in juvenile rats have suggested a role for catecholamines and opiates. Early studies showed a dose-dependent inhibition of pinning by peripheral administration of amphetamine, suggesting a role for dopamine (Beatty, Dodge, Dodge, White, & Panksepp, 1982). This effect was later confirmed by treatment with different doses of apomorphine, a dopamine receptor agonist (Niesink & Van Ree, 1989). This reduction was partially reversed by treatment with haloperidol, a dopamine receptor antagonist (Niesink & Van Ree, 1989). Finally, the possible inhibitory role of dopamine in play activity was recently supported by acute treatment with cocaine (Ferguson, Frisby, & Ali, 2000). Interestingly, similar inhibitory effects have also been observed after treatment with clonidine (an α-2-adrenergic agonist) which could be partially reversed by treatment with yohimbine (an α-2 receptor antagonist), suggesting that the inhibitory effect of dopamine may be generalized to catecholamines (Normansell & Panksepp, 1985a). In addition, play could also be reduced by treatment with quizapine, a serotonin receptor agonist (Normansell & Panksepp, 1985b). These data suggest that a number of monoaminergic systems can modulate the expression of play in the nervous system.

The modulation of play is not limited to monoaminergic drugs. Opiates also alter play activity in rats. However, the effect is opposite to that of catecholamines (Niesink & Van Ree, 1989). Play activity can be enhanced by treatment with morphine or β-endorphin and inhibited by treatment with naltrexone or naloxone (both opioid receptor antagonists) (Panksepp, Jalowiec, DeEskinazi, & Bishop, 1985).

It is important to note that these behavioral observations focused on pinning frequency and allogroming and may not be specific to play. Furthermore, these observations provide no information relating to how and where monoamines or opiates participate in the modulation of play or play activity in rats. Further studies will require more specific manipulations and the identification of a neural circuitry.

As a first approach to identifying the neural circuitry controlling play in rats, studies focused on specific lesions of brain areas. Lesions of the parafascicular thalamic area, the dorsomedial thalamus, and the ventrolateral portions of the brainstem had specific inhibitory effects on play activity (mostly pinning frequency), without impairing indices of play motivation (Siviy & Panksepp, 1985, 1987a). In addition, lesions of the amygdala extending to the medial, central, and cortical amygdaloid nuclei also inhibit play activity (Meaney, Dodge, & Beatty, 1981). However, this inhibition is limited to males, reducing their play activity to the levels observed in females (Meaney et al., 1981). This sex-specific role of the amygdala in play has been further reinforced by implantation of testosterone within the area (Meaney & McEwen, 1986). Implantation of testosterone within the amygdala during the neonatal period was sufficient to raise the play fighting activity of females to the levels observed in males (Meaney & McEwen, 1986).

A more recent study attempted to confirm the role of these areas in play activity in rats through quantification of c-*fos* gene expression in the brain (Gordon, Kollack-Walker, Akil, & Panksepp, 2002). However, none of these areas contained enhanced expression in animals after play. Instead, enhanced c-*fos* expression was noted within the deep and dorsolateral tectum, inferior colliculus, and dorsal part of the midbrain central gray. In addition, enhanced expression was also noted in the ventromedial hypothalamus, dorsal and ventral striatum, and somatosensory cortex. This study remains unique and it is unclear whether the enhanced expression was specific to play. Further studies on this topic would need to include comparisons with rough play fighting or just enhanced activity. Further studies could also include additional labeling for neurotransmitters suspected to be involved in the control of play activity, such as dopamine or enkephalin.

Comparative studies with species performing simplified forms of play or play fighting may be useful to determine the specific roles of particular neurotransmitters in brain areas. At this point, studies with animals such as hamsters are useful because of the apparent lack of play in this species. However, little is presently known of the neural systems controlling play fighting in hamsters. It has been hypothesized that the same neural systems controlling the activation of offensive responses in adults would also control the activation of offensive responses in juveniles (Delville et al., 2003). In male hamsters, offensive aggression is activated by vasopressin and inhibited by serotonin release in the hypothalamus (Delville et al., 1996a; Delville, Mansour, & Ferris, 1996b; Ferris et al., 1997, 1999). A preliminary study was designed along the lines of these findings (Delville et al., 2003). If similar neural systems control offensive responses in juvenile hamsters, then acute peripheral treatment with fluoxetine (a serotonin reuptake inhibitor) should inhibit play fighting activity in juveniles. As predicted, fluoxetine treatment inhibited play fighting activity in hamsters tested around P-35 (Delville et al., 2003). This effect appeared specific to play fighting, as it did not inhibit locomotor activity tested in the LAT maze (Delville et al., 2003). Of course, these studies were very preliminary and will require further confirmation through central injections of serotonin or vasopressin, as well as comparison of neural activation between juveniles and adults sacrificed after an offensive response.

Controlling the Time Course of the Maturation of Agonistic Behavior

A variety of factors are capable of affecting play fighting behavior and its maturation into adult agonistic behavior. As mentioned above, deprivation of play can impair normal social behavior (van den Berg et al., 1999). Other factors, such as illumination and prenatal stress, have been associated with decreased play in rats (Vanderschuren, Niesink, Spruijt, & Van Ree, 1995; Ward & Stehm, 1991). In contrast, environmental enrichment enhances play activity in rats (Morley-Fletcher, Rea, Maccari, & Laviola, 2003). However, these studies did not focus on the time course of the maturation of agonistic behavior, nor did they include rough play fighting. The following examples focus on the maturation of agonistic behavior from one to the other, rather than the expression of one behavior (figure 14.5).

Stress During Puberty

If manipulation of glucocorticoids during puberty can accelerate or delay the maturation of agonistic behavior in hamsters, then stress exposure early in puberty (P-28 to P-42) should also affect the behavior. Male hamsters do not habituate to repeated exposure to social subjugation (Wommack & Delville, 2003). After 2 weeks of repeated exposure to social subjugation,

Stress in Early Puberty

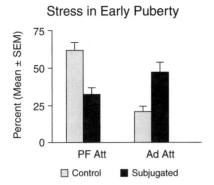

Perinatal Stress

Lead Exposure

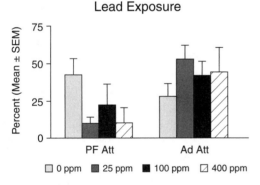

FIGURE 14.5 The development of agonistic behavior is accelerated in animals exposed to daily social subjugation during early puberty (subjugated) (stress in early puberty), in the offspring of dams stressed before parturition (stressed) (perinatal stress), or in animal exposed to various does of lead (lead acetate in parts per million [ppm] in the drinking water) throughout development (lead exposure). Tests were performed for 10-min periods in the presence of a smaller and younger intruder. Data presented show tests performed on P-45, at midpuberty. Play fighting attacks (PF Att) were targeted at the face and cheeks. Adult attacks (Ad Att) were targeted at the lower belly and rump. Side attacks (Side Att) were targeted at the flanks.

male hamsters keep having elevated plasma cortisol levels. This elevation is associated with an acceleration in the maturation of agonistic behavior from play fighting attacks to adultlike attacks (Wommack et al., 2003; Wommack & Delville, 2003) (figure 14.5). Such acceleration is not observed after repeated exposure to another stressful stimulation, placement in an unfamiliar environment (Weinberg & Wong, 1986). Indeed, after 2 weeks of repeated exposure to an unfamiliar environment, hamsters no longer have elevated plasma cortisol levels (Wommack & Delville, 2003). As hamsters were capable of habituating to repeated exposure to an unfamiliar environment, this stimulus did not affect the maturation of agonistic behavior (Wommack et al., 2003; Wommack & Delville, 2003). While repeated exposure to social subjugation affects the maturation of offensive responses, no effect was observed on defensive responses (Wommack et al., 2004). As explained above, it is unclear that defensive responses change during peripubertal development in hamsters.

In addition, differences were observed between individuals exposed to daily social subjugation in early puberty (Wommack & Delville, 2003). Some individuals were more likely to respond to social subjugation by remaining immobile while on a supine position, thus exposing themselves to any attack. The relative occurrence of these on-back submissive displays was associated with individual differences in the acceleration of the maturation of agonistic behavior in subjugated animals. Individuals least likely to display on-back submission during subjugation were also most likely to be accelerated. Individuals most likely to display on-back submission were least accelerated. Although the stress responses these animals was not characterized, it is expected that animals least likely to display on-back submission had greater or longer lasting elevations in plasma cortisol levels.

One may wonder about the ecological significance of accelerated development of agonistic behavior. Accelerated hamsters initiate adultlike aggressive behavior earlier in life. These animals undergo normal gonadal development, but they also are particularly aggressive toward smaller and younger individuals (Wommack et al., 2003). The consequences of this enhanced aggression may depend on population density (Delville et al., 2003). Previous studies on aggression have established a relationship between population density and aggression (Brown, 1953; Greenberg, 1972; Southwick, 1955). In mice, as population increases, the level of aggression also increases. Under conditions of elevated population density, juvenile hamsters are most likely to become socially sub-jugated by adults. Consequently, they themselves become more aggressive, therefore increasing the level of aggres-sion in the population (Delville et al., 2003).

In contrast, stress during late puberty does not alter the development of agonistic behavior, as it has already reached an adult stage (Delville et al., 2003). Instead, hamsters exposed to repeated social subjugation during late puberty and in adulthood become submissive even to smaller and younger individuals (Delville et al., 2003; Huhman, Moore, Ferris, Moughey, & Meyerhoff, 1991; Huhman et al., 2003; Potegal et al., 1993). This effect is long lasting (Huhman et al., 2003). Such animals would be the least likely to defend a territory or compete for females. In a wild population, such animals would be least likely to participate in the next generations.

Role of the Perinatal Environment

If exposure to stress in early puberty accelerates the matu-ration of agonistic behavior, how about stress during ear-lier time periods? A number of studies have addressed effects of stress during perinatal development (Sanchez, Ladd, & Plotsky, 2001). These are associated with differ-ences in stress responsiveness later in life (Sanchez et al., 2001). Prenatal stress has been associated with increased stress responsiveness (Meaney et al., 1991; Sherrod, Meier, & Connor, 1977; Vallee et al., 1997), while post-natal handling or increased maternal care has been asso-ciated with decreased stress responsiveness (Takahashi, Haglin, & Kalin, 1992; Vallee et al., 1997). Such differ-ences in stress responsiveness could result in individual differences in the development of agonistic behavior and explain part of the variability of the behavior in a popula-tion of hamsters. A first study was performed with animals raised by females exposed to a mild stress late in gestation (Taravosh-Lahn & Delville, manuscript in preparation). As predicted, the offspring of such stressed females were faster to initiate adultlike attacks (figure 14.5). These data support the relationship between stress responsiveness and the development of agonistic behavior in hamsters.

These data also have an ecological relevance, again in relation to enhanced aggression under increased population density. Under enhanced population den-sity, it is likely that lactating and pregnant females would be exposed to some stressful pressure. This stress-ful pressure would contribute to enhanced aggression in the population through the acceleration of adult aggression in young individuals. In addition, these data show that the effects of perinatal stress are not limited

to altering stress responsiveness. Perinatal manipula-tions altering stress responses also alter the develop-ment of social and agonistic behavior.

Role of Substances in the Environment

Beside stress, exposure to a number of substances dur-ing development affects aggressive behavior early in adulthood (Delville, 1999; Ferris, Shtiegman, & King, 1998; Harrison, Connor, Nowak, & Melloni, 2000; Melloni et al., 1997). In hamsters, exposure to low doses of lead throughout development (Delville, 2000) and exposure to alcohol (Ferris et al., 1998), anabolic steroids (Melloni et al., 1997), or cocaine (Harrison et al., 2000) during puberty enhance aggression dur-ing early adulthood. However, these studies did not ad-dress the development of agonistic behavior. The effect of one such environmental substance was recently tested in our laboratory on the development of agonis-tic behavior in hamsters (Cervantes et al., in press). Adult female hamsters were exposed to various doses of lead for a period of time to allow stabilization of blood lead levels. Later, the females were mated, be-came pregnant, and were allowed to raise their pups. Afterward, the pups were weaned and tested for offen-sive responses during peripubertal development. In such studies it is important to test the effect of expo-sure to low doses of lead. The effects of exposure to low doses of such contaminants are still being tested to establish the toxicity of such substances and to influ-ence environmental policy. In this study, animals ex-posed to the lowest doses of lead were more likely to be aggressive as adults. Interestingly, these animals also had an accelerated development of agonistic behav-ior, maturing into adultlike aggression faster than their controls or animals exposed to higher lead doses (fig-ure 14.5). In this study, plasma cortisol levels were not tested. These data are interesting as they suggest that a variety of neurobiological factors may participate in the maturation of agonistic behavior from play fighting to adult aggression.

Comparison With Humans

Normal Development

Human aggression changes both qualitatively and quantitatively during development. During childhood (up to age 11), aggression changes from physical to verbal and becomes more hostile (e.g., Caplan, Vespo, Pedersen, & Hay, 1991; Goodenough, 1931; Hartup, 1974). By the age of 11, the majority of aggressive acts are retaliatory in nature (Sancilio, Plumert, & Hartup, 1989). Several studies suggest that children (especially boys) of this age view retaliation as a normal reaction to being wronged (Astor, 1994; Coie, Dodge, Terry, & Wright, 1991; Sancilio et al., 1989). The occurrence of retaliatory aggression peaks with the onset of puberty and then declines through the end of adolescence and into adulthood (Cairns, Cairns, Necerkman, Ferguson, & Gariepy, 1989; Loeber, 1982). However, it appears that adolescents are simply more adept at channeling their overt hostilities into covert and antisocial behavior. Teenage girls are more likely to deal with adversaries through ostracism and teasing (Bjorkqvist, Lagerspetz, & Kaukainen, 1992; Cairns et al., 1989), whereas teenage boys are more likely to express their anger through delinquent acts (Newcombe & Bentler, 1989; U.S. Department of Justice, 1992).

Threats to Normal Development

Adolescence has been described as a time of "storm and stress" (Hall, 1904), when individuals try to find a balance between their biological maturity and their social dependence. Tremblay (2003) has argued that the socialization process consists of *un*learning aggressive behavior and learning alternative problem solving strategies. However, development does not always go as planned. A number of risk factors can derail the socialization process, and Tremblay groups these into "individual" and "environmental" categories. Individual risk factors can be *physiological* (e.g., higher testosterone, lower serotonin) or *psychological* (e.g., cognitive deficits, poor anger control in childhood). Environmental risk factors can be *physical* (e.g., exposure to toxins, poor nutrition) or *social* (e.g., aggressive peers, poor social relationships). If social relationships play an important role in normal development, then we would expect threats to social relationships to have negative consequences for later development. In some recent work, we have used bullying as a model to study the role that social stress during puberty plays in the development of aggressive human behavior.

Bullying as a Stressor

According to most estimates, 30% of children have been victims of bullying at some point, and between 5 and 10% are victims on a regular basis (e.g., Nansel et al., 2001; Olweus, 1993; Perry, Kusel, & Perry, 1988; Rigby & Slee, 1991). Boys are more likely than girls to be physically bullied (e.g., Arora & Thomson, 1987; Nansel et al., 2001; Siann, Callaghghan, Glissov, Lockhart, & Rawson, 1994; Slee & Rigby, 1993), but boys and girls are equally likely to be teased verbally (e.g., Crick, 1995). Being a victim of bullying has been associated with a number of negative psychological outcomes, including anxiety (e.g., Bond, Carlin, Thomas, Rubin, & Patton, 2001; Craig, 1998; Perry et al., 1988) and depression (e.g., Craig, 1998; Neary & Joseph, 1994).

The link between victimization and aggressive behavior is less clear. A handful of laboratory studies have subjected participants to teasing and found that people willingly take revenge on their tormentors and others (e.g., Gaertner & Iuzzini, 2002; Twenge, 2001). In the real world, being victimized by bullies appears to increase the risk that one will be involved in violent behavior (e.g., bringing a weapon to school, fighting; Nansel, Overpeck, Haynie, Ruan, & Scheidt, 2003). A number of high-profile school shootings captured the headlines in the mid to late 1990s, and many of the perpetrators had been teased by their peers. Indeed, a recent case study of several school-shooting perpetrators found that nearly all had been rejected and bullied (Leary, Kowalski, Smith, & Phillips, 2003). However, given the percentage of children who are victimized by bullies, it is clear that being bullied, per se, does not "cause" aggression.

How might victimization by bullies lead to violent behavior? Several theorists have argued that aggression is a natural instinct, which most people learn to control (e.g., Lorenz, 1966; Tremblay, 2003). Thus, if victimization leads people to be aggressive, it must be interfering with this "unlearning" process. Indeed, there is evidence that victimization interferes with the ability to regulate emotions and to altered perceptions of both the appropriateness and the effectiveness of acting aggressively (Schwarz & Proctor, 2000). One possibility is that the stress of victimization is the first step in a chain of events leading to impaired cognition and emotion. Aggressive behavior may be limited to those who suffer the greatest impairments and who have the fewest resources to cope with these impairments. Many stressful situations create physiological arousal, but an emotional or behavioral response often depends on one's interpretation of the situation (cf. Schachter & Singer, 1962). Thus, if bullying victims are more likely to respond violently, it stands to reason that they might be both (a) more likely to view violence as an acceptable response and (b) more physiologically aroused in a stressful situation.

Bullying and the Hamster Model

The research on aggression in hamsters provides a good starting point for making predictions about humans. As mentioned above, the timing of subjugation is a critical factor in hamsters. However, the issue of timing has not yet been examined in a human population. This may be because victimization by bullies tends to decline with age (e.g., Boulton & Underwood, 1992; Olweus, 1993; Whitney & Smith, 1993), and researchers have devoted more attention to early bullying.

A set of specific predictions emerges from the hamster model about the consequences of being bullied. First, people bullied early in puberty (i.e., before high school) should view aggression as more normal and appropriate, and they report more stress and depression symptoms. Second, people bullied later in puberty (i.e., during high school) should view aggression as less appropriate, but report even more stress and depression symptoms. These predictions were tested in two recent studies in which college freshmen completed a set of questionnaires over the internet.

Study 1: Victimization and the Appropriateness of Aggression

The predictions about perceptions of aggression were tested in Study 1 (N = 1483, 68% females; Newman, Holden, & Delville, 2004). First, they were asked about their *victimization experiences*, both during high school and before. Second, they were asked to evaluate the likelihood that males of different ages would respond aggressively to an insult. We then examined the link between victimization at each time period and perceptions of the appropriateness of aggression. According to the hamster model, those bullied before high school should see aggression as more appropriate, and those bullied during high school should see it as less appropriate.

Across both time periods, females thought males would act more aggressively than males did. Contrary to our hypotheses, early victimization did not affect perceptions of the likelihood of aggression. However, consistent with predictions, males who were bullied frequently in high school saw aggression as less normal (figure 14.6).

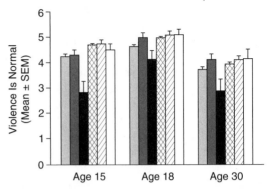

Violence as a Normal Response

Gender and Frequency of Victimization in High School

- ☐ Males—Not at All
- ◼ Males—Occasional
- ◼ Males—Frequently
- ⊠ Females—Not at All
- ▨ Females—Occasional
- ☐ Females—Frequently

FIGURE 14.6 Belief that violence is a normal response to an insult. Participants were asked to rate the likelihood that males of different ages would respond violently to an insult, on a 1–7 Likert scale. Participants reported their experiences with being bullied as "not at all," "occasionally," or "frequently." Victimized participants were bullied only during high school.

Study 2: Victimization and Stress Symptoms

The predictions about stress symptoms were tested in Study 2 (N = 853, 59% females; Newman, Holden & Delville, in press). Participants completed two questionnaires. Participants again completed the measure of *victimization experiences*. They were also asked about their current frequency of several *stress and trauma symptoms* (TSC-33; Briere & Runtz, 1989). We then examined the link between victimization at each time period and stress symptoms.

Those who were bullied more frequently *before high school* reported more stress symptoms. Females also reported more of these symptoms than males, but there was no interaction between victimization and gender. Those who were bullied more frequently *during high school* reported more stress symptoms than those bullied less frequently. Females also reported more of these symptoms than males, but there was no interaction between gender and victimization. Finally, we compared the effects of victimization at each time period on current stress. When both were entered into a regression analysis, high school victimization (β = .173) had a stronger association with stress than earlier victimization (β = .056). This was consistent with our predictions.

Summary

The data from these two studies provide partial support for our hypothesis. Males victimized during high school (i.e., in late puberty) saw aggression as less appropriate than those not bullied. However, those victimized before high school did not see aggression as any *more* appropriate than those not bullied. It may be the case that the consequences of early victimization fade by the time participants reach college. It may also be the case that timing plays a larger role in the development of aggressive behavior or of other attitudes toward aggression, but future research is needed to explore this possibility. Victimization was also associated with a higher number of stress symptoms, and this association was strongest for bullying that occurred in high school (i.e., in late puberty).

These data suffer the same problems as any self-report, retrospective study. Namely, reports of victimization may reflect people's perceptions, rather than their actual experiences. As such, it is difficult to determine whether experiences or perceptions are associated with long-term stress symptoms. Future research could address these concerns with a prospective design, by identifying victims and their degree of isolation or support during school and then conducting follow-up assessments to determine stress symptoms.

Coping With Threats to Development

One final question is whether people are able to cope with the stress of being bullied and with other environmental threats to normal development. A large body of research supports the idea that people use a variety of coping strategies for dealing with a stressor (for a review, see Carver, Scheier, & Weintraub, 1989). One of the best coping strategies appears to be a strong social support network (for reviews, see Leavy, 1983; Schradle & Dougher, 1985; Uchino, Cacioppo, and Kiecolt-Glaser, 1996). In times of stress, both acute and chronic, social support has been shown to lower blood pressure, strengthen immune response, and decrease the secretion of stress hormones (Uchino et al., 1996).

In the study of victimization and stress symptoms discussed above (Newman et al., in press), we also included a measure of perceived isolation. We predicted that the effects of being bullied would be magnified

in those without a social support network. Results confirmed this prediction. In a multiple regression analysis, the best predictor of current stress symptoms was the interaction between high school victimization and perceived isolation in high school (β = .37, p = .02). Isolation appears to magnify the effects of being bullied frequently (figure 14.7). Or, more optimistically, the link between victimization and stress symptoms was much weaker among those who did not feel isolated. Importantly, the correlation between victimization and isolation was only .17, suggesting that one can be victimized with or without feeling isolated.

The most intriguing question raised by this finding is the meaning of "perceived isolation." We see two possibilities, both of which are likely to provide a buffer against the stress of being bullied. First, perceived isolation may reflect differences in actual available social support. It is certainly plausible that individuals with a larger support network would be less affected by bullying. Second, perceived isolation may reflect individual differences in coping styles. For example, some individuals may be less prone to feeling alone or may find it easier to seek comfort from others. According to Sarason, Sarason, and Pierce (1994), those who believe others are around to help them are more optimistic and have a higher sense of self-efficacy. Consequently, these individuals may be more resilient in dealing with stress,

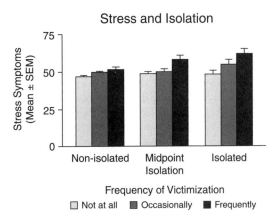

FIGURE 14.7 Total experience with stress symptoms. Frequencies of 32 items were evaluated on a 0–3 Likert scale. Isolation was rated on a 1–5 Likert scale, where "nonisolated" = 1 or 2 on the isolation scale (N = 680); "midpoint" = 3 on the isolation scale (N = 125); and "isolated" = 4 or 5 on the isolation scale (N = 45). Participants reported their experiences with being bullied as "not at all," "occasionally," or "frequently."

and this may remove a critical link in the chain between victimization and later violence.

Summary and Conclusions

Puberty is a critical period in the development of aggressive behavior in most mammals. Typically, elements of the adult aggressive responses start appearing early and become fully integrated in mature behavior in late puberty. There is little evidence for a role of gonadal hormones in the maturation of aggressive behavior during this developmental period. However, the maturation of aggressive behavior is also correlated with the maturation of the HPA axis. Our data show that the HPA axis controls the maturation of aggressive behavior during puberty. It is also likely that adrenarche, the onset of the activity of the HPA axis, controls the appearance of aggressive responses before puberty. This regulation mechanism may provide an explanation for interactions between genes and the environment, as the activity of the HPA axis differs between individuals and can be affected by external stimuli, such as stress. In addition, the maturation of the HPA axis and its relevance to the control of the maturation of aggressive behavior during puberty can also explain differential consequences of stress exposure between early and late puberty in animals, as well as in humans.

Note

The studies described in this review and originating from our laboratory were supported by Grant ES10385 from the NIH (awarded to Y.D.). Matt Newman was supported by Postdoctoral Fellowship MH65728–1 from the NIH. Joel Wommack was supported by a continuing predoctoral fellowship awarded by the University of Texas at Austin. The authors are grateful to George Holden for helpful discussions on the studies on bullying.

References

Albers, H. E., Huhman, K. L., & Meisel, R. L. (2002). Hormonal basis of social conflict and communication. In D. W. Pfaff, A. P. Arnold, A. M. Etgen, S. E. Farhbach, & R. T. Rubin (Eds.), Hormones, brain and behavior (Vol. 1, pp. 393–433). San Diego: Academic Press.

Albers, H. E., Karom, M., & Smith, D. (2002). Serotonin and vasopressin interact in the hypothalamus to control communicative behavior. Neuroreport, 13, 931–933.

Albert, D. J., Walsh, M. L., Gorzalka, B. B., Siemens, Y., & Louie, H. (1986). Testosterone removal in rats results in a decrease in social aggression and a loss of social dominance. Physiology and Behavior, 36, 401–407.

Arora, C. M. J., & Thomson, D. A. (1987). Defining bullying for a secondary school. Education and Child Psychology, 4, 110–120.

Astor, R. A. (1994). Children's moral reasoning about family and peer violence: The role of provocation and retribution. Child Development, 65, 1054–1067.

Barfield, R. J., Auerbach, P., Geyer, L. A., & McIntosh, T. K. (1979). Ultrasonic vocalizations in rat sexual behavior. American Zoologist, 19, 469–480.

Beanninger, L. P. (1967). Comparison of behavioral development in socially isolated and grouped rats. Animal Behaviour, 15, 312–323.

Beatty, W. W., Dodge, A. M., Dodge, L. J., White, K., & Panksepp, J. (1982). Psychomotor stimulants, social deprivation and play in juvenile rats. Pharmacology, Biochemistry and Behavior, 16, 417–422.

Beatty, W. W., Dodge, A. M., Traylor, K. L., & Meaney, M. J. (1981). Temporal boundary of the sensitive period for hormonal organization of social play in juvenile rats. Physiology and Behavior, 26, 241–243.

Bjorkqvist, K., Lagerspetz, K. M., & Kaukainen, A. (1992). Do girls manipulate and boys fight? Developmental trends in regard to direct and indirect aggression. Aggressive Behavior, 18, 117–127.

Blanchard, R. J., Wall, P. M., & Blanchard, D. C. (2003). Problems in the study of rodent aggression. Hormones and Behavior, 44, 161–170.

Bolles, R. C., & Woods, P. J. (1964). The ontogeny of behaviour in the albino rat. Animal Behaviour, 12, 427–441.

Bond, L., Carlin, J. B., Thomas, L., Rubin, K., & Patton, G. (2001). Does bullying cause emotional problems? A prospective study of young teenagers. British Medical Journal, 323, 480–484.

Boulton, M. J., & Underwood, K. (1992). Bully/victim problems in middle-school children: Stability, self-perceived competence, peer perceptions and peer acceptance. British Journal of Developmental Psychology, 62, 73–87.

Bradbury, J. W., & Vehrencamp, S. L. (1998). Principles of animal communication. Sunderland, MA: Sinauer.

Briere, J., & Runtz, M. (1989). The Trauma Symptom Checklist (TSC-33): Early data on a new scale. Journal of Interpersonal Violence, 4, 151–163.

Brown, R. E. (1953). Social behaviour, reproduction and population changes in the house mouse (Mus musculus L.). Ecology Monographs, 23, 217–240.

Brown, R. E. (1979). The 22-kHz pre-ejaculatory vocalizations of the male rat. *Physiology and Behavior, 22,* 483–489.

Brudzynski, S. M., & Pniak, A. (2002). Social contacts and production of 50-kHz short ultrasonic calls in adult rats. *Journal of Comparative Psychology, 116,* 782–798.

Cairns, R. B., Cairns, B. D., Necerkman, J. J., Ferguson, L. L., & Gariepy, K. (1989). Social networks and aggressive behavior: Peer support or peer rejection. *Developmental Psychology, 24,* 815–823.

Caplan, M., Vespo, J., Pedersen, J., & Hay, D. F. (1991). Conflict and its resolution among small groups of one- and two-year-olds. *Child Development, 62,* 1513–1524.

Carver, C. S., Scheier, M. F., & Weintraub, J. K. (1989). Assessing coping strategies: A theoretically based approach. *Journal of Personality and Social Psychology, 56,* 267–283.

Cervantes, M. C., David, J. T., Loyd, D. R., Salinas, J. A., & Delville, Y. (in press). Lead exposure alters the development of agonistic behavior in hamsters. *Developmental Psychobiology.*

Christensen, F., & Dam, H. (1953). A sexual dimorphism of the Harderian glands in hamsters. *Acta Physiologica Scandinavica, 27,* 333–336.

Clabough, J. W., & Norwell, J. E. (1973). Effects of castration, blinding, and the pineal gland on the Harderian glands of the male golden hamsters. *Neuroendocrinology, 12,* 344–353.

Coie, J. D., Dodge, K. A., Terry, R., & Wright, V. (1991). The role of aggression in peer relations: An analysis of aggression episodes in boys' play groups. *Child Development, 62,* 812–826.

Craig, W. M. (1998). The relationship among bullying, victimization, depression, anxiety, and aggression in elementary school children. *Personality and Individual Differences, 24,* 123–130.

Crick, N. R. (1995). Relational aggression: The role of intent attributions, feelings of distress, and provocation type. *Development and Psychopathology, 7,* 313–322.

Cutler, G. B., Jr., Glenn, M., Bush, M., Hodgen, G. D., Graham, C. E., & Loriaux, D. L. (1978). Adrenarche: A survey of rodents, domestic animals, and primates. *Endocrinology, 103,* 2112–2118.

Deanesly, R. (1938). The reproductive cycle of the golden hamster (*Cricetus auratus*). *Proceedings of the Zoological Society, London, 108,* 31–37.

Delville, Y. (1999). Exposure to lead during development alters aggressive behavior in golden hamsters. *Neurotoxicology and Teratology, 21,* 445–449.

Delville, Y., David, J. T., Taravosh-Lahn, K., & Wommack, J. C. (2003). Stress and the development of agonistic behavior in golden hamsters. *Hormones and Behavior, 44,* 263–270.

Delville, Y., Mansour, K. M., & Ferris, C. F. (1996a). Serotonin blocks vasopressin-facilitated offensive aggression: Interactions within the ventrolateral hypothalamus of golden hamsters. *Physiology and Behavior, 59,* 813–816.

Delville, Y., Mansour, K. M., & Ferris, C. F. (1996b). Testosterone facilitates offensive aggression by modulating vasopressin receptors in the hypothalamus. *Physiology and Behavior, 60,* 25–29.

Dieterlen, F. (1959). Das Verhalten des Syrischen Goldhamsters (*Mesocricetus auratus* Waterhouse). *Zeitschrift fur Tierpsycholgie, 16,* 47–103.

Elmlinger, M. W., Kuhnel, W., & Ranke, M. B. (2002). Reference range for serum concentrations of lutropin (LH), follitropin (FSH), estradiol (E2), prolactin, progesterone, sex hormone-binding globulin (SHBG), dehydroepiandrosterone sulfate (DHEAS), cortisol and ferritin in neonates, children and young adults. *Clinical Chemistry and Laboratory Medicine, 40,* 1151–1160.

Ferguson, S. A., Frisby, N. B., & Ali, S. F. (2000). Acute effects of cocaine on play behaviour of rats. *Behavioral Pharmacology, 11,* 175–179.

Ferris, C. F., Albers, H. E., Wesoloswki, S. M., Goldman, B. D., & Leeman, S. E. (1984). Microinjection of vasopressin into a discreet hypothalamic site triggers a complex stereotypic behavior in golden hamsters. *Science, 224,* 521–523.

Ferris, C. F., Axelson, J. F., Shinto, L. H., & Albers, H. E. (1987). Scent marking and the maintenance of dominant/subordinate status in male golden hamsters. *Physiology and Behavior, 40,* 661–664.

Ferris, C. F., & Delville, Y. (1994). Vasopressin and serotonin interactions in the control of agonistic behavior. *Psychoneuroendocrinology, 19,* 593–601.

Ferris, C. F., Delville, Y., Brewer, J. A., Mansour, K. M., Yules, B., & Melloni, R. H., Jr. (1996). Vasopressin and the developmental onset of flank marking behavior in golden hamsters. *Journal of Neurobiology, 30,* 192–204.

Ferris, C. F., Melloni, R. H., Jr., Kopel, G., Perry, K. W., Fuller, R. W., & Delville, Y. (1997). Vasopressin/serotonin interactions in the anterior hypothalamus control aggressive behavior in golden hamsters. *Journal of Neuroscience, 17,* 4331–4340.

Ferris, C. F., Shtiegman, K., & King, J. A. (1998). Voluntary ethanol consumption in adolescent hamsters increases testosterone and aggression. *Physiology and Behavior, 63,* 739–744.

Ferris, C. F., Stolberg T., & Delville, Y. (1999). Serotonin regulation of aggressive behavior in male golden hamsters (*Mesocricetus auratus*). *Behavioral Neuroscience, 113,* 804–815.

Festing, M. F. (1986). Hamsters. In T. P. Poole (Ed.), *The UFAW handbook on the care and management of laboratory animals* (6th ed., pp. 242–256). New York: Longman Scientific & Technical.

Field, E. F., Whishaw, I. Q., & Pellis, S. M. (1996). A kinematic analysis of evasive dodging movements used during food protection in the rat. Evidence of sex differences in movement. *Journal of Comparative Psychology, 110*, 298–306.

Floody, O. R., & Pfaff, D. W. (1977). Communication among hamsters by high-frequency acoustic signals: I. Physical characteristics of hamster calls. *Journal of Comparative and Physiological Psychology, 91*, 794–806.

Floody, O. R., Pfaff, D. W., & Lewis, C. D. (1977). Communication among hamsters by high-frequency acoustic signals: II. Determinants of calling by females and males. *Journal of Comparative and Physiological Psychology, 91*, 807–819.

Foroud, A., & Pellis, S. M. (2003). The development of "roughness" in the play fighting of rats: A Laban Movement Analysis perspective. *Developmental Psychobiology, 42*, 35–43.

Gaertner, L., & Iuzzini, J. (2002, January). *Social rejection and perceived groupness as antecedents of mass violence.* Paper presented at the annual meeting of the Society for Personality and Social Psychology, Savannah, GA.

Gerall, H. D., Ward, I. L., & Gerall, A. A. (1967). Disruption of the male rat's sexual behaviour induced by social isolation. *Animal Behaviour, 15*, 54–58.

Goldman, L., & Swanson, H. H. (1975). Developmental changes in pre-adult behavior in confined colonies of golden hamsters. *Developmental Psychobiology, 8*, 137–150.

Gomez, F., Houshyar, H., & Dallman, M. F. (2002). Marked regulatory shifts in gonadal, adrenal, and metabolic system responses to repeated restraint stress occur within a 3-week period in pubertal male rats. *Endocrinology, 143*, 2852–2862.

Goodenough, F. L. (1931). *Anger in young children.* Minneapolis: University of Minnesota Press.

Gordon, N. S., Kollack-Walker, S., Akil, H., & Panksepp, J. (2002). Expression of c-*fos* gene activation during rough and tumble play in juvenile rats. *Brain Research Bulletin, 57*, 651–659.

Gray, G. O., & Leavitt, W. W. (1987). RU486 is not antiprogestin in the hamster. *Journal of Steroid Biochemistry, 28*, 493–497.

Greenberg, G. (1972). The effects of ambient temperature and population density on aggression in two inbred strains of mice, Mus musculus. *Behaviour, 42*, 119–130.

Gruendel, A. D., & Arnold, W. L. (1969). Effects of early social deprivation on reproductive behavior of male rats. *Journal of Comparative and Physiological Psychology, 67*, 123–128.

Guerra, R. F., Vieiria, M. L., Takase, E., & Gasparetto, S. (1992). Sex differences in the play fighting activity of golden hamster infants. *Physiology and Behavior, 52*, 1–5.

Hall, G. S. (1904). *Adolescence: Its psychology and its relations to physiology, anthropology, sex, crime, religion, and education* (Vol. I). New York: Appleton-Century-Crofts.

Hamilton, J. B., & Montagna, W. (1950). The sebaceous glands of the hamster: I. Morphological effects of androgens on integumentary structures. *American Journal of Anatomy, 86*, 191–233.

Harrison, R. J., Connor, D. F., Nowak, C., & Melloni, R. H., Jr. (2000). Chronic low-dose cocaine treatment during adolescence facilitates aggression in hamsters. *Physiology and Behavior, 69*, 555–562.

Hartup, W. W. (1974). Aggression in childhood: Developmental perspectives. *American Psychologist, 29*, 336–341.

Hole, G. H., & Heinon, D. F. (1984). Play in rodents. In P. K. Smith (Ed.), *Play in animals and man* (pp. 95–117). Oxford, UK: Blackwell.

Huhman, K. L., Moore, T. O., Ferris, C. F., Moughey, E. H., & Meyerhoff, J. L. (1991). Acute and repeated exposure to social conflict in male golden hamsters: Increase in plasma POMC-peptides and cortisol decreases in plasma testosterone. *Hormones and Behavior, 25*, 206–216.

Huhman, K. L., Solomon, M. B., Janicki, M., Harmon, A. C., Lin, S. M., Israel, J. E., et al. (2003). Conditioned defeat in male and female Syrian hamsters. *Hormones and Behavior, 44*, 293–299.

Jasnow, A. M., Huhman, K. L., Bartness, T. J., & Demas, G. E. (2002). Short days and exogenous melatonin increase aggression of male Syrian hamsters (*Mesocricetus auratus*). *Hormones and Behavior, 42*, 13–20.

Johnston, R. E. (1975). Scent marking by male golden hamsters (*Mesocricetus auratus*): I. Effects of odors and social encounters. *Zeitschrift fur Tierpsychologie, 37*, 75–98.

Johnston, R. E. (1977). The causation of two scent marking behaviors in female golden hamsters. *Animal Behaviour, 25*, 317–327.

Johnston, R. E. (1985). Communication. In H. I. Siegel (Ed.), *The hamster* (pp. 121–154). New York: Plenum.

Jonetz-Mentzel, L., & Wiedemann, G. (1993). Establishment of reference ranges for cortisol in neonates, infants, children and adolescents. *European Journal of Clinical Chemistry and Clinical Biochemistry, 31*, 525–529.

Knutson, B., Burgdorf, J., & Panksepp, J. (1998). Anticipation of play elicits high-frequency ultrasonic vocalizations in young rats. *Journal of Comparative Psychology, 112*, 65–73.

Laviola, G., & Alleva, E. (1995). Sibling effects on the

behavior of infant mouse litters (*Mus musculus*). *Journal of Comparative Psychology, 109,* 68–75.

Leary, M. R., Kowalski, R. M., Smith, L., & Phillips, S. (2003). Teasing, rejection, and violence: Case studies of the school shootings. *Aggressive Behavior, 29,* 202–214.

Leavy, R. L. (1983). Social support and psychological disorder: A review. *Journal of Clinical Child and Adolescent Psychology, 11,* 3–21.

Lisk, R. D., Ciacco, L. A., & Catanzaro, C. (1983). Mating behavior of the golden hamster under seminatural conditions. *Animal Behaviour, 310,* 659–666.

Loeber, R. (1982). The stability of antisocial behavior: A review. *Child Development, 53,* 1431–1446.

Lorenz, K. (1966). *On aggression.* New York: Harcourt, Brace, & World.

Meaney, M. J., Dodge, A. M., & Beatty, W. W. (1981). Sex-dependent effects of amygdaloid lesions on the social play of prepubertal rats. *Physiology and Behavior, 26,* 467–472.

Meaney, M. J., & McEwen, B. S. (1986). Testosterone implants into the amygdala during the neonatal period masculinize the social play of juvenile female rats. *Brain Research, 398,* 324–328.

Meaney, M. J., Mitchell, J. B., Aitken, D. H., Bhatnagar, S., Bodnoff, S. R., Iny, L. J., et al. (1991). The effects of neonatal handling on the development of the adrenocortical response to stress: Implication for neuropathology and cognitive deficits in later life. *Psychoneuroendocrinology, 16,* 85–103.

Meaney, M. J., Sapolski, R. M., & McEwen, B. S. (1985). The developmental of the glucocorticoid receptor system in the rat limbic brain: II. An autoradiographic study. *Developmental Brain Research, 18,* 165–168.

Meaney, M. J., & Stewart, J. (1979). Environmental factors influencing the affiliative behavior of male and female rats (*Rattus norvegicus*). *Animal Learning and Behavior, 7,* 397–405.

Meaney, M. J., & Stewart, J. (1981a). A descriptive study of social development in the rat (*Rattus norvegicus*). *Animal Behaviour, 29,* 34–45.

Meaney, M. J., & Stewart, J. (1981b). Neonatal-androgens influence the social play of prepubescent rats. *Hormones and Behavior, 15,* 197–213.

Meaney, M. J., Stewart, J., & Beatty, W. W. (1985). Sex differences in social play: The socialization of sex roles. *Advances in the Study of Behavior, 15,* 1–58.

Meaney, M. J., Stewart, J., Poulin, P., & McEwen, B. S. (1983). Sexual differentiation of social play in rat pups is mediated by the neonatal androgen-receptor system. *Neuroendocrinology, 37,* 85–90.

Melloni, R. H., Jr., Connor, D. F., Hang, P. T., Harrison, R. J., & Ferris, C. F. (1997). Anabolic-steroid exposure during adolescence and aggressive behavior in golden hamsters. *Physiology and Behavior, 61,* 359–364.

Morley-Fletcher, S., Rea, M., Maccari, S., & Laviola, G. (2003). Environmental enrichment during adolescence reverses the effects of prenatal stress on play behaviour and HPA axis reactivity in rats. *European Journal of Neuroscience, 18,* 3367–3374.

Nansel, T. R., Overpeck, M. D., Haynie, D. L., Ruan, J., & Scheidt, P. C. (2003). Relationships between bullying and violence among U.S. youth. *Archives of Pediatric and Adolescent Medicine, 157,* 348–353.

Nansel., T. R., Overpeck, M. D., Pilla, R. S., Ruan, W. J., Simons-Morton, B., & Scheidt, P. (2001). Bullying behaviors among US youth: Prevalence and association with psychosocial adjustment. *Journal of the American Medical Association, 285,* 2094.

Neary, A., & Joseph, S. (1994). Peer victimization and its relationship to self-concept and depression among schoolgirls. *Personality and Individual Differences, 16,* 183–186.

Newcombe, N., & Bentler, P. M. (1989). Substance use and abuse among children and teenagers. *American Psychologist, 44,* 242–248.

Newman, M. L., Holden, G. W., & Delville, Y. (2004). It's all in the timing: Cognitive and emotional consequences of bullying during puberty. Unpublished manuscript.

Newman, M. L., Holden, G. W., & Delville, Y. (in press). Isolation and the stress of being bullied. *Journal of Adolescence.*

Niesink, R. J., & Van Ree, J. M. (1989). Involvement of opioid and dopaminergic systems in isolation-induced pinning and social grooming of young rats. *Neuropharmacology, 28,* 411–418.

Normansell, L., & Panksepp, J. (1985a). Effects of clonidine and yohimbine on the social play of juvenile rats. *Pharmacology, Biochemistry and Behavior, 22,* 881–883.

Normansell, L., & Panksepp, J. (1985b). Effects of quipazine and methysergide on play in juvenile rats. *Pharmacology, Biochemistry and Behavior, 22,* 885–887.

Olioff, M., & Stewart, J. (1978). Sex differences in the play behavior of prepubescent rats. *Physiology and Behavior, 20,* 113–115.

Olweus, D. (1993). *Bullying at school: What we know and what we can do.* Oxford, UK: Blackwell.

Panksepp, J. (1981). The ontogeny of play in rats. *Developmental Psychobiology, 14,* 327–332.

Panksepp, J., & Burgdorf, J. (2003). "Laughing" rats and the evolutionary antecedents of human joy? *Physiology and Behavior, 79,* 533–547.

Panksepp, J., Jalowiec, J., DeEskinazi, F. G., & Bishop, P. (1985). Opiates and play dominance in juvenile rats. *Behavioral Neuroscience, 99,* 441–453.

Payne, A. P. (1973). A comparison of the aggressive behaviour of isolated intact and castrated male golden hamsters towards intruders introduced into the home cage. *Physiology and Behavior, 10*, 629–631.

Payne, A. P. (1974). A comparison of the effects of androstenedione, dihydrotestosterone and testosterone propionate on aggression in the castrated male golden hamster. *Physiology and Behavior, 13*, 21–26.

Payne, A. P. (1977). Pheromonal effects of Harderian gland homogenates on aggressive behaviour in the hamster. *Journal of Endocrinology, 73*, 191–191.

Pellis, S. M. (2002). Sex differences in play fighting revisited: Traditional and nontraditional mechanisms of sexual differentiation in rats. *Archives of Sexual Behavior, 31*, 17–26.

Pellis, S. M., Field, E. F., Smith, L. K., & Pellis, V. C. (1997). Multiple differences in the play fighting of male and female rats. Implications for the causes and functions of play. *Neuroscience and Biobehavioral Reviews, 21*, 105–120.

Pellis, S. M., Field, E. F., & Whishaw, I. Q. (1999). The development of a sex-differentiated defensive motor pattern in rats: A possible role for juvenile experience. *Developmental Psychobiology, 35*, 156–164.

Pellis, S. M., & McKenna, M. (1992). Intrinsic and extrinsic influences on play fighting in rats: Effects of dominance, partner playfulness, temperament and neonatal exposure to testosterone propionate. *Behavioural Brain Research, 50*, 135–145.

Pellis, S. M., & Pasztor, T. J. (1999). The developmental onset of a rudimentary form of play fighting in C57 mice. *Developmental Psychobiology, 34*, 175–182.

Pellis, S. M., & Pellis, V. C. (1987). Play fighting differs from serious fighting in both targets of attacks and tactics of fighting in the laboratory rat (*Rattus norvegicus*). *Aggressive Behavior, 13*, 227–242.

Pellis, S. M., & Pellis, V. C. (1988a). Identification of the possible origin of the body target that differentiates play fighting from serious fighting in Syrian golden hamsters (*Mesocricetus auratus*). *Aggressive Behavior, 14*, 437–449.

Pellis, S. M., & Pellis, V. C. (1988b). Play-fighting in the Syrian golden hamster *Mesocricetus auratus* Waterhouse, and its relationship to serious fighting during postweaning development. *Developmental Psychobiology, 21*, 323–337.

Pellis, S. M., & Pellis, V. C. (1989). Targets of attacks and defense in the play fighting by the Djungarian hamster (*Photopus campbelli*): Links to fighting and sex. *Aggressive Behavior, 15*, 217–234.

Pellis, S. M., & Pellis, V. C. (1990). Differential rates of attack, defense, and counterattack during the developmental decrease in play fighting by male and female rats. *Developmental Psychobiology, 23*, 215–231.

Pellis, S. M., & Pellis, V. C. (1991). Attack and defense during play appear to be motivationally independent

behaviors in muroid rodents. *Psychological Records, 41*, 175–184.

Pellis, S. M., & Pellis, V. C. (1992). Juvenilized play fighting in subordinate male rats. *Aggressive Behavior, 18*, 449–457.

Pellis, S. M., & Pellis, V. C. (1993). Influence of dominance on the development of play fighting in pairs of male Syrian golden hamsters (*Mesocricetus auratus*). *Aggressive Behavior, 19*, 293–302.

Pellis, S. M., & Pellis, V. C. (1997). The prejuvenile onset of play fighting in laboratory rats (*Rattus norvegicus*). *Developmental Psychobiology, 31*, 193–205.

Pellis, S. M., Pellis, V. C., & McKenna, M. M. (1993). Some subordinates are more equal than others: Play fighting amongst adult subordinate male rats. *Aggressive Behavior, 19*, 385–393.

Pellis, S. M., Pellis, V. C., & McKenna, M. M. (1994). Evidence for a feminine dimension in the play fighting of rats *Rattus norvegicus*. *Journal of Comparative Psychology, 108*, 68–73.

Pellis, S. M., Pellis, V. C., & Whishaw, I. Q. (1992). The role of cortex in play fighting by rats: Developmental and evolutionary implications. *Brain, Behavior and Evolution, 39*, 270–284.

Pellis, S. M., & Uwaniuk, A. N. (1999). The roles of phylogeny and sociality in the evolution of social play in muroid rodents. *Animal Behaviour, 58*, 361–373.

Pellis, S. M., & Uwaniuk, A. N. (2000). Comparative analyses of the role of postnatal development on the expression of play fighting. *Developmental Psychobiology, 36*, 136–147.

Perry, G. D., Kusel, S. J., & Perry, C. L. (1988). Victims of peer aggression. *Developmental Psychology, 24*, 807–814.

Potegal, M., Huhman, K. L., Moore, T., & Meyerhoff, J. (1993). Conditioned defeat in the Syrian golden hamster (*Mesocricetus auratus*). *Behavioral and Neural Biology, 60*, 93–102.

Rigby, K., & Slee, P. T. (1991). Bullying among Australian school children: Reported behavior and attitudes towards victims. *Journal of Social Psychology, 131*, 615–627.

Romeo, R. D., Schulz, K. M., Nelson, A. L., Menard, T. A., & Sisk, C. L. (2003). Testosterone, puberty, and the pattern of male aggression in Syrian hamsters. *Developmental Psychobiology, 43*, 102–108.

Sales, G. D. (1972). Ultrasound and mating behaviour in rodents with some observations on other behavioural situations. *Journal of Zoology, 168*, 149–164.

Sanchez, M. M., Ladd, C. O., & Plotsky, P. M. (2001). Early adverse experience as a developmental risk factor for later psychopathology: Evidence from rodent and primate models. *Developmental Psychopathology, 13*, 419–449.

Sancilio, M. F. M., Plumert, J. M., & Hartup, W. W.

(1989). Friendship and aggressiveness and determinants of conflict outcomes in middle childhood. *Developmental Psychology, 25,* 812–819.

Sarason, I. G., Sarason, B. R., & Pierce, G. R. (1994). Social support: Global and relationship-based levels of analysis. *Journal of Social and Personal Relationships, 11,* 295–312.

Schachter, S., & Singer, J. E. (1962). Cognitive, social, and physiological determinants of emotional state. *Psychological Review, 69,* 379–399.

Schoenfeld, T. A., & Leonard, C. M. (1985). Behavioral development in the Syrian golden hamster. In H. I. Siegel (Ed.), *The hamster* (pp. 289–321). New York: Plenum.

Schradle, S. B., & Dougher, M. J. (1985). Social support as a mediator of stress: Theoretical and empirical issues. *Clinical Psychology Review, 5,* 641–661.

Schwartz, D., & Proctor, L. J. (2000). Community violence exposure and children's social adjustment in the school peer group: The mediating roles of emotion regulation and social cognition. *Journal of Consulting and Clinical Psychology, 68,* 670–683.

Sherrod, K. B., Meier, G. W., & Connor, W. H. (1977). Open-field behavior of prenatally irradiated and/or postnatally handled C57BL/6 mice. *Developmental Psychobiology, 10,* 195–202.

Siann, G., Callaghchan, M., Glissov, P., Lockhart, R., & Rawson, L. (1994). Who gets bullied? The effect of school, gender, and ethnic group. *Educational Research, 36,* 123–134.

Siegel, H. I. (1985). Aggressive behavior. In H. I. Siegel (Ed.), *The hamster* (pp. 261–286). New York: Plenum.

Simon, N. G. (2002). Hormonal processes in the development and expression of aggressive behavior. In D. W. Pfaff, A. P. Arnold, A. M. Etgen, S. E. Farhbach, & R. T. Rubin (Eds.), *Hormones, brain and behavior* (Vol. 1, pp. 339–392). San Diego: Academic Press.

Siviy, S. M., & Panksepp, J. (1985). Dorsomedial diencephalic involvement in the juvenile play of rats. *Behavioral Neuroscience, 99,* 1103–1113.

Siviy, S. M., & Panksepp, J. (1987a). Juvenile play in the rat: Thalamic and brain stem involvement. *Physiology and Behavior, 41,* 103–114.

Siviy, S. M., & Panksepp, J. (1987b). Sensory modulation of juvenile play in rats. *Developmental Psychobiology, 20,* 39–55.

Slee, P. T., & Rigby, K. (1993). Australian school children's self appraisal of interpersonal relations: The bullying experience. *Child Psychiatry and Human Development, 23,* 273–282.

Smith, L. K., Fantella, S.-L. N., & Pellis, S. M. (1999). Playful defensive responses in adult male rats depend on the status of the unfamiliar opponent. *Aggressive Behavior, 25,* 141–152.

Smith, L. K., Field, E. F., Forgie, M. L., & Pellis, S. M. (1996). Dominance and age-related changes in the play fighting of intact and post-weaning castrated male rats (*Rattus norvegicus*). *Aggressive Behavior, 22,* 216–226

Smith, L. K., Forgie, M. L., & Pellis, S. M. (1998a). Mechanisms underlying the absence of the pubertal shift in the playful defense of female rats. *Developmental Psychobiology, 33,* 147–156.

Smith, L. K., Forgie, M. L., & Pellis, S. M. (1998b). The postpubertal change in the playful defense of male rats depends upon neonatal exposure to gonadal hormones. *Physiology and Behavior, 63,* 151–155.

Southwick, C. H. (1955). Regulatory mechanisms of house mouse populations: Social behavior affecting litter survival. *Ecology, 36,* 627–634.

Takahashi, L. K., Haglin, C., & Kalin, N. H. (1992). Prenatal stress potentiates stress-induced behavior and reduces the propensity to play in juvenile rats. *Physiology and Behavior, 51,* 319–323.

Takahashi, L. K., & Lore, R. K. (1983). Play fighting and the development of agonistic behavior in male and female rats. *Aggressive Behavior, 9,* 217–227.

Taravosh-Lahn, K., & Delville, Y. (2004). Aggressive behavior in female golden hamsters: Development and the effect of repeated social stress. *Hormones and Behavior, 46,* 428–435.

Taylor, G. T. (1980). Fighting in juvenile rats and the ontogeny of agonistic behavior. *Journal of Comparative and Physiological Psychology, 94,* 953–961.

Taylor, G. T., Frechmann, T., & Royalty, J. (1986). Social behaviour and testicular activity of juvenile rats. *Journal of Endocrinology, 110,* 533–537.

Terranova, M. L., Laviola, G., & Alleva, E. (1993). Ontogeny of amicable social behavior in the mouse: Gender differences and ongoing isolation outcomes. *Developmental Psychobiology, 26,* 467–481.

Thiessen, D. D., Clancy, A., & Goodwin, M. (1976). Harderian gland pheromone on the Mongolian gerbil, *Meriones unguiculatus. Journal of Chemical Ecology, 2,* 231–238.

Thor, D. H., & Holloway, W. R., Jr. (1984). Sex and social play in juvenile rats (*Rattus norvegicus*). *Journal of Comparative Psychology, 98,* 276–284.

Thor, D. H., & Holloway, W. R., Jr. (1985). Play soliciting behavior in prepubertal and postpubertal male rats. *Animal Learning and Behavior, 13,* 327–330.

Tonjes, R., Docke, W., & Dorner, G. (1987). Effects of neonatal intracerebral implantation of sex steroids on sexual behaviour, social play behaviour and gonadotropin secretion. *Experimental and Clinical Endocrinology, 90,* 257–263.

Tremblay, R. E. (2003). Why socialization fails: The case of chronic physical aggression. In B. B. Lahey, T. E. Moffitt, & A. Caspi (Eds.), *Causes of conflict disor-*

der and juvenile delinquency (pp. 182–224). New York: Guilford Press.

Twenge, J. M. (2001). If you can't join them, beat them: Effects of social exclusion on aggressive behavior. *Journal of Personality and Social Psychology, 81,* 1058–1069.

Uchino, B. N., Cacioppo, J. T., & Kiecolt-Glaser, J. K. (1996). The relationship between social support and physiological processes: A review with emphasis on underlying mechanisms and implications for health. *Psychological Bulletin, 119,* 488–531.

U.S. Department of Justice. (1992). *Crime in the United States.* Washington, DC: U.S. Government Printing Office.

Vallee, M., Mayo, W., Dellu, F., Le Moal, M., Simon, H., & Maccari, S. (1997). Prenatal stress induces high anxiety and postnatal handling induces low anxiety in adult offspring: Correlation with stress-induced corticosterone secretion. *Journal of Neuroscience, 17,* 2626–2636.

Van den Berg, C. L., Hol, T., Van Ree, J. M., Spruijt, B. M., Everts, H., & Koolhaas, J. M. (1999). Play is indispensable for an adequate development of coping with social challenges in the rat. *Developmental Psychobiology, 34,* 129–138.

Vandenbergh, J. G. (1973). Effects of gonadal hormones on the flank gland of the golden hamster. *Hormones and Behavior, 4,* 28–33.

Vanderschuren, L. J. M. J., Niesink, R. J. M., Spruijt, B. M., & Van Ree, J. M. (1995). Influence of environmental factors on social play behavior of juvenile rats. *Physiology and Behavior, 58,* 119–123.

Van Kampen, M., & Fuchs, E. (1998). Age-related levels of urinary free cortisol in the tree shrew. *Neurobiology of Aging, 19,* 363–366.

Vomachka, A. J., & Greenwald, G. S. (1979). The development of gonadrotropin and steroid hormone patterns in male and female golden hamsters from birth to puberty. *Endocrinology, 105,* 960–966.

Ward, I. L., & Stehm, K. E. (1991). Prenatal stress feminizes juvenile play patterns in male rats. *Physiology and Behavior, 50,* 601–605.

Weinberg, J., & Wong, R. (1986). Adrenocortical responsiveness to novelty in the hamster. *Physiology and Behavior, 37,* 669–672.

Whitney, L., & Smith, P. K. (1993). A survey of the nature and extent of bullying in junior/middle and secondary schools. *Educational Research, 35,* 3–25.

Wommack, J. C., & Delville, Y. (2003). Repeated social stress and the development of agonistic behavior: Individual differences in coping responses in male golden hamsters. *Physiology and Behavior, 80,* 303–308.

Wommack, J. C., Salinas, A., Melloni, R. H., Jr., & Delville, Y. (2004). Behavioral and neuroendocrine adaptations to repeated social stress during puberty in male golden hamsters. *Journal of Neuroendocrinology, 16,* 767–775.

Wommack, J. C., Taravosh-Lahn, K., David, J. T., & Delville, Y. (2003). Repeated exposure to social stress alters the development of agonistic behavior in male golden hamsters. *Hormones and Behavior, 43,* 229–236.

15

Neurobiology of Aggression in Children

R. James R. Blair, Karina S. Peschardt, Salima Budhani, & Daniel S. Pine

More than 3 million violent crimes are committed in the United States annually, and the majority of offenders are under 18 years of age (Reiss, Miczek, & Roth, 1994). Clinically, maladaptive aggression in youth is one of the most common and troublesome reasons for referrals to child psychiatrists (Steiner, Saxena, & Chang, 2003). In this chapter, we review neurobiological risk factors for aggression in children. First, we consider two general positions that have received considerable attention with respect to aggression in children: the frontal lobe and fear dysfunction positions. Second, we consider a fundamental difficulty with these types of general account of aggression in children, that they implicitly assume all aggression is mediated by the same neural architecture. We argue that a distinction must be made between reactive and instrumental aggression. Third, we consider neurobiological risk factors for reactive and instrumental aggression.

General Accounts of Aggression in Children

The Frontal Lobe Dysfunction Hypotheses

Frontal lobe and consequent executive dysfunction have long been related to antisocial behavior (Barratt, 1994; Elliot, 1978; Gorenstein, 1982; Moffitt, 1993a; Raine, 1997, 2002a). This has led to suggestions that antisocial behavior in childhood and adulthood is due to frontal lobe dysfunction (Gorenstein, 1982; Moffitt, 1993a; Raine, 2002a, 2002b). These suggestions have been prompted by three sets of data: (a) data from neuropsychological studies of individuals presenting with antisocial behavior, (b) data from patients with acquired lesions of the frontal cortex, and (c) data from neuroimaging studies of individuals presenting with antisocial behavior.

Data From Neuropsychological Studies of Individuals Presenting With Antisocial Behavior

There are considerable data indicating that individuals with antisocial behavior show impaired performance on measures of executive functioning (see, for reviews of this literature, Kandel & Freed, 1989; Morgan & Lilienfield, 2000). This association between executive dysfunction and antisocial behavior is observed in children, as well as adults (Moffitt, 1993a, 1993b; Pennington & Ozonoff, 1996; Raine, 2002a).

Data From Patients With Acquired Lesions of the Frontal Cortex

There is a consistent literature indicating that patients with acquired lesions of the frontal cortex may present with emotional and personality changes, such as euphoria, irresponsibility, lack of affect, lack of concern for the present or future, and increased aggression (Hecaen & Albert, 1978; Stuss & Benson, 1986). This is the case even if the lesions are acquired very early in life (Anderson, Bechara, Damasio, Tranel, & Damasio, 1999; Pennington & Bennetto, 1993). Analysis of the lesion locations of patients presenting with increased levels of aggression has shown that only lesions of the orbital (ventral) and medial frontal cortices, but not the dorsolateral prefrontal cortex, are associated with an increase in aggression (Damasio, 1994; Grafman, Schwab, Warden, Pridgen, & Brown, 1996; Volavka, 1995).

Data From Neuroimaging Studies of Individuals Presenting With Antisocial Behavior

A series of brain imaging studies of aggressive individuals have examined neural responding in aggressive individuals relative to comparison individuals. Typically, these studies have examined neural responding when the participants were at rest; they were not conducting a cognitive task. These studies strongly suggest that aggressive individuals are marked by reduced frontal functioning (see Scarpa & Raine, ch. 18 in this volume; Critchley et al., 2000; Goyer et al., 1994; Raine, Buchsbaum, & LaCasse, 1997; Raine, Buchsbaum, Stanley, Lottenberg, Abel, & Stoddard, 1994; Raine, Lencz, Bihrle, LaCasse, & Colletti, 2000; Raine, Meloy, et al., 1998; Raine, Phil, Stoddard, Bihrle, & Buchs-

baum, 1998; Schneider et al., 2000; Volkow & Tancredi, 1987; Volkow et al., 1995; Wong et al., 1997). Importantly, all of these studies to date have been conducted on adults.

Although there are reasons to believe that frontal dysfunction can increase the probability of aggression, the frontal lobe dysfunction positions face some serious difficulties. Typically, they do not distinguish between different regions of the prefrontal cortex, different forms of executive function, or, at the behavioral level, different forms of aggression. Moreover, the frontal lobe positions usually fail to provide any detailed cognitive account as to why damage to functions mediated by the frontal cortex should lead to an increased risk of aggression. Reference is made to difficulties with inhibition or working memory, but without the development of a full theory as to why these difficulties should result in increased risk of aggression. Finally, particularly for studies among children, the potentially confounding effects of attention-deficit hyperactivity disorder (ADHD) have not been sufficiently evaluated. Studies in children with ADHD document strong associations with both antisocial behavior and frontal lobe dysfunction (Moffitt, 1993a, 1993b; Pennington & Ozonoff, 1996). Therefore, an association between antisocial behavior and frontal lobe dysfunction might be attributable to the confounding effects of ADHD.

The Fear Dysfunction Hypotheses

There have been repeated suggestions that children and adults marked by elevated levels of aggression are marked by dysfunction in neurophysiological systems modulating fear behavior (Cleckley, 1976; Eysenck, 1964; Fowles, 1988; Gray, 1987; Lykken, 1995; Mealey, 1995; Patrick, 1994; Pichot, 1978; Trasler, 1973, 1978). These suggestions generally assume that moral socialization is achieved through the use of punishment (Eysenck & Gudjonsson, 1989; Trasler, 1978). In essence, they assume that healthy individuals are frightened by punishment and associate this fear with the action that resulted in the punishment, thus making such individuals less likely to engage in the action in the future. The suggestion is that antisocial children, because they are less aversively aroused by punishment, make weaker associations and thus are more likely to engage in the punished action in the future than healthy individuals.

The variants of the fear dysfunction hypothesis have generated a considerable body of empirical literature.

For example, antisocial children and adults show impaired aversive conditioning (Flor, Birbaumer, Hermann, Ziegler, & Patrick, 2002; Lykken, 1957; Raine, 2002a). In fact, Raine and colleagues have reported a relationship between the ability to perform aversive conditioning and the probability of a healthy prognosis in boys at high risk for antisocial behavior (Raine, Venables, & Williams, 1996). In addition, antisocial children and adults show impaired passive avoidance learning; they fail to learn to avoid stimuli that give rise to punishment (Newman & Kosson, 1986; Newman, Widom, & Nathan, 1985; Scerbo et al., 1990). Moreover, from the clinical perspective, considerable research implicates low levels of anxiety in the persistence of conduct problems (see Raine, 1993, for a review).

However, despite this empirical success, the variants of the fear dysfunction hypothesis face several problems. First, for the most part, the variants are underspecified at both the cognitive and neural levels. The various authors do not provide many details concerning the computational properties of the fear system. For example, it is difficult to be certain about the range of inputs to any putative fear system or how the fear system operates in response to these inputs. Second, there is the related difficulty that many variants of fear dysfunction hypothesis assume a unitary fear system. However, the empirical literature suggests that there is no single fear system, but rather a series of at least partially separable neural systems that are engaged in specific forms of processing that can be subsumed under the umbrella term fear (Amaral, 2001; Blair & Cipolotti, 2000; Killcross, Robbins, & Everitt, 1997; Prather et al., 2001). Third, the fundamental assumption of the fear dysfunction positions, that conditioned fear responses play a crucial role in moral socialization, can be challenged (Blackburn, 1988; Blair & Morton, 1995). The developmental literature indicates that moral socialization is not achieved through the formation of conditioned fear responses, but rather through the induction and fostering of empathy (Hoffman, 1984). Studies have shown, for example, that moral socialization is better achieved through the use of empathy induction (reasoning that draws children's attention to the effects of their misdemeanors on others and increases empathy) than through harsh authoritarian or power assertive parenting practices which rely on the use of punishment (Baumrind, 1971, 1983; Hoffman & Saltzstein, 1967). Indeed, there have been suggestions that while empathy facilitates moral socialization, fear actually hinders it (Brody & Shaffer, 1982; Hoffman,

1994). Fourth, there is a well-documented positive correlation in cross-sectional studies between anxiety and antisocial behavior in children (Pine, Cohen, Cohen, & Brook, 2000; Russo & Beidel, 1993; Zoccolillo, 1992) and adults (Robins, Tipp, & Pryzbeck, 1991); i.e., more anxious children may be more aggressive than less anxious children. This result is in apparent direct contradiction of the fear dysfunction hypotheses.

Reactive and Instrumental Aggression

A major assumption implicitly made by the frontal lobe and fear dysfunction hypotheses is that all aggression is mediated by the same neural architecture. The frontal lobe dysfunction hypotheses basically argue that frontal lobe damage can disinhibit this architecture. The fear dysfunction positions assume that this neural architecture develops differently in antisocial children; they do not learn to avoid antisocial behavior. However, the assumption that all aggression is mediated by the same neural architecture does not receive strong support. A distinction between reactive and instrumental aggression generates more consistent associations with underlying neurobiology (Barratt, Stanford, Dowdy, Liebman, & Kent, 1999; Barratt, Stanford, Kent, & Felthous, 1997; Berkowitz, 1993; Linnoila et al., 1983). These two forms of aggression are mediated by at least partially separable neural systems.

In reactive aggression (also referred to as affective aggression), a frustrating or threatening event triggers the aggressive act and frequently also induces anger. Importantly, the aggression is initiated without regard for any potential goal (for example, gaining the victim's possessions or increasing status within the hierarchy). In contrast, instrumental aggression (also referred to as proactive aggression) is purposeful and goal directed. The aggression is used instrumentally to achieve a specific desired goal (Berkowitz, 1993). This is not usually the pain of the victim but rather possession of the victim's possessions or to increase status within a group hierarchy. Bullying is an example of instrumental aggression and, unsurprisingly, individuals who engage in bullying behaviors frequently engage in other forms of instrumental antisocial behavior in other contexts (Roland & Idsoe, 2001).

It is important to note here that reactive aggression is not inappropriate per se. Reactive aggression is, in many respects, the appropriate response to a highly threatening stimulus. However, reactive aggression can be inappropriate, and will gain clinical attention, if it is expressed to stimuli that are not conventionally considered sufficiently threatening. In other words, reactive aggression directed toward an individual who has cornered you in a dark alley is appropriate, and reactive aggression directed toward an individual who has accidentally knocked into you on the street is not. The explosive aggression may be mediated by the same neural architecture in both situations (see below). However, the aggression in the second situation suggests that the architecture has become dysregulated. A similar argument can be made for instrumental aggression. Instrumental aggression is aggression used to achieve a particular goal. This can occur in an antisocial context (e.g., during a robbery) or in a socially sanctioned context (e.g., corporal punishment).

There has been criticism of the distinction between reactive and instrumental aggression because of some difficulty in characterizing the nature of specific human aggressive episodes (Bushman & Anderson, 2001). However, there are considerable data suggesting that there are two relatively separable populations of aggressive children, children who present with mostly reactive aggression and children who present with very high levels of instrumental aggression and also reactive aggression (Barratt et al., 1999; Crick & Dodge, 1996; Linnoila et al., 1983). We are not suggesting here that instrumental aggression and reactive aggression are not highly correlated. Indeed from our neurobiological analysis, we would predict that if children engage in elevated levels of instrumental aggression due to the neurobiological risk factors described below, they should also present with an elevated risk for reactive aggression. The suggestions here are twofold. First, that the neural systems that mediate reactive aggression are at least partially dissociable from those that mediate instrumental aggression. Second, that there is a population of children who present almost exclusively with reactive aggression.

Reactive Aggression

The expression of reactive aggression is thought to be mediated by a dedicated neural circuit that humans share with other mammalian species (Gregg & Siegel, 2001; Panksepp, 1998; see figure 15.1). This circuit runs from the medial amygdaloidal areas downward, largely via the stria terminalis to the medial hypothalamus, and from there to the dorsal half of the periaqueductal gray (PAG) (Bandler, 1988; Gregg & Siegel, 2001; Panksepp, 1998). The animal's basic response to threat is mediated by this circuit. When activated at a low level, by a distant threat, it initiates freezing. When the level of activation increases, by a closer threat, it initiates escape behaviors. At maximal activation, when the threat is very close and escape is impossible, it initiates reactive aggression (Blanchard, Blanchard, & Takahashi, 1977).

Two neurochemical systems that respond to stress/threat and are likely to contribute to reactive aggression are depicted in figure 15.1 (Charney, 2003; Francis

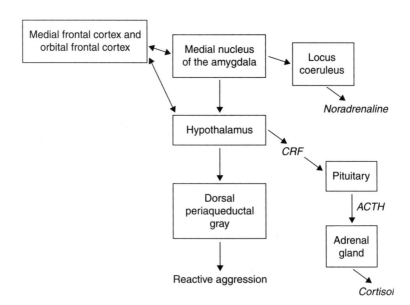

FIGURE 15.1. Neural and neurotransmitter systems involved in the basic response to threat.

& Meaney, 1999). These are (a) the hypothalamic-pituitary-adrenal (HPA) axis and (b) the noradrenergic (NE) system. With respect to the HPA axis, stress stimulates the paraventricular nucleus (PVN) of the hypothalamus, leading to the release of corticotropin releasing factor (CRF). CRF is released into the portal blood supply of the anterior pituitary, where it provokes the pituitary, leading to the synthesis and release of adrenocorticotropin hormone (ACTH). The release of ACTH increases cortisol release from the adrenal gland. With respect to the NE system, there is a second population of CRF neurons in the central nucleus of the amygdala. These neurons project to the locus coeruleus. Their activation increases NE release from the terminal fields of this ascending NE system.

In short, reactive aggression can be elicited by strong activation, by a highly aversive stimulus, of the basic neural architecture that organizes the animal's response to threat. However, if the basic neural architecture becomes dysregulated, reactive aggression may be inappropriately expressed to a less threatening stimulus. We now consider four ways in which this dysregulation might occur.

Heightened Threat Circuitry Sensitivity Due to Prior Significant Threat Exposure

Exposure to environmental threats may change the baseline activation of the basic threat circuitry. For example, repetitive electrical stimulation of the superior colliculus, a region of the threat basic response circuitry (Gregg & Siegel, 2001; Panksepp, 1998), can have long-term (at least 3 months) effects on anxiety-related behavior (King, 1999). By changing the baseline activation of the threat circuitry, prior environmental threats may increase the probability of future reactive aggression; less of a threat is needed to activate the threat circuitry to the level sufficient for reactive aggression.

Prior threat experience, particularly it this occurs early in life, can profoundly affect the neurochemical response to threat. Thus, stressors in early life may have profound and long-term effects on HPA function (Bremner & Vermetten, 2001; Charney, 2003). In rodents, both prenatal and early deprivation stress result in increases in glucocorticoid responses to subsequent stressors (Levine, Wiener, & Coe, 1993; Stanton, Gutierrez, & Levine, 1988). Early postnatal adverse experiences alter hypothalamic CRF mRNA, hippocampal glucocorticoid receptor mRNA, median eminence CRF content, and stress-induced CRF, corticosterone,

and ACTH release (Heim, Owens, Plotsky, & Nemeroff, 1997; Liu et al., 1997; Plotsky & Meaney, 1993). Similarly, chronic stress in rodents is also associated with potentiated release of norepinephrine following exposure to subsequent stressors (Nisenbaum, Zigmond, Sved, & Abercrombie, 1991) and a general lifelong increase in the sensitivity of the noradrenergic system (Francis, Caldji, Champagne, Plotsky, & Meaney, 1999). Repetitive stress is associated with an increased turnover and release of NE in the cortex, hippocampus, amygdala, hypothalamus, and locus coeruleus (Nisenbaum et al., 1991; Tanaka, Yoshida, Emoto, & Ishii, 2000).

While more research in human children is needed, these neuroscientific findings may have direct relevance to the known association between physical and sexual abuse and increased risk of aggression (Farrington & Loeber, 2000) and posttraumatic stress disorder (PTSD) (Silva, Derecho, Leong, Weinstock, & Ferrari, 2001). Physical and sexual abuse are highly significant stressors that elevate the baseline neural and neurochemical response to threat. Both are associated with PTSD (Charney, 2003). Patients with PTSD show clear indications of greater baseline activity in the basic threat system, that is, an elevated startle, relative to comparison individuals, to basic aversive stimuli (Morgan, Grillon, Lubin, & Southwick, 1997; Morgan, Grillon, Southwick, Davis, & Charney, 1996).

In animals, repetitive stimulation of the basic threat response circuitry can give rise to hypervigilance, a heightened alertness for threat (King, 1999). This phenomenon parallels the processing style of many children presenting with heightened levels of reactive aggression, that is, the hostile attribution bias described by Dodge and colleagues (Crick & Dodge, 1994, 1996; Dodge, 1991; Quiggle, Garber, Panak, & Dodge, 1992). According to Dodge and colleagues, children with reactive aggression are more likely than comparison children to direct their attention selectively toward hostile social cues and have difficulty diverting attention away from these cues (Gouze, 1987), leading these children to interpret ambiguous stimuli as hostile and to react accordingly (Crick & Dodge, 1994). Studies have repeatedly shown that reactively aggressive children are about 50% more likely to infer hostile intent than comparison children in situations where a provacateur's actual intent is ambiguous (Crick & Dodge, 1996; Dodge, 1980, 1991; Dodge & Coie, 1987; Quiggle et al., 1992). In line with the position developed here, that prior repeated, significant environmental threats may change the baseline activation levels of the basic threat circuitry and lead to hypervigilance, are results of an elegant longitudinal study conducted by Dodge and colleagues (Dodge, Pettit, Bates, & Valente, 1995). In this study, almost 600 children were assessed for the lifetime experience of physical abuse through clinical interviews with mothers prior to the child's matriculation in kindergarten. Abuse was associated with the formation of hostile attribution biases which, in turn, predicted externalizing outcomes in grades 3 and 4 (Dodge et al., 1995).

Heightened Threat Circuitry Sensitivity as a Result of Innate Biological Predispositions

As stated above, the probability that a child or adult will display reactive aggression is presumed to vary as a function of the degree of current threat, as well as the baseline level of activation of the threat circuitry. As described above in studies using rodents, the baseline activation level can be increased by prior threat exposure. In addition, it is likely that the baseline activation level of the threat circuitry is influenced by innate biological predispositions, that is, genetic factors may predispose an individual's basic threat responsiveness to be elevated. Recent positions on depression and anxiety stress the role of overactivity in the basic threat circuitry, particularly within the amygdala (Drevets, 2003; Kagan & Snidman, 1999). It is plausible that this overactivity has a genetic basis (Hettema, Neale, & Kendler, 2001; Johnson, McGue, Gaist, Vaupel, & Christensen, 2002). In line with the suggestion that elevated responsiveness of basic threat circuitry can increase the risk of aggression, children and adults with depression and anxiety are at heightened risk for the display of reactive aggression. Moreover, as reported above, a positive correlation between anxiety and antisocial behavior has been well documented in children (Pine et al., 2000; Russo & Beidel, 1993; Zoccolillo, 1992) and adults (Robins et al., 1991).

Reduced Regulation of Threat Circuitry Due to Disturbance of Orbital and Medial Frontal Cortical Regions

Earlier, we described accounts that have linked frontal lobe dysfunction to an increased risk of aggression. These accounts have generated a considerable body of data. However, they face significant difficulties. Most especially, they do not distinguish between reactive and instrumental aggression, different forms of executive function, or different regions of the prefrontal cortex.

However, we would suggest that the current empirical literature allows considerable constraint of these positions. First, damage to the frontal lobes leads to increased irritability and reactive aggression but not an increase in instrumental aggression (Anderson et al., 1999; Blair & Cipolotti, 2000; Grafman et al., 1996; Rolls, Hornak, Wade, & McGrath, 1994). Second, it is damage to the medial frontal and orbital frontal cortices, but not the dorsolateral prefrontal cortex, that is associated with a particularly heightened risk for the display of reactive aggression (Anderson et al., 1999; Grafman et al., 1996; Pennington & Bennetto, 1993). Moreover, we suggest that a region of the lateral orbital frontal cortex (Brodmann's Area 47—also known as the ventrolateral frontal cortex) may be particularly important for the regulation of reactive aggression. We suggest this for two reasons: (a) One of the very few studies to dissociate functional regions of the frontal cortex with regard to aggression found that there was lower normalized cerebral blood flow (CBF) in BA 47 that correlated with a history of reactive aggression (Goyer et al., 1994) and (b) the executive functions that currently have been most tightly linked to reactive aggression both rely on BA 47. These are systems that allow response reversal and social response reversal (Blair, 2004).

Response Reversal

Frustration has long been linked to the display of reactive aggression (Berkowitz, 1993). Frustration occurs following the initiation of a behavior to achieve an expected reward and the subsequent absence of this reward. Both the medial and orbital frontal cortices are involved in expectation violation computations and the error detection necessary to induce frustration (Blair, 2004; Rolls, 2000). BA 47, in particular, has been associated with these computations through work with response reversal paradigms (Cools, Clark, Owen, & Robbins, 2002; Kringelbach & Rolls, 2003). We therefore suggest that the medial and orbital frontal cortices (and BA 47 in particular) may increase neuronal activity in the subcortical systems mediating reactive aggression under conditions when an expected reward has not been achieved and suppress neuronal activity when the expected reward is achieved.

Social Response Reversal

The display of social cues by others and the expectations of others' emotional reactions are stimuli that regulate behavior, including reactive aggression (Blair, 2001; Blair & Cipolotti, 2000). For example, an individual may reverse a current response following another person's display of anger or the expectation that they will become angry. In neuroimaging work, both the medial (including anterior cingulate) and orbital frontal cortices (particularly BA 47) are activated by negative emotional expressions, in particular anger, but also fear and disgust (Blair, Morris, Frith, Perrett, & Dolan, 1999; Kesler/West et al., 2001; Sprengelmeyer, Rausch, Eysel, & Przuntek, 1998).

It is important to note that the consequences of damage to the medial and orbital frontal cortices are comparable whether the damage occurs in childhood or adulthood (Anderson et al., 1999; Grafman et al., 1996; Pennington & Bennetto, 1993). In other words, though there must be developmental implications to early medial and orbital frontal cortex damage that are additional to the on-line processing effects, the patient with damage early in life does not present markedly differently, at least as regards antisocial behavior, to those whose damage occurs late in life.

Two psychiatric conditions appear to be related to disruption of the regulatory systems described here: intermittent explosive disorder/ impulsive aggressive disorder (Coccaro, 1998) and childhood bipolar disorder (McClure, Pope, Hoberman, Pine, & Leibenluft, 2003). In neither of these conditions is there strong evidence of neurological trauma. Yet both are associated with dysfunction in the computational systems allowing response reversal and social response reversal. Patients with both intermittent explosive disorder/ impulsive aggressive disorder and childhood bipolar disorder show difficulty on response reversal paradigms requiring expectation violation computations and error detection (Best, Williams, & Coccaro, 2002; Gorrindo, Blair, Budhani, Pine, & Leibenluft, in press). In addition, they show impairment in the ability to recognize facial expressions, suggesting difficulties with social cue processing (Best et al., 2002; McClure et al., 2003). Patients with both disorders express irritability and are at higher risk for reactive aggression.

Reduced Regulation of Threat Circuitry Due to Serotonergic Abnormalities

Serotonin (5-hydroxytryptamine, or 5-HT) has long been implicated in the modulation of aggression, in particular reactive aggression (Lee & Coccaro, 2001). Experimental manipulations that increase 5-HT receptor activa-

tion generally decrease aggression, and those that decrease receptor activation generally increase aggression (Bell, Abrams, & Nutt, 2001; Shaikh, De Lanerolle, & Siegel, 1997). Indeed, animal work has demonstrated a selective suppressive action of $5\text{-}HT_{1A}$ receptors on the PAG neurons mediating reactive aggression (Gregg & Siegel, 2001). In work with humans, low cerebrospinal fluid (CSF) concentrations of 5-hydroxyindoleacetic acid (5-HIAA) have been consistently associated with increased risk of reactive aggression, and the CSF concentration of 5-HIAA has been successfully used to predict the risk of aggression (Virkkunen, De Jong, Bartko, & Linnoila, 1989).

Specific gene knockout studies on mice have reported increased aggressiveness for several knockouts affecting serotonergic functioning, including the $5\text{-}HT_{1B}$ receptor (Ramboz et al., 1996) and MAO (monoamine oxidase) A but not B (Shih, Chen, & Ridd, 1999). In addition, a human family with a stop codon of the MAO_A gene has been reported in which the males were affected by mild mental retardation and sexually aggressive behaviors (Miczek, Maxson, Fish, & Faccidomo, 2001). Interestingly, recent work with rodents suggests that such genetic effects may be modulated by developmental stage. For example, the 5-HT1a knockout mouse exhibits an anxious phenotype, but this phenotype is only expressed when the knockout occurs in the first 3 weeks of life, as opposed to in adulthood. Preliminary data in humans note some comparable evidence of developmental fluctuations in the relationship between 5-HT function and behavior. For example, aggressive behavior in some populations of children may be associated with enhanced as opposed to reduced activity in the 5-HT system (Halperin et al., 1994; Pine et al., 1997). Moreover, these findings were moderated by the effects of psychosocial stress on 5-HT activity (Pine et al., 1997). This emphasizes the need to examine complex interplay among development, aggressive behavior, neurochemistry, and environmental adversity.

Consistent with such an emphasis, recent work in humans has suggested the possibility that the emergence of an increased risk for aggression might be a necessary interaction of environmental stressors with particular genetic contributions to the functioning of the serotonergic system (Moffitt, Caspi, Harrington, & Milne, 2002). Thus, Moffitt et al. (2002) observed that a functional polymorphism in the gene encoding MAO_A moderated the effect of maltreatment. Maltreated children with a genotype conferring high levels of MAO_A expression were less likely to develop antisocial problems than maltreated children with a genotype conferring low levels of MAO$_A$ expression.

Summary

There is a population of children who present with predominantly reactive aggression. This reactive aggression can be severe and repetitive.

Animal work has identified a neural circuit that runs from the medial nucleus of the amygdala to the medial hypothalamus and from there to the dorsal half of the PAG. This circuitry allows the expression of reactive aggression in mammalian species, including humans.

This circuitry can become dysregulated. We identified four potential ways in which this can occur. The first two relate to the basic neural circuit that responds to threat and allows the expression of reactive aggression. Children for whom the sensitivity of this basic circuitry is elevated, as a result of either physical/sexual abuse or endogenous factors, are at greater neurobiological risk of displaying reactive aggression. The third and fourth relate to regulatory systems for this circuitry. Thus, the functioning of medial and orbital frontal systems involved in the regulation of the basic threat circuitry can be compromised. This appears to occur in children who present with bipolar disorder and intermittent explosive disorder. Alternatively, or perhaps as a contributory factor to the compromising of the frontal regulatory systems, the serotonergic system may be disturbed.

Instrumental Aggression

Instrumental aggression is a goal-directed motor activity. From this perspective, there are strong similarities between using a card in an ATM machine to extract money from it and waving a knife in the face of a victim to demand money. Both are examples of goal-directed motor behavior. We argue that instrumental aggression recruits the same cortical neural systems as other goal-directed motor activities. These include the temporal cortex and the striatal and premotor cortical regions (Passingham & Toni, 2001). We argue that elevated levels of instrumental behavior in specific individuals are unlikely to be due to pathology in the neural systems directly mediating motor behavior; individuals presenting with heightened levels of instrumental aggression do not show general motor impairment. In contrast, we suggest that

the pathology will be related to the decision to utilize antisocial, rather than social, motor behavior.

A child faced with the goal "obtain $50" will have a range of behavioral choices available (e.g., to simplify: "find a job," "beg," "mug someone," and "steal from an untended bag"). Choosing between these options will be a function of (a) whether they are indeed available (Can a job be found? Is there a potential victim available?) and (b) the costs associated with these actions (in the case of the antisocial actions, social punishment and the distress of the victims; highly salient with respect to the mugging option and less salient with respect to the stealing option). A child might choose to achieve a goal through antisocial behavior because (a) it is the most viable option available or (b) the child's calculation of the costs related to the actions is deficient. We will consider a specific form of the first option before turning our attention to the second.

Adolescent Limited Antisocial Behavior

When official rates of crime are plotted against age, there is a sharp rise in both the prevalence and incidence of offending that begins in early adolescence. Indeed, several studies have indicated that it is statistically aberrant to refrain from some level of rule violation during adolescence (Hirschi, 1969; Moffitt & Silva, 1988). This rise in offending peaks at the age of 17 and then drops precipitously in young adulthood; by the early 20s, the number of active offenders has decreased by over 50%, while by age 28, almost 85% of former delinquents have stopped offending (Blumstein & Cohen, 1987; Farrington, 1986). Moffitt has labeled the individuals who begin to offend in their early teens, but who are no longer offending by their early twenties, *adolescent limited* offenders (1993a).

Adolescent limited offenders engage in instrumental antisocial behavior. This means that while biological accounts of adolescent limited offenders could be proposed (e.g., based on hormone/neurotransmitter level changes occurring around puberty), they are unlikely to be successful. Why should temporary hormonal/neurotransmitter levels increase the probability that a child will choose one form of instrumental behavior (antisocial acts) to achieve goals rather than another, non-antisocial form of instrumental behavior? If the increase in antisocial behavior was predominantly reactive aggression, such accounts might be plausible. The responsiveness of the basic threat response architecture which mediates reactive aggression is sensitive to a variety of hormones/neurotransmitters (Gregg & Siegel, 2001; Panksepp, 1998). However, the antisocial behavior is instrumental. It is unclear how a biological variable could evoke this specific form of goal-directed behavior for the adolescent period. We would argue that a social account is more plausible.

Moffitt has provided an interesting social account of adolescent limited offending (1993a). She argues that teenagers face a 5- to 10-year role vacuum, the "maturity gap," where they are "biologically capable and compelled to be sexual beings, yet they are asked to delay most of the positive aspects of adult life" (Moffitt, 1993a, p. 686); they have to live with their parents, cannot own significant material possessions, are constrained in their romantic lives, and their decisions may not be regarded as consequential by adults. She argues that adolescent limited youths learn to mimic the lifestyles of their *life-course-persistent* peers (Moffitt's term for individuals who begin their offending at younger than 10 years of age and continue to offend long after the age of 20; see below). The life-course-persistent youths are not seen to suffer from the maturity gap by their peers; they can steal for possessions and are likely to have engaged in sexual activity. "Viewed from within contemporary adolescent culture, the antisocial precocity of life-course-persistent youths becomes a coveted social asset" (Moffitt, 1993a, p. 687). In line with Moffitt's position, whereas life-course-persistent individuals are ignored and rejected by their peers when they are children because of their unpredictable, aggressive behavior (Coie, Belding, & Underwood, 1988; Dodge, Coie, & Brakke, 1982), they are no longer rejected by their peers when they become adolescents (Coie, Dodge, & Kupersmidt, 1988). According to Moffitt, adolescent limited offenders stop engaging in antisocial behavior because as young adults they have many other ways to demonstrate their value beyond antisocial behavior.

Deficient Cost Calculation

Moral socialization is the term given to the process by which caregivers, and others, reinforce behaviors that they wish to encourage and punish behaviors that they wish to discourage. We would argue that moral socialization helps the developing child appropriately represent the costs of antisocial behavior.

The ease with which a child can be socialized is related to the temperamental variable of fearfulness (Kochanska, 1993, 1997). Fearful children show higher

levels of moral development/conscience than less fearful children (Asendorpf & Nunner-Winkler, 1992; Kochanska, 1997; Kochanska, De Vet, Goldman, Murray, & Putman, 1994; Rothbart, Ahadi, & Hersehey, 1994). A crucial punisher, with respect to instrumental antisocial behavior, is the victim's pain and distress; empathy induction, focusing the transgressor's attention on the victim, particularly fosters moral socialization (Eisenberg, 2002; Hoffman, 1994).

We, and others, have argued that dysfunction in the processes underlying socialization might give rise to an individual who presents with an increased risk of instrumental antisocial behavior (Blair, 1995; Eysenck, 1964; Trasler, 1978). Viewed from this perspective, instrumental antisocial behavior is strongly tied to deficient functioning in processes and associated brain systems that facilitate empathy and fear. We argue that children with psychopathic tendencies represent such individuals. Individuals with psychopathic tendencies show markedly elevated levels of instrumental antisocial behavior (Cornell et al., 1996; Williamson, Hare, & Wong, 1987). The syndrome of psychopathy itself involves both affective-interpersonal (e.g., such as lack of empathy and guilt) and behavioral components (e.g., criminal activity and poor behavioral controls) (Forth, Kosson, & Hare, in press; Frick & Hare, 2001; Frick, O'Brien, Wootton, & McBurnett, 1994; Hare, 1991; Harpur, Hare, & Hakstian, 1989; Kosson, Cyterski, Steuerwald, Neumann, & Walker-Matthews, 2002). In appropriately developing children the increased use of positive parenting techniques, including empathy induction, is associated with reduced antisocial behavior in the child. However, the form of parenting strategy adopted by the parent has no significant impact on the level of antisocial behavior expressed by children who present with the emotional dysfunction associated with psychopathy (Wootton, Frick, Shelton, & Silverthorn, 1997).

We have developed an emotion-based account of psychopathy (Blair, 1995; Blair, 2001; Blair, 2002; Blair, 2003b; Blair, 2004; Frith & Blair, 1998). We assume a genetic contribution to the emotional dysfunction seen in psychopathy, an assumption borne out by recent data (Blonigen, Carlson, Krueger, & Patrick, 2003; Viding, Blair, Moffitt, & Plomin, in press). For example, Viding et al. (in press) examined the callous and unemotional affective-interpersonal component of psychopathic tendencies at age 7 in almost 3,500 twin pairs within the Twins Early Development Study. Significant group heritability ($h^2_g = .67$) but no shared environmental influence were found for this component.

We assume that the genetic contribution influences the functioning of a neurotransmitter(s) involved in specific aspects of amygdala functioning, in particular coding punishment information (Peschardt, Leonard, Morton, & Blair, submitted for publication; Peschardt, Richell, et al., submitted for publication). Polymorphisms of particular genes can alter the functioning of specific neurotransmitter systems (Lichter et al., 1993; Shih et al., 1999; Vandenbergh et al., 1992). While it is currently unclear which neurotransmitter systems might be dysfunctional in psychopathy, one possibility is that the noradrenergic response to stress/threat stimuli, described above, is disturbed (Blair, 2003b; Peschardt, Leonard, et al., submitted for publication). Noradrenaline appears to mediate the impact of aversive cues in human choice (Rogers, Lancaster, Wakeley, & Bhagwager, 2004). Moreover, recent pharmacological data imply that noradrenergic manipulations selectively impact the processing of sad expressions (Harmer, Perrett, Cowen, & Goodwin, 2001; Sustrik, Coupland, & Blair, manuscript in preparation). With respect to antisocial behavior, numerous studies have linked reduced noradrenalin (NA) levels to aggression in children and adults (Raine, 1993; Rogeness, Cepeda, Macedo, fischer, & Harris, 1990; Rogeness, Javors, Mass, & Macedo, 1990). Interestingly, with reference to the low fear positions outlined earlier and findings that ease of socialization is linked to the temperamental variable of fearfulness (Kochanska, 1993, 1997) while NA function may be decreased in antisocial children (Raine, 1993), it is *increased*, at least in adults, among patients with a range of anxiety disorders (Charney, Heninger, & Brier, 1984).

The amygdala is crucially involved in the formation of stimulus-reward and stimulus-punishment associations (Baxter & Murray, 2002). We suggest that the genetic contribution disrupts the ability of the amygdala to form the stimulus-punishment associations (Blair, 2003b; Peschardt, Leonard, et al., submitted for publication; Peschardt, Richell, et al., submitted for publication). Lesions of the amygdala disrupt functions reliant on the formation of stimulus-punishment associations, such as (a) aversive conditioning (Bechara, Damasio, Damasio, & Lee, 1999; Bechara et al., 1995; LaBar, Gatenby, Gore, LeDoux, & Phelps, 1998), (b) the augmentation of the startle reflex to visual threat primes (Angrilli et al., 1996; Funayama, Grillon, Davis, & Phelps, 2001), (c) passive avoidance learning (Ambrogi Lorenzini, Baldi, Bucherelli, Sacchetti, & Tassoni, 1999), and (d) fearful expression recognition (Adolphs, 2002; Blair, 2003a). Adults with psychopathy show impair-

ment in all of these functions (Flor et al., 2002; Levenston, Patrick, Bradley, & Lang, 2000; Lykken, 1957; Newman & Kosson, 1986; Newman & Schmitt, 1998). Children with psychopathic tendencies present with impaired passive avoidance learning and fearful expression recognition (Blair, Colledge, Murray, & Mitchell, 2001; Budhani, Johnston, & Blair, in press; Newman et al., 1985; Stevens, Charman, & Blair, 2001). Although aversive conditioning and the augmentation of the startle reflex have not been indexed in children with psychopathic tendencies, the ability to perform aversive conditioning at age 15 can be used to predict the probability that the child will display antisocial behavior in adulthood (Raine et al., 1996). Direct evidence of amygdala dysfunction in individuals with psychopathology has been provided by recent neuroimaging work. In adults with the disorder, reduced amygdala activation has been found during emotional memory (Kiehl et al., 2001) and aversive conditioning tasks (Veit et al., 2002). However, there has as yet been no neuroimaging work with children with psychopathic tendencies.

According to our position, disruption of the ability of the amygdala to form stimulus-punishment associations reduces the efficacy of standard socialization practices (Blair, 2003b). Within this model, the impact of the temperamental variable of fearfulness, related to the ease to which the child can be socialized (Kochanska, 1993, 1997), can be understood as an index of the integrity of the amygdala (Blair, 2003b). Though fear conditioning is not considered important in socialization (Brody & Shaffer, 1982; Hoffman, 1994), it is argued that the amygdala's response to the fear and sadness of victims, during empathy induction, is crucial for socialization (Blair, 1995). The developing child needs to associate moral transgressions (transgressions that result in harm to others) with the punishment of the distress of the victim. Children with psychopathic tendencies are less able to form these associations and so are at greater risk to choose antisocial behavioral options.

Additional neural systems to the amygdala may be affected in children with psychopathic tendencies. In particular, psychopathy has been associated with dysfunction in both the anterior cingulate (Kiehl et al., 2001) and orbital frontal cortex (Damasio, 1994; LaPierre, Braun, & Hodgins, 1995; Mitchell, Colledge, Leonard, & Blair, 2002). Little work has as yet focused on the anterior cingulate, but there are indications that children with psychopathic tendencies show impairment on functions that recruit the orbital frontal cortex.

Children with psychopathic tendencies show difficulties with some response reversal and extinction tasks
(Blair, Colledge, & Mitchell, 2001; Newman et al.,
1987; O'Brien & Frick, 1996). Performance on these
tasks is known to recruit the orbitofrontal cortex and
particularly BA 47 (Cools et al., 2002; Kringelbach &
Rolls, 2003; Rolls et al., 1994; Swainson et al., 2000).
The ability to achieve response reversal and extinction
is related to the computation of expectations of reward
and identifying if these expectations have been violated
(Rolls, 2000). Earlier we suggested that this computational process was related to the presentation of frustration-induced reactive aggression. Indeed, children
with psychopathic tendencies show heightened levels
of reactive aggression. In line with our earlier suggestions regarding reactive aggression, we suggest that
their difficulties in computing reward expectations/
violations may be related to their elevated levels of
reactive aggression.

Summary

There are neurobiological risk factors for instrumental antisocial behavior. One biological risk factor is
adolescence itself. Adolescents engaging in antisocial
behavior may be perceived by peers to be successful
and worthy of emulation. But there are also neurobiological factors that put the developing child at risk
of a significantly elevated level of instrumental aggression. Such an elevation is not limited by adolescence
but will persist throughout the life span. We suggest
that there are genetic factors that can suppress emotional responsiveness. Amygdala functioning may be
compromised such that the coding of punishment
information is impaired. This impairment reduces the
efficacy of parenting techniques, resulting in the
developing child less efficiently coding the costs, particularly in terms of the distress of the victims, of antisocial behavior.

General Summary and Conclusions

We began this chapter by considering two general accounts of antisocial behavior, the frontal lobe and fear
dysfunction positions. We suggested that such accounts
need greater specification. Without increased specification, apparent contradictions, such as aggression's
being linked to both elevated and reduced levels of fear,
cannot be reconciled.

Within this chapter we have considered neural and
neurochemical systems involved in the mediation and
regulation of childhood and adulthood reactive and
instrumental aggression. With respect to reactive aggression, we considered the neural circuit running
from the medial nucleus of the amygdala to the medial hypothalamus and from there to the dorsal half
of the PAG and the ways in which it can become dysregulated. This can occur because the sensitivity of this
basic circuitry can become elevated (as a result of either physical/sexual abuse or endogenous factors) or
because the medial and orbital frontal systems involved
in the regulation of this basic threat circuitry can be
compromised (perhaps, in some cases, due to serotonergic disturbance).

Whereas reactive aggression can be considered an
emotional response to an extreme threat, instrumental aggression is simply one type of instrumental behavior. Children's decisions to use antisocial behavior are
a result of their goals, current abilities to achieve these
goals, and prior learning history. There are periods in
an individual's history when instrumental antisocial
behavior may become particularly advantageous, such
as adolescence. There need be nothing pathological
in the antisocial behavior. The behavior may be, or at
least seems to be, the most efficient course of action to
achieve that particular goal at that time.

However, there are neurobiological risk factors that
put a child at risk of displaying inappropriate levels of
very severe instrumental aggression (psychopathic tendencies). There appear to be genetic factors that give
rise to a child whose emotional responsiveness is suppressed. In such children, the amygdala's ability to code
punishment information is impaired. This impairment
interferes with their ability to be socialized. When
evaluating the appropriateness of antisocial behavior,
the coding of the costs of this behavior (particularly the
distress of victims) will be inadequate and instrumental aggression will more likely be expressed.

It is important to note that, from the perspective of
affective cognitive neuroscience, it is clear that aggression is not a unitary construct. There is at least a partial architectural divide between the systems that
mediate reactive and instrumental aggression. Moreover, even within this dichotomy there are different
forms of neurobiological risk factors, for example, in
the context of reactive aggression, factors that affect the
sensitivity of the basic threat circuitry as opposed to
factors that determine the functioning of systems that
regulate the activity of this basic threat circuitry. These

differences in pathology suggest that treatment options need to become far more refined.

Currently, children with antisocial behavior, whatever their pathology, are diagnosed with conduct disorder (CD). CD is defined as "a repetitive and persistent pattern of seriously anti-social behavior usually criminal in nature" (American Psychiatric Association [APA], 1994). CD is a highly prevalent disorder, with the *Diagnostic and Statistical Manual of Mental Disorders* (1994) fourth edition (*DSM-IV*) suggesting rates in the general American population ranging from about 6 to 16% for males and 2 to 9% for females (APA, 1994). There have been concerns that CD, as many conditions in the *DSM-IV*, identifies a highly heterogeneous population (Steiner et al., 2003). This is even recognized in the *DSM-IV*, where a subdivision of CD into childhood- and adolescent-onset types is made (those emerging before and after age 10, respectively) (APA, 1994). Moreover, CD frequently presents together with a variety of other conditions, such as post-traumatic stress disorder, mood disorders, and bipolar disorder (Steiner et al., 2003), a confirmation of the heterogeneity. We have presented six different pathologies in this chapter. All of them would lead to a diagnosis of CD. Yet treatment appropriate for one type of pathology may not be appropriate for another. Treatments designed to increase the emotional responsiveness of children with psychopathic tendencies may exacerbate the reactive aggressive symptomatology of the child whose pathology is related to elevated responsiveness of the basic threat architecture.

References

Adolphs, R. (2002). Neural systems for recognizing emotion. *Current Opinions in Neurobiology, 12,* 169–177.

Amaral, D. G. (2001). Society for Research in Child Development, Minneapolis, MN.

Ambrogi Lorenzini, C. G., Baldi, E., Bucherelli, C., Sacchetti, B., & Tassoni, G. (1999). Neural topography and chronology of memory consolidation: A review of functional inactivation findings. *Neurobiology of Learning and Memory, 71,* 1–18.

American Psychiatric Association. (1994). *Diagnostic and statistical manual of mental disorders* (4th ed.). Washington, DC: Author.

Anderson, S. W., Bechara, A., Damasio, H., Tranel, D., & Damasio, A. R. (1999). Impairment of social and moral behaviour related to early damage in human prefrontal cortex. *Nature Neuroscience, 2,* 1032–1037.

Angrilli, A., Mauri, A., Palomba, D., Flor, H., Birhaumer, N., Sartori, G., et al. (1996). Startle reflex and emotion modulation impairment after a right amygdala lesion. *Brain, 119,* 1991–2000.

Asendorpf, J. B., & Nunner-Winkler, G. (1992). Children's moral motive strength and temperamental inhibition reduce their immoral behaviour in real moral conflicts. *Child Development, 63,* 1223–1235.

Bandler, R. (1988). Brain mechanisms of aggression as revealed by electrical and chemical stimulation: Suggestion of a central role for the midbrain periaqueductal gray region. In A. N. Epsein & A. R. Morrison (Eds.), *Progress in psychobiology and physiological psychology* (pp. 135–233). San Diego: Academic Press.

Barratt, E. S. (1994). Impulsiveness and aggression. In J. Monahan & H. Steadman (Eds.), *Violence and mental disorders: Developments in risk assessment* (pp. 61–79). Chicago: University of Chicago Press.

Barratt, E. S., Stanford, M. S., Dowdy, L., Liebman, M. J., & Kent, T. A. (1999). Impulsive and premeditated aggression: A factor analysis of self- reported acts. *Psychiatry Research, 86,* 163–173.

Barratt, E. S., Stanford, M. S., Kent, T. A., & Felthous, A. (1997). Neuropsychological and cognitive psychophysiological substrates of impulsive aggression. *Biological Psychiatry, 41,* 1045–1061.

Baumrind, D. (1971). Current patterns of parental authority. *Developmental Psychology Monographs, 4,* 1–103.

Baumrind, D. (1983). Rejoinder to Lewis's interpretation of parental firm control effects: Are authoritative families really harmonious? *Psychological Bulletin, 94,* 132–142.

Baxter, M. G., & Murray, E. A. (2002). The amygdala and reward. *Nature Reviews in Neuroscience, 3,* 563–573.

Bechara, A., Damasio, H., Damasio, A. R., & Lee, G. P. (1999). Different contributions of the human amygdala and ventromedial prefrontal cortex to decision-making. *Journal of Neuroscience, 19,* 5473–5481.

Bechara, A., Tranel, D., Damasio, H., Adolphs, R., Rockland, C., & Damasio, A. R. (1995). Double dissociation of conditioning and declarative knowledge relative to the amygdala and hippocampus in humans. *Science, 269,* 1115–1118.

Bell, C., Abrams, J., & Nutt, D. (2001). Tryptophan depletion and its implications for psychiatry. *British Journal of Psychiatry, 178,* 399–405.

Berkowitz, L. (1993). *Aggression: Its causes, consequences, and control.* Philadelphia: Temple University Press.

Best, M., Williams, J. M., & Coccaro, E. F. (2002). Evidence for a dysfunctional prefrontal circuit in patients with an impulsive aggressive disorder. *Proceedings of the National Academy of Sciences USA, 99,* 8448–8453.

Blackburn, R. (1988). On moral judgments and personality disorders: The myth of psychopathic personality revisited. *British Journal of Psychiatry, 153,* 505–512.

Blair, R. J. (2003a). Facial expressions, their communicatory functions and neuro-cognitive substrates. *Philosophical Transactions of the Royal Society London, Series B, Biological Sciences, 358,* 561–572.

Blair, R. J. (2003b). Neurobiological basis of psychopathy. *British Journal of Psychiatry, 182,* 5–7.

Blair, R. J., Colledge, E., & Mitchell, D. G. (2001). Somatic markers and response reversal: Is there orbitofrontal cortex dysfunction in boys with psychopathic tendencies? *Journal of Abnormal Child Psychology, 29,* 499–511.

Blair, R. J., Colledge, E., Murray, L., & Mitchell, D. G. (2001). A selective impairment in the processing of sad and fearful expressions in children with psychopathic tendencies. *Journal of Abnormal Child Psychology, 29,* 491–498.

Blair, R. J. R. (1995). A cognitive developmental approach to morality: Investigating the psychopath. *Cognition, 57,* 1–29.

Blair, R. J. R. (2001). Neuro-cognitive models of aggression, the antisocial personality disorders and psychopathy. *Journal of Neurology, Neurosurgery and Psychiatry, 71,* 727–731.

Blair, R. J. R. (2002). A neuro-cognitive model of the psychopathic individual. In T. Robbins & M. Ron (Eds.), *Disorders of brain and mind II.* Cambridge: Cambridge University Press.

Blair, R. J. R. (2004). The roles of orbital frontal cortex in the modulation of antisocial behavior. *Brain and Cognition, 55,* 198–208.

Blair, R. J. R., & Cipolotti, L. (2000). Impaired social response reversal: A case of "acquired sociopathy." *Brain, 123,* 1122–1141.

Blair, R. J. R., Morris, J. S., Frith, C. D., Perrett, D. I., & Dolan, R. (1999). Dissociable neural responses to facial expressions of sadness and anger. *Brain, 122,* 883–893.

Blair, R. J. R., & Morton, J. (1995). Putting cognition into sociopathy. *Brain and Behavioral Science, 18,* 548.

Blanchard, R. J., Blanchard, D. C., & Takahashi, L. K. (1977). Attack and defensive behaviour in the albino rat. *Animal Behaviour, 25,* 197–224.

Blonigen, D. M., Carlson, R. F., Krueger, R. F., & Patrick, C. J. (2003). A twin study of self-reported psychopathic personality traits. *Personality and Individual Differences, 35,* 179–197.

Blumstein, A., & Cohen, J. (1987). Characterizing criminal careers. *Science, 237,* 985–991.

Bremner, J. D., & Vermetten, E. (2001). Stress and development: Behavioral and biological consequences. *Development and Psychopathology, 13,* 473–489.

Brody, G. H., & Shaffer, D. R. (1982). Contributions of parents and peers to children's moral socialization. *Developmental Review, 2,* 31–75.

Budhani, S., Johnston, K., & Blair, R. J. R. (in press). Passive avoidance learning in boys with psychopathic tendencies: Effects of attention deficit/hyperactivity disorder, memory load and level of punishment/reward. *Journal of Abnormal Child Psychology.*

Bushman, B. J., & Anderson, C. A. (2001). Is it time to pull the plug on the hostile versus instrumental aggression dichotomy? *Psychological Review, 108,* 273–279.

Charney, D. S. (2003). Neuroanatomical circuits modulating fear and anxiety behaviors. *Acta Psychiatrica Scandanavia Supplements,* 38–50.

Charney, D. S., Heninger, G. R., & Breier, A. (1984). Noradrenergic function in panic anxiety. Effects of yohimbine in healthy subjects and patients with agoraphobia and panic disorder. *Archives of General Psychiatry, 41,* 751–763.

Cleckley, H. M. (1976). *The mask of sanity* (5th ed.). St Louis, MO: Mosby.

Coccaro, E. F. (1998). Impulsive aggression: A behavior in search of clinical definition. *Harvard Review of Psychiatry, 5,* 336–339.

Coie, J. D., Belding, M., & Underwood, M. (1988). Aggression and peer rejection in childhood. In B. Lahey & A. Kazdin (Eds.), *Advances in clinical child psychology.* Cambridge: Cambridge University Press.

Coie, J. D., Dodge, K. A., & Kupersmidt, J. (1988). Peer group behavior and social status. In S. R. Asher & J. D. Coie (Eds.), *Peer rejection in childhood.* Cambridge: Cambridge University Press.

Cools, R., Clark, L., Owen, A. M., & Robbins, T. W. (2002). Defining the neural mechanisms of probabilistic reversal learning using event-related functional magnetic resonance imaging. *Journal of Neuroscience, 22,* 4563–4567.

Cornell, D. G., Warren, J., Hawk, G., Stafford, E., Oram, G., & Pine, D. (1996). Psychopathy in instrumental and reactive violent offenders. *Journal of Consulting and Clinical Psychology, 64,* 783–790.

Crick, N. R., & Dodge, K. A. (1994). A review and reformulation of social information-processing mechanisms in children's social adjustment. *Psychological Bulletin, 115,* 74–101.

Crick, N. R., & Dodge, K. A. (1996). Social information-processing mechanisms on reactive and proactive aggression. *Child Development, 67,* 993–1002.

Critchley, H. D., Simmons, A., Daly, E. M., Russell, A., van Amelsvoort, T., Robertson, D. M., et al. (2000). Prefrontal and medial temporal correlates of repetitive violence to self and others. *Biological Psychiatry, 47,* 928–934.

Damasio, A. R. (1994). *Descartes' error: Emotion, rationality and the human brain.* New York: Putnam (Grosset Books).

Dodge, K. A. (1980). Social cognition and children's aggressive behaviour. *Child Development, 51,* 162–170.

Dodge, K. A. (1991). The structure and function of reactive and proactive aggression. In *The development and treatment of childhood aggression* (pp. 201–218). Hillsdale, NJ: Erlbaum.

Dodge, K. A., & Coie, J. D. (1987). Social information processing factors in reactive and proactive aggression in children's peer groups. *Journal of Personality and Social Psychology, 53,* 1146–1158.

Dodge, K. A., Coie, J. D., & Brakke, N. P. (1982). Behavior patterns of socially rejected and neglected preadolescents: The roles of social approach and aggression. *Journal of Abnormal Child Psychology, 10,* 389–409.

Dodge, K. A., Pettit, G. S., Bates, J. E., & Valente, E. (1995). Social information-processing patterns partially mediate the effect of early physical abuse on later conduct problems. *Journal of Abnormal Psychology, 104,* 632–643.

Drevets, W. C. (2003). Neuroimaging abnormalities in the amygdala in mood disorders. *Annals of the New York Academy of Sciences, 985,* 420–444.

Eisenberg, N. (2002). Empathy-related emotional responses, altruism, and their socialization. In R. J. Davidson & A. Harrington (Eds.), *Visions of compassion: Western scientists and Tibetan Buddhists examine human nature* (pp. 131–164). New York: Oxford University Press.

Elliot, F. A. (1978). Neurological aspects of antisocial behavior. In W. H. Reid (Ed.), *The psychopath* (pp. 146–189). New York: Bruner/Mazel.

Eysenck, H. J. (1964). *Crime and personality.* London: Routledge & Kegan Paul.

Eysenck, H. J., & Gudjonsson, G. H. (1989). *The causes and cures of criminality.* London: Plenum.

Farrington, D. P. (1986). Age and crime. In M. Tonry & N. Morris (Eds.), *Crime and justice: An annual review of research* (pp. 189–250). Chicago: University of Chicago Press.

Farrington, D. P., & Loeber, R. (2000). Epidemiology of juvenile violence. *Child and Adolescent Psychiatry Clinics North America, 9,* 733–748.

Flor, H., Birbaumer, N., Hermann, C., Ziegler, S., & Patrick, C. J. (2002). Aversive Pavlovian conditioning in psychopaths: Peripheral and central correlates. *Psychophysiology, 39,* 505–518.

Forth, A. E., Kosson, D. S., & Hare, R. D. (in press). *The Psychopathy Checklist: Youth Version* Toronto, Ontario, Canada: Multi-Health Systems.

Fowles, D. C. (1988). Psychophysiology and psychopathy: A motivational approach. *Psychophysiology, 25,* 373–391.

Francis, D. D., Caldji, C., Champagne, F., Plotsky, P. M., & Meaney, M. J. (1999). The role of corticotropin-releasing factor–norepinephrine systems in mediating the effects of early experience on the development of behavioral and endocrine responses to stress. *Biological Psychiatry, 46,* 1153–1166.

Francis, D. D., & Meaney, M. J. (1999). Maternal care and the development of stress responses. *Current Opinion in Neurobiology, 9,* 128–134.

Frick, P. J., & Hare, R. D. (2001). *The antisocial process screening device.* Toronto, Ontario, Canada: Multi-Health Systems.

Frick, P. J., O'Brien, B. S., Wootton, J. M., & McBurnett, K. (1994). Psychopathy and conduct problems in children. *Journal of Abnormal Psychology, 103,* 700–707.

Frith, U., & Blair, R. J. R. (1998). Editorial: Does antisocial personality disorder have a neurological basis and can it be treated? *Criminal Behaviour and Mental Health, 8,* 247–250.

Funayama, E. S., Grillon, C., Davis, M., & Phelps, E. A. (2001). A double dissociation in the affective modulation of startle in humans: Effects of unilateral temporal lobectomy. *Journal of Cognitive Neuroscience, 13,* 721–729.

Gorenstein, E. E. (1982). Frontal lobe functions in psychopaths. *Journal of Abnormal Psychology, 91,* 368–379.

Gorrindo, T., Blair, R. J. R., Budhani, S., Pine, D. S., & Leibenluft, E. (in press). Probabilistic response reversal deficits in pediatric bipolar disorder. *American Journal of Psychiatry.*

Gouze, K. R. (1987). Attention and social problem solving as correlates of aggression in preschool males. *Juornal of Abnormal Child Psychology, 15,* 181–197.

Goyer, P. F., Andreason, P. J., Semple, W. E., Clayton, A. H., King, A. C., Compton-Toth, B. A., et al. (1994). Positron-emission tomography and personality disorders. *Neuropsychopharmacology, 10,* 21–28.

Grafman, J., Schwab, K., Warden, D., Pridgen, B. S., & Brown, H. R. (1996). Frontal lobe injuries, violence, and aggression: A report of the Vietnam head injury study. *Neurology, 46,* 1231–1238.

Gray, J. A. (1987). *The psychology of fear and stress* (2nd ed.). Cambridge: Cambridge University Press.

Gregg, T. R., & Siegel, A. (2001). Brain structures and neurotransmitters regulating aggression in cats: Implications for human aggression. *Progressions in Neuropsychopharmacological Biological Psychiatry, 25,* 91–140.

Halperin, J. M., Sharma, V., Siever, L. J., Schwartz, S. T., Matier, K., Wornell, G., et al. (1994). Serotonergic function in aggressive and nonaggressive boys with attention deficit hyperactivity disorder. *American Journal of Psychiatry, 151,* 243–248.

Hare, R. D. (1991). *The Hare Psychopathy Checklist-Revised.* Toronto, Ontario, Canada: Multi-Health Systems.

Harmer, C. J., Perrett, D. I., Cowen, P. J., & Goodwin, G. M. (2001). Administration of the beta-adrenoceptor blocker propranolol impairs the processing of facial expressions of sadness. *Psychopharmacology, 154,* 383–389.

Harpur, T. J., Hare, R. D., & Hakstian, A. R. (1989). Two-factor conceptualization of psychopathy: Construct validity and assessment implications. *Psychological Assessment: A Journal of Consulting and Clinical Psychology, 1,* 6–17.

Hecaen, H., & Albert, M. L. (1978). *Human neuropsychology.* New York: Wiley.

Heim, C., Owens, M. J., Plotsky, P. M., & Nemeroff, C. B. (1997). Persistent changes in corticotropin-releasing factor systems due to early life stress: Relationship to the pathophysiology of major depression and post-traumatic stress disorder. *Psychopharmacological Bulletin, 33,* 185–192.

Hettema, J. M., Neale, M. C., & Kendler, K. S. (2001). A review and meta-analysis of the genetic epidemiology of anxiety disorders. *American Journal of Psychiatry, 158,* 1568–1578.

Hirschi, T. (1969). *Causes of delinquency.* Berkeley: University of California Press.

Hoffman, M. L. (1984). Empathy, its limitations, and its role in a comprehensive moral theory. In J. Gewirtz & W. Kurtines (Eds.), *Morality, moral development, and moral behavior* (pp. 283–302). New York: Wiley.

Hoffman, M. L. (1994). Discipline and internalisation. *Developmental Psychology, 30,* 26–28.

Hoffman, M. L., & Saltzstein, H. D. (1967). Parent discipline and the child's moral development. *Journal of Personality and Social Psychology, 5,* 45–57.

Johnson, W., McGue, M., Gaist, D., Vaupel, J. W., & Christensen, K. (2002). Frequency and heritability of depression symptomatology in the second half of life: Evidence from Danish twins over 45. *Psychological Medicine, 32,* 1175–1185.

Kagan, J., & Snidman, N. (1999). Early childhood predictors of adult anxiety disorders. *Biological Psychiatry, 46,* 1536–1541.

Kandel, E., & Freed, D. (1989). Frontal lobe dysfunction and antisocial behavior: A review. *Journal of Clinical Psychology, 45,* 404–413.

Kesler/West, M. L., Andersen, A. H., Smith, C. D., Avison, M. J., Davis, C. E., Kryscio, R. J., et al. (2001). Neural substrates of facial emotion processing using fMRI. *Cognitive Brain Research, 11,* 213–226.

Kiehl, K. A., Smith, A. M., Hare, R. D., Mendrek, A., Forster, B. B., Brink, J., et al. (2001). Limbic abnormalities in affective processing by criminal psychopaths as revealed by functional magnetic resonance imaging. *Biological Psychiatry, 50,* 677–684.

Killcross, S., Robbins, T. W., & Everitt, B. J. (1997). Different types of fear-conditioned behaviour mediated by separate nuclei within amygdala. *Nature, 388,* 377–380.

King, S. M. (1999). Escape-related behaviours in an unstable, elevated and exposed environment. II. Long-term sensitization after repetitive electrical stimulation of the rodent midbrain defense system. *Behavioral Brain Research, 98,* 127–142.

Kochanska, G. (1993). Toward a synthesis of parental socialization and child temperament in early development of conscience. *Child Development, 64,* 325–347.

Kochanska, G. (1997). Multiple pathways to conscience for children with different temperaments: From toddlerhood to age 5. *Developmental Psychology, 33,* 228–240.

Kochanska, G., De Vet, K., Goldman, M., Murray, K., & Putman, P. (1994). Maternal reports of conscience development and temperament in young children. *Child Development, 65,* 852–868.

Kosson, D. S., Cyterski, T. D., Steuerwald, B. L., Neumann, C. S., & Walker-Matthews, S. (2002). The reliability and validity of the psychopathy checklist: Youth version (PCL:YV) in nonincarcerated adolescent males. *Psychological Assessment, 14,* 97–109.

Kringelbach, M. L., & Rolls, E. T. (2003). Neural correlates of rapid reversal learning in a simple model of human social interaction. *Neuroimage, 20,* 1371–1383.

LaBar, K. S., Gatenby, J. C., Gore, J. C., LeDoux, J. E., & Phelps, E. A. (1998). Human amygdala activation during conditioned fear acquisition and extinction: A mixed-trial fMRI study. *Neuron, 20,* 937–945.

LaPierre, D., Braun, C. M. J., & Hodgins, S. (1995). Ventral frontal deficits in psychopathy: Neuropsychological test findings. *Neuropsychologia, 33,* 139–151.

Lee, R., & Coccaro, E. (2001). The neuropsychopharmacology of criminality and aggression. *Canadian Journal of Psychiatry, 46,* 35–44.

Levenston, G. K., Patrick, C. J., Bradley, M. M., & Lang, P. J. (2000). The psychopath as observer: Emotion and attention in picture processing. *Journal of Abnormal Psychology, 109,* 373–386.

Levine, S., Wiener, S. G., & Coe, C. L. (1993). Temporal and social factors influencing behavioral and hormonal responses to separation in mother and infant squirrel monkeys. *Psychoneuroendocrinology, 18,* 297–306.

Lichter, J. B., Barr, C. L., Kennedy, J. L., Van Tol, H. H., Kidd, K. K., & Livak, K. J. (1993). A hypervariable segment in the human dopamine receptor D4 (DRD4) gene. *Human Molecular Genetics, 2,* 767–773.

Linnoila, M., Virkkunen, M., Scheinin, M., Nuutila, A., Rimon, R., & Goodwin, F. K. (1983). Low cerebrospinal fluid 5-hydroxy indoleacetic acid concentration differentiates impulsive from nonimpulsive violent behavior. *Life Sciences, 33,* 2609–2614.

Liu, D., Diorio, J., Tannenbaum, B., Caldji, C., Francis, D., Freedman, A., et al. (1997). Maternal care, hippocampal glucocorticoid receptors, and hypothalamic-pituitary-adrenal responses to stress. *Science, 277,* 1659–1662.

Lykken, D. T. (1957). A study of anxiety in the sociopathic personality. *Journal of Abnormal and Social Psychology, 55,* 6–10.

Lykken, D. T. (1995). *The antisocial personalities.* Hillsdale, NJ: Erlbaum.

McClure, E. B., Pope, K., Hoberman, A. J., Pine, D. S., & Leibenluft, E. (2003). Facial expression recognition in adolescents with mood and anxiety disorders. *American Journal of Psychiatry, 160,* 1172–1174.

Mealey, L. (1995). The sociobiology of sociopathy: An integrated evolutionary model. *Behavioral and Brain Sciences, 18,* 523–599.

Miczek, K. A., Maxson, S. C., Fish, E. W., & Faccidomo, S. (2001). Aggressive behavioral phenotypes in mice. *Behavioral Brain Research, 125,* 167–181.

Mitchell, D. G., Colledge, E., Leonard, A., & Blair, R. J. (2002). Risky decisions and response reversal: Is there evidence of orbitofrontal cortex dysfunction in psychopathic individuals? *Neuropsychologia, 40,* 2013–2022.

Moffitt, T. E. (1993a). Adolescence-limited and life-course-persistent antisocial behavior: A developmental taxonomy. *Psychological Review, 100,* 674–701.

Moffitt, T. E. (1993b). The neuropsychology of conduct disorder. *Development and Psychopathology, 5,* 135–152.

Moffitt, T. E., Caspi, A., Harrington, H., & Milne, B. J. (2002). Males on the life-course-persistent and adolescence-limited antisocial pathways: Follow-up at age 26 years. *Development and Psychopathology, 14,* 179–207.

Moffitt, T. E., & Silva, P. A. (1988). Self-reported delinquency: Results from an instrument for New Zealand. *Australian and New Zealand Journal of Criminology, 21,* 233–240.

Morgan, A. B., & Lilienfeld, S. O. (2000). A meta-analytic review of the relation between antisocial behavior and neuropsychological measures of executive function. *Clinical Psychology Review, 20,* 113–136.

Morgan, C. A., III, Grillon, C., Lubin, H., & Southwick, S. M. (1997). Startle reflex abnormalities in women with sexual assault-related posttraumatic stress disorder. *American Journal of Psychiatry, 154,* 1076–1080.

Morgan, C. A., III, Grillon, C., Southwick, S. M., Davis, M., & Charney, D. S. (1996). Exaggerated acoustic startle reflex in Gulf War veterans with posttraumatic stress disorder. *American Journal of Psychiatry, 153,* 64–68.

Newman, J. P., & Kosson, D. S. (1986). Passive avoidance learning in psychopathic and nonpsychopathic offenders. *Journal of Abnormal Psychology, 95,* 252–256.

Newman, J. P., Patterson, C. M., & Kosson, D. S. (1987). Response perseveration in psychopaths. *Journal of Abnormal Psychology, 96,* 145–148.

Newman, J. P., & Schmitt, W. A. (1998). Passive avoidance in psychopathic offenders: A replication and extension. *Journal of Abnormal Psychology, 107,* 527–532.

Newman, J. P., Widom, C. S., & Nathan, S. (1985). Passive avoidance in syndromes of disinhibition: Psychopathy and extraversion. *Journal of Personality and Social Psychology, 48,* 1316–1327.

Nisenbaum, L. K., Zigmond, M. J., Sved, A. F., & Abercrombie, E. D. (1991). Prior exposure to chronic stress results in enhanced synthesis and release of hippocampal norepinephrine in response to a novel stressor. *Journal of Neuroscience, 11,* 1478–1484.

O'Brien, B. S., & Frick, P. J. (1996). Reward dominance: Associations with anxiety, conduct problems, and psychopathy in children. *Journal of Abnormal Child Psychology, 24,* 223–240.

Panksepp, J. (1998). *Affective neuroscience: The foundations of human and animal emotions.* New York: Oxford University Press.

Passingham, R. E., & Toni, I. (2001). Contrasting the dorsal and ventral visual systems: Guidance of movement versus decision making. *Neuroimage, 14,* S125–S131.

Patrick, C. J. (1994). Emotion and psychopathy: Startling new insights. *Psychophysiology, 31,* 319–330.

Pennington, B. F., & Bennetto, L. (1993). Main effects or transaction in the neuropsychology of conduct disorder? Commentary on "The neuropsychology of conduct disorder." *Development and Psychopathology, 5,* 153–164.

Pennington, B. F., & Ozonoff, S. (1996). Executive functions and developmental psychopathology. *Journal of Child Psychology and Psychiatry, 37,* 51–87.

Peschardt, K. S., Leonard, A., Morton, J., & Blair, R. J. R. Differential stimulus-reward and stimulus-punishment learning in individuals with psychopathy. Manuscript submitted for publication.

Peschardt, K. S., Richell, R. A., Mitchell, D. G. V., Leonard, A., Morton, J., & Blair, R. J. R. Primed up for positive, but not negative, words: Affective priming in individuals with psychopathy. Manuscript submitted for publication.

Pichot, P. (1978). Psychopathic behavior: Approaches to research. In R. D. Hare & D. S. Schalling (Eds.), *Psychopathic behavior: A historical review—reverse* (pp. 55–70). Chichester, UK: Wiley.

Pine, D. S., Cohen, E., Cohen, P., & Brook, J. S. (2000). Social phobia and the persistence of conduct problems. *Journal of Child Psychology and Psychiatry, 41,* 657–665.

Pine, D. S., Coplan, J. D., Wasserman, G. A., Miller, L. S., Fried, J. E., Davies, M., et al. (1997). Neuroendocrine response to fenfluramine challenge in boys. Associations with aggressive behavior and adverse rearing. *Archives of General Psychiatry, 54,* 839–846.

Plotsky, P. M., & Meaney, M. J. (1993). Early, postnatal experience alters hypothalamic corticotropin-releasing factor (CRF) mRNA, median eminence CRF content and stress-induced release in adult rats. *Brain Research. Molecular Brain Research, 18,* 195–200.

Prather, M. D., Lavenex, P., Mauldin-Jourdain, M. L., Mason, W. A., Capitanio, J. P., Mendoza, S. P., et al. (2001). Increased social fear and decreased fear of objects in monkeys with neonatal amygdala lesions. *Neuroscience, 106,* 653–658.

Quiggle, N. L., Garber, J., Panak, W. F., & Dodge, K. A. (1992). Social information processing in aggressive and depressed children. *Child Development, 63,* 1305–1320.

Raine, A. (1993). *The psychopathology of crime: Criminal behavior as a clinical disorder.* San Diego: Academic Press.

Raine, A. (1997). *The psychopathology of crime.* New York: Academic Press.

Raine, A. (2002a). Annotation: The role of prefrontal deficits, low autonomic arousal, and early health factors in the development of antisocial and aggressive behavior in children. *Journal of Child Psychology and Psychiatry, 43,* 417–434.

Raine, A. (2002b). Biosocial studies of antisocial and violent behavior in children and adults: A review. *Journal of Abnormal Child Psychology, 30,* 311–326.

Raine, A., Buchsbaum, M. S., & LaCasse, L. (1997). Brain abnormalities in murderers indicated by positron emission tomography. *Biological Psychiatry, 42,* 495–508.

Raine, A., Buchsbaum, M. S., Stanley, J., Lottenberg, S., Abel, L., & Stoddard, J. (1994). Selective reductions in prefrontal glucose metabolism in murderers. *Biological Psychiatry, 15,* 365–373.

Raine, A., Lencz, T., Bihrle, S., LaCasse, L., & Colletti, P. (2000). Reduced prefrontal gray matter volume and reduced autonomic activity in antisocial personality disorder. *Archives of General Psychiatry, 57,* 119–127.

Raine, A., Meloy, J. R., Birhle, S., Stoddard, J., LaCasse, L., & Buchsbaum, M. S. (1998). Reduced prefrontal and increased subcortical brain functioning assessed using positron emission tomography in predatory and affective murderers. *Behaviour Science and Law, 16,* 319–332.

Raine, A., Phil, D., Stoddard, J., Bihrle, S., & Buchsbaum, M. (1998). Prefrontal glucose deficits in murderers lacking psychosocial deprivation. *Neuropsychiatry Neuropsychology and Behavioral Neurology, 11,* 1–7.

Raine, A., Venables, P. H., & Williams, M. (1996). Better autonomic conditioning and faster electrodermal half-recovery time at age 15 years as possible protective factors against crime at age 29 years. *Developmental Psychology, 32,* 624–630.

Ramboz, S., Saudou, F., Amara, D. A., Belzung, C., Segu, L., Misslin, R., et al. (1996). 5-HT1B receptor knock out—behavioral consequences. *Behavioral Brain Research, 73,* 305–312.

Reiss, A. J., Miczek, K. A., & Roth, J. A. (1994). *Understanding and preventing violence.* Washington, DC: National Academy Press.

Robins, L. N., Tipp, J., & Pryzbeck, T. (1991). Antisocial personality. In L. N. Robins & D. A. Regier (Eds.), *Psychiatric disorders in North America* (pp. 258–290). New York: Free Press.

Rogeness, G. A., Cepeda, C., Macedo, C. A., Fischer, C., & Harris, W. R. (1990). Differences in heart rate and blood pressure in children with conduct disorder, major depression, and separation anxiety. *Psychiatry Research, 33,* 199–206.

Rogeness, G. A., Javors, M. A., Mass, J. W., & Macedo, C. A. (1990). Catecholamines and diagnoses in children. *Journal of the American Academy of Child and Adolescent Psychiatry, 29,* 234–241.

Rogers, R. D., Lancaster, M., Wakeley, J., & Bhagwager, Z. (2004). The effects of beta-adrenoceptor blockade on components of human decision-making. *Psychopharmacology, 172,* 157–164.

Roland, E., & Idsoe, T. (2001). Aggression and bullying. *Aggressive Behavior, 27,* 446–462.

Rolls, E. T. (2000). The orbitofrontal cortex and reward. *Cerebral Cortex, 10,* 284–294.

Rolls, E. T., Hornak, J., Wade, D., & McGrath, J. (1994). Emotion-related learning in patients with social and emotional changes associated with frontal lobe damage. *Journal of Neurology, Neurosurgery, and Psychiatry, 57,* 1518–1524.

Rothbart, M., Ahadi, S., & Hershey, K. L. (1994). Temperament an social behavior in children. *Merrill-Palmer Quarterly, 40,* 21–39.

Russo, M. F., & Beidel, D. C. (1993). Co-morbidity of childhood anxiety and externalizing disorders: Prevalence, associated characteristics, and validation issues. *Clinical Psychology Review, 14,* 199–221.

Scerbo, A., Raine, A., O'Brien, M., Chan, C. J., Rhee, C., & Smiley, N. (1990). Reward dominance and passive avoidance learning in adolescent psychopaths. *Journal of Abnormal Child Psychology, 18,* 451–463.

Schneider, F., Habel, U., Kessler, C., Posse, S., Grodd, W., & Muller-Gartner, H. W. (2000). Functional imaging of conditioned aversive emotional responses in antisocial personality disorder. *Neuropsychobiology, 42,* 192–201.

Shaikh, M. B., De Lanerolle, N. C., & Siegel, A. (1997). Serotonin 5-HT1A and 5-HT2/1C receptors in the midbrain periaqueductal gray differentially modulate defensive rage behavior elicited from the medial hypothalamus of the cat. *Brain Research, 765,* 198–207.

Shih, J. C., Chen, K., & Ridd, M. J. (1999). Monoamine oxidase: From genes to behavior. *Annual Review of Neuroscience, 22,* 197–217.

Silva, J. A., Derecho, D. V., Leong, G. B., Weinstock, R., & Ferrari, M. M. (2001). A classification of psychological factors leading to violent behavior in posttraumatic stress disorder. *Journal of Forensic Science, 46,* 309–316.

Sprengelmeyer, R., Rausch, M., Eysel, U. T., & Przuntek, H. (1998). Neural structures associated with the recognition of facial basic emotions. *Proceedings of the Royal Society of London, Series B, 265,* 1927–1931.

Stanton, M. E., Gutierrez, Y. R., & Levine, S. (1988). Maternal deprivation potentiates pituitary-adrenal stress responses in infant rats. *Behavioral Neuroscience, 102,* 692–700.

Steiner, H., Saxena, K., & Chang, K. (2003). Psychopharmacologic strategies for the treatment of aggression in juveniles. *CNS Spectrum, 8,* 298–308.

Stevens, D., Charman, T., & Blair, R. J. R. (2001). Recognition of emotion in facial expressions and vocal tones in children with psychopathic tendencies. *Journal of Genetic Psychology, 162,* 201–211.

Stuss, D. T., & Benson, D. F. (1986). *The frontal lobes.* New York: Raven Press.

Sustrik, R., Coupland, N., & Blair, R. J. R. Noradrenergic drugs and emotion recognition. Manuscript in preparation.

Swainson, R., Rogers, R. D., Sahakian, B. J., Summers, B. A., Polkey, C. E., & Robbins, T. W. (2000). Probabilistic learning and reversal deficits in patients with Parkinson's disease or frontal or temporal lobe lesions: Possible adverse effects of dopaminergic medication. *Neuropsychologia, 38,* 596–612.

Tanaka, M., Yoshida, M., Emoto, H., & Ishii, H. (2000). Noradrenaline systems in the hypothalamus, amygdala and locus coeruleus are involved in the provocation of anxiety: Basic studies. *European Journal of Pharmacology, 405,* 397–406.

Trasler, G. B. (1973). Criminal behaviour. In H. J. Eysenck (Ed.), *Handbook of abnormal psychology* (pp. 273–298). London: Pitman.

Trasler, G. B. (1978). Relations between psychopathy and persistent criminality—methodological and theoretical issues. In R. D. Hare & D. Schalling (Eds.), *Psychopathic behaviour: Approaches to research* (pp. 67–96). Chichester, UK: Wiley.

Vandenbergh, D. J., Persico, A. M., Hawkins, A. L., Griffin, C. A., Li, X., Jabs, E. W., et al. (1992). Human dopamine transporter gene (DAT1) maps to chromosome 5p15.3 and displays a VNTR. *Genomics, 14,* 1104–1106.

Veit, R., Flor, H., Erb, M., Hermann, C., Lotze, M., Grodd, W., et al. (2002). Brain circuits involved in emotional learning in antisocial behavior and social phobia in humans. *Neuroscience Letters, 328,* 233–236.

Viding, E., Blair, R. J. R., Moffitt, T. E., & Plomin, R. (in press). Psychopathic syndrome indexes strong genetic risk for antisocial behaviour in 7-year-olds. *Journal of Child Psychology and Psychiatry.*

Virkkunen, M., De Jong, J., Bartko, J., & Linnoila, M. (1989). Psychobiological concomitants of history of suicide attempts among violent offenders and impulsive fire setters. *Archives of General Psychiatry, 46,* 604–606.

Volavka, J. (1995). *Neurobiology of violence.* Washington, DC: American Psychiatric Press.

Volkow, N. D., & Tancredi, L. (1987). Neural substrates of violent behaviour. A preliminary study with positron emission tomography. *British Journal of Psychiatry, 151,* 668–673.

Volkow, N. D., Tancredi, L. R., Grant, C., Gillespie, H., Valentine, A., Mullani, N., et al. (1995). Brain glucose metabolism in violent psychiatric patients: A preliminary study. *Psychiatry Research, 61,* 243–253.

Williamson, S., Hare, R. D., & Wong, S. (1987). Violence: Criminal psychopaths and their victims. *Canadian Journal of Behavioral Science, 19,* 454–462.

Wong, M., Fenwick, P., Fenton, G., Lumsden, J., Maisey, M., & Stevens, J. (1997). Repetitive and non-repetitive violent offending behaviour in male patients in a maximum security mental hospital—clinical and neuroimaging findings. *Medicine, Science and Law, 37,* 150–160.

Wootton, J. M., Frick, P. J., Shelton, K. K., & Silverthorn, P. (1997). Ineffective parenting and childhood conduct problems: The moderating role of callous-unemotional traits. *Journal of Consulting and Clinical Psychology, 65,* 292–300.

Zoccolillo, M. (1992). Co-occurrence of conduct disorder and its adult outcomes with depressive and anxiety disorders: A review. *Journal of the America Academy of Child and Adolescent Psychiatry, 31,* 547–556.

PART V

PHARMACOLOGY AND PSYCHOPHYSIOLOGY

16

Drugs of Abuse and Aggression

Jill M. Grimes, Lesley Ricci, Khampaseuth Rasakham,
& Richard H. Melloni, Jr.

There is a growing body of evidence indicating that drug abuse is associated with escalated states of aggressive responding. Considerable debate exists, however, regarding whether the escalated aggressive states associated with drug abuse are due to direct pharmacologic and/or neurologic effects of the drug or to environmental circumstances surrounding drug attainment. It is not surprising, then, that little clinical research to date has been carried out examining whether drugs of abuse stimulate aggressive behavior directly, in the absence of socioeconomic factors and environmental pressures that correlate with drug acquisition. The influences these factors have in the decision to use aggression in humans are difficult to separate from forces that may represent the direct activation of aggressive response patterns. By using animal models, researchers can circumvent social motivations that relate to the requirement for drug attainment, facilitating the investigation of whether drugs of abuse directly alter aggressive drive. This chapter summarizes studies examining the link between drugs of abuse and the behavioral neurobiology of aggressive behavior in animal models. Throughout the chapter, we consider studies examining how drugs of abuse affect the aggressive response patterns of animals, as well as the development, activity, and function of neural systems implicated in aggression control.

The clinical literature and studies from the National Institute on Drug Abuse (NIDA) indicate that drug abuse is most prevalent in adult populations (NIDA, n.d.; see also Cherek, Tcheremissine, & Lane, ch. 17 in this volume). Accordingly, the majority of animal studies considered in this chapter investigate the link between drugs of abuse and aggression in adult animal models. However, survey studies from NIDA also report that drug abuse is increasing in youth (i.e., adolescent) populations worldwide and others report that use during this sensitive developmental period is associated with elevated aggression and violence (NIDA, n.d.). Given this trend, it is surprising that comparatively few studies to date have examined the developmental effects of drugs of abuse on the behavioral neurobiology of aggression. Thus, in this chapter, the effects of developmental exposure to drugs of abuse on aggression are considered when appropriate, including gestational, prepubertal, and pubertal exposure. In addition to age of exposure, there are a number of other important factors to consider when reviewing the literature investigating the link between drugs of abuse and aggression, including pharmacological factors, such as the class (e.g., form and type) of drug, dosing regimen, exposure time, and route of administration, and the choice of experimental aggression paradigm and animal species studied. In addition, one must take into account the influence of epigenetic factors, such as social influence and structure, when considering the literature investigating the link between drugs of abuse and aggression. Each of these factors has significant potential to alter the experimental outcome(s) of studies examining the effects of drugs of abuse on aggressive responding; thus they are critically important issues to consider when evaluating the results of studies reviewed here. The drugs included in this chapter are restricted to those (a) classified as drugs of abuse by NIDA and (b) that have been shown to influence aggression in the preclinical literature. In the event that individual drugs fit multiple classifications, we combine those for ease of review. We consider studies examining the effects of both common drugs of abuse and drugs classified as prescribed medications. Throughout the course of this review, we consider studies in a systematic fashion beginning with age of drug exposure (i.e., adult, adolescent, gestational). At each time of drug exposure we review studies employing different experimental aggression paradigms examining multiple aggression subtypes (i.e., resident/intruder tests for territorial aggression, neutral arena tests for intermale aggression, and maternal aggression tests to name a few) in a number of different animal species and strains.

Anabolic-Androgenic Steroids

Testosterone and its synthetic derivatives, collectively termed anabolic androgenic steroids (AAS), are compounds known to have both tissue building (anabolic) and masculinization (androgenic) effects (Clark & Henderson, 2003; Kuhn, 2002; NIDA, n.d.). The commonly abused AAS fall into three distinct classes, including (a) testosterone esters (e.g., testosterone cypionate and testosterone proprionate), (b) 19-nor-testosterone (e.g., nandrolone decanoate), and (c) 17α-alkyl AAS (e.g., 17α-methyltestosterone, methandrostenolone, northandrolone, danazol, fluoxymesterone, oxandrolone, oxymetholone, and stanzolol). Drugs in each class of AAS have been examined for their effects on aggressive responding in preclinical animal models. With notable exceptions, the preclinical literature linking AAS and aggression provides strong evidence for a stimulatory role for AAS in aggression despite significant differences in

experimental design. For instance, pharmacological factors, which include the class of AAS, dosing regimen, exposure time, and route of administration, have a dramatic effect on the experimental findings, as do the animal model used and the experimental aggression paradigm employed.

The majority of studies that have examined the effects of AAS on aggression have focused on adult male rats as an animal model in both territorial (i.e., resident-intruder) and intermale (i.e., neutral arena) aggression testing paradigms. Long, Wilson, Sufka, and Davis (1996) examined the effect of nandrolone decanoate (ND, 2 mg/kg daily or 20 mg twice weekly) on aggression in adult, male Sprague–Dawley rats using the resident-intruder paradigm. Experimental animals underwent aggression testing twice weekly for 2 weeks prior to drug administration to determine baseline aggression levels. Starting after 1 full week of administration and through 4 full weeks of treatment, ND-treated rats displayed heightened levels of aggression when compared to controls, as indicated by the composite aggression score assigned to each animal (calculated based on the number of lateral and lunge attacks + attack duration + number of bites + on top duration + piloerection). The effects of housing conditions and gonadal status of opponents were examined on AAS-induced aggression in adult, male Long–Evans rats (Breuer, McGinnis, Lumia, & Possidente, 2001). In this study, three AAS were tested individually in gonadally intact rats: testosterone propionate (TP), ND and stanozolol (ST) (5 mg/kg five times per week for 12 weeks). Each experimental rat was tested for aggression, in a counterbalanced fashion, in a variety of testing situations that differed regarding testing environment (i.e., home cage, neutral cage, opponent's cage) and gonadal status of opponent (castrate vs. intact). A composite score was determined for each animal and was derived from adding the frequency of attack/fights, threats, mounts, and dominance postures. Only TP-treated rats showed increases in the mean composite aggression score when compared to control rats. ST-treated rats displayed the least aggression of all the groups, and this decrease was statistically significant from TP-, ND-, and control-treated males. TP-treated rats were more likely to aggress toward an intact opponent versus a gonadectomized one when compared to ND- and ST-treated rats, but not to controls. ST treatment eliminated all aggressive behaviors toward both intact and gonadectomized opponents when compared to all other treatment groups, including controls. Regarding environmental conditions, TP-treated rats displayed increased aggression in both their home cage and the opponent's cage when compared to their responses in the neutral arena. In contrast, ND-treated rats and controls only exhibited increases in aggression in their home cage when compared to the neutral cage. In a study of the effects of daily injections of three AAS on aggression using the resident-intruder paradigm, resident, adult, male Long–Evans rats were castrated at 90 days of age 3 weeks prior to the first aggression test (Clark & Barber, 1994). Daily injections of methyltestosterone (3 mg/day), ST (400 µg/day), TP (400 µg/day), or vehicle were administered starting on the day of castration. Two weeks after castration, resident male rats were housed with an intact female with aggression testing beginning 1 week after pairing. Aggression testing was conducted for 3 weeks, with one test per week. For each aggression test, a lighter, intruder male rat was injected with 0.50 mg of diazepam (shown to decrease the defensive behaviors of intruder males) and behaviors were recorded for 15 min and a composite aggression score was calculated as described (Breuer et al., 2001). Total attack time did not differ between any treatment groups during all three tests. During Weeks 2 and 3 of testing, castrated rats treated with methyltestosterone displayed a significant increase in bites when compared to controls and TP-treated rats showed a similar increase at Week 3. No differences were observed between control and any AAS for total attack frequency and on top posture; however, both methyltestosterone- and TP-treated castrated rats had higher mean aggression composite scores when compared to controls. ST failed to increase any measure of aggression in castrated male rats. Frye, Rhodes, Walf, and Harney (2002) examined whether the aggression-enhancing effects of testosterone are modulated by its 5α-reduced metabolite, 3α-diol, by testing mice deficient in the 5α-reductase type I enzyme for aggression using the resident-intruder paradigm. In a first experiment, the effects of both testosterone and 3α-diol on aggression in gonadectomized, C21 adult male mice were measured. Mice received testosterone (1000 µg), 3α-diol (1000 µg), or vehicle 1 hr prior to aggression testing. Both testosterone and 3α-diol increased the number of aggressive acts (attacks, bites, threats, and tail rattles) toward a conspecific when compared to control. In a second experiment, both wild-type (WT) and 5α-reductase-deficient mice were administered either testosterone (1000µg) or vehicle 1 hr prior to aggression testing. WT mice administered testosterone had significantly shorter latencies to the first aggres-

sive act and a significantly greater number of aggressive acts when compared to both 5α-reductase-deficient mice and controls. Authors speculate that both testosterone and its metabolite, 3α-diol, can enhance aggression and that the metabolism of testosterone by 5α-reductase may be involved in the aggressive response observed in these mice.

The effects of withdrawal from AAS on aggression were recently examined in adult, male Long–Evans rats (McGinnis, Lumia, & Possidente, 2002). Gonadally intact, male rats were administered TP, ND, ST, or vehicle at a dose of 5 mg/kg, five days per week for 12 weeks. For all animals, aggression was assessed against a gonadally intact or gonadectomized opponent in the experimental animal's home cage, a neutral cage, or the opponent's home cage following either 3 or 12 weeks withdrawal from the AAS. TP-treated rats displayed significantly more attack/fights, threats, and mounts than controls following short-term withdrawal. Short-term withdrawal from ND did not alter aggressive responding when compared to controls, whereas rats treated with ST displayed lower levels of aggression than controls. In addition, the gonadal status of the opponent and the location of aggression testing influenced composite aggression scores. Specifically, TP-treated rats displayed increased aggression (i.e., composite aggression score) toward the intact opponent in both its home cage and the opponent's home cage when compared to aggression directed toward the castrated opponent. ND-treated rats only displayed increased aggression toward intact opponents while being tested in the opponent's home cage. After 12 weeks withdrawal from AAS, aggressive behavior of TP- and ST-treated rats returned to control levels, indicating that AAS-induced aggression is reversible following the cessation of treatment.

McGinnis, Lumia, Breuer, and Possidente (2002) also examined whether mild physical provocation, a tail pinch, altered the aggressive response of gonadally intact male Long–Evans rats that had been treated with one of three AAS. Rats were administered TP, ND, ST, or vehicle in a dose of 5 mg/kg, 5 days per week for 12 weeks. Injections continued while animals were being tested for aggression. Six tests were conducted and each experimental animal was confronted with a gonadally intact and a gonadectomized opponent in its home cage, the opponent's home cage, and a neutral cage to obtain baseline aggression scores. In a second series of tests, the experimental animal received a brief tail pinch (1 s long, once per minute) in each of the conditions. In baseline conditions, TP-treated rats displayed significantly higher threat frequencies in the neutral cage against a castrated opponent, while ST-treated rats showed significantly fewer attacks in their home cages and fewer threats in the neutral cage against intact opponents when compared to controls. The mean composite aggression score was significantly enhanced in TP-treated males receiving a tail pinch in every condition when compared to all other groups. In other words, TP-treated rats displayed increased aggression regardless of the gonadal status of the opponent and the testing location following tail pinch. In contrast, ND-treated and control animals only displayed increased aggression in their home cages against an intact opponent.

The effects of long-term exposure of TP (1 mg/rat 3 times per week for 10 weeks) were examined in intact, Long–Evans rats on aggression when confronted with a gonadally intact, conspecific in a neutral cage (Lumia, Thorner, & McGinnis, 1994). Aggression testing started following 5 weeks of TP exposure and continued weekly throughout the 10 weeks of treatment. Exposure to TP increased the frequency of dominance postures and threats and decreased the frequency of submissive postures when compared to controls; however, TP-treated rats did not differ from controls in the frequency of attack/fights over the 5-week testing period. The behavioral and physiological effects of a combination of AAS were reported in male and female mice (Bronson, 1996; Bronson, Nguyen, & De La Rosa, 1996). In these studies, CF-1 female mice were administered low and high doses of an AAS cocktail (testosterone, testosterone cypionate, methyltestosterone, norethandrolone) via subcutaneous silastic tubes for 7 weeks (Bronson et al., 1996). Dosages were calculated based on previous doses found to restore androgenic properties in castrated male mice. A low dose of the combined AAS is representative of 5 times the dose required to restore androgenic properties in castrated male mice. A high dose is 20 times the dose required to restore androgenic properties in castrated male mice. Two females of different treatments (i.e., pairs of control vs. low dose, control vs. high dose, low dose vs. high dose) were tested for aggression in a neutral arena for 10 min. No specific pairing of doses tested produced any significant effect on aggression; however, AAS-treated female mice (at both low and high doses) showed an increase in aggressive behavior, as reflected by numbers of threats and attacks when paired with controls. Similar results were observed in a follow-up study in female mice

(Bronson et al., 1996); however, when AAS were administered to male mice, no effect on aggression was observed.

The effects of AAS on aggression have also been examined using an isolation-induced aggression paradigm. For example, the effects of chronic treatment with TP on aggression were examined in intact, adult, male OF-1 mice (Martinez-Sanchis, Salvador, Moya-Albiol, Gonalez-Bono, & Simon, 1998). Mice were individually housed for 3 weeks prior to receiving one of four doses of TP: 3.75, 7.5, 15, or 30 mg/kg/week for 10 weeks. During the last 3 weeks of treatment, behavior testing was conducted in a neutral arena with an anosmic opponent. Some differences in threat and attack behaviors between groups were found across the 3-week testing period. Specifically, the latency to first threat decreased in TP-treated groups, whereas this measure increased in control animals. Significant decreases in latency to first threat were observed in the 3.75 and 30 mg/kg groups on the first week of behavior testing when compared to the second and third weeks, whereas mice treated with 7.5 mg/kg of TP showed a significant decrease in latency to threat in the first week when compared to the third week of behavior testing. Across all doses tested, the number of attacks increased over time; however, not one dose significantly differed from another or from control in this behavioral measure. Thus, in general, exposure to TP in adult, intact male CF-1 mice did not produce any profound effects on aggressive behavior in this particular study.

In one of the few reports to assess aggression following treatment with AAS in a competition task, daily injections of ND were administered at a dose of 15 mg/kg for 2 weeks to intact adult, male Wistar rats (Lindqvist, Johansson-Steensland, Nyberg, & Fahlke, 2002). One week following the last injection of ND, experimental rats were paired and housed with an oil-treated conspecific. Animals had 3 days to acclimate to the new environment and were subjected to a 1-hr water restriction per day. On the fourth day, rats had to compete for access to the water spout and various behaviors were recorded (i.e., time rats spent drinking, number of pushes, number of lunge attacks, number of paw strikes) during the 4-min testing period. No differences in numbers of pushes, attacks, or paw strikes between AAS- and vehicle-treated rats were observed during the water competition task.

The effects of anabolic steroids were examined on aggression in cynomolgus monkeys, allowing researchers to gain an understanding of the effects of these drugs in a complex social setting (Rejeski, Brubaker, Herb, Kaplan, & Koritnik, 1988). Ten adult male cynomolgus monkeys were housed in two groups of five, with control and experimental animals being housed separately. Monkeys were provided 4 weeks prior to behavioral observation to allow for the development of social stability within the groups. Behavior was observed for 2 weeks (30 min/day) prior to 8 weeks of exposure to TP (4 mg/kg/2 times per week) or vehicle. Behavior was reassessed after TP administration for 2 weeks to obtain post-test aggression scores. Various aggressive and social behaviors were recorded during the three testing sessions, including contact aggression (i.e., slap, push, grapple, bite), noncontact aggression (i.e., open-mouth threat, stare threat, chase), and affiliation (i.e., groom, play). Monkeys receiving TP exhibited more contact and noncontact aggression when compared to the control group. Interestingly, the effects of TP on aggression appear to be influenced by the social status of the animal. Although both dominant and subordinate monkeys displayed more contact aggression when treated with TP, the increases in aggression from pre- to post-test in the dominant monkeys were 3 times those of the subordinate monkeys. When analyzed separately, TP-treated dominant monkeys displayed more noncontact aggression when compared to controls, whereas subordinate monkeys treated with TP did not differ from the control group.

The effects of adolescent AAS exposure on aggression has been examined in male Syrian hamsters (*Mesocricetus auratus*) using the resident-intruder paradigm. In a first study, Melloni, Connor, Hang, Harrison, and Ferris (1997) examined the effects of a subchronic exposure to a high-dose cocktail of AAS on the aggressive behavior of adolescent, male Syrian hamsters. On Postnatal Day (P) 27, individually housed hamsters were treated with a cocktail of AAS consisting of 2 mg/kg of testosterone cypionate, 2 mg/kg of nandrolone decanote, and 1 mg/kg of boldenone undecylenate or sesame oil vehicle for 14 consecutive days (P-27–P-42). On P-43, experimental hamsters were tested for offensive aggression (i.e., number of attacks and bites and latency to first bite) by placing a stimulus animal in their home cage. Results from this study showed that after 2-week exposure to high-dose AAS in the midst of adolescent development, hamsters were significantly more aggressive than controls, as indicated by increases in the total number of attacks and bites. In addition, adolescent AAS-treated hamsters displayed a quicker

aggressive response than controls, as indicated by the latency to first bite. In a second set of studies, Harrison, Connor, Nowak, Nash, and Melloni (2000) further characterized the aggression-stimulating effects of adolescent AAS exposure, in addition to examining the role of the neuropeptide arginine vasopressin (AVP) in this phenomenon. A similar treatment regimen was used as described (Melloni et al., 1997); however, adolescent, male Syrian hamsters were treated with AAS throughout the entire period of adolescent development (P-27–P-56). Young adult hamsters were then tested for offensive aggression on the day following the last AAS injection (P-58) using the resident-intruder paradigm. As seen in animals treated with AAS during the first 2 weeks of adolescent development (Melloni et al., 1997), long-term exposure to high doses of AAS during adolescence increased offensive aggression (i.e., increased the number of bites and attacks and decreased the aggressive response time) in early adulthood. In a subsequent set of experiments, the involvement of anterior hypothalamic AVP (AH-AVP) signaling in adolescent AAS-stimulated aggression was examined. In a first experiment, this phenomenon was examined pharmacologically through local administration of an AVP receptor antagonist (AVP V1A) into the anterior hypothalamus (AH) of AAS-treated hamsters (figure 16.1). Adolescent hamsters were pretreated with AAS as described and stereotaxically implanted with a microinjection cannulae directed toward the AH to allow for the administration of the AVP V1A antagonist. Antagonist was administered to the AH 1 hr prior to aggression testing, which was conducted as described. Microinjection of an AVP V1A receptor antagonist into the AH significantly decreased the intensity of the aggressive response (i.e., the numbers of bites and attacks) in AAS-treated hamsters compared to saline-treated controls. However, the latency to first aggressive response was not altered, indicating that the AH-AVP neural system may not be involved in the initiation of the aggressive response.

In a second experiment, adolescent Syrian hamsters were treated with AAS or vehicle for 30 days as described and their brains were labeled for AVP immunoreactivity (AVP-ir) by immunohistochemistry to investigate for differences in the distribution and/or number of AVP-containing cells between groups. Interestingly, no differences in the distribution and/or number of AVP-containing cell groups were observed in AH-AVP-ir between AAS-treated and control hamsters (figure 16.2). However, an examination of AVP

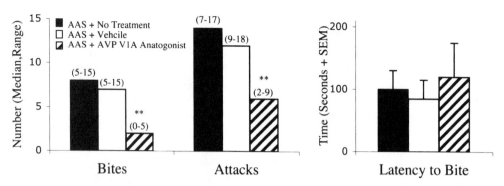

FIGURE 16.1 Microinjection of arginine vasopressin (AVP) V1A receptor antagonists into the anterior hypothalamus (AH) regulates anabolic steroid (AAS)-facilitated aggression. Aggressive AAS-pretreated animals were given each of three treatments and tested for offensive aggression. The treatments were (a) no microinjection (black bars), (b) microinjection of vehicle into the AH (open bars), and (c) microinjection of AVP V1A receptor antagonists into the AH (striped bars). $**p < .01$, Kruskal–Wallis followed by Mann–Whitney U tests (two-tailed). From "Chronic Anabolic-Androgenic Steroid Treatment During Adolescence Increases Anterior Hypothalamic Vasopressin and Aggression in Intact Hamsters," by R. J. Harrison, D. F. Connor, C. Nowak, K. Nash, and R. H. Melloni, Jr., 2000, *Psychoneuroendocrinology*, 25(4). Copyright 2000 by Elsevier. Reprinted with permission.

FIGURE 16.2 Dark-field photomicrographs showing immunoreactive labeling for AVP in the AH of (A) anabolic steroid- and (B) vehicle-treated hamsters; oc, optic chiasm. Bar, 250 μm. From "Chronic Anabolic-Androgenic Steroid Treatment During Adolescence Increases Anterior Hypothalamic Vasopressin and Aggression in Intact Hamsters," by R. J. Harrison, D. F. Connor, C. Nowak, K. Nash, and R. H. Melloni, Jr., 2000, *Psychoneuroendocrinology*, 25(4), p. 326. Copyright 2000 by Elsevier. Reprinted with permission.

fiber density within the AH revealed that hamsters treated with AAS throughout adolescence displayed a 2.3- to 2.5-fold increase in the mean area covered by AVP-ir fibers when compared to controls.

To examine this difference in a more quantitative fashion, total protein was extracted from the AH of control and AAS-treated hamsters and AVP levels were determined by enzyme immunoassay (EIA). Levels of AVP peptide were statistically higher in the AH of AAS-treated hamsters compared to vehicle controls, with AAS-treated hamsters displaying a greater than 2.5-fold increase. To determine whether the observed increase in AH-AVP by AAS is a result of alterations in AVP mRNA expression, in situ hybridization and RNA blot analysis were performed using RNA from the AH of aggressive, AAS-treated hamsters and nonaggressive, vehicle-treated counterparts. Despite increases in AVP-ir fiber density and peptide content in the AH of AAS-treated hamsters, neither the intensity of AVP mRNA-specific hybridization signal nor RNA blot levels of AVP mRNA differed between AAS- and vehicle-treated hamsters, indicating that the observed increases in AVP-ir fiber density and peptide content in the AH were not likely due to transcriptional responses of the AVP gene. In a later study from this laboratory, DeLeon, Grimes, and Melloni (2002) examined whether aggressive, adolescent AAS-treated hamsters display alterations in AVP V1A receptor binding in brain regions implicated in the control of offensive aggression. Following behavioral testing for offensive aggression using the resident-intruder paradigm, brains of hamsters pretreated with AAS as described above (Harrison et al., 2000) were processed for AVP V1A receptor in situ receptor autoradiography and the AVP V1A receptor binding density was compared between aggressive, AAS-treated hamsters and nonaggressive, vehicle-treated littermates in regions of the brain known to express this receptor subtype, including the bed nucleus of the stria terminalis (BNST), central amygdaloid nucleus (CeA), corticomedial amygdaloid nucleus (CoMeA), lateral septum (LS), lateral aspects of the medial preoptic area to the anterior hypothalamus (MPOA-AH), paraventricular nucleus (PVN), and ventrolateral hypothalamus (VLH). AVP V1A receptor binding was altered in several area of the hamster brain important for aggression control in aggressive, AAS-treated hamsters. In particular, AAS-treated hamsters displayed significantly greater (~ 20%) AVP V1A receptor labeling in the VLH when compared to controls. Significant increases in AVP V1A receptor binding were also observed in the BNST, LS, and PVN of AAS-treated hamsters compared to vehicle-treated controls. However, not every brain region implicated in the control of aggressive behavior showed changes in AVP V1A receptor binding following adolescent AAS exposure, including the CeA, MPOA-AH, and the CoMeA.

In an attempt to further characterize the neurobiological changes that may occur as a result of exposure to AAS during adolescent development, Grimes and Melloni (2002) examined the role of the serotonin neural system in regulating AAS-induced aggression in adolescent Syrian hamsters. In a first experiment, to determine whether serotonin (5-HT) signaling played a significant role in adolescent AAS-facilitated attack, an acute dose of the selective 5-HT reuptake inhibitor fluoxetine (20 mg/kg, ip) or saline was administered to hamsters (P-58) stimulated to respond aggressively by pretreatment with AAS throughout adolescence as described (DeLeon et al., 2002; Harrison et al., 2000) 1 hr prior to resident-intruder aggression tests. AAS-treated hamsters that received an acute injection of saline prior to aggression testing displayed heightened levels of offensive aggression (i.e., numbers of attacks and decreased latency to first attack), although aggressive, AAS-treated hamsters pretreated with fluoxetine displayed significant decreases in the total number of attacks and an increase in the latency to first attack. In a second experiment, brains of aggressive, AAS-treated hamsters and nonaggressive, vehicle-treated littermates were removed and processed for 5-HT immunohis-

tochemistry to determine whether exposure to AAS during adolescence alters the normal development of the serotonergic neural system. In aggressive, AAS-treated hamsters, the immunohistochemical staining pattern for 5-HT was altered in several brain areas when compared to vehicle-treated controls (figure 16.3).

Specifically, hamsters treated with AAS throughout adolescence displayed a statistically significant decreased pattern of staining for 5-HT-immunoreactive (5-HT-ir) varicosities and fibers in the AH, VLH, MeA, and CeA when compared to controls. However, not every brain region implicated in the aggressive response showed changes in 5-HT afferent innervation following exposure to AAS during adolescence, including the BNST, LS, CoMeA, and medial preoptic nucleus (MPN).

Recently, Grimes and colleagues (2003) examined whether the gamma-aminobutyric acid (GABA) neural system is involved in adolescent AAS-induced aggression in Syrian hamsters by examining the immunohistochemical localization of glutamic acid decarboxylase (GAD_{65}) in brains of aggressive, AAS-treated hamsters and nonaggressive, vehicle-treated littermates. Adolescent, male Syrian hamsters were treated with AAS throughout adolescent development as described (DeLeon et al., 2002; Grimes & Melloni, 2002; Harrison et al., 2000). On P-58, hamsters were tested for offensive aggression and sacrificed 24 hr later, and brains were removed and processed for immunohistochemistry for GAD_{65}. As in other studies from this laboratory, hamsters treated with AAS throughout adolescence displayed significantly escalated levels of offensive aggression when compared to vehicle-treated controls. In particular aggressive, AAS-treated hamsters showed significant increases in very specific behavioral components of the aggressive response, including the number of lateral attacks, upright offensive postures, and chases when compared to controls. In addition, AAS-treated hamsters displayed decreases in both attack and bite latencies when compared to controls (figure 16.4).

Chronic, high-dose AAS throughout adolescent development led to alterations in the density of GAD_{65}-ir puncta in various brain regions. Specifically, aggressive, AAS-treated hamsters displayed significant increases in GAD_{65}-ir in the AH, VLH, and MeA, while showing a significant decrease in the LS when compared to nonaggressive, vehicle-treated controls. Together, these studies in adolescent hamsters support a functional role for AVP, 5-HT, and GABA in adolescent AAS-facilitated aggression. Further, they suggest a role for alterations

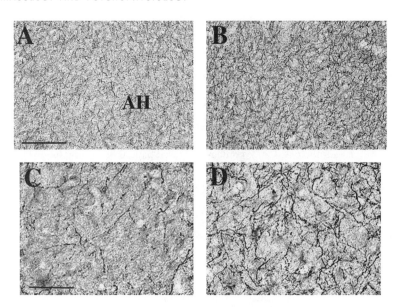

FIGURE 16.3 Bright-field photomicrographs showing 5-HT-ir varicosities and fibers in the AH of (A and C) AAS- and (B and D) oil- treated hamsters. Bars, 20 μm (A and B) and 2 μm (C and D). From "Serotonin Modulates Offensive Attack in Adolescent Anabolic Steroid-Treated Hamsters," by J. M. Grimes and R. H. Melloni, Jr., 2002, *Pharmacology, Biochemistry and Behavior*, 73(3), p. 717. Copyright 2002 by Elsevier. Reprinted with permission.

in AVP, 5-HT, and GABA development and neural signaling (AVP through the AVP V1A receptor) in specific brain regions, namely, the AH, VLH, and MeA, that is, brain regions implicated in aggression control in hamsters.

Using Long–Evans rats, Farrell and McGinnis (2003) examined the effects of AAS exposure during puberty on aggressive behavior. Rats were individually housed on P-35 and for the duration of the study. Rats (P-40) were injected with 5 mg/kg of T, ND, ST, or vehicle (5×/week) for 12 weeks. Following 2 weeks of testing for copulatory behavior, scent marking, and vocalizations, all rats were tested for aggression once a week for 6 weeks against either a castrated intruder with no hormonal implant (i.e., castrated) or one that had been implanted with testosterone (i.e., intact) in the experimental animal's home cage, the opponent's home cage, and a neutral cage. A composite score was determined for each animal and was derived from adding the frequency of attack/fights, threats, mounts, and dominance postures. Overall, a nonsignificant increase in the mean aggression/dominance score was observed in T-treated rats, whereas ND-treated males showed

scores similar to those observed in controls. ST-treated rats showed decreased aggression when compared to controls in all testing sessions; however, this only reached statistical significance in the home cage against both types of intruders (castrated and intact) and in the neutral cage against castrated opponents. When aggression data were analyzed to reveal differences based on the gonadal status of the opponent, only ST-treated males showed statistically lower levels of aggression than controls toward both castrated and intact opponents; however, rats in all treatment groups showed more aggression toward the intact than the castrated opponents. With respect to behavior testing location, T-treated rats displayed significantly higher levels of aggression in the opponent's cage when compared to controls. ND-treated males showed no differences and ST-treated rats displayed significantly reduced aggression in all three test environments when compared to controls.

The effects of AAS on aggressive behavior have also been examined in intact, adolescent Alderley Park male albino mice using an isolation paradigm for aggression (Martinez-Sanchis, Brain, Salvador, & Simon, 1996).

P-29 mice were isolated for 8 days prior to the be-ginning of drug treatment and isolation continued throughout the 21-day treatment period. Groups were administered a high (7.0 mg/kg), moderate (0.7 mg/kg), or low (0.07 mg/kg) dose of ST or vehicle on alternate days from P-29 to P-50. Animals were tested for aggres-sion 24 hr after the last injection by placing both the experimental animal and a standard opponent into a neutral cage. Although no significant differences in ag-gression were observed between any dose, a trend toward an increase in attack and threat behaviors was seen at the higher doses of ST. These results are in contrast to those of previous studies and to a second experiment within this study, which had examined the effects of ST on aggressive behavior in adult animal models.

Central Nervous System (CNS) Stimulants

Cocaine

Studies examining the effects of cocaine exposure dur-ing adulthood have employed a variety of dosing regi-mens and testing paradigms subsequently leading to conflicting results. Using an intruder-evoked model of aggression in both isolated and nonisolated adult male Swiss–Webster mice, treatment with acute exposure to cocaine dose dependently decreased attack behavior (attack, tail rattle, and pursuit), with the effective ag-gression-reducing doses of cocaine being 8.0 mg/kg in isolated mice and 2.0 mg/kg in nonisolates (Miczek &

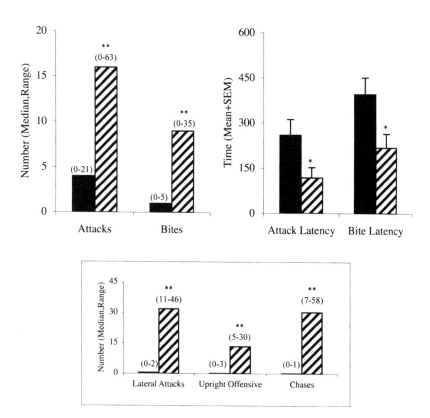

FIGURE 16.4 Adolescent AAS treatment increases offensive aggression. The number of total attacks and bites and the latency to first attack and bite, as well as lateral attacks, upright offensive attacks, and chases (inset), in AAS- and vehicle-treated residents are shown. Bars denote SEM. Solid columns = vehicle, striped columns = adolescent AAS. $*p < .05$, $**p < .01$, Mann–Whitney two-tailed test (number measures) and Student's t test, two-tailed (latency measures). From "Glutamic Acid Decarboxylase (GAD65) Immunoreactivity in Brains of Aggressive, Adolescent Anabolic Steroid-Treated Hamsters," by J. M. Grimes, L. A. Ricci, and R. H. Melloni, Jr., 2003, *Hormones and Behavior, 44*(3), p. 275. Copyright 2003 by Elsevier. Reprinted with permission.

O'Donnell, 1978). Miczek (1979) also tested the effects of acute cocaine exposure in adult rats using the resident-intruder paradigm. These studies found that administration of cocaine at any dose tested (0.5, 2.0, 8.0, or 32.0 mg/kg) failed to increase aggressive behavior; however, at the high end of this dose curve (i.e., 8.0 and 32.0 mg/kg) aggression was significantly decreased, with no other behaviors (i.e., locomotion) being affected. Contrary to these findings, Hadfield, Nugent, and Mott (1982) examined the effects of acute exposure to high doses (i.e., 10 and 35 mg/kg) of cocaine on isolation-induced fighting in adult male mice and found that both doses significantly increased fighting, including biting, pummeling, and sparring, compared to saline-treated controls. The acute and chronic effects of cocaine were examined on isolated-induced aggression in adult male mice (Darmani, Hadfield, Carter, & Martin, 1990). Mice were individually housed for 6 weeks and received 0.5, 1.0, 5.0, 10, or 20 mg/kg of cocaine or saline 20 min prior to testing for the acute studies. At high doses (i.e., 10 and 20 mg/kg), acute cocaine exposure significantly reduced the number of attacks and increased the latency to first attack toward the intruder when compared to animals in the lower dose cocaine treatment groups and controls. At the end of the acute cocaine studies, the same animals were further treated two times per day for 7 days with the dose of cocaine they had received during the acute studies and were behavior tested on the eighth day. Chronic low-dose cocaine exposure (0.5 and 1.0 mg/kg) significantly increased the number of attacks and decreased the latency to first attack toward intruders when compared to controls and higher dose groups. In addition, as in acute studies, chronic exposure to high doses of cocaine (i.e., 10 and 20 mg/kg) significantly decreased the number of attacks compared to all other treatment groups.

The effects of chronic cocaine on aggressive behavior have also been examined in male, adolescent Syrian hamsters using the resident-intruder paradigm. A low (0.5 mg/kg), moderate (5.0 mg/kg), or high (15 mg/kg) dose of cocaine was administered to Syrian hamsters throughout adolescent development (i.e., P-27–P-56), followed by resident-intruder tests for offensive aggression on P-57 (Harrison et al., 2000). Chronic low-dose cocaine (0.5 mg/kg/day) exposure during adolescence significantly increased the total number of attacks and bites toward intruders and significantly decreased latency to first bite of cocaine-treated animals compared to vehicle-treated controls and higher dose

groups. Although medium- and high-dose cocaine-treated animals displayed slightly increased numbers of attacks and bites on intruders compared to control animals, comparisons between these groups did not achieve statistical significance. To investigate whether 5-HT function influenced the aggressive phenotype of adolescent cocaine-treated animals, they were given the aggression-facilitating dose of cocaine (0. 5 mg/kg/day) throughout adolescence (P-27–P-56) and then tested for offensive aggression using the resident-intruder paradigm on P-57 following the systemic administration of fluoxetine (i.e., a selective 5-HT reuptake inhibitor (DeLeon, Grimes, Connor, & Melloni, 2002). Fluoxetine significantly diminished the aggressive response of adolescent cocaine-treated animals, as reflected by the decrease in the number of attacks and bites toward an intruder and the increase in attack and bite latencies when compared to cocaine-treated littermates which had received saline prior to the aggression test (figure 16.5).

Authors subsequently examined the brains of aggressive, cocaine-treated hamsters for differences in 5-HT afferent innervation to regions of hamster brain implicated in aggressive responding. Chronic, low-dose cocaine treatment throughout adolescence led to significant decreases in the number of 5-HT-ir varicosities and fibers in the AH, the LS, the bed nucleus of the BNST, and the MeA. However, not every brain area implicated in the aggressive response showed significant changes in 5-HT afferent innervation following adolescent cocaine exposure. For instance, no differences in 5-HT-ir were observed the CoMeA, the VLH, the CeA, and the MPN between treatment groups, nor were there differences in 5-HT-ir noted in the caudate putamen (an area not implicated in the control of offensive aggression) of cocaine-treated animals versus controls. Together, these results support a role for 5-HT innervation and function in adolescent cocaine-facilitated offensive aggression. In more recent work from this laboratory, the role of 5-HT type 3 ($5\text{-}HT_3$) receptors was examined in adolescent cocaine-facilitated offensive aggression in Syrian hamsters (Ricci, Grimes, & Melloni, 2004). In this study, adolescent, male Syrian hamsters were treated with the aggression-facilitating dose of cocaine (0.5 mg/kg/day × 28 days) as described previously (Harrison et al., 2000). In a first experiment on the day following the last injection of cocaine, hamsters received one of six doses (0.01, 0.05, 0.1, 0.3, 0.6, or 1.2 mg/kg) of the $5\text{-}HT_3$ receptor antagonist tropisetron or one of three doses (5, 10, or 15 mg/kg) of the $5\text{-}HT_3$ agonist mCPBG, 30 min prior to

A

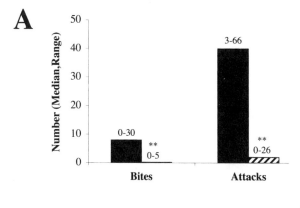

B

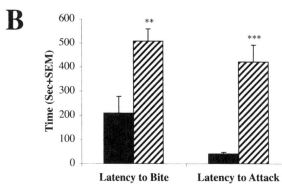

FIGURE 16.5 Fluoxetine pretreatment decreases offensive aggression in adolescent cocaine-treated hamsters. (A) Aggression intensity (i.e., number of attacks and bites) in saline- and fluoxetine-pretreated residents. $**p < .01$, Mann–Whitney, two-tailed. (B) Aggression initiation (i.e., mean latencies to first attack and bite) in saline- and fluoxetine-pretreated residents. Bars denote *SEM*. Solid columns = saline, striped columns = fluoxetine. $***p < .001$, $**p < .01$, Student's t test, two-tailed. From "Adolescent Cocaine Exposure and Offensive Aggression: Involvement of Serotonin Neural Signaling and Innervation in Male Syrian Hamsters," by K. R. DeLeon, J. M. Grimes, D. F. Connor, and R. H. Melloni, Jr., 2002, *Behavioural Brain Research*, 133(2), p. 214. Copyright 2002 by Elsevier. Reprinted with permission.

being tested for offensive aggression in the resident-intruder paradigm. Tropisetron dose dependently blocked offensive aggression in cocaine-treated hamsters, with an effective dose of 0.3 mg/kg of tropisetron. Specifically, tropisetron decreased the number of attacks and bites toward intruders when compared to saline-treated controls and when compared with lower (0.025 mg/kg) and higher (1.2 mg/kg) doses of tropisetron. By comparison, administration of the 5-HT₃ receptor agonist mCPBG to aggressive, cocaine-treated hamsters produced no effect on either attack or bite behaviors compared to controls. The specificity of the aggression-reducing effects of tropisetron was examined by administering a noneffective dose (10 mg/kg) of mCPBG 10 min prior to administration of an effective dose (0.3 mg/kg) of tropisetron, followed by behavior testing. Following pretreatment with mCPBG, a higher dose of tropisetron (1.2 mg/kg) was required to reduce lateral attacks and bites and increase in latency to first attack and bite when compared to hamsters that had received only mCPBG prior to aggression testing (figure 16.6).

To further characterize the role of this receptor in adolescent cocaine-facilitated aggression, a third study was performed to examine any differences in immunohistochemical localization of the 5-HT₃ receptor in brains of aggressive cocaine-treated hamsters versus nonaggressive controls. Chronic, low-dose cocaine exposure during adolescence significantly increased 5-HT₃-ir in the AH, VLH, CeA, and LS, while a significant decrease in 5-HT₃-ir elements was observed in the BNST when compared to controls. Together, results from these studies implicate an important role for 5-HT neural signaling through the 5-HT₃ receptor in cocaine-facilitated aggression in Syrian hamsters. Further, they suggest a role for alterations in 5-HT and 5-HT₃ receptor development and signaling in specific brain regions, namely, the AH, LS, and BNST, that is, brain regions implicated in aggression control in hamsters (figure 16.7).

The effects of cocaine exposure on maternal aggression and on the aggressive behavior of prenatally exposed offspring have also been studied using Sprague–Dawley rat dams and female and male pups as adult and developmental animal models. Wood and Spear (1998) assessed the frequency of aggressive attack using a water competition paradigm in adolescent and adult Sprague–Dawley rats that had been exposed to 40 mg/kg of

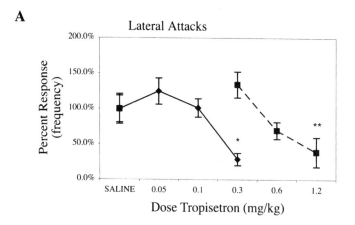

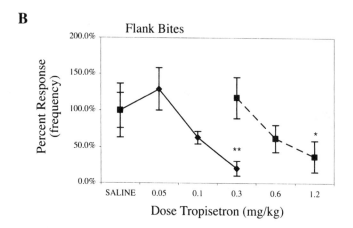

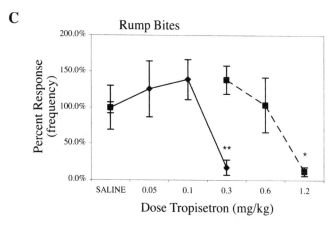

FIGURE 16.6 Effects of tropisetron on the frequency of lateral attacks and flank and rump bites in adolescent cocaine-treated residents. Diamond symbols represent data after treatment with the antagonist alone. Square symbols represent data from tests when the antagonist was given tropisetron after pretreatment with 10 mg/kg of mCPBG. Data are represented as mean percentages of response. Asterisks denote statistically significant differences relative to vehicle. $^*p < .05$, $^{**}p < .01$, ANOVA followed by Fischer's *PLSD* post hoc (two-tailed). Bars denote *SEM*. From "Serotonin Type-3 Receptors Modulate the Aggression-Stimulating Effects of Adolescent Cocaine Exposure," by L. A. Ricci, J. M. Grimes, & R. H. Melloni, Jr., 2004, *Behavioral Neuroscience, 118*(5). Reprinted with permission.

FIGURE 16.7 Bright-field photomicrographs of a coronal section through the Syrian hamster hypothalamus. Shown are 5-HT$_3$ immunoreactive puncta within the ventrolateral hypothalamus (VLH) of (A) cocaine-treated and (B) saline-treated hamsters. Bar, 500 μm. From "Serotonin Type-3 Receptors Modulate the Aggression-Stimulating Effects of Adolescent Cocaine Exposure," by L. A. Ricci, J. M. Grimes, & R. H. Melloni, Jr., 2004, *Behavioral Neuroscience, 118*(5), p. 1105. Copyright 2004. Reprinted with permission.

cocaine during Gestation Days 8–20. This study showed that adolescent, male rats (P-33) exposed to cocaine during gestation showed an increased incidence of attack and boxing compared to controls but not to females in the same treatment group. In the adult competition studies, both male and female rats were examined for aggression between P-60 and P-70. Adult male rats prenatally exposed to cocaine showed an increased incidence of boxing compared to controls and to female counterparts; however, the number of attacks was not analyzed in the adult group in this study due to the decreased amount of overall attacking across all treatment groups. The effects of cocaine exposure were also examined on the social/aggressive behavior of prenatally exposed offspring in addition to examining the effects of cocaine exposure on maternal aggression in dams (Johns et al., 1998). This study employed biological assays, including radioimmunoassay and receptor binding, to examine the activity of neural systems that may play a role in maternal aggression and the aggres-

sive behavior of prenatally exposed offspring. Rat dams received 15 mg/kg of cocaine or vehicle twice daily from Gestation Days 1–20 and then were tested for aggression using the resident-intruder paradigm on postpartum days 6, 8, and 10. The authors found that aggression levels toward an intruder were significantly increased in chronic cocaine-treated dams on postpartum days 6, 8, and 10. Following behavior testing, dams were sacrificed on postpartum days 8 or 11 and the ventral tegmentum area (VTA), hippocampus, and amygdala were removed for oxytocin radioimmunoassay. Aggressive dams treated with chronic cocaine had decreased oxytocin in the amygdala compared to controls. In addition to testing the dams for aggression, prenatally exposed offspring were tested for aggression, using the resident-intruder paradigm, on P-30, P-60, P-90, and P-180. Male rats that were exposed to cocaine during Gestation Days 1–20 chased the intruder more, for a longer period of time, and earlier in the test at P-180 compared to controls. Several of these aggressive pups were killed on P-1, P-4, and P-10 and brains were processed for 5-HT$_{1A}$ receptor binding. The authors found that at P-10, aggressive male pups that had been chronically exposed to cocaine during prenatal development displayed decreased 5-HT$_{1A}$ receptor binding in brain. A later study examined the dose-related effects of chronic gestational cocaine treatment in maternal aggression of Sprague–Dawley rats on postpartum days 2, 3, and 5 (Lubin, Meter, Walker, & Johns, 2001a). Pregnant rats were administered twice daily injections of 3.5, 7.5, or 15 mg/kg of cocaine or saline for 20 consecutive days throughout gestation (20 days). On postpartum days 2, 3, and 5, the aggressive behavior of the rat dams was assessed by placing a male intruder into their home cages with their pups present. Rat dams receiving 30 mg/kg displayed significant increases in the frequency of threats during all three postpartum tests when compared to the 7.5 mg/kg cocaine group and the non-yoke-fed saline controls. No differences were observed regarding the frequency or latency of fight attacks. Additionally, immediately following the aggression test (5 days following the last injection), female rats were decapitated and the hippocampus, amygdala, and VTA were removed for radioimmunoassay to measure the levels of the neuropeptide oxytocin. No significant differences in oxytocin were observed in the amygdala or VTA of lactating dams. However, dams treated with 15 mg/kg of cocaine had significantly higher hippocampal oxytocin levels when compared to the saline-treated yoke-fed controls. Lubin, Meter, Walker, and Johns (2001b) subsequently examined the effects of chronic cocaine exposure on aggressive behavior in adult, virgin female Sprague–Dawley rats using the same treatment and behavioral testing regimen as described (Lubin et al., 2001a). Although significant main effects of group in the frequency of fight attacks and aggressive postures were observed, subsequent comparisons revealed that the saline-treated group had nonsignificantly higher rates of fighting compared to each of the cocaine-treated groups. Additionally, immediately following the aggression test (5 days following the last injection), female rats were decapitated and the hippocampus, amygdala, and VTA were removed for oxytocin radioimmunoassay. Following cocaine or saline administration to virgin female rats, no differences in oxytocin levels in the amygdala or VTA were observed. Rats treated with 30 mg/kg of cocaine did, however, show significant decreases in hippocampal oxytocin when compared to the 15 mg/kg cocaine group. In a more recent study from this group (Lubin, Elliott, Black, & Johns, 2003), the effects of local administration of an oxytocin antagonist into the central nucleus of the amygdala (CNA) and cocaine administration on maternal aggression were studied in Sprague–Dawley rat dams. On Gestation Day 15, pregnant females had bilateral cannulas implanted into the CNA or VTA (control brain region). One group of females with CNA cannulae was given twice daily injections of 15 mg/kg of cocaine throughout gestation (20 days), while all other females remained untreated. On Postpartum Day 6, drug-naive rat dams were given bilateral infusions of vehicle or 250 or 500 ng of an oxytocin antagonist (OTA), therefore receiving a total dose of either 500 or 1,000 ng of OTA. Rat dams receiving cocaine throughout gestation were bilaterally infused with buffer. Rat dams infused with 1,000 ng of OTA into the CNA displayed significantly more attacks when compared to dams infused with buffer and those infused with either 500 or 1,000 ng of OTA into the VTA and this measure was similar to that observed in rat rams receiving cocaine throughout gestation.

ᴅ-Amphetamine and Methamphetamine

Amphetamine is found in two basic isoforms, ʟ-amphetamine and ᴅ-amphetamine. The most commonly abused form of amphetamine, the ᴅ form, dextroamphetamine, therefore, is the primary drug form considered in this section. Methamphetamine differs from amphetamine due to the presence of a methyl group on the terminal amino group.

A number of studies have investigated the effects of ᴅ-amphetamine on aggressive behavior, utilizing a variety of species, testing paradigms and doses, and producing divergent results. Using an intruder-evoked model of aggression in both isolated and group-housed adult male Swiss–Webster mice, Miczek and O'Donnell (1978) examined the effects of acute ᴅ-amphetamine (0.125, 0.5, 2.0, and 8.0 mg/kg) administration on fighting behavior. In these studies, acute administration of high-dose (i.e., 8.0 mg/kg) ᴅ-amphetamine decreased aggression (attack, tail rattle, and pursuit) in isolated mice, whereas the effective aggression-reducing dose in group-housed mice was only 2.0 mg/kg. Additional studies from this laboratory showed that both acute (2, 4, 6, and 8 mg/kg) and chronic (16 mg/kg/day for 2 weeks) administration of ᴅ-amphetamine dose dependently (acute exposure) decreased the frequency of attack bites when compared to saline controls (O'Donnell & Miczek, 1980). In a study using adult, male CFW mice, Miczek and Haney (1994) examined the effect of a variety of doses of ᴅ-amphetamine (0.1–10.0 mg/kg) on aggression in animals that had been trained to perform in an operant task of acquiring a food-reinforced nose poke response. In these studies, mice were confronted by an intruder in their home cages for 5 min in the middle of a 60-min conditioning session (i.e., subjects were subjected to two cycles of a fixed interval 10-min fixed ratio 30 schedule, returned to their home cage for aggression testing, and returned to the conditioning chamber for the rest of the session). ᴅ-Amphetamine was administered immediately prior to the beginning of this 60-min session. A moderate dose of amphetamine (6.0 mg/kg) was able to significantly decrease the frequency of attack bites displayed by these mice, while the frequency of attack bites and sideways threats was increased by smaller doses of ᴅ-amphetamine (0.3 and 1.0 mg/kg). The effects of acute intracranial injections of ᴅ-amphetamine on agonistic responses have been studied in a species of fish, the cichlids (Munro, 1986). Adult male cichlids were isolated in their individual observation tanks for 2 weeks prior to the start of the experiment and were administered 10 and 20 μg via intracranial injection 20 min prior to a mirror being lowered into the tank and the fish observed for the frequency and duration of frontal and lateral displays and attempted bites. As seen in rodent studies, ᴅ-amphetamine induced a dose-dependent decrease in both the duration of aggressive displays and the frequency of bites relative to saline controls.

Several studies have examined the effects of social structure/experience on the effects of amphetamine on aggression. For example, Miczek and Gold (1983) examined whether the social status in established groups of squirrel monkeys influenced amphetamine effects on social and agonistic behaviors. Low doses of amphetamine (0.1 and 0.3 mg/kg; 5 min prior to behavior testing) decreased the amount of agonistic behavior initiated by dominant monkeys. At higher doses, administration of amphetamine (0.6 and 1.0 mg/kg) to the dominant monkeys resulted in their being the target of agonistic behaviors from the other monkeys in their social group. In addition, administration of D-amphetamine at all tested doses (0.06, 0.1, 0.3, and 0.6 mg/kg) decreased the amount of aggressive behavior displayed by subdominant monkeys toward other monkeys in the group, as well as decreasing the amount of agonistic behavior being displayed toward them by the other monkeys. In contrast to these results are data from studies that examined the effects of D-amphetamine on aggressive behaviors in a complex social setting using adult, male stump tail macaques (Smith & Byrd, 1984, 1985). In these studies male subjects were treated with one of several doses of D-amphetamine ranging from 0.003 to 0.56 mg/kg, and the aggressive behaviors of these animals toward other members of their social groups were recorded. D-Amphetamine increased aggressive behaviors initiated by the highest and lowest socially ranking monkeys and had little effect on the midranking monkeys. The effect of D-amphetamine administration on aggressive behaviors of these male monkeys toward both adult and nonadult members of the social group was examined, finding that D-amphetamine uniformly increased aggressive behaviors toward nonadult members of the group and decreased aggressive behaviors toward adult monkeys. Along similar lines, in a resident-intruder test, Miczek (1979) reported that administration of a very low dose of D-amphetamine (0.063 mg/kg) to resident alpha rats resulted in these animals displaying an increase in the frequency of attacks, sideways threats, and pursuits toward an intruder compared to control animals. Yet, higher doses of D-amphetamine (0.25–1.0 mg/kg) effectively decreased attack and threat behavior; however, these decreases in agonistic behaviors were also accompanied by increases in nonagonistic behaviors, such as rearing and walking.

Various studies have examined the effects of D-amphetamine on predatory aggression using adult animal models. The effects of acute amphetamine (0.5, 1, 2, or 4 mg/kg) administration was examined on spontaneous mouse killing (i.e., muricide) by adult cats (Leaf, Wnek, Lamon, & Gay, 1978). In these studies, D-amphetamine, administered 20 min prior to the start of the behavioral test, dose dependently decreased mouse killing in these cats, with an effective muricide blocking dose of 0.5 mg/kg. Similarly, Barr, Moyer, and Gibbons (1976) investigated the effects of D-amphetamine on frog and mouse killing in the rats. All rats were tested in their home cage and D-amphetamine (2 mg/kg) was administered 30 min and 2, 4, and 24 hr prior to the start of behavior testing. D-Amphetamine significantly reduced the number of attacks the rats directed toward both mice and frogs, effectively blocking both mouse and frog killing behavior. Additional work from this laboratory (Barr, Gibbons, & Bridger, 1977) evaluated the effects of acute and chronic administration of amphetamine on mouse killing in rats. In acute experiments, rats were injected with D-amphetamine 20 or 60 min prior to the introduction of a mouse into the home cage of the resident rat. D-Amphetamine inhibited mouse killing by rats at both time points in a dose-dependent manner, with an effective muricide blocking dose of 1.9 mg/kg. In the chronic D-amphetamine experiment, prior to the first test for muricide, rats were given a pretest dose of amphetamine (1.9 mg/kg) to block mouse killing (Day 1). Chronic amphetamine (2.4 mg/kg/day) was then administered for 8 days (Days 2–9) prior to a post-test injection of 1.9 mg/kg of amphetamine and subsequent testing for muricide (Day 10). The previously observed inhibition of mouse killing by D-amphetamine was decreased by chronic administration of the drug, indicating that, in contrast to acute treatment, chronic administration of D-amphetamine was effective at increasing muricide behavior in rats.

In addition to the studies that have focused on the effects of D-amphetamine on aggression in adult animal models, several studies have examined the effects of D-amphetamine on aggression in peripubertal subjects in a number of different species and in both sexes. In one study, Miller (1976) examined the effects of D-amphetamine on social behavior in feral-born male juvenile monkeys with lesions of the dorsolateral frontal cortex and nonlesioned controls. All monkeys were placed together and observed for 60 days to allow for social patterns and group structure to develop. In a dose range (0.5–2.0 mg/kg) of D-amphetamine, 1 mg/kg produced the most predictable motor response stereotype pattern at the lowest reliable dose and was therefore used throughout the study. One animal was injected with 1 mg/kg of D-amphetamine 15 min prior to the 30-min observation period and then scored for social behaviors, including social behaviors (i.e., allogrooming), aggressive behaviors (i.e., threatening, biting, hitting, chasing) and nonsocial behaviors (i.e., autogrooming). Nonlesioned monkeys showed an increased in agonistic behavior following D-amphetamine administration, whereas D-amphetamine decreased the number of agonistic incidents in lesioned animals. However, the authors attribute this decrease in agonistic activity in the lesioned monkeys to increases in pacing behavior, (i.e., hyperactivity directly related to the lesion and not to the drug itself). Other experiments using peripubescent rodents have investigated the effect of D-amphetamine exposure on play fighting behavior. A dose-response study was conducted to examine the effects of acute amphetamine administration on play fighting in male albino rats (Beatty, Dodge, Dodge, White, & Panksepp, 1982). Pairs of male rats (between P-26 and P-42) were tested in 10-min sessions at one of four drug conditions (0, 0.25, 0.5, or 1.0 mg/kg of D-amphetamine; 20 min prior to testing). Administration of D-amphetamine decreased the occurrence of play fighting in a dose-dependent manner; however, doses of 0.5 mg/kg or greater reliably depressed play fighting and pinning. At the lowest dose (0.25 mg/kg) D-amphetamine only decreased pinning behavior. Similarly, the effects of acute D-amphetamine exposure were tested on play fighting in female Long–Evans rats (Field & Pellis, 1994). Pairs of female rats (between P-30 and P-45) were isolated for 24 hr prior to testing and testing began by placing the isolated pairs in the test chamber for a 10-min period. Of each pair, only one rat was assigned to the treatment condition (0.15, 0.5, or 1.0 mg/kg of D-amphetamine; 20 min prior to the trial). Amphetamine at the two higher doses tested (0.5 and 1.0 mg/kg) decreased the frequency of attack. Acute treatment with D-amphetamine in peripubertal male OF-1 mice using similar doses produced contradictory results on aggression (Moro, Salvador, & Simon, 1997). In this study, mice were tested for aggression at P-42 in a neutral arena with a standard group-housed anosmic opponent. Mice were injected with one of three doses of D-amphetamine (0.25, 1.5, or 3 mg/kg) 30 min prior to the behavior test and were scored for both aggressive and nonaggressive behaviors. The total duration of attack was decreased at all doses tested, although this result was only significant in the two higher doses

when compared to saline controls. However, an increase in offensive behaviors (i.e., threat and attack) was observed at the lowest dose of D-amphetamine, with no significant differences in the latency to first attack between any dose and the saline-treated control group.

Few studies have examined the effects of methamphetamine on aggression. In one of the first reports to assess aggression after methamphetamine exposure, Panksepp (1971) examined how administration of methamphetamine at 2 mg/kg in adult male albino rats affected stimulus-bound attack. Rats were fitted with 24 electrode placements yielding stimulus-bound attack where stimulation at 5 electrode sites yielded quick biting attack versus the other 19 sites, which yielded affective attack. Test periods consisted of five successive 30-s trials with 1-min intertrial intervals. During each trial three live mice were placed into the test chamber with the rat and behaviors of the rat were scored following administration of 2 mg/kg of methamphetamine or saline 45 min prior to testing. This study found that methamphetamine significantly increased affective attack, with quick biting attack being slightly attenuated with methamphetamine. Also, methamphetamine increased the level of current necessary to produce an attack. Using another type of behavior testing paradigm, Shintomi (1975) examined the effects of various psychotropic drugs on methamphetamine-induced behavioral excitation in group-housed adult male mice. Mice treated with 5 mg/kg of methamphetamine 90 min prior to behavioral observation showed significant increases in behavioral excitation, including increased fighting among group members. The purpose of this study was to examine the effects of various classes of drugs on this methamphetamine-induced behavior excitation in grouped mice. Both the major tranquilizers (i.e., butyrophenones, phenothiazines, and thioxanthenes) and the minor tranquilizers (i.e., benzodiazepines) depressed methamphetamine-induced fighting behavior in these mice at relatively low doses. However, none of the tested antidepressant drugs and adrenergic blocking agents blocked increased fighting behavior in the methamphetamine-treated mice.

The effects of methamphetamine exposure were examined on fighting behavior in adult male Swiss–Webster mice that had been either group or singly housed (Miczek & O'Donnell, 1978). Mice were confronted in their home cages or in a neutral arena with standard opponents 30 min following administration of methamphetamine (0.125, 0.5, 2.0, or 8.0 mg/kg). In contrast to the aforementioned studies, methamphetamine exposure decreased attack behavior (attack, tail rattle, and pursuit) in isolated and in nonisolated mice in a dose-dependent manner, with the dose-response curve being shifted to the right in isolated mice, that is, the observed decrease in attack behavior in methamphetamine-treated mice required a higher (8.0 mg/kg) dose in isolated mice when compared to the effective aggression-reducing dose in nonisolates (2.0 mg/kg). Causes for the discrepant results between studies may be related to several factors, including the testing paradigm and the dose of drug tested. These differences may also be attributed to the species tested or even the strain used for the experiment. In an attempt to examine the effects the strain used in an experiment may have on the results, the acute and chronic behavioral effects of methamphetamine were examined in related species and strains of mice treated with constant and increasing doses of the drug (Richardson, Karczmar, & Scudder, 1972). In these experiments, seven types of mouse were used, including (a) male, ICR albino mice, (b) *Onychomys leucogaster* (grasshopper mouse), (c) *Peromyscis maniculatus* Bairdii (deer mouse), (d) *Microtus ochogaster* (meadow vole), (e) *Mus musculus* "Missouri," (f) *M. musculus* C57 Bl/J6, and (g) *M. musculus* CF-1. All experiments were conducted in a "mouse city" consisting of a Plexiglas apparatus with six small chambers connected with a central compartment by means of tubular runways. A pair of mice consisting of either one male and one female or two males of each species or strain were placed in each of the small chambers. The chambers opened and all 12 mice were allowed to roam in the mouse city for 75 min. Both the acute effects of methamphetamine (i.e., a single dose of methamphetamine; 7 mg/kg, 15 min prior to testing) and the chronic effects of methamphetamine (i.e., 2, 4, 6, 8, 16, or 32 mg/kg; one dose, twice daily, with doses increasing each day for ICR mice, and 3, 6, 12, 24, or 48 mg/kg for all other mouse types) on various social and aggressive behaviors were examined in these animals. Acute methamphetamine exposure in all mice tested abolished aggressive behavior; however, as expected, stereotypy was increased in all strains. In the chronic treatment regimen, aggression decreased and remained low at all doses, except in *Onychomys*, where aggression was inhibited on the first day of treatment (3 mg/kg, twice), then showed a significant increase on the next 2 days of treatment (6 and 12 mg/kg, twice each), and then decreased and remained low on the fourth and fifth days of treatment (24 and 48 mg/kg, twice each). Interestingly, the grasshopper mouse differs markedly from other mouse strains with regard to monoamine and acetylcholine brain levels (with *Onychomys* exhibiting higher levels of both compared to *Mus*), which may explain the differences in the observed behavioral response to chronic methamphetamine exposure.

Nicotine

The effects of nicotine on aggressive behavior have been examined in various species; however, the vast majority of this research is on aggression in adult rats. In addition, as with other studies examining the effects of drugs of abuse on aggression, the effects of nicotine on aggression have been examined in various testing paradigms, including shock-induced fighting, predatory attack, and intermale aggression. However, in contrast to the varied and rather inconclusive nature of the data on the relationship between other drugs of abuse and aggression, the effects of nicotine on aggressive appear to remain consistent across all testing paradigms and species. Rodgers (1979) examined the effects of nicotine on shock-induced fighting in adult, male Sprague–Dawley rats. In this study, weight-matched pairs of male rats, one treated with nicotine (0.25, 0.5, or 1.0 mg/kg; 15 min prior to testing) and one nontreated rat were placed in the test chamber for 2 min. The pair was subjected to 60 foot shocks and the incidence of fighting was recorded between treated and nontreated rats. This study found that shock-induced fighting was significantly reduced by nicotine (0.5 and 1.0 mg/kg) when compared to controls. Similarly, Driscoll and Baettig (1981) examined the effects of various doses of nicotine on shock-induced fighting in adult, male and female Roman high-avoidance rats. Following two initial foot shock sessions to establish fighting between the permanently paired rats, pairs were subjected to four additional shock sessions preceded by administration of saline or one of three doses of nicotine (0.1, 0.2, or 0.4 mg/kg) and behaviors were scored. In this study, a dose-dependent decrease in fighting behavior was observed in male and female rats treated with nicotine; however, this decrease in fighting was accompanied by an increase in freezing behavior when compared to controls. Waldbillig (1980) examined the effects of nicotine on both shock-induced fighting and muricide. For the shock-induced fighting studies, pairs of Long–Evans rats underwent 10 trials with 8 levels of foot shock. Fifteen minutes prior to the test, the rats received either saline or 800 µg/kg of nicotine and behaviors were analyzed in terms of the threshold for the elicitation of the aggressive response. Nicotine treatment increased the threshold for the elicitation of attack when compared to controls. The local effects of nicotine in brain were also examined in these animals. The purpose of this study was to examine the effects of intracerebralventricular (icv) injections of nicotine on foot shock-induced attack. For this study, Long–Evans rats were fitted with a cannula placed unilaterally in the lateral ventricle. Pairs of rats were subjected to 10 trials of 10 levels of foot shock. During the behavioral test, animal were scored for foot shock-induced aggressive responses (i.e., threat, attack, bite, latency to attack) immediately following treatment with saline (vehicle control) or one of two doses of nicotine (27.0 or 55.0 µg). This study found that icv administration of nicotine could suppress threat behavior and increase attack latency compared to controls.

Waldbillig (1980) also examined the effects of nicotine and nicotinic antagonists on mouse killing in rats. "Mouse killing" Long–Evans rats (determined by the ability of the rat to kill mice in 10-min tests on each of 4 successive days) underwent two attack tests. In a first experiment, rats were tested for mouse killing during the first trial 15 min after treatment with saline. Forty-five minutes later and 15 min prior to the second trial, the rats received either saline or one of six doses of nicotine (100–1000 µg/kg). Nicotine inhibited mouse killing (as reflected by attack latency) in a dose-dependent manner. In a second set of experiments, effects of the nicotinic antagonists mecamylamine (a central nicotinic blocking agent) and hexamethonium (a peripheral nicotinic blocking agent) on mouse killing were examined. Following experimental procedures similar to those above, rats were tested for mouse killing following administration of nicotine alone and mecamylamine (30 mg/kg) or hexamethonium (30 mg/kg) in combination with nicotine or saline. Attack latency was compared between the groups that received the nicotinic blocking agent plus nicotine and the nicotine alone group. Hexamethonium did not inhibit the suppressive effects of nicotine on attack latency, while mecamylamine significantly reduced the suppressive effects of nicotine on attack latency. No change in attack behavior was observed when this nicotinic antagonist was paired with saline rather than nicotine. These data indicate that central action of nicotine is essential for the suppressive effects of the drug on mouse killing. Another study investigated the role of cholinergic activity in the control of biting attack behavior

in adult cats and, subsequently, the effect(s) of nicotine on this behavior (Berntson, Beattie, & Walker, 1976). In a first experiment, cats were administered either the muscarinic agonist arecoline alone or arecoline 10 min following the administration of either nicotine or saline and were observed for various aggressive behaviors. Arecoline decreased the latency to biting attack toward the stimulus and increased vocalized aggressive acts (i.e., hissing and growling). Pretreatment with nicotine significantly reduced the arecoline-induced biting attack and increased the latency and decreased the frequency of vocalized aggression. In a second experiment, the effects of nicotine on spontaneous muricide were examined in adult, female cats which had previously demonstrated this behavior. Each cat underwent five attack tests 10 min following nicotine injections. Each cat received two saline control tests and three tests with one of three doses (0.075, 0.2, and 0.5 mg/kg) of nicotine; the tests were separated by 48 hr. The results from this study are in agreement with those of other studies, finding that nicotine significantly decreased spontaneous muricide in cats as measured by bite latency (the highest dose of nicotine, 0.5 mg/kg, significantly increased bite latency compared to controls).

The effects of a "smoking dose" (25 µg/kg) of nicotine administration on the social behavior of albino ("Alderley Park" Wistar) and black-hooded rats paired with a member of the other strain in a test of social aggression toward a conspecific (Silverman, 1971). One rat was removed from the pairing for 5–6 hr every weekday and returned early in the 12-hr dark phase. Observations of aggressive behavior were made weekly for 6 min immediately following the return of the rat to the pairing. For nicotine treatment each rat served as its own control and received both nicotine and saline treatments during the study. One rat of each pair was removed, treated with either nicotine or saline, and scored for aggression. As previously observed in various species and testing situations, nicotine was found to decrease aggression and these effects were compounded through each trial, that is, after each subsequent dose of nicotine, aggressive behavior decreased further.

3,4-Methylenedioxymethamphetamine (MDMA)

Very few studies have examined the effects of the stimulant/hallucinogen MDMA on aggressive behavior. In one study, Miczek and Haney (1994) examined the effects of MDMA on aggressive behavior in mice following an operant task of acquiring a food-reinforced nose poke response. In these studies, mice were confronted by an intruder in their home cage for 5 min in the middle of a 60-min conditioning session (i.e., mice were subjected to two cycles of a fixed interval 10-min, fixed ratio 30 schedule, returned to their home cage for aggression testing, and returned to the conditioning chamber for the rest of the session). MDMA was administered immediately prior to the beginning of this 60-min session. Adult, male CFW mice were confronted by an intruder in their home cages for 5 min and observed for aggression following administration of a dose of MDMA (0.3–10.0 mg/kg). This study found that MDMA significantly decreased the combined frequency of attacks and sideways threats at 3.0, 6.0, and 10.0 mg/kg compared to controls. Similarly, the effects of MDMA on agonistic behavior were examined in male mice using an animal model of isolation-induced aggression (Navarro & Maldonado (1999). Adult, albino male mice of the OF-1 strain underwent an isolation period of 30 days before behavioral testing. Mice were assigned to groups and received one of the following treatments: vehicle or 0.5, 1.25, 2.5, 5, 10, 15, or 20 mg/kg of MDMA 30 min prior to testing. Experimental animals were confronted with a standard opponent in a neutral cage for a 10–min period. MDMA reduced the time spent in threat and attack behaviors when compared to the control group, with no increase in immobility; however, avoidance and defensive behaviors were increased in mice treated with the higher doses of MDMA (5–20 mg/kg) compared to controls. In a later study from this laboratory, the effects of acute, subchronic, and intermittent exposure to MDMA were examined on aggressive behavior in isolated, adult male OF-1 mice (Navarro & Maldonado, 2004). Individually housed mice were subjected to one of the following drug schedules: (a) acute treatment with MDMA (vehicle for 6 days and one of three doses of MDMA [1.25, 2.5, or 5 mg/kg] on Day 7); (b) subchronic treatment (daily injection of 1.25, 2.5, or 5 mg/kg of MDMA for 7 days); (c) intermittent treatment (1.25, 2.5, or 5 mg/kg of MDMA on Days 1 and 7; vehicle on Days 2 and 6); (d) vehicle (daily injection for 7 days). Thirty minutes after the last injection, experimental animals were tested for aggression in a neutral cage against a standard opponent. All doses of MDMA in all treatment schedules significantly reduced attack when compared to controls. However, exposure to the highest

dose of MDMA (5 mg/kg) also increased defensive/submissive and avoidance/flee behaviors, indicating that MDMA at this dose may produce anxiogenic like activity in mice.

CNS Depressants

Marijuana

Marijuana, cannabis, and hashish are characterized by the chemical constituents cannabinoid, cannabidiol, and cannabigerol, with the main active ingredient common to all agents being the cannabinoid tetrahydrocannabinol (Δ9-THC). The effects of Δ9-THC on aggression have been described using a variety of paradigms assessing various types of aggressive behavior. Moreover, as with most drugs of abuse, it appears that Δ9-THC enhances and suppresses aggressive behavior, depending on experimental design. In isolated adult TO mice, the effects of acute exposure to various doses of Δ9-THC were examined on territorial offensive aggression using the resident-intruder paradigm (Dorr & Steinberg, 1976). One hour before aggression testing mice were treated with Δ9-THC at 1.25, 2.5, 5, 10, or 20 mg/kg in either 1% Tween-80 saline or propylene glycol (10% propane-1,2-diol–1% Tween saline). Data from these studies show that the frequency of aggressive acts decreased in a dose-dependent fashion in animals exposed to Δ9-THC in either vehicle solution. However, mice that had received Δ9-THC in 1% Tween-80 saline showed significantly decreased aggression only at the three highest doses tested (i.e., 5, 10, or 20 mg/kg). Interestingly, mice that had received Δ9-THC in propylene glycol showed decreased aggression at all doses of drug tested. Similarly, using the resident-intruder paradigm in pair-housed male adult C3H/HeJ mice, Sieber, Frischknecht, and Waser (1980) found that acute exposure to hashish extract (20 mg/kg) by oral gavage to both residents resulted in a depression of aggressive behavior, as well as nonsocial activities, social investigation, and sexual behavior. In oil-treated pairs, dominant mice more frequently attacked intruders compared to submissive mice. However, in pairs receiving a single exposure to hashish extract (20 mg/kg), both dominant and subordinate mice showed suppression of aggressive behavior toward intruders (aggressive groom and offensive sideways), as well as other social and nonsocial behaviors. Additionally, after subchronic exposure to hashish extract (20 mg/kg), that is, three consecutive treatments alternately administered over 6 days, aggressive behavior was reinstated and hashish-treated animals displayed behaviors like oil-treated controls, that is, increases in nonsocial, social investigation, sexual, and aggressive behaviors.

Studies examining the effects of chronic exposure to marijuana during adulthood on aggressive behavior have assessed interspecies aggression within the home cages of group-housed animals. Food-deprived female Wistar rats experiencing chronic exposure to cannabis extract (10 mg/kg for 22 days) increased spontaneous fighting on the day following the last injection (Day 23) compared to food-deprived rats treated with vehicle alone (Carlini & Masur, 1969). In a subsequent experiment using a separate group of food-deprived female Wistar rats, the authors (1969) showed that over a time course of 15 days of chronic exposure to cannabis extract (10 mg/kg) spontaneous fighting could be observed after only 7 days of treatment. Further examination of the effects of chronic cannabis exposure (i.e., 10 mg/kg/day for 32 days) on spontaneous fighting in food-deprived male and female Wistar rats revealed that the duration of spontaneous fighting was much longer in female pairs than in male pairs receiving cannabis extract treatment when tested on Days 16 and 32 of treatment. Further experiments within the same study showed a dose-dependent increase in aggression (i.e., duration of spontaneous fighting) following chronic cannabis extract exposure in food-deprived female Wistar rats administered cannabis extract at 2.5, 5, 10, and 20 mg/kg daily for 20 days. The lowest effective dose producing aggressive behavior was 5.0 mg/kg, at which spontaneous fighting was apparent after 10 days of treatment. At higher doses (10 and 20 mg/kg), the occurrence of spontaneous fighting was observed after 8 days of treatment.

To study the effects of temperament on cannabis-induced spontaneous aggression in food-deprived rats, male Wistar rats were divided into two types of temperaments, high and low anxiety based upon observations in an open-field test (Palermo Neto & Carvalho, 1973). After temperaments were determined rats were subjected to daily 22-hr food deprivation and treated with cannabis extract (20 mg/kg/day) for 30 days. Spontaneous aggression was assessed daily immediately after drug treatment. The authors found that chronic 30-day treatment with cannabis extract increased aggressive behavior in both low and high anxiety rats. However, the effects were found to be more prominent in high anxiety rats, with effects apparent after only 5 days of

treatment, while in low anxiety rats, effects were observed after 15 days of treatment. Rats were killed 3 hr after the last exposure to cannabis and 5-HT levels in the cerebellum, medulla oblongata, hypothalamus, midbrain, and cerebral cortex were determined. These data revealed significantly decreased 5-HT levels in the hypothalamus, midbrain, and cerebral cortex in both high and low anxiety, aggressive, cannabis-treated rats compared to nonaggressive saline-treated controls, as well as nonaggressive low and high anxiety rats treated with cannabis extract, indicating that effects of chronic cannabis exposure on serotonergic function are dependent on temperament.

Palermo Neto and Carlini (1972) observed the effects of the chemical stressors p-chlorophenylalanine (PCPA), a 5-HT-depleting compound, and dihydroxyphenylalanine (DOPA), a precursor in dopamine metabolism, on cannabis-induced spontaneous fighting in food-deprived male rats. In these studies, food-deprived rats were treated with cannabis extract (20 mg/kg/day) for 20 days, during which, on Days 11, 15, 16, 17, and 20, they received intraperitoneal injections of DOPA (40 mg/kg) prior to cannabis extract, while on Days 14 and 19 they received saline injections. Behavior was observed daily for 3 hr after drug treatment. The authors found that DOPA and cannabis extract in combination increased the duration of spontaneous fighting in food-deprived rats. In a subsequent experiment, food-deprived rats were chronically treated with cannabis extract (20 mg/kg/day) for 30 days, but on Days 10, 15, 20, and 25 were treated with a single dose of (a) saline, (b) DOPA (40 mg/kg), (c) PCPA (300 mg/kg), or (d) a combination of DOPA and PCPA. Aggressive behavior assessed daily revealed that pretreatment of PCPA alone and in combination with DOPA potentiated cannabis-induced aggression compared to cannabis-treated rats pretreated with saline. In a final experiment, rats were chronically food deprived and treated with cannabis extract (20 mg/kg/day) for 27 days, but on Day 22 were pretreated as above. Aggressive behavior was measured on the same day (Day 22) and then 3 (Day 25) and 5 (Day 27) days later. Treatment with PCPA alone or the combined DOPA and PCPA prior to administration of cannabis extract potentiated the cannabis-induced aggressive behavior for up to 3 days postinjection (i.e., until Day 25). However, at Day 27, aggressive behavior returned to levels seen on Day 22, (i.e., prior to treatment with chemical stressors). These studies suggest an important, perhaps facilitory, role for brain catecholamines in cannabis-induced aggression.

Another study investigated the role of acetylcholine (Ach) in modulating aggressive behavior in rapid eye movement (REM) sleep-deprived female Wistar rats treated with cannabis extract (De Souza & Neto, 1978). In the first session, housed pairs of rats were deprived of REM sleep and treated with cannabis extract (20 mg/kg) 10 min prior to the ending of REM sleep deprivation, and baseline spontaneous fighting was observed for 100 min in their home cage. Sixteen days after baseline, rats were subjected to the same procedure of REM sleep deprivation and acute cannabis treatment, but prior to spontaneous aggression tests, rats were pretreated with the acetylcholine blocking drugs atropine (25, 50, or 100 mg/kg), scopolamine (10 or 20 mg/kg), or atropine methyl nitrate (50 mg/kg) or a control solution of distilled water. A third session was conducted 16 days after the second session following the same procedure. With the exception of atropine, all acetylcholine blocking drugs significantly decreased cannabis-induced aggressive behavior. However, scopolamine was only effective at the highest dose (20 mg/kg). The authors propose two possible mechanisms of action; anti-Ach drugs may nonspecifically block dopamine (DA) receptors and/or acetylcholine blocking drugs may shift the balance between Ach and DA systems, decreasing the activity of DA, suppressing its facilitory role in cannabis-induced aggression.

Researchers have also examined the effects of marijuana on intraspecies aggressive behavior using a neutral arena., Decreasing noradrenaline (NE) activity and increasing DA activity promotes the aggression-inducing effects of cannabis extract (10 mg/kg) or Δ9-THC (10 or 20 mg/kg) in adult male Wistar rats in a neutral arena (Carlini, Hamaoui, Bieniek, & Korte, 1971). REM sleep-deprived rats were treated acutely with cannabis extract (10 mg/kg) prior to the end of REM sleep deprivation followed by aggression testing in a neutral arena for 2(15 min. Immediately after the second 15-min observation, cannabis extract-treated rats received a single intraperitoneal injection of the β-adrenergic agonist clonidine at 0, 50, or 100 μg/kg and aggression testing was observed for eight additional sessions of 15 min. At both doses of clonidine a significant decrease in aggressive behavior was observed in cannabis-treated REM sleep-deprived rats.

In a later study chemical lesions by intraventricular injection of 6-hydroxydopamine (6-OHDA) prior to REM sleep deprivation and acute cannabis extract exposure (10 mg/kg) in adult male Wistar rats further potentiated cannabis-induced aggressive behavior that could be reversed by increasing brain NE (Musty, Lindsey, & Carlini, 1976). One week following 6-OHDA lesions rats were sleep deprived for 96 hr. Immediately following sleep deprivation rats received an acute dose of cannabis extract (10 mg/kg) or saline. Thirty minutes after drug treatment rats were paired and observed in a neutral arena for 3 hr, after which the rats were sacrificed and brains were analyzed for NE and DA content. In rats that did not receive 6-OHDA lesions, the REM sleep-deprived, cannabis-treated rats showed increased duration of fighting and normal levels of NE and DA. Rats treated with 6-OHDA alone showed no fighting, but had lower levels of both NE and DA, and the ratio of DA to NE was increased compared to that in control rats that were non 6-OHDA lesioned and not subjected to REM sleep deprivation, as well as those subjected to REM sleep deprivation. However, the combination of 6-OHDA lesion and REM sleep deprivation resulted in an increase in duration of fighting behavior that was associated with the same biological changes observed in the above 6-OHDA lesioned rats, (i.e., low levels of NE and DA with an increase in the ratio of DA to NE). Last, rats with 6-OHDA lesions, REM sleep deprivation, and cannabis extract treatment showed the highest fighting time associated with a large drop in NE and DA and an increase in the ratio of DA to NE. To assess whether restoring catecholamine depletion could reverse these behavioral trends, the authors treated rats with either NE (5 and 10 μg) or DA (5 and 10 μg) by intraventricular injections following cannabis treatment in 6-OHDA lesioned and REM sleep-deprived rats, prior to aggression testing. At both doses of NE the duration of fighting behavior was significantly reduced but was associated with a decrease in locomotor activity, while treatment with DA had no effect on aggressive behavior.

Treatment of subordinate male Wistar albino rats with an acute dose of Δ9-THC (10 mg/kg) prior to the end of 96 hr of REM sleep deprivation resulted in a reversal of dominance in spontaneous fighting tests (Carlini, 1977). In this study, baseline aggression and ranks were determined in paired rats that were subjected to 96 hr of REM sleep deprivation. Then, subordinate rats were treated with an acute dose (10 mg/kg) of Δ9-THC, while dominant rats received an equal volume of saline, and both groups underwent another bout of REM sleep deprivation for 96 hr. Treatment with Δ9-THC in subordinate rats resulted in a reversal of rank, where subordinate rats displayed more aggressive postures (i.e., upright offensive, extending the forepaws, and exposing teeth) and previously dominant rats displayed an increase in submissive supine postures (i.e., lying on their back with all four feet extended and belly exposed). In a subsequent experiment, following the same as procedure as experiment 1, drug-treated pairs were randomized, that is, REM sleep-deprived Δ9-THC-treated rats were paired with sleep-deprived saline-treated or non-sleep-deprived Δ9-THC-treated controls. When REM sleep-deprived rats treated with Δ9-THC (10 mg/kg) were paired with saline-treated REM sleep-deprived or non-REM sleep-deprived Δ9-THC-treated controls, they displayed an increase in defensive attack, upright mutual posture, attack, submissive posture, and aggressive posture after three sessions of assessing fighting behavior relative to initial testing. When drug treatment was removed on the fourth session, REM sleep-deprived Δ9-THC-treated rats no longer displayed aggressive behavior. Further analysis of the dose response to Δ9-THC revealed a dose-dependent increase in aggressive behavior (i.e., aggressive posture, submissive supine, and bites) following acute administration of Δ9-THC (1.25, 2.5, or 5.0 mg/kg) in REM sleep-deprived rat pairs and in the single treated rat within a pair of REM sleep-deprived rats.

In contrast to the above studies that report that acute marijuana exposure increases aggression in assessed rats, several other studies report a decrease in aggression in other species. In isolated adult male Swiss–Webster mice, aggressive behavior (i.e., number of fighting episodes and total fight time) decreased following acute exposure to high doses of Δ9-THC (10 or 25 mg/kg) and another cannabinoid, Δ8-THC (10 or 25 mg/kg), compared to baseline levels assessed prior to drug treatment (Ten Ham & De Jong, 1974). In adult *Betta splendens* (Siamese fighting fish), the same effects followed chronic exposure to low doses of Δ9-THC and cannabis extract (Gonzalez, Matsudo, & Carlini, 1971). Here, exposure to Δ9-THC (0.5 µg/ml) or cannabis extract (1 µg/ml) resulted in a decrease in aggressive behavior when assessed in a neutral tank. In this study, individually housed fish were removed from their home tanks and paired into a tank divided by a removable plate for exposure to Δ9-THC (0.5 µg/ml), cannabis extract (1 µg/ml), or control solution daily for 2 hr a day for 31 days. After drug exposure, plates were removed and aggressive behavior (i.e., duration of fighting, gill opening or expansion of fins, frontal approach, and side by side undulating movements) was observed. Fish that were exposed to Δ9-THC or cannabis extract showed a depression of aggressive behaviors, as well as

locomotor activity (slower swimming but without signs of motor incoordination). Suppressed aggressive behavior (duration of fighting) was also observed in isolated adult male albino mice administered an acute dose of Δ9-THC (2.5, 5, 10, or 20 mg/kg), with an effective dose of 5 mg/kg that was unassociated with motor deficits (the ED_{50} of motor deficits for Δ9-THC was found to be 62.1 mg/kg) (Dubinsky, Robichaud, & Goldberg, 1973).

The effect of marijuana on shock-induced aggression is less cohesive than that shown in studies that have assessed aggression using the resident-intruder paradigm and neutral arena. Chronic exposure to cannabis extract (10 mg/kg/day) for a minimum of 7 days effectively increased the duration of fighting in rats when administered an electric shock of 0. 5 milliamps (mA) 50–60 min postinjection (Carlini & Masur, 1969). A dose-dependent decrease in frequency of fighting followed acute Δ9-THC (0.12, 0.25, 0.5, 1.0, or 2 0 mg/kg) exposure at various electric shock intensities (0.8, 1.0, 1.2, 1.5, 1.8, 2.0, 2.2, 2.3, 2.4, and 2.5) in adult male Sprague–Dawley rats (Carder & Olson, 1972). Although lower doses of Δ9-THC (0.12–0.5 mg/kg) produced an increase in fighting, higher doses (1.0 and 2.0 mg/kg) suppressed fighting behavior. When tested 7 and 14 days after treatment, rats showed a significant decrease in shock-induced fighting. Dubinsky et al. (1973) reported a dose-dependent decrease in shock-induced fighting in adult male albino mice and adult male Long–Evans rats following acute Δ9-THC exposure. In this study, mice received acute exposure to Δ9-THC at 12.5, 25, or 50 mg/kg followed by shocks administered at 2 mA, whereas rats received an acute exposure of Δ9-THC at 2.5, 5, 10, 15, 30, or 60 mg/kg followed by three electric shocks administered at 3 mA. On the contrary, no effects of Δ9-THC were observed on shock-induced aggression in isolated adult male Walter Reed rats (Manning & Elsmore, 1972). After baseline aggression was assessed, (i.e., the average number of fighting episodes elicited following administration of 2.0-mA electric shocks), rats were treated with Δ9-THC or oil prior to each weekly run in sequentially increasing doses of Δ9-THC at 6.4, 200, 400, 800, 1,600, 3,200, and 6,400 mg/kg. At all doses of Δ9-THC there were no changes in frequency of fighting observed compared to oil-treated controls, (i.e., fighting behavior remained stable). Further examination on the effects of time of testing revealed no difference when tested 1 or 2 hr post drug treatment.

The very few studies that have examined the effects of marijuana on aggression using operant conditioning paradigms have shown marijuana to decrease aggressive behavior. In Balb/cJ (aggressive) mice, Δ9-THC exposure suppressed aggressive behavior in reward- and learning-based aggression paradigms, while having no impairment on learning or motor activity (Kilbey, Fritchie, McLendon, & Johnson, 1972). Briefly, prior to running a T maze, adult Balb/cJ (aggressive) mice were primed with C57BL/6J (passive) mice in the start box for 2 min until an attack was initiated and lasted 5 s. After priming, aggressive mice were allowed to traverse the runway until they reached the end, where a choice between a left or right goal box was made. Aggressive mice were trained to choose a goal box that rewarded the mice with the opportunity to attack and fight a passive mouse for 10 s, while choosing the wrong goal box resulted in confinement for 15 s. After 16 days of training, aggressive Balb/cJ mice received acute exposure to Δ9-THC (0.6, 1.25, or 2.5) 30 min prior to testing. Δ9-THC-treated mice showed a decrease in attack initiation, as demonstrated by increased latency to attack primed passive mice in the start box. When given the opportunity to fight, the number of attacks onto passive mice was significantly decreased. Furthermore, analysis of brain amines found no difference in DA, NE, or 5-HT. Cherek and Thompson (1973) also found a decrease in aggressive behavior following acute Δ9-THC exposure using an operant conditioning task of key pecking behavior in adult white male *Carneaux* pigeons. Pigeons were trained to key peck on a fixed interval schedule to receive food pellets and at the same time were primed to attack a restrained target pigeon that was physically inaccessible. After training, pigeons were administered Δ9-THC (0.125, 0.25, 0.5, or 1.0 mg/kg) 2 hr before testing. Δ9-THC treatment produced a dose-dependent decrease in the rate of attack and the rate of key pecking. At lower doses (0.125 and 0.25 mg/kg) of Δ9-THC, there was no effect on food reinforcement but decreased aggressive behavior was observed. However, because the rate of key pecking behavior (40–95 pecks/minute) was much higher than attack rates (4–12 attacks/minute), a subsequent experiment aimed to equate the rates of behavior to efficiently measure the change in behavior. Therefore, to decrease the rate of key pecking behavior the researchers added a differential reinforcement of low rate responding reinforcement (6–8 s) after a key pecking response. Once reshaping was established, Δ9-THC was administered at 0.25, 0.5, or 1.0 mg/kg. At a low dose of Δ9-THC, 0.25 mg/kg, no effect on key pecking was observed, but attack behavior was decreased.

At 1.0 mg/kg of Δ9-THC, attacks were completely abolished, while no effects on key pecking were observed.

Studies that have examined the effects of marijuana on predatory aggression have shown conflicting results that may be attributed to individual differences and type of species used as prey. Chronic cannabis exposure (20 mg/kg/day) for 40 days increased mouse killing (muricide) behavior (80%) after only 10 days of daily muricide testing in nonkiller male Wistar rats subjected to isolation and food deprivation, whereas cannabis treatment without food deprivation induced muricide only 20% of the time (Alves & Carlini, 1973). Acute exposure to Δ9-THC (6 mg/kg) 30 min or 1 hr prior to predatory aggression tests using a mouse as prey resulted in 60% of isolated adult male Wistar King A rats committing muricide (Yoshimura, Fujiwara, & Ueki, 1974). Subsequently, Ach was measured in the cortex, striatum, amygdala, diencephelon, and brain stem, revealing an increase in Ach in the striatum and amygdala in nonkiller and killer rats treated with Δ9-THC compared to control rats treated with vehicle. Fujiwara and Ueki (1979, p. 30) observed the time course of muricide behavior following acute Δ9-THC exposure in the same strain of rats. Here, isolated and food-deprived female Wistar King A rats received a single injection of Δ9-THC (6 mg/kg), followed by a predatory aggression test observed 1 hr later on Day 1, and subsequently were tested on Days 2, 3, 5, 7, 10, 15, 20, 25, 30, 40, 50, 60, 80, and 100 after the last injection. One hour after Δ9-THC treatment, 70% of rats committed muricide, decreasing to only 30% 24 hr later (on Day 2). Fujiwara and Ueki (1978) examined the time course of acute exposure to various doses of Δ9-THC in adult male Wistar King A rats. Isolated and food-deprived rats received a single injection of Δ9-THC (2, 4, 6, 8, or 16 mg/kg) and muricide behavior was assessed at 1 hr and 1, 3, 5, 7, 10, 15, 20, and 30 days. Muricide behavior was increased in a dose-dependent manner, with the lowest dose (2 mg/kg) of Δ9-THC able to produce muricide behavior (20%) 1 hr after drug treatment. Over time, beginning at 3 days postinjection, the increased muricide behavior remained stable for all doses. Miczek (1976) also examined the dose and time effects of repeated administration of Δ9-THC on muricide behavior in adult male Sprague–Dawley rats. Isolated and socially housed nonkiller rats received daily injections of Δ9-THC (2, 10, 20, or 50 mg/kg)/day for 60 days (35 days for the low dose of 2 mg/kg) and were tested weekly for muricide behavior 1 hr after drug injection. In a dose-dependent manner, Δ9-THC was found to increase muricide behavior; however, at the highest dose of 50 mg/kg, 50% of the treated rats died. Over time, the proportion of killers also increased. An effect of housing was found on Δ9-THC-induced muricide behavior in female Wistar King A rats (Ueki, Fujiwara, & Ogawa, 1972). Chronic exposure (30 days) to Δ9-THC (6 mg/kg/day) in chronically food-deprived and isolated rats increased muricide behavior, apparent immediately after the first treatment, whereas in group-housed rats muricide behavior was not observed until after 15 days of treatment. Bac, Pages, Herrenknecht, and Paris (1998) examined the time course of each phase of muricide behavior in Δ9-THC-treated naive and nonkiller, as well as untreated natural killer, male Long–Evans rats. Naive and nonkiller rats were food deprived and isolated for 48 hr prior to an acute exposure to Δ9-THC (11 mg/kg) followed by muricide testing 1, 2, 4, 6, 12, 24, and 24 hr later. The durations of the following three phases were observed: attack latency, attack, and attack on a dead mouse. One hour after Δ9-THC treatment nonkiller rats showed a muricide rate of 18%, but after 12 hr this was decreased to normal levels. Naive rats treated with Δ9-THC showed a muricide rate of 70% after 1 hr, but it progressively decreased over time. In naive and nonkiller rats treated with Δ9-THC, further analysis showed that the duration of each phase was increased compared to that in natural killer rats. After repeated exposure, naive rats treated with Δ9-THC began to show killing patterns similar to those of natural killer rats. Contrary to these findings, cannabis extract exposure (20 mg/kg/day) for up to 4 days reduced muricide behavior (i.e., by increasing latency to attack and kill) in killer male Wistar rats (Alves & Carlini, 1973). Further studies showed a decrease in predatory aggression in food-deprived and isolated female Holtzman rats treated with Δ9-THC (Kilbey & Moore, 1973). In contrast to assessing muricide behavior, the prey used in this study was a 2- to 3-in. frog (Rana pipens). A stable baseline of predatory aggression was assessed prior to 3 days of treatment with Δ9-THC (0, 0.25, 0.5, 1.25, 1.5, and 2.5 mg/kg) 30 min prior to testing. The authors found a dose-dependent decrease in predatory aggression (increase in the latency to attack and kill) following Δ9-THC exposure. Immediately after the last aggression tests, rats were sacrificed and 5-HT, NE, and Ach contents in whole brain were measured. Biological assays revealed that 5-HT and NE levels were increased at higher doses of

Δ9-THC (i.e., at 1.0 and 1.5 mg/kg, respectively), suggesting a role for 5-HT and NE in inhibiting predatory aggression. Predatory aggression was suppressed in isolated male albino Walter Reed rats after acute Δ9-THC (6. 4 mg/kg) treatment with turtles (Pseudomys ornate) as prey (McDonough, Manning, & Elsmore, 1972). Rats were treated with alternating injections of Δ9-THC (6.4 mg/kg) and saline every other day for 7 days. Predatory aggression was assessed daily 1, 2, 4, and 8 hr after drug treatment. The study revealed a decrease in aggression (wounding on turtle) after only 1 and 2 hr postinjection relative to controls (i.e., from 40 to 22.5% and after 2 hr from 47.5 to 25%).

Studies have also examined the effects of marijuana exposure on aggressive behavior using social aggression paradigms. Acute exposure to Δ9-THC (1, 2, or 4 mg/kg) resulted in opposing effects on several indices of aggressive behavior in subordinate and dominant Sprague–Dawley rats in a runway competition task (Miczek & Barry, 1974). Food-deprived rats were trained to run a narrow runway to receive a food pellet reward. Once trained, rats were paired and placed to enter the runway on opposite ends, enabling them to meet halfway. Subordinate rats were those that retreated back to their start positions, to which dominant rats followed, and fighting behavior occurred in the subordinate rats' start chambers. Once baseline ranks were assessed, rats received drug treatment 30 min prior to testing. Treatment with Δ9-THC at all doses of subordinate rats resulted in an increase in the number of wounds and submissive postures (i.e., submissive supine and immobile crouch) and an increase in the dominant animal's attack. In contrast, treatment with Δ9-THC, effective at the lowest dose of 1. 0 mg/kg, of dominant rats dose dependently decreased the duration of submissive postures (i.e., submissive supine and immobile crouch) and the frequency of mutual upright posture and biting attack. Hashish extract (20 mg/kg) disrupted social dominance and food dominance hierarchies in colony-housed C3H/HeJ mice (Sieber et al., 1980). After 3 days of treatment with hashish extract (20 mg/kg/day), socially dominant mice showed a decrease in dominance behavior after the third day of treatment, but by 24 hr after exposure, dominance was regained. In a food competition task, mice were trained to retrieve a piece of chocolate in a food dispenser, accessible by one mouse at a time. After the first exposure to 20 mg/kg of hashish extract, no discrete changes were observed in dominant mice, but after the second and third treatments, previously dominant mice were no longer able to obtain chocolate. The disruption in food hierarchy persisted up to 3 days post drug treatment.

Studies examining the effects of cannabis on aggressive behavior in a younger aged population have revealed inconclusive data. Carlini and Masur (1969) observed the effects of chronic cannabis extract exposure on spontaneous fighting and shock-induced fighting in female Wistar rat pairs beginning as young as 1 month. Female Wistar rat pairs aged 1–4 months, at the start of the study, were chronically treated with daily injections of cannabis extract (10 mg/kg) for 26 days. Immediately following treatment, observations of spontaneous fighting and electric shock-induced fighting were measured every other day. At 1 month of age, cannabis extract was able to induce low levels of aggressive behavior (i.e., duration of fighting and frequency of fighting behavior). However, the effects of cannabis treatment are more prominent with increasing age, that is, older rats showed an increase in duration of fighting and number of fighting episodes. In another study of primates using naturalistic observations, the effects of oral administration of Δ9-THC (2.5 mg/kg) administered daily in diet for up to 1 year were examined in indoor and outdoor group-housed pubertal male and female macaques (*Macaca mulatta* or *Mac. fasicularis*) (Sessenrath & Chapman, 1975). A summation of aggressive behavior over the course of the 24-month Δ9-THC treatment of indoor macaques revealed that drugged macaques displayed an increase in aggressive behavior (spontaneous fighting, hitting, biting, or chasing) compared to aggression levels prior to drug treatment. Additionally, Δ9-THC treatment caused a disruption of social hierarchy, in which drugged dominant macaques displayed a decrease in aggressive behavior, resulting in spontaneous fighting among nondrugged subordinate cage mates. In contrast to drugged dominant macaques, drugged subordinate macaques displayed an increase in submissive postures, which resulted in increases in wounding received from dominant animals. The authors also found that with Δ9-THC exposure in indoor-housed subordinate females there was an initial drop in social rank (between 0 and 2 months) that then rose to second rank dominance, that is, immediately below the alpha male, observed between 6 and 8 months. The authors propose that the rise in dominance is a result of irritable aggression produced by tolerance to chronic Δ9-THC exposure.

In pups that have been prenatally exposed to Δ9-THC, the effects of Δ9-THC on aggressive behavior have been shown to be short lived (Vardaris, Weisz, Fazel, & Rawitch, 1976). Pregnant Sprague–Dawley rats were administered radioactively labeled Δ9-THC (2 mg/kg) beginning on Embryonic Day 3 until parturition. At birth, radioactively labeled Δ9-THC concentrations averaged 553 ng in pups. Aggressive behavior was assessed using a push-tube competition task. In this task, pups were placed on opposite ends of a tube and were then required to force each other out. Three trials were conducted each at P-21 and P-90. At P-21, pups that were exposed to THC showed a shorter latency to win, marked by an increase in aggressive behavior compared to controls. At P-90, performance on the competition task remained the same as assessed on P-21.

Alcohol

Studies examining the effects of alcohol on aggression have produced results that highlight the complexity of its actions in the central nervous system. Alcohol has been shown to both increase and decrease aggressive behaviors in several animal species and in various models of aggression. While there is still no conclusive evidence, there is a vast research base suggesting that various factors play an integral role in the valid assessment of the effects of alcohol on a complex behavior such as aggression, including species-specific behavioral patterns, social context, and time of exposure during neural development. Several neurobiological substrates have been implicated in the physiological effects of alcohol, as they have been correlated with coincident alterations in aggressive responding.

The majority of preclinical research investigating the link between alcohol and aggression has been conducted using adult rats and mice using the resident-intruder paradigm. Acute alcohol exposure, at doses ranging from 0.4 to 2.4 g/kg, produced a biphasic effect on aggression in mice using the resident-intruder test (Krisiak, 1976). Specifically, low doses of alcohol (ethyl alcohol) produced increases in tail rattling, aggressive unrest, and attack behaviors in residents when the intruder was present, while these same behaviors were decreased at higher doses of alcohol. Miczek and O'Donnell (1980) sought to further characterize the acute effects of alcohol on aggression and administered one of several doses of alcohol (300, 600, or 1,200 mg/kg) to individually housed adult, male Swiss–Webster mice and observed the behavior of these mice after an intruder was placed into the home cage of the experimental animal or in a neutral cage. No change in fighting was observed at any dose of alcohol when the resident was confronted with an intruder in his home cage. However, 300 mg/kg of alcohol increased fighting in the neutral arena. Using the resident-intruder paradigm, one of several doses of alcohol (0.1, 0.3, 1.0, 1.7, or 3.0 g/kg) was administered to adult male Swiss–Webster mice 15 min prior to aggression testing (DeBold & Miczek, 1985). Interestingly, a behavioral pattern similar to that observed in the neutral arena emerged. Specifically, mice treated with a low dose of alcohol (0.3 g/kg) increased pursuits during the testing period, while the highest dose tested, 3.0 g/kg, significantly decreased the frequency of attack and threat, increased attack latency, and decreased pursuits. In an attempt to determine the effects of mouse strain on the acute effects of alcohol on aggression, Everill and Berry (1987) administered one of two doses of alcohol (i.e., 0.5 or 1.0 g/kg) 20 min prior to a resident-intruder test to three mouse strains (i.e., C57BL/10, DBA/2, and BALB/C) that had been isolated for either 14 or 28 days. A significant effect of strain and time of isolation was observed regarding the effects of alcohol on offensive aggression. Specifically, control mice from the DBA strain showed more overall aggression when compared to the other two strains. Within the DBA strain, mice that had been isolated for 14 days showed increased aggression after receiving vehicle and 0.5 g/kg of alcohol when compared to 28-day isolates in the same conditions and when compared to 14-day isolates receiving 1.0 g/kg of alcohol. In addition, no effects of alcohol on offensive aggression were observed in any of the other strains tested, leading to the conclusion that exposure to alcohol does not potentiate aggression in these mouse strains. Although the majority of studies on the effects of alcohol on aggression lead to the conclusion that alcohol exerts a biphasic effect on aggression (i.e., low doses of alcohol increase aggression, whereas high doses decrease aggression). To examine the relationship between blood alcohol levels and aggression in isolated, adult male TO mice were injected with either saline or one of three doses of alcohol (0.5, 1.0, or 2.0 g/kg) and two animals that received the same drug treatment were placed together into the home cage of one of the mice (Benton & Smoothy, 1984); fighting was monitored for 23 hr. In order to determine blood alcohol levels following these doses of alcohol, experimentally naive TO male mice were administered

0.5, 1.0, or 2.0 g/kg of alcohol prior to blood extraction under anesthesia. Contrary to previous reports, at no time during the first 3 hr after alcohol injection did any dose of alcohol produce a significant increase in aggression. In fact, the dose of alcohol that had previously been shown to increase aggression (0.5 g/kg) initially had an antiaggressive effect in this study.

The effects of alcohol on aggression of adult, male Long–Evans rats, selected for different baseline levels of aggressive behavior, were examined in individually housed animals given two preliminary 10-min resident-intruder tests to provide fighting experience (Blanchard, Hori, Blanchard, & Hall, 1987). Rats were then subjected to four additional resident-intruder tests 30 min following administration of saline or 0.3, 0.6, or 1.2 g/kg of alcohol. Animals were then placed into a zero, low-intermediate, or high aggression group based on the total frequency of offense during the saline test. Animals in the zero aggression group did not show any increase in aggression at any dose of alcohol tested. In the low-moderate aggression group, aggression was increased at the 0.3 and 0.6 g/kg alcohol doses, while aggression levels decreased to slightly below baseline at the 1.2 g/kg dose. However, offensive aggression dose dependently decreased in animals in the high aggression group. Weerts, Tornatzky, and Miczek (1993) examined how acute alcohol influenced aggressive responding in both adult, male Long–Evans rats and adult, male squirrel monkeys in confrontations with conspecifics and how these effects were influenced by treatment with various benzodiazepine antagonists. First, resident rats were administered alcohol (0.1, 0.3, 1.0, 1.7, or 3.0 g/kg) or vehicle 15 min prior to behavioral testing. As with previous studies in mice, alcohol produced a biphasic effect on offensive aggression in adult, male Long–Evans rats. Attack bites, sideways threats, and aggressive postures were increased following administration of low doses of alcohol (0.1 g/kg), while being decreased following high doses (3.0 g/kg). Rats that displayed alcohol-heightened aggression (AHA) were further tested to examine the ability of specific benzodiazepine antagonists to suppress this increase in aggressive responding. Either ZK93426 (5-isopropoxy-4-methyl-b-carboline-3-carboxylic acid ethyl ester) or flumazenil (Ro 15-1788) was administered (3 mg/kg) along with the individuals' peak aggression-enhancing dose or aggression-reducing dose of alcohol prior to behavioral tests for aggression. Pretreatment with ZK93426 significantly antagonized alcohol-enhanced frequencies and durations of sideways threats and reduced bites;

however, there was no effect on behavior when tested with the aggression-reducing dose of alcohol (3 g/kg). Similarly, pretreatment with flumazenil antagonized the proaggressive effects of low-dose alcohol by decreasing sideways threats, with no effect on the aggression-reducing dose of alcohol (figure 16.8).

In the second study, both dominant and subordinate squirrel monkeys were observed for aggressive behaviors following alcohol treatment in two settings: (a) within their complex social group and (b) during a dyadic confrontation with a rival monkey. Dyad tests were conducted to assess drug effects on agonistic displays by dominant squirrel monkeys. For this experiment, dominant, male squirrel monkeys were administered alcohol (0.1, 0.3, 0.6, 1.0, or 1.5 g/kg) 15 min prior to confronting a rival male monkey who was contained in an adjacent cage, thereby allowing both monkeys to receive sensory cues through a mesh wall but preventing physical contact. As with research in mice and rats, alcohol produced a biphasic effect on agonistic displays in the squirrel monkey. Specifically, alcohol increased aggressive actions displayed by the dominant male at low doses (i.e., 0.1 and 0.3 g/kg), while at higher doses (i.e., 1.0 and 1.5 g/kg) alcohol reduced these behaviors. As with the rats, pretreatment with 3 mg/kg of ZK93426 blocked the increase in aggression produced by 0.1 and 0.3 g/kg of alcohol, but had no effect on the reductions in aggression at the higher doses. Finally, these same doses of alcohol were administered to dominant and subordinate monkeys and their behavior was observed while in their established colony. In dominant males, the low dose of alcohol (0.1 g/kg) significantly increased aggressive threats, grasps, and displays, while the high doses (1.0 and 1.5 g/kg) reduced these behaviors and pretreatment with 10 mg/kg of flumazenil could reduce these increases in aggression. The dose-dependent effects of alcohol on aggression have also been characterized in territorial, male convict cichlids (*Cichlasoma nigrofasciatum*) (Peeke, Ellman, & Herz, 1973). Adult, male cichlids were individually placed into an aquarium and allowed to acclimate for 4 days before the introduction of alcohol into the tank at concentrations of 0.07, 0.18, or 0.33%. Six hours later, the resident fish was presented with a live male conspecific that was confined to a clear glass tube, and the frequency of aggressive displays by the resident was recorded. All subjects in the control group and the low-dose alcohol group attacked the intruder, while >85% of fish in the medium-dose and >45% of fish in the high-dose group attacked.

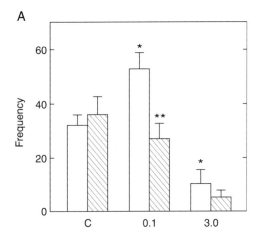

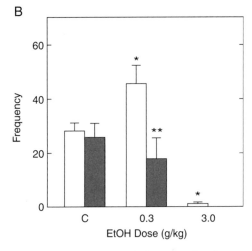

FIGURE 16.8 Effects of alcohol (EtOH white bars) and (A) ZK93426 (striped bars) (3 mg/kg) pretreatment ($n = 6$) and (B) flumazenil (black bars) (10 mg/kg) pretreatment ($n = 6$) on sideways threats in resident male rats ($n = 6$) directed toward an untreated male intruder. $^*p < .05$ compared to vehicle control. $^{**}p < .05$ compared to the same dose of EtOH alone. From "Prevention of the Pro-Aggressive Effects of Alcohol in Rats and Squirrel Monkeys by Benzodiazepine Receptor Antagonists," by E. M. Weerts, W. Tornatzky, and K. A. Miczek, 1993, *Psychopharmacology, 111*(2), p. 147. Copyright 1993 by Springer-Verlag. Reprinted with permission.

A slightly different pattern emerged when only the fishes that attacked intruders were included in the analysis. No significant differences in frequencies and duration of aggressive behaviors were observed between the control and low-dose alcohol groups; however, the medium-dose alcohol group showed a higher level of aggression and the highest dose alcohol group showed a lower level of aggression when compared to all other groups. Using this behavioral selection method, Peeke, Peeke, Avis, and Ellman (1975) showed that fish that received a medium dose of alcohol (0.15%) showed the greatest frequency of displays and bites, followed by control fish and then by fish that received the highest dose of alcohol (0.30%). All groups were statistically different from each other. This set of results further lend weight to the theory that alcohol produces biphasic effects on aggression and this effect is observable across many species.

Hormones are known to play an integral role in modulating many behaviors, including aggression in various species (see Simon & Lu, ch. 9 in this volume, and Ogawa, Nomura, Choleris, & Pfaff, ch. 10 in this volume). Alcohol has been shown to both increase and decrease aggressive responding in male mice; however, the influence of the hormonal milieu on this phenomenon had not been investigated. The extent to which androgen levels in male mice influence the effects of acute alcohol on aggressive responding has been examined (DeBold & Miczek, 1985). Castrated male Swiss–Webster mice were assigned to one of three testosterone groups (0.0-, 2.5-, or 7.7-mm capsules) filled with 75 mg/kg of testosterone or cholesterol (0.0 mm) and subsequently separated into seven acute alcohol exposure conditions (0.0, 0.1, 0.3, 1.0, 1.7, 3.0, and 5.6 g/kg). Mice were tested for offensive aggression in the resident-intruder paradigm. Both controls (castrated with cholesterol capsule) and animals that had received low testosterone showed suppressed aggression after receiving the highest doses of alcohol tested (3.0 and 5.6 g/kg). However, the high-testosterone group displayed a significant enhancement of attack bites and pursuits following administration of 1.0 g/kg of alcohol. This effect was also observed for attack bites and sideways threats at 1.7 g/kg. In addition, the high-testosterone group was less sensitive to the aggression-reducing effects of high alcohol concentrations. Specifically, the 3.0 g/kg dose of alcohol inhibited aggression in all other groups (unaltered, castrates/cholesterol, and castrates/low testosterone), but had no effect on aggressive behavior in the high-testosterone group, although at the highest alcohol dose (5.6 g/kg dose) aggression was suppressed the high-testosterone animals. Another study from this laboratory examined the effects of acute alcohol exposure on aggressive behavior in squirrel monkeys and the influence of testosterone and social context in this phenomenon. Dominant

and submissive adult, male squirrel monkeys were selected from four established groups and were administered TP (25 mg/kg/day), resulting in significantly elevated plasma levels of testosterone. Two to three weeks after the beginning of testosterone treatment, monkeys were administered one of three doses of alcohol (0.1, 0.3, or 0.6 g/kg) prior to being observed for aggressive behavior. Administration of low doses of alcohol to TP-treated subordinate males significantly increased the frequency (0.1 g/kg of alcohol) and duration (0.1 and 0.3 g/kg of alcohol) of aggressive behaviors, but had no effect on aggression at the higher doses. Interestingly, these effects were seen only when the dominant male was present in the colony. If the dominant male was removed from the group, there was no statistically significant effect of alcohol on the aggressive behavior of TP-treated subordinates. In TP-treated dominant monkeys, both low and moderate doses of alcohol (0.3 and 0.6 g/kg) produced a significant increase in the frequency and duration of aggressive behaviors, with no effect observed at the highest dose of alcohol administered. In a later study, Lisciotto, DeBold, and Miczek (1990) examined the influence of sexual differentiation on the effect of acute alcohol exposure on aggression by manipulating the hormonal state of neonatal male and female Swiss–Webster mice, both as neonates and during adulthood. On the day of birth, mice were assigned to one of six testing conditions: male offspring were bilaterally gonadectomized or sham operated, and female offspring were injected with either 250 μg of TP or vehicle. At 75 days of age, all of the animals that had not been gonadectomized at birth were gonadectomized as adults and all of the neonatally castrated males and half of the neonatally TP-treated females were implanted with 7.5-mm capsules containing testosterone, while the other half did not receive the capsules. Animals were then tested for offensive aggression using the resident-intruder paradigm following the administration of one of five doses of alcohol (0.1, 0.3, 1.0, 1.7, or 3.0 g/kg) 15 min prior to the behavioral test. Results showed that the effects of alcohol on aggression largely depended upon neonatal and adult hormonal treatment and that males and females responded differently to alcohol. Oil-treated females (controls) did not show increases in aggression at any dose of alcohol tested; however, they did show a suppression of attack bites, sideways threats, and pursuits at the highest dose of alcohol (i.e., 3.0 g/kg). Sham-operated males showed a statistically significant enhancement of attack bites at medium doses of alcohol (i.e., 1.0 g/kg), and contrary to prior research from this laboratory, these mice did not exhibit a significant suppression of aggression at the high 3.0 g/kg dose. Neonatally gonadectomized males, independently of whether they received testosterone during adulthood, displayed aggression patterns similar to that of control females, that is, aggression was not increased by any tested dose of alcohol and was in fact suppressed at 3.0 g/kg. This set of experiments shows a sex-specific effect of alcohol on offensive aggression and indicates that the presence of the testes during postnatal development is necessary for the induction of an adult male-typical behavioral response to alcohol, specifically in regard to offensive aggression. Hilakivi-Clarke and Goldberg (1995) examined the influence of 17β-estradiol (E_2) on the behavioral response of highly aggressive, transgenic CD-1 male mice overexpressing transforming growth factor-α (TFG-α) and moderately aggressive, nontransgenic CD-1 male mice to alcohol in the resident-intruder test. At 8 weeks of age, transgenic TFG-α mice and nontransgenic CD-1 controls were castrated or sham operated, with some of the castrated mice being implanted with E_2 pellets. After surgery, mice were individually housed for 4–7 weeks and 20 min prior to being confronted by an intruder in their home cage, animals received an acute exposure to alcohol (0, 0.6, 1.2, or 2.0 g/kg). In the control condition, nontransgenic CD-1 mice displayed increased aggressive behavior following the acute exposure to low doses of alcohol (i.e., 0.6 g/kg) while high doses (i.e., 2.0 g/kg) reduced aggression; however, none of the doses of alcohol given to the transgenic TFG-α mice altered their aggressive responding in any of the conditions (i.e., sham operated, castrated, or castrated with E_2). Interestingly, although castration can reduce the aggressive behavior observed in TFG-α mice under the influence of alcohol, E_2 treatment returns aggression to the levels seen in intact TFG-α mice. The interpretation provided is that the elevated E_2 plasma levels in TFG-α mice may be responsible for the lack of response to alcohol in the resident-intruder test, supported by the observation that castrated, nontransgenic animals that had been exposed to E_2 also show no changes in aggression following alcohol administration.

Several studies that have been conducted in rats, dogs, and primates have taken advantage of the complex social groups these species form in order to examine the effects of alcohol administration under varied social conditions on aggressive behavior. Blanchard, Hori, Flannelly, and Blanchard (1987) examined the effects of acute alcohol administration on aggression in adult, male Long–Evans rats during colony formation, which is a complex social setting involving both inter- and intrasex interactions. In these studies, one male rat was treated with one of three doses of alcohol (0.3, 0.6, or 1.2 g/kg) prior to being introduced into a group consisting of three male and three female rats. Behavioral observations were made over the first 6 hr of group formation. In accord with previous research in mice, male rats exposed to a high dose of alcohol (i.e., 1.2 g/kg) showed decreased aggression when compared to saline-treated controls. In addition, while rats in the saline and low-dose alcohol groups directed fewer attacks toward the females in the group (15–25% of total attacks), rats treated with the high dose directed a majority of their attacks toward the females. In similar studies in dogs, the effect of acute alcohol exposure on the agonistic behaviors of Telomian dogs was examined within a social structure (Pettijohn, 1979). Telomian dogs were tested for aggression while in their established groups of two males and one female. Alcohol (0.8 or 1.6 g/kg) or vehicle was administered to one dog or to all the dogs within the group 30 min prior to behavioral observations. Interestingly, the alcohol effects on aggression were influenced by the social rank of the individual dogs. In top- and middle-ranking dogs, the high dose of alcohol (1.6 g/kg) significantly decreased the frequency of attacks, while the low dose of alcohol (0.8 g/kg) increased attacks in low-ranking dogs. High-dose alcohol decreased aggression when compared to controls and to the low-dose groups, independently of whether only one dog received the alcohol or all dogs in the group did. Conversely, the frequencies of attacks for the top- and middle-ranking dogs increased in the control (vehicle) condition, but greatly decreased in the low- and high- alcohol (i.e., 0.8 and 1.6 g/kg) conditions, while the frequency of attacks for the low-ranking dogs increased initially in the control condition and even more so in the 0. 8 g/kg condition. Last, as in top- and middle-ranking dogs, the frequencies of attacks significantly decreased in the high-dose alcohol (1.6 g/kg) condition in low-ranking dogs. The effects of acute alcohol exposure on aggression in both male and female, dominant and subordinate, members of established groups of squirrel monkeys have also been studied (Winslow & Miczek, 1985). In first part of these studies, monkeys (i.e., four dominant males, one dominant female, two subordinate males, and six subordinate females) were subjected to several behavioral tests to establish baseline behavioral responding.

Then, prior to testing, the animal to be treated was removed from the group and received a specific dose of alcohol (0, 0.1, 0.3, 0.6, or 1.0 g/kg), and observation began 5 min after alcohol administration. All animals received all doses of alcohol in different sequences. In baseline testing conditions, alcohol administration did not alter aggressive behaviors in subordinate monkeys. The effects of alcohol in the dominant monkeys were more variable. Forty percent of dominants displayed increases in aggressive behavior at the low doses (0.1 and 0 3 g/kg); however, the highest dose of alcohol (1.0 g/kg) reduced aggression in all dominant monkeys. Under experimental conditions, dominant monkeys exhibited increased aggression during the first 45 min following low to moderate doses of alcohol. As in the baseline experiment, none of the doses tested altered aggressive behavior in any of the subordinate monkeys.

Van Erp and Miczek (1997) examined the effects of chronic (i.e., self-administered) alcohol on aggression. Adult, male Long–Evans rats were trained to drink a 10% alcohol solution using a sucrose-fading technique. The fading procedure took 4–5 weeks, followed by a 10-day period to stabilize self-administration of the 10% alcohol solution when the solution was presented daily for 15 min. Resident-intruder tests were conducted immediately following the 15-min access period and a blood sample was taken immediately following the behavioral testing to determine blood alcohol levels of the experimental animals. Although there was a trend toward an increase in some categories of aggressive behavior, no significant effects were found after low or moderate amounts of alcohol when compared to control. However, despite the lack of significance in behavioral data when all animals were analyzed together, the authors noted that there appeared to be significant individual differences in various aggressive behaviors. Because of these differences, animals were divided into an AHA group and an alcohol-nonheightened aggression ANA group. Posthoc analysis revealed that the AHA group showed significant increases in aggressive behavior after alcohol self-administration when compared to the ANA group. The 5-HT$_{1B}$ receptor was studied to understand the neural substrates involved in the effect of chronic alcohol on aggression (Miczek & de Almeida, 2001). Individually housed, adult, male CFW mice learned to self-administer specific concentrations of alcohol (0.6, 1.0, 1.7, or 3.0 g/kg) on a fixed ratio schedule using standard operant conditioning techniques. Following task acquisition, mice were tested for aggressive behavior in the resident-intruder paradigm following acute administration of the 5-HT$_{1B}$ receptor agonist anpirtoline (0.125, 0.25 or 0.5 mg/kg; 15 min prior to testing) or vehicle. Self-administration of 1.0 and 1.7 g/kg of alcohol significantly increased the frequency of attack bites, sideways threats, and tail rattles, while self-administration of 3.0 g/kg of alcohol reduced these behaviors. Although pretreatment with anpirtoline significantly decreased low-dose alcohol-induced aggression, this aggression-reducing effect does not appear to be specific to the effects of alcohol since anpirtoline also reduced aggression after sucrose-reinforced responding.

A number of studies have examined the effects of alcohol on aggression in the neutral arena in mice and have yielded different results. The interaction between acute alcohol exposure and housing condition (i.e., group housed vs. isolated) on aggression in a neutral arena test was studied in adult, male NIH Swiss mice (Hilakivi & Lister, 1989). Mice were group housed, isolated for 5 days, or isolated for 10 days prior to receiving one dose of alcohol (0.8 or 2.0 g/kg) 30 min prior to being confronted with a conspecific in a neutral arena. In vehicle-treated mice, isolation increased the amount of time spent displaying aggressive behaviors and the proportion of mice exhibiting these behaviors when compared to group-housed mice. Although exposure to alcohol did not affect the aggressive behavior of group-housed mice, 0.8 g/kg of alcohol significantly enhanced the aggressive behavior in 5-day isolates and 2.0 g/kg significantly reduced these behaviors. In 10-day isolates, alcohol dose dependently decreased the duration of aggressive behavior and decreased the proportion of mice displaying these behaviors. Paivarinta (1992) administered 0.8 g/kg of alcohol to adult, group-housed male Swiss–Webster mice 30 min prior to aggression testing in a neutral arena. No increases in aggression were observed following this moderate-high dose of alcohol. To study the effects of alcohol on aggression in adult, group-housed female Swiss–Webster mice, females were given a single injection of 0, 0.5, 1.0, or 2.0 g/kg of alcohol 20 min prior to aggression testing in a neutral cage by introducing an anosmic male into the cage with the female (Smoothy, Brain, Berry, & Haug, 1986). In this study, control mice were not aggressive and none of the alcohol doses tested altered this behavioral pattern.

Although there appear, in general, to be different effects of acute and chronic alcohol on aggression measured in the resident-intruder and neutral arena paradigms, particular social contexts seem to provide reliable increases in the probability that alcohol-induced aggression will be observed regardless of animal species or model of aggression utilized. The effects of acute alcohol exposure on aggression in dominant and submissive pairs of adult, male Sprague–Dawley rats have also been studied (Miczek & Barry, 1977). Dominance and submissiveness were determined between pairs by placing both rats within the testing apparatus and observing the interaction during consecutive testing sessions. Dominant rats were administered both 0.5 and 1.0 g/kg of alcohol and tested for attack and threat behaviors. Administration of the lower dose in these rats significantly increased the frequency of attacks and increased the duration of aggressive posturing, while the higher dose (1.0 g/kg) inhibited attack behavior. Walker and Gregory (1985) assessed acute alcohol effects on aggression under winner and loser conditions in the Syrian hamster. After habituation to the testing cage, individually housed adult male hamsters were confronted with a conspecific to determine dominance relationships. A "winner" was characterized as the hamster that successfully defeated the other during a 3-min encounter. Once this stable dominance relationship was established, pairs of hamsters were assigned to one of two groups. In one group, winners received a high dose of alcohol (i.e., 2.0 g/kg) 15–60 min prior to behavior testing, whereas in the other group the losers received 2.0 g/kg of alcohol. In this study, the effects of alcohol were dependent on the social status of the animal within a dyad. Specifically, administration of alcohol to a previous winner decreased aggression toward the other hamster, while administration of alcohol to a previous loser had no effect on aggression when compared to administration of saline.

The interaction between acute alcohol administration and the size of the intruder was also studied on maternal aggression in adult, female Long–Evans rats (Blanchard, Flannelly, Hori, Blanchard, & Hall, 1987). In this study, a rat dam received saline or 0.5 or 1.2 g/kg of alcohol and was tested for aggression on postpartum days 2 and 3 by placing either a large or a small male intruder into her home cage without the pups being present. During the 30-min testing period, saline-treated rat dams displayed an intermediate level of offensive aggression toward both small and large intruders that declined over the next 15–20 min, only to be followed by another increase toward the end of the testing period. Rat dams treated with 0.5 g/kg of alcohol displayed a higher level of aggression toward large intruders and a much higher level toward smaller intrud-

ers when compared to controls. Animals in the high-dose (1.2 g/kg) group, however, displayed very little aggression toward either type of intruder throughout the 30-min test period.

The effects of alcohol on aggression have also been examined using a shock-induced paradigm for aggression following both acute and chronic exposure to alcohol in adult, food-restricted, male albino rats (Tramill, Gustavson, Weaver, Moore, & Davis, 1983). Rats in the chronic alcohol condition received a 30% alcohol solution each day for 15 days, while animals in the acute alcohol condition received a saline injection for 14 days and an injection of 30% alcohol on the 15th day. In the control condition, animals received an injection of saline every day for 15 days. For testing, rats received a 6-min period of tail shocks that consisted of 2-mA shocks of 300-ms duration at 3-s intervals and the number of aggressive responses during the shock trial was recorded. Chronic administration of alcohol increased shock-induced aggressive responding when compared to both the control group and the acute condition. It was also observed that animals in the control condition displayed increased aggressive behavior when compared to rats in the acute alcohol condition, leading to the conclusion that acute administration of alcohol decreases shock-induced aggressive responding in rats. In another examination of chronic alcohol exposure on shock-induced aggression, adult, male Wistar rats were treated with 10 g/kg of alcohol over a 24-hr period for 13 days via intragastric catheter (Rouhani et al., 1991). Rats were administered 50 shocks per session (i.e., 1.20-mA intensity for 0.5 s, with a 6-s interval between shocks), during which animals were observed for aggressive reactions toward a conspecific. An increase in shock-induced fighting was observed in rats chronically treated with alcohol when compared to controls. On the day following the last administration of alcohol, animals received an acute injection of either muscimol (i.e., a $GABA_A$ receptor agonist, 0.25 mg/kg) or homotaurine (i.e., a GABA mimetic, 140 mg/kg) in order to examine the influence of the GABA system on this shock-induced increase in aggression. The number of attacks was decreased in alcohol-dependent rats that received both muscimol and homotaurine, suggesting that alcohol may potentiate shock-induced aggressive responses by decreasing GABA signaling, perhaps acting through the $GABA_A$ receptor.

Although a large number of studies have examined acute and chronic alcohol effects on aggressive behavior in adult animal models, relatively few have examined the effects of alcohol on aggression in the developing brain, particularly following adolescent and prenatal exposure to this drug. The studies that do consider this important time of exposure without exception study the effects of chronic alcohol exposure on aggressive responding. Ferris, Shtiegman, and King (1998) examined the effects of chronic alcohol exposure during early puberty on levels of testosterone and aggression in male Syrian hamsters. From P-25 to P-43 (early–mid adolescence), animals were allowed free access to a 15% alcohol solution (an average of 13 g/kg/day) and 72 hr after the cessation of alcohol availability, adolescent hamsters were tested for aggression in the resident-intruder paradigm. Plasma testosterone levels were also measured from animals that received alcohol or vehicle at various times betweenP-30 and P5-3. Adolescent hamsters that were administered alcohol were significantly more aggressive than vehicle-treated controls. Specifically, the majority (> 95%) of alcohol-treated hamsters bit intruders, whereas only half of the controls directed bites toward intruders. In addition, alcohol-treated hamsters showed significantly decreased latency to bite when compared to controls. A significant difference in plasma testosterone levels was also found between alcohol-treated hamsters and controls. On P-35, alcohol-treated hamsters showed higher plasma testosterone levels than controls, although this difference disappeared by P-41, a time point well before aggression testing.

The effects of prenatal and postnatal exposure to alcohol were examined on aggressive behavior in two mouse strains, C57 and DBA (Yanai & Ginsburg, 1977). In these studies, male and female mice in the experimental condition received a 10% alcohol solution from P-28 to P-60. Females were then bred, individually housed, and maintained on their nutritional regimen until 14 days postparturition. At this time, the alcohol solution was replaced with tap water so that the offspring were never directly administered alcohol. Offspring of both mouse strains (i.e., C57 and DBA) whose parents were exposed to alcohol displayed significant increases in latency to attack when compared to controls. Among these offspring, there was also a significant reduction in the number of 20-s periods spent fighting compared to controls; however, there was no difference in the number of fighting bouts, tail rattles, or attacks between offspring exposed to alcohol during gestation and controls. Because the contributions of prenatal versus postnatal exposure to alcohol (through the dams' milk) on aggression could not be determined

by this study, an additional group of DBA parents received alcohol from P-28 until the offspring were born and in another group from the day the offspring were born until 14 days postparturition. DBA offspring which received alcohol during gestation showed aggressive displays similar to those of control mice; however, mice that were exposed to alcohol during the postnatal period with no prenatal exposure displayed increased attack latency and decreases in the number of 20-s periods spent in fighting, attacks, and number of fighting bouts. These results suggest the critical period for the aggression-eliciting effects of alcohol on the developing brain may be during early postnatal, not prenatal, development. In contrast to this study, there have been findings that both male and female Sprague–Dawley rats were more aggressive as juveniles engaging in play fighting when exposed to alcohol during gestation (Royalty, 1990). Rat dams were exposed to 95% alcohol/kg of body weight on each of Gestation Days 6–19 via stomach intubation. Juvenile play behavior was assessed in prenatally exposed offspring over P-32–P-34, followed by 5 days of individual housing. Both male and female rats exposed to alcohol during gestation were significantly more aggressive than controls during bouts of play fighting. In addition, females initiated more play fighting responses when compared to male counterparts. Postpubertal aggressive responses were assessed in male offspring over P-78–P-83. Males exposed to alcohol during gestation were significantly more aggressive than controls and the play fighting behavior displayed by these males was correlated with these adult forms of aggression, indicating long-term effects of prenatal alcohol exposure on aggression.

Krsiak, Elis, Poschlova, and Masek (1977) examined aggressive behavior and the level of brain monoamines in adult mice that had been exposed to alcohol during prenatal development. Alcohol (1 g/kg) was administered to pregnant albino mice throughout gestation (21 days). At 10 weeks of age, mice exposed to alcohol during gestation and control offspring were individually housed, with social interactions beginning after 5 weeks of isolation. Male offspring of alcohol-treated dams were significantly more aggressive than controls and this difference increased with repeated interactions. Brain concentrations of norepinephrine, DA, and 5-HT between offspring exposed to alcohol and controls were also examined both following an aggressive encounter and without confrontation. In alcohol-treated offspring that engaged in an aggressive encounter, significant reductions in 5-HT levels were observed compared to controls, with no differences in the other amines. The experience of an aggressive encounter had no influence on this effect, as alcohol-treated mice that did not engage in a social interaction test also had decreased 5-HT levels when compared to controls. These data suggest that prenatal exposure to alcohol may disrupt the development of the 5-HT neural system, facilitating the development of a long-lasting aggressive phenotype.

The effects of prenatal exposure to alcohol on shock-induced aggression has been studied in rats (Davis et al., 1984). Rat dams had unrestricted access to a 10% alcohol solution throughout pregnancy and the alcohol solution was removed upon birth of the offspring. From birth until weaning (P-21), pups were either raised with their natural mother or cross-fostered and were placed in individual cages at P-45. Shock-elicited aggression tests were conducted when the offspring were 81 days old. Following habituation to the testing apparatus, the rats received 100, 2.0-mA tail shocks of 300 ms duration at 3-s intervals for a 5-min testing period. As in other paradigms, both male and female rats exposed to alcohol during gestation showed significantly more aggressive responses when compared to controls, with no cross-fostering differences observed, supporting the notion that prenatal exposure to alcohol facilitates the development of a long-lasting aggressive phenotype.

Benzodiazapines

The nonmedical use of prescription psychotropics has become a serious health problem. Benzodiazepines (BZs) such as diazepam (Valium), chlordiazepoxide (Librium, or CDP), and alprazolam (Xanax) are CNS depressants that have been classified as commonly abused drugs. Many studies have examined the link between exposure to benzodiazepines and aggression in various testing paradigms for aggression, in many species, and in many treatment paradigms, with divergent results.

CDP (Librium)

CDP, or Librium, has been shown to increase and decrease aggressive behavior in various species and these effects may be due to the treatment regimen used (i.e., chronic or acute exposure). Specifically, many studies have examined the effects of acute CDP exposure on territorial aggression using the resident-intruder test in adult mice and in monkeys. Although as little

as 5 mg/kg of CDP increases attacks and sideways threats in adult male Swiss–Webster mice in a neutral arena test, this same effect was not observed for mice tested for aggression in their home cage using the resident-intruder test (Miczek & O'Donnell, 1980). However, as seen in mice tested for aggression in the neutral arena, higher doses (i.e., 10 and 20 mg/kg) of CDP were found to decrease attack and threat behavior in the resident-intruder test. Another study also examined the effects of a range of doses of CDP (1, 4, or 8 mg/kg; 30 min prior to testing) on both resident-intruder aggression and intermale aggression (neutral arena), and as above, these studies produced divergent results (Gao & Cutler, 1993). The authors found that whereas 8 mg/kg of CDP could significantly increase aggression between adult male, CD-1 mice in the neutral arena, no dose of the drug could affect aggression in these animals in the resident-intruder test. In another study of the effects of acute CDP exposure on territorial aggression using the resident-intruder test, Ferrari, Parmigiani, Rodgers, and Palanza (1997) administered one of three doses of CDP (5, 10, or 20 mg/kg; 30 min prior to testing) to adult male, Swiss albino mice which experienced one of two conditions after weaning: (a) group housing with same-sex conspecifics and then screening for aggression with an unfamiliar same-sex conspecific or (b) single housing for 1 month. In this examination 20 mg/kg of CDP significantly reduced the proportion of attacking mice among the isolates while increasing attack latency. At the lowest dose tested (5 mg/kg), CDP increased accumulated attack time among aggressive, group-housed mice and at the highest dose tested (20 mg/kg), CDP decreased accumulated attacking time only in isolates. As with the increase in total attacking time in aggressive, group-housed mice, 5 mg/kg also increased the bite frequency; however, this measure was reduced at the 10 and 20 mg/kg doses. The results of this study show many parallels to another study (Miczek & O'Donnell, 1980) that characterized the effect of acute CDP exposure on intermale aggression in animals which had experienced different housing conditions following weaning. Squirrel monkeys treated with acute CDP exposure displayed dose-dependent effects on aggressive behavior similar to those previously observed in mice (Weerts & Miczek, 1996). In these studies, a dominant, resident male was removed from his social group and administered one dose of CDP ranging from 0.3 to 10.0 mg/kg. Monkeys were returned to their colony room and put into a cage, while a nondrugged dominant male (intruder) from another social group was placed into an identical cage immediately adjacent to the experimental animal's cage, thereby preventing physical contact. The frequency of aggressive displays was increased by acute CDP administration at 0.3 and 3.0 mg/kg compared to controls, yet these displays were significantly reduced at higher doses (i.e., 10 mg/kg) of CDP.

Many studies have also examined the effects of acute CDP exposure in mice and hamsters using the neutral arena test for aggression. Adult, male OF-1 mice were treated with various doses of CDP (0.3, 1.0, and 3.0 mg/kg; 60 min prior to testing) (Zwirner et al., 1975); CDP increased aggressive behavior (as measured by the number of attacks during the test) without altering motor behavior. Similarly, using adult Swiss–Webster mice, 5 mg/kg of CDP produced a trend toward increasing attack and sideways threat behavior when animals were tested versus a standard opponent in a neutral arena, whereas at higher doses (20 mg/kg), CDP decreased attacks and threats (Miczek & O'Donnell, 1980). In a later study of adult mice that were selectively bred for either high or low aggression, the effects of CDP on aggression and the activity of the GABAergic neural system were examined (Weerts et al., 1993).

Adult, male ICR mice selected from two lines that had been bred for low and high aggression, as well as unselected control mice, were singly housed and administered an acute dose of CDP (1, 3, 10, 17, and 30 mg/kg) 25 min prior to aggression testing in a novel cage. CDP was found to dose dependently decrease sideways threats and attacks in mice that had been selected for high aggression, with an effective aggression-suppressing dose of 17 mg/kg. In contrast, the unselected control mice showed a trend toward increasing the frequency and duration of sideways threats and pursuits at 3 mg/kg of CDP, while showing a reduction of these behaviors at 30 mg/kg. Interestingly, brains of high and low aggressive mice showed large differences in GABAergic specific uptake of [³H]Ro-15-1788, indicative of variations in BZ receptor binding. In the high aggressive line, decreases in BZ receptor binding were observed in various brain regions, including the hippocampus, hypothalamus, and cortex, when compared to the low aggressive line. In contrast, the low aggressive line showed a significant increase in BZ binding in the hypothalamus and cortex when compared to unselected controls (figure 16.9).

The three lines also differed significantly with regard to Cl⁻ uptake in cortical synaptoneurosomes

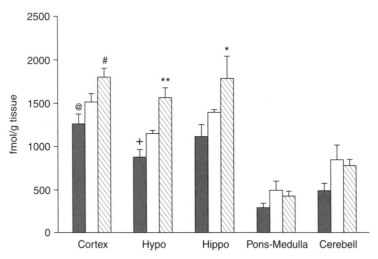

FIGURE 16.9 Benzodiazepine binding in vivo in high ($n = 9$) and low aggressive ($n = 9$) lines compared to the unselected line ($n = 5$). Binding was determined by specific uptake of [³H]Ro15-1788 as fmol/g of tissue in five brain regions. Results are means ± SEM. #$p < .05$ compared to the high aggressive line and $p < .10$ compared to the unselected line. +$p < .05$ compared to the low line and $p < .10$ compared to the unselected line. *$p < .05$ when compared to the high aggressive line. **$p < .05$ compared to the low aggressive line and unselected lines. @$p < .05$ compared to the low aggressive line and $p < .15$ compared to the unselected line. High (black bars); unselected (white bars); low (striped bars). From "Increased GABAA-Dependent Chloride Uptake in Mice Selectively Bred for Low Aggressive Behavior," by E. M. Weerts, L. G. Miller, K. E. Hood, and K. A. Miczek, 1992, *Psychopharmacology* (Berl.), 108(1–2), pp. 196–204. Copyright 1992 by Springer-Verlag. Reprinted with permission.

treated with muscimol, indicative of differences in GABA$_A$ receptor function in these mice. At 50 μM muscimol, the low aggressive line showed a 41% increase in GABA-dependent chloride uptake when compared to unselected controls, whereas the high aggressive line showed a 66% reduction in Cl⁻ uptake. Together, these results indicate that trait differences in aggressive responding may be the result of altered GABA activity and function through BZ-sensitive GABA receptors. Using a similar behavioral selection design, Sulcova and Krisiak (1989) examined the effect of a wider range of doses of CDP (5.0–90 mg/kg) on isolation-induced aggression in adult male albino mice in a neutral arena. Following testing, mice were separated into two groups, aggressive and timid (nonaggressive) isolates and were analyzed separately. This study found that in timid mice, CDP reduced defensive behaviors and escapes while increasing social sniffing. However, in aggressive mice, 30 mg/kg of CDP was the lowest dose that significantly decreased attacks, but this dose also decreased locomotion; thus the aggression-reducing effects of CDP in aggressive mice may be nonspecific. Poole (1973) examined the effects of CDP on the social and aggressive behavior of socially experienced adult, male Syrian hamsters. For this study, aggressive behavior was established between two hamsters through repeated interactions in a neutral cage. CDP was administered to one hamster at a dose of 50 mg/kg. Behavior data were analyzed after hamsters were classified as "losers," "winners," or "intermediates" following the repeated interactions. In all "winning" animals, CDP increased social investigation and decreased aggression (i.e., attack and chase).

Although the aforementioned experiments examined the effects of acute exposure to CDP on aggression, other studies have examined the effects of chronic CDP administration on aggression. In one study, a diet supplemented with low-dose CDP (0.3 mg/g of chow) was administered to singly housed, adult wild strain brown house mice for 6 days (Fox, Tuckosh, & Wilcox, 1970). After 6 days of treatment, mice were placed in a novel cage with three other mice that had undergone the same experimental treatment, and they each were scored for aggressive behavior 40 min later. Males that received the CDP-supplemented diet fought more during the 40-min observation period, as indicated by an increase in the mortality rate compared to the control group that received a normal nonsupplemented rodent diet. In a second experiment, mice underwent a similar treatment regimen as above; however, after the 6 days of treatment, mice were group housed and maintained on their respective diets (0.3 mg/g of food or control) for 8 weeks. CDP significantly increased the mortality rate of mice when compared to the control group during the 8-week treatment period. Similarly, Cutler, Rodgers, and Jackson (1997) administered CDP (1.0, 4.0, or 8.0 mg/kg) once per day for 21 days to adult, male CD-1 mice. On Day 21 of treatment, mice received CDP 30 min prior to testing for aggression in a neutral cage with an untreated group-housed unfamiliar DBA/2 mouse. At the medium dose (4.0 mg/kg), aggressive behaviors (i.e., attacks/bites, chases, and upright offensive postures) were significantly increased in frequency and duration in CDP-treated mice compared to controls.

The effects of CDP have also been examined on maternal aggression in rats and mice (Olivier, Mos, & van Oorschot, 1985; 1986). Several doses of CDP (5, 10, or 20 mg/kg) were given to rat dams 60 min prior to aggression testing. Parturient females were tested for aggression in a neutral cage against a naive male intruder on postpartum days 3, 5, 7, and 9. In both studies, 5 mg/kg of CDP increased aggression, including increases in on top posture, biting (head and body) and upright posture, and total time of aggression when compared to controls. At 10 mg/kg, CDP also increased aggression, as indicated by on top posture and total time of aggression compared to control. Interestingly, in one study (Olivier et al., 1989), 20 mg/kg of CDP also increased the total amount of time the dams spent in aggressive acts when compared to controls, while in the other study the behavior of animals treated with 20 mg/kg of CDP aggression was not statistically significantly different from controls. The source of this discrepancy is unknown, as all conditions appear to be similar, if not identical, between the two studies. The effects of CDP on maternal aggression was examined in a later study, taking into account the size of the male intruder (Mos, Olivier, & van Oorschot, 1987). Aggression tests were performed in an observation cage on postpartum days 4, 6, 8, and 10 against either a heavy or a light intruder male. CDP treatment increased aggression frequency and duration when the male opponent was heavier. CDP treatment did not increase the frequency of bite attacks and other aggressive components if the opponent was a light-weight male, although the duration of total time spent displaying aggressive behaviors was significantly increased under these conditions. This study shows that CDP treatment increases maternal aggression; however, these effects may be context dependent, (i.e., influenced by the nature of the threatening stimulus). Various studies of the effects of CDP on maternal aggression have also been conducted in mice. The effects of both acute and chronic CDP exposure on aggressive behavior have been studied in mouse dams (Yoshimura & Ogawa, 1989). In the acute treatment studies, parturient mice (i.e., postpartum days 5 and 7) were presented with an intruder male in the home cage 30 min after they had been injected with one of several doses of CDP (5, 10, or 15 mg/kg). Data from this study showed that treatment with 10 mg/kg of CDP could significantly increase the frequency of bites toward intruders compared to predrug levels, while 15 mg/kg significantly decreased the frequency of bites. In chronic treatment studies, CDP treatment started immediately following the removal of the male partner and terminated on postpartum days 3 (treatment varied from 20 to 22 days). Although acute treatment with CDP affected the aggressive response of these mouse dams, chronic treatment with 5 or 10 mg/kg of CDP did not alter the frequency of bites when compared to vehicle controls. Finally, Palanza, Rodgers, Ferrari, and Parmigiani (1996) investigated the effects of CDP on offensive aggression in lactating Swiss albino mice, taking into account the aggressive characteristics and prior experience of the animals. Lactating female mice were prescreened for aggression while being confronted in their home cage with either a male or a female intruder. This test allowed mice to be characterized as aggressive if they attacked and delivered at least one bite to the opponent. Following testing, aggressive dams were kept in their home cage for 24 hr prior to being put into the testing apparatus, which consisted of an open field and two chambers into which the experimental female and intruder were placed. On the test day, both prescreened and nonscreened dams were allocated to four treatment conditions: (a) saline, (b) 2.5 mg/kg of CDP, (c) 5.0 mg/kg of CDP, or (d) 10.0 mg/kg of CDP, with injections given 20 min prior to behavioral testing. Nonscreened females were further divided to receive either a sexually naive male or female intruder and prescreened females confronted the same sex intruder they encountered during prescreening. CDP had no effect on the aggression displayed by screened dams; however, in nonscreened dams, 10.0 mg/kg of CDP significantly reduced the proportion of male intruders that were attacked and increased attack latencies. Interestingly, in screened dams, CDP dose dependently increased accumulated attack time toward male intruders, with a peak effective dose of 10 mg/kg, but against female intruders, this

same dose reduced total attacking time. Similarly, in screened dams, 10 mg/kg of CDP reduced biting against female intruders, while this dose increased the bite frequencies toward male intruders.

Quenzer and Feldman (1975) examined the effects of chronic CDP administration on muricide in rats. In the first of two experiments, a mouse was placed into the home cage of an adult male, Sprague–Dawley rat and the latency to kill was recorded. After three no-drug (saline) trials, each rat received CDP (25, 50, or 75 mg/kg) 30 min prior to each of eight successive, daily muricide tests. In this study, all doses suppressed muricide, with no effect of drug on muricide latency. In a second experiment, rats were given a saline injection on Days 1–3, followed by a muricide test 30 min later. On Days 4–10 of testing, rats were given an injection of CDP or saline, with no muricide tests being conducted on these days. On Day 11, each rat was given the usual dose of CDP and subjected to a muricide test 30 min later and the rats which received saline on Days 4–10 now received 50 mg/kg of CDP. All rats killed the mice during the first of three saline tests and all CDP-treated rats killed mice during the test on Day 11. Among the saline-treated rats who received CDP on Day 11, four failed to kill the mice; however, two killed after 70 and 90 s. There was a significant increase in kill latency for the 25 and 75 mg/kg groups, but no increase for the 50 mg/kg group on Day 11, when compared to the behavior on the third no-drug test day. Leaf, Wnek, and Lamon (1984) examined the effect of acute CDP on muricide in adult, Holtzman strain albino male rats. Rats received 7.5 mg/kg of CDP prior to a mouse being placed into their home cage and this study showed that CDP induced significant killing at this 7.5 mg/kg dose. Therefore, both chronic and acute exposure to CDP can increase mouse killing behavior; however, it appears as though, when given acutely, CDP affects mouse killing behavior differently at high and low doses.

Finally, the effects of CDP on shock-induced aggression in mice have been examined (Kostowski, 1966). Mice were administered CDP prior to being subjected to foot shocks with a voltage that was 10 V less than the pain threshold for the animal. A dose of 1 mg/kg of CDP abolished shock-induced aggression in these mice. Similarly, Irwin, Kinoi, Van Sloten, and Workman (1971) evoked 20-ms-long foot shocks with four to five pulses per second at a maximum voltage of 1,500 V to adult, female Swiss–Webster mice 60 min after they were treated with CDP and confronted with a conspecific; 5 mg/kg of CDP decreased fighting in these animals without inducing a change in locomotion.

Alprazolam

Although few studies exist, the majority of studies examining the effects of alprazolam on aggression have been conducted using neutral arena tests (i.e., intermale aggression paradigms), using both acute and chronic treatment regimens, and several examined the effects of alprazolam withdrawal on aggressive behavior. The effects of acute alprazolam exposure on aggression were studied in both timid and aggressive male albino mice (Sulcova & Krisiak, 1989). In this study, mice were tested for aggression in a neutral cage against a nonaggressive group-housed mouse following 3 weeks of isolation. Three to five interactions were repeated 1 week apart, with the experimental animals receiving alprazolam (0.05–2.5 mg/kg) 30 min prior to the interaction. In aggressive mice, acute alprazolam exposure significantly reduced attacks at doses that did not affect locomotor behaviors (1.25 mg/kg). Conversely, in a study using the neutral arena test for maternal aggression, Mos and Olivier (1989) found that acute exposure to alprazolam (i.e., 1.25 mg/kg) 30 min prior to confrontation with a male conspecific increased the total time rat dams spent displaying aggressive behaviors. This increase in aggression was suppressed by higher doses of alprazolam, with 2.5 mg/kg reducing on top posture, head bites, and lateral threats displayed by rat dams compared to controls. These same measures were further decreased with higher doses of alprazolam (i.e., 5 mg/kg); however, these effects were accompanied by muscle relaxation, therefore preventing adequate functioning in these animals.

In an attempt to delineate the neural mechanisms by which alprazolam decreases aggression, the effect of chronic treatment with alprazolam was examined on aggression induced by either clonidine or apomorphine (Kostowski, Valzelli, & Baiguerra, 1986). Adult, male Swiss albino mice were group housed while receiving 5 mg/kg/day of alprazolam for 21 days. Two hours following the last dose of alprazolam, mice were injected with clonidine (10 mg/kg) immediately before being placed in a cylinder with three other mice for a 30–min observation period. Chronic alprazolam completely abolished biting attacks and vocalizations in mice that had been made aggressive by clonidine treatment. In addition, in similar studies rats were treated as above with alprazolam; however, they were injected

with apomorphine (10 mg/kg) instead of clonidine prior to being tested for aggression. In contrast to the clonidine experiment in mice, chronic treatment with alprazolam had no effect on apomorphine-induced aggression. Together, these data point to an important relationship between the GABAergic and noradrenergic neural systems in the modulation of aggression. In another study examining the effects of chronic exposure to alprazolam and withdrawal from this drug on aggression, isolated male, albino mice were assessed for intermale aggression prior to being treated with 1 mg/kg/2×/day of alprazolam for 8 days and 24 and 72 hr following the last dose of alprazolam (the 9th and 11th days of the experiment; Krisiak, Podhorna, & Miczek, 1998). Mice treated with 2 mg/kg/day for 8 days showed less aggressive behavior than control animals, as reflected by the number of attacks and the latency to first attack. However, mice that were treated with alprazolam for 8 days and subsequently withdrew from the drug for 72 hr prior to being tested for aggression showed increased aggression when compared to the level of aggression they displayed during the prewithdrawal phase. Further characterizing the phenomenon of alprazolam withdrawal-induced aggression, Votava, Krsizk, Podhorna, and Miczek (2001) treated mice with 1 mg/kg/2×/day for 21 days and tested for intermale aggression as described above. Following a 72-hr withdrawal period from chronic alprazolam treatment, the total duration spent in aggressive acts significantly increased when compared to control mice. These data suggest an important, yet not well studied, phenomenon, that withdrawal from chronic treatment with alprazolam may lead to altered aggressive states

Diazepam

Contrary to the discrepant results obtained from studies examining the acute effects of CDP and alprazolam on aggression, the general consensus is that acute diazepam treatment effectively decreases aggressive responding in different testing paradigms and in various animal models. Research on the acute effects of diazepam on intermale aggression has shown that in both mice and marmosets, diazepam can reduce aggression toward a conspecific. Kudryavtseva and Bondar (2002) examined how acute treatment with a low dose of diazepam (0.5 mg/kg, 2.5 hr prior to testing) affected the aggressive response of adult male C57B1/B6 mice toward an untreated partner. In this experiment, mice had 3 or 20 days of aggressive experience consisting of wins during social interactions prior to the test day.

Results showed that in mice with 3 days of aggressive experience, diazepam decreased the total number of attacks and increased the latency to first attack when compared to control animals. In addition, diazepam decreased the total and mean durations of attacks and increased the latency to first attack in animals with 20 days prior aggressive experience, but did not affect the total number of attacks in these animals compared to controls. In line with these findings, two doses of diazepam (1 and 3.5 mg/kg, 30 min prior to testing) significantly decreased the frequency of aggressive behaviors in pair-housed marmosets during confrontations with unfamiliar conspecifics in a neutral arena when compared to control animals (Cilia & Piper, 1997). Although the neural mechanisms underlying the ability of diazepam to decrease aggression are unknown, the involvement of adenosine receptors has been examined in this phenomenon (Ushijima, Katsuragi, & Furukawa, 1984). In this study, aggressive behavior was stimulated in adult male albino mice via acute administration of clonidine. Diazepam (2.5 mg/kg) was administered 15 min prior to clonidine administration and mice were tested for aggression through confrontation with a conspecific in a neutral cage. Clonidine-induced aggression was significantly reduced by pretreatment with diazepam. The authors speculate that an inhibition of adenosine uptake may be an important factor in the antagonistic action of diazepam on clonidine-induced aggressive behavior in mice.

While there is agreement that acute diazepam treatment effectively decreases aggression across different testing paradigms and in various animal species and strains, in contrast, studies that have investigated the effects of chronic diazepam on aggressive behavior have produced divergent results. Fox and Snyder (1969) administered a low-dose diazepam-supplemented diet (0.1 mg diazepam/gram of food) to group-housed male, brown house mice for 6 days and recorded the mortality rates and the frequency of aggressive encounters among experimental animals. In this study, diazepam-fed mice displayed higher rates of mortality, and aggressive encounters were more frequent in males in this group when compared to control mice. A study similar to that of Ushijima and colleagues (1984) was conducted in which the effects of chronic diazepam treatment on clonidine-induced aggression were examined using adult, male albino Swiss mice (Kostowski et al., 1986). In this study, mice were administered 5 mg/kg/day of diazepam for 21 days. Two hours after the last dose of diazepam and immediately prior to being tested

for aggression by confrontation with a familiar mouse, mice were injected with 10 mg/kg of clonidine to induce an aggressive response. In accord with results observed by Ushijima et al. (1984), treatment with diazepam effectively prevented clonidine-induced increases in biting attacks. An effect of chronic diazepam treatment on aggression is difficult to generalize based on these two studies due to the mechanisms by which each produced aggressive behavior in their subjects. Although both acute (Ushijima et al., 1984), and chronic (Kostowski et al., 1986) treatments with diazepam have been shown to decrease clonidine-induced aggression, this type of aggression may be due to the activation of different neural mechanisms and pathways than aggression resulting from other epigenetic factors (e.g., social experience), perhaps explaining why chronic administration with diazepam increases intermale aggression in one study but not another.

Additional studies in mice and rats have examined the effects of diazepam on isolation-induced aggression and have produced results similar to those observed in intermale aggression paradigms. Specifically, Malick (1978) examined acute and subchronic effects of diazepam (10 mg/kg) on isolation-induced aggression in adult, male mice. Mice were tested for aggression by confrontation with a conspecific in the home cage of the isolate 30 min following diazepam administration on each of the 5 days the animals received the drug. After the first dose of diazepam, fighting between the pairs was inhibited in 60% of the mice; however, this effect was accompanied by ataxia in 52.5% of subjects. The ataxic effect of diazepam was eliminated by the fifth day of drug treatment, whereas the antiaggressive effect of diazepam did not show tolerance. Simply, diazepam inhibited aggression on all 5 days of treatment without affecting motor behavior. Skolnick, Reed, and Paul (1985) administered a lower, acute dose of diazepam (4 mg/kg, 30 min prior to testing) to isolated, adult male mice and tested for aggression against a conspecific in a neutral arena. In this study, diazepam significantly reduced the number of attacks, with no obvious impairments in motor behavior. Wongwitdecha and Marsden (1996) examined the effects of even lower doses of diazepam (1 and 2.5 mg/kg, 30 min prior to testing) on isolation-induced aggression in adult, male Lister hooded rats. Isolated rats were confronted with an unfamiliar rat in a novel testing apparatus. As with previous reports, pretreatment with diazepam dose dependently reduced aggressive behavior in isolated rats, as indicated by the frequency of biting and boxing the partner. Unlike that seen with clonidine-induced aggression, both acute and chronic administration of diazepam decreased both intermale and isolation-induced forms of aggressive behavior in various species.

In maternal aggression paradigms, diazepam administration has been shown to both increase and decrease aggressive responding regardless of the testing paradigm used or animal species chosen. Mos and Olivier (1989) administered various doses of diazepam (1.25, 2.5, or 5 mg/kg, 60 min prior to testing) to parturient rat dams on postpartum days 3, 5, 7, and 9 and tested them for aggression when confronted with a naive male conspecific in a novel observation cage in the absence of rat pups. Compared to controls, total aggression time and on top posture were increased in dams that received 1.25 mg/kg of diazepam, whereas only on top posture was increased at a higher dose of diazepam (i.e., 2.5 mg/kg), while the highest dose produced no effects on aggressive behavioral. The acute effects of similar doses of diazepam were also examined on maternal aggression using ICR albino mice dams (Yoshimura & Ogawa, 1991). Aggression testing was conducted in the home cage of the lactating female with pups present by placing a naive male intruder in the cage 30 min following diazepam administration (0.5, 1, or 2.5 mg/kg) on postpartum days 5 and 7. In this study, 1 mg/kg of diazepam significantly increased bite frequency when compared to control animals. A higher dose of diazepam (2.5 mg/kg) significantly decreased this same measure of behavior, in addition to decreasing tail rattles. However, this decrease was observed in the context of decreased motor activity and therefore may not be specific to aggression. In contrast to these studies, maternal aggression in Wistar rats (i.e., the total number of attacks, lateral postures, and bites) was significantly decreased after acute treatment with both 1 and 2 mg/kg of diazepam (administered 20 min prior to testing) compared to control animals using a similar resident-intruder model with pups present during testing (Ferreira, Picazo, Uriarte, Pereira, & Fernandez-Guasti, 2000). Since all three studies administered similar doses of diazepam, the divergent results reported here may not be due to a dosing phenomenon, but may be attributed to either the species/strain of animals used and/or the presence or absence of pups during the aggression test.

In the only study of its kind, Grimm, McAllister, Brain, and Benton (1984) examined the effects of perinatal exposure to diazepam on the aggressive behavior of peripubescent male mice. In this study, pregnant mouse dams were injected daily with 2.5 mg/kg of diazepam or vehicle (for 1–6 days depending upon the day of parturition), in addition to receiving daily injections after giving birth. Mice were weaned 22 days after birth and housed in individual cages. Fourteen days after individual housing, male mice were confronted with an unfamiliar, group-housed intruder in their home cages and scored for aggression. Male mice that received both pre- and postnatal exposure to diazepam showed an increase in the frequency of sideways offensive posture when compared to control mice; however, there was no influence of this exposure on more overt measures of offensive aggression.

As with other measures of aggression, the influence of diazepam on mouse killing behavior has produced disparate results. Various doses of diazepam (0.5, 1, 2, or 4 mg/kg) had no effect on mouse killing in adult male and female cats (Leaf et al., 1978). In this study, cats continued to kill mice despite diazepam pretreatment; however, Pellis et al. (1988) found that acute diazepam (4 mg/kg, 30 min prior to testing) exposure increased attack patterns compared to controls in cats with various temperaments. Specifically, in cats which did not kill mice in pretest situations, pretreatment with diazepam induced attacking behavior in these animals toward a live mouse in its cage. In addition, in cats that had tentatively interacted with mice but did not kill, a stronger form of attack was induced by diazepam treatment, resulting in the mouse being killed. Also, in a group of cats that had previously killed mice after an initial period of nonaggressiveness, acute exposure to diazepam decreased the latency for the kill to occur. Results of these studies indicate that this particular dose of diazepam can induce and intensify muricide in cats. However, in mouse killing experiments in rats, acute administration (10 mg/kg) of diazepam inhibited muricide in olfactory bulbectomized, male Wistar rats (Shibata, Nakanishi, Watanabe, & Ueki, 1984). In addition, an examination of the effects of chronic diazepam administration (10 mg/kg/day, 21 days) on mouse killing revealed that the inhibition of muricide observed 1 hr after treatment was reduced by chronic treatment. In other words, chronic treatment with diazepam increased mouse killing behavior back to levels observed prior to drug administration. Behavioral testing was again conducted on Days 7 and 14 following the cessation of the chronic treatment regimen. On Days 7 and 14, there were no lingering effects of chronic diazepam exposure, as muricide in the experimental animals was 100% of that seen in controls.

Opioids

Morphine

In adult models, several studies have examined the effects of morphine withdrawal on territorial aggression using the resident-intruder paradigm. A time-dependent increase in offensive aggression following withdrawal from acute morphine (75 mg) exposure was reported in adult, male CFW mice (Tidey & Miczek, 1992a). Males housed in pairs with female counterparts for 3–4 weeks were scored for baseline aggression toward a male conspecific. Once baseline aggression was established, males received drug treatment. In addition to testing the hypothesis that morphine withdrawal increased offensive aggression, these studies examined the dopaminergic modulation of this aggressive state. In these studies, at 5, 48, or 96 hr after morphine treatment mice received either saline or D-amphetamine (0.3, 1, 3, or 10 mg/kg), followed by aggression tests 30 min later. In mice undergoing morphine withdrawal alone a time-dependent increase in aggressive (i.e., attack and threat) and motor (i.e., walking, rearing, and grooming) behavior was observed, which remained stable over time. However, treatment with d-amphetamine after 5 or 48 hr of withdrawal showed a dose-dependent decrease in aggressive behavior induced by morphine withdrawal, suggesting an inhibitory role for dopaminergic systems in this behavioral response. Accordingly, in a subsequent study Tidey and Miczek (1992b) explored the hypothesis that increases in dopaminergic activity inhibit offensive aggression induced by morphine withdrawal. In these studies, adult, male CFW mice were exposed to morphine (75 mg) or placebo for 72 hr and then treated with the DA D1 receptor agonist SKF 38393 (3, 10, 56, or 100 mg/kg), the DA D2 receptor agonist quinpirole (0.2, 0.3, 0 6, or 1.0 mg/kg), a combination of 1–2–D1 and D2 receptor agonists (3 mg/kg and between 0.1 and 3.0 mg/kg, respectively), or saline 4 hr after morphine treatment. During morphine withdrawal, D1 and D2 agonists dose dependently decreased morphine withdrawal-induced aggressive behavior. Specifically, compared to results with saline-treated placebo controls, D1 agonist SKF 38393 dose dependently reduced the frequency of threats, attacks, and bites, while having no effect on locomotor activity (i.e., frequency and duration of walking) (figure 16.10).

In contrast, while treatment with the D2 agonist quinpirole also decreased morphine withdrawal-induced aggression (i.e., the frequency of attack bites

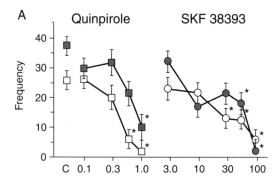

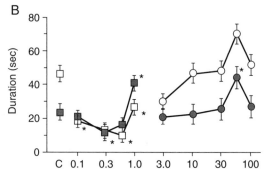

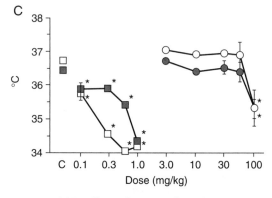

FIGURE 16.10 Effects of quinpirole and SKF 38393 on attack biting (A), walking (B), and core temperature (C) in morphine-withdrawn (solid symbols) and placebo (open symbols) mice. Error bars denote *SEM*, and asterisks denote $p < .05$ compared to saline control values. From "Morphine Withdrawal Aggression: Modification With D1 and D2 Receptor Agonists," by J. W. Tidey and K. A. Miczek, 1992, *Psychopharmacology*, *108*(1–2). Copyright 1992 by Springer-Verlag. Reprinted with permission.

and sideways threat) in a dose-dependent manner, this behavioral response was associated with an increase in locomotor activity and body temperature. Furthermore, the combination of D1 and D2 agonists produced results similar to those of D2 alone, by decreasing both aggressive and motor behavior. These studies indicated that only D1 receptor activation was specific in reducing aggression induced by morphine withdrawal, implicating a role for this receptor in morphine withdrawal-induced aggressive behavior.

Several other studies have also examined the effects of withdrawal following subchronic and chronic exposure to morphine on offensive aggression. Isolated, aggressive Swiss male mice chronically treated with morphine (beginning at 10 mg/kg/day and increasing at 10 mg/kg/day up to a terminal dose of 80 mg/kg on the eighth day) adjusted aggressive behavior in a time-dependent manner (Sukhotina, 2001). After 24 hr of withdrawal, no differences in aggression were observed. However, at this time significant increases in social nonaggressive behavior (i.e., sniffing and grooming) were observed in morphine-treated mice compared to saline-treated controls. In contrast, after 48 hr of morphine withdrawal mice displayed increased levels of aggression (i.e., duration of attack and threats), while no differences in social nonaggressive behaviors were observed. After 72 hr of withdrawal, the increased aggression observed in morphine-withdrawing mice dissipated to levels observed in saline controls. In an additional experiment, using the same strain of mouse, Sukhotina (2001) demonstrated that after 48 hr of morphine withdrawal from the same chronic treatment regimen as described, a subcutaneous injection of saline effectively reduced aggressive behavior (i.e., duration of attacks and threats) compared to an intraperineal injection of saline, suggesting the effects of morphine withdrawal to be context dependent and modulated by stressful stimuli.

In another study conducted by Sukhotina and Bespalov (2000), adult male SHR mice withdrawing from chronic morphine exposure showed increased offensive aggression that could be reduced by glutamate N-methyl-D-aspartate (NMDA) receptor antagonists. In these studies, group-housed male mice were isolated for 8 days, followed by the first resident-intruder test. Isolation continued for an additional 4 weeks, with intermittent aggression testing (i.e., two times per week) during the last 2 weeks. Isolated aggressive mice received morphine for 8 days, beginning at a dose of 10 mg/kg and increasing in increments of 10 mg/kg/day to a

terminal dose of 80 mg/kg. Aggression testing took place at 24, 48, or 72 hr after the cessation of morphine treatment. Additional groups of morphine-treated mice were administered the selective NMDA receptor antagonists memantine (1-amino-3, 5-dimethyladamanta; 1, 3, 10, or 30 mg/kg), MRZ 2/579 (1-amino-1, 3, 3, 5, 5-pentamethyl-cyclohexan; 1, 3.2, 5.6, or 10 mg/kg), or vehicle after 48 hr of morphine withdrawal and tested for aggression. As previously observed after 24 and 72 hr of morphine withdrawal, mice displayed no significant differences in aggression between treatment groups. After 48 hr of morphine withdrawal, however, isolated mice displayed escalated levels of offensive aggression (i.e., mean duration of attack, latency to bite, threats, and tail rattling) compared to saline-treated mice. The increase in aggressive behavior after 48 hr of morphine withdrawal was blocked by pretreatment (prior to aggression testing) with memantine and MRZ 2/579 in a dose-dependent manner. In comparison to saline-treated mice, memantine- and MRZ 2/579-treated mice showed no significant differences in aggressive or nonaggressive social behaviors. However, in comparison to baseline aggression, memantine and MRZ 2/579 treatment significantly reduced aggression (i.e., duration of attacks, bites, threats, and tail rattlings), with effective low doses of 3 and 5.6 mg/kg of memantine and MRZ 2/579, respectively. As opposed to the inhibitory role of DA in morphine withdrawal-induced aggressive behavior, this study provides evidence that glutaminergic systems facilitate morphine withdrawal-induced offensive aggression.

The studies presented above show that offensive aggression is affected by withdrawal from morphine after acute and chronic exposure, during which withdrawal was induced by the spontaneous removal of treatment. In an early study, the effects of morphine withdrawal on aggression resulting from chronic morphine treatment were dependent on the method of withdrawal (Kantak & Miczek, 1986). In these studies, male CFW mice received subcutaneous implants of morphine (75 mg) for 5 days, and the behavioral effects of withdrawal were examined by cessation of treatment (spontaneous removal via pellet withdrawal) or treatment with 1 mg/kg of naloxone. Aggression tests performed 48 hr after spontaneous removal showed an increase in offensive aggression (i.e., sideways threat postures and biting attacks) compared controls, whereas a decrease in offensive aggression (tail rattle, sideway threat postures, bite, attack, and chase) was observed in morphine-treated mice after only 15 min of naloxone-induced withdrawal. However, morphine pellet removal did not affect offensive aggression (i.e., sideway threat postures and bite attacks) in experienced fighters.

Studies that examined the effects of morphine withdrawal on intermale aggression assessed in a neutral arena have found conflicting results that may be attributed to the type of species used. Using isolated "timid" male albino Swiss–Webster mice, acute exposure to morphine (0.5, 1.0, 2.5, or 5 mg/kg) 15 min prior to testing resulted in a significant increase in the frequency of offensive ambivalent aggression (i.e., offensive sideways and upright postures) at 1.0, 2.5, and 5.0 mg/kg and an increase in the frequency of defensive ambivalent aggression (i.e., defensive sideways and upright postures) at 2.5 and 5.0 mg/kg compared to isolated, saline-treated control mice (D'Amato & Castellano, 1989). Further analysis of the effects of housing revealed no difference in aggression (i.e., offensive ambivalent, defensive ambivalent, and crouch posture) between isolated and group-housed mice treated with morphine (2.5 mg/kg), whereas in saline-treated mice, housing condition produced a prominent effect on aggression (i.e., an increase in defensive ambivalent and crouch posture and a decrease in offensive ambivalent behavior). Thus, morphine treatment of isolated "timid" mice suppresses the behavioral effects induced by isolated housing conditions, (i.e., by reducing timidity and increasing aggression in this strain of mice). In contrast, acute administration of morphine reduced intermale aggression in cats, and this reduction was mediated by cholinergic mechanisms (Krstic, Stefanovic-Denic, & Beleslin, 1982). In these studies, adult male cats received icv injections of carbachol (i.e., a cholinergic agonist, 5 and 30 μg) followed by morphine (0.2 or 1.0 mg/kg), methadone (0.2 or 1.0 mg/kg), or pethidine (i.e., also known as the prescribed opioid Demerol; 0.2 or 2.0 mg/kg) treatment just prior to aggression testing in a neutral arena. A separate group of cats received drug treatment in the reversed order, (i.e., morphine, methadone, or pethidine followed by carbachol at the same doses as above). Aggressive behavior (duration of fighting) was significantly increased at the higher dose of carbachol (30 μg), but was also associated with an increase in motor activity, as well as several autonomic behaviors, such as salivation, tremor, and rigidity. Morphine, methadone, and pethidine treatment following carbachol treatment had no effect on aggressive behavior, whereas administration of analgesics prior to carbachol treatment effectively reduced the duration of fighting behavior. However, because this study assessed the immediate effects of morphine treatment on aggressive behavior, whether morphine withdrawal can further potentiate carbachol-induced aggression remains unknown.

Chronic exposure to morphine (2.5 mg/kg/day for 14 days) increased intermale aggression (i.e., threats and attacks) after 48 hr of withdrawal or 10 min after withdrawal induced by acute naloxone (1 mg/kg) treatment in isolated male albino OF-1 mice (Rodriguez-Arias, Pinazo, Minarro, & Stinus, 1999). Administration of DA D1– (SCH 23390, 0.5 mg/kg), D2- (raclopride, 0.3 mg/kg), or the nonselective D1 and D2 (haloperidol, 0.1 mg/kg) receptor antagonists 30 min prior to aggression testing after 48 hr of withdrawal, or 10 min after or 20 min before naloxone treatment, effectively suppressed aggressive behavior (i.e., increased latency to attack and decreased threat and attack) induced by morphine withdrawal, suggesting a facilitory role for dopaminergic activity in morphine withdrawal-induced intermale aggression. Using isolated Sprague–Dawley rats, a time stable dose-dependent increase in aggression (i.e., number of fighting episodes) was observed over 6 days of withdrawal from chronic morphine (5 mg/kg increasing at 5 mg/kg every 6 hr until terminal doses reached 100, 200, or 400 mg/kg/day maintained for 3 days) compared to handled and sterile water-treated controls (Thor & Teel, 1968). The reported increase in morphine withdrawal-induced aggression appeared 60–70 min following drug exposure and continued until 50 hr post-treatment.

In contrast to the above studies, Haney and Miczek (1989) found that acute exposure to low doses of morphine (1, 3, 6, 10, or 30 mg/kg by subcutaneous injections) reduced maternal aggression in female CFW mice during the 3-week lactation period. Aggression tests administered 30 min after morphine treatment revealed that in the first week of lactation morphine treatment (10 mg/kg) reduced only one index of aggressive behavior, (i.e., pursuit frequency). However, there was a dose-dependent trend toward a decrease in several other indices of aggressive behavior (i.e., attack frequency, attack latency, and sideways threat postures).

The effect of morphine on aggressive behavior has also been observed using social aggression paradigms. Acute morphine (1, 10, 20, or 30 mg/kg) or morphine (20 mg/kg) plus naloxone (2 mg/kg) increased aggressive behavior (i.e., number of fighting, wounding, and killed conspecifics) 18 hr following drug treatment in group-housed naked mole rats (Kanui & Hole, 1990). After 18 hr, all animals that received 10 and 30 mg/kg of morphine had been mortally wounded due to their participation in highly aggressive encounters. In contrast, naked mole rats treated with morphine plus naloxone showed no aggressive behavior nor attrition in numbers. Extending these results, Towett and Kanui (1993), using the same experimental design, observed the same effects on aggressive behavior following treatment with the prescribed opioid Demerol (20 or 30 mg/kg).

In isolated 70-day-old male Long–Evans hooded rats, chronic morphine (13.3 mg/kg increasing three times per day at increments of 133 mg/kg/injection to a terminal dose of 400 mg/kg and maintained for 5 days) treatment during a 30–min socialization period decreased aggressive behavior (i.e., attacks, vocalizations, and rearing time) in a neutral cage compared to isolated and group-housed mice treated with morphine but not allowed to socialize (Miksic, Smith, & Lal, 1976). After 72 hr of withdrawal, isolated and group-housed mice that were not allowed to socialize during treatment showed a significant increase in the number of attacks, duration of vocalization, and rearing compared to rats that received injections during a 30-min socialization period. This study further supports a role for the context-dependent effects on aggressive behavior following morphine withdrawal.

Using male Long–Evans hooded rats in another paradigm assessing social aggression, Gellert and Sparber (1979) found that treatment with high doses of morphine reversed established food competition hierarchies. Food-deprived isolated rats were trained to press a lever to obtain a food pellet at a fixed ratio of 1:20. Once training was complete, rats were paired until a stable hierarchy was observed. Dominant rats were characterized as those that won 20 of 21 bouts of observed fighting behavior. Subsequently, both rats in a pair received chronic exposure to increasing doses morphine (two injections of each dose of 25, 50, and 100 mg/kg every 12 hr) over a course of 9 days. Food competition tests were alternated between each dose, that is, food retrieval was assessed at each dose in a paired and an unpaired situation. Morphine treatment at 25 and 50 mg/kg impaired food retrieval in singly tested rats. In paired rats, morphine treatment (100 mg/kg) resulted in decreased food pellet retrieval in dominant rats and increased retrieval of food pellets in submissive rats for up to 6 days of withdrawal. Furthermore, the reversal of food hierarchy during morphine withdrawal was associated with an increase in the duration of fighting. However, after 14 days of morphine withdrawal, escalated aggressive behavior was no longer observed, although submissive rats obtained equivalent food retrieval pellets compared to dominant rats.

Hallucinogens

Phencyclidine (PCP)

PCP is a hallucinogen with profound effects on the CNS, including psychostimulation, analgesia, anesthesia, depression, and hallucinations. In one of three reports on the effects of acute PCP exposure on isolation-induced aggression in adult mice, male albino Swiss–Webster mice were isolated for either 14 or 28 days and then tested for aggression 15 min following administration of saline, 1 mg/kg of PCP, or 5 mg/kg of PCP (Rewerski, Kostowski, Piechocki, & Rylski, 1971). For behavior testing, three mice were placed together in a neutral arena for 5 min and aggression was scored. After 14 days of isolation, the group which had received 1 mg/kg of PCP showed no fighting, whereas the group which received 5 mg/kg was significantly more aggressive, with a lower latency for the first aggressive response when compared to controls. After 28 days of isolation, there were no significant effects of PCP exposure on aggression, with the exception of a higher latency to aggressive response in the group that received 1 mg/kg of PCP compared to controls. Thus, these data revealed that PCP caused opposite effects at low and high doses; the high dose of PCP increased aggression, whereas the low dose eliminated aggressive behavior in isolated male Swiss–Webster mice. The effects of acute PCP administration on isolation-induced aggression were also examined in male ICR albino mice (Burkhalter & Balster, 1979). In this study, isolated residents were treated with either saline or 1 or 3 mg/kg of PCP and then tested for aggression 30 min later using a resident-intruder test. This study reported that 1 mg/kg of PCP was sufficient to increase attack bites in these animals, with no effects observed at the 3 mg/kg dose. Similarly, the effects of acute PCP administration on isolation-induced fighting have been examined in adult male CF-1 mice that had been individually housed for 5, 10, 19–21, or 32–35 days (Wilmot, Vanderwende, & Spoerlein, 1987). Twelve to fifteen minutes prior to a resident-intruder test, mice were either handled but not treated or treated with saline or one of two doses of PCP (1.25 or 2.5 mg/kg). As isolation time increased, aggression increased in control mice and in mice that had been treated with the low dose of

PCP (1.25 mg/kg). A significant decrease in the number of mice fighting was observed in the 2.5 mg/kg PCP group after 19–21 and 32–35 days of isolation. Interestingly, both doses of PCP significantly decreased the latency to the first fighting bout after 32–35 days of isolation, with no effect observed after other isolation times. Overall, this study found that PCP increased total fighting time and PCP-treated mice tended to continue fighting even after the intruder displayed a submissive posture. Contrary to these results, PCP significantly decreased aggression in group-housed adult male Swiss–Webster CFW mice administered 0.3, 1.0, 3.0, 6.0, or 10.0 mg/kg of PCP prior to the twice weekly aggression tests versus an intruder (Tyler & Miczek, 1982). Acute PCP administration significantly decreased attack frequencies at the highest dose tested (i.e., 10 mg/kg) without affecting locomotor activity. In an attempt to delineate the neural mechanisms behind the PCP-induced decrease in aggression in these mice, the authors administered either the DA D2 receptor antagonist haloperidol (1 mg/kg) or the 5-HT$_2$ receptor antagonist methysergide (3 mg/kg) in combination with either saline or PCP (10 mg/kg). Neither haloperidol nor methysergide blocked the suppressive effects of PCP on aggressive behavior, implicating a minimal role for DA and 5-HT neural signaling (at least through the DA D2 and 5-HT$_2$ receptors) in this phenomenon.

The effects of acute PCP administration on the display of muricide by adult male Wistar rats have been reported (Rewerski et al., 1971). In this study, following 3 weeks of isolation, rats were treated with saline or PCP (5 mg/kg) either 30 or 120 min prior to being exposed to mice for a 5-min test period. Acute PCP exposure decreased mouse killing behavior in rats, although not significantly compared to controls (attributed to small sample size, $n = 7$ rats in the PCP group). Thus, together with the above studies, the dose-dependent effects of PCP on isolation-induced aggressive behavior appear to be influenced by the species and/or strain used and the effects of this drug on behavior are greatly influenced by the type of aggression being examined (i.e., isolation-induced aggression, intermale aggression, and muricide).

In one of two reports on the effects of acute PCP exposure on shock-induced aggression, Cleary, Herakovic, and Poling (1981) used adult male rats to examine whether PCP administration affected shock-induced fighting versus conspecifics and the biting of inanimate targets placed in the home cage. For the fighting experiment, adult Sprague–Dawley rats were housed as

fighting pairs throughout the experiment. Rats were placed together in a darkened chamber for 5 min, followed by lights on and a 30-min shock session. Shocks were delivered for 0.5 s at 1.5 mA every 4 s. Thirty minutes prior to each session, rats received 0 (saline), 0.5, 1.0, or 2.0 mg/kg of PCP. PCP significantly reduced shock-induced fighting in a dose-dependent manner, with an effective dose of 1.0 mg/kg. Similarly, adult Wistar rats were used to examine the effects of PCP on tail shock-induced biting of inanimate objects placed in the home cage. In this study, rats received 13, 0.5-s 4-mA shocks to the tail every 2 min. Thirty minutes prior to testing, rats received 0 (saline), 0.25, 0.5, 1.0, or 2.0 mg/kg of PCP. PCP significantly reduced tail shock-induced biting in a dose-dependent manner, with an effective dose of 1.0 mg/kg. Altogether, the authors concluded that shock-elicited fighting bouts and tail shock-induced bites were significantly reduced by PCP; however, due to the analgesic effects of PCP, the effects on shock-induced aggression may not be specific and/or selective to this behavior alone. Indeed, contrary to these results are data from Emley and Hutchinson (1983) that explored the effects of PCP on shock-induced aggressive behavior in squirrel monkeys. In this experiment, adult monkeys were given 15 tail shocks at 200 ms, 400 V every 4 min, or no shock at all. All monkeys received saline injections 30 min prior to the experiment, while PCP was administered on one particular day of the week in mixed doses (0.01, 0.025, 0.05, 0.1, 0.2, 0.4, and 1.0 mg/kg). This dosing regimen was repeated until each monkey had received each dose once. The aggressive response was measured by the occurrence of preshock lever presses and postshock hose bites. In monkeys which had not received any shock, hose biting was rarely observed. Monkeys treated with increasing doses of PCP displayed increased numbers of postshock bites, with this effect decreasing with repeated exposure to the drug. In short, higher doses of PCP caused increased biting in squirrel monkeys but subsequent retesting did not show as much of an increase in this behavior. Also, although unshocked PCP-treated monkeys did not bite any more than unshocked, untreated monkeys, administration of a shock did cause more biting in PCP-treated monkeys than in untreated monkeys.

Lysergic Acid Diethylamide

Lysergic acid diethylamide (LSD) is another hallucinogen with the ability to significantly alter mood and induce hallucinations in the human user. The role of LSD in aggressive behavior has received little attention in the literature; however, earlier reports have examined this phenomenon in various adult models of aggressive behavior with divergent results. In one of the earliest studies, the effects of acute LSD exposure were examined on social interactions in adult mice, including the incidence of aggressive behaviors (Siegel & Poole, 1969). In this very narrative report, male CF-1 mice were housed in large colonies and used for three experiments investigating the effects of LSD on behavior in a variety of social settings. In a first experiment, mice were injected with an acute dose of LSD (ranging from 2 to 30 µg/kg) and placed into a colony of untreated strangers and scored for social behavior, including aggression. In a second experiment, entire colonies of mice were treated with LSD by putting the drug in the water supply, and in a third experiment, an untreated mouse was placed into a colony of mice in which all of the mice had been treated with LSD. In each of these latter experiments all individuals or selected individuals were scored for aggressive responding. In all of these experiments, regardless of social situation and which individual or group received the drug treatment, treatment with LSD produced significant decreases in aggression and group aggregation. In contrast, Sheard, Astrachan, and Davis (1977) examined the effects of acute LSD exposure on shock-induced fighting in adult rats. One rat of a pair was treated with water and the other with one of five doses of LSD (20, 40, 80, 160, or 640 µg/kg) immediately prior to an aggression test. Pairs were placed in the chamber 10 min post-treatment and received 40, 1-s-long shocks at each of four intensities (1, 1.5, 2, and 2.5 mA), with 15-s intervals, and fighting behavior was measured. Data from this study showed that at low doses (20–160 µg/kg), LSD significantly increased fighting behavior when compared to controls, although this effect was not seen at the highest dose (640 µg/kg). In a similar study using shock-induced aggression, one of three doses of LSD (25, 100, or 400 µg/kg) was administered to adult male rats 20 min prior to placing them into a test chamber (Sbordone, Wingard, Gorelick, & Elliott, 1979). Although this study found no effect of any dose of LSD on the severity or frequency of aggression, an increase in fight duration and biting was observed at the two higher doses (100 and 400 µg/kg) of LSD when compared to control animals which displayed no biting, although this increase was statistically nonsignificant.

Mescaline

As with other hallucinogenic drugs, very few studies have examined the effects of mescaline on aggressive behavior in animal models; however, the studies that have been conducted and are reviewed here have concluded that at certain doses, acute mescaline exposure can induce aggressive behavior in different species/ strains and in different testing paradigms. In a first study of shock-induced aggression, Sbordone and Carder (1974) assigned individually housed adult male, Sprague–Dawley rats to one of three experimental conditions in which each pair in the testing situation received an injection of water or 10 or 50 mg/kg of mescaline 20 min prior to aggression testing. For behavior testing, each pair of rats was placed on the grid floor of the experimental chamber and received electric shocks 1.5 s in duration every 30 s. The authors found that in control rats, a brief fighting episode was observed following the onset of the shock, but fighting was rarely observed during the intershock interval. Rats which had received 10 mg/kg of mescaline fought frequently during the intershock interval, although severe biting was never observed in this group. However, in rats that had received 50 mg/kg of mescaline, fighting behavior was more intense and appeared to be unrelated to the onset of shock compared to the two other treatment groups. Also, in general rats that had been pretreated with mescaline fought for longer periods of time when compared to controls. In a similar study, Sbordone, Wingard, Elliott, and Jervey (1978) examined whether aggression was a generalized and ubiquitous response to acute mescaline exposure by administering the drug to rats of different ages and different strains. Male Sprague– Dawley and Long–Evans rats at P-40–50, P-90–110, and P-180–200 were paired within strains tested for shock-induced aggression 20 min following an injection of 50 mg/kg of mescaline. Aggression was scored during a trial comprising of 100 shocks of 2.0 mA for 1.5 s duration every 30 s. High levels of aggressive behavior were observed in all animals following 50 mg/kg of mescaline treatment, regardless of age or strain, when compared to controls. Therefore, the authors concluded that the effects of mescaline on aggression are generalizable and appear to be independent of the strain of animal and/or the age of the animal at the time of exposure.

In another different model of aggression, how changing the properties of a target could change the aggressive response of a mescaline-treated rat was examined

(Carder & Sbordone, 1975). In this study, rats were confronted in the test cage with one of five targets following mescaline administration (15 or 50 mg/kg; 15 min prior to testing). The targets consisted of a normal target which had received no treatment prior to testing, a target which had its forepaws and hind paws taped together, a target which had been anesthetized with 40 mg of pentobarbital, a recently deceased rat, and finally and inanimate model of a rat. The test rat was exposed to each target for 15 foot shocks. Control rats and rats treated with 15 mg/kg were similarly more aggressive toward the target which was more like itself (i.e., the normal target which had received no treatment elicited the greatest aggressive response); however, treatment with 50 mg/kg of mescaline induced a great number of attacks toward the anesthetized rat. While the control rats displayed very few bites toward any target, 15 mg/kg of mescaline increased biting toward targets with taped paws and anesthetized targets, whereas 50 mg/kg induced severe biting toward both targets with taped paws and the recently deceased rat.

Summary and Conclusions

In summary, the effects of many commonly abused drugs, illegal and prescribed, on aggression are dependent upon the sex and species of the animal, the dosing and treatment regimen, and the behavioral testing paradigm. Although very few drugs, or drug classes, have been shown to consistently influence aggressive behavior regardless of the aforementioned factors (i.e., species, age, sex, dosing, testing paradigm), there are notable exceptions, including some AAS, nicotine, MDMA, and mescaline. Specifically, the administration of various types of AAS, with the notable exception of ST, has consistently increased aggression in various animal species of varying ages regardless of experimental paradigm, whereas nicotine, MDMA, and mescaline have been shown to consistently decrease aggressive responding. Although the abovementioned drugs of abuse appear to produce an invariable effect on aggression, the effect of exposure to most drugs on aggression, including cocaine, marijuana, alcohol, most hallucinogens, and prescribed benzodiazepines, seems more influenced by various experimental methods (i.e., dosing, species of animal used, age of animal used, and/or testing paradigm), naturally leading to divergent results and conclusions throughout the scientific literature.

From a neurobiological standpoint, studies in various animal species have provided considerable evidence that exposure to drugs of abuse during all stages of development (i.e., neonatal, pubertal, and adulthood) produce considerable changes in many key neural systems, and many forms of drug-induced aggression can be decreased using pharmacological agents which target these neurotransmitters in the brain. Specifically, there appears to be much evidence for the involvement of serotonin, GABA, dopamine, norepinephrine, and acetylcholine in control of drug-induced aggression, and exposure to drugs of abuse elicits significant changes in the function and/or expression of these neural systems.

The National Institute on Drug Abuse has compiled significant data suggesting that drug abuse among human adolescents remains high and, in some instances, is rising. While the majority of studies examining the effects of exposure to drugs of abuse on aggression have been performed in adult, male subjects, it is imperative that further studies be conducted to understand how drug insult during a critical period of neural development, such as adolescence, affects not only the manifestation of the aggressive phenotype but also potential short-term and/or permanent alterations in brain chemistry and function. Furthermore, the effects these drugs of abuse have on the aggressive behavioral state and neural system(s) of female subjects remains largely unexplored.

References

Alves, C. N., & Carlini, E. A. (1973). Effects of acute and chronic administration of *Cannabis sativa* extract on the mouse-killing behavior of rats. *Life Sciences*, 13(1), 75–85.

Bac, P., Pages, N., Herrenknecht, C., & Paris, M. (1998). Measurement of the three phases of muricidal behavior induced by delta9-tetrahydrocannabinol in isolated, fasting rats. *Physiology and Behavior*, 63(5), 815–820.

Barr, G. A., Gibbons, J. L., & Bridger, W. H. (1977). Inhibition of rat predatory aggression by acute and chronic D- and L-amphetamine. *Brain Research*, 124(3), 565–570.

Barr, G. A., Moyer, K. E., & Gibbons, J. L. (1976). Effects of imipramine, d-amphetamine, and tripelennamine on mouse and frog killing by the rat. *Physiology and Behavior*, 16(3), 267–269.

Beatty, W. W., Dodge, A. M., Dodge, L. J., White, K., & Panksepp, J. (1982). Psychomotor stimulants, social deprivation and play in juvenile rats. *Pharmacology, Biochemistry and Behavior, 16*(3), 417–422.

Benton, D., & Smoothy, R. (1984). The relationship between blood alcohol levels and aggression in mice. *Physiology and Behavior, 33*(5), 757–760.

Berntson, G. G., Beattie, M. S., & Walker, J. M. (1976). Effects of nicotinic and muscarinic compounds on biting attack in the cat. *Pharmacology, Biochemistry and Behavior, 5*(3), 235–239.

Blanchard, D. C., Flannelly, K., Hori, K., Blanchard, R. J., & Hall, J. (1987). Ethanol effects on female aggression vary with opponent size and time within session. *Pharmacology, Biochemistry and Behavior, 27*(4), 645–648.

Blanchard, R. J., Hori, K., Blanchard, D. C., & Hall, J. (1987). Ethanol effects on aggression of rats selected for different levels of aggressiveness. *Pharmacology, Biochemistry and Behavior, 27*(4), 641–644.

Blanchard, R. J., Hori, K., Flannelly, K., & Blanchard, D. C. (1987). The effects of ethanol on the offense and defensive behaviors of male and female rats during group formation. *Pharmacology, Biochemistry and Behavior, 26*(1), 61–64.

Breuer, M. E., McGinnis, M. Y., Lumia, A. R., & Possidente, B. P. (2001). Aggression in male rats receiving anabolic androgenic steroids: Effects of social and environmental provocation. *Hormones and Behavior, 40*(3), 409–418.

Bronson, F. H. (1996). Effects of prolonged exposure to anabolic steroids on the behavior of male and female mice. *Pharmacology, Biochemistry and Behavior, 53*(2), 329–334.

Bronson, F. H., Nguyen, K. Q., & De La Rosa, J. (1996). Effect of anabolic steroids on behavior and physiological characteristics of female mice. *Physiology and Behavior, 59*(1), 49–55.

Burkhalter, J. E., & Balster, R. L. (1979). Effects of phencyclidine on isolation-induced aggression in mice. *Psychological Reports, 45*(2), 571–576.

Carder, B., & Olson, J. (1972). Marihuana and shock induced aggression in rats. *Physiology and Behavior, 8*(4), 599–602.

Carder, B., & Sbordone, R. (1975). Mescaline treated rats attack immobile targets. *Pharmacology, Biochemistry and Behavior, 3*(5), 923–925.

Carlini, E. A. (1977). Further studies of the aggressive behavior induced by delta9–tetrahydrocannabinol in REM sleep-deprived rats. *Psychopharmacology, 53*(2), 135–145.

Carlini, E. A., Hamaoui, A., Bieniek, D., & Korte, F. (1970). Effects of (–) delta-9-trans-tetrahydrocannabinol and a synthetic derivative on maze performance of rats. *Pharmacology, 4*(6), 359–368.

Carlini, E. A., Lindsey, C. J., & Tufik, S. (1977). Can-

nabis, catecholamines, rapid eye movement sleep and aggressive behaviour. *British Journal of Pharmacology, 61*(3), 371–379.

Carlini, E. A., & Masur, J. (1969). Development of aggressive behavior in rats by chronic administration of *Cannabis sativa* (marihuana). *Life Sciences, 8*(11), 607–620.

Cherek, D. R., & Thompson, T. (1973). Effects of delta1-tetrahydrocannabinol on schedule-induced aggression in pigeons. *Pharmacology, Biochemistry and Behavior, 1*(5), 493–500.

Cilia, J., & Piper, D. C. (1997). Marmoset conspecific confrontation: An ethologically-based model of anxiety. *Pharmacology, Biochemistry and Behavior, 58*(1), 85–91.

Clark, A. S., & Barber, D. M. (1994). Anabolic-androgenic steroids and aggression in castrated male rats. *Physiology and Behavior, 56*(5), 1107–1113.

Clark, A. S., & Henderson, L. P. (2003). Behavioral and physiological responses to anabolic-androgenic steroids. *Neuroscience and Biobehavioral Reviews, 27*(5), 413–436.

Cleary, J., Herakovic, J., & Poling, A. (1981). Effects of phencyclidine on shock-induced aggression in rats. *Pharmacology, Biochemistry and Behavior, 15*(5), 813–818.

Cutler, M. G., Rodgers, R. J., & Jackson, J. E. (1997). Behavioural effects in mice of subchronic chlordiazepoxide, maprotiline, and fluvoxamine. I. Social interactions. *Pharmacology, Biochemistry and Behavior, 57*(1–2), 119–125.

D'Amato, F. R., & Castellano, C. (1989). Behavioral effects of morphine in mice: Role of experimental housing. *Pharmacology, Biochemistry and Behavior, 34*(2), 361–365.

Darmani, N. A., Hadfield, M. G., Carter, W. H., Jr., & Martin, B. R. (1990). Acute and chronic effects of cocaine on isolation-induced aggression in mice. *Psychopharmacology, 102*(1), 37–40.

Davis, S. F., Nielson, L. D., Weaver, M. S., Dungan, D. S., Sullivan, P. K., & Tramill, J. L. (1984). Shock-elicited aggression as a function of early ethanol exposure. *Journal of General Psychology, 110*(Pt. 1), 93–98.

DeBold, J. F., & Miczek, K. A. (1985). Testosterone modulates the effects of ethanol on male mouse aggression. *Psychopharmacology, 86*(3), 286–290.

DeLeon, K. R., Grimes, J. M., Connor, D. F., & Melloni, R. H., Jr. (2002). Adolescent cocaine exposure and offensive aggression: Involvement of serotonin neural signaling and innervation in male Syrian hamsters. *Behavioural Brain Research, 133*(2), 211–220.

DeLeon, K. R., Grimes, J. M., & Melloni, R. H., Jr. (2002).

Repeated anabolic-androgenic steroid treatment during adolescence increases vasopressin V(1A) receptor binding in Syrian hamsters: Correlation with offensive aggression. *Hormones and Behavior, 42*(2), 182–191.

De Souza, H., & Neto, J. P. (1978). Effects of anti-acetylcholine drugs on aggressive behaviour induced by *Cannabis sativa* in REM sleep-deprived rats. *Journal of Pharmacy and Pharmacology, 30*(9), 591–592.

Dorr, M., & Steinberg, H. (1976). Effects of delta9-tetrahydrocannabinol on social behaviour in mice: Comparison between two vehicles. *Psychopharmacology, 47*(1), 87–91.

Driscoll, P., & Baettig, K. (1981). Selective inhibition by nicotine of shock-induced fighting in the rat. *Pharmacology, Biochemistry and Behavior, 14*(2), 175–179.

Dubinsky, B., Robichaud, R. C., & Goldberg, M. E. (1973). Effects of (-)9-trans-tetrahydrocannabinol and its selectivity in several models of aggressive behavior. *Pharmacology, 9*(4), 204–216.

Emley, G. S., & Hutchinson, R. R. (1983). Effects of phencyclidine on aggressive behavior in squirrel monkeys. *Pharmacology, Biochemistry and Behavior, 18*(2), 163–166.

Everill, B., & Berry, M. S. (1987). Effects of ethanol on aggression in three inbred strains of mice. *Physiology and Behavior, 39*(1), 45–51.

Farrell, S. F., & McGinnis, M. Y. (2003). Effects of pubertal anabolic-androgenic steroid (AAS) administration on reproductive and aggressive behaviors in male rats. *Behavioral Neuroscience, 117*(5), 904–911.

Ferrari, P. F., Parmigiani, S., Rodgers, R. J., & Palanza, P. (1997). Differential effects of chlordiazepoxide on aggressive behavior in male mice: The influence of social factors. *Psychopharmacology, 134*(3), 258–265.

Ferreira, A., Picazo, O., Uriarte, N., Pereira, M., & Fernandez-Guasti, A. (2000). Inhibitory effect of buspirone and diazepam, but not of 8-OH-DPAT, on maternal behavior and aggression. *Pharmacology, Biochemistry and Behavior, 66*(2), 389–396.

Ferris, C. F., Shtiegman, K., & King, J. A. (1998). Voluntary ethanol consumption in male adolescent hamsters increases testosterone and aggression. *Physiology and Behavior, 63*(5), 739–744.

Field, E. F., & Pellis, S. M. (1994). Differential effects of amphetamine on the attack and defense components of play fighting in rats. *Physiology and Behavior, 56*(2), 325–330.

Fox, K. A., & Snyder, R. L. (1969). Effect of sustained low doses of diazepam on aggression and mortality in grouped male mice. *Journal of Comparative and Physiological Psychology, 69*(4), 663–666.

Fox, K. A., Tuckosh, J. R., & Wilcox, A. H. (1970). Increased aggression among grouped male mice fed chlordiazepoxide. *European Journal of Pharmacology, 11*(1), 119–121.

Frye, C. A., Rhodes, M. E., Walf, A., & Harney, J. P. (2002). Testosterone enhances aggression of wildtype mice but not those deficient in type I 5alpha-reductase. *Brain Research, 948*(1–2), 165–170.

Fujiwara, M., & Ueki, S. (1978). Muricide induced by single injection of delta9–tetrahydrocannabinol. *Physiology and Behavior, 21*(4), 581–585.

Fujiwara, M., & Ueki, S. (1979). The course of aggressive behavior induced by a single injection of delta 9-tetrahydrocannabinol and its characteristics. *Physiology and Behavior, 22*(3), 535–539.

Gao, B., & Cutler, M. G. (1993). Buspirone increases social investigation in pair-housed male mice: Comparison with the effects of chlordiazepoxide. *Neuropharmacology 32*(5), 429–437.

Gellert, V. F., & Sparber, S. B. (1979). Effects of morphine withdrawal on food competition hierarchies and fighting behavior in rats. *Psychopharmacology, 60*(2), 165–172.

Gonzalez, S. C., Matsudo, V. K., & Carlini, E. A. (1971). Effects of marihuana compounds on the fighting behavior of Siamese fighting fish (*Betta splendens*). *Pharmacology, 6*(3), 186–209.

Grimes, J. M., & Melloni, R. H., Jr. (2002). Serotonin modulates offensive attack in adolescent anabolic steroid-treated hamsters. *Pharmacology, Biochemistry and Behavior, 73*(3), 713–721.

Grimes, J. M., Ricci, L. A., & Melloni, R. H., Jr. (2003). Glutamic acid decarboxylase (GAD65) immunoreactivity in brains of aggressive, adolescent anabolic steroid-treated hamsters. *Hormones and Behavior, 44*(3), 271–280.

Grimm, V. E., McAllister, K. H., Brain, P. F., & Benton, D. (1984). An ethological analysis of the influence of perinatally-administered diazepam on murine behaviour. *Comparative Biochemistry and Physiology C, 79*(2), 291–293.

Hadfield, M. G., Nugent, E. A., & Mott, D. E. (1982). Cocaine increases isolation-induced fighting in mice. *Pharmacology, Biochemistry and Behavior, 16*(2), 359–360.

Haney, M., & Miczek, K. A. (1989). Morphine effects on maternal aggression, pup care and analgesia in mice. *Psychopharmacology, 98*(1), 68–74.

Harrison, R. J., Connor, D. F., Nowak, C., Nash, K., & Melloni, R. H., Jr. (2000). Chronic anabolic-androgenic steroid treatment during adolescence increases anterior hypothalamic vasopressin and aggression in intact hamsters. *Psychoneuroendocrinology, 25*(4), 317–338.

Hilakivi, L. A., & Lister, R. G. (1989). Effect of ethanol on the social behavior of group-housed and isolated mice. *Alcoholism, Clinical and Experimental Research*, 13(5), 622–625.

Hilakivi-Clarke, L., & Goldberg, R. (1995). Gonadal hormones and aggression-maintaining effect of alcohol in male transgenic transforming growth factor-alpha mice. *Alcoholism, Clinical and Experimental Research*, 19(3), 708–713.

Irwin, S., Kinoi, R., Van Sloten, M., & Workman, M. P. (1971). Drug effects on distress-evoked behavior in mice: Methodology and drug class comparisons. *Psychopharmacologia*, 20(2), 172–185.

Johns, J. M., Noonan, L. R., Zimmerman, L. I., McMillen, B. A., Means, L. W., Walker, C. H., et al. (1998). Chronic cocaine treatment alters social/aggressive behavior in Sprague-Dawley rat dams and in their prenatally exposed offspring. *Annals of the New York Academy of Sciences*, 846, 399–404.

Kantak, K. M., & Miczek, K. A. (1986). Aggression during morphine withdrawal: Effects of method of withdrawal, fighting experience, and social role. *Psychopharmacology*, 90(4), 451–456.

Kanui, T. I., & Hole, K. (1990). Morphine induces aggression but not analgesia in the naked mole-rat (*Heterocephalus glaber*). *Comparative Biochemistry and Physiology C*, 96(1), 131–133.

Kilbey, M. M., Fritchie, G. E., McLendon, D. M., & Johnson, K. M. (1972). Attack behaviour in mice inhibited by -9-tetrahydrocannabinol. *Nature*, 238(5365), 463–465.

Kilbey, M. M., & Moore, J. W., Jr. (1973). Delta9-tetrahydrocannabinol induced inhibition of predatory aggression in the rat. *Psychopharmacologia*, 31(2), 157–166.

Kostowski, W. (1966). A note on the effects of some psychotropic drugs on the aggressive behaviour in the ant, *Formica rufa*. *Journal of Pharmacy and Pharmacology*, 18(11), 747–749.

Kostowski, W., Valzelli, L., & Baiguerra, G. (1986). Effect of chronic administration of alprazolam and adinazolam on clonidine- or apomorphine-induced aggression in laboratory rodents. *Neuropharmacology*, 25(7), 757–761.

Krsiak, M. (1976). Effect of ethanol on aggression and timidity in mice. *Psychopharmacology*, 51(1), 75–80.

Krsiak, M., Elis, J., Poschlova, N., & Masek, K. (1977). Increased aggressiveness and lower brain serotonin levels in offspring of mice given alcohol during gestation. *Journal of Studies on Alcohol*, 38(9), 1696–1704.

Krsiak, M., Podhorna, J., & Miczek, K. A. (1998). Aggressive and social behavior after alprazolam withdrawal: Experimental therapy with Ro 19–8022. *Neuroscience and Biobehavioral Reviews*, 23(2), 155–161.

Krstic, S. K., Stefanovic-Denic, K., & Beleslin, D. B. (1982). Effect of morphine and morphine-like drugs on carbachol-induced fighting in cats. *Pharmacology, Biochemistry and Behavior*, 17(2), 371–373.

Kudryavtseva, N. N., & Bondar, N. P. (2002). Anxiolytic and anxiogenic effects of diazepam in male mice with different experience of aggression. *Bulletin of Experimental Biology and Medicine*, 133(4), 372–376.

Kuhn, C. M. (2002). Anabolic steroids. *Recent Progress in Hormone Research*, 57, 411–434.

Leaf, R. C., Wnek, D. J., & Lamon, S. (1984). Oxazepam induced mouse killing by rats. *Pharmacology, Biochemistry and Behavior*, 20(2), 311–313.

Leaf, R. C., Wnek, D. J., Lamon, S., & Gay, P. E. (1978). Despite various drugs, cats continue to kill mice. *Pharmacology, Biochemistry and Behavior*, 9(4), 445–452.

Lindqvist, A. S., Johansson-Steensland, P., Nyberg, F., & Fahlke, C. (2002). Anabolic androgenic steroid affects competitive behaviour, behavioural response to ethanol and brain serotonin levels. *Behavioural Brain Research*, 133(1), 21–29.

Lisciotto, C. A., DeBold, J. F., & Miczek, K. A. (1990). Sexual differentiation and the effects of alcohol on aggressive behavior in mice. *Pharmacology, Biochemistry and Behavior*, 35(2), 357–362.

Long, S. F., Wilson, M. C., Sufka, K. J., & Davis, W. M. (1996). The effects of cocaine and nandrolone co-administration on aggression in male rats. *Progress in Neuro-Psychopharmacology and Biological Psychiatry*, 20(5), 839–856.

Lubin, D. A., Elliott, J. C., Black, M. C., & Johns, J. M. (2003). An oxytocin antagonist infused into the central nucleus of the amygdala increases maternal aggressive behavior. *Behavioral Neuroscience*, 117(2), 195–201.

Lubin, D. A., Meter, K. E., Walker, C. H., & Johns, J. M. (2001a). Dose-related effects of chronic gestational cocaine treatment on maternal aggression in rats on postpartum days 2, 3, and 5. *Progress in Neuro-Psychopharmacology and Biological Psychiatry*, 25(7), 1403–1420.

Lubin, D. A., Meter, K. E., Walker, C. H., & Johns, J. M. (2001b). Effects of chronic cocaine administration on aggressive behavior in virgin rats. *Progress in Neuro-Psychopharmacology and Biological Psychiatry*, 25(7), 1421–1433.

Lumia, A. R., Thorner, K. M., & McGinnis, M. Y. (1994). Effects of chronically high doses of the anabolic androgenic steroid, testosterone, on intermale aggression and sexual behavior in male rats. *Physiology and Behavior*, 55(2), 331–335.

Malick, J. B. (1978). Selective antagonism of isolation-induced aggression in mice by diazepam following chronic administration. *Pharmacology, Biochemistry and Behavior, 8*(4), 497–499.

Manning, F. J., & Elsmore, T. F. (1972). Shock-elicited fighting and delta-9-tetrahydrocannabinol. *Psychopharmacologia, 25*(3), 218–228.

Martinez-Sanchis, S., Brain, P. F., Salvador, A., & Simon, V. M. (1996). Long-term chronic treatment with stanozolol lacks significant effects on aggression and activity in young and adult male laboratory mice. *General Pharmacology, 27*(2), 293–298.

Martinez-Sanchis, S., Salvador, A., Moya-Albiol, L., Gonzalez-Bono, E., & Simon, V. M. (1998). Effects of chronic treatment with testosterone propionate on aggression and hormonal levels in intact male mice. *Psychoneuroendocrinology, 23*(3), 275–293.

McDonough, J. H., Jr., Manning, F. J., & Elsmore, T. F. (1972). Reduction of predatory aggression of rats following administration of delta-9–tetrahydrocannabinol. *Life Sciences I 11*(3), 103–111.

McGinnis, M. Y., Lumia, A. R., Breuer, M. E., & Possidente, B. (2002). Physical provocation potentiates aggression in male rats receiving anabolic androgenic steroids. *Hormones and Behavior, 41*(1), 101–110.

McGinnis, M. Y., Lumia, A. R., & Possidente, B. P. (2002). Effects of withdrawal from anabolic androgenic steroids on aggression in adult male rats. *Physiology and Behavior, 75*(4), 541–549.

Melloni, R. H., Jr., Connor, D. F., Hang, P. T., Harrison, R. J., & Ferris, C. F. (1997). Anabolic-androgenic steroid exposure during adolescence and aggressive behavior in golden hamsters. *Physiology and Behavior, 61*(3), 359–364.

Miczek, K. A. (1976). Mouse-killing and motor activity: Effects of chronic delta9-tetrahydrocannabinol and pilocarpine. *Psychopharmacology, 47*(1), 59–64.

Miczek, K. A. (1979). A new test for aggression in rats without aversive stimulation: Differential effects of d-amphetamine and cocaine. *Psychopharmacology, 60*(3), 253–259.

Miczek, K. A., & Barry, H., III. (1974). Delta9-tetrahydrocannabinol and aggressive behavior in rats. *Behavioral Biology, 11*(2), 261–267.

Miczek, K. A., & Barry, H., III. (1977). Effects of alcohol on attack and defensive-submissive reactions in rats. *Psychopharmacology, 52*(3), 231–237.

Miczek, K. A., & de Almeida, R. M. (2001). Oral drug self-administration in the home cage of mice: Alcohol-heightened aggression and inhibition by the 5-HT1B agonist anpirtoline. *Psychopharmacology, 157*(4), 421–429.

Miczek, K. A., & Gold, L. H. (1983). d-Amphetamine in squirrel monkeys of different social status: Effects on social and agonistic behavior, locomotion, and stereotypies. *Psychopharmacology, 81*(3), 183–190.

Miczek, K. A., & Haney, M. (1994). Psychomotor stimulant effects of d-amphetamine, MDMA and PCP: Aggressive and schedule-controlled behavior in mice. *Psychopharmacology, 115*(3), 358–365.

Miczek, K. A., & O'Donnell, J. M. (1978). Intruder-evoked aggression in isolated and nonisolated mice: Effects of psychomotor stimulants and L-dopa. *Psychopharmacology, 57*(1), 47–55.

Miczek, K. A., & O'Donnell, J. M. (1980). Alcohol and chlordiazepoxide increase suppressed aggression in mice. *Psychopharmacology, 69*(1), 39–44.

Miksic, S., Smith, N., & Lal, H. (1976). Reduction of morphine-withdrawal aggression by conditional social stimuli. *Psychopharmacology, 48*(1), 115–117.

Miller, M. H. (1976). Behavioral effects of amphetamine in a group of rhesus monkeys with lesions of dorsolateral frontal cortex. *Psychopharmacology, 47*(1), 71–74.

Moro, M., Salvador, A., & Simon, V. M. (1997). Changes in the structure of the agonistic behavior of mice produced by D-amphetamine. *Pharmacology, Biochemistry and Behavior, 56*(1), 47–54.

Mos, J., & Olivier, B. (1989). Quantitative and comparative analyses of pro-aggressive actions of benzodiazepines in maternal aggression of rats. *Psychopharmacology, 97*(2), 152–153.

Mos, J., Olivier, B., & van Oorschot, R. (1987). Maternal aggression towards different sized male opponents: Effect of chlordiazepoxide treatment of the mothers and d-amphetamine treatment of the intruders. *Pharmacology, Biochemistry and Behavior, 26*(3), 577–584.

Munro, A. D. (1986). The effects of apomorphine, d-amphetamine and chlorpromazine on the aggressiveness of isolated *Aequidens pulcher* (Teleostei, Cichlidae). *Psychopharmacology, 88*(1), 124–128.

Musty, R. E., Lindsey, C. J., & Carlini, E. A. (1976). 6-Hydroxydopamine and the aggressive behavior induced by marihuana in REM sleep-deprived rats. *Psychopharmacology, 48*(2), 175–179.

Navarro, J. F., & Maldonado, E. (1999). Behavioral profile of 3,4-methylenedioxy-methamphetamine (MDMA) in agonistic encounters between male mice. *Progress in Neuro-Psychopharmacology and Biological Psychiatry, 23*(2), 327–334.

Navarro, J. F., & Maldonado, E. (2004). Effects of acute, subchronic and intermittent MDMA ("ECSTACY") administration on agonistic interactions between male mice. *Hormones and Behavior, 30*(1), 84–91.

National Institute on Drug Abuse (NIDA). (n.d.). NIDACapsules. Available at http://www.nida.nih.gov/NIDACapsules/NCIndex.html.

O'Donnell, J. M., & Miczek, K. A. (1980). No tolerance to antiaggressive effect of d-amphetamine in mice. *Psychopharmacology, 68*(2), 191–196.

Olivier, B., Mos, J., & van Oorschot, R. (1985). Maternal aggression in rats: Effects of chlordiazepoxide and fluprazine. *Psychopharmacology*, 86(1–2), 68–76.

Olivier, B., Mos, J., & van Oorschot, R. (1986). Maternal aggression in rats: Lack of interaction between chlordiazepoxide and flupramine. *Psychopharmacology*, 88, 40–43.

Paivarinta, P. (1992). Lack of increased intermale fighting behavior in mice after low ethanol doses. *Pharmacology, Biochemistry and Behavior*, 42(1), 35–39.

Palanza, P., Rodgers, R. J., Ferrari, P. F., & Parmigiani, S. (1996). Effects of chlordiazepoxide on maternal aggression in mice depend on experience of resident and sex of intruder. *Pharmacology, Biochemistry and Behavior*, 54(1), 175–182.

Palermo Neto, J., & Carlini, E. A. (1972). Aggressive behaviour elicited in rats by *Cannabis sativa*: Effects of p-chlorophenylalanine and DOPA. *European Journal of Pharmacology*, 17(2), 215–220.

Palermo Neto, J., & Carvalho, F. V. (1973). The effects of chronic cannabis treatment on the aggressive behavior and brain 5-hydroxytryptamine levels of rats with different temperaments. *Psychopharmacologia*, 32(4), 383–392.

Panksepp, J. (1971). Drugs and stimulus-bound attack. *Physiology and Behavior*, 6(4), 317–320.

Peeke, H. V., Ellman, G. E., & Herz, M. J. (1973). Dose dependent alcohol effects on the aggressive behavior of the convict cichlid (*Cichlasoma nigrofasciatum*). *Behavioral Biology*, 8(1), 115–122.

Peeke, H. V., Peeke, S. C., Avis, H. H., & Ellman, G. (1975). Alcohol, habituation and the patterning of aggressive responses in a cichlid fish. *Pharmacology, Biochemistry and Behavior*, 3(6), 1031–1036.

Pellis, S. M., O'Brien, D. P., Pellis, V. C., Teitelbaum, P., Wolgin, D. L., & Kennedy, S. (1988). Escalation of feline predation along a gradient from avoidance through "play" to killing. *Behavioral Neuroscience*, 102(5), 760–777.

Pettijohn, T. F. (1979). The effects of alcohol on agonistic behavior in the Telomian dog. *Psychopharmacology*, 60(3), 295–301.

Poole, T. B. (1973). Some studies on the influence of chlordiazepoxide on the social interaction of golden hamsters (*Mesocricetus auratus*). *British Journal of Pharmacology* 48(3), 538–545.

Quenzer, L. F., & Feldman, R. S. (1975). The mechanism of anti-muricidal effects of chlordiazepoxide. *Pharmacology, Biochemistry and Behavior*, 3(4), 567–571.

Rejeski, W. J., Brubaker, P. H., Herb, R. A., Kaplan, J. R., & Koritnik, D. (1988). Anabolic steroids and aggressive behavior in Cynomolgus monkeys. *Journal of Behavioral Medicine*, 11(1), 95–105.

Rewerski, W., Kostowski, W., Piechocki, T., & Rylski, M. (1971). The effects of some hallucinogens on aggressiveness of mice and rats. I. *Pharmacology*, 5(5), 314–320.

Ricci, L. A., Grimes, J. M., & Melloni, R. H., Jr. (2004). Serotonin type-3 receptors modulate the aggression-stimulating effects of adolescent cocaine exposure. *Behavioral Neuroscience*, 118(5), 1097–1110.

Richardson, D., Karczmar, A. G., & Scudder, C. L. (1972). Intergeneric behavioral differences among methamphetamine treated mice. *Psychopharmacologia*, 25(4), 347–375.

Rodgers, R. J. (1979). Effects of nicotine, mecamylamine, and hexamethonium on shock-induced fighting, pain reactivity, and locomotor behaviour in rats. *Psychopharmacology*, 66(1), 93–98.

Rodriguez-Arias, M., Pinazo, J., Minarro, J., & Stinus, L. (1999). Effects of SCH 23390, raclopride, and haloperidol on morphine withdrawal-induced aggression in male mice. *Pharmacology, Biochemistry and Behavior*, 64(1), 123–130.

Rouhani, S., Emmanouilidis, E., Payan, C., Tran, G., Castresana, A., Soulairac, A., et al. (1992). Effects of alcohol dependence on shock-induced fighting: Action of muscimol and homotaurine. *Pharmacology, Biochemistry and Behavior*, 41(1), 49–51.

Royalty, J. (1990). Effects of prenatal ethanol exposure on juvenile play-fighting and postpubertal aggression in rats. *Psychological Reports*, 66(2), 551–560.

Sassenrath, E. N., & Chapman, L. F. (1975). Tetrahydrocannabinol-induced manifestations of the "marihuana syndrome" in group-living macaques. *Federation Proceedings*, 34(8), 1666–1670.

Sbordone, R. J., & Carder, B. (1974). Mescaline and shock induced aggression in rats. *Pharmacology, Biochemistry and Behavior*, 2(6), 777–782.

Sbordone, R. J., Wingard, J. A., Elliott, M. K., & Jervey, J. (1978). Mescaline produces pathological aggression in rats regardless of age or strain. *Pharmacology, Biochemistry and Behavior*, 8(5), 543–546.

Sbordone, R. J., Wingard, J. A., Gorelick, D. A., & Elliott, M. L. (1979). Severe aggression in rats induced by mescaline but not other hallucinogens. *Psychopharmacology*, 66(3), 275–280.

Sheard, M. H., Astrachan, D. I., & Davis, M. (1977). The effect of D-lysergic acid diethylamide (LSD) upon shock elicited fighting in rats. *Life Sciences*, 20(3), 427–430.

Shibata, S., Nakanishi, H., Watanabe, S., & Ueki, S. (1984). Effects of chronic administration of antidepressants on mouse-killing behavior (muricide) in olfactory bulbectomized rats. *Pharmacology, Biochemistry and Behavior*, 21(2), 225–230.

Shintomi, K. (1975). Effects of psychotropic drugs on methamphetamine-induced behavioral excitation in grouped mice. *European Journal of Pharmacology*, 31(2), 195–206.

Sieber, B., Frischknecht, H. R., & Waser, P. G. (1980). Behavioral effects of hashish in mice. III. Social interactions between two residents and an intruder male. *Psychopharmacology, 70*(3), 273–278.

Siegel, R. K., & Poole, J. (1969). Psychedelic-induced social behavior in mice: A preliminary report. *Psychological Reports, 25*(3), 704–706.

Silverman, A. P. (1971). Behaviour of rats given a "smoking dose" of nicotine. *Animal Behaviour, 19*(1), 67–74.

Skolnick, P., Reed, G. F., & Paul, S. M. (1985). Benzodiazepine-receptor mediated inhibition of isolation-induced aggression in mice. *Pharmacology, Biochemistry and Behavior, 23*(1), 17–20.

Smith, E. O., & Byrd, L. D. (1984). Contrasting effects of d-amphetamine on affiliation and aggression in monkeys. *Pharmacology, Biochemistry and Behavior, 20*(2), 255–260.

Smith, E. O., & Byrd, L. D. (1985). d-Amphetamine induced changes in social interaction patterns. *Pharmacology, Biochemistry and Behavior, 22*(1), 135–139.

Smoothy, R., Brain, P. F., Berry, M. S., & Haug, M. (1986). Alcohol and social behaviour in group-housed female mice. *Physiology and Behavior, 37*(5), 689–694.

Sukhotina, I. A. (2001). Morphine withdrawal-facilitated aggression is attenuated by morphine-conditioned stimuli. *Pharmacology, Biochemistry and Behavior, 68*(1), 93–98.

Sukhotina, I. A., & Bespalov, A. Y. (2000). Effects of the NMDA receptor channel blockers memantine and MRZ 2/579 on morphine withdrawal-facilitated aggression in mice. *Psychopharmacology, 149*(4), 345–350.

Sulcova, A., & Krsiak, M. (1989). Differences among nine 1,4-benzodiazepines: An ethopharmacological evaluation in mice. *Psychopharmacology, 97*(2), 157–159.

Ten Ham, M., & De Jong, Y. (1974). Tolerance to the hypothermic and aggression-attenuating effect of delta 8- and delta 9-tetrahydrocannabinol in mice. *European Journal of Pharmacology, 28*(1), 144–148.

Thor, D. H., & Teel, B. G. (1968). Fighting of rats during post-morphine withdrawal: Effect of prewithdrawal dosage. *American Journal of Psychology, 81*(3), 439–442.

Tidey, J. W., & Miczek, K. A. (1992a). Heightened aggressive behavior during morphine withdrawal: Effects of d-amphetamine. *Psychopharmacology, 107*(2–3), 297–302.

Tidey, J. W., & Miczek, K. A. (1992b). Morphine withdrawal aggression: Modification with D1 and D2 receptor agonists. *Psychopharmacology, 108*(1–2), 177–184.

Towett, P. K., & Kanui, T. I. (1993). Effects of pethidine, acetylsalicylic acid, and indomethacin on pain and behavior in the mole-rat. *Pharmacology, Biochemistry and Behavior, 45*(1), 153–159.

Tramill, J. L., Gustavson, K., Weaver, M. S., Moore, S. A., & Davis, S. F. (1983). Shock-elicited aggression as a function of acute and chronic ethanol challenges. *Journal of General Psychology, 109*(Pt. 1), 53–58.

Tyler, C. B., & Miczek, K. A. (1982). Effects of phencyclidine on aggressive behavior in mice. *Pharmacology, Biochemistry and Behavior, 17*(3), 503–510.

Ueki, S., Fujiwara, M., & Ogawa, N. (1972). Mouse-killing behavior (muricide) induced by delta 9-tetrahydrocannabinol in the rat. *Physiology and Behavior, 9*(4), 585–587.

Ushijima, I., Katsuragi, T., & Furukawa, T. (1984). Involvement of adenosine receptor activities in aggressive responses produced by clonidine in mice. *Psychopharmacology, 83*(4), 335–339.

Van Erp, A. M., & Miczek, K. A. (1997). Increased aggression after ethanol self-administration in male resident rats. *Psychopharmacology, 131*(3), 287–295.

Vardaris, R. M., Weisz, D. J., Fazel, A., & Rawitch, A. B. (1976). Chronic administration of delta-9-tetrahydrocannabinol to pregnant rats: Studies of pup behavior and placental transfer. *Pharmacology, Biochemistry and Behavior, 4*(3), 249–254.

Votava, M., Krsiak, M., Podhorna, J., & Miczek, K. A. (2001). Alprazolam withdrawal and tolerance measured in the social conflict test in mice. *Psychopharmacology, 157*(2), 123–130.

Waldbillig, R. J. (1980). Suppressive effects of intraperitoneal and intraventricular injections of nicotine on muricide and shock-induced attack on conspecifics. *Pharmacology, Biochemistry and Behavior, 12*(4), 619–623.

Walker, D. L., & Gregory, E. H. (1985). Differential effect of alcohol on aggressive behavior in dominant and subordinate hamsters. *Psychological Reports, 56*(1), 275–282.

Weerts, E. M., & Miczek, K. A. (1996). Primate vocalizations during social separation and aggression: Effects of alcohol and benzodiazepines. *Psychopharmacology, 127*(3), 255–264.

Weerts, E. M., Miller, L. G., Hood, K. E., & Miczek, K. A. (1992). Increased GABAA-dependent chloride uptake in mice selectively bred for low aggressive behavior. *Psychopharmacology (Berl.), 108*(1–2), 196–204.

Weerts, E. M., Tornatzky, W., & Miczek, K. A. (1993). Prevention of the pro-aggressive effects of alcohol in rats and squirrel monkeys by benzodiazepine receptor antagonists. *Psychopharmacology, 111*(2), 144–152.

Wilmot, C. A., Vanderwende, C., & Spoerlein, M. T. (1987). The effects of phencyclidine on fighting in differentially housed mice. *Pharmacology, Biochemistry and Behavior, 28*(3), 341–346.

Winslow, J. T., & Miczek, K. A. (1985). Social status as determinant of alcohol effects on aggressive behavior in squirrel monkeys (*Saimiri sciureus*). *Psychopharmacology*, 85(2), 167–172.

Wongwitdecha, N., & Marsden, C. A. (1996). Social isolation increases aggressive behaviour and alters the effects of diazepam in the rat social interaction test. *Behavioural Brain Research*, 75(1–2), 27–32.

Wood, R. D., & Spear, L. P. (1998). Prenatal cocaine alters social competition of infant, adolescent, and adult rats. *Behavioral Neuroscience*, 112(2), 419–431.

Yanai, J., & Ginsburg, B. E. (1977). Long term reduction of male agonistic behavior in mice following early exposure to ethanol. *Psychopharmacology*, 52(1), 31–34.

Yoshimura, H., Fujiwara, M., & Ueki, S. (1974). Biochemical correlates in mouse-killing behavior of the rat: Brain acetylcholine and acetylcholinesterase after administration of delta9-tetrahydrocannabinol. *Brain Research*, 81(3), 567–570.

Yoshimura, H., & Ogawa, N. (1989). Acute and chronic effects of psychotropic drugs on maternal aggression in mice. *Psychopharmacology*, 97(3), 339–342.

Yoshimura, H., & Ogawa, N. (1991). Ethopharmacology of maternal aggression in mice: Effects of diazepam and SM-3997. *European Journal of Pharmacology*, 200(1), 147–153.

Zwirner, P. P., Porsolt, R. D., & Loew, D. M. (1975). Inter-group aggression in mice: A new method for testing the effects of centrally active drugs. *Psychopharmacologia*, 45(2), 133–138.

17

Psychopharmacology of Human Aggression: Laboratory and Clinical Studies

Don R. Cherek, Oleg V. Tcheremissine, & Scott D. Lane

Over the past 75 years, per capita violent crime in the Unites States increased during the 1930s, the early 1960s through mid 1970s, and the early 1980s and finally reached a peak in the early 1990s (LaFree, 1999). Violent crime rates have steadily decreased during the past 10 years (U.S. Department of Justice, 2002). As noted earlier in this volume, owing in part to the dramatic increase in violent crime in the early 1990s, human aggression has during the past decade captured the attention of the general public, government officials, and the scientific community. Violence has become a major media and public health concern; both the *Journal of the American Medical Association* (1992) and *Science* (2000) have devoted special issues to the subject. Former Surgeon General C. Everett Koop called it a public health emergency (Koop & Lundberg, 1992).

Aggression, both verbal and physical, is commonplace in human society. Many conflicts are resolved without excessive or permanent harm, and aggression sometimes serves an adaptive function. However, extreme and persistent forms of aggression often have devastating consequences on both individuals and communities—escalating beyond adaptation to psychopathology. Maladaptive human aggression thus presents a continuing dilemma for the biobehavioral sciences, as

well as for the public health and criminal justice systems. Interest in aggressive and violent behavior cuts a wide path of concern across public, social, and scientific sectors.

The identification of drug effects on human aggression is important to the biological, behavioral, and public health sciences. Controlled laboratory studies may potentially benefit all three. Aggressive behavior occurs at a relatively low frequency in the natural environment, and it thus presents logistical problems for direct measurement in nonlaboratory settings. Laboratory studies provide opportunities not afforded by naturalistic observation techniques (Cherek & Pietras, 2003). A more rigorous study of factors involved in human aggression under controlled laboratory conditions may provide useful information. This chapter focuses on the psychopharmacology of human aggression.

Association Between Drugs and Human Aggression

A powerful and undeniable association exists between alcohol and illicit drug use and human aggression and violence. Indeed, some studies link public drug policy and drug use rates to trends in violent crime rates (see

LaFree, 1999). However, there appears to be confusion among both the general public and the scientific community regarding both the causality and direction of this relationship. The historical sequence (or emergence) of aggressive behavior and substance use is commonly misunderstood or confounded. Several epidemiological studies show that individuals with a history of aggressive behavior consume alcohol more heavily than nonaggressive cohorts (Leonard, Bromet, Parkinson, Day, & Ryan, 1985; Murdoch, Pihl, & Ross, 1990). Aggressive behavior during childhood has repeatedly been established as the most significant risk factor for later life substance abuse and dependence (Dawes, Tartar, & Kirisci, 1997; Kellam, Stevenson, & Rubin, 1983; Loeber et al., 1993). Additionally, violent crimes among heroin users were found to be much more likely when a history of criminal behavior predated heroin use than when heroin use preceded criminal and violent activity (Kaye, Darke, & Finlay-Jones, 1998). Despite such clear evidence, some authors have noted that some relationships may be a direct function of the pharmacological effect of the drug (e.g., alcohol), whereas many others suggest a more complex influence of factors, including psychiatric/individual differences, neurotoxicity, and withdrawal effects (Hoaken & Stewart, 2003).

The epidemiological evidence linking alcohol to aggressive behavior is overwhelming. Alcohol intoxication, abuse, and dependence are highly associated with criminal activity (Ensor & Godfrey, 1993; Lanza-Kaduce, Bishop, & Winner, 1997; Martin, 2001). The non-health-related costs of alcohol abuse to society, for example, those resulting from criminal behavior, are estimated at $13 billion annually (Martin, 2001). A substantial proportion of these crimes are of a violent nature; alcohol may be involved in 40 to 50% of all violent crimes, including homicide and assault (Collins & Messerschmidt, 1993; Murdoch et al., 1990). This pattern is present in adolescents and young adults (Galanter, 1997; Milgram, 1993). Data also indicate that alcohol is related to increased sexual aggression (Seto & Barbaree, 1995).

Some reports have noted an occasional association between benzodiazepine use and aggressive /violent behavior (Bond, Lader, Carlos, DaSilveira, & Blackburn, 1998; Pihl & Peterson, 1995). Extended use of alprazolam resulted in loss of self-control and violence in some patient populations for whom it had been prescribed (Bond, Curran, Bruce, O'Sullivan, & Shine, 1995; Cole & Kando, 1993; Gardner & Cowdry, 1985).

A cross-sectional survey of adolescent and young adult women found that recreational flunitrazepam (Rohypnol) use significantly increased the odds of experiencing a physical or sexual assault (Rickert, Wiemann, & Berenson, 1999). Documented adverse consequences following use of flunitrazepam include sexual assault and motor vehicle accidents (Calhoun, Wesson, Galloway, & Smith, 1996). A survey of drug users in Mexico City reported an association between flunitrazepam abuse and street fights, robbery, and rape (Galvan et al., 2000). A study of forensic psychiatric patients found that flunitrazepam abuse was more common in offenses involving robbery, weapons, and drugs than among nonabusers (Daderman & Edman, 2001). Another report found that use of flunitrazepam (in combination with alcohol) among juvenile offenders was related to acts of impulsive violence and that among flunitrazepam abusers, nearly all had been sentenced for a serious violent offense (Daderman & Lidberg, 1999).

A 1977 review of the literature linking marijuana to violence concluded that there was little evidence suggesting that marijuana use was directly associated with aggressive behavior (Abel, 1977). However, Abel (1977) concluded that the presence of certain personality dimensions or disorders, certain settings and events (e.g., provoking or socially charged contexts), coupled with a marijuana-related increase in anxiety may precipitate increases in aggressive behavior. Contrary to Able's review, recent data suggest that marijuana use may be related to increased likelihood of violence. One study of 612 inner city low-SES (socioeconomic status) youth found (after controlling for many confounding variables) that frequency of marijuana use was associated with an increased likelihood to commit weapons offenses and with attempted homicide (Friedman, Glassman, & Terras, 2001). A large-scale longitudinal study of 2,226 Columbian adolescents found that marijuana use during early adolescence predicted violence experiences in later adolescence (Brook, Brook, Rosen, & Rabbitt, 2003). Among delinquent adolescents categorized into those that committed only property offenses versus those that committed violent offenses toward other people, frequent use/abuse of marijuana was the most predictive drug (among a range of classes) of membership in the violence toward people category (Simonds & Kashani, 1980). This finding emphasizes the complex interaction between behavioral history and drug effects—all the boys in this study had a history of conduct problems that may have preceded their drug use. In a similar manner, a prospective longitudinal study indicated that violent behavior during adolescence was associated marijuana use and dependence in early adulthood, again highlighting the frequent difficulty of clearly rendering the direction of the drug use–aggression relationship (Poulton, Brooke, Moffitt, Stanton, & Silva, 1997). Further complexity is added by studies suggesting that aggressive behavior may increase during periods of marijuana withdrawal (Hoaken & Stewart, 2003; Kouri, Pope, & Lukas, 1999).

A number of studies have reported a relationship between aggressive behavior and the use of central nervous system (CNS) stimulants. One longitudinal study examined day-to-day substance use in males and violence toward female partners and found that the use of cocaine and/or alcohol was associated with increases in physical aggression, even after controlling for the presence of antisocial personality disorder (Fals-Stewart, Golden, & Schumacher, 2003). Denison, Parades, and Booth (1997) reported in regular cocaine users that the incidence of violent behavior increased during periods of cocaine and/or cocaine-alcohol use and that the nature of the violent behavior changed after cocaine use escalated into cocaine dependence. Structured phone interviews documented that cocaine-dependent individuals reported committing violent acts, including murder and rape, while acutely intoxicated (Miller, Gold, & Mahler, 1991). The authors speculated that dysregulation of the limbic system following chronic cocaine use may be a neurobiological mechanism related to heightened aggression (Miller et al., 1991). The dysregulated limbic system hypothesis of cocaine and aggression was also suggested by Davis (1996), who further proposed that chronic cocaine use may produce a kind of kindling effect in the limbic region that could trigger aggressive behavior. Correspondingly, cocaine-dependent individuals were more aggressive than controls based on psychometric and laboratory measures of aggression and showed a significant correlation between measures of aggression and growth hormone response to a buspirone challenge, which was not observed in controls (Moeller et al., 1994). In a subsequent study, however, Moeller and colleagues (1997) reported that, after controlling for the presence of antisocial personality disorder in cocaine-dependent subjects, there was no relationship between aggressive behavior and cocaine craving, withdrawal, or use levels. In addition to cocaine, violent and aggressive behavior has been linked to the abuse of other psychostimulants, including methamphetamine (National Institute on Drug Abuse, 1998;

Richards, Johnson, Stark, & Derlet, 1999) and 3,4-methylenedioxy-methamphetamine (MDMA or Ecstasy) (Bond, Verheyden, Wingrove, & Curran, 2004; Gerra, Zaimovic, Ampollini, et al., 2001).

Opiate dependence is related to heightened aggression in response to neurochemical challenges on both laboratory measures (Gerra, Zaimovic, Raggi, et al., 2001) and psychometric scales (Gerra et al., 1995). A large-scale study of heroin addicts in the Baltimore area showed that violent crimes were most likely during the onset of initial addiction and violent, as well as all other, criminal activity decreased substantially during periods of abstinence (Ball, Shaffer, & Nurco, 1983). As with other drugs of abuse, additional studies highlight the complexity of the relationship between drug use and aggressive behavior. For example, Bovasso, Alterman, Cacciola, and Rutherford (2002) reported that among individuals on methadone maintenance, increased risk for violent criminal activity was associated primarily with the presence of antisocial personality disorder. Among heroin-dependent incarcerated individuals, violent behavior was more likely when a history criminal behavior preceded heroin use (termed "primary antisocials") than vice versa (Kaye et al., 1998). Furthermore, one epidemiological study examining the use of heroin and the onset of criminal behavior found little evidence for a relationship between the onset of crime, violent crime, and heroin use (Taylor & Albright, 1981). These authors also noted that once regular heroin use developed, crimes were typically focused on obtaining money rather than aggressive behavior intended to produce harm.

Several large catchment-based epidemiological studies have shown that the presence of any *DSM-IV* disorder (*Diagnostic and Statistical Manual of Mental Disorders*, fourth edition; American Psychiatric Association, 1994) places an individual at increased risk for violent behavior. This risk is greatly increased by the presence of substance abuse symptoms (Robins, 1993; Steadman et al., 1998; Swanson, Holzer, Ganju, & Jono, 1990). Consistent with the preceding paragraphs, and perhaps most notable, is the finding that the combined presence of substance use disorders and Axis II personality disorders (particularly conduct, antisocial personality, and borderline personality disorders) increases the risk for violent behavior and violent crime well above that of either disorder alone; by one account comorbid substance use and personality disorders increase the odds of violent criminal behavior by 15–20:1 compared to community-matched base rates (Steadman et al., 1998). Adding further complexity, another study noted that adolescent drug users were not only more prone to fighting and assault than nondrug users, they were also more significantly more likely to be victims of violent behavior (Kingery, Pruitt, & Hurley, 1992). The collective implication of such data is that, at least in natural settings, rather than a direct pharmacological effect of (most) drugs on aggressive behavior, there are important interactions with concomitant factors, such as history or aggressive behavior and the presence of psychiatric disorders, that must be understood.

The foregoing is intended, in part, to highlight the range of interacting variables involved in connecting drug use and aggressive behavior. The apparent confluence of factors underscores the complex nature of the relationship between psychopathology, behavioral history, and drug effects on aggressive behavior and speaks to the importance of laboratory-based experiments. Controlled laboratory studies allow for the isolation of relevant variables that may be involved in drug effects on aggressive behavior. The ensuing sections of this chapter detail the outcomes of such laboratory experiments in human populations.

Laboratory Studies of Human Aggression

Defining the Aggressive Response

The primary problem facing laboratory studies of human aggression is establishing an operational definition of an aggressive response. Investigators have historically distinguished between verbal and physical aggression. Physical aggression is defined as behavior which produced or was intended to produce physical injury to or pain in another person. Lack of agreement regarding definitions of aggressive behavior has been a significant impediment to the progress of research in this area.

Before the laboratory studies of human aggression could proceed, the operational definition of the aggressive response and the development of an objective measure of such a response had to be established. The aggressive response could not result in any physical injury. Buss (1961) operationally defined aggressive responses as responses which result in the actual or ostensible delivery of a noxious, aversive stimulus to another person. The term noxious or aversive stimulus indicated that the subject would respond to avoid or escape the presentation of such a stimulus. The aversive stimulus employed by Buss was electric shock. The presentation of an aversive stimulus (e.g., electric shock) was thought to be directly analogous to the presentation of aversive stimuli, such as physical blows, in the natural environment. The research subject presented the aversive stimulus to the other person by pressing a button, which allowed automatic and objective recording of the aggressive response.

Procedures Used to Measure the Aggressive Response

Three basic methodologies have been developed to study human aggressive behavior under controlled laboratory conditions: the Buss procedure, Taylor's Competitive Reaction Time Task, and the Point Subtraction Aggression Paradigm. All three of these paradigms employ the same operational definition of the aggressive response, that is, the actual or ostensible delivery of an aversive stimulus to another person. The aggressive response is recorded in these procedures by requiring subjects to press buttons to deliver the aversive stimulus.

Buss Aggression Machine

In the Buss procedure, subjects are told that the study involves the assessment of the effects of punishment on learning. The research subjects are instructed to present an electric shock to another subject whenever the subject makes an error on a learning task. The research subject chooses the intensity of the shock by pressing one of a series of buttons representing increasing shock intensities. The measures of the aggressive response are (a) the shock intensity selected for presentation to the other subject and (b) the shock duration, the amount of time the subject presses the shock delivery button. In contrast to the other two procedures, the Buss procedure does not involve provocation.

Zeichner and Pihl (1979, 1980) modified the basic Buss procedure to include a retaliatory response involving provocation of the research subject. When the research subject ostensibly administered an electric shock to the fictitious other person following an error, this other person was able to present an auditory tone

PHARMACOLOGY AND PSYCHOPHYSIOLOGY

of varying intensity via headphones to the research subject.

Taylor's Competitive Reaction Time Task

Taylor (1967) developed a second procedure, the Competitive Reaction Time Task (CRT), which also involved the ostensible presentation of electric shock to another fictitious person. Research subjects were instructed that they were competing with another subject in a reaction time task. Before each reaction time trial, the research subject selected a shock intensity, which might be delivered to the other subject, and presumably the other subject did the same. At the end of each trial, the subject with the slowest reaction time received the electric shock. The investigator controlled outcomes, since there was no other competing subject, and the research subject received electric shock on half of the trials. Research subjects also received feedback after each trial regarding the shock intensity selected by the other subject whether or not the electric shock was presented. To maintain aggressive responses (setting shock intensities for the other subject), the research subject was given feedback which indicated that over trials the other subject set higher shock intensities for the research subject.

This presented the research participant with another person acting in an increasingly more aggressive manner over the course of the test session. As with the Buss procedure, the measure of aggression is the intensity of electric shock the research subject sets for the other person on each trial. Bond and Lader (1986) modified Taylor's CRT by substituting white noise for electric shock, and other researchers have also employed noise (Bushman, Baumeister, & Phillips, 2001). For a recent review of aggression research using the Taylor CRT procedure see McCloskey and Berman (2003).

Point Subtraction Aggression Paradigm

A third procedure, the Point Subtraction Aggression Paradigm (PSAP), altered the type of aversive stimulus from electric shock to the subtraction of money (Cherek, 1981, 1992). More detailed descriptions have been provided in a recent chapter devoted to the PSAP (Cherek, Lane, & Pietras, 2003). The subtraction of money will maintain avoidance and escape respond-

ing and functions as an aversive stimulus similar to electric shock. This change in the type of aversive stimulus has advantages which are discussed in the following section. The PSAP procedure provides both aggressive and nonaggressive response options to subjects. One nonaggressive response option is a monetary reinforced response which allows subjects to accumulate money on a computer screen, which is paid to the subjects at the end of their participation each day. Subtracting money from their counter and attributing this to the behavior of a fictitious subject paired with the research subject during that particular session provokes subjects. The research subject is told that the other subject gets to keep money which is subtracted from the research subject's earnings. The subject has an aggressive response option available, which allows the research subject to retaliate and subtract money from the other subject's earnings. Such responses meet the operational definition of ostensible delivery of an aversive stimulus to another person. The research subject does not keep money subtracted from the other person. A third option, an escape option, is also typically available that protects the subject's earnings from subtractions initiated by the other person. Participants are provoked throughout each experimental session, and both aggressive and escape responses produce temporary periods of time during which research subjects are not provoked (termed provocation-free intervals/ PFIs). At least one provocation, that is, monetary subtraction, must occur before a PFI can be initiated by either aggressive or escape responses, ensuring that research subjects will be provoked across the session. The measure of aggression is simply the number of times the subject presses the aggressive response option button. A recent review of PSAP research has been published (Cherek et al., 2003).

Comparisons of These Three Procedures

Because the Buss procedure did not include provocation to engender aggressive responding, this procedure quickly fell into disuse. The Taylor CRT procedure has continued to be used over the ensuing 35 years. The newest procedure, the PSAP, has not enjoyed as widespread use by researchers, but does provide a number of advantages over the Taylor CRT procedure.

The use of the subtraction of money as an aversive stimulus to increase the likelihood of aggressive responding can be presented across sessions repeatedly, while electric shock presentations are limited to one session. In addition, the use of monetary subtractions as a provoking stimulus greatly expands the types of subjects who may participate, for example, children and patients. The intensity of possible electric shock presentations is increased across blocks of trials in the Taylor CRT procedure, whereas provocation frequency remains relatively constant during and across sessions with the PSAP procedure. This would result in very large changes in aggressive responses within blocks of trials, making it more difficult to detect possible drug effects. Another factor contributing to increased sensitivity is the use of rate of aggressive responses as the dependent measure with PSAP. The Taylor CRT procedure cannot use frequency as a measure, since the number of trials, that is, the opportunity to aggress, is controlled by the experimenter. With the PSAP procedure, the number of aggressive responses per session can vary from zero to several hundred.

The PSAP procedure also provides alternative response options to the subject. In the Taylor CRT procedure, the subject must respond aggressively and no other options are provided. The subject can vary the intensity of the shock, but the subject must choose to administer a shock to the fictitious other person. The PSAP procedure provides two additional response options (a) the monetary reinforced response option which allows the subject to accumulate money and (b) an escape option which protects the subject's earnings, but does not aggress toward the other person.

Tedeschi and Quigley (1996) and colleagues have criticized laboratory studies of human aggression. Their principal criticism is that laboratory procedures do not provide a nonaggressive response option. This criticism does apply to the Buss and Taylor procedures, but the PSAP procedure provides a monetary reinforced option and an escape response option. However, more recent studies using the Taylor CRT have included a zero shock intensity the equivalent of a nonaggressive response (Zeichner, Frey, Parrott, & Butryn, 1999). These authors have criticized laboratory procedures because of a failure to establish external validity, (i.e., providing data that aggressive individuals respond more under laboratory conditions than nonaggressive subjects).

There are in fact studies supporting the external validity of both the Taylor CRT and PSAP procedures. Gustafson (1985, 1992) provided evidence of the validity of the Taylor CRT procedure. The external va-

lidity of the PSAP procedure has been established in studies comparing violent and nonviolent male parolees (Cherek, Moeller, Schnapp, & Dougherty, 1997; Cherek, Schnapp, Moeller, & Dougherty, 1996) and female parolees (Cherek, Lane, Dougherty, Moeller, & White, 2000). Others have established significant correlations between diagnostic categories or rating scales/questionnaires and aggressive responding on the PSAP (Coccaro, Berman, Kavoussi, & Hauger, 1996; Dougherty, Bjork, Huckabee, Moeller, & Swann, 1999). Other researchers have established similar relationships for aggressive responses on the Taylor CRT procedure (Wolfe & Baron, 1971; Zeichner et al., 1999).

Effects of Drugs on Human Aggression Under Laboratory Conditions

All three procedures have been used to assess the effects of alcohol and other drugs on human aggression. The PSAP procedure has a number of advantages, particularly when evaluating the effects of drugs on human aggression. The major advantage for drug studies is the ability to evaluate the specificity of drug effects. With the PSAP procedure, the investigator can compare the effects of the particular drug on aggressive, escape, and monetary reinforced responding. Drugs found to decrease both aggressive and escape responding, that is, d-fenfluramine, can possibly have some affect on participants' reactions to provocation or on its aversiveness, thereby reducing the ability of the provocation to engender aggressive and escape responses. A generalized sedative or stimulant action would be indicated by a decrease or increase in monetary reinforced responding. If the aggressive and monetary reinforced responding both decreased or increased, this would most likely be the result on a nonspecific drug action. The Taylor CRT procedure can also evaluate specificity to some extent by examining the effects of the drug on the reaction times of the subjects.

One major problem hinders pharmacological investigations employing the Taylor CRT (i.e., the inability to do repeated testing within subjects and determine dose-response relationships). This was clearly evidenced in a study (Lau & Pihl, 1994) which attempted to compare placebo and a high alcohol dose on aggressive responding using the Taylor CRT within subjects. The authors could not demonstrate an alcohol effect, because the effect on two CRT sessions was greater than any effect attributed to alcohol. The placebo and alcohol treatments were balanced across participants.

Alcohol

Bennett, Buss, and Carpenter (1969) conducted the first laboratory study of the effects of alcohol on laboratory measures of human aggression using the Buss procedure. Acute administration of relatively low doses of alcohol (0.24 and 0.5 g/kg) result in small nonsignificant increases in the shock intensity selected for delivery to the other person, the measure of aggression. Zeichner and Pihl (1979, 1980), using a modified version of the Buss procedure, observed significant increases in the intensity and duration of shocks presented by research subjects after administration of a high dose of alcohol (1.2 g/kg) compared to subjects given a placebo drink or no beverage.

The first study using the Taylor CRT reported increased aggressive responses following administration of a more moderate alcohol dose of approximately 0.5 g/kg (Shuntich & Taylor, 1972). Participants receiving this alcohol dose set higher shock intensities for the other subjects than subjects receiving a placebo drink or no beverage. A subsequent study, comparing the same alcohol dose, 0.5 g/kg, and a high dose, 1.2 g/kg, found that individuals given the higher alcohol dose set higher shock intensities for the other subject during the first trial before they were provided with any information about shock intensities selected by the other fictitious subject (Taylor & Gammon, 1975). In addition, individuals given the higher alcohol dose were more likely to select the highest available shock intensity for the other subject. Another study reported that subjects given the 1.2 g/kg dose were more likely to choose an extreme shock intensity added to the usual selection panel which was described as very painful and potentially injurious to the other subject (Taylor, Schmutte, Leonard, & Cranston, 1979).

Chermack and Taylor (1995) compared the effects of the subject's expectancies regarding the effects of alcohol on aggression and the actual administration of alcohol. The highest alcohol dose increased aggressive responses on the Taylor CRT independently of the subjects' reported expectancies. Gender effects have also been examined, and alcohol produced more consistent increases in aggressive responses on the Taylor CPT among men when compared to women (Giancola & Zeichner, 1995). A review of earlier studies of alcohol effects on human aggression presents investigations

of a number of additional variables (Taylor & Chermack, 1993; Taylor & Leonard, 1983).

The PSAP has also been used to investigate the effects of alcohol on human aggression under laboratory conditions. The basic research design is very different, consisting of a within-subject repeated measures design, with each subject receiving placebo and three different doses of alcohol. With the Taylor CRT, the procedure employed group designs in which each subject received a single dose, usually a placebo and one alcohol dose.

Using the PSAP, the first study reported dose-dependent increases in the number of aggressive responses per session following administration of 0, 0.12, 0.23, and 0.46 g/kg of alcohol. Two early studies of the effects of alcohol on aggressive responding (Cherek, Steinberg, & Manno, 1985; Cherek, Steinberg, & Vines, et al., 1984) reported dose-related increases following alcohol administration. Kelly, Cherek, Steinberg, and Robinson (1988) reported that alcohol (0.25, 0.5, and 0.75 g/kg) increased aggressive responding across different provocation frequency conditions. Alcohol doses of 0.25, 0.5, and 1.0 g/kg also produced increased aggressive responses on the PSAP in female subjects (Dougherty, Cherek, & Bennett, 1996).

Increasing the response requirement for monetary reinforcement produced increases in aggressive responding, and the increased aggressive responding resulting from administration of 0.5 g/kg of alcohol was greater at higher monetary reinforcement response requirements (Kelly, Cherek, & Steinberg, 1989). Alcohol produces the characteristic increases in aggressive behavior when subjects are provided with a social context, that is, they will be paired with other people, but it has no effect when subjects are instructed that they are paired with a computer (Kelly & Cherek, 1993).

With all three laboratory procedures, it was found that acute administration of alcohol increases measures of human aggression under laboratory conditions. As discussed in a review (Kelly & Cherek, 1993) the effect may be due to large increases in aggression evidenced by a small proportion of subjects, with many subjects showing no changes following alcohol administration. An earlier study (Cherek, Steinberg, Kelly, Robinson, & Spiga, 1990) reported different effects of D-amphetamine and diazepam on aggressive responding when provocations were attributed to another person compared to a computer.

A meta-analysis of the results of several laboratory studies concluded that alcohol caused an increase in aggressive behavior (Bushman & Cooper, 1990); however, this too is influenced by data from a small subset of the group data.

Marijuana

Historically, there has been continued controversy in the scientific literature regarding the relationship between marijuana use and aggressive behavior. Only a few studies have been conducted. The first study employed the Taylor CRT procedure (Taylor et al., 1976), with Δ-9-tetrahydrocannabinol (THC) administered orally, the active principle in marijuana, and subjects were assigned to a low (0.1 mg/kg) or a high (0.3 mg/kg) dose. Subjects receiving the higher THC dose set lower shock intensities for the fictitious other subjects than subjects given the low THC dose. This same effect was observed during the first trial before subjects received any information regarding shock intensities set for the research subject by the other fictitious subject, that is, before any provocation. A subsequent study (Myerscough & Taylor, 1985) also administered THC orally in three different doses: 0.1, 0.25, and 0.4 mg/kg. In contrast to the earlier THC study, the other fictitious person set high shock intensities for the subject thorough out the series of trials. The mean shock intensities set by the research subjects were not changed across the three oral THC dose conditions. A very intense potentially injurious shock intensity could also be selected, in addition to the usual 10 shock intensities. At the end of the second trial, subjects were informed that the other person had selected the very intense shock for presentation to the research subject. Following this specific intense provocation, subjects receiving the lowest oral THC dose increased their shock settings for the fictitious subject, but there was no change in subjects receiving the middle and high oral THC doses.

Two studies have been conducted on the effects of smoked marijuana of different potencies on aggressive responding employing the PSAP. The first study, of participants with histories of drug abuse, reported that marijuana produced increases in aggressive responding, while escape and monetary reinforced responding was decreased (Cherek et al., 1993). A second study determined that the effects of acute marijuana smoking on aggressive responding depended on the frequency of provocation (high vs. low) during the test session (Cherek & Dougherty, 1995).

A study of chronic marijuana smokers under hospital conditions examined the effects of acute marijuana withdrawal over a 28-day detoxification period (Kouri et al., 1999). Significant elevations in aggressive responding using the PSAP procedure were noted during the first week of observation. These differences did not persist beyond the first week.

Tobacco

Only a few studies have looked at the effects of tobacco smoking and tobacco deprivation on human aggression in the laboratory. Schechter and Rand (1974) compared aggressive responses in tobacco smokers and nonsmokers using the Buss procedure. Only tobacco smokers increased the intensity and duration of electric shocks ostensibly presented to fictitious subjects, and this only occurred when they were not allowed to smoke. The increased aggressive responding was associated with acute tobacco deprivation.

In our initial PSAP study (Cherek, 1981) the effects of not smoking or smoking low or high nicotine cigarettes were compared within tobacco smoking subjects. When subjects smoked tobacco cigarettes they emitted fewer aggressive responses compared to nonsmoking conditions. The decreased aggressive responding was also dose related, with the high nicotine cigarettes resulting in a larger decrease compared to the low nicotine cigarettes. Both of these studies produced results which are consistent with the view that acute tobacco deprivation may increase aggressive responding, rather than acute tobacco smoking reducing aggressive responding.

One additional study focused upon acute tobacco deprivation and its possible effects on aggressive responding. Individuals undergoing acute tobacco deprivation were studied under three conditions: nicotine gum, placebo gum, and no gum. Aggressive responding increased under conditions of no gum and placebo gum compared to nicotine gum conditions or when subjects were allowed to smoke cigarettes (Cherek, Bennett, & Grabowski, 1991).

Opiates

Two studies have been reported on the effects of opiates on human aggression. The first examined the effects of 45 mg of oral morphine using the Taylor CRT and found that morphine increased aggressive responses (Berman, Taylor, & Marged, 1993). A second study assessed the effects of codeine (25, 50, and 75 mg/70 kg) on aggressive responding using the PSAP. Slight increases in aggressive responding occurred at the middle dose and no effects were seen at the highest codeine dose (Spiga, Cherek, Roache, & Cowan, 1990).

Benzodiazepines

Studies utilizing the Taylor CRT and the PSAP have examined the effects of several benzodiazepines. The first Taylor CRT study (Wilkinson, 1985) used the standard paradigm and assigned subjects to placebo or 10 mg of diazepam. As is typical with the Taylor procedure, subjects were provoked with increasing shock intensity across blocks of trials. This was accomplished by providing the research subjects with information of increasing shock intensities selected for presentation to the research subject by the other person. During the initial trials when low shock intensities were set for the research subject, subjects receiving 10 mg of diazepam set higher shock intensities than those receiving placebo. Small differences were observed as the provoking shock intensity increased across blocks of trials. Overall, the subjects receiving 10 mg of diazepam set significantly higher shock intensities for the fictitious other subject, (i.e., acute diazepam increased aggression). A more recent study (Ben-Porath & Taylor, 2002) replicated the effect of 10 mg of diazepam to increase aggressive responding, and the effect was most reliable in subjects who reported high levels of hostility.

A study compared the effects of oxazepam (15 and 30 mg) and lorazepam (1 and 2 mg) on aggressive responses using the Taylor CRT and found that the higher lorazepam dose increased aggressive responses (Bond & Lader, 1988). Alprazolam (1 mg) increased aggressive responses on the Taylor CRT, and when combined with alcohol (0.5 g/kg) the effect of this combination in increasing aggressive responses was greater than the effects of alprazolam or alcohol alone (Bond & Silveira, 1993). In addition, alprazolam administered to patients with panic disorder with agoraphobia resulted in increased aggressive responses on the Taylor CRT (Bond et al., 1995). Comparisons of three benzodiazepines (clorazepate, diazepam, and oxazepam) at a single dose indicated that only diazepam reliably produced increased aggression on the Taylor CRT (Weisman, Berman & Taylor, 1998).

A study of the effects of acute diazepam administration on human aggression using the PSAP procedure produced very different results. The PSAP study (Cherek, Steinberg, Kelly, & Robinson, 1986) used a within-subject repeated measures design, with each subject receiving placebo and 2.5, 5, and 10 mg per 70 kg of diazepam. Seven of eight subjects decreased aggressive responding following the highest diazepam dose, and three subjects also decreased at the middle 5-mg dose. This reduction in aggressive responses is the result of a diminished ability of provocation (monetary subtractions) to reliably produce aggressive responses (see Cherek & Steinberg, 1987). One subject increased aggressive responding following diazepam administration, an observation subsequently noted with other benzodiazepines. A study of triazolam at doses of 0.125, 0.25, and 0.5 mg/kg produced similar results: dose-dependent decreases in monetary reinforced responding and escape responding and variable effects on aggressive responding (Cherek, Spiga, Roache, & Cowan, 1991). An unpublished study of lorazepam also produced one individual with large increases in aggressive responding and nine participants who decreased aggressive responding.

Our effects with diazepam, triazolam, and lorazepam are consistent with clinical reports of paradoxical increases in aggression in a small group of patients receiving benzodiazepine therapy (Bixler, Kales, Brubaker, & Kales, 1987; Hall & Zisook, 1981). Results of diazepam effects using the Taylor CRT procedure and the PSAP are conflicting, the PSAP reporting decreased aggressive responses in almost all subjects and the Taylor CRT procedure reporting increases. Taylor's CRT procedure employs a group design with only one treatment condition for each subject and does not determine dose-response effects. Both of these factors would limit the sensitivity of the CRT procedure. In addition, differences in provocation may also contribute to the different results. In the Taylor CRT procedure, the intensity of the shock set for the research subject increases across trials, in contrast with the PSAP procedure, in which the frequency of provocation remains relatively constant across sessions and experimental days.

CNS Stimulants

Initial studies with the PSAP looked at acute effects of caffeine (in capsules) and a comparison of drinking decaffeinated and regular coffee. Both of these studies reported modest decreases in aggressive responding in regular caffeine users (Cherek, Steinberg, & Brauchi, 1983, 1984). Since subjects reporting higher caffeine consumption had larger decreases in aggressive responding, these effects could be attributed to acute caffeine withdrawal similar to the tobacco results.

D-amphetamine has been studied with the PSAP procedure (Cherek et al., 1986). D-amphetamine resulted in increased aggressive responding at the 5 and 10 mg per 70 kg doses. At the highest dose (20 mg per 70 kg), D-amphetamine decreased aggressive responding relative to the lower doses to a level at or slightly below those observed at placebo administration.

Oral doses (1 and 2 mg/kg) of cocaine were given to subjects participating in Taylor CRT trials. The highest cocaine dose produced more intense shock selection (more aggression) by these subjects than by subjects receiving the lower cocaine dose or placebo (Licata, Taylor, Berman, & Cranston, 1993).

Tryptophan Depletion

Tryptophan, an essential amino acid, is necessary for the synthesis of serotonin. Administering a drink containing a mixture of amino acids (excluding tryptophan) stimulates protein synthesis that will deplete the body stores of tryptophan required for such synthesis, but not present in the drink. This rapid depletion of tryptophan will greatly diminish serotonin synthesis for some period of time. Thus, the tryptophan depletion procedure is used to examine the short-term effects of reducing serotonin synthesis and in turn function.

An initial study of the effects of tryptophan depletion using a modified Buss procedure produced negative results (Smith, Pihl, Young, & Ervin, 1986). Studies using both Taylor's CRT and the PSAP have reported increased aggression following consumption of an amino acid drink which resulted in a depletion of available stores of tryptophan. Four studies using the Taylor CRT procedures reported nonsignificant increases in aggressive responding (LeMarquand et al., 1998; LeMarquand, Benkelfat, Pihl, Palmour, & Young, 1999; Pihl et al., 1995; Young, Pihl, & Ervin, 1988). Four studies employing the PSAP procedure (Bjork, Dougherty, Moeller, Cherek, & Swann, 1999; Bjork, Dougherty, Moeller, & Swann, 2000; Dougherty, Moeller, Bjork, & Marsh, 1999; Moeller et al., 1996) all reported significant increases in aggressive responding following tryptophan depletion procedures. These comparisons clearly indicate that the PSAP procedure is more sensitive to the effects of tryptophan depletion than Taylor's CRT, probably due in part to the measure of response frequency as opposed to the selection of shock intensity. In addition, the effects of tryptophan depletion in increasing aggressive responses on Taylor's CRT

have also been shown in female subjects (Bond, Wingrove, & Critchlow, 2001).

Serotonin Releasing and Reuptake Inhibitors

Many studies have established a consistent relationship between serotonin and aggressive behavior (see Manuck, Kaplan, & Lotrich, ch. 4, and Miczek & Fish, ch. 5, in this volume; Eichelman, 1990; Miczek, Weerts, Haney, & Tidey, 1994; Zubieta & Alessi, 1993). The PSAP procedure has been used in a series of studies to examine the relationship between serotonin and human aggression. Some of these studies involved a neuroendocrine challenge test in which a drug was administered to stimulate serotonin receptors and plasma prolactin was measured to assess the functional serotonergic activity. One study compared the neuroendocrine challenge response in two groups of male and female parolees based upon their self-reported history of aggression (Cherek, Moeller, Kahn-Dawood, Swann, & Lane, 1999). The challenge agent was an oral dose of baclofen, 0.4 mg/kg, and plasma prolactin levels were measured. Prolactin release was suppressed among the violent parolee subjects, indicating a diminished CNS serotonergic activity. In a subsequent study (Moeller, Cherek, Dougherty, Lane, & Swann, 1998), subjects participated in PSAP testing and were then given the neuroendocrine challenge agent ipsapirone. Subjects with the greatest frequency of aggressive responses during PSAP sessions demonstrated the smallest changes in plasma prolactin indicative of diminished serotonin function. Coccaro et al. (1996) used d-fenfluramine (a serotonin releasing agent) as a challenge drug in 14 personality disordered males with a history of aggressive behavior. The prolactin response to d-fenfluramine challenge was significantly negatively correlated to the subject's frequency of aggressive responding during PSAP sessions.

Additional studies with the PSAP have been conducted which involve administration of drugs that directly interact with serotonin. In the initial study (Cherek & Lane, 1999), male parolees with a history of childhood conduct disorder (CD) as children and adolescents, as well as continued antisocial behavior as adults, received placebo and three doses of d,l-fenfluramine (0.2, 0.4, and 0.8 mg). This drug stimulates the release of serotonin and also dopamine in the CNS (Rowland & Carlton, 1986). The results indicated that aggressive responding was significantly decreased at the highest *d,l*-fenfluramine dose. Simultaneous monetary responding was unchanged, indicating that the decreased aggressive responding could not be attributed to nonspecific sedative effects.

A subsequent study (Cherek & Lane, 2001) administered three doses of *d*-fenfluramine, 0.1, 0.2, and 0.4 mg, in two groups of male parolees. *D*-fenfluramine is a more specific releaser of serotonin, with little or no effect upon dopamine. One group had a history of CD and adult antisocial behavior, and the other had no history of CD. At the highest *d*-fenfluramine dose, aggressive responding with the PSAP procedure was significantly reduced among the CD subjects and the non-CD control subjects were unchanged.

Another study (Cherek, Lane, Pietras, & Steinberg, 2002) relating to serotonin function was conducted with the serotonin reuptake inhibitor paroxetine. Male parolees with a history of CD were assigned to placebo or paroxetine, 20 mg per day, treatment. The study consisted of 1 week of baseline, 2 weeks of placebo treatment, followed by 4 weeks of either paroxetine or placebo treatment, and finally 2 weeks of placebo treatment for both groups. During the period of paroxetine treatment, subjects decreased aggressive responding in comparison to the placebo subjects; however, the differences were not statistically significant.

Collectively, all these studies, which have examined effects of perturbing serotonin function, suggest a role for serotonin in the regulation of human aggressive behavior. In addition, drugs which increase serotonin function result in reductions in aggressive behavior, and this effect may be more pronounced in subjects with a lifetime history of antisocial behavior which begins in childhood.

GABA Agents

More recently, our laboratory has begun to investigate drugs which interact with the γ-aminobutyric acid (GABA) neurotransmitter system. The GABA system is another potential inhibitory system which has been implicated in the possible control of aggression based upon studies with nonhuman subjects (see Miczek & Fish, ch. 5 in this volume). Our initial study (Cherek, Lane, Pietras, Sharon, & Steinberg, 2002) examined the effects of acute doses of baclofen, a $GABA_B$ agonist, which does not interact with the $GABA_A$ benzodiazepine receptor complex. Again male parolees were separated into those with and without a history of CD. Across days, three acute doses of 0.07, 0.14, and 0.28

mg/kg of baclofen were administered with intervening placebo days. No effects on monetary reinforced responding were observed in either group, indicating no evidence of a generalized, nonspecific stimulation or sedation. Escape responding was decreased slightly in both groups. Major differences were observed on the effects of baclofen on aggressive responding. Baclofen decreased aggressive responding among the CD group, but increased aggressive responding in the non-CD group. In both cases, maximal effects were observed at the highest baclofen dose.

The next study (Cherek, Tcheremissine, Lane, & Pietras, 2004) examined the effects of gabapentin, which promotes the release of GABA, affecting all types of GABA receptors. Gabapentin was administered acutely in doses of 200, 400, and 800 mg with intervening placebo days. These effects were observed in two groups of CD or non-CD male and female parolees. The effects of gabapentin were not different in the two groups. No changes in monetary reinforced responding were seen, indicating no evidence for nonspecific sedative effects. Both aggressive and escape responding were decreased at the highest doses, while the lowest baclofen dose produced slight increases in both responses.

At the present time, studies are examining the effects of lorazepam, a $GABA_A$ agonist, flumazenil, a $GABA_A$ receptor antagonist, and tiagabine, a GABA reuptake inhibitor.

Clinical Studies

Aggressive behavior is common in psychiatric disorders and accounts for significant morbidity and mortality. The treatment of aggressive behavior is a part of the practice of clinical psychiatry and an active area of research. Although a variety of psychopharmacological agents (aimed at modifying aggression) have been studied in different patient populations, there is yet no agent with an FDA-established indication for aggression. Importantly, most of the current treatments of human aggressive behavior tend to focus primarily on impulsive aggression. Thus, current therapeutic modalities do not address issues related to premeditated aggression, with the exception of specific circumstances associated with delusional beliefs (Buchanan et al., 1993).

Excessive patterns of human aggressive behavior are extremely heterogeneous phenomena present across a variety of diagnostic categories, ranging from brain injury to schizophrenia and personality disorders. The effectiveness of treatment varies greatly with the diagnosis. Certain medications may be the treatment of choice for certain neurological and psychiatric conditions associated with aggressive behavior and may, at the same time, be ineffective in the treatment of aggressive patients with other neuropsychiatric disorders (Fava, 1997). Although there are no specific antiaggressive agents currently available, the large body of existing literature supports therapeutic applications of a variety of psychotropic agents, including mood stabilizers and anticonvulsants, antidepressants, anxiolytics, antipsychotics, and β-blockers. Much of the current knowledge is based on clinical case reports and uncontrolled studies. This chapter, however, focuses on the results of more systemic treatment outcomes from double-blind, placebo-controlled trials.

Mood Stabilizers and Anticonvulsants

Lithium may be the first treatment reported to have a specific, nonsedative effect on aggressive behavior. Lithium affects multiple neurotransmitter systems. No neurotransmitter has been shown to be unaffected by lithium. As a result, serotonin, norepinephrine, dopamine, acetylcholine, and GABA and a variety of neuropeptides have been implicated both singly and in combination to explain the therapeutic effects of lithium. (Jefferson & Greist, 2000). Lithium has a gradual onset of action; therefore, it is mainly used for subacute or chronic, but not acute, treatment. Lithium reduces aggression across a range of psychiatric diagnoses in different patient populations, including prisoners, patients diagnosed with major psychiatric illnesses (i.e., bipolar disorder, major depression, and schizophrenia) or personality disorders, and children and adolescents with a history of conduct disorder. One of the first double-blind, placebo-controlled studies of the effect of lithium on aggressive behavior was conducted by Sheard, Marini, Bridges, and Wagner (1976). Sixty-six male subjects, who were prisoners in a medium security institution, ranging in age from 16 to 24 years, received lithium or placebo daily for up to 3 months. After final analysis, lithium was shown to reduce infractions involving aggressive behavior. These results were confirmed in another double-blind, placebo-controlled trial (Craft et al., 1987). Five centers participated in the trial, contributing a total of 42 patients. In the lithium-treated group, 73% of patients showed a reduction in aggression during treatment. One of the few double-

blind, placebo-controlled studies to examine the pharmacological treatment of children and adolescents with conduct disorder compared lithium and placebo (Malone, Delaney, Luebbert, Cater, & Cambell, 2000). Eighty-six patients were initially enrolled in the study; 40 children and adolescents, with a median age of 12.5 years and diagnosed with conduct disorder, entered and completed the inpatient treatment. Lithium's antiaggressive properties were clinically and statistically superior to those of a placebo. Although lithium has been reported to be safe and effective in the treatment of children and adolescents, its use was associated with adverse side effects, including nausea, vomiting, and urinary frequency.

A growing body of literature supports a role for divalproex in the treatment of impulsive aggression, agitation, hostility, and irritability in a variety of psychiatric disorders (Horne & Lindley, 1995; Kavoussi & Coccaro, 1998). The pharmacological effects of divalproex sodium on impulsive aggressiveness and irritability were examined (Frankenburg & Zanarini, 2002). In a 6-month, double-blind, placebo-controlled study of 30 female subjects with borderline personality disorder and comorbid bipolar II disorder, divalproex was significantly more effective than placebo in reducing anger, irritability, and impulsive aggressiveness. In general, these symptoms declined about 30 to 40% for those treated with divalproex sodium and about 15% for those treated with placebo. The results of this study are limited to female patients diagnosed with borderline personality disorder. Therefore, additional research was needed to replicate these results. A study conducted by Hollander and colleagues (2003) was the first large, multicenter, randomized, double-blind, placebo-controlled trial conducted on the efficacy of divalproex sodium treatment on impulsive aggression. The data showed divalproex sodium to be superior to placebo in the treatment of aggression and irritability in a large subgroup of patients ($N = 96$) with cluster B personality disorders (i.e., borderline, antisocial, histrionic, and narcissistic). These data raise the interesting possibility that divalproex sodium may be effective in treating impulsive aggression across a range of heterogeneous patient populations.

Phenytoin has a long and controversial history as an antiaggressive agent. Initially, the suggestions of the antiaggressive effects of phenytoin were based on a series of clinical observations and reports published from samples of epileptic patients and patients with abnormal electroencephalograms (Looker & Connors,

1970; Ross & Jackson, 1940; Walker & Kirkpatrick, 1947). Over a period of a few decades, studies of the effects of phenytoin on human aggression produced equivocal results, with almost even numbers of positive (Haward, 1982; Stevens & Shaffer, 1970, 1973) and negative reports (Gottschalk, Covi, Ultana, & Bates, 1973; Uhlenhath, Stephens, Dim, & Covi, 1972). More recently, the effects of phenytoin on impulsive and premeditated aggression were examined in a double-blind, placebo-controlled trial (Barratt, Stanford, Felthous, & Kent, 1997). Of 126 inmates that completed the drug/placebo phases of the study, two groups of 30 inmates each were selected for the final analysis based on the pattern of their aggressive acts: primarily impulsive versus nonimpulsive or premeditated. The results suggested that phenytoin significantly reduces impulsive aggression but not premeditated aggressive acts. The mechanisms by which phenytoin may modify aggressive behavior were further examined (Stanford et al., 2001). In a double-blind, placebo-controlled crossover design, male subjects with a history of impulsive aggression were administered phenytoin and placebo. The results indicated a significant decrease in the frequency of impulsive-aggressive outbursts during phenytoin administration compared to baseline and placebo. Physiological measures (evoked potentials) were taken at baseline and at the end of each 6-week condition. As hypothesized, the impulsive-aggressive individual is better able to regulate sensory and early attentional processing and thus is more effective in evaluating and reacting to eliciting stimuli. Concomitant with this increased efficiency in processing was a reduction in impulsiveness/irritability and a decrease in aggressive behavior.

The antiaggressive effects of carbamazepine as an adjunctive treatment in the treatment of schizophrenia and schizoaffective disorder were suggested based on the results from two double-blind, placebo-controlled trials (Neppe, 1988; Okuma et al., 1989). The results of the Neppe study are limited by its having a heterogeneous patient population and a small sample size. Okuma and colleagues reported no significant difference between carbamazepine and placebo on symptoms of psychosis, but carbamazepine demonstrated better effects than placebo on agitation and aggression. However, this evidence appears inconclusive because the final analysis incorporated data from both behaviors. Carbamazepine has been used to treat aggressiveness in children with conduct disorder in a double-blind, placebo-controlled study (Cueva et al.,

1996), but significant effects versus placebo were not found.

Antidepressants

A large corpus of scientific evidence supports a relationship between central serotonergic system dysfunction and human impulsive aggression. Therefore, pharmacological enhancement of serotonin activity has often been used by practitioners to decrease irritability and aggression across a variety of diagnostic categories. The antiaggressive effects of fluoxetine, a selective serotonin reuptake inhibitor (SSRI), were examined in a study comparing 40 patients diagnosed with personality disorders who had current histories of impulsive-aggressive behavior and irritability (Coccaro & Kavoussi, 1997). The results of this double-blind, placebo-controlled trial confirmed that fluoxetine treatment diminished impulsive aggression in this group. The effect of fluoxetine in these subjects was primarily on verbal and indirect forms of aggression (e.g., aggression against objects). The absence of an effect on aggression against others may have been related to infrequently reported baseline levels. These results were not influenced by the secondary measures of depression, anxiety, or alcohol use. Similar conclusions were reached based on the outcomes from a double-blind, placebo-controlled, randomized trial using the SSRI fluvoxamine for 6 weeks, followed by a blind half-crossover for 6 weeks and an open follow-up for another 12 weeks, in 38 female patients with borderline personality disorder (Rinne, van den Brik, Wouters, & van Dyck, 2002). The outcome measures were the rapid mood shift, impulsivity, and aggression subscales from the Borderline Personality Disorder Severity Index (Weaver & Clum, 1993). Fluvoxamine produced a robust and long-lasting reduction in the scores on the subscale for rapid mood shifts. In contrast, no difference between the fluvoxamine and placebo groups was observed in the effect on the impulsivity and aggression scores.

Patients with chronic schizophrenia and a history of aggressive behavior, who remained symptomatic while receiving their daily antipsychotics, were enrolled into a double-blind, crossover study in which the patients were treated for 24 weeks with placebo and 24 weeks with citalopram. The results revealed that during citalopram treatment, the frequency of aggressive incidents was significantly lower and mental status did not deteriorate (Vartiainen et al., 1995).

Antipsychotics

Antipsychotic drugs are among the most frequently used pharmacological strategies in reducing acute agitation and aggression. Current data lack direct evidence for their specificity as antiaggressive agents beyond their sedative effects in acutely agitated patients or patients whose aggression is directly related to psychosis (Yudofsky, Silver, & Schneider, 1987). Furthermore, the traditional antipsychotic drugs (i.e., haloperidol, fluphenazine, and droperidol) are effective in the control of aggressive behavior when used on a short-term basis. Long-term use results in possible serious side effects, such as tardive dyskinesia, making chronic administration a less attractive alternative. On the other hand, atypical antipsychotics (i.e., clozapine, olanzapine, risperidone, ziprasidone, and quetiapine) have clinically effective antiaggressive effects that may be independent of their antipsychotic effects. Clozapine, the prototype of the second generation of atypical antipsychotics, is known to have a broad spectrum of clinical effects. A large study ($N = 137$) evaluated the impact of clozapine on aggression in an inpatient population over a period of 12 months (Chengappa et al., 2002). Using a mirror-image study design, seclusion and restrain rates were computed per patient-month and compared during clozapine treatment. Statistically significant reductions in seclusion and restraint rates supported the emerging data on the benefits of clozapine for aggressive and violent patients with psychoses.

Preliminary data from a smaller double-blind, placebo-controlled study provided evidence that a low dose of risperidone may have efficacy in the treatment of aggression in children and adolescents (ages 6–14) with conduct disorder (Findling et al., 2000). Although atypical antipsychotics can cause sedation in young patients treated with this class of medication, its authors noted that the reduction in aggression observed during the course of this study was not solely due to sedation.

In summary, although the behavioral specificity of the atypical antipsychotics remains promising, the behavioral assessment of aggression and the ethical difficulties of conducting well-controlled studies using neuroleptics continue to be problematic areas (Volavka & Citrome, 1999).

Benzodiazepines

Although little scientific evidence exists to support the use of benzodiazepines for the management of acute aggressive episodes, these agents may be particularly useful if anxiety is contributing to agitation or some degree of sedation is needed. In a double-blind study of 60 acute psychotic patients with a history of aggressive behavior, Guz, Moraes, and Sartoretto (1972) reported a significant trend suggesting that a combination of haloperidol and lorazepam was therapeutically superior to haloperidol alone for the treatment of severe agitation. However, one limitation that always should be considered is the paradoxical agitation that can occur with benzodiazepines. Several controlled laboratory studies and numerous clinical reports have documented an increase in aggressive behavior in normal volunteers and in clinical populations (Bond et al., 1995; Bond & Lader, 1988; Bond & Silveira, 1993; Salzman et al., 1974; Tobin, Bird, & Boyle, 1960). For example, triazolam has received significant criticism because of an alleged association with serious dose-dependent aggressive behavioral manifestations. These effects of triazolam on human aggressive behavior were tested by Cherek, Spiga, et al. (1991) under controlled laboratory conditions. The results confirmed that triazolam might produce substantial variability across human subjects in aggressive responding. Although understanding of the basic mechanisms by which triazolam can produce states of behavioral disinhibition in some individuals is not entirely clear, triazolam was banned in Great Britain in 1991. Perhaps a key determinant for the increase in aggressive behavior after benzodiazepine administration is the individual's personal history of aggression. Specifically, those with more extensive aggressive histories may be more prone to exacerbation following benzodiazepine administration.

The long-term use of benzodiazepines is associated with a variety of problems, including high potential for abuse and dependence, sedation, withdrawal symptoms, and altered cognitive function, making benzodiazepines a questionable choice for the pharmacological treatment of aggression.

β-Adrenergic Blockers

The first report of the antiaggressive properties of propranolol in humans did not provide any proposed mechanism of action (Elliott, 1977). To date, the exact mechanism of the antiaggressive effects of β-adrenergic agents is still not clear. It has been found that the onset of the antiaggressive effects of propranolol can be seen 4–8 weeks after the effective dose is reached (Yudofsky, Silver, & Holes, 1990). The dose of propranolol perceived as effective by researchers and clinicians ranges between 30 and 1,600 mg/day. However, a dose-dependent response relationship has not been systematically studied. Additionally, most of the studies involving propranolol did not include a placebo control. Greendyke, Kanter, Schuster, Vestreate, and Wootoon (1986) have completed a double-blind, crossover, placebo-controlled study of nine patients with dementia who had a high frequency of violent behavior and difficulties with impulse control. All patients were on neuroleptics and other medications before the study. All medications were discontinued 2 weeks prior to the study, except for oral paraldehyde and intramuscular sodium phenobarbital. Patients in treatment group were given propranolol in doses gradually increased to 520 mg/day and were treated for 11 weeks. The groups were then crossed over, with patients in the new treatment group receiving propranolol in the same dose for the same period of time. The results of the study indicated that that the intensity and duration of aggressive episodes were diminished. However, this study employed only subjective measures. Greendyke and Kanter (1986) have examined the antiaggressive properties of pindolol, a β-blocker with a partial agonistic effect. Eleven patients who were diagnosed with severe dementia and had a history of impulsive-aggressive and hostile behavior participated in this study. As measured by incident reports and a rating scale designed to measure hostility, communicativeness, and repetitious behavior, nine patients showed a 20% decrease in hostility and uncommunicativeness and a 27% reduction in repetitive behavior on doses ranging from 40 to 60 mg/day. Four patients improved enough to be transferred to hospital units providing a lower level of care; one was later discharged.

A more recent randomized double-blind study examined the effectiveness of nadolol in controlling aggressive behavior in 41 in patients with heterogeneous diagnoses (Ratey et al., 1992). The study included a 4-week washout period and a 12-week treatment phase. Using the Overt Aggression Scale (Yudofsky, Silver, Jackson, Endicott, & Williams, 1986), the Brief Psychiatric Rating Scale (BPRS) (Overall & Gorham, 1988), and the Clinical Global Impression Scale (Guy, 1976) in their assessments, Ratey and colleagues showed that nadolol significantly decreased a number of episodes involving aggressive behavior from baseline compared to placebo. Furthermore, a number of subfactors in the BPRS were also affected: hostility-suspicion, negative symptoms, and signs of hyperarousal/tension decreased.

In summary, the antiaggressive properties of β-blockers have been demonstrated in several different groups of patients. Therefore, it appears that β-blockers can be considered a reasonable treatment option in clinical practice.

Conclusions and Future Directions

Methodological difficulties often prevent unequivocal interpretations of the outcomes of pharmacological treatments of aggression. Conducting well-designed placebo-controlled studies in an inpatient setting is difficult, as drug-free washout periods may be unsafe for both patients and staff. Crossover study designs may be problematic due to the intermittent nature of human impulsive aggression and its unpredictable frequency and intensity, which may change over time. Importantly, aggression is not conceptualized as a discrete disorder in the DSM-IV (1994); it is more likely to be seen as secondary symptom without regard for its possible biological and psychological causes. Therefore, aggression is often treated along with the primary illness. Thus, it is clinically difficult to assess whether a reduction in aggression is a specific effect of the pharmacological agent or of nonspecific effects of medications such as neuroleptics and benzodiazepines commonly used for the management of specific Axis I and Axis II disorders. Furthermore, nonpharmacological factors, such as the therapeutic milieu, also can affect treatment outcome and should be considered when evaluating the efficacy of a pharmacotherapeutic intervention for aggression.

The future study of human aggression will require an approach able to translate the knowledge acquired through laboratory studies of aggressive behavior to naturalistic and inpatient settings. Pathological aggression is an extremely heterogeneous phenomenon. Such heterogeneity makes it difficult to predict an individual's need for treatment interventions and to assess clinically relevant outcomes based on diagnosis alone. In this context, a dimensional approach (as opposed to the more traditionally used categorical approach) to diagnostic categories might be more specific in examining novel pharmacological and molecular mechanisms. This raises the possibility of applying a dimensional approach in a formal manner in clinical research, including clinical trials, and the clinical practice of psychiatry in general. One way to assess the relative clinical validity of symptom-based and syndrome-based approaches to psychopathology is to identify groups of correlated symptoms or symptom dimensions in patient populations comprising a range of diagnostic groups (Everitt, Gourlay, & Kendell, 1971; Fleiss, Gurland, & Cooper, 1971; McGorry, Bell, Dudgeon, & Jackson, 1998). Such designs will allow a direct comparison of the utility of categorical and dimensional approaches (Kendell, 1993). One advantage of such an approach directly comparing dimensional and categorical representations of psychopathology is that there is no need to rely on indirect parameters, such as statistical evidence of bimodality, which may be difficult to interpret (Grayson, 1987). Furthermore, the dimensional approach to clinically relevant outcomes does not preclude the simultaneous use of the traditional diagnostic categories and holds promise as an adjunctive source of information.

Ideally, a specific antiaggressive agent should not interfere with any behavior dimensions other than aggression. Furthermore, desirable characteristics of anti-aggressive drugs should include rapid onset of action; a low potential for drug-drug interaction; and low potential drug abuse, low toxicity, and availability in different forms (i.e., oral and intramuscular). Several preclinical experimental protocols have begun to model the distinction between the proposed subtypes of human aggression, namely, impulsive-reactive-hostile-affective versus controlled-proactive-instrumental-predatory (Vitiello & Stoff, 1997). Future human studies (both lab and clinical trials) should include individuals with these contrasting aggressive subtypes in order to better understand their specificity of action.

Note

This research was supported by Grant DA 03166 from the National Institute on Drug Abuse.

References

Abel, E. L. (1977). The relationship between cannabis and violence: A review. *Psychological Bulletin, 84,* 193–211.

American Psychiatric Association. (1994). *Diagnostic and statistical manual of mental disorders* (4th ed.). Washington, DC: Author.

Ball, J. C., Shaffer, J. W., & Nurco, D. N. (1983). The day-to-day criminality of heroin addicts in Baltimore—a study in the continuity of offence rates. *Drug and Alcohol Dependence, 12,* 119–142.

Barratt, E. S., Stanford, M. S., Felthous, A. R., & Kent, T. A. (1997). Effects of phenytoin on impulsive and premeditated aggression: A controlled study. *Journal of Clinical Psychopharmacology, 17,* 341–349.

Bennett, R. M., Buss, A. H., & Carpenter, J. A. (1969). Alcohol and human physical aggression. *Quarterly Journal of Studies on Alcohol, 30,* 870–876.

Ben-Porath, D. D., & Taylor, S. P. (2002). The effects of diazepam (valium) and aggressive disposition on human aggression: An experimental investigation. *Addictive Behavior, 27,* 167–177.

Berman, M., Taylor, S., & Marged, B. (1993). Morphine and human aggression. *Addictive Behaviors, 18,* 263–268.

Bixler, E. O., Kales, A., Brubaker, B. H, & Kales, J. D. (1987). Adverse reactions to benzodiazepine hypnotics: Spontaneous reporting system. *Pharmacology, 35,* 286–300.

Bjork, J. M., Dougherty, D. M., Moeller, F. G., Cherek, D. R., & Swann, A. C. (1999). The effects of tryptophan depletion and loading on laboratory aggression in men: Time course and a food restricted control. *Psychopharmacology, 142,* 24–30.

Bjork, J. M., Dougherty, D. M., Moeller, F. G., & Swann, A. C. (2000). Differential behavioral effects of plasma tryptophan depletion and loading in aggressive and nonaggressive men. *Neuropsychopharmacology, 22,* 357–369.

Bond, A. J., Curran, H. V., Bruce, M. S., O'Sullivan, G., & Shine, P. (1995). Behavioural aggression in panic disorder after 8 weeks treatment with alprazolam. *Journal of Affective Disorders, 35,* 117–123.

Bond, A. J., & Lader, M. (1986). A method to elicit aggressive feelings and behavior via provocation. *Biological Psychology, 22,* 69–79.

Bond, A. J., & Lader, M. (1988). Differential effects of oxazepam and lorazepam on aggressive responding. *Psychopharmacology, 95,* 369–373.

Bond, A. J., Lader, M. H., Carlos, J., DaSilveira, C., & Blackburn, R. (1998). Aggression: Individual differences, alcohol, and benzodiazepines. *Personality and Individual Differences, 25,* 397–397.

Bond, A. J., & Silveira, J. C. (1993) The combination of alprazolam and alcohol on behavioral aggression. *Journal of Studies on Alcohol, 11*(Suppl.), 30–39.

Bond, A. J., Verheyden, S. L., Wingrove, J., & Curran, H. V. (2004). Angry cognitive bias, trait aggression and impulsivity in substance users. *Psychopharmacology, 171,* 331–339.

Bond, A. J., Wingrove, J., & Critchlow, D. G. (2001). Tryptophan depletion increases aggression in women during the premenstrual phase. *Psychopharmacology, 156,* 477–480.

Bovasso, G. B., Alterman, A. I., Cacciola, J. S., & Rutherford, M. J. (2002). The prediction of violent and nonviolent criminal behavior in a methadone maintenance population. *Journal of Personality Disorders*, 16, 360–373.

Brook, J. S., Brook, D. W., Rosen, Z., & Rabbitt, C. R. (2003). Earlier marijuana use and later problem behavior in Columbian youths. *Journal of the American Academy of Child and Adolescent Psychiatry*, 42, 485–492.

Buchanan, A., Reed, A., Wessely, S., Garety, P., Taylor, P., Grubin, D., et al. (1993). Acting on delusions: 2. The phenomenological correlates of acting on delusions. *British Journal of Psychiatry*, 163, 77–81.

Bushman, B. J., Baumeister, R. F., & Phillips, C. M. (2001). Do people aggress to improve their mood? Catharsis beliefs, affect regulation opportunity, and aggressive responding. *Journal of Personality and Social Psychology*, 81, 17–32.

Bushman, B. J., & Cooper, H. M. (1990). Effects of alcohol on human aggression: An integrative research review. *Psychological Bulletin*, 107, 341–354.

Buss, A. H. (1961). The psychology of aggression. New York: Wiley.

Calhoun, S. R., Wesson, D. R., Galloway, G. P., & Smith, D. E. (1996). Abuse of flunitrazepam (Rohypnol) and other benzodiazepines in Austin and south Texas. *Journal of Psychoactive Drugs*, 28, 183–189.

Chengappa, K. N. R., Vasile, J, Levine, J., Ulrich, R., Baker, R., Gopalani, A., et al. (2002). Clozapine: Its impact on aggressive behavior among patients in a state psychiatric hospital. *Schizophrenia Research*, 53, 1–6.

Cherek, D. R. (1981). Effects of smoking different doses of nicotine on human aggressive behavior. *Psychopharmacology*, 75, 339–345.

Cherek, D. R. (1992). Point Subtraction Aggression Paradigm (PSAP). Houston: University of Texas.

Cherek, D. R., Bennett, R. H., & Grabowski, J. (1991). Human aggressive responding during acute tobacco abstinence: Effects of nicotine and placebo gum. *Psychopharmacology*, 104, 317–322.

Cherek, D. R., & Dougherty, D. M. (1995). Provocation frequency and its role in determining the effects of smoked marijuana on human aggressive responding. *Behavioural Pharmacology*, 6, 405–412.

Cherek, D. R., & Lane, S. D. (1999). Effects of d,l-fenfluramine on aggressive and impulsive responding in adult males with a history of conduct disorder. *Psychopharmacology*, 146, 473–481.

Cherek, D. R., & Lane, S. D. (2001). Acute effects of d-fenfluramine on simultaneous measures of aggressive, escape and impulsive responses of adult males with and without a history of conduct disorder. *Psychopharmacology*, 157, 221–227.

Cherek, D. R., Lane, S. D., Dougherty, D. M., Moeller, F. G., & White, S. (2000). Laboratory and question-naire measures of aggression among female parolees with violent and nonviolent histories. *Aggressive Behavior*, 26, 291–307.

Cherek, D. R., Lane, S. D., & Pietras, C. J. (2003). Laboratory measures: The Point Subtraction Aggression Paradigm. In E. F. Coccaro (Ed.), *Aggression: Psychiatric assessment and treatment* (pp. 215–228). New York: Dekker.

Cherek, D. R., Lane, S. D., Pietras, C. J., Sharon, J., & Steinberg, J. L. (2002). Acute effects of baclofen, a GABA B agonist, on laboratory measures of aggressive and escape responses of adult males with and without a history of conduct disorder. *Psychopharmacology*, 164, 160–167.

Cherek, D. R., Lane, S. D., Pietras, C. J., & Steinberg, J. L. (2002). Effects of chronic paroxetine administration on measures of aggressive and impulsive responses of adult males with a history of conduct disorder. *Psychopharmacology*, 159, 266–274.

Cherek, D. R., Moeller, F. G., Kahn-Dawood, F., Swann, A., & Lane, S. D. (1999). Prolactin response to buspirone was reduced in violent compared to nonviolent parolees. *Psychopharmacology*, 142, 144–148.

Cherek, D. R., Moeller, F. G., Schnapp, W., & Dougherty, D. M. (1997). Studies of violent and nonviolent male parolees: I. Laboratory and psychometric measurements of aggression. *Biological Psychiatry*, 41, 514–522.

Cherek, D. R., & Pietras, C. J. (2003). Human aggression: Biological correlates and environmental influences. In M. A. Ron & T. W. Robbins (Eds.), *Disorders of brain and mind* (Vol. 2, pp. 375–399). Cambridge: Cambridge University Press.

Cherek, D. R., Roache, J. D., Egli, M., Davis, C., Spiga, R., & Cowan, K. (1993). Acute effects of marijuana smoking on aggressive, escape and point-maintained responding of male drug users. *Psychopharmacology*, 111, 163–168.

Cherek, D. R., Schnapp, W., Moeller, F. G., & Dougherty, D. M. (1996) Laboratory measures of aggressive responding in male parolees with violent and nonviolent histories. *Aggressive Behavior*, 22, 27–36.

Cherek, D. R., Spiga, R., Roache, J. D., & Cowan, K. A. (1991). Effects of triazolam on human aggressive, escape, and point-maintained responding. *Pharmacology Biochemistry and Behavior*, 40, 835–839.

Cherek, D. R., & Steinberg, J. L. (1987). Effects of drugs on human aggressive behavior. In G. D. Burrows & J. S. Werry (Eds.), *Advances in human psychopharmacology* (pp. 239–290). Greenwich, CT: JAI Press.

Cherek, D. R., Steinberg, J. L., & Brauchi, J. T. (1983). Effects of caffeine on human aggressive behavior. *Psychiatry Research*, 8, 137–145.

Cherek, D. R., Steinberg, J. L., & Brauchi, J. T. (1984). Consumption of regular or decaffeinated coffee and subsequent human aggressive behavior. *Psychiatry Research, 11*, 251–258.

Cherek, D. R., Steinberg, J. L., Kelly, T. H., & Robinson, D. E. (1986). Effects of d-amphetamine on human aggressive behavior. *Psychopharmacology, 88*, 381–386.

Cherek, D. R., Steinberg, J. L., Kelly, T. H., Robinson, D. E., & Spiga, R. (1990). Effects of acute administration of diazepam and d-amphetamine on aggressive and escape responding of normal male subjects. *Psychopharmacology, 100*, 173–181.

Cherek, D. R. Steinberg, J. L., & Manno, B. R. (1985). Effects of alcohol on human aggressive behavior. *Journal of Studies on Alcohol, 46*, 321–328.

Cherek, D. R., Steinberg, J. L., & Vines, R. V. (1984). Low doses of alcohol affect human aggressive responses. *Biological Psychiatry, 19*, 263–267.

Cherek, D. R., Tcheremissine, O. V., Lane, S. D., & Pietras, C. J. (2004). Acute effects of gabapentin on laboratory measures of aggressive and escape responses of adult parolees with and without a history of conduct disorder. *Psychopharmacology, 171*, 405–412.

Chermack, S. T., & Taylor, S. P. (1995). Alcohol and human physical aggression: Pharmacological versus expectancy effects. *Journal of Studies on Alcohol, 56*, 449–456.

Coccaro, E. F., Berman, M. E., Kavoussi, R. J., & Hauger, R. L. (1996). Relationship of prolactin response to d-fenfluramine to behavioral and questionnaire assessments of aggression in personality-disordered men. *Biological Psychiatry, 40*, 157–164.

Coccaro, E. F., & Kavoussi, R. J. (1997). Fluoxetine and impulsive aggressive behavior in personality-disordered subjects. *Archives of General Psychiatry, 54*, 1081–1088.

Cole, J. O., & Kando, J. C. (1993). Adverse behavioral events reported in patients taking alprazolam and other benzodiazepines. *Journal of Clinical Psychiatry, 54*, 49–63.

Collins, J. J., & Messerschmidt, P. M. (1993). Epidemiology of alcohol-related violence. *Alcohol Health and Research World, 17*, 93–100.

Craft, M., Ismail, I. A, Krishnamurti, D., Mathews, J., Regan, A., Seth, R. V., et al. (1987). Lithium in the treatment of aggression in mentally handicapped patients: A double-blind trial. *British Journal of Psychiatry, 150*, 685–689.

Cueva, J. E., Overall, J. E., Small, A. M., Armenteros, J. L., Perry, R., & Campbell, M. (1996). Carbamazepine in aggressive children with conduct disorder: A double-blind and placebo controlled study. *Journal of the American Academy of Child and Adolescent Psychiatry, 35*, 480–490.

Daderman, A. M., & Edman, G. (2001). Flunitrazepam abuse and personality characteristics in male foren-

sic psychiatric patients. *Psychiatry Research, 103*, 27–42.

Daderman, A. M., & Lidberg, L. (1999). Flunitrazepam (Rohypnol) abuse in combination with alcohol causes premeditated, grievous violence in male juvenile offenders. *Journal of the American Academy of Psychiatry and the Law, 27*, 83–99.

Davis, W. M. (1996). Psychopharmacologic violence associated with cocaine abuse: Kindling of a limbic dyscontrol syndrome? *Progress In Neuro-Psychopharmacology and Biological Psychiatry, 20*, 1273–1300.

Dawes, M. A., Tarter R. E., & Kirisci, L. (1997). Behavioral self-regulation: Correlates and 2 year follow-ups for boys at risk for substance abuse. *Drug and Alcohol Dependence, 45*, 165–176.

Denison, M. E., Paredes, A., & Booth, J. B. (1997). Alcohol and cocaine interactions and aggressive. *Recent Developments in Alcoholism, 13*, 283–303.

Dougherty, D. M., Bjork, J. M., Huckabee, H. C. G., Moeller, F. G., & Swann, A. C. (1999). Laboratory measures of aggression and impulsivity in women with borderline personality disorder. *Psychiatry Research, 85*, 315–326.

Dougherty, D. M., Cherek, D. R., & Bennett, R. H. (1996). The effects of alcohol on the aggressive responding of women. *Journal of Studies on Alcohol, 57*, 178–186.

Dougherty, D. M., Moeller, F. G., Bjork, J. M., & Marsh, D. M. (1999). Plasma l-tryptophan depletion and aggression. *Advances in Experimental Medical Biology, 467*, 57–65.

Eichelman, B. S. (1990). Neurochemical and psychopharmacologic aspects of aggressive behavior. *Annual Review of Medicine, 41*, 149–158.

Elliott, F. A. (1977). Propranolol for the control of belligerent behavior following acute brain damage. *Annals of Neurology, 5*, 489–491.

Ensor, T., & Godfrey, C. (1993). Modeling the interactions between alcohol, crime and the criminal-justice system. *Addiction, 88*, 477–487.

Everitt, B., Gourlay, A., & Kendell, R. E. (1971). An attempt at validation of traditional psychiatric syndromes by cluster analysis. *British Journal of Psychiatry, 119*, 399–412.

Fals-Stewart, W., Golden, J., & Schumacher, J. A. (2003). Intimate partner violence and substance use: A longitudinal day-to-day examination. *Addictive Behaviors, 28*, 1555–1574.

Fava, M. (1997). Psychopharmacologic treatment of pathologic aggression. *Psychiatric Clinics in North America, 20*, 427–451.

Findling, R. L., McNamara, N. K., Branicky, L. A., Schluchter, M. D., Lemon, E., & Blumer, J. L. (2000). A double-blind pilot study of risperidone in the treatment of conduct disorder. *Journal of American*

Academy of Child and Adolescence Psychiatry, 39, 509–516.

Fleiss, J., Gurland, B., & Cooper, J. (1971). Some contributions to the measurement of psychopathology. *British Journal of Psychiatry, 119,* 647–656.

Frankenburg, F. R., & Zanarini, M. C. (2002). Divalproex sodium treatment of women with borderline personality disorder and bipolar II disorder: A double-blind, placebo-controlled pilot study. *Journal of Clinical Psychiatry, 63,* 442–446.

Friedman, A. S., Glassman, K., & Terras, B. A. (2001). Violent behavior as related to use of marijuana and other drugs. *Journal of Addictive Diseases, 20,* 49–72.

Galanter, M. (1997). Alcohol and violence: Epidemiology, neurobiology, psychology, family issues. In *Recent developments in alcoholism.* New York: Plenum.

Galvan, J., Unikel, C., Rodriguez, E. M., Ortiz, A., Soriano, A., & Flores, J. C. (2000). General perspective of flunitrazepam (Rohypnol) abuse in a sample of drug users of Mexico City. *Salud Mental, 23,* 1–7.

Gardner, D. L., & Cowdry, R. W. (1985). Alprazolam-induced dyscontrol in borderline personality disorder. *American Journal of Psychiatry, 142,* 98–100.

Gerra, G., Fertonani, G., Zaimovic, A., Rota-Graziosi, I., Avanzini, P., Caccavari, R., et al. (1995). Hostility in heroin abusers subtypes: Fluoxetine and naltrexone treatment. *Progress in Neuro-Psychopharmacology and Biological Psychiatry, 19,* 1225–1237.

Gerra, G., Zaimovic, A., Ampollini R., Giusti, F., Delsignore, R., Raggi, M. A., et al. (2001). Experimentally induced aggressive behavior in subjects with 3,4-methylenedioxy-methamphetamine ("Ecstasy") use history: Psychobiological correlates. *Journal of Substance Abuse, 13,* 471–491.

Gerra, G., Zaimovic, A., Raggi, M. A., Giusti, F., Delsignore, R., Bertacca, S., et al. (2001). Aggressive responding of male heroin addicts under methadone treatment: Psychometric and neuroendocrine correlates. *Drug and Alcohol Dependence, 65,* 85–95.

Giancola, P. R., & Zeichner, A. (1995). An investigation of gender differences in alcohol-related aggression. *Journal of Studies on Alcohol, 56,* 573–579.

Gottschalk, L. A., Covi, L., Ultana, R., & Bates, D. E. (1973). Effects of diphenylhydation on anxiety and hostility in institutionalized prisoners. *Comprehensive Psychiatry, 14,* 503– 511.

Grayson, D. A. (1987). Can categorical and dimensional views of psychiatric illness be distinguished? *British Journal of Psychiatry, 151,* 355–361.

Greendyke, R. M., & Kanter D. R. (1986). Therapeutic effects of pindolol on behavior disturbances associated with organic brain disease: A double-blind study. *Journal of Clinical Psychiatry, 47,* 423–428.

Greendyke, R. M., Kanter, D. M., Schuster, D. B.,

Vestreate, S., & Wootoon, J. (1986). Propranolol treatment of assaultive patients with organic brain disease. *Journal of Nervous and Mental Disease, 174,* 290–294.

Gustafson, R. (1985). Alcohol and aggression: A validation study of the Taylor Aggression Paradigm. *Psychological Reports, 57,* 667–676.

Gustafson, R. (1992). Alcohol and aggression: A replication study controlling for potential confounding variables. *Aggressive Behavior, 18,* 21–28.

Guy, W. (1976). *ECDEU assessment manual for psychopharmacology* (rev. ed., U.S. Department of Health, Education and Welfare Publication Publication No. ADM 91–338). Rockville, MD: National Institute of Mental Health.

Guz, I., Moraes, R., & Sartoretto, J. N. (1972). The therapeutic effects of lorazepam in psychotic treated with haloperidol: A double-blind study. *Current Therapeutic Research, 14,* 767–774.

Hall, R. C., & Zisook, S. (1981). Paradoxical reactions to benzodiazepines. *British Journal of Clinical Pharmacology, 11,* 99S–104S.

Haward, L. R. C. (1982). The use of phenytoin in neurotic disorders treated in general practice. *Current Medical Research Opinion, 8,* 134–138.

Hoaken, P. N., & Stewart, S. H. (2003). Drugs of abuse and the elicitation of human aggressive behavior. *Addictive Behaviors, 28,* 1533–1554.

Hollander, E., Tracy, K. A., Swann, A. C., Coccaro, E. F., McElroy, S. L., Wozniak, P., et al. (2003). Divalproex in the treatment of impulsive aggression: Efficacy in cluster B personality disorders. *Neuropsychopharmacology, 28,* 1186–1197.

Horne, M., & Lindley, S. E. (1995). Divalproex sodium in the treatment of aggressive behavior and dysphoria in patients with organic brain syndrome. *Journal of Clinical Psychiatry, 56,* 430–431.

Jefferson, J. W., & Greist, J. H. (2000). Lithium. In B. J. Sadock & V. A. Sadock (Eds.), *Comprehensive textbook of psychiatry* (pp. 2377–2390). Philadelphia: Lippincott, Williams & Wilkins.

Kavoussi, R. J., & Coccaro, E. F. (1998) Divalproex sodium for impulsive-aggressive behavior in patients with personality disorder. *Journal of Clinical Psychiatry, 59,* 676–680.

Kaye, S., Darke, S., & Finlay-Jones, R. (1998). The onset of heroin use and criminal behaviour: Does order make a difference? *Drug and Alcohol Dependence, 53,* 79–86.

Kellam, S. G., Stevenson, D. L., & Rubin, B. R. (1983). *How specific are the early predictors of teenage drug use?* (NIDA Research Monograph 43, pp. 329–334). Washington, DC: U.S. Government Printing Office.

Kelly, T. H., & Cherek, D. R. (1993). The effects of alcohol on free-operant aggressive behavior. *Journal of Studies on Alcohol, 11*(Suppl.), 40–52.

Kelly, T. H., Cherek, D. R., & Steinberg, J. L. (1989). Concurrent reinforcement and alcohol: Interactive effects on human aggressive behavior. *Journal of Studies on Alcohol, 50,* 399–405.

Kelly, T. H., Cherek, D. R., Steinberg, J. L., & Robinson, D. (1988). Effects of provocation and alcohol on human aggressive behavior. *Drug and Alcohol Dependence, 21,* 105–112.

Kendell, R. E. (1993). Diagnostic and classification. In R. E. Kendell & A. K. Zeally (Eds.), *Companion to psychiatric studies* (5th ed., pp. 277–295). London: Churchill Livingstone.

Kingery, P. M., Pruitt, B. E., & Hurley, R. S. (1992). Violence and illegal drug use among adolescents: Evidence from the U.S. National Adolescent Survey. *International Journal on Addictions, 27,* 1445–1464.

Koop, C. E., & Lundberg, G. D. (1992). Violence in America: A public health emergency. *Journal of the American Medical Association, 267,* 3075–3076.

Kouri, E. M., Pope, H. G., Jr., & Lukas, S. E. (1999). Changes in aggressive behavior during withdrawal from long-term marijuana use. *Psychopharmacology, 143,* 302–308.

LaFree, G. (1999). Declining violent crime rates in the 1990s: Predicting crime booms and busts. *Annual Review of Sociology, 25,* 145–168.

Lanza-Kaduce, L., Bishop, D. M., & Winner, L. (1997). Risk/benefit calculations, moral evaluations, and alcohol use: Exploring the alcohol-crime connection. *Crime and Delinquency, 43,* 222–239.

Lau, M. A., & Pihl, R. O. (1994). Alcohol and the Taylor Aggression Paradigm: A repeated measures study. *Journal of Studies on Alcohol, 55,* 701–706.

Leonard, K. E., Bromet, E. J., Parkinson, D. K., Day, N. L., & Ryan, C. M. (1985). Patterns of alcohol use and physically aggressive behavior in men. *Journal of Studies on Alcohol, 46,* 279–282.

Loeber, R., Wung, P., Keenan, K., Giroux, B., Stouthamer-Loeber, M., Van Kammen, W. B., et al. (1993). Developmental pathways in disruptive child behavior. *Developmental Psychopathology, 5,* 103–133.

LeMarquand, D. G., Benkelfat, C., Pihl, R. O., Palmour, R. M., & Young, S. N. (1999). Behavioral disinhibition induced by tryptophan depletion in nonalcoholic young men with multigenerational family histories of paternal alcoholism. *American Journal of Psychiatry, 156,* 1771–1779.

LeMarquand, D. G., Pihl, R. O., Young, S. N., Tremblay, R. E., Seguin, J. R., Palmour, R. M., et al. (1998). Tryptophan depletion, executive functions, and disinhibition in aggressive adolescent males. *Neuropsychopharmacology, 19,* 333–341.

Licata, A., Taylor, S., Berman, M., & Cranston, J. (1993). Effects of cocaine on human aggression. *Pharmacology, Biochemistry and Behavior, 45,* 549–552.

Looker, A., & Connors, C. K. (1970). Diphenylhydation in children with severe temper tantrums. *Archives of General Psychiatry, 23,* 80–90.

Malone, R. P., Delaney, M. A., Luebbert, J. F., Cater, J., & Cambell, M. (2000). A double-blind placebo-controlled study of lithium on hospitalized aggressive children and adolescents with conduct disorder. *Archives of General Psychiatry, 57,* 649–654.

Martin, S. E. (2001). The links between alcohol, crime and the criminal justice system: Explanations, evidence and interventions. *American Journal on Addiction, 10,* 136–158.

McCloskey, M. S., & Berman, M. E. (2003). Laboratory measures: The Taylor Aggression Paradigm. In E. F. Coccaro (Ed.), *Aggression: Psychiatric assessment and treatment* (pp. 195–213). New York: Dekker.

McGorry, P. D., Bell, R., Dudgeon, P., & Jackson, H. (1998). The dimensions of first episode psychosis: An exploratory factor analysis. *Psychological Medicine, 28,* 935–947.

Miczek, K. A., Weerts, E., Haney, M., & Tidey, J. (1994) Neurobiological mechanisms controlling aggression: Preclinical developments for pharmacotherapeutic interventions. *Neuroscience and Biobehavioral Reviews, 18,* 97–110.

Milgram, G. G. (1993). Adolescents, alcohol and aggression. *Journal of Studies on Alcohol, 11*(Suppl.), 53–61.

Miller, N. S., Gold, M. S., & Mahler, J. C. (1991). Violent behaviors associated with cocaine use: Possible pharmacological mechanisms. *International Journal on Addiction, 26,* 1077–1088.

Moeller, F. G., Cherek, D. R., Dougherty, D. M., Lane, S. D., & Swann, A. C. (1998). Ipsapirone neuroendocrine challenge: Relationship to aggression as measured in the human laboratory. *Psychiatry Research, 81,* 31–38.

Moeller, F. G., Dougherty, D. M., Rustin, T., Swann, A. C., Allen, T. J., Shah, N., et al. (1997). Antisocial personality disorder and aggression in recently abstinent cocaine dependent subjects. *Drug and Alcohol Dependence, 44,* 175–182.

Moeller, F. G., Dougherty, D. M., Swann, A. C., Collins, D., Davis, C. M., & Cherek, D. R. (1996). Tryptophan depletion and aggressive responding in healthy males. *Psychopharmacology, 126,* 97–103.

Moeller, F. G., Steinberg, J. L., Petty, F., Fulton, M., Cherek, D. R., Kramer, G., et al. (1994). Serotonin and impulsive/aggressive behavior in cocaine-dependent subjects. *Progress in Neuro-Psychopharmacology and Biological Psychiatry, 18,* 1027–1035.

Murdoch, D., Pihl, R. O., & Ross, D. (1990). Alcohol and crimes of violence: Present issues. *International Journal of Addiction, 25,* 1065–1081.

Myerscough, R., & Taylor, S. P. (1985). The effects of marijuana on human physical aggressive behavior. *Journal of Personality and Social Psychology, 49,* 1541–1546.

National Institute on Drug Abuse. (1998). *NIDA research report—methamphetamine abuse and addiction* (NIH Publication No. 02–4210). Rockville, MD: Author.

Neppe, V. M. (1988) Carbamazepine in nonresponsive psychosis. *Journal of Clinical Psychiatry, 49*(Suppl. 4), 22–28.

Okuma, T., Yamashita, I., Takahashi, R, Itoh, H., Otsuki, S., Watanabe, S., et al. (1989). A double-blind study of adjunctive carbamazepine versus placebo on excited states of schizophrenic and schizoaffective disorders. *Acta Psychiatrica Scandinavica, 80,* 250–259.

Overall, J. E., & Gorham, D. R., (1988). The Brief Psychiatric Rating Scale (BPRS): Recent developments in ascertainment and scaling. *Psychopharmacology Bulletin, 24,* 97–99.

Pihl, R. O., & Peterson, J. (1995). Drugs and aggression—correlations, crime and human manipulative studies and some proposed mechanisms. *Journal of Psychiatry and Neuroscience, 20,* 141–149.

Pihl, R. O., Young, S. N., Harden, P., Plotnick, S., Chamberlain, B., & Ervin, F. R. (1995). Acute effects of altered tryptophan levels and alcohol on aggression in normal male subjects. *Psychopharmacology, 119,* 353–360.

Poulton, R. G., Brooke, M., Moffitt, T. E., Stanton, W. R., & Silva, P. A. (1997). Prevalence and correlates of cannabis use and dependence in young New Zealanders. *New Zealand Medical Journal, 110,* 68–70.

Ratey, J. J., Sorgi, P., O'Driscoll, G. A., Sands, S., Daenict, M. L., Fletcher, J. B., et al. (1992). Nadolol to treat aggression and psychiatric symptomatology in chronic psychiatric inpatients: A double-blind, placebo-controlled study. *Journal of Clinical Psychiatry, 53,* 41–46.

Richards, J. R., Johnson, E. B., Stark, R. W., & Derlet, R. W. (1999). Methamphetamine abuse and rhabdomyolysis in the ED: A 5-year study. *American Journal of Emergency Medicine, 17,* 681–685.

Rickert, V. I., Wiemann, C. M., & Berenson, A. B. (1999). Prevalence, patterns, and correlates of voluntary flunitrazepam use. *Pediatrics, 103,* E61–E65.

Rinne, T., van den Brik, W., Wouters, L., & van Dyck, R. (2002). SSRI treatment of borderline personality disorder: A randomized, placebo-controlled clinical trial for female patients with borderline personality disorder. *American Journal Psychiatry, 159,* 2048–2054.

Robins, L. (1993). Childhood conduct problems, adult psychopathology, and crime. In S. Hodgins (Ed.), *Mental disorder and crime* (pp. 173–193). London: Sage.

Ross, A. T., & Jackson, V. (1940). Dilantin sodium: Its influence on conduct and on rating of institutionalized epileptics. *Annals of Internal Medicine, 14,* 770–773.

Rowland, N. E., & Carlton, J. (1986). Neurobiology of an anorectic drug: Fenfluramine. *Progress in Neurobiology, 27,* 13–62.

Salzman, C., Koshansky, G. E., Shader, R. I., Porrino, L. J., Harmatz, J. S., & Sweet, C. P. (1974). Chlordiazepoxide-induced hostility in a small group setting. *Archives of General Psychiatry, 31,* 401–405.

Schechter, M. D., & Rand, M. J. (1974). Effect of acute deprivation of smoking on aggression and hostility. *Psychopharmacology, 35,* 19–28.

Seto, M. C., & Barbaree, H. E. (1995). The role of alcohol in sexual aggression. *Clinical Psychology Review, 15,* 545–566.

Sheard, M., Marini, J., Bridges, C., & Wagner, E. (1976). The effect of lithium on impulsive aggressive behavior in man. *American Journal of Psychiatry, 133,* 1409–1413.

Shuntich, R. J., & Taylor, S. P. (1972). The effects of alcohol on human physical aggression. *Journal of Experimental Research on Personality, 6,* 34–38.

Simonds, J. F., & Kashani, J. (1980). Specific drug use in delinquent boys. *American Journal of Dug and Alcohol Abuse, 7,* 305–322.

Smith, S. E., Pihl, R. O., Young, S. N., & Ervin, F. R. (1986). Elevation and reduction of plasma tryptophan and their effects on aggression and perceptual sensitivity in normal males. *Aggressive Behavior, 12,* 393–407.

Spiga, R., Cherek, D. R., Roache, J. D., & Cowan, K. A. (1990). The effects of codeine on human aggressive responding. *International Journal of Clinical Psychopharmacology, 5,* 195–204.

Stanford, M. S., Houston, R., Mathias, C. W., Greve, K. W., Villemarette-Pittman, N. R., & Adams, D. (2001). A double-blind placebo-controlled crossover study of phenytoin in individuals with impulsive aggression. *Psychiatry Research, 103,* 193–203.

Steadman, H. J., Mulvey, E. P., Monahan, J., Robbins, P. C., Appelbaum, P. S., Grisso, T., et al. (1998). Violence by people discharged from acute psychiatric inpatient facilities and by others in the same neighborhoods. *Archives of General Psychiatry, 55,* 393–401.

Stevens, J. H., & Shaffer, J. W. (1970). A controlled study of the effects of diphenylhydation on anxiety, irritability, and anger in neurotic patients. *Psychopharmacologia,* *117*, 169–181.

Stevens, J. H., & Shaffer, J. W. (1973). A controlled replication of the effectiveness of diphenylhydation in reducing irritability and anxiety in selected neurotic outpatients. *Journal of Clinical Pharmacology, 13,* 351–356.

Swanson, J. W., Holzer, C. E., Ganju, V. K., & Jono, R. T. (1990). Violence and psychiatric disorder in the community: Evidence from the Epidemiologic Catchment Area surveys. *Hospital and Community Psychiatry, 41,* 761–770.

Taylor, P. L., & Albright, Jr. W. J., (1981). Nondrug criminal behavior and heroin use. *International Journal on Addictions, 16,* 683–696.

Taylor, S. P. (1967) Aggressive behavior and physiological arousal as a function of provocation and the tendency to inhibit aggression. *Journal of Personality, 35,* 297–310.

Taylor, S. P., & Chermack, S. T. (1993). Alcohol, drugs and human physical aggression. *Journal of Studies on Alcohol, 11*(Suppl.), 78–88.

Taylor, S. P., & Gammon, C. B. (1975). Effects of type and dose of alcohol on human physical aggression. *Journal of Personality and Social Psychology, 32,* 169–175.

Taylor, S. P., & Leonard, K. E. (1983). Alcohol and human physical aggression. In R. G. Geen & E. I. Donnerstein (Eds.), *Aggression: Theoretical and empirical reviews* (Vol. 2, pp. 77–101). New York: Academic Press.

Taylor, S. P., Schmutte, G. T., Leonard, K. E., & Cranston, J. W. (1979). The effects of alcohol and extreme provocation on the use of a highly noxious electric shock. *Motivation and Emotion, 3,* 73–81.

Taylor, S. P., Vardaris, R. M., Rawtich, A. B., Gammon, C. B., Cranston, J. W., & Lubetkin, A. I. (1976). The effects of alcohol and delta-9-tetrahydrocannabinol on human physical aggression. *Aggressive Behavior, 2,* 153–161.

Tedeschi, J. T., & Quigley, B. M. (1996). Limitations of laboratory paradigms for studying aggression. *Aggressive and Violent Behavior, 1,* 163–177.

Tobin, J. M., Bird, I. F., & Boyle, D. E. (1960). Preliminary evaluation of Librium (Ro 5–0690) in the treatment of anxiety reactions. *Disorders of Nervous System, 21,* 11–19.

Uhlenhath, E. H., Stephens, J. H., Dim, B. H., & Covi, L. (1972). Diphenylhydation and phenobarbital in the relief of psychoneurotic symptoms: A controlled comparison. *Psychopharmacologia, 27,* 67–84.

U.S. Department of Justice. (2002). *The National Crime Victimization Survey report: Criminal victimization, 2002* (Office of Justice Programs, Bureau of Justice Statistics Document NCJ-199994). Washington, DC: Author.

Vartiainen, H., Tiihonen, J., Putkonen, A., Koponen, H., Virkkunen, M., Hakola, P., et al. (1995). Citalopram, a selective serotonin reuptake inhibitor, in the treatment of aggression in schizophrenia. *Acta Psychiatrica Scandinavica, 91,* 348–351.

Vitiello, B., & Stoff, D. M. (1997). Subtypes of aggression and their relevance to child psychiatry. *Journal of Academy of Child and Adolescent Psychiatry, 36,* 307–315.

Volavka, J., & Citrome, L. (1999). Atypical antipsychotics in the treatment of persistently aggressive psychotic patient: Methodological concerns. *Schizophrenia Research, 35,* S23–S33.

Walker, C., & Kirkpatrick, B. B. (1947). Dilantin treatment for behavior problem children with abnormal electroencephalograms. *American Journal of Psychiatry, 103,* 484–492.

Weaver, T. L., & Clum, G. A. (1993). Early family environments and traumatic experiences associated with borderline personality disorder. *Journal of Consulting and Clinical Psychology, 61,* 1068–1075.

Weisman, A. M., Berman, M. E., & Taylor, S. P. (1998). Effects of chlorazepate, diazepam, and oxazepam on a laboratory measurement of aggression in men. *International Clinical Psychopharmacology, 13,* 183–188.

Wilkinson, C. J. (1985). Effects of diazepam (Valium) and trait anxiety on human physical aggression and emotional state. *Journal of Behavioral Medicine, 8,* 101–114.

Wolfe, B. M., & Baron, R. A. (1971). Laboratory aggression related to aggression in naturalistic social situations: Effects of an aggressive model on the behavior of college student and prisoner observers. *Psychonomic Science, 24,* 193–194.

Young, S. N., Pihl, R. O., & Ervin, F. R. (1988). The effect of altered tryptophan levels on mood and behavior in normal human males. *Clinical Neuropharmacology, 11*(Suppl. 1), S207–S215.

Yudofsky, S. C., Silver, J. M., Jackson, W., Endicott, J., & Williams, D. (1986). The Overt Aggression Scale for the objective rating of verbal and physical aggression. *American Journal of Psychiatry, 143,* 35–39.

Yudofsky, S. C., Silver, J., & Schneider, S. (1987). Pharmacologic treatment of aggression. *Psychiatry Annals, 17,* 397–407.

Yudofsky, S. C., Silver, J. M., & Holes, R. E. (1990). Pharmacological management of aggression in elderly. *Journal of Clinical Psychiatry, 51*(Suppl.), 22–26.

Zeichner, A., Frey, F. C., Parrott, D. J., & Butryn, M. F. (1999). Measurement of laboratory aggression: A new response-choice paradigm. *Psychological Reports, 85,* 1229–1237.

Zeichner, A., & Pihl, R. O. (1979). Effects of alcohol and behavior contingencies on human aggression. *Journal of Abnormal Psychology, 88,* 153–160.

Zeichner, A., & Pihl, R. O. (1980). Effects of alcohol and instigator intent on human aggression. *Journal of Studies on Alcohol, 41,* 265–276.

Zubieta, J. K., & Alessi, N. E. (1993). Is there a role of serotonin in the disruptive behavior disorders? A literature review. *Journal of Child and Adolescent Psychopharmacology, 3,* 11–35.

18

The Psychophysiology of Human Antisocial Behavior

Angela Scarpa & Adrian Raine

There is little doubt that social and psychological factors contribute to the development of crime and other antisocial behavior, and there is an extensive body of research established in those areas and reviewed elsewhere (e.g., Bartol, 1991; McCord, 1979; Scarpa, 2003; Visher & Roth, 1986; Widom, 1989). There is a growing body of literature to suggest, however, that biological individual differences may also predispose to antisocial behavior. These include a wide range of findings on genetics, biochemistry, neuropsychology, brain imaging, and psychophysiology (Mednick, Moffitt, & Stack, 1987; Raine, 1993; Scarpa & Raine, 1997a, 1997b), and these factors often interact with environmental events in a dynamic interplay (Raine, 2002; Raine, Brennan, Farrington, & Mednick, 1997; Scarpa & Raine, 2003; Walsh, 2002). While acknowledging at the outset that environmental factors play a clearly important role in the development and expression of antisocial behavior, this chapter focuses on one area of biological influences on antisocial behavior, namely, psychophysiology.

Psychophysiology involves the study of cognitions, emotions, and behavior as related to physiological principles and events (i.e., the mind-body relationship), using measures that are typically noninvasive (Cacioppo

& Tassinary, 1990). This chapter reviews the major psychophysiological findings and theories regarding antisocial behavior, with a specific focus on skin conductance (SC), heart rate (HR), electroencephalogram (EEG), and startle blink research. The goal is to provide evidence of psychophysiological relationships with antisocial behavior and overview theories regarding the meaning of these relationships.

It is important to note that antisocial behavior encompasses a wide range of behaviors and diagnoses where the main characteristic is a violation of the basic rights of others. This includes human aggression, crime, violence, psychopathy, antisocial personality disorder, conduct disorder, and delinquency, among others. Though most of the psychophysiological findings converge, considerable variability in behavior exists both across and within these forms of antisocial expression. Studies of criminal behavior, for example, may include acts ranging from robbery to rape and murder. Studies of aggression and conduct disorder may include behaviors that are not necessarily illegal (e.g., lying, slapping, or pushing) or individuals that have never been charged or convicted of a crime. The findings reviewed below are in relation to any of these antisocial behaviors or diagnoses. As such, they can be considered pervasive across many different kinds of antisocial behavior, but must also be viewed as broad evidence that increasingly needs clarification.

Last, the view of antisocial behavior as having biological underpinnings has another implication. That is, for a small proportion of individuals in the general population, this behavior is part of an underlying disorder that leads to serious repetitive antisocial acts. This is consistent with the definition of a mental disorder as described by the *Diagnostic and Statistical Manual of Mental Disorders*, fourth edition (*DSM-IV*; American Psychiatric Association, 1994) under the diagnosis of Conduct Disorder; specifically, the "behavior in question [must be] symptomatic of an underlying dysfunction within the individual and not simply a reaction to the immediate social context" (p. 88). The perspective of repeat criminality as a psychopathology also has been argued by Raine (1993), who suggests that these individuals are influenced by biological, social, and psychological factors over which they have little, if any, control. Thus, the study of psychophysiological contributions to antisocial behavior is important in helping to explain and clarify this putative underlying dysfunction.

Skin Conductance (SC)

Definition and Description

SC measures the electrical conductance of a small current that is passed through two electrodes on the hand as sweat rises in the glands. Conductivity generally increases as a person becomes more aroused or attentive. Changes in the electrical activity of the skin generally occur in response to the presentation of novel stimuli in one's environment. For example, the presentation of a new tone generally causes an orienting response that is accompanied by increased electrical activity in the skin and thus a change in skin conductance levels called the skin conductance orienting response (SCOR). SCORs also increase if a novel stimulus is recognized as significant and needs further processing. In either case, augmented controlled processing of information would produce a SCOR (Ohman, 1979, 1985). Thus, the SCOR is a useful index of how one attends to and processes novel environmental stimuli (Dawson, Filion, & Schell, 1989).

Besides measuring SC phasically (in response to a stimulus), as discussed above in the description of the SCOR, SC can also be measured tonically (in a resting state). In this regard, SC is measured in terms of level (SCL) or number of nonspecific SC fluctuations (NSF). NSFs are changes in SC that look like orienting responses, but do not occur in response to a known stimulus. Both SCL and NSF are thought to reflect a baseline level of physiological sympathetic arousal and thus have often been associated with fear emotions in the fight/flight response.

Tonic Findings

With regard to SC underarousal, both SCL and NSFs are generally reduced in antisocial groups in a number of studies, though this has not been entirely consistent. The findings are primarily found in uninstitutionalized subjects with mild forms of aggressive or other antisocial behavior, but seem to predict later institutionalization. For example, in a study of behavior disordered children, low SCL measured at age 11 predicted institutionalization at age 13 (Kruesi, Hibbs, Zahn, & Keysor, 1992). Also, a prospective study revealed that reduced numbers of NSFs at age 15 years predicted criminal behavior 9 years later (Raine, Venables, & Williams, 1990a). Raine and colleagues suggested that this pattern, along with low resting HR, reflected autonomic underarousal in future criminals. More recently, a study of 335 boys from the community who self-reported serious delinquency found that this classification was characterized by low SCL measured at 16 years of age (Gatzke-Kopp, Raine, Loeber, Stouthamer-Loeber, & Steinhauer, 2002), consistent with the notion of reduced SC arousal in antisocial boys.

In an early review of the literature on psychopathy, Hare (1978) concluded that these individuals are characterized by reduced SCL. Thus, it is possible that reduced SC arousal is also related to criminal and other antisocial behavior in adulthood. This conclusion has recently been confirmed in a study showing that adults with antisocial personality disorder show reduced SC activity during a social stressor (Raine, Lencz, Bihrle, LaCasse, & Colletti, 2000).

Phasic Findings

Regarding SCORs, Hare (1978) had concluded that the research to that date showed reduced SC responses to aversive (loud), but not neutral, tones (i.e., a reduced defensive response but no difference in orienting response). This pattern of findings, however, has not consistently been replicated in research conducted after that review. On the other hand, deficits in SCOR have been consistently observed in individuals who display both antisocial behavior and features of schizotypal personality disorder (characterized by odd behavior, interpersonal deficits, and cognitive/perceptual distortions). For example, antisocial adolescents with schizotypal features had significantly lower SCORs relative to those with only schizotypal features (Raine & Venables, 1984a). In his review, Raine (1993) also noted that, with the exception of one study, reduced frequency of SCORs was found only in studies where antisocial behavior was combined with schizotypal or schizoid characteristics. This conclusion was supported and extended in a study in which adolescents with schizotypal tendencies who later became criminal were characterized by reduced SCORs relative to those who were nonschizotypal or did not become criminal (Raine, Bihrle, Venables, Mednick, & Pollock, 1999). Thus, it seems that SCOR deficits may be specific to schizotypal criminals.

In a study using magnetic resonance imaging, fewer orienting responses were related to reduced prefrontal area in normal subjects (Raine, Reynolds, & Sheard, 1991). Because the number of SCOR responses may be related to frontal lobe functioning, Raine and colleagues (1991) interpreted the results in schizotypal criminals as reflecting frontal dysfunction in this particular subgroup of antisocial individuals. Further support for interpreting reduced SC activity in terms of prefrontal deficits comes from a recent study showing that individuals with antisocial personality disorder have both reduced prefrontal gray matter and reduced SC activity, although this study measured SC levels rather than SCOR (Raine et al., 2000). Furthermore, when antisocials were divided into those with and without reduced prefrontal gray, it was the subgroup of individuals with prefrontal gray deficits who showed SC deficits compared to those without prefrontal deficits. If the attentional function of frontal brain areas is considered, these findings are also consistent with the notion of reduced attentional resources in individuals characterized by low SCOR responsivity.

Other findings, however, have indicated increased SC reactivity in relation to antisocial behavior. For example, in a study of second grade boys and girls, reac-

tive (i.e., defensive), but not proactive (i.e., instrumental), aggression was positively related to SC reactivity, as well as to angry nonverbal behaviors, in response to a frustration challenge (Hubbard et al., 2002). Similarly, in an analog aggression task, male undergraduates who were subjected to an uncontrollable noise showed increased SC responsivity and, if also previously provoked, gave the most persistent shocks to a confederate (Green & McCown, 1984). In contrast, Zahn and Kruesi (1993) found no difference in SCORs to a series of tones in boys with or without a diagnosis of conduct disorder.

SC Conditioning

Perhaps the strongest findings for SC activity lie with respect to reduced classical conditioning in antisocial populations. Classical conditioning involves learning that an initially neutral event (i.e., a conditioned stimulus, or CS) when closely followed in time by an aversive event (i.e., an unconditioned stimulus, or UCS) will develop the properties of this UCS. Eysenck (1977) argued that the socialization process and development of a "conscience" stems from a set of classically conditioned negative emotional responses to situations that have previously led to punishment. In this way, socialized individuals develop a feeling of uneasiness at even contemplating antisocial behavior, presumably because such thoughts elicit representations of punishment earlier in life. Furthermore, according to Eysenck's theory, arousal levels are related to conditionability, such that low levels of arousal predispose to poor conditionability and high levels to good conditionability.

The central idea in Eysenck's theory is that antisocial people will be characterized by poor classical conditioning. Classical conditioning has frequently been assessed using SC: a neutral, nonaversive tone (CS) is presented to the subject, followed a few seconds later by either a loud tone or an electric shock (UCS). The key measure is the size of the SC response elicited by the CS after a number of CS-UCS pairings. In one review, 13 of 14 studies reported significantly poorer SC conditioning in antisocial populations (Hare, 1978). In a review of post-1978 studies by Raine (1993), all six studies showed some evidence of significantly poorer SC conditioning in antisocial groups, including psychopathic gamblers, other psychopaths, conduct disordered children from high social class backgrounds, and criminals from good homes.

Heart Rate (HR)

Definition and Description

The HR reflects both sympathetic (i.e., activation) and parasympathetic (i.e., conservation) nervous system activity and can be measured both tonically (i.e., beats per minute at rest) or phasically (i.e., change in response to a stimulus). Accelerations in HR to a stimulus are thought to reflect sensory rejection or "tuning out" of noxious environmental events, whereas decelerations are thought to reflect sensory intake or an environmental openness (Lacey & Lacey, 1974). As such, accelerations in HR in response to a stimulus are considered defensive responses and decelerations are considered orienting responses.

Emotionally, high resting or tonic HR has been associated with the experience of anxiety. As such, high tonic HR is thought to reflect fear or an inhibited temperament characterized by behavioral avoidance and shyness, while low tonic HR may reflect fearlessness or disinhibition (Kagan, Reznick, & Snidman, 1987, 1988; Scarpa, Raine, Venables, & Mednick, 1997). A related explanation is that heightened HR activity reflects a well-functioning autonomic nervous system, which cues an individual to avoid risky or threatening situations and thus facilitates adaptive behavior (Bechara, Tranel, Damasio, & Damasio, 1996; Damasio, 1994). Last, low HR may suggest a pattern of stimulation seeking (Gatzke-Kopp et al., 2002). According to this perspective, individuals with low arousal levels attempt to maintain an optimal level of arousal by seeking out thrill and excitement. Indeed, in a prospective study, both fearlessness and stimulation seeking at age 3 predicted aggressive behavior at age 11 (Raine, Reynolds, Venables, Mednick, & Farrington, 1998).

Another cardiovascular measure that is gaining popularity is heart rate variability (HRV), which is the normal variation in interval that occurs between heartbeats as a function of respiration. Whereas HR has both sympathetic and parasympathetic influences, HRV is vagally mediated and controlled primarily by the parasympathetic branch of the autonomic nervous system. In other words, the parasympathetic nervous system helps to slow the heart, which creates more beat-to-beat variability in HR. Because of its parasympathetic influence, increased HRV is thought to reflect emotion regulation capacity in the sense of being able to self-soothe when experiencing a strong emotion (Katz & Gottman, 1995; Porges, Doussard-Roosevelt, & Maiti, 1994).

Tonic Findings

One of the best-replicated psychophysiological findings to date is that of reduced resting HR in antisocial individuals. In his review of this topic, Raine (1993) noted that of 14 relevant studies, there were no failures to replicate the finding of reduced resting HR in the antisocial groups. Low heart rate is a robust marker independent of cultural context, with the relationship having been established in England (Farrington, 1987), Germany (Schmeck & Poustra, 1993), New Zealand (Moffitt & Caspi, 2001), the United States (Rogeness, Cepada, Macedo, Fischer, & Harris, 1990), Mauritius (Raine, Venables, & Mednick, 1997), and Canada (Mezzacappa et al., 1997). It is also diagnostically specific (i.e., not found in other disorders) and for which multiple confounds have been controlled (Raine, Venables, et al., 1997). Furthermore, in a recent study of childhood aggression, a negative relationship was found between HR and proactive (i.e., goal driven), but not reactive (i.e., defensive, impulsive), forms of aggression (Van Voorhees & Scarpa, 2002), suggesting that HR underarousal may be specific to instrumental displays of aggression.

All of these studies used child or adolescent samples but, consistent with this finding, low HR also recently has been associated with self-reported aggression in uninstitutionalized young adults (Scarpa, Fikretoglu, & Luscher, 2000). In addition, adults from the community with a diagnosis of antisocial personality disorder had low HR during a social stressor (Raine et al., 2000).

Reviews by Hare (1970, 1975, 1978) revealed no successes and at least 15 failures to obtain low resting HR in institutionalized, psychopathic criminals. More recently, however, low resting HR has been found to characterize life-course-persistent offenders (Moffitt & Caspi, 2001), as well as convicted psychopathic criminals (Ishikawa, Raine, Lencz, Bihrle, & LaCasse, 2001), indicating that low HR is related to a pervasive pattern of severe rule violations. It also seems to reflect some risk factor in children and adolescents that preface more serious violations later in life. For example, in one of the few prospective studies examining this issue, psychophysiological measures were obtained at age 15 years in an unselected sample of male schoolboys, and government records were obtained 9 years later to measure any criminal violations. The criminals were found to have significantly lower resting HR than the noncriminal controls, indicating reduced cardiovascular arousal as measured 9 years earlier (Raine et al., 1990a). Low HR at age 3 years is also predictive of aggressive behavior at age 11 years in both males and females (Raine, Venables, et al., 1997).

Reduced HR may reflect autonomic underarousal and sensation seeking, as suggested by Raine et al. (1990a), and/or fearlessness in novel situations (Kagan, 1989; Venables, 1987), which theoretically could predispose a child to early social transgressions that cycle into later serious antisocial behavior. Heightened HR arousal, on the other hand, may reflect a well-functioning autonomic nervous system that serves a protective function by aiding individuals to avoid maladaptive and risky behaviors (Damasio, 1994). In support of this contention, successful (i.e., unconvicted) psychopaths from the community had increased HR reactivity to an emotional task relative to convicted psychopaths and controls (Ishikawa et al., 2001). Other studies have also found increased autonomic arousal (i.e., both HR and SC) in at-risk males who resisted or desisted from engaging in later crime (Brennan et al., 1997; Raine, Venables, & Williams, 1995), indicating that high arousal can protect some children from a criminal outcome.

Phasic Findings

Regarding studies on phasic HR changes, the literature is less extensive, but suggests that psychopathic criminals exhibit anticipatory HR acceleration prior to an aversive event. In general, the findings of early studies indicated that psychopaths gave significantly larger acceleratory HR responses in anticipation of a signaled aversive stimulus, such as a loud noise or electric shock, followed by reduced SC responses to the aversive stimulus itself (Hare, 1982; Hare & Craigen, 1974; Hare, Frazelle, & Cox, 1978). Hare (1978) interpreted these findings to suggest that psychopathic individuals have a very proficient active coping mechanism that allows them to "tune out" aversive events. Although interesting, there has been very little further research on this phenomenon. One prospective study found that reduced HR and SC orienting to neutral tones (as opposed to the defensive HR responses found in psychopaths) in adolescents predicted a later criminal outcome (Raine et al., 1990a; Raine, Venables, & Williams, 1990b). In terms of theories of socialization, the pattern of sensory rejection of aversive stimuli found in psychopaths may lead to poor conditioning in response to cues of punishment and thus decreased learning of appropriate social behavior (Eysenck, 1977). The pattern of HR and

SC orienting deficits in criminals, on the other hand, may reflect a general failure to allocate attentional resources to stimulus processing (Dawson et al., 1989), especially if the stimulus is not very interesting.

HR Variability Findings

In general, HRV findings in relation to antisocial behavior tend to be mixed. Consistent with the literature showing an association between low HR and antisocial behavior, some studies have found a relationship between increased HRV and aggression (Catipovic-Veselica et al., 1999; Scarpa et al., 2000), particularly in uninstitutionalized samples. These results suggest that the robust findings of HR underarousal in antisocial samples may be mediated by the parasympathetic nervous system. Indeed, Venables (1988) has suggested that antisocial individuals may be characterized by vagotonia (i.e., increased vagal tone), which would be consistent with reports of both low HR and increased HRV. Emotionally, vagotonia may reflect a reduced fear response and increased control over emotional reactivity. In support of this notion, a recent study found increased HRV to be related to proactive, but not reactive, aggression, where proactive aggression was defined as a relatively unemotional display of aggression that is instrumentally motivated or goal directed (Van Voorhees & Scarpa, 2002).

Others, however, have shown inverse relationships between antisocial behavior and HRV. In other words, these studies indicate that reduced HRV is related to increased levels of aggressive behavior in boys exposed to marital conflict (Katz & Gottman, 1995), externalizing behavior in younger brothers of adjudicated delinquents (Pine et al., 1998), and psychopathic characteristics in institutionalized security patients (Hinton & O'Neill, 1978). The inconsistency in findings suggests that although some antisocial individuals may be quite adept at emotional control, others may be deficient in such emotion regulatory capacity and thus be prone to high negative affect.

Electroencephalogram (EEG)

Definition and Description

The EEG reflects the electrical activity of the brain recorded from electrodes placed at different locations on the scalp according to the standardized International

10–20 system. EEG can be broken down into different frequency components, most commonly delta (0–4 Hz), theta (4–8 Hz), alpha (8–12 Hz), and beta (13–30 Hz). A predominance of low-frequency activity (e.g., delta and theta) indicates low tonic levels of arousal, whereas high-frequency activity (e.g., beta) is more indicative of an aroused cortex. Alpha and beta are also often subdivided into slow and fast components. EEG can be either clinically scored by eyeballing the chart record for excessive slow-wave activity or subjected to a more quantitative computerized analysis which more objectively delineates the EEG into different components.

EEG frequency has been aligned with a continuum of consciousness, with delta associated with sleep, theta associated with drowsiness and low levels of alertness, alpha associated with relaxed wakefulness, and beta associated with alertness and vigilance. As such, individuals with a predominance of delta, theta, or slow alpha activity would be viewed as having relatively reduced levels of cortical arousal, whereas those with relatively faster alpha and beta activity would be viewed as relatively more aroused. In this way, EEG frequency is reflective of tonic levels of cortical arousal.

When EEG is used to measure phasic activity, it is referred to as the event-related potential (ERP), which reflects averaged changes of electrical activity of the brain in response to specific stimuli. ERP responses typically follow a sequence of early, middle, and late components that are thought to reflect the psychological processes of environmental filtering, cortical augmenting, and attention, respectively.

Tonic Findings

In a review by Mednick, Volavka, Gabrielli, and Itil (1982), the authors concluded that there is a high prevalence of EEG abnormalities in violent criminals (ranging from 25 to 50%), especially in recidivistic offenders, compared with 10–15% normally found in the general population. Other reviews have drawn similar conclusions for crime in general and violent crime in particular (Milstein, 1988; Volavka, 1987, 1990), and EEG abnormalities continue to be reported in more recent studies (Evans & Claycomb, 1999; Wong, Lumsden, Fenton, & Fenwick, 1994). Reviews of the EEG literature on psychopathy are less consistent. Hare (1970) initially concluded that psychopaths are characterized by excessive slow-wave activity. Later reviews, however, argued that evidence of EEG abnormalities

in psychopaths is inconsistent (Blackburn, 1983; Syndulko, 1978), with one study even showing the opposite pattern that primary psychopaths were *more* aroused than secondary (schizoid) psychopaths.

The reported EEG abnormalities have been localized most often to either the temporal or frontal regions of the brain (Deckel, Hesselbrock, & Bauer, 1996; Mednick et al., 1982; Volavka, 1995). The temporal lobes are involved in audition, visual perception, sexual behavior, and social behaviors. The frontal lobes are involved in planning, decision making, reasoning, fear conditioning, emotion regulation, and regulation of sympathetic activity. Thus, damage to these areas may give rise to poor self-regulation and lack of inhibitory control over antisocial, violent behavior. Although it is still unclear if EEG reflects cerebral cortical functioning or is controlled by subcortical regions of the brain (e.g., the amygdala, hippocampus, etc.), Volavka (1995) hypothesized that early brain injuries may have interfered with normal neural development, thus leading to the observed EEG slowing.

Phasic Findings

ERP studies of antisocial behavior have primarily involved psychopathic populations, and a review of this literature (conceptually broken down into early, middle, and late latency studies) is presented by Raine (1989). The main conclusions of this review are findings of (a) long early latency brainstem averaged evoked responses, reflecting excessive environmental filtering and reduced arousal, (b) increased middle latency ERP amplitudes to stimuli of increasing intensity, which has been linked to sensation seeking, and (c) enhanced late latency ERP P300 amplitudes to stimuli of interest, suggesting enhanced attention to stimulating events. Raine suggested that these processes may be causally linked, such that individuals with chronically low levels of arousal (possibly caused by excessive filtering of stimuli) would seek out stimulating events (including risky situations) in order to increase their levels of arousal to more optimal levels. This stimulation seeking may partly account for the enhanced attention shown to events of interest.

There is reason to believe that impaired EEG and ERPs may reflect early risks for later criminal behavior. As reflected in a prospective study (Raine et al., 1990a, 1990b), criminals versus noncriminals had significantly more slow-frequency EEG theta activity and larger N100 ERPs to target stimuli as measured 9 years earlier. These findings are consistent with notions of underarousal (increased theta activity) and enhanced early stimulus attention (larger N100) in criminals and psychopaths.

Relationship to Neuropsychological and Brain Imaging Findings

Findings of excessive slow-wave EEG functioning in the frontal and temporal brain regions is consistent with neuropsychological findings in antisocial samples. For example, there is some evidence that generalized frontal dysfunction is characteristic of antisocial and criminal behavior. Recent studies examining damage to the frontal cortex in noncriminal samples have shown a pattern of personality changes including argumentativeness, lack of concern for consequences of behavior, loss of social graces, impulsivity, distractibility, shallowness, lability, violence, and reduced ability to utilize symbols. This pattern has been termed frontal lobe syndrome (Silver & Yudofsky, 1987). More direct evidence comes from neuropsychological studies that have implicated anterior and frontal dysfunction in violent adult criminals using the Halstead-Reitan Neuropsychological Test Battery (Flor-Henry, 1973; Yeudall & Fromm-Auch, 1979) and the Luria-Nebraska Neuropsychological Battery (Bryant, Scott, Golden, & Tori, 1984). Consistent findings of frontal dysfunction have not been found, however, in violent juvenile delinquents (Yeudall, Fromm-Auch, & Davies, 1982) or adult psychopaths (Gorenstein, 1982; Hare, 1984). Thus, it has been suggested that generalized frontal dysfunction may be specific to adult violent offenders (Moffitt & Henry, 1991), whereas psychopaths may have more selective frontal deficits (Raine & Venables, 1992).

As with EEG findings, the temporal lobe has also been implicated in antisocial behavior. For example, one influential theory of brain dysfunction in criminals suggests left hemisphere damage and, in particular, disruption to frontal and temporal cortical-limbic (i.e., hippocampal/amygdala) systems (Flor-Henry, 1973; Yeudall et al., 1982). Yeudall and Flor-Henry (1975), for instance, found that 76% of aggressive criminals had dysfunction localized to the frontal and temporal regions of the brain. Of these, 79% showed frontotemporal abnormalities lateralized to the left hemisphere.

In general, brain imaging studies that show significant effects in criminals support the neuropsychological findings of frontal and temporal deficits. Frontal dysfunction tends to be found in violent offenders (Raine, Buchsbaum, Stanley, Lottenberg, Abel, & Stoddard, 1994; Volkow & Tancredi, 1987), child sexual assaulters (Hendricks et al., 1988), or sex offenders containing a large proportion of rapists (Wright, Nobrega, Langevin, & Wortzman, 1990). Of those studies that found deficits partly localized to the temporal lobe, samples contained a larger proportion of sex offenders, including more passive sex offenders, such as pedophiles and incest offenders (Hucker et al., 1986, 1988; Wright et al., 1990). Because of this pattern in findings, it has been tentatively suggested that frontal dysfunction is associated with violent offending and rape, whereas temporal dysfunction is associated more with sexual offending, such as incest or pedophilia (Raine, 1993).

Startle Blink

Definition and Description

Startle blink activity measures the automatic eyeblink response that occurs to a startling probe, such as a loud noise or a puff of air to the eye. The magnitude of the startle blink response varies with the valence of an ongoing emotional state; it is typically magnified when viewing unpleasant stimuli, but diminished when viewing pleasant stimuli (see Patrick, 1994, for a review). Moreover, because the startle response is a reflex, it is thought to index emotional reactions at a very basic and primitive level. At this level, affective reactions have either an appetitive or a defensive motivational function. Startle potentiation (i.e., increased startle magnitude), therefore, is thought to reflect defensive reactivity, negative affect, and temperamental differences in negative emotionality (Cook, Stevenson, & Hawk, 1993; Lang et al., 1993).

Findings

In a study of criminals that were classified according to their level of antisocial behavior and emotional detachment, differences were found in startle blink potentiation while anticipating an aversive stimulus (Patrick, Bradley, & Lang, 1993). Criminals with high emotional detachment (including psychopaths) exhibited reduced startle potentiation, while criminals with low emotional detachment exhibited robust startle potentiation. The authors' main conclusion was that psychopaths display a core emotional deficit in fear potentiation and defensive response modulation.

There have since been several replications of this finding in criminal (Herpertz et al., 2001; Levenston, Patrick, Bradley, & Lang, 2000; Patrick, 1994) and noncriminal (Vanman, Mejia, Dawson, Schell, & Raine, 2003) male psychopathic samples, as well as in women with psychopathy (Sutton, Vitale, & Newman, 2002). That is, the typical linear increase in startle response from pleasant to neutral to unpleasant stimuli is not found in psychopaths compared to nonpsychopathic controls, and the deficit in affective startle modulation is particularly tied to the personality feature of emotional detachment. This has been interpreted as suggesting that the core personality traits of psychopathy are associated with a temperamental predisposition of reduced responsivity to emotional cues, especially if they are aversive or threatening.

In addition to the clarification of psychopathic tendencies, these startle modulation studies also give some insight into nonpsychopathic antisocial criminal behavior. In general, all of the abovementioned studies found that high levels of antisocial behavior, without emotional detachment, was associated with normal or even increased affective startle modulation. Furthermore, negative affect was related to high antisocial behavior and low emotional detachment in these individuals (Patrick et al., 1993; Patrick, Zempolich, & Levenston, 1997). Although some criminals and psychopaths are characterized primarily by an emotional deficit, these studies therefore also suggest that others with high levels of antisocial behavior (particularly angry outbursts and reactive aggression) may be characterized by heightened negative affect. This notion is further supported in a study using a laboratory analog aggression task where participants with high trait negative emotionality (NEM) showed more tonic distress, as evidenced by startle sensitization, than low NEM participants. Moreover, those with high NEM delivered more intense shocks (Verona, Patrick, & Lang, 2002). The authors suggest that high sustained negative affect may bias some individuals toward more intense acts of aggression.

Summary and Conclusions

A great deal of evidence has accumulated on psychophysiological correlates of antisocial behavior in youth and adults, including aggression, crime, violence, psychopathy, antisocial personality disorder, conduct disorder, and delinquency. In particular, low autonomic

and central nervous system arousal has been implicated in terms of reduced resting HR and SC measures and increased slow-wave EEG activity (Raine et al., 1990a). Low resting HR, in particular, is one of the best-replicated psychophysiological measures that characterize antisocial behavior. Such underarousal may index a fearless/disinhibited temperament and/or a tendency toward stimulation seeking, characteristics that have both been found to be predictive of antisocial outcomes (Raine et al., 1998). Evidence for a fear deficit has also been implicated in studies of psychopaths who show reduced startle blink potentiation to aversive stimuli, and this deficit has been specifically pronounced in those who score high on the dimension of emotional detachment (Patrick et al., 1993).

It has also been suggested that a well-functioning nervous system serves a protective function by facilitating learning of adaptive behaviors (Damasio, 1994). Findings of poor SC classical conditioning to aversive stimuli in various antisocial populations lends some support to this view (Raine, 1993). Eysenck (1977), for example, argued that socialization occurs through the process of being conditioned to avoid punishment. If the nervous system is not functioning properly in order to fully experience the fear or discomfort associated with punishment, then normal socialization will be impaired.

Findings of reduced SC orienting responses in antisocial individuals with schizotypy and EEG abnormalities localized to the frontal and temporal lobes have implicated frontal dysfunction in antisocial groups, particularly in relationship to violence (Mednick et al., 1982; Volavka, 1995). Damage to this area of the brain has been associated with personality and behavioral characteristics that are similar to what is observed in psychopathic individuals, thus leading Damasio (1994) to coin the term "acquired sociopathy" in people who suffer these sorts of injuries. Even in the absence of visible lesions, subtle impairment in frontal lobe functioning may exist, which can lead to antisocial behavior by interrupting fear conditioning, regulation of autonomic arousal, emotional control, and executive cognitive functioning (i.e., planning, decision making, consideration of future consequences to guide behavior, reasoning, etc.).

Last, some contrasting findings of increased SC reactivity (Hubbard et al., 2002), robust startle blink potentiation (Patrick, 1993, 1994), and decreased HRV (Pine et al., 1998) in some antisocial populations suggest that further clarification of the underlying physiological dysfunction in antisocial individuals is needed.

These findings are often associated with situations and analog aggression tasks that involve provocation, anger, and heightened negative emotionality, providing support to the suggestion that psychophysiological profiles will differ depending upon the type of antisocial behavior studied (e.g., reactive vs. proactive aggression, psychopathic vs. nonpsychopathic criminal behavior) and the temperamental qualities expressed (Patrick et al., 1997; Scarpa & Raine, 1997b). Indeed, in light of the extreme variation in antisocial behaviors manifested and studied, it would be overly simplistic to assume that they are all characterized by the same underlying biological dysfunction and concomitant psychophysiological correlates.

A Comprehensive View of Antisocial Behavior

As stated in the introduction, it is widely acknowledged that psychological and social variables contribute to the development and expression of antisocial behavior. A comprehensive view of antisocial behavior, therefore, must necessarily take such variables into account, while also recognizing the importance of biological influences. With this in mind, we have argued that psychophysiological relationships to antisocial behavior differ depending upon one's history of experiences, including factors such as child abuse, family atmosphere, social class, and adult violence victimization (Scarpa & Raine, 2003).

Overall, there appear to be two primary findings in regard to biosocial interactions. One finding shows stronger psychophysiology-antisocial behavior relationships in antisocial populations with a history of relatively benign or "good" home backgrounds, such as high social classes, privileged environments, intact homes, and absence of exposure to violence or parental conflict (e.g., Raine & Venables, 1984b). In other words, antisocial individuals from good versus bad backgrounds can be distinguished by their psychophysiological functioning, with greater psychophysiological deficits found in those from good backgrounds. For example, reduced SC conditioning has been found in antisocial adolescents from high but not low social classes (Raine & Venables, 1981) and adult criminals without a childhood history of parental absence or domestic conflict (Hemming, 1981). Similarly, low resting HR is a particularly strong characteristic of antisocial people from higher social classes (Raine & Venables, 1984b; Raine, Venables, et al., 1997), privileged middle-class backgrounds attending private schools (Maliphant, Hume, & Furnham, 1990), and intact but not broken homes (Wadsworth, 1976); high HRV predicted aggression only in adults who did not have a history of violence victimization (Scarpa & Ollendick, 2003). These findings lend support to the "social push" hypothesis, which suggests that biological bases of antisocial behavior are most clear in the absence of the push toward antisociality typically received from psychosocial risks (Mednick, 1977; Raine, 2002; Raine & Venables, 1981).

The second primary finding is that the antisocial outcome seems greatest when psychophysiological risks are combined with psychosocial risks relative to having either set of risks alone. For example, Farrington (1997) reports that boys with low resting HRs are more likely to become adult violent criminals if they also have a poor relationship with their parents and come from a large family. He also reports that boys with low HRs are more likely to be rated as aggressive by their teachers if their mother was pregnant as a teenager, they come from a low social class family, or they were separated from a parent before age 10. This is consistent with transactional models of development which posit that behavior problems arise out of contributions from both intrinsic and extrinsic risk factors that cannot be readily separated from each other (Sameroff, 1995). These findings also converge with those involving many other biological systems, including genetics, obstetric and birth complications, hormones, neurotoxins, and neurotransmitters (see Raine, 2002, for a review). Of note, the combined literature suggests that biological influences increase the risk for an antisocial outcome regardless of an individual's background and serve to compound the risk when coupled with psychosocial adversity.

Research and Clinical Implications

What implications do psychophysiological findings on antisocial behavior have for both research and clinical practice? Regarding research implications, these findings indicate a need for more refined analysis. At the outset, it was argued that psychophysiological findings can help inform us about the underlying dysfunction within chronically antisocial individuals. Have we achieved this goal? In part, yes. Psychophysiological findings are leading us toward understanding effects of the peripheral and central nervous systems on some forms of antisocial behavior. For example, results of reduced startle blink and fear conditioning to aversive stimuli in psychopathic samples suggest that these individuals may have a deficit in primitive subcortical structures that subserve basic emotional functions. Findings from SCOR and EEG studies suggest subtle frontotemporal brain dysfunction in the absence of clear lesions. Moreover, studies finding tonic autonomic and central underarousal suggest difficulties with stimulation seeking and disinhibition.

Findings are mixed, however, and sometimes contradictory, suggesting that there is variability in antisocial behavior and its underlying qualities that need further explication. To this end, psychophysiological research needs to move toward specifying the processes and contexts that might influence psychophysiology and why or how this is related to various antisocial outcomes. For example, is the motivation behind an antisocial act (i.e., instrumentally verus emotionally driven) differentially related to psychophysiology? Do the same profiles characterize individuals who solely abuse family members versus those who also aggress against strangers? Do other factors, such as temperamental qualities or prior experiences with victimization, distinguish which antisocial individuals exhibit psychophysiological underarousal, defensive reactivity, or emotional dyscontrol? Moreover, how do these psychophysiological profiles develop? Are they genetic predispositions, or are they by-products of violent experiences these individuals have had (e.g., frontal injuries from child maltreatment; emotional desensitization and underarousal from chronic violence exposure)? Future research would also benefit from considering the role of additional factors, such as attention-deficit hyperactivity or alcoholism, in clarifying the relationship of biology and environmental experience to antisociality. Regarding clinical implications, research on the psychophysiology of antisocial behavior indicates that the biological influence on such behavior can no longer be ignored in its amelioration. Thus, it is clear that the most effective prevention and treatment programs and the greatest understanding of antisocial development will include multiple modes of treatment and information from both biological and psychosocial perspectives.

Directly altering biological functioning through interventions such as good prenatal care, nutrition and health programs, biofeedback training, or psychotropic medication would be helpful. Early intervention might also benefit children who experience psychosocial hardship but do not yet show behavioral difficulties by indirectly changing their psychophysiological functioning. For example, an environmental preschool enrichment program similar to Head Start resulted in significant increases in SC and EEG activity and attention 8 years later (Raine et al., 2001).

Interventions may need to differ depending upon the kind of psychophysiological functioning that is noted. Programs that help individuals to form emotional connections to their actions (e.g., social perspective taking), increase conditionability (e.g., behavior modification), and understand both the immediate as well as long-term consequences of their behavior may directly benefit those with general underarousal, fearlessness, or emotional detachment. Programs that address stress reactivity, anger, and emotional control may be beneficial to those with autonomic and startle-blink overactivity and frontal/temporal dysfunction.

Last, the findings on biosocial interactions suggest that treatment to reduce conflict in the home or create a more stable environment could have a protective influence on children who have biological deficits. For example, one study found that a stable home environment protected children with fetal alcohol syndrome from developing antisocial behavior (Streissguth, Barr, Kogan, & Bookstein, 1996). Other programs that aim to improve parenting skills, promote stronger parent-infant attachments, eliminate child maltreatment, or redirect stimulation seeking to more prosocial activities may similarly suppress a biological predisposition toward antisociality.

Summary

In sum, psychophysiological findings in relation to antisocial behavior provide support for the notion that chronic serious antisocial behavior is a disorder that partly arises from a biological dysfunction within the individual. Despite the heterogeneity of antisocial behaviors covered in the literature, several themes emerge. The strongest evidence suggests that antisocial individuals are characterized by fearlessness or emotional detachment, reflected in reduced levels of tonic autonomic (i.e., HR and SC) arousal, increased HRV, greater slow-wave EEG activity, and reduced startle blink potentiation to unpleasant stimuli. There is also growing evidence of other antisocial behavior that is characterized more by defensiveness, stress reactivity, and negative emotionality as reflected in decreased HRV, increased SC reactivity, normal or increased affective startle modulation, and left frontotemporal dysfunction. Of course, this is a simplification. All behaviors are subject to context and so it is conceivable that both patterns can be observed within the same individual at different times or in different situations, and multiple biosocial interactions may ensue. Nonetheless, the literature reviewed here and in the previous chapters of this book provides compelling evidence that a comprehensive view of antisocial behavior, which incorporates both biological and psychosocial influences, is needed to fully understand this phenomenon and develop effective preventive and interventive strategies.

References

American Psychiatric Association. (1994). *Diagnostic and statistical manual of mental disorders* (4th ed.). Washington, DC: Author.

Bartol, C. R. (1991). *Criminal behavior: A psychosocial approach* (3rd ed.). Englewood Cliffs, NJ: Prentice Hall.

Bechara, A., Tranel, D., Damasio, H., & Damasio, A. (1996). Failure to respond autonomically to anticipated future outcomes following damage to prefrontal cortex. *Cerebral Cortex, 6,* 215–225.

Blackburn, R. (1983). Psychopathy, delinquency, and crime. In A. Gale & J. A. Edwards (Eds.), *Physiological correlates of human behavior* (Vol. 3, pp. 187–205). London: Academic Press.

Brennan, P. A., Raine, A., Schulsinger, F., Kirkegaard-Sorensen, L., Knop, J., Hutchings, B., et al. (1997). Psychophysiological protective factors for male subjects at high risk for criminal behavior. *American Journal of Psychiatry, 154,* 853–855.

Bryant, E. T., Scott, M. L., Golden, C. J., & Tori, C. D. (1984). Neuropsychological deficits, learning disability, and violent behavior. *Journal of Consulting and Clinical Psychology, 53,* 323–324.

Cacioppo, J. T., & Tassinary, L. G. (1990). Psychophysiology and psychophysiological inference. In J. T. Cacioppo & L. G. Tassinary (Eds.), *Principles of psychophysiology: Physical, social, and inferential elements* (pp. 3–33). New York: Cambridge University Press.

Catipovic-Veselica, K., Amidzic, V., Durijancik, J., Kozmar, D., Sram, M., Glavas, B., et al. (1999). Association of heart-rate variability with scores on the Emotion Profile Index in patients with acute coronary heart disease. *Psychological Reports, 84,* 433–442.

Cook, E. W., Stevenson, V. E., & Hawk, L. W. (1993). *Enhanced startle modulation and negative affectivity.* Paper presented at the annual meeting of the Society for Research in Psychopathology, Chicago.

Damasio, A. R. (1994). *Descartes' error: Emotion, reason, and the human brain.* New York: Avon Books.

Dawson, M. E., Filion, D. L., & Schell, A. M. (1989). Is elicitation of the autonomic orienting response associated with the allocation of processing resources? *Psychophysiology, 26,* 560–572.

Deckel, A. W., Hesselbrock, V., & Bauer, L. (1996). Antisocial personality disorder, childhood delinquency, and frontal brain functioning: EEG and neuropsychological findings. *Journal of Clinical Psychology, 52,* 639–650.

Evans, J. R., & Claycomb, S. (1999). Abnormal QEEG patterns associated with dissociation and violence. *Journal of Neurotherapy, 3,* 21–27.

Eysenck, H. J. (1977). *Crime and personality* (3rd ed.). St. Albans, UK: Paladin.

Farrington, D. P. (1987). Implications of biological findings for criminological research. In S. A. Mednick, T. E. Moffitt, & S. A. Stack (Eds.), *The causes of crime: New biological approaches* (pp. 42–64). Cambridge: Cambridge University Press.

Farrington, D. P. (1997). The relationship between low resting heart rate and violence. In A. Raine, P. A. Brennan, D. P. Farrington, & S. A. Mednick (Eds.), *Biosocial bases of violence* (pp. 89–106). New York: Plenum.

Flor-Henry, P. (1973). Psychiatric syndromes considered a manifestation of lateralized-temporal-limbic dysfunction. In L. Laitiner & K. Livingston (Eds.), *Surgical approaches in psychiatry.* Lancaster, UK: Medical and Technical Publishing.

Gatzke-Kopp, L. M., Raine, A., Loeber, R., Stouthamer-Loeber, M., & Steinhauer, S. R. (2002). Serious delinquent behavior, sensation seeking, and electrodermal arousal. *Journal of Abnormal Child Psychology, 30,* 477–486.

Gorenstein, E. E. (1982). Frontal lobe functions in psychopaths. *Journal of Abnormal Psychology, 91,* 368–379.

Green, R., & McCown, E. J. (1984). Effects of noise and attack on aggression and physiological arousal. *Motivation and Emotion, 8,* 231–241.

Hare, R. D. (1970). *Psychopathy: Theory and practice.* New York: Wiley.

Hare, R. D. (1975). Psychophysiological studies of psychopathy. In D. C. Fowles (Ed.), *Clinical applications of psychophysiology* (pp. 77–105). New York: Cambridge University Press.

Hare, R. D. (1978). Electrodermal and cardiovascular correlates of psychopathy. In R. D. Hare & D. Schalling (Eds.), *Psychopathic behavior: Approaches to research* (pp. 107–144). New York: Wiley.

Hare, R. D. (1982). Psychopathy and physiological activity during anticipation of an aversive stimulus in a distraction paradigm. *Psychophysiology, 19,* 266–271.

Hare, R. D. (1984). Performance of psychopaths on cognitive tasks related to frontal lobe function. *Journal of Abnormal Psychology, 93,* 133–140.

Hare, R. D., & Craigen, D. (1974). Psychopathy and physiological activity in a mixed motive game situation. *Psychophysiology, 11*, 197–206.

Hare, R. D., Frazelle, J., & Cox, D. (1978). Psychopathy and physiological responses to threat of an aversive stimulus. *Psychophysiology, 15*, 165–172.

Hemming, J. H. (1981). Electrodermal indices in a selected prison sample and students. *Personality and Individual Differences, 2*, 37–46.

Hendricks, S. E., Fitzpatrick, D. F., Hartmann, K., Quaife, M. A., Stratbucker, R. A., et al. (1988). Brain structure and function in sexual molesters of children and adolescents. *Journal of Clinical Psychiatry, 49*, 108–112.

Herpertz, S. C., Werth, U., Lucas, G., Qunaibi, M., Schuerkens, A., Kunert, H., et al. (2001). Emotion in criminal offenders with psychopathic and borderline personality disorders. *Archives of General Psychiatry, 58*, 737–745.

Hinton, J. W., & O'Neill, M. T. (1978). Pilot research on psychophysiological response profiles of maximum security hospital patients. *British Journal of Social and Clinical Psychology, 17*, 103.

Hubbard, J. A., Smithmyer, C. M., Ramsden, S. R., Parker, E. H., Flanagan, K. D., Dearing, K. F., et al. (2002). Observational, physiological, and self-report measures of children's anger: Relations to reactive and proactive aggression. *Child Development, 73*, 1101–1118.

Hucker, S., Langevin, R., Dickey, R., Handy, L. Chambers, J., Wright, S., et al. (1988). Cerebral damage and dysfunction in sexually aggressive men. *Annals of Sex Research, 1*, 33–47.

Hucker, S., Langevin, R., Wortzman, G., Bain, J., Handy, L., Chambers, J., et al. (1986). Neuropsychological impairment in pedophiles. *Canadian Journal of Behavioral Science, 18*, 440–448.

Ishikawa, S. S., Raine, A., Lencz, T., Bihrle, S., & LaCasse, L. (2001). Autonomic stress reactivity and executive functions in successful and unsuccessful criminal psychopaths from the community. *Journal of Abnormal Psychology, 110*, 423–432.

Kagan, J. (1989). Temperamental contributions to social behavior. *American Psychologist, 44*, 668–674.

Kagan, J., Reznick, J. S., & Snidman, N. (1987). The physiology and psychology of behavioral inhibition. *Child Development, 58*, 1459–1473.

Kagan, J., Reznick, J. S., & Snidman, N. (1988). Biological bases of childhood shyness. *Science, 240*, 167–171.

Katz, L. F., & Gottman, J. M. (1995). Vagal tone protects children from marital conflict. *Development & Psychopathology, 7*, 83–92.

Kruesi, M. J., Hibbs, E. D., Zahn, T. P., & Keysor, C. S. (1992). A 2-year prospective follow-up study of children and adolescents with disruptive behavior disorders: Prediction by cerebrospinal fluid 5-hydroxy-indoleacetic acid, homovanillic acid, and autonomic measures? *Archives of General Psychiatry, 49*, 429–435.

Lacey, B. C., & Lacey, J. I. (1974). Studies of heart rate and other bodily processes in sensorimotor behavior. In P. A. Obrist, A. H. Black, J. Brener, & L. V. DiCara (Eds.), *Cardiovascular psychophysiology: Current issues in response mechanisms, biofeedback, and methodology* (pp. 538–564). Chicago: Aldine.

Lang, P. J., Bradley, M. M., Cuthbert, B. N., et al. (1993). Emotion and psychopathology: A startle probe analysis. In L. Chapman & D. Fowles (Eds.), *Progress in experimental personality and psychopathology research* (Vol. 16, pp. 163–199). New York: Springer.

Levenston, G. K., Patrick, C. J., Bradley, M. M., & Lang, P. J. (2000). The psychopath as observer: Emotion and attention in picture processing. *Journal of Abnormal Psychology, 109*, 373–385.

Maliphant, R., Hume, F., & Furnham, A. (1990). Autonomic nervous system (ANS) activity, personality characteristics, and disruptive behavior in girls. *Journal of Child Psychology and Psychiatry and Allied Disciplines, 31*, 619–628.

McCord, J. (1979). Some child-bearing antecedents of criminal behavior in adult men. *Journal of Personality and Social Psychology, 9*, 1477–1486.

Mednick, S. A. (1977). A bio-social theory of the learning of law-abiding behavior. In S. A. Mednick & K. O. Christensen (Eds.), *Biosocial bases of criminal behavior.* New York: Gardner.

Mednick, S. A., Moffitt, T. E., & Stack, S. A. (Eds.). (1987). *The causes of crime: New biological approaches.* Cambridge: Cambridge University Press.

Mednick, S. A., Volavka, J., Gabrielli, W. F., & Itil, T. (1982). EEG as a predictor of antisocial behavior. *Criminology, 19*, 219–231.

Mezzacappa, E., Tremblay, R. E., Kindlon, D., Saul, J. P., Arsenault, L., Seguin, J., et al. (1997). Anxiety, antisocial behavior, and heart rate regulation in adolescent males. *Journal of Child Psychology and Psychiatry, 38*, 457–469.

Milstein, V. (1988). EEG topography in patients with aggressive violent behavior. In T. E. Moffitt & S. A. Mednick (Eds.), *Biological contributions to crime causation* (pp. 40–54). Dordrecht, Netherlands: Nijhoff.

Moffitt, T. E., & Caspi, A. (2001). Childhood predictors differentiate life-course persistent and adolescent limited pathways among males and females. *Development and Psychopathology, 13*, 355–375.

Moffitt, T. E., & Henry, B. (1991). Neuropsychological studies of juvenile delinquency and juvenile violence. In J. S. Milner (Ed.), *Neuropsychology of aggression* (pp. 131–146). Boston: Kluwer.

Ohman, A. (1979). The orienting response, attention, and learning: An information processing perspective. In H. D. Kimmel, E. H. van Olst, & J. F. Orlebeke (Eds.), *The orienting reflex in humans* (pp. 443–471). Hillsdale, NJ: Erlbaum.

Ohman, A. (1985). Face the beats and fear the face: Animal and social fears as prototypes for evolutionary analyses of emotions. *Psychophysiology, 23,* 123–145.

Patrick, C. J. (1994). Emotion and psychopathy: Startling new insights. *Psychophysiology, 31,* 319–330.

Patrick, C. J., Bradley, M. M., & Lang, P. J. (1993). Emotion in the criminal psychopath: Startle reflex modulation. *Journal of Abnormal Psychology, 102,* 82–92.

Patrick, C. J., Zempolich, K. A., & Levenston, G. K. (1997). Emotionality and violent behavior in psychopaths: A biosocial analysis. In A. Raine, P. A. Brennan, D. P. Farrington, & S. A. Mednick (Eds.), *Biosocial bases of violence* (pp. 145–161). New York: Plenum.

Pine, D. S., Wasserman, G. A., Miller, L., Coplan, J. D., Bagiella, E., Kovelenku, P., et al. (1998). Heart period variability and psychopathology in urban boys at risk for delinquency. *Psychophysiology, 35,* 521–529.

Porges, S. W., Doussard-Roosevelt, J. A., & Maiti, A. K. (1994). Vagal tone and the physiological regulation of emotion. In N. A. Fox (Ed.), *The development of emotion regulation: Biological and behavioral considerations.* Monographs of the Society for Research in Child Development (Vol. 59, pp. 167–186). Ann Arbor, MI: Society for Research in Child Development.

Raine, A. (1989). Evoked potentials and psychopathy. *International Journal of Psychophysiology, 8,* 1–16.

Raine, A. (1993). *The psychopathology of crime: Criminal behavior as a clinical disorder.* San Diego: Academic Press.

Raine, A. (2002). Biosocial studies of antisocial and violent behavior in children and adults: A review. *Journal of Abnormal Child Psychology, 30,* 311–326.

Raine, A., Bihrle, S., Venables, P. H., Mednick, S. A., & Pollock, V. (1999). Skin-conductance orienting deficits and increased alcoholism in schizotypal criminals. *Journal of Abnormal Psychology, 108,* 299–306.

Raine, A., Brennan, P. A., Farrington, D. P., & Mednick, S. A. (Eds.). (1997). *Biosocial bases of violence.* New York: Plenum.

Raine, A., Buchsbaum, M. S., Stanley, J., Lottenberg, S., Abel, L., & Stoddard, J. (1994). Selective reductions in pre-frontal glucose metabolism in murderers assessed with positron emission tomography. *Biological Psychiatry, 36,* 365–373.

Raine, A., Lencz, T., Bihrle, S., LaCasse, L., & Colletti, P. (2000). Reduced prefrontal gray matter volume and reduced autonomic activity in antisocial personality disorder. *Archives of General Psychiatry, 57,* 119–127.

Raine, A., Reynolds, G. P., & Sheard, C. (1991). Neuroanatomical mediators of electrodermal activity in normal human subjects: A magnetic resonance imaging study. *Psychophysiology, 28,* 548–558.

Raine, A., Reynolds, C., Venables, P. H., & Mednick, S. A., & Farrington, D. P. (1998). Fearlessness, stimulation-seeking, and large body size at age 3 years as early predispositions to childhood aggression at age 11 years. *Archives of General Psychiatry, 55,* 745–751.

Raine, A., & Venables, P. H. (1981). Classical conditioning and socialization—a biosocial interaction. *Personality and Individual Differences, 2,* 273–283.

Raine, A., & Venables, P. H. (1984a). Electrodermal nonresponding, schizoid tendencies, and antisocial behavior in adolescents. *Psychophysiology, 21,* 424–433.

Raine, A., & Venables, P. H. (1984b). Tonic heart rate level, social class, and antisocial behaviour in adolescents. *Biological Psychology, 18,* 123–132.

Raine, A., & Venables, P. H. (1992). Antisocial behavior: Evolution, genetics, neuropsychology, and psychophysiology. In A. Gale & M. Eysenck (Eds.), *Handbook of individual differences: Biological perspectives* (pp. 287–312). London: Wiley.

Raine, A., Venables, P. H., Dalais, C., Mellingen, K., Reynolds, C., & Mednick, S. A. (2001). Early educational and health enrichment at age 3–5 years is associated with increased autonomic and central nervous system arousal and orienting at age 11 years: Evidence from the Mauritius Child Health Project. *Psychophysiology, 38,* 254–266.

Raine, A., Venables, P. H., & Mednick, S. A. (1997). Low resting heart rate at age 3 years predisposes to aggression at age 11 years: Findings from the Mauritius Joint Child Health Project. *Journal of the American Academy of Child and Adolescent Psychiatry, 36,* 1457–1464.

Raine, A., Venables, P. H., & Williams, M. (1990a). Relationships between CNS and ANS measures of arousal at age 15 and criminality at age 24. *Archives of General Psychiatry, 47,* 1003–1007.

Raine, A., Venables, P. H., Williams, M. (1990b). Relationships between N1, P300, and CNV recorded at age 15 and criminal behavior at age 24. *Psychophysiology, 27,* 567–575.

Raine, A., Venables, P. H., & Williams, M. (1995). High autonomic arousal and electrodermal orienting at age 15 years as possible protective factors against criminal behavior at age 29 years. *American Journal of Psychiatry, 152,* 1595–1600.

Rogeness, G. A., Cepada, C., Macedo, C. A., Fischer, C., & Harris, W. R. (1990). Differences in heart rate and blood pressure in children with conduct disorder, major depression, and separation anxiety. *Psychiatry Research, 33,* 199–206.

Sameroff, A. J. (1995). General systems theories and developmental psychopathology. In D. Cicchetti & D. J. Cohen (Eds.), *Developmental psychopathology: Vol. 1. Theory and methods* (pp. 659–695). New York: Wiley.

Scarpa, A. (2003). Community violence exposure in young adults. *Trauma, Violence, and Abuse: A Review Journal, 4,* 210–227.

Scarpa, A., Fikretoglu, D., & Luscher, K. A. (2000). Community violence exposure in a young adult sample: II. Psychophysiology and aggressive behavior. *Journal of Community Psychology, 28,* 417–425.

Scarpa, A., & Ollendick, T. H. (2003). Community violence exposure in a young adult sample: III. Psychophysiology and victimization interact to affect risk for aggression. *Journal of Community Psychology, 31,* 321–338.

Scarpa, A., & Raine, A. (1997a). Biology of wickedness. *Psychiatric Annals, 27,* 624–629.

Scarpa, A., & Raine, A. (1997b). Psychophysiology of anger and violent behavior [special issue on anger, aggression, and violence]. *The Psychiatric Clinics of North America, 20,* 375–394.

Scarpa, A., & Raine, A. (2003). The psychophysiology of antisocial behavior: Interactions with environmental experiences. In A. Walsh & L. Ellis (Eds.), *Biosocial criminology: Challenging environmentalism's supremacy* (pp. 209–226). New York: Nova Science.

Scarpa, A., Raine, A., Venables, P. H., & Mednick, S. A. (1997). Heart rate and skin conductance in behaviorally inhibited Mauritian children. *Journal of Abnormal Psychology, 106,* 182–190.

Schmeck, K., & Poustra, F. (1993). Psychophysiologische reacktionsmuster und psychische auffalligkeiten im kindesalter. In P. Baumann (Ed.), *Biologische psychiatrie der gegenwart.* Vienna, Austria: Springer-Verlag.

Silver, J. M., & Yudofsky, S. C. (1987). Aggressive behavior in patients with neuropsychiatric disorders. *Psychiatric Annals, 17,* 367–370.

Streissguth, A. P. Barr, H. M., Kogan, J., & Bookstein, F. L. (1996). *Understanding the occurrence of secondary disabilities in clients with fetal alcohol syndrome (FAS) and fetal alcohol effects (FAE).* Seattle: Washington Publication Services.

Sutton, S. K., Vitale, J. E., & Newman, J. P. (2002). Emotion among women with psychopathy during picture perception. *Journal of Abnormal Psychology, 111,* 610–619.

Syndulko, K. (1978). Electrocortical investigations of sociopathy. In R. D. Hare & D. Schalling (Eds.), *Psychopathic behavior: Approaches to research* (pp. 145–156). Chichester, UK: Wiley.

Vanman, E. J., Mejia, V. Y., Dawson, M. E., Schell, A.

M., & Raine, A. (2003). Modification of the startle reflex in a community sample: Do one or two dimensions of psychopathy underlie emotional processing? *Personality and Individual Differences, 35,* 2007–2021.

Van Voorhees, E., & Scarpa, A. (2002). Psychophysiological variables in childhood proactive and reactive aggression. *Psychophysiology, 39*(Suppl.), 82.

Venables, P. H. (1987). Autonomic and central nervous system factors in criminal behavior. In S. A. Mednick, T. E. Moffitt, & S. A. Stack (Eds.), *The causes of crime: New biological approaches* (pp. 110–136). Cambridge: Cambridge University Press.

Venables, P. H. (1988). Psychophysiology and crime: Theory and data. In T. E. Moffitt & S. A. Mednick (Eds.), *Biological contributions to crime causation* (pp. 3–13). Dordrecht, Netherlands: Nijhoff.

Verona, E., Patrick, C. J., & Lang, A. R. (2002). A direct assessment of the role of state and trait negative emotion in aggressive behavior. *Journal of Abnormal Psychology, 111,* 249–258.

Visher, C. A., & Roth, J. A. (1986). Participation in criminal careers. In A. Blumstein, J. Cohen, J. A. Roth, & C. A. Visher (Eds.), *Criminal careers and career criminals* (pp. 211–291). Washington, DC: National Academy Press.

Volavka, J. (1987). Electroencephalogram among criminals. In S. A. Mednick, T. E. Moffitt, & S. Stack (Eds.), *The causes of crime: New biological approaches* (pp. 137–145). Cambridge: Cambridge University Press.

Volavka, J. (1990). Aggression, electroencephalography, and evoked potentials: A critical review. *Neuropsychiatry, Neuropsychology, and Behavioral Neurology, 3,* 249–259.

Volavka, J. (1995). *Neurobiology of violence.* Washington, DC: American Psychiatric Association.

Volkow, N. D., & Tancredi, L. (1987). Neural substrates of violent behavior: A preliminary study with positron emission tomography. *British Journal of Psychiatry, 151,* 668–673.

Wadsworth, M. E. J. (1976). Delinquency, pulse rate, and early emotional deprivation. *British Journal of Criminology, 16,* 245–256.

Walsh, A. (2002). *Biosocial criminology: Introduction and integration.* Cincinnati, OH: Anderson.

Widom, C. S. (1989). The cycle of violence. *Science, 244,* 160–166.

Wong, M. T. H., Lumsden, F., Fenton, G. W., & Fenwick, P. B. C. (1994). Electroencephalography, computed tomography and violence ratings of male patients in a maximum-security mental hospital. *Acta Psychiatrica Scandinavica, 90,* 97–101.

Wright, P., Nobrega, J., Langevin, R., & Wortzman, G.

(1990). Brain density and symmetry in pedophilic and sexually aggressive offenders. *Annals of Sex Research*, 3, 319–328.

Yeudall, L. T., & Flor-Henry, P. (1975). *Lateralized neuropsychological impairments in depression and criminal psychopathy*. Paper presented at the Conference of the Psychiatric Association of Alberta, Calgary, Alberta, Canada.

Yeudall, L. T., & Fromm-Auch, D. (1979). Neuropsychological impairments in various psychopathological populations. In J. Gruzelier & P. Flor-Henry (Eds.), *Hemisphere asymmetries of function and psychopathology* (pp. 5–13). New York: Elsevier/North–Holland.

Yeudall, L. T., Fromm-Auch, D., & Davies, P. (1982). Neuropsychological impairment of persistent delinquency. *Journal of Nervous and Mental Disease, 170*, 257–265.

Zahn, T. P., & Kruesi, M. J. P. (1993). Autonomic activity in boys with disruptive behavior disorders. *Psychophysiology, 30*, 605–614.

Author Index

Appearances of the author in captions are indicated by italic page numbers.

Fields, H. L., 52
Fiero, P. L., 87
Figler, M. H., 39, 42, 43
Figueiredo, H. F., 285
Fikretoglu, D., 450
File, S. E., 168
Filion, D. L., 448
Findlay, A., 254
Findling, R. L., 437
Fink, G., 218, 241
Finkel, D., 27, 29
Finkelstein, E. R., 126
Finkelstein, J. E., 42
Finlay-Jones, R., 425
Finn, P. R., 96
Finsberg, J. P., 67
Fiorella, D., 125, 167
Fischer, C., 360, 450
Fish, E. W., 4, 8, 11, 117, *118*, 119, 120, *120*, 124, *124*,
    133, 134, *134*, 154, 219, 240, 263, 357, 433, 434
Fishbein, D. H., 87
Fisher, L. A., 303
Fisher, R. A., 21
Fishman, M. C., 155
Fiske, D. W., 32
Fitzgerald, H. E., 82
Fitzpatrick-McElligott, S., 168
Fivizzani, A. J., 194
Flannelly, K. J., 251, 254, 256, 257, 258, 259, 264, 275,
    282, 284, 399, 401
Flannelly, L., 251, 256, 257, 264, 282
Fleagle, J. G., 71
Fleiss, J., 438
Fleming, A. S., 264
Fleshner, M., 297
Fletcher, P. J., 124
Floody, O. R., 297, 330
Flor, H., 353, 360
Flores, T., 11
Florey, E., 49
Flor-Henry, P., 453
Flory, J. D., 31, 65, 70, 85, 91, 92, 97, 222
Flugge, G., 285, 296
Foch, T., 23
Foch, T. T., 23
Foidart, A., 197, 213
Foldes, A., 168
Foley, D. L., 92
Fonnum, F., 130
Fontenot, M. B., 75, 79, 126
Ford, J. J., 282
Foresberg, A. J. L., 283
Forgie, M. L., 335, 336
Foroud, A., 329
Forth, A. E., 359
Foster, R. H., 129
Foster, T. C., 232
Fowler, S. C., 129
Fowles, D. C., 352
Fox, H. E., 296

Fox, K. A., 405, 408
Fox, N. A., 31
Frady, R. L., 168
Francis, D. D., 157, 354–355, 355
Francis, R. C., 187
Frank, L. G., 195, 200
Franke, L., 94
Frankenburg, F. R., 435
Franklin, M., 67
Frantz, A. G., 262
Frazelle, J., 451
Frechmann, T., 336
Fredericson, E., 116
Freed, D., 352
Freeman, S., 197
Freese, R., 154
French, L. R., 253
Frenguelli, B., 315
Frey, F. C., 429
Frick, P. J., 359, 361
Fricke, R. A., 43
Friedman, A. S., 425
Frisby, N. B., 337
Frisch, C., 155
Frischknecht, H. R., 168, 297, 389
Fritchie, G. E., 393
Frith, C. D., 357
Frith, U., 359
Fritzsche, P., 285
Frohm, K. D., 26
Fromm-Auch, D., 453
Frye, C. A., 373
Fuchs, E., 285, 296, 303, 336, 337
Fugger, H. N., 232
Fujita, O., 11
Fujiware, M., 393, 394
Fukunaga-Stinson, C., 251, 282, 284
Fulker, D. W., 26, 27
Fuller, J. L., 12
Funayama, E. S., 360
Funk, D., 263
Furlong, R., 222
Furnham, A., 455
Furukawa, T., 408
Fusani, L., 198
Fuxe, K., 127

Gabel, S., 82
Gabriel, S., 86, 122
Gabrielli, W. F., 25, 452
Gaertner, L., 341
Gahr, M., 197, 198
Gaist, D., 356
Galanter, M., 425
Galdzicki, Z., 153
Gale, M. C., 131
Galeno, T. M., 300
Gallagher, M., 301
Galloway, G. P., 425
Galvan, J., 425

Irwin, S., 406
Isaenko, 12
Isaksson, K., 46, 125
Iseki, E., 154
Ishida, N., 130
Ishii, H., 355
Ishii, K., 67
Ishikawa, S. S., 450, 451
Isom, G. E., 130
Israel, J. E., 298
Issa, F. A., 41, 43, 45, 46, 47, 50, 54
Itil, T., 128, 452
Ito, T., 241
Itzik, A., 300
Iuzzini, J., 341
Iwasaki, Y., 168
Iwata, J., 301

Jacklin, C. N., 28
Jackson, A., 218
Jackson, D. N., 166, 222
Jackson, H., 438
Jackson, J. E., 126, 405
Jackson, V., 436
Jackson, W., 438
Jacobowitz, D., 126
Jacobs, B. L., 123
Jacobs, J. D., 182, 183, 187, 194, 197, 199, 214
Jacobs, P. A., 21
Jacobson, B., 187
Jacobson, S., 42, 47, 48
Jaffe, J. H., 87
Jaggard, D., 191
Jalowiec, J., 337
Jamot, L., 10
Janowsky, A., 218
Jasnow, A. M., 152, 153, 168, 285, 297, 298, 303, 305, 306, 309, 310, 311, 315, 336
Javors, M., 300, 360
Jaynes, J., 254
Jefferson, J. W., 435
Jefferson, K. K., 70
Jefferson, W. N., 217
Jegalian, K. G., 212
Jellestad, F. K., 301
Jellinck, P. H., 213
Jenck, F., 303
Jenkins, G. L., 70
Jennes, L., 217
Jennings, D. H., 185, 193
Jennings, R. K., 132
Jennions, M. D., 41
Jensen, G. C., 43
Jervey, J., 415
Jessop, T. S., 186, 193
Jivoff, P., 40
Johansson-Steensland, P., 374
Johns, J. M., 258, 261, 383, 384
Johnson, B. H., 282
Johnson, E. B., 426

Johnson, K. M., 393
Johnson, R. E., 296
Johnson, R. G., 125, 167
Johnson, S. K., 256
Johnson, W., 22, 28, 356
Johnston, J. B., 299
Johnston, K., 360
Johnston, R. E., 243, 244, 297, 298, 300, 327, 328, 332, 333
Jolly, A., 286
Jones, D. N., 303
Jones, G., 31
Jones, K. A., 52
Jonetz-Mentzel, L., 336, 337
Jonik, R. H., 219, 252, 253, 282
Jono, R. T., 426
Jonsson, E. G., 70, 91, 94
Joppa, M. A., 122, 163, 220
Jorgensen, M. J., 78, 120, 164
Jorm, A. F., 91, 92
Joseph, S., 341
Jouvet, M., 67, 262
Joyce, P. J., 87
Jummonville, J. E., 4
Jurgens, J. K., 262
Jurkovic, G., 168, 220
Juutistenaho, P., 251

Kaada, B., 300
Kagan, J., 356, 450, 451
Kahn, R. S., 83, 86
Kahn-Dawood, F., 85, 433
Kales, A., 432
Kales, J. D., 432
Kalin, N. H., 277, 303, 304, 340
Kalivas, P. W., 131
Kalynchuk, L. E., 130
Kamali, M., 79
Kamboh, M. I., 31
Kamis, A. B., 166, 232
Kandel, E., 352
Kandel, E. R., 314
Kandel, F. L. M., 190
Kando, J. C., 425
Kaneda, Y., 155
Kant, R., 129
Kantak, K. M., 115, 122, 128, 411
Kanter, D. M., 438
Kanter, D. R., 438
Kanui, T. I., 412, 413
Kao, M. H., 296
Kaplan, J. K., 79
Kaplan, J. R., 14, 31, 75, 77, 78, 79, 96, 98, 120, 126, 164, 216, 219, 222, 263, 285, 375, 433
Kapp, B. S., 300
Kappeler, P. M., 190, 219, 222
Kaprio, J., 28
Karanth, S., 155, 156, 263
Karavanich, C., 44, 48
Karczmar, A. G., 120, 387

Subject Index

Appearances of the subject in captions are indicated by italic page numbers.

AAS. *See* anabolic androgenic steroids
abuse, 355
ACTH (adrenocorticotropic hormone), 155–156
additive genetic effects, 21–22
ADHD (attention-deficit hyperactivity disorder)
  fenfluramine challenge studies of, 81–82
  frontal lobe dysfunction and, 352
  serotonin levels and, 81–82
adolescence
  AAS exposure in, 375–378, *376*, *379*
  aggression in
    biological predisposition to, 88–89
    fenfluramine challenge studies of, 88–89
    genetic and environmental influences on, 23–25, 29
    heritability in, 23–24, 32
    stability of, 27
  alcohol exposure in, 402
adoption studies, 22–23, 29
adrenal steroid hormones, 165–168
  in play fighting, 336–337, *337*
β-adrenergic blockers, in clinical studies of aggression, 437–438
adrenocorticotropic hormone (ACTH), 155–156
adult aggression
  genetic and environmental influences on, 25–27
  stability of, 28
  transition into, 331–333
affective aggression. *See* impulsive aggression
aggression. *See also specific types*
  AAS and, 372–379
  abuse and, 355
  alcohol and, 395–403, *397*

alprazolam and, 407
D-amphetamine and, 384–386
and antisocial behavior, 352
appropriateness of, victimization and, *342*, 342–343
behavior patterns of, 116–119, *181*, 181–182
benzodiazepines and, 403–409
biological predisposition to, 88–89
CNS depressants and, 389–409
CNS stimulants and, 379–389
cocaine and, 379–384
comparative genetics of, 4–15
contexts of, 39–43, 182, 191
definition of, 275
development of, 4
  olfactory communication in, 327–328
  play fighting in, 328–331
  scent marking in, 327–328
  sex differences in, 334–335
  threats to, 341, 343–344
  time course of, 338–340
diazepam and, 407–409
dimensions of, 71–74
drug abuse and, 371–372
dynamic nature of, 276
enhancement of, GABA and, 131
ethology of, finite state machine theory applied to, 183, *184*
etiology of
  in adults, 25–27
  in children and adolescents, 23–24
  moderating effects in, 28–30
evolution of, 4